1990

SECOND EDITION

PSYCHOLOGY
The Study of Human Experience

SECOND EDITION

PSYCHOLOGY
The Study of Human Experience

Robert Ornstein

Harcourt Brace Jovanovich, Publishers

San Diego   New York   Chicago   Austin   Washington, D.C.
London   Sydney   Tokyo   Toronto

Cover photo by Frank Whitney, The Image Bank

Text art by John and Judith Waller, Acurate Art Inc., Alex Mendoza, and Noel Malsberg

ISBN: 0-15-572680-3
Library of Congress Catalog Card Number: 87-81165
Printed in the United States of America

Copyrights and Acknowledgments and Illustration Credits appear on pages 747–749, which constitute a continuation of the copyright page.

Preface

It can be difficult to say when the writing of a book begins. This one is easy to date. When I sat in my first introductory psychology class 25 years ago, I decided to study the field in more depth and to learn enough about it to write my own book. I thought, smugly, that I could easily write one. But it took, at this reckoning, 25 years.

Why all that time? Well, it took some experiences in my own life, some research of my own, and much reading in the field and meeting with the contemporary psychologists who were doing all that famous research. Then, 10 years ago, I finally thought I could give it a try.

We are all the stars in our own lives, but we each see the world from only one viewpoint, from one culture, through one set of parents, one sex, one time and place. We learn much from our own experience, but the experiences of others and of scientists can deepen our understanding of ourselves and our lives. We want to know how human life evolved and what makes us think, act, feel, live, love, and learn the way we do. There are pieces to this human puzzle, but they are scattered throughout many studies and disciplines: archeological studies of the dawn of our ancestors, genetic analyses of the transmission of physical characteristics, neuroscience and psychophysiology, and studies of our intricate sensory system. There are clues in the analyses of how we think; how we make mistakes in remembering and learning; how we assess others' intelligence; how emotions are expressed by

peoples of various cultures; and how we face stress, depression, and old age.

There was no book, either in or out of the field of psychology, that assembled these pieces into one coherent story. Yet, there is a real story to tell, I found, and it is the story of our lives. It begins where human life first emerges and continues, in each of us, until we die. In it there are glimpses of the human condition and of human possibilities.

This is a book written for the student who wants to know more about why he or she does "stupid" things, what going "crazy" is like, how stress can be reduced, how the brain evolved in different eras, and how the dazzling mechanisms of maturation coalesce to produce the miracle of a 3-year-old who can speak sentences never heard before. This book is written, too, to explore and explain those miracles that seem beyond ordinary understanding: how populations can physically grow and change; how every cell of the body contains the information necessary to make every other cell; and how the senses routinely screen out most of the information that reaches us and yet transform the external world—silent, colorless, odorless—into a rich world of sight, sound, smells, and tastes. I hope to show clearly how extraordinary the ordinary experience of life really is.

This is a book for students, but there are many aspects directed at teaching and teachers. Information is presented from many viewpoints throughout the book so that students can recall what they have learned in different contexts. This principle, called "multiple encoding," is an important concept, and I have tried to put it to use here. Concepts are developed throughout the book to increase familiarity, but also to offer slightly different views so that students can connect what they have learned with their own experience.

This leads to a second principle I have used here: everything is learned better if it is related to oneself. The examples are drawn from personal experiences that have happened to me and to others. The brain is described as an organ with a purpose that students can follow and relate to

themselves. Memory is described as a functioning system designed to aid us in operating in the world, not as a wiring diagram of a nonexistent machine. There are glimpses of other's experiences: creative moments, dreams, being unemployed, and getting married. Questions many students ask are addressed: Does everyone dream? What happens to children when their parents divorce? Can I improve my intelligence? Are whites and blacks different in intelligence? Who stays healthy under stress? Why am I shy? Would I be able to resist harming another?

These are among the great questions with which psychology must constantly deal. And yet some of them remain mysterious, and all give up their answers slowly. We learn more by our continuing investigation as we put together more pieces of the puzzle. But the process is by no means complete, and this second edition, while remaining true to the overall themes established in the first edition, reflects that state of affairs—how things have changed in the last two or three years.

Working with the suggestions of many students and instructors who have used the book, I have been able to improve it in many ways.

I have been able to put in much new material, including discussions of Alzheimer's disease, the social genesis of homosexuality, Bronfenbrenner's and Stern's views of child development, psychoimmunology, Type A behavior, and Oliver Sacks's description of brain diseases related to the nature of self-centeredness. There is new work on the modular view of mental activities; new views of intelligence by Fodor, Gazzaniga, Ornstein, and Sternberg; Gardner's view of the "frames of mind"; and Marr's approach to vision expert systems. I have included expanded treatments of defense mechanisms and of self-monitoring. An analysis of terrorism is presented and why evolved mental mechanisms influence our response to the news. The viewpoint on evolution is strengthened throughout, from the inception of our response to terrorism to living in modern society.

The major change in the book is the addition of Chapter 18, Living in a High-Tech Society, which includes a new view of stress, the latest research on blood pressure and the heart in the new field of health psychology, new ideas on how we are adapting to computers, and some thoughts on our changing society.

Of course, I could not have done it alone. I have had the pleasure of collaborating on many new works since the first edition, and my collaborators, notably David Sobel and Paul Ehrlich, have left a strong imprint. Others at the Institute for the Study of Human Knowledge have helped revise and extend the book, and I want to thank them all. Carolyn Aldwin, Linda Garfield, Stephen LaBerge, Tom Malone, and Charles Swencionis all contributed significant extracts or working drafts for me. Shane DeHaven, Warren Davis, and Lauren LaBerge helped put the last edition into the computer when it couldn't be done mechanically and made the task of revision much easier, allowing me to

incorporate much more new material and to rewrite what remained. Lauren helped greatly on the galley proofs as well. Mary Ann Cammarota contributed much to the difficult problem of tracking down and organizing hundreds of new references. The work of Nancy Hechinger on the first edition still infuses the spirit of the second.

I am fortunate to have had a wise and lucid editor in Marc Boggs and an enthusiastic manuscript editor in Kathy Walker. Maggie Porter selected great photographs and managed to improve the art immeasurably, while Cheryl Solheid continued and refined the fine design.

Robert Ornstein

Acknowledgments

Christopher M. Aanstoos
West Georgia College

Harry H. Avis
Sierra College

Pamela Birrell
University of Oregon

Peter C. Brunjes
University of Virginia

Robert Cialdini
Arizona State University

Stanley Coren
University of British Columbia

Frank Costin
University of Illinois, Champaign-Urbana

Lynette Crane
City College of San Francisco

Aaron Ettenberg
University of California, Santa Barbara

Scott Fraser
University of Southern California

Albert R. Gilgen
University of Northern Iowa

William J. Gnagey
Illinois State University

Michael Godsey
Indian Valley Colleges

Ronald Growney
University of Connecticut, Storrs

Patrick R. Harrison
U.S. Naval Academy

Elizabeth S. Henry
Old Dominion University

Earl Hunt
University of Washington

John P. Keith
Clark County Community College

Michael J. Lambert
Brigham Young University

Ross J. Loomis
Colorado State University

Elizabeth Matarazzo
Camden County College

Rick McNeese
Sam Houston State University

John W. Nichols
Tulsa Junior College

Patricia Owen
St. Mary's University

A. Christine Parham
San Jacinto College Central

Robert Pellegrini
San Jose State University

James L. Phillips
Oklahoma State University

Alan Randich
The University of Iowa

Duane Reeder
Glendale Community College

Frederick Rhodewalt
University of Utah

Gary Schaumburg
Cerritos College

Thomas R. Scott
University of Delaware

Michael H. Siegel
State University of New York, Oneonta

John W. Somervill
University of Northern Iowa

Tim Stringari
Canada College

Charles Swencionis
Yeshiva University

Charles Van Dyne
Ohio State University

Paul J. Wellman
Texas A&M University

Barbara Williams
Palomar College

John W. Wright
Washington State University

Contents

4

The Brain and Nervous System   132

5

Sensory Experience   176

Part II
The Mental World   212

6

Perceiving the World   214

Part IV
The Social World of the Adult 576

SECOND EDITION

PSYCHOLOGY
The Study of Human Experience

Chapter *1*

The Study of Human Experience

H ere is a tale called "The Elephant in the Dark" about a town in which everyone was blind.

One day, an elephant appeared in the town square. No one in town had ever heard of or knew of this strange animal. The King of the Blind sent his three wisest men to find out what manner of creature this elephant was. Each sage approached the elephant from a different side. The one whose hand had touched the ear reported back that he had discovered the true nature of the elephant. "It is large and flat, rough — like a rug." The second, who had felt only the trunk, said, "That's not it at all — I know the answer. It is like a trumpet, but capable of dramatic movement." The third touched only the legs, and he disagreed vehemently with the other two, "No, no, no. You've got it all wrong. The elephant is mighty and firm like a pillar." Needless to say, none of the single observations could reveal the true nature of the elephant. (Adapted from *Tales of the Dervishes* by Idries Shah, 1970)

Suppose *you* were curious about the discovery of a "strange creature," but instead of an elephant, it was a human being. How would you find out what it is

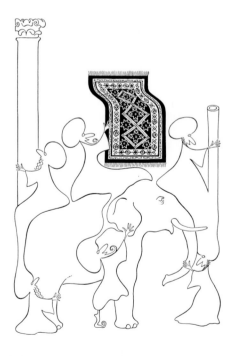

like? You would need to understand where it came from, its past, its family history, its physiology. You would ask, how does its brain work? How does it behave and communicate? What is its sex? What pleases it? How does it act with others? How do culture, groups, and family affect it? How is it like all other individuals of its species?

You would have to ask all these questions—and many more. Each question answered could lead to more questions. One that seems quite simple such as "What is sleep?" might remain unanswered, even after years of inquiry.

Psychologists are in this situation. They approach their study from numerous directions, ask different questions, and use diverse methods. Each aspect of psychology tries to shed some small light on some previously mysterious part of being human: to illuminate the "person in the dark." Psychology tries to answer many of the questions we have about ourselves, other people, and the nature of human life: Why do I feel lonely? What is "going crazy" like? What makes someone "creative"? What happens when I take drugs? What is a mystical experience? What makes someone help another?

Psychology can be broadly defined as a complete science of human experience and behavior. The science involves the study of the brain and nervous system, mental life, behavior, stresses, and disorders. What all this means will take this chapter to start to define and the rest of the book to begin to flesh out.

Selected Moments from the History of Psychology

Psychology is a recent addition to the sciences. In 1900 there were about 125 psychologists in the United States, while there are now more than 60,000. Psychology borders and draws from many different disciplines—from biology and genetics to philosophy and sociology—since psychologists may work probing a gene or a group, a child's thoughts, or a politician's popularity.

It is a fertile science and its sources are abundant. For centuries, inquiry regarding the mind, behavior, and human nature was the dominion of philosophical schools. But after the Renaissance, many thinkers speculated that direct observation of human conduct, as well as inspection of the structure of the human brain and body, might illuminate the perennial questions of philosophy: Is thinking

---

WHO AM I?

How do you know what you are like? Often our personal deliberations about our own identity do not suffice. Nasrudin, an essential folk character, tried many ways to know himself. We will become acquainted with more of them as this book goes on.

Psychology is both a science and a method of understanding yourself and others from a collection of viewpoints.

> Nasrudin went into a bank with a check to cash.
> "Can you identify yourself?" asked the clerk.
> Nasrudin took out a mirror and peered into it.
> "Yes, that's me all right," he said.

innate or learned? Do human beings apprehend reality directly through their senses? How is knowledge gained? Is thought affected by others?

The beginnings of the modern attempt to find in the structure of the human nervous system the answers to many long-standing philosophical questions began with Rene Descartes (1596–1650). After a great deal of deliberation, Descartes came to believe that much human knowledge was innate; it existed within the structure of the brain and nervous system. He then proposed that there exists an inherent set of abilities through which the "Mind" directs the automaton of a body. He even proposed a physical location for this interaction — the *pineal* of the brain, for it is one organ of the brain whose structure is single rather than dual. Descartes was most important because he set the modern study of mind–brain relationships in motion. He wrote:

> What must be the fabric of the nerves and muscles of the human body in order that the animal spirits therein should have the power to move the members . . . what changes are necessary in the brain to cause wakefulness, sleep and dream; how light, sounds, smells, tastes, and all other qualities pertaining to external objects are able to imprint on it various ideas by the intervention of the senses.

Descartes' voice was not the only one to be heard on this matter. The British empiricists held that the human mind was not so prepared for such knowledge but rather gained it through associations. Association is one of psychology's oldest principles. The exploration began with the Greek philosophers and was revived in the seventeenth century. John Locke, David Hume, and John Stuart Mill believed that the "association of ideas" (a sensation or a thought) connects experience. "Ideas" become associated when they occur close to each other in space or in time. John Locke (1670) wrote:

> A man has suffered pain or sickness in a place; he saw his friend die in such a room, though these have in nature nothing to do with one another, yet when the idea of the place occurs to mind, it brings (the impressions being once made) that of pain and displeasure with it, he confounds them in his mind and can as little bear the one as the other.

The empiricists, who have been quite influential in science's view of the human mind, believed that all knowledge came from experience. They assumed that the mind was

> . . . white paper void of all characters, without any ideas — How comes it to be furnished? Whence comes it by that vast store which the busy and boundless fancy of man has painted on it with an almost endless variety? Whence has all the materials of reason and knowledge? To this I answer, in one word, from EXPERIENCE. (Locke, 1670)

This was Locke's colorful account, not looking to the structure of the nervous system, but to the world in which the person lives. These different proposals spawned later schools of psychology, notably the behaviorists and the physiological approach. The behaviorists are the heirs to Locke and the empiricists.

In the late nineteenth century when psychology originated, the predominant consideration was the mind. Researchers used the technique of **introspection;** they studied how their own minds worked and dissected the contents of their

John B. Watson
(1878–1958)

(See Chapter 2, section
on Process of
Adaptation and
Evolution.)

experience. The problem was that the investigators could not agree. John Watson (1914) proposed that introspection was therefore useless if psychology was to become a science and that the study of observable *behavior* was a more defensible subject for psychology. **Behaviorism,** an approach that deals with association, maintains that our knowledge is largely learnt and comes from experience.

Other sciences inspired psychology. For almost all of human history it was assumed that human beings were at the center of the universe. After all, anyone can see that the sun goes around the earth. But Copernicus showed that this was not so, that the earth was but one planet around its sun and there were many more suns as well. Humanity was not special.

The next great blow came from a young British naturalist named Charles Darwin (1809–1882) who showed that human beings evolved along with the rest of life on earth and were descended from a common ancestor. Before the advent of modern science, it was generally believed that all creatures were individually created to suit their special environments. By the nineteenth century, the commonly held scientific view was that all animals did change and had developed from earlier forms of life. Darwin proposed a theory of how this change, or adaptation, occurs, called *natural selection.* Darwin's theory, combined with modern genetics, is the basis of the modern *theory of evolution,* now the generally accepted explanation of how organisms change through time.

Darwin began the modern era in biology and had great influence on psychology: Sigmund Freud's psychoanalysis, Jean Piaget's work on child development (Darwin wrote the first "baby biography"), and the study of emotions were all consequences of evolutionary thinking. Since human beings and other animals descended from a common ancestor, then much wisdom could be gained from studying animals. So comparative psychology and ethology owe their debt to Darwin, too.

Psychology owes its systematic beginnings to two men: William James (1842–1910) and Wilhelm Wundt (1832–1920). James, the first great synthesizer of psychology, wrote *The Principles of Psychology* in 1890, taking 20 years to do it. It remains perhaps the most eloquent description of the science of psychology, but one which has been superseded by later scientific investigation. The tradition of scientific investigation is due largely to Wundt, who established the first laboratory of psychology, thus putting psychology on a scientific basis. Modern psychologists combine a general understanding of their subject with the analysis of scientific data.

Today, many of these distinct early strands weave together: while Descartes may have been wrong in detail, the search for the machinery of the mind is one of the most important components of psychology; while Locke may have overstated the case, teaching by association is the main method of instruction; laboratory, clinical, and speculative insights routinely give rise to new treatments and studies. Every psychologist draws from the scientific study of behavior, physiology, perception, psychotherapy, and the like. Human experience and behavior is distressingly complex, and its determinants—biology, society, personal interactions, learning, associations, and difficulties—all are combined in our modern understanding.

The present distinctions between types of psychologists concern mainly *what they study* and which method they use, rather than which doctrine they hold or what school they belong to. Psychologists study associations, but assume that the organism has built-in capabilities. Psychotherapists may approach a problem through talking or through biology. Social psychologists may base their analysis on the structure of thought or on society. It is a young science, our science of human experience and action, but one which is just out of its infancy and beginning to challenge entrenched ideas from medicine through philosophy. We will describe some of these in this book.

Psychologists evaluate human experience from many viewpoints: biology, development, mental system, how the person behaves, the influence of society and the environment, the experiences of disordered people, and the achievements of exceptional ones. All these distinct sides merge to form a scientific assessment of the "person in the dark."

BEHAVIORISM: WHAT PEOPLE DO

Behaviorists assume that people do what they do because of conditions (defined precisely as "prerequisite circumstances") in their environment. Behaviorists reason that if the conditions change, behavior can also change. Underlying behaviorism is an optimistic belief in betterment through alteration of the environment.

> Give me a dozen healthy infants, well-formed, and my own specified world to bring them up in and I'll guarantee to take any one at random and train him to become any type of specialist I might select—doctor, lawyer, artist, merchant-chief, and yes, even beggar-man and thief, regardless of his talents, penchants, tendencies, abilities, vocations, and race of his ancestors. (Watson, 1925)

"Control the conditions and you will see the order," the influential behaviorist B. F. Skinner wrote (1972). Thus, behaviorists often modify the conditions and observe variations in behavior which follow. Through behavioral studies animals have learned to choose between difficult alternatives and to perform complicated tricks. Using a complicated series of learning trials, pigeons can even become quality control inspectors (Figure 1-1). Every psychologist has been influenced by behaviorism, and it has led to important discoveries about learning and remembering and about how people act alone, with other people, and in society at large.

FIGURE 1-1
Conditioned Behavior
The scientific alteration of the conditions in their environment can shape the responses of animals so they learn various new ways of behaving. Left: Pidgeon being trained in a "Skinner box." Right: A killer whale performing at Sea World.

FIGURE 1-2
Imitating Violent Behavior
Hitting and kicking an inflated doll were among the ways nursery school children like this little girl responded to seeing a film showing adults and other children acting violently.

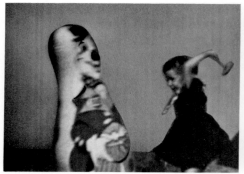

Consider this important issue: Why do people act violently? Some recent investigations concern the effect of television on violent behavior. Any given child of age 10 has seen thousands of acts of violence on television, such as robberies, rapes, murders, and fights. Do these "conditions" affect how aggressive a child will be? A study of the behavior of people in different circumstances is the best way to find out.

Some psychologists propose that watching "fictional" violence may be constructive because the viewer experiences a **catharsis;** that is, viewing violence allows the fierce feelings to be discharged and the viewer will then be *less* likely to act aggressively. Other psychologists believe that people learn by observation and imitation; they propose that the more violence a child sees, the *more* likely he or she will act violently.

In an important study, children of several ages were shown films of adults (and other children) hitting dolls and other people. After the movie the children's behavior was monitored (Figure 1-2). Children who watched violence afterward acted *more* aggressively (see Bandura, 1986, for a discussion of learning by observation).

BIOLOGICAL APPROACH

People are the product of millions of years of evolution. Each person comes into the world with an amazing inheritance — a complex brain and nervous system. Studies of the structure and operations of the brain, the **biological approach,** provide clues for psychologists. In 1942, Wilder Penfield, a neurosurgeon, made a startling discovery while working on a patient with a brain tumor. To study which parts of the brain were active, he stimulated the brain at different locations with electrical current (Figure 1-3). Penfield probed one location and the patient did not respond; he probed another and the fingers twitched. Here is the rest of the record (the numbers corresponding to those on Figure 1-3):

11 —"I heard something, I do not know what it was."

11 — (Probe repeated without warning the patient) "Yes, Sir, I think I heard a mother calling her little boy somewhere. It seemed to be something that happened years ago." When asked to explain, she said, "It was somebody in the neighborhood where I live." Then she added that she herself "was somewhere close enough to hear."

12 —"Yes, I heard voices down along the river somewhere — a man's voice and a woman's voice calling. . . . I think I saw the river."

15 —"Just a tiny flash of a feeling of familiarity and a feeling that I knew everything that was going to happen in the near future."

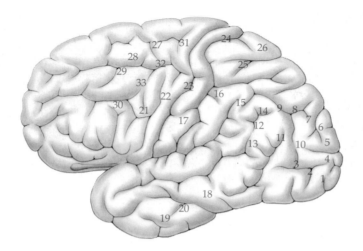

FIGURE 1-3
Electrical Stimulation of the Brain
The numbers indicate the locations at which Penfield stimulated the brain with his electrode.
(After Penfield, 1975)

17c— . . . Oh! I had the same very, very familiar memory, in an office somewhere. I could see the desks. I was there and someone was calling to me, a man leaning on a desk with a pencil in his hand." I warned her I was going to stimulate, but I did not do so. "Nothing."

18a—(Stimulation without warning) "I had a little memory—a scene in a play—they were talking and I could see it—I was just seeing it in my memory." (Penfield, 1975)

Each time Penfield's electrode was inserted into the particular spot, a similar experience was stimulated. Penfield writes: "I was more astonished each time my electrode brought forth such a response. How could it be? This had to do with the mind. I called such responses 'experiential'" (Penfield, 1975).

So, disturbances of the *brain's* electrical activity can influence the *mind* dramatically. There are other ways this comes about. Injuries to the brain, surgery, and drugs that affect the chemistry of the brain all have striking effects on the mind. The biological underpinnings of experience are an increasingly important part of psychology, a part that has developed greatly over the past 20 years, but one which has a long history (Ornstein & Sobel, 1987).

See Chapter 4, section on Creating Anew: The Cerebral Cortex.

COGNITIVE APPROACH

The word *cognitive* comes from the Latin verb "to know," and the central object of study in **cognitive psychology** is the mind. But the mind is *not* a physical organ like the brain. Rather, it involves many activities such as thinking, memory, language, and consciousness.

Cognitive psychologists attempt to observe, as directly as possible, the operations of the mind. One question that would interest a cognitive psychologist is: "How many things can a person do at once?" The common wisdom is that "you can't do two things at once." But is that "wisdom" true?

Ulric Neisser decided to see if it were possible to do two extremely complex activities at once: reading one subject while writing on another (Figure 1-4). Two students, Diane and John, were enlisted as subjects. They read short stories while copying down a list of words that was being dictated to them rapidly. At first Diane and John found the task impossible. They read slowly, and when they were tested later for story comprehension, they did poorly. But after six weeks of training, they could perform both tasks easily.

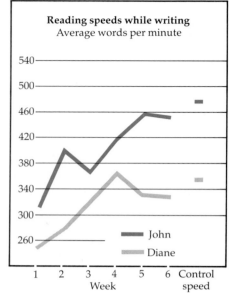

FIGURE 1-4
Learning To Do Two
Things at Once
John and Diane steadily
improved their ability to
read while writing. After a
few weeks their reading
speeds were close to their
normal rates, as this record
of their progress in the
experiment shows.
(After Hirst et al., 1978)

Later the demonstration was extended. While Diane and John were reading, they took dictation, not simply of words, but of whole sentences. Again, it was difficult at first, but within weeks they were reading one subject and writing on another at the same time, at normal speed, and with normal comprehension (Hirst, Neisser, & Spelke, 1978).

It is thus possible to learn to increase mental capacity and to divide attention. Cognitive psychologists also examine mental limitations, such as our tendency to judge through comparison. Suppose you were buying a toaster, and it cost $30 at the store you were at. Then you discovered that it cost $20 at a store 20 minutes away. Would you make the trip? Most people say they would. Suppose, again, that you were going to buy a car that cost $14,320. You discover that another dealer (also 20 minutes away) is selling the same car for $14,310. Would you go? Most likely not.

The situation is actually the same. In *both* instances you are being asked to drive 20 minutes for a savings of $10. The savings is the same; the drive is the same. But the $10 *seems* like a lot compared with the $30 for the toaster and almost nothing compared with the price of the car (Kahneman, Slovic, & Tversky, 1982). We judge things by *comparing* them with others.

Cognition in Contemporary Society

Part of the discovery of modern psychology, which you will read about, is that we do not perceive the world as it really is. In the summer of 1986, hundreds of thousands of American tourists stayed away from Europe because of the perceived threat of terrorism — 25 people had been killed that year. Certainly no one wanted to get gunned down in an airport shootout. But was staying away from Europe effective? Consider this set of statistics from *Newsweek* (June 2, 1986):

43,500 killed in automobile accidents in the US (1985)
1,384 murdered in New York City (1985)

36 murdered in Honolulu (1985)
150 died in their own bathtubs (1984)
1,063 killed in boating accidents (1984)
3,100 died choking on food (1984)

During the next half day, if current trends continue, more people will die in automobile accidents in the United States than have *ever* (up until the writing of this book) been killed by terrorists. In fact, more people are murdered every *two hours* in the United States than were killed by terrorists during the entire summer of 1986. Certain events, because of their new and surprising nature, become automatically emphasized in the mind (Ehrlich & Ornstein, in press).

There are countless examples of our notice of sudden news—the murder of hostage Leon Klinghoffer in 1985; the poisoning of Tylenol® capsules in late 1985; the explosion of the space shuttle in early 1986. All of these and many similar events commanded national and international attention when they occurred. But about 300 murders occur in the United States *every day,* most of which remain almost unnoticed by the general population.

The nature of the human system of cognition makes terrorism very effective. Terrorism taps into the nervous system program which originally functioned to register short-term changes in a steady state. When a ''noise'' continues, the nervous system stops responding to it. When a new noise appears, automatic emphasis is given in the form of an increased response. A sudden threat, even insignificant, is thus registered intensely. A continuing threat, just like a continuing noise, becomes part of the background. This analysis, which draws together social and cognitive psychology, will be examined in Chapter 18.

SOCIAL ENVIRONMENT

Suppose you heard a scream from the room next door. Would you help? If you were alone, the chances are that you would, but if you were with six other people who did not help, the chances are that you would not! (Darley & Latane, 1968). Human beings are quite dependent on one another; other people *intensify* actions. Runners are faster when they run with others; people behave more aggressively in crowds than when alone. The investigation of how other people and our environment affect us is the **social environmental perspective.**

Some social psychological studies are stimulated by life events. In 1964 a young woman named Kitty Genovese was mugged and stabbed to death in New York City. The murder of a woman is, unfortunately, not unusual, but what made this case horribly remarkable was that Kitty Genovese screamed repeatedly and was heard by at least 38 people who watched the crime from the safety of their homes. No one tried to help her; no one even called the police. This apathy shocked many psychologists who initiated many studies of what makes a person stop to help.

Recent research (Cialdini, 1985) has shown that in this case and others like it, it is *not* apathy that makes bystanders not help, but rather simple innocent confusion. Everyone thinks someone else will help. Another reason is that everyone remains calm so as not to appear socially inappropriate, giving the appearance that nothing is really wrong! This points out an interesting social characteristic of human beings: we base our behavior in large part on the behavior of those around us.

In one experiment, a divinity student was told to go to a certain building and give a sermon that was to be taped. On the way he found a man, slumped and

What Makes a Person Stop to Help? Psychologists study the social environment to discover factors accounting for bystander apathy, bystander intervention, and similar behavior that can affect our lives.

groaning, in a doorway (who was actually one of the psychologists acting the part). Would the student stop to help, and under what conditions?

Sixty divinity students were divided into three groups: one-third were told that they were late and had to hurry; one-third were told to go to the building, but not necessarily to hurry; one-third were told that there was a delay in the taping and to take their time. All the students were assigned a topic for their sermon. Half were to talk on the biblical parable of the Good Samaritan; half were assigned a nonreligious topic. The experimenters wanted to know if either the pressure of time or what they were thinking about influenced "helping behavior."

Only 40 percent of the divinity students stopped to help; 60 percent did not. The pressure of time seemed to have more influence on their behavior than what they had just read. Of the students who were in no hurry, 63 percent stopped, but only 10 percent of the rushed students did; 53 percent of those thinking about the Good Samaritan paused. Analysis of the results of this experiment suggest that if people are in a hurry, they are not likely to stop to help.

Psychologists also analyze *social biases*, which are inherent tendencies in the mind that guide our behavior. One of these is a partiality toward immediately valuing and searching out scarce items, short-term thinking at its purest. Social psychologist Robert Cialdini (1985) noticed this reaction in himself.

The city of Mesa, Arizona, is a suburb in the Phoenix area where I live. Perhaps the most notable features of Mesa are its sizable Mormon population—next to Salt Lake City, the largest in the world—and a huge Mormon temple located on exquisitely kept grounds in the center of the city. Although I had appreciated the landscaping and architecture from a distance, I had never been interested enough in the temple to go inside, until the day I read a newspaper article that told of a special inner sector of Mormon temples to which no one has access but faithful members of the church. Even potential converts must not see it. There is one exception to the rule, however. For a few days immediately after a temple is newly constructed, nonmembers are allowed to tour the entire structure, including the otherwise restricted section.

The newspaper story reported that the Mesa temple had been recently refurbished and that the renovations had been extensive enough to classify it as "new" by church standards. Thus, for the next several days only, non-Mormon visitors could see the temple area traditionally banned to them. I remember quite well the effect this article had on me: I immediately resolved to take a tour. But when I phoned a friend to ask if he wanted to come along, I came to understand something that changed my decision just as quickly.

After declining the invitation, my friend wondered why I seemed so intent on a visit. I was forced to admit that, no, I had never been inclined toward the idea of a temple tour before, that I had no questions about the Mormon religion I wanted answered, that I had no general interest in church architecture, and that I expected to find nothing more spectacular or stirring than what I might see at a number of other churches or cathedrals in the area. It became clear as I spoke that the special lure of the temple had a sole cause: If I did not experience the restricted sector soon, I would never again have the chance. Something that, on its own merits, held little appeal for me had become decidedly more attractive merely because it was rapidly becoming less available.

A sensitivity to the scarcity of resources — especially a sudden change leading to scarcity — is clearly important. However, in the modern social world these biases can lead to baffling behaviors. In part, social psychology studies these kinds of influences on behavior, for example, in how we choose partners, how we work, and how we act in the courtroom (Hatfield & Sprecher, 1986).

RANGE OF HUMAN EXPERIENCE

Three other perspectives on human experience yield much data: the analysis of disorders, called the **clinical approach;** the study of how mental events affect the body, called **health psychology;** and the study of the important positive attributes of people, called the **humanistic approach.**

Clinical Approach

The clinical approach is based on the idea that observing a person who is unable to perform a function can offer information on how that function usually operates. Here are several examples.

1. *Biological malfunction.*   A man is interviewed in a hospital. His interviewer asks: "Can you tell me what work you have been doing?" He answers: "If you had said that, poomer, near the fortunate, tamppoo all around the fourth of marz. Oh, I get all confused!" (Gardner, 1975) This man has a variety of *aphasia,* or loss of language, caused by damage to part of the brain. If people with damage to the front of the left hemisphere of the brain have specific difficulties with language, we presume that this part of the brain has an important role in normal language.

See Chapter 10, section on Language.

2. *Mental errors.*   Psychologists analyze mental errors to diagnose the workings of normal thought. One class of errors is called *capture errors.* Suppose that you planned to stop at a fish store on your way home and then find that you have driven past it and have just driven into your driveway. The route home was such a well-formed habit that it *captured* you. Another example would be: "I was using a copying machine and I was counting the pages. I

found myself counting: 1, 2, 3, 4, 5, 6, 7, 8, 9, 10, Jack, Queen, King" (Norman, 1983). In both cases, the intended action was replaced by the normal operation of mind, presumably stronger than the chosen action. While some psychologists assume that anything one does has a "hidden" meaning, these capture errors show that there may sometimes be a simpler explanation of why, for example, when you move to a new house in a city, you automatically drive back to the old home for the first few days. It does not necessarily mean that you wish to return there.

3. *Multiple personality.* In a college town in the Midwest, a young man named Billy Milligan was arrested for raping a woman. The psychologist interviewing him asked for his social security number.

> He shrugged. "I don't know."
> The psychologist read his number to him.
> . . . "That's not my number, it must be Billy's."
> . . . "Well aren't you Billy?"
> "I'm *David*."
> "Well, where's Billy?"
> "He's asleep."
> "Asleep where?"
> He pointed to his chest. "In here, he's asleep."
> . . . "I have to talk to Billy."
> "Well, *Arthur* won't let you. Billy's asleep. Arthur won't wake him up, 'cause if he does, Billy'll kill himself." (Keyes, 1982)

One might dismiss all these different "people" inside as a criminal's elaborate ruse to avoid conviction, but the Ohio authorities finally did not. Although "Billy Milligan" committed the crime, it was judged that another "person" inside him was responsible and *Billy* as a whole could not be punished for the crime of one of his parts. A program of treatment to attempt to "fuse" the different personalities was prescribed. It was successful. While they are exotic and controversial, multiple personalities shed light on the many diverse systems, minds, traits, or selves that live within one person.

Health, the Mind, and the Brain

Recently, psychological, physiological, and medical knowledge are merging into the study of how mental events affect the body. This *health psychology* promises to become a major way in which psychological knowledge can be used to improve (and possibly lengthen) the lives of many people. Many of the indicators of the role of the brain and nervous system in health are found in reactions to daily events.

Suppose you received a telephone call late at night from the police telling you that your spouse (or a loved one) had just been killed in a train wreck. Imagine your reaction to this very personal disaster.

We know what happens after a train wreck. The dead are pulled away, and their bodies are identified and buried. But a train wreck also has disastrous effects on the lives of many others. Close members of the family and friends grieve.

There is the pain of the loss and the real problems of those who are left behind, who must learn to live without their husband or wife, father or mother. And it is now known that there is another unexpected effect from an accident like this: it also wrecks the immune system of those who feel the loss!

The discovery of the link between a shocking tragedy and subtle internal changes in susceptibility to disease began with a newspaper story that was similar to many we see each day:

> SYDNEY, AUSTRALIA. A train heading for Melbourne derailed at a crossing killing 33 and injuring scores of passengers. The cause of the accident is not yet known but is under intense investigation.

After the Melbourne train wreck, many of the spouses of those who died suffered greatly and almost all grieved for their loss. Many were offered counseling services and the help of sympathetic friends to help them adjust. But this time there was a difference: many of those so affected were studied to determine how the stress of their grief affected the functioning of their immune system.

In a pioneering study, a group of psychiatrists and immunologists in New South Wales, Australia, followed the lives of the spouses and families affected by the deaths in the train wreck. R. W. Bartrop and colleagues took blood samples from 26 of the spouses within three weeks. The immune systems of the grieving spouses were shown to have been considerably weakened.

The clinical measures showed lower levels of activity of those cells in the blood which attack "foreign bodies"—the lymphocytes. This study was the first to show that there is a measurable depression of immune function following severe psychological stress in a real life setting. The findings may also contribute to understanding the tremendous increase in illness and death which often follows loss of a spouse (Bartrop et al., 1977; Ornstein & Sobel, 1987). These studies and others have sparked the field of *psychoimmunology,* which is the assessment of the effect of mental events on the immune system of the body.

Humanistic Approach

The study of disorders yields much information on the workings of the normal mind. But to achieve a full understanding of the nature of the human mind and experience, one must also know the full extent of its capabilities as well. Some of the first questions you might ask that "person in the dark" would be: "What are you really good at? What is the best you can do?"

This emphasis on the important positive aspects of human experience is called **humanistic.** Abraham Maslow, its founder and leading theorist, believed that human beings have an inherent inclination toward "growth" and "development," that is, toward improvement in health, creativity, achievement, love, and understanding (Frager & Fadiman, 1987).

Maslow presumed that we all have within us genuine "potentials," and given the opportunity, we strive to make those potentials "actual," a process called **self-actualization.** Maslow studied people who seemed to develop their potential to its fullest—scientific geniuses such as Einstein and world leaders such as Gandhi.

SOME UNIVERSAL PSYCHOLOGICAL CHARACTERISTICS: PRIORITIES AND POLICIES

In going through this book, you will find detailed accounts of development, of sensation, of the workings of the brain and mind, of motives and social life, and more. It may help to keep in mind throughout all this that people need to act quickly even though many different things happen to them. Numerous stimuli reach the person every moment. Many are filtered out by the senses, which respond to only a small portion of the array of stimulation. Those that remain are organized and simplified by the numerous processes of perception, thinking, and memory: a roaring noise outside may presage that a son has come home, or ice on the road may mean that a crop is destroyed. Of the many experiences we had last year, only a few remain in memory.

There are still too many things happening at one moment for us to act on all of them. We must simplify the world and act on only the most important ones, and those that are the highest priority to us are in our consciousness. Throughout this book, particularly in our treatment of the brain, senses, perception, consciousness, and motivation, we will touch on an internal priority system that is part of the operation behind the scenes of our experiences. Here is just an introductory look at this system for you to keep in your mind.

You can feel this system working when you are in the middle of a "hot" conversation while driving. Suddenly the brake lights of the car in front of you go on. Immediately the conversation goes out of your mind and you attend to the potential threat. Extreme hunger crowds out ideas; pain preempts plans. We constantly shift up and down along a set of priorities that are governed by conscious and unconscious brain processes.

There is a definite hierarchy in the priority of plans and behaviors. Starting at the bottom, and taking priority, are the physiological needs, then come the needs for safety, love, and belonging. Higher up are the needs for esteem, cognitive needs, aesthetic needs, and the needs of self-actualization and transcendence. So in our example, avoiding the car ahead automatically takes precedence over what you are talking about.

Events and ideas come in and out of consciousness via neurological processes governed by the brain. We consciously select information inside and outside of ourselves; we oversee our own actions and resolve discrepancies.

The brain "minds" the body. It controls body temperature, blood flow, digestion, and heartbeat, among many other bodily processes; it responds to internal and external changes through an immense network of sensory systems and adapts to changes in the world.

When the most basic and immediate physiological needs, such as hunger and thirst, are met, other "higher" ones need to be satisfied. Safety is maintained, pain avoided, pleasure sought, and social needs, like belonging, are met.

Similarly, we reduce the amount of information to which we attend by certain "policies" of the mind, as are listed here. Keep in mind that these are only very general and somewhat whimsical descriptions of tendencies of the mind, with which you will become familiar.

1. *What have you done for me lately?*
   People are extremely sensitive to recent information; emotional upsets like bad feelings last for a while, then are forgiven. Terrible disasters like an aircrash force attention on airliners, and for a while, all sorts of reforms are initiated, and then the spotlight dims.
2. *Don't call me unless anything new and exciting happens.*
   Most mental operations focus upon "the news," a sudden appearance of something unknown. Unexpected or extraordinary events seem to have fast access to consciousness, while an unchanging

background noise or a constant weight, such as a chronic problem, soon gets shunted into the background. It is easy to raise money for emergencies, such as for the few victims of a well-publicized disaster, but it is much more difficult to raise money for the many victims of continuous malnutrition. We quickly respond to scarcity and danger.

Gradual changes in the world go unnoticed while sharp changes are immediately seized upon by the mind. Gasoline prices increased in the 1970s from about $0.30 per gallon to about $0.95 with little decrease in consumption. When prices went over $1.00 there was an immediate decline in consumption, as we had been "awakened" somehow by the change. This happens too on the simple sensory registration of information: for example, a sudden loud noise is commanding, but the continual low din in the factory next door is well (probably too well) tolerated.

3. The comedian Henny Youngman was asked, "How do you like your wife?" *"Compared to what?"* he responded. Youngman's answer points out two phenomena: we constantly judge by comparison, and our judgment of any item depends upon what we are comparing it to at that moment. Suppose that your boss hands you $1,000 at the end of the year. You are delighted because you are expecting nothing. But suppose he had told you that he was going to give you $10,000 and then changed his mind? It is very doubtful that you would be delighted. Your reaction is different because the basis of comparison has changed. The same is true of Youngman's wife or anybody's spouse. Our standards for other people are very different: actions that are alluring in others might be regarded as unbecoming in a spouse. Comparison processes span

everything from judgments of primitive sensations, such as heaviness and heat, to social status.

4. *What does this mean to me?*

The mental system determines the meaning of any event and its relevance to a person. In the process it throws out almost all the information that reaches us. Of the billions of leaves you saw last summer, how many do you remember? A flash of red crossing your view may mean that your wife has driven home in her red car, but you hardly notice the visual stimulus, just the meaning. A siren is frightening because it *means* that the police want you to stop. Almost automatically new information is processed in terms of what we have to do next. We remember things better, for instance, when we can relate them to ourselves. Because this book is written to be understood, it often gives examples of personal relevance so that abstract principles become more meaningful.

All these "policies" and procedures exist to simplify the amount of information current in the mind. "What have you done for me lately" allows a focus on only the most recent events. "Don't call me . . ." allows much of the real changes in the world to go ignored, and only when they are great do they enter the system. Most people do not "mind" the slow increases in the prices they pay for milk, bread, wine, meat, and other items that they buy every day. However, the increase in car prices meets with great dismay, even though car prices have increased less than the average of the consumer price index. The reason lies in "policy" number 2: we don't notice the slow monthly price increases in an item like milk, but a car, which we buy only every 3 or 4 years, contains the accumulated price increase—and we notice that quickly!

"What does this mean to me?" allows us to operate on and to (cont.)

remember only the meaning or the "gist" of conversations, meetings, and different situations. "You mean you talked for three hours and you only decided to paint the house blue?"

Our own understanding of ourselves is also processed by the policies and procedures system, thus we don't always know ourselves directly. We hold a well-organized and simplified version of our environment, of the nature of other people, and even *of our own lives and our own beliefs* in our minds.

We are constantly sifting through evidence, making decisions, inferring from information, deciding what a person is talking about, sorting through different hypotheses, deciding whether the situation is an emergency, whether resources are scarce, whether that noise needs action, whether

something is larger (or brighter or smaller) than something else, and countless more. All this goes on "behind the scenes" of the mind. We are aware of the specific contents of our mind but are most often unaware of all the wheeling and dealing of the "system of mind." One aim of psychology is to go behind the scenes and to understand the processes of perception, memory, thought, and language, not only their products.

Most of the chapters in the beginning of this book introduce more formal "principles of psychology" which carry out functions of the organism. They include processes like comparison, as well as more general life processes like adaptation. Remembering these "principles" will help make sense of the data of psychology. (from Ornstein, 1986)

If we want to answer the question how tall can the human species grow, then obviously it is well to pick out the ones who are already tallest and study them. If we want to know how fast a human being can run, then it is no use to average out the speed of a "good sample" of the population: it is far better to collect Olympic gold medal winners and see how well they can do. If we want to know the possibilities for spiritual growth, value growth, or moral development in human beings, then I maintain that we can learn most by studying our most moral, ethical or saintly people.

On the whole I think it fair to say that human history is a record of the ways in which human nature has been sold short. The highest possibilities of human nature have practically always been underrated. Even when "good specimens": the saints and sages and great leaders of history, have been available for study, the temptation too often has been to consider them not human but supernaturally endowed. (Maslow, 1970)

Humanistic psychologists also treat people with difficulties, but they emphasize the positive elements, the possibilities for growth and development.

A Concluding Note

Unfortunately, for individuals trying to understand themselves, and even worse for psychologists, human beings are very complex animals. Many factors determine our lives, so it is through more and more observations from different viewpoints—biological, cognitive, behavioral, social and environmental, clinical, and humanistic—that a complete picture can begin to emerge. But how these observations *themselves* are made is important to the study of psychology as a science, and it is to this we now turn.

Most of us act like psychologists each day and try to understand ourselves and others. Why do I make so many mistakes? How intelligent am I? Some of the questions we have are more general. Is personality formed in the first few years of life? Is an aggressive person always aggressive? The difference between "everyday psychologists" and the scientific psychologist is a matter of degree. In ordinary life we often cannot control what happens, and so guesses are imprecise. In science, many researchers may study the same problem for years in carefully controlled environments, painstakingly checking their deductions.

Science Goes Beyond Personal Experience

You are the star of your own life: you see things from the point of view of only yourself, one woman or man, born into only one family, in one era of history, in one country, rich or poor, old or young. A person's ordinary knowledge is limited by the situations encountered and by particular life circumstances, for example, where we were born, whom we meet, and what our opportunities are. Most people base their "everyday psychology" upon their particular set of experiences. In contrast, scientific psychology examines human behavior and experience from many different viewpoints (such as the perspectives mentioned in the previous section), and its knowledge is more generally applicable and reliable.

Everyday life is full of quick responses to specific situations. We may like or dislike someone or something on a whim or the flimsiest evidence. But in scientific psychology, judgments are slow, measured, and tentative. The knowledge of science is gathered slowly; it is the most conservative and stable form of knowledge.

Personal and Scientific Knowledge of Dreams

Sometimes our understanding of ourselves is wrong. For instance, many people are convinced, based on their own experience, that they do not dream every night. They are wrong. In a pioneering experiment in 1953, researchers brought people into a lab and observed them while they slept (Figure 1-5). About every 90 minutes throughout the night, every sleeper's eyes moved rapidly. If these people were awakened during these "rapid eye movement" periods, they said that they were dreaming. In the morning, they had no recollection of the past night's events—either that they had been awakened or reported a dream (Aserinsky & Kleitman, 1953).

See Chapter 7, section on Dreams.

In this case, scientific knowledge is more accurate about people's experience than people are themselves. This experiment has been repeated often over the past 40 years, and the relationship of rapid eye movement periods of sleep to dreams has been observed in every sleeping person. All of us, no matter what we may believe, dream every night.

Some Aims and Virtues of Science

Regular people, not inhuman calculating machines, do science, and they do it the way they do everything else: they make guesses and mistakes, argue, try out ideas to see what works, and discard what doesn't work. Science has a reputation for being difficult to learn and to do, but it is basically quite simple. Scientific methods

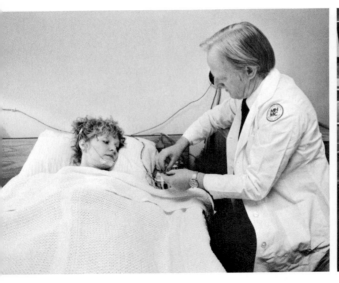

FIGURE 1-5
The Scientific Study of Sleep
Sleep is studied in the laboratory by recording the subject's brain waves, eye movements, and heart activity through the night.

are extensions and refinements of methods people use every day to answer questions about ourselves and about the world we live in. Individual scientists make the same mistakes everyone else does (Kahneman, Slovic, & Tversky, 1982). But science differs from ordinary inquiry in that it is a systematic and formal process of gathering information—with rules for testing ideas, interpreting results, and correcting mistakes.

Order, Simplicity, and Unity

The world often seems chaotic: things happen all at once and we have to "make sense" out of it. The first assumption of science is that there is *order* in the world, and the second is that there is *unity* in it. Einstein (1956) wrote, "The great aim of science is to cover the greatest number of phenomena with the fewest number of ideas."

Scientific discoveries build on one another; one generation's knowledge is superseded in the next. The first task of the young scientist is to know what has already been discovered. If not, trouble can result. Suppose, while sitting under an apple tree, you realized that the fall of an apple and the movement of the planets were related; you would not be heralded as a genius as was Isaac Newton 300 years ago. You would instead be criticized for not doing your homework and considered somewhat of a dolt for not boning up on what was already known.

Each generation of scientists can begin where the last left off. Even though this is an introductory text, it contains information on the human brain, mental operations, development, social behavior, and therapies unknown to the most learned investigator of the 1940s. Isaac Newton said, "If I have seen farther than others, it is because I have stood on the shoulders of giants."

Corrections and Replication

In communicating results, scientists expose the "scaffolding" that supports their discoveries—what they were trying to do, how they did it, and how they interpreted the results. A scientific discovery has to be as repeatable as a recipe. Aserinsky and Kleitman first discovered in 1953 that people dream every night. They published their findings in a scientific journal, and their findings have been repeated, or **replicated,** in many labs around the world.

Because you read about advancements, psychology may seem a certain, even boring, step-by-step process with everything neatly in place. But for every "solution," for every successful experiment, there have been scores of blind alleys, mistakes, and failures. Science, although it strives to be objective and unbiased in *understanding,* is not cool and detached in *operation.* For example, there is great disagreement on such issues as the role of race in intelligence, whether intelligence itself can even be measured, how important the early years of childhood are to adult life, and whether or not sex differences are biologically determined.

Scientific Ideas and Tests

In everyday psychology ordinary guesses are vague, and we do not always have all the information, so confirmation is haphazard. Scientific psychology is more specific; ideas are defined and tested by three methods: observation, demonstration, and experimentation.

Of the three, observation is closest to real life; occurrences are recorded but not interfered with. Demonstrations are the most compelling: a phenomenon is presented to other people so it can be determined how they experience it. The experimental method is the most creative. The experimenter intervenes, arranges a situation, controls all the parts of an experience, and records the results. While observation is the most representative of life, experimentation is the most precise and repeatable.

Observation

Direct observation without interference is sometimes the only way to understand a phenomenon. If you want to discover how city life affects experience, you must observe people in crowded cities. The observation of people's reaction (or lack of reaction!) to the murder of Kitty Genovese is an example of recording an occurrence without interfering.

One important associated observation is that people walk faster in cities than in the country. The larger the city, the faster people walk (Freedman, Sears, & Carlsmith, 1984). The faster walk of city dwellers may mean they are in a hurry or that they notice less of what is going on around them, or both. This is one reason why people are less likely to stop and help in cities.

Formal observations in scientific psychology are made in three ways: (1) *case histories,* (2) *measurements and tests,* and (3) *questionnaires.*

Case Histories

A **case history** is an elaborate form of observation in which a particular subject is studied in depth. Here is an example.

Autism is a childhood disorder in which children seem lost in fantasy. They create and inhabit a world of their own and are usually inaccessible through the normal channels of communication — speech and gestures. For years researchers and therapists could find no way to reach them. In some rare cases, children have

The Pace of City Life
The observation that people in cities move at a faster pace helps psychologists understand such phenomena as bystander apathy.

found a way to break through the barrier and communicate with the outside world. Nadia does it in drawings (Figure 1-6). They give us a glimpse into the world of an autistic child and clues to the operation of an otherwise impenetrable mind. Nadia's drawings have been extremely helpful to psychologists in reaching and helping these children (Selfe, 1977).

Measurements

Measurement is as central to psychology as it is to all science; it enables psychologists to make **quantitative** as well **qualitative** distinctions. An example of a qualitative distinction would be X is an aggressive person, Y is not. A

FIGURE 1-6
Art and Autism: A Case History
Nadia's precocious artistic ability (this drawing was done when she was only 5½ years old) showed that she could perceive and conceptualize complex ideas and images her autism prevented her from formulating verbally.
(Selfe, 1977)

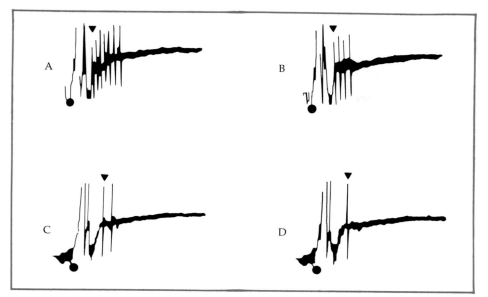

FIGURE 1-7
Measuring Habituation
The brain's ability to "tune out" background noises is called habituation. It can be measured by noting the decreasing firing rate, as shown here, of a neuron under constant stimulation. (Thompson, 1986)

quantitative distinction would tell us *how much more* aggressive X is than Y and in which situations.

Some measurements concern subtle physiological processes. When you walk into a room, you may hear a clock ticking or a fan whirring, but after a while you do not notice these noises; you seem to tune them out. Psychologists have measured the changing response of the brain to recurring external noises. They have found that it begins to ignore them and other continuously present stimuli. When we first hear the tick of a clock, the brain responds one way. If continued, the same noise a few minutes later causes a different reaction (Figure 1-7). The brain ceases to respond to the continuous presence of the ticking. This "tuning out" process is called *habituation* and it is the simplest form of learning (Thompson, 1986).

Tests

Tests can be used to measure psychological abilities: intelligence, verbal and spatial ability, and the ability to get along well with others. The SAT® you took to get into college was devised by educators and psychologists to measure your verbal and mathematical abilities to predict how well you would do at college. Each college has its own expectations of students and tries to select students who will fulfill those expectations. SAT scores are a kind of guide; they help in the selection process. The SAT score is not merely the number of items answered correctly. It is a comparison: your test results are compared to a standard set of scores of high school seniors.

Like the measurement of the brain's electrical activity, test scores indicate the presence of an ability or quality. Achievement tests measure academic progress. An aptitude test may help you select a career. Personality tests measure such qualities as sociability, helpfulness, and leadership. Personality tests might be useful to an employer who may be looking for a manager for a sensitive position

FIGURE 1-8
Demonstration of the
Rules of Perspective
Notice how the figure on
the right appears to be
larger than the one on the
left, even though they are
the same size.
(After Gombrich, 1969)

Look at the three people in Figure 1-8. Which one is the largest? Now take out a ruler and measure them. They are the same! These figures *appear* to be different sizes because the converging lines give the impression of depth. The drawing is composed of two main elements: the people and the lines. Without the lines, the people appear as they are, that is, the same size.

If you had merely read the boring textbook sentence, "The rules of perspective, which generally allow us to make accurate guesses about an object's relative size and distance, can also trick perceptions," you might not have been convinced or even interested. A *demonstration* of the fact is much more compelling.

and wants someone who can get along with people and who also shows qualities of leadership and initiative. Personality tests are also used by psychotherapists to measure the depth of their client's feelings and attitudes.

Questionnaires

If you want to know how people feel about something, the most direct way to find out is to ask them. A **questionnaire** is a formal way of asking specific questions. Charles Tart (1971) wanted to find out about the general experience of marijuana intoxication and asked people to report what happened to them after they had smoked marijuana. He then compared the reports to see which experiences were universally shared. These are the effects reported:

Low intoxication: people are less noisy at parties than when drunk—they hear more subtle changes in sounds.

Fair or moderate intoxication: people are noisier, experience new qualities to taste, enjoy eating a lot, experience insights about self, and their need for sex goes up.

Strong intoxication: people are easily distracted, are more here and now, feel emotions more strongly, experience new qualities to sexual orgasm, and forget the start of conversations. (Tart, 1971)

In a questionnaire, people report in a controlled manner. Researchers want to know only about the factors they are studying, so a questionnaire ensures that they will get the information they need. A survey or poll is a large-scale variety. The information provided on a questionnaire becomes the data that scientists analyze and interpret. The questions may only require yes or no answers (have you ever been in an automobile accident?), or people may be asked to rank their opinions or feelings (how do you think the president is doing?).

Experimental Method

Experiments allow the scientist to *intervene* in a situation and *control* its components. The essence of a good experiment is selection: what to include and what to exclude. In life things happen in unplanned combinations and all at once. We cannot, in our ordinary experience, always tell what caused someone to act in a certain manner nor can we see an "instant replay" to observe what happened more carefully.

Hypotheses

The first step in an experiment is the development of an **hypothesis,** a specific statement about what the experimenter thinks will happen if certain events take place. Then the experimenter begins to act like a playwright: sets the stage, outlines the plot, and assembles the characters. But unlike the playwright, the experimenter does not decide *what* will happen, but instead sets events in motion and records what unfolds.

Variables

Life is chaotic—things change or "vary" all the time. In an experiment most conditions are kept constant. Those few things that are allowed to vary in an experiment are thus called the *variables.* There are two kinds of variables: those the experimenter changes, called **independent variables**—for instance, an experimenter may vary the number of hours that an animal is deprived of food—and those the experimenter measures, called **dependent variables,** which in this case might be how much the animal eats.

The Sample: Experimental and Control Groups

People (and sometimes animals) are often part of the experiment; they are called **subjects.** Whatever subjects are used, they must be selected to *represent accurately* the entire population under study. The group of subjects is called the **sample.**

However, the appropriate number of subjects necessary for the study, called the **sample size,** varies depending on what is being studied. The smaller the differences from individual to individual on the specific measure, the smaller the sample size has to be. For example, to study the effect of light on pupil dilation, a few subjects, perhaps fewer than ten, are enough. This is because the purely physical aspects of vision are fundamentally the same for all human beings. Although eyes are similar, opinions are not. To determine something such as the most popular television shows or voter preferences in polls taken before a national election, a sample of about 1,200 people is used. Here individuality, personal preference, prejudices, background, and geography play important roles. The sample has to be large enough to average out individual differences.

The sample is usually divided into two groups: the **experimental group** and the **control group** (Figure 1-9). The experimental group is the one that is intervened with, the one that is studied to judge the effect of those elements that are changed and manipulated. The control group is similar to the experimental group in every respect *except* the independent variable. A control group is necessary because we have to know what would have happened had the experimenter *not* intervened. When the experiment is over, the outcomes from the two groups are compared.

Suppose you want to know if a certain psychotherapy is effective. The findings are that two years after treatment, 75 percent of the people who had undergone psychotherapy are improved. These results sound great. But could you then

136, 403

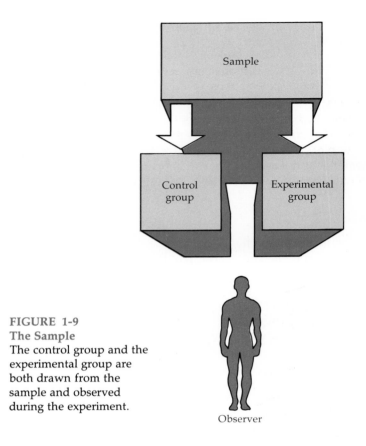

FIGURE 1-9
The Sample
The control group and the experimental group are both drawn from the sample and observed during the experiment.

Observer

report in a scientific journal that this psychotherapy is effective? Not yet, because (and here is the big difference between everyday life and science) *you do not know what would have happened to these people if they had not received psychotherapeutic treatment,* and in life you never do.

In this case, a control group would have to be included—a similar group of people who want to have psychotherapy, but for some reason are unable to obtain it. Suppose that after the same two years, *95 percent* of the people in this control group are improved. That figure would certainly change your opinion on the benefits of psychotherapy! It would mean that psychotherapy is *less* effective than doing nothing! Alternatively, you might find that only 35 percent of the control group improved; then you would conclude that psychotherapy is effective, and you would have a good idea just how effective. Please note that in these two examples the *results* of the psychotherapy you are studying (that is, 75 percent improvement) are the same, but the scientific judgment of its effectiveness depends on what would have happened if there had been no therapy.

In experiments the control group represents "what would have happened anyway." The control group is one more way to ensure sound and measured judgments; it is the standard for scientific comparison.

Thinking Like an Experimental Psychologist

Let's look at the development of one study that was comprised of several experiments. Recall that the experimenter's job is to select a few variables to alter and observe and that the procedures for doing an experiment derive from normal common sense.

Suppose you wanted to find out which factors make one person sexually attracted to another? The complete answer is quite complex: it includes the background of the person, expectations, whether the person is involved with someone else, and so on. However, to think like an experimental psychologist, you might try to isolate one part of the puzzle. One major factor that you may not have considered is the circumstances of a meeting. In films or novels it is the daring hero, the one who takes chances, who always gets the girl. More people fall in love and get married during disasters and wartime than during times of quiescence. People go to horror movies, drive like maniacs, and ride on roller coasters on dates. These situations have in common the element of danger, and danger is arousing (Figure 1-10). Could a dangerous *location* contribute to sexual arousal?

Experiment I.   What happens when a man and a woman are put in exciting circumstances? The actual experiment used a wobbly bridge as the setting (Dutton & Aron, 1974). A woman interviewed two groups of men, each on a different bridge in Vancouver, British Columbia. One bridge was safe, the other was very precarious. The first was a solid wood structure only 10 feet above a stream; this was the "control bridge." The other was the Capilano Suspension Bridge, which is 450 feet long, 5 feet wide, and sways and wobbles over a 230-foot drop to rapids and rocks below. This was the "experimental bridge."

The experimenters compared meeting a person of the opposite sex in both dangerous and safe circumstances. Men crossing both the experimental and control bridges were met by an attractive woman interviewer. She was asked to tell each man that she was researching "the effects of scenic attraction on creative expression." Then, while still on the bridge, she asked each man to write a brief story based on a picture she showed him of a young woman covering her face with one hand while reaching out with the other.

FIGURE 1-10
Does Danger Contribute to Sexual Arousal?
Psychological experiments have been conducted to determine whether or not dangerous situations play a role in sexual arousal.

When he finished, she gave the man her name and number and invited him to call her if he wanted more information about the experiment. Experimenters hypothesized that if there were fewer calls from the men who crossed the solid control bridge than from those who crossed the wobbly experimental bridge, then arousing circumstances are a factor in sexual attraction. The stories written by the men were also scored for sexual imagery.

The *independent variables* were the two bridges. The *dependent variables* were the number of phone calls and the men's scores for sexual imagery. Since the hypothesis was that men on the experimental bridge would be more sexually aroused than men on the control bridge, they should (1) telephone the assistant more often than the "controls" and (2) write stories with more sexual imagery.

The results were that 12.5 percent of the men who were on the secure bridge called the woman for more information, but *50 percent* of the men who were on the wobbly bridge called. Also, those who met the woman on the wobbly bridge wrote stories with far more sexual imagery than those on the secure bridge.

Therefore we *could* conclude that these results support the hypothesis that dangerous circumstances can lead to arousal and to increased sexual attraction. However, psychologists are rarely convinced by one study. To think like an experimental psychologist means that you must consider whether the results could have come about in another way. In most studies, there are other possible interpretations of the findings. For example, consider another possible interpretation: it could be that the men who *chose* to cross the wobbly bridge were more daring than the ones who chose to cross the secure control bridge. If so, these men might also be more daring about calling a strange woman for a date than were the possibly more timid control bridge travelers, and they might also be more sexually daring. Therefore, the results might be due to existing differences in the *men* who crossed the bridges, not the *effect* of crossing a dangerous bridge. So, another experiment is necessary.

Experiment II.   The second experiment was designed to rule out any differences in the two groups of men. This time the sample was composed entirely of men who crossed the wobbly bridge, but they were divided into "aroused" and "nonaroused" groups. The aroused group was interviewed as before — just as they crossed the bridge. The nonaroused group was interviewed at least 10 minutes later, when the exciting effects of the bridge had worn off.

The same experiment was done. If the original results were due to *differences* in the men who crossed the bridge, we would expect both groups in this second experiment to be *equally* attracted to the woman. If the original results were due to the arousal of crossing the bridge, then we should expect that the group interviewed *on* the bridge would be *more* attracted to the woman. The results showed the latter to be the case, and this provides further evidence for the idea that general arousal can lead to sexual arousal.

This makes the conclusion clearer. But, again, an experimental psychologist would then wonder whether this result applies to a limited situation or whether it is more general. Is this finding true only under certain conditions (a "damsel in distress" on a wobbly bridge)? Is it just a curiosity or is the relationship between excitement and attraction more basic?

Experiment III.   A third experiment was run, this time in the laboratory. A man sat in a room and was told that he was participating in a study to "measure the effect of pain on learning." A woman entered and was introduced as the other subject in the experiment. Actually she was in cahoots with the experimenters.

The pair were told that if they gave an incorrect answer on their test, they would receive an electric shock. The experimenter would assign one of them to receive a mild shock and the other a severe shock. They were told that the experimenter would be measuring which shock level was the more effective learning tool. Now, thinking like a psychologist, how would you make sure that brave men might choose the severe shock and be likely to call the woman, too?

Before the tests and shocks were to begin, each subject was sent to a different room and asked to fill out a questionnaire "on your present feelings and reactions, since they often influence performance on the learning task." *This was the critical part of the experiment.* There were actually no tests or shocks. The first part of the questionnaire measured anxiety. As you might expect, the subjects who expected to receive a strong shock reported much more anxiety than those who anticipated a weak shock. The second part of the questionnaire related directly to arousal and sexual attraction. The men who expected severe shocks and were anxious about them also expressed more attraction for the woman than the calmer men expecting a mild shock.

This series of experiments contributes a little more evidence to the hypothesis that a man who meets a woman in a dangerous or anxiety-producing circumstance is *more likely* to interpret the feeling of arousal as attraction to the other person. In this experiment we go from an everyday observation — that exciting people and situations are attractive — to a slightly more comprehensive understanding of the general experience. We know a *little* more about the whys of sexual attraction because of our analysis of one of its components and, I hope, a little more about how to think like a psychologist. Of course, this experiment would need to be replicated many times and others like it done before we could conclude that arousal of any kind has an effect on sexual attraction. Then, of course, there would be many other new questions. Some of these will be treated later in this book.

Some Problems of Experiments: Further Help in Learning to Think Like a Psychologist

Even with all the rules of doing an experiment, there is the possibility that the experimenter may subtly and unconsciously influence or *bias* the results. Because experimenters so often find what they are looking for, the psychologist Robert Rosenthal thought that some subtle and unconscious influence was occurring. He ran a famous experiment that clearly demonstrated the presence of this so-called **experimenter bias.** A group of students were told to run rats through a maze. Half were told that their rats were bred to be especially smart, called (in the trade) *maze bright,* and the other group were told that their rats were *maze dull.* In fact, there was no difference: the rats were selected at random and both groups were equal in ability. The independent variable was the expectation of the students. That expectation turned out to be an important difference: the "maze bright" rats learned the maze faster than their supposedly "dull" counterparts (Rosenthal, 1986).

There are two methods psychologists use to minimize the problem of experimenter bias.

1. **Replication.** Every experiment must be able to be replicated (reproduced) in another laboratory. The new investigator may have a different bias — perhaps even the desire to disprove the finding.

2. **Double-blind procedure.** The subject of an experiment is usually kept in the dark about the object of an experiment. A double-blind procedure keeps the experimenter in the dark, or "blind," as well—unaware of which is the experimental group and which is the control group until after the experiment is over and the results have been tabulated.

Suppose you invent a new sleeping pill called "Snoozie" and you want to test its effect. If the drug works and is a commercial success, you stand to make a lot of money. Suppose further that you give one group Snoozie and another group a sugar pill. Then you interview both groups to determine the drug's effects. If the people who took the pill knew that the pill was supposed to make them drowsy, they might report feeling that way. Subjects in experiments generally try to be cooperative, and the expectation of the feeling might lead to the feeling itself.

Similarly, if *you know* who has taken Snoozie and who has taken the sugar pill, you might influence the results by your questions during the interview: "Don't you feel slightly sleepy? Not even a teensy-weensy bit?" But if you do not know who took which pill, you cannot influence the results with your questions. In the Dutton and Aron wobbly bridge experiment, the attractive female *confederate* (the one who asked the questions) was kept in the dark about the real purpose of the experiment.

WHAT DOES IT MEAN? STATISTICS

See Appendix, "Statistics: Making Sense of Fallible Data."

Psychologists use these methods—demonstration, observation, and experiment—to gather data. Once the evidence is in hand, the next steps are to *evaluate* and *interpret* it. **Statistics** is the formal set of rules for evaluation of evidence. It enables scientific judgments to be more precise and quantitative than ordinary judgments. If a study shows a difference in results between groups, as we saw in the wobbly bridge experiment, we need to know if it is a **significant difference.**

Suppose you are interested in improving the mathematical skills of third graders. You have two gadgets designed to encourage the learning process, and you want to see which works better. One is a computer that flashes and wiggles when the child gives a correct answer. The other is a set of mathematical instruments that make noise and project the problems on the ceiling.

You assemble two groups of children, and you give the computer to one group, the mechanical toy to the other. You find that both groups show an average of 15 percent improvement in learning over their previous work (and over a third control group, which was given no toy to play with). Would you say that both methods are equally effective? At first glance, it seems so, but a statistical analysis shows that they are not.

Take a closer look at the evidence provided below. In the first group, all the children using the computer made some improvement. The computer's effect on

---

Group 1 (computer) percent improvement for each of the children
10, 20, 15, 10, 25, 15, 15, 10, 20, 10

Group 2 (mechanical)
50, −10, −20, 85, 55, −30, 60, −15, −25, 0

INDIVIDUAL AND GROUP DIFFERENCES

Most scientific conclusions are not about individual differences, but about average group differences. These differences, while important, need to be understood. They mean that *on the average* one group scored higher, was more attracted, made more mistakes, or did something differently than the average of another group. This sounds fine, but sometimes average differences have a way of becoming thought of as true of all of those in the group.

Let's use a nonpsychological example to explore this. Do males run faster than females? Yes, on average. All world records for running at any distance are held by males. The average marathon winner of the male race finishes 20 minutes ahead of the female winner. The same is true of many different distances.

Does this mean that any given female is slower than any given male? Of course not! Look at it from the point of view of a fast female runner, say the female winner of the Boston Marathon. She runs faster than 99+ percent of all men! When we discuss group differences, we refer to the average of a large range of observations. Here it is male and female running, but it could be height, intelligence scores on a test, compliance to a directive, and so on.

So the differences scientific psychologists report are averages, and there is much room for maneuvering. And remember that most psychological differences are much less than differences in running speed.

learning, as the statistical test showed, is constant and meaningful. But in the second group, four of the ten children were helped by the mechanical toy, but six of the ten showed no improvement or worsened. Both gadgets were *not* equally effective as learning tools, even though the *average* difference is the same. A good psychologist would continue to work, however, to find out *why* the mechanical instrument toy provided such different results for different children.

Mean and Median

There are two measures scientists use to analyze data: the mean and the median. The **mean** is the arithmetic average. **Median** comes from the Latin word for middle, and that is what the median is. If you rank the results in numerical order, the figure in the middle of the lists is the median. It usually differs from the mean, as shown in the following example.

In the table below, which is the more well-to-do street, Avenue A or Avenue B? The average, or mean, income is the same for both streets, $22,500. But 10 of the 11 families in Avenue B have higher incomes than their corresponding families in Avenue A. Therefore the more accurate measure is the median. For Avenue A, the

Avenue A (in thousands of dollars)
    10, 10, 15, 15, 15, 17.5, 20, 20, 25, 25, 75

Avenue B
    15, 15, 20, 20, 20, 22.5, 24, 25, 27, 29, 30

median is $17,500, but for B it is $22,500. That figure better reflects the consistent difference in income for the residents of the two streets. The median is used when an extreme value on one end or the other of the range might unduly influence the average, as when a high scorer on a test might affect the average or, as in this case, one family's income ($75,000) might elevate the average of the incomes of the families on Avenue A.

Correlation

Is there any *relationship* between a person's high school SAT score and college grades? Between years of drinking and decline of intelligence? Between a father's intelligence and his son's? We cannot do experiments to find out these things, but we can measure the statistical relationships that already exist between them. When the relationship of two things is important to measure, psychologists compute a statistic called a **correlation** (the word comes from "co," which means *with*, and "relation").

Correlation is an important tool, for there are many studies that do not allow experimentation. Suppose you want to determine how much brain damage affects speech. Obviously, you could not produce brain damage in your subjects for this purpose, but you could study people with brain damage to determine the relationship of the amount of damage to speech impairment.

The Natural Experiment

Sometimes things happen in life that cannot be duplicated but that can provide important evidence, and the correlation method can be used to interpret the results. To find out which is the more important factor in human intelligence —

FIGURE 1-11
Experiments and Natural Experiments
This flow chart shows that the principal difference between the two types of experiments is that in a natural experiment — such as the one conducted by Scarr and associates — the creation of the independent variable involves assessment of specified characteristics like occupations, IQs, and interests.

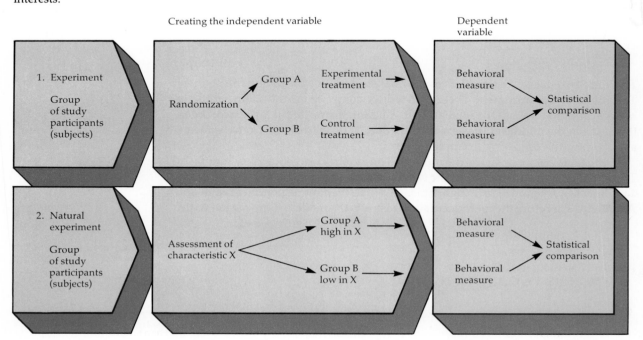

heredity or the environment in which a person grows up—the most obvious thing to do would be to study a pair of identical twins (who are as close genetically as two human beings can possibly be). Separate them at birth and let one child grow up in an intellectually enriched environment and the other in a similarly deprived one; then observe what happens. This is unthinkable—no one would manipulate people's lives for the sake of psychological knowledge; but, again, a psychologist might use correlation to study circumstances where this has actually occurred.

In one study, Sandra Scarr and associates studied groups of adopted children for whom the occupations, IQs, and interests of the natural parents were known and who were raised by couples with children of their own. Scarr and her team then compared the IQs and interests of the adopted children with the natural children raised in the same family, using correlations (see Figure 1-11). They found startling evidence that *IQ and even interests seem to be inherited* (Scarr & Carter-Saltzman, 1983).

See Chapter 11, section on Testing Intelligence.

Another example of the use of correlation is shown in Figure 1-12. Is there a relationship between high school and college grades? First, we plot one person's high school grades on one axis of a graph and his or her college grades on the other. If the college grades are relatively low and the high school grades high, the graph will look approximately like Figure 1-12A. If the high school grades are low and the college grades high, it will look something like B. If both are high, then like C; if both are low, then D. Then we plot the grades of a very large sample of students on the graph (E).

If everyone who did well in high school got high grades in college and everyone who did poorly in high school got low grades in college, that would be a perfect correlation. The relationships displayed in Figures 1-12A–D are high correlations, but not perfect ones. A perfect correlation would indicate a perfect relationship: whenever X happens, Y happens; the more X, the more Y. On the

FIGURE 1-12
Correlation
Plotting data on scatter diagrams is one way to reveal possible correlations between sets of data.

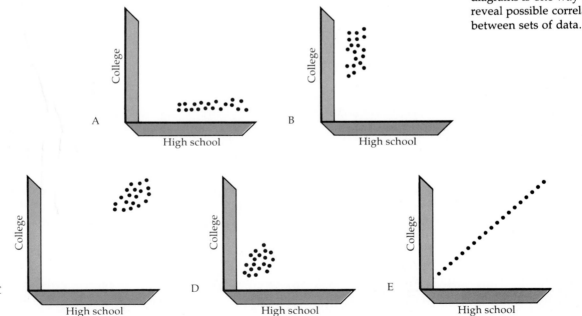

graph a perfect correlation would look like Figure 1-12E. This 100 percent relationship is written in statistics as a correlation of 1.0, either positive or negative. Such a perfect correlation is almost never found.

"No correlation" means there is no relation between X and Y—for example, there is no correlation between grades in high school and eye color. This lack of relationship is written as 0.0. Most correlations fall somewhere between 0.0 and 1.0. There has to be a certain degree of relationship, usually at least 0.2, to be considered statistically significant. The relationship may be positive or negative. A *positive correlation* means the more X happens, the more Y happens. A *negative correlation* means the more X happens, the *less* Y happens (for example, the more food you eat, the less weight you lose). A negative correlation is distinguished from a positive correlation by a minus sign in front of the figure, such as -0.4. A positive correlation would be written simply 0.4.

A CONCLUDING NOTE

Considering all that we have covered, we can now begin a definition of psychology. It is the science of human experience, and it involves specific perspectives, methods of study, and statistical rules of interpretation.

The *perspectives* that psychology encompasses include studies of our biological inheritance, of the mind, of our behavior and the social environment, and of the full range of disorders (the clinical perspective) and great achievements (the humanistic perspective).

Psychologists use numerous methods to go beyond ordinary experience. These include systematic observation, such as measurements and tests; demonstrations, such as illusions; and experiments, such as the study at the wobbly bridge.

HOW THIS BOOK IS ORGANIZED

Psychology tells a story, and that story follows the course of our lives—where we come from, how each person grows from an infant to an adult, how people learn, think, and remember, what consciousness is like, how we argue with and love other people, how groups affect us, how we develop as we get older, and much more. This book follows that story, which is our story.

Think of it this way: in the beginning ("center") is biology (inner circle of Figure 1-13), followed by the normal processes of development from which develops the mind (second circle). Then comes our life as individuals and with other individuals: how we communicate, how we express our feelings, how we get into trouble (third circle). Finally, there is the world of society and our lives as adults. Each stage is more complex and filled with more challenges than the previous one.

The first part of this book is called The Biological World, and it begins where human beings first developed, in East Africa about four million years ago (Chapter 2). It then continues with the development of a person, from birth to adolescence (Chapter 3). This part ends with the study of the most complex thing in the universe, the human brain, and how the senses act to inform the brain (Chapter 4).

The second part is called The Mental World. It begins with perception and how we organize the world (Chapters 5 and 6), and it continues with the study of how our consciousness changes and how we can change consciousness (Chapter 7). This part continues with the basic processes of learning to associate things in the

world with things in the mind (Chapter 8), and then goes on to the mystery of how we remember (Chapter 9). It ends with a chapter on thinking, how we create and make mistakes (Chapter 10), and one on intelligence — can we assess intelligence and can we increase it (Chapter 11).

The third part is called The World of the Individual, and it begins with our feelings and our relationships with other people. The first chapters in this part are on what "moves" us: our emotions (Chapter 12) and our motives (Chapter 13) — *why* we do what we do. Then we deal with a most complex subject: what one's personality is "really" like (Chapter 14). If you have ever tried to understand another person (let alone yourself), you will not be surprised to find that the answer is puzzling. The final two chapters of this part deal with our problems. The first deals with the abnormal, with such disorders as when sadness becomes debilitating depression and when withdrawal becomes catatonia (Chapter 15). The last chapter covers the psychotherapies — the attempts to relieve these difficulties (Chapter 16).

The final part, called The Social World of the Adult, is even more complex: it deals with our life in current society. The first chapter deals with the effect other people have on us, in small groups, in crowds, and in cities (Chapter 17). The next chapter gives a modern view of living in a high-tech society (Chapter 18). The final chapter deals with the process of growing up that lies ahead: job, marriage, family, aging, and, finally, death (Chapter 19).

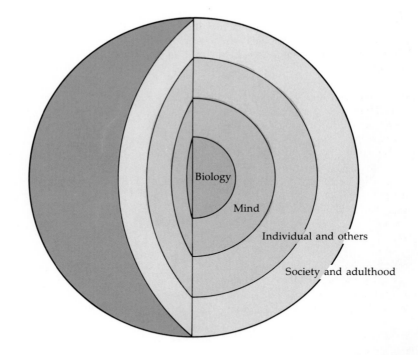

FIGURE 1-13
The Organization of This Book and of Human Experience
Our study of psychology —like the course of our individual lives—starts with the biological world before moving on to the mental world, the world of the individual, and the social world of the adult. Each stage augments and amplifies the others.

Biology

Mind

Individual and others

Society and adulthood

So, our story actually begins *before* our birth and ends after our death. In it we can obtain a few glimpses of why we are the way we are and what we can become. There are a few myths dispelled; blacks and whites do not differ as much as many think. Some obvious facts are analyzed closely: why we "naturally" will assist our own family at the expense of others, why we have great difficulty losing weight, why emotions are universal. Some surprising findings show the importance of psychological factors in health: we know that cigarette smoking is dangerous to our health, but we do not realize that the effect on the heart of someone who has just been divorced is equal to smoking two packs a day; and just watching a comedian has immediate effects on your immune system. It is a long story, our story, and I hope you find something illuminating, here and there, in these chapters.

1. Psychology is the complete science of human experience. It involves the study of the brain and nervous system, our mental life, behavior (both alone and in society), stresses, and disorders. It deals with the nature of human experience from many different viewpoints — cognitive, behavioral, social, environmental, clinical, and humanistic.

2. Behaviorists assume that people do what they do because of conditions in the environment. They reason that if the conditions change, behavior can also change. Thus, behaviorists often modify conditions in experiments and observe variations in the behavior that follows. All psychology depends on behaviorism, and it has guided psychologists to important discoveries about learning and remembering.

3. The biological approach looks for the keys to human behavior in the nature of the nervous system. Evidence comes from many sources: injuries to the brain, surgery, drugs, and studies of evolution and development. The biological foundations of experience are a critical part of psychology, one that has developed greatly in the past 20 years.

4. The main object of study in *cognitive psychology* is the mind. One discovery of modern psychology is that we do not perceive the world as it really is. Cognitive psychologists attempt to observe, as directly as possible, the operations of the mind, the way we perceive and remember, and the way the outside world is represented in the mind.

5. Social psychology studies the influences on behavior of other people, for example, how we choose partners and how we act at work or in the courtroom. It studies how attitudes develop and change and the conditions under which people will help or not help others, as in the case of Kitty Genovese, and the Good Samaritan experiment.

6. The clinical approach observes people who are unable to perform certain functions, which can help the understanding of how that function usually operates. Aphasia and multiple personality are two examples. Psychologists are also beginning to study how mental events affect the body. For instance, one study showed a measurable depression of immune function following severe psychological stress resulting from a real-life tragedy.

7. An emphasis on the important positive aspects of human experience is called *humanistic.* Abraham Maslow, its founder and leading theorist, believed that human beings have an inherent inclination toward growth and development. Maslow presumed that we all have within us genuine potentials, and given the opportunity, we strive to make those potentials actual — a process called *self-actualization.* He studied people who seemed to develop their potential to its fullest, such as Einstein and Gandhi.

8. The difference between scientific psychology and everyday psychology is the manner in which it is approached. Scientific psychology goes beyond individual experience and is more comprehensive; judgments are objective. Science differs from ordinary inquiry in that it is a *systematic formal* process of gathering information with specific rules for testing ideas and interpreting the results.

9. Scientific knowledge is *cumulative,* and it involves specific procedures for *correction* and *replication.* The scientific method involves observation and uses such techniques as case histories, measurements, tests, questionnaires, demonstrations, and experiments.

SUMMARY

10. Experiments involve the development of a *hypothesis,* manipulation of independent variables, and measurement of dependent variables. An important part of an experiment is to obtain a *sample* of the population under study. This sample is usually divided into an *experimental* and a *control* group.

11. Statistics enable psychologists to go beyond personal experience by giving them a way to *evaluate* and *interpret* the information gained. An important statistical test is whether a difference that is measured is *significant:* how unlikely it was that the observed difference would have occurred by chance.

12. *Correlation* is an important statistical procedure that measures the relationship between two factors. Zero correlation means that there is *no* relationship between two factors. A positive correlation means that an increase in one factor is associated with an increase in the other. For example, high SAT scores are positively correlated with high college grades. A negative correlation means an increase in one factor is associated with a decrease in the other.

13. Psychology, like this book, can be roughly divided into four parts, each one concerning a different perspective on the human condition. The first part is the biological world; the second, the mental world; the third, the world of the individual; and the fourth, the social world of the adult.

TERMS AND CONCEPTS

arousal
autism
average
behaviorism
biological approach
case history
catharsis
clinical approach
cognitive psychology
comparison processes
consciousness
control group
correlation
dependent variable
Descartes
double-blind procedure
empiricism
experimental group
experimenter bias
humanistic approach
hypothesis
independent variable
introspection

James
Locke
mean
measurements
median
multiple personality
nativism
natural selection
negative correlation
neurosurgeon
psychoimmunology
qualitative
quantitative
questionnaire
replication
sample
self-actualization
significant difference
social environmental perspective
statistics
subjects
tests
Wundt

Hilgard, E. R. (1986). *Psychology in America: A historical survey.* San Diego: Harcourt Brace Jovanovich.

> The monumental survey of the origins and development of psychology by one of its foremost and longest lived practitioners. Contains much first-hand material.

Here are five readable and important books which introduce some of the diversity of psychology.

Bruner, J. S. (1986). *Actual minds, possible worlds.* Boston: Harvard University Press.

> An eminent cognitive psychologist's attempt to understand how the mind reflects (or doesn't reflect) the world outside. Not easy to read, but worth trying for a look at how one psychologist thinks about problems.

Cialdini, R. (1984). *Influence.* Chicago: Scott, Foresman.

> The most readable account of the social psychological perspective. Excellent introduction.

Erdelyi, M. H. (1985). *Psychoanalysis: Freud's cognitive psychology.* New York: Freeman.

> An attempt to give Freud's ideas a contemporary treatment, written in fairly plain language.

Gardner, H. (1985). *The mind's new science.* New York: Basic Books.

> How cognitive psychology came into being.

Shah, I. (1982). *Seeker after truth.* San Francisco: Harper & Row.

> A modern account, in story and tale, of a different perspective on psychology.

At the beginning each of us is a cell so small that it is invisible to the naked eye.

From this cell, formed by the joining of mother and father, comes an organism controlled by the most complex organ in the biological world — the human brain. A brain so complex that no computer, no matter how large, could ever mimic its functions.

If that cell has an extravagant future, it also has an extravagant past. It contains the genetic code developed over millions of years. That cell grows in sequence: embryo to fetus, infant to toddler, child to adolescent.

Many human behaviors are rooted in the mold of the nervous system, which has evolved to adapt to the world.

This part contains the beginnings of the common human story: where we come from, what is in us at birth, how we grow, and what the structures are that underlie knowledge.

Part I

The Biological World

Chapter 2

Where We Come From: Evolution and Genetics

There is a footprint in Africa that was impressed into the sand more than three and a half million years ago (Figure 2-1). It preserves an occasion when our ancestors began to diverge from the great apes. The footprint is of a creature who could stand on two legs. Those pioneering steps taken by that creature made present human beings possible.

The adjustment from walking on four limbs to two encouraged our predecessor's reliance on vision. The weight of the body that was previously supported by the front limbs then shifted to the legs and pelvis, so that the front limbs were freed for other responsibilities, such as toolmaking and tool carrying. The pelvis thickened to haul around the weight of the upper body; this refashioned childbirth, making human beings a species born "immature." This evolution then set off an explosion of growth in the brain as it swiftly became larger, and ultimately words were spoken.

Modern human beings (the species *Homo sapiens*) are the result of these changes and we thus have certain distinct physical features. We stand up on two legs and walk erect. We are the most sexual primate; although other animals typically mate a few times a year when they are in heat, human beings have intercourse repeatedly at any time of the year. We have the largest brain of any animal in relation to body size and have hands capable of fine movements.

These unique physical features are *not* the only things that make us such an extraordinary animal. The lion has its mane, the penguin its feathers, the deer its antlers. But most animals are able to survive only in their own original habitat. A lion abruptly transported to New York would not survive the winter; a penguin could not survive a New York summer. However, human beings can and do live successfully in every environment in the world, in the bleak heights of the Himalayas, in the deserts of Africa, in the frozen north of Alaska, and in crowded cities. *We are an animal that lives far outside our original habitat* and that makes drastic changes in the environment to suit itself. Think of the differences between your life, with television and air travel, and the life of a Stone Age tribesman.

How did we become such a novel animal? First, we will look at the long sweep of human history, a history of *millions* of years; then we will look at the scientific theory of how our ancestors changed over time, a process known as *evolution;* and then we will discuss the distinctive features of the human organism and human life, and the dilemmas of living in a world unlike that of our ancestors 25,000 years ago. Finally, this chapter ends with a description of the instruments of inheritance, how physical characteristics are conveyed from one generation to the next.

In all this sweep of history, taking millions of years, one occasion is noteworthy—that first time our human ancestors stood upright and began to

FIGURE 2-1
The footprint of one of our prehuman ancestors, left in the sands of Africa more than three and a half million years ago and discovered by Mary Leakey.

move away from the trees into a new world, one filled with new circumstances and challenges. In a way, we are still doing that. Sometimes we meet new challenges well, other times not. We respond strongly to sudden upsets in our lives, such as a terrorist attack, but not to steadily increasing dangers, like those from chemical pollution — because of the way we evolved. The evolutionary understanding of human thought makes it possible to know in what ways we are matched, and in what ways we are mismatched to the world in which we live (Barash, 1986; Ehrlich & Ornstein, in press).

Principles and Issues in Human Origins

Most chapters in this book begin with a discussion of major issues and principles of psychology. These issues and principles are important because they provide a general understanding of many of the specialized topics presented here in the book.

Nature–Nurture

Are human beings "naturally" violent? Are women more fluent than men? Do men want sex more than women do? Are white people more intelligent than black? These questions reflect one of the oldest controversies in the study of psychology. This argument centers around how much a person is determined by "nature" and how much by "nurture."

The "pure" **nature** view holds that human beings are dominated by *innate* characteristics such as instinct. Instincts are inborn, fixed patterns of behavior, such as the salmon's inevitable return to the river of its birth. Love or attachment of a mother for her child is thought by many to be a human instinct. Because human behavior is more complex than that of other animals, advocates of the nature view presume the existence of hundreds of instincts to account for behavior. The "pure" **nurture** view asserts that people are almost totally the result of their environment and that it is only life circumstances that make one person a thief and another a respected banker (Skinner, 1972; Watson, 1925).

Both these views are, of course, too extreme. Neither is sufficient to explain the full range of human behavior. Human beings have certain universal patterns of behavior in common, such as their emotions, the use of language, and the ability to make tools. At the same time, an individual's specific experience affects the

FIGURE 2A
Upright Posture and Locomotion: A Human Inheritance
Apes can walk upright better than monkeys, but the human ability to stand and travel efficiently on two legs is far greater, having resulted from numerous anatomical adaptations over hundreds of generations.
(After Leakey & Lewin, 1977)

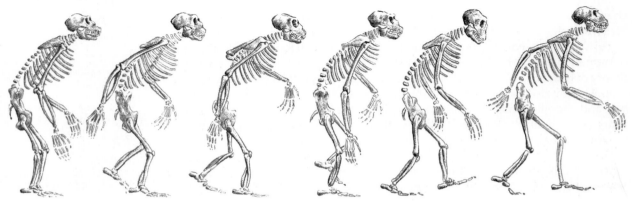

way in which these universal patterns are expressed in one's own life. The interplay goes like this: all normal human beings are capable of learning language (nature), but the *particular* language they learn depends on their specific experiences (nurture). Most behavior is the *product of both factors,* as the area of a rectangle is determined by the product of its length *and* width. Some behaviors may be more determined by "nature" and some by "nurture," but all are shaped by differing combinations of both.

The nature versus nurture argument has taken on a new form. While most psychologists accept some biological background to different behaviors, there is great controversy now over *just how much behavior is specified in the genes* and how far conscious influence pulls us away from our heritage.

The Principle of Adaptation

The first order of business in life is to survive. To endure, an individual must be able to function in its environment. **Adaptation** is the routine whereby an organism changes—adapts—to fit better into its environment. A trait such as color vision or speech has **adaptive value** if it assists an organism to function in its environment. Human adaptation is very intricate; it takes many unlikely forms because a human being is a very complicated animal and is always adjusting to meet new circumstances.

Different forms of human adaptations involve different mechanisms. Enter a darkened theater and your eyes will gradually adapt to the change in illumination. This is a form of **sensory adaptation** called dark adaptation. Put on a new set of glasses and the world seems bent at first, but then you adjust. This is a form of **perceptual adaptation.** Many kinds of adaptations will be treated in later chapters in the book, such as adapting to different temperatures and adapting to a high-tech world, as well as the failure to adapt, which results in stress.

This chapter concerns how our human ancestors, through a long series of *physical* changes called **evolution,** developed unique characteristics like walking on two legs and talking, which enabled them to adapt to their environment.

See Chapter 5, section on Sensory Adaptation and Comparison, and Chapter 6, section on Adapting to the Environment.

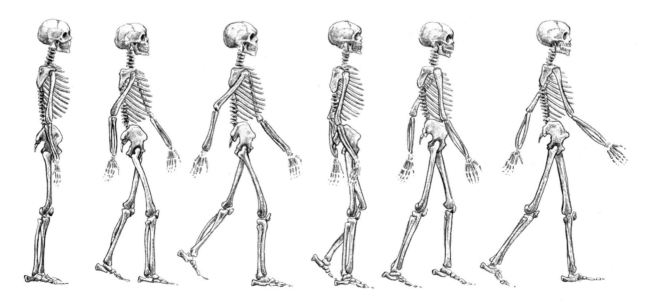

Feedback and Systems

It is necessary in science, including psychology (and certainly in textbook writing), to present individual topics separately and in a sequence. There would be no way to make sense of all the different findings in psychology without describing unlike topics in different chapters. But events in the world are not separate from one another and not isolated. How do different events affect one another?

Systems

Each person is part of many systems at once: biological, educational, social, legal, cultural, political, ecological, and many others. A **system** is any group of things that *function together for a common purpose* (Miller, 1978)—it is an important and very general concept.

Systems can be as widely dispersed and complex, as is the "educational system" of the United States, which includes the activity of individual schools, colleges, teachers, government agencies, and even textbook writers. A system can exist within a single organism, such as the human visual system in which eyes, the optic nerve, and the brain function together for the common purpose of sight.

Feedback

Feedback connects information about separate operations together into a system to attain its goals. There is a cycle of feedback: information from one part of the system (A) affects other parts of the system (B), which affect the initial part (A). This recurrent action is known as a **feedback loop** (Figure 2-2). Negative feedback keeps a system in a predetermined condition. Positive feedback allows it to change, sometimes in unexpected directions.

Negative Feedback. Important to any living organism is the upkeep of the body's internal state, the need to eat, drink, and maintain a certain body temperature to survive. The brain monitors blood temperature in much the same way as a thermostat monitors heat (Figure 2-3). The brain monitors blood sugar levels in a similar way. A low blood sugar level triggers activity aimed at restoring the proper level: hunger pangs occur and these "tell" the person to look for food.

Homeostasis, which is a condition of steady-state or equilibrium, operates through a **negative feedback** loop. "Negative" refers to the way in which the

FIGURE 2-2
Basic Feedback Loop
Information from one component of the system (A) affects some other part (B), which in response feeds back information that affects the part (A) that began the interaction.

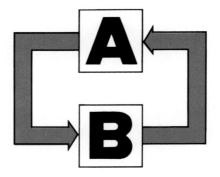

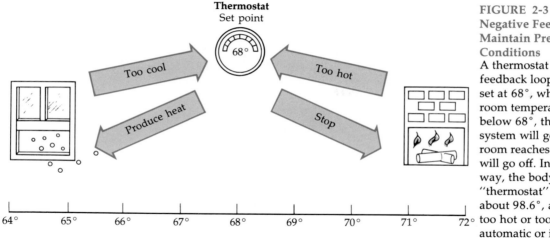

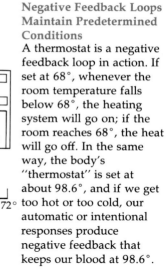

FIGURE 2-3
Negative Feedback Loops Maintain Predetermined Conditions
A thermostat is a negative feedback loop in action. If set at 68°, whenever the room temperature falls below 68°, the heating system will go on; if the room reaches 68°, the heat will go off. In the same way, the body's "thermostat" is set at about 98.6°, and if we get too hot or too cold, our automatic or intentional responses produce negative feedback that keeps our blood at 98.6°.

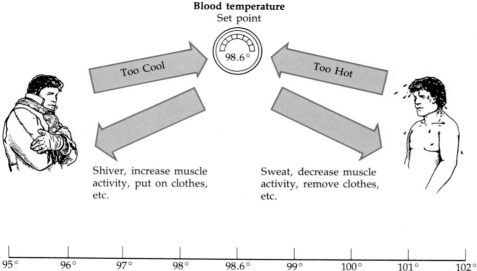

information is "fed back" into the system. In the case of hunger, the information triggers changes in the *opposite* (−) direction: *low* blood sugar signals us to *increase* our food intake, while high blood sugar signals the reverse reaction.

Positive Feedback. Instead of keeping things constant, a positive feedback loop is a process by which things may change significantly: changes in one element of the system first transform other parts of the system, which then change the first element and the routine repeats again and again.

While negative feedback keeps a system at a steady-state, **positive feedback** *is the mechanism of adaptation and change.* In Figure 2-4, one response changes the situation so that the other person is now willing to give a friendly response. This makes it possible for the original person to be even more friendly in return. The

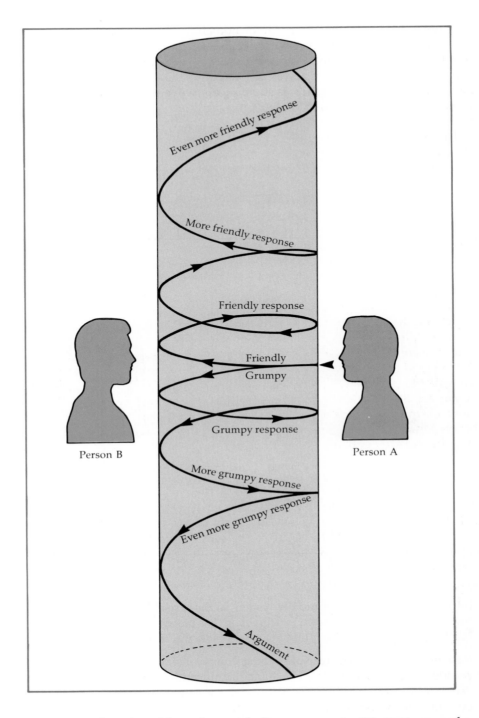

FIGURE 2-4
Positive Feedback: The Mechanism of Adaptation and Change
In positive feedback loops, things change rapidly and in the same direction. Friendliness elicits a friendly response, which prompts an even friendlier response in turn—in an escalating cycle. The opposite is also true: just as friendliness begets more friendliness, grumpiness breeds increasingly grumpy responses. Human development has involved a long, ongoing process of positive feedback in which interacting changes and responses have created adaptations to new situations and to the adaptive changes themselves.

Even more friendly response

More friendly response

Friendly response

Friendly

Grumpy

Grumpy response

More grumpy response

Even more grumpy response

Argument

Person B

Person A

same loop can also arise with unpleasant feelings: a grumpy statement can evoke a similarly grumpy response, which can lead quickly to an argument. Positive feedback loops clarify how things can change rapidly and dramatically. In positive feedback, the change is in the *same* direction (+); thus friendliness begets friendliness.

This is an unverifiable story about human origins, because we cannot be completely sure of events that occurred millions of years ago. Scientists now have a reasonably good idea how our human ancestors, over millions of years, underwent successive physical changes to adapt better to their new circumstances. Each change, such as standing on two legs, the growth of a bigger brain, and the uniquely human style of sex, fed into a positive feedback loop. Modern human beings are the result of this long process of feedback.

The only records of these important changes are a few fragments of tools and some skeletons preserved as fossils. But with new evidence being discovered, the full story of human history is emerging—the line of the species from four million years ago to the present day.

A Note on Evolutionary Time

Before beginning the story that spans millennia, it is necessary to reset one's idea of time. In evolutionary time, a few million years, give or take a few thousand, is not very much. Given the vast time scale of the history of the earth, humanity has developed and bred with unprecedented speed. In only a few million years, human beings have spread from the African plains to inhabit every part of the planet, and have grown from a population of a scattered few thousand to well over four billion.

If we were to chart earth history on a single year's calendar, with midnight on December 31 representing the present, the first form of life on earth would appear about April 1 (Figure 2-5). Fish appear about November 20. The first recognizable human ancestor would not come forth until the *morning of December 31*. The first human being would emerge at about 11:45 P.M. All that has happened in human history would occur in the final *minute* of the year. The forces that fashion our lives are much older than we usually think!

Prehuman Beings

Between 13 and 25 million years ago a succession of events occurred that finally led to the divergence of two primates: human beings and chimpanzees. Prehuman ancestors descended from tree-dwelling animals in East Africa. Sometime before 13 million years ago, the forests of East Africa began to thin out, forcing many of the tree-dwelling primates out of their homes and inviting others to try living in new ecological niches on the ground.

Those that had no trouble holding on to their tree homes evolved into chimpanzees. Of those who were forced or attracted out, some did not adapt and became extinct (Lancaster, 1978), while others learned to live out of the trees. They took up residence in the surrounding grasslands, prospered and survived, and eventually evolved into prehuman beings and the first members of the hominid family. **Hominids** include us and all our humanlike ancestors. The change from prehuman to human involved the development of four important hominid characteristics: a progressively upright stance, an increased use of tools, the growth of the brain, and the emergence of a cooperative society.

Prehuman beings had both apelike and humanlike characteristics. The first humanlike ancestor was *Ramapithecus,* who appeared sometime between nine and thirteen million years ago. Tiny *Australopithecus* (three to four million years ago) was the first direct ancestor.

ORIGINS AND DEVELOPMENT OF HUMAN BEINGS

FIGURE 2-5
The History of Life on Earth
Representing the entire history of the earth on a one-year calendar puts human beings' short stay on our planet in a new perspective.

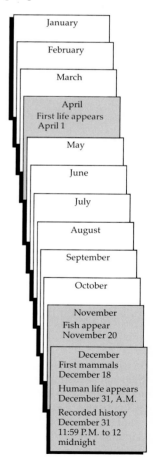

| January |
| February |
| March |
| April
First life appears
April 1 |
| May |
| June |
| July |
| August |
| September |
| October |
| November
Fish appear
November 20 |
| December
First mammals
December 18
Human life appears
December 31, A.M.
Recorded history
December 31
11:59 P.M. to 12
midnight |

Of these species, **Homo habilis** (Latin for "handy men") seems to have prevailed, although this is not certain. The advantages that might have ensured the survival of *Homo habilis* or similar species were the capacity to use tools and to hunt. In addition to having these social skills, these hominids were physically more nearly human: their brains were larger and they walked more upright (Figure 2-6).

Tool use probably made *Homo habilis* a more efficient worker. Tools would have made it possible to build shelters and construct primitive settlements. Perhaps more important, *Homo habilis* hunted in groups. Feeding a group on fruits and berries is difficult; most of the day must be spent foraging for food. But a group of hunters can bring home enough food for several families for days. Food sharing allowed *Homo habilis* to begin to establish a stable home base and a more permanent cooperative society.

Consider what hunting requires: speed and accuracy are obvious, but the ability to plan, communicate, and cooperate are even more important. These abilities foretell superior intelligence: to think and reason, to speak a language, and to create a culture.

Human Beings

Why do human beings have the talents they have? How did the grunts and gestures of our ancestors grow into the precision and grace of modern language? How did the human brain enlarge to its present great size? How did some apparent disadvantages, such as the helplessness of human children, turn into important advantages?

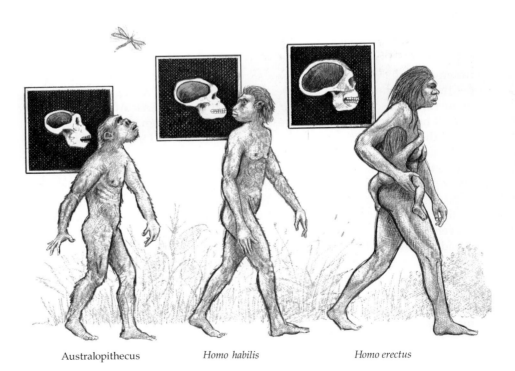

FIGURE 2-6
From Prehuman to Human
The characteristics and abilities that distinguish modern human beings gradually emerged over millions of years of adaptation by our humanlike ancestors.

Australopithecus   *Homo habilis*   *Homo erectus*

It took six to nine million years for the prehuman brain to grow significantly, for some communal living to develop, and for the invention and use of tools (Figure 2-7). But once these things happened, *they affected one another* and began to work together. As would be expected in a positive feedback loop, this process spurred further and more rapid change. It has only been about one and a half million years since the emergence of *Homo erectus* (see next section). In this time the brain has doubled in size, primitive tools have developed into complex technology, and civilizations have risen and fallen.

Physical differences between prehuman and human beings are obvious (Figure 2-6). The human skull is greater to contain a larger brain (Table 2-1). The brain of *Australopithecus* was 450 cubic centimeters (cc); human brains are presently between 1,000 and 2,000 cc (Campbell, 1982). Human beings stand more fully erect and walk and run better than prehumans. As human evolution progressed, society became increasingly stable; home bases were permanent and more central to life. Social organization grew in complexity.

See Chapter 4 on the brain.

Homo erectus: 1.6 Million to About 500,000 Years Ago

Homo erectus (Latin for "upright man") stood erect and walked on two legs. What most distinguished them from their predecessors was a large brain and a greater complexity of behavior. Their appearance was generally modern: they were probably over five feet tall and their skeletons were very similar to ours, at least from the neck down. *Homo erectus* migrated and settled in places as far north as present-day Germany and as far east as China.

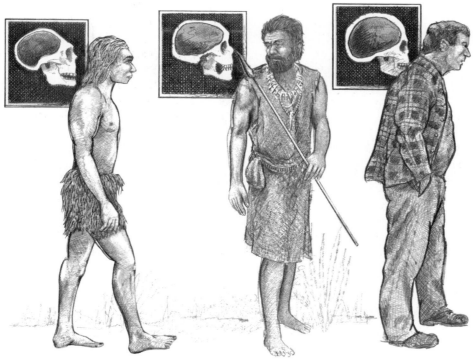

Neanderthal   Cro-Magnon   Modern *Homo sapiens*

TABLE 2-1 Comparison of Cranial Capacities

	Range of Cranial Capacity (cc)	Average Cranial Capacity (cc)
Lemur	10–70	—
Chimpanzee	282–500	383
Gorilla	340–752	505
Australopithecus africanus	435–530	450
A. robustus	—	500
A. boisei	506–530	515
Homo habilis	600–752	666
H. erectus	775–1,225	950
Modern adult human	1,000–2,000	1,330

SOURCE: Campbell, 1982.

FIGURE 2-7
Brain Size
Progressive increase in the size of the cerebrum in vertebrates is evident in these drawings, which show a representative selection of vertebrate brains all drawn to the same scale. Note the dramatic increase in size and complexity of the primate brains over lower vertebrates.

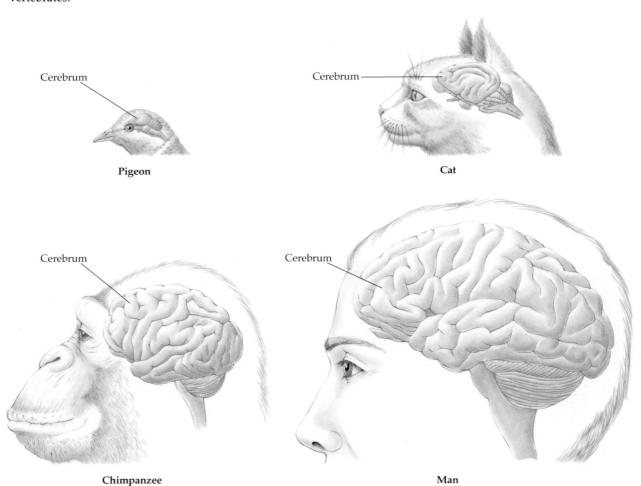

Cerebrum

Pigeon

Cerebrum

Cat

Cerebrum

Chimpanzee

Cerebrum

Man

In 1965 archaeologists uncovered a preserved settlement called Terra Amata, which unlocked many of the mysteries of *Homo erectus* (de Lumley, 1969). Today, in a housing complex built on that same site, people engage in many of the same activities as their ancestors did 400,000 years ago. The remains at Terra Amata indicate that the culture of *Homo erectus* was very advanced. Cooking pots, skins, marrow scrapers, and other advanced tools have been unearthed.

Homo erectus built elaborate shelters, invented clothing, and used fire in a controlled manner. The taming of fire is an important landmark in human history. Along with the inventions of clothing and shelter, it made life in cold climates possible. Even today 75 percent of people use fire as their primary source of warmth. Cooked food does not spoil as quickly as raw and it is more versatile. Fire is also a social landmark. People are drawn to fires not only for warmth but also for socializing. Because brain size had increased considerably by the time *Homo erectus* had evolved and because of the increased time spent around a fire, it is possible that *Homo erectus* was the first to use speech.

Neanderthal: From About 250,000 to 40,000 Years Ago

Neanderthals are the cavemen of popular folklore. They have been portrayed as brutish and dim-witted (possibly because of their physical appearance), but that idea now seems to be wrong.

Neanderthals first appeared during the Ice Age about 250,000 years ago. The geographic range they inhabited was similar to that of *Homo erectus*: probably from Germany to China and predominantly in northern regions. They had adapted primarily to cold weather and some scientists think they became extinct when the Ice Age ended. More likely they merged into the group of modern humanity.

Figure 2-8 depicts an important event in human history. A cave near what is now Shanidar, Iraq, marks where, on a day 60,000 years ago, a Neanderthal man

FIGURE 2-8
A Neanderthal Funeral
Such organized ceremonies indicate that Neanderthals had an advanced— identifiably human— culture.
(After Leakey & Lewin, 1977)

was buried. But this was not merely a burial, but a funeral — an organized ceremony. The fossilized remains of several kinds of flowers and grains are distributed in an orderly fashion around the skeleton. The bones of the deceased lie on a woven bed.

Evidence of a deliberate burial so far in the past is impressive. Evidence of an organized ceremony is even more impressive. What is most impressive is that the particular species of flowers located at the burial are still used today in local herbal medicine, which indicates that Neanderthals probably understood the medicinal properties of plants (Leakey & Lewin, 1977).

Neanderthal culture was advanced. There was division of labor, increased inventiveness (as seen by the tools and other artifacts found), and even organized conflict. It is possible that Neanderthals were the first to wage wars and the first to conceive of a spiritual life. There is documentation of both worship and ritual: bear skulls and bones are carefully placed in caves.

Neanderthals probably refined the inventions of *Homo erectus*. Their shelters were more elaborate. They clothed themselves in skin for warmth and created quite complex tools. Early forms of cooperation had evolved into a genuine society. Thus, Neanderthals were not very different from us (and their brains, at 1,500 cc, were larger than ours).

Homo sapiens

Cro-Magnon. In 1868 railway workers were cutting through a hillside in the south of France when they came upon four human skeletons. The skeletons looked modern, but what was next to them did not: stone tools, seashells, and animal teeth with holes drilled in them, apparently for stringing as ornaments. These skeletons are verified as the earliest remains (from sometime about 50,000 years ago) of *Homo sapiens* (Latin for "intelligent human being").

These people were called "Cro-Magnon" after the site of their discovery. There are critical distinctions in the shape of the skull of a Cro-Magnon and a Neanderthal (see Figure 2-6). Between their eras the entire shape of the face altered and the physiological apparatus for producing a great range of sounds expanded. The brain did not change much but was elevated in the skull. The palate (inside the mouth) enlarged, which allowed greater precision in speech.

Speech is the most sophisticated "tool" human beings have. With the emergence of language, the pace of evolution, which had quickened since *Homo erectus*, began to accelerate even more. Because of their language skill, Cro-Magnons had a tremendous advantage over Neanderthals: they could plan, organize, and cooperate much more efficiently. The tools Cro-Magnons used were more elaborate than those of Neanderthals. Shelters and settlements, too, were more complex.

Art and language are both critical milestones in human evolution because they signify a mind capable of abstraction, symbolism, and invention. Making art is an abstraction of a world not present and often a representation of a world view or a spiritual system. The Cro-Magnon paintings found in the caves of Lascaux in France, done 15,000 years ago, are as beautiful as anything ever created (Figure 2-9). Language, too, is abstract, involving the use of arbitrary sounds in arbitrary sequences to represent real objects in the world. Fifteen thousand years ago, one researcher has said, our ancestors were fully human (Marshak, 1978).

FIGURE 2-9
Cro-Magnon Art
The Cro-Magnon paintings
from the caves of Lascaux,
France, reveal highly
developed artistic ability
and sensibility, powers of
abstraction, and both an
appreciation of the realistic
details and the spiritual
essence of life and living
things.

Hunting, Gathering, and the Agricultural Revolution

Hunter-Gatherers

For most of history, human beings have lived in hunting and gathering societies; many still do. In this form of society there are two main activities: the search for meat and the gathering of available fruits, vegetables, and grains. Such **hunter-gatherers** lead a nomadic existence, moving as grains become scarce or following the seasonal migration of animals. But their lives are not necessarily impoverished; one anthropologist (Figure 2-10) found that an individual in a contemporary hunter-gatherer tribe—an "original affluent society"—spends less time working and has more leisure time than an average Frenchman today (Johnson, 1978). Still, the life of hunter-gatherers does not make for a very *stable* society—their life changes greatly as they migrate.

Agricultural Revolution

The creation of agriculture unshackled human beings from the vulnerability of the nomadic life of hunter-gatherers. The first crops planted about 10,000 years ago were the first extensive effort to prevail over the environment. A hunter-gatherer is at the mercy of nature; a farmer can harness it to some extent.

The cultivation of crops transformed human societies from mobile hunting and gathering ones to stable groups. Freed from the recurring search for food, people

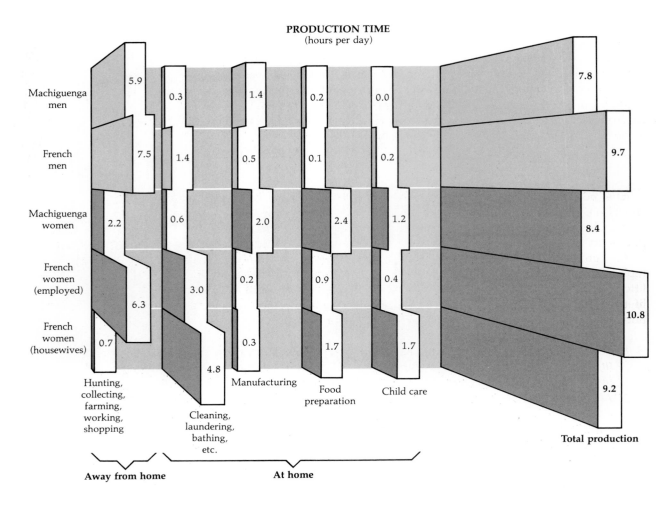

PRODUCTION TIME
(hours per day)

	Hunting, collecting, farming, working, shopping	Cleaning, laundering, bathing, etc.	Manufacturing	Food preparation	Child care	Total production
Machiguenga men	5.9	0.3	1.4	0.2	0.0	7.8
French men	7.5	1.4	0.5	0.1	0.2	9.7
Machiguenga women	2.2	0.6	2.0	2.4	1.2	8.4
French women (employed)	6.3	3.0	0.2	0.9	0.4	10.8
French women (housewives)	0.7	4.8	0.3	1.7	1.7	9.2

Away from home — At home

FIGURE 2-10
The Affluence of Hunting and Gathering Societies
Hunter-gatherers, such as the Machiguenga, lack the material wealth of modern French men and women, but—as this chart shows—they spend less time working and caring for their homes and possessions, so they are richer in leisure time than the average member of our modern technological society.
(After Johnson, 1978)

now literally "put down roots." Agriculture made possible the origin of civilization as we know it. In what is now Iran and Iraq, our recent ancestors began to grow grains and to domesticate animals and build permanent settlements. These first tentative settlements later developed into communities and, still later, into cities.

Then, almost in an instant (in an evolutionary time sense), the great ancient civilizations emerged in those regions where agriculture was first developed—in China, India, and the Near East. The pace of change quickened. In a few thousand years, human society transformed from nomadic to settled, and the foundations of advanced human culture were cemented.

Process of Adaptation and Evolution

Before the origin of modern science, it was usually believed that all creatures were individually created to suit their special environments. Organisms were thought fixed—human beings were created as human beings, monkeys were created monkeys, and so on. But by the nineteenth century, the commonly held scientific view was that all animals did change and had developed from earlier forms of life.

Evolution of organisms was an accepted theory, but its mechanism remained a riddle.

The answer appeared when the English naturalist Charles Darwin (1809–1882) proposed his theory of how adaptation occurs. He called the process "descent with modification." In 1859 he published a revolutionary book, *The Origin of Species*, in which he described the mechanism by which organisms adapt to the environment—**natural selection.** Darwin's theory, joined with modern genetics, is the basis of the modern **theory of evolution.**

Charles Darwin
(1809–1882)

Natural Selection

How populations change over time is their *evolution;* natural selection is the crucial mechanism that makes it work. A *population* is a group of similar organisms who can produce fertile offspring. For a group of animals to survive as a population, each generation must replace itself through sexual reproduction.

Any group of organisms produces far more offspring than are needed to replace itself. One salmon lays thousands of eggs, a cat can give birth to several litters of six or more kittens, a woman can have ten or even more children in her lifetime. But populations usually remain at a fairly constant size from one generation to the next. That observation led to two important insights.

1. Some individuals produce more surviving offspring than others. Therefore, *the individuals who do survive must in some way be more fit, better able to live in and adapt to their environment.*
2. Although the offspring have much in common with their parents, they also *differ from them* in many important respects.

Sexual reproduction and occasional mutation yield offspring that are *combinations* of two different *individuals,* not exact copies. Variations that permit the offspring to adapt better and to reproduce more would be likely to be passed on to the next generation, and thus that generation would change, or evolve (Darwin, 1859).

Consider, as did Darwin, the selective breeding of animals: to breed a small poodle, one needs the smallest female and the smallest male poodle. The dogs in the resulting litter will probably be smaller on average than the parents. If we repeat this process, each succeeding generation, *on average,* will be smaller than the previous one by this *artificial* selection.

In nature, there is no such calculated manipulation. There is *natural* selection, in which successful organisms are "chosen" by the environment. Animals more or less choose their own mates and produce offspring that, because they are combinations of their parents' characteristics, diverge slightly from their parents. Adaptive traits are passed on.

Adaptive Value and Fitness

Darwin's idea thus became known as the *survival of the fittest.* A popular misconception regarding the "survival of the fittest" is that life is a struggle between different *individuals* to survive. But that is incorrect. The struggle for survival referred to in the theory of evolution is the struggle of a *species,* not an individual.

The advantage of a new trait is not seen in the individual who inherits the trait, but in *succeeding generations.* The process works like this: individuals born with characteristics that enable them to adapt better to their environment reproduce more successfully and pass on those characteristics to others. ''Fitness'' in this context refers to *a match between the traits of a population and its environment.* The greater the fitness, the more surviving offspring.

Here is an example of how it works. Sunlight stimulates synthesis of vitamin D, which is a necessary nutrient for humans. Human beings can absorb sunlight through their skin. In a tropical environment where there is an abundance of sunlight, human beings run the risk of producing excessive vitamin D; thus a mechanism blocking the sun's rays would have *adaptive value.* In a northerly environment, where there is not much sunlight, individuals with a mechanism for stimulating production of vitamin D would be more ''fit'' to survive.

This is possibly why there are different skin colors in human populations. As human beings settled farther and farther north, those who survived better had lighter skin color, which allows sunlight to be absorbed through the skin at a higher rate. The closer to the equator, the darker the skin.

Darwin's insight enabled later scientists to comprehend evolution: to understand how our ancestors became us and how populations could change over time. To recap, the process by which the environment ''selects'' the individuals best adapted to it is *natural selection.* The change in the composition of the population that follows is its *evolution.*

Impact of Darwin's Theory

Although the principles of evolution are straightforward, they have probably had more impact than any others in the human sciences. The theory of evolution shifted the conception of human nature and our place in the universe. It provides the paradigm for most research in the life sciences and has greatly influenced psychology.

Our View of Ourselves

For most of history the prevailing view was that human beings were at the center of the universe: the sun and the planets revolved around the earth and the earth was the center of the universe. It was thought that human beings were specially created to dwell at the center of creation.

This conception first was attacked in 1543 when the Polish astronomer Nicolaus Copernicus demonstrated that the planets did *not* revolve around the earth and that, instead, the earth was one of many planets that revolved around the sun. The Catholic Church considered this theory heretical for many years, until the evidence supporting the theory was undeniable and it had to be accepted. Still, Copernicus did not upset the belief that human beings were unique creatures especially created to rule the earth.

Then came Darwin, whose theory placed human beings under the same rules of life that applied to all creatures. All organisms, it was thought, have a common ancestor, and adding insult to injury, human beings are directly descended from apes. The Victorian world was appalled. There is a vast distinction between thinking of yourself as ''created in God's own image'' and ''descended from the apes.'' One proper Victorian lady said, on learning of Darwin's theory, ''I pray that it is not true, but if it is true, I pray that it does not become widely known" (Leakey & Lewin, 1977).

Darwin was the subject of ridicule; he was lampooned in cartoons and attacked in sermons, debates, and editorials. His theory has continued to be controversial to this day. In 1925, an American biology teacher was fired for teaching the principles of evolution in a Tennessee school in violation of a state law. The controversy ended in the famous "Monkey Trial." Today, in the United States, many fundamentalist Christian groups protest the teaching of the theory of evolution in public schools, at least in the absence of any teaching of "creationism," the conception that God created the world as written in the Bible.

Darwin's work and the later development of evolutionary theory did more than shock the world. It placed human beings as members of the animal kingdom subject to the same forces that act on all animals, and, more than any other scientific contribution, it launched the scientific inquiry of human nature. It produced a different view of human beings in the universe. The complexity of the world is taken, not as an example of God's works but as an evolved system without general direction (Dawkins, 1986). In this view, if there is a controlling force, it is, as in the title of a new book, *The Blind Watchmaker.*

H uman beings have many physical, behavioral, and mental characteristics that set us off from all other animals. One physical characteristic, the ability to stand up, was very crucial in human evolution: it led to increased reproduction. Somewhat later (although it is an oversimplification to separate each characteristic) came tool use, an increasingly large brain, and self-awareness.

These physical changes resulted in countless behavioral changes, among them the development of a cooperative society. The physical developments and the resulting developments in the human style of life in turn prompted vast changes in human society so that cultures and behavior changed rapidly over a very short time.

Several characteristics set human beings apart from other animals. We present them here in the rough order in which they evolved, but it is better to think of the process of **human adaptation** as the *simultaneous* development of all these characteristics, in a positive feedback loop (Figure 2-11). The effects of the loop have continuously increased the difference between us and our nearest ancestors.

Bipedalism: Standing Up and Walking

Human beings are **bipedal,** that is, they walk on two feet instead of all four. Chimps and gorillas can stand upright at times, but when they move they typically do so on all fours. A fossil skeleton called Lucy, the first known hominid that showed evidence of bipedal locomotion, dates from about 3.75 million years ago, about 1 million years before the use of tools (Johansen & Edey, 1981).

Walking

Bipedal walking and running are efficient modes of locomotion. People can cover greater distances over time than any other animal. We are the only animals that can climb a tree, swim a mile across a river, and walk 20 miles in a day

(Haldane, 1986). Walking enabled our ancestors to travel into new and unexplored territory, which in turn led them into new and often dangerous situations. Almost all other animals live their lives in the environment in which they are born.

Get down on all fours and look around. The view is more limited than when you stand. To four-legged animals smell is important. A standing animal can see farther than it can smell. Since standing animals can spot approaching danger as well as opportunities farther away, a more sophisticated visual system developed

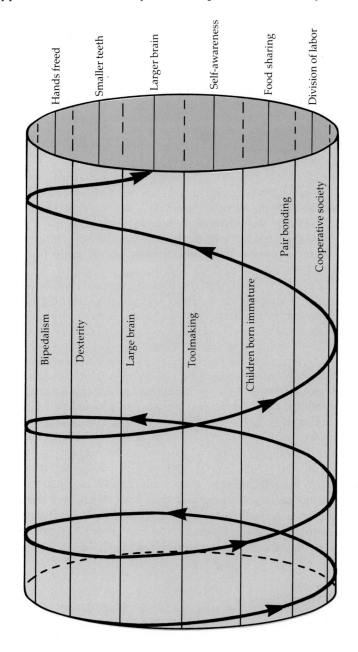

FIGURE 2-11
Human Adaptation and the Power of Positive Feedback
Unique human characteristics include the following: (1) we stand on two legs and walk; (2) children are born immature and need care for a long time; (3) females are biologically sexually receptive all the time and usually pair off with one male; (4) we have forelimbs capable of fine motor control and use tools; (5) our human brain is the largest (relative to body size) and is capable of sophisticated communication; (6) our society is cooperative and organized around food sharing and division of labor; and (7) we have the capacity to change our environment and live anywhere on earth.

along with upright posture. Hands were freed from weight-bearing responsibilities, making tool use possible. Erect posture also led to profound changes in human sexuality and social systems. Although we cannot be sure, this complex of factors surrounding bipedalism was probably our first adaptive advantage (Johansen & Edey, 1981).

Immaturity at Birth and Its Consequences

With the freeing of the front limbs, the hind limbs had to bear the entire weight of the body. The human back was not originally "designed" to support upright posture (which partially explains why back pains are a common complaint). To support the additional weight, the human pelvis grew thicker than that of the great apes (Washburn, 1960). The thickened pelvis made the birth canal, the opening through which infants are born, much smaller.

But here is the problem: while the birth canal was becoming smaller, the brain and head were growing larger. If there had been no correction for this new disadvantage, the human species would have eventually died out because of inefficient childbirth. The "solution" was to have human babies born very early in their development.

At birth a chimp's brain is about 45 percent of its adult weight, while a human baby's brain is only 25 percent of its adult weight (Lovejoy, 1974). Human children have the longest infancy in the animal kingdom (Figure 2-12); they are not as competent and independent as baby chimps or baboons. Within a day, baby baboons can hold onto their mothers by themselves (Campbell, 1982). The human child is helpless and will die if not taken care of for years.

The Brain.   The major portion of the brain's development occurs outside the womb, exposed to and influenced by many different environments, events, and people. The "environment" plays a much greater role in the development of the human brain than in any other animal's brain development. And because the environment is different for each person, the specific abilities each of us develops differ considerably.

The Mother – Father – Infant Relationship.   A helpless infant requires at least one caretaking parent to survive. In other species, newborns can fend for themselves within a relatively short time, and the mother can almost immediately resume her place in the group while still providing her young with food and protection. But taking care of a human infant is a full-time job.

For most of human history, child care has been the mother's job. In subsistence societies, like hunter-gatherers, a nursing mother would have a hard time getting enough food for herself while caring for a child (Benshoof & Thornhill, 1979). But parents working together can form an efficient team. The father can hunt for meat and bring it home to the mother, who stays close to home gathering fruits and vegetables. Human fathers take an active role in feeding their young (Alexander et al., 1979).

Evolution of Love

As far as we can tell, love appears to be unique to human beings. The love "bond" between people is important to human adaptation and to humans as a race.

FIGURE 2-12

Long Infancy

With the longest infancy of any animal, human young are wholly dependent upon their parents for twice as long as baby chimpanzees. But the long period of protecting the helpless infants gives human family groups greater cohesion and the infants have the time to learn all that is involved in being human.

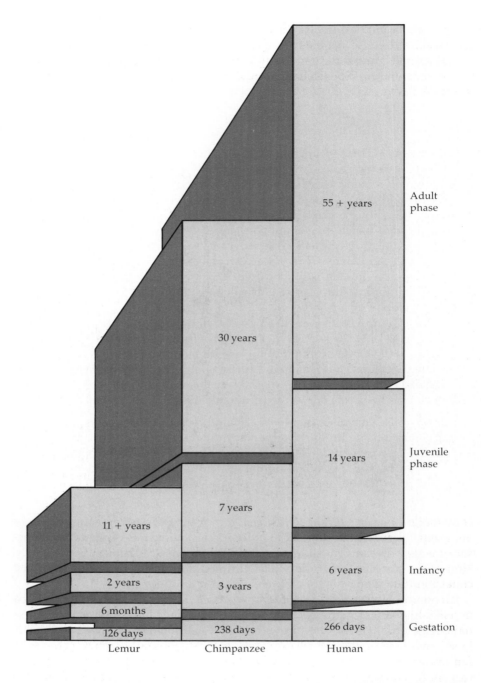

		55 + years	Adult phase
	30 years		
11 + years	14 years	Juvenile phase
	7 years		
2 years		6 years	Infancy
6 months	3 years		
126 days	238 days	266 days	Gestation
Lemur	Chimpanzee	Human	

Because of our upright posture, the birth canal is small, and this leads to human infants being born immature and helpless. The love and attachment between the father and the mother have a key biological role: they ensure that the father remains with the mother and helps care for the offspring. Human fathers are the only males among primates who take a significant role in the care of their own offspring.

The father–mother–child unit is bonded by love into the family unit that is typical of our species. Any analysis of the nature of our love, far from being trivial, is of the utmost importance to our understanding of ourselves. The analysis of love and its evolutionary history is rather new (Mellen, 1981), and the current studies of love and loving are also in their infancy.

Sexuality

One result of bipedalism is that human beings are very sexual mammals. All female mammals except humans are sexually excitable only when "in heat," that is, when *ovulating*. **Ovulation** is the time when the female's egg is released from the ovaries, and thus the only time when she is fertile. The period of ovulation is called **estrus.** Most female mammals, other than humans and some higher primates, have an *estrus cycle*, which means that they ovulate usually only a few times a year. In addition, males are generally excited by a female in estrus and a female can only physically receive the male when she is ovulating.

A female animal in estrus communicates her sexual excitability (or receptivity) by emitting certain odors from the vagina. Without estrus, however, males cannot tell by smell when females are ovulating. With menstrual cycle in which ovulation occurs every month, a woman is always sexually receptive, or (to put it a less potentially offensive way) sex is possible at almost any time. Humans thus can have intercourse frequently throughout the year.

Pair Bonding

Human sexual signals are more visual than those of other animals. Woman's breasts are sizable, even when they are not nursing. In other mammals this is not the case. The man's penis is much larger, relative to body size, than that of any of the great apes. Humans face each other during intercourse; in other mammals the male mounts the females from the rear (Goody, 1976).

The frequency of sex, combined with the eye contact during sex and the continual presence of visual sex signals, may be the basis for attachments based on sexual pleasure. There is good evolutionary basis for the pleasure derived from sex; it encourages sexual relations and thus increases the chance of conception. Human beings customarily like to have sex much more than the demands of conception require.

The human style of sex allows a foundation for a stable society built on family units (Sahlins, 1972). The place sex occupies in human life is unique: we do not have sex merely to replace ourselves in the next generation. Instead, we "fall in love" and "make love." The sexual bond, or **pair bonding,** is the basis of the family: fathers stay with, care for, and care about their families. The mother can care for several small children at home if the father brings home most of the food (Benshoof & Thornhill, 1979).

Consider the female chimpanzee. She lives from 18 to 40 years, but because she bears all the responsibility for her children—nursing, feeding, and protection—it takes her about 16 years to produce and raise two offspring (Gallup, 1977). Because of the support and help of the family unit, a human female could theoretically produce and raise one child per year from the onset of

SEX DIFFERENCES AND DIVISION OF LABOR

In all 800 primitive societies that have been studied, the men hunt and the women gather (Friedl, 1978). It is impossible to be an effective hunter while pregnant or while nursing or carrying a child (Washburn, 1960). Also, males are physically bigger and stronger than females and are usually faster runners.

Males do the fighting in every society. This is not only because of their greater physical strength, but is also because of the most basic requirement of a species: survival of the next generation. In a population of ten males and ten females, if nine females died in battle, probably only one child would be born to the group during the next year, and survival of the population would be in peril. But if nine men died in battle, the ten surviving females could each produce a child in the next year. So, *males are the more expendable* (Leutenegger, 1977).

Even so, in virtually every society men have held and continue to hold the most powerful and respected positions. Why has this *male dominance* occurred?

This question brings up the issue of nature–nurture. Are males "naturally" dominant? Many theorists (males) have contended that males are not only physically stronger but also intellectually superior. But studies in recent years, by both men and women, have not supported this.

One theory suggests that control of a society's most valued resources determines who dominates (Friedl, 1978). We need protein to live, and meat is a much more concentrated source of protein than fruits and vegetables. A large gazelle, caught and brought home by a hunting party, can feed several families for several days.

Thus, many can eat well for a long period of time from the labor of a few. With larger brains, language skills, and increased dexterity, males became more skillful hunters, and meat became the most valued resource. Males who procured and distributed it became the dominant members of the community. Today males do not always command protein resources directly, but because men in the past have controlled the supply of the most valuable resource, they have amassed dominant status. As women gain control over valuable resources, this "tradition" of male dominance is changing.

menstruation to menopause. One important part of the adaptive value of bipedalism may lie in the human style of sexuality, which creates the family unit and cooperation (Lovejoy, 1981), although this view has been challenged, in that male and female sexual strategies may be different (Symons, in press).

Differences in Sexuality

The description in the text so far has emphasized the harmonious and cooperative nature of the human sexual bond, the monogamous couple–family unit. However, anyone who has had even a small interest in sexual matters cannot fail to see that all is not smooth and harmonious. One new view on the discord in sexual relationships comes from evolutionary biology. It emphasizes that males and females, because of their different roles in reproduction, have different ways of behaving sexually so that they gain the greatest advantage: the advantage for the male is not the same as for the female (Symons, in press).

Dorothy Parker wrote, in her "General Review of the Sex Situation":

Woman wants monogamy;
Man delights in novelty
Love is woman's moon and sun;
Man has other forms of fun.
Woman lives but in her lord;
Count to ten and man is bored.
With this gist and sum of it;
What earthly good can come of it?

While this poem written in 1926 may be a bit outmoded, especially about "woman living for her lord," it contains some truth about sex differences in sexual expression and desire. There are fundamental differences in the sexual conduct of males and females in all societies and in most animals.

In Figure 2-13, which shows the average frequency of orgasms of men and women, note that at all ages, men have more sex per week than females do. One consistent difference in sexuality is this: in all cultures studied, men on the average desire more sex and more variety in sex than women do. In their monumental survey of human sexual activity, Kinsey, Pomeroy, and Martin (1953) wrote:

Among all peoples, everywhere in the world, it is understood that the male is more likely than the female to desire sexual relations with a variety of partners.

As a whole, men seek sexual arousal more often than women do. Although the recent preference for free sexual expression has narrowed this difference somewhat, men on the average still seek vicarious, visual, and other sexual stimulation far more than women. The industry in X-rated films and sex-oriented books and magazines, which in the United States alone does over $1 billion in business a year, is almost entirely geared to male interests. Prostitution has almost exclusively male clients.

The pattern of sex differences holds in homosexuality. Male homosexuality is thought to be a "hypermale" sexuality, uninhibited by females (Symons, in

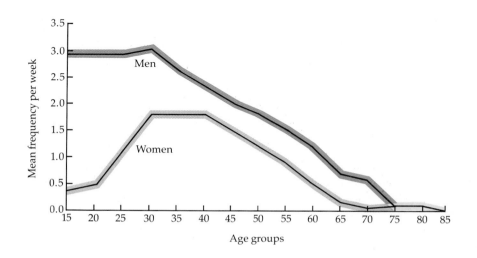

FIGURE 2-13
Frequency of Orgasm
At all ages, men are more active sexually than women of the same age. However, men's highest level of sexual activity is achieved in their teens and 20s, whereas women just begin reaching their highest level in their 30s.
(After Kinsey, Pomeroy, Gebhard, & Martin, 1953)

press). Male homosexuality is usually characterized by many sexual encounters; female homosexuality, by long, stable relationships. Male homosexual prostitution is quite common in large cities; female homosexual prostitution is almost unknown (Symons, in press).

While experience (environment and cultural conditions) undoubtedly sharpens, develops, and exaggerates the differences between male and female sexuality, *there are fundamental biological differences in the sexual natures of the sexes.* In every known human society, and in primate societies too, there is a very basic divergence of sexual interest. This may be due to the differences between the reproductive strategies of the male and female. The male can father a large number of children in a year, but the female can carry usually only one. In biological terms, it is "cheap" for males to father offspring, while much more "expensive" for females to mother offspring, which leads to very different strategies: it is more advantageous for a male to mate with a greater number of partners.

With changes in society, such as the acceptability of female sexual expression, the increasing ability of single parents to care adequately for their children, and contraceptives that allow a woman to have sex without worrying about pregnancy, these differences will probably continue to decrease in the coming years, but it is unlikely they will disappear entirely (Symons, in press).

Cooperation and Human Society

In the mating systems of other animals, which are governed by estrus, the female is available only at specific times and is available to many males at those times. Mating in most other animal societies is preceded by aggressive competition among males for the females in heat. With the replacement of an estrus cycle by a menstrual cycle and the emergence of pair bonding in human society, this continual sexual competition among males is lessened. Increased cooperation took place, not only within the pair bond but also among members of the society (Johansen & Edey, 1981; Lovejoy, 1981). One characteristic of all human societies studied so far is their cooperation, as defined by food sharing and division of labor. The complex and interdependent human society has a biological basis in cooperation.

Every individual begins life dependent on the mother. As humans mature, they recognize increasingly complex networks of interdependence: from family to group to nation to the entire world. Even organized aggression depends on cooperation. Hunting, which is a primary human adaptation, requires planning, division of labor, complex signaling, cooperative carrying home of the kill, and a sharing of the prize with those at home (Lancaster, 1978).

Dexterity and Tool Use

Because most primates are tree-dwelling animals, both the front and hind limbs are needed to grasp branches and vines. Once human beings became bipedal and the forelimbs were freed from their weight-bearing function, the limbs developed into hands having great **dexterity** capable of more precise movements, such as those needed for fashioning and **using specialized tools.** It is thought that human beings began to make tools as early as three million years ago.

Specialized tools for chopping, digging, killing, cooking, washing, and skin-

Primitive
pebble chopper

Early *Homo erectus*
hand ax

Cro-Magnon knife

Late *Homo erectus*
hand ax

Neanderthal knife

ning led to specialized labor by those who used them. Some people gathered wood or nuts, others dug for roots, and still others killed animals (Washburn, 1960). Axes made the hunt more efficient; choppers and scrapers were used to butcher a large animal at the kill. At home, tools helped scrape the nutritious marrow out of the bones; animal hides were scraped to make warm clothing.

One mark of improved dexterity is the modification in the tools themselves. Those made by *Homo erectus* about one million years ago took 35 blows to make. The knives of Cro-Magnon, made about 20,000 years ago, were more delicately fashioned, requiring at least 250 separate blows (Figure 2-14).

About 5000 B.C., human beings began to extract and use metals. This step further advanced the technology and created the need for more specialized labor. Specialization led inevitably to greater interdependence among individuals.

The Brain

Pivotal to human adaptation is our large brain, which has evolved faster than any other human organ. (See Chapter 4.) It took hundreds of millions of years to create the 400 cc brain of *Australopithecus*, yet in only a few million years the brain grew to 1250–1500 cc and had developed the capacity for abstract thought —the key to human adaptation. It has helped us to adapt to every kind of geography and climate, and it enables us today to transcend our biological inheritance.

The brain underlies mental life: to learn, to create, to invent, to think, and to say things no one has ever thought. The brain increased in size radically from *Ramapithecus* to *Homo sapiens*. It is the largest, relative to body size, of all land mammals, but it is not the size of the brain that matters. What is crucial is *what parts* of the brain expanded. Although the anatomy of much of our brain is identical with that of other primates, our cerebral cortex, the uppermost part of the brain, is the largest and most elaborate of all primates. The cortex is the area of the brain devoted to learning, organizing, planning, and other mental activities.

All primates have developed varying degrees of fine motor control. The main mode of locomotion of nonhuman primates is swinging through trees, which requires the ability to grasp tightly onto branches. To do this, an animal must have

FIGURE 2-14
The Increasing Complexity of Toolmaking
The growing sophistication of human stone implements, and of their manufacture, is illustrated here. Each wedge symbol represents a blow struck in making the tool and the clusters of symbols stand for the different operations during manufacture.
(After Campbell, 1979)

extremely well-developed motor control in the fine muscles of his limbs. A "kind of grammar" is necessary to know how to get from one place to another, which hand to use, where and how tightly to grasp. Those areas of the brain that control fine motor movements, and which became further developed in toolmaking, are the same ones involved in language (Gallup, 1977). The increasing size of the cerebral cortex thus gave our ancestors great advantages—from control of delicate muscle movements to the development of speech and written language.

Ethology and Biological Fixed Action Patterns

If humans (and all other organisms) are the result of such an extended evolutionary process, then it is likely that many behaviors are the direct result of evolution. Many of the significant studies of such inborn behaviors have been the domain of **ethology:** the study of behavior under natural conditions.

Imprinting

When a newly hatched duckling is 12 to 18 hours old, something remarkable happens: if it recognizes something moving and follows it for about 10 minutes, it becomes **imprinted** on it (Figure 2-15). It will continue to follow the object anywhere (Hess, 1973). In nature, of course, the most likely "object" that a baby duckling sees is its mother, so this "prepared reaction" is a *stable strategy*—it leads to a greater chance of survival.

However, if a scientist wishing to examine the routine intervenes and shows the duckling anything at that period, be it a rectangle or a decoy on wheels, the duckling will follow that object. In the most dramatic demonstration, Konrad Lorenz, one of the world's most influential ethologists, *himself* appeared in front of some baby geese at the right time. Presto! The tiny goslings followed him as if he were the mother, crying when he was not around (Figure 2-16). So, a predisposition to bond to the mother is encouraged by this innate reaction.

FIGURE 2-15
Imprinting and the Critical Period
The curve shows the relation between imprinting and the age at which a duckling was exposed to a male moving model. The imprinting score represents the percentage of trials on which the duckling followed the model on a later test.
(From Hess, 1958)

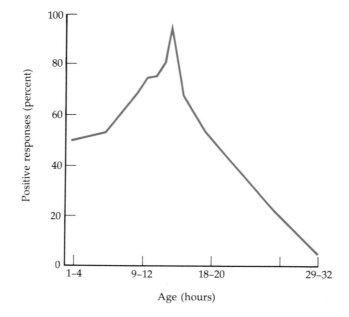

Age (hours)

FIGURE 2-16
Imprinting
This is the classic photo of
the famous ethologist
Konrad Lorenz and his
imprinted graylag geese.

Fixed Action Patterns: Stickleback Attack

The "neural program" for imprinting is actually simpler than the behavior. A baby duckling usually attaches to the mother, but the only instructions from the brain are something like "follow anything that appears within 12 to 18 hours after you are hatched." By observing animals closely, additional simple innate patterns such as these have been observed. These *fixed action patterns* are unlearned behavior, generic to a species, which appear or are released in the presence of certain sign stimuli.

Tinbergen (1951) identified the simple stimuli that cause the three-spined stickleback to attack. If the fish is shown a perfect model of a stickleback (Figure 2-17), it will not attack. But if the belly of the model is painted red, this seems to be the sign to attack. As you can see, the models that spark stickleback attack do not have to look at all like the fish, but have to have the critical sign. The guiding principle here seems to be this: it is probably more economical in the world of the stickleback to instigate attacks against anything with a red belly.

In these ethological analyses we see two points: that many reactions are built in and that they can be quite simple in their composition (Tinbergen, 1951). David Barash (1986) comments:

> . . . male European robins will attack a tuft of red feathers mounted on a stick and placed inside their territory, while ignoring a much more realistic stuffed robin that lacks the color red, which apparently releases robin aggressiveness. Crows will sometimes attack someone carrying a bit of black cloth, apparently because the unwitting victim has stimulated the "crow in distress" releasing mechanism normally reserved for predators such as hawks or owls. . . . [the reactions] can be produced by simple models with only the vaguest resemblance to a live animal, so long as the appropriate releaser is present.
>
> . . . if the appropriate characteristics that make up a releaser are artificially exaggerated by an experimenter, animals will often prefer them to the naturally occurring signal, or will perform their particular behavior more intensely or for a

FIGURE 2-17
Stickleback Attack
Of the five models used to provoke a fighting response in male sticklebacks, only the four above on the right with red bellies worked, even though the left one is shaped most like a stickleback. It lacked the critical sign stimulus of a red belly.
(Based on Tinbergen, 1951)

longer time. These exceptionally successful manmade signals are called "supernormal" releasers. Many nesting birds . . . prefer to sit on the biggest egg possible, ignoring their own in favor of a larger experimental model. The oystercatcher, a common robin-sized shorebird, will apparently forget her own eggs and perch ridiculously on top of a huge artificial egg the size of a watermelon.

Attachment and Cuteness

The success of child rearing is the end-product of evolution and is too important to be left to finicky individual choices: what if the mother doesn't like the child? Many innate reactions of the child, among them *distress calls*, bring up the "correct" reaction in the mother! There is, in addition, a network of attachments which persist between mothers (or caregivers) and their offspring (see Chapter 3 for a more complete discussion).

One of the ways evolution bestows an attachment between mother and baby is by the *cuteness* of the baby. Babies have much larger foreheads, eyes, and cheeks than adults (Figure 2-18). This is called the *neotenic face*; the more a face approaches that of the proportions of a baby, the more we want to hold and cuddle and say gaa-gaa goo-goo.

These same facial proportion relationships exist in other animals as well (Lorenz, 1943). Our seemingly built-in tendency to like and respond to these facial proportions is taken advantage of in the media. Mickey Mouse is beloved throughout the world, not only because of his antics, but also because of his brow and eyes. Attractive female faces show similar proportions: large eyes and forehead.

Notice the evolution of cute features in Mickey Mouse.

FIGURE 2-18
Cuteness
Cute features of babies of many species, including a round head, protruding forehead, and large eyes, trigger a nurturing, caring response in adults.

Self-Awareness

We are conscious of our existence and our mortality — we know who we are and we have a sense of personal self. Other animals show little evidence of **self-awareness** (although a variation of it can be experimentally induced in the pigeon [Skinner, 1981]). If you put a cat in front of a mirror, it will approach its own reflection as if its reflection were another animal.

A chimpanzee, however, who has a considerably larger brain and a more developed cortex, shows some self-recognition. When Gallup (1977) put chimps in front of a mirror, they acted as though they knew it was a reflection of themselves. In an experiment, Gallup put a red mark on a chimp's forehead, then put him in front of a mirror. The chimp touched the mark on himself — not on the mirror. This action indicated that he recognized himself and knew that something was unusual. All sighted human beings, from the age of 10 months on, can recognize themselves in the mirror.

Awareness of one's own existence can lead to further questionings about the nature of existence: where do we come from, what will happen when we die? It can also lead to philosophical questions and to a search for universal principles of human life — morality, spirituality, and religion.

Social-Cultural Evolution

Our ability to change the environment has also enhanced human evolution. Clothing, fire, dwellings, and agriculture all enabled human beings to live where none had lived before, such as in the colder climates of northern Europe. However, this inventiveness has also created problems. Once an invention becomes widespread, everyone is under pressure to *adapt* to the new situation it creates. And it seems that *our ability to judge lags behind our ability to create.*

Our mental system may have been helpful in coping with the early environment of humans, but in the complex world of today people are often upset by and unable to cope with new situations and changes in their lives (Holmes & Rahe, 1967). This leads to stress-related or physical ailments such as ulcers and high blood pressure (Selye, 1978). We are thus *always adapting* to our own creations — airplanes, television, computers, nuclear power.

Three and a half million years ago certain primates stood up. One to two million years ago prehuman beings had begun fashioning tools out of stone; 10,000 years ago, human beings were planting seeds. Since then the rate of human cultural and intellectual development has been dazzling. Although children born today are biologically the same as those born 25,000 years ago, they are born into a very different world.

Think of it this way: 25,000 years ago the human population was at most a few million, surviving mainly by hunting and gathering. The invention of agriculture 10,000 years ago revolutionized the human experience. Settlements grew up along the fertile flood plains of the Nile, in the Fertile Crescent of the Middle East, and around the Ganges Delta and Huang Ho (Yellow River) in Asia.

The statistics on the rise of the human population, the measure of our reproductive success, are astonishing. At the time of the agricultural revolution, the total human population was less than ten million. Today, almost that many people are born *each month*. It took from the beginnings of humanity about a million years ago to produce the first billion people, and it took only the last 14 years to produce the most recent billion! In 10,000 years, the population has exploded from ten million to five billion (Figure 2-19) (Ehrlich, Holdren, & Ehrlich, 1977).

Since surviving offspring are one measure of a species' success, human beings are a notably successful species. The basis for this is adaptability. Natural selection favors those who adapt to changing conditions. Physical changes, bipedalism, a larger brain, dexterity, visual acuity — combined with the propensity to cooperate and invent — enabled humans to transform their world.

The world has changed more in the last 10,000 years than in the preceding four million. On our calendar of human life, science, civilizations, religions, technology, and architecture all appeared in the last few minutes before midnight of December 31 (see Figure 2-5). Our ancestors had thousands, sometimes millions, of years to adapt to smaller changes in the environment than those we now face daily. Modern human development is *cultural*, not physical, evolution (Campbell,

FIGURE 2-19
The Human Population Explosion of Modern Times

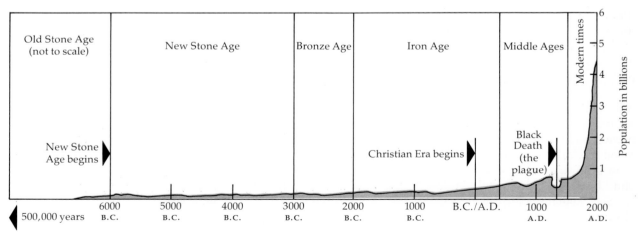

1982); 25,000 years is too fleeting a time for there to be physical adaptation to the radical changes in the environment (Dubos, 1978).

Y ou are your parents' donation to human evolution. You can probably see a lot of them in your looks and bearing. Human heritage is manifold: all human beings inherit certain characteristics: a large brain, erect posture, color vision, manual dexterity. But each human being is also one of a kind — at once like all others and also like no other person who has ever lived. Human individuality is the subject of **genetics,** which is the science of heredity. This chapter now shifts from a broad view of evolution to a microscopic focus on the mechanisms of evolution.

Each person is "dealt a complex genetic hand" at birth, a set of biological instructions for fabricating a human body and brain. There is an individual inheritance: specific physical traits, such as sex and eye color. These are set at conception and are unaffected by the environment or experience. There is also a more subtle inheritance: dispositions toward discrete traits, such as tallness; toward different diseases, such as diabetes or schizophrenia (a severe form of mental disturbance); and even toward certain interests and attitudes (Scarr & Weinberg, 1978).

The single cell composed at the moment of conception by the female egg and the male sperm incorporates all these potentials. For biological inheritance to take place, something must control the transmission from each of the parents to the offspring. That is the *gene.* Genetics is the study of how characteristics are transferred from one generation to the next.

Genetic Code

The **gene** is the basic component of heredity in all living things. Genes are made of a substance called **DNA** (deoxyribonucleic acid). The DNA molecule is shaped like a long flexible ladder twisted into a spiral. The rungs of the ladder contain the genetic information encoded on four special nitrogen-containing chemicals called *amines,* the chemical "building blocks" of life: adenine, thymine, guanine, and cytosine.

Virtually every living thing is made up of these chemicals. What creates the difference between living things is only the arrangement of the four amines on the double helix of the DNA molecule. The order in which these substances appear along the double helix is called the **genetic code.** Thus, the fundamental difference between human beings and turtles, at the molecular level, is *only in the pattern of the four chemical substances deriving from the DNA molecule.*

Organisms grow by cell division, a process called **mitosis** (Figure 2-20). One cell divides into two, two into four, and so forth. In mitosis, the DNA spirals separate, yet each new cell has the same genetic code as the original cell. That is because each DNA spiral has the ability to "replicate" the instructions of the other spiral.

In 1953 two molecular biologists at Cambridge University in England, Watson and Crick, clarified how this operates. Each fragment on a DNA strand contains specific *pairs* of the four chemicals that make up DNA: guanine and cytosine are always linked; adenine is always connected with thymine. Thus, the presence of

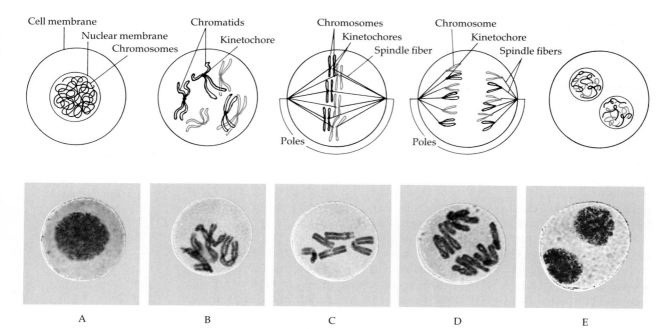

FIGURE 2-20
Chromosomes during the
Phases of Mitosis

one, such as adenine, is in itself an instruction: ''thymine goes next.'' Each strand has all the information needed to reproduce a complementary strand and conceive a new double helix (Figure 2-21).

Chromosomes

Genes are arranged, like beads on a string, on a **chromosome.** Human beings have 46 chromosomes; half the chromosomes (23) come from each parent. These chromosomes carry an individual's entire genetic program. Each human chromosome contains thousands of genes; human beings have a total of about a million genes. All of them exist in the nucleus of every cell of the body. *Each cell of the body contains all the information necessary to produce all the other cells of the body.* There is so much DNA entwined in there that each cell could unwind to thousands of times its length.

Dominant and Recessive Genes

Each parent has a set of genes for eye color. At conception, the pair is split. The ''eye color gene'' from the mother pairs up with the ''eye color gene'' from the father. Now the child has his own set of ''eye color genes.'' But a mother may donate a gene for brown eyes and a father a gene for blue eyes. Which gene will win out and be *expressed* in the child's appearance?

All the genes an individual carries are called the **genotype.** But not all genes in an individual are expressed. The portion of our genotype that is expressed is called the **phenotype.**

Genes are selected on the basis of whether they are **dominant** or **recessive.** When *one dominant* gene is present, the trait it governs appears in the person's physical makeup. In this case, the child's eyes will be brown because genes for brown eyes are dominant over those for blue eyes. However, even though only the gene for brown eyes is *expressed,* the gene for blue eye color is still part of the child's genetic makeup. Later, when the child grows up and becomes a parent, his or her own child could have blue eyes, but only if that parent contributes a "blue eye" gene. A *recessive* trait, such as blue eyes, will normally be expressed only if *both* parents contribute the recessive gene.

Sex

An important effect of chromosomes is the sex of the animal. The chromosomes of pair number 23 (Figure 2-22) determine an individual's sex. Chromosomes have two different shapes: one looks like an X, the other like a Y and thus they are designated X and Y. A female has two X chromosomes in pair 23, and a male has one X and one Y chromosome. Thus, because he can contribute either kind of chromosome, *the sex of the child is determined by the father:* if he contributes the X chromosome, the child will be a girl; if he contributes the Y chromosome, the child will be a boy.

One might assume, therefore, that the chances of conceiving a male or a female are 50-50, but this is not so. For every 100 females conceived, 130 males are conceived. Sperm carrying Y chromosomes may be more mobile than those carrying X chromosomes and reach the egg first. But this disparity is evened out: the XY (male) unit is more fragile than the XX (female) unit in the womb. Thus, only 106 boys are born for every 100 girls. This fragility continues: *more males than females die at every age level in infancy, childhood, and adulthood.* Thus, women typically live longer than men, and there are more females in the population than males (Table 2-2) (Singer & Hilgard, 1978).

Abnormal Chromosomes and Birth Defects

Sometimes a mistake occurs in the process of combining the parents' chromosomes in the fertilized egg. A chromosome can be lost, broken, turned around, or an extra one can be added. If a chromosome is lost at the first cell division (that is, one parent donates only 22, not 23, chromosomes), the fertilized egg almost never develops. Sometimes an extra chromosome can be present. This happens when either the sperm or the egg donates more than one member of one of the 23 pairs.

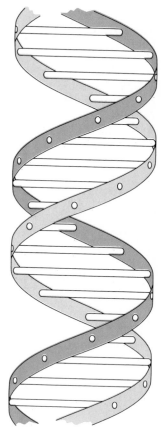

FIGURE 2-21
DNA Molecule
The rungs of the double-helix structure of the DNA molecule are formed by four different amines—adenine (A), guanine (G), thymine (T), and cytosine (C). The order in which these chemicals appear forms the genetic code.

TABLE 2-2   Approximate Sex Ratio for the Human Species

Conception	120 to 150 males for every 100 females
Birth	105 males for every 100 females
Age 15	100 males for every 100 females
Age 50	90 males for every 100 females
Age 60	70 males for every 100 females
Age 70	60 males for every 100 females
Age 80	50 males for every 100 females
Age 100	20 males for every 100 females

SOURCE: Berger, 1980, as adapted from McMillen, 1979; Nagle, 1979.

Events that occur on the microscopic level during fertilization drastically affect the nature of the children who are born. An extra chromosome will produce a child with Down's syndrome (left); a split in the fertilized egg will produce monozygous (identical) twins (right).

With this abnormality, the egg generally develops with tragic results. Note in Figure 2-23 that there is an extra chromosome in pair 21. If a child with three chromosomes (a trisome) in pair 21 is born, that individual will have **Down's syndrome:** he or she will be very short, have a malformed heart, and be severely mentally retarded. Down's syndrome is a common birth defect; it occurs in 1 out of every 600 live births.

In pair 23, the sex chromosomes, another trisome can occur. If the father donates *both* X and Y chromosomes, in addition to the mother's X chromosome, a

FIGURE 2-22
The 23 Pairs of Human Chromosomes
The 23rd pair, XX (right) shows that individual to be a female, while the one on the left has an XY 23rd pair, indicating those are the chromosomes of a male.

A1	A2	A3		B4-B5

C6-C12

D13-D15	E16	E17	E18

F19-F20	G21-G22	XY

A1	A2	A3		B4-B5

C6-C12

D13-D15	E16	E17	E18

F19-F20	G21-G22	XX

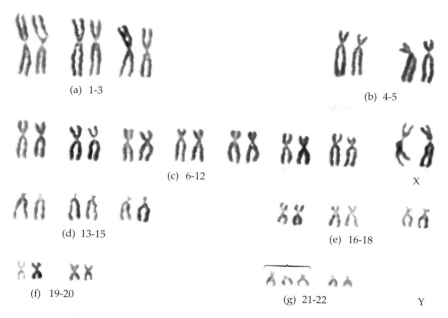

FIGURE 2-23
Chromosomal
Abnormality in Down's
Syndrome
The extra chromosome in
pair 21, called trisomy 21,
is responsible for this
relatively common birth
defect.

(a) 1-3

(b) 4-5

(c) 6-12

X

(d) 13-15

(e) 16-18

(f) 19-20

(g) 21-22

Y

male child with feminine characteristics (enlarged breasts, feminine body contours) will be born. In a few recent Olympic contests, the Russians entered males with this abnormal chromosome composition in women's events. Their performances were unusual for females and so were their genes!

Mutations

Offspring can differ in characteristics from their parents in two ways: through the sexual recombinations that occur when each parent donates half of the child's chromosomes and through mutations. A **mutation** is a spontaneous change in the structure of one or more genes. Mutations are "accidents" in the normal functioning of genetic replication, but they differ from abnormal chromosomes. Mutations can occur in a variety of ways: from a mistake when the chromosomes from the mother and father are combined at conception, from mistakes in DNA replication, and from physical damage to DNA molecules, which can be caused by environmental events such as radiation.

Mutations can affect the life of an individual in different ways: negatively, positively, or not at all. Some mutations have no effect on the individual, but most mutations are decidedly negative. They result in serious diseases, physical deformity, or mental retardation. Although dire for the individual, these mutations have little or no effect on the evolution of the species, because these individuals do not often reproduce successfully. Mutations with a positive adaptive value obey the laws of natural selection. In fact, it is thought that positive mutations are the basic mechanism by which changes in species eventually occur.

Twins

The only exception to the rule of genetic uniqueness is identical twins. **Identical twins** are **monozygotic,** that is, they develop from the same fertilized egg. (**Fraternal twins** develop when the mother releases two eggs and each is fertilized by different sperm; fraternal twins are genetically no more alike than any other two siblings.) Because genetic makeup determines much of an individual's behavior and abilities, in addition to physical appearance, genetic similarity is important to psychologists in tracing the role of genetic factors in intelligence, disease, and personality. Because identical twins offer the only possible instance of identical heredity, they are prized as subjects by psychologists interested in tackling the nature versus nurture issue. The group next most similar in genetic makeup is siblings, who share many of the same genes from their parents.

There is some degree of genetic similarity between all relatives: parents, aunts, uncles, half-brothers, and so on. When we speak of "blood relatives," we are actually speaking about genetic relatives.

Heredity and Environment

Some inherited traits may not show up right away, such as myopia (hereditary nearsightedness). Eye color is determined by one gene or at the most a pair of genes, but most human traits are determined by a combination of many. It is possible for a child to have nostrils like the mother's and the bridge of the nose like the father's. Some characteristics are so strong that they come to characterize a family: the Hapsburgs, the ruling family of the Austrian Empire for generations, had a characteristic lip (Figure 2-24). Some are rather inconsequential: whether you have attached or detached earlobes, whether or not you can roll your tongue, or whether your second toe is longer than your big toe.

FIGURE 2-24
Hereditary Traits
The characteristic Hapsburg lip gives most of these relatives a strong family resemblance.

Genetic Potential

We are certainly dealt a hand at birth, but how we play the hand is important. Most complex human abilities are determined by an interplay between inheritance and the environment; these are the kinds of abilities governed by what is called the **range of reaction.** The range of reaction is contained in a person's **genetic potential.** The specific genetic endowment may predispose an individual to an ability or a trait. Whether the predisposition develops into a reality depends largely on experience. There is probably a genetic component in intelligence, but another influence on the development of intelligence is environment. Height too may be influenced by environment (nutrition). A genetic predisposition for a particular disease may or may not express itself, depending on specific experiences (diet, stress, and culture) (Figure 2-25).

The interaction of the *genotype* (the individual's genetic potential) with the environment determines what part of the genotype will be expressed in the *phenotype.* Every organism, even the simplest bacterium, contains more genetic potential than can be expressed. The expression depends on circumstance and opportunity. Caucasians are generally taller than Orientals because the genetic potential for height in the Caucasian gene pool produces taller people. However, a study of Japanese brought up in North America showed that, with better nutrition, these Japanese grew taller than their countrymen in Japan. Therefore, it can be said that Japanese-Americans express the upper range of their height potential (Gottesman, 1974).

It is easy to analyze the comparative contributions of heredity and environment in a physical trait, such as height. Mental abilities or disabilities are much more difficult to spell out in this way. **Schizophrenia** is a severe mental disorder, affecting about one percent of the world's population; it has a genetic component as well as social causes.

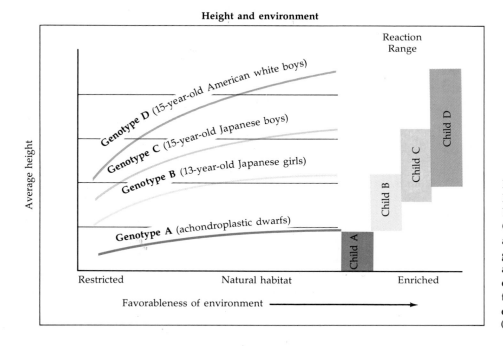

Height and environment

Reaction Range

Genotype D (15-year-old American white boys)

Genotype C (15-year-old Japanese boys)

Genotype B (13-year-old Japanese girls)

Genotype A (achondroplastic dwarfs)

Average height

Child A   Child B   Child C   Child D

Restricted   Natural habitat   Enriched

Favorableness of environment ⟶

FIGURE 2-25
Range of Reaction to the Environment
One individual may have a genetic potential for greater height than another, but the height each achieves depends on the environment in which each develops.
(After Gottesman, 1974)

TABLE 2-3 Concordance Rates in Recent Twin Studies of Schizophrenia (%)

	Identical Twins	Fraternal Twins
Norway	45	15
Denmark	56	26
United States	43	9
Finland	35	13
United Kingdom	58	12

SOURCE: Data from Gottesman & Shields, 1972.

The genetic contribution was discovered by examining the family histories of schizophrenics and correlating them with those of nonschizophrenics. That comparison revealed an additional schizophrenia within the schizophrenic's families than among the families of nonschizophrenics. Moreover, within schizophrenic families, the greater the genetic similarity, the greater the incidence of schizophrenia (Table 2-3) (Kessler, 1980). The identical twin of a schizophrenic is more likely to suffer from the disorder than a fraternal twin; a sibling of a schizophrenic has a greater chance of being one than a cousin. The child of a schizophrenic has 12 to 13 times the average chance of being a schizophrenic (Table 2-4) (Kessler, 1980). This is a predisposition only; in a favorable and healthy environment, the serious disorder of schizophrenia stands less of a chance of being expressed.

TABLE 2-4 Estimates of the Risk for Schizophrenia among Relatives of Schizophrenics (%)

	Rosenthal (1970)	Slater & Cowie (1971)
Parents	4.2	4.4
Sibs (neither parent affected)	6.7	8.2
Sibs (one parent affected)	12.5	13.8
All Sibs	7.5	8.5
Children	9.7	12.3
Children (both parents affected)	35.0*	36.6–46.3
Half-Sibs	—	3.2
Aunts and Uncles	1.7	2.0
Nephews and Nieces	2.3	2.3
Grandchildren	2.6	2.8
First Cousins	1.7	2.9

* Excludes Kallmann's (1938) study.
SOURCE: Data from Rosenthal, 1970; Slater & Cowie, 1971.

Do Our Genes "Wear" Us?: Sociobiology

Genetic mechanisms explain how characteristics of one individual can be passed on to succeeding generations. It was only because Darwin's theory of evolution was consistent with the findings of modern genetics in the 1930s and 1940s that evolution became dominant in modern science.

One important question in evolution remains highly controversial: What does natural selection "select"? Darwin's idea was that natural selection is a process involving countless individuals struggling for survival and that these individuals pass on their genes to the succeeding generation. Other investigators have hypothesized that natural selection can work on a *group* of related organisms or on the entire *population* of organisms themselves (the species). Thus, anything that helps a *family unit* to survive will be selected, or anything that helps humans as a whole will also be selected.

Recently, to these three factors—the individual, the group (such as a tribe), and the population—a fourth has been added: the gene itself. The role of the gene in evolution is crucial to a new scientific theory called sociobiology.

Sociobiology attempts to account for *social* behavior in *biological* terms. There are, however, many different approaches that attempt to understand the biological basis of social behavior. What is different is that sociobiology concentrates on the *gene* as the determinant of our behavior. According to this view, much of our social behavior can be considered as the outcome of our genes trying to ensure their *own survival* through their temporary hosts, us. This idea is well stated as "A hen is an egg's way of making another egg."

Inclusive Fitness and the Concept of Altruism

If you consider the chicken and egg statement, this turns the normal inquiry around: instead of looking at the individual as the central element in evolution, the focus shifts to the gene, operating through the individual. This viewpoint has given rise to the important concept of **inclusive fitness.** To understand this we must go back to Darwin. His "survival of the fittest" focuses on the individual's ability to produce genetically related surviving offspring. However, many human behaviors seem to make no sense with respect to survival of the species: Why do people give up their lives to save others? Why do Eskimos commit suicide when they are no longer viable? Why is infanticide common to many cultures? (Barash, 1986)

The concept of inclusive fitness widens that of reproductive fitness. It states that an individual will act in such a way as to maximize not only his offspring, but *the number of copies of his genetic material.* This would include actions that benefit his or her family and those closely related. This means that motives other than sexual ones are important in evolution.

An important example of inclusive fitness is the analysis of **altruism.** In some extreme situations an individual will give up his or her life for that of others. Why, if the individual is the unit of natural selection, would anyone do this? This behavior could eradicate any chance of that individual passing on his or her characteristics to the next generation. From the point of view of the individual, such behavior would make no sense.

But it might make sense from the "point of view" of the *gene:* an altruistic act would ensure the survival of those genes that the individual has in common with the others. In fact, an inclusive fitness analysis reveals that the *closer the relationship,* and thus the more genes in common, *the higher the probability of altruism.* In studies of nonhuman beings this seems to be the case: almost all instances of altruism occur between immediate family members (Hamilton, 1964). Haldane (1986) quipped, "I would give up my own life for three of my children, or eight cousins. In each case, the number of one's own genes is increased."

Another example is schizophrenia; it is difficult to see how such a devastating disorder could persist. However, as we shall see later in Chapter 16, it has been found that relatives of schizophrenics have a high probability of being unusually creative, and thus of value to society. This fits the sociobiological concept: the inclusive fitness of the gene that manifests as schizophrenia is of value to the population (Wenegrat, 1984).

Parental Investment

The concept of reproductive fitness, although important, does not completely take into account all the actions and decisions that take place after conception. Sometimes a parent must weigh the benefits of supporting one child well versus supporting many less well, or must weigh one child against the other. **Parental investment** is any "investment" (of care, food, support, risk, and resources) that enhances the survival potential of an offspring. The analysis draws from and is similar to economic cost–benefit analyses (Trivers, 1971).

At very low levels of parental investment, with little daily care of an infant, the offspring may die. But at very high levels of investment, when parents devote almost all of their resources to one infant, the parent's ability to invest in *another* offspring is limited. Such high investment may not be in the parent's genetic interest, for it would be better to have more survivors (Figure 2-26).

Of course, it is to the child's benefit for parental investment to be increased because the child is acting (in this analysis) to maximize his or her genes. If this analysis is true, it provides a feasible underpinning for many of the common conflicts between parents and children. As a child, it would be to one's advantage to get the greatest investment, even at the expense of siblings. But when one is grown, one's *own* children will similarly seek more investment than one is willing to give. Individuals will act differently at different stages of their lifespan (Wenegrat, 1984). Because of different parental investments, males and females will also have differing priorities.

Note on Sociobiology, Evolution, and the Gene-centered Viewpoint

While it is important to note that the gene-centered view of evolution does provide a good explanation of several puzzles, it seems that natural selection in human beings works mainly on the individual, who exercises conscious choices and passes on a *very large number* of different genes to the offspring (Hamilton, 1964). It is unlikely that *one* individual gene of the million or so within us could have a major effect on our behavior.

However, there is more to the evolutionary viewpoint than this specific doctrine. Psychology is beginning to draw from the vast literature on evolution in many ways, and when major traditions, such as biology and psychology, begin to merge, there are often some misconceptions. One is that sociobiology *is* evolution.

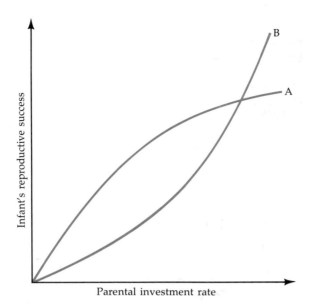

FIGURE 2-26
Parental Investment
Inclusive fitness benefits
(curve A) and costs (curve
B) as functions of parental
investment rate (horizontal
axis).

More reasonably, we could distinguish the *phylogenetic* and the *selectionist* viewpoints. The phylogenetic view simply assumes the fact of evolution, that organisms evolved to suit their environment. This means that some characteristics of perception and cognition are more probable than others. So such psychologists as Shepard (1984), Marr (1982), and Chomsky (1980) look to *specialized computational mechanisms* in the nervous system which allow the person to decode important components of the world, for instance, syntax and the constancies of sensation and vision. Others look to the universal expression of emotions (Ekman, 1984) as another part of the program. Chomsky (1980) compares the mind to a collection of different organs, such as exist in the body. Even Skinner (1986), an ardent behaviorist, now feels that modern life has eroded the original, built-in relationship between an organism's actions and their consequences.

See Chapter 8, section
on Operant
Conditioning.

The selectionist viewpoint is slightly more complex: it assumes that some specific selection mechanisms are at work in human judgment and choice. Some psychologists use this approach to analyze biases in moral judgments (Cosmides & Tooby, 1986).

BEYOND OUR INHERITANCE

At the end of this swift history, it seems that the unique characteristics of the human animal are the source of our greatest triumphs and obstacles. Human beings are the only animals who have gone beyond their original "birthplace" to live under almost any conditions on earth—in the desert, on frozen mountains, on the sea, in small settlements, in large cities—and even beyond the boundaries of the earth to live in space, for a while. We inherit many physical characteristics as do other animals, but our most important is this: *the ability to go beyond our inheritance.*

Human beings have created their own environment and are constantly adapting to this created world. This is why we are plagued with the pervasive physical and mental "disorders of civilization." It is as if our "feet" are rooted in the inheritance we share with other animals, but we are reaching beyond ourselves. In this aspiration we sometimes break in the middle. A new kind of adaptation is now necessary: one that will call on all the capacities of our minds and that will require new adaptations in behavior. For much of the rest of this book we will try to understand how we behave and think, judge and speak, learn and forget. From this we may discover what new steps, following from those of our ancestor's, we might now take.

SUMMARY

1. The question of *nature–nurture* concerns whether our biology, thoughts, and behavior are completely determined by either "nature" or "nurture." The nature view holds that we are governed by our innate characteristics such as instincts. Instincts are inborn fixed patterns of behavior. The nurture view emphasizes that people are the product of their environmental circumstances and that these circumstances determine, for example, whether one person becomes a beggar and another a banker. More recent thinking in psychology holds that people are a product of *both* factors. Nature sets certain limits and predispositions, and then nurture determines the outcome.

2. Adaptation occurs when an organism changes to fit better in its environment. There are several varieties. *Sensory* adaptation occurs when we walk into a dark room and we can see better after a period of time has passed. When we put on a new pair of glasses, the world seems curved at first, but then we adjust. This is *perceptual* adaptation. An important form of adaptation took place when our ancestors, through a long series of physical changes called *evolution,* developed specific characteristics like walking and talking, which allowed them to adapt better to their environment.

3. A *system* is any group of things that function together for a common purpose. What connects them together is *feedback,* which is information about the operation of a system, used within the system to attain its goals. There are two different kinds. Negative feedback produces changes in a direction *opposite* to an initial change. A thermostat is an example. Positive feedback produces change in the *same* direction as the initial change: smiling at a person produces a greater smile by that other person, which, in turn, might produce an even greater smile by oneself.

4. The ancestors of human beings emerged over the last 25 million years. The first species that now seems close to being our direct ancestor was *Australopithecus,* who appeared 3 to 4 million years ago. The first recognizable human ancestor was probably *Homo erectus.* They had large brains and fairly complex behavior: they cooked, used skins for covering, had advanced tools, and built elaborate shelters. Neanderthals, the cavemen of popular folklore, appeared during the Ice Age about 250,000 years ago. They developed much more elaborate rituals and social organization, including ceremonial burial of their dead. Cro-Magnon, about 60,000 years ago, was almost indistinguishable from modern human beings. They had art (as seen in the paintings of the caves of Lascaux) and developed language.

5. Hunter–gatherers lead a nomadic existence, searching for game and for fruits, vegetables, and grains to gather. It is probable that most human cultures, until quite recently, were characterized by such a nomadic existence. The invention of agriculture enabled

our ancestors to live in permanent settlements and develop stable social organizations and the beginnings of civilization.

6. How populations change over time is their *evolution. Natural selection* is the key element. Organisms in any given situation vary; those organisms with the most "adaptive fitness" to their environment have more surviving and successful offspring. This causes the population to change. Therefore, the environment "selects" the species best adapted to it by natural selection.

7. Characteristics of *human adaptation* are bipedalism, children born immature, females sexually receptive all the time, forelimbs capable of fine motor control (dexterity), large brain, cooperative social life, and an interdependent society.

8. *Bipedalism* (standing on the hindlimbs) led directly to a more delicate set of forelimbs that could become hands, which, in turn, could develop tools to use. Bipedalism also led to a thickened pelvic structure, which led to a narrower birth canal and thus the need for infants to be born at a comparatively immature stage in their development.

9. Human beings are the most sexual mammal. All female mammals except human beings are sexually excitable only when in *estrus* (when ovulating), but with human females there is no time when sex is not possible. Human beings can thus have intercourse frequently throughout the entire year. Human sexual signals are more visual than other animals' and are more obvious. The human style of sex lays the foundation for a stable society built of family units.

10. An important aspect of being human is that we seem to inherit the ability to go beyond our inheritance. Individual learning can be transmitted quickly between individuals, through language and through other communication instruments. This, however, leads to an important and continual human problem: biological evolution cannot match the speed of cultural evolution—the sum of developments in science, arts, humanities, and technology. Thus, many of today's most serious psychological problems—such as stress due to crowding—have their roots in our evolutionary history.

11. The *gene* is the basic unit of heredity. Genes are made of DNA molecules consisting of two chains twisted into a double spiral of four chemical building blocks. The order in which these chemicals appear along the spiral, called a double helix, is the *genetic code.*

12. Organisms grow by cell division in a process called *mitosis.* One cell divides into two, two into four, and so on. Genes are arranged, like beads on a string, on a *chromosome.* Human beings have 46 chromosomes that carry the individual's entire genetic program. All the genes that an individual carries are called the *genotype,* but not all genes in an individual actually appear in the characteristics of that individual. That portion of a genotype that does appear is called the *phenotype.*

13. Most complex human activities are determined by an interplay between their genetic inheritance and the environment with which a person comes in contact. Human abilities are governed by the range of reaction. A person's genetic inheritance may predispose him or her to a certain potential, but the environment determines just how much of that potential is developed.

TERMS AND CONCEPTS

adaptation
adaptive value
altruism
amniocentesis
Australopithecus
bipedalism
chromosome
Cro-Magnon
cultural evolution
Darwin
dexterity
DNA
dominant gene
Down's syndrome
estrus
ethology
evolution
feedback loop
fixed action pattern
fraternal twins
gene
genetic code
genetic potential
genetics
genotype
hominids
Homo erectus
Homo habilis
Homo sapiens
human adaptation

hunter–gatherers
identical twins
imprinting
inclusive fitness
innate
Lascaux
mitosis
monozygotic
mutation
natural selection
nature–nurture
Neanderthal
negative feedback
ovulation
pair bonding
parental investment
phenotype
positive feedback
prehuman beings
range of reaction
recessive gene
schizophrenia
self-awareness
sensory adaptation
sociobiology
stable strategy
system
Terra Amata
tool use

SUGGESTIONS FOR FURTHER READING

Barash, D. (1986). *The tortoise and the hare.* New York: Viking Penguin.
An interesting analysis of human behavior from the sociobiological perspective.

Cosmides, L., & Tooby, J. (1986). From evolution to behavior: Evolutionary psychology as the missing link. In J. Dupre (Ed.), *The latest on the best: Essays on evolution and optimality.* Cambridge, MA: MIT Press.
An essay in a new collection which tries to carry the evolutionary view further into psychology.

Dawkins, R. (1986). *The blind watchmaker.* New York: Norton.
A brilliantly written work by the author of The selfish gene, *which portrays the human world as an interconnected set of evolved actions, unguided. Very controversial, especially to religious viewpoints, but worth knowing about.*

Ehrlich, P., & Ornstein, R. (in press). *New world new mind.* New York: Doubleday.
The mismatches between the world that made us and the world we made. Amplifies much of this discussion.

Haldane, J. B. S. (1986). *On being the right size.* London: Oxford.
The great evolutionary biologist's essays, edited by Maynard Smith. It allows the reader to begin to think like a biologist and look at common phenomena in a different way.

Johansen, D., & Edey, M. A. (1981). *Lucy: The beginnings of humankind.* New York: Simon & Schuster.

The discovery of what is perhaps our oldest ancestor, written in an engaging "detective story" style.

Wenegrat, B. (1984). *Sociobiology and mental disorder: A new view.* Boston: Addison Wesley.

Excellent source material for the ideas, drawn from evolutionary biology, which are now influencing psychology and psychotherapy.

Zahn-Waxler, C., et al. (Eds.). (1986). *Altruism and aggression: Social and biological origins.* New York: Cambridge University Press.

Cross disciplines and cross species, this is a collection of scientific articles about how altruism and aggression relate.

Early Development: Birth to Adolescence

The most dazzling biological achievement in nature begins when one of the hundreds of millions of male sperm finds and unites with the female egg (Figure 3-1). It is the first moment of a new life; that single cell divides, and the new cells divide again and again to form the brain, organs, muscles, skin, and bones. Only about 50 doublings of that first cell beget a baby! No one knows how this happens—why some cells become "brain" and others "tongue."

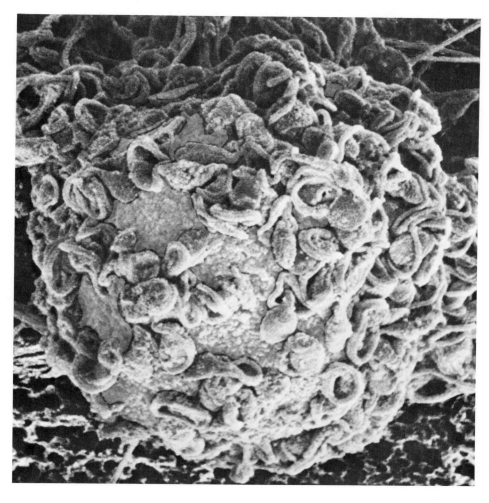

FIGURE 3-1
Sperm Swarming over the Female Egg at the Moment of Conception

FIGURE 3-2
The Interaction of
Heredity and
Environment
In geneticist Conrad
Waddington's analogy of
heredity and environment,
the landscape represents
possibilities determined by
genetic factors, and forces
such as wind, gravity, and
so on represent
environmental influences.
The path the ball takes
indicates the course of
development. There are
various paths open, but
once development is
moving along a particular
path—down one of the
valleys—it is difficult to
change to another course.
The analogy helps explain
how both heredity and
environment play
important roles in shaping
an individual's personality
and abilities.
(After Waddington, 1957)

What we do know is that a speck starting so small that it is barely detectable under a microscope bursts upon the scene in 40 weeks in the form of a seven-pound baby. Even though life inside the womb is the period of the most rapid growth, development has just begun. From conception to adulthood a baby changes form so drastically and so often that it almost seems to be a succession of very different organisms: the ovum, embryo, fetus, newborn, infant, child, and adolescent.

Although babies are helpless and immature at birth, the seeds of adult abilities are present at the beginning (Figure 3-2). Those seeds begin to bear fruit. Growth and development is a process of widening capacities, which allow the child to widen his or her "world." A helpless baby blossoms into an adult capable of an extraordinary range of motor abilities, from running to writing. Mentally, a newborn, who can only recognize its mother's odor and face and barely follow a light, blooms into an adult who can invent and imagine things never before dreamt of.

Socially, the world expands—from the moment the umbilical cord is cut—from a singular attachment to mother to many attachments to family, friends, and, finally, community and work. As a child grows, life becomes less fixed by biology and more by the family, friends, and choices. This chapter follows development from a single cell to the self, while the last chapter of the book ends the progression of the widening spheres of development. What begins here continues on, just as the processes of thought inaugurated in the child later mature and become the basis for perception, cognition, and reasoning, which ripen further in old age.

Principles and Issues

Nature–Nurture

Human development offers a powerful way of studying the nature versus nurture issue. By observing newborns, psychologists can see what human beings know without "experience" in the environment. As people age, the environment increasingly influences innate abilities. Nature has potent influence early in life. By about the age of 25, individual experiences, such as language, schooling, profession, and culture, become the center of influence.

Maturation

Maturation is the emergence of individual characteristics through normal growth processes. *Physical* maturation is controlled by the information contained in the genes and is relatively unaffected by experience. It follows a universal pattern: children all over the world crawl before they walk, have milk teeth before permanent teeth, and mature sexually in puberty.

Behavior appropriate at one age may not be at another. Imagine that you are seated at dinner and the person next to you gets up, runs around the room, and asks everyone at the table for food. This individual finally sits down, but interrupts every conversation with deafening yells. If your partner were 25 years old, you might look for the nearest psychotherapist. If your companion were 2 years old, you would no doubt think the behavior was "understandable."

Psychological maturation is the development of mental abilities that result from the normal growth of the brain and nervous system. Due to the long period of immaturity, experiences such as language, family, and culture can have profound effects on psychological maturation (Kagan, 1984).

Adaptation

Chapter 2 showed how our earliest ancestors, through successive physical adaptations over thousands of years, evolved to meet the demands of a changing world. Although changes occur much more rapidly in an individual's development (years rather than millennia), the changes are extreme and require continual adaptation.

Egocentrism

Egocentric literally means "self-centered." Although this term is usually used to criticize someone, practically speaking, it is impossible not to be self-centered. The principle of **egocentrism** differentiates stages in human development, as the infant matures from an initially strong egocentrism to realizing that other people exist outside of themselves and thus have separate minds.

Life Before Birth

The mother and the unborn child are the "closest human relationship," a single biological unit for nine months. For the unborn child, physical development is the most rapid and vulnerable in the 40 weeks inside the mother's womb. There are three distinct periods *in utero* (in the womb): the period of the ovum, of the embryo, and of the fetus. The period of the *ovum* begins at the moment of fertilization and ends about two weeks later when the fertilized egg (ovum) is implanted in the uterus. Once attached to the uterine wall, the ovum becomes an embryo (Plate 1).

The **embryonic period** lasts until about the ninth week of pregnancy. It is the critical stage of development for the nervous system. In about the ninth week, the period of the fetus begins with the baby's first independent reaction to the world: the fetus responds to upsets by flexing its torso and extending its head.

The First Two Weeks of Life

Newborns have some important abilities that seem to be the seeds from which adult capacities grow. They identify with other human beings almost immediately—they imitate, coo, and smile at the sight of other people.

Reflexes

When babies are born they face new experiences such as sounds, hot and cold temperatures, movements, and pain. Babies are ready for these changes; they turn toward interesting noises and away from unpleasant events (Newman & Newman 1987). Newborns know how to signal distress: they cry. A baby's cry gets the attention of the caretaker, usually the mother, who tries to comfort him.

Only two hours after birth, newborns can follow a slowly moving light in front of their eyes. If a nipple or a finger is put into their mouths, they begin to suck on

FOOD, DRUGS, AND THE UNBORN CHILD

The many physical and psychological changes the mother undergoes during pregnancy can affect the baby. The mother's emotional state, the drugs she takes, and the food she eats all affect the unborn child. For example, a woman who is exposed to or contracts German measles during the first two months of pregnancy runs a high risk of having a severely retarded or physically deformed child. If she has measles in her ninth month, the child is far less likely to be affected.

Certain basic nutrients are needed by the fetus to develop properly. If the nervous system does not develop well, there can be impairment of mental abilities in the child: insufficient protein during pregnancy can lead to mental retardation. In a seven-year study in Guatemala, children of mothers who had been given dietary supplements in pregnancy scored higher on intelligence tests (Kagan, 1985).

Because the fetus is especially sensitive at certain periods of development, drugs the mother takes may affect the child. The baby of a heroin addict may be born addicted to heroin and go through withdrawal at birth. Babies born of alcoholic mothers suffer **fetal alcoholic syndrome:** they are small, have cone-shaped heads, and may be mentally retarded. Even moderate alcohol consumption, such as two drinks per day, can cause malformation of the fetus. Women who smoke are twice as likely to have a miscarriage as nonsmokers. Children of smokers weigh less at birth and are more likely to die of crib death than others.

Hormones taken by the mother during pregnancy may have long-term consequences. Anke Ehrhardt and her colleagues (1981) studied children whose mothers had taken *estrogen,* the female sex hormone, as a supplement during pregnancy. Eight years later the boys were judged to be less masculine and the girls more feminine. *Perhaps the best advice pregnant women can be given is to take as few drugs as possible.*

it. This sucking response is very strong; because it is the only way for them to obtain food, it is an important survival technique. If you gently stroke their cheeks or the corner of their mouths, they will turn their heads in that direction; this is called "rooting" and it is an attempt to find their mother's nipple. Such unlearned responses of newborns are called **reflexes** and are part of an inborn, unlearned program (Figure 3-3).

Many of these inborn movements are the building blocks of sophisticated motor skills, such as walking and speech. Trevarthen (1981) recorded the unforced lip movements of newborns and found that they were the same as those required for adult speech. In the first few months of life, an infant makes most of the sounds of every known language (Miller, 1981).

Cognition

William James (1890) wrote that the experience of the newborn is a "blooming, buzzing confusion." Jean Piaget characterized it as a transitory world: "There are no permanent objects, only perceptual pictures which appear, dissolve and sometimes reappear" (Piaget, 1952).

These portrayals are in part accurate. The world to the infant probably appears to be more disorganized than to the adult and most likely seems unstable and meaningless. Because the sensory systems are relatively well developed at birth

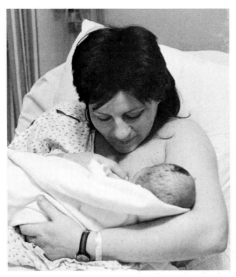

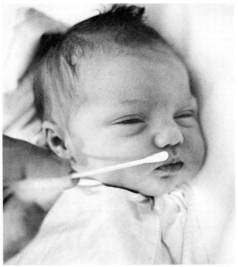

(Coren & Poirac, 1984), the newborn's world probably consists of a sequence of sounds, lights, and other sensations with less stability than adult perception.

My own view is that the world of the infant is not so much confused as it is *simpler* and more *selective* than the adult world. Newborns are biologically unprepared to function in the adult world, on their own, but they *are* prepared to function in their *limited* world. Their extreme egocentrism, for example, can be thought of as adaptive: an extremely narrow perspective is important for survival.

They seem designed to recognize the mother by smell. Newborns notice objects that are *very close* to them, things that are a part of their very small world. Later on, the newborns' world expands, and so does their thought and perspective. They become less egocentric. At birth newborns can focus up to only ten inches away, about the distance from the breast to the mother's face. Later on, their range of vision expands. Newborns can distinguish between figures and the ground, have some depth perception, and can respond to different smells (Haith, 1980).

Even very young babies are interested and interactive observers of the world around them.

Preferences in Perception

Robert Fantz (1961) showed newborns a set of six discs (Figure 3-4). The babies looked longer at patterned discs than at single-color discs and *longest* at the pictures of a face. At first, babies look primarily at the areas of most contour and change, that is, the edges of objects. By six weeks they look at peoples' mouths, especially at mother's mouth when she is talking (Bower, 1978). This inborn preference exists because being attracted to human beings is important to survival.

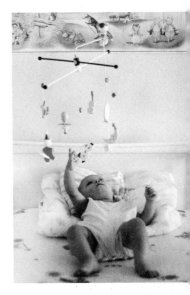

Babies seem to be born with a set of rules to look at the world with: (1) if awake and alert, open your eyes; (2) if you find darkness, search the environment; (3) if you find light, but not edges, begin a broad uncontrolled search of the environment; and (4) if you find an edge, look near the edge and try to cross the edge (Haith, 1980). It seems likely that the infant comes into the world with a predisposition to search out new features of the environment.

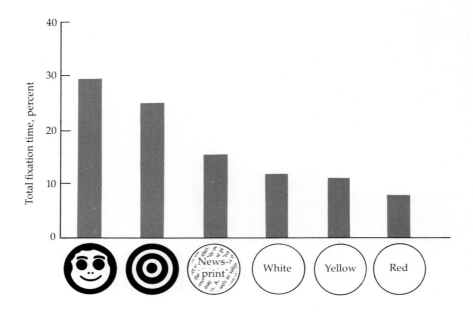

FIGURE 3-4
Visual Preference of Newborns
In experiments exposing infants to various visual stimuli, newborns as young as 10 hours old to 5 days old looked longer at the disc with the black-and-white face than at simpler discs showing a bull's-eye, newsprint, or solid colors.
(After Fantz, 1961)

PHYSICAL GROWTH IN THE EARLY YEARS

Sequence of Motor Development

Figure 3-5 and Table 3-1 show when children achieve important motor skills. An infant may skip one or another stage in the sequence (for example, some babies never crawl), but the order in which these skills appear is the same for all children. No one walks before sitting up or standing. Each element in the sequence builds to the next. Although there is some variation in the age at which any one of the particular skills may appear, there are limits: no baby walks at six months or sits up at three weeks.

Adjustments to Growth

The first two years are marked by such rapid physical growth that the child must constantly adapt to a changing body (Figure 3-6). Children at two are almost twice as tall as they were at birth and are half their adult height. If adults grew at the same rate as babies do in their first two years, in two years we would be 11 feet tall. Imagine the number of adaptations you would have to make! An infant's experience may be a gradual version of Alice's experience in Wonderland when she took the drink that suddenly made her tall. She had to adjust constantly her relationship to such familiar objects as tables and chairs.

To lift a cup to your mouth, you must know not only where the cup is and how to move it toward you, but you must also know *where you are* — where your arm is, how long it is, how far to stretch it, and where your mouth is. Growth affects all sensory systems. As the head grows, the eyes grow farther apart, which makes it difficult to judge the distance between oneself and an object accurately (Bower, 1981). These constant changes contribute to the instability of the perceptual and mental worlds of the infant.

FIGURE 3-5
The Achievement of Motor Skills
Not all children achieve these motor skills at exactly these ages. But this sequence is most often
observed, as are the milestones of language development described in Table 3-1. (After Shirley, 1933)

TABLE 3-1   Developmental Milestones in Motor and Language Development[1]

Age	Motor Development	Vocalization and Language
12 weeks	Supports head when in prone position; weight is on elbows; hands mostly open; no grasp reflex.	Markedly less crying than at 8 weeks; when talked to and nodded at, smiles, followed by squealing-gurgling sounds usually called *cooing*, which is vowellike in character and pitch-modulated; sustains cooing for 15–20 seconds.
16 weeks	Plays with a rattle placed in hands (by shaking it and staring at it); head self-supported; tonic neck reflex subsiding.	Responds to human sounds definitely; turns head; eyes seem to search for speaker; occasionally some chuckling sounds.
20 weeks	Sits with props.	The vowellike sounds begin to be interspersed with more consonant sounds; labial fricatives, spirants, and nasals are common; acoustically, all vocalizations are very different from the sounds of the mature language of the environment.
6 months	Sitting: bends forward and uses hands for support; can bear weight when put into standing position, but cannot yet stand holding on; reaching: unilateral grasp; no thumb opposition yet; releases cube when given another.	Cooing changes into babbling resembling one-syllable utterances; neither vowels nor consonants have very fixed recurrences; most common utterances sound somewhat like *ma, mu, da,* or *di.*
8 months	Stands holding on; grasps with thumb opposition; picks up pellet with thumb and fingertips.	Reduplication (or more continuous repetitions) becomes frequent; intonation patterns become distinct; utterances can signal emphasis and emotions.
10 months	Creeps efficiently; takes side steps, holding on; pulls to standing position.	Vocalizations are mixed with sound-play such as gurgling or bubble blowing; appears to wish to imitate sounds, but the imitations are never quite successful; begins to differentiate between words heard by making differential adjustments.
12 months	Walks when held by one hand; walks on feet and hands, knees in air; mouthing of objects almost stopped; seats self on floor.	Identical sound sequences are replicated with higher relative frequency of occurrence, and words ("mamma" or "dadda") are emerging; definite signs of understanding some words and simple commands ("Show me your eyes").

Age	Motor Development	Vocalization of Language
18 months	Grasp, prehension, and release fully developed; gait stiff, propulsive, and precipitated; sits on child's chair with only fair aim; creeps downstairs backward; has difficulty building tower of three cubes.	Has a definite repertoïre of words—more than 3, but less than 50; still much babbling but now of several syllables with intricate intonation pattern; no attempt at communicating information and no frustration for not being understood; words may include items such as "Thank you" or "Come here," but there is little ability to join any of the lexical items into spontaneous two-item phrases; understanding is progressing rapidly.
24 months	Runs, but falls in sudden turns; can quickly alternate between sitting and standing; climbs stairs up or down.	Vocabulary of more than 50 items (some children seem to be able to name everything in environment); begins spontaneously to join vocabulary items into two-word phrases; all phrases appear to be own creations; definite increase in communicative behavior and interest in language.

[1] Note: these skills are given for the age at which *almost all* children will have accomplished them.
SOURCE: Lenneberg, 1967.

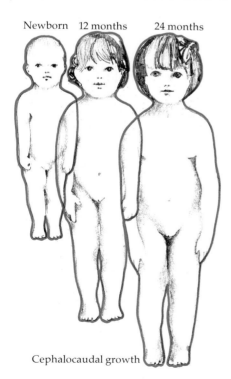

Newborn   12 months   24 months

Cephalocaudal growth

Proximodistal growth

FIGURE 3-6
The Direction of Growth and Development
Children grow physically and develop their motor abilities in two directions at the same time. They experience cephalocaudal growth (from top to bottom) and proximodistal growth (from the center to the periphery).
(After Hall et al., 1982)

COGNITIVE DEVELOPMENT: PIAGET'S THEORY

A father reads a book to his 2-year-old and 2-week-old children. The 2-year-old laughs, helps turn the pages, points to things and identifies them, asks questions, and asks for the book to be read again. The newborn coos, looks around the room, and dozes off. The infant is oblivious. The 2-year-old and the newborn are closer in age than the 2-year-old is to the father, yet in terms of cognitive abilities, the 2-year-old and the father are more nearly alike. They share the same world, one which the newborn has not yet entered. The 2-year-old has attachments to people, can organize activities around a goal, and is concerned with competence.

During the early years, a child gradually becomes more organized and more able to focus and direct attention for longer periods. Children who are 3 years of age and younger focus attention on an exciting event or object and are easily distracted by the next exciting event; they attend to irrelevant events. A 6-year-old's attention is more under control, less distractible by outside stimuli.

From one month after conception to birth, the human brain grows at an amazing rate and is fully developed at birth (Figure 3-7). By about 5 years of age the brain is 95 percent of adult size. The maturation and growth of the brain and nervous system allow better coordination and motor control, including the fine control needed to draw, color, and write and the hand-eye coordination needed to catch balls and thread needles.

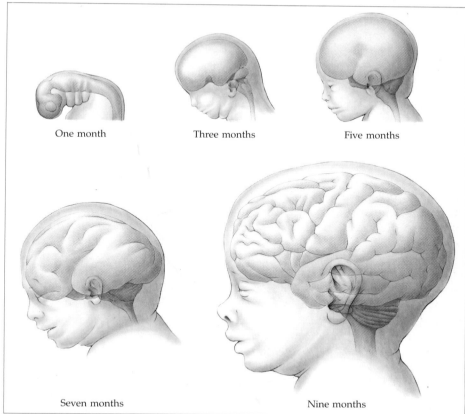

One month

Three months

Five months

Seven months

Nine months

FIGURE 3-7
Embryonic Growth of the Human Brain
Note that the characteristic convolutions of the brain's surface do not appear until about mid-pregnancy. The brain grows amazingly fast: it is calculated that neurons are generated in the embryonic brain at a rate of 250,000 per minute! (Source: Cowan, W. M., 1979, Development of the Brain. *Scientific American*)

Jean Piaget
(1896–1980)

By 7 years of age, children have made great cognitive leaps. They know right from left, their memories improve dramatically, and they can distinguish between *p* and *q*, *b* and *d*. A 5-year-old uses simple reasoning, but is not very good at making and carrying out plans. A 7-year-old uses complex reasoning, plans, and works to "get the right answer."

Piaget's Assumptions and Terms

The most influential theory of cognitive development was proposed by a biologist turned psychologist, Jean Piaget (1896–1980). It is impossible to do full justice here to as comprehensive a theory as Piaget's. Nevertheless, we will outline the important premises and concepts of his theory. The theory is evolutionary in nature; Piaget thought that *mental abilities* are adaptive and might be understood by studying how the child's mind becomes "assembled" during development.

Piaget assumed that *knowledge guides action*. The world we experience becomes more complex and detailed as we develop new structures. He also felt that *knowledge develops through experience and action*. Babies find out about the world by exploring things with their mouths; young children use their hands and their senses.

Also, in Piaget's view, *the complexity of mental structures is determined largely by biological age*. The difference between a child at 10 and one at 3 is not merely that the older child has more information, but that the older child has a more complex and capable mind. This growth of capacity, or *mental structures*, is cognitive development.

Schema

Piaget assumes that the unit of mental life is the **schema. Schemata** (plural of schema) are the knowledge of how things are organized and relate to each other. This organization may relate actions to one another, relate different stimuli to one another, or relate outside stimuli to specific actions. Knowing that the general sequence of movements used in picking up a ball is similar to that used in picking up a pencil might be a general schema for "picking things up."

A schema may organize parts of an object onto a whole — for example, knowing that a nose, two eyes, and a mouth arranged in a certain way constitute a "face." A face schema would explain why babies prefer to look at the elements of an organized face rather than a disorganized one (Figure 3-8). A schema may also relate perceptions to actions; a baby smiles when it sees another face smile.

Assimilation and Accommodation

Schemata *change* and grow by the processes of **assimilation** and **accommodation.** When children encounter a new event, they attempt to *assimilate* it into their existing knowledge structure (the schema) (Figure 3-9). A young child learns that the family pet is called "dog." During a walk the child sees a German shepherd and says "dog"—collies, Chihuahuas, and poodles are all assimilated into this schema. But the child may also say "dog" when seeing a cat or a cow. Then it is clear that the schema was "all animals are dogs."

When new events cannot be assimilated into existing schemata, there is *disequilibrium* (imbalance). A change occurs to *accommodate* the new information

FIGURE 3-8
Innate Form Preferences
By turning their heads to look at the "face" with the features in the right places, rather than at the other "faces," babies less than 1 day old showed an innate preference that could indicate they were born with a "face" schema.

and restore equilibrium. This usually involves changing or expanding the existing schemata. The child's parent may say, "That's wrong. There are many different kinds of animals. Only some are dogs." Then the schema "all animals are dogs" changes and expands to include the new knowledge. Each time the child accommodates the schemata to new information, the intellectual world expands. Schemata, which shape experience, become more comprehensive and adaptive as the child matures.

Operations

As the child learns about the world, schemata join together to form repeated mental routines, called **operations.** Operations are rules for transforming and manipulating information. Operations are *reversible.* Consider the simple arithmetic operation, "If you add 2 of anything to 2 of anything, you will have 4 of anything." The reverse is, "If you have 4 of anything and take 2 away, you will have 2." This operation reflects a basic fact about the physical world—that quantities change when combined with other quantities.

Operations grow more complex as cognition develops. Piaget proposed that children gain concepts by *performing operations* on things. As simple as $2 + 2 = 4$ is, it is nevertheless an abstract mental concept, the understanding of which requires much repeated experience with counting things. Thus, physical manipu-

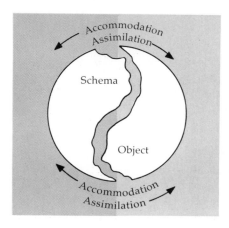

FIGURE 3-9
Assimilation and Accommodation in Piaget's Theory
Children continually develop their thought processes by assimilating new information about objects and events and accommodating it by changing their existing schemata.

lation of the environment leads to knowledge. Piaget developed many experiments to ascertain the level of a child's use of operations.

Stages of Cognitive Development

Piaget assumed that all children, regardless of culture, go through the same stages of cognitive development in the same four stages: the *sensorimotor, preoperational, concrete operational,* and *formal operational.*

Sensorimotor Stage (Birth to 2 Years)

In the **sensorimotor stage** children learn primarily through motor and sensory play. Babies are born with *reflexes,* innate motor programs, which develop in the first 18 to 24 months into complex and controlled movements. During this time, practical intelligence of one's effect on the world is developed: the baby may find that crying brings mother or that splashing in the bathtub makes all the bath toys move around. At around 18 months children begin to develop a sense of self and begin to be capable of **representational** or **symbolic thought.**

One important form of symbolic thought is the use of language. By 2 years of age, a bubbling infant has a vocabulary of about 200 words, which are used effectively in two-word sentences. Another indication of representational thought is metaphoric play, such as pretending to stroke a cat or pretending to be an elephant.

One of the most important attainments of the early phase of this sensorimotor stage is **object permanence:** babies discover that something continues to exist even when they cannot see it. If you hide an object that a 5- to 7-month-old infant is reaching for behind a screen or under a cloth, the child will stop reaching (Figure 3-10). At 8 months the baby will look behind the screen or under the cloth. This new ability to search and find is a great advance, an important cognitive step. It is also a source of fun for the child (peek-a-boo, basically a game of object permanence, is a favorite game).

Piaget first discovered this when he showed his 7-month-old daughter his watch on a chain and she reached for it. When he put his watch back in his pocket,

FIGURE 3-10
Object Permanence
Because this infant does not yet have the concept of object permanence, it acts as if an object merely hidden from view has ceased to exist.

she acted as if the watch had disappeared into thin air. But at 8 months, the child began to reach for and search in his pocket. She now knew the watch still existed, even though she could not see it.

Preoperational Stage (2 to 7 Years)

In the **preoperational stage,** children use symbols — they can *represent* objects in drawings and words (Figure 3-11). Schemata that were just being arranged in the sensorimotor stage become more coordinated in the preoperational stage, but are not yet fully organized. Children at this stage are quite fluent in the use of language, but rely primarily on their senses, on what they see or hear, rather than on what they know or imagine. They are unable to use *mental operations* — to reason, to deduce, to wonder about what *might* be.

Conservation.   Piaget did some important experimentation with children in this stage on one basic operation called conservation. **Conservation** means that an object is understood to be the same even if it appears different. Piaget contended that before the age of 6 or 7, the child has not formed the conservation rule. If you give one 3-year-old a sandwich cut into quarters and another 3-year-old a sandwich cut in half, the child with the two pieces may complain that he has ''less'' than the child with four pieces.

In Piaget's conservation of volume experiments, the experimenter shows the child two tumblers, one short and squat and the other tall and thin. He fills the short, squat one with water and then pours the water from that tumbler into the other (Figure 3-12, p. 105). He asks the child, who has watched this whole procedure, if there is the same amount of water in both tumblers. Because of the

---

WIT AND WISDOM OF 2- TO 5-YEAR-OLDS

A look at the way 2-year-olds express themselves offers a glimpse of the mental capabilities of the child. Studies of German, French, Russian, Samoan, and many other languages have shown that there is remarkable universality in the kinds of words 2-year-olds use and how they use them (Slobin, 1970). A 2-year-old can identify objects (''big car''), note their location (''book here''), demand repetition (''more milk''), note what kind of action is taking place (''man sit''), and can ask questions (''where ball?'').

Chukovsky (1963) assessed the language of children between the ages of 2 and 5. After 5, children become less inventive with words as they become more precise and realistic in their use of language. Below are some remarks of toddlers and young children less than 5 years of age. Many of them, you will note, show how important it is for children to have some explanation, *any* explanation, of how the world works.

''Our Granny killed the geese in the wintertime so that they would not catch cold.''

''Mommie, I'm so sorry for the baby horses — they cannot pick their noses.''

''I sing so much that the room gets big and beautiful.''

''Daddy, please cut this pine tree — it makes the wind. After you cut it down the weather will be nice and Mother will let me go for a walk.''

''Mothers give birth to boys too? Then what are fathers for?'' (Chukovsky, 1963)

**FIGURE 3-11
Cognitive Development
Revealed by
Children's Art**
Children's cognitive
development is apparent
in drawings like these. The
simple face (top left)
drawn by a 3-year-old
lacks the action and
relatively complex
composition of the work
(top right) by a 6-year-old.
And although the sports
picture (center) by a
9-year-old is exciting and
evocative, it is crude
compared to the bottom
drawing by a 12-year-old.
Artistic skill, like cognitive
ability, emerges in stages.

difference in shapes, the water is closer to the top of the long, thin tumbler. It appears to be full, unlike the short, squat one. Because of this, a young child will usually say "no." An older child, however, understands the deeper principle of constancy: "If you started out with the same amount of water, then it must be the same in each container." Piaget would conclude that the younger child is influenced more by appearances: information directly obtained through the senses dominates over reasoning.

Concrete Operations (7 to 12 Years)

In the **concrete operational stage** of cognitive development, thinking is no longer dominated by sensory information. Children begin to reason abstractly and can carry a task through to completion and understand some of the basic characteristics of things in the world: number, weight, and order.

The child becomes more organized and able to plan, and consequently can focus and direct attention for longer periods. There are large differences between the ways preoperational and concrete operational children direct attention (Newman & Newman, 1987). Younger children direct attention to whichever event or object is most exciting to them and are thus easily distracted. A 7-year-old's attention is more focused, more under control, and less distracted by novel stimuli, more to information relevant to a *plan*.

Formal Operations (12 Years to Adult)

Higher order thinking begins in the **formal operational stage.** Adolescents are capable of thinking abstractly and thinking through situations logically and systematically. They can follow a complex scientific experiment from start to finish and can sometimes formulate hypotheses and test them. For the first time, children in the formal operational stage are able to envision things as they *might be* instead of how they *are.* Their new capacity of conjectural thought launches them into the adult world. However, this is a somewhat idealized description, since not all adults possess this capacity, and it is not evident in all of the various skills of adulthood.

Egocentrism and Decentration

Important indicators of cognitive development, according to Piaget, are **egocentrism** and **decentration.** At each stage, children become more aware of the world outside and less focused on themselves. Infants are totally egocentric: they know no differences between themselves and other people or objects in the world. Between 18 and 24 months, children become aware that they are single individuals among many. They *decenter,* that is, move away from thinking they are the center of the world and grow increasingly concerned with life outside themselves. Decentration continues throughout development in the following stages:

1. The sensorimotor phase of life is totally egocentric: "The world is me." It is not that the baby experiences itself as the center of the world, rather that it *is* the world. In this phase of life, babies are *thought* to be unable to tell the difference between themselves and any external object.

2. As they grow, children discover that there is a world apart from them. At first they think this world revolves around them and their family. In the

FIGURE 3-12
Conservation of Volume
Around age six or seven, children start to understand the concept of conservation. Without it, they do not realize that equal amounts of a liquid in different-shaped containers are still equal, or that equal amounts of clay rolled into different shapes remain equal. Piaget repeatedly demonstrated that lack of this concept characterized preoperational children.

preoperational stage, children are aware of other people and things, but they cannot see or imagine the world from any viewpoint but their own: "The world is as I see it." If children see that their mother is sad, they may bring her a toy to cheer her up because that is what cheers *them* up.

3. In the concrete operational stage, children recognize that there are ways of looking at things other than their own, but they think *their* way is the only *valid* one: "I have the right view of the world."

4. In the formal operational stage, adolescents characteristically believe that the way they view the world is the *right* way for *everyone*. "The world *should* be as I view it."

Most adults perceive that they are but one among many. Billie Jean King, the tennis star, said, after entering her 35th Wimbledon tournament, "When you're young, you think you're the center of the universe. When you're older, you realize that you're just a little speck" (*Time,* July 11, 1983). We become progressively less egocentric as we develop.

Review and Criticism of Piaget's Theory

Jean Piaget was one of the first to construct a comprehensive theory of the acquisition of knowledge through the development of specific mental structures. But, as with many pioneering theories, Piaget's has limitations.

Piaget often seems to underestimate the reasoning abilities of children and overestimate their verbal abilities. Piaget's preoperational child is incapable of conservation and is unable to see things from another point of view. This assertion, however, depends on Piaget's particular experiments.

Consider the conservation experiments. Since young children are easily distracted, perhaps too much information confuses them. Bruner (1978) performed the same conservation experiment as above with one difference: before he emptied liquid from one tumbler into the other, he placed a screen between the tumblers and the child to block the child's view.

When he asked, "Is there the same amount of water now?" the 4-year-olds, unable to *see* the pouring of water into the tumblers, answered "yes." When there is no information overload, constancy can be achieved, even at this early stage. Other investigators have changed the experimental situation so that the tasks are more fully explained. In these cases children as young as 3 years are able to solve conservation problems and to see things from another point of view (see Kagan, 1984).

Stages of cognitive development are not as fixed as Piaget assumed. Although development does seem to proceed generally the way Piaget proposed (that is, formal operations come later than sensorimotor, and the ability to think abstractly comes after the ability to perform operations), the idea of discrete "stages of thought" may be too rigid.

According to Piaget, each stage of cognition builds upon an earlier stage, in the way a house is constructed: first the foundation is laid, then the walls, and finally the roof. Thus, the formal operational child experiences a dramatic transformation of his cognitive abilities, leaving the previous stage behind.

However, children differ from one another, and life experiences may hasten or slow the appearance of one or another component of a stage (Brainerd et al.,

1985). Not all of a child's cognitive abilities develop at the same time, and *some develop independently of one another.*

Whether development is "continuous" or "discrete" and in stages according to Piaget depends upon the point of view. From one viewpoint, abilities required, for example, to ride a bike develop at different rates: leg strength to pedal, eye-to-hand coordination, balance. However, *when these skills operate in unison, the child is at a different stage:* he or she can now bicycle to school, to the store, to a friend's house, and do many things that he or she could not do before. Similarly, the development of abstract thought enables the child to entertain fanciful ideas and to explore others' thoughts, which he or she had been unable to do previously.

Piaget's "stages" are useful as *descriptions* of the thinking of an "ideal" child at different points of development, but they are not accurate *explanations* of the course of intellectual growth (Gelman & Galistel, 1986).

Piaget focuses too much on the cognitive aspects of development. He sees the child as a miniature scientist and logician, perhaps one in his own mold. This concentration leads to a neglect of other significant components such as social relationships, personality, emotions, fantasy, creativity, intuition, and other important aspects of experience.

It is only natural that many of Piaget's conceptions would prove too rigid, some ideas too narrowly based. But it is to his breadth of vision that we owe the most complete description of intellectual growth from birth to adolescence.

Morality is the knowledge of what is right and wrong. A child's morals undergo development that is dependent on the stage of thought. Piaget (1932) reasoned that moral judgments reflect a child's cognitive abilities at different stages. By observing children's games and recording their reactions to stories about children breaking windows and stealing apples, he described stages of moral development related to cognitive stages.

Kohlberg (Colby & Kohlberg, 1986), like Piaget, also assumed that moral reasoning is based on cognitive abilities. However, he thought that moral development was a process that continues throughout adolescence and adulthood. Kohlberg's focus is on people's *reasons* for doing what they think is right and how moral reasoning and behavior shift as schemata become more complex. There are three basic levels of moral reasoning, each of which has two stages:

Level I—Premoral
    Stage 1. Obey rules to avoid punishment (punishment and obedience orientation).
    Stage 2. Conform to obtain rewards, to have favors returned.
Level II—Conventional morality
    Stage 3. Conform to avoid disapproval, dislike by others ("good boy" morality, approval by others).
    Stage 4. Conform to avoid "censure" by legitimate authorities and resultant guilt (authorities maintain morality)—obedience to laws.
Level III—Postconventional morality
    Stage 5. Conform to maintain the respect of the impartial spectator in judging in terms of community welfare (the morality of social contract, of individual rights, and of democratically accepted law).

MORAL DEVELOPMENT: KOHLBERG'S THEORY

Stage 6. Conform to avoid self-condemnation (morality of individual principles of conscience) (Colby & Kohlberg, 1986).

These three levels represent a progression of *sociomoral perspective*. The development of this perspective in an individual is illustrated by one of Kohlberg's long-term subjects, "Joe" (Kohlberg, 1969).

Joe was asked at ages 10, 17, and 24 the same question: "Why shouldn't you steal from a store?" His replies show the changes in his moral reasoning.

At age 10, he replied,

> It is not good to steal from the store. It's against the law. Somebody might see you and call the police.

The reason not to steal is that you might get caught; the law can be enforced by the police. Joe's motivation is to avoid punishment. This level of moral reasoning is **premoral:** Joe considers only his own interests.

At age 17, he responded,

> It is a matter of law. It's one of our rules that we're trying to help protect everyone, protect property, not just to protect a store. It's something that's needed in our society. If we didn't have these laws, people would steal, they wouldn't have to work for a living and our whole society would get out of kilter.

At this stage the concept of law is extended: not so much as rules *against* as rules *for* something. Law is made for the good of society. Joe thinks the law should be maintained. His perspective is **conventional.** He has gone beyond individual considerations and takes the view of society as a whole.

At age 24, Joe responded this way to the questions:

A: It is violating another person's rights, in this case to property.
Q: Does the law enter in?
A: Well, the law in most cases is based on what is morally right, so it's not a separate subject, it's a consideration.
Q: What does 'morality' or 'morally right' mean to you?
A: Recognizing the rights of other individuals, first to life, and then to do as he pleases as long as it doesn't interfere with someone else's rights.

Joe's perspective has again widened. Stealing is wrong because it violates the *moral rights* of individuals. Property rights are universal human rights, and the purpose of society is to secure these rights for the individuals who live in it. This is the final, **postconventional** level.

Criticism of Kohlberg's Theory

Kohlberg's theory is complex, as is his way of assessing the stages of morality. Both of these characteristics have been at the center of controversies, which has resulted in numerous changes by Kohlberg to his theory and assessments.

Some critics point out that Kohlberg's stages are very "western" in their emphasis on democracy and individual judgment. His stages might not hold true in a culture in which there is less emphasis on individual rights. Others point out flaws in his methodology; Kohlberg's measurements are not very reliable and do not work in the way his theory says (Kurtines & Grief, 1974).

Kohlberg and Nisan (1982), however, analyzed the sequence of moral development in youths in Turkey, with the "moral dilemmas" adapted to the Turkish setting. They found the same sequence of moral development, especially in the urban youths, as found in the studies in the West. This validates somewhat the conception that a "sociomoral progression" is, if not universal, at least possible in many different cultures (see Colby & Kohlberg, 1986).

Other critics say that the stages of moral development are not fixed and can be greatly modified by experience at both young (Bandura & McDonald, 1963) and older ages (Prentice, 1972). Also, a person at a certain level of moral development may exhibit several different kinds of action (Kurtines & Grief, 1974; Colby & Kohlberg, 1986).

There seems to be a bias in the ranking of Kohlberg's stages: political liberals would rank at the highest classifications (stages 5 and 6), while conservatives would rank only at stage 4. It could be that Kohlberg found this because his subjects tended to come of age during the time of the civil rights movement and protests over the war in Vietnam. If so, this would not reflect a true picture of morality at all because of the biased sample (Rest, Davison, & Robbins, 1978).

Aren't Females as Moral as Males?

A more serious criticism has been made by Carol Gilligan (1982). She believes that the stages of morality described by Kohlberg are descriptive of a male concept of development and a male sample bias in Kohlberg's work. And if one examines not only Kohlberg, but many other developmental psychologists' work, one does see this bias. Theories of development, child and adult, are largely male in their choice of subjects and in their orientation.

What does this mean about morality? Gilligan believes that females value relationships between people more than abstract rights, which are more characteristic of the male world. Thus, reasons for not stealing, in our example, might be overridden if a greater good could be achieved.

In one of Kohlberg's most famous dilemmas, a choice is given between stealing a drug to save a person and obeying authority. Should a loved one die for the sake of the law? Clearly, there are different possible interpretations here. However, Gilligan points out that the highest levels of moral development in Kohlberg's system are traditionally masculine values, such as individuality, rationality, detachment, and the like. Other values such as caring and responsibility for others (those more traditionally feminine) are assigned lower moral value by Kohlberg.

Of course, this argument will continue. It is clear that many concepts in psychology, including development, thought, and personality, will have to be analyzed again in the light of this criticism. For too long, psychologists and other scientists have used the white, western male as the standard against which all others are judged.

Moral Behavior

Another question is, Does *knowing* what is right and wrong ensure moral *behavior?* Some psychologists feel that the correlation between what people think and what they do, between moral principles and moral actions, may not always be strong (Mischel, 1981).

Numerous studies have tried to link moral judgment and moral behavior. The results have been mixed, but the bulk of evidence indicates that individuals at higher levels of development assessed by Kohlberg's scales appear to *behave* more "morally" than those at lower levels and tend to be more honest and altruistic, at least in their moral judgments. Juvenile delinquents are more likely to be at lower stages of moral development than nondelinquents. Thus, there seems to be a *general* progression in moral understanding close to the one Kohlberg describes (Blasi, 1980).

PSYCHOSOCIAL DEVELOPMENT

At age 2, children walk and talk and have begun to become part of society. But what children say, what they do, how they play, and how they think of themselves varies. **Psychosocial development** is the way personality and response to various groups (family, school, community, nation, and so on) matures in an individual.

Erikson's Stages

Erik Erikson divides psychosocial development into "the eight ages of man" (Roazin, 1986). Each stage has a characteristic "crisis," and the way that crisis is resolved influences the individual's later experience.

1. *First year.* The most important influence in the first year of life is the primary caregiver. The crisis of this year is *basic trust versus mistrust.* Whether the infant has a sense of basic trust or confidence in the outside world depends on his relationship with his mother or other primary caregiver.

2. *Second year.* The important influence at this stage is both parents. The crisis is *autonomy versus shame and doubt.* A child must learn self-control (toileting, frustration, anger, and so on). If his parents are overly critical, the child may come to doubt his own adequacy (resulting in shame). If they allow him to work through difficult problems himself, he develops a sense of self (autonomy).

3. *Third to fifth years.* The major influence in life at this stage is the family. The crisis is *initiative versus guilt.* How the family reacts to a child's individuality will affect the degree to which he or she feels free to express themselves. If initiative or innovation is condemned, the child will suffer guilt.

4. *Sixth year to puberty.* The important influences in life at this stage are neighborhood and school. The crisis is *industry versus inferiority.* Children during this stage try to find out how things work. If they succeed, they are likely to become more industrious. If they do not, they may consider themselves inferior.

5. *Adolescence.* Friends are the dominant influences on life in adolescence. The crisis is *identity versus role confusion.* Adolescents are on the brink of adulthood. They have achieved the flexible thinking of the formal operational stage. They can imagine many possibilities for their own life. The choices they make now will determine who they will become. The danger is

role confusion: if adolescents do not succeed in making a choice (distinguishing among the many possibilities), they may not be able to establish their own sense of identity.

6. *Early adulthood.* The "job" of early adulthood is to establish intimate bonds of love and friendship. These bonds typically include marriage and children. The crisis is *intimacy versus isolation,* whether one will develop lasting intimate relationships or remain isolated.

7. *Middle adulthood.* At this age, the primary relationships of a person's life are the people he or she lives and works with. The crisis in this period is *generativity versus self-absorption.* The choice is between concern for others, one's family, and a preoccupation with oneself. The danger is becoming too self-absorbed, of becoming concerned primarily with self and not others.

8. *The aging years.* The crisis is *integrity versus despair.* A person can have a sense of satisfaction looking back over his or her life, a sense of fulfillment, or he or she can have a sense of despair at lost opportunities and regrettable actions. At this stage the dominant influence is a sense of "mankind is my kind." How one faces the approach of death is largely determined by one's assessment of having lived a worthwhile life or having wasted possibilities.

Erikson's theory is considered by most psychologists an idealized narration of development and not an explanation. However, Erikson's ideas have stimulated research in attachment in infancy, the search for identity in adolescence, and psychology's concerns with adulthood.

See Chapter 19, section on Theories of Adult Development.

Systems of the Child's World: Bronfenbrenner's Approach

All the theories discussed so far, of Piaget, Kohlberg, and Erikson, and many other theories as well, center around the development of the individual through various stages of life. But is life simply a series of problems? Also, is it adequately addressed by having a child come into a laboratory to have its behavior tested? Obviously, laboratory studies can give only a partial picture.

In most studies of development, there is little mention of the complex world that the child inhabits. Urie Bronfenbrenner (1970; Bronfenbrenner & Crouter, 1983) sees it differently. His horizon is the *systems approach* (see Chapter 2), which looks at all the different kinds and levels of determinants of a child's life. This is an important approach for it shows how development can be considered as an adaptation, not to *the environment*, but to all the *different environments* of a life, child or adult.

In Bronfenbrenner's approach, there is a "nested hierarchy" of systems (Figure 3-13) which influence one's life. What this means is that many different factors, from one's immediate family to society, are important and influential.

First is the *microsystem,* those relationships of everyday life, home, and family. How, for instance, does the marriage affect how the parents behave toward their child? What happens when the father is late for dinner?

Next is the *mesosystem,* the family structure at different stages of development. As with other views, Bronfenbrenner emphasizes that the world of the infant expands as he or she grows older. The infant's world of mommie and daddy and brother or sister widens to include school friends, athletic groups, and social clubs in late childhood. The network of relationships becomes larger and larger.

The *exosystem* is those elements of society that affect the individual: for example, the media, jobs, and political movements and currents. Because these levels are nested, changes on this level can affect those below it. Something that happens in the microsystem, such as how much time the father spends with the child, can be affected by trends like unemployment.

Finally, the *macrosystem* is the cultural norms that guide behavior. In our culture, children are special and are protected and given great advantages. They are not called upon at age 6 to work, for instance. Many societies simply have made childhood a time for silent observance of adult life (Aries, 1962). This is a startling conception to a Westerner, wanting to produce a superkid! However, such a component of the *macrosystem* obviously influences many facets of life.

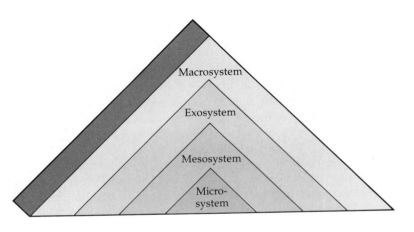

FIGURE 3-13
Bronfenbrenner's Nested
Hierarchy of Systems

This perspective is important, for it allows us to see the child developing in the world, and if extended, allows us to see how well the child is adapted to his or her ever-changing environment, from the "small world" of the infant, bounded by the primary caregiver, to the expanding worlds of childhood, and thence to adulthood. The same viewpoint can (and, as you might guess, will) be applied to the further development of the adult.

Attachment

As the child matures, his or her social world expands from only the parents to friends, religion, nationality, and so on. But, due to human beings' long period of immaturity, the relationships formed in the first few years have a special quality.

That special quality is called the **attachment** between the infant and the mother or primary caregiver. Even a young infant can tell the difference between the mother and other people: the baby's eyes follow her more than anyone else and it smiles more enthusiastically at her. By eight months, most infants have a strong attachment to their mothers. They smile, coo, and attempt to stay close to her. When frightened, they go to her and try to cling to her leg or demand to be picked up. As long as she is near, an infant feels free to explore.

At about eight months, the infant often shows extreme distress when the mother leaves (Figure 3-14). When the mother returns, the child will often cling to her desperately. The child cannot be comforted by just anyone — only the mother

FIGURE 3-14
Separation Anxiety
Beginning about 8 months of age, most infants become so strongly attached to their mothers that they become extremely distressed when left with anyone else, even a grandparent or other person they know, like, and trust.

or primary caregiver brings relief. This bonding and early attachment serves to keep the helpless infant close to the mother where it can be protected. Early in our evolutionary history, infants who wandered too far probably did not survive to reproduce.

Before infants develop separation anxiety, they also become afraid of strangers, a fear called **stranger anxiety.** At four or five months, infants smile at people almost indiscriminately; they can be comforted by almost anyone, even a stranger. By the last quarter of the first year, however, they are likely to scream and cry if a stranger approaches, especially if they are in a strange place or if their mothers are not around (Bretherton & Waters, 1985).

Why Do Infants Attach to Their Mothers?

The attachment of the baby to the mother is an important event in development and involves many different factors. It is probably (1) an innate bond which develops due to (2) the necessity for mother love, (3) the gratification of needs, (4) the infant's cognitive development, and (5) the communication between mother (or caregiver) and child.

1. John Bowlby (1982) and Mary Ainsworth (1982) believe that attachment is innate and that strong attachments have a survival function. Because an infant relies for protection on his primary caregiver, it is safer for the infant to spend most of his time clinging to or close by the mother. Babies do not necessarily become attached solely to their primary caregivers, but to people who interact with them socially. The connection to others is stimulated early.

   Bowlby also noted that separation from an affectional attachment such as the mother–child bond has three stages: (1) anxiety, disbelief, and searching for the lost one; (2) depression, withdrawal, and despair; and (3) acceptance and recovery. These stages have physiological effects, similar in the first two stages to the physiological arousal of the flight or fight response. Reite and his colleagues (Reite & Fields, 1985) implanted telemetry equipment in infant monkeys to record their physiology when they were separated from their mothers. On the first day, there was agitation and increased heart rate. A day later the infants settled into depression, marked by decreased heart rate and low body temperature. After four days, the physiological signs returned to normal. Similar attachments occur in adult human beings, although it is not under such strict genetic control. But the same agitation, the same arousal, and the same feelings of grief occur. There are also dire health consequences of losing a loved one — breaking attachments can affect the immune system and the heart.

2. Harlow and Harlow (1966) tested the hypothesis that attachment was due to a necessity for love and care. They raised rhesus monkeys with two surrogate mothers made out of wire mesh. One wire mesh "mother" had the feeding bottle attached to its chest; the other was covered with terry cloth. The infant monkeys spent most of their time clinging to the terry cloth mothers. They would go to the wire mother when hungry, but then return to the cloth mother. When frightened, they would run to the cloth mother rather than to the one that fed them (Figure 3-15). So food is not the primary basis for attachment.

FIGURE 3-15
Love Is Soft
Harlow and Harlow showed that infant monkeys would go to a wire mesh surrogate mother for food, but were more attached to their soft terry cloth surrogate mother, to whom they clung for warmth, security, and a semblance of affection.

A million, million spermatozoa,
    All of them alive
Out of their cataclysm but one poor Noah
    Dare hope to survive
And among that billion minus one
    Might have chanced to be
Shakespeare, another Newton, a new Donne
But the One was Me.

Aldous Huxley
"Fifth Philosopher's Song"

PLATE 1A
The Moment of Conception

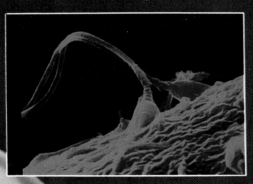

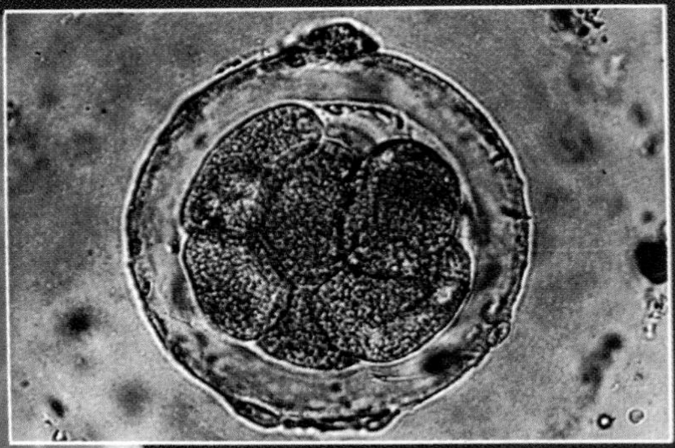

PLATE 1B
The Period of the Ovum
The cells of the fertilized ovum immediately begin to divide (above). This period lasts about 2 weeks, ending when the ovum is implanted in the uterine wall and the embryonic period begins.

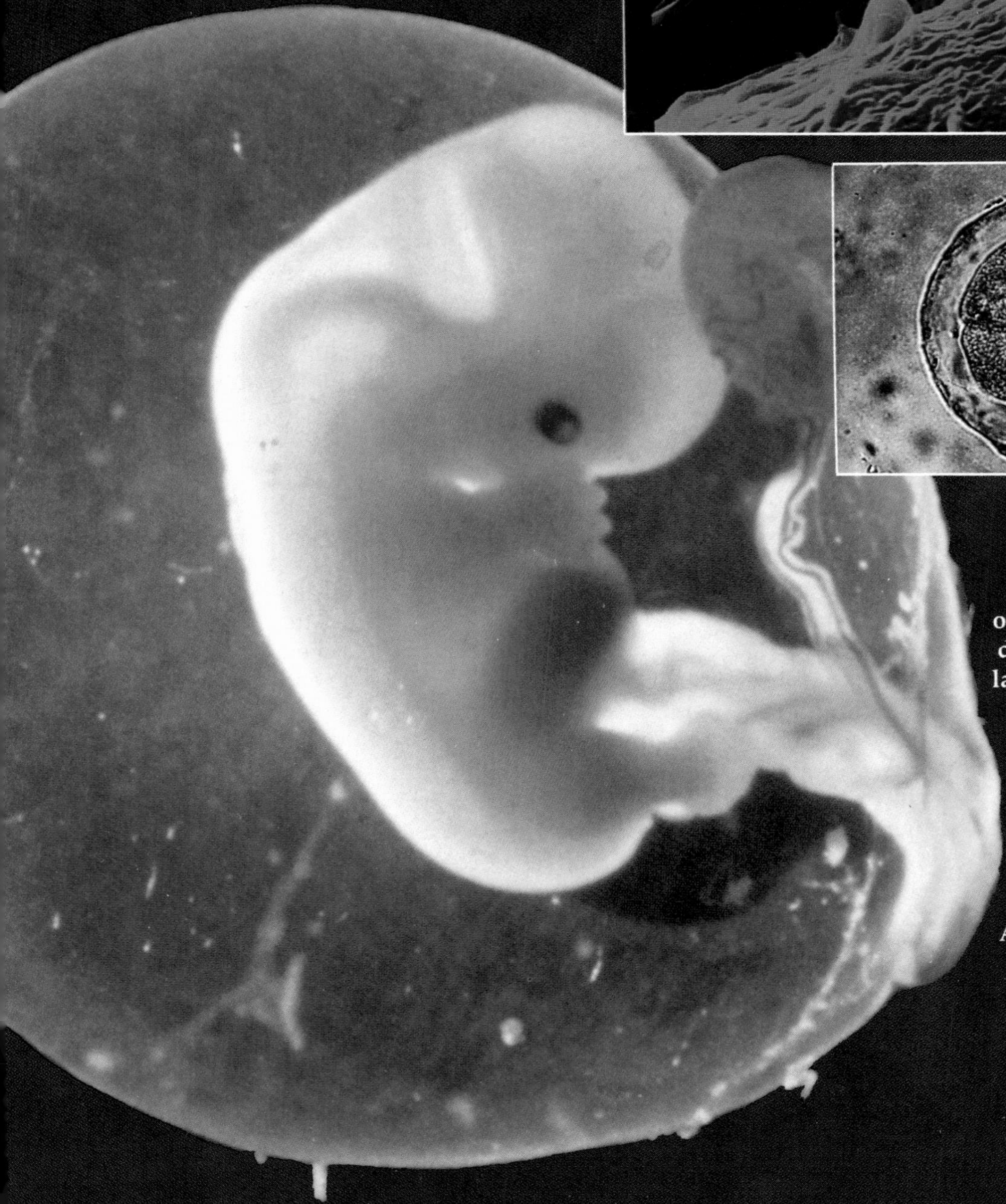

PLATE 1C
The Embryonic Period
At 5 to 6 weeks the embryo (left) is mostly head and heart. The heart has begun to beat; the head and brain can be discriminated.

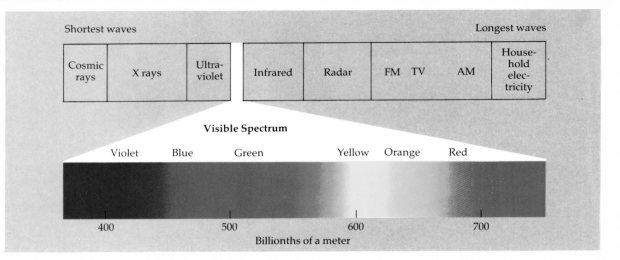

PLATE 2
The Spectrum of Electromagnetic Energy
The visible spectrum—what our unaided senses
can detect—is a small fraction of the
total range of radiation around us.

PLATE 3
The Spreading Effect
Because we judge sensory
stimuli largely by
comparison, even if the red
or blue in an illustration is
actually all one shade, the
so-called spreading effect of
the adjacent lines can make
you perceive the red or blue
as lighter or darker in
different parts of the
drawing.

PLATE 4
Child Development
One facet of the broad field of psychology is the study of the growth and
development of children, one of the miracles of everyday life.

PLATES 5A AND B
The Human Brain
These computer-generated displays were made from the cut surfaces
of a human brain sliced at regular intervals in a giant microtome. The
images of the surfaces were traced into computer memory,
reassembled, and displayed in color as a three-dimensional object. In
the left image, the cerebral cortex is shown in dark blue, the
cerebellum in pink (or yellow where not superimposed on other
organs), and the brain stem in light blue. The right image shows
these same structures using other colors.

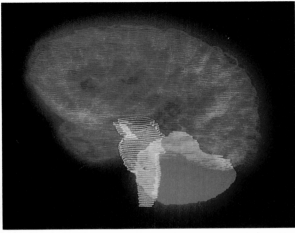

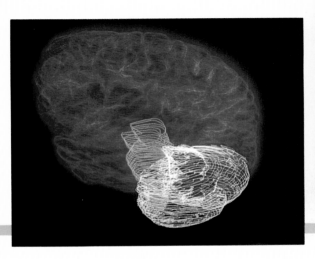

PLATES 6A AND B
The World to a Color-blind Person
The view at the left is what would be seen by a person with red-green color blindness, the most common form of defect in the color-sensing system. The right view is what this same scene would look like to a person with normal vision.

PLATE 7
Human Taste Buds
Taste buds, here magnified greatly, are collections of taste cells concentrated in various places on the surface of the tongue to respond to the four basic elements of taste: sour, sweet, bitter, and salty.

3. Sigmund Freud believed that the basis for attachment lies in the fact that the mother gratifies the baby's needs, especially for food. Similarly, ''learning theorists'' believe that the pleasure infants feel at having their needs gratified becomes associated with the mother and that such emotional needs are important.

4. Piaget (1932) believed that attachment of the child depends on object permanence. A baby must be far enough along in his cognitive development to be able to have a permanent conception of his mother before he can miss her when she is gone. He has to recognize that something is strange or different before he can think there may be something to be afraid of.

5. Babies do not necessarily become attached solely to their primary caregivers (Schaffer & Emerson, 1964). Generally, human infants become more attached to *people who interact with them socially*, whether or not they provide any caregiving functions. Many researchers believe that communication is the primary ingredient in the development of attachment (Maccoby, 1980).

Mary Ainsworth

The Strange Situation

Ainsworth and colleagues have experimented extensively with attachment, separation anxiety, and stranger anxiety, in the home and the laboratory (Ainsworth, Blehar, Waters, & Wall, 1978). She developed an experiment called the **strange situation,** which has become a classic test of the nature of mother–child attachment. In this experiment a stranger enters a room where a baby and his mother are playing with toys. The mother then leaves the room, so that the child is alone with the stranger and the toys. The experimenter observes how the child reacts to mother's departure, how much the child plays with the toys, and how he or she responds to the stranger and to the mother upon her return (Figure 3-16). Ainsworth found three basic patterns of attachment:

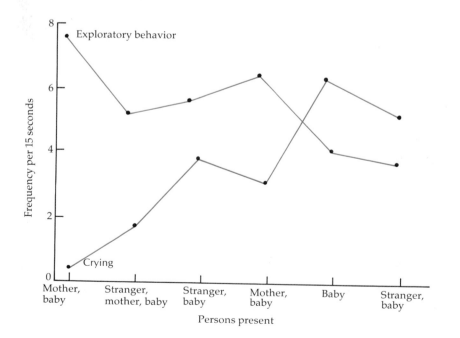

FIGURE 3-16
An Infant's Reaction to the Strange Situation
A 1-year-old child will cry more and explore its environment less when a stranger enters the room. Presence of a stranger combined with absence of the mother increases these negative effects. Such interactions, over a period of about a half an hour, are charted here.
(After Ainsworth & Bell, 1970)

- *Unattached infants* showed little or no interest in either the mother or the stranger and exhibited little or no separation or stranger anxiety.
- *Securely attached infants* appeared to be very happy around their mothers, using her as a "security base" for exploration. When the mother left the room, they showed varying amounts of distress, but always greeted her happily when she returned.
- *Insecurely attached infants* explored less and stayed close to their mothers, especially when the stranger was there and showed great distress when the mother left the room.

Attachment and Competence

Being securely attached may be an advantage in early development. At 20 months of age, securely attached children are more advanced in cognitive and social skills. They play more intensely and more enjoyably than babies who were judged either unattached or insecurely attached 10 months earlier (Main, 1973).

Experiments with children 2 years of age showed that secure children were more adept at problem solving and approached problems with enthusiasm, interest, and pleasure. Unattached and insecure children, however, were easily frustrated and gave up on problems. They seldom asked for help; they simply clung to their mothers (Matas, Arend, & Sroufe, 1978). At $3\frac{1}{2}$ years, children who at $1\frac{1}{2}$ had been judged securely attached, played well with others and tended to be leaders, whereas insecurely attached children tended to be more anxious, withdrawn, and less curious (Richards & Light, 1986).

The quality of attachments in the first two years of life leads to competence and social adjustment for a few years afterward. Better adjustment in later life may not be due to attachment in the first year, but to a *continuing* good relationship with parents.

Play

For a young child, all the world is a plaything. Children play with their bodies, language, objects, ideas, animals, and other people. *How* they play reflects the degree of their motor, cognitive, and social development. A toddler shrieks with delight at being able to roll a ball back and forth to his mother; a few years later he may hit the winning homerun for his little league team.

As the child ages, play becomes more complex and is combined with other aspects of play. A 9-year-old playing baseball plays with more objects, uses more skilled motions, and uses more cognitive skills than a toddler rolling a ball back and forth to his mother.

The concrete properties of materials become less important as fantasy and imaginative play become more complex. To a 2-year-old a toy is usually the focus of play. The child dials and talks into a toy telephone. An 8-year-old is more likely to use a toy as a prop in a complex situation: the toy telephone may be part of a supermarket he or she has built.

As children gain more experience with the outside world, they incorporate new people, situations, and skills into fantasy play. A common activity of 3-year-olds is to play house; they pretend to cook, iron, or maybe drive to work. The fantasy play of 8-year-olds is more complicated and imaginative; they play *Star Wars*, using sticks as laser guns and chairs as spaceships to fly to other planets.

Development of Sex Roles

"It's a girl!" "It's a boy!" The first words spoken about a baby are about its sex. From the first moments of life, sex has important influences on identity, behavior, and personality. One's **gender identity** means that a child knows and identifies with what sex he or she is. A **sex role** is society's expectations of how a male or female should behave. In all cultures some behaviors are considered "masculine" and others "feminine."

Biological Factors

There are a few consistent biological differences in occupations. In primitive tribes, men's greater strength allows them to be warriors, hunters, and fishermen. Women's childbearing capacity often ties them more to activities centered around the home: child care, cooking, and gardening. What biological differences there are between men and women, however, can be almost completely changed by the culture. Among the Guatemalan Indians agriculture is considered a man's work; in Kenya women work the fields. In the United States the majority of physicians are men; in Russia almost all physicians are women.

Social Factors: The Newborn

A few obvious behavioral differences between boys and girls at birth have been documented. Newborn boys are more active than girls; they are awake more and grimace more. They are more irritable, as well. However, these differences are not always found. Some studies have found no differences in activity level, crying, or "soothability" between boy and girl babies.

However, from the first day of life there is an enormous difference in how parents perceive and treat their children. Parents, especially fathers, are more likely to rate their 1-day-old daughters as soft, small, delicate, and weak and their boys as strong, firm, and hardy (Rubin, Provenzano, & Luria, 1974), whether they are or not. When asked to interpret their baby's crying, parents generally interpreted their son's crying as anger and their daughter's as fear.

Social Factors: Toddlers and Preschoolers

Parents and other adults also encourage sex-typed behavior in children through the toys and clothes they choose for them, by how they play with them, and by what types of play they encourage (Figure 3-17) (Fausto-Sterling, 1986). In a hospital nursery, girls are often covered in pink blankets, boys in blue. At 1 year of age there is no difference between boys and girls in the toys they prefer. Boys and girls are equally happy with a doll or a truck. But parents give girls dolls, doll houses, and stuffed animals, while boys are given blocks, trucks, and sports equipment. By age 3, children begin to show a clear preference for sex-typed toys.

Parents also play with their infant sons and daughters differently. Mothers touch their little girls more and prefer to keep them close by. By age 2, girls generally prefer to play closer to their mothers than do boys. Little boys also receive more gross motor stimulation than girls; they are more likely to be tossed, swung, and chased.

FIGURE 3-17
Sex Roles and Sex-typed Behavior
Children of both sexes will happily play with toys and engage in behavior traditionally identified with their own or the other gender. The critical factor is whether and how early adults encourage children in their care to engage in sex-typed behavior.

From the age of 2 on, boys show a higher activity level in their play and are more likely to engage in rough and tumble play. In most cultures they are also more likely to be aggressive than girls, to get into more confrontations (Fausto-Sterling, 1986). Fathers tend to perpetuate sex roles in their children more than do mothers (Block, 1979). They are more likely to reward their daughters for playing with other girls but punish their sons for playing with girls (Langlois & Downs, 1980).

The Middle Years

Parents place different expectations on their sons and daughters, expectations that are often echoed by the children's teachers. Boys are likely to be encouraged to compete and achieve, to be independent and responsible, and to control their feelings. Fathers, especially, are stricter with their sons than with their daughters and punish them more readily. Girls generally get more warmth and physical closeness from their parents; they are more trusted and receive less punishment. They are also encouraged to be nurturant and obedient and are more likely to be closely supervised than boys (Block, 1979).

With all this encouragement, sex roles become much more pronounced in the middle school years. Children play in groups of the same sex; girls form small, quiet groups of two or three; boys move in larger, more active groups and differ in the way they play team games. Boys choose teammates on the basis of skill, whereas girls prefer to play with those they like. This pattern has been observed in Swiss and African children alike (Omark & Edelman, 1973).

Concluding Note on Sex Roles

In all societies men and women assume different roles. Something this consistent must involve *both* biological and social factors. It is likely that social factors *exaggerate* biological differences. The large behavioral differences between the sexes may be, in part, the result of a positive feedback loop.

Slight differences between male and female infants in the early months of life can be amplified by the special way parents treat children of different sexes. Girl babies react more to the human voice; they are more likely to cry in response to another baby's cry and to vocalize in response to their parents' voices. Their response, in turn, encourages the parents, especially the mother, to talk more to their daughters than to their sons. By three months, mothers speak more to their girl infants than to their boy infants (Lewis & Freedle, 1973).

Both mothers and fathers spend more time encouraging infant daughters to smile and talk than they do their sons. This may explain why little girls learn to talk earlier than little boys and by 2 years of age do better on vocabulary tests. Girls and boys as toddlers and young children may then go down different developmental paths, where further social expectations continue the process.

Effects of Divorce on Children

One important part of the child's social world is whether his or her parents stay together. Currently, the rate of divorce is at an all-time high. In 1964, there was one divorce for every four marriages, but by 1976 there was one divorce for every two marriages (Wallerstein & Kelly, 1980). Between one-third and one-half of all children growing up in the 1970s experienced the separation or divorce of their parents.

Not surprisingly, childless couples are most likely to divorce, and the more children a couple have, the more stable their marriage is. But surprisingly, having either sons or daughters seems to be related to how stable the marriage is. Couples who have only daughters are the most likely to divorce, whereas couples who have only sons are the least likely (Glick & Norton, 1977).

It has been assumed that divorce is better for children than living in a family environment characterized by strife and bitterness. Indeed, parents usually feel that they and their children are better off after the divorce. However, the *children themselves* may not feel that way.

In a study of the effects of divorce on children, Wallerstein and Kelly (1980) found that 18 months after break-up, two-thirds of the children in the study did not see their family as better off than before the divorce. More children accepted the divorce with time, especially the adolescents and those who maintained a good relationship with both parents. Five years later, however, 56 percent still did not feel their family life was better.

Initial Reactions to Divorce

Nearly all children show some degree of distress at the news of parental separation, although it may not be initially apparent. Children feel frightened and more vulnerable; they may feel an enormous sense of loss and may worry about the state of their parents, who will feed them, and where they will live. They also worry about their relationship with their parents—if their parents could stop loving each other, why not them, too? Will their father prefer his new girlfriend to them, or maybe the stepchildren? The children and adolescents may feel angry and rejected and be torn by conflicting loyalties to both parents.

Most of all, the children feel lonely. One parent, generally the father, has left the household, and the mother is less available to them, due to her own anxiety and often the need to work full time. How children respond to the divorce depends greatly upon their age and how the parents handle the divorce.

Preschool children react with fear, guilt, bewilderment, and regression. Few children of this age are prepared for such a separation and, in essence, awake one morning to find a parent gone. This stimulates intense fear of abandonment by both parents and macabre fantasies to explain the loss of one parent.

Children in the middle years (from 6 to 8 years), on the other hand, respond mostly with grief. They may cry a great deal and express intense yearning for the departed parent. Boys, especially at this age, may express considerable anger at the mother for either causing the divorce or driving the father away.

Children 9 to 12 years of age are more able to handle grief, but they also express intense anger at their parents. They are also most likely to become involved in the battles between their parents, often taking sides with one against the other, which is particularly detrimental to smooth adjustment to postdivorce life.

Adolescents with a relatively separate identity and strong peer support appear to be able to cope well and mature more rapidly. Others, however, especially those with low self-esteem, tend to regress or "act out" through sexual promiscuity, drugs, or alcohol.

Continued conflict between the parents and their inability to nurture can have a devastating impact on the children. The children who do best are those who have easy access to the separated parent (generally the father) and maintain a good relationship with them, and whose custodial parent (generally the mother) is able to regain her own internal equilibrium and provide a reasonably well-organized and secure household and also be emotionally available to her children (Wallerstein, in press).

How Much Does Early Experience Affect Us?

Human beings are born helpless and have a long period of immaturity. This period, childhood, is of great concern to society and to parents because it is widely believed that the early years determine later experiences. This idea has also been important in psychology. Sigmund Freud asserted that most of the major problems of adulthood stem from events in the first few years (Freud, 1920). Erikson proposed that the basic outlook on the world (trusting or mistrusting) is formed in the first two years.

Physical Development

For physical development, the first few years *are* especially important. Improper nutrition can cause permanent damage to the brain, resulting in mental retardation and slowed physical growth. McConnell and Perry (1978) found that severe protein deficiency in the fetus interferes with the normal development of the brain and can lead to mental retardation. Animals deprived of normal environmental stimuli have smaller brains than those not deprived (Diamond, 1980).

Cognitive Development

Although laboratory deprivations are extreme and beyond what may occur in normal life, the cognitive development of children deprived of normal stimulation is profoundly affected. Children in radically deprived environments show a much slower growth rate and become mentally retarded as well. There are children who have been prohibited, for some tragic reason, from learning a language in the early years of their life. For these children, the longer they are deprived, the harder it is for them to ever learn to speak.

However, children can *recover* from deprivation to a remarkable extent. Dennis (1960) observed a group of babies in a Lebanese orphanage. These children were given hardly any stimulation; they laid on their backs all day in bare rooms in bare cribs. They were touched only when their diapers were changed. At the age of 1 year, the children's development was about that of a 6-month-old.

Some of these babies were later adopted and Dennis was able to compare their development with that of the children still left in the orphanage. Those in the orphanage remained retarded, but those who were adopted caught up with other children in many aspects of development. This and many other studies show that we are capable of overcoming early deprivations *if later experience compensates.*

Birth Order

One early experience that has persistent effects is **birth order.** For millennia the firstborn (male, at least) has been regarded as the heir, the favored one, the one destined to assume family leadership upon death of the father. Recent evidence somewhat surprisingly confirms that firstborns are better leaders, but also shows that later birth has its advantages, too.

Intellect. Robert Zajonc and his colleagues (Zajonc, 1986) propose that a child's intellectual development is related to the intellectual abilities of the people in his immediate environment, namely the family. To determine the intellectual value of that environment, Zajonc used a mathematical formula in which he assigned the parents "intelligence values" of 30 each and newborns a value of 0. Thus, the first child is born into an environment of

$$\frac{30 + 30 + 0}{3} = 20$$

If the next child is born when the first child has an intellectual level of four, the intellectual value of his or her environment is

$$\frac{30 + 30 + 4 + 0}{4} = 16$$

The intellectual environment for later children will be lower still. The first child is born into the highest intellectual environment. Each new child is born into a successively lower one. Most older children teach their younger siblings in many ways—games, behavior, language. Zajonc hypothesized that this informal teaching experience increases the older child's intellectual abilities.

Family size also has an effect on intellectual development. One study examined the scores of almost 800,000 participants in National Merit Scholarship programs from 1962 to 1965 (Breland, 1977). Average scores declined as family size increased. Firstborns have higher verbal IQs than second-borns, and second-borns in turn score higher than third-borns. Thus, birth order and family size are two aspects of early experience that seem to have a lasting effect, at least on those aspects of intelligence measured by IQ tests. One example of this is that many more eminent scientists are firstborns than would be expected from their number in the population. In a recent review Zajonc (1986) shows that SAT scores have decreased during the period from 1963 to 1980 when there were increases in family size. The trend reversed itself in 1980 when family size declined.

Personality and Psychosocial Development. Firstborns tend to be more cautious, nervous, and anxious than those born later. Firstborn and later born children are treated differently by their parents, and these effects continue into later life. Generally, mothers pay more attention to their firstborns. They are more strict with and protective of their firstborns, preventing them from doing things for fear of harm. At just less than 4 years of age, firstborns obey their parents more than those born later (Maccoby, 1980). Later in life, firstborns seem to be more inhibited.

Firstborns are also more *conformist* on the average, less likely to express antisocial sentiments. They remain a little more physically fearful as well, generally preferring safer sports such as swimming to gymnastics or skiing. They are also usually more nervous. During a power blackout in New York City, people were asked, "How nervous and uneasy were you during the experience?" Firstborns reported more anxiety and distress (Schacter, 1959). Those born later, being less anxious and inhibited, are more likely to be socially popular, but they are also more likely to harbor doubts about themselves. The reason for this may be that because they do not have as much of their parents' attention as they want, they feel that others do not like them very much.

Early experience is quite important in several respects. There are lasting effects on the brain, on intelligence, and on personality. However, early experience does *not* completely determine lives. The important thing is this: people are not so susceptible to one-time traumas, stages, or fixed reactions as has been thought (Kagan, 1985). Instead, a *continuing pattern* of mother–child–society interaction seems to be what determines a life (Stern, *in* Goleman, 1986). People probably remember isolated events as important because they are typical of an era, not because the specific incident meant much. Even an extremely deprived environment can be overcome if later experience compensates.

A fter late childhood a major developmental change occurs. Increases in the level of sex hormones transform the child's appearance into that of an adult. Sex organs and secondary sex characteristics begin to develop at about the same time. There is a "growth spurt." Although growth in the first few years of life is also rapid, young children are not aware enough of themselves or the world to be aware of the physical changes. But teenagers are aware of their growth, and this awareness is often upsetting.

Another source of instability is cognitive: adolescents have just entered the formal operational stage, which involves a more abstract way of thinking and problem solving. These new mental abilities often cause conflicts between themselves and their family and society.

Other factors are personal and social. Adolescents are for the first time preparing to leave home and family. And perhaps most important, for the first time, adolescents are aware of and concerned with sexuality, leading to new desires and exploration. Nevertheless, society and family still regard adolescents as children. Being considered as children allows for greater protection (by families and from the law) and also imposes restrictions (curfews, drinking age), which are further causes of conflict.

Physical Growth and Puberty

Adolescence is marked by a sudden increase in physical growth, the *growth spurt*, which lasts about three years (see Figure 3-18). Boys at about age 12 and girls at age 10 begin to gain weight. Bones grow thicker and wider and muscle bulk and weight increase (especially around the hips in girls). This "pudginess" is a sign that the changes of puberty are fast approaching.

At the peak of their growth spurt, girls may gain 20 pounds and boys as much as 26 pounds in a year. A sharp increase in height follows the weight gain. The stored fat is then redistributed, particularly in boys. Typically, adolescents gain two to five inches in height during the growth spurt, fueled by a dramatic increase in caloric intake. Many teenage boys consume as many as 6,000 calories per day (about twice what a normal adult eats).

The body during adolescence does not change uniformly and simultaneously. Hands, head, and feet grow more than the central trunk, which causes many adolescents to feel awkward or "gangly." More upsetting, sometimes one side of

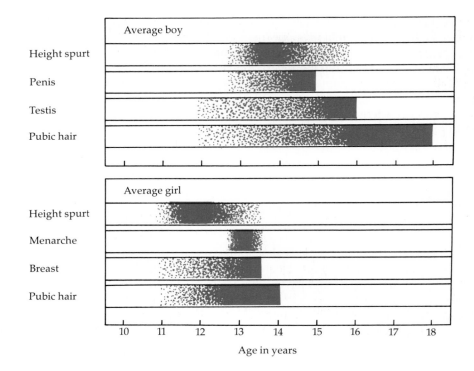

FIGURE 3-18
Physical Development in Puberty
The darkest areas on this chart indicate growth spurts during which adolescent boys and girls grow and change most. Individual patterns of development may vary greatly from these averages. (After Tanner, 1962)

Average boy

- Height spurt
- Penis
- Testis
- Pubic hair

Average girl

- Height spurt
- Menarche
- Breast
- Pubic hair

10 11 12 13 14 15 16 17 18

Age in years

the body develops a bit more quickly than the other (for example, one breast or one ear). Almost 50 percent of all adolescents are dissatisfied with their appearance. Boys wish they were taller, girls that they were thinner.

Puberty

The word *puberty* comes from the Latin "to be covered with hair," and the appearance of darkened hair on the legs, genitals, and underarms for both sexes, and on the face and chest for boys, is one of the first signs of puberty. In males, the larynx lengthens and the voice deepens (sometimes "cracking").

Puberty officially begins for boys when they produce live sperm cells. The scrotum, testes, and penis grow and eventually ejaculation is possible. For girls, puberty officially begins at **menarche,** the onset of menstruation. Their breasts and pubic hair develop simultaneously with the growth of the uterus, vagina, clitoris, and labia. Although a girl's menstrual periods may be regular, it may be some time before she produces fertile eggs.

Cognitive Development

At adolescence there is a major shift in thinking — the emergence of *formal operations,* the ability to transform information received. For many adolescents the emergence of this new mental ability causes a radical break in their previous schemata. For the first time they realize that the way they have done things and the way their parents, school, or country operates is not necessarily the only or "true" way.

Questioning and Idealism

The first exercise of the new level of abstract thought is often an intense period of questioning, searching, and rebellion. The adolescent begins to see that there are many possible choices in life — of careers, of life-style, of identity: "Who am I? What do I want to do?" On the threshold of adult life, adolescents imagine it to be ideal; experience inevitably tempers some of this idealism. Because teenagers cannot reconcile the fact that their parents are less than ideal, adolescence is often a difficult time for both parents and children.

Adolescents become idealistic because for the first time they can imagine what an ideal world and an ideal society might be like. This ability can also lead toward ideologies and organizations that claim to offer an "ideal" life, such as cults led by gurus.

Psychosocial Development

Egocentrism

Although adolescents tend to be idealistic, at the same time they remain emotionally egocentric. They imagine that their new and thrilling experiences, discoveries, and feelings are unique. A young girl may reproach her mother saying, "But Mother, you don't know how it feels to be in love." Adolescents are often so preoccupied with their physical appearance that they assume that everyone else notices minute details about them.

They are extremely self-conscious; they may even avoid going to a party when they have a pimple. It may be years before such egocentrism abates, before a young person can acknowledge that others feel as deeply as he does (even those who disagree) and before he can realize that no one pays as much attention to him as he pays himself.

Identity and Turbulence

As children move into young adulthood, they begin to realize that their actions may have long-range consequences on their lives. How well you do in high school determines the college you go to, which in turn is important to your career. Adolescents begin to make their own choices for their lives. Thus, adolescence and young adulthood are often marked by a search for one's own identity. "Who am I? What makes me different from other people? Do I want to be like my parents? What am I going to do with my life?"

Not knowing who you are or what you are going to do can be at once exhilarating and anxiety provoking. College or military service may provide a testing ground for the young person to explore his or her possibilities. Questioning, searching, and conflicts, especially with parents (Figure 3-19), are characteristic of the teenager's search for identity. This search is made more urgent by changes in the body and by developments in cognition that occur in adolescence. Adolescence is characteristically a very turbulent time. The rate of juvenile delinquency and heavy drug use attests to that. In recent years the rate of teenage suicide attempts and successes has increased.

Some adolescents, however, never question their predefined roles and travel through adolescence without anxiety; for these teenagers adolescence is not dramatically turbulent. In a recent study of a sample of teenagers who could be characterized, 35 percent had reported rather smooth sailing through adolescence, indicating that not everyone experiences such crises and storms (Berger, 1984).

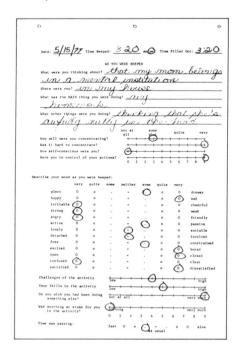
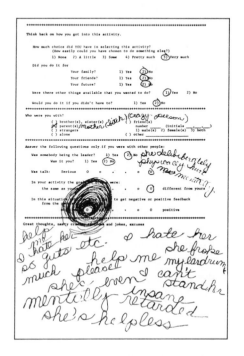

FIGURE 3-19
Adolescent Anger
Teenagers often have angry feelings about their parents, which is well shown on this questionnaire filled out by an angry teenager.

Teenage Sexuality

In the last few decades, attitudes toward sex have changed, and all adolescents, girls in particular, have become more sexually active than before. The first major reports on sexual habits of normal people were published in 1948 and 1953 by Kinsey and his colleagues. Their reports were based on interviews with white middle-class people in the 1940s. They found that only 3 percent of women and 40 percent of the men interviewed had sex by the age of 16 (Kinsey, 1953).

However, in the mid-1970s a survey of people having the same age and background asked teenagers when they would like to first have sexual intercourse. In response, 23 percent of 15- to 16-year-old boys but only 0.5 percent of the girls said, ''On a first or second date.'' Even with the liberalizing of attitudes in the society, losing virginity seems to be a different experience for boys and girls.

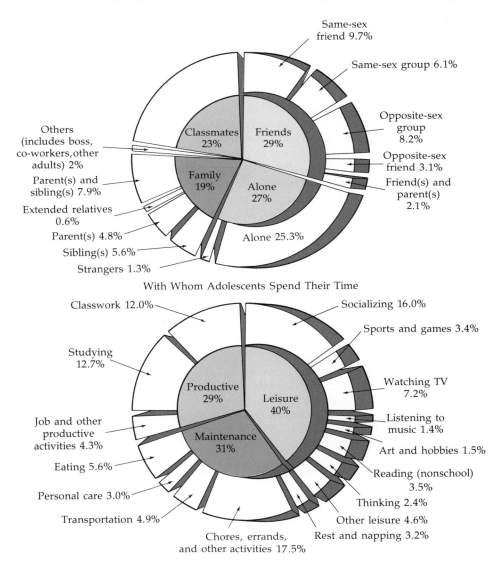

With Whom Adolescents Spend Their Time

How Adolescents Spend Their Time

For boys it is almost a rite of passage into manhood. Their attitudes about it are overwhelmingly positive (Haas, 1978).

Emotional involvement with the sexual partner is often more important for young women than it is for young men. In one study, almost half of the young men interviewed said they were not emotionally involved with their sex partner; however, over 80 percent of the women said they were in love with their first partner (Simon, Berger, & Gagnon, 1972). This distinction is also reflected in the patterns of male and female sexual activity. Young men typically have more sexual partners than young women, while young women generally have more enduring relationships.

A CONCLUDING NOTE: THE SEEDS AND FRUITS OF DEVELOPMENT

Psychology considers an organism, the human organism, from its biological inheritance, through life in society, to maturity, and to death. But nowhere is the continuity between the different parts more clear than in the development of a child into an adult. The adaptation of the infant to her small world gradually widens into the social worlds of adulthood.

The same cognitive processes that the child uses to make sense of its small world continue on in life. Schemata developed in childhood become important for thinking, for relating to others, and for operating intelligently. The processes of mental growth involved in assimilating and accommodating to new experiences change as perception and thought become more sophisticated. Slight differences among infants grow into separate and distinct personalities.

Remember, it is the *same organism* who grows up and then grows old; the same one who first tries to put things together and who later gets a job in a factory. The person who makes childhood friends is the same one who gets married and has children, letting the cycle begin again. Chapter 19 picks up the story of development in the adult.

SUMMARY

1. *Maturation* is the emergence of individual characteristics through normal growth processes. *Physical* maturation is controlled by the information in the genes and is relatively unaffected by learning or experience. *Psychological* maturation is the development of mental abilities that result from the normal growth of the brain, nervous system, and experience.

2. When babies are born they have many innate *reflexes*. Only two hours after birth, they can follow a slowly moving light and if a nipple or finger is put into their mouths, they will begin to suck automatically. Newborns also have many visual preferences. They prefer to look at faces, and prefer small amounts of change and variation. Babies open their eyes when awake and alert. They look away from darkness and toward light. They look along edges.

3. The most influential theory of cognitive development was proposed by Piaget. Piaget assumes (a) knowledge guides action, (b) knowledge develops through experience and action, and (c) the complexity of mental structures is determined largely by biological age.

4. *Schemata* are the knowledge of how things are organized and how they relate to one another. Other important concepts of Piaget's are *assimilation* and *accommodation*. When children encounter a new event, they may attempt to assimilate it into their existing knowledge structure. As long as there is an acceptable fit between the new

information and the existing schemata, information can be assimilated. If it cannot be assimilated, they *accommodate* this new knowledge by changing their knowledge structure. As they learn about the world, schemata join to form repeated mental routines that Piaget calls *operations* — rules for transforming and manipulating information in the world.

5. Piaget's theory involves several stages of cognitive development. In the sensorimotor stage (birth to 2 years) children learn through motor and sensory play. The preoperational stage (2 to 7 years) finds children less bound by their senses and able to represent objects in drawings and words. Schemata that were just being organized are now able to be used intentionally. Concrete operations (7 to 12 years) is when thinking abstractly is possible. Children can carry a task through to completion and can understand some of the basic characteristics of things in the world, such as number, weight, and order. Formal operations (12 years to adult) concerns higher level thinking: thinking abstractly, thinking through situations logically and systematically, and being able to imagine worlds that do not exist.

6. Important indicators of cognitive development are *egocentrism* and *decentration*. At each stage of development children become increasingly aware of the world outside themselves and less focused on only their thoughts and points of view.

7. Piaget's theory has been criticized by many, although it is generally accepted as the most useful one. Some of the criticisms are that (a) Piaget underestimates the reasoning abilities of children and overestimates verbal abilities, (b) stages of cognitive development are not exactly fixed, and (c) Piaget focuses too much on the cognitive aspects of development and not enough on social and emotional factors in development.

8. *Morality* is the knowledge of what is right and wrong. Like other aspects of cognition, a child's morals also undergo development. Kohlberg's theory suggests there are three levels of moral reasoning, each with different stages. The first stage is premoral, in which rules are obeyed to avoid punishment; the second is conventional morality, in which rules are obeyed for the good of all; and the third is postconventional morality, in which rules are obeyed because of respect for individual rights.

9. One criticism of Kohlberg's stages is that they seem to describe only male development. In fact, many theories of development, child and adult, are largely male. Females value relationships between people more than abstract rights, which are more characteristic of the male world. The reasons against stealing might be overridden if a greater good could be achieved. Gilligan points out that the highest stages of moral development are traditionally masculine values, such as individuality, rationality, and detachment. Other values such as caring and responsibility for others (traditionally feminine) are accredited lower moral value by Kohlberg.

10. Erikson's theory divides psychosocial development into eight stages, each associated with a characteristic "crisis." In the first year of life the crisis is trust versus mistrust; in the second year, autonomy versus shame and doubt; in the third to fifth years, initiative versus guilt; in the sixth year to puberty, industry versus inferiority; in adolescence, identity versus role confusion; in early adulthood, intimacy versus isolation; in middle adulthood, generativity versus self-absorption; and in the aging years, integrity versus despair.

11. Bronfenbrenner offers a different perspective on development involving a "nested hierarchy" of systems. Many different factors, from one's immediate family to society are important and influential. The hierarchy contains these levels: the *microsystem*, relationships of everyday life, home, and family; the *mesosystem*, the family structure

at different stages of development; the *exosystem*, elements of society that affect the individual; and the *macrosystem*, cultural norms.

12. An important part of child development is *attachment*—the quality of the relationship between the infant and the mother or other caregivers. Attachment is probably an innate bond that develops due to the necessity for maternal love, the gratification of needs, the infant's cognitive development, and communication between the primary caregiver and the child. Attachment is studied in the "strange situation." A stranger enters a room where a baby and mother are playing with toys; the mother leaves and the child is alone with the stranger and toys. Three basic patterns of attachment are observed: (a) unattached infants, (b) securely attached infants, and (c) insecurely attached infants.

13. Children's play reflects four developmental trends: (a) biological maturation permits increasing skill; (b) play becomes more complex; (c) play becomes more abstract; and (d) children incorporate new people, situations, and skills into their fantasies.

14. Sex roles also develop. *Gender identity* means that a child knows and identifies with what sex he or she is. A *sex role* is society's expectations of how a male or female should behave. Fathers are more likely to rate their 1-day-old daughter as soft, small, delicate, and weak, and their son as strong, firm, and hardy, whether they are or not. Parents also encourage sex-typed behavior through the toys and clothes they choose, how they play with their children, and what types of play they encourage. It is likely that social factors emphasize and exaggerate the innate biological differences.

15. Children have different reactions to divorce, depending on their stage of development. Preschool children may react with fear, guilt, bewilderment, and regression. Children in the middle years (6 to 8) respond mostly with grief, while 9- to 12-year-olds are more able to handle grief but express intense anger. Adolescents are often able to cope well.

16. The effects of early life experience vary. In physical development, the first few years are especially important. Improper nutrition can cause permanent damage to the brain, resulting in mental retardation and slowed physical growth. In cognitive development children deprived of normal stimulation are profoundly affected, but many studies show that they can recover if later experience compensates.

17. Birth order affects intellectual abilities—the later the child is born, the lower the IQ—and has an effect on personality as well. Later in life, firstborns tend to be more inhibited and more conforming than later borns, less likely to express antisocial sentiments, and remain a little more physically fearful.

18. At the beginning of adolescence (puberty), there is a characteristic growth spurt and major shift in thinking—the emergence of formal operations. The first exercise of this new level of abstract thought is questioning, searching, and rebelling, commonly called the "identity crisis." It is occasioned by the emergence of the ability to imagine a world as the adolescent thinks it *ought* to be rather than the world as it is.

TERMS AND CONCEPTS

accommodation
adolescence
assimilation
attachment
birth order
Bronfenbrenner

cognition
competence
concern with standards
concrete operational stage
conservation
conventional morality

decentration
egocentrism
embryonic period
Erikson
exosystem
fetal alcohol syndrome
formal operational stage
gender identity
Kohlberg
macrosystem
maturation
menarche
mesosystem
microsystem
morality
nested hierarchy
object permanence
operations

ossification
Piaget
planning
postconventional level
premoral level
preoperational stage
psychosocial development
puberty
reflexes
representational thought
schema
schemata
sensorimotor stage
separation anxiety
sex roles
strange situation
stranger anxiety
symbolic thought

SUGGESTIONS FOR FURTHER READING

Bretherton, J., & Waters, I. (1985). *Growing points of attachment theory and research.* SRCD monographs.

A collection of up-to-date papers on research on attachment.

Chess, S., & Thomas, A. (1987). *Know your child.* New York: Basic Books.

An important contribution to child rearing in that it presents the modern evidence on the inheritance of temperament and its importance in childhood.

Colby, A., & Kohlberg, L. (1986). *The measurement of moral behavior.* New York: Cambridge.

An enormous compendium of the testing procedure for classifying behaviors as moral or not.

Gelman, R., & Galistel, C. R. (1986). *The child's understanding of number.* Boston: Harvard.

Update of the classic study of how children understand.

Kagan, J. (1984). *The nature of the child.* New York: Basic Books.

A controversial analysis of the ability of the child to recover from early experiences.

Newman, B. N., & Newman, P. R. (1987). *Development through life.* Chicago: Dorsey.

Richards, M., & Light, P. (1986). *Children of social worlds.* Boston: Harvard.

Two up-to-date accounts of the "psychosocial" perspective on development throughout the life cycle.

Roazin, P. (1986). *Erik Erikson.* New York: The Free Press.

A perceptive introduction to Erikson.

Scarr, S. (1984). *Mothercare/othercare.* New York: Basic Books.

An attempt to analyze how different styles of upbringing affect the child.

Skolnick, A. (1986). *The psychology of human development.* San Diego: Harcourt Brace Jovanovich.

Perhaps the best balanced of the current texts on development.

Zajonc, R. (1986). The decline and rise of Scholastic Aptitude scores. *American Psychologist,* 41(8), pp. 862–867.

A recent update of the "confluence model" and how it predicts changes in SAT scores.

The Brain and Nervous System

I t is a little larger than a grapefruit and it weighs about half as much as this book. It is the one organ we cannot transplant and still be ourselves. It regulates all body functions, controls our most primitive behavior, and is the source of all our most sophisticated creations of civilization, including music, art, science, and language. Hopes, thoughts, emotions, and personality all nest — somewhere — in the brain. Even though thousands of scientists have studied it for centuries, it still remains, in some ways, an awesome mystery. In a single human brain the number of *potential* interconnections between cells is greater than the number of atoms in the known universe (see Plate 5).

Although psychologists may never unravel all the mysteries of the brain, much is known about how it evolved, how brain cells communicate with one another, and how injuries to certain areas of the brain affect behavior. Individuals' brains are different from one another, even different between the sexes. Changes in diet and in the air we breathe affect brain chemistry, which in turn influences mood. The brain is a pharmacy; it produces more chemical substances than any other organ of the body. Some of these chemicals stop pain and aid in healing. The brain can recover from damage, grow in response to new experience, and can grow and develop in old age.

There is a kind of architecture to the brain because the brain evolved partly by "design" and partly by accident over hundreds of millions of years. So think of it like an old ramshackle house, one originally built long ago for a small family, then added on to over generations of growth and change. Like such a house, the original structure remains basically intact. Some of the original functions moved elsewhere, as when one builds a modern kitchen and converts the old one into a pantry.

The brain contains room after room of unequal structures united only because they are side by side in the same skull. The brain is not like a well-designed modern house, with each cubic foot well planned and organized. We just were not built that way. The brain has an irregular design, embodying some structures adapted to the needs of animals and situations long gone.

People carry their evolution within them, within the various structures of the brain, structures built over many eras. This chapter reveals the complex architecture of the brain. It begins with the overall shape of the house, then the design of the rooms, their columns, and finally the components, the bricks, and the chemicals. *It is in this structure that our experience resides.*

"Architecture" of the Brain

Here is a way to help you visualize the "rooms" of the brain. Place your fingers on both sides of your head beneath the earlobes. In the center of the space between your fingertips is the oldest part of the brain, called the *brain stem*. Now imagine an area in the very center of your head. That is the *limbic system*, which governs emotions and regulates the internal workings of the body. To visualize the whole brain, make two fists and join them at the heels of the hands. This is about the size and shape of the entire brain, which is divided into two hemispheres, each about the size of one fist. The front of the brain is where your little fingers are; the back, your thumbs. The middle fingers represent the area where the brain controls movement, and the index fingers where the brain receives sensory information. Now imagine your hands covered with thick gray gloves. This is the *cortex* (Latin for "bark") (Figure 4-1). The cortex was the last part of the brain to evolve and produces the most distinctive human activities, such as language and art.

"Archaeology" of the Brain

In addition to an architecture, the brain has what we could call an "archaeology" that resulted from the development of the brain over millions of years. Like an archaeological dig, there are "layers" to the brain — four different levels of functions that developed. But we did not end up with four brains, rather, a highly complex organ with many specialized and interdependent units.

FIGURE 4-1
The Human Brain
This drawing shows the major structures of the brain and their relative positions.

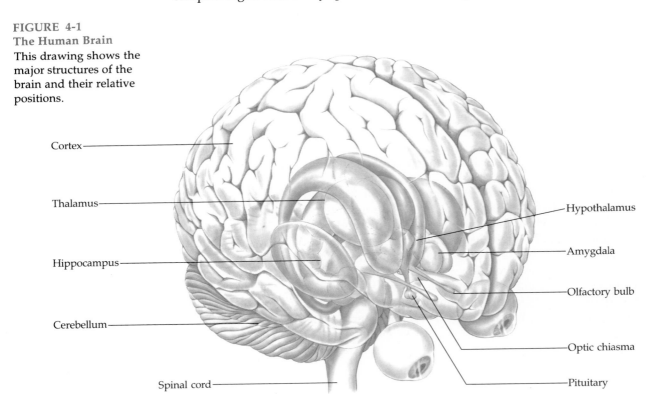

Cortex

Thalamus

Hippocampus

Cerebellum

Spinal cord

Hypothalamus

Amygdala

Olfactory bulb

Optic chiasma

Pituitary

The brain is theorized to have been "built" over a period of more than 500 million years, and it comprises several separate structures. They seem laid on top of each other, like a ramshackle house continuously being remodeled. It is a multilevel brain that seems to have been built in different eras, for differing priorities. Many of these separate parts of the brain have, loosely speaking, "minds of their own." There are minds for alertness, for emotions, for danger, for comparing sensory information, for avoiding scarcity, and many, many others.

The human brain is in part archaic. Many scientists think that its ground plan evolved on the neural mechanisms of primates, earlier mammals, and before that, more primitive vertebrates. The structure of the codfish's brain contains many of the same basic elements as the human brain. The codfish even has a cerebral cortex (although it is small), a pituitary gland for controlling hormone production, a cerebellum, and most of the other parts of the brain that we possess. In turn, vertebrates like the codfish obtained many of their neural circuits and routines from earlier and simpler multicelled creatures.

Many of our commonplace preferences stem from the archaic nature of the nervous system. Our bodies seem to want to return to the original environments of our ancestors. We maintain concentrations of trace minerals in internal fluids appropriate in a fish living deep in the Mediterranean Sea. We prefer weather like that of the East African plains from which our first true ancestors came — 60 to 85°F, if possible. We experience a "work slump" in the late afternoon because of the ancient body rhythms of our savanna-dwelling precursors; they took their "siesta" at that time. Even in Norway in November, this same slump occurs.

The cerebral hemispheres of the human brain control the opposite sides of the body. Why? Hundreds of millions of years ago, simple creatures evolved specialized programs, stored in nerve nets, to move *away* from an attack. If the attack and the means of movement were on the same side of their body, the creatures would have been unable to get away. So the nerves on the side of the organism opposite from the attack developed the ability to sense information and move the body away! Millions of years later, these elaborate crossovers in the nervous system remain.

Our "hackles" raise during a business meeting because our ancestors fluffed their hair when threatened to appear larger and menacing. We raise up gooseflesh to provide an insulating layer of air in fur that disappeared millions of years ago. This response would make us (if we had fur) look larger to an attacker if we were frightened.

Keeping Alive: The Brain Stem

What may be the oldest part of the brain evolved over 500 million years ago, before the evolution of mammals (MacLean, 1978). The **brain stem** is primarily concerned with basic life support. It governs the control of breathing and heart rate. In the center of the brain stem and traveling its full length is a core of neural tissue known as the **reticular activating system** (RAS) (Figure 4-2). Like a bell, the RAS alerts the cortex to arriving information (such as, "visual stimulus on its way"). When a sleeping dog is stimulated by electrodes in the RAS, it awakens immediately and searches the environment. The RAS also controls the general level of arousal, such as wakefulness, sleep, attention, excitement, and so on (Thompson, 1986).

FIGURE 4-2
The Reticular Activating System (RAS)
The RAS, buried in the brain stem, communicates with wide areas of the cortex, informing it of incoming stimuli and controlling its general level of arousal.
(After Ornstein, Thompson, & Macaulay, 1984)

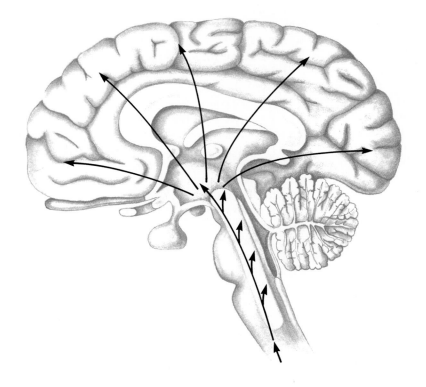

Most sensory information from the outside world enters the lower brain stem. The **thalamus** then relays the information to the *appropriate* part of the cortex (Figure 4-1). The thalamus makes preliminary classifications of external information (such as, "is it visual or auditory?"). Points in the thalamus receive particular kinds of sensory information, which they then relay to the cortex.

Stuck to the side of the brain stem is the **cerebellum.** It originally developed to improve control of balance, body position, and movement in space. Its job has changed throughout the course of evolution. Now, the memory for certain types of simple learned responses is stored there. The change in responsibility of the cerebellum is typical of how the brain evolved: original structures took over new functions as evolution proceeded.

Keeping Alive: The Limbic System

A person in a coma cannot respond to or interact with the outside world. He or she continues to live because the area of the brain that regulates vital body functions continues to operate. This area of the brain is the **limbic system** (Figure 4-3), which is a group of cell structures in the center of the brain immediately atop the brain stem. It probably evolved from 200 to 300 million years ago, during the transition from sea-dwelling to land animals. In human beings, this older part of the brain has changed its function. The limbic system now stores memories of life experiences.

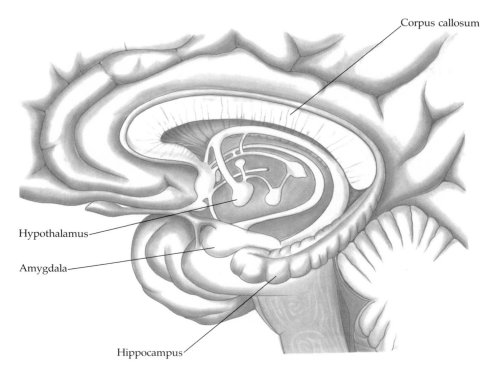

Corpus callosum

Hypothalamus

Amygdala

Hippocampus

FIGURE 4-3
The Limbic System in Relation to the Cerebral Cortex
Centrally located between the cerebral hemispheres —which are connected by the corpus callosum—and in touch with the frontal lobes and the brain stem, the limbic system is ideally placed for coordinating many of the brain's operations.

The limbic system is the area of the brain that helps to maintain **homeostasis,** a constant environment in the body. Homeostatic mechanisms located in the limbic system regulate such functions as the maintenance of body temperature, blood pressure, heart rate, and blood sugar level. Without a limbic system, we would be like "cold-blooded" reptiles. We would be unable to adjust our internal state to maintain its constant climate.

The limbic system also directs emotional reactions such as self-protection through fighting or escaping. One way to remember limbic functions: they are the four *f*'s of survival: feeding, fighting, fleeing, and sexual reproduction. It includes many of the most important structures of the brain: the hypothalamus, the pituitary gland, the hippocampus, the amygdala, and part of the frontal lobes of the cortex, which will be treated later.

The Hypothalamus and the Pituitary

The **hypothalamus** is the most intricate and amazing structure of the brain. It is small and weighs about 4 grams. It regulates eating, drinking, sleeping, waking, body temperature, chemical balances, heart rate, hormones, sex, and emotions. It operates through negative feedback. Body temperature is registered in the hypothalamus via blood temperature. If the blood becomes too cool, the hypothalamus stimulates heat production and conservation of energy. With an injured hypothalamus, an animal may not eat or drink, no matter how long it has been deprived of food or water. Conversely, stimulation or destruction of points of the hypothalamus cause incessant eating, which can be fatal.

Through a combination of electrical and chemical messages, the hypothalamus

See section on The Brain's Chemical System, this chapter.

directs the master gland of the brain, the **pituitary.** This gland regulates the body through **hormones.** These are chemicals manufactured and secreted by special neurons in the brain. Hormones flow through the blood to specific "target cells" in the body. The pituitary gland synthesizes most brain hormones that inform the other glands of the body (Figure 4-4).

The Hippocampus and Amygdala

The word **hippocampus** is Greek for "sea horse," which is what it looks like (Figure 4-3). Information coming to the brain streams through the hippocampus, which determines whether it is new or whether it matches stored information. The hippocampus involves three related limbic functions: learning, the recognition of novelty, and the storage of recent events into memory.

The **amygdala** is a small structure between the hypothalamus and the hippocampus. Its functions are not completely understood, but it is basically a large relay, like the thalamus. Surgery on the amygdala results in emotional deficiencies in humans.

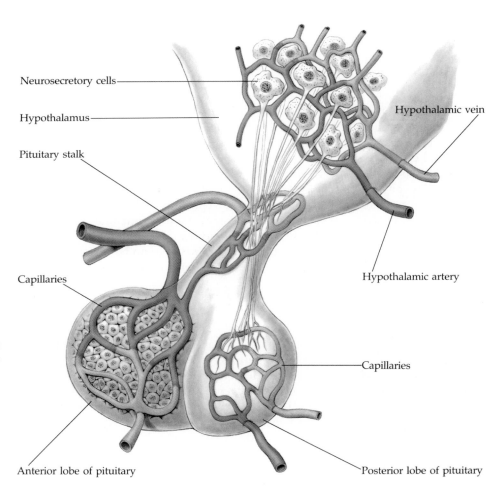

Neurosecretory cells

Hypothalamus

Pituitary stalk

Hypothalamic vein

Hypothalamic artery

Capillaries

Capillaries

Anterior lobe of pituitary

Posterior lobe of pituitary

FIGURE 4-4
The Vital Hypothalamus–Pituitary Link
The hypothalamus is able to integrate functions of the neuroendocrine and nervous systems because it is structurally connected to the cerebral cortex and to the pituitary gland, with which it communicates both by nerve impulses and by chemical messages sent directly or through the general bloodstream. (After Vannini & Pogliani, 1980)

Creating Anew: The Cerebral Cortex

The top level of the brain, the **cerebral cortex,** developed in vertebrates about 50 million years ago. It performs the functions that have increased human adaptability and which make us uniquely human. In the cortex, decisions are conceived, the world is organized, individual experiences are stored in memory, speech is produced and understood, paintings are seen, and music is heard.

The cortex is only about one-eighth of an inch thick and is convoluted and folded (Figure 4-5). If it were unfolded and spread out smooth, it would be about the size of a newspaper page. Of all mammals, human beings have the most enfolded cortex, perhaps because such a large cortex had to fit into a head small enough to survive birth.

The cortex is built in an interesting manner, with specialized cells arranged in columns. The columns each have specific functions, such as the visual detection of corners and edges. They act as *data processing centers* in the cortex and serve as

EARLY TWENTIETH CENTURY VIEWS OF THE BRAIN

Even after the discovery of the neuron, the brain was still thought to act as one single system. Some of the first influential experiments done on brain function and learning were in the laboratory of Karl Lashley, a great physiologist. He proceeded to remove pieces of cortex and chart the effects on learning of simple associations. The more cortex removed from an animal, the greater the impairment of the learning process.

So, the earliest understanding of the brain was the simplest. First generation neurophysiologists believed the brain, especially the cells of the cortex, to be "equipotential." They thought that any part of the brain had an equal role in any action. The brain was thought to be an aggregate of undifferentiated tissue; it acted like a simple and single mass.

The early and influential "learning theorists" like B. F. Skinner found this simplified understanding of the brain quite congenial. The contemporary doctrine of learning (following Locke) held that anything could be conditioned as easily as anything else. Skinner considered the brain as a single system and thought everything in the mind was equal.

This simplified physiology was well in accord with contemporary social movements and political theorizing, especially among respected academics in America. This view of learning and of the brain was eagerly promoted because it agreed with the principally optimistic approach in American education. While the social aims of equality of *opportunity* are quite laudable, the idea of equality of *ability* is a mistake. These two ideas do not necessarily go together, even though people have associated them in the past.

The viewpoint of "a single and equal brain for all" was an important idea politically. The excitement of the idea that anyone could learn anything did enhance the quality of the work that went into education. It provided an acceptable rejoinder to the brutal "genetic determinism" of the "physicians" of Nazi Germany. Today in the United States mention of the influence of the inheritance of specific abilities can call up immediate cries of "fascism."

People are not equal in ability. It is obvious to anyone that people differ greatly, for example, in their preference for visual versus auditory information, in their reading and reasoning ability, and in their ability to know what colors look good together. Psychologists and brain scientists have discovered that there is no standard individual with a standard mind.

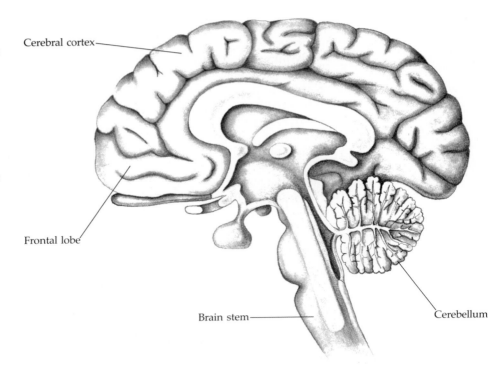

FIGURE 4-5
The Cerebral Cortex
The visible part of the brain is the surface of the cortex, which is thin and enfolded compactly to fit inside the skull. Fifty percent of the cortex is enfolded. The cortex is shown here in relation to the brain stem and cerebellum and to the limbic system, to which it is linked and which it surrounds.

Cerebral cortex

Frontal lobe

Brain stem

Cerebellum

"modules" for the basic interpretation of information. So, the "rooms" of the brain have "columns"!

These columns of cells, some of which are modules, do the basic analysis work of the mind. For example, they interpret a pattern of sounds and translate them into language. They analyze millions of bits of visual information to determine size, shape, and position. They decode a set of squiggles such as $2 + 2 = 4$ into meaningful abstract mathematical symbols. They track the position of the limbs to allow you to turn and avoid an oncoming car. They interpret the sounds of music, and much, much more. There are probably modules for specific reactions and patterns of activity, too (Thompson, 1986; Gazzaniga, 1985).

Side by side inside the cortex lie separate centers of what I call "talents." This may be an unusual word to use in this context, but I think it describes this level of brain operation. Most people probably have more of one "talent" than another. These abilities, such as the ability to move gracefully or to speak fluently, seem to exist as coherent mental and behavioral units as well as specific anatomical units.

If you imagine the brain in this way, it divides into different and well-defined areas. Each has a rich concentration of certain abilities. If you imagine each of these areas as a "patch," the cortex would look much like a folded patchwork quilt.

The cortex is the "executive branch" of the brain, responsible for making decisions and judgments on all the information coming into it from the body and the outside world. It performs three distinct functions. First, it receives information from the outside world. Second, it analyzes and compares it with stored information from prior experiences and knowledge and then makes a decision.

Third, it sends its own messages and instructions out to the appropriate muscles and glands.

The cortex is divided into two hemispheres, each of which has four lobes: the frontal, parietal, temporal, and occipital. These lobes are discussed first, followed by a detailed look at the two hemispheres and their significance.

Frontal Lobes

The **frontal lobes** lie just behind the forehead. They are the largest of the four lobes and oversee much of the rest of the brain's activity. Information about the inside and outside world as well as plans and controls are all assembled by a uniquely human talent—a system concerned with the maintenance of the individual self. While it is not possible to find an actual location for the "self" in the brain, many of the functions of this system are probably dependent on decisions carried out in the frontal lobes.

The frontal lobes are a crossroads. They lie at the intersection of the neural pathways that convey information from the parietal areas of the brain about people and events in the world, and information from the limbic system about one's own state. They also contribute to the control of basic systems such as heart rate. They are so intimately connected to limbic functions that many psychobiologists classify the frontal lobes as part of the limbic system. Certainly there are different forms of emotions represented within each of the lobes, as well as some control of the expression of emotions. In tragic cases, damage to the frontal areas results in the inability to carry out plans and to know on a long-term basis who one is.

The first and still the most famous case of such frontal lobe damage was to a railroad worker named Phineas Gage, who in 1868 accidentally had a piece of a rail line permanently embedded in his skull (Figure 4-6). He survived, but his personality and sense of self disappeared. Here is a record of his condition from one of his doctors:

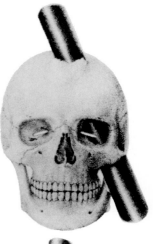

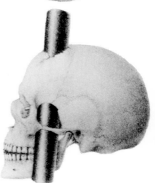

FIGURE 4-6
Frontal Lobe Damage
Phineas Gage, a railroad worker, suffered severe damage to the left frontal lobe of his brain when a device to set tamping irons accidently exploded and lodged the spike in his skull. He survived, but his personality was drastically altered.

> His physical health is good, and I am inclined to say that he has recovered. . . . The equilibrium or balance, so to speak, between his intellectual faculty and animal propensities, seems to have been destroyed. He is fitful, irreverent, indulging at times in the grossest profanity (which was not previously his custom), manifesting but little deference for his fellows, impatient of restraint or advice when it conflicts with his desires, at times pertinaciously obstinate, yet capricious and vacillating, devising many plans of future operation, which are no sooner arranged than they are abandoned in turn for others appearing more feasible. A child in his intellectual capacity and manifestations, he has the animal passions of a strong man. Previous to his injury, though untrained in the schools, he possessed a well-balanced mind, and was looked upon by those who knew him as a shrewd, smart business man, very energetic and persistent in executing all his plans of operation. In this regard, his mind was radically changed, so decidedly that his friends and acquaintances said he was "no longer Gage." (Heilman & Satz, 1984)

Feelings are perhaps the most central readout in the brain, and the self-system involving decision centers in the frontal lobes probably influence every brain process. They may cause us to seek out different information, remember things differently, think and evaluate differently. They also cause health problems, among them cancer and sudden heart attacks, which we will discuss later.

The frontal lobes participate in planning, decision making and purposeful behavior. If they are destroyed or removed, the individual becomes incapable of planning, carrying out, or comprehending a complex action or idea and is unable to adapt to new situations. Such people are unable to focus attention and become distracted by irrelevant stimuli (Luria, 1973). Their language and consciousness are fine. However, the loss of the ability to adapt and plan ahead makes those abilities useless.

Loss of Self. In a wonderfully titled book, *The Man Who Mistook His Wife for a Hat,* neurologist Oliver Sacks describes a woman with frontal lobe problems.

> Mrs B., a former research chemist, had presented with a rapid personality change, becoming "funny" (facetious, given to wisecracks and puns), impulsive —and "superficial" ("You feel she doesn't care about you," one of her friends said. "She no longer seems to care about anything at all.") At first it was thought that she might be hypomanic, but she turned out to have a cerebral tumour. At craniotomy there was found, not a meningioma as had been hoped, but a huge carcinoma involving the orbitofrontal aspects of both frontal lobes.
>
> When I saw her, she seemed high-spirited, volatile—"a riot" (the nurses called her)—full of quips and cracks, often clever and funny.
>
> "Yes, Father," she said to me on one occasion.
>
> "Yes, Sister," on another.
>
> "Yes, Doctor," on a third.
>
> She seemed to use the terms interchangeably.
>
> "What *am* I?" I asked, stung, after a while.
>
> "I see your face, your beard," she said, "I think of an Archimandrite Priest. I see your white uniform—I think of the Sisters. I see your stethoscope—I think of a doctor."
>
> "You don't look at *all* of me?"
>
> "No, I don't look at all of you."
>
> "You realise the difference between a father, a sister, a doctor?"
>
> "I *know* the difference, but it means nothing to me. Father, sister, doctor—what's the big deal?"
>
> Thereafter, teasingly, she would say: "Yes, father-sister. Yes, sister-doctor," and other combinations.
>
> Testing left-right discrimination was oddly difficult, because she said left or right indifferently (though there was not, in reaction, any confusion of the two, as when there is a lateralising defect of perception or attention). When I drew her attention to this, she said: "Left/right. Right/left. Why the fuss? What's the difference?"
>
> "*Is* there a difference?" I asked.
>
> "Of course," she said, with a chemist's precision. "You could call them *enantiomorphs* of each other. But they mean nothing to *me*. They're no different for *me*. Hands . . . Doctors . . . Sisters . . ." she added, seeing my puzzlement. "Don't you understand? They mean nothing—nothing to me. *Nothing means anything* . . . at least to me."
>
> "And . . . this meaning nothing . . . " I hesitated, afraid to go on. "This meaninglessness . . . does *this* bother you? Does *this* mean anything to you?"
>
> "Nothing at all," she said promptly, with a bright smile, in the tone of one who makes a joke, wins an argument, wins at poker.
>
> Was this denial? Was this a brave show? Was this the "cover" of some unbearable emotion? Her face bore no deeper expression whatever. Her world had been

voided of feeling and meaning. Nothing any longer felt "real" (or "unreal"). Everything was now "equivalent" or "equal"—the whole world reduced to a facetious insignificance.

I found this somewhat shocking—her friends and family did too—but she herself, though not without insight, was uncaring, indifferent, even with a sort of funny-dreadful nonchalance or levity.

Mrs B., though acute and intelligent, was somehow not present—"de-souled"—as a person. (Sacks, 1986)

People seem to lose "themselves" in a most terrifying and disheartening way when something in the frontal lobes is destroyed. But also important, and keep this in mind, is that this "self" is separate from other mental faculties, which are governed by another component of the brain.

Sensory and Motor Areas

The **sensory** and **motor areas** are at the juncture of the frontal and parietal lobes (Figure 4-7). They are proportionately smaller in human beings than in other animals (Figure 4-8). The sensory areas receive information about body position, muscles, touch, and pressure from all over the body. The motor areas control the movements of the different parts of the body.

Figure 4-9 shows the body as it is represented proportionally in the brain. In the **homunculus,** various parts of the body are distorted out of proportion to their physical size. *The more complex the function, the more space the brain devotes to it.* Although the back is much larger than the tongue, it makes fewer intricate movements and is less sensitive, thus it seems "smaller" to the brain. Our hands are terribly important to us. They process information about touch and pressure and are also capable of extremely complex movements. But this is different for other species: in the homunculus of a cat's brain, paws have little space, but the more sensitive whiskers have a very large area (Thompson, 1986). Whiskers are

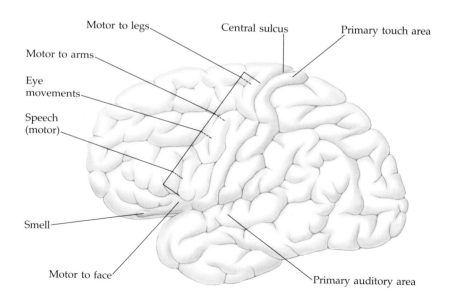

FIGURE 4-7
Sensory and Motor Areas of the Brain
Control of the senses and body movements is located in an area of the brain between the frontal and parietal lobes.

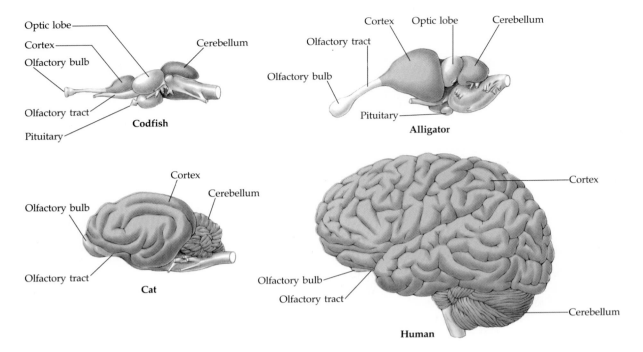

FIGURE 4-8
The Range of Complexity
of Animal Brains
Although not drawn to
scale, the differences
between human and
subhuman brains are
obvious, particularly the
proportionally smaller
human sensory and motor
areas and the vastly larger
human cortex.
(After Truex & Carpenter, 1964)

also important to a mouse, and the corresponding area of the animal's cortex reflects this (Figure 4-10).

Parietal Lobes

The **parietal lobes** *analyze* sensory input. It is probably here where letters come together as words and where words are put together into thoughts.

Damage to the parietal lobes can result in a form of *agnosia* (which means "not knowing"). Mountcastle (1976) studied a person with parietal lobe damage who was unaware of a whole side of his body. This is a condition called *amorphosynthesis*. Because he had right parietal lobe damage, he ignored or did not "know" the left side of his body or the left side of anything. Drawings by Mountcastle's patient are shown in Figure 4-11. Notice how the numbers of the clock squeeze into the right half. Most everything on one side of the world is ignored. A person with damage to half the parietal lobe may only dress and groom one side of his or her body (Figure 4-12). Some individuals lose the ability to follow audio or visual cues and cannot recognize familiar objects by touch.

Temporal Lobes

The **temporal lobes** (Figure 4-13) have several important functions. A small area in each lobe (the auditory cortex) interprets sound information. Other temporal lobe functions involve perception, memory, and dreaming.

Most of our knowledge of temporal lobe functions comes from people who have suffered some sort of damage to this region. Sometimes dramatic hallucinations occur, while in other cases, memories of events occurring after the damage disappear.

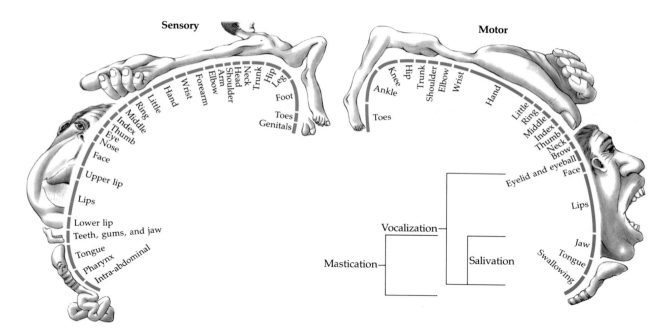

Sensory

Motor

FIGURE 4-9
A Homunculus of the
Sensory and Motor Areas
A cross section of the
cortex is diagrammed to
show the relative space
devoted to different
functions. Parts of the
body that engage in
important activities
involving great sensitivity
—such as speech, touch,
and dexterity—are shown
much larger proportionally
than their real relative size
in the body.
(After Penfield & Rasmussen, 1950)

Aphasia and Other Temporal Lobe Deficits. Severe damage to certain areas of the left temporal lobe may result in **aphasia,** language impairment. Here is an example of how a person with temporal lobe damage may act. Howard Gardner describes an interview with a Coast Guard operator.

> I asked Mr. Ford about his work before he entered the hospital.
>
> "I'm a sig . . . no . . . man . . . uh, well, . . . again." These words were emitted slowly, and with great effort. The sounds were not clearly articulated; each syllable was uttered harshly, explosively, in a throaty voice. With practice, it was possible to understand him, but at first I encountered considerable difficulty in this.
>
> "Let me help you," I interjected. "You were a signal . . . "
>
> "A sig-nal man . . . right," Ford completed my phrase triumphantly.
>
> "Were you in the Coast Guard?"
>
> "No, er, yes, yes . . . ship . . . Massachu . . . chusetts . . . Coast-guard . . . years." He raised his hands twice, indicating the number "nineteen."
>
> "Oh, you were in the Coast Guard for nineteen years."
>
> "Oh . . . boy . . . right . . . right," he replied.

This was a man who had normal speech before his left hemisphere injury. He clearly wants to communicate but cannot find the words to do it.

That there are clearly separate verbal abilities is shown by another type of brain injury to a different portion of the left hemisphere. The tragic result is called *Wernicke's aphasia.* Gardner gives an example:

> "What brings you to the hospital?" I asked the 72-year-old retired butcher four weeks after his admission to the hospital.

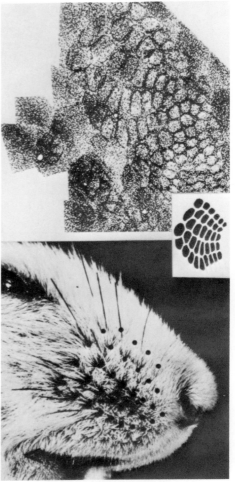

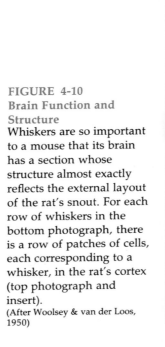

FIGURE 4-10
Brain Function and Structure
Whiskers are so important to a mouse that its brain has a section whose structure almost exactly reflects the external layout of the rat's snout. For each row of whiskers in the bottom photograph, there is a row of patches of cells, each corresponding to a whisker, in the rat's cortex (top photograph and insert).
(After Woolsey & van der Loos, 1950)

"Boy, I'm sweating, I'm awful nervous, you know, once in a while I get caught up, I can't mention the tarripoi, a month ago, quite a little, I've done a lot well, I impose a lot, while, on the other hand, you know what I mean, I have to run around, look it over, trebbin and all that sort of stuff."

I attempted several times to break in, but was unable to do so against this relentlessly steady and rapid outflow. Finally, I put up my hand, rested it on Gorgan's shoulder, and was able to gain a moment's reprieve.

"Thank you, Mr. Gorgan. I want to ask you a few—"

"Oh sure, go ahead, any old think you want. If I could I would. Oh, I'm taking the word the wrong way to say, all of the barbers here whenever they stop you it's going around and around, if you know what I mean, that is tying and tying for repucer, repuceration, well, we were trying the best that we could while another time it was with the beds over there the same thing. . . ." (Gardner, 1975)

In the first example, there is meaning, but no words to carry it. In the second example, there are words but no meaning, just sounds roughly coherent, unconfined by any direction. These are probably two separate verbal talents, producing the words and producing the meaning.

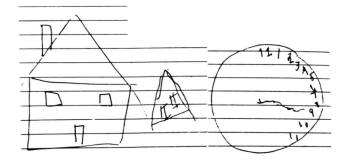

FIGURE 4-11
A One-sided View of the World

A patient with right parietal damage is unaware of the left side of things. The drawings of the watch—the top one made two days after the injury and the bottom one seven days later—in which all the numbers are crowded into the right half of the watch face, show that the patient ignores left-hand external reality. (The house drawings on the far left are the physician's, which the patient tried to duplicate.) (After Mountcastle, 1976)

FIGURE 4-12
A Shattered Mind

Lovis Corinth, an important turn-of-the-century German artist, did the portrait of his wife on the left in 1910. The portrait on the right was done in 1912 after he had suffered a right-hemisphere stroke that, among other deficits, impaired his ability to render the left side of his subject.

FIGURE 4-13
The Temporal Lobes
The left temporal lobe is
shown here as a darker
patch in relation to the rest
of the left hemisphere.

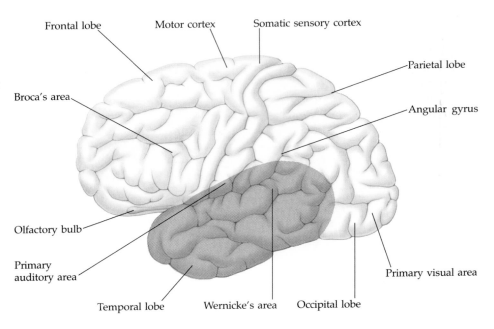

Frontal lobe   Motor cortex   Somatic sensory cortex

Parietal lobe

Broca's area

Angular gyrus

Olfactory bulb

Primary
auditory area

Primary visual area

Temporal lobe   Wernicke's area   Occipital lobe

Temporal lobe damage is not restricted to loss of language. In one test, people with right temporal lobe damage could not recognize portraits they had studied closely only two minutes before (Kimura, 1963).

After temporal lobe stimulation, some people report the feeling of being in two places at once. The memory of an event and the present *coexist* in the person's consciousness. While fully conscious and aware of the activity of the moment, a person might suddenly feel elsewhere. He may also be in a kitchen, 30 years ago, and the sounds and smells seem real. Recall Penfield's dramatic finding of memory in the brain during electrical stimulation of the temporal lobe. (See Chapter 1, Figure 1-3.) A person seems to *relive* specific past experiences.

Occipital Lobes: The Visual Cortex

At the rear of the brain are the **occipital lobes.** Because this area analyzes vision, it is often called the *visual cortex.* Visual information leaves the eyes and enters the visual cortex for analysis of orientation, position, and movement. Damage to the occipital lobes can result in blindness even if the rest of the visual system is unaffected.

Two Hemispheres

The cerebral cortex is divided into two hemispheres connected by a large structure of 300 million neurons called the **corpus callosum.** Only in human beings do these hemispheres specialize for different functions. This *lateral specialization* is the fourth level of brain organization. It is the most recent development in human evolution, less than four million years old, and perhaps "only" about one million years old.

The left hemisphere controls the right side of the body. It also controls language and logical activities, in other words, things that happen in a specific order. The right hemisphere controls the left side of the body. It directs spatial, simultaneous things—which happen all at once—and artistic activities. These differences in function probably appeared at the time human beings began to make and use symbols (both language and art). One commentator has named this level of brain organization the "asymmetric–symbolic level" (Brown, 1977).

The two hemispheres look about the same, but they have significant anatomical differences. In 95 percent of fetuses the left hemisphere is larger than the right (Geschwind & Levitsky, 1976). The enlarged area is the *planum temporale* in the temporal lobe. The planum temporale governs speech and written language (Figure 4-14). Damage to the temporal lobe of the left hemisphere causes aphasia, the loss of the ability to speak language. Damage to the right hemisphere results in impaired performance of spatial tasks, such as the ability to draw or to recognize faces.

Although each hemisphere specializes for different tasks, the division between them is not absolute. Rather, they are in constant communication with each other. Rarely is one hemisphere completely idle and the other frantic with activity. The left hemisphere is much more involved and more proficient in language and logic than the right. The right is much more involved in spatial abilities and "gestalt" thinking than the left.

The two hemispheres are not *separate* systems, nor "two brains." An activity as complex as language involves both hemispheres interacting with each other. If either hemisphere is damaged, the remaining "intact" hemisphere can take over, but this becomes less easy as we age. If the left hemisphere is damaged at birth, the right will take over language. However, the person may be less adept at language than he or she would have otherwise been (Kohn & Dennis, 1974).

EDUCATION, SOCIETY, AND THE HEMISPHERES OF THE BRAIN

Some critics have seized on the results of research on hemispheric specialization to justify their rejection of conventional science and educational systems. Like many new discoveries, the nature of the brain's specialization has often been misrepresented. Many concerned people in psychology, education, medicine, and environmental sciences realize that those of us in industrialized societies have not developed our abilities to think in terms of whole systems.

Some people seem to believe that it is all quite simple. They hope that all the world's problems would be solved if we simply suppressed our left hemispheres and ran ourselves and society with only the "intuitive" thought of the right hemisphere. Although such conclusions are simplistic, much of our education focuses on an oversimplified "rational" view of intelligence. The brain is divided into more independent centers of thought and feeling than just the two hemispheres. There are centers of movement, of calculation, of sensory analysis. There are divergent computations of the external world and divergent decisions made inside the brain. There thus exist many different centers of judgment and analysis, each of which is important to education. The nature of these divisions will be addressed later in the book, concerning the question of intelligence.

FIGURE 4-14
Asymmetry of the Cortex
In most people the left hemisphere of the cortex is larger than the right, which is thought to be due to the left hemisphere's linguistic dominance. The shaded areas in the boxed drawings show the temporal lobes in the left (top) and right (bottom) hemispheres. Cross sections of the two lobes show differences in the sizes of Wernicke's area and the planum temporale, which contribute to the brain's asymmetry.

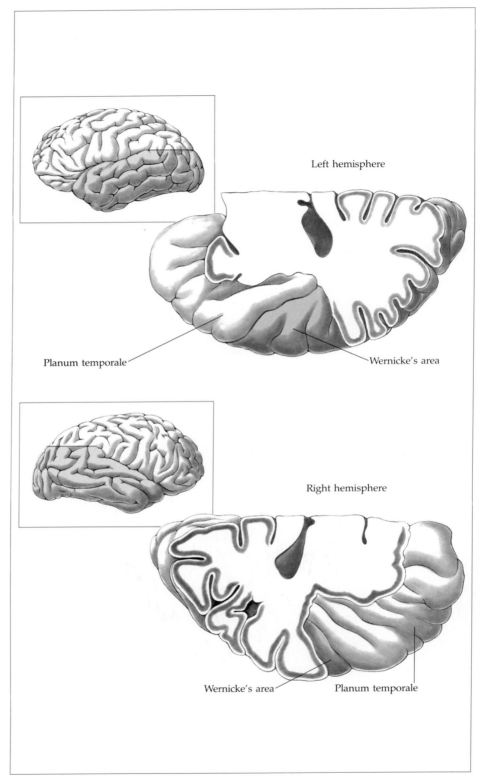

Left hemisphere

Planum temporale

Wernicke's area

Right hemisphere

Wernicke's area

Planum temporale

The "Split Brain"

The two cerebral hemispheres communicate through the corpus callosum, which joins the two sides anatomically (Figure 4-15). Roger Sperry and Joseph Bogen initiated radical treatment for severe epilepsy in human beings. They cut the callosum, producing a so-called **split brain** (Sperry, 1982).

After the surgery, if patients held an object, such as a pencil, hidden from sight in the right hand, they could describe it verbally. However, if the object was in the left hand, they could not describe it at all. Recall that the left hand informs the right hemisphere, which has a limited capability for speech. With the corpus callosum severed, the verbal (left) hemisphere is no longer connected to the right hemisphere, which communicates largely with the left hand. Here the *verbal apparatus literally does not know what is in the left hand.* Sometimes, however, the patients were offered a set of objects out of sight, such as keys, books, pencils, and so on. They were asked to select the previously given object with the left hand. The patients chose correctly, although they still could not say verbally just what object they were taking. It was as if they were asked to perform an action and someone else was discussing it.

The right half of each eye sends its messages to the left hemisphere, the left half to the right hemisphere. In an experiment using divided visual input, the word "heart" flashed before the patients. The "he" was to the left of the eye's fixation point and the "art" to the right. A normal person would report seeing the word "heart." The split-brain patients responded differently, depending on which

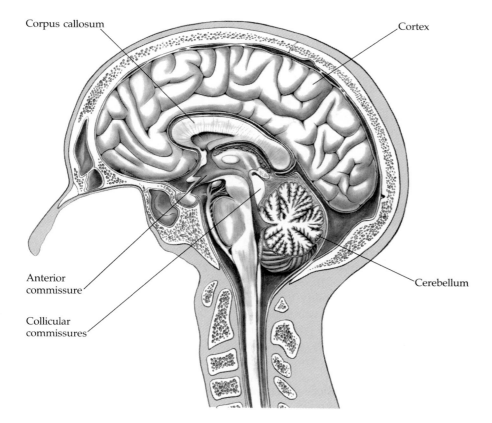

FIGURE 4-15
Splitting the Brain
In split-brain operations, called commissures, the connective nerve tissue of the corpus callosum, through which the two hemispheres communicate, is severed. This procedure has caused radical changes in patients' perception and behavior.
(After Sperry, 1982)

Corpus callosum

Cortex

Anterior commissure

Collicular commissures

Cerebellum

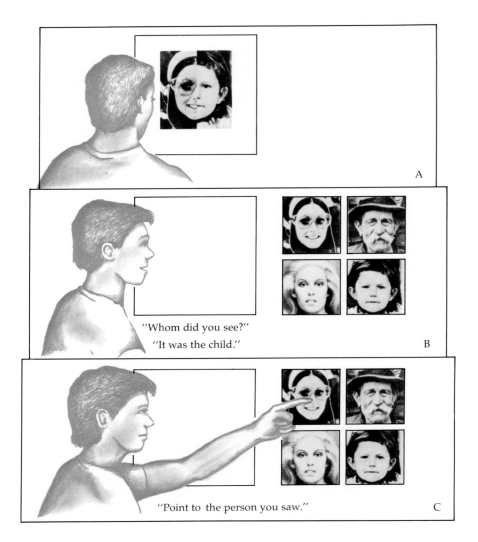

FIGURE 4-16
Hemisphere Specialization and Visual Input
A composite photograph of two different faces is flashed before a split-brain subject (A). When shown a group of photographs and asked to pick out the person he saw in the composite, he will *say* it is the face from the *right* half of the composite (B). But if asked to *point out* which one he originally saw, he will indicate the picture from the *left* side of the composite (C). Such experiments suggest the two hemispheres are independent to some degree, each performing different functions in different ways.
(After Sperry, 1982)

"Whom did you see?"
"It was the child."   B

"Point to the person you saw."   C

hemisphere was controlling the response. When asked to point with the left hand to the word seen, the patients pointed to "he," but with the right hand, they pointed to "art." The experience of each hemisphere was independent of each other in these patients. The verbal hemisphere gave one answer, the nonverbal hemisphere another (Figure 4-16).

Most right-handed people write and draw with the right hand only. However, many can also write and draw to some extent with their left. After surgery, Dr. Bogen tested the ability of the split-brain patients to draw with either hand. The right hand retained the ability to write, but it could no longer draw very well (Figure 4-17). The left hand was able to convey the relationship of the parts, even though the line quality was poor. Note the right hand's performance: the cross contains the correct elements, yet the ability to link the disconnected elements is lacking. Normally, a square would never be considered as a set of disconnected corners!

Recent tests of hemisphere functioning confirm that the right hemisphere is superior at part to whole relationships. Robert Nebes (1972) asked split-brain

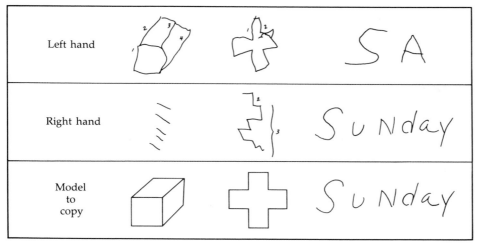

Left hand			
Right hand			
Model to copy			

FIGURE 4-17
The Role of the Hemispheres in Controlling Writing and Drawing
After split-brain surgery, the right hand, which is controlled by the left hemisphere of the cortex, cannot integrate the elements of a drawing as well as the left hand, which is controlled by the right hemisphere, the one that specializes in dealing with spatial relationships and other visual information.
(After Bogen, 1969)

patients to match arcs of circles to completed circles, which requires the ability to generalize from a segment to the whole. The right hemisphere was superior in doing this.

Workings of the Normal Brain

As startling as the split-brain studies are, an important question remains. How do the hemispheres operate in *normal* people doing *normal* things? One way to find out what an intact brain is doing measures electrical activity in the brain through an electroencephalograph (EEG) (Figure 4-18). Brain activity produces various kinds of electrical waves on the scalp: alpha wave activity indicates an awake brain on "idle" and beta waves indicate an awake brain actively processing information.

In one study (Galin & Ornstein, 1972) the right hemisphere showed more alpha activity than the left while the subject was writing a letter. The left hemisphere showed more beta activity. While arranging blocks, the left hemisphere showed more alpha than the right and the right hemisphere showed beta waves. When people write, they "turn off" the right side of the brain. While arranging blocks in space, they "turn off" the left hemisphere.

The primary component of hemispheric specialization is *not* the *type* of information processed (words and pictures versus sounds and shapes). What is important is *how* the brain processes the information. A recent study compared subjects' brain activity while reading technical passages versus folk tales. There was no change in the level of activity in the left hemisphere from the technical material to the other. However, the right hemisphere activated while the subjects read the folk stories, but it did not while they read the technical material (Ornstein, Herron, Johnstone, & Swencionis, 1979). Technical material is almost exclusively logical. Stories, on the other hand, are simultaneous; many things happen at once. The sense of a story emerges through style, plot, images, and feelings. Thus, it appears that language *in the form of stories* can stimulate activity of the right hemisphere.

Another experiment recorded brain activity while subjects mentally rotated objects in space. This normally involves the right hemisphere. When asked to do

FIGURE 4-18
Studying the Workings of the Brain with an Electroencephalograph (EEG)
The electrodes in the skull cap worn by this subject are connected to an electroencephalograph (EEG) that measures the brain's electrical impulses, which are recorded as various kinds of brain waves during different kinds of brain activity.

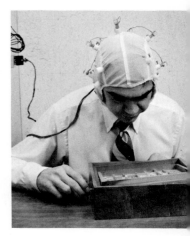

the task analytically, by counting the boxes, subjects by and large "switched over" to their left hemisphere (Ornstein & Swencionis, 1985). Thus, in problem solving, people can apparently use their hemispheres at will.

So there are two systems at the "top" of the human brain. They govern our abilities to create, in language and in art, and to discover new connections in the world. These two hemispheres appeared in our ancestors as *specialized systems* sometime during the long period of human evolution. There is evidence for them at least 100,000 years ago and probably earlier. They are the most distinctively human part of the brain (Ornstein, Thompson, & Macaulay, 1984).

HOW THE BRAIN "MINDS" THE BODY

The most recently developed areas of the brain contain the "rational" abilities that we human beings prize and develop. But the brain as a whole is *not* primarily designed for thinking. Those attributes we consider most human— language, perception, intelligence—represent only a *small fraction of the brain's functions*. What the brain does is to regulate or "mind" the body. It controls temperature, blood flow, and digestion. It monitors every sensation, each breath and heartbeat, every movement, every blink and swallow. It directs movement: walk this way, take the hand off the stove, lift the arm to catch the ball, smile.

Running the Body

The brain translates several worlds: the internal molecules, the organs, the individual, other people, and more. The brain has separate and independent "modular systems," which maintain cellular, organ, and individual health. If you think about the brain this way, its evolution and functions become more clear. Its basic job is health and running the body. The brain directs all voluntary and involuntary movements. It communicates with the body via the glands of the *endocrine system* and three interconnected systems of nerves. They are the *central nervous system (CNS)*, the *peripheral nervous system (PNS)*, and the *autonomic nervous system (ANS)*, which is a portion of the PNS. The brain and spinal cord comprise the CNS.

The brain is the control center of all the neural networks. The spinal cord is the central trunk through which all neural communications pass on the way to the brain. The somatic PNS is a two-way communication system between the brain and muscles for controlling *voluntary* movements. *Involuntary* movements, such as heart beat, digestion, blood flow, and heat regulation, are regulated by the autonomic PNS and the glands of the endocrine system.

The brain responds to changes in the external and internal worlds. Through the

FIGURE 4-19
The Brain's Response to the Unexpected
The left hemisphere of the brain responds to an inappropriate word inserted at the end of an otherwise ordinary sentence by registering a marked change in its pattern of electrical activity.
(After Kulas & Hillyard, 1980)

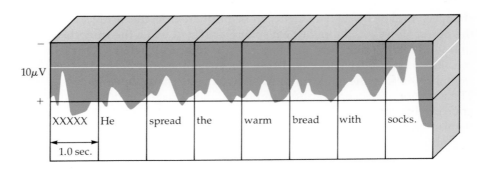

senses the brain receives information about occurrences in the outside world. The endocrine system controls the internal state of the body, the blood sugar level and pain.

Stimuli that gets the brain's attention signal a change from the existing state. The change may be as subtle as a change in air pressure or as jarring as a strange and unexpected statement. Read the sentence, "He spread the warm bread with jam." A record of the electrical activity of the brain as someone reads this sentence shows little disruption. Now read the sentence, "He spread the warm bread with socks." Brain activity changes significantly at the last word (Figure 4-19), which is an indication of surprise (Kutas & Hillyard, 1980).

As a health system, the brain is the major organ of adaptation. It tells the body what to do based on its information of the changing state of the world. The ability to respond quickly to change and to be flexible in responding are the primary ingredients of adaptability. Consider what happens when a frog is confronted by a fallen tree. The frog has a very specialized sensory system and brain. It probably will not even notice the tree unless it runs into it. A human, however, can cut it, play seesaw on it, make tables out of it, even make paper for this book. This greater flexibility of action is in part due to a larger brain.

Language of the Brain

Whether an activity is simple or complex, voluntary or involuntary, the brain has *only one way of communicating.* The brain works by sending and receiving information in electrical and chemical codes. That "language" of the brain is the action of very simple signals sent at varying rates among billions of neurons. It is in the *pattern of firing* of the neurons of the brain that all experience is to be read — if we can learn to read it.

Neurons

Neurons, the nerve cells that are the major constituent of the brain, are the most remarkable of all biological cells (Figure 4-20). They are the building blocks that make up the "rooms" of the brain. The nucleus of the neuron is the *cell body.* It contains the biochemical apparatus for powering the electrical charge and for maintaining the life of the cell. The **axon** extends outward from the cell body (Figure 4-20). The axon is the "transmitter" end of the neuron; signals sent from the neuron exit through the axon. The **dendrites** look like the branches of a tree (Figure 4-21). They are the "receiving" end; they receive information from the axons of other neurons. Because of the extensive branching of the dendrites, one neuron is able to communicate with thousands of other neurons (Figure 4-22).

The Neural Impulse: Action Potential

If you could see the brain working, you would see millions of miniature explosions going on and off each instant. Neurons fire, then stop, and then fire their electrical charges again and again. In the pattern and composition of those explosions lie our thought and individuality. An enormous amount of research over the past few years has begun to uncover the secrets of this neural code.

Minute quantities of chemical transmitter molecules are the ultimate unit of action of the nervous system. Different concentrations of these various

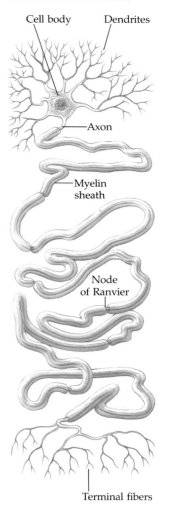

FIGURE 4-20
The Parts of a Neuron

Cell body

Dendrites

Axon

Myelin sheath

Node of Ranvier

Terminal fibers

FIGURE 4-21

**The Dendrites of a Single
Neuron**
This highly magnified
photograph shows the
axons and branching
dendrites through which
the neuron can receive
information from many
other neurons.

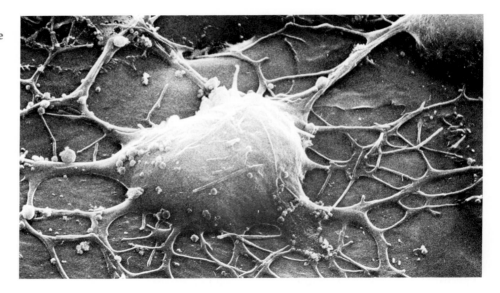

neurotransmitters in the brain may well determine activity level, temperament,
and mood. They also seem to influence the healing systems of the brain.

Earlier neuroscientists thought there were only a very few such chemicals,
perhaps three or four. It now appears there may be hundreds of different chemical messenger molecules. These neurotransmitters are the "words" with which
the brain uses to communicate. These transmitters, including acetylcholine, norepinephrine, serotonin, dopamine, and endorphins, govern excitability, sleep and
dreams, hallucinations, pain regulation, mood, and thought. In short, these
chemicals underlie all the different brain functions.

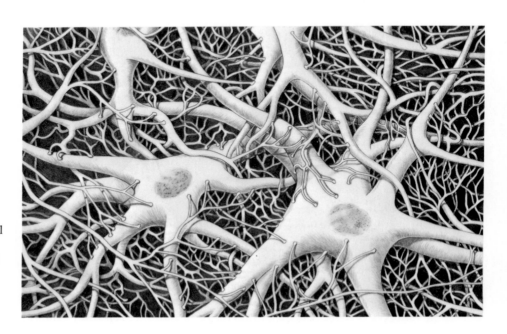

**FIGURE 4-22
A Living Network of
Brain Cells in Continual
Communication**
This sketch shows only a
tiny section of the cerebral
cortex, giving you an idea
of the intricacy and extent
of the network of cells
communicating with one
another through
neurotransmission.

The Neuron and Neurotransmission

Suppose you could get inside a neuron itself. You would see scores of chemicals being released, going from cell to cell and back again. In the pattern and the chemical composition of those explosions lie our thoughts and our brain's control of our body.

The brain communicates with and controls the body through this continuous flow of chemical messages. Neurotransmitter molecules convey messages between cells, and neurohormones produced and secreted by the brain carry messages through the bloodstream to distant target organs. In this sense each nerve cell and the brain itself is like an internal pharmacy. It dispenses a stream of powerful drugs to influence and control moods, thoughts, and bodily functions (Thompson, 1986).

Communication between neurons occurs by **neurotransmission** which is accomplished through the release of chemical molecules *(neurotransmitters)*. Like a battery, a neuron at rest has an electrical charge called the *resting potential.* When the neuron is adequately stimulated by another neuron, it fires. The firing of the neuron releases its stored energy.

The neural impulse of a firing neuron is the **action potential.** The action potential sweeps down the axon. Once it fires, the neuron is temporarily depleted of energy and does not immediately fire again. This period of time is the *absolute refractory period.* In this period, firing is possible only if there is a greater than normal stimulus. These refractory periods are not long; they are measured in thousandths of a second.

Myelin Sheath

The axons of many neurons are coated with a fatty substance called the **myelin sheath.** This sheath begins to develop in infancy and contributes to the weight added to the brain after birth. It has three main functions:

1. *Insulation.* The sheath covers the neuron and prevents loss of electrical potential, just as a cable protects an electrical wire from "leaking" its signals.
2. *Acceleration of transmission.* There are periodic gaps in the surface of the sheath. The electrical impulses leap across the gaps and move directly to the next gap. These gaps thus speed up the rate of neural conduction.
3. *Isolation.* For a system to function, the right information must get to the right place. The myelination prevents a neuron from communicating randomly with other neurons.

Neurotransmission

The action potential inside a neuron is *electrical,* but the transmission of the neural impulse from one neuron to the next is *chemical.* Between the axon of one neuron and the dendrite of the next is a tiny space called the **synapse** (Greek for "connection"). The neuron sending the information is the *presynaptic* neuron. The neuron receiving information is the *postsynaptic* neuron (Figure 4-23). A neuron transmits its signal to the next neuron at the synapse between the two. The transmitter chemicals are stored in pouches, called *synaptic vesicles,* at the termi-

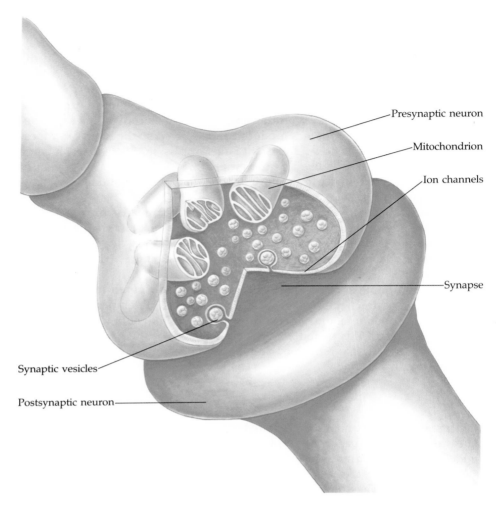

FIGURE 4-23
Neurotransmission
The presynaptic neuron and the postsynaptic neuron meet at a tiny gap called the synapse across which the transmitter chemicals "jump" to transmit their signals.

Presynaptic neuron

Mitochondrion

Ion channels

Synapse

Synaptic vesicles

Postsynaptic neuron

nal of the axon. When the action potential arrives at the synapse, it starts a sequence of steps that eventually convey the signal from one neuron to another.

1. Neurotransmitters are stored inside synaptic vesicles in the terminal button of the presynaptic neuron. When the action potential reaches the synapse, it causes some of these neurotransmitters to be released into the synaptic opening, called the *synaptic cleft.*
2. The transmitters cross the cleft and either *stimulate* or *inhibit* the firing of the postsynaptic neuron (the neuron receiving the message).
3. After the transmission, the whole process is deactivated (the refractory period). Some transmitters may break down, while some return to the axon of the presynaptic neuron; this process is called *reuptake.*

Neurotransmitters

The brain probably has hundreds of different transmitters—new ones are discovered almost monthly. The chemical compound **acetylcholine** (ACh) is one of the major transmitters in the nervous system. It relates to the arousal of the organism and is most concentrated in the brain during sleep. ACh conveys information from the brain to the muscles. The Amazon Indians knew the results, though not the mechanism, of interfering with neurotransmission when they dipped their arrows in the poison curare. Curare is fatal because it interferes with ACh transmission and paralyzes the victim. Such a victim will die quickly without some assistance in breathing.

Individual neurotransmitters cluster into different "chemical pathways." These networks connect parts of the brain in complex mosaics unimagined even a few years ago. The following pathways are especially noteworthy.

Norepinephrine.   Norepinephrine (formerly called adrenaline) is important in the coding of memory and in the reward system of the brain. This is a group of structures that is activated in pleasurable moments. The pathway connects the outer brain stem to the cortex. Norepinephrine exists outside the brain in the autonomic nervous system.

Dopamine.   The dopamine pathway connects the limbic system to the cortex. It also participates in the brain's reward system and in the control of motor activity. Parkinson's disease is one in which the sufferer exhibits severe motor tremors. It is caused by a lack of dopamine and can be aided by the administration of the drug L-dopa, transformed by the brain into dopamine (Figure 4-24).

Serotonin.   The serotonin pathways are widespread in the brain. They connect the brain stem and the reticular activating system to the cortex and to the limbic system at the hypothalamus and hippocampus. Serotonin controls sleep and many activities associated with sleep. Loss of serotonin causes insomnia.

The drug LSD seems to affect the serotonin system by blocking the firing of serotonin neurons. Because hallucinations are common in LSD "trips," serotonin may be involved in hallucinations and even in psychosis. Since serotonin is an inhibitor of neural firing, blocking its transmission speeds up sensory transmission. The great increase in all kinds of neuronal activity leads to a breakup of the normal mode of perception.

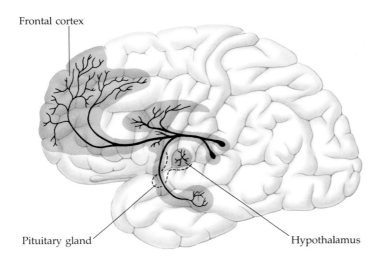

Frontal cortex

Pituitary gland

Hypothalamus

FIGURE 4-24
Dopamine Pathways in
the Brain

Mood and Neurotransmitters

People have long believed that internal substances affect mood, disposition, and even personality. The ancient Greeks mistakenly believed that there were specific body *humors* that determined mood. A characteristically angry person was thought to have an excess of *bile,* and a calm one, too much *phlegm;* hence, the descriptions "bilious" and "phlegmatic." Perhaps different concentrations of various neurotransmitters may affect temperament and mood. Many of the transmitters are involved in excitability, sleep and dreams, and hallucinations.

THE BRAIN'S NEURAL AND CHEMICAL SYSTEMS

The complexities of the neural and chemical organization of the brain and its four different levels of organization all serve one master: the body. The end point of brain activity is action: plans and ideas as well as walking, turning, dancing, or following something with the eyes. The brain, through its neural and chemical connections, monitors activity in every cell in the body. The brain communicates with and controls the body via two kinds of systems: the nervous system and the neuroendocrine system (Figure 4-25).

The Nervous Systems

The nervous systems that link the brain to the body are the central nervous system and the peripheral nervous system.

Central Nervous System

The brain and spinal cord together make up the **central nervous system** (CNS). Just below the brain and physically joined to it is the *spinal cord.* It is the central trunk of the nervous system. It delivers both the brain's commands to the body and the body's messages to the brain.

Reflexes that protect the body from damage are commanded from the spinal cord. A reflex is an immediate, inborn response. Place your hand on a hot stove and you will immediately withdraw it, literally "without thinking." The spinal cord handles such emergencies without involving the brain. These are the only movements that take place without the brain.

The spinal cord contains all the basic elements of the nervous systems. There are three types of neurons in the spinal cord:

1. **Afferent neurons** bring information to the brain from the sensory system.
2. **Efferent neurons** take messages from the brain and activate muscles and glands.
3. **Interneurons** connect the afferent and efferent neurons.

The spinal cord is encased in the vertebrae. It is further protected by the spinal fluid, which acts as a shock absorber. The spinal cord is subject to thousands of shocks during the course of a day. The average person is a half inch shorter at night than in the morning.

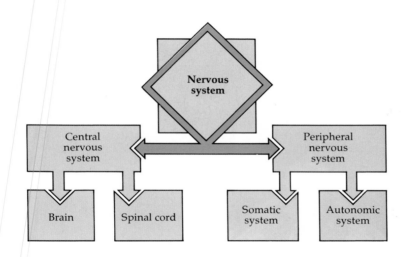

FIGURE 4-25
Subdivisions of the
Human Nervous System

Peripheral Nervous System

Commands to the muscles move through the **peripheral nervous system** (PNS). Nerves flow from the spinal cord into the muscles and organs of the body. Information is gathered about body states, muscle and limb position, and the internal states of organs. If something is awry, action will be taken.

The vast network of nerves in the PNS (Figure 4-26) ultimately reach every organ and muscle of the body. The PNS is divided into two parts: the somatic and autonomic.

FOOD FOR THOUGHT

The brain is precious tissue and is specially protected from the outside world. The skull is a barrier against blows. There are also internal barriers to guard the brain. A special network of cells called the "blood–brain barrier" keeps toxins in the blood from reaching the brain. Because of such protections, the inner workings of the brain have been thought to be almost completely isolated from the state of the body or the external world.

This view is now challenged. Some recent experiments have found striking short-term changes in brain chemistry associated with diet. In an early study, eating substances rich in choline increased ACh throughout the brain. This is true particularly in the brain stem and cerebral cortex (Wurtman & Wurtman, 1984). Choline is present in egg yolks (1.7 percent by weight), meat (0.6 percent), and in lesser amounts in fish, cereal, and legumes.

Whether specific diets can help learning and memory is far from proven, but research may show that this is possible. Other foods also have specific effects on the workings of the brain. A high carbohydrate diet increases serotonin levels (Wurtman & Wurtman, 1984). Tryptophan, a neurotransmitter active in sleep, is also increased by a high carbohydrate intake. The brain seems much more responsive to its internal environment than has been thought, even to the short-term environment of the last meal.

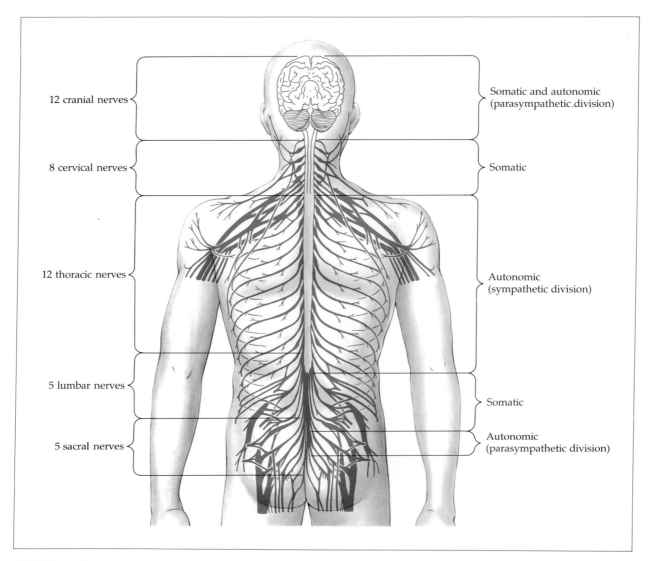

12 cranial nerves

8 cervical nerves

12 thoracic nerves

5 lumbar nerves

5 sacral nerves

Somatic and autonomic
(parasympathetic.division)

Somatic

Autonomic
(sympathetic division)

Somatic

Autonomic
(parasympathetic division)

FIGURE 4-26
The Network of Nerves
in the Peripheral Nervous
System

1. The **somatic nervous system** (SNS) controls the voluntary movements of the body, such as reaching for a glass or picking up a pencil. These movements begin in the sensory motor area of the brain. *Afferent* nerves convey information about the skin, sensory organs, muscles, and joints to the brain, and *efferent* nerves bring instructions from the brain to the muscles.

2. The **autonomic nervous system** (ANS) is primarily responsible for running the automatic processes of the body (Figure 4-27). The heart beats about 70 times per minute without us instructing it to beat. The kidneys purify the blood without us telling them to. The liver and gastrointestinal tract also work outside conscious control. The ANS is largely under the direct control of the limbic system (usually without the involvement of the cortex). It regulates emotional reactions, such as crying, sweating, and stomach pains.

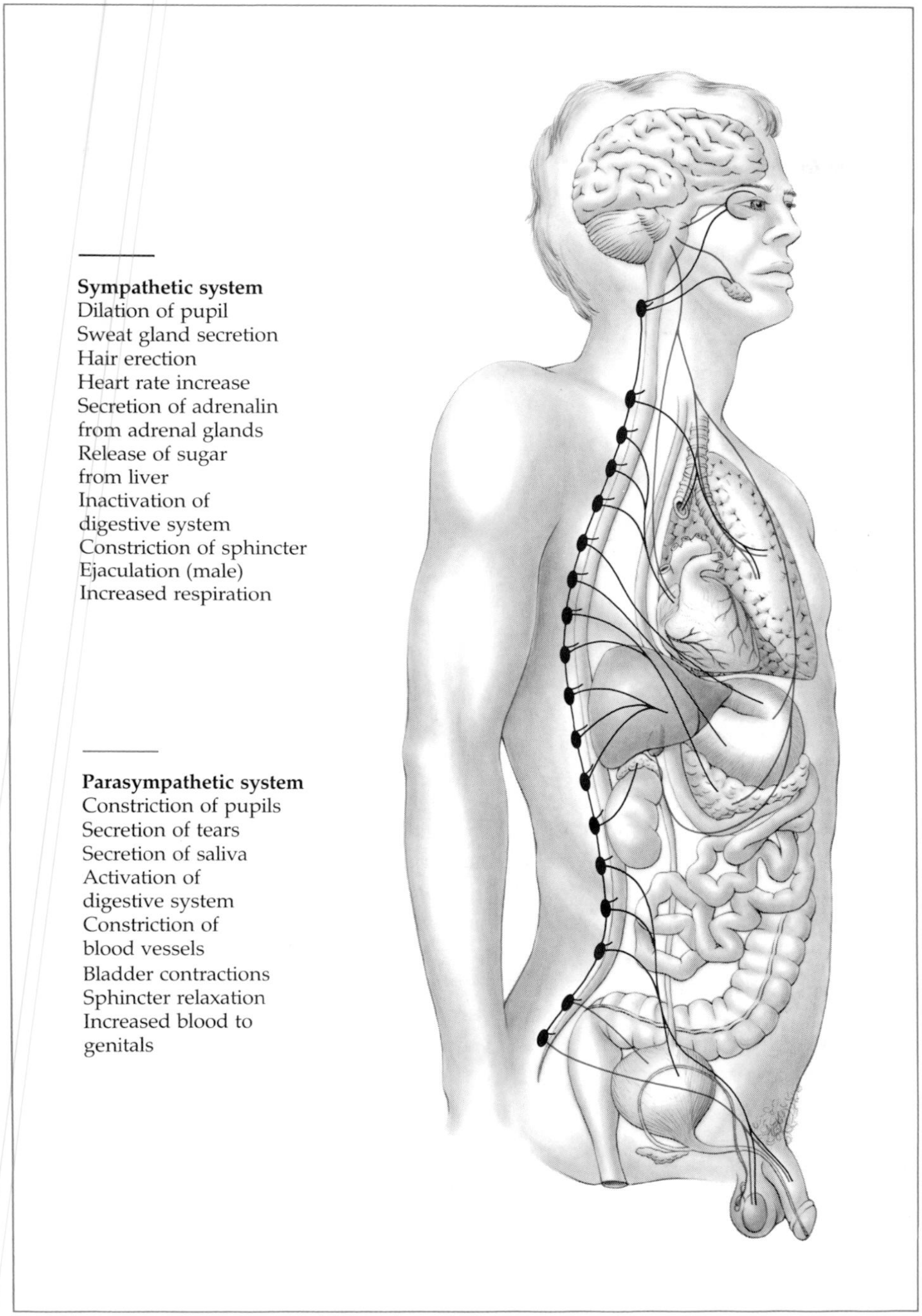

FIGURE 4-27
Autonomic Nervous
System
This simplified diagram
shows the different
functions of the two
systems of the autonomic
nervous system: the
sympathetic system (black
lines) and the
parasympathetic system
(red lines).

Sympathetic system
Dilation of pupil
Sweat gland secretion
Hair erection
Heart rate increase
Secretion of adrenalin
from adrenal glands
Release of sugar
from liver
Inactivation of
digestive system
Constriction of sphincter
Ejaculation (male)
Increased respiration

Parasympathetic system
Constriction of pupils
Secretion of tears
Secretion of saliva
Activation of
digestive system
Constriction of
blood vessels
Bladder contractions
Sphincter relaxation
Increased blood to
genitals

The ANS is divided into two systems. The **sympathetic system** prepares the internal organs for emergencies, when there are extra demands on the body. It operates "in sympathy" with the emotions, like an accelerator, telling the body to "go." Signs of sympathetic activation include sweating and other symptoms of

FIGURE 4-28
Hormone Regulation
This schematic drawing
exemplifies the feedback
process that regulates
hormone production. The
level of thyroxin in the
blood may trigger the
pituitary to produce
thyroid-releasing hormone
(TRH); this signals the
thyroid to produce
thyroxin, thereby raising
the level of that hormone
in the blood, which on
reaching the pituitary,
informs it that TRH
production can be reduced.

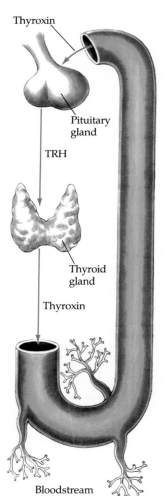

Thyroxin

Pituitary
gland

TRH

Thyroid
gland

Thyroxin

Bloodstream

arousal. The sympathetic nervous system is usually activated by unusual circum-stances: emergencies, ecstasy, excitement.

The **parasympathetic system** is more conservative. It acts like a brake on the sympathetic system and returns the body to normal after an emergency. Typi-cally, when an exciting event has passed, the heart rate slows and dryness of the mouth begins to cease. These changes occur because sympathetic activation ceases and the parasympathetic system actively slows heart rate and deactivates internal organs.

The two forms of signals, "go" and "slow down," are carried by different nerve circuits. The messages move via different neurotransmitters. Norepinephrine carries the sympathetic message, ACh the parasympathetic message. The sympa-thetic neurons are centralized in the brain, acting on their target from a distance. The parasympathetic system is decentralized; each ganglion (collection of neurons) is located near the organ it serves.

The Brain's Chemical System

Neuroendocrine System

Another way the brain controls the body is via the **neuroendocrine system,** which includes the ANS and the endocrine glands. Think about the brain this way: each neuron is like a little gland. So the brain is a great organ of secretion. The understanding of this final level of the brain's operations has come about only in the past two decades. It will provide the key to the ultimate workings of the brain.

Hormones and the Pituitary

The **pituitary** is the control gland of the endocrine system. It lies below the hypothalamus in the limbic system of the brain. Many important behaviors, such as sex, are under its direct control. The pituitary also controls many other glands, such as the adrenal and thyroid glands, and it synthesizes a wide variety of hormones.

A **hormone** is a chemical messenger molecule secreted by specialized cells called *neurosecretory cells.* Hormones are larger molecules than neurotransmit-ters. Molecules of hormones migrate within the bloodstream to locations where they stimulate production of other hormones. Neuroendocrine communication operates on the lock-and-key principle (see box). A hormone secreted into the bloodstream passes many organs until it fits into the intended receptor. This receptor identifies itself by its shape.

Hormone regulation works through feedback. To stimulate the thyroid gland, the pituitary produces *thyroid-releasing hormone* or TRH. When the thyroid re-ceives TRH, it produces its own hormone, *thyroxin,* which it releases into the bloodstream. Some thyroxin reaches the pituitary, which then measures the amount of the hormone and either increases or decreases production of TRH (Figure 4-28). Similar feedback processes operate for other hormones.

Adrenal Glands

The adrenal glands start up in emergency situations. They have two parts: the outer *adrenal cortex* and the inner *adrenal medulla.* When activated by the ANS,

LOCK AND KEY: ARCHITECTURE OF MOLECULES

Heroin produces exultation; LSD, even in minute quantities, can produce hallucinations. How does this happen? We are born with certain "locks" within our nervous system. Drugs such as heroin are the "keys" that open these locks; that is why they are so powerful.

Specific molecules have many different effects on their cells, but they can exert these effects only when their messenger molecules (or drugs that mimic the messenger molecules) combine with them. If the molecule "fits," the receptor will attach it and be triggered into action. This is the reason why very tiny amounts of many drugs have such powerful effects on the brain and mind. Their shapes resemble the shapes of normal synaptic transmitter chemicals. The similar shapes fool the receptors into believing that they are receiving their normal messenger molecules. The nature of this relationship has been discovered only in the past few decades. It is fundamental to our research into how the brain works. It allows scientists to understand how drugs affect the brain and how psychological disorders can be treated chemically.

On the surfaces of cell membranes are hundreds, perhaps thousands, of different types of molecular structures called *receptors*. Each type of receptor has a characteristic three-dimensional shape, and like a lock, can only be opened or activated by a chemical key. The *shape* of the drug or the neurotransmitter molecule is the "key." It "fits" a receptor whose shape matches it, as a key fits into a lock. This lock-and-key relationship describes how the chemical messages of the body connect with their target cells. The messenger molecules move through the bloodstream or across synapses until they fit the receptors designed for them. Once the receptor activates, the activity of the cell is either stimulated or inhibited. Drugs stimulate body processes because they mimic the shape of naturally existing substances in the body. Every neurotransmitter and hormone molecule has a specific shape which can fit only specific receptors.

Many mental disorders, such as schizophrenia, may be due to alterations in neurotransmission. Many psychoactive drugs, such as cocaine, work because they affect the process of neurotransmission. Cocaine may prevent reuptake, so that the firing of the neurons involved does not cease. This seems to be how cocaine functions as a stimulant. See Chapter 7, section on Drugs.

---

the adrenal medulla secretes epinephrine and norepinephrine. Both of these stimulate the cardiovascular (heart-lung) system. Adrenal gland activity is coordinated with the ANS during emergency situations. If there is injury to the body, adrenal cortisol, an antiinflammatory agent, travels to the site of the injury.

The Healing Brain

Endorphins and the Intrinsic Pain Relief System

The brain has its own pharmacy. It controls pain and has a significant function in healing. It regulates the conveyance of hormones to wounds, regulates the internal state of organs, and maintains homeostasis. The brain also produces a number of specific chemicals related to the direct relief of pain.

For centuries it has been known that opium and its derivatives relieve pain. Such drugs as morphine and codeine are routinely used to relieve the pain of injury on the battlefield or after surgery. The brain contains specific receptors for opiates, which fit the receptors by the lock-and-key principle. These receptors are mainly located in the limbic system and the spinal cord. During pregnancy there are many opiate receptors in the placenta to protect the fetus from pain and shock.

Opium is the extract of the poppy plant. People have used it for thousands of years to relieve pain and to induce feelings of intense pleasure. The major active ingredient of opium is morphine, which was first purified in the early nineteenth century and later synthesized in the laboratory. Morphine is the best understood of all drugs that act on the brain; it is a relatively simple molecule consisting of several atoms having a particular shape.

Similar chemical molecules are made in the laboratory that have very specific *antagonistic* actions to morphine, that is, they oppose the action of morphine. Naloxone is the most potent of these—at very low doses it rapidly and completely reverses the effects of morphine. A heroin addict who is about to die from an overdose of heroin will be fully awake and recovered in minutes after an injection of naloxone. He will also then immediately exhibit severe withdrawal symptoms. However, it has no detectable effect at all if injected into a normal person who is not addicted to morphine. Interestingly, morphine-related drugs and their antagonists, such as naloxone, are structurally very similar.

The Search for the Endorphins

The opiate receptors in the brain that "fit" the morphine molecules were found in 1974 by Solomon Snyder and Candace Pert working at Johns Hopkins University. Because of the similar structure of morphine and naloxone, they used naloxone in their experiments. Snyder and Pert made naloxone radioactive so it could later be identified with a radiation counter. It attached or bound very specifically to receptors on neurons in several regions of the brain.

The opiate molecules block pain by fitting receptors in areas of the limbic system that seem to be pathways of pain. The discovery of the opiate receptors in the brain led inevitably to a question. What is the brain doing with receptors for a substance extracted from a poppy? It is unlikely that our evolution was directed toward providing the human brain with receptors for refined products that would be synthesized 150 million years later. The answer is that the brain *produces its own pain-blocking compounds* and that the opiates work because they happen to fit the receptors for that built-in system (Figure 4-29).

The search was on. Several groups of scientists around the world began work to find these "natural opiates." John Hughes and Hans Kosterlitz (1975) in Scotland were the first to succeed. They isolated a substance from the brains of pigs that had the same action as morphine. These substances are a class of peptide proteins called **endorphins** (*endo*genous mor*phines*), which are both synaptic transmitter chemicals and hormones. Several varieties of endorphins have been identified, including *enkephalins,* which were the ones discovered by Hughes and Kosterlitz. Enkephalins seem to act as general *modulators* of nervous system activity: they enhance or suppress responsiveness to stimuli. It was initially thought that if endorphins could be extracted in quantity they would provide a safe, nonaddicting painkiller. Unfortunately, at least one endorphin, beta-endorphin, is even more addictive than refined opiates such as heroin.

At first glance, these brain "morphines" do not seem to resemble the drug morphine at all. The enkephalins, for example, are peptides, made up of a string of five amino acids. The morphine molecule, in contrast, is not a peptide and has a very different chemical make-up. In fact, there are no natural biological sub-

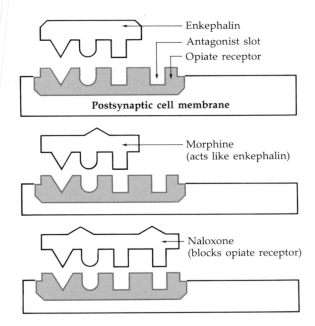

FIGURE 4-29
Opiate Receptors in the
Brain
The shapes of special
molecules in the brain
allow them to act as
receptors to natural opiates
produced by the brain
(enkephalin, top); to opiate
drugs made from the
poppy plants (morphine,
middle); and to a drug
antagonistic to morphine
but having the same basic
shape (naloxone, bottom).

stances in the body or brain that are chemically similar to the morphine compounds. There must be other brain chemicals that have an *architectural* (shape) similarity. Some part of the molecule of a naturally occurring substance must have the same shape as the opiate drugs, a molecular shape that fits into the receptor.

In its three-dimensional shape, one end of the morphine molecule closely resembles one end of the enkephalin molecule. The "opiate" receptors in the brain are, of course, not opiate receptors at all. They are enkephalin receptors, acted on by the naturally occurring brain opioids. It just happens that morphine and the closely similar synthetic drugs have a shape that fits the opiate receptor.

Indeed, naloxone, the drug that antagonizes morphine, fits the opiate receptor in the brain even better than morphine. This is why it antagonizes the actions of morphine so effectively. It literally knocks the morphine molecule off the receptor and attaches to the receptor. However, its shape is such that although it attaches to the receptor, it does not activate the receptor. Naloxone simply attaches and prevents morphine and other opiates from acting on the receptor.

The actions of the brain opioids seem identical to the actions of morphine — they relieve pain and induce feelings of pleasure. One might think that these substances would prove to be the ideal painkillers. After all, they are naturally occurring substances in our bodies. Unfortunately, these brain opioids are just as addicting as morphine and heroin. Any substances that join with the opiate receptors to relieve pain and induce pleasure are potentially addicting.

Opiates Within Us

What do we do with these opioid substances in our brains? Animal studies have shown that stress causes these substances to be released into the bloodstream, mostly from the master endocrine gland at the base of the brain, the pituitary. They are released to help counter the pain and suffering induced by stress. In an emergency situation we don't even notice minor injuries that would otherwise be painful.

Naloxone not only antagonizes morphine, it also antagonizes the naturally occurring brain opioids. Injection of naloxone causes clear increases in pain in both animals and humans. Normal people in nonstressful situations given naloxone report no particular subjective feelings. However, experiments in which people have to come back for daily doses of naloxone often run into problems. The subjects don't show up after the first dose. They don't report any unpleasant feeling, but their behavior seems to indicate they don't like it.

Pain Relief

At about the same time endorphins were discovered, another dramatic series of studies was taking place. Electrical stimulation of various specific sites in the brain was shown to enhance and reduce the experience of pain. The most relief from pain came when areas containing the most endorphin receptors were stimulated. Stimulation in those areas produced marked relief in patients with intractable pain. Repeated stimulation brought increased relief (Beer, 1979). For one patient, the need for stimulation became less and less until minimal and infrequent stimulation was necessary.

This discovery, that the brain produces its own painkillers and that it possesses an intrinsic analgesia (pain relief) system, was important. It has encouraged new research about the many social and psychological factors that directly affect brain chemistry, health, and healing. In one study that has come out of this new research, young patients with strong postoperative dental pain were given *placebos*. This is a nonactive substance whose curative effect lies solely in the taker's belief that it will help. Many of the patients reported reductions in pain. After the placebo was given, students were given the drug naloxone, which normally blocks the effect of opiates and endorphins. The students then felt pain again, so, in essence, the naloxone removed the "painkilling" effect of the placebo. That means that the patients must have stimulated their own endorphin production just by believing they had taken real painkilling drugs (Levine & Fields, 1979).

Naloxone also blocks other effects, such as pain relief from acupuncture (Berger, Watson, Akil, Barchas, & Li, 1980). Perhaps emotional state, mood, "will to live," and the doctor–patient relationship may be as important as drugs in promoting the synthesis of endorphins in the brain. The healing rituals of "primitive" societies may have real biological effects by stimulating the brain's own healing system.

THE INDIVIDUAL BRAIN

People's brains are as different as their noses. The brain can respond and grow depending on different experiences. The environment determines the languages that one speaks, and early experience can affect brain size. There are even temporary reactions caused by changes in the local environment, such as nutrition and air quality.

Brain Growth with Experience

Environmental conditions play a greater role in the brain development of human beings than in any other animal. It is commonly thought that at birth the neurons begin to make connections and these connections increase as we age and acquire

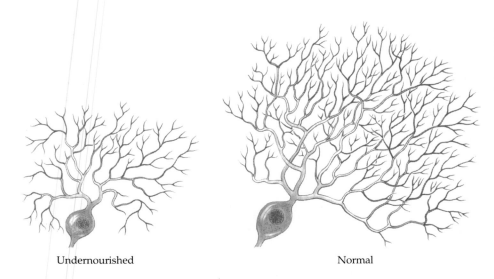

FIGURE 4-30
Malnutrition and the Brain
A brain cell from an undernourished rat is clearly less developed, with fewer and smaller dendrites.
(After McConnell & Berry, 1978)

Undernourished   Normal

experience. The opposite is actually the case (Greenough, 1975). There are many *more* connections in the brain of an infant than in an elderly adult. Development seems to be a matter of "pruning" original connections rather than making new ones. Consider this about infant babbling. In the first months of life, a baby utters almost *every sound of every known language* (Miller, 1951) and later on *loses* the ability to make sounds that are not in the language he or she has learned to speak. There is thus a universe of potential sound patterns available to us at birth, but we *learn* only a few of them. Similarly, the brain may be "set up" at birth to do a myriad of different things, but we only get around to doing a few of them.

Severe malnutrition may cause inadequate brain development, a smaller brain than normal, and severe mental retardation (Livingston, Callaway, MacGregor, Fischer, & Hastings, 1975). Rats deprived of normal food show distortions in brain structure and even shrinkage of certain brain structures. The left illustration in Figure 4-30 shows a brain cell from a deprived rat.

The brain, like a muscle, grows in response to certain experiences: the neurons actually become larger. Rats brought up in an enriched environment have a larger cortex than rats brought up in a deprived one. This developmental process goes on as long as the organism lives and is active. Brain growth can be increased in *old* rats who are stimulated for as little as one week (Connors & Diamond, 1982). The brain is *modifiable* and it grows with experience and stimulation.

The Brain of the Left-Hander

In most right-handed people, language and other sequential abilities are present in the left hemisphere. Spatial abilities and simultaneous thinking reside primarily in the right hemisphere. In left-handed people, brain organization is often different (Herron, 1980).

There are three types of hemispheric organization in left-handers: (1) those whose cortical organization is similar to right-handers, (2) those whose organization is reversed, and (3) those who have language and spatial abilities in both hemispheres. Electroencephalograph studies of left-handers show all three patterns of hemisphere organization in different individuals (Galin, Ornstein, Herron, & Johnstone, 1982).

Left-handers are a distinct minority (about 10 percent of the population is left-handed). They face some difficulty living in a right-handed world. For example, it is sometimes difficult for them to write alphabet languages because these were designed by and for right-handers. Some left-handers write in a "hooked" position, while others write in the same way as right-handers (Figure 4-31).

There is controversy about whether being left-handed affects intellectual abilities. A great percentage of left-handers have "mixed dominance" (language in both sides of the brain). Many investigators argue that spatial ability is interfered with. However, most investigators who have studied many subjects show equivocal results (Miller, 1971). What is less equivocal is the cultural bias against things

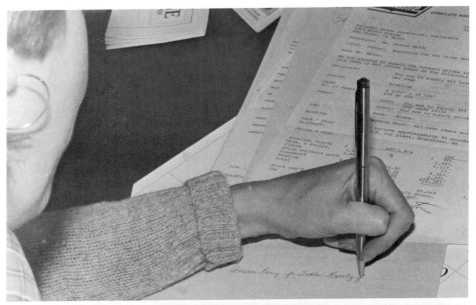

FIGURE 4-31
The Trials of Being Left-handed
Whether using the so-called hooked position or the ordinary way of writing, trying to write a language designed for right-handers is but one of the problems of left-handed people in a largely right-handed world.

of the left. The word *gauche* (meaning "awkward") is the French word for left. The word *sinister* comes from the Latin for left *(sinistra)*.

Whether brain differences manifest themselves as personality or intellectual traits is unknown, but the existence of strong brain differences is certain.

Sex Differences in the Brain

There are many physical differences between the sexes in adulthood. The most notable differences are in the reproductive systems, body size and weight, and muscle mass. Males on the average are more physically active at an earlier age than are females (Barsley, 1979). Males are characteristically superior to females in gross motor control and spatial abilities (Witelson, 1976).

Behavioral differences between the sexes have a physical expression in the brain. Boys show earlier right hemisphere development than girls. Witelson (1976) asked boys and girls 3 to 13 years old to match held objects to visually presented shapes. At age 5, boys showed a superiority at the task with objects held in the left hand (compared to their right hand). Girls did not show a similar superiority until age 13.

Girls, however, are slightly better than boys at left hemisphere tasks in the grade school years (Buffrey & Gray, 1972). Bryden (1973) presented spoken syllables to boys and girls in kindergarten, second, fourth, sixth, and eighth grades. The girls showed a clear right ear (left hemisphere) advantage by the fourth grade; boys were much later in developing this asymmetry.

The two hemispheres in males are also more specialized than those in females. The representation of analytic and sequential thinking is more clearly present in the left hemisphere of males than in females. Damage to the left hemisphere interferes more with verbal abilities in males than in females (McGlone, 1980).

The Changing Brain

The brain continuously changes in response to a changing environment. Some alterations are in response to temporary, short-term conditions, while some are to long-range, permanent conditions.

Short-term Changes in the Brain

The concentration of neurotransmitters changes rapidly after a meal. A meal of eggs increases the available levels of ACh in the brain. A meal rich in carbohydrates increases the brain's supply of serotonin (Wurtman & Wurtman, 1984). Neurotransmitters also respond to changes in the air. Hot, dry winds (such as the Santa Ana in southern California) often precede outbreaks of violence, including suicide (Krueger, 1978). These "ill winds" contain a preponderance of positive ions. An ion is the electrical charge attached to a gaseous molecule. In contrast, air full of negatively charged ions has a refreshing and stimulating effect. Negative ions predominate around waterfalls, in clean mountain air, and at beaches, but disappear in polluted urban centers or enclosed spaces. Ionization of the air has a direct effect on the serotonin system of the brain (Krueger, 1978) and the growth of the cortex. Rats raised in a negatively ionized atmosphere have a cortex 9 percent larger than those in a nonionized atmosphere (Diamond, 1980). An increase in negative ionization seems to elevate mood (Krueger, 1978).

Long-term Alterations

The brain also changes its chemistry and size in response to long-term conditions. It can often rearrange its organization to compensate for accidents. People with left hemisphere damage can learn to produce language using the right hemisphere, although this flexibility decreases with age. The right hemisphere takes over language functions in young children who have suffered severe damage to the left hemisphere (Kohn & Dennis, 1974). In deaf people, areas of the temporal cortex normally used for the processing of speech sounds are used instead for processing visual information (Neville, 1977).

When a person learns a second language, the brain's representation of language changes. In some people, when the second language is learned, the first language *may migrate from the left hemisphere to the right.* In others, the second language may occupy only the right hemisphere or may be represented in both (Albert & Obler, 1978).

The brain is continually changing and developing, responding to influences ranging from the language one hears in infancy to the meal just eaten. The brain has evolved to adapt to conditions in a changing world; our brains still change continuously to aid us in our adaptation to an unpredictable world.

SUMMARY

1. The brain runs the body—controlling temperature, blood flow, digestion, and heartbeat, among many other bodily processes. It responds to internal and external changes through an immense network of sensory systems. It adapts to respond in a flexible manner to changes in the world. The brain evolved over millions of years and consists of four different levels of organization: the brain stem, the limbic system, the cortex, and the divided hemispheres.

2. The *brain stem* evolved earliest and operates basic systems of life support. The *reticular activating system* (RAS) of the brain stem alerts the cortex to arriving information through the *thalamus*. The *limbic system* governs more advanced systems of life support and maintains *homeostasis* (constant conditions) in the body. It is also involved in emotional reactions. It includes the *hypothalamus*, which regulates the *pituitary*.

3. The *cortex* is the "executive branch" of the brain. It is responsible for making decisions and judgments on the information reaching it. It is divided into four lobes each with a separate function. The *frontal* lobes plan actions, act in decision making, and control purposeful behavior. The sensory and motor areas (between the frontal and parietal lobes) process sensory information and issue motor commands. The *parietal* lobes integrate and analyze sensory input. This is probably where letters come together to make words and words join to make thoughts. The *temporal* lobes are responsible for hearing and are involved with perception, memory, and dreaming. The *occipital* lobes process and analyze visual information.

4. The division of the brain into two hemispheres is not unique to human beings, but their division of functions is. The left hemisphere controls the ability to produce spoken and written language. The right hemisphere controls the ability to produce art

and to recognize faces. Evidence for hemispheric duality comes from studies of *split-brain* patients who have had the connection between the two hemispheres, the *corpus callosum*, severed. Further evidence comes from EEG studies of normal people: results show that the two hemispheres are activated individually depending on the situation. In speaking, for instance, the left hemisphere is active, while the right is relatively idle.

5. The brain operates in electrical and chemical codes. Every brain process works through the action of a single specialized cell called a *neuron*. Neurons fire electrical charges and secrete chemicals across *synapses*, the gaps between two neurons. Neurons have transmitter ends *(axons)* and receiving ends *(dendrites)*.

6. Transmission from one neuron to another is chemical—a process called *neurotransmission*. The transmitter chemicals are stored in synaptic vesicles, tiny pouches within the neuron. When the electrical *action potential* reaches the synapse, it causes some of these neurotransmitter chemicals to be released into the synaptic opening. The transmitters cross this opening and stimulate or inhibit the firing of the *postsynaptic* neuron (the neuron receiving the message). After transmission, the process is deactivated.

7. Neurotransmitters organize into "chemical pathways" within the brain, the most noteworthy of which are (a) the *norepinephrine* pathway, which helps code memory and connects the brain stem to the cortex; (b) the *dopamine* pathway, which connects the limbic system to the cortex and aids control of motor activity; and (c) the *serotonin* pathways, which are widely dispersed in the brain and connect the reticular activating system to the cortex and limbic system.

8. The brain communicates with the body through the *central* and *peripheral nervous systems*. The central nervous system (CNS) includes the brain and spinal cord. It controls reflexes, which are actions that do not involve the cortex. The peripheral nervous system (PNS) carries information to and from the muscles and is divided into two parts. The *somatic* nervous system controls voluntary movements such as picking up a glass, and the *autonomic* nervous system controls the autonomic processes of the body such as heartbeat.

9. The *neuroendocrine* system also allows communication of the brain with the body. The *pituitary* is the master gland of the neuroendocrine system. Neuroendocrine regulation of the body is accomplished when the pituitary secretes special chemical messengers called *hormones*. These are released into the bloodstream and stimulate further activity in their target locations. Neuroendocrine communication works on the lock-and-key principle. A hormone secreted into the bloodstream will move through the body until it finds its intended receptor molecule, into which it fits perfectly.

10. The brain produces a wide variety of chemicals, most of which are yet to be discovered. One class of chemicals is the *endorphins* (including the enkephalins), which seem to act as general moderators of activity. They affect pain relief and also have profound effects on mood. Their molecular shape is similar to drugs that are taken to alter mood and relieve pain, such as morphine.

11. There are individual differences in people's brains. One example is that left-handers' brains differ from right-handers' brains. Some have hemispheric specialization reversed, while others have language and spatial abilities dispersed in both hemispheres. Another example is that male and female brains differ. Boys show earlier right hemisphere development than girls, but girls show earlier left hemisphere development. The two hemispheres of males seem more specialized than those of females.

12. The brain responds to short-term changes in the world. Air ionization affects the serotonin system and mood. Ingested food can change brain chemistry; a meal rich in carbohydrates can also affect serotonin. The brain can also change dramatically over the long term. A stimulating environment can stimulate brain growth even in very old organisms. Learning a new language can affect the existing organization of function in the brain.

TERMS AND CONCEPTS

acetylcholine
action potential
afferent neurons
agnosia
amygdala
aphasia
autonomic nervous system
axon
brain stem
central nervous system
cerebellum
corpus callosum
cortex
dendrites
dopamine
efferent neurons
electroencephalogram
endorphins
evoked potential
frontal lobes
hippocampus
homeostasis
homunculus
hormones

hypothalamus
interneurons
limbic system
myelin sheath
neuroendocrine system
neurons
neurotransmission
norepinephrine
occipital lobes
parasympathetic nervous system
parietal lobes
peripheral nervous system
pituitary
positron emission tomography
reticular activating system
sensory-motor areas
serotonin
somatic nervous system
split brain
sympathetic nervous system
synapse
temporal lobes
thalamus

SUGGESTIONS FOR FURTHER READING

The Behavioral and Brain Sciences. (1978–present).

A quarterly journal that presents important research areas such as cortical function and intelligence and presents commentary from many scientists. Difficult, but gives a good view of the controversies in the field.

Gazzaniga, M. (1985). *The social brain.* New York: Basic Books.

One attempt to describe the different systems within the human brain.

Kolb, B., & Whishaw, I. Q. (1984). *Fundamentals of human neuropsychology* (2nd ed.). San Francisco: W. H. Freeman.

A good summary of the field.

Searle, J. (1984). *Minds, brains and science.* Boston: Harvard.

An interesting brief book which analyzes many of the developments and the follies of mind/ brain relations from a philosopher's perspective.

Ornstein, R., Thompson, R., & Macaulay, D. (1984). *The amazing brain.* Boston: Houghton Mifflin.

Describes in drawings how the brain was "built" and the functional architecture of the cortex. Amplifies material in the text.

Sacks, O. (1986). *The man who mistook his wife for a hat.* New York: Simon & Schuster.

A brilliant set of clinical vignettes which portray brain-injured people as distinct individuals. A good read.

Thompson, R. (1986). *The brain.* New York: W. H. Freeman.

An excellent basic text.

Wurtman, R., & Wurtman, J. (1984). *Nutrition and the brain* (Vol. 7). New York: Raven.

Recent reviews of the new research linking ingestion of different foods with changes in brain chemistry.

Sensory Experience

For years my house had been plagued by squirrels. They nested under the eaves of the roof and held meetings in the recesses of the attic. When they got hungry, they made a nice meal out of the side of my house. For years I harbored the most destructive thoughts about them. Then one day I saw an advertisement for a "rodent eliminator." "Rids you once and for all of all pesty rodents!" I was not only delighted, but filled with ideas of how the rodent eliminator would torture the critters that brought me such grief.

The gadget arrived. It was not a giant flame thrower or an electric cage, but a miniature box with an on–off switch. The instructions advised to set the box near the "rodent infestation" and "watch the rodents disappear forever."

When I turned the machine on, nothing happened as far as I could tell. But suddenly there was a great scurrying commotion! The squirrels were running over one another to get out. There were so many that they had to eat a *new* hole in the house to escape. Even so, I was delighted.

The rodent eliminator works by emitting a very high frequency sound wave, one that is beyond the range of human hearing but within the sensitivity of most rodents. Our worlds are different: I heard nothing, but the squirrels, in the words of the manual, "will feel that a 747 jet has landed inside their heads." No sound to me and, now, no squirrels either.

The world appears to us as it does because we are built the way we are. Every organism lives in a unique world determined by its senses. Consider yourself and a cat responding to a chocolate cake. When you see a brown cake, you savor sweetness. The cat does not usually see colors or taste sweetness. A cat, however, can see things at night that you cannot, because it has a reflective layer in its eye that doubles the intensity of light.

The senses are the outposts of the brain. They connect the physical and psychological worlds. The job of the senses is to "catch" a small and specific bit of the outside world and to reject the rest. To function, all organisms need to know about the world outside. Although there is an amazing variety of ways to extract information from the world, human beings are limited to sight, hearing, smell, taste, and touch. We also have senses that keep us informed of the internal world of our bodies: they maintain balance, coordinate and control body movements, and sense internal conditions such as pain and nausea.

It is easy for any organism, especially an intellectual one, to ignore how limited it is. After all, the eyes reveal a brilliant colorful world, and through the ears we can appreciate the complexities of Mozart. But although it is seemingly limitless, the world of human experience and the world of any animal's experience is in truth very small. It is here that the modern analysis of the nervous system and the mind yields a surprising conclusion: instead of experiencing the world as it is, most animals (including humans) experience only about one-trillionth of outside events, a miniature world indeed!

Evolution has served most animals well: those external events that are consequential to an organism typically become part of its experience. Each organism's mental system blinds it to most of reality so that it can avoid dangers and exploit opportunities.

The outside world is silent and dull in and of itself. There is no color in nature, no sound, no touch, no smell or feel. All these wonders exist inside the nerve circuits. The human sensory, brain, and mental system allows some events fast access to consciousness, but prevents access to other events to insulate us.

Principles of Sensory Experience

Deconstruction.   The world seems, to the casual observer, to consist of different objects: cats and chocolate cakes, shoes and sealing wax. But think about it, even if this is the first time you have done so. How could a cat, or an image of a cat, get inside the brain? It doesn't enter directly; there are no "cat paths" inside us. And if there were such paths, what about buildings, trees, grass, and the sky? Obviously, it doesn't happen like that.

How does it happen, then? No one really knows for sure, but psychologists do know that there must first be a process of *deconstruction* of the physical world so that selected parts of it enter the nervous system (Marr, 1982). Deconstruction means just what it sounds like, a breakup or decomposition of a whole object into its components. The technical task for psychologists and other analysts of sensation is to determine how that deconstruction is done, which components of the outside world are analyzed, and later, how they are assembled again in a process of reconstruction. This is a complex subject with a complex analysis, and it will take the next two chapters just to begin it. But you may never think the same way about your own experience again.

See Chapter 6, section on Deconstruction, Computation, and Reconstruction.

The human brain simplifies our experience by selecting only important stimuli for the brain to respond to. Otherwise, we would not be able to function under conditions of sensory overload, such as shown in this busy Christmas scene.

REFLECTING IMPORTANT EVENTS IN THE WORLD

The first problem for all animals is to know what is happening in the world and what to do about it. The world is full of events, be they simple wind shifts, sunrises, miniscule movement of particles in the air, or the sudden alighting of hawks. The earth shifts on its large surface plates, rotates upon its axis, and moves around the sun. On the skin are millions of tiny particles and vast populations of bacteria. Pressure waves (sounds) move through the air and, in the modern world, radiant electromagnetic energy fills the air. If you had the proper sensory equipment, you could receive television programs directly, as well as all the telephone calls in your area.

However, if you were trying to make a telephone call, you would not want to hear all possible human voices. The mind needs to limit information received to very little of what is actually present in the outside world. It extracts from the cacophony of the entire "big world" a specialized "small world" in which an individual organism can act and live. This radical mind blindness has been successful.

Organisms, for the most part, adapt to their small world, in their particular environmental niche. Thus, sensory systems reflect the regularities of the world (Shepard, 1984).

The first part of the filtering is done by the structure of the nervous system itself. The nervous system evolved to reduce radically the information transmitted to the brain. From a trickle of sensory information a simplified small world is computed. The brain monitors the sensory input to scan for information that doesn't fit a preset model of the world and that would signal a significant change or threat to which the brain must react.

The nervous system organizes information so that relatively few actions, appropriate ones, can take place. Much of the intricate network of receptors, ganglia, and analysis cells in the cortex serve as part of the selection system. The few meaningful elements of all the stimuli that reach us are organized into occurrences that are probable, and only a small sample are remembered or acted upon.

Selectivity. The senses are both *sensors* and *censors.* Obviously, our senses convey the outside world, but if we experienced *all* sensations in the world, experience would be extremely chaotic. The air in the room you are in is filled with various forms of energy: radiant electromagnetic, infrared, sound and radio waves, and more. Yet you are aware of only a small portion of that energy. "Light" is actually just a small portion of the band of radiant **electromagnetic energy** (see Plate 2 in color insert). Selection, then, involves both *inclusion* and *exclusion.* The senses select what is important and keep the rest of the world out. And each sense is "designed" to extract a very specific kind of information. You *see* light, you do not hear it. You cannot taste an apricot by squeezing it into your ear!

Each organism's sensory system simplifies the world to which it needs to attend. The cat is a nocturnal animal and so needs its reflective eye; insects *see* infrared radiation, which we feel as warmth; a frog sees only things that move.

Change. The senses transmit information concerning *changes* in the external environment; what is important to us are *new events:* the sun coming up, a sudden loud noise, a change in the weather. The sensory systems are designed to notice beginnings and endings of events. When an air conditioner is turned on in a room, you notice the hum. Soon you become *habituated* to the noise. When the machine is turned off, you again take note, this time because of the *absence* of the noise. The senses are thus interested in news; loosely speaking, "call me when something new happens."

Comparison. How do the senses recognize change? A sensory change is a *difference* in a stimulus from one moment to the next. One sensation always follows and precedes another, so one stimulus is louder, softer, brighter, dimmer, warmer, colder, greener, or redder than *something else* (Figure 5-1).

We compare *relative* differences between stimuli. Try this demonstration. Put a three-way bulb (50-100-150 watt) in a lamp in a dark room. Turn on the lamp; the difference between darkness and the 50-watt illumination is great. But the next two increases in light, from 50 to 100 watt and from 100 to 150 watt, do not have the same effect. Although the change in the physical stimulus is the same each time, you hardly notice the difference.

HOW THE SENSES SIMPLIFY AND ORGANIZE THE WORLD

Simplification and Selectivity

William James wrote:

> We see that the mind is at every stage a theatre of simultaneous possibilities. Consciousness consists in the comparison of these with each other, the selection of some, and the suppression of others, of the rest by the reinforcing and inhibiting agency of attention. The highest and most celebrated mental products are filtered from the data chosen by the faculty below that, which mass was in turn sifted from a still larger amount of simpler material, and so on. The mind, in short, works on this block of stone. In a sense, the statue stood there from eternity. But there were a thousand different ones beside it. The sculptor alone is to thank for having extracted this one from the rest. . . . Other minds, other worlds, from the same monotonous and inexpressive chaos! My world is but one in a million, alike embedded and alike real to those who may abstract them. How different must be the world in the *consciousness* of ants, cuttle-fish, or crab! (James, 1890)

FIGURE 5-1
Stare at the dot at the center of this figure. Those shadowy squares at the intersections of the white lines do not actually exist in the drawing. They are "seen" only because of the way your sensory systems work.
(After Verheijen, 1961)

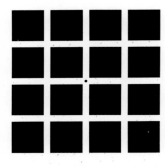

"Our world" is much simpler than the physical complexity of the entire external world. A primary job of the sensory systems is to discard irrelevant stimuli and to select for transmission to the brain only that small portion of stimuli that is relevant.

The first major basis of selection is the biological nature of the senses themselves. We have only the operations of sight, hearing, taste, smell, and touch available to us. Second, within each sense only a limited range of stimuli is received. The eye responds to only a minute portion (one-trillionth) of radiant electromagnetic energy. What we see, then, is less than *one-trillionth* of the energy that actually meets the eye. Like other creatures, we are economical; we sense only what is necessary for our survival.

Consider an animal that simplifies even more than we do. Jerome Lettvin and his associates (1959) at Massachusetts Institute of Technology devised an experiment in which visual stimulation was offered to one eye of an immobilized frog. The frog was placed so that its eye was at the center of a hemisphere seven inches in radius. Small objects were placed in different positions on the inner surface of this hemisphere by means of magnets and could be moved around in the space inside the hemisphere.

The investigators measured "what the frog's eye tells the frog's brain"—the electrical impulses sent to the brain by the eye. Unlimited different visual patterns could be presented to a frog—colors, shapes, movements, and various combinations of all these. However, when various objects, colors, and patterns were shown to the frog, the investigators noticed a remarkable phenomenon. Out of *all* the different kinds of stimulation present, *only four kinds of "messages" were sent to the brain.*

These four messages contained information relating directly to the two most important aspects of a frog's survival: obtaining food and escaping danger. The first message provided a general outline of the environment. Two of the messages formed a kind of bug-perceiving system: one detected moving edges and the other responded to small, dark objects entering the field of vision. Frogs only trap and eat live bugs. A frog surrounded by food that did not move would starve to death because it has no means for detecting nonmoving objects. The fourth message responded to sudden decreases in light, as would happen when a large enemy approaches. The frog's brain is thus "wired" to ignore all but extremely limited types of information. Although higher level animals, ourselves included, are not as restricted in sensory experience as the frog, sensory systems of *all* animals simplify their organism's world by the act of selection.

Sensory Adaptation and Comparison

Adaptation

Once messages from the outside world are selected for transmission to the brain, they are *further simplified.* The senses respond vigorously to beginnings and endings of events; they respond less to constant stimulation. This decline in response is called *sensory adaptation.* Sensory adaptation reduces the number of irrelevant sensations, allowing us to focus on new events in the environment.

Comparison

Although each sensory system can discriminate millions of different gradients of stimuli, there is not a specific receptor for each shade of color or sound tone. This is an important part of how we are built: we rarely, if ever, experience the same situation twice, so it would be uneconomical to have a system that responded anew to each stimulus. Thus, sensory systems operate primarily by comparison. Judgments are comparative: the color seen at one moment is brighter or redder than the previous one; a sound is louder or more complex than an earlier one (see Plate 3).

Here is a demonstration of sensory adaptation, change, and comparison. Fill three bowls with water, one hot, one cold, and one tepid. Put one hand in the hot water and the other in the cold water. Wait a few moments. Now place both hands in the tepid bowl. Notice that the hand that was in the hot water feels cold, while the hand that was in the cold water feels warm. Both hands had *adapted* to their relative temperatures. Then, when the hands were put in the tepid bowl, they signaled a *change.* Although both hands were in the same bowl of water, each responded differently to it. The particular message of change each hand signaled to the brain was based on a *comparison* of two events.

How Physical and Psychological Worlds Are Related

The senses relate the external physical world and internal psychological experience. The measurement of this relationship, called *psychophysics,* was the first

HUMAN SENSITIVITY

Average absolute thresholds for the five senses have been determined by careful measurement; they are approximately as follows (Galanter, 1962):

Vision: a single flame 30 miles away on a dark, clear night.

Hearing: a watch ticking 20 feet away in a quiet place.

Taste: one teaspoon of sugar dissolved in two gallons of water.

Smell: one drop of perfume in a six-room apartment.

Touch: the wing of a fly alighting on your cheek from a height of one centimeter.

idea of investigation of scientific psychology in the late nineteenth century. Using the methodology and techniques of physics as their model, the first psychologists tried to determine precisely how changes in the outside world affected the internal world of human experience. They pursued their investigations in a rather straightforward way: they clanged bells and shined lights of varying degrees of brightness at people and then measured how much a stimulus had to change in order for a person to report a change in experience.

Thresholds

There are some absolute limits to what we can sense, limits set by the range of physical energy to which the senses respond. A light must attain a certain intensity before we notice it; a sound must be loud enough for us to hear it. The least amount of physical energy necessary for us to notice a stimulus is called the **absolute threshold.** The absolute threshold is defined as the minimum strength for a stimulus to be *noticed* by an observer 50 percent of the time.

The absolute threshold is not the amount of energy required to *activate* the sensory system, but that is required for us to *experience* the stimulus. Although the senses have absolute limits, they can be activated with little energy. The eye will respond to the smallest quantity of light and the ear to movements in the air only slightly greater than those of the air molecules themselves, but we rarely, if ever, notice these phenomena.

The minimum increase in a physical stimulus necessary for us to notice a difference is called the **difference threshold** or, more commonly, the **just noticeable difference (j.n.d.).** Unlike the absolute threshold, the j.n.d. is not constant. If it takes one additional candle to notice a difference in illumination in a room with 10 candles, then in a room with 100 candles, there would need to be 10 additional candles to notice a difference. There would be no noticeable difference if 101 rather than 100 candles were lit (Coren, Dorac, & Ward, 1984).

The Discoverers of General Principles of Sensation

Weber's Law.   A single candle flame emits a fixed amount of physical energy, but it is experienced differently depending on the surrounding circumstances. In a darkened room, it provides much illumination; in a bright room, it is hardly noticed.

This first principle of sensation was discovered by Ernst Weber (1834). He noted that *equal changes in physical intensity do not produce equal changes in experience.* This means that the relationship between the inner world and the external world is not a simple one. Although the psychological world does not have a one-to-one relationship with the physical world, Weber noted that there is a consistent relationship between them. The amount of added energy in a stimulus required to produce a just noticeable difference is always the same *proportion* of the stimulus. If a 64-watt light is required to notice a change in illumination from 60 watts, then 128 watts would be needed to detect a change from 120 watts. This consistent proportional relationship, known as Weber's Law, can be stated mathematically as follows:

$$\frac{\text{change in stimulus}}{\text{stimulus}} = \text{constant}$$

$$\text{In our example,} \quad \frac{4}{60} = \frac{1}{15}$$

$$\text{and} \quad \frac{8}{120} = \frac{1}{15}$$

Fechner.   Gustave Fechner continued Weber's search to discover how the mind responds to external reality. Fechner's insight was that senses are not designed to notice the *absolute* differences between lights and sounds, but rather their *relative* intensity. Thus, when danger is approaching, the important thing to know is *how fast* it is approaching, that is, how *much* louder one threatening sound is than another, *not* the absolute volume of any given sound. A system built to notice differences provides great flexibility and makes good sense from an evolutionary point of view. On sensory psychologist writes:

> Our sensory systems are designed to weigh heavily the ratios between stimulus intensities rather than the differences between them. It is not too difficult to understand why such a sensory system is useful. . . . Imagine yourself sitting in front of a fire surrounded by forests, without any effective weapons, listening to the growl of a large and hungry animal. The most important information would be the ratio between the loudness of two successive growls. If the present growl is twice as loud as the last one, you know that the animal has covered half the distance toward you in that time. So you know that it will be arriving in just that much time! That information is really much more important than estimating the actual loudness of each growl or the actual difference in loudness of two growls. (Ludel, 1978)

Stevens.   A third principle, discovered by S. S. Stevens, is that *different senses transform the information they select differently.* This principle, called the **Power Law,** states that within each sensory system equal ratios of stimulus intensity produce equal ratios of change in experience. When these relationships are charted on a graph, they produce characteristic curves. Note in Figure 5-2 that the curves for the experience of length, brightness, and pain are very different (Stevens, 1956).

Plotting sensory experience reveals much about the function of different sensory systems. The straight line that represents the experience of length in Figure 5-2 indicates that the relationship between the experience of length and actual

FIGURE 5-2
Power Curves for
Different Stimuli

There is great variation in
the power curves charting
the magnitude of your
experience of such stimuli
as pain (electric shock),
apparent length, and
brightness.
(After Stevens, 1961)

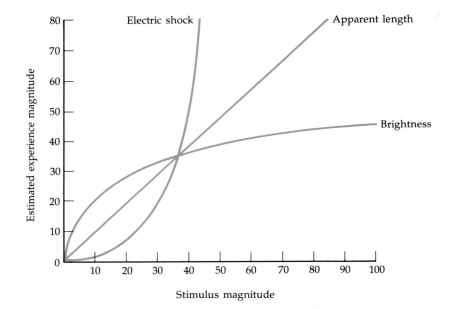

physical length is a direct correlation. This makes sense because we do not often have to estimate very long distances visually.

We do, however, encounter an extremely large range of brightness: we can see a single candle flame on a clear night 30 miles away and are able to glance at the sun, which is about 1,000 billion times brighter. Since there is such an enormous range of brightness to judge daily, our sensory system has to attenuate, or reduce, that range. The flattened curve of brightness on the graph indicates that brightness information is indeed compressed.

The pain curve in Figure 5-2 reflects our experience of pain. Because it is important to be aware of potential injury as fast as possible, the experience of pain is *amplified,* not attenuated—*a small amount of pain gets our undivided attention very quickly.* The upward curve of pain on the graph shows this. Our amplified response to pain makes it an extremely effective early warning system for possible bodily harm.

Summary. Psychophysics has thus revealed four major related principles: (1) there is a consistent relationship between changes in the physical world and changes in experience; (2) these relationships are proportional; (3) each sense system has a different internal representation of the outside world; and (4) the internal representation of these relationships reveals how closely tied our senses are to survival.

How Physical Energy Is Changed into Experience: Transduction

Although each sense responds to a different form of physical energy, the brain has only one way of receiving and responding to information: *neural firing.* Thus, another function of the senses is to transform specific kinds of physical energy, such as waves in the air and mechanical pressure (touch), into the electrical or chemical activation of nerve cells.

Even a little bit of pain
gets an immediate reaction.

The senses routinely perform two miracles. First, each sensory organ transforms a particular kind of physical energy into neural firing. This process is called **transduction.** Each sense has specialized receptors responsible for the transduction of external energy into the language of the brain. The eye transduces light, the ear transduces sound waves, and the nose transduces gaseous molecules.

At some point in the sensory and brain system, there is a second transformation: all of these electrical and chemical reactions in the brain somehow become human experience. The "trees" of experience are not present in the brain; there are no birds, no light, no sound, no thoughts—only constant electrical and chemical activity. These two miracles occur every moment of life and are so routine that we are unaware of them. Psychologists are on the way to understanding the first miracle, but everyone remains mystified by the second.

V ision is the dominant sense of human beings, responsible for the control of almost all the basic actions necessary for living in the human world. James Gibson (1966) classified the basic functions of vision.

VISION

- *Detecting the layout of the surroundings.* This involves the ability to notice large features of the environment and to distinguish objects and other animals.
- *Detecting change or sequence.* We can distinguish between day and night, between fine and gross movements, and between motion and events in the world.
- *Detecting and controlling movement.* We are able to see what we are doing and where we are going. If we did not have visual feedback, movements would be uncontrolled.

The Eye

Where is the "image" that a human being sees? One can see what a camera does by looking through its lens, but the eye does not work like a camera. The brain does not "see" the image on the retina; neural impulses, not images, are received by the brain. The visual system of the eye works more like television. Your television set does not receive a whole picture, but only coded patterns of radiant electromagnetic energy that are translated into colors and shapes.

The eye is the most complex of all the sense organs. In the *retina,* a single layer inside the eye, there are over 120 million receptor cells called *rods* and 6 million receptor cells called *cones.* The *optic nerve* that connects the eye to the brain contains more than one million nerve cells (Figure 5-3).

Light first enters the eye through the **cornea,** a transparent membrane that covers the front of the eye. It travels inside the eye through the *pupil,* which is an opening in the *iris,* the colored part of the eye. The iris is composed of two kinds of muscles, circular and radial. The circular muscles make the pupil smaller; the radial muscles open it up to make the pupil larger. As with the aperture of a camera, the size of the opening of the pupil determines the amount of light that is let in.

Light then passes through the *lens* which focuses it. The lens is held in place by the interocular ("inside the eye") muscles, which pull the lens and thus change its

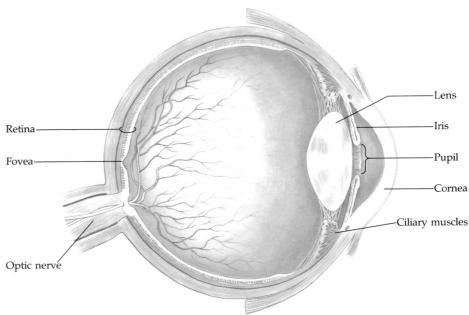

FIGURE 5-3
Major Structures of the Human Eye

Retina

Fovea

Optic nerve

Lens

Iris

Pupil

Cornea

Ciliary muscles

shape to focus on objects at different distances. If all is working well, the light is put into sharp focus on the retina at the back of the eye.

The Retina

The **retina** is the key structure of vision. It begins its development as part of the brain, but buds out to become part of the eye in the embryonic stage. It is comprised of *neural tissue* that is about the thickness of this page. It transduces waves of light energy (which arrive at the eye as electromagnetic radiation) into neural impulses. The retina has three main layers of nerve cells:

1. **Photoreceptors** (*photo* comes from the Greek word for "light"). There are two types of photoreceptors: *rods* and *cones.* They contain photochemicals that respond to light. (They are discussed in the following section.)

2. **Intermediate layer.** Three kinds of cells in the intermediate layer make connections to the other cells. The *bipolar cells* take information from the rods and cones to the third layer of cells, called *ganglia* (singular, ganglion). The *horizontal cells* transfer information from rods and cones horizontally. The *amacrine cells* transfer information from rods and cones and all cells in the intermediate layer and send it to other intermediate layer cells or to cells in the ganglia (Figure 5-4).

3. **Ganglion cells.** The third layer is composed of ganglion cells. Each cell has a long *axon,* the part of a neuron that carries information from the cell to other neurons. All the axons from the eye's ganglion cells leave the eye at the same point, where they are bundled together to form the optic nerve. This tiny spot where the ganglion cells exit the eye on the way to the brain is commonly called the *blind spot.* There are no photoreceptor cells here, so this part of the eye cannot respond to light (Plate 9). We are not normally aware of the blind spot because we are not aware of what we do not see (Figure 5-5).

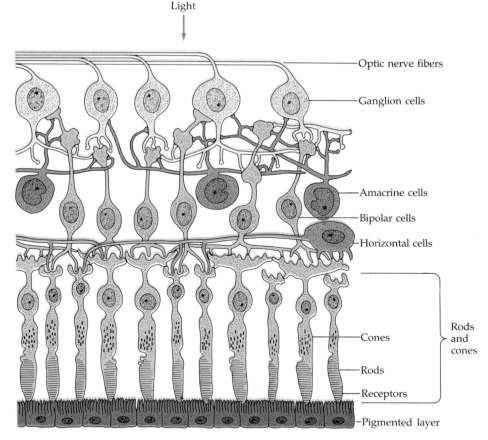

Light

Optic nerve fibers

Ganglion cells

Amacrine cells

Bipolar cells

Horizontal cells

Cones

Rods

Receptors

Rods
and
cones

Pigmented layer

Photoreceptors: Rods and Cones

The rods and cones are shaped as their names imply (Plate 8). And though their shapes are different, their internal structures are similar: like stacks of discs. The photochemicals are inside the discs. The major differences between rods and cones are the kind of light they respond to and their distribution in the eye.

Rods respond most to light energy at low levels. They respond best to wavelengths of 480 nanometers (nm), or billionths of a meter, which register in vision

LOOKING THROUGH BLOOD VESSELS: A DEMONSTRATION

Blood cells lie between the retina and the outside. Because we are structured to repsond to changes, we never see these blood cells, since they are always there. But you can see for yourself that you do look at the world through blood vessels. Get a pen flashlight, a blank piece of paper, and a pencil.

Turn on the flashlight and hold it near the outer edge of your eye and jiggle it around. You will see a luminous red spider web, which is a reflection of the blood vessels. By looking at the paper immediately, you can trace a map of these vessels.

FIGURE 5-5

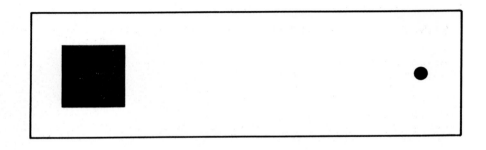

FIGURE 5-5
Finding Your Blind Spot
Close your right eye and stare at the circle on the right. Holding the book about one foot from your face, slowly move it back and forth until the square on the left disappears. The square cannot be seen at that point because its image falls on your blind spot.

as a blue-green color. About 120 million rods are distributed over the retina, with the heaviest concentration at the sides. Light vision is most sensitive slightly to the side of the eye rather than dead center. The rods are like black-and-white television; they sense all the "colors" in the world as relative shades of blue-green "grays." They allow us to see when the illumination is low, as at night.

Cones are responsible for color vision and are less sensitive than rods. They need bright light to be activated. There are three different kinds of cones, each of which responds to a range of wavelengths, but responds best to certain ones (Figure 5-6). One responds best to 575 nm, which is seen as red-orange, another to 550 nm, seen as green, and the last to 440 nm, seen as blue-violet.

The greatest concentration of cones is in the center of the retina. This area, which has no rods, is called the **fovea.** To examine an object closely, you move your head, body, and eyes until the image of the object falls on your fovea. The fovea is especially well represented in the brain; more brain cells receive input from the fovea than from any other part of the eye. The cones operate like a color television camera, which also has sensors for three colors of light: red-orange, green, and blue-violet. These are the colors from which all other colors can be made.

The rods and cones are the first cells to receive light, yet they face *away* from the light and are at the *innermost* layer of the retina. The reason for this surprising arrangement is the need for oxygen. Although all parts of the eye require oxygen

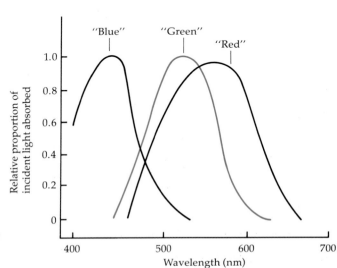

FIGURE 5-6
Relative Wavelength Absorption of Different Kinds of Cones in the Human Eye

(supplied by blood vessels throughout the eye), the photochemicals of the rods and cones need much more.

If the rods and cones were at the *front* of the eye, there would have to be many more blood vessels, which would block so much light that it would be impossible to see. So, the layer of cells right behind the retina has an additional network of blood vessels that supply the rods and cones with the necessary amount of oxygen (Figure 5-4).

Dark Adaptation

It is difficult to see upon entering a darkened movie theater. Minutes later the outlines of people and seats become visible. The eyes, through the process of *dark adaptation*, become sensitive to the dark.

The cones quickly adapt to the dark, but after 10 minutes they stop adapting. The rods continue becoming increasingly sensitive to less light stimulation, reaching their maximum in 30 to 40 minutes (Figure 5-7). At first you see objects

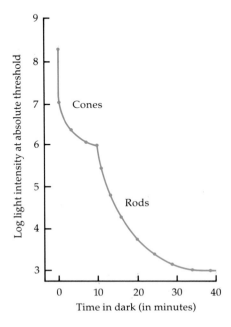

FIGURE 5-7
Testing Dark Adaptation
Subjects whose eyes had become adapted to bright light were then placed in darkness. The curve shows how their retinas adapted to the dark. They became more sensitive to even fainter flashes of light. The abrupt turn at about 10 minutes is called the rod-cone break, indicating where the cones have reached their maximum sensitivity while the rods continue becoming more sensitive over another half hour or so.

only in black and white, then in shades of blue-green. After 15 minutes some color becomes visible.

Basis of Color Vision

Human beings can make roughly eight million distinctions in color! As might be expected, color vision has adaptive value. Seeing in color enables us to make more precise judgments about the outside world. For example, the bright color of fruit made it very easy for our primitive ancestors to find it while foraging in the forest.

There is no color in nature. What is seen as color is actually variations in the wavelengths of light reflected from different surfaces. These wavelengths activate one of three different kinds of cones, which in turn send their coded information to the brain. *The experience of color,* unique to human beings, *is a product of our sensory systems.*

Coding of Color

Figure 5-8 shows a wiring diagram for the retina which has been proposed to explain how it codes color information. The nature of this coding process determines much of color experience. Four colors are seen as primary: red, green, blue, and yellow, and they are seen as "pure"; these are called psychological primaries. These colors, like all others, are associated with specific wavelengths of light. What makes these colors seem pure is not the colors themselves. It is the way the visual system responds to different wavelengths of light.

Three systems of color information are sent from the eye to the brain. Each sends information on two opposite dimensions; therefore, the brain's method for

FIGURE 5-8
How the Retina Codes Color Information
We see primary colors (red, green, blue, yellow) and their variations, as well as experiencing brightness (dark and light, white and black), because of the way our visual system responds to different wavelengths of light. This diagram represents connections in an opponent process that elicits responses from various cone cells. The round and the flat connections may arbitrarily be considered either excitatory or inhibitory and the numbers indicate the wavelength of the cones' maximum sensitivity.
(After Hurvich & Jameson, 1974)

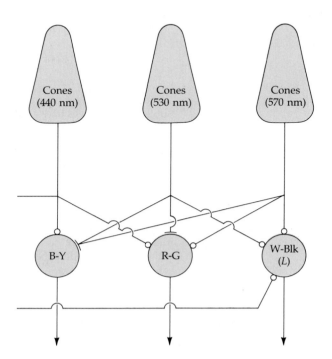

color coding is called an *opponent process.* The first two systems are transmitted only by cone cells and relay information about hue: one transmits the blue-yellow component of color, the other, the red-green. The third system, in which both cones and rods have a part, provides information about the color's brightness (dark-light).

Afterimages

Stare at a red square against a white background for a minute. Then take the square away and look at the background. You will see an afterimage of its complementary color, green. Staring at a black square produces white, and blue produces a yellow afterimage. The color of these afterimages results from the brain's opponent process of coding information.

Color Blindness

Color blindness is a genetic defect of one of the color systems and occurs predominantly in males. Seven out of 100 men have some form of color blindness, while only about one woman in 1,000 suffers from this defect (see Plate 6). The most common form is red-green color blindness, while blue-yellow is rare. But because of opponent processing, there is no such thing as red-blue color blindness. Many of the tests for color blindness involve discriminating figures composed of color circles against a background composed of other color circles.

What the Eye Tells the Brain

Sight does not take place *in* the eyes, but with the *assistance* of the eyes. The first part of visual experience is what the eye tells the brain; the second is what the brain tells the eye.

In each eye there are about 126 million photoreceptor cells whose impulses are channeled into about one million ganglion cells. Information from the outside world is increasingly simplified and abstracted as the information travels from the outside to the visual cortex of the brain (Figure 5-9).

Information from the left eye travels via the left *optic nerve* and information from the right eye goes through the right optic nerve. But notice in Figure 5-10 that a change takes place at an intersection called the *optic chiasma:* some of the axons cross over. Those from the left sides of both eyes go off to the right and vice versa. Only the arrangement, not the structure, of the axons changes. But the name also changes. After the crossover, the optic nerve is called the *optic tract.*

Lateral Geniculate Nucleus

The million nerve fibers in each of the two optic tracts reach the brain first at the *lateral geniculate nucleus* (LGN) in the thalamus (*lateral* means "sideways"; a *geniculate* is a bend or joint). The visual cortex is alerted to visual input via the LGN. Because of the similarity between LGN cells and ganglion cells, it appears that the LGN is a kind of switching station relaying messages to the visual cortex. While in the LGN, the messages from the two eyes are still separate. The LGN also analyzes color signals. The neural fibers that leave the LGN fan out to inform the visual cortex.

FIGURE 5-9

Detail of the Visual Cortex
A cross section of the visual cortex shows its six-layered construction, I–VI, in which each layer contains cells of certain shapes and complexity that specialize in responding to different kinds of information. The black and white stripes on the surface represent the tendency of each eye to dominate alternating areas of cells—those dominated by the right eye are shown by white stripes and those by the left eye, black stripes.

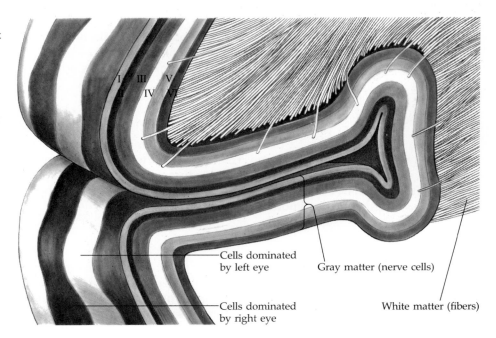

Cells dominated by left eye

Gray matter (nerve cells)

Cells dominated by right eye

White matter (fibers)

Receptive Fields in the Retina and Visual Cortex

The rate of firing in a single axon can be measured and recorded by a hairlike electrical probe. By flashing a light at an animal's eye and recording the response to individual nerve cells, neuropsychologists can find out which cells respond to the stimulus. The area of stimulation that a cell responds to is called the **receptive field** (Figure 5-11). The function of the cells in the cortex is different from that of cells in the optic tract—they respond best to specific features in the environment and are called **feature analyzers.** (However, the cells may actually serve other functions unknown to us.)

There are over 100 million neurons in the human visual cortex, and it is currently hard to know the extent of their specialization. Isolating and identifying receptive fields is one way that investigators can determine what features specific cells are designed to notice. It appears that each species of animal possesses a special set of feature analyzers that pick out the objects and events that are important for it. Recall that the frog responds to only four specialized aspects of the environment. The visual system of the cat, which so far is the most thoroughly studied (Hubel, 1979; Hubel & Wiesel, 1962), selects for edges, angles, and objects moving in different directions. In monkeys, some cells seem to respond to specific features of the environment.

Gross, Rocha-Miranda, and Bender (1972) experimented with one rhesus monkey. They probed a single cell in the cortex and tried to find out what would make that particular cell respond. They placed food in front of the monkey, showed it cards, moving objects, and so on. They tried everything they could think of and found no response. Finally, one of the experimenters began waving his hand "good-bye" to the monkey; there was an immediate response from the cortical cell. They then began showing lots of new stimuli to the monkey. The more similar a stimulus was to a monkey's hand, the greater was the response in

T. N. Wiesel and D. H. Hubel

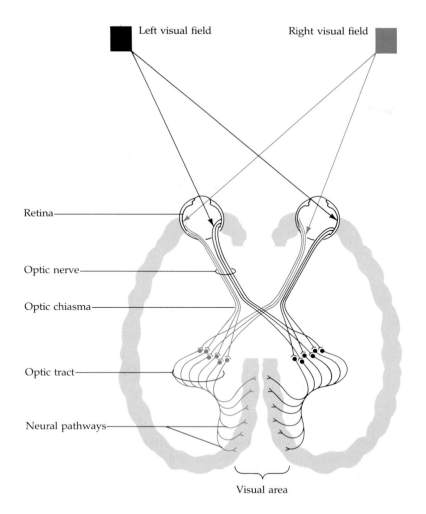

Left visual field   Right visual field

Retina

Optic nerve

Optic chiasma

Optic tract

Neural pathways

Visual area

FIGURE 5-10
Visual Pathways
in the Brain
The right half of each
retina picks up light rays
from the left visual field
and those from the right
visual field fall on the left
half of each retina. The
optic nerves meet at the
optic chiasma, where
information from the right
sides of both retinas is
channeled to the occipital
cortex of the right cerebral
hemisphere and that from
the left sides of both
retinas goes to the left
hemisphere.

the cell (Figure 5-12). So, at least in the monkey, there is a single cell that responds strongly to an extremely specific feature.

Three kinds of cells have been identified, in the visual cortex of cats, each of which detects specific kinds of patterns (Ornstein, Thompson, & Macaulay, 1984).

1. *Simple cells* respond to a bar, line, or edge. Figure 5-13 shows the different kinds of receptive fields of simple cells and the stimulus that can cause them to fire at maximum strength. Because simple cells respond most strongly to particular angles, they are called *orientation detectors*. They are arranged in columns in the visual cortex; each column contains cells that respond to a particular orientation.
2. *Complex cells* respond to orientation and to movement, such as a diagonal line moving from left to right (Figure 5-14).
3. *Hypercomplex cells* respond to bars of light in any orientation. It may well be that other cells will be found that respond to even more specialized features of the environment (such as the hand-responding cell of the monkey).

FIGURE 5-11

Feature Analyzers' Responses to Different Receptive Fields

The response of single cortical cells to various stimuli can be measured by an oscilloscope. When bars of light (left) are flashed in the subject's eye, the most vigorous neural response is to the vertical bar. This suggests that this particular cell is a feature analyzer intended to detect and react to visual stimuli that have a vertical orientation.

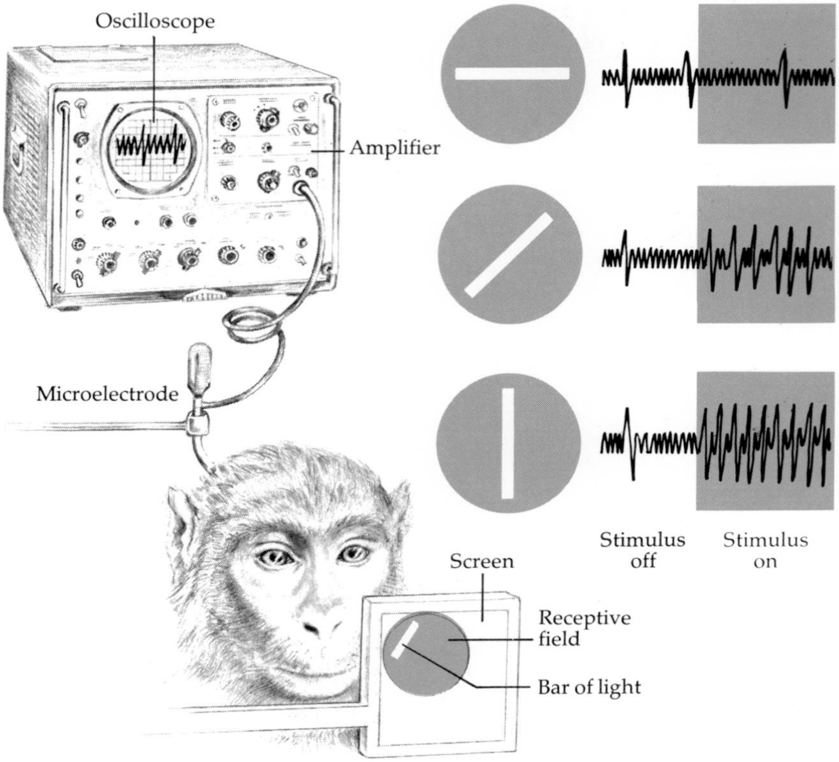

Oscilloscope

Amplifier

Microelectrode

Screen

Stimulus off

Stimulus on

Receptive field

Bar of light

FIGURE 5-12

The Monkey Paw Detector

These shapes are arranged in order of their ability to make a single cell in a monkey's brain respond to the sight of them. Some shapes (1) produced no response; some made a neuron react a little (2 and 3). Those shapes somewhat like a monkey's paw (4 and 5) produced a greater response, and the maximum neural response was to the shape most closely resembling a monkey's paw (6). Clearly, there are brain cells intended to detect and react to very complex, highly specific features. (After Gross, 1973)

Modules of Sensory Analysis

The discovery of these cells in the visual cortex has had a great effect on neuropsychology and psychology. The cells are arranged in columns, each column corresponding to one kind of analysis, such as edges and corners. As electrophysiology becomes more and more precise, it is thought by many that more and more complex "modules" will be discovered. The word *module* means a fixed plan or program, as when a house is described as modular, signifying that the components are standard.

It is now thought by many psychologists (Fodor, 1983; Gazzaniga, 1985; Ornstein, 1986a) that there exist many different kinds of sensory modules in the brain and that they are *encapsulated,* that is, they do not communicate with other modules. It is also thought that they are *domain specific* — the analysis routine for smell, for instance, may be very different from the analysis for shape or for language. Just how complex and how "hard-wired" these modules are is the subject of much current research.

Lateral Inhibition

Every sensory experience depends on the previous sensory experience. A lump of coal in bright sunlight reflects more light than this page in the shade. But the

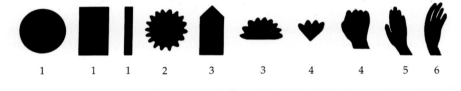

1 1 1 2 3 3 4 4 5 6

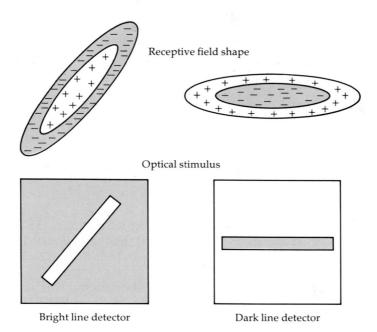

Receptive field shape

Optical stimulus

Bright line detector

Dark line detector

FIGURE 5-13
Receptive Fields of Simple Cells
These cells, from the visual cortex of cats, are arranged in receptive fields whose elongated central regions are oriented for the cells' maximal response to stimuli—dark or light bars, lines, or edges—at particular angles.
The + sign shows that a cell gives an on response and a − sign indicates an off response.
(After Hubel & Wiesel, 1962)

coal is always experienced as dark and the page as light because the coal is darker than its surroundings and the page is lighter. In Figure 5-15 all the central squares are exactly the same shade of gray, but the darker the surrounding figure is, the brighter each square appears. An edge or corner or sharp change in color is a clear demarcation between two objects or planes. Things appear brighter at edges and corners than in the middle.

The physiological mechanism by which certain cells inhibit or stimulate one another is called **lateral inhibition.** Most of the evidence on lateral inhibition comes from studies on the horseshoe crab *Limulus,* whose visual system is both simple and large. Retinal cells respond to light by firing: the brighter the light, the more they fire. Whenever a cell fires, it inhibits the cells next to it (laterally) from

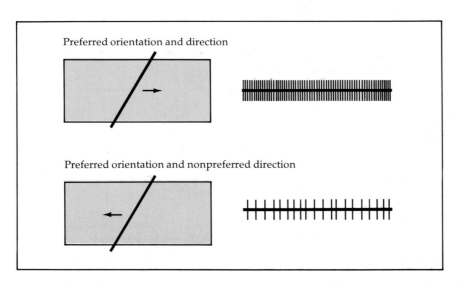

Preferred orientation and direction

Preferred orientation and nonpreferred direction

FIGURE 5-14
The Preference of Complex Cells
Like simple cells, these cortical cells respond best to bars and edges at certain angles, but they are especially sensitive to stimuli moving within their receptive field. The preference of these cells for extremely specific stimuli is revealed in this drawing, which shows a complex cell responding vigorously to an angled slit of light moving left to right (top), but with less vigor to the same slit of light moving in the opposite direction (bottom).
(After Hubel & Wiesel, 1962)

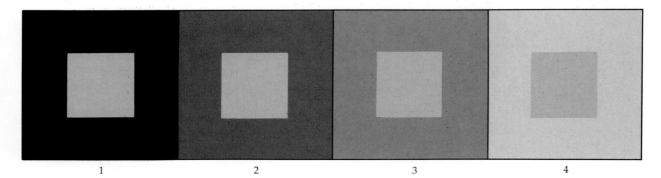

1	2	3	4

FIGURE 5-15
How Simultaneous Brightness Contrast Fools Your Eye
All the central squares are the same shade of gray. But how each contrasts with its lighter or darker background triggers the lateral inhibition mechanism of retinal cells and alters your perception so the central squares seem to be of different shades.

firing. In Figure 5-16 you can see that the brighter the stimulus, the greater the inhibition. Thus, the basic mechanism of lateral inhibition is that the more a retinal cell fires, the more it inhibits neighboring cells from firing. The firing of cell A inhibits the firing of cell B.

Lateral inhibition helps us see sharp changes, like corners, in the environment (Figure 5-17). It may enhance discrimination between two slightly different figures. Because it exaggerates changes in the environment, we can be fooled. Look at the two illustrations in Figure 5-18. If you stare at the center of the left illustration, the fuzzy-edged circle disappears. This does not happen if you stare at the center of the well-defined circle on the right.

What the Brain Tells the Eye

So far, this analysis has considered visual experience as if it occurred to a stationary observer looking straight ahead. But an observer is rarely stationary; both the head and the eyes move to look at something. The eye is never still. When we look at a painting or photo, our eyes seem to trace the outline of the figure (Figure 5-19).

FIGURE 5-16
A Demonstration of Lateral Inhibition
The onset of light striking cell A causes neural response; the onset of light striking cell B does not. This is because while a retinal cell is responding to the initial stimulus, neighboring (lateral) cells are inhibited from responding. And the brighter the stimulus, the greater the inhibition.
(After Lindsay & Norman, 1977)

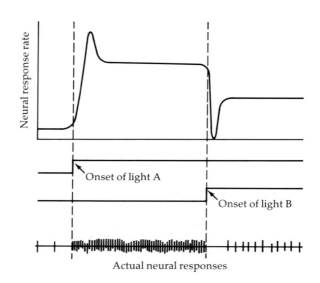

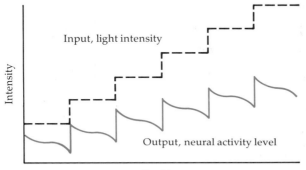

FIGURE 5-17
Lateral Inhibition Accentuates Change
There is a uniform progression of changes between successive steps in this photograph. But you do not perceive the changes as uniform. Lateral inhibition makes nerve cells in the retina respond so that changes are accentuated—the relationship between the input (light intensity) and the output (neural activity level) is not uniform.
(After Cornsweet, 1970)

Eye Movements and the Brain

For an organism to see, it must relate body movements and visual experience. Held and Hein (1963) investigated this relationship using kittens. They raised a group of kittens in total darkness except for one hour each day. During this hour, one group was allowed to move freely around a patterned cylinder; another sat passively in a gondola pulled by a cat from the active group. Later, both groups were exposed to the same visual stimulation. The kittens with an "active" experience in light learned to see normally, but the vision of the other kittens was

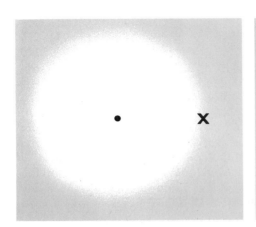
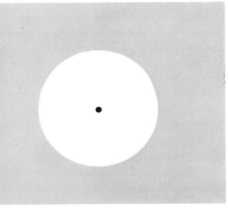

FIGURE 5-18
Sensitivity to the Changes Presented by Stabilized Images
Your visual system is especially sensitive to the sharp-edged circle on the right, so if you stare at it, the photoreceptors continue firing and it remains sharp. In contrast, the fuzzy circle on the right disappears as you stare at the dot. But it will come back into view if your gaze shifts to the "X."

FIGURE 5-19
Your Roving Eye
The pattern of lines trace the eye movements of someone who looked at this picture of the little girl for 3 minutes. The lines not only outline the picture, they indicate points of fixation where the subject's eye paused over areas of visual interest
(After Yarbus, 1967)

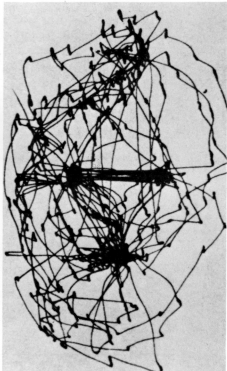

permanently impaired. Visual information coming into the brain must in some way be correlated, through experience, with an organism's movements.

Sensory experience is in part determined by movements. Look straight ahead, then move your eyes sharply to the left. Your *view* of the scene has changed dramatically, but the "world" remains stable. The brain keeps a record of current movements to account for the changes in the *movement-produced stimulation*. Now, gently tap your right eye on the right side with your right index finger so that your eye jumps slightly to the left. When it does, the world seems to "jump." The difference between this and the previous movement is that we rarely, if ever, move our eye with our hand, so there is no record of movement signals to account for the change in stimulation.

Eye movements stimulate change in the information reaching retinal receptors. Normally eyes move in sweeps called *saccades*. We hardly ever stare at any one point very long. Even if you try to fix vision at one point on an object, very small involuntary movements occur. These movements are called *nystagmus*. Portions of the retina are constantly stimulated as a result of both types of eye movements, although at any given moment only some receptor cells are stimulated.

Close your eyes, then open them. What you just saw is a result of all the processes discussed here. Light enters, passes through the retina, and is transduced to the brain. Orientation analyzers and color analyzers do their jobs. A neuropsychologist can follow the sequence from light to the firing of cells on the visual cortex and understand some of the workings of the cells. But how all of this becomes visual experience somewhere in the brain is still a great mystery.

Hearing is our second most important sense. The external ear we see (called the *pinna*) has little to do with hearing itself. Its function is to direct sound waves into the auditory channel. The process of hearing begins in the middle and inner ear. The stimuli for hearing are sound waves — vibrations of air. Sound waves are invisible, but you can see their effects on the surface of a drum as it is beaten.

The ear, like other sensory organs, is both highly sensitive and highly selective. The loudest sounds are millions of times louder than the softest. The ear transmits only a fraction of the energy reaching it, but it is precise in what it does transmit. A mosquito buzzing around your ear can keep you up all night, yet the energy in that buzz would have to be 100,000,000,000,000,000 times greater to light a small lamp (Stevens, 1956).

The Ear and How It Works

The ear picks up vibrations in the air. The auditory system performs the two routine miracles mentioned earlier: it transduces the mechanical energy of sound waves from the outside world into chemical or electrical activity in nerve cells, which in turn becomes the raw material for the experience of sound.

Hearing allows us to locate events and discriminate between quite disparate sounds — a bird's song, a car approaching from the left or right, a musical note. When an exciting event occurs, we try to focus on it visually by moving the image onto the fovea. The ear helps guide the eye to that positioning by sensing differences in loudness. A sound to one side will cause us to turn our heads until the sound is equal in both ears; at that point we will be looking straight at the object.

Hearing gives us feedback on the sounds we make and is especially important for speech. If the auditory feedback from speech is interrupted, distorted, or delayed by even one second, it may completely disrupt the ability to speak coherently.

Sound Waves

Sound waves have two major characteristics: amplitude and frequency. *Amplitude* refers to the height of the wave; *frequency* refers to the number of cycles the wave makes each second. Amplitude governs the experience of loudness; the higher the amplitude, the louder the sound. Frequency governs the pitch; a high frequency results in high-pitched tones. The beat in music is the overlapping of the frequencies of two waves. Sound waves must travel through a medium such as air, water, or a solid material; there is no sound in a vacuum. Sound waves travel through the ear under pressure; sound that is too intense can therefore be painful because of the pressure on sensitive tissue in the ear.

The Ear

The ear is a marvelous physical system of great complexity (Figure 5-20). It includes a wide-range sound wave analyzer, an amplification system, a two-way communication system, a relay unit, a multichannel transducer that converts mechanical into electrical energy, and a hydraulic balance system. All this is compressed into two cubic centimeters (Stevens, Warshofsky, & Staff, 1965).

FIGURE 5-20
The Structure of the
Human Ear

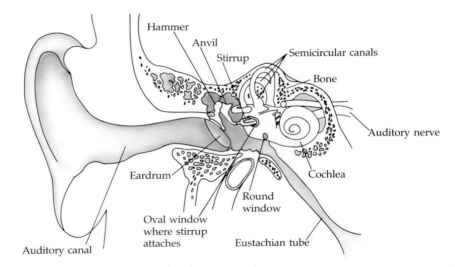

Pressure moves sound waves down the auditory canal to the eardrum, causing it to vibrate. The vibration of the eardrum causes the three bones of the middle ear to vibrate. These bones, named after their shapes, are the hammer, the anvil, and the stirrup. Their vibrations match the original signal in frequency, but are of greater amplitude (25 times greater). The pressure of that amplification forces the waves into the inner ear, where it is transduced into electrical energy in the nerve cells.

The Cochlea

Hearing really begins in the **cochlea** (named for its shape; it is the Latin word for *snail*). The liquid that fills the cochlea is an ideal medium for transmitting sound waves. The cochlea has an impressive auditory response range that can be compared to that of a piano (Figure 5-21).

At the base of the cochlea is a structure called the **basilar membrane.** When the stirrup beats on the cochlea at the *oval window* (see Figure 5-20), the basilar membrane moves just like a whip being cracked. This whipping movement creates a *traveling wave* (Von Bekesy, 1949). A short wave produces a high frequency; its bulge is closer to the oval window. On top of the basilar membrane is the *organ of Corti.* The membrane's movements bend the outer hair cells of the organ of Corti and its cells fire. Here the pressure waves are transduced into neural firing, sent up the auditory nerve, and then to the brain. The pressure from all this banging is finally released through the *round window.*

What the Ear Tells the Brain

Although there are far fewer neurons in the auditory nerve than in the optic nerve (28,000 versus 1 million), the number of sound discriminations is about equal to the number of visual discriminations. A typical auditory receptor has a "tuning curve" (Figure 5-22), which represents its ability to respond to tones of different frequencies. The nerve cells in the ear are as sensitive and specific in the kinds of stimuli they respond to as those in the eye. Some cells respond only to complex sounds, others to pure tones, and so on. Each auditory neuron is generally

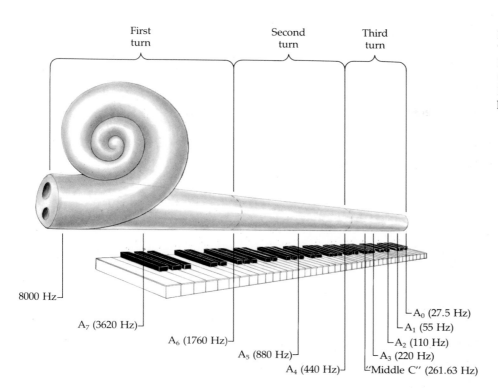

First turn Second turn Third turn

FIGURE 5-21
The Auditory Response Range of the Cochlea Compared to That of a Piano
Hz = hertz.

8000 Hz

A_7 (3620 Hz)

A_6 (1760 Hz)

A_5 (880 Hz)

A_4 (440 Hz)

A_0 (27.5 Hz)
A_1 (55 Hz)
A_2 (110 Hz)
A_3 (220 Hz)
"Middle C" (261.63 Hz)

thought to collect information from a specific place in the basilar membrane. As the amplitude of the sound wave increases, the rate of firing of the neurons increases. As the frequency of the wave changes, different neurons begin to fire.

Auditory Cortex

The first stop after a signal has left the ear on its way to the brain is the *cochlear nucleus*. Many of the fibers of the auditory nerve end here. The axons of the

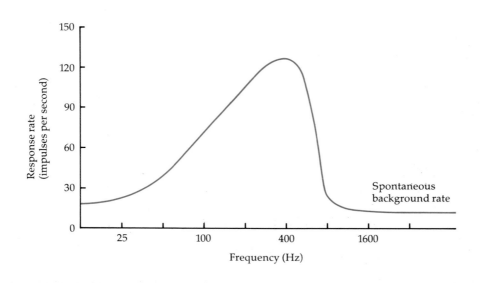

FIGURE 5-22
The Tuning Curve of a Typical Auditory Receptor
When an auditory neuron is presented tones of various frequencies, the pattern of its responses traces a tuning curve such as this one. The point of the receptor's peak response is called the *critical frequency*—in this example, about 400 Hz—which departs most from the neuron's spontaneous background rate.
(After Lindsay & Norman, 1977)

cochlear nucleus of each ear carry the information to the *superior olive* on the opposite side of the brain, where they enter the auditory cortex through the *medial geniculate.* These nerve fibers respond similarly in amplitude and frequency to the "tuned" neurons.

Selection and analysis take place in the auditory cortex; 60 percent of the cortical cells there respond to specific tones. These cells behave in much the same way as those in the visual cortex. There are three types: *on cells* respond when a tone starts, *off cells* respond when the tone stops, and *on-off cells* respond when there is any change. The other 40 percent are more specialized. They respond to bursts of specific waves, sharp sounds, or clicks. For example, *frequency sweep detectors* respond to the small changes in frequency produced in normal speech. Some auditory cells with even more specific functions have been found in other animals. Whitfield (1976) found cells in the auditory system of the squirrel monkey that respond most strongly to the sounds of other squirrel monkeys.

Like the visual system, the auditory system is one of great selectivity and sensitivity. In both systems, physical stimulation of the body by the outside world — the radiation of light or the movement of sound waves — is translated in the body until it somehow becomes the inner world of experience: sight and sound, luminance and tone.

CHEMICAL, SKIN, AND INTERNAL SENSES

Senses of smell, taste, and touch and the internal senses are much simpler systems than sight and hearing, but they are a substantial part of our sensory experience. Without smell and taste we could not judge if food were fresh or spoiled. People born without a sense of touch feel no pain and must be specially protected from injuring themselves.

The senses we are least aware of are the *internal senses.* These senses keep us standing up, help us maintain balance while moving, inform us of internal feelings, and let us know where each part of the body is in relation to every other part. Without information on body position or movements we could not do something as "simple" as walking.

Chemical Senses: Smell and Taste

Smell

Our sense of smell helps discriminate tastes and also is useful in judging distance, location, and danger. For example, people usually smell something burning before they see a fire. The nose is the sensory organ for smell, and the stimulus it responds to is gaseous molecules carried on currents of air. The receptors for smell, the **olfactory cilia,** are located at the end of the nasal cavity in the outer surface of the *olfactory epithelium* (which means "smell skin") (Figure 5-23). These receptors also analyze food. It is difficult to taste the difference between an apple, an onion, and a potato if the nose is blocked.

Smell is the most direct sense. The neural information about smell is sent directly to the brain without any intermediate nerves. Since it is a "straight line" into the brain, smell information is less complex than other sensory information reaching the brain. The direct connection of the nose to the brain may explain certain phenomena: memory for odors is very good, much better than visual or other kinds of memory. Once a smell has been presented, it is rarely forgotten.

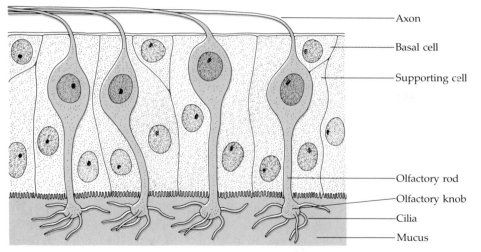

- Axon
- Basal cell
- Supporting cell
- Olfactory rod
- Olfactory knob
- Cilia
- Mucus

FIGURE 5-23
The Structure of the Olfactory Epithelium Smells reaching the surface of the olfactory epithelium stimulate the olfactory cilia, which are embedded in mucus secreted by glands situated only in that part of the nasal passage. The cilia protrude from the olfactory knobs, expanded portions of the olfactory rods that extend from the receptors' cell bodies, which are attached by their axons to the brain.

Smell is not the dominant sense in humans as it is in other animals. Recall that one result of the development of erect posture was that as the nose became further elevated from the earth there was increased reliance on vision. The size of an animal's nose is directly related to the importance of that sense. A dog not only has a much larger snout than we do, but a much larger area of the dog's brain is devoted to smell. Dogs are therefore used to track down a wide variety of things, including specific chemical substances to which human noses are not particularly sensitive. However, there is much speculation about the possible unconscious effect of smell in humans.

Pheromones

Smell may have a more direct effect on behavior than was previously thought. Most animals communicate their sexual receptivity through odors. During estrus, the female of a species produces an odor that arouses the male. Such chemical substances that convey information are called **pheromones.** They have been found in insects and in many mammals. Female mice secrete a substance, *copulin,* which arouses the male.

The evidence in humans is beginning to become clear. A difference between the smells of women and men can also be discriminated. People have described the male smell as "musky" and the female as "sweet." Some recent evidence indicates that smell plays a role in human sexual behavior and that people can distinguish their own body odor from others. Scent glands in the armpits seem to be part of a human pheromone system.

Females unconsciously respond to the odor of other females. In one study, it was shown that the menstrual cycles of women living together were synchronized. One woman can even influence the cycles of other women by smell even if she is absent (McClintock, 1971). If women sniff the scent of the absent woman, their cycles will become synchronized (Preti et al., in press).

Unlike other animals, the human male is more odorous than the female. In a new and potentially revolutionary set of studies, the effects of human male pheromones on women have been confirmed. Women who have intimate contact (usually sexual intercourse) with men at least once a week, have longer menstrual

Because of their superior sense of smell, dogs are used to sniff out illegal drugs brought into the country by drug traffickers.

cycles, fewer infertility problems, and a less difficult menopause. As in the previous study, the effect can be produced by sniffing male "essence" from pads worn underarm by male volunteers. Women whose menstrual cycles were longer than 33 days or shorter than 26 days synchronized to the normal 29.5 days after the "treatment." It was also found that the pheromones of males and females act differently: the female scent can diffuse through a room and be effective, while the male one requires close contact (Preti et al., in press).

Obviously, human sexuality is not completely determined by chemical messages. But the portrayal of scent in sexual experience will have to be expanded. People who say they feel "the right chemistry" with someone of the opposite sex may be right!

Taste

A professional wine taster can often tell the vintage, type of grape, and vineyard of a wine from a single sip. Coffee, tea, and liquor manufacturers employ professional tasters. Human ability to discriminate and remember tastes is remarkably precise. What is especially interesting about human taste is that complex taste sensations are built up on an extremely simple receptor system.

Look at your tongue in the mirror. Its surface is covered with small bumps called *papillae*. Each has 200 *taste buds* in and around it (see Plate 7). Taste buds are a collection of taste cells. They do not live very long and are replaced every few days. When you burn your tongue on hot food, you cannot taste anything in that spot for a few days. This is because the taste buds have been killed and new ones have not yet replaced them.

There are four basic taste elements in our palate: sour, bitter, sweet, and salty. As with the other senses, taste stimuli are "coded" into these basic categories and are transmitted to the brain as one of these four. Each cell has a different threshold for each taste (Figure 5-24). Different parts of the tongue are more sensitive to one taste than another. The tip of the tongue is most sensitive to sweet and salty, while the sides are most sensitive to sour, and the back to bitter (Figure 5-25) (Coren et al., 1984). The taste buds also respond to temperature—hot, warm, and cold.

FIGURE 5-24
Taste Buds' Response Thresholds
The single taste bud whose responses are charted here is highly responsive to sweet tastes and fairly sensitive to salt tastes. It is such relatively low thresholds that characterize individual taste buds, not their high thresholds, because taste receptors often have no reaction to certain tastes and therefore have infinitely high thresholds for such stimulation.
(After Ludel, 1978)

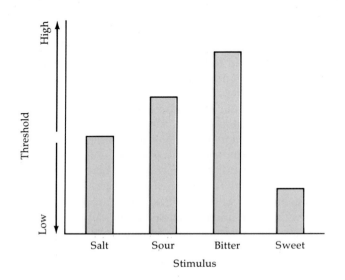

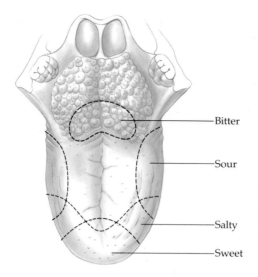

FIGURE 5-25
Areas of the Human
Tongue and Their
Relative Sensitivity to
the Four Basic Tastes
(After Ludel, 1978)

— Bitter

— Sour

— Salty

— Sweet

All other senses develop more complexity and sensitivity with age, but the opposite occurs in taste. An adult has fewer taste cells than a child. This difference means that children are more sensitive to taste, which helps explain why children are "picky" eaters and why adults add seasoning to food.

Touching and Feeling

Touching informs and communicates. The skin is the primary sensory organ for touch, and it responds to three dimensions of stimuli: *pressure, pain,* and *temperature.* The skin is the largest sense organ of the body, and one of its most important functions is to define the boundary between ourselves and the outside world. We also obtain information about the surface textures of the outside world through the skin. Touch gives us feedback on motor movements: whether we are holding a pencil correctly, grasping a screwdriver or losing our grip. Touch also communicates. In our culture a good indicator of the closeness of two people is how much they touch each other. Sex is largely an experience of touching, as is the bond between mother and infant.

Different parts of the body are more sensitive to touch than others. The most sensitive regions of the body are the fingers, cheeks, nose, lips, genitals, and soles of the feet. Least sensitive are the arms, back, thighs, and calves.

The skin has many types of receptors, each of which responds to a different kind of stimulation. One is the *pacinian corpuscle* (Lowenstein, 1960), which has an internal structure much like the layers of an onion (Figure 5-26). It seems to respond directly to *mechanical pressure,* which directly stimulates the nerve. Although there are many different kinds of nerve endings in the skin, they all send their information to the brain via one of two systems, one fast and one slow. The fast one, the *lemniscal system,* is comprised of large nerve fibers that conduct information directly into the cortex. The *spinothalamic system* is slow and diffuse, is regulated through the reticular activating system, and reaches the brain at the limbic system. These two systems seem to be specialized for the transmission of two types of pain information: the immediate pain of a blow is sent quickly to the brain by the lemniscal system. The slow spinothalamic system conveys chronic

FIGURE 5-26
The Pacinian Corpuscle
Sensitive to touch, such receptors respond to direct mechanical pressure, adapt to it, and then are ready to respond again soon after the pressure is removed.
(After Ludel, 1978)

Capsule of connective tissue

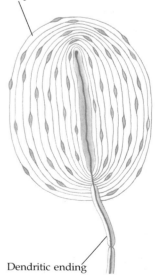

Dendritic ending

FIGURE 5-27

Pain Pathways

The fast pathway (lemniscal system) carries information on such sudden pain as that from a blow or a pinprick, conducting it directly to the cerebral cortex. Information on chronic pain travels the slow pathway (the spinothalamic system), being routed through the limbic system before coming to the attention of the cortex.
(After Snyder, 1977)

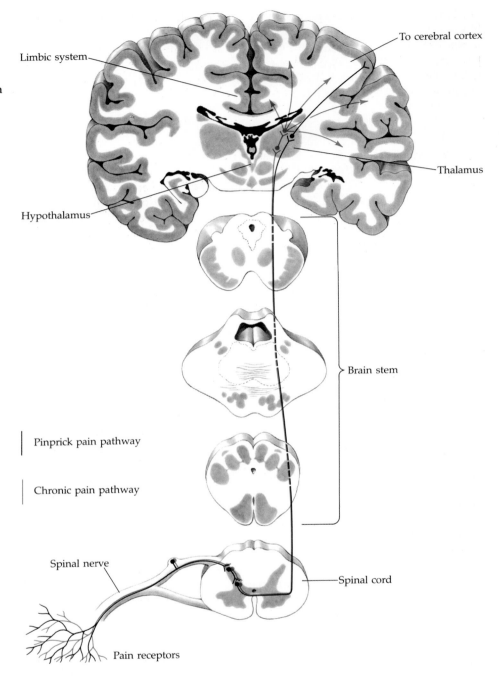

Limbic system

To cerebral cortex

Thalamus

Hypothalamus

Brain stem

Pinprick pain pathway

Chronic pain pathway

Spinal nerve

Spinal cord

Pain receptors

pain from long-term injuries and ailments, as well as internal pains such as those resulting from surgery or a toothache (Figure 5-27).

Internal Senses

While the eyes, ears, nose, and skin inform us primarily of events coming at us, the internal senses relay information on movements and bodily functions. We need to be aware of internal processes to maintain balance and to move. The sense of movement is called *kinesthesis;* the sense of balance is one of the *vestibular senses.* The **somesthetic system** conveys to the brain information concerning sensations in the internal environment, such as deep pain or nausea. We also need to know where each part of the body is in relation to all other parts. The sense that performs that function is called **proprioception.**

Kinesthesis

Close your eyes and concentrate on each movement you must make to walk across the room. The legs must flex, then extend a certain distance, while movements of the arms and back must be coordinated. At every instant you know precisely the position of your body. The sense that makes all this possible is **kinesthesis** (from the Greek word *kine,* meaning "movement"). Even when we are not moving through space — when we are sitting, lying down, or relaxed — we have kinesthetic feedback. At every moment of life we respond to the unseen force of gravity. You know, without looking at them, where your limbs are, their angle, and what they are doing. Special nerve cells in the muscles, called *joint position receptors,* relay information on movements of the muscles, and nerve endings in the skin and muscles respond to these signals.

As with all other senses, habituation occurs in the neurons that signal the location of limbs: if the hand is held in one place, the neurons stop firing. We receive no information if we do not move.

Vestibular Senses

The **vestibular system** consists of organs sensitive to motion, position, and balance. Our organs of balance are in the inner ear next to the cochlea. They are called the *otolith organs* (meaning "ear stone," from their shape), and they are the exception to the rule that sensory systems respond only to *changes* in stimuli. The otolith organs contain three semicircular canals that lie in different planes so that movement of the head in any direction is registered in the canals. The enlarged area at the end of the canals is called the *ampulla,* inside of which are hair cells like those in the organ of Corti. When we tilt our heads, the fluid in the canals stimulates certain hair cells to fire. The firing of the cells signals specific directions of the movements.

These organs signal the actual position of the head. They respond constantly so that the head and body are always oriented to the only constant force in the world of sensation — gravity. They do not adapt because their stimulus, the force of gravity, never changes through an organism's lifetime.

S ensory experiences do not occur separately. We may see "red" but do not see only pure red alone; it may be on the surface of an automobile, in bright or dim light, or next to a green car. We always see red in comparison to other colors and objects. A photograph of a white car at sunset may be much redder than a tomato at noon.

Animals are always adapting. We reset the level of adaptation according to the situation. In winter 50°F is experienced as "warm," while the same temperature in summer is "cold." I visited Hawaii one winter when the temperature was 68°F. On the beach were tourists from Minnesota in bathing suits; the weather they had

THE RELATIVITY OF SENSORY EXPERIENCE

HOW JUDGMENTS ABOUT NEWS ARE BASED ON THE CHARACTERISTICS OF THE SENSES

One reason it is important to study the nature of the sensory systems and the "old wiring" of the nervous system is that the same neural processes that originally developed to judge brightness and weight are also used in modern times to judge current events. This makes some of the ways we respond to events more comprehensible. Simply because of the normal processes of the nervous system—the transmission to the brain of sharp changes in the world—human beings are not easily able to register threatening changes that are not immediate emergencies. Such changes are not perceived in the same way as are other threats, and they are often incorporated wrongly into our culture. The typical response is to attend closely to the first occurrence of an event, then tune out. This happens in responding to a noise, to a sudden appearance of the sun, and to extreme danger.

This may seem not to apply to you, but consider the responses to atomic threats. People were more afraid of the first few small atomic bombs than they are of the tens of thousands of much more powerful nuclear weapons that are now in U.S. and Soviet arsenals. The first atomic bombs were kept secret and then were unveiled *suddenly*. The mushroom cloud over Hiroshima and the unparalleled destruction signaled a sharp change in the world—it was easily noticed and properly feared. In contrast, nuclear bombs have accumulated *gradually* until they now number in the tens of thousands, each one much more powerful than the first ones. These arsenals have hardly been given the notice of the first weapons. Yet the growth of these arsenals as well as countless other alterations in the environment of the contemporary world are dangers of a dimension that humanity has never known.

It happens like this because the same general processes that evolution developed to judge sensory information are used to judge more complex information. This is one reason why understanding basic neural processes is important. This kind of perception (and thousands of examples can be given) is a misapplication of a system designed, like a frog's, to respond only to immediate and local phenomena.

left was −20°F. At the end of the beach were Hawaiian workers wearing heavy sheepskin coats. The native workers were experiencing the low end of their temperature range, the tourists the high end (in winter). That we constantly maintain and interpret experience by comparison to a standard, is a principle to keep well in mind, not only for sensory judgments, but for all kinds of judgments, from wealth to people to politics.

Adaptation Level Theory

In trying to adjust to the changes in the external world, an organism sets an **adaptation level** which is determined by three factors (Helson, 1964).

1. *Focal stimuli.* These stimuli are at the center of our attention; they constitute immediate experience.
2. *Background stimuli.* These are the contextual stimuli in which the focal stimuli are embedded, such as the different sequences in brightness contrast and the constant sounds in a room.

FIGURE 5-28
Adaptation Level
Look at the left-hand photograph. You will quickly form the impression that one man is "tall," that he is probably above average height. Now look at the right-hand photograph. The "tall" man from the other picture is obviously the shorter of the two here. From the initial sensory experience you set an adaptive level, a conviction about what "average" and "tall" are. But the second picture forced you to modify it. We judge people and things against such internal standards, which can be altered by new experience that shows them to be in error.

3. *Residual stimuli.*These are stimuli that the observer has experienced in the past.

If you look at a television sportscaster of normal height interviewing a jockey, you are likely to judge the sportscaster as tall. If you see him interviewing a basketball star, he seems short. The height of the sportscaster is the focal stimulus. The heights of the jockey and the basketball player are the background stimuli. The residual stimulus is the range of experienced human heights. They all combine to create the adaptation level in this situation. You can see an example of this in Figure 5-28.

The adaptation level approach allows us to quantify comparative sensory experience. One important finding is the **anchoring effect,** which is the effect of the *preceding* stimuli on the judgment of *subsequent* stimuli. In one experiment people were given either heavy (400 to 600 grams) or light (100 to 300 grams) weights to judge. Then half of each group switched. Those going from the heavy to the light weights experienced the light weights as lighter than those who had lifted light weights all along.

Adaptation levels occur in most sensory and judgmental processes. An apple tastes sweet with cheese but sour after ice cream. Sensory judgments of magnitude are also made in comparison to previous experience. As Ernst Weber, the first psychophysicist, pointed out, an inch seems longer compared to a foot than to a yard.

Sensory experience involves a process of *selection, adaptation,* and *comparison.*

The senses are at the intersection of the biological world and the world of perception, consciousness, thought, and intelligence. It is to these subjects that we now turn.

SUMMARY

1. The senses of sight, sound, smell, taste, and touch use the processes of deconstruction, selection, adaptation, and comparison to simplify information entering the nervous system.

2. The least amount of energy necessary to notice a stimulus is the *absolute threshold*. The minimum increase in energy necessary to notice a difference in stimuli is the difference threshold, or more commonly, the *just noticeable difference* (j.n.d.).

3. Weber's Law was the first principle of sensation. It states that equal changes in physical intensity do not produce equal changes in experience.

4. Fechner discovered that it is the *relative* intensity of the physical differences that senses are designed to notice, not the *absolute* differences.

5. Stevens discovered that different senses transform the information they select differently. Pain is greatly amplified, while brightness is attenuated.

6. Senses function to transform physical energy into *neural firing* in the brain, a process called *transduction*. The physics and chemistry of the brain then transform into human experience.

7. Light strikes the *retina*, the center of the visual system, after passing through the cornea and lens. The retina transduces light energy into neural impulses. *Rods* in the retina respond most to light energy at low levels. *Cones* are primarily responsible for color vision. There are three types of cones: one that responds primarily to red-orange wavelengths, one to green, and one to blue-violet.

8. In each eye there are about 126 million *photoreceptor* cells whose impulses are channeled to the brain via the *ganglion* cells. On their way to the brain they pass through the *lateral geniculate nucleus* (LGN). Each cell has a *receptive field* — the area of stimulation on the retina to which it is most sensitive.

9. Specialized cells in the brain respond individually to complex features presented on the retina. These features range from bars, lines and edges, to orientation, movement, and other specific features of the environment. One animal study even found that a single cell responded specifically to the shape of the hand. It is currently thought that many different kinds of cortical modules analyze the sense's output.

10. Lateral inhibition, a mechanism by which cells inhibit or stimulate one another, helps us to distinguish objects in our environment.

11. The ear responds to vibrations in the air, and like the visual system, the auditory system transduces what it receives into neural impulses. Pressure waves in the air move down the auditory canal to the eardrum, causing it to vibrate. This causes three bones of the middle ear to vibrate: the hammer, the anvil, and the stirrup. The stirrup beats on the *cochlea* at the oval window and causes the *basilar membrane* to vibrate. These vibrations are transduced into neural signals at the organ of Corti. Although not as well studied as the selection and analysis process of the visual system, that of the auditory system is similar.

12. The *olfactory cilia* are the receptors for our most direct sense—smell. Memories of odors are better than for any other sense. Smell has a direct effect on our behavior through *pheromones,* chemicals secreted in our sweat that affect our sexual behavior.

13. Human taste ability is complex and discriminating, although it is built on a simple receptor system of taste buds which sense four basic tastes—sour, bitter, sweet, and salty.

14. Skin is the largest organ of the body and allows us to communicate and gather information through touching using the *lemniscal system* for fast transmission and the *spinothalamic system* for slow transmission.

15. The *vestibular senses* include the sense of balance. The sense of movement is called *kinesthesis.* The somesthetic system conveys to the brain information concerning sensations in the internal environment.

16. An *adaptation level* is set by an organism to adjust to differences in its environment; it is determined by focal, background, and residual stimuli. The effect of preceding stimuli on the judgment of subsequent stimuli is called the *anchoring effect.*

TERMS AND CONCEPTS

absolute threshold
adaptation level
anchoring effects
auditory cortex
basilar membrane
cochlea
comparison
cones
cornea
deconstruction
difference threshold
electromagnetic energy
feature analyzers
fovea
ganglion cells
just noticeable difference (j.n.d.)
kinesthesis
lateral geniculate nucleus (LGN)
lateral inhibition

module
neural firing
olfactory cilia
optic nerve and optic tract
pheromones
photoreceptors
Power Law
proprioception
psychophysics
receptive field
retina
rods
selectivity
simplification
somesthetic system
transduction
vestibular system
visual cortex
Weber's Law

SUGGESTIONS FOR FURTHER READING

Coren, S., Porac, C., & Ward, L. M. (1984). *Sensation and perception.* New York: Academic Press.

  The best textbook on the senses.

Kosslyn, S. (1986). *Image and mind.* Boston: Harvard.

  A chance to read through a leading psychologist's analysis of mental processing.

Pinker, S. (Ed.) (1985). *Visual cognition.* Cambridge, MA: MIT/Bradford.

  An excellent current collection about the analysis of the computations of vision.

The mind is hard to grasp.

Biology is at least tangible: fossils, neurons, sense organs.

The mind, however, cannot be so easily uncovered. It can be analyzed using concepts like those of chemistry before atomic particles were discovered. The "atoms" of the mind are the basic associations: seeing a red light means stop. The "elements" are the schemata, linked associations that simplify actions: walking, talking, dancing. The "compounds" are prototypes and categories which instantly decode the information that arrives.

The mind is not a single entity, but is made up of a multitude of components, which combine and recombine differently in different people. The nature of those components is becoming clear, just as particles, once only theories, became understood as science progressed.

The Mental World

Perceiving the World

How does experience compose within the mind? All that the neural networks do is gather and transform various forms of energy. Here is a simplified and abbreviated example of sensory information as it is transmitted to the brain: "increasing 700 nanometer waves to the right, accompanied by increasing pressure of sound waves of 60–80 hertz at 40° to the left." Information in this form does not mean much to us. The message "a bear is coming, and fast, on the left" certainly does. The difference is that this message has *meaning*.

Perception is not a description of the actions of specific neurons, like sensation, but is *the organization of sensory information into simple, meaningful patterns*.

Usually the transformation of individual sensations into perception is so quick and automatic that we are unaware of the difference. Occasionally, however, you may experience it. I did one morning when I awoke, slowly. I seemed surrounded by bright grayness. I felt a certain heaviness and my back was very warm. I could hear a low pitched sound close by and a lower one farther away. I smelled an odd mixture of aromas. Then these disconnected sensations became organized. I was home in bed on a cloudy morning, my cat was on my back purring, and a lawn mower was working in the distance. Breakfast was on in the kitchen and the toast was burnt.

When I realized the *meaning* of the disconnected sensations, I had shifted between two worlds—from disconnected "raw" sensations, to understanding the nature of the world. This process goes on all the time; it is the difference between seeing a group of letters printed on a page and recognizing the meaning of the message "I love you."

Perception is an active and complex process. It begins with the information the senses receive and involves *reception* and *selection* as well as *computation* and *creation*. This chapter considers the diverse mechanisms through which mental processes harvest meaning. It then examines the primary achievement of perception: the stable, "constant" experience of the world, even though nature is in continuous change. Finally, the perception of the external world is considered: place, space, and time.

Principles and Issues

To interpret meaning from raw sensory information, the mental system uses a basic rule of thumb: what is the simplest meaningful thing that the sensory stimuli can be organized into? We do not experience a "semirectangular expanse of red," but rather a "red book"; when we hear sounds getting louder, we experience an object approaching; when an object looks smaller and smaller, this means it is moving away from us. Two important components of perceptual analysis are *organization* and *interpretation*.

Perceptual Organization.   The fusion and coordination of separate stimuli into something meaningful is **perceptual organization.** The disorganized sensations that I felt on awakening were *organized* into one experience: "I'm at home in bed on a cloudy morning." This organization "made sense" of all the different sensory information reaching me.

Once a number of stimuli are organized into a precept, it becomes difficult to see them once again as separate and disorganized. Look at Figure 6-1 for a few moments. At first it seems to be only a collection of dots strewn at random. At some moment you will organize them into a scene of a Dalmatian dog near a tree. Once so organized, it is almost impossible to see the picture as a "random" collection of dots again.

Interpretation.   The second step in constructing meaning is **interpretation.** Consider the bear approaching: first the information from the senses is organized into the perception "bear." But what is the meaning of "a bear" in your presence? What action do you take? Suppose the "bear" suddenly says "Trick or treat!" Now you remember that it is Halloween, and the significance of "bear" becomes quite different than if you had been camping in the woods and heard a growl!

Simplicity.   When something is organized, it is simplified. The experience of many different "dots" on a page is quite complex, but a Dalmatian near a tree is organized and simple. Because there is a vast amount of information in the world, it is important that we simplify it so that we can act quickly.

Our experience of the world is far simpler than the external world itself. Our senses select and simplify the physical stimulation to which our bodies are exposed. Perception continues this simplification process. *In any situation we tend to*

FIGURE 6-1
Organizing Sensory Stimuli
It takes your perception to make a meaningful pattern emerge from what at first seems to be a random collection of spots and dots. And once you have made sense of it, it is hard to recapture your impression of the picture as random or meaningless.
(After Carraher & Thurston, 1966)

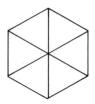 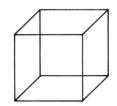

FIGURE 6-2
**Three Dimensionality
and Organizational
Simplicity**
The continuous lines in
each drawing make it
easier to perceive one as a
two-dimensional pattern
(left) and the other as a
three-dimensional cube
(right), although both are
views of a cube.
(After Hochberg & McAlister,
1953; Kopfermann, 1930)

experience the simplest meaningful organization of the stimuli registered. Look at the two drawings in Figure 6-2: both are of a cube, but from different angles. The simplest interpretation of the one on the top is to see it as a two-dimensional hexagon rather than a cube viewed from one of its corners. We see the drawing on the bottom as a cube in three dimensions because this is simpler than seeing it as a group of rectangles.

PROCESS OF PERCEPTION

I f you don't stop to analyze it, nothing seems simpler than perceiving the environment. At this moment I see grass and the sky beyond, I hear kids playing in the street, and I smell the musty odor of old books in my study. Let us consider a simple, typical scene. I walk into a room and see my friend Dennis. I might speak to him, perhaps ask him about a project he is working on. This is a simple, ordinary experience, not worthy of much analysis — or so it would seem.

It takes a lot of work to keep things simple. It might interest you to know that no computer, no matter how large and sophisticated, can accomplish this simple feat. I know hundreds of people, and it is not extraordinary that I know what to talk about with each one. A computer could not even identify Dennis, let alone hold a conversation with him. This simple and ordinary experience is actually the result of many difficult and complex operations. We may be aware of *what* we perceive, but we are not normally aware of the mental processes "behind the scenes" that make perception possible. The analysis of these processes is the subject of perception, and more generally, of cognition, the study of how we know the world.

Let's go back to Dennis in the room. To see Dennis, you first "pick up" information from the environment. Only a few of the millions of stimuli reaching the sense receptors yield any information about Dennis and the room. This raw sensory information is first picked up and organized. That expanse of red is perceived as the couch and the gray as his shirt; the voice identifies Dennis, not Fred. But your perception of Dennis also goes beyond what meets the eyes and ears. Once you have assembled Dennis, you go beyond that immediate information and make assumptions — that he is the same person he was before, with the same memories, interests, and experiences. Further, perception is continuous. The world changes: Dennis may move around, you may move as well, someone else may enter the room, you may leave.

See Chapter 5, section on Simplification and Selectivity.

Perception thus involves "picking up" information about the world, organizing it, and making inferences about the environment in a continuous cycle. Each of these processes will be considered in this section.

Picking Up Information about the World

Perception begins with the environment to be perceived. To be useful, perceptions must accurately reflect the world around us. People approaching must be seen if we are to avoid bumping into them. We have to be able to identify food before it can be eaten. The senses act as information gatherers and selectors for perception. They select information about color, taste, and sound relevant for survival. What an organism perceives depends on what elements the environment "affords." These characteristics of the environment have been analyzed extensively by specialists called *ecological psychologists;* two of them are:

1. **Affordance.** Each object in the environment offers, or *affords,* a rich source of information (Doner & Lappin, 1980). A wooden post "affords" information about its right angles; a tomato affords information about its roundness, color, and taste; a tree, about its greenness, the color of its fruit, and its height.

2. **Invariance.** The external environment contains many different objects. Each offers to the perceiver certain *invariant* features, which are constant patterns of stimulation (Michaels & Carello, 1981). For example, look at the photo of the rows of grave markers in Figure 6-3. Although the markers appear different from one another in the photo, each presents invariant (unchanging) information about itself to the perceiver: each is white, rectangular, and perpendicular to the ground. These invariant characteristics remain constant no matter what angle or distance they are viewed from. Because perceivers are always in motion, they have the chance to "pick up" many of the invariant features of the environment. There are invariant patterns that are common to all objects: all objects get smaller as their distance from the perceiver increases; lines converge at the horizon; when one object is nearer it blocks out another.

Perception thus involves an organism "picking up" the information afforded by the environment and using it.

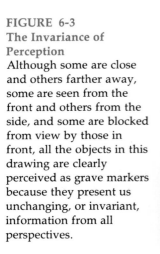

FIGURE 6-3
The Invariance of Perception
Although some are close and others farther away, some are seen from the front and others from the side, and some are blocked from view by those in front, all the objects in this drawing are clearly perceived as grave markers because they present us unchanging, or invariant, information from all perspectives.

FIGURE 6-4
Resistance to Stable
Organization
Op art such as this can
present many different and
changing meaningful
patterns of organization.
This runs counter to our
perceptual preference for
stable, invariant patterns
of organization.
(After Carraher & Thurston, 1968)

Rules of Organization

Sensory information is very often so complex that it must be simplified and organized. The perceptual system is so specialized for organizing sensory information that it attempts to organize disconnected things into a pattern even when there is none. We look up at a cloud and see shapes in it—a whale or a bird.

"Op art," popular in the 1960s, played with this predisposition to organize. Op art is at once intriguing and unsettling because we try continually to organize certain figures that are designed by the artist to have no organization (Figure 6-4).

Gestalt: Principles of Organization

The rules of perceptual organization are the basis of the *gestalt* approach to psychology. **Gestalt** is a German word with no direct English equivalent (which is why it has entered English in its original form), but it roughly means *to create a form.* A gestalt is the immediate organization of the form of an object. In gestalt psychology, an object is more than the sum of its parts. For example, in Figure 6-5 you instantly perceive the lines as a square. You do not see four individual lines,

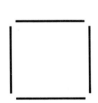

FIGURE 6-5
Perception of the Whole
We tend to organize our
perceptions immediately
into wholes, rather than
seeing them as their
constituent parts—which
is why you first see this
figure as one square, not
four individual lines.

FIGURE 6-6
Seeing Figure and Ground
Because you can perceive either the light or the dark portions of these drawings as figures against a background of the opposite shade, the meaning of what you see can vary dramatically even as you gaze at them.

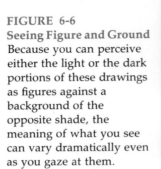

then later notice they are all at right angles to one another, then judge that they are of equal length, and then count them and say, "Gee, that's a square." The figure is *immediately* perceived as a whole, not as the sum of its parts.

Gestalt psychologists have identified a number of rules governing the organizing principles of perception. Four of the principles of organization are figure-ground, proximity, similarity, and good continuation (Rock, 1985).

Figure-ground.   What you see in Figure 6-6 depends on which color you decide is the background and which is the "figure." These drawings are called "ambiguous figures" because it is not clear which is the figure and which is the background. Depending on what you decide, you see a chalice or two human profiles and some stones from an ancient ruin or the word "TIE."

Proximity.   When elements are close together, they tend to be perceived as a unit, that is, they seem to describe a form (Figure 6-7).

Similarity.   Like elements tend to be grouped together (Figure 6-8).

Good Continuation.   It is simpler to see *continuous* patterns and lines. In Figure 6-9, it is much easier to perceive the whole and parts of the continuous figure at

FIGURE 6-7
Organization by Proximity
Separate elements placed close together tend to be perceived as a unit and seem to describe a form rather than being seen as distinct and unrelated.

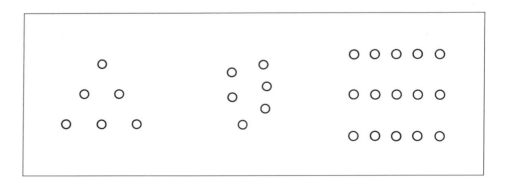

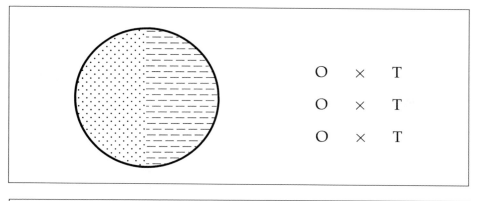

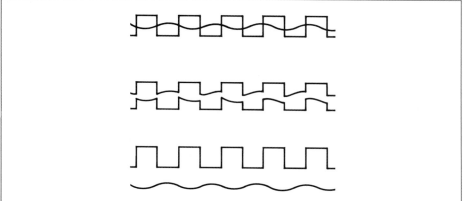

FIGURE 6-8
Organization by Similarity
Our perception tends to recognize similar elements and group them with one another. Thus, you are likely to see the two halves of the spheres as separate and different and to perceive three groups of the *same* letters rather than groups of the letters OXT.

FIGURE 6-9
Organization by Continuity
It is much easier to perceive the whole and the parts of the top figure than to see those identical elements presented in the other two discontinuous drawings.

the top than to perceive the identical elements in the other two discontinuous figures.

Interpretation: Going Beyond the Information Given

In spite of the fact that there is a great richness of sensory information reaching us, the information we receive at any one moment is often incomplete. We may catch but a glimpse of Dennis's shirt or hear only a word or two of his voice, yet we recognize him. In order to organize experience of the world we often need to go beyond the immediate information we receive. In order to act quickly and flexibly in the world, we fill in the gaps of missing information (Hochberg, 1978). This is why, for example, it is so easy to miss typographical errors when you are writing a term paper.

One of the most common perceptual operations is one that "cleans up" information and "straightens it out." Look at Figure 6-10 for a moment; now, before reading on, cover up the figure and draw the shapes. You probably drew the slanted ellipse as a circle, made the "square" with straight sides, completed and

FIGURE 6-10
Cleaning up Perceptual Information
After looking at these figures for a few seconds, cover them and draw what you saw. What does your drawing indicate about how you interpret what you perceive?

FIGURE 6-11
Filling in Perceptual
Information
Look at the first three
figures in the sequence:
you don't see a triangle
overlaid. But when you see
the figure as a whole
(lower right), you see two
overlying triangles. You
are interpreting or
subjectively "filling in" the
white central one, which
does not actually exist.
(After Coren, 1972)

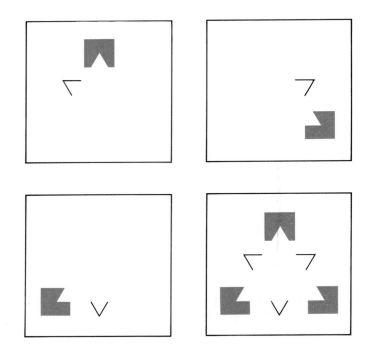

connected the sides of the "triangle," and made the "X" with two straight lines. You cleaned up, corrected, and connected the figures to match your interpretation of them.

The final diagram in Figure 6-11 is composed of three acute angles spaced equidistantly between three squares, each square with a small piece missing at the corners. What you probably "saw" instead was three squares with two overlapping triangles. However, the topmost "white" triangle is something you "filled in" by the process of interpretation. We experience things in the best form available to us.

Unconscious Inferences

We are usually unaware of the acts of perception and the rules of organization. Rather, we make what is called in psychology **unconscious inferences.** We draw conclusions about reality on the basis of the suggestions and cues brought in by the senses. The nineteenth century scientist Hermann Helmholtz compared the perceiver to an astronomer, forced to fill in the gaps in his information.

An astronomer, for example, comes to real conscious conclusions of this sort, when he computes the positions of the stars in space, their distances, etc., from the perspective images he has had of them at various times and as they are seen from different parts of the orbit of the earth. His conclusions are based on a conscious knowledge of the laws of optics. In the ordinary acts of vision this knowledge of optics is lacking. Still it may be permissible to speak of the (psychological) acts of ordinary perception as unconscious conclusions, thereby making a distinction of some sort between them and the common so-called conscious conclusions.

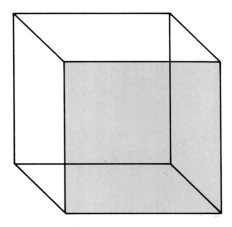

FIGURE 6-12
Inference and Perceptual Ambiguity
The shaded part of this so-called Necker cube seems to shift from the front to the back as you look at it. But, of course, the figure is not changing, only your perception of it, which changes as your brain organizes and interprets the ambiguous perceptual information it receives.
(After Gregory, 1986)

Many classic demonstrations in perception show the effect of inferences on our experience. As you look at the cube in Figure 6-12, its structure may seem to shift before your eyes. Is the shaded portion at the rear or front of the cube? The figure itself does not change, of course. What does change is your *perception* of the cube. The eyes send the brain bits of information about the arrangement of a set of lines. The next step is to *organize* the information and *interpret* what it is. Your perception of the cube shifts because the interpretation changes; indeed the shift in *experience* is actually a shift in interpretation. Normally we are not aware that perception involves such inferences because few figures are ambiguous and it is usually easy to settle on one correct inference.

Assumptive World

For us to act and react at our usual rapid pace, we must assume much about the world we perceive. If I say that Dennis is in a room, you immediately assume the room has four walls, a floor, a ceiling, and probably furniture. Upon entering a room you do not inspect it to determine whether the walls are at right angles, nor do you run back to check if the room is still there after you leave it. If you constantly verified everything in the environment, there would be no time to do anything. Thus, perceptual experience, such as "Dennis in the room," involves many *assumptions*.

If much of experience is assumed, then it follows that *if assumptions change, perceptions will, too.* This was the hypothesis of Adelbert Ames and his colleagues at Dartmouth in the late 1940s and early 1950s (Ittleson, 1952). They analyzed perception involving a transaction between an organism and its environment. Hastorf (1950) showed that judgment of the distance of a thing depends on how big we assume it to be. A ping-pong ball up close might look instead like a volley ball farther away. How we experience the ball and judge distance from it depends on assumptions of what it is.

Another demonstration involves the shapes of rooms. Space is three-dimensional, but representations of space on paper, such as a photograph, are only two-dimensional. Thus, sometimes our assumptions are wrong, such as in the left and center photos of Figure 6-13. Because we assume that a room is rectilinear, we see the boy and dog as impossible sizes. This trick room fools us and distorts our perception of reality.

See section on Cultural Effects on Perception, this chapter.

FIGURE 6-13
Perceptual Assumptions
Because we assume rooms are rectilinear, a trick room like this, shaped to exploit that assumption, can destroy our perception and fool us into seeing the boy and the dog as impossibly different sizes. The last photo shows how the room actually looks.

Needs and Values

Other determinants of perception are *needs* and *values.* Bruner and Goodman (1946) conducted an experiment in which they compared the perceptual experiences of children from poor and well-to-do families. When shown a certain coin, children from poor homes experienced it as larger than did the richer children. This finding has been repeated in other cultures, such as in Hong Kong (Dawson, 1975). In another similar study, students in a class were asked to draw a picture of their teacher. The honor students drew the teacher as being shorter than themselves, while the poorer students drew themselves as smaller than the teacher. Thus, needs and values determine perception in many ways.

Perceptual Cycle

Picking up information, organizing it, and filling in gaps all help explain how we might perceive static objects and events. These processes also help explain how we recognize things we have experienced before. The world is constantly changing, however, and to get along we must be able to discover the meaning of new things and information we encounter. The concept of a *perceptual cycle* helps explain how we handle new information about undiscovered parts of the world.

The **perceptual cycle** is based on the idea that perception is a continuous process directed by schemata (Neisser, 1976). When one person says a glass is "half empty" and another says it is "half full," we have an example of how people look at their environment differently. One person is looking at what is gone (the empty space); the other is looking at what is left (the liquid).

See Chapter 3, section on Schemata.

Schemata, the first factor of the cycle, not only link past experience with present events, they also direct discovery of the world. The second factor is movements and manipulations of the world; the third is the incoming information about changes in the external world. Figure 6-14 is a diagram of the cycle.

The schemata direct exploration: sensory information provided by these exploratory movements modifies the view of the world produced by the brain, which in turn changes the schema. New movements are directed and exploration begins anew. This continuous cycle produces continually changing experience, and thus different people may "carve out" different perceptual experiences.

Consider the different experiences of a child, an artist, and a botanist as each walks across a park. The child sees everything at the knee level of adults. He or she

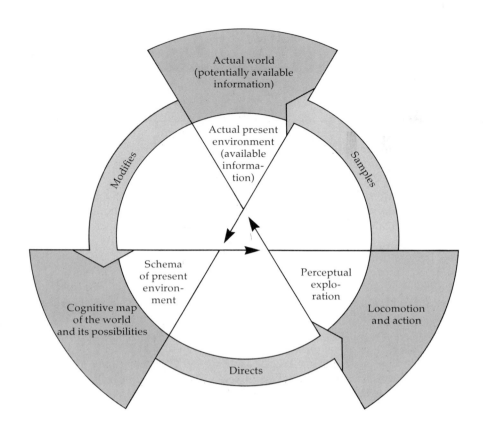

FIGURE 6-14
The Perceptual Cycle
This diagram represents
the theory that perception
is a continuous process of
changing experience
directed by schemata,
themselves modified by
sensory information
provided by the selective
exploration of the
environment.
(After Neisser, 1976)

Actual world
(potentially available
information)

Actual present
environment
(available
informa-
tion)

Modifies

Samples

Schema
of present
environ-
ment

Perceptual
explo-
ration

Cognitive map
of the world
and its possibilities

Locomotion
and action

Directs

may notice balls that roll nearby and other children (especially if they have balloons); the bell of the ice cream truck is compelling. The artist notices the different colors of green on the grass and trees, the play of light, the shape of the clouds. If in need of a dark-haired woman to model for a painting, every dark-haired woman in view will be examined as a potential model. When the botanist looks at the trees, the scientific name of each one may come to mind and the progress of some spring blossoms seen the week before will be noted. The child may pick up a leaf unconsciously and begin to tear and fold it. The botanist may pick up the same leaf exclaiming, "My God! This is the first time the *Fernicus imaginarius* has been seen outside Europe!" Although the three park strollers are afforded the same sensory stimuli, their experiences are very different. Schemata direct the selection of events and carve out a "small world" for each of them (Rock, 1985).

How Perceptual Experience Changes

Perceptual experience changes in the same ways that children's schemata change as they get older: assimilation and accommodation. In the perceptual cycle, schemata are constantly updated as the search of the external environment relays information that requires new interpretation.

We interpret incoming information to match existing schemata through **assimilation.** Read the message in Figure 6-15. You probably had no trouble deciphering "I do what I please." But notice that the *l* in "please," the *I*, and the *d* in the

I do what I please.

"do" are identical. That same element is experienced differently, and appropriately, in each case. We do not perceive the individual letters of words, but rather the words they signify. Similarly, Figure 6-16 is experienced as a rabbit if seen with rabbits, a bird if among birds.

Accommodation is the process by which schemata are changed to fit new information. If the discrepancy between the outside world and schemata is too great, then the schemata must change to accommodate the new information. Look *quickly* at the playing cards in Plate 12 and then turn away. (Do this before reading any more of this paragraph.) How many aces of spades are there? Now look again, but this time keep in mind that for this illustration, an ace of spades can be red or black. Now how many are there? The difference in the two answers was due to a change in "playing card schema," which in turn changed the perception of the future, of what you were prepared to see the second time. Normal "playing card schema" directs us to look for black spades only. When schemata change, we see things more "as they are." The same process holds in the evaluation of other people and even of scientific theories. Scientific "facts" are actually interpretations of events according to some theory. When events occur that cannot be explained by the theory, the theory is discarded and replaced with a new, more encompassing one.

Perceiving is a very complex act. It begins with the picking up of information from the environment. That information is simplified and organized, and we determine its meaning through assumptions and unconscious inferences. We then search out new information as the cycle of perceptual experience continues, and we come to know a stable, continuing, meaningful world.

FIGURE 6-16
Context and Ambiguity
Depending on its context, this ambiguous figure can be perceived as either a duck or a rabbit.

Perception involves determining the meaning of outside information, but how do we accomplish this? Do we receive, invent, or compute the external world? There are three major theoretical approaches to the process of perception. The *ecological approach* emphasizes the relevance of the external information in perception. A comparison is made between the perceiver and a radio set; they both "tune into" the environment and pick up information they are built to receive (Gibson, 1979). The *constructivist approach* emphasizes the role of the schemata in perception. This view likens the perceiver to a computer, making judgments and decisions about the external world according to past experience or "programs." Finally, the *computational approach* tries to analyze the mechanisms of how perception works.

Ecological Approach

The **ecological approach** emphasizes the richness of the information available to the perceiver. In this view perception is a direct function of stimulation (Michaels & Carello, 1981; Shepard, 1984). The information for color vision is *directly* present at the receptors, it stimulates the receptors, and we experience color. The proponents of this view say that information about distance, relative size, shape, and perspective are all similarly available to the human perceiver.

This process of human perception is similar to that of other organisms. The worm, the fish, the eagle, the tiger, and the human being all live in quite different environments. Different organisms have evolved differently in different environments, and each organism has evolved specialized perceptual systems to pick up information that is relevant to the organism. This part of the ecological approach is called *evolutionism* (Turvey & Shaw, 1979). This is an important point and deserves emphasis. According to the ecological view, the *environment is different for each organism,* thus the information that is appropriate for each organism is different to varying extents. Insofar as perception is successful, it responds directly, as does a radio, to the specific features of the world it is designed to pick up (Gibson, 1979).

See Chapter 2, section on Process of Adaptation and Evolution.

Constructivist Approach

This approach asserts that perception is a process of constructing a *representation* or model of the world (as an ordinary globe is fashioned to represent the earth). Hence, the information from the senses "sparks off" the creation of an image of what could have caused this sensation. Many of the classic demonstrations, such as the figure-ground illustrations (Figure 6-6) and the distorted room (Figure 6-13), support the view that perception involves an act of creation as well as "passive" reception of information. We process, infer, and analyze information until we arrive at a reliable solution, the percept. Of course, percepts must also be correct when checked out in the real world: they should keep us from bumping into walls or drinking boiling hot fluids.

Criticism of the Ecological and Constructivist Approaches

Each of these views emphasizes different aspects of the perceptual process. The ecological approach deals with the adaptive nature of perception. Like all other organisms, we have evolved in response to a physical environment. It is thus highly likely that we would possess some built-in systems for the reception of external information, things of importance to survival, like color. However, disappointingly few cells or neural networks have been found that pick up more organized and complex features of the world, like a monkey's paw cell (Marr, 1982).

Many psychologists feel that the view that *all* of perception is "direct" is too extreme, that it cannot account for actual human perception in the complex, invented environment (Hayes-Roth, 1980; Ullman, 1980). The ecological view does not account well for the fact that the same stimulus can mean different things to different people; the meaning of a police siren is not the same to a thief as it is to the victim. It also ignores the role of assumptions. The ecological approach, then, does not account for the elements of meaning that depend on interpretation.

The constructivist approach assumes that we must invent a stable world anew, each moment, and that this invention is the product of trial and error. This view, too, is extreme. It ignores evolutionary history, which causes an organism to select important information in the environment. Obviously, most organisms evolved to take advantage of their environment, and human beings did as well.

Perception involves both processes and much more than these viewpoints have allowed. The "primary" qualities of the environment are "picked up" directly by the perceiver. But even these must be interpreted. What is the *meaning* of the man approaching or of an object disappearing into the distance? We need not restrict ourselves to a one-track view of a complex process like perception; we are probably a little like a radio and a little like a computer, but neither satisfies the student looking for an idea of how it might work.

Deconstruction, Computation, and Reconstruction

The first two classical approaches to perception just described have dominated psychology for a long time. The argument continues between these approaches in large part because neither of them really answers in a satisfactory and scientific manner the question, "How does experience compose in the mind?"

While it might be useful to assume that humans must construct a model of the world, and that the world also "affords" information for us, the scientist is left with many questions. From what information does the mind do all this composing, constructing, and interpreting? Which elements of the outside world are transformed in the brain? It cannot be, for instance, that we "pick up" an entire post or leaf or cat somewhere in our heads, nor can we construct a perfect model based upon nothing inside the nervous system.

Marr's Theory

David Marr, among others, began to see the limits of these classical approaches and set out to analyze how perception actually happens: the mechanisms of the way the outside world is decomposed into elements that the nervous system can deal with, and later composed into the representations an organism needs to survive. It is obvious that some internal methodology has to *compute* the way the outside world gets represented inside; it can't be magic.

Thus, Marr began to develop a "computational" approach to visual perception. If this analysis also seems lacking in completeness, there are two reasons: it is at its beginnings, and Marr died a tragic and premature death before he could fully develop his theory.

According to Marr, vision cannot be understood by looking only at the cells of the sensory system (as we did in Chapter 5) or at the environment. It all has to work together: the sensors, the neural networks, the computer models of the networks (the approach he favored), the necessity of the organism, and the nature of the world.

He wrote in his book, *Vision:*

> It is not enough to be able to predict locally the results of psychophysical experiments. Nor is it enough even to be able to write computer programs that perform in the desired way. One has to do all these things at once and also be very aware of the additional level of explanation that I have called the level of computational theory. (Marr, 1982)

To carry out perception, the nervous system does not produce a picture that we "see" of the outside world within. Very few cells have been found like the "monkey paw" cell to account for perception. So another process must take place. How does it happen? While the computational approach is technical in nature, I will try to outline it here. Marr tried to assess the specific *process of deconstruction* in which a visual image is first broken down (decomposed) and then analyzed.

See Chapter 5, Figure 5-12.

In Marr's view the first operation of the break up of a visual stimulus is the "raw primal sketch" in which the general intensity changes are computed. The major points of change from light to dark, and the reverse, seem to be important, as well as the rough geometry of a scene (Figure 6-17). The places on a visual

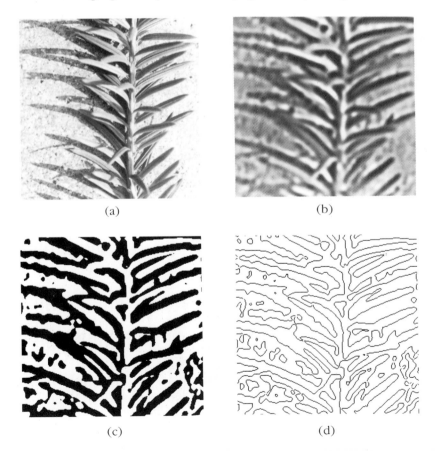

(a) (b)

(c) (d)

FIGURE 6-17
Decomposition
A visual scene such as this branch of a pine tree (a) is *decomposed* (or broken up) by the brain into its most basic elements: first, simple blurs (b) and then blacks and whites (c). The places where zero-crossings occur (where light goes to dark) are shown in the final figure (d). (From Marr, 1982)

scene where the light goes from positive to negative (that is, light to dark) are called *zero-crossings.* Registering these points is an important part of the deconstruction of a scene. Further analysis is done to produce what is called a two-dimensional sketch. For this, the zero-crossings are further analyzed, and other features such as edges, bars, and "blobs" are noted. This produces a sketch centered from the viewpoint of the viewer of the basic extent and orientation of the surfaces in its surroundings.

The progression of internal analysis follows from (1) the "raw primal sketch" to what Marr calls the "full primal sketch," to (2) the two-dimensional sketch, and finally (3) to a full three-dimensional representation. The details of all these steps are not important, but only that a similar procedure of analysis in the nervous system in some form of computations probably occurs.

If this theory is right, then there should be cells or networks of cells in the brain that respond to the relative size of two objects, to the convergence at the horizon, and other features of the natural world, just in the same way that cells in the visual system respond to colors and corners. If such networks are discovered, we would have a more precise understanding of what is *built in* and what is *built up* in the perceptual process.

The details are not worked out in Marr's system and won't be for a long time, but this kind of analysis goes a long way toward actually answering the questions about how experience comes to be composed by the nervous system. Marr's theory is only at its beginnings, but it is one that might some day have the power to bring together much of what is known about sensation and perception.

Neural Spatial Frequency Channels

Some confirmation of the computational approach has been found in studies of the way the nervous system responds to different frequencies of stimulation.

FIGURE 6-18
How Brain Cells Analyze Frequencies of Waves
Cells in the visual cortex analyze wave forms of particular wavelengths and frequencies. If the part of the cell marked in the diagram with a "+" coincides with the size of the wave, as in the two middle figures, it will fire, thus detecting that wave frequency.
(From Coran, Porac, & Ward, 1984)

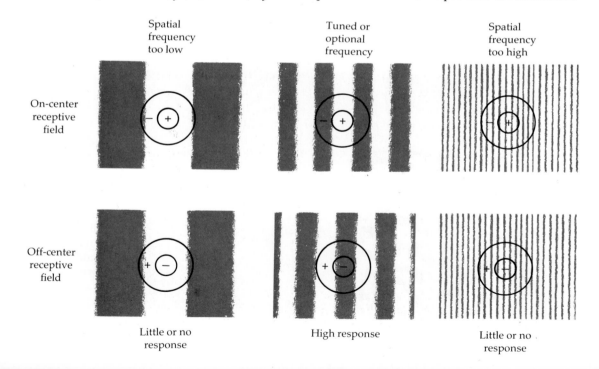

Spatial frequency too low   Tuned or optional frequency   Spatial frequency too high

On-center receptive field

Off-center receptive field

Little or no response   High response   Little or no response

For the zero-crossings to be computed, there must be cells which respond. The *spatial frequency* of any wave is how often it crosses zero, that is, how fast the waves move. High spatial frequency refers to a fast wave, which can be represented by a pattern of closely spaced stripes, while a low frequency pattern would have fewer stripes (Figure 6-18).

Now, how could the nervous system respond to this? Recall the circular receptive fields discussed in Chapter 5 (see Figure 5-12). Each has an *on* region, which when stimulated by light gives rise to increased firing, as well as an *off* field that decreases response to light. If we have an *on* receptive field that is exactly the size of the spatial frequency, then it will respond at its maximum. If the field is a bit larger, it will respond less, and if smaller, it will also respond less (Figure 6-18).

Thus, in much the same way as hearing, each frequency of zero-crossings could be easily identified by the neural networks, yielding much information for the "raw primal sketch" (Derrington & Fuchs, 1981; DeValois, Albrecht, & Thorell, 1982; Coren, Porac, & Ward, 1984).

Of course, just because these cells exist does not necessarily mean that they work this way. There is much speculation about this kind of neural analysis, which often causes hasty rejection of other worthwhile theories. However, Marr's viewpoint offers a welcome addition to the timeworn approaches to perception and might provide the system that finally cracks the neural codes of experience.

W e experience little change even though the sensory information reaching us changes radically. A building may appear as a small dot on the horizon or may completely fill our visual world. Yet we perceive the building to be the same size and shape regardless of our vantage point. The main purpose of all the receiving, organizing, and interpreting that goes on in the perceptual processes is to achieve **constancy,** a stable, constant world.

CONSTANCY: COMPUTING THE STABLE WORLD

Types of Constancy

You can easily demonstrate three kinds of perceptual constancies with your hand. Hold it with the palm facing toward you; then turn the palm away; then turn it so that you see the side of the hand. Even though the sensory impression of the hand is very different in each orientation, you perceive the same shape. That is *shape constancy.*

Now hold your hand close to your face; then hold it at arm's length. Even though the image on the retina is very different in each case, the hand seems to be the same size. That is *size constancy.* Now hold your hand under a lamp; then turn the lamp out. What color is your hand? You experience the hand as having the same underlying color and brightness, even though the information is different. That is *brightness* and *color constancy.*

Shape Constancy

The same object presented in very different aspects is experienced as the same. In Figure 6-19, a cup is seen from several different angles. Even though the actual image is different, you see the same cup. Changes in the slant of an object cause the retinal image to change, but not your experience of the object.

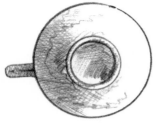

FIGURE 6-19
Shape Constancy
Like most objects we perceive, this cup, though viewed from various angles, is always recognized as a cup. Such changes of orientation may alter the retinal image, but not what is experienced.

Size Constancy

The size of the object can be accurately judged whether it is near or far away. As someone walks toward you from the horizon, that person's "image" on your retina can increase by more than 100 times (Figure 6-20), but you do not think the person is actually growing larger before your eyes.

Brightness and Color Constancy

Although the brightness and color of an object vary in different illuminations, they are perceived to be the same. The whiteness of the pages of this book will look about the same in sunlight as it does in an unlit room at twilight. In experiments on brightness constancy, people are asked to adjust a light source to match the brightness of a test object.

The subjects are shown a test object (A in Figure 6-21). The outer circle is assigned a brightness level of 200, the inner circle, 100. Then drawing B is presented; here the outer circle has a brightness level of 200. The subjects are asked to produce the gray that matches the inner circle of the test object (A). The subjects usually choose accurately, producing a gray with 100 units of brightness.

Then they are shown another drawing (C) in which the outer circle has a brightness of 100. Again, they are asked to match the gray of the inner circle to the

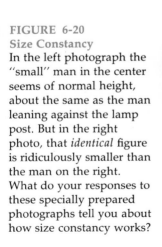

FIGURE 6-20
Size Constancy
In the left photograph the "small" man in the center seems of normal height, about the same as the man leaning against the lamp post. But in the right photo, that *identical* figure is ridiculously smaller than the man on the right. What do your responses to these specially prepared photographs tell you about how size constancy works?

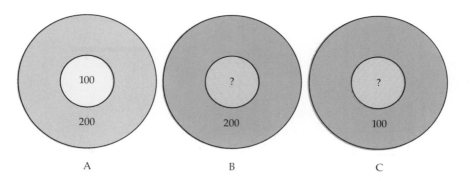

FIGURE 6-21
Brightness Constancy
As explained in the accompanying text, it is the relativity of brightness, not absolute values, that remain constant in perception.

test object (A). This time they are most likely to produce a gray with brightness level 50. This demonstrates that people do not perceive absolute values of brightness, but instead judge the *relative* brightness of objects to achieve a sense of constancy.

Likewise with color. A white car at sunset reflects the red color of the setting rays of the sun. But it appears white because we see it as relatively whiter than the surrounding environment.

Illusions

Perceptual mechanisms work so quickly and so well that we are unaware of the operations involved. Illusions are prized by psychologists not only for their fun, but because they reveal the normal processes of perception. Many illusions elicit a misapplication of the rules that govern constancy. Sometimes we may go from the process of "filling in the gaps" to "jumping to conclusions" as a consequence of the speed necessary to make quick judgments, and we often make mistakes.

Comparative Size

The central circle on the left of Figure 6-22A looks larger than the central circle on the right, although they are the same size. They are perceived incorrectly because the circle surrounded by larger circles is smaller relative to its context than the other central circle. Recall that we ordinarily perceive in a comparative way rather than according to absolute values. This is a basic principle of all cognitive processes, from perception to decision making (Rock, 1985).

Ponzo Illusion

Look at the two lines at the top of Figure 6-22B. You can see that they are the same length. Now look at the illustration below. Putting two converging lines next to these lines makes the top line seem longer. The rules of perspective that normally help us to judge size and distance accurately have in this case misled us.

Müller–Lyer Illusion

Although both lines in Figure 6-23A are equal in length, the figure with the arrows pointing toward its center looks longer than the figure with the arrows pointing toward its ends. The arrows may be taken as "depth cues" by the brain:

FIGURE 6-22
The Illusion of
Comparative Size
The central circle on the
left (A) only looks bigger
because it is surrounded by
smaller circles than the
identical central circle next
to it. Likewise, the upper
horizontal line in the lower
part of the right-hand
drawing (B) seems longer
no matter how you look at
it—even turning the book
sideways or upside down
does not destroy the
illusion. Even knowing
that the lines are the same
length cannot overcome
the power of the rules of
perspective and the
principle of comparative
values.

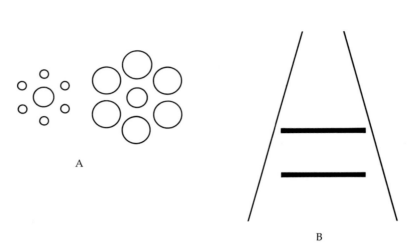

A

B

the arrows pointing inward probably cause us to judge the lines as farther away and thus longer (Gregory, 1973). Figure 6-23 is an example of this illusion in the world. The central vertical line of the corner in the left photo looks longer and appears to be farther away than that in the right photo. In this illusion, two schemata, "the appearance of things that recede into the background" and "things that approach and open up toward us," have probably been activated and misapplied.

FIGURE 6-23
The Müller–Lyer Illusion
Depth cues can alter our
perception of lines of
equal length. Because the
arrows in the sketch below
and the arrowlike
intersecting lines at the
corners in the photographs
make us judge the vertical
lines as closer or farther
away, we see each line as
shorter or longer than the
other.

A

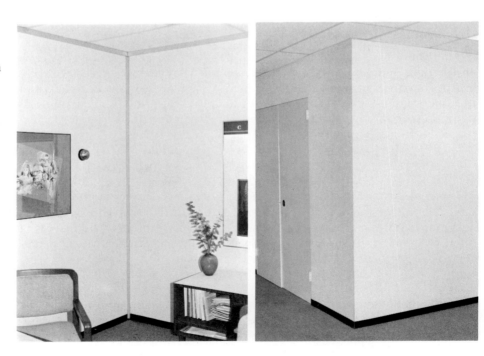

Controlled laboratory experiments can uncover some of the basic perceptual processes, but these processes normally operate in a much more complex and changeable environment than that of the laboratory. How these processes work in the real world is the subject of this section.

Adapting to the Environment

The optical image on the retina is upside down from what we "see." How is it that we see the world "right side up?" Where is the image reversed? The answer reveals an important principle of perception: the "image" is never actually turned right side up. We do not need such an image; all we need to adapt to the external world is consistent information. The image on the retina is, in fact, inverted and consistently obscured by blinks, blind spots, and blood vessels, yet we adapt to all of this.

Adaptation to Distortion

In the late nineteenth century the psychologist George Stratton reasoned that if perception is a process of adaptation to the environment, then it ought to be possible to learn to adapt to an entirely different arrangement of visual information, *as long as it is consistent.* To test this hypothesis, Stratton wore a special prism lens over one eye, so that he saw the world inverted 180°: the world was upside down, so that up-down and left-right were reversed. Stratton had great difficulty at first in doing even simple things like reaching for or grasping an object. He felt very dizzy when he walked, and he bumped into things. But within days he began to adapt. After only three days of wearing the inverted lens, he wrote, "Walking through the narrow spaces between pieces of furniture required much less art than hitherto. I could watch my hands as they wrote, without hesitating or becoming embarrassed thereby."

By the fifth day he could move around the house easily. On the seventh day he enjoyed his evening walk as usual. On the eighth day he removed the lens and wrote, "The reversal of everything from the order to which I had grown accustomed during the last week gave the scene a surprisingly bewildering air which lasted for several hours." Once Stratton had adapted to the new relationship between information and perception, it took some time to unlearn it.

Stratton wrote (1896) of his results:

> The different sense-perceptions, whatever may be the ultimate course of their extension, are organized into one harmonious spatial system. *The harmony is found to consist in having outer experiences meet our expectations.* [Italics added for emphasis.]

More than 60 years later, Ivo Köhler conducted further experiments on the effects of optical rearrangement. His observers wore various kinds of distorting lenses for weeks. At first they all had great difficulty in seeing the world. But in a few weeks they had adapted. One of Köhler's subjects was able to ski while wearing distorting lenses! People can also adapt to color distortions. In another of Köhler's demonstrations, his subjects wore glasses in which one lens was green and one red. Within a few hours they sensed no difference in color between the lenses (Köhler, 1962).

Is Perception Innate or Learned?

Suppose a blind person were suddenly able to see after years of blindness. What would he or she experience? The question of what is innate and what is learned in perception has been studied in many ways, using children, people from various cultures, blind people, and even a person born blind who had an operation to restore sight.

We come into the world with many abilities that enable us to perceive right away. Children prefer to look at faces. They are disturbed when the facial elements are rearranged. They seem to be born with, at the very least, the preference to perceive other human beings before other things in the world. (See Chapter 3, Figure 3-8.) The newborn's ability to imitate others, to discriminate between the mother's odor and that of other women, to turn toward sounds, as well as other abilities all point to the likelihood of innate perceptual abilities.

Visual Cliff

Some perceptual abilities are probably innate but only develop with maturation. Recall that the "world" of the infant or young child is narrow, a very limited physical and social environment. Eleanor Gibson established that depth perception seems to develop only along with a baby's ability to move around.

One day, Gibson was having a picnic on the rim of the Grand Canyon when she began to wonder if a baby would perceive the danger of the cliff or blithely ignore it and fall off. To test this question, she constructed an apparatus in her laboratory that she called the "visual cliff" (Figure 6-24).

FIGURE 6-24
Visual Cliff
Babies will not crawl over a "cliff" onto a solid glass surface below which they can see a lower surface to which it appears they could fall. Both crawling infants and young animals seem able to perceive depth and its potential dangers.
(After Gibson & Walk, 1960)

The **visual cliff** is the effect created by two surfaces under glass, both of which have a checkerboard pattern. One is directly underneath the glass, the other is several feet below. Another patterned board is placed on the glass top along the "break" between the upper and lower checkerboard surfaces, that is, at the "cliff's edge." If babies old enough to crawl are placed on this board, they will not crawl to their mothers if it means "falling" to the lower surface, even though the glass top is solid and perfectly safe. The babies will leave the center board only if they can crawl across what is perceived by them to be a safe surface (Gibson & Walk, 1960).

Recovery from Blindness

What would be the visual experience of a person who had been born blind but was suddenly able to see? Richard Gregory had the good fortune to study such a case. At 52 a man called S. B., blind from birth, had a successful corneal transplant. When the bandages were removed, he heard the voice of the surgeon, turned to look at him, and saw nothing but a blur. Within a few days his sight had improved and he could walk around the hospital corridors without touching the walls and could tell time from a wall clock. Even so, he could not see the world as crisply as a normally sighted person does. He was, however, able almost immediately to recognize objects for which he had already developed an "internal picture" through touch (Gregory, 1973).

He was surprised by the appearance of the moon. He could see and draw objects that he had known previously by touch, but had difficulty with those objects that he had not had the opportunity to touch while blind. His drawings of a London bus even a year after the operation omitted the front of the bus, which he had never touched. Windows and wheels, however, were drawn in pretty fair detail right from the beginning (Figure 6-25). When Gregory showed S. B. a lathe, which was a tool S. B. was experienced in using, he had no idea what it was. Then S. B. was asked to touch a lathe; he closed his eyes, examined it thoroughly with his hand, and said, "Now that I have felt, it I can see." Although S. B. had been deprived of sight, he had not been deprived of perception.

We began this book with the story of "The Elephant in the Dark." In a study that echoes this story, Kennedy gave blind children pictures of parts of an

FIGURE 6-25
Blindness and Perception Regaining his sight after an operation did not instantly enable the man who drew these pictures to perceive the world as it is. Both the left-hand drawing, done 48 days after the operation, and the other, done a year later, show more detail for parts of the bus the man used — and especially touched — while he was blind. His perceptions from when he was blind still influenced his experience of the world.

FIGURE 6-26
Drawings by Blind People
The crossed fingers (top), a runner (middle), and a boy (bottom) were drawn by people blind from birth, yet they show awareness of perspective and even of such artistic subtleties as the need to foreshorten one leg of a running person.

SEEING WITHOUT EYES

What do blind people think the world looks like? Are their mental images of people and things very different from those of sighted people? Over the past 10 years John Kennedy has conducted experiments that begin to answer these questions. He asked people, blind since birth, to draw pictures. At first you might think that was a ridiculous request; most of the blind people thought it was. A picture is, after all, a two-dimensional representation of a three-dimensional object, and the blind sense their world primarily through touch, a strictly three-dimensional experience. Kennedy gave each subject a plastic sheet that makes a raised line when a ballpoint pen is moved across it. He first asked them to draw simple objects—a cup, a hand, a table—and later, more complicated scenes (Figure 6-26).

To his surprise, Kennedy found that the blind realized almost immediately that some aspects of reality must be sacrificed in a drawing. You cannot draw a cup from all sides at once; a point of view must be selected. The blind artists devised ways to convey their meaning. Their solutions were easily understood by sighted people either at a glance or with brief captions, such as, "This is how it would look from the side." What most

surprised Kennedy was that his blind artists understood perspective (Kennedy, 1974).

There is more to seeing than meets the eye, and more to visual perception than sight. Although we rarely *experience* the difference, sensation and perception are not the same. Perception fills in the gaps left by incomplete sensory information. We recognize a cup even though we see only one side; we are not likely to check for a bottom before pouring coffee. The properties of weight, size, texture, form, function, and color all figure into the final perception of what a thing is. Through touch, a blind person can gain almost all the same information as a sighted person.

In fact, the sense of touch appears to be part of the visual perceptual system. It definitely is for blind people. Carter Collins and his colleagues on the Tactile Sensory Replacement (TSR) project at the Smith–Kettlewell Institute of Visual Sciences in San Francisco have devised a machine that capitalizes on a blind person's fine-tuned sense of touch. The machine impresses "televised" images onto the skin using electrical stimulation (Figure 6-27). The felt pattern of the image allows individuals to recognize objects in front of them. In fact, blind people

elephant (the lines in the pictures were raised, in relief, so they could be felt). In 39 out of 41 cases the children recognized that together the pieces made up a picture of an elephant. These children lacked *sight,* but not perception; the wise men in the story had sight, but not perception.

Cultural Effects on Perception

Although we appear to have some innate perceptual abilities, a completely pre-wired, built-in perceptual system seems unlikely. Humans live in all types of environments in the world and have lived in many cultures. It is almost certain that much perceptual experience is learned. Pygmies of the Congo of Africa dwell primarily in dense forest and thus rarely see across large distances. As a result they do not develop as strong a concept of size constancy as we do. Colin Turnbull, an anthropologist who studied pygmies, once took his pygmy guide on a trip out of the forest. As they were crossing a wide plain, they saw a herd of buffalo in the distance.

have been able to "see" and work with instruments as precise as an oscilloscope, using the TSR device.

The reason Collins and his co-workers chose touch instead of another sense is that of all senses, touch is the closest to vision. Collins says:

No matter how acute your hearing is, it is a cue for location and distance only—not forms. But the thing about vision and touch is that they are both three-dimensional systems. What you see in front of you is essentially a frame on which patterns of light and shadow are played. You see in three dimensions because you move your neck and eyes and you have binocular vision. When a person wears the TSR vest, the camera moves just as the eyes do in sighted people.

Still I could not understand how such representations might actually "look." So I went to the Institute and tried it myself. I sat blindfolded in the chair, the cones cold against my back. At first I felt only formless waves of sensation. Collins said he was just waving his hand in front of me so that I could get used to the feelings. Suddenly I felt, or saw, I wasn't sure which, a black triangle in the lower left corner of a square. The sensation was

hard to get a fix on. I felt vibrations on my back, but the triangle appeared in a square frame in my head. Although there was no color, there were light and dark areas. If you close your eyes and face a strong light or the sun and pass an object in front of your eyes, a difference appears in the darkness. That difference is approximately what I saw. The TSR image was fuzzy at first, but within 10 minutes of sitting in the chair it became clearer. When Collins confirmed that he was indeed holding a triangle, it became clearer still.

For me, believing that there is a difference between sensation and perception has always required an enormous leap of faith. It is hard to believe that I do not see with my eyes or hear with my ears. Although we are taught that there is a difference between sensation and perception, at the TSR lab I *experienced* the difference for the first time. The sensation was on my back, the perception was in my head. Feeling is believing.

(This report was researched and written by Nancy Hechinger, Institute for the Study of Human Knowledge, especially for this textbook.)

FIGURE 6-27
The Tactile Sensory Replacement Device that enables blind people to "see" by television-guided electrical stimulation of their skin.

FIGURE 6-28
Culture and Perception
People who live in round houses do not experience the Müller–Lyer illusion (Figure 6-23) as strongly as people who live in square houses.

Kenge looked over the plain and down to a herd of buffalo some miles away. He asked me what kind of insects they were, and I told him buffalo, twice as big as the forest buffalo known to him. He laughed loudly and told me not to tell him such stupid stories. . . . We got into the car and drove down to where the animals were grazing. He watched them getting larger and larger, and though he was as courageous as any pygmy, he moved over and sat close to me and muttered that it was witchcraft. . . . When he realized they were real buffalo he was no longer afraid, but what puzzled him was why they had been so small, and whether they had really been small and suddenly grown larger or whether it had been some kind of trickery. (Turnbull, 1961)

People from different cultures may not be "fooled" by the same optical tricks because they do not share the same schemata. Illusions such as the Müller–Lyer and the Ponzo illusions depend to a certain extent on living in a world in which right angles and straight lines predominate. Our world is a "carpentered world." By contrast, some African tribes, such as the Zulus, live in round huts with round doors (Figure 6-28) and plough their fields in circles; they do not experience the

Müller–Lyer illusion as strongly as we do (Segal, Campbell, & Herskovits, 1963).

Look at Figure 6-29. Is the hunter closer to the baboon or the rhinoceros? The baboon. However, many Africans, who do not share Western perspective in drawing and do not make the same assumptions we make regarding the representation of three dimensions, answer that the rhinoceros is closer. This seems odd to us. However, if you look at the drawing as it is, in two dimensions, the rhinoceros *is* closer to the hunter.

The conventions for representing three dimensions on a two-dimensional surface can lead to some interesting confusions. Look at the "impossible" object in Figure 6-30, sometimes called the Devil's tuning fork, and try to draw it from memory. The figure itself is obviously not impossible — after all, it's there on the page. But most Western people cannot reproduce the drawing because we interpret it as an object that could not exist in three dimensions. It is our *interpretation*, not the figure itself, that is impossible. Schemata for translating two-dimensional drawings into three-dimensional figures prevent us from seeing the figure as it is. Africans who do not share these conventions have little difficulty in reproducing this figure from memory (Deregowski, 1987).

Perception of Space

How do we perceive objects and events in space? How do we know when an object is far away from us? In 1790 Bishop George Berkeley initiated the modern argument over space perception. He stated that information regarding distance must be inferred. "We cannot sense distance in and of itself," he wrote. According to this view, distance must be constructed from a set of cues, such as the relative

FIGURE 6-29
Cultural Assumptions and Three Dimensionality
Most of us would say the hunter is closer to the baboon, while many Africans would say the rhinoceros is closer.
(After Hudson, 1962)

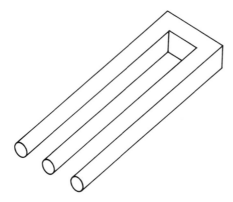

FIGURE 6-30
The Devil's Tuning Fork

size of an object. This view is now thought to be incorrect. Recent research has shown that there is a great amount of distance information directly available to the perceiver.

Internal Cues to Distance

To focus the lens of a camera you adjust the angle at which incoming light is bent and falls on the film. You do this so that the object of interest will be clear and in focus. As a result, things in front of or behind the object will be less clear.

The eye works in a similar way. When we look at objects at different distances, contractions of the ciliary muscles cause the width of the lens to change. This change is called **ocular accommodation.** To demonstrate this for yourself, hold a pen about 10 inches in front of your face. Choose a distant object to look at. When you focus on the far object, the pen becomes blurred. When you focus on the pen, the background becomes blurred. Changes in the width of the lens are monitored by the brain and coupled with other information to develop distance information. This other information includes the convergence of the eyes (the eyes are turned more sharply inward as they look as closer objects) and the difference between the information reaching the left versus right eye and ear.

Binocular Disparity. Because the eyes are in different locations in the head, each eye receives slightly different information (Figure 6-31). This difference in information—**binocular disparity**—increases the closer we get to something

What the
left eye
sees

What both
eyes see
together

What the
right eye
sees

FIGURE 6-31
Binocular Disparity

we are looking at. The difference in the left and right images is analyzed by the brain to provide information on distance (Coren, Porac, & Ward, 1984).

Binaural Disparity. Likewise, the difference in location of the two ears also provides us with distance information. A sound directly in front of us strikes both ears at the same time; one to the left strikes the left ear before the right. Also, since sound is composed of physical pressure waves, the wave can strike the two ears at different points in its cycle, producing **binaural disparity.** This information, too, is used to judge distance (Kaufman, 1974).

External Cues to Distance: Stationary Cues

A great amount of information in the external environment contributes to the perception of distance. These "cues" include interposition, perspective, size, texture gradient, and relative brightness.

Interposition. Because most objects are not transparent, an object in front of another will block part of the one behind. This is called **interposition.** In most cases interposition is a simple, reliable, and unambiguous cue to depth, so much so that when the cues are unusual and misleading, the rule of interposition governs judgment. In Figure 6-32, the balloon that blocks parts of those behind is perceived as the closest one. In looking at Figure 6-33 you probably assumed, like most subjects in laboratory experiments, that the small playing card was in front of the large card.

Perspective. When you look at a long stretch on a road or railroad tracks, the parallel lines seem to converge on the horizon. This apparent convergence is called **perspective.** Because it is a powerful cue for judging distance, it is crucial in two-dimensional representations of three dimensions. Artists manipulate perspective to create different impressions and evoke different emotions. The exaggerated perspective in Van Gogh's *Hospital Corridor* expresses tension and a

FIGURE 6-32
Interposition
The largest balloon appears closest because of its size and also because it blocks parts of balloons behind it.

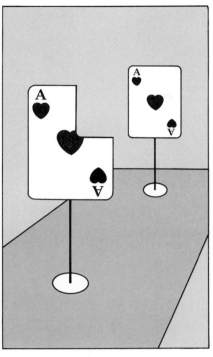

FIGURE 6-33
Interposition Assumed
The normal assumption is that the smaller playing card is in front of the larger one (left) because interposition provides a perceptual cue. But the picture on the right shows the same scene from a different angle, revealing that this assumption can be wrong and our perception confounded by interposition used as a misleading cue.

closed-in, cramped feeling (Figure 6-34, top). M. C. Escher uses perspective and other depth cues to create an "impossible" world in which water runs uphill (Figure 6-34, bottom).

Size. The size of objects on the retina gets smaller as objects recede into the distance. These size variables are valuable depth cues.

Brightness. The closer an object is, the brighter it appears. The amount of light from distant objects that hits the eyes is less because particles in the eye diffuse the intensity of light. In the absence of other cues, the brighter of the two objects will be judged to be closer (Figure 6-35).

Texture Gradient. As you look over a uniform surface, like a pebbled beach or grassy field, the *density* of the texture increases with distance (Figure 6-36). A change in density, or **texture gradient,** can also signal a change in the angle of the surface (Figure 6-37). Consequently, information about distance may be directly available to the perceiver.

Movement Cues to Distance

However, as we move around the world, the stimulus information changes. This change of information gives us additional and important information about distance.

Motion Parallax. When you look out the window of a moving car, stationary objects outside the car appear to move. However, objects at varying distances move in different directions at different speeds. Some objects in the far distance

FIGURE 6-34
The Power of Perspective
Perspective is normally used to judge distance, but artists also rely on it to make their paintings more evocative. Van Gogh's *Hospital Corridor* (top) uses perspective to create a constricting view, capturing his feelings about the place. Escher's *Waterfall* (bottom) shows the artist's habit of using perspective and other depth cues to fashion scenes in which the laws of nature are playfully violated.

FIGURE 6-35
Brightness as a Depth Cue
(Top, left) The brighter, sunlit building here appears closer even though it is further away.

FIGURE 6-36
Texture Gradients as Depth Cues
(Top, right) Because the density of the texture of a uniform surface increases with distance, such texture gradients can help you judge distance.

FIGURE 6-37
Changes in Texture Gradient
(Bottom) Changes in the angle, tilt, or level of an otherwise uniform surface (here due to an earthquake) change the density of texture, providing a texture gradient cue to depth.

FIGURE 6-38
Optical Expansion — the Looming Effect
The fact that objects you approach or that are approaching you appear to be moving faster when closer than when farther away gives you cues to speed of approach, angle of approach, and relative distance between objects in the scene affected by optical expansion.

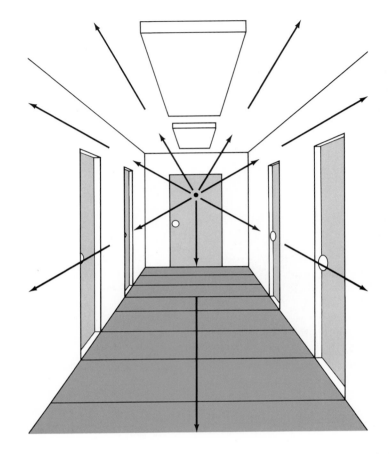

seem to move in the same direction — the moon may even appear to be following you. Objects quite close, however, move in the opposite direction. This difference in movement is called **motion parallax.**

Optical Expansion.   As you approach a scene, close objects appear to be moving toward you faster than those far away (Figure 6-38). This apparent difference —**optical expansion,** or the "looming effect" — provides information on how fast you are approaching, at what angle, and the relative distances of objects in the scene.

A Note on Space

Although many sources of spatial information are available to us, we probably use only some of them at any given time. It is probably only when the environment is extremely limited, as in the case of Kenge, the pygmy, that we do not learn all the relevant cues. Berkeley probably underestimated our ability to "pick up" the information in the environment that is available to us (Gibson, 1979).

Experience of Time

Time is an invisible dimension that underlies perceptual experience. Perceptual, intellectual, and emotional events take place in time. We may feel these events passing quickly or dragging on. We say we have a "sense" of time, but there is no actual sensory organ (like the eye) for the experience of time. Time is not a physical stimulus in the external world, like the wavelength of light, which can be isolated and measured by scientific analysis.

Kinds of Time

We experience two kinds of time: the time that is *now* and the time that has *passed.*

Time That Is Now — The Present.   The time that is experienced as the present is literally gone the moment you speak of it. As one anonymous poet wrote, "The moment of which I speak is already far away." Generally, however, present time varies, depending on perspective. "Now" can be this moment, this day, or this year.

Time That Has Passed — Duration.   The experience of time passing is based primarily on the perception of the duration of events. Albert Einstein once explained his theory of relativity this way: "When you sit with a pretty girl for two hours, it seems like two minutes; when you sit on a hot stove for two minutes, it seems like two hours. That's relativity." Thus, duration is perceived according to the nature of the events taking place. Enjoyable activity seems to go by quickly. Judgment of duration, however, is also based on the number of things that occur during that time. The fewer the number of events in a given time, the shorter it will seem when you remember it later (Ornstein, 1969). People who have taken mind-stimulating drugs (like LSD) report later that time seems to be expanded under the drug. If you wait an hour with nothing to do, it may seem like an eternity while you are waiting, but that hour will probably disappear from memory and in retrospect seem quite short.

Storage Space and Time

The more that is remembered of a given situation, the longer it seems. A piece of music that contains 40 sounds per minute is experienced as shorter than one with 80 per minute (Ornstein, 1969). In one study, people were given 30 seconds to look at Figure 6-39A; then they were given 30 seconds to look at Figure 6-39B. Later they were asked which time period was longer. The subjects estimated that the time spent looking at the more complicated figure (B) was 20 percent longer that the time looking at the simple figure (A).

Ultimately, the sense of time is constructed out of memory of experience. Periods of time are judged by how much is remembered about them, that is, how much **storage space** they take up. If you are on an interesting vacation, each day is filled with new experiences, people, and places. At the end of a couple of weeks, it is as if you have been on vacation forever. When you return home, at first your memories and descriptions of the experience are quite complex: "We went to Waikiki Beach, ate mahi-mahi in a famous restaurant, listened to Dorman's orchestra, traveled by sailboat to Maui, stayed in a little cottage. . . ." Later memory may change. It may be simply, "I went to Hawaii for two weeks last year and had a great time." In a study that bears on this, people perceived and remembered an interval containing a successful event as shorter than one with a failure (Harton, 1938). Increased organization and automatization decrease the storage space

FIGURE 6-39
Time Worth Remembering
The same amount of time spent looking at the simpler pattern (A) will be recalled as shorter than the same period spent contemplating the more interesting figure (B). The effect holds true for experiences of all kinds.
(After Ornstein, 1969)

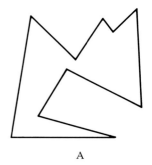

A

B

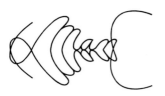

FIGURE 6-40A
Time and Memory
Experiment
Study this figure for a few
moments then cover it.
Now try to draw it from
memory (do this *before* you
look at the next page).
Difficult, isn't it?

DECOMPOSITION, COMPOSITION, AND THE MODEL OF THE WORLD

required and the time needed to recall a memory. Automatic experiences, such as driving an automobile over familiar terrain, seem shorter than the same amount of time in unfamiliar territory.

I conducted an experiment on the effect of organizing memory on the experience of time. Look at Figure 6-40A. Before reading on or turning the page to look at Figure 6-40B, try to describe it. Groups of subjects were also asked to look at and describe this figure. One group was given no organizing principle, the second group was told the figure was the word *Man* written on top of its mirror image, and the third group was told that it was an insect. Those who were told it was the word *Man* were able to reconstruct it much faster than the other two groups. The more organized the figure was in memory, the easier and faster it was described, in other words, the experience of duration shortened. Time experience, then, seems to be based on how much we remember and how that memory is organized (Ornstein, 1969).

This chapter began with what might have seemed an odd question: how does experience *compose* in the mind? Why, you might have asked, would "experience" be composed? Our experience of the world seems so stable and continuous: rich with color, shapes, thoughts, and ideas. The house we live in is the same from day to day; friends are the same; the world of colors, lights, and sounds goes on; the robins come back every year; the smell of autumn is the same.

But the analysis of brain processes, perception, and sensation shows that the human experience of a stable outside world is a *consistent illusion that the brain creates*. It is an illusion that was "designed" long before we arrived on earth for the purpose of biological survival. The illusion begins at the first neuron. Our senses grab only a little of reality; the eye takes in one-trillionth of the energy that reaches it, the ear similarly. So, experience of the world as stable is so only because of the way the brain is organized, not because of the way the world is.

As the primitive brain of lower organisms evolved throughout evolutionary time, a strategy gradually emerged. The nervous system evolved to radically reduce and limit the information transmitted to the early brain. Otherwise the brain would have been flooded with information. It would not have "known" which changes in the environment were relevant and which were not, that is, which represented threats to survival of the organism.

Human beings have inherited this ability of the brain. From a trickle of sensory information, a simplified model of the world is constructed. The brain then monitors the sensory input to scan for information that doesn't fit the model so that it can signal a significant change or threat to which it must react. Thus, the nervous system organizes information so that a few actions, the appropriate actions, can take place. Much of the intricate network of receptors, ganglia, and analysis cells in the cortex serve to simplify. Our senses select only a few meaningful elements from all the stimuli that reach us, organize them into the most likely occurrence, and remember only a small organized sample of what has occurred.

We select the items of highest priority to us at any given time. They may be real emergencies, such as "the house is on fire!" Some may be immediate concerns, such as "watch that car in the left lane, it's weaving all over the road." Some may be chronic concerns, such as earning enough money, while some may be simply new events, such as a person entering the room.

At each step in the pathway from sensory nerve cell to the brain the world becomes more organized and simplified in the mind. A network of schemata is developed to represent the world so that the external world, so chaotic and changing, becomes stable, simplified, and seemingly coherent in the mind. Instead of thousands of reflecting bits of glass, gray stone, scores of doors opening and closing, many high ceilings, and so on, we perceive *one* building. The parts fit together as a coherent whole.

The information from the senses is then somehow decomposed, by a process probably similar to that described by Marr, then further analyzed until an adequate representation is composed.

These percepts are useful insofar as they correspond closely enough with reality that they help us survive. But, as difficult as it is to imagine, they are not really a *complete* portrait of the outside world, much more than the frog's four programs completely represent the outside world.

FIGURE 6-40B
This figure contains the same basic elements as Figure 6-40A only moved further apart so that the organizing principle emerges. It now would be much easier and faster to draw from memory.

---

1. The distinction between sensation and perception lies in *meaning*. Disconnected and chaotic sensory impressions are *organized* by the processes of perception into a meaningful whole. Another important aspect of perceptual analysis is interpretation, which is the judgment of the most likely phenomena that are behind the observed stimuli. In any situation, we tend to experience the simplest meaningful organization of the stimuli registered.

2. The complex process of perception requires many separate operations "behind the scenes" so that the simple "performance" on the "stage" is experienced. The perceptual process involves *picking up* information about the world, *organizing* it, and making *inferences* about the environment in a *continuous cycle*.

3. Ecological psychologists have extensively analyzed two characteristics of the environment: (1) *Affordance*. Each object in the environment offers, or *affords*, a rich source of information available to be perceived. (2) *Invariance*. The external environment contains many different objects, each one offering the perceiver certain *invariant* features. A fence post presents unchanging information about itself as we walk around it, including its right angles and that it is perpendicular to the earth.

4. The concept that there are certain rules that *organize* our perceptual experience is the basis of the gestalt school of psychology. Four principles of organization are figure-ground, proximity, similarity, and good continuation.

5. An important aspect of perception is that we go *beyond* the information given, that we *interpret* the sensory information offered to us. This interpretation is performed in *unconscious inferences*. A person may see a little splotch of red in the distance and register that it is a car belonging to a friend. The car being there at that time could in turn mean that the friend is home from school early or is sick. Needs and values are important determinants of inferences. When shown a certain coin, children from poor families experienced it as larger than did children of rich families.

SUMMARY

6. Perception operates in a cycle—a concept proposed by Neisser. Three factors are involved in the *perceptual cycle*. First, because the *schemata* we already possess allow us to perceive things as connected to one another, we can act in an organized way. Schemata not only link past experience with present events, they also direct discovery of the world. Second, as we move through the world, the information we receive is changed by movements and exploration. Third, the sensory information provided by these exploratory movements modifies the view of the world produced by the brain, which, in turn changes the schemata. New movements are directed and exploration begins again. This perceptual cycle is a description of how experience continually changes and becomes refined.

7. Two important theories of perception concern whether we directly *receive* or *invent* the external world. The *ecological approach* emphasizes that there is an enormous amount of information directly available to the perceiver. Information for color vision, for example, is directly present at the receptors, as is the information for corners, edges, lines, and so on. Similarly, information for distance, relative size, shape, and perspective is all directly available to the human perceiver.

8. The second theory is the *constructivist approach* which asserts that because sensory information reaching the brain is incomplete and disorganized, perception must be a process of constructing a representation or model of the world. In this view, the information we receive from the sensors "sparks off" the creation of an image of what might have caused this sensation.

9. The constructivist view has been dominant in psychology for many decades but is now being challenged by the ecological approach. Perception most likely involves both processes. Perhaps some of the basic or primary qualities of the environment are directly picked up by the perceiver; however, these still need to be interpreted, probably by the processes described in the constructivist approach.

10. The two classic approaches don't answer how experience composes in the mind. Marr developed a *computational approach* to visual perception to analyze how the outside world is *decomposed* into elements the nervous system can deal with, which are later composed into the kinds of experiences an organism needs to have to survive. Confirmation of the computational approach has been found in *spatial frequency* analysis cells. This is a beginning approach, whose importance lies in integrating many of the previous attempts at understanding perception.

11. An important result of all the perceptual processes is how little change we experience, even though the sensory information reaching us changes radically. The main purpose of the receiving, organizing, and interpreting processes is to achieve a stable, *constant* world. Several forms of constancy have been described. In *shape* constancy the same form seen from different angles is still seen as the same shape. In *size* constancy one perceives an object as being the same size no matter what the image on the retina is. In *brightness* and *color* constancy the luminance and saturation of an object may vary in different lighting, but they are still perceived to be the same.

12. The question of whether perception is innate or learned has been studied using children from various cultures, blind people, and even a person born blind who had an operation to restore sight. The findings show that there are some features, such as the ability to distinguish a figure from the background, that seem to be built into the perceptual process at birth, while other, more specific features of the environment seem to be learned.

13. There are many internal and external cues governing space perception. Among them are binocular and binaural disparity, interposition, perspective, size, brightness, texture gradient, and the cues provided by movement.

14. Time is an invisible dimension that underlies perceptual experience. We experience both time that is *now* and time that has *passed* (duration). Duration is perceived according to the nature and number of events taking place. Time experience is based on how much we remember (storage space) and on how that memory is organized.

15. We have a large innate ability to pick up information in the environment. It is probably only when the environment is extremely limited that we do not learn all the relevant cues that we need.

TERMS AND CONCEPTS

accommodation
affordance
assimilation
assumptions
binaural disparity
binocular disparity
computational approach
constancy
constructivist approach
deconstruction
ecological approach
gestalt
illusions
interposition
interpretation
invariance

Köhler
Marr
motion parallax
ocular accommodation
optical expansion
perceptual cycle
perceptual organization
prototypes
representation
simplicity
storage space
Stratton
tactile sensory replacement
texture gradient
unconscious inference
visual cliff

SUGGESTIONS FOR FURTHER READING

Freeman, N., & Cox, C. (1986). *Visual order.* Boston: Cambridge: University Press.

One approach to how pictures get represented in the mind. Not an easy read, but worth considering.

Marr, D. (1982). *Vision.* New York: W. H. Freeman.

The beginnings of the computational approach to perception, to be continued by Marr's successors, owing to his tragic early death.

Michaels, C. F., & Carello, C. (1981). *Direct perception.* Englewood Cliffs, NJ: Prentice-Hall.

A recent outline of the emerging ecological viewpoint in perception.

Rock, I. (1985). *Perception.* New York: Scientific American.

Well-illustrated and compelling. A good treatment of perception as traditionally understood.

Chapter *7*

The Varieties of Consciousness

Consciousness is the "front page" of the mind.

It is compiled like a newspaper: what is most important is on the front page. This includes immediate crises, such as a breakdown in transportation or a terrorist attack, or new and unexpected situations that require action, such as a flood or a death. Consider the sequence of headlines just before, during, and after the explosion of the space shuttle in 1986. One important event such as this can move everything else off the front page. Countless ordinary events each day never make the headlines. We would never see the headline "75 Million Pleasant Dinners Served Last Evening." Instead, newspaper editors who select the front page ask, Is it unexpected? Is it important? Is it new? Is it a threat?

A similar process goes on in the mind. Numerous stimuli are filtered out by the senses and then organized and simplified by perception. What is in consciousness at any given moment are the high priority items most needing action: emergencies, threats to safety, and immediate concerns, such as "watch that car weaving into your lane." Some may be chronic concerns, such as solving an intellectual problem, and some may be new events, such as a person entering the room.

Since situations and needs for action are constantly changing, our consciousness changes continually within a day: from sleeping and dreaming to "borderline" states upon awakening; from tiredness to excitement; from daydreaming to directed thinking. These daily alterations in consciousness are much more extreme than we normally realize.

It is possible to deliberately alter consciousness. Techniques for doing so have been developed in almost every culture. Meditation turns down the normally active consciousness and allows a more receptive, inward state to emerge. Under hypnosis, the control of consciousness is given over to another. A person in hypnosis can withstand normally intolerable levels of pain and can uncover lost memories. Mind-altering drugs, such as LSD and cocaine, also affect consciousness by altering the neurotransmitters of the brain.

William James, in a now classic passage, described the potential varieties of consciousness:

> Our normal waking consciousness, rational consciousness as we call it, is but one special type of consciousness, whilst all about it, parted from it by the filmiest of screens there lie potential forms of consciousness entirely different. We may go through life without suspecting their existence; but apply the requisite stimulus, and at a touch they are there in all their completeness, definite types of mentality which probably somewhere have their field of application and adaptation. No account of the universe in its totality can be final which leaves these other forms of consciousness quite disregarded. How to regard them is the question—for

William James
(1842–1910)

they may determine attitudes though they cannot furnish formulas, and open a region though they fail to give a map. At any rate, they forbid a premature closing of our accounts with reality. (James, 1890)

Principles

Automatization

New information enters consciousness because well-learned actions become automatized. **Automatization** takes place when a series of movements or actions are repeated, as in writing a set of letters to make a word. Automatization occurs in

FIGURE 7-1
Automatization
The division of attention to deal simultaneously with a variety of stimuli requires both conscious processing and automatization, or automatic processing.

FIGURE 7-2
Automatization of
Complex Tasks
Activities such as playing a
musical instrument,
assembling devices,
driving a car, or flying an
airplane involve
automatization that
permits you to accomplish
such demanding routine
tasks without really
thinking or worrying about
how you are performing
the many separate actions
that go into accomplishing
these tasks.

difficult skills that are practiced or repeated, such as sports and musical activities (Figures 7-1 and 7-2). Familiar actions are accomplished "without thinking," without much involvement of consciousness, leaving us free to notice new events (Wolman & Ullman, 1986).

Behold a baby learning to walk. Notice how he or she concentrates on the movements required. Eventually, the complex coordination involved in walking is automatized. Do you remember how it was when you first learned to drive a car? "Let's see. Press the left foot down on the clutch. Move the stick shift into first gear. Let the left foot off the clutch. Press on the gas with the right foot." While learning to operate a car it is very hard to think about anything else — including driving somewhere! But once the movements become automatized, you can carry on a conversation, sing, or admire the scenery without being conscious of operating the car. Shifting gears, even the total activity of driving, becomes automatized.

Adaptation, Selection, and Egocentrism

Consciousness is adaptive in that it enables us to be flexible enough to initiate the correct action at the correct moment. It is selective in that it focuses on the item with the highest priority for survival at any given moment. Consciousness is egocentric because it is geared to individual needs.

Functions of Consciousness

The functions of consciousness differ among animals. A frog sees only a few selected features of the physical world and responds automatically to them. A cat can respond to many more features of the world, but it lacks much of human flexibility.

In addition to simplifying and selecting information, consciousness guides and oversees actions. At any moment the *content* of consciousness is what we are prepared to act on next. In consciousness the priority system of the brain is administered. This priority system gives events that affect survival fast access to

See Chapter 13, section
on Physiological and
Safety Needs.

FIGURE 7-3
Consciousness and Discrepancies
Because consciousness tends to be stimulated by change, contrast, and the unusual, we are sure to become conscious of a perceptual discrepancy, such as seeing a man wearing a suit on the beach.

consciousness. Although hunger will not intrude as dramatically as does pain, the need to eat will be felt strongly if you do not eat.

When there is a discrepancy between existing knowledge about the world (schemata) and an event, it is more likely to come to consciousness. A man in a suit is hardly noticeable on a city street, but if he wore a suit on the beach it would certainly be noticed (Figure 7-3). You may straighten out a crooked painting on the wall because it doesn't "fit" with the others, thus resolving a discrepancy.

STRUCTURE OF CONSCIOUSNESS

Continuing the newspaper analogy, the contents of consciousness are those few important events demanding immediate action. But consciousness is only the "front page" of the mind; behind it are many different **levels of awareness** that contain plans and expectations, assumptions, and basic knowledge of how to operate in the world (Figure 7-4).

So the mind is divided in two ways a newspaper is divided. The first is the division between the front page and the rest of the paper, that is, between consciousness and other forms of awareness. The second is the division of the front page (consciousness) itself (see Plate 10).

Conscious and Subconscious Levels of Awareness

Subconscious Awareness

When something is only in awareness *it means that we are keeping track of it.* We are aware of a great deal, much more than we are conscious of. To walk we must be aware of our movements, our feet on the pavement, and whether there is a crack, a curb, or a stone to step over. But we are not *conscious* of these things as we walk, nor are we conscious of breathing, arm movements, the background noises, or traffic.

There is a difference between awareness and consciousness. When we *know* we are aware of something, we are conscious of it. But we may be aware of something without being conscious to it. During sleep, for example, when consciousness is shut down, we are nevertheless aware of sounds. If the sounds have a particular significance, consciousness can be aroused. Sleepers will awaken to

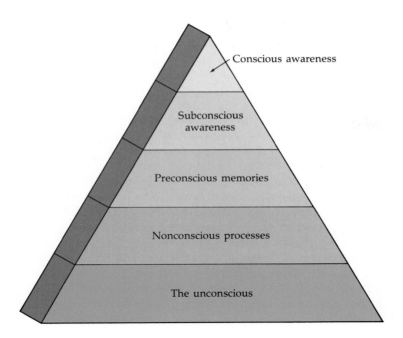

FIGURE 7-4
Levels of Awareness
There are various levels in the structure of our conscious and subconscious.

their own names or to a word like "fire," although they will not awaken to random words spoken. A mother sleeps through the noise of sirens in the streets, but awakens at the far softer sound of her baby crying. For that to occur, she must have been *aware* of the words and sounds of the environment and have selected only the important ones to enter consciousness.

Preconscious Memories

At a more basic level of awareness are **preconscious memories.** These are memories that enable us to operate in the world, and they include two kinds. *Episodic memory* consists of specific memories in life. *Representational memories* are stored knowledge of the world, such as the knowledge of language and where Scotland is. Preconscious memories become conscious only when the situation stimulates them, such as meeting an old friend. Suddenly you may remember things that had been forgotten for years.

Nonconscious Processes

Nonconscious processes include the automatic functioning of the body, including pumping of the heart, regulation of blood circulation and blood pressure, and neurotransmitter production. However, if something goes wrong with one of these processes, for example, if your heart suddenly speeds up, these processes can enter consciousness.

Unconscious

A more controversial level of awareness is called the **unconscious.** The unconscious is the "place" postulated by Sigmund Freud (1900) in which memories and thoughts that are difficult to deal with are hidden. For example, someone who hates a parent but cannot face this might try to prevent the feeling from entering consciousness. As interesting as this idea is, however, attempts to validate it have not been successful.

Division of Consciousness: Dissociation

Past experiences are not usually in consciousness, but many are retrievable. Your high school graduation was not in consciousness a moment ago. Now you are conscious of it and can recall specific experiences associated with it. Some experiences, however, can only be recovered under specific conditions.

This division in consciousness is called **dissociation.** Pierre Janet, a nineteenth-century psychiatrist who used hypnosis in his therapy, first introduced the term dissociation in 1899. He suggested to one of his patients under hypnosis that she would write letters to certain people when she came out of her hypnotic state. Later, when she was shown the letters, she had no recollection of having written them and accused Janet of forging her signature. The act of writing had been dissociated, "split off," from normal consciousness.

We all experience splits in consciousness. Have you ever felt "out of it" and just snapped back, with no recollection of the time, as if you had just lost a half hour? When such splits become extreme or a permanent condition, a **multiple personality** may result. A multiple personality is a person in whom two or more distinct consciousnesses coexist. The consciousnesses are so well developed and distinct that they are more like separate personalities than simply shifting states of consciousness or mood. Such people are usually unaware of the other personalities inside them. Their normal consciousness is dissociated when one of the others emerges.

VARIATIONS IN CONSCIOUSNESS

Borderline States

Borderline states are just what their name implies — receptive states of consciousness that "border" on lower levels of awareness. They include daydreams and the times just before sleep and just before waking. When in a borderline state, we experience a decline in active performance but are more imaginative.

Daydreaming

Everyone daydreams almost daily. Daydreams usually occur when external events are boring, automatized, or unchanging (such as riding in a car or listening to a dull lecture). At these times consciousness tunes out the outside world and tunes in an inside world.

We routinely simplify sensory information by tuning out unchanging events to direct attention to novel events. But since consciousness does not turn off when novel events are absent in the environment, *we create our own.* During daydreams we lose consciousness of the external world and our effectiveness is diminished. Even so, daydreaming may have some important functions. During daydreams, thoughts are more free flowing and uncensored, making us more receptive to new courses of action and new ideas, even to reflecting "honestly" on faults and mistakes. Such thoughts are less likely to enter consciousness in a normal active state (Singer, 1984).

Singer classifies daydreams into general and specific types. General daydreams are wide-ranging fantasies with a limitless variety of content. Specific daydreams fall into clearer categories (Singer, 1976):

1. *Self-recriminating.* These daydreams are prompted by the question, "What should I have done (or said)?"
2. *Well-controlled and thoughtful.* These daydreams are a form of planning—the day is organized, a party is planned, and so forth.
3. *Autistic.* In these daydreams, material usually associated with nighttime dreams breaks through and disrupts consciousness—for example, seeing a horse flying through the lecture hall.
4. *Neurotic or self-conscious.* These daydreams include fantasies: "How I can score the winning point and become revered by all the fans," or "How I can be discovered by a Hollywood director."

Although parents, teachers, and bosses keep telling us not to daydream, everyone does.

The Daydream in Art
I and My Village, by Marc Chagall

States before Sleep and Waking

The state of consciousness we enter just before complete awakening is called **hypnopompic;** the state before sleep is called **hypnagogic** (*hypno* is Greek for "sleep"). The mode of consciousness in both states is receptive. Our images at these times have four qualities: vividness, originality, independence of conscious control, and changeableness. Many people report that creative insight frequently occurs during these moments.

Sleep

We undergo a most radical and dramatic alteration in consciousness each night—we go to sleep. The outside world is shut off; the content of consciousness is generated entirely from within. During sleep we continue to have conscious experience called dreams. The nature of sleep and dreams has fascinated people for millennia. Why sleep? Why dream? What do dreams mean?

Every animal sleeps, but, surprisingly, no one is sure why. Most people assume sleep is restorative because we commonly go to sleep tired and awake refreshed. There are two kinds of tiredness, each requiring a different kind of sleep. *Physical tiredness* follows intense physical effort and is usually pleasant because of the relaxed state of the muscles. *Mental tiredness* comes after intense intellectual or emotional activity and is usually an unpleasant feeling of having been "drained."

Sleep Deprivation and the Functions of Sleeping

There has been little direct evidence to back up the assumption that sleep is restorative. The specific functions of sleep, and therefore of dreaming, remain a mystery. However, some real progress has been made in the last few years on both of these questions. One way to figure out the functions of sleep is to deprive people of it. In 1959 a New York City disc jockey, Peter Tripp, tried to stay awake for 200 hours to raise money to benefit charity. For this marathon he was surrounded by psychologists and medical specialists; his physiological and psychological functioning were monitored continuously.

> Almost from the first the overpowering force of sleepiness hit him. Constant company, walks, tests, broadcasts helped, but after about five days he needed a stimulant to keep going. . . . After little more than two days as he changed shoes in the hotel, he pointed out to [a psychiatrist] a very interesting sight. There were cobwebs in his shoes—to the eyes at least. . . . Specks on the table began to look like bugs. . . . He was beginning to have trouble remembering things. By 100 hours . . . he had reached an inexorable turning point. . . . Tests requiring attention or nominal mental agility had become unbearable to him. . . . By 70 hours the tests were torture. By 110 hours there were signs of delirium. Tripp's world had grown grotesque. A doctor walked into the recording booth in a tweed suit that Tripp saw as a suit of furry worms. By about 150 hours he became disoriented, not realizing where he was, and wondering who he was. . . . Sometimes he would back up against a wall and let nobody walk behind him. Yet from 5 to 8 p.m. all his forces were mysteriously summoned, and he efficiently organized his commercials and records and managed a vigorous patter for three hours. . . . On the final morning of the final day [of the 200-hour period] a famous neurologist arrived to examine him. The doctor carried an umbrella although it was a bright day, and had a somewhat archaic mode of dress. . . . [Tripp] came to the morbid conclusion that this man was an undertaker, there for the purpose of burying him. . . . Tripp leapt for the door with several doctors in pursuit. (Luce & Segal, 1966)

With some encouragement, Tripp managed to get through the day, gave his broadcast, and then, following an hour of tests, sank into sleep for 13 hours. When he awakened, the terrors, ghoulish illusions, and mental agony had vanished.

There have been other cases of sleep deprivation, though most have been less extreme than Tripp's. Randy Gardiner, who now holds the record for staying awake, suffered much less. He spent most of his time playing pinball. Except for some mild hallucinations, his performance on the pinball machines was unimpaired. One of the sleep researchers who stayed with Gardiner reported that on the morning of the final day the two played 100 games of pinball and Gardiner won them all (Dement, 1974). A large study of sleep deprivation in 359 servicemen showed that by the third sleepless day 70 percent experienced hallucinations and 7 percent behaved abnormally. However, a good night's sleep restored all to normal. Thus, when people are deprived of sleep there can be a profound disorganization of normal mental processes.

REM Sleep

In 1953 Eugene Aserinsky and Nathaniel Kleitman made a chance observation in the course of studying the sleep patterns of infants: periods of eye movements and bodily activity seem to alternate regularly with periods of "quiet" sleep. These regular periods of rapid eye movements, called **REM sleep,** were precisely observed by attaching electrodes near the subjects' eyes. People of all ages experience some REM sleep every night.

Whenever test subjects are awakened just after periods of REM sleep, they give vivid reports of their dreams. When awakened after other stages of sleep (collectively called "non-REM" or NREM), they report dreams only a third of the time.

William Dement has been trying to discover the relationship of REM sleep to dreaming. He has produced evidence for a precise correspondence between REM sleep behavior and dream gaze changes. One subject who showed many side-to-side eye movements reported dreaming of a tennis match!

Stages of Sleep

Determining what stage of sleep a person is in is quite involved and requires recording of three physiological measures using three different devices: the electroencephalograph (EEG), which measures brain waves; the electrooculogram, (EOG), which records the movements of the eyes; and the electromyogram (EMG), which measures muscle tension in the chin. When a subject lies awake in bed before going to sleep, the EEG is likely to exhibit alpha rhythm, the EOG reveals blinks and occasional REMs, and the EMG level is relatively high. This state is called "relaxed wakefulness" (Figure 7-5A).

When drowsy, the EEG alpha rhythm is gradually replaced by the low-voltage EEG activity characteristic of "stage 1 sleep" (Figure 7-5B). The EOG usually shows slow eye movements and the EMG may decrease. Stage 1 sleep lasts only a few minutes.

Stage 2 sleep is marked by the appearance of 12 to 14 hertz rhythms on the EEG called **sleep spindles** (Figure 7-5C). EOG activity is minimal and the EMG usually decreases still further. Gradually, high-amplitude slow waves begin to appear on the EEG. When 20 to 50 percent of the EEG is these (delta) waves, stage 3 is reached (Figure 7-5D). Eventually, delta activity dominates the EEG. When the proportion of delta activity exceeds 50 percent, the "deepest" stage of sleep (stage 4) is reached (Figure 7-5E). During these stages there are no eye movements and the EMG is normally low.

After about an hour and a half, the sequence is reversed. By the time the EEG indicates that stage 1 has been reached, however, the EMG is at the lowest level of the night and REMs occur. This is "stage 1 REM," or REM sleep. REM sleep is extremely curious; many contradictory phenomena occur at once. The EOG shows the eyes moving rapidly (Figure 7-5, bottom); breathing and heart rate become irregular; erection in the male and vaginal engorgement in the female occurs; and the vestibular system is activated.

During all this activation, however, *all other commands for voluntary movement emanating from the brain are blocked* from reaching the muscles at the spinal cord. You might dream that you are running, but your legs do not move. Breathing, heart rate, and cerebral blood flow are all activated, but the rest of the body is momentarily paralyzed.

Here's how it works. Immediately preceding and during REM sleep there is increased "spiking" activity in cells of the *pontine reticular formation,* a network of cells located in the *pons* of the brain, which is a mass of nerve fibers at the end of the medulla oblongata. These cells in turn activate eye movement neurons. At the same time, the activity in the pontine reticular formation inhibits a nearby group of cells, the *locus cerulus,* which affects muscle tone and blocks muscle movements. REM sleep lasts on average about 10 minutes.

The cycle of sleep stages repeats three or four times a night, although the same stage is slightly different at each occurrence. The depth of sleep decreases throughout the night, and there is less stage 3 and stage 4 sleep. Successive REM periods increase in length, and the interval between REM periods decreases from

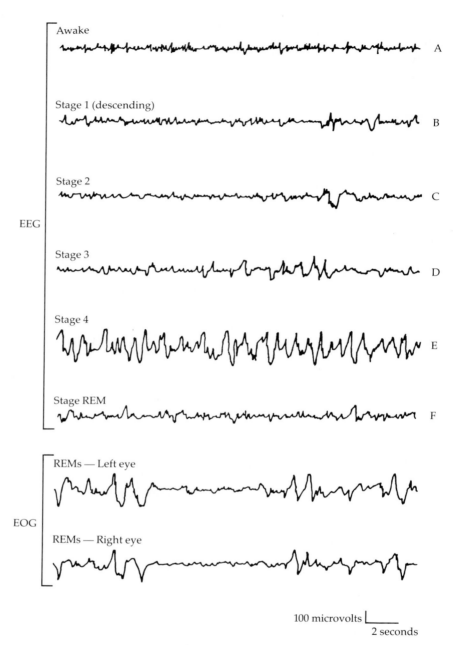

FIGURE 7-5
Stages of Sleep
These electroencephalograph (EEG) records (A – F) show brain wave activity during the five stages of sleep. The electrooculogram (EOG) records at the bottom record eye movement during the REM stage.

90 minutes early in sleep to as little as 40 minutes. The typical sequence of sleep stage changes during the night is illustrated in Figure 7-6.

Dreams

REM sleep was an important discovery not only for the insights it provided on sleep, but because it was one of the first physiological measures psychologists and

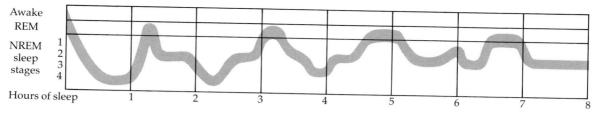

Awake
REM
NREM
sleep
stages 1 2 3 4
Hours of sleep   1   2   3   4   5   6   7   8

FIGURE 7-6
Sequence of Sleep Stages
This graph shows how the brain cycles through REM sleep and the four stages of non-REM (NREM) sleep throughout the night.
(After Van de Castle, 1971)

psychiatrists could use to correlate internal events with external experiences. Recording REM, researchers have been able to answer many basic questions about dreams. *We all dream every night, whether or not we can recall the content of our dreams.* Most people have four or five dream periods per night at about 90-minute intervals; dream periods become longer throughout the night. Dreams are more frequently recalled if the sleeper is awakened immediately after a REM period.

The content of dreams can be influenced by outside stimuli. Many people have dreamt of a loud noise only to awaken to the alarm clock. Dement and Wolpert (1958) sprayed water on subjects' faces during REM periods. When awakened, many subjects reported water imagery in their dreams.

REM sleep may be involved in the reorganization of mental structures (schemata) to accommodate new information. People in an experiment were placed in a ''disturbing and perplexing'' atmosphere four hours just before sleep and asked to perform difficult tasks with no explanation. REM time increased during their subsequent sleep. REM sleep increases after people have had to learn complex tasks. This might explain why REM sleep decreases with age (Figure 7-7): as less and less new information is accommodated, there may be less need for REM sleep.

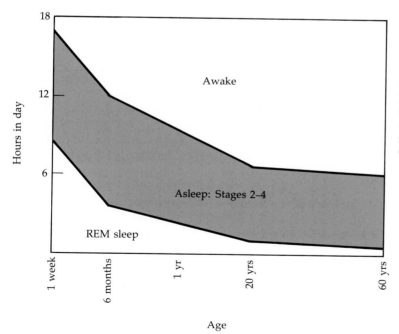

FIGURE 7-7
Need for Sleep Decreases with Age
Over a lifetime (but especially from birth to 20 years), the average person spends more time awake each day and needs less sleep, especially REM.
(After Hartmann, 1967)

What Dreams Mean

The meaning of dreams has been the subject of much philosophical and, more recently, scientific thought. The belief that the contents of dreams are important is virtually universal. Within psychology there have been several dream theories. The most influential theory of the meaning of dreams is Freud's, presented in a brilliant book, *The Interpretation of Dreams* (Freud, 1900). Freud's analysis is rich and complex, so only two main points are given here.

Wish Fulfillment. During dreams, normal controls are released, allowing unconscious wishes to be expressed directly. For Freud, dreams are the "royal road to the unconscious" because normally forbidden desires rise into consciousness. A hungry person might dream of food, the sexually deprived of sex. These "pent up" desires are diminished to some extent simply by being expressed in dream consciousness, and they are then less likely to disturb waking consciousness and influence behavior.

Dreams Guard Sleep. However, a dream about killing a rival or sleeping with a friend's spouse might be disturbing. If a dream is upsetting enough, a person may wake up. Since that rarely happens, Freud felt that dreams "guard" sleep by transforming the unconscious desires into disguised symbols. It was the aim of Freudian *psychoanalysis* to uncover what these disguised symbols meant to dreamers by encouraging them to free associate to the dream content.

See Chapter 16, section on Psychoanalysis.

Activation Synthesis. A more recent and scientific theory of dreaming is based on observations of the unique state of the brain and nervous system during REM sleep. During REM the brain stem produces neuronal "spikes," the signals to the muscles are blocked at the brain stem, and the vestibular system is stimulated. The brain may be reshuffling schemata. This theory is called **activation synthesis** because it assumes that the brain is *activated* in REM sleep and that dreams are a conscious interpretation or *synthesis* of the information in consciousness during dreams (see Plates 11A and B).

See Chapter 5, section on Simplification and Selectivity.

During wakefulness the mental operating system organizes sensory information into the simplest meaningful interpretation. This theory assumes that the *same system* is at work during dreaming. In dreams, therefore, mental processes attempt to organize diverse material: falling (from the vestibular activation), the inability to move (from the blocking of motor output), and the specific events of the day needing to be assimilated or accommodated. The "simplest meaningful experience" of all these events becomes the dream (Hobson & McCarley, 1977).

Many common dream experiences may be the *interpretation* of the brain's state (Table 7-1). Being chased, unable to avoid the pursuer, tied up, locked up, or frozen with fright may all well be interpretations of the blocked motor commands to muscles during REM. Floating, flying, and falling experiences in dreams may be the interpretation of the vestibular activation. The sexual content of dreams may be an easy and meaningless interpretation of vaginal engorgement or penile erection.

Freud is reported to have said that "Sometimes a cigar is just a cigar," responding to criticism that not everything is symbolic of sexual activity and sexual organs all the time. With respect to the theory just described, similarly, a dream may be just a dream.

Dreams are often incoherent, even bizarre. One minute you may be speaking to your boss, the next you may be singing in a cabaret in some exotic city. Such

TABLE 7-1   Common Dreams

The 20 most common dreams of 250 college students are listed here with the percentage of students having each type of dream

Type of Dream	Percentage of Students
Falling	83
Being attacked or pursued	77
Trying repeatedly to do something	71
School, teachers, studying	71
Sexual experiences	66
Arriving too late	64
Eating	62
Being frozen with fright	58
A loved person is dead	57
Being locked up	56
Finding money	56
Swimming	52
Snakes	49
Being dressed inappropriately	46
Being smothered	44
Being nude in public	43
Fire	41
Failing an examination	39
Flying	34
Seeing self as dead	33

SOURCE: R. M. Griffith, O. Miyago, & A. Tago. The universality of typical dreams: Japanese vs. Americans. *American Anthropologist*, 1958. 60, pp. 1173–1179.

abrupt shifts in imagery may simply be the brain's "making the best of a bad job in producing partially coherent dream imagery from the relatively noisy signals sent up . . . from the brainstem" (Hobson & McCarley, 1977). If activation synthesis is correct, then the experience of dreams can be understood as a product of the nature of the mental operating system when the brain is generating its own "raw" information. Of course, dreams still *may* have specific meanings, but these meanings may lie in the *interpretation* of events.

If deprived of dreaming, we tend to have dreams during the day: first as daydreams, then as hallucinations, then as more extreme difficulties. "The madman is a waking dreamer," wrote Immanuel Kant. Sleep and dreams are certainly a common and yet dramatic alteration of consciousness. Sleeping is almost instantaneous, and dreams are often fully orchestrated, elaborate hallucinations that *each of us experiences every night.*

Practices to change consciousness are found in every society. These changes may be undertaken simply for amusement, as in recreational drug taking, or as a disciplined way of deepening one's understanding of reality.

DELIBERATE ALTERATIONS IN CONSCIOUSNESS

Since normal consciousness is geared to action, reducing the requirements for action can offer consciousness a chance to change. In laboratory studies, consciousness can be changed by removing the normal requirements for action, as in sensory deprivation, or by very weak stimulation, as in subliminal studies. In meditation and in many religious practices, the practitioner is removed from normal routines.

Sensory Deprivation and Isolation

If the ordinary consciousness responds to changes in the environment, then the absence of such changes may cause it to alter. For centuries techniques to eliminate awareness of changes have been known: mystics remove themselves to a cave or to the desert or they perform repetitive movements or sounds. These situations have been duplicated in isolation rooms designed to keep perceived changes to a minimum.

In early experiments in sensory deprivation, people reported unusual experiences, temporal disorientation, hallucinations, and extreme pathology. Yet those bizarre results depend on the expectations of the subjects and the experimenter.

People try to keep the same level of stimulation going into consciousness. It seems that different people like different "levels" of stimulation, in the same way that different people prefer their music at different volumes or different amounts of spice in their food. Much research has been done on changing the level of sensory stimulation, since as you might expect, this would change consciousness. When people are put into sensory deprivation situations, they will immediately try to seek stimulation. They may begin to move about, or brush their hand against their leg, or make noises vocally. It seems that consciousness, accustomed to a steady supply of stimulation, needs its "fix" to keep going.

What happens when people are prevented from stimulating themselves? They rapidly become disorganized, they lose intellectual ability and concentration, and their coordination declines. For some, the condition mirrors daydreams or night dreams: they begin to create their own world. The hallucinations are often in vivid color and detail. They range from slight sensations to complex objects and scenes, experienced in a progression from simple to complex. Feelings of anxiety, boredom, and restlessness are common (Suedfield, 1983).

However, the "disorienting" effects of sensory deprivation and isolation may be potentially beneficial. Sensory isolation has been used for relaxation and in clinics for the control of smoking. The radical shift in the environment may cause consciousness to change in line with expectations. There may be both pathology and benefit in boredom, depending on what we expect from it.

Subliminal Perception

As there are gradations in consciousness throughout the day, there are gradients in how conscious one is of any stimulus at any moment. Below consciousness are several levels of awareness, and it is obviously not necessary for us to be *conscious* of everything in our world all the time. Some things seem to seep into the mind indirectly under the threshold of conscious awareness.

While sleeping we will awaken when *our* name is called but not someone else's. When sleeping people listen to recordings of names, they show a profound cortical response to their name, but not to others'.

Even when we are awake there are many indications that we react to informa-

Isolation tank used in sensory deprivation experiments

tion at a level below consciousness—changes in skin resistance, heart rate, and other measures of activation. There is a growing, but still controversial, research showing that we may be profoundly affected by this *subliminal perception*. The effects of these indirect stimuli are often indirect as well.

When some words are flashed quickly to a person, those that are "taboo" take longer to recognize. *Whore* takes longer, for instance, than *shore*. Also, people tend to develop specific feelings toward stimuli even though they cannot recognize the stimulus itself. In one experiment geometric shapes were flashed to a person faster than they could be recognized, and the person was asked, "How much do you like them?" The subject responded that he liked the figures he had seen before, while at the same time insisting that the question was nonsensical!

In one important series of studies, the stimulus MOMMY AND I ARE 1 was flashed to people who were unaware of the message being flashed. When groups who had seen this message were later tested on a variety of tasks, such as achievement, exam scores, and aspirations, all seemed to be enhanced! These studies were done with the idea of supporting the psychoanalytic point of view that the experience of such "oneness" will enhance performance. While it is not necessary to accept such an implausible idea, certainly the phenomenon is important enough to merit a change in our ideas of the permeability and multiplicity of our consciousness (Silverman, 1983).

Meditation

The aim of **meditation** is knowledge of oneself and one's place in the world. These techniques aim at shifting consciousness from the active to the receptive. Instead of coming to an intellectual understanding of "different mechanisms of attention," meditation seeks to teach individuals to experience the world differently. Meditation is used by nearly all traditional psychologies of the East— among them Sufism, Zen, and Yoga—and in the West by religious orders such as the Franciscans.

Meditation is often practiced during pregnancy to aid in relaxation and increased body awareness.

Concentrative Meditation

The instructions for concentrative meditation are strikingly similar in different traditions. In the book *What the Buddha Taught*, the Buddhist monk Rahula (1969) gives these instructions:

> Breathe in or out as usual, without any effort or strain. Now, bring your mind to concentrate on your breathing-in and breathing-out. Let your mind watch and observe your breathing in and out. . . . Forget all other things, your surroundings, your environment; do not raise your eyes and look at anything. . . .
>
> At the beginning, you will find it extremely difficult. . . . You will be astonished how your mind runs away. It does not stay. You begin to think of various things. You hear sounds outside. Your mind is disturbed and distracted. You may be dismayed and disappointed. But if you continue to practice this exercise twice a day . . . you will experience just that split second when your mind is fully concentrated on your breathing, when you will not hear even sounds nearby, when no external world exists for you.

The process of concentrative meditation is similar throughout the world, which suggests that there may be a common experience stimulated by this process. It does not seem to matter what actual practice is followed, or whether one

TEACHING STORIES

Another technique for upsetting routine and for deepening consciousness is a narrative containing paradoxes and unusual events. Such a tale is often called a **teaching story** (Shah, 1982). One aim of many esoteric traditions is to experience unfamiliar ideas and information. Teaching stories are said to contain certain specially chosen patterns of events that encourage openness to new ideas. Repeated reading of the story allows these patterns to become strengthened in the mind of the person reading them, thus slowly changing the mind (Shah, 1986).

The Man with the Inexplicable Life

There was once a man named Mojud. He lived in a town where he had obtained a post as a small official, and it seemed likely that he would end his days as Inspector of Weights and Measures.

One day when he was walking through the gardens of an ancient building near his home, Khidr, the mysterious Guide of the Sufis, appeared to him, dressed in shimmering green. Khidr said: "Man of bright prospects! Leave your work and meet me at the riverside in three days' time." Then he disappeared.

Mojud went to his superior in trepidation and said that he had to leave. Everyone in the town soon heard of this and they said: "Poor Mojud! He has gone mad." But, as there were many candidates for his job, they soon forgot him.

On the appointed day, Mojud met Khidr, who said to him, "Tear your clothes and throw yourself into the stream. Perhaps someone will save you."

Mojud did so, even though he wondered if he were mad.

Since he could swim, he did not drown, but drifted a long way before a fisherman hauled him into his boat, saying, "Foolish man! The current is strong. What are you trying to do?"

Mojud said: "I do not really know."

"You are mad," said the fisherman, "but I will take you into my reed-hut by the river yonder, and we shall see what can be done for you."

When he discovered that Mojud was well-spoken, he learned from him how to write.

After a few months, Khidr again appeared, this time at the foot of Mojud's bed, and said: "Get up now and leave this fisherman. You will be provided for."

Mojud immediately quit the hut, dressed as a fisherman, and wandered about until he came to a highway. As dawn was breaking, he saw a farmer on a donkey on his way to market. "Do you seek work?" asked the farmer. "Because I need a man to help me to bring back some purchases."

Mojud followed him. He worked for the farmer for nearly two years, by which time he had learned a great deal about agriculture but little else.

One afternoon when he was baling wool, Khidr appeared to him and said: "Leave that work, walk to the city of Mosul, and use your savings to become a skin merchant."

Mojud obeyed. In Mosul he became known as a skin merchant, never seeing Khidr while he plied his trade for three years. He had saved quite a large sum of money, and was thinking of buying a house, when Khidr appeared and said: "Give me your money, walk out of this town as far as distant Samarkand, and work for a grocer there." Mojud did so.

Presently he began to show undoubted signs of illumination. He healed the sick, served his fellow men in the shop during his spare time, and his knowledge of the mysteries became deeper and deeper.

symbol or another is used, the experience is the same. The important factor common to all is *the same information is cycled through the nervous system over and over.*

The sensory systems are specialized to detect changes in the environment; concentrative meditation defeats these systems by producing unchanging stimulation. Normal conscious experience ceases and is replaced by a state of receptiv-

Clerics, philosophers and others visited him and asked: "Under whom did you study?"

"It is difficult to say," said Mojud.

His disciples asked: "How did you start your career?"

He said: "As a small official."

"And you gave it up to devote yourself to self-mortification?"

"No, I just gave it up."

They did not understand him.

People approached him to write the story of his life.

"What have you been in your life?" they asked.

"I jumped into a river, became a fisherman, then walked out of his reed-hut in the middle of one night. After that, I became a farmhand. While I was baling wool, I changed and went to Mosul, where I became a skin merchant. I saved some money there, but gave it away. Then I walked to Samarkand where I worked for a grocer. And this is where I am now."

"But this inexplicable behavior throws no light upon your strange gifts and wonderful examples," said the biographers.

"That is so," said Mojud.

So the biographers constructed for Mojud a wonderful and exciting history; because all saints must have their story, and the story must be in accordance with the appetite of the listener, not with the realities of the life.

And nobody is allowed to speak of Khidr directly. That is why this story is not true. It is a representation of a life. This is the real life of one of the greatest Sufis.

The High Cost of Learning

Nasrudin is interested in learning to play the lute. He searches out the lute master and asks, "How much do you charge for lessons?" The lute master replies, "Ten gold pieces for the first month, one gold piece for the succeeding months." "Excellent," says Nasrudin. "I shall begin with the second month."

See What I Mean?

Nasrudin was walking on the main street of a town, throwing out bread crumbs. His neighbors asked, "What are you doing, Nasrudin?"

"Keeping the tigers away."

"There have not been tigers in these parts for hundreds of years."

"Exactly. Effective, isn't it?"

I Believe You Are Right

During Nasrudin's first case as a magistrate, the plaintiff argues so persuasively that he exclaims, "I believe you are right." The clerk of the court begs him to restrain himself, for the defendant has not yet been heard. Nasrudin is so carried away by the eloquence of the defendant that he cries out as soon as the man has finished his evidence, "I believe you are right." The clerk of the court cannot allow this. "Your honor, they cannot both be right." "I believe you are right," says Nasrudin. (Shah, 1986)

These stories, collected for years by Idries Shah, are important "documents" of a different type of psychology than the one we are studying. The insights and conclusions about the different divisions of the mind, or the different personalities within an individual, are here given full voice. Done so, the interested reader can begin to see the different "selves" within, and perhaps understand the nature of his or her mind, composed of diverse, and often opposed forces.

ity. The purpose of "heightening" consciousness in this way is to restructure schemata and thus *de-automatize* one's response to the world.

One aim of many forms of conscious development is to remove "blindness," to awaken a fresh perception. *Enlightenment* or *illumination* are words often used for progress in these disciplines. The psychological term is **de-automatization,** an undoing of the normal automatization of consciousness (Deikman, 1966).

Opening-up Meditation

A second form of meditation is much more closely related to daily activity. These exercises do not isolate the practitioner, but attempt to involve everyday events in the training of consciousness. In these exercises, called "just sitting" in Zen, "mindfulness" in Yoga, and "self-observation" in Sufism, consciousness is "opened up" to everything that occurs.

Opening-up exercises emphasize the difference between the information that reaches consciousness and the interpretation of that information. This has also been attempted in psychology. The early "introspectionist" psychologists attempted to analyze the elements of their own consciousness—in our terms the difference between sensation and perception. In philosophical and religious traditions the purpose is different: to disassociate one's "models" of the world from the actual outside world. In Zen this is stated as "to stop conceptualizing while remaining fully awake."

Opening-up meditation attempts to change what consciousness selects. For example, one exercise might be to listen to all the sounds inside and outside of the room you are in: the noises of the buildings and traffic, static on the radio, creaks in the walls. They are ever present but almost never noticed. Because consciousness evolved as an adaptive advantage for survival, this exercise is extremely hard to do and could be dangerous if it were done all the time. Opening-up meditation exercises also attempt to de-automatize perception, to undo some of the selectivity and interpretation that take place in normal perception.

Religious Experiences

Many meditation and spiritual exercises result in what are called *religious experiences.* In his classic *The Varieties of Religious Experience,* William James (1917) cited the analysis and description of a mystical experience by a Canadian psychiatrist, which James called "cosmic consciousness."

> I was walking in a state of quiet, almost passive enjoyment. . . . All at once, without warning of any kind, I found myself wrapped in a flame-colored cloud. For an instant I thought of fire, an immense conflagration somewhere close by in that great city; the next, I knew that the fire was within myself. Directly afterward there came upon me a sense of exultation, an immense joyousness accompanied or immediately followed by an intellectual illumination impossible to describe. Among other things, I did not merely come to believe but I saw that the universe is not composed of dead matter, but is, on the contrary, a living Presence; I became conscious in myself of eternal life. It was not a conviction that I would have eternal life, but a consciousness that I possessed eternal life then; I saw that all men are immortal; that the cosmic order is such that without any peradventure all things work together for the good of each and all; that the foundation principle of the world, of all the worlds, is what we call love, and that the happiness of each and all is in the long run absolutely certain. . . . That view, that conviction, I may say that consciousness, has never, even during periods of the deepest depression, been lost.

James (1890) defines four characteristics of the mystical or religious experience.

1. *Unity or oneness.* Experience becomes comprehensive rather than fragmented; relationships between things normally separate are seen.

2. *A sense of "realness."* The person has the sensation that the relations between things he or she experiences are closer to truth than ordinary experiences.
3. *Ineffability.* The experience is said to be impossible to communicate in ordinary words.
4. *Vividness and richness.* Events take on a glow of freshness and clarity, not present in ordinary consciousness.

Hypnosis

Two hundred years ago Franz Anton Mesmer claimed he had discovered the property of "animal magnetism," a force of nature through which he could control and influence another person's experience. Miraculous healing cures were claimed. His technique was called *mesmerism*. It was essentially what we now call hypnosis.

Hypnosis is a form of dissociation in which individuals relinquish the normal control of their consciousness to another person. Through a variety of techniques, a hypnotist engages and relaxes the subject's waking consciousness. People under hypnosis have been able to recall events otherwise inaccessible to their waking consciousness; they have also been able to withstand extreme pain.

Although the idea of a "force" transmitted through hypnosis is no longer popular today, there is as yet no accepted scientific explanation of how hypnosis works. This makes many psychologists uncomfortable with the phenomenon and has stimulated fierce attempts to discredit it. In the nineteenth century, a British surgeon, Esdaile, demonstrated hypnosis to an audience of the Royal College of

This woman is being hypnotized prior to dental work.

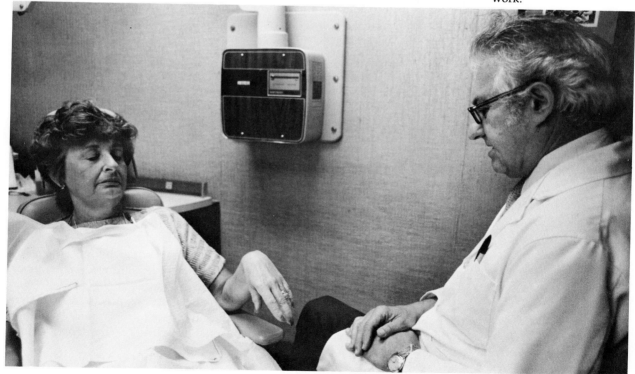

WARTS AND ALL

There are remarkable examples, anecdotal as well as experimental, which demonstrate how the body can be altered in profound ways through hypnosis and suggestion.

Holly, a 9-year-old fourth grader began to develop warts during her first year in grammar school. The growths started on her left hand, but to her considerable dismay, they began to spread. She was unmercifully teased by her schoolmates, and consequently her grades at school declined. At last count she had 31 warts on her hands and face. These warts had survived the best conventional medical treatment had to offer, so she agreed to participate in a study of hypnotic treatment of warts.

Holly didn't know much about hypnosis but readily agreed to participate in this novel "kind of game," as it was presented. She took to the hypnosis avidly. She was told under hypnosis to feel a tingling sensation in the warts. After she felt the tingling she was told that the warts would go away in a week or possibly longer. The warts began to disappear after the first session. By the fifth session only five remained, and by three months only two small warts persisted on her left hand.

Controlled studies have shown that warts can sometimes indeed be wished away. Sinclair-Gieben and Chalmers reported (1959) success in hypnotic treatment of 14 patients with intractable generalized warts on both sides of their bodies. The subjects were hypnotized and instructed that the warts on one side of their body would disappear, while the other side would serve as the control. Within several weeks the warts in 9 of the patients had regressed significantly but only on the treated side. The untreated side had as many warts as ever, except in one subject, whose warts on the untreated side also showed spontaneous disappearance six weeks after the treated side had been cured.

In a later study at Massachusetts General Hospital, 9 of 17 patients treated with hypnosis demonstrated significant wart regression, while none of an untreated control group showed any improvement (Surman, Gottlieb, Hackett, & Silverberg, 1973).

So why get excited about the disappearance of a few warts by suggestion? The virus that causes warts is ubiquitous, and since not everyone develops warts, some type of immune defense must protect the majority of people. The mental wart cures presumably work by either activating the immune system or by altering the blood flow to these growths, or both.

Consider how elegant the mind's approach is: quick, painless, no side effects, and no scars compared to the crude freezing, burning, cutting, and cautery employed in the modern medical treatment of warts. Furthermore, think what is involved in the mental cures. The brain must translate such vague suggestions as "warts go away" into detailed battle plans. Chemical messengers are sent to marshal the cells of the immune system in an assault on the virus-induced tumor. Or perhaps small arterioles are selectively constricted, strangling the wart but sparing neighboring healthy skin. A remarkable feat.

Physicians. The demonstration was dramatic: a man under hypnosis had his gangrenous leg amputated without anesthetic! The patient showed no evidence of pain and was wheeled away after the successful surgery. Still, Esdaile was ridiculed. In the *Lancet*, a respected British medical journal, it was asserted that "the patient was an imposter who had been trained not to show pain." Another nonplussed observer reported that Esdaile must have hired a "hardened rogue" to undergo the operation for a fee!

Hypnotic Suggestibility

Suggestible people share several characteristics; among them is the capacity for imaginative involvement. Typical forms of such involvement include reading science fiction or drama; adventurousness in physical activities, such as exploration; and adventurousness of a mental nature, such as experimentation with drugs.

Hidden Observer in Hypnosis

In 1960 Kaplan hypnotized a college student and induced "automatic writing" in which the subject's right hand was able to "write anything it wanted to, not subject to control or restriction of the 'conscious' personality." Then the hypnotist told the subject he would feel no pain in his left hand. He began pricking the left hand with pins, which ordinarily would have been unbearable. The student showed and reported no pain (Kaplan, 1960). This demonstration was one of the first and most important examples of dissociation of consciousness. In dissociation one part of the person is conscious of experiences (and can report them) and another part is not.

Even in a dissociated state normal consciousness is not cut off or "unconscious" of what is happening. In another study, Hilgard hypnotized a man and gave him the suggestion that he would become completely deaf at the count of three. The man did not react to the sound. Hilgard said to the man, "Although you are hypnotically deaf, perhaps some part of you is hearing my voice and processing this information. If there is, I should like the index finger of your right hand to rise as a sign that this is the case." To Hilgard's amazement, the finger rose! Hilgard called this phenomenon the **hidden observer** (Hilgard, 1978).

The hidden observer is an important demonstration of the hypothesis that many experiences below consciousness may enter consciousness through hypnosis. We may be instructed under hypnosis not to feel pain and indeed report no pain. But because the hidden observer *does* report pain (Figure 7-8), it may be assumed that the hypnotic state is only one part of awareness.

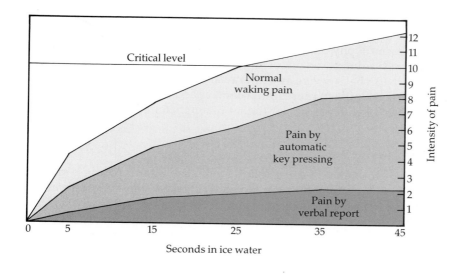

FIGURE 7-8
The Hidden Observer
People hypnotized not to feel pain while their hands are in ice water signal pain during an experiment by automatic key pressing or by reporting it later. This is done through the hidden observer, a level of awareness apparently not affected by hypnosis.
(After Hilgard, 1978)

Hypnotic Condition

Under hypnosis warts have been removed, migraine headaches relieved, people have stopped smoking, and episodes have been forgotten. Many people are concerned that hypnosis is dangerous because unethical hypnotists might make subjects do things they would not do in a normal waking state. But that is more the stuff of movies and fiction than reality; a person will not do anything under hypnosis that goes against his or her moral code.

The general characteristics of the hypnotic condition are:

1. Attention can be changed, narrowed, or broadened according to instructions.
2. Distortions of reality can be accepted. Hypnotized persons can imagine and act as if they were young children (age regression).
3. They will act out roles suggested by the hypnotist.
4. They can be given suggestions about posthypnotic behaviors (Hilgard, 1966).

Later, when acting out the suggestions, they may not realize they are following directions.

Drugs

In nearly every culture, drugs and other biochemical agents have been deliberately used to affect consciousness. These substances range from coffee to the psychedelic drug LSD. Generally, drugs work by stimulating, depressing, or altering neurotransmission.

The effects of drugs are not only pharmacological but social. Taking a drug can be an expression of a desire for social change, a protest against society, an exploration of taboo areas, or simply "mental adventurousness." Adolescents often experiment with drugs as part of their general exploration of forbidden activities.

The social acceptability of a drug often influences the experience. At a conference on drug abuse, concerned professionals discuss the dangers of marijuana, heroin, and amphetamines, while at the same time they smoke cigarettes and drink coffee and alcohol, three drugs that not only alter consciousness but also have very harmful physical effects. Smoking tobacco leads to severe health consequences such as increased risk of lung cancer and heart attacks, and withdrawal from tobacco can be as severe as withdrawal from heroin (Brecher, 1974). Excessive alcohol consumption causes brain damage and liver degeneration. The physiological effect of coffee is similar to that of amphetamines.

Pattern of Drug Taking

The social acceptance of drugs follows a similar pattern. A drug is often introduced into a culture by a minority primarily interested in the drug's effects on consciousness. The drug is then condemned, confiscated, and finally, taken up by the culture (Brecher, 1974). Coffee provides a good illustration of both this process and the effect of interpretation. At first coffee was banned throughout Europe. An early Arabic writer comments:

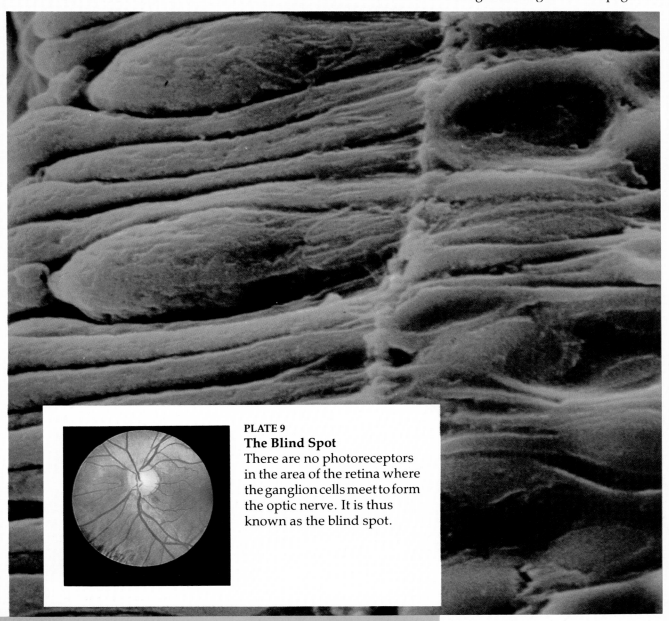

PLATE 8
Rods and Cones in the Retina
This photomicrograph
(a photograph taken through a light microscope)
shows the thicker cones among the slender rods.
Compare this real view with the schematic
diagram in Figure 5-4 on page 187.

PLATE 9
The Blind Spot
There are no photoreceptors
in the area of the retina where
the ganglion cells meet to form
the optic nerve. It is thus
known as the blind spot.

PLATE 10
Multiple States of Consciousness
This painting by Joan Miró, entitled *Woman, Bird by Moonlight* (1949), vividly represents the various levels of consciousness in the human mind. Miró often created his images in a state of semi-self-hypnosis, apparently tapping into his own various conscious and subconscious states.

PLATES 11A AND B
Dream Images
In dreams, objects can take on multiple meanings and forms. Dream images are common themes in many fine art works, beautifully exemplified here by Salvador Dali's *Apparition of a Face of a Fruit-Dish on a Beach* (top) and by Giorgio de Chirico's *The Anguish of Departure* (bottom).

PLATES 12A, B, AND C
Computer Graphics
Modern computer technology assists us in learning because it allows us to create images that were never before possible. This beautiful still life (top left) is a computer graphic that was created by an artist to simulate a painting. This frostlike pattern (top right) was created on a computer screen by a program using fractal geometry. This computer-generated image (bottom) of a woman pulling a gun helps to test the reaction of a policeman under pressure in a real-life situation.

The sale of coffee has been forbidden. The vessels used for this beverage . . . have been broken to pieces. The dealers in coffee have received the bastinado, and have undergone other ill-treatment without even a plausible excuse. . . . The husks of the plant . . . have been more than once devoted to the flames and in several instances persons making use of it . . . have been severely handled. (Brecher, 1974)

If coffee is offered under conditions of secrecy and great expectation, its effect will be very different than if the same substance is offered in plastic cups in vending machines. The *interpretation* of drug experiences may make us underestimate the danger of the familiar and overestimate the danger of the unfamiliar.

Classification of Drugs

Drugs that affect consciousness can be divided into five classes:

1. **Analgesics** such as morphine reduce the experience of pain.
2. **Sedatives** induce relaxation and sleep. Barbiturates are a class of sedative.
3. **Stimulants** elevate mood and increase alertness. Amphetamines and cocaine are two well-known stimulants.
4. **Psychoactive drugs** change the overall structure of consciousness. Marijuana, mescaline, and LSD are psychoactive drugs.
5. **Psychiatric drugs** such as antidepressants, antipsychotics, and lithium help to "normalize" consciousness by correcting neurochemical imbalances.

These five classes are not entirely mutually exclusive. For instance, many psychoactive drugs are also stimulants, and some have depressive effects.

Analgesics

Morphine (from *Morpheus,* the Greek god of dreams) is the most widespread analgesic. Morphine is the active ingredient in opium, long used in east and northeast Asia to relieve pain as well as to induce extraordinary dreamlike experiences. More recently opiates have become a major recreational drug in the West.

Opium is an unrefined extract of the poppy seed pod; morphine is a refined extract of opium and is stronger in its effects. Heroin is derived from morphine and is even more potent in its pure form. ("Street" heroin, however, is usually diluted to below the strength of opium.) The opiate class of drugs kills pain by blocking neurotransmission. They fit into "opiate receptors" in the limbic system and stop pain from reaching the cortex. But the molecular structure of the opiates fits the brain's own opiate receptors imperfectly. It may also fit into other receptors in the limbic system.

See Chapter 4, section on The Healing Brain.

Because the limbic system is involved with emotion, the opiates can have a major effect on emotion. Immediately after injection, the opiates produce a pronounced feeling of intoxication and euphoria, called a "rush." The opiates seem to block so many afferent impulses to the cortex (at the limbic system) that the user not only feels no pain but also no signals of normal physiological needs, such as hunger. So while physical pain is relieved, there is also a decrease in anxiety and often in the motivation for food, sex, and work.

But heroin is more dangerous psychologically than physiologically. The real physical danger of heroin is that people who use it often neglect their health by not eating or drinking, or attending to pain. It is not, however, in itself an extremely dangerous substance; alcohol, in contrast, *is* dangerous. Much of the danger of heroin is that it is addicting and it is illegal. In England people addicted to heroin and other opium derivatives are registered and receive regular oral doses; consequently, there are fewer physiological difficulties than in the United States, although this has changed with the widespread addiction in the 1980s (Brecher, 1974).

Sedatives

Sedatives, including alcohol, are nonselective depressants of the central nervous system, which results first in relaxation, then drowsiness, and finally sleep. When taken together, they add to one another's effects. The most common use of sedatives is to induce sleep. Barbiturates are the drugs most commonly prescribed as sleeping pills. They are also sometimes taken, although not prescribed, to produce a state of "sedated inebriation," which some people find pleasant. Quaaludes are also a medically designed sedative commonly abused as a so-called recreational drug.

The most widely used (and abused) sedative is a nonprescription drug — alcohol. Alcohol is the major "drug of choice" in most Western societies. However, it is so dangerous that it is banned in many places, notably in all Moslem societies and by Hindu communities in India. In the first stages of drunken behavior, people commonly feel euphoric and uninhibited. Dancing in the streets, wild parties, and other drunken behavior are expressions of these stages. Later stages are characterized by depression and withdrawal.

Alcohol first acts as a depressant on the brain stem, which explains the loss of inhibitions on behavior — rowdiness, bawdiness, and so on. It later acts on the cortex, which explains loss of muscular control and depressing thoughts. Doses sufficient to depress activity in the brain stem probably do not at first depress

cortical activity; this releases the cortex from the regulatory controls exerted by the brain stem, such as the excitatory signals from the reticular activating system (Julien, 1978).

Alcohol is used by about 70 percent of people in the United States, and most of them have little trouble with it. There is even evidence that moderate drinking may benefit health. Perhaps because it aids relaxation, moderate drinkers have fewer heart attacks than nondrinkers (Darby, 1978). But alcohol can be addicting. Among the effects of alcohol addiction, or "alcoholism," are liver damage, ulcers, and hypertension. An excess of alcohol during pregnancy may result in birth defects. Withdrawal from alcohol dependence is a difficult and severe experience. The user may suffer delirium tremens ("DTs"), frightening visions, auditory hallucinations, and severe trembling. Alcohol withdrawal can be a more frightening experience than heroin withdrawal.

Stimulants

Stimulants and drugs such as amphetamines elevate mood, increase alertness, and reduce fatigue. Since one of their effects is loss of appetite, they are commonly used as diet pills. Amphetamines stimulate neurotransmission at the synapse. Recall that when a neuron fires, the chemical neurotransmitters jump from one neuron to the next at the synapse. After firing there is a *refractory* period when the neuron is inactive, giving the neurotransmitter time to return to the first neuron. This process is called *re-uptake.*

Amphetamines interfere with the re-uptake of dopamine and norepinephrine, causing erratic and uncontrolled neural impulses, which can eventually disrupt consciousness. With continued use, the disruptions can become permanent, resulting in a condition known as *amphetamine psychosis.* Chronic use of amphetamines (or colloquially, "speed") may result in schizophrenia. Among the first signs of an amphetamine breakdown are paranoid delusions, such as, "The CIA is after me." People also often become violent, which may be attributable more to the delusions than the drug itself. "An amphetamine party may begin with everyone very elated and talkative, and may end with each person stationed silently at a window, peeking through the curtains for signs of the police" (Snyder, 1980).

Cocaine is becoming increasingly popular in affluent Western societies. The leaves of the coca plant, from which cocaine is derived, have been chewed by the Indians of Bolivia and Peru for thousands of years to banish fatigue and boredom. The drug was introduced to North America and Europe in the late nineteenth century. "Tonics" and patent medicines containing cocaine or other coca extract were widely used in the United States until the early twentieth century. One of the most popular of these was Coca-Cola®, a drink that contained cocaine for 20 years until it became illegal in the early 1900s.

Sigmund Freud experimented with cocaine and was extremely enthusiastic about it at first. Later, however, he became disillusioned with the drug when he discovered that overuse could lead to severe depression, addiction, and even psychosis. Governments became alarmed at the harmful and dangerous aspects of cocaine. By World War I, cocaine was viewed as a dangerous drug and made illegal. Abuse of cocaine then declined until the early 1970s. Its use has been increasing since then, stimulated at first by the revival of interest in psychoactive drugs.

CYCLE OF ADDICTION

Any drug that gives pleasure or relief from pain or anxiety is potentially addicting. Pleasure-giving or pain-relieving drugs are potentially addicting because their effects on mood are produced by altering brain chemistry. Addiction is a cycle, often controlled by the principle of feedback. Consider morphine as a painkiller. Normally, the brain produces its own "opiates," the endorphins, which serve to kill pain. When this supply is inadequate, as in recovery from surgery, additional opiates in the form of morphine may be given.

However, since brain chemistry operates on a feedback system, the presence of the morphine is registered in the pituitary and a signal is sent to decrease production of the brain's own painkillers. When the morphine wears off, the pain is even more excruciating, requiring the administration of more morphine the next time, which leads to a still further reduction in the production of internal painkillers. Eventually, the drug no longer gives pleasure but instead only *relief from the unpleasant state that develops during abstinence*. Nothing else gives quite the same pleasure either. The addict becomes so conditioned to the intense effect of the drug that lesser stimuli like food and sex are uninteresting.

Cocaine, or "coke" as it is commonly called, is usually ingested by sniffing ("snorting") the white powder. This produces a sense of exhilaration and relief from fatigue that lasts approximately one-half hour. Most cocaine use is moderated by the high cost of the substance—as much as $100 per half-hour high. Cocaine intoxication is similar to *mania*, a psychological disorder characterized by an extremely frantic high mood. Lithium, a drug that can alleviate acute mania, blocks the euphoric effects of cocaine.

See Chapter 16, section on Severe Mental Disorders: Depression.

Psychoactive Drugs

Marijuana

Although illegal, marijuana is in common use in the United States; it is probably the most common drug used for altering consciousness. More than 60 percent of people under 35 have tried marijuana (Davison & Neale, 1982). The use of marijuana among young people is increasing rapidly. More than one in four people of age 18 to 25 now use marijuana regularly, and three out of five have tried it. Women tend to use the drug less often than men.

The leaf of the *Cannabis sativa* plant is the source of marijuana. The leaves are often dried and smoked. When the oil from the plant is collected and dried, this produces hashish, a substance that is more powerful in effect than marijuana. Marijuana or hashish is usually smoked, although some prefer to eat it in cookies and cakes.

Marijuana is an extremely complex substance; it contains more than 400 identified compounds, but the active agent is THC, one of a variety of "cannabinoids." There may well be other active cannabinoids in marijuana, but this has yet to be demonstrated. The THC content of different preparations of marijuana varies. Prior to 1973, "street" marijuana typically possessed less than one percent THC; now a THC content of 5 percent or more is common.

Marijuana is smoked for pleasure, and its users often report that it elevates mood and enhances enjoyment of music and other sensual experiences, including sex. In one survey, Charles Tart interviewed 150 experienced marijuana users in 1968–1969. Tart's sample of marijuana smokers distinguished three levels of marijuana intoxication. At low levels, they reported being quiet at parties, "more quiet than if drunk," and interested in subtle musical sounds. At medium levels, they reported they were more noisy and boisterous, experienced new qualities about themselves, and their need for the enjoyment of sex increased. At strong intoxication they became easily distracted, had poorer memory, felt emotions more strongly, and experienced heightened qualities to sexual orgasm (Tart, 1971).

For many, marijuana is primarily a social drug, to be used as an alternative to alcohol at parties. Users often prefer it to alcohol because they prefer the alteration of consciousness it produces and because they feel that marijuana is not as serious a health hazard as alcohol. In this latter point they are, unfortunately, wrong.

Smoking marijuana impairs memory. Something learned during marijuana intoxication is difficult to recall when not under the influence. Smoking marijuana seems to interfere with the transfer of information into permanent memory (Tinkelberg & Darley, 1975). Marijuana intoxication is also quite detrimental to driving. It interferes with driving as tested on the road and increases the rate of fatal accidents (Sterling-Smith, 1976). Marijuana interferes with normal lung functioning (Taskin, Calvarese, Simmons, & Shapiro, 1978) and decreases sperm count and motility. Although no definitive studies have been done, pregnant women should avoid it.

LSD

LSD is derived from a fungus that grows on rye, called *ergot.* When ergot-infected rye bread is eaten, a disease known as ergotism results. One symptom of the disease is hallucinations.

LSD is one of the most powerful drugs known. Albert Hoffman first synthesized it in 1943. In a test, he took what he thought was an infinitesimal dose, about 250 micrograms (250-millionths of a gram) and wrote down his experience:

> After 40 minutes, I noted the following symptoms in my laboratory journal: slight giddiness, restlessness, difficulty in concentration, visual disturbances, laughing . . . [Later:] I lost all count of time, I noticed with dismay that my environment was undergoing progressive changes. My visual field wavered and everything appeared deformed as in a faulty mirror. Space and time became more and more disorganized and I was overcome by a fear that I was going out of my mind. The worst part of it being that I was clearly aware of my condition. My power of observation was unimpaired. . . . Occasionally, I felt as if I were out of my body. I thought I had died. My ego seemed suspended somewhere in space, from where I saw my dead body lying on the sofa. . . . It was particularly striking how acoustic perceptions, such as the noise of water gushing from a tap or the spoken word, were transformed into optical illusions. I then fell asleep and awakened the next morning somewhat tired but otherwise feeling perfectly well. (Hoffman, 1968)

As little as 10 micrograms can produce noticeable effects: mild euphoria and de-automatization (the unravelling of normally associated schemata), very simi-

FIGURE 7-9

Drawings Made under the Influence of LSD
The first drawing (A), made 25 minutes after the first dose, shows the drug had not yet taken effect. After a second dose (B), the man had little control of his hand's movements. The man was unhappy with the third drawing (C), and 2 hours and 45 minutes after the first dose the full effect of the LSD was discernible in the highly distorted fourth drawing (D). After 5 hours and 45 minutes the drug's influence was still obvious (E), but the effects were starting to wear off. Eight hours after the first dose the intoxication had worn off, but the quality of the last drawing (F) was not on par with that of the first.

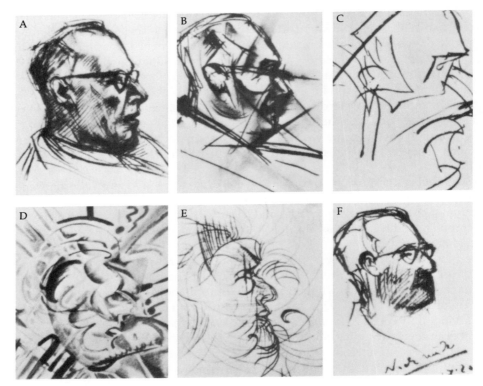

lar to the effect of marijuana. A dose of 250 micrograms causes major effects, which increase up to the usual high dose of 500 micrograms. The lethal dose of LSD is unknown. In the only reported case of death due to the drug's direct physiological effects, an autopsy suggested that 320,000 micrograms (about 1,000 times the normal dose) had been injected intravenously (Grinspoon & Bakalar, 1979).

The drug has a dramatic effect on conscious experience: sensation is enhanced, de-automatization occurs, emotions are greatly amplified, and thought processes are transformed (Figure 7-9). Users may identify themselves with everything from animals to God.

There are four forms of LSD experiences (Barr, Langs, Holt, Goldberger, & Klein, 1972):

1. Elation, loss of inhibition, and loss of control of attention.
2. Feelings of unreality and of being dissociated, the ability to observe one's self, fear and suspicion, loss of control, and regression to infancy.
3. Body image alterations and physical symptoms.
4. Anxiety and fear of losing control.

The effect of LSD on an individual is influenced by the interpretation: when people take the drug and do not know that they are taking it, the effects can be disastrous. The perceptual distortions that might occasion great interest in those who know they have taken the drug can be terrifying to someone who is ignorant of that fact. Suicides have resulted from failure to interpret the experience of an LSD ''trip'' properly.

New Approach to Dream Research

Since we are unconscious of the external world during sleep, dreams have often been considered the most involuntary and unconscious of mental processes. Recent research, however, indicates that at times we can be fully conscious in our dreams while remaining soundly asleep. People have long reported sometimes knowing that they are dreaming while dreaming and being able to control their dreams. LaBerge, Nagel, Dement, and Zarcone (1981) devised a method for testing claims for such ''lucid'' dreaming in the sleep laboratory. Relying on the correspondence between the pattern of dream gaze changes and actual eye movements, they asked five self-reported lucid dreamers to signal by means of regular eye movements whenever they became conscious that they were dreaming. The results showed that lucid dreams occurred during bona fide REM sleep.

The ability of proficient lucid dreamers to communicate in this way has made possible a new approach to dream research. Trained subjects can remember to carry out previously agreed-upon experimental tasks during their lucid dreams. In this way the relationship between subjectively experienced dream events and corresponding objectively measured physiological processes can be studied.

LaBerge (1985) has described a series of such studies showing striking physiological correlation for a variety of dreamed behaviors, including time estimation, breathing, singing, counting, and sexual activity. The strength of the psychophysiological correlations observed in these studies suggests that, from the brain's perspective, dreaming of doing something is more similar to actually doing it than merely imagining doing it. Perhaps that is why dreams seem so real while they last.

Parapsychology

Parapsychology is a field of psychology dealing with the study of extraordinary experiences. It is an extremely controversial area of research attracting both ardent believers and extreme skeptics.

In almost everyone's life are moments of extraordinary coincidence. You ''knew'' the phone was going to ring before it did. You have a dream about a friend who is in trouble and you wake to find that he has been in an accident. Over the centuries there have been accounts of people who could ''read'' others' minds, who dreamt of events that occurred in the future, who could move objects at will. These are called *paranormal phenomena.* If they could be demonstrated scientifically, the implications would be enormous. If people can foresee events, if they can communicate through thought alone over great distances, if they can influence others' actions or events at a distance, then it would be necessary to completely revise our notions of space, time, and human consciousness. Since there is so much at stake, it is not surprising that the scientific community sets a high standard of proof regarding these phenomena.

Paranormal abilities (called *psi abilities*) are classified into two categories: **extrasensory perception (ESP),** the ability to communicate and acquire information about the world by means other than those familiar to us (such as talking and reading); and **psychokinesis (PK),** the ability to affect the physical world by mental force alone, such as transporting objects merely by willing.

Experiments in Parapsychology

The first major obstacle to parapsychological research was how to go about studying a phenomenon that might not even exist. Parapsychological research began in the 1930s in the United States in the laboratory of J. B. Rhine at Duke University. To rid parapsychology of the "freak show" stigma, Rhine instituted a card-guessing paradigm. Subjects were asked to guess which cards the experimenter was holding. If the subject guessed accurately several times, that would be evidence of ESP. However, in a series of well-controlled experiments over 30 years of extensive research, few positive results were obtained. Few scores were above chance; these results could mean that paranormal phenomena do not exist; they could also mean that these kinds of experiments will not discover them.

More recently, researchers in parapsychology have attempted to develop more sophisticated methods than those used by Rhine and to look at more subtle phenomena. Attempts to produce repeatable scientific investigations have fallen into several categories (Beloff, 1978):

1. A conducive state of mind. REM sleep and borderline states have been investigated (Honorton, 1974; Ullman, Krippner, & Vaughn, 1973).
2. A method of training psi ability. Such methods include feedback on right and wrong choices (Tart, 1977).
3. People with psi. Often "psychics" and "mediums" with spectacular claims have been studied. The most famous modern psychic is Uri Geller, who claims he can receive telepathic (mental) communication and perform psychokinesis (Figure 7-10). Most of his "feats," however, have been repeated by professional magicians (Randi, 1975; Targ & Puthoff, 1977).

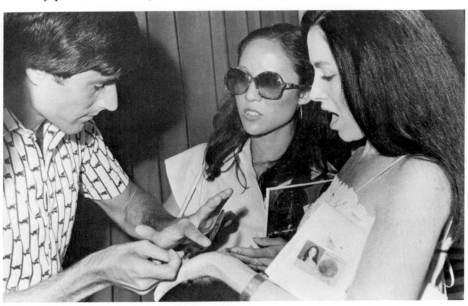

FIGURE 7-10
"Demonstration" of Paranormal Abilities
The famous psychic Uri Geller, shown here bending a spoon, claims to have psychokinetic ability, but most of his "feats" have been shown to be elaborate magic tricks.

4. A dependable physiological reaction to extrasensory signals. Perhaps ESP is unavailable to normal consciousness, but can be injected into awareness. Experiments have been conducted in an attempt to influence such processes as heart rate (Tart, Puthoff, & Targ, 1979).

Two major difficulties continually beset parapsychological researchers who report some positive findings: (1) there are no repeatable effects, and (2) when there are mild successes, their effects seem to decline with practice, which is the opposite of what would normally be expected.

Unfortunately, there have not been as yet any reliable demonstrations of paranormal abilities. Perhaps you, the current or next generation of researchers, will come up with convincing demonstrations of the existence of paranormal abilities. Until then, whether some individuals have "special gifts" or whether all humans have "hidden" mental abilities remains a fascinating, elusive, unproven area of research.

Self-Regulation

For centuries there have been reports from India of extraordinary self-control by Yogis. These adepts were said to be able to control their experience of pain when lying on a bed of nails or walking across hot coals. Recently, developments in both consciousness research and technology have made it possible to evaluate these claims, which have been confirmed in precise studies (Bagchi & Wenger, 1957).

Control of Internal Processes

Several internal processes can be consciously controlled. These include the electrical potential of the skin, heart rate, blood pressure, muscle tension, and electrical activity of the brain (Miller, 1980). Perhaps other controls will be uncovered.

Studies in self-regulation have led to experimental clinical treatments to control seizures without using drugs (Sterman, 1978). Tension headache and anxiety have also been treated experimentally using biofeedback techniques, specifically by reducing tension in the frontalis muscle of the forehead (Budzynski, 1981). Migraine headaches have been successfully treated by redirecting blood flow from the head to the hands.

Biofeedback

The method of training people to control internal processes not normally controlled by consciousness is called **biofeedback** (Figure 7-11). Glandular and muscular activity, brain waves, and blood pressure have all been controlled through these techniques (Miller, 1978). In biofeedback, individuals' physiological processes, such as heart rate, are converted into easily perceived information and then communicated to them. Their heartbeats may be amplified so they can easily hear the sounds. If they want to slow their heartbeat, they breathe differently, concentrate, and try to relax. If they succeed, they will immediately hear a slower heartbeat. When previously unconscious information is vividly brought to consciousness, action can be taken and the internal processes can be altered.

FIGURE 7-11
Biofeedback
Modern equipment is used
for self-regulation of
internal processes through
biofeedback.

Biofeedback is of interest to researchers because it is a drug-free therapy (free of unwanted side effects) and it is a new way to study consciousness.

Concluding Remarks

Consciousness is so difficult to study objectively that researchers had to wait for the development of new and sophisticated techniques such as biofeedback, the analysis of REM sleep, and studies of the physiology of meditation. Investigations so far reveal that human consciousness is much more diverse and variable than most people have thought. Consciousness changes radically each day because there exist many divisions of consciousness, each activated by different circumstances. We may have more control over internal environment than has been thought.

SUMMARY

1. Consciousness (a) selects information from the inner and outer world, (b) guides and oversees actions, (c) sets priorities for actions, and (d) detects and resolves discrepancies.

2. The structure of the mind can be compared to that of a newspaper. Consciousness is the "front page" of the mind, and below it are many different levels of awareness: (a) *Subconscious awareness.* When something is in awareness, it means that we are keeping track of it. We are aware of a great deal, much more than we realize. (b) *Preconscious memories.* These enable us to operate in the world. Episodic memory consists of specific memories of our lives, and representational memory is our stored, general knowledge of the world. (c) *Nonconscious processes.* These are concerned with regulating the automatic functioning of the body. (d) *Unconscious processes.* The unconscious is the part of the mind, postulated by Freud, in which memories and thoughts that are difficult to deal with consciously are hidden.

3. *Dissociation* is a division in consciousness in which an experience can only be recovered under specific conditions. Dissociation includes hypnotic trances and multiple personality, thought by many psychologists to be an extreme version of the divisions of consciousness in every person's mind.

4. Consciousness goes through borderline states each day when the mode of consciousness is receptive. These include *daydreams* in which individuals, unable to receive enough outside stimulation, create their own internal world, and *hypnopompic* and *hypnagogic* states, which occur just before waking and just before sleep, respectively.

5. During sleep, periods of involuntary rapid eye movement (REM) and intense bodily activity alternate regularly with periods of quiet sleep. During REM, the eyes move rapidly, breathing and heart rate become irregular, there is erection in the male and vaginal engorgement in the female, and the vestibular system is activated. All other commands for voluntary muscle movement are blocked. REM periods occur every night and are strongly associated with dreaming.

6. Sequential stages of sleep occur throughout the night. Stage 1 sleep is the entrance into sleep and is a drowsy period lasting only a few minutes. Stage 2 sleep is marked by the appearance of "sleep spindles" on the EEG and a further relaxation in muscle tension. Stage 3 is reached when 20 to 50 percent of the EEG record is filled with high-amplitude, slow (delta) waves. When delta activity is more than 50 percent, the deepest stage of sleep (stage 4) is reached. During these stages there is no REM and EMG is normally low. The stages then reverse, but instead of stage 1, a period of REM and dreaming occurs, lasting about 10 minutes. The cycle of sleep stages is repeated three or four times each night.

7. Freud thought that dreams served two functions. The first is *wish fulfillment;* dreams are one of the few times when normally forbidden desires rise to the surface of consciousness. These pent-up desires are diminished to some extent by being expressed in dream consciousness. Second, he thought that dreams guard sleep. The expression of these unconscious desires may become frightening to the sleeper. If the dream is upsetting enough, the person will wake up. Freud felt that dreams guard sleep by transforming the unconscious desires into disguised symbols; for instance, a snake might represent the penis.

8. Another, more scientific, dream theory is *activation synthesis* in which dream phenomena are interpreted as derived from the unique state of the brain and nervous system during sleep. Dreams are the attempt of the perceptual processes to organize the diverse information in consciousness that needs to be assimilated or accommodated. The commonly reported dream of being chased and unable to avoid the pursuer may be an interpretation of the blocked motor commands to our muscles during REM sleep. Floating experiences may be the interpretation of vestibular activation. Dreams are often incoherent, and such abrupt shifts in imagery may be the brain's attempt to integrate many diverse signals.

9. Throughout history people have tried to deliberately alter consciousness through several basic methods. Meditation includes a number of techniques aimed at knowledge of oneself and one's place in the world rather than intellectual knowledge. Important in these is *concentrative meditation,* in which a person restricts attention to one unchanging source of stimulation, such as their breathing or a repeated word. This form of meditation seems to produce measurable change in the brain's activity, a shutting off of response to the external world.

10. Many techniques open up and de-automatize consciousness and produce what has been called *religious* or *mystical experiences*. Among these techniques are upsets of routine, unsolvable problems, and tales of the Sufi tradition, called *teaching stories*. These stories contain specifically chosen patterns of events that encourage openness to new ideas. Characteristics of the mystical experience include a sense of unity, realness, ineffability, and vividness and richness.

11. An important technique to alter consciousness is *hypnosis,* which is a deliberate, voluntary form of dissociation. The individual relinquishes normal control of consciousness to another person. General characteristics of the hypnotic condition are that attention can be changed—narrowed or broadened—according to instructions. Distortions of reality are accepted; the person can act out roles suggested by the hypnotist and can be given suggestions about posthypnotic behavior.

12. Drugs that alter consciousness can be divided into five classes: (a) *analgesics* (e.g., morphine and heroin) reduce the experience of pain; (b) *sedatives* (e.g., barbiturates) induce relaxation and sleep; (c) *stimulants* (e.g., amphetamines) elevate mood and increase alertness; (d) *psychoactive drugs* (e.g., marijuana and LSD) change the overall structure of consciousness; and (e) *Psychiatric drugs* (e.g., lithium) help to normalize consciousness by correcting neurochemical imbalances.

13. Parapsychology is the study of extraordinary experiences. Paranormal abilities (*psi abilities*) are classified into two categories: *extrasensory perception* (ESP), and *psychokinesis* (PK). Most studies of parapsychology have failed to convince the scientific community of the validity of the phenomena. Several things are sought: a conducive state of mind, such as REM sleep; a method of training psi ability; special people with psi; and dependable physiological reactions to extrasensory signals. Two problems in parapsychology are that there seem to be no repeatable effects, and when there are mild successes, they seem to decline with practice.

14. Several internal processes can be consciously controlled: the electrical potential of the skin, heart rate, blood pressure, muscle tension, and the electrical activity of the brain. It is the hope of researchers that many of the previously "involuntary" processes of the body may be brought under conscious control.

TERMS AND CONCEPTS

activation synthesis
analgesics
automatization
biofeedback
borderline states
daydreaming
dissociation
extrasensory perception
hidden observer
hypnagogic
hypnopompic
hypnosis
levels of awareness
meditation
multiple personality
nonconscious

parapsychology
pontine reticular formation
preconscious memories
psychiatric drugs
psychoactive drugs
psychokinesis
religious experiences
REM sleep
sedatives
sensory deprivation
sleep spindles
stages of sleep
stimulants
subliminal perception
teaching story
unconscious

LaBerge, S. (1986). *Lucid dreaming.* New York: Ballantine.

A well-written and even lucid account of teaching self-control of dreams.

Ornstein, R. (1986). *The psychology of consciousness* (3rd ed.). New York: Penguin Books.

An attempt to bring together much of the diverse literature on consciousness for students who wish to take matters in this chapter further.

Shah, I. (1982). *Seeker after truth.* New York: Harper & Row.

One of many of Idries Shah's books for persons seriously interested in developing a more comprehensive personal understanding. Highly recommended.

Wolman, B. B., & Ullman, M. (Eds.). (1986). *Handbook of states of consciousness.* New York: Van Nostrand–Reinhold.

A collection of diverse approaches to the study of consciousness.

The Basics of Learning

I don't eat Mexican food. My friends always make fun of me because of this. You're so inconsistent, they tell me, you love hot food, like Indian curry. You love tomatoes, onions, garlic, and avocadoes. It is strange to me too. It's not just that I don't care for the food, I simply can't bear the thought of eating it, no matter what. Until I did the research for this chapter, I never understood *why* I feel this way about Mexican food.

I certainly do know *when* and *where* I developed my problem. About 20 years ago I was working as a deckhand on a freighter. It stopped at the port of Zihuatenejo, on the west coast of Mexico. We arrived one night and I went ashore to enjoy a meal given for the ship's crew. The ship was going to leave the port early the next morning. That night it was my turn to stand watch on the bow. Before the sun came up a terrific storm arose; the rain poured and the wind blew. The bow of the ship heaved again and again out of the water, crashing back into the sea. The only way I could stand up on deck was to tie myself onto the little perch on the bow. So I bounced and heaved (in more than one sense of the word!) along with the ship itself.

When all had calmed down, I returned to my quarters, sick and completely exhausted. I slept for 12 hours. When I awoke I was afraid of returning to the bow of the ship. I was also completely disgusted by the idea of Mexican food. My fear of the bow was completely understandable, and I got over it fast. I returned to my regular watch two or three days later. However, I have never been able to eat Mexican food again. Although I "knew" the cause of my sickness was the storm and not the dinner, my *association* of the dinner with the sickness was too deep.

Association

The experience just described is quite unusual, but what we know of our world consists in large part of associating things that occur together. If a traffic light flashes red, you hit the brakes without thinking because the light has come to "mean" STOP. When the music begins to swell in a movie, you know that a big clinch is coming. You can almost anticipate the heroine rushing into the hero's arms. When the music becomes low and menacing, you know the hero is in trouble. The dinner bell conjures up the taste and smell of food: the sound has become associated with the idea of food. These simple **associations** form the basis of our knowledge of the world. They underlie our ability to know what events occur together, how events are linked to actions, and how actions are linked to one another.

Associations are basic to the mind. How they are formed has been the subject of more research in psychology than any other topic. We know the specific conditions under which simple associations occur; in fact, the process of forming

Much of the advertising industry is based on the idea of forcing an association between a desirable image and a product.

associations is called *conditioning*. We even know that certain kinds of associations, especially those involving food, are probably built into us.

Association is one of psychology's oldest principles. The study of associations began with the Greek philosophers and was revived by the British empiricists in the seventeenth century. Such philosophers as John Locke, David Hume, and John Stuart Mill felt that the "association of ideas" is the bond that connects all experience. What they meant by "idea" is what we might now call a sensation or a thought. "Ideas" become associated when they occur close to each other in space or time. John Locke (1670) wrote:

> A man has suffered pain or sickness in a place; he saw his friend die in such a room, though these have in nature nothing to do with one another, yet when the idea of the place occurs to mind, it brings (the impressions being once made) that of pain and displeasure with it, he confounds them in his mind and can as little bear the one as the other.

The empiricists, who have been quite influential in science's view of the human mind, believed that knowledge came from experience. They felt that, at birth, the mind is a blank slate and that our specific experiences are "written" on this slate. Of course, the "blank slate" has to have the innate ability to learn from experience, so something still has to be built in (Cosmides & Toohy, 1986).

It isn't necessary to accept that we are a blank slate to understand the importance of associations. There is much evidence that some of our abilities and "knowledge" *are* built in. Infants are *prepared* to react to their world in a certain way, and different species are prepared biologically to learn different things. Human beings, for instance, learn language easily, while other species do not. Associations are learned, but various organisms are biologically "prepared" to learn some things more easily than others.

CLASSICAL OR RESPONDENT CONDITIONING

A student of mine was once watching a television program about how bees make honey from flowers. At one point in the program, the narrator shook a box of flowers to demonstrate how much pollen there is in them. When the yellow stuff appeared on the screen, my student began to sneeze violently. Of course, she was allergic to pollen itself, not to the *sight* of it. But a long period of

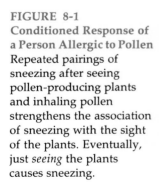

FIGURE 8-1
Conditioned Response of a Person Allergic to Pollen Repeated pairings of sneezing after seeing pollen-producing plants and inhaling pollen strengthens the association of sneezing with the sight of the plants. Eventually, just *seeing* the plants causes sneezing.

experiencing bouts of sneezing after seeing and inhaling pollen made her associate sneezing with seeing pollen. Her response had become "conditioned" to the sight of pollen (Figure 8-1).

We all have similar experiences. One man underwent psychotherapy because of a learned fear. He was in his car, waiting for a red light to change, when his car was struck by another from the rear. His head went into the windshield. Afterward, he became extremely fearful not only of driving a car, but even of sitting in one. One woman, who was laughed at once when she spoke in class, was fearful of ever speaking in a group again (Wolpe, 1981).

But exactly how do these associations develop? What are the rules governing the formation of associations? Once formed, do associations disappear? Some of the earliest scientific experiments designed to answer these questions were by Ivan Pavlov (1849–1936).

Pavlov's Experiments

Pavlov was a Russian physiologist whose work on digestive processes earned him a Nobel Prize in 1904. Today, he is most remembered for his contribution to the psychology of learning. This work, like many important experiments, began by accident. To study the role of salivation in digestion, Pavlov invented a procedure that allowed him to measure saliva precisely. He cut a small slit in each laboratory dog's cheek and inserted one end of a tube into the salivary glands. The other end he inserted into a measuring device (Figure 8-2). When a piece of meat or meat powder was put into the dog's mouth, the saliva was caught and measured.

The dogs soon began to ruin Pavlov's experiment. After a few trials with the same dog, the salivation began *before* the food was put in the dog's mouth. The dogs even went so far as to salivate at the sight of the person who usually brought the food or when they heard the rattling of the food trays. The dogs were learning to anticipate the arrival of food. Pavlov realized that he could study the process of "association" with this experimental setup. At the time, studying associations was the realm of philosophy or psychology—both of which were deemed

Ivan Pavlov
(1849–1936)

FIGURE 8-2
Apparatus Used by Pavlov in His Experiments in Classical Conditioning

unscientific by Pavlov. Yet, this procedure allowed him to produce an observable, measurable response (salivation) that could objectively be used as an index of "associative strength." That is, Pavlov set out to discover the *conditions* under which a dog would come to associate a previously "neutral" stimulus with food. Hence, he gave his research the name **conditioning.** In fact, over 60 percent of the terms we use today in animal learning were first coined by Pavlov (Bower & Hilgard, 1981).

First, he designed a special environment in which he could control all the stimuli. The environment included the apparatus shown in Figure 8-2. The dog was harnessed so that it couldn't move and was forced to see the experimental stimulus. The laboratory was soundproof. Pavlov delivered the food by remote control and watched the dog from behind a silvered mirror. He then flashed a light. The dog noticed it, but did not salivate. Food was presented and the dog ate and salivated as normal. Then again the light was flashed and food was presented. After a number of repetitions or "trials," the dog salivated when the light was flashed but *before* the food was presented. Later, the dog salivated when the light was flashed, even if the food was not presented at all. The change in the response is evidence that the dog has learned to associate the flash of light with the food.

Some Definitions

When food is in the mouth, salivation always occurs. This salivary reflex is called an **unconditioned response (UCR).** The taste of food is the **unconditioned stimulus (UCS)** that elicits the UCR. The flash of light had an important effect on the dog's behavior but only under a specific condition: after it had been paired temporally with tasting the food (UCS). The flash of light is called the **conditioned stimulus (CS).** When the dog salivated at the sight of the light, it was a **conditioned response (CR).** Pavlov used the word "conditional," meaning that the response is conditional upon the presence of the stimulus. The term now used is *conditioned.*

How a previously neutral stimulus (NS) comes to have a significant effect on an organism's behavior is called **classical** or **respondent conditioning** (Figure 8-3). The process works this way. An unconditioned stimulus (UCS), such as the taste of meat, always elicits the unconditioned response (UCR), such as salivation. The CS, such as a bell, is repeatedly paired with the UCS. Eventually it elicits a response equivalent to the UCR, which is designated as a CR. The unconditioned and conditioned responses are often the same physiological response, as in the salivating dog. In this example, associations in the dog's mind trigger a response

FIGURE 8-3
Relationship of Stimuli to Responses Before, During, and After Classical Conditioning

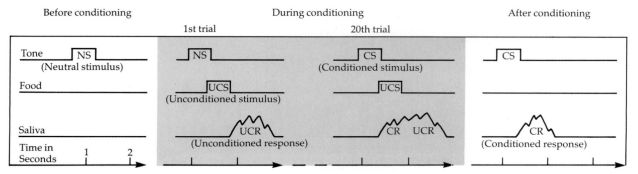

that is normally physiologically initiated. However, the conditioned response is not always identical to the unconditioned response. For instance, if a dog is shocked, it will jump and flinch (UCR). But if a light is used as the conditioned stimulus to the shock, the dog will crouch or freeze (CR) when the light is flashed instead of flinching.

Importance of Basic Conditioning

Pavlov was able to explain how new behaviors can be acquired. This process of building new connections allows an organism more flexibility than if it were limited to the few reflexes with which it was born. *If we could not be conditioned, we would not be able to survive.* In Pavlov's words:

> The complex conditions of everyday existence require a much more detailed and specialized correlation between the animal and its environment than is afforded by the inborn reflexes alone. This more precise correlation can be established only through the medium of the cerebral hemispheres; and we have found that a great number of all sorts of stimuli always act through the medium of the hemispheres as temporary and interchangeable signals for the comparatively small number of agencies of a general character which determine the inborn reflexes, and that this is the only means by which a most delicate adjustment of the organism to the environment can be established. (Pavlov, 1927)

Conditions of Conditioning

Stimulus Significance

If you were sitting in a library reading and someone dropped a book nearby, you might automatically turn and think, "What is it?" Numerous physiological changes would take place preparing you for possible action. You would stop doing what you were doing. Your senses would sharpen and your muscles would tense. This set of responses is called the **orienting reflex.** It occurs in response to any perceived novel or unexpected stimulus.

If a stimulus loses its novelty by repetition, the orienting reflex habituates unless the stimulus is made significant by conditioning. Pavlov found that only stimuli that initially elicited an orienting reflex could be made conditioned stimuli. This was Pavlov's way of making certain the animals were perceiving the stimuli he used.

There are two classes of stimuli that are significant: those the organism seeks to *approach* and those it tries to *avoid.* There are two corresponding kinds of conditioning called appetitive and aversive. Food, sex, and water are unconditioned stimuli that an organism might like to approach (when hungry, aroused, or thirsty). Shock, pain, and loud noises are stimuli that an organism would usually try to avoid. *Appetitive conditioning* refers to the procedure in which an organism is conditioned to positive, pleasant stimuli. *Aversive conditioning* refers to conditioning that avoids painful events.

Timing and Frequency of Stimuli

There are bound to be many stimuli in the environment when a UCS is presented. Consequently, which stimulus comes to acquire the status of a CS is contingent on when and how often it is paired with the UCS. These contingencies are known as the principles of *recency* and *frequency.*

Recency.   There are five different temporal arrangements of CS and UCS.

1. Simultaneous—the CS and the UCS are presented at the same time.
2. Delay—the CS is presented and continues until the UCS is presented.
3. Trace—the CS is presented but is discontinued before presentation of the UCS.
4. Backward—the CS is presented after the UCS.
5. Temporal—the CS in this case is time; the UCS is simply presented at precisely regular intervals.

Delay is the most effective arrangement, and backward conditioning is the least effective. This is probably because stimuli presented just before the UCS can be used to prepare the organism for the UCS. Stimuli presented after the UCS are of no such use. Given that the stimulus to be conditioned must occur *before* the UCS, does it matter how much earlier? If the stimulus precedes the UCS by too much time, for example, half an hour, then it will not effectively predict exactly when the UCS will be presented. On the other hand, if the stimulus precedes the UCS by too little time, for example, one-thousandth of a second, then the organism will not be able to react in time to take advantage of the warning. The optimal *interstimulus interval* is between these extremes. It is usually about 0.5 second for such responses as an eye blink or a foot jerk, but longer for automatic responses such as salivation, about 5 to 30 seconds.

Frequency.   How often a CS must be presented before it elicits a CR depends on the nature of both the stimulus and the response. Some associations are so easily formed that they require only one trial or a very few. For example, the relationship between food and sickness is so strong that anyone who gets sick is likely to associate the illness with a particular food, even if the experience happens only once (Revusky & Garcia, 1970). This is something I know well!

Acquisition and Extinction

Other characteristics of the stimulus affect classical conditioning as well. Because of habituation, a constant stimulus such as a shining light is not as effective as an irregular one such as a flashing light. The intensity of competing stimuli is another factor in the acquisition of a CR. Moderate stimuli are most easily conditioned, but a weak stimulus may take longer. An extremely strong stimulus may prevent classical conditioning altogether by producing disruption. The more often a neutral stimulus is paired with an unconditioned stimulus (UCS), the faster the conditioned response (CR) will be acquired.

As discussed previously, most conditioned responses are acquired by repeated pairing of UCS and CS, but what happens to a CR if it is no longer reinforced? What if the bell continues to sound, but no food is presented? If after a conditioned response has been acquired, the CS is presented *without* the UCS, the CR gradually decreases (Figure 8-4). This procedure is called **extinction.** The CR has not been completely eliminated, however, if when the CS is presented after some time has elapsed, the CR reappears. This is *spontaneous recovery.*

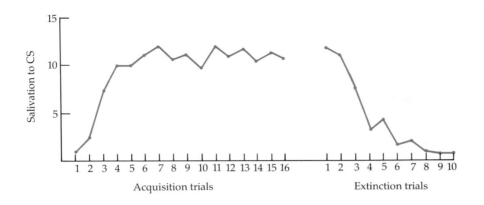

FIGURE 8-4
Acquisition and
Extinction
A CR is gradually acquired
by repeated pairings of
UCS and CS. But when the
reinforcement in the form
of the UCS is removed and
the CS is presented alone,
the CR steadily decreases,
which is called extinction.

Generalization and Discrimination

Respondent conditioning would have little importance in learning if an organism did not transfer knowledge from one situation to another. We know someone is at the door whether the signal is a bell, buzzer, knocker, or chimes. **Generalization** means that once a specific stimulus has become a CS, *similar* stimuli will elicit the conditioned response. The more similar the stimuli, the stronger the transfer of the conditioned response.

Generalization is common to all forms of learning. Watson and Raynor (1920) gave a 1-year-old baby named Albert a white rat to play with. As Albert crawled to the rat to pet it, Watson stood behind the baby and banged a steel bar. They repeated the procedure until Albert began to cry (CR) as soon as he saw the rat (CS). Although Albert was only conditioned to fear white rats, this fear *generalized* to a white dog, a rabbit, a fur coat, and even a Santa Claus mask.

Gregory Razran (1939) demonstrated the principle of generalization in an experiment on *semantic conditioning*—the alteration of responses to words. Razran conditioned college students to salivate to certain words. He flashed the words "style, urn, freeze" on a screen as they sucked on lollipops. Soon, when those words appeared on the screen, the students salivated (CR). New words were then flashed that were either homonyms or synonyms of the original list. There was little salivary response to the homonyms "stile, earn, frieze," but the synonyms "fashion, vase, chill" did elicit the CR. Thus, the conditioned response can generalize to the *meaning* of words.

Generalization tests the ability to observe similarities. It is also important for organisms to know differences between stimuli; this ability is called **discrimination.** If a dog is conditioned to salivate to a certain tone, according to the principle of generalization, it will salivate to a similar tone. But if food does not follow the similar tone for several pairings, the dog will no longer respond to that tone. It will still respond to the original. In this example, we would say that the dog has learned to *discriminate* between the tones (Pavlov, 1927).

Human discrimination appears in infants' learning of language (Brown, 1965). Initially, infants are positively reinforced for saying "da-da" and "ma-ma" in the presence of parents. These words are then generalized and applied to all adults, strangers included. Since infants are not reinforced for these responses, they learn to discriminate and use the words correctly.

What happens if impossible discriminations are demanded? Pavlov and a student in his laboratory found that extremely fine discriminations can cause an animal to become "neurotic." First, they conditioned a dog to salivate (CR) to the sight of a circle (CS) projected on a screen. Then they projected a picture of an elongated ellipse, not followed by food. The dog soon learned to discriminate between the ellipse and the circle. Then Pavlov began presenting the dog with increasingly circular ellipses. The dog was able to make discriminations, but at the same time, the whole behavior of the animal underwent an abrupt change. The hitherto quiet dog began to squeal in its apparatus. It kept wriggling about, and with its feet, tore off the apparatus for mechanical stimulation of the skin. It also bit through the tubes connecting the animal's room with the observer, a behavior that never had happened before. On being taken into the experimental room, the dog began barking violently, which was also contrary to its usual custom. In short, it presented all the symptoms of a condition of acute neurosis.

Applications of Respondent Conditioning

It is possible that Albert (the subject of Watson and Raynor's experiment, who would now be in his late 60s) may still be afraid of white rats and Santa Claus beards and psychologists in white coats. It is more likely, however, that his fear underwent extinction as he met many white furry things throughout his life that were not followed by terrifying sounds. It is also possible that fear can be so intense that it generalizes to representations or even thoughts of the CS. Some people are so terrified of flying that they become frightened even thinking about it.

Mary Cover Jones (1924) discovered a method, using extinction and generalization, to help people overcome their fears. The method is called **counterconditioning.** In counterconditioning, an unwanted CR is eliminated by conditioning the subject to another stimulus (CS). The CS elicits a new conditioned response (CR) that is less disruptive than the unwanted CR. Jones found a child named Peter who was afraid of rabbits. In an experiment, Peter was put in a high chair and given some candies to eat. While he was enjoying the candy, she brought a rabbit close to the high chair. When Peter screamed, Jones moved the rabbit back until he was appeased. Each day she inched the rabbit closer and closer. After six weeks of trials, the rabbit sat on the high chair with Peter. Once the boy even asked for the rabbit when it wasn't there. What had happened was that the rabbit was no longer a CS associated only with a fearful CR. It became associated with an enjoyable CR, that is, eating candy.

Another useful application of respondent conditioning comes from taste aversion research. Alcoholics given Antabuse will suffer a violent nausea if they drink alcohol. In many cases the taste of alcohol is later avoided because it was paired with sickness.

OPERANT OR INSTRUMENTAL CONDITIONING

Respondent (classical) conditioning describes how we learn to associate different events in the world. *Instrumental conditioning* describes how we learn to *act* in the world to get what we want. One major principle of instrumental conditioning is very familiar: *we act in such a way as to seek pleasure and avoid pain.* In psychology this is called the *Law of Effect.*

Law of Effect

Edward Thorndike (1874–1949) was an early investigator of how an organism learns new behaviors. One of his experiments involved cats trying to escape a locked cage to get food. The cat could escape the cage by unlatching a string that held the door closed. A hungry cat will move around and claw the cage. Eventually it will accidentally loosen the string that releases the door and escape. Each time it is put in the cage, its behavior will become increasingly organized. Instead of random clawing, it will head right for the string and unlatch the door. This is evidence that the cat has learned to open the cage. This process is called **instrumental conditioning** because the cat's actions were *instrumental* in getting what the cat wanted (Hilgard & Marquis, 1940).

Thorndike proposed that learning is governed by the **Law of Effect:** any action that is followed by a "satisfying state of affairs" is likely to be repeated. Similarly, any action that results in an "annoying state of affairs" probably will not be. The Law of Effect is a useful way to predict behavior. If you put your hand into a fire, you get burned and you are unlikely to do it again. If while wandering, you find a beautiful stream, you may go there straight away the next time you are out walking.

B. F. Skinner

Operant Conditioning

In a very important series of studies in the late 1930s, B. F. Skinner described two kinds of learning. This famous behaviorist gave respondent conditioning its name because it is the *response* of the organism that is conditioned. He renamed instrumental conditioning to **operant conditioning** because it is the organism's *operations* or actions that are conditioned in this case. In respondent or classical conditioning the UCS both *precedes* and *reflexively elicits* the response, while in operant conditioning the UCS (reinforcement) *follows* the response which is *voluntarily emitted*. Operant conditioning involves feedback: the organism's responses are part of the system, unlike respondent conditioning. Operant conditioning is based on a principle similar to the Law of Effect. All actions have certain consequences, and those consequences increase or decrease the possibility of recurrence of that action. Consequences of actions that increase the probability of the recurrence of those actions are called *reinforcements*. Reinforcements are central to the operant conditioning approach and are discussed in the next section.

The Skinner Box

Skinner invented a controlled environment commonly known as the "Skinner box." It contains a food tray, a lever, and a water spout. A rat is placed inside the box (Figure 8-5). Food pellets dropped into the tray by a mechanical device make a clicking sound as the pellets are released. Quickly the rat shows a conditioned response to the click and runs to the tray. At this stage of the experiment, the lever is not connected to the food dispenser. This is because it is necessary to determine how often the rat presses the bar by chance. The number of times this response is made before conditioning is called the **operant level** of the response.

Once the operant level is determined, the lever is hooked up to the food dispensing device. When the rat again presses the bar, it will hear the click of the food dispenser. It takes a few such bar pressings for most rats to begin to change their behavior. Once the connection between bar pressing and food is made, the rat's behavior becomes notably reorganized. Since food is a desirable consequence to a hungry rat, it is likely that bar pressing will be repeated.

The experimenter measures the rate at which the rat presses the bar after conditioning. This measurement indicates the strength of the association between

FIGURE 8-5
A Skinner Box
This apparatus provides the controlled environment in which a rat (or other animal) can receive operant or instrumental conditioning by emitting responses that are measured, shaped, and reinforced.

bar pressing and food. The measure of the rate of response is called the **operant strength** of the response.

Reinforcement: The Carrot and the Stick

Popular wisdom holds that there are two basic ways to motivate behavior. The first way is reward—the "carrot." How do we know whether something is rewarding for someone or not? The Law of Effect suggests how. If a consequence of an action increases the frequency of the action, the consequence is rewarding or reinforcing. If, on the other hand, the consequence decreases the frequency of the behavior, the consequence is punishing—the "stick."

A **reinforcement** is something that strengthens the possibility that a certain response will recur. There are two kinds of reinforcements: positive and negative (Figure 8-6). When something pleasant is *given* to an animal or person after a desired response, this is *positive reinforcement.* Press the bar, get food; deposit a quarter, get a soda. When something unpleasant is *taken away* after a desired response, this is *negative reinforcement.* Press the bar, the electric shock stops; take an aspirin, your headache goes away. The terms positive and negative may be confusing. Here the terms are not used in the judgmental sense of good or bad, but rather in a purely arithmetic sense. Positive reinforcement is something added (+); negative reinforcement is something subtracted (−).

Punishment is the opposite of reinforcement. It is a consequence that *decreases* the likelihood that a response will recur. Press the bar, get a shock. Go through a red light, get a ticket. Punishments, like reinforcements, can be positive or negative. "Positive punishment" means something is added to decrease the likelihood that a response will be repeated. Press the bar, get a shock. Swear at your mother, get slapped. "Negative punishment" means that something that has been rewarding is taken away. Press the bar, no food to eat. Swear at your mother, no car to drive.

Characteristics of Reinforcers

In classical conditioning the word "reinforcement" simply means strengthening: each time the CS and the UCS are paired, the CR is reinforced. Because the UCS is usually something that directly causes a reflexive response, almost any stimulus can become a CS under the right conditions. The critical contingency in classical conditioning is timing, including frequency and recency (how closely the CS and UCS are paired). Although timing is important in operant conditioning too, the *value* of the reinforcement to the organism also plays an obvious role.

FIGURE 8-6
Relationship of Events with Reinforcement and Punishment
These graphs show how responses such as bar presses (spikes) relate to pleasant or unpleasant events (solid areas).

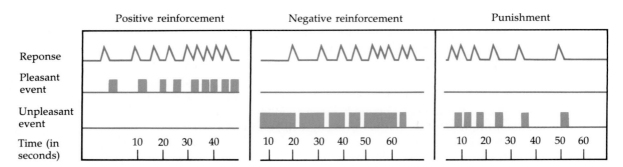

CONDITIONING CAN BE THE MOTHER OF INVENTION

Skinner was a graduate student when he developed the first "Skinner box." In the experiment he was working on, a rat had to repeatedly run an eight-foot maze. At the completion of the maze, Skinner gave the rat food and carried the rat back to the beginning. He redesigned the apparatus so that he did not personally have to give the rat food each time it ran the maze. Now the rat automatically received its reward. Skinner also wanted to avoid the task of recording the rat's responses. There was a notched wheel on the food box that turned each time the rat got food. Skinner realized that since the wheel turned one notch per trial, all he had to do was wind a string around the wheel's spindle, attach a pen to the string, and place the pen on a moving drum of paper.

He then had an accurate record of the animal's behavior. More importantly, this was done automatically, and Skinner did not have to stick around through long nights of continuous experimentation.

In Skinner's own theoretical terms, his own reinforcement was the avoidance of lab drudgery. The behaviors within young Skinner's repertoire (attaching strings to wheels and designing levers) were reinforced and therefore persisted. The "invention" of the Skinner box, although ingenious, was merely a new combination of existing behaviors, called up by the contingencies of the environment. Skinner could spend a night on the town and collect his data at the same time.

Relativity of Reinforcement. Reinforcements are relative. One hundred dollars is a lot of money to a poor man, but not very much to a rich one. Working for $10,000 a year is perceived differently if it is a first job than if one's last salary was $25,000. One person's reinforcement may be another person's punishment. A hungry rat will press a bar for food, but a satiated one will not. A job I might be eager to take may be turned down by a millionaire.

To change behavior through operant conditioning, an appropriate reinforcement has to be determined. Psychologists have recently rediscovered what parents have long known: behaviors themselves can be reinforcers. For example, "You can watch TV if you finish your homework first."

David Premack (1965) has studied this form of reinforcement. *Premack's principle* states that a more favored behavior can be used to reinforce a less favored behavior. He demonstrated his principle with a group of elementary school children in a room with a pinball machine and chocolate. Some children preferred to play pinball; he called these children "manipulators." The ones who preferred the chocolate he called the "eaters."

A few days later the children went back to the room, but this time their play was restricted. Before the "manipulators" were allowed to play pinball, they had to eat a piece of chocolate. The result was an increase in their consumption of chocolate. Likewise, the "eaters" had to play pinball first, which caused a parallel increase in manipulating.

Ayllon and Azrin (1968) used Premack's principle on psychotic patients in an Illinois State Hospital. Their goal was to teach the patients behaviors and social skills so that they could live in the community. Ayllon and Azrin observed the patients carefully and discovered the favorite behaviors of each individual. One liked to sit in a certain chair, another hid things under his mattress, and some liked to sit alone hidden from others. The project was designed so that these favored behaviors had to be earned. The price for indulging in them was participation in a new social activity or the practice of a new skill: for example, asking questions, following directions, keeping appointments, keeping clean, and so on. The project was quite successful and has been repeated in a variety of situations in institutions.

Primary and Conditioned Reinforcers.　There are two broad categories of reinforcers: primary and conditioned. *Primary reinforcers* include food, water, and relief from pain. They need no training because they are inherently reinforcing. A *conditioned* (or secondary) *reinforcer* is something that is not innately reinforcing but has come to be associated with a primary reinforcer. The most common conditioned reinforcer in human life is money. Although we all work indirectly so that we can eat, our bosses hand us our paychecks at the end of the week, not a bag of groceries! We work for money, which allows us to obtain the primary reinforcers.

In one study, Wolfe (1936) taught chimps to put poker chips into a machine to get grapes (Figure 8-7). Soon, the chimps performed other tasks to earn poker chips. Conditioned reinforcers are especially important when there is a delay between a behavior and a primary reinforcer. Wolfe's chimps were only allowed to use the grape dispensing machine at certain times, but they could earn the chips at all times. When a chimp deposited a chip and had to wait a long time for a grape, the operant strength of the new behavior decreased. As long as the chimp could do something while it waited, like earn chips, the operant strength was maintained. The importance of conditioned reinforcement is enormous. It enables us to wait for payday, to work hard, and save for the future.

Physiological Reinforcers.　It appears that electrical stimulation to cetain locations of the brain is itself reinforcing. Olds and Milner (1954) implanted electrodes in specific areas of a rat's brain and ran electrical current through them. The rats began to repeat actions that immediately preceded the stimulation. Thus, stimulation to a site in the brain was a reinforcer. There are many stimulation sites in the brain that might be reinforcing, especially those related to hunger, thirst, and sex. Electrode implantation has also been tried on people suffering from neurological disorders like epilepsy. The patient sits in front of a display of buttons; each of the buttons sends electrical stimulation to a different part of the brain. Heath (1963) found that certain buttons were pressed more than others. The patients reported sensations ranging from intoxication to specific tastes to the intense feeling right before orgasm.

Schedules of Reinforcement

In the last section, the qualities and characteristics of reinforcers were discussed. Now we turn to another important factor affecting reinforcement—timing. In general, the best time for a reinforcer or punishment to be presented is *immediately following the response*. In this way no random stimuli become inadvertently associated with the reinforcement. No animals can learn if there is too much of a delay between a response and a reinforcer or punishment. Grice (1948) had rats run a maze for food. The reinforcement delays for different groups of rats ranged from 0 to 10 seconds. The shorter the delay, the faster the rat learned. The rats who faced a 10-second delay showed no improvement after even hundreds of

FIGURE 8-7
Conditioned Reinforcers, Chimpanzees, and People
This chimpanzee earned poker chips (conditioned reinforcers) in a learning experiment and is now using one to get food (primary reinforcer). Most people are rewarded in this way, being paid later for work done now, with money that can be converted into primary reinforcers of their choice.

trials. Likewise, when administering a punishment, it is more effective to do so as soon as the inappropriate response is made. Thus, a young child who misbehaves should be punished immediately, not made to wait until daddy comes home.

Continuous and Partial Reinforcement

For conditioning to occur, a reinforcer need not be presented each time a response is made. There are two patterns of reinforcement: continuous (or constant) and partial. **Continuous reinforcement** means that each time the animal makes the correct response, it is reinforced. **Partial reinforcement** means that reinforcement does not always follow the response.

Continuous reinforcement, as you might imagine, makes learning very fast. It is almost essential if an animal is to learn a very complex new behavior beyond the bounds of its species' normal behavior. A seal must be reinforced with a fish every time it balances a ball on its nose. Continuous reinforcements, however, are not necessary for humans to acquire new skills. In life outside the laboratory or the circus there is not always someone to throw a fish for a job well done. A child who gets an award for reading new words in class may also read well alone with no decrease in operant strength.

Partial Reinforcement Schedules

There are four kinds of partial reinforcement schedules.

1. **Fixed Interval (FI).** On a fixed interval schedule, reinforcement is presented at regular intervals after the correct response. The interval is written as a number; for example, a pigeon who knows how to peck for food may be put on FI-7, which is a fixed interval (FI) of seven seconds. The pigeon pecks and receives food. Then, no matter how many times it pecks, it will receive no food until seven seconds have elapsed. As a rule, response on an FI schedule increases just before reinforcement and decreases immediately following it.

   Mawhinney, Bostow, Laws, Blumenfeld, and Hopkins (1971) asked their students to use a special room for study. The experimenters observed the actual amount of time the students spent studying in the special room. Once the operant level of studying was determined, manipulation of the conditions began. The teachers gave a test every day. The observers noted that about the same amount of studying went on every day. Later the teachers gave a test once every three weeks (FI-3 weeks). They noted a distinct difference in study habits. Little studying was done immediately after a test, but it increased noticeably later in the three-week interval. Most studying was done in the few days before the test. When the teachers returned to giving a daily test, studying was once again regular.

2. **Variable Interval (VI).** On this schedule, the intervals between reinforcement vary randomly about an average. It is impossible for an animal to adjust its response rate to match the schedule. The schedule is independent of the number of responses it makes. A VI-5 (minute) schedule means that the intervals could vary from a few seconds to a few minutes, but the average of all the intervals is 5 minutes. When you keep trying to call

someone and the line is busy, you are on a VI schedule. Sometimes the call goes through immediately and sometimes the line is busy for hours. The time you dial when the line is free is the only response that is reinforced (by talking to your friend). "Superstitious" behavior often develops in animals (humans included!) on a VI schedule (see "box" on Superstitions, next section).

3. **Fixed Ratio (FR).** On a fixed ratio schedule, reinforcement is given after a certain number of responses. A rat on an FR-5 schedule is reinforced every fifth time it presses the bar. Some people are paid on an FR schedule. Farm workers may be paid a specified amount for a certain number of bushels. Piece workers are paid when they have finished making a certain number of objects. A farm worker who picks seven bushels of lettuce to receive payment is on an FR-7 schedule.

4. **Variable Ratio (VR).** On this schedule, reinforcement occurs after a randomly varying number of responses. A VR-5 schedule means that, on the average, every fifth response will be reinforced. People who gamble on slot machines are on a VR schedule.

The closer a schedule is to continuous reinforcement, the faster the learning. A response conditioned on a continuous schedule will undergo extinction the fastest. An animal may be switched from a continuous to a partial reinforcement schedule when adequate operant strength has been reached. The same thing happens to people. If one takes tennis lessons, at first the instructor may say "good shot" each time the ball is hit well. Later he or she may only comment occasionally.

An animal's response patterns vary with the kind of schedule it is on. On an FI, the response rate decreases immediately after the reinforcement and gradually increases. On a VI schedule there is not much change in response rate from

Gamblers are rewarded on a variable ratio schedule, because if they win it is after a randomly varying number of bets—but this also allows them to expect to win at *any* time.

reinforcement to reinforcement. On both FR and VR schedules, the rate of response is rapid. This indicates that the animal knows that reinforcement has something to do with the number of responses. In a lab, conditions can be tightly controlled, but in life things are more haphazard. The four schedules of partial reinforcement are analogous to the way things happen in life. As a rule, you cannot always be rewarded for every good thing you do. But intermittent rewards for your efforts are enough to keep you trying and they enable you to learn.

The most important effect of partial reinforcement is the increased persistence of the resultant learning. An organism will respond for a longer time without reinforcement when it has received partial rather than continuous reinforcement during learning. Variable ratio schedules are particularly resistant to extinction. This helps account for why gamblers may lose all their money to "one-armed bandits." They expect to "win big" each time they put a quarter into the slot. If one learns to expect reward "now and then" (partial reinforcement), one cannot be sure that the situation has changed to "never." On the other hand, under continuous reinforcement one has learned to expect reward every time. So the first unrewarded response informs you that the contingency has changed.

Practical Applications of Operant Conditioning

Many of the principles of operant conditioning have been used effectively in classrooms: for example, in changing behavior or in the use of teaching machines that makes individualized learning possible. The principles have been useful in many kinds of psychotherapy. They are used in bringing up children, settling labor disputes, and even healing.

See Chapter 17, section on Behavior Therapy

Skinner designed for his daughter Deborah a controlled environment based on operant conditioning principles. This "heir conditioner" (so named because it conditioned Skinner's "heir") was an enclosed box in which all needs were immediately met. Skinner also invented a toilet-training device. He wired a music box to the toilet so that it began to play when his child urinated into the toilet.

Another practical application of operant conditioning is a posture-improving device. It makes use of "slump straps" that are a specially wired apparatus worn under clothing. If the person is not standing up straight, a buzzer sounds. The only way to turn off the buzzer is to stand up straight. As you might imagine, the wearer's posture would improve greatly, but only as long as the embarrassing apparatus is worn.

Respondent and Operant Conditioning Compared

There are many similarities between respondent and operant conditioning. In both cases what is learned is an association between relatively contiguous events. In both cases some sort of reinforcement is required for learning to occur. The unconditioned stimulus in respondent conditioning is equivalent to the reinforcer in operant conditioning. The phenomena of discrimination, generalization, and extinction are similar for both.

There are, however, differences between the two types of conditioning. Respondent conditioning involves involuntary responses in the organism elicited by stimuli. Operant conditioning involves voluntary responses emitted by the organism operating on the environment and followed by reinforcing stimuli. But how deep are these distinctions? As you may have realized already, there are situations

SUPERSTITIONS

When a behavior is *accidentally associated* with reinforcement, a superstition may be the result. Skinner created superstitious behavior in pigeons by dispensing food randomly, entirely independently of the birds' responses. The pigeons, however, all made associations between their actions and the dropping pellet. When Skinner returned to the laboratory after a weekend, he found pigeons exhibiting a variety of behaviors. For example, some were turning in circles, some jumping up and down, and some pecking. None of these behaviors was related to the actual consequence. Whatever the pigeons happened to be doing at the time of the reinforcement, they continued to do.

Baseball players, too, exhibit quite a bit of superstitious behavior. After winning a game or playing well, they often isolate one specific action or series of actions as the cause of their success. Some players have developed an elaborate ritual.

On each pitching day for the first three months of a winning season, Dennis Grossini, a pitcher on a Detroit Tiger farm team, arose from bed at exactly 10 A.M. At 1 P.M. he went to the nearest restaurant for two glasses of iced tea and a tuna fish sandwich. Although the afternoon was free, he changed into the sweat shirt and supporter he wore during his last winning game. One hour before the game, he chewed a wad of Beech-Nut chewing tobacco. During the game, he touched his letters (the team name on his uniform) after each pitch. He also strained his cap after each ball. Before the start of each inning, he replaced the pitcher's rosin bag to the spot where it was the inning before. And after every inning in which he gave up a run he would wash his hands. (Gmelch, 1978)

Baseball players are renowned for their superstitious behavior. Here are the Mets in their dugout trying to get a rally going.

in which these distinctions break down, such as in biofeedback, which can be considered as the voluntary or operant conditioning of autonomic responses.

It is supposed by some researchers that operant conditioning affects the organism's future but respondent does not. Yet it has been shown that respondent conditioning can be viewed as preparing the organism for a future response. Salivation, for example, occurs in expectation of food; the respondent has features of an operant.

I f you suspect there is more to learning than classical and operant conditioning, you are right. These two forms of learning are important, but people have additional ways of learning.

Insight

Much learning, from Thorndike's cats escaping their cage to human problem solving, is accomplished by trial and error. There is, however, another experience of learning: when the solution to a problem seems to appear in a flash of **insight.**

In one experiment that demonstrates insight, a chimp was placed in a cage with a short stick (Figure 8-8). A few feet outside the cage was a longer stick, beyond which was some enticing fruit. The chimp immediately tried to reach the fruit, but discovered that his arms were too short. Next he tried using the short stick to get the fruit and failed—it was not long enough either. Then he seemed to stop all overt activity for a while. All of a sudden the solution seemed to pop into his mind. He picked up the short stick and used it to get the long stick, then used the long stick to get the fruit. What was learned in this case was not a specific association between a stimulus and a response, but rather the organization of objects and

FIGURE 8-8
Chimpanzee Insight
After apparent contemplation, this chimpanzee used a short stick to pull a longer stick into his cage and then used it to reach some fruit.

events in the environment. The chimp learned to combine familiar objects and behaviors into a new solution to a problem.

In a similar experiment, a bunch of bananas was suspended from the ceiling of a room. The room contained nothing but a few boxes. The chimp jumped in vain, then stopped, pondered, and perused the room. It then piled the boxes one upon the other, climbed up, and got the bananas (Köhler, 1925).

Köhler points out that the chimp who learned to use the two sticks had learned a *relationship*, not a response. Thus, learning will *generalize* to new situations. If there were no stick around, but there was instead a long wire, the chimp would have picked up the wire. Once a new relationship has been learned, it becomes part of an organism's behavioral repertoire.

Latent Learning

Performance is the ultimate test of learning. If an organism shows consistent reductions in errors while performing a task, we say learning has taken place. However, there is evidence that learning can occur without being manifested in performance improvement. Such **latent learning** amounts to a change in ability not yet demonstrated by performance.

The classic demonstration of latent learning was by Tolman and Honzik (1930). Three groups of rats ran a complex maze once a day for two to three weeks. Group A always found food in its goal box. Group B never found food. Group C found no food for the first 10 days. On the 11th day, group C rats found food in their box, and then food was presented every day thereafter. Figure 8-9 shows the results. The performance of group C rats was, for the first 10 days, like that of group B. After the 11th day, it was immediately equal to or *better* than group A's performance. This demonstrated that group C had learned during the previous 10 days and that their performance had been low only because of the lack of reward.

FIGURE 8-9
Latent Learning
The rats in this experiment ran a maze like the one on the left. The graph charts the different performance curves of the three groups discussed in the text.
(After Tolman & Honzik, 1930)

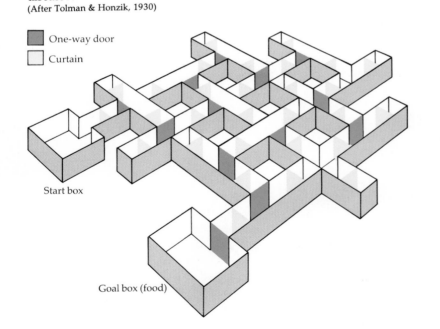

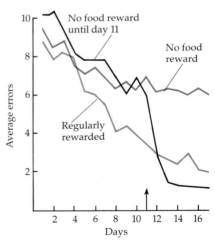

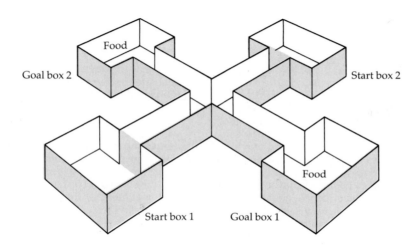

FIGURE 8-10
Learning by Developing
Cognitive Maps
The rats who had to run
this cross-shaped maze in
a natural foraging pattern
learned the maze faster
than those who always
found food by turning one
way after leaving their
start box. Tolman believed
that the more successful
foraging group developed
wider expectations and a
kind of cognitive map of
the relationships in their
environment.

In Köhler's experiments, the chimps had learned that sticks could be used to reach things, even though chimps usually use sticks only for digging food. Tolman (1930) believed that learning goes far deeper than what overt behavior expresses, and he conducted an experiment to prove the point.

Two groups of rats were to run a cross-shaped maze, such as the one in Figure 8-10. The maze was open so that the rats could see any objects in the experimental room. There were two start boxes and two goal boxes with food. Half the time the rats began in start box 1 and half the time in 2. Group A rats always found food in goal box 1 no matter which start box they left from. Sometimes they needed to make a right turn to get food and sometimes left. Group B rats found food in goal box 1 only when they left start box 1 and in goal box 2 only when leaving start box 2. Group B rats always turned right to get food.

There was a great difference in the rate at which these two groups learned the maze. One group learned in about eight runs, while some rats in the other group never learned. From a strict conditioning point of view, the prediction would be that group B should have learned faster, since the learning was simple: "turn right for food." However, group A learned faster, not B. Tolman argued that the way an organism naturally finds food in the environment is through foraging. It comes to know the lay of the land by random exploration. Specifically, Tolman noted that organisms learn not only by responding to simple stimuli but also by developing a set of expectations about the relationship of elements in the environment, a sort of *cognitive map*.

Learning How to Learn

Practice with a learning task will often lead to improved performance on subsequent similar learning tasks. For example, Ward (1927) arranged for subjects to learn 16 word lists of equal length with one new list being learned on each of 16 successive days. The subjects showed a striking decrease in the number of trials required to learn the lists as a function of practice: they needed nearly 40 trials to learn the first list but less than 20 trials to learn the last list. Obviously, they had learned something about what strategies to use in the task of learning word association lists; for this task at least, they had learned how to learn.

MAKING THINGS FUN TO LEARN

According to Plato, "No compulsory learning can remain in the soul. . . . In teaching children, train them by a kind of game and you will be able to see more clearly the natural bent of each" (from *The Republic*, Book VII). While Plato's prescription may not always be appropriate, many students would certainly like their learning in school to be more enjoyable.

Whenever people engage in any activity for its own sake rather than to achieve some external goal, they are said to be *intrinsically motivated*. Computer games are a new activity in which many people are highly intrinsically motivated to learn complex skills. Studies of why people find these games captivating have led to the illumination of the following features that make educational environments more enjoyable and interesting (Malone, 1981; Malone & Lepper, 1987).

Challenge

For an activity to be challenging, it should have a *goal* whose *outcome is uncertain*. Explicit goals are important in the appeal of simple computer games. Open-ended learning environments (such as art studios or computer programming systems) often have many *emergent goals* that people generate for themselves (Csikszentmihalyi, 1975).

Just having a goal is not enough. If the goal is too easy or too difficult, it will not be challenging. Most highly motivating activities (such as games, artistic creation, and scientific research) have *multiple levels of goals* for different people at different times.

Sometimes the difficulty level of an activity can be increased automatically as you become more skilled. Most video games get harder as you continue to play, and sometimes you can choose the difficulty level yourself. In any game that has scores, people at many different skill levels can be challenged by goals they choose for themselves, such as beating their own previous best score.

Fantasy

Many activities can be made more appealing by incorporating fantasy. It is probably no accident that successful arcade video games often involve vivid fantasies of combat and destruction. Some educational computer games take advantage of this by having fantasies that are not related to the material being learned. For example, a spaceship advances toward the moon

Observational Learning: Multiprocess Analysis

Primates are social animals; remember that an important function of a group is to teach the young how to act in society. This process is called socialization. Implicit in socialization is the ability to *learn from the experience of others*. One child watches another touch a hot stove and get burned. In the future, they both are less likely to put their hands on the hot stove. The child with the burned finger has learned the lesson by operant conditioning; the other has learned by painless observation.

Albert Bandura, a leading theorist in **observational learning** (also called social learning), says that people would not learn much if they had to rely only on the effects of their own actions to inform them what to do. People can learn behavior by observing others, at least in approximate form, before performing any behavior themselves (Bandura, 1986).

What an organism learns in classical and operant conditioning is clear enough: in the former it is the association between events in the world and, in the latter, an association between one's actions and their effect on the environment. One is the depending on how many right answers a student makes in an arithmetic drill. It is probably better, however, to use educational fantasies that are related to the skill being taught. For example, students can learn about gravity by piloting spaceships in imaginary universes with different amounts of gravity.

Fantasies probably derive much of their appeal from the emotional needs they help to satisfy (see Freud, 1950). They allow people to experience satisfactions—from power, success, or aggression—in ways that would be impossible otherwise. Different people, however, have very different emotional needs and find very different kinds of fantasies appealing. Learning environments that let students choose the fantasies they want may therefore appeal to many more different kinds of people.

Control

The desire to control one's environment is fundamental (Rodin, 1986). Learning environments can exploit this motivation by giving learners choices. Students may be able to choose which problems to solve and how difficult a goal to set. They may choose which game format to use, or what fantasy to overlay on the instructional material.

A very common explanation for why people find computer games captivating is that the games give their players a powerful sense of control. Computer environments can often "empower" their users by, for example, making spectacular audio and visual displays depend on very simple actions.

Interpersonal Motivations

When more than one person is included in a learning situation, three additional kinds of motivation are possible: *competition, cooperation,* and *recognition.* Sometimes these are simply external motivators. At other times, however, they are intrinsic to the task itself. For instance, in one teaching technique that draws on the cooperation motivation, each student on a team is given different information about a famous person. Then the team members work together to write a biographical report (Aronson, 1984). As another example, students write for a class newspaper rather than just for their teacher. Some of their motivation to do so may come from a desire for recognition. (After Malone & Lepper, 1987)

This young Peruvian woman learned the art of weaving intricate patterns entirely through observation.

result of frequent pairing, the other the result of reinforcements. In observational learning, what the observing organism acquires is an organized set of associations: schemata that direct behavior. These schemata can then direct behavior at appropriate times. Among Peruvian weavers, for example, young girls are taught to weave solely by observing others. For years, the girls simply watch their mothers while they weave the traditional patterns. They do not work on a loom until their teens. Everything from the setting up of the loom to weaving itself, even creating the intricate patterns that set each tribe apart, is learned entirely by observation (Franquemont, 1979).

According to the social cognitive perspective (Bandura, 1986), four processes are involved in observational learning. *Attentional* processes determine the perception and exploration of the modeled behavior; *retention* processes involve the development of mental models or schemata to guide the *production* processes whereby schemata are organized into action; and *motivational* processes determine whether or not the observationally acquired behaviors will actually be performed.

Attentional Processes

It hardly needs to be stated that observational learning requires observation. **Attentional processes** determine what exactly is observed about the modeled behavior. It is not always obvious to the learner which elements of the modeled behavior are crucial to performance and which are irrelevant. Consequently, observational learning can be facilitated by drawing attention to the most important components of the action being modeled: parents tend to expressively dramatize actions to attract their children's attention to the actions they are modeling. The attractiveness of the model also determines the degree of attention paid. This is one of the reasons that television is so effective at modeling behavior (Bandura, 1986).

Enhancing attention can lead to improved observational learning. Observer's attention can be directed to the important elements of the modeled behavior by physical emphasis or verbal instruction. Modeling of both good and poor performances helps to focus the observer's attention on the crucial aspects of superior performance (Debus, 1970). When people attempt to observe whole performances, they may miss important details; hence observational learning can be enhanced by subdividing complicated modeled actions into a number of simpler actions (Sheffield & Maccoby, 1961).

Retention Processes

We cannot repeat actions that we have observed if we do not remember them. To reproduce an observed behavior we must draw on a symbolic representation or mental model of the behavior stored in our memories. The importance of symbolic representations for observational learning is shown by studies that show that observers who encode their perceptions of modeled behavior by means of vivid imagery or concise verbal descriptions learn more effectively than those who do not.

Cognitive rehearsal is one means of aiding **retention processes** in observational learning. Although cognitive rehearsal by itself improves performance, physical practice is usually more effective. However, a combination of cognitive and physical rehearsal has been shown to lead to faster mastery of skilled action

COMPARISON OF THEORIES: COGNITIVE VERSUS BEHAVIORAL

The cognitive approach to learning emphasizes that the learner is an active part of the process. Thus, the processes of perception, memory, consciousness, and decision making are important intermediary events between a stimulus and response. Human learning depends to a great degree on the ability to recall similarities and relationships among situations, to recombine information, and to weigh alternative courses of action. This agrees with much of modern psychology and certainly follows from our analyses of sensation, perception, and consciousness. However, the behavioral approach to learning of Pavlov and Skinner emphasizes only the study of observable actions, that is, measurable responses such as paw presses and the like.

The differences between the cognitive and behavioral approaches produced a bitter controversy that lasted more than a generation and centered on one question: Could psychologists study anything other than external, observable responses? With the advent of new technology enabling scientists to make many internal processes observable — such as brain waves and blood pressure — the flood gates opened. Psychology now studies observable behavior, internal physiological processes, and the unobservable mind all together (Bandura, 1986). Although observational learning has been reported in many species, the capacity is most highly developed in the primates.

than physical practice alone (Rawlings, Rawlings, Chen, & Yilk, 1972). Preparatory cognitive rehearsal also improves performance of well-learned skills; if you visualize yourself performing an action you are about to do, you will probably be more successful than otherwise (Richardson, 1967). The usefulness of cognitive rehearsal will depend on the nature of the task being performed. For example, complex performances benefit more from cognitive rehearsal than simple performances (Feltz & Landers, 1983).

Production Processes

To perform an observed behavior pattern we need to have the component actions in our behavioral repertoire and we need to know how to organize them into a smoothly connected sequence of action. The response **production processes** governing this stage of observational learning are mainly a matter of conception matching (Bandura, 1986), in which sensory feedback during performance is compared with conceptions or mental models.

Performance errors can come from a number of sources. One problem may involve faulty conceptions of the modeled task due to incorrect observation. Practice reveals which parts of the behavior pattern have been inadequately observed and need further study. Another problem may be that the learner lacks the component subskills required for performance of the behavior pattern.

Here the solution is modeled practice of the component actions. For example, autistic children were unable to learn modeled sentences until they were first taught the speech components by rewarded modeling (Lovaas, 1966). Another source of difficulty in observational learning is that it is difficult to match action to conception if we cannot adequately observe our own behavior. Videotaped feedback can provide a solution to this kind of problem, provided that learners observe their performance after having correctly conceptualized the modeled action.

Motivational Processes

People do not typically imitate every behavior they have observed. Whether or not observationally learned behaviors are transformed from potential to action depends on **motivational processes.** In general, we are more likely to imitate behavior we have seen rewarded in others than to imitate behavior we have seen punished or unrewarded. The kinds of motivation that affect observational learning and performance depend on the individual's level of development. For example, young children are mainly motivated by the immediate sensory and social consequences of their actions. As development proceeds, children are increasingly motivated by abstract incentives such as personal satisfaction and a sense of the power to produce an effect (Bandura, 1986).

Abstract Modeling

If we only learned actions we had previously observed, our abilities would be much more limited than they are. Children don't just learn how to say the sentences modeled by their parents; they learn generalizable rules allowing the unlimited production of classes of grammatical sentences. In this process of **abstract modeling,** observers generate and test hypotheses about the rules guiding the performance of models. Modeling plays a crucial role in the highest forms of human behavior. Creativity is an example. You might think that it is contradictory to view innovation as the product of modeling, but the fact is that creative achievements are based on the preceding creations of others. Creative thinking is

largely a matter of combining familiar elements in a new way, and creativity can itself be learned through modeling. People who have observed innovative models perform more creatively than people who have observed conventional models (Belcher, 1975; Harris & Evans, 1973).

Imitation

The visible behavior resulting from observational learning is called **imitation.** The ability to imitate is not as simple as it might seem. To imitate, observers must be able to recognize similarities between the model's behavior and their own and must be able to recreate that behavior. The processes of attention, retention, motivation, and reproduction are involved in even the simplest imitation. Imitation may be the earliest form of human complex learning. A 4-day-old baby can imitate the mother smiling or sticking out her tongue.

Humans also imitate behavior when the model is not present. Rosekrans and Hartup (1967) conducted an experiment that showed this imitation in the form of aggression. How does the observation of violence on television affect later behavior? Children watched a videotape in which an adult model punched a Bobo doll, shouting, "Wham, bam, I'll knock your head off." Some saw a version in which the model's behavior was punished by another adult's reprimands, while others saw a different version showing the model being rewarded by the other adult's praise. A control group saw a nonviolent tape.

All the children were later taken to a playroom with lots of normal nursery school toys and a Bobo doll. They were left alone and observed through a one-way mirror. The children's behavior was greatly influenced by their observation of the model. The group that had seen aggression rewarded acted much more aggressively than the group that saw no aggression. Both of these groups were more aggressive than the group that saw aggression punished.

See Chapter 1, Figure 1-2.

Many psychologists feel that children *learn* to behave aggressively and that many of their lessons in aggression come from television. Their concern is shared by many parents, some of whom have founded Action for Children's Television (ACT). ACT monitors children's television shows and commercials and has been instrumental in banning extremely violent shows.

Concluding Note

Observational learning is a latecomer in the psychology of learning. The exact conditions under which it takes place and the kinds of schedules of reinforcement have not been firmly established. Generalization and discrimination take place just as in other forms of learning. Observational extinction can be used (watching someone perform an action not punished) to help people overcome fears.

The most important factors in observational learning are the hardest to pin down: the characteristics of the model and the learner and the interaction between the two. So the process of observational learning is certainly not as well understood as conditioning.

Up to this point, we have been emphasizing how associations are formed, how they gain strength and decline, and how they become organized. But learning is also influenced by the basic differences between different organisms at birth. Each organism comes into the world with some inborn abilities: birds learn

WHAT WE ARE "PREPARED" TO LEARN

to fly, human beings do not; we read and write, birds do not. The set of abilities each organism is born with is its **behavioral repertoire.** This repertoire varies greatly among species. There is, however, a more subtle question that psychologists have recently addressed: Are some things easier to learn than others?

Assumption of Equivalence of Associability

This question could also be asked, are all events equally associable? Most students of conditioning, Pavlov, for instance, have assumed that any CS and any UCS could be associated with equal facility. He wrote:

> Any natural phenomenon chosen at will may be converted into a conditional stimulus . . . any visual stimulus, any desired sound, any odor, and the stimulation of any part of the skin. (Pavlov, 1928)

Similarly, Skinner assumed that any response could be conditioned by any reinforcer. It was believed that the laws of learning governing the association of arbitrary events such as we have considered would apply to *all* events. The problem, as we shall see, is that these laws may only apply to arbitrary associations in the lab and not to more normal and biologically adaptive associations in nature.

Continuum of Preparedness

In an influential paper, Martin Seligman (1970) questioned the assumption of equivalence of associability and suggested that organisms are more predisposed (prepared) to associate some events than others. He proposed that there is a continuum of **preparedness** ranging from prepared to unprepared to counterprepared.

Response Difference

One of the first indications that something was wrong with the classical assumptions about learning came from the Brelands' experiences with the "misbehavior of organisms." They had difficulties in teaching a pig to deposit a coin in a "piggy bank." They termed the phenomenon **instinctive drift:** "learned behavior drifts toward instinctive behavior" (Breland & Breland, 1961).

Many other studies have shown difficulties with getting organisms to learn arbitrary responses. Cats in experiments by Thorndike (1954) had great difficulty learning to escape by scratching or licking themselves. Moreover, when they did learn, the response degenerated to a "mere vestige of a lick or scratch." Other experiments showed that dogs found it extremely difficult, if not impossible, to learn to yawn for food. Neither rats nor pigeons are prepared to avoid shock by lever pressing. On the other hand, pigeons easily learned to escape shock by flying and rats by running. Bolles (1970) suggested that the easily learned responses in avoidance situations are closely related to innate *species-specific defense reactions* (SSDRs). The idea behind SSDRs is that the organisms do not usually have the opportunity to learn how to escape from predators. A rat cannot afford to try "pressing levers" when it sees a cat. It is counterprepared to do so. It must run if it is to survive. Any avoidance response inconsistent with an organism's specific defenses will be difficult or impossible to condition.

Stimulus Difference

We know that some responses are easier to condition than others, but what about *stimuli?* Again, the assumption of equivalence of associability appears to be mistaken — that is, some things *are* more easily learned than others. For example, dogs are counterprepared to learn to associate different locations of the trainer's voice with responding to commands, yet they easily learn to use voice tone as a discriminative stimulus, as with "Go!" or "Stay!" (Dobrzecka & Konorowski, 1968).

An important series of experiments showing differences in the associability of different stimuli and reinforcers was performed by Garcia and Koelling (1966). They arranged for rats to drink saccharin-flavored ("tasty") water or to drink unflavored water while lights flashed and clicking noises were heard ("bright-noisy"). The bright-noisy and tasty water were made aversive in three ways: rats were shocked as they drank, the water was slightly poisoned, or they were given doses of radiation. Afterward the rats were tested with tasty water and bright-noisy water separately. The rats that had been made ill by poison or radiation avoided the tasty water but not the bright-noisy water. The rats that had been shocked showed exactly the opposite result, avoiding the bright-noisy water but not the tasty water (Figure 8-11).

These results can be understood from an evolutionary perspective. Organisms that survived developed either adaptive fixed action patterns or the ability to master their environment. Garcia and Koelling's experiment makes this point clear. The rats were "prepared" to associate one external event (foot shock) with another external event (bright-noisy water) but not with nausea, an internal event. They were also prepared to associate nausea with an internal event (tasty water), but not with a shock. Doesn't this make sense? How well would a rat (or a human being, for that matter) survive that decided it was sick because of something it heard or saw? Or a rat that reacted to a sore foot with "it must be something I ate"?

Human Preparedness

You might be thinking that the notion of preparedness applies only or mainly to "animal" learning. But the evolutionary history of *Homo sapiens* has selectively prepared human beings for certain kinds of learning as well. Some of the things we find easy to learn are common to other species, while others appear to be uniquely human.

FIGURE 8-11
The "Bright-Noisy"
Water Experiment
Whether or not a rat avoided the water depended on the water's characteristics and on the consequences that followed drinking it. Avoidance developed if tasty water and illness were paired (both internal) or if bright-noisy water was paired with shock (both external) — but not if these pairings were reversed.
(After Garcia & Koelling, 1966)

		Consequences	
		Illness	Shock
Cues	Taste	Avoid	Not avoid
	Sound-sight	Not avoid	Avoid

An example of one kind of prepared learning is taste aversion—the "sauce bearnaise" phenomenon. Seligman (1970) describes how the problem of preparedness first became compelling to him. One evening he had gone to the opera with his wife. For dinner, he had one of his favorite dishes—a filet mignon with bearnaise sauce. In the middle of the night, Seligman became violently ill. As a result, he developed an aversion to the taste of what had been his favorite sauce. This was in spite of knowing that the cause of his sickness was not food, but flu. Moreover, he did *not* develop an aversion to the opera, his wife, or the friend he caught the flu from. The connection between nausea and prior food taste is so strongly prepared in us that it defies reason. Similarly, ocean voyagers may acquire aversions to food eaten prior to seasickness, in spite of "knowing" that the cause of their sickness is the ship's motion, not the food (Garcia & Koelling, 1966).

So, now you know why I have, for all these years, been unable to eat Mexican food. Of the particular combination of events I experienced, only the meal and the stomach upset—not the storm and the tossing ship—became strongly associated because the relationship between food and stomach upset is strongly built into us. I behaved like a subject in one of Garcia's experiments. Even now that I know *why* I can't eat Mexican food, I still can't do anything about it. My "prepared associations" are stronger than my logic, so that even conscious knowledge of why this happened has made little difference.

This tendency for highly prepared learning to result in superstitious behavior is perhaps demonstrated by phobias as well. A little girl saw a snake while playing in the park. Some hours later she accidentally slammed a car door on her hand. The result? A fear of snakes! Evidently human beings are more highly prepared to fear snakes than cars, all logic aside (Seligman & Hager, 1972).

See Chapter 10, section on Language.

As a final, and more positive example of human preparedness, consider language acquisition. Our species appears to be uniquely prepared to learn language with ease (Lenneberg, 1967). With very informal training, children in all cultures learn the complicated contingencies involved in language use. The conditions under which normal children fail to learn to speak and understand language must be impoverished indeed—amounting essentially to complete linguistic isolation. Otherwise, willy-nilly, they learn.

LEARNING THEORY AND MODERN-DAY BEHAVIOR

See Chapter 2, section on A New Theory: Sociobiology.

But how do all these laboriously won principles of learning contribute to our knowledge of what governs behavior in modern-day society? If you work in a large company, for example, whether your job is around next year or not might have little to do with you. Similarly, you might get welfare or an inheritance without doing anything. Where do the contingencies of reinforcement come into play in situations like these in the modern world? You might expect these questions to be raised by a critic of Skinner's behaviorism, but instead they are raised in a recent article by Skinner (1986) himself, entitled, "What Is Wrong with Behavior in the Western World?"

The problem, as Skinner sees it, is that current society has eroded the normal feedback between actions and consequences. People in the work force often get no feedback from their bosses and co-workers. People are helped who could help themselves. Bureaucracies make rules that must be followed no matter what the outcome. Governments and organizations control individual behaviors and delay rewards, such as retirement. People get rewarded for not working (such as in welfare). People work for wages, but their production does not reinforce their behavior. How much of a building can a construction worker feel pride about?

All these are effects of more and more people living far beyond what they were "evolved" to do. Even Skinner, who for a long time was a proponent of "pure" behaviorism, now recognizes that human beings evolved to meet far different circumstances than they now face. Many people's lives are out of control, and their behavior drifts far from what is desirable in a society.

Human beings evolved to suit a world long gone, a world of perhaps 20,000 years ago. Some of the problems in today's modern world are due to a mismatch between our adaptations to this ancient world and the nature of the modern world human beings have made (see Chapter 2). People thus feel out of control because the laws of learning no longer hold. Chapter 18 presents what many psychologists are now doing to reduce the mismatch between these worlds, which may eventually lead to making people aware of the problems, which in turn may lead to giving control back to people and changing the way people act in society.

See Chapters 2 and 18.

Concluding Note

We have learned much about the basic processes of learning. Organisms learn to associate events that occur together by simple and repeatable procedures in the lab and, sometimes, in life. These simple associations form the groundwork of our knowledge of what goes on in the world; they allow us to understand why particular experiences such as being embarrassed once in class affect us strongly, why we have superstitions, and why we behave the way we do—from calling someone on the phone to playing a slot machine that once hit the jackpot. Some of us even know why we cannot eat certain things, even though there is no "rational" reason for it. How we remember and organize these learned associations is the topic of the next chapter.

SUMMARY

1. *Association* is one of psychology's oldest principles. It began with the Greek philosophers and was revived by British empiricists such as John Locke, who wrote that the "association of ideas" is the bond that connects all experience. In more recent times the study of association has become more precise, and evidence shows that we are biologically "prepared" to make certain associations.

2. Pavlov set out to discover the underlying conditions under which an animal could come to associate a previously neutral stimulus with food. He gave his research the name *conditioning*. In Pavlov's experiments with dogs, an innate reflex, such as salivation at the sight of food (called an *unconditioned response* or UCR), came to be associated with a new stimulus, such as a bell (*conditioned stimulus* or CS). The dog, after repeated pairings of the bell and the food, soon tended to associate the bell with the food and to salivate in response to the bell even without the presentation of the food. When the dog salivated at the sound of the bell alone, that was a *conditioned response* (CR).

3. Pavlov's long series of experiments are the basis of such principles in conditioning as acquisition, extinction, discrimination, generalization, reinforcement, and the timing of conditioned and unconditioned stimuli.

4. *Generalization* is one of the more important principles discovered by Pavlov. It is common to all forms of learning. We know someone is at the door whether the signal is a bell, buzzer, knocker, or chime. Generalization means that once a specific stimulus has become a CS, similar stimuli will elicit the conditioned response.

5. Skinner extended Pavlov's methods through his study of *operant conditioning*—how we learn to *act* in the world to get what we want. One of its primary principles is that we act in such a way to seek pleasure and avoid pain—the "Law of Effect." Operant conditioning, unlike Pavlov's *classical conditioning,* involves feedback within a system that includes the organism's responses. In operant conditioning, the consequences of any actions (responses) that increase the probability of the recurrence of those actions are called *reinforcements.*

6. A reinforcement is something that strengthens the probability that a certain response will occur. There are two kinds of reinforcement—positive and negative. Something given to the animal after a desired response is a *positive* reinforcement; something unpleasant taken away from the animal after a desired response is a *negative* reinforcement.

7. Schedules of reinforcement are central to operant conditioning. Continuous reinforcement means that every time the animal makes the correct response, it is reinforced. Partial reinforcement means that reinforcement does not always follow the response. In partial reinforcement, responses persist long after a reward is terminated. There are four kinds of partial reinforcement schedules: fixed interval, variable interval, fixed ratio, and variable ratio.

8. The laws of associative learning have prepared psychologists for an investigation into more complex forms, such as *cognitive learning,* although for a long period the existence of two different kinds of learning was controversial. However, it has recently been well established that animals as well as people can learn by virtue of *insight.* A chimp who is able to use two sticks to draw a banana into a cage has learned a *relationship,* not a response.

9. Another important form of learning is *observational learning.* Most animals learn from the experience of others through a process known as *modeling.* Observational learning is guided primarily by attention, retention, reproduction of the action, and motivation. The visible behavior that results from observational learning is called *imitation.*

10. The assumption of early investigators was that any response can be equally associated with any stimulus. However, a more subtle question psychologists have recently addressed is, Are all events equally associable? The concept of *preparedness* suggests that organisms are more predisposed or "prepared" to associate certain events than others. Seligman proposes that there is a continuum of preparedness encompassing responses that an organism is prepared, unprepared, and counterprepared to perform. Some animals simply *cannot* learn certain arbitrary responses; for example, cats have great difficulty learning to escape from their boxes by scratching or licking themselves. An example of a strongly prepared association is taste aversion—the strong reaction to the taste of food associated with stomach upset.

abstract modeling
association
attentional processes
behavioral repertoire
classical conditioning
conditioned response (CR)
conditioned stimulus (CS)
conditioning
continuous reinforcement
counterconditioning
discrimination
extinction
fixed interval (FI)
fixed ratio (FR)
generalization
imitation
insight
instinctive drift
instrumental conditioning
latent learning

Law of Effect
motivational processes
observational learning
operant conditioning
operant level
operant strength
orienting reflex
partial reinforcement
preparedness
production processes
punishment
reinforcement
respondent conditioning
retention processes
superstitions
unconditioned response (UCR)
unconditioned stimulus (UCS)
variable interval (VI)
variable ratio (VR)

Bandura, A. (1986). *Social foundations of thought and action.* Englewood Cliffs, NJ: Prentice-Hall.

> *A masterful and readable account of observational learning.*

Chance, P. (1987). *Learning and behavior* (2nd ed.). San Francisco: Wadsworth.

> *A very good current introduction to more contemporary viewpoints on learning.*

Johnston, T. (1981). Contrasting approaches to a theory of learning. *Behavioral and Brain Sciences, 4,* 125-139.

> *Shows the wide range of contemporary thought on learning.*

Leahey, T. H., & Harris, R. J. (1985). *Human learning.* Englewood Cliffs, NJ: Prentice-Hall.

> *An excellent current introduction to the field.*

Lynch, G. et al. (Eds.). (1984). *Neurobiology of learning and memory.* New York: Guilford.

> *An important collection on the new biological analysis of the basics of learning.*

Norman, D. (1983). *Learning and memory.* San Francisco: W. H. Freeman.

> *A well-written introduction to the joint analysis of learning and remembering.*

Pavlov, I. P. (1927). *Conditioned reflexes.* New York: Oxford University Press.

Skinner, B. F. (1938). *The behavior of organisms.* New York: Appleton-Century-Crofts.

> *This book and the Pavlov book are the major classics in the discovery of the basic laws of learning. It may be very useful to see how these men wrote and how they related their discoveries to contemporary knowledge.*

Snow, R. E., & Farr, M. J. (Eds.). (in press). *Aptitude, learning, and instruction: III. Conative and affective process analysis.* Hillsdale, NJ: Erlbaum.

> *A modern analysis of learning, in which psychologists try to apply their research to different problems such as making things fun to learn.*

Remembering and Forgetting

One night a friend put on a record that was popular when I was in graduate school. I hadn't listened to the record for 15 years, and as soon as I heard the first note I had a strange experience. I was instantly flooded with vivid memories from that whole period of my life. I could smell once again the orchard that I lived in, and I could see the faces of friends who I hadn't seen (or even thought of) in 15 years. I saw my old blue '56 Chevy convertible; it had a top that never worked, I remembered. I often drove that car to the beach at night. When I heard that song, I could once again smell the night air, see the night sky, and feel the car slipping around the winding curves of the road out to the beach. As I listened to the music, I was transported back in time.

I once worked in a mental hospital. One day I was taking care of Michael S., a patient who suffered from amnesia, due in this case to a blow to the head. He told me a story I will never forget. "This morning a woman came to see me in my room. I felt attracted to her. She was very pretty, and I liked talking to her. I asked her for her name. 'Ellen,' she said. I asked why she had come to visit me, as I thought she was a hospital volunteer. She slumped and burst into tears. She said, 'Michael, I'm your *wife*. We've been married for 20 years!' I just didn't know what to say. I don't remember her at all."

And consider Clive Waring, a Renaissance music conductor. He contracted encephalitis, which left him with a memory span of only a few seconds. He cannot remember the meal he just ate or the conversation he just had, but he can still conduct a choir (Sacks, 1986).

Memory is a great mystery. How can a song suddenly bring up memories of an orchard, an automobile, a lost era? How can someone forget a spouse of 20 years? How can someone remember a performance long ago, yet not his last spoken sentence? No one really knows, but the answers must lie in the nature of our system of memory. There are *different kinds* of memory, too. Michael lost his memory of Ellen, but not of the English language.

Our memories give meaning to our life, a sense of continuity between the past and present. To live and function, we must be able to remember our friends, our house, how to drive, how to walk, and even who we are. And at the end, what do we have but memories. Thanks to our memory, one poet wrote, "we can have roses in December."

Some Principles of Memory

This chapter discusses the principles and operation of memory, that is, our "system of memory," and not our specific personal memories. The analysis here is like that of perception — not an examination of what is on stage, but of the operations

See Chapter 6.

"behind the scenes." Many of the principles that underlie perception — such as simplicity, organization, and meaning — also hold true for memory.

Three important principles of memory processes are described by William James (1890):

> The more other facts a fact is associated with in the mind, the better possession of it our memory retains. Each of its associates becomes a hook to which it hangs, a means to fish it up when sunk beneath the surface. Together they form a network of attachments by which it is woven into the tissue of our thought. The "secret of a good memory" is the secret of forming diverse and multiple associations with every fact we care to retain. . . . Most men have a good memory for facts connected with their own pursuits. . . . The merchant remembers prices, the politician other politicians' speeches and votes. . . . The great memory for facts which a Darwin and a Spencer reveal in their books is not incompatible with the possession on their part of a brain with only a middling degree of physiological retentiveness. . . . Let a man early in life set himself the task of verifying such a theory as that of evolution, and facts will soon cluster and cling to him like grapes to their stem. Their relations to the theory will hold them fast, and the more of these the mind is able to discern, the greater the erudition will become.

1. *Memory involves associations.* The mind, in the modern analysis, is a network of associations formed from past experiences. The more we associate an event with something we already know, the more our memory of it will "stick" with us. For example, a car, friends, an orchard, and the beach are all associated for me with a song. When I hear that song now, I am reminded of past experiences I had while listening to the song. If you listened to that same song, there is no way you could have the same memories as I do. You may never have heard the song, or it may not have been associated with specific events in your life.

2. *Memory selects and simplifies reality.* Because there is simply too much information available to us at any one moment to act on, the senses, the perceptual process, and consciousness all simplify events by selecting only immediately important information, usually information that is relevant to what we are doing. Even after all the filtering out, there are still too many experiences in our past to handle. We remember a few of the many things that happen to us. How many of the billions of momentary experiences you had last summer do you remember? Perhaps one glorious day at the beach, some fine times lazing about, but certainly not every bite of food, every right turn, every conversation, every moment of every day. *Memories are much simpler than actual experience.*

3. *We remember meaningful events.* Perhaps the most important criterion for remembrance is what an event means to us. We remember events of personal importance or aspects of events that at the time appeared important to us. For example, your notes of a lecture transcribe the meaning of the lecture, not the shape of the room.

Since we remember meaningful details, we often overlook "familiar" details of everyday life. For instance, which of the drawings in Figure 9-1 is an accurate representation of a penny? Most people cannot readily tell, although we see pennies daily. The reason we cannot tell is that most of the specific details of the penny are meaningless to us. We need to remember little more about a penny than

A PERFECT MEMORY

Just about everyone would like to have a better memory. But an absolutely perfect memory, one permitting us to remember everything that ever happened to us, would paralyze us. The Argentine writer Jorge Luis Borges, in his story "Funes the Memorius," describes what that would be like:

We, at one glance, can perceive three glasses on a table; Funes, all the leaves and tendrils of fruit that made up a grape vine. He knew by heart the forms of the southern clouds at dawn on the 30th of April, 1882, and could compare them in his memory with the mottled streaks on a book in Spanish binding he had only seen once and with the outlines of the foam raised by an oar in the Rio Negro the night before the Quebracho uprising. These memories were not simple ones; each visual image was linked to muscular sensations, thermal sensations, etc. He could reconstruct all his dreams, all his half-dreams. Two or three times he had reconstructed a whole day; he never hesitated, but each reconstruction had

required a whole day. He told me: "I alone have more memories than all mankind has probably had since the world has been the world." And again: "My dreams are like you people's waking hours." And again, toward dawn: "My memory, sir, is like a garbage heap." A circle drawn on a blackboard, a right triangle, lozenge—all these are forms we can fully and intuitively grasp; Ireneo could do the same with the stormy mane of a pony, with the herd of cattle on a hill, with the changing fire and its innumerable ashes, with the many faces of a dead man throughout a long wake. I don't know how many stars he could see in the sky. (Borges, 1966)

Because of Funes's extraordinary memory, it took him the same amount of time to recall events as the events themselves took—an entire day to remember an entire day. As a result, Funes forfeited the future. In ordinary life, we need to act quickly. Memory serves this need by retaining only a "simplified version" of events.

that it is a small copper coin with Lincoln on it. Whether Lincoln faces left or right and where the date is placed are meaningless details to us, and they are normally not remembered.

FIGURE 9-1
Which drawing of the penny is accurate? It may be hard to pick the correct one because the few details that identify it are not sufficiently meaningful that you would remember them.
(After Nickerson & Adams, 1979)

FUNCTIONS OF MEMORY

Memory records specific *episodes* in life, but it also contains the general rules for operating in the world, called *representational* memory. Memory is continuously updated as new events occur, which allows us to respond to continuous changes in the world. Memory allows us to organize past experiences and to make them accessible when needed (Baddeley, 1986).

Episodic Memory

Episodic memory is a record of individual experiences. These memories include a movie we saw, a hike in the woods, a certain book, and experiences shared with others. They are a continuing "autobiographical reference" (Tulving, 1972). Episodic memory can be remarkably precise. In a study of memory, Lindsay and Norman (1977) asked students the question, "What were you doing on Monday afternoon in the third week of September two years ago?" Before reading on, try to answer the question yourself (write down your thoughts as you try to recall the event). The following was a typical exchange between a subject (S) and one of the experimenters (E) (Lindsay & Norman, 1977):

> S: Come on. How should I know?
> E: Just try it anyhow.
> S: OK. Let's see. Two years ago . . . I would be in high school in Pittsburgh. . . . That would be my senior year. Third week in September —that's just after summer—that would be the fall term. . . . Let me see. I think I had chemistry lab on Mondays. I don't know. I was probably in chemistry lab. Wait a minute—that would be the second week of school. I remember he started off with the atomic table—a big fancy chart. I thought he was crazy trying to make us memorize that thing. You know, I think I can remember sitting. . . .

Episodic memory records the major events of our lives and is a continuing autobiographical reference for each of us.

Episodic memory records quite specific details of particular events. The evidence suggests that specific episodes can endure in memory a long time, sometimes for decades.

Updating Information about the World

Because our world is always changing, memory would be useless if its content did not also change; it must be updated. Episodic memory is updated more frequently than representational memory. We must be able to remember where we parked "today," who is going out with whom "this" week, and countless other temporary episodes (Bjork & Landauer, 1979).

Representational Memory

Representational memory is a record of general knowledge of the world, common sense, and skills. Representational memory thus underlies episodic memory. Episodic memory is specific to one individual. However, people who share the same culture have a basically similar representational memory, for example, about the rules of language, inference, and logic and about general facts of the world, such as the effects of gravity, how to ride a bicycle, and who the president is. This memory underlies perception because it allows us to "fill in the gaps" when we get new information and to assume "facts" on the basis of partial information. You know, for example, that people living in Timbuktu eat and sleep, have children, and work. You know this even though you may never have visited Timbuktu and witnessed these facts firsthand (Wickelgren, 1977).

Representational memory is of two types: semantic and perceptual–motor memory.

Semantic Memory

Semantic memory includes the knowledge of a specific language, of what words mean and how they are used (Tulving, 1972). This semantic knowledge is vast; the average college student has a vocabulary of about 50,000 words in semantic memory. Semantic memory also includes "commonsense" inferences, so simple that they go unnoticed. Suppose you ask mother where her keys are and she says, "They are either in the bag or on the mantel." You look in the bag and they are not there; you then know without any further information they are on the mantel. Semantic memory also contains the rules for everyday, informal inferences. If someone says, "I hate country music," you know immediately not to invite that person to the next Willie Nelson concert. The rules for deducing these things are in semantic memory, as are the rules of formal logic and inference.

Perceptual–Motor Memory

Perceptual–motor memory contains the automatized schemata for performing routine actions, whether they are simple, like throwing a ball or getting dressed, or complex, like driving a car or playing baseball. It also guides our movements in space, using the knowledge of perspective and constancy. This kind of memory also underlies much of our ordinary perceptual experience: that

Perceptual-motor memory permits easy performance of routine actions, both simple and complex.

we are drinking coffee, not tea, that the milk is sour, or that someone is singing off key.

Sometimes our representational memory can cause us to make errors in perception, such as the common mistake shown in Figure 9-2. We represent Los Angeles as on the "coast," and Reno (in Nevada) as "inland." Therefore, anything on the coast "has to be" west of anything inland. But as the map shows, this is not the case.

Memory Organizes and Makes Past Experience Accessible

Although the information stored in memory is a severe reduction of all the experiences that pass in and out of consciousness, there are still an enormous number of events stored in memory. There would be no point in retaining all these memories if the ones we wanted could not be called up at the appropriate time. We would become confused by the irrelevant information. Thus, perhaps

FIGURE 9-2
Errors in Representational Memory
Which map is correct? Most people choose the one on the left because Reno is "represented" in our minds as inland from Los Angeles, therefore we think it must be east of Los Angeles. But, believe it or not, Reno is actually *west* of Los Angeles.

the most important function of memory is that it is organized to make information accessible.

Organization

Memory is organized around relating associated events to one another. When you think about your father, you recall things that relate to your knowledge of him. Memories of people and events unrelated to him do not intrude (Baddeley, 1986).

If memory were a random collection of bits of information, you would have to rifle through millions of memories simply to recognize a face or the voice of someone calling your name. Let's use the analogy of a library. Suppose you wanted the book *The Theory of the Leisure Class* by Thorstein Veblen, and suppose that the library you went to was a random collection of books, that is, no book had an assigned place. The only way you would be able to find Veblen's book would be to look at one book after another, perhaps tens of thousands, until you found it. Even in a small town library with a few thousand books, it might take days to find.

In reality, however, libraries are not just buildings that house books; they are *organized systems* for locating books. You could find Veblen's book in a number of ways. You could look up the author's name, or, if you had forgotten the author's name, you could do a quick search through a subject catalog. If the book had been assigned for class, you might even go directly to a special reserved book section.

Human memory is similarly richly interrelated and organized. If I ask you to tell me what you know about U.S. presidents, a variety of information may come to mind: names of presidents, what the powers of the president are, and important policies of past presidents.

If memory becomes disorganized, efficiency is impaired. Consider the simple question, "What are the months of the year?" You would probably answer by reciting the months in chronological order, beginning with January. This takes about 5 seconds, because the months are usually organized in that order in your memory. Now, try to name the months of the year in reverse order. This usually

---

WHAT DAY IS IT?

Consider this simple question: What day is it? To answer this question a representational knowledge of the days of the week is required and it is necessary to update—today's answer is not the same as yesterday's or tomorrow's.

If our memory system were simple, like a date counter on a digital watch, we would be able to answer the question just as quickly on one day as on any other. However, if people are asked what day it is on Wednesday, it takes twice as long to answer as when they are asked on Sunday (Figure 9-3).

However, our memory is not only updated and stored in simplified schemata. Weekdays take longer to recall than weekends, probably because there are five weekdays and only two weekend days. The closer the weekday is to the weekend, the faster it is recalled (Shannon, 1979). In the real world, the length of every day is equal, but their meaning to us is not. Weekends are perhaps more central to our lives and therefore we may represent our weeks largely with reference to weekends.

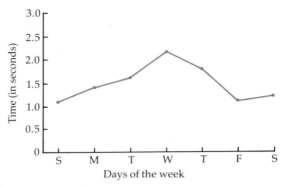

FIGURE 9-3
Memory and Meaning
In timed responses to the question, ''What day of the week is it?'' people take longer to respond in the middle of the week, perhaps showing that we represent our weeks with reference to the more ''meaningful'' weekends.

takes about 12 to 15 seconds. Finally, name the months of the year in alphabetical order. Although you know the months and know how to alphabetize, you probably have rarely had to use these two pieces of knowledge together. There is, in effect, no organization to speed the response. It generally takes more than a minute to answer this question and most people make several mistakes.

Accessibility

Only a limited amount of information in memory is accessible at any one time, and this information constantly changes. This helps us to adapt to different situations: for example, an old song makes certain memories accessible to me or talking to a good friend may bring forth the memory of shared experiences.

The schemata associated with whatever is in consciousness becomes accessible at that time. During exam week you may have tests in English literature, psychology, and history one right after the other. When you are writing your English exam, the information relevant to English literature is easily accessible. That information recedes when you plunge into your psychology exam.

One analogy for this ''dynamic'' aspect of memory is a storehouse: often-ordered items are at the front where they are easy to get to, and items that are rarely called for are tucked away in corners and are less accessible. In one experiment, subjects were asked to name any fruit that begins with the letter *a*; next, they were asked to name fruits that begin with the letter *p*. The second question was answered faster. The first question summoned up the storehouse of information about fruits, making the names of fruits more readily accessible for the second question (Loftus & Loftus, 1975).

PROCESSES OF MEMORY

Although distinguishing between the functions of memory is a relatively straightforward matter, how these functions are performed is a question of much debate. This section describes the overall processes of memory in terms of the *memory cycle* and the *memory system*. The memory cycle describes the process by which we experience something, retain it, and later retrieve it. The memory system includes the different divisions of memory from momentary visual impressions to the lifelong retention of important moments in our lives.

Memory Cycle

Recall of a specific event depends on three prior processes. First, of course, is *perception:* the event must be sensed, transduced into neural language, and perceived. The second process is *retention:* the new information must be stored and kept. *Retrieval* is the third process, by which the stored information is brought forward into consciousness at the appropriate time.

Perceptual Encoding

To be remembered, an event must be perceived. This occurs when information brought in by the senses stimulates appropriate receptors, which then relay it by neural firing to the brain. Sensory information is then organized by perceptual processes into the simplest meaningful percepts; this process is called *encoding*.

Retention

The theory of retention states that a remembered event is retained as long as needed. The retention time may be a few seconds, a few years, or an entire lifetime. Occasionally, we consciously direct retention ("I am going to remember that term"), but usually we select things on the basis of a few rules: something is striking or new, related to other memories, important to our career, and so on.

Specialists have not yet pinpointed the locations in the brain of specific memories or even different kinds of memories. Childhood memories do not seem to be stored in one corner of the brain and memories of songs in another. But the mere fact that we do have memories means that there must be physical changes that occur somewhere in the brain when we remember something.

Retrieval

When a past event is brought into consciousness, we regain or *retrieve* information previously stored. Two types of retrieval are recognition and recall.

Recognition is the ability to correctly identify an object or event. This identification involves a match between present perception and your memory of the information presented to you. The word *recognize* comes from the Latin "to know again." Recognition is the most common experience of memory.

Recall is the ability to summon up stored information in the absence of the actual event or object. An exam question such as "Which of Shakespeare's plays is concerned with the emotion of jealousy?" tests *recall*. The same question presented with a choice of answers would test recognition: "Jealousy is the central theme of which Shakespeare play? (a) *Merchant of Venice,* (b) *Macbeth,* (c) *All's Well That Ends Well,* or (d) *Othello.*"

It is easier to recognize something than to recall it because in recognition the stimulus is present and calls up all the relevant associated schemata. This is why multiple-choice tests are easier than tests that require recall. The capacity of recognition memory is enormous. Haber and Standig (1966) showed subjects 2,560 photographs for 10 seconds each. A few days later recognition of the pictures was greater than 90 percent.

Memory System

Some information, like the name or phone number of someone you have just met, is remembered for only a brief time before it is forgotten altogether. Other information that we use continually, like our own name and address, we do not forget.

This difference has led many psychologists to hypothesize that memory has two distinct components: short-term and long-term memory.

Short-term Memory

Information that is retained temporarily, for only a few seconds, is thought to be stored by a specific process called **short-term memory.** The storage capacity of short-term memory is about seven items, such as a seven-digit number. Short-term memory can be regarded as "scratch paper," on which immediate information for a specific purpose is written and continuously erased as new information comes into consciousness. When you look up a phone number, you only have to remember the number long enough to dial it. If you encounter interference—a busy signal or a loud noise next to you—you may have to look the number up again. That act can be thought of as constantly replacing the number in short-term memory or nudging it into the more permanent component of the memory system: long-term memory.

Long-term Memory

Information retained for more than a few seconds is stored in what is termed **long-term memory.** You do not have to look up your *own* telephone number when you call home, nor do you have to repeat your name over and over to remember it. Both episodic and representational memories are stored as long-term memories. The storage capacity of long-term memory is huge; many psychologists consider it limitless. In a subsequent section we look in more detail at this amazing ability.

Alternative Interpretations of Memory Cycle and System

Although many psychologists accept the twin concepts of a memory cycle and memory system, some recent theorists have challenged both ideas as inadequate descriptions of how memory works.

Memory Changes with Experience

The concept of a memory cycle is appealing. It describes in a clear manner how an event enters consciousness and is remembered through the stages of encoding, storage, and recall. The findings of many experiments that test the recall of specific kinds of information support this hypothesis. Nevertheless, it is quite unlikely that our memory operates this way all the time. One important cognitive psychologist, William Estes, describes a different view: "Human memory does not, in a literal sense, store anything; it simply changes as a function of experience" (Estes, 1980).

So far in the discussion, memory has been likened to a computer: acquiring information, filing it, and bringing it back. The alternative idea, that memory simply produces changes in us, is similar to the ecological and computational approaches. According to this experiential view, changes that take place in response to experience are analogous to changing the dial on a radio set: when the "tuning" is changed, new stations can be received. The changes that we call "memory" are more like physical changes to the body that occur because of our experiences. When we exercise, for example, muscles change shape and change their performance.

See Chapter 6, section on Theories of Perception.

Both views are probably partially accurate. Both interpretations agree that experiences change us and that the resultant changes are reflected in memory. They differ on the question of how those changes are reflected in memory. A part of memory is probably a little like a computer, storing words, phrases, and specific events that can later be described. But for much of our life, we are not storing information simply because we might need it in the future. Rather, our general concern is adaptation: being able to change behavior as a result of experience. For example, we may wish to avoid someone who once caused us pain. Previous experience with that person produced changes in us. We then begin to pick up information about other people who we think may also cause us pain, by noticing similarities between them and the person who has hurt us before. But in these cases we are not retrieving specific information as a computer does. Instead, we have become "tuned" differently; we perceive and act differently. Probably no single machine analogy is sufficient to explain the complexity of the human mind, even a machine as complex as a computer.

Memory as a Continuous Process

Many psychologists do not believe that *separate* processes for short-term and long-term memory are plausible. Instead, they think of the memory system as a *single* and *continuous* process. In this view, each repetition of an event causes an increase in the strength of the association of that event and increases the probability that it will be remembered later on.

The single or continuous process hypothesis seems to be an accurate description of real life (Wickelgren, 1977). There is no sharp distinction between not remembering and fully remembering. You may forget a phone number the first time you dial it, then remember a few of the numbers the next time, and finally the whole thing if you keep using it.

The single process hypothesis regards short-term and long-term memory not as separate mechanisms, but as the extreme ends of a single process. Each exposure to a situation increases the probability of its being remembered. In this view, all memories are generated by the same system. Because the continuous memory approach postulates only a single process for all normal memory experience, it has the advantage of being simpler and more inclusive. The majority viewpoint now seems to be shifting toward this hypothesis.

No matter how much controversy surrounds the question of how to conceptualize the processes of memory, our observable experience is unmistakable: new information fades quickly in our memory, while at the same time we have a relatively stable and permanent knowledge of the world.

The modern scientific study of memory began 100 years ago with controlled experiments designed to uncover the fundamental characteristics of human memory by determining the basic rate of forgetting. More recently, the emphasis has been on research outside the laboratory, on determining how and what we remember and forget of real-life events.

HOW WE FORGET AND WHAT WE REMEMBER: LONG-TERM MEMORY

Factors of Forgetting

The first paradigm for controlled research on memory was developed in 1885 by Hermann Ebbinghaus. He devised long lists of **nonsense syllables,** such as "dof," "zam," and "fok." By using such nonsense syllables to test memory, Ebbinghaus hoped to eliminate any effect subjects' personal experience might have on their ability to recall information. In this way, he hoped to obtain a precise measure of learning and memory independent of previous experience.

His method was heroic; he used himself as a subject through long hours of investigations. He learned a list of syllables by heart, well enough to recite it two times in a row. He then tested his recall of the list over several days. He designated his measure of forgetting as the time needed to relearn the list until he recalled it perfectly. This method yielded a precise measurement of the rate of forgetting. He discovered that the rate of forgetting is described by a predictable curve; most forgetting occurs immediately and tapers off as time goes on (Figure 9-4). Ebbinghaus' curve is a general description of the rate at which material with no previous associations is forgotten.

Decay of Memory

In movies, scenes of the distant past are commonly shot in dulled, faded colors. Although the idea of memory literally fading with time is appealing, this use of imagery is an oversimplification of a very complex process. For instance, a senile person may not be able to recall the day's events, but may clearly remember events from youth. The memory of motor skills, like how to ride a bicycle, does not fade away over time, even without practice.

In one important test of the "fading" notion, Jenkins and Dallenbach (1924) asked two groups to learn lists of nonsense syllables in the same way Ebbinghaus had done. Immediately after the memorization task, one group was allowed to go to sleep, while the second was required to stay awake. It was reasoned that if memory fades with time alone, then there should be no difference in recall between the two groups if both groups are tested for recall at the same time. The results showed, however, that those who slept retained far more than those who had stayed awake. The most likely explanation for this result is that the "awake" group had experiences that *interfered* with retention. The decay of memory is not just a matter of time: the particular events that occur during that time are also a factor.

FIGURE 9-4
Curve of Forgetting
Ebbinghaus showed that at first we forget quickly, but then our rate of forgetting evens out and becomes stable.

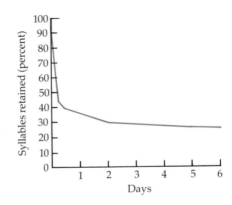

Interference

Some kinds of events interfere with memory more than others. Two kinds of interference have been studied in the laboratory. **Proactive interference** occurs when previous knowledge interferes with present memory. The term *proactive* is a combination of "pro," meaning forward, and "active," which together means that the interference *moves forward* from previous to present knowledge. Proactive interference is easily demonstrated in the following test. Two groups learn the same list (B). However, the first group has learned another list (A) before. Both groups are tested for their ability to recall list B.

	Learn	Learn	Test
Group 1	A	B	B
Group 2	—	B	B

On testing, Group 2 can remember more of list B than Group 1 can.

Retroactive interference occurs when new information interferes with previous memories. It can be demonstrated as follows. Two groups learn list C. The first group then learns list D, the other does not. Both groups are tested for their memory of list C.

	Learn	Learn	Test
Group 1	C	D	C
Group 2	C	—	C

On testing, Group 1 will remember less of list C than will Group 2. Similarly, suppose you are making a list of people to invite to a party. You are about to write down John's name, but before you do, someone interrupts with, "Hey don't forget we have to invite June and Sally." You write their names down but then find that you cannot remember the name of the person you had thought of before.

Two general factors in interference are (1) the *longer* the interval between the first and second event, the *less* interference; and (2) the more *similar* the items, the *more* interference. For example, suppose you are trying to remember the phone numbers of two people. If the first number is 524-5318 and the second is 883-2299, there will be less interference than if the second number is 542-5218.

Primacy and Recency

We seem to be structured, even at the most rudimentary physiological level, to notice and retain elements at transition points. Recall that the senses respond most vigorously at the beginnings and endings of stimuli; in between they habituate, or stop responding.

See Chapter 5, section on Sensory Adaptation and Comparison.

REMEMBERING PHONE NUMBERS

Telephone numbers have proved useful in some simple experiments on memory. Although it is not clear exactly what phone number memory tells us about real-world memory, it is clear that memory research has provided some important information to telephone companies. Phone numbers have seven numbers, but the first three are a prefix that designates the exchange in a certain area of town. These prefixes are remembered as a single unit, or chunk, not as three separate numbers. Shepard and Sheenan (1963) thought, therefore, that it would be easier for people to remember phone numbers if the last four digits were dialed first, when the memory of these numbers was freshest. They showed that this method reduced the time needed for dialing by 20 percent and that errors made in dialing were cut in half. However, the telephone companies cannot take advantage of this research because the cost of switching their equipment over to such a method is prohibitive. It does point out, however, the need for people who design machines and equipment to be aware of relevant psychological research.

We remember the beginning and ending of an event better than the middle and the ending better than the beginning. A word at the beginning of a list is recalled 70 percent of the time, words in the middle less than 20 percent, and words at the end almost 100 percent (Loftus & Loftus, 1975). Our enhanced recall of beginnings is an example of the effect of **primacy.** Our enhanced recall of endings is an example of the effect of **recency.** The principles of primacy and recency in memory have been extensively demonstrated experimentally using lists of nonsense syllables. They also hold as general principles in many areas of life, from the basic characteristics of the sensory systems to our involvement in political campaigns, love affairs, and theater performances. In 1980, presidential candidate Ronald Reagan illustrated these principles by saying, "Politics is just like show business. You need a big opening. Then you coast for a while. Then you need a big finish."

Memory for Life Experiences

Although studies in the laboratory make clear some of the basic operations of the memory system, they shed little light on our real-life memories; lists of syllables and numbers are not important parts of our lives. The most memorable events of your life would be impossible to duplicate in the lab. When I was 6 years old I almost drowned trying to learn how to swim. I remember, as if it just happened, the blue water turning to black as I lost consciousness and the blinding light when my father pulled me out. I will never forget it. If you ask people of your parents' generation where they were when President Kennedy was shot, they will probably remember every detail. But in pursuit of scientific knowledge, we cannot deliberately create such powerful events and then check on people 20 years later to see what they remember about them.

Psychologists are now trying to develop methods to study what kinds of things people recall in the normal course of their lives. Some psychologists use themselves as subjects and sometimes they use a common experience as a focus. Some of the studies discussed here involve considerable amounts of time (sometimes decades) between the event and the recall test, while others involve memory for visual scenes, faces, and odors. Another question that has been recently investigated is the nature of differences between one individual's memory and another's.

Memory for Real-World Events after Six Years

The forgetting curve of Ebbinghaus (Figure 9-4) shows that the greater part of relatively meaningless information, such as nonsense syllables, is quickly forgotten. But how long do you remember a tennis victory, a good movie, or a passionate kiss? Marigold Linton studied her memory of her life events over a period of six years (Neisser, 1982). During this time she recorded 5,500 events and tested some of them for recall every two months. Her record includes such items as "narrowly beat HEO at tennis today" and "received a call from Maureen, Strassberger's secretary, indicating that she will make the travel arrangements to Washington."

She expected that her rate of forgetting would follow the Ebbinghaus curve. Surprisingly, it was much less rapid. Where Ebbinghaus found that forgetting was rapid at first, Linton's loss of memory for the details of her own life proceeded at a slower, more constant rate. Although there are many differences in the two test situations, the key difference may be that because events in your life have *personal meaning*, they are not quickly forgotten. Many laboratory tests are designed to have no meaning, so there is no reason to remember them when the experiment is over.

Memory for Very Old Events

To investigate memory for events long past, Bahrick, Bahrick, and Wittlinger (1975) tested the ability of high school graduates to recognize the names and faces of their former classmates. They chose nine groups from a variety of graduating classes (the youngest had graduated 3.3 months before, and the oldest, 47 years before). Each group had about 50 people. All groups were shown photographs and asked to pick out any pictures they recognized. The data were quite surprising (Figure 9-5). Recognition of the faces of old classmates remained at over 90 percent for intervals up to 34 years! However, name recognition was not as durable; it dropped after 15 years (still a considerably long interval). This finding suggests that memory for names might be organized differently from memory for faces.

In another test of what is often called "very long-term" memory, Rubin (1977) tested elementary and college students on their recall of passages most of us learn in school: Hamlet's soliloquy, the Preamble to the Constitution, and the Twenty-third Psalm. There seem to be certain words and phrases that are remembered of each passage, although individuals differ in how many of them they remember. Figure 9-6 shows how many words 50 people remembered of Hamlet's soliloquy "To be or not to be."

Recognition of Pictures and Odors

Our ability to remember our high school classmates for so long is impressive. We have an enormous capacity in recognition memory for pictures. In one study, Shepard (1967) selected 612 familiar pictures and allowed subjects to review the

FIGURE 9-5
Remembering Faces and
Names from the Past
When high school
graduates were tested on
their ability to recall the
faces of former classmates,
even very old subjects
showed remarkable
memory. The retention in
various categories is
shown here; the test is
discussed in the
accompanying text.
(After Bahrick, Bahrick, &
Wittlinger, 1975)

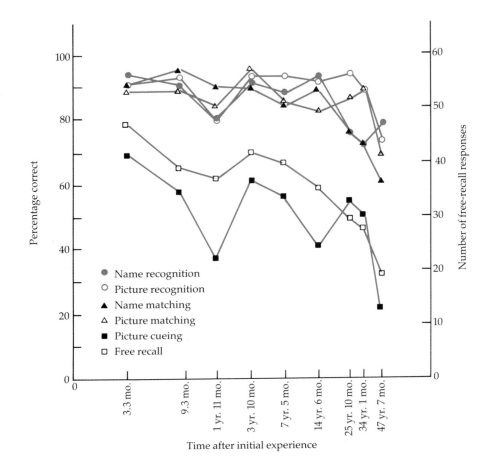

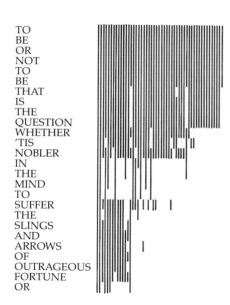

TO
BE
OR
NOT
TO
BE
THAT
IS
THE
QUESTION
WHETHER
'TIS
NOBLER
IN
THE
MIND
TO
SUFFER
THE
SLINGS
AND
ARROWS
OF
OUTRAGEOUS
FORTUNE
OR

FIGURE 9-6
Very Long-term Memory
Fifty subjects tested on
how much of Hamlet's
soliloquy they remembered
showed the results charted
here: each vertical line
represents recall by one
subject. How much do you
recall of such material
learned when you were in
high school?
(After Rubin, 1977)

pictures (on slides) at their own pace. A recognition test was given immediately afterward; recognition was 96.7 percent. After 120 days more than 50 percent of the pictures were recognized (Figure 9-7).

Are other kinds of information remembered as vividly as pictures? Smell is our most direct sense, so an important component of real-world memories is odor. Marcel Proust, in the famous passage from *Swann's Way*, describes how the smell of madeleine cookies summoned up details of his childhood. Cities have characteristic odors. The London underground has an unpleasant but distinctive odor; I always feel I am *really* in London when I smell it.

Brown University has a collection of more than 100 different odors, ranging from a skunk's scent to whiskey. In one experiment, subjects sniffed 48 cotton balls, each saturated with a different odor. Afterward, a second group of odors was presented, including many from the first group; 69 percent of the odors were recognized (Engen & Ross, 1973). While this is very high, it is not as high as

See Chapter 5, section on Chemical Senses: Smell and Taste.

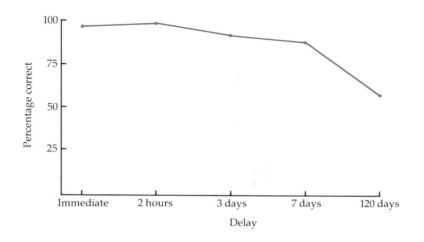

FIGURE 9-7
Recognition of Pictures
People have a great ability to recognize photographs, even long after they are first seen.
(After Shepard, 1967)

picture recognition. However, there seems to be no decline in odor recognition; recognition was 70 percent one week later and 68 percent one month later.

Individual Differences in Memory

We all know people who seem to have a good memory for faces but not for numbers. Other people can remember stories well but not directions. "Absent-minded professors" may remember specific details of the Peloponnesian War but cannot remember to pick up their laundry. That individuals differ in memory is a universal observation and is one that is attracting new interest among researchers. In a very early study, Francis Galton (1874) surveyed an eminent group of subjects: British men of science. He found that some relied primarily on vision, while others relied more on words to remember things. In a more recent (though still exploratory) study, Herrmann and Neisser (1978) have developed a questionnaire called the Inventory of Memory Experiences (IME), which asks respondents how often they remember and forget different kinds of things. Their analysis reveals eight characteristics that distinguish individual memories:

1. *Rote memory.* Forgetting such things as numbers and addresses and having to recheck them.
2. *Absentmindedness.* Forgetting what one has just done or intended to do.
3. *Names.* The ability or inability to recall people's names.
4. *People.* Recognizing individuals by their appearance.
5. *Conversation.* Remembering jokes, stories, and conversations.
6. *Errands.* Remembering "things to do."
7. *Retrieval.* Inability to recall why something seems familiar.
8. *Place.* Where things are.

Although these findings are very tentative, they suggest that an individual's memory may be "assembled" out of these components. One person may have a great memory for jokes and names but forget "things to do." Another may easily remember where things are but have difficulty in remembering why someone's face is familiar. Further research may reveal which of these components of memory are associated with one another.

MEMORY DISORDERS

Different forms of damage to the brain can affect the storing and retrieval of memory. This search for how memory is distributed in the brain is one of psychology's most exciting pursuits.

Epileptic seizures often overstimulate and damage parts of the limbic system. When the hippocampus is affected, either by the epilepsy or by subsequent surgery, there are profound effects on memory. Here is an example of an interview with such a patient:

YOU: Good morning Mr. H. M.
H. M.: Good morning.
YOU: I wonder whether you could answer a few questions?
H. M.: Fine, go ahead.

YOU:	Who was president of the U.S. during World War II?
H. M.:	Franklin Roosevelt, later Truman.
YOU:	What did Truman do when a national rail strike was threatened?
H. M.:	He nationalized the railways, or he threatened to.

The questions and answers continue, until you begin to wonder whether there is any deficit in memory. Then the phone rings and you excuse yourself to take an urgent call. You return.

| YOU: | Sorry, H. M., to interrupt our session. |
| H. M.: | I beg your pardon, have we met before? I don't seem to remember you. (Ornstein, Thompson, & Macaulay, 1984) |

It hits you: H. M. cannot remember what is happening to him *now;* he lives in a kind of perpetual present. Everything he has learned since his surgery is forgotten almost immediately, just as when you jot down a phone number and then quickly forget it. But note that H. M. has retained his previous memories, such as language and what an interview is. Perhaps the damage to the hippocampus has affected his ability to lay down new memories, while leaving alone his ability to retrieve old ones.

Amnesia

Although unusual, the case of H. M. is not unique. **Amnesia,** the general name for deficits in learning and memory that occur abruptly, can take many different forms and can involve many different brain mechanisms. This multiplicity of causes suggests that there are a great variety of pathways for memory storage in the brain (Squire, 1987). Amnesia can occur from damage to the frontal lobe, from damage due to electroconvulsive shock, and from lesions to the hippocampus and amygdala. Lesions can occur only in one hemisphere of the brain or can involve both sides.

Thus, all amnesia is not the same, just as all memory is not one system. People may be deficient in recalling past events or current events, in learning new distinctions or remembering old ones, or in recognizing people or places. All these distinctions, confusing as they may be to the student and the scientist, are nevertheless of great excitement. For the first time, different forms of memory (such as those distinctions proposed by Herrmann and Neisser) have been identified by different lesions in the brain (Squire, 1987; Lynch, McGaugh, & Weinberger, 1984). It is likely that there will soon be a breakthrough in the neural coding of memory. Many theories have now been proposed (Thompson, 1986; Squire, 1987; Lynch et al., 1984), but none yet can encompass even one of the different forms of memory considered in this chapter.

The most basic principle of memory is that we remember *meaningful* events. Of all the information we receive, of all the experiences we have, the things we remember are those that are most meaningful to us. The word *mnemosyne* would be extremely difficult to remember if it had no meaning; "It's Greek to me," we would say. (In fact, Mnemosyne is the Greek goddess of memory.) The word

MEANINGFUL-
NESS AND
ORGANIZATION
IN MEMORY

memory is easier to remember because we know what it *means*. For the same reason, a jumble of words such as "The for time now come good party all men to their to aid the is of" is much harder to remember than the well-known sentence "Now is the time for all good men to come to the aid of their party," even though they both contain the same words.

See Chapter 6, section on Perceptual Cycle.

Meaning differs from individual to individual. Recall how a child, a botanist, and an artist have different perceptual experiences during a walk in the park. They see only those things that interest them as individuals. The botanist is likely to perceive and remember a plant in detail because it is of particular professional interest. Meaningful events and nonmeaningful events are distinguished by their strength of association with other items in memory (Winograd, 1980).

Importance of Context

Quickly read the following story (Dooling & Lachman, 1971) and then, before reading on, jot down what you remember of it.

> With hocked gems financing him, our hero bravely defied all scornful laughter that tried to prevent his scheme. "Your eyes deceive," he had said. "An egg, not a table, correctly typifies this unexplored planet." Now three sturdy sisters sought proof. Forging along, sometimes through calm vastness, yet more often very turbulent peaks and valleys, days became weeks as many doubters spread fearful rumors about the edge. At last from nowhere welcome winged creatures appeared, signifying momentous success.

You probably remembered next to nothing of this passage. Now read the story again, but this time, consider the context: the story is about Columbus's voyage to America. Dooling and Lachman (1971) found that people who had been given this context remembered much more than those who had not. The main function of *context* is to provide a way of organizing information *beforehand,* therefore making it more memorable. A title, for example, usually announces an overall context and makes what is read more accessible, as naming fruits aids recall of other fruits.

The context of a story can affect what is remembered. Because of context, some events are better remembered, some less well. Although it is difficult to study how different people organize information into a meaningful memory, here is a demonstration of how context, when deliberately altered, can affect memory. Read the following story (Bransford & Johnson, 1974) *once* and do not reread any part of it. Then write down or recite what you remember of it.

> *Watching a Peace March from the 40th Floor*
>
> The view was breathtaking. From the window one could see the crowd below. Everything looked extremely small from such a distance but the colorful costumes could still be seen. Everyone seemed to be moving in one direction in an orderly fashion, and there seemed to be little children as well as adults. The landing was gentle, and luckily the atmosphere was such that no special suits had to be worn. At first there was a great deal of activity. Later, when the speeches started, the crowd quieted down. The man with the television camera took many shots of the setting and the crowds. Everyone was very friendly and seemed glad when the music started.

Did you write down anything about the sentence "The landing was gentle, and luckily the atmosphere was such that no special suits had to be worn"? In one experiment, only 18 percent of the subjects recalled something about the sentence. With a different context, however, recollection of this sentence is improved. Now reread the story, but this time under the title "A Space Trip to an Uninhabited Planet." Now the sentence "The landing was gentle . . . " makes sense. Of the subjects who read the story with this title, 53 percent recalled the sentence. You might try this out on a couple of friends, giving both of them the story, but each one a different title. Then compare their recollections.

The word *context* comes from the Latin word meaning "to weave together." When information is presented in a context that is meaningful to an individual, it is remembered more easily. Information is "weaved" into an already meaningful background. All the schemata associated with the new information are activated.

How Information Is Organized into Meaningful Units

In this section we will examine three processes of organization:

1. How existing schemata influence and often change what we remember.
2. How incoming information is organized into meaningful units or "chunks."
3. How some memory can be reconstructed on the basis of these two processes.

Effect of Schemata on Memory

In 1932 F. C. Bartlett wrote an important book on remembering in which he demonstrated the important effects of a person's existing knowledge structure on memory. The method he used in his experiments is similar to the children's games "telephone" and "whisper down the lane." A subject is given an "original stimulus," either a drawing or a story, and asked to reproduce it. That person then passes on his or her reproduction to the next person, who reproduces it, and so on. Bartlett called this method *serial reproduction*. The stimuli Bartlett chose were deliberately exotic, unfamiliar to residents of Cambridge, England, where he did his research.

One example of serial reproduction is a series of drawings that begin with an African drawing, *Portrait d'Homme* (Figure 9-8). In these drawings, the subjects transformed figures to correspond with what was already in their memories. According to Bartlett, unfamiliar features "invariably suffer transformation in the direction of the familiar," that is, people have a tendency to transform odd or unfamiliar figures into conventional or familiar ones. In each successive reproduction of the African drawing, the original unconventional characteristics are dropped. The final figure is an ordinary schematic representation of a face. It is interesting, however, that the exotic qualities of the original drawing are retained in the transformation of the name *Portrait d'Homme* (portrait of a man) to *L'Homme Egyptien* (Egyptian man).

Bartlett also presented an unusual story to his students, an Indian tale called "The War of the Ghosts." Again, each subject was asked to reproduce what he or she remembered from the previous subject's version of the story. The original story is recounted here.

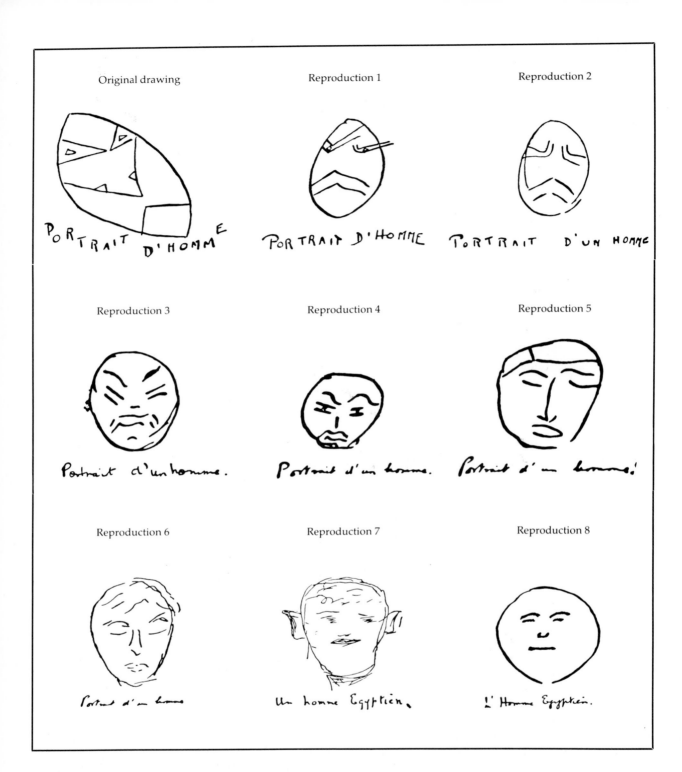

FIGURE 9-8
Portrait d'Homme
These successive drawings show the transformation of the unfamiliar in the direction of the familiar.

The War of the Ghosts

One night two young men from Egulac went down to the river to hunt seals, and while they were there it became foggy and calm. Then they heard war-cries, and they thought: "Maybe this is a war-party." They escaped to the shore, and hid behind a log. Now canoes came up, and they heard the noise of the paddle, and saw one canoe coming up to them. There were five men in the canoe, and they said:

"What do you think? We wish to take you along. We are going up the river to make war on the people."

One of the young men said: "I have no arrows."

· "Arrows are in the canoe," they said.

"I will not go along. I might be killed. My relatives do not know where I have gone. But you," he said, turning to the other, "may go with them."

So one of the young men went, but the other returned home.

And the warriors went on up the river to a town on the other side of Kalama. The people came down to the water, and they began to fight, and many were killed. But presently the young man heard one of the warriors say: "Quick, let us go home: that Indian has been hit." Now he thought: "Oh, they are ghosts." He did not feel sick, but they said he had been shot.

So the canoes went back to Egulac, and the young man went ashore to his house, and made a fire. And he told everybody and said: "Behold I accompanied the ghosts, and we went to fight. Many of our fellows were killed, and many of those who attacked us were killed. They said I was hit, and I did not feel sick."

He told it all, and then he became quiet. When the sun rose he fell down. Something black came out of his mouth. His face became contorted. The people jumped up and cried.

He was dead.

Now here is an example of one of the final reproductions of the story.

Two Indians from Momapan were fishing for seals when a boat comes along containing five warriors. "Come with us," they said to the Indians, "and help us to fight the warriors further on." The first Indian replied: "I have a mother at home, and she would grieve greatly if I were not to return." The other Indian said, "I have no weapons." "We have some in the boat," said the warriors. The Indian stepped into the boat.

In the course of the fight further on, the Indian was mortally wounded, and his spirit fled. "Take me to my home," he said, "at Momapan, for I am going to die." "No, you will not die," said a warrior. In spite of this, however, he died, and before he could be carried back to the boat, his spirit had left this world. (Bartlett, 1932)

The effects of the English student's organization are clear: the story has been transformed into a more conventional one. The original distinctive names are gone, although "Momapan" has been added. Bartlett says, "The story has become more coherent, as well as much shorter. No trace of any odd or supernatural element is left: we have a perfectly straightforward story of a fight and a death." Things that do not match the common schemata of an Englishman are omitted or transformed into the familiar: canoes become boats and references to ghosts are omitted. What occurred here is similar to what happened in your recollection of "Watching a Peace March from the 40th Floor." We tend to omit elements that do not "fit in" with what we know already.

Chunking and Coding

A unit of memory is called a *chunk*. In perceiving and remembering bits of information, **chunking** is the process of using a *code* to organize individual items into units of memory. GEAIMNN is a "list" of seven bits that you can probably retain only briefly. MEANING is a list of the same seven bits, but you have a code (in this case, the English language) that organized them into a chunk (in this case, the word "MEANING"). The ability to chunk information greatly expands the storage capacity of memory because small chunks can be combined into larger chunks that are then more easily remembered (Figure 9-9).

Knowing a code increases the capacity of memory and the ability to remember. Read the following list of numbers quickly: 41236108324972. Now write down what you remember; most likely you remembered only about seven of the numbers. Now, here is a code to follow: begin with 4, then multiply it by 3; then multiply this product by 3 again; repeat this multiplication three more times. With these instructions, you need not *memorize* any of the numbers; the code tells you where to begin, what to do, and where to stop.

Here is another example. Read the following lists quickly and see if you can devise a code to help you remember them.

IB MF BI TW AJ FK

816 449 362 516 941

If you had to reproduce the two lists locational, the simple way would be to notice that the top line includes four well-known acronyms (such as IBM) and that the bottom row includes the squares of all single-digit numbers in descending order from 9. We could easily reproduce the lists as

IBM FBI TWA JFK

81 64 49 36 25 16 9 4 1

The Reconstructive Nature of Remembering

Various kinds of information can color or change our memory of the past. In one study designed by Elizabeth Loftus, researchers showed people a reddish orange disc. One group was told it was a tomato; the other group was told it was an orange. Later the two groups were shown colors and were asked to select the

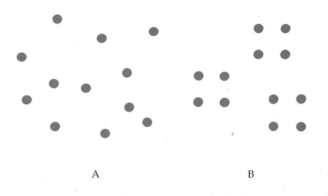

FIGURE 9-9
Chunking
It is easier to count the dots on the right (B) because they are arranged in groups, or chunks.

A   B

color that most closely matched the color they saw. The group that had been told the disc was an orange selected a color close to orange; the group that had been told the disc was a tomato selected a color closer to red (Loftus, 1978). In another demonstration two groups of subjects were presented with ambiguous doodles (Figure 9-10). Each drawing was labeled with a word. Although both groups saw the same drawings, they were each given a different set of word labels. For example, the same doodle was presented with the word *eyeglasses* or with the word *dumbbell.* Immediately after each presentation, the subjects were asked to reproduce, as accurately as possible, the figure they had seen. The result was that the subjects' drawings were influenced by the label they had been given; there was an obvious effort to draw pictures according to the verbal labels. For example, the subjects attempted to reproduce eyeglasses or a dumbbell rather than the original ambiguous figure (Carmichael et al., 1932).

Eyewitness Testimony

The reconstructive nature of memory is sufficient for everyday life. We do not need to know things in complete detail, nor are we capable of recalling literally *every* detail of an experience, even what a penny looks like. But when details are important, perhaps a matter of life and death, the reconstructive nature of memory can become a problem.

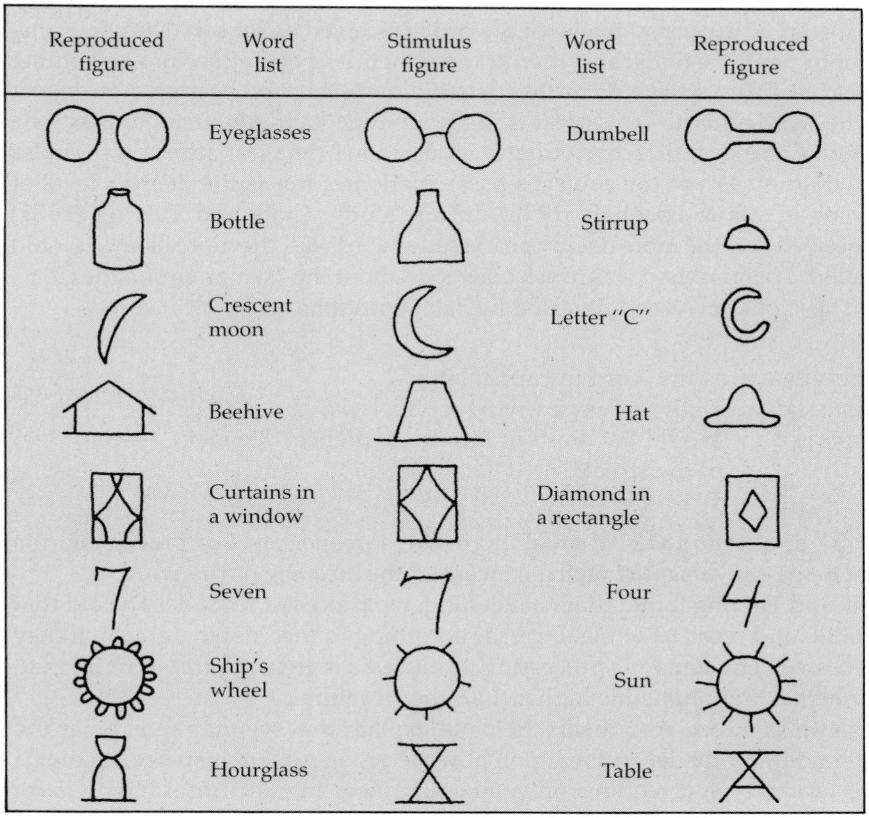

Reproduced figure	Word list	Stimulus figure	Word list	Reproduced figure
	Eyeglasses		Dumbell	
	Bottle		Stirrup	
	Crescent moon		Letter "C"	
	Beehive		Hat	
	Curtains in a window		Diamond in a rectangle	
	Seven		Four	
	Ship's wheel		Sun	
	Hourglass		Table	

FIGURE 9-10
Labeling and Remembering
The name something is given influences our memory of it, as this chart demonstrates. Subjects in an experiment recalled and reproduced ambiguous doodles as more like the labels given them than did subjects given different labels for the same doodles. (After Carmichael, Hogan, & Walters, 1932)

FIGURE 9-11
Eyewitness Testimony
Memory can be influenced by what is experienced between perceiving an event and when it is recalled. Thus, being told two cars collided or bumped into each other will make us recall a milder accident (top) than if we were told the cars "smashed" (bottom).
(After Loftus & Loftus, 1975)

No courtroom testimony is more effective than a witness who stands, points a finger at someone, and says, "It's him. I saw him do it with my own eyes." We have such confidence in our memory that the power of an eyewitness's testimony is not easily overcome, even if it is successfully challenged by other testimony. But an understanding of the malleability of memory should make us more wary. Many innocent people have been accused and sentenced to prison on the basis of the testimony of an eyewitness.

Memory is influenced not only by previous knowledge but also by events that happen between the time an event is perceived and the time it is recalled. In one experiment, people were shown a film of a traffic accident and later asked questions about what they had seen (Figure 9-11). The key question in the first part of the test was, "How fast were the cars going when they *smashed* into each other?" For some groups the word *smashed* was replaced by less aggressive verbs, such as hit, bumped, or collided. A week later the groups were asked, "Did you see any broken glass?" More of those who had been asked the question with the word smashed in it answered yes, although no broken glass was shown in the film (Loftus, Miller, & Burns, 1978).

Levels of Processing

No one theory has yet been able to tie together all the complex phenomena of memory. One recent attempt at such a theory is called **levels of processing.** This theory states that all information presented to us is *processed* at different *depths* or *levels.*

For instance, the visual image of a word is received as sensory stimuli, transduced into neural signals, and then transformed by perception into something meaningful. This stage would be the first, shallow level of processing. At a deeper level, the word and the sentence it is in are identified and understood. Next, the meaning of the sentence may trigger associations (images, stories, or similar events) on the basis of the subject's past experience; this is the deepest level of processing (Craik & Lockhart, 1972). In one study, Craik and Tulving (1975) hypothesized that the more deeply processed a word was, the more likely it would be recalled. Their method was to ask questions about the "semantic qualities" of a word. These qualities were revealed by such questions as:

STRUCTURAL:	Is the word in capital letters?
PHONEMIC:	Does the word rhyme with *weight*?
SEMANTIC:	Would the word fit into the sentence "He met a ——— in the street?"

Each type of question was intended to evoke a deeper level of processing, the deepest being the *semantic,* which concerned the *meaning* of the word.

Craik and Tulving found that it takes longer to process a word deeply, but that recognition and recall of words increase according to the "depth" at which they are processed. The semantic processing produced a higher amount of recall than the phonemic, the phonemic higher than the structural.

The level-of-processing theory helps to explain that we may remember the same item differently depending upon how we process it. For instance, reading a page of text to type it requires only shallow processing; less information is remembered than if it were being read to understand it.

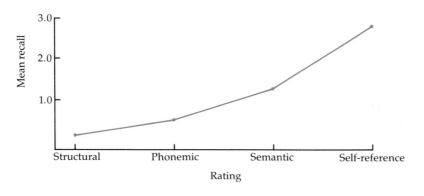

FIGURE 9-12
Memory and Self-
Reference
You can deepen the
processing of what you
perceive and want to recall
if you relate that
information to yourself or
to an event in your life.
(After Rogers, Kulper, & Kirker,
1977)

Relating Information to Yourself

An important way to "deepen" processing is to try to relate the information to yourself. To the list of questions in Craik and Tulving's experiment, Rogers and his colleagues (1977) added the question "Describes you?" They found that people best remembered words they could relate to themselves (Figure 9-12). Asking yourself such questions as "What would have made me do that?" and considering whether or not "That happened to me once" both increase the likelihood of recall. The reason for this increase in remembering may be that the richest set of associations in memory relate to ourselves. When information can be referred to an event in your own life, it is remembered longer (Bower, Gilligan, & Monteiro, 1981).

Why Are Meaningful Events Better Remembered?

Although the idea of levels of processing offers a useful framework for understanding memory, it has been criticized as circular reasoning: "Deep processing leads to better memory because we remember something that is deeply processed." A possibly simpler, and therefore preferable, explanation is that successfully remembering an event depends primarily on the number of associations that that particular event calls up. One dominant view in psychology, which began with the British empiricists such as Locke and Hume and continued with James and many current researchers, is that the mind is best described as a network of associations. When something arises in consciousness, all associated schemata arise with it. Associations may be semantic, visual, or emotional.

Something is meaningful to us because it evokes many associations. Because the most meaningful information has the most associations, it is remembered better. They cluster, as James wrote, "like grapes to a stem." Each time a particular event occurs, the number of associations to it increases, and memory of that event is improved. Thus, relating information to yourself serves to increase the number of associations to that event because we have the most items associated with ourselves. Generally, then, the more meaningful something is, the more associations it has, thus the more memorable it is.

T echniques for improving memory change the way information is organized in our minds so that it becomes more accessible. It is always easier to remember something according to a rule than by rote. For example, it is simpler to

**IMPROVING
MEMORY**

remember the spelling rule "*i* before *e* except after *c*" and the few exceptions than to learn to spell every word containing *ie*.

More than any other group, students probably have the greatest self-interest in improving memory. A successful student is usually one who can retrieve the correct information easily at exam time. Several of the principles discussed in this chapter may help you remember things better.

Improving Memory by Changing Encoding

It is not useful to have learned something "by heart" if the information cannot be retrieved when needed. Exams test your ability to retrieve information, either by recognition or by recall. Have you ever heard someone say after an exam, "I knew the answer, but not the way the question was asked"? Concerning this problem, one psychologist writes:

> The critical thing for most of the material you learn in school is to *understand* it, which means encoding it in a way that makes it distinctive from unrelated material and related to all the things it ought to be related to in order for you to use it. . . . The time you spend thinking about material you are reading and relating it to previously stored material is about the most useful thing you can do in learning any new subject matters. (Wickelgren, 1977)

Instead of simply memorizing "by heart," ask "What does this mean?" Talking to a friend about what you have read is a good way to make sure you have grasped the central meaning.

Relating Information to Yourself

As discussed previously, the self is the most efficient context for remembering. Try to relate material to your own past experience and knowledge. Psychology is almost tailor-made for efficient studying, since its subject is you. The demonstrations and examples in this book have been selected to help you relate concepts to your own experience. So far, every chapter concerns information that bears on your life in some way. As we progress into the more individual aspects of psychology, you may have to associate information to a less familiar concept. For example, most people do not suffer from severe psychological abnormalities. However, noticing how you *differ* from someone who is seriously disturbed will help you retain the information.

SQ3R Method

Learning progresses with active use. The more ways information is encoded, the better it will be retained and, simultaneously, the more access routes there will be to its retrieval. One successful study method that attempts to improve encoding is called **SQ3R,** which stands for "Survey, Question, Read, Recite, Review."

A student who crams for an exam at the last minute may need to improve his study habits and develop recall techniques using a method such as SQ3R.

1. *Survey* a chapter before reading it. Look at the outline, the general headings, and the chapter summary; this way you will get an idea of what will be covered. In addition, the length of a section should indicate how important the topic is in relation to other topics covered. Notice the organization of the

book you are studying. In this book, the introduction at the beginning of each chapter provides an overall context for reading the chapter; important concepts are highlighted and topics covered in the chapter are previewed. The chapter summary also provides schemata for improving your understanding.

2. *Question* the material *before* you read it. Ask such questions as, "I wonder what this means?" "Is this related to what I read in an earlier chapter?" Such questioning ignites curiosity and demands answers. Your active questioning will lead to an active search for answers.

3. *Read* the material only after a framework for encoding is in place.

4. *Recite* what you have learned from your reading. Try to answer the questions you asked before reading. Make sure you understand important concepts and facts featured in the introduction and summary.

5. *Review* the material after you have retained the important information. Implicit in the SQ3R method are *rehearsal* and *relearning.* The greater the familiarity or number of associations, the greater the retention and retrieval. The more time you spend attending to and concentrating on the material, the better your retention will be.

Mnemonics

As discussed before, the best way to remember material with no apparent meaning is to *impose a context* that will serve as an aid to memory or will convert the material into something meaningful. Here is one of two methods for improving memory of meaningless events.

Mnemonics (the first *m* is silent) is a straightforward, and sometimes fun, technique for aiding memory. For example, there is nothing about the names of the months of the year that gives clues to the number of days they have. The rhyme "Thirty days hath September . . . " is a mnemonic to help you retrieve that information when you need it. To remember which way to change your clocks for Daylight Savings Time, a useful mnemonic is "Spring forward, fall back." People often use mnemonics to remember names. To remember someone named Scott McDonald, you might remember that his last name is the same as the fast food restaurant.

Mnemonics is often useful in remembering lists in a certain order. Try associating each item with a previously learned, organized set of "peg words," such as in this example:

One is a bun	Six is sticks
Two is a shoe	Seven is heaven
Three is a tree	Eight is a gate
Four is a door	Nine is wine
Five is a hive	Ten is a hen

Now let's say you want to buy the following at the grocery store: lettuce, soup, paper towels, tomatoes, and chicken. Try to visualize these items with the locational peg words. The more outrageous the association, the more likely it will be remembered. For example, imagine lettuce on a bun, soup spilling out of your

How many times have you heard someone say, "I'll never forget the time I . . . "? Even though we often forget new things we learn, many important events in our lives and facts about the world seem almost impossible to forget. Here is a story that illustrates an extreme form of this phenomenon:

I'll Make You Remember

One day Latif the Thief ambushed the commander of the Royal Guard, captured him and took him to a cave.

"I am going to say something that, no matter how much you try, you will be unable to forget," he told the infuriated officer.

Latif made his prisoner take off all his clothes. Then he tied him, facing backwards, on a donkey.

"You may be able to make a fool of me," screamed the soldier, "but you'll never make me think of something if I want to keep it out of my mind."

"You have not yet heard the phrase which I want you to remember," said Latif. "I am turning you loose now, for the donkey to take back to town. And the phrase is: 'I'll catch and kill Latif the Thief, if it takes me the rest of my life!'"(Shah, 1982).

Why is Latif so sure the commander will remember the phrase? First of all, the phrase is highly meaningful. Most psychologists would explain this in terms of the number and strength of associations between the new phrase and the other knowledge in the commander's mind. All the words in the phrase are associated in his mind with their meanings and with all sorts of other information—both semantic and episodic memories. The associations to the concept of the commander's "self" are especially rich.

But more importantly, Latif knows that the commander will go on thinking about the phrase, constructing more and stronger associations between it and other knowledge all the time. Every time the commander looks at himself, the donkey, or anything else as he rides back to town, he will be reminded of how he got to be in this humiliating situation. And every time he thinks of that, he is likely to think again about how he will get revenge on Latif. Every image in his mind of another way of catching and killing the thief will add more and stronger associations to the phrase Latif wants him to remember. Thus, the phrase will be "processed" very deeply indeed and will be associated so

shoe, a tree with paper towels for leaves, eggs splattered all over the door, a hive-full of tomatoes, and a chicken picking up sticks.

A word to the wise: choose your mnemonic carefully. A friend of mine, Betty Cone, said she knew exactly how the principal of her school tried to remember her name, because he always called her Betty Pine.

Method of Loci

In addition to mnemonics, visualizing items to be recalled is another powerful aid to memory of meaningless events (Bower, 1973). An example of the use of visualization is in the **method of loci,** a memory trick devised by the Greeks. The trick here is to create new and different associations to improve recall. Select a group of places that have some relationship with one another. For example, every day you awaken in your bedroom, wash up in the bathroom, have breakfast in the kitchen or dining room, and walk or drive along a certain route. Associate the items in order with the different places, such as your bed, the sink, the dining strongly with so many other things that it will be almost impossible to forget.

Trying Not to Remember

Can you go for one minute without thinking of the word *elephant?* If you have ever tried it, you know it is very difficult. To understand this phenomenon (and much else about memory), you can imagine that each concept in your mind is like a dot (or "node") and the associations between concepts are like lines (or "links") between the dots. When you think about a concept, you "activate" that dot and the activation spreads along the lines to other concepts with which it is associated. In this way, you remember the other concepts as well (Collins & Quillian, 1972).

Now, when you are trying not to think about an elephant, you will have remembered your task by creating links between the concept of "what I am trying to do" and the concept of "elephant." Every time you think of what you are trying to do, activation spreads to the concept of elephant, and you are reminded of it whether you want to be or not.

In general, memory seems to depend mostly on the kinds of links you create in your mind and very little on your direct intentions to remember. If you are trying to remember something, you can process it more deeply and thus establish more associations with it, but unless you do establish these associations, you probably will not remember it any better than if you had not tried to remember it at all (Nelson, 1976).

Implications for Teaching

This story has a lesson for teachers, too. If you are trying to get someone to learn something (whether the person wants to learn it or not), you should try to construct a situation in which the learner's own interests and inclinations will lead to the thoughts you want to encourage. For example, students' inclinations to be competitive are harmful in some situations, just as the commander's tendency to be vengeful was sometimes harmful. But, in the same way that Latif "harnessed" this vengefulness to achieve his goals, good teachers can sometimes harness their students' competitiveness for constructive purposes. Spelling bees use this competitive motivation to encourage students to learn spelling.

room wall, and a tree that you pass. For the shopping list used in the previous section, you could imagine that the sheets on your bed are lettuce, that you are eating soup out of the sink, that paper towels are on the dining room table, and so on. The method of loci is effective because human memory is associative, and "putting things in their place" increases the number of associations.

Great Feats of Memory

A knowledge of how memory operates will help you improve your memory. But, as with every human ability, there are some people who are simply born with extraordinary memories. Some people can play as many as 60 games of chess at once. Some people can multiply long numbers in their heads as fast as a calculator (for example, $789054.78 \times 657483.86$). One man could look at 70 unrelated words and recall them perfectly a day later, and sometimes even a year later. These feats are made possible by applying the principles of memory and the memory improvement techniques described in this section.

Chunking in Chess

The chess masters who can play several games at once blindfolded are not necessarily possessed of supernatural memory, but are simply able to combine or "chunk" larger units of a chess game than ordinary chess players (see section on Chunking and Coding). Figure 9-13 shows a fairly common arrangement of chess pieces during an actual game. Look at it briefly and, if you have a board, try to reproduce it quickly without referring back to the book. In one study, chess masters were able very quickly to reproduce most common chess arrangements; beginners could not (Chase & Simon, 1973). All positions on the board form one meaningful chunk of information to the masters. When Chase and Simon placed the chess pieces on a board at random, masters and beginners were equally inept at reproducing the positions.

The Great Russian Mnemonist

The most famous case of memorization is "S." studied by the Russian psychologist Luria (1968). To gain a sense of the greatness of his feats, study this table of numbers for three minutes.

```
563908972

878992111

389763009
```

Now try to reproduce it without looking. S. was able to do it in 40 seconds. Even more impressively, he could repeat it several months later! Luria writes: "The only differences in the two performances was that for the later one he needed time to revive the entire situation in which the experiment had been carried out; to 'see' the room in which he had been sitting; to 'hear' my voice; to 'reproduce' an image of himself looking at the board." S. thus encoded information with as *many meaningful associations as possible* to aid retrieval. He was especially adept at

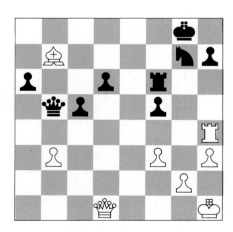

FIGURE 9-13
Chunking in Chess
Look briefly at the positions of the chess pieces and try to reproduce them without looking back at the page.

associating information with specific visual imagery. When trying to recall a particular list, he once said: "Yes . . . yes, that was a series you gave to me once when you were sitting in your apartment. You were sitting at the table and I was in the rocking chair. . . . You were wearing a gray suit and you looked at me like this" (Luria, 1968).

S. also used the method of loci in remembering, and this sometimes led to interesting mistakes. Trying to recall a particular list of words, he imagined a "mental walk" but missed the words *pencil* and *egg*.

> I put the image of the pencil near a fence . . . , the one down the street, you know. But what happened was that the image fused with that of the fence and I walked right on past without noticing it. The same thing happened with the word "egg." I had put it up against a white wall and it blended in with the background. How could I possibly spot a white egg up against a white wall? (Luria, 1968)

S. had an extraordinary ability to visualize, but even so his methods are merely extensions of the principles discussed in this chapter: *making the associations between information meaningful by making those associations rich and complex.* Thus, as in the quotation from James at the beginning of the chapter, facts will "cluster and cling" in the mind.

SUMMARY

1. Memory involves associations, selection, and simplification of reality and is organized around meaningful events.

2. Memory records specific episodes in our lives, but it also contains rules for operating in the world; the latter is called *representational memory*. Memory is continuously updated as new events occur, which allows us to respond to continuous changes in the world. Memory allows us to organize past experiences and to make them accessible as needed.

3. New information must be stored and kept in our memories. The *retention* time may be a few seconds, a few years, or a lifetime. In *retrieval*, a past event is brought into consciousness; thus, we regain or "retrieve" information previously stored. Two types of retrieval are recognition and recall.

4. Some psychologists make the distinction between short- and long-term memory. Information retained temporarily, like a telephone number for a few seconds, is thought to be stored by *short-term memory*. Its storage capacity is about seven items, such as a seven-digit number. Information that is retained for more than a few seconds is stored in *long-term memory*. You do not need to look up your own telephone number when you call home, and you certainly do not need to continuously remember your own name. These memories are relatively permanent. Both episodic and representational forms of memory are stored in long-term memory.

5. Although many psychologists accept the concepts of short- and long-term memory as a specific system, recent theorists have challenged these ideas. Estes does not feel, for instance, that memory actually stores or retrieves anything, but rather acts more like other changes in the body that result from experience, such as strengthening muscles through exercise.

6. Many psychologists do not believe that separate processes for short- and long-term memory are plausible. Instead, they think of the memory system as a single and continuous process. In this view, each repetition of an event simply causes an increase in the associative strength of that event, thereby increasing the probability that it will be remembered.

7. Some kinds of events *interfere* with memory more than others. Two kinds of interference have been studied in the laboratory. *Proactive* interference occurs when previous knowledge interferes with present memory. *Retroactive* interference occurs when new information interferes with memory of old. Two general factors in interference are (1) the longer the interval between the first and second event, the less interference, and (2) the more similar the items, the more interference.

8. Linton found that the loss of memory for details of one's own life proceeds at a very slow, constant rate, unlike the quick decay of memory for meaningless events learned in laboratory tests. Bahrick and his colleagues found that memory for names might well be organized differently from memory for faces, and other studies have found that odor memory may also differ from other forms of memory. In an important study, Herrmann and Neisser developed a list of eight characteristics that distinguish individual memories: rote memory, absentmindedness, names, people, conversation, errands, retrieval, and places.

9. Different forms of damage to the brain can affect the storage and retrieval of memory, sometimes in strange ways. One patient could remember details of presidential policy from 40 years ago but couldn't remember the last sentence he spoke. Amnesia is caused by a sudden injury to the brain, but other specific types of memory loss can also be caused by brain tumors and epilepsy. Study of memory disorders is an exciting new field, as psychologists attempt to discover how and where the various forms of memory are controlled in the brain.

10. The most basic principle of memory is that we remember the most *meaningful* events. Meaning differs from individual to individual. Important determinants of memory include how existing schemata influence and often change what we remember; how information is organized into meaningful units or *chunks;* and how memories can be reconstructed on the basis of these two processes. Bartlett's book on remembering demonstrated the important effects of a person's existing knowledge structure on memory. He used the method of serial production, in which a drawing or a story was given to successive people in the manner of the children's game "telephone." According to Bartlett, unfamiliar features "invariably suffer transformation in the direction of the familiar."

11. A unit of memory is called a *chunk.* In perceiving and remembering bits of information we organize individual items into chunks by using a *code.* Knowing a code (such as a language) increases the capacity of memory and the ability to remember.

12. One theory that attempts to tie together the complex phenomena of memory is called *levels of processing.* This states that information is processed at different depths or levels, such as the structural, the phonemic, and the semantic. This view holds that the deeper the level of processing, the more likely it is that the event will be remembered. It also helps explain why you can deepen processing by trying to relate information to the rich associations in your memory of personal experiences.

13. Several techniques useful in improving memory include mnemonics, method of loci, and SQ3R. *Mnemonics* is the use of a silly game or rhyme to remember meaningless

information. Visualization is used in the *method of loci,* a memory trick that takes advantage of our ability to visualize the arrangement of things, such as the rooms in our house. The *SQ3R* method emphasizes that the more ways information is encoded, the better it will be retained and the more access routes there will be to its retrieval. It involves surveying, questioning, reading, reciting, and reviewing material to be remembered, such as a textbook. Implicit in the SQ3R method are rehearsal and relearning; the greater the familiarity (number of associations), the greater the retention and the retrieval. This is a useful lesson for studying this and other chapters in this book.

amnesia
chunking
context
continuous process memory
encoding
episodic memory
levels of processing
long-term memory
memory cycle
memory system
method of loci
mnemonics
nonsense syllables

perceptual–motor memory
primacy
proactive interference
recall
recency
recognition
representational memory
retention
retrieval
retroactive interference
semantic memory
short-term memory
SQ3R

Baddeley, A. (1986). *Working memory.* New York: Oxford.

A useful, somewhat technical account of how memory operates.

Neisser, U. (1982). *Memory observed: Remembering in natural context.* San Francisco: W. H. Freeman.

A compendium of the different aspects of memory—aspects that have too often been forgotten by psychologists. Includes articles on testifying, forgetting, performing, getting things done, and people who have special memories. Highly recommended for those who wish to absorb some of the phenomena of memory as opposed to the theories.

Squire, L. (1987). *Memory and the brain.* New York: Oxford.

One of the leading theorists about how memory is stored in the brain presents his theories.

Chapter *10*

Thinking and Language

I magine the following chain of events. You are an executive of your town council. One day you receive a report saying that a large capital expense is essential to correct hazards on the highway near your town. Repaving is needed and a guardrail should be put up at Goose Curve. But during the town council meeting financial consultants caution you that the $100,000 assessment would raise property taxes. You feel it is irresponsible to spend so much at a time when money is tight, so you decide against the improvements for now and go on to other issues.

After the budget meeting, you drive home thinking it's too bad the funds aren't there for the highway safety measures. You know they are important; you think, maybe next year. You decide to go two miles out of your way and look at Goose Curve yourself. It's gotten dark and it's begun raining; the boring budget battles still pack your mind.

Then suddenly you see something: skid marks all over the road. You follow slowly and hope all is well. It is probably old Johnson drunk again, you think, most likely driving too fast under the influence. You hope that he didn't go over the edge of the cliff.

But he did. Wild slashing tire tracks lead to a spot where the lip of the gully has been broken off very recently. It's pouring and late, but you slam on the brakes and leap out of the car, your mind filled with fear. You begin to climb down the hill, and then you see Johnson, lying in a pool of blood, thrown out of his car, his arm and head bleeding.

You struggle up the hill carrying Johnson on your shoulder, blood pouring over your suit and shoes, but you don't care. Your heart is pounding, and a surge of adrenaline gives you the strength to make it to the top of the hill. You breathe a sigh of relief and gently lay Johnson in the back seat of your car and you race to the hospital. The whole way to the hospital you think, if only that guardrail had been there, this could have been prevented. You make a firm resolve that tomorrow you will convene a special session of the town council and push to get the guardrail issue passed immediately.

Now, follow the trains of thought during both the budget meeting and the emergency. In both circumstances the thought processes seem logical and lead to obvious conclusions. From the perspective of the town council, the matter of the guardrail was of minor concern and did not seem to warrant any increase in expenditures in an already tight budget. Most people would agree that this makes sense. But an individual's point of view can shift drastically from encounter to encounter. In the emergency, this same issue (of putting in a guardrail) is suddenly magnified to fill one's perspective. It becomes impossible not to help someone who is badly injured, and the issue of putting in a guardrail suddenly becomes paramount.

Comparable shifts in thought and judgment occur all the time, for example, in the way we respond to the media and in the way we understand others. The preceding story is only one example that helps to contrast the inconsistencies in our thought processes. These processes are often mismatched and even "overmatched" in the modern world. Some errors of misperception and misjudgment are silly, some are stupid, and some are serious. The problem is that human beings, who have the same kind of nervous system as frogs, cats, and chimps, have evolved to respond to single events, not to long-term changes.

We should not argue about whether human beings are complete geniuses or complete fools. In fact, we are *both* miraculously inventive and continuously stupid because of the nature of our thought processes. Remember, the same kinds of neural processes that developed to judge brightness and taste are also used by us to judge prices and politics.

See Chapter 5, section on Characteristics of the Senses.

Like other aspects of the mind, thinking involves a great deal of simplification. As there are fixed ways the senses deal with external information, as well as fixed rules of organization in perception and memory, so people develop set strategies for solving problems and making decisions. A limited amount of information is selected on which to base judgments and direct fixed strategies for contemplating that information, which makes us overgeneralize from what little information we obtain. When the news reports a murder in a distant city, we tend to think of the world as a more murderous place. When someone famous contracts breast cancer, it becomes a national concern. These single instances fill our attention.

An analysis of the mind must shift when it comes to the study of thinking. Mental processes, as we have seen, are simplifying processes. But in thought processes, something different also happens: the information we have is sifted, combined, and changed, so that *new* ideas and new combinations of ideas result. These creative acts seem to be as characteristic of us as simplification and generalization. The processes examined in this chapter share a common theme: a few simplified elements are selected, which can be combined and recombined to create new and diverse possibilities. A similar process underlies language. English has only a few elements — 26 letters — but those few elements can be combined to form an almost infinite number of different sentences. The use of language seems to be an almost automatic process, and yet every sentence we utter is a new creation.

Generalization and Overgeneralization

The ability to generalize saves effort. We need not waste time discriminating one car horn from another to get out of the way; different-sounding door bells all mean the same thing. Also, we are conscious of only a few things at once. Thus, what happens is that *whatever enters our consciousness is overemphasized.* It does not matter how the information enters, whether it is a television program, a newspaper story, a friend mentioning something, or a strong emotional reaction — it all gets overemphasized. We ignore other more compelling evidence to overemphasize and overgeneralize from the information at hand. Consider this example:

Let us suppose that you wish to buy a new car and have decided [on] either a Volvo or a Saab. . . . *Consumer Reports* informs you that the consensus of their experts is that the Volvo is mechanically superior, and the consensus of their readership is that the Volvo has the better repair record. Armed with this information, you decide to go and strike a bargain with the Volvo dealer before the week is over. In the interim, however, you go to a cocktail party where you announce this intention to an acquaintance. He reacts with disbelief and alarm: "A Volvo! You've got to be kidding. My brother-in-law had a Volvo. First, that fancy fuel injected computer thing went out. $250. Next he started having trouble with the rear end. Had to replace it. Then the transmission and the clutch. Finally he sold it in three years for junk." (Nisbett & Ross, 1981)

How would you feel about a Volvo now? Most likely you would strongly reconsider buying one. But think about it; the information you received is that *one* person out of thousands does not like the Volvo, but nevertheless, you are strongly influenced by this single case.

However, all is not lost with overgeneralization. It probably reflects a tendency to emphasize the most recent information, even at the cost of ignoring past knowledge. In 1985 there was a toxic leak from a chemical plant in Bhopal, India. Would you have gone into the country at that time? Probably you would have cancelled any plans. Here our tendency to overgeneralize is clearly adaptive: it helps to protect against dangers associated with *changing circumstances.* This kind of mechanism has the tendency to trip the emergency reaction, and it may have gotten our ancestors out of a lot of trouble.

See Chapter 1, section on The Cognitive Approach, and Chapter 2, section on Human Adaptation.

The tendency to overgeneralize is an important part of the system of thought, with advantages and disadvantages; it simplifies, it allows us to adapt quickly to changes in the world, and it makes mistakes in a stable situation.

CHARACTERISTICS OF THOUGHT

Helping us to cut our way through the complex world are the simplifying mental structures that underlie thought. Psychologists have defined two different structures of thought: how we classify things into *categories* and how we simplify judgments using *heuristics,* or "fast paths" of the mind.

Classification into Categories

People love to classify. The process of classifying, or assigning things to groups, may be as concrete as deciding that something is an antique, or as nebulous as mulling over whether a person is dishonest or trustworthy.

Classification is a major simplifying factor in mental life. Without it we would have to identify and decide on *each* shading of color, *each* idea, and *each* feeling every time it was encountered. For example, the range of colors we encounter is huge; the human visual system can discriminate 7,500,000 colors; however, only 8 color names are commonly used (Brown & Lenneberg, 1954). We consider a sunset "red," an apple "red," and a tomato "red." Here we use a single category (red) to classify a large number of different objects. A *category,* then, is a number of objects that can be considered equivalent in an important dimension (Rosch, 1978).

A NONEXISTENT CATEGORY SYSTEM

Here is a classification of the animal kingdom attributed to an ancient Chinese encyclopedia, the *Celestial Emporium of Benevolent Knowledge*:

On these remote pages it is written that animals are divided into a. Those that belong to the emperor, b. Embalmed ones, c. Those that are trained, d. Suckling pigs, e. Mermaids, f. Fabulous ones, g. Stray dogs, h. Those that are included in this classification, i. Those that tremble as if they were mad, j. Innumerable ones, k. Those drawn with a very fine camel's hair brush, l. Others, m.

Those that have broken a flower vase, n. Those that resemble flies from a distance. (Borges, 1966).

It is clear that this is an impossible, nonexistent category system (in fact, it is an excerpt from a story by the Argentine writer Jorge Luis Borges). The reason this type of categorization system is not found in any culture is that it does not help anyone to understand the world.

Function of Categories

The first function of categorizing is to *simplify* — to give the most information with the least effort. It is simpler to call a tomato, a sunset, and an apple "red" than to identify them by "orangey red," "luminescent red-orange with streaks of blue and black," and "pure red speckled with green." We *can* do all this, but it is unnecessary and wasteful unless we are writing poetry; the word "red" is enough.

Second, categories are not random and arbitrary, but are part of a mental model that reflects events and occurrences in the world. Most objects in our world are made up of a combination of predictable features (Garner, 1974). Wings are more likely to have feathers on them than fur; legs are found on animals, not trees. Rooms do not move on their own; people breathe, buildings do not. Certain aspects of the world seem to "go together" and categories reflect this: dogs are thought to be more similar to cats than to airplanes.

Thus, categories aid us in interacting with the world; they simplify experience and reflect the actual structure of the world. Any system of classification, called **taxonomy,** organizes things by similarities and differences. By doing so, relationships become explicit. Categories help us make relationships and associations among many disparate objects and events.

Natural and Artificial Categories

Some categories are universal, probably because there are universal "truths" in the world. These categories of natural phenomena are called **natural categories.** Color, for example, is a natural category because it is a universal and innate response to the external environment. Our receptive apparatus for color is reflected in the categories most languages use for colors. Recall that the human visual system codes information in two ways: in black-white, and in color combinations of red, yellow, green, and blue. In a study of almost 100 languages, Berlin and Kay (1969) determined that color terms always appear in the following sequence:

See Chapter 5, section on Basis of Color Vision.

$$\left\{ \begin{array}{l} \text{white} \\ \text{black} \end{array} \right\} \rightarrow \text{red} \rightarrow \left\{ \begin{array}{l} \text{green} \\ \text{yellow} \\ \text{blue} \end{array} \right\} \rightarrow \text{brown} \rightarrow \left\{ \begin{array}{l} \text{purple} \\ \text{pink} \\ \text{orange} \\ \text{gray} \end{array} \right\}$$

If a language has only two color terms, they will be black and white; if it has three, they will be black, white, and red. If there is a fourth color term, it will be green, yellow, or blue. The fifth and sixth terms will be the remaining two of green, yellow, and blue. The final terms come last and fill the gaps between the other more general terms.

In addition to these basic natural categories, there are other **artificial categories** that refer to the attributes of constructed objects such as chairs or buildings. In the case of natural categories, people usually have no trouble judging the relative qualities of the category. There is more disagreement and difficulty in artificial categories; for example, it is easier to judge whether something is "more red" than whether something is "more of a chair" than another.

Categories not only reflect the structure of the physical world, but many are peculiar to the culture in which they originate and are used as standards for judgments. An American traveling in Italy would probably have to convert 15,000 lira into dollars to find out if that was a good price for a pair of shoes. In the United States the most commonly used measures are inches, feet, yards, miles, Fahrenheit, and so on. If the weather report said it was going to be 28 degrees Celsius, most of us would have to "translate" that figure into Fahrenheit to know if it was hot or cold.

Characteristics of Categories

Basic Level.   Categories are arranged hierarchically from extremely broad to quite detailed. An example of a broad category is furniture. Furniture is relatively abstract; there are few specific features common to all items of furniture, but furniture may be many different things: chairs, beds, cabinets, tables. Each of these is also a category itself (Figure 10-1). "Tables" have clear perceptual distinctions: they have legs, a flat top, and other features in common that differentiate them from chairs. Tables even have subdivisions: dining room tables, coffee tables, wood tables, antique tables. The category *table*, however, seems to be the level at which we most naturally divide the world, thus it is called a **basic level category.** Basic level categories such as table, apple, and dog, are the categories first learned by children (Rosch, Mervis, Gray, Johnson, & Boyes-Braem, 1976).

Typicality and Prototypes.   A category is arranged around a **prototype,** which is the best example that most typifies the category (Rosch & Mervis, 1975). **Typical** examples of a category are closest to the prototype, as when a strong, agile man is considered a "typical athlete" or when an attitude like the love of wine is considered "typically French." Nonetheless, a typical example may not always be the one we meet most frequently. Consider this: which bird do you think is mentioned most often in written English? Most people think it is the robin. A robin flies, has feathers, tugs at worms, makes a nest, sings, announces the arrival of spring; this fits our prototype of a "bird." True, but the bird that is most

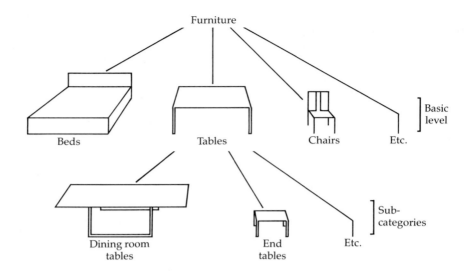

FIGURE 10-1
Categories
This diagram shows how the category "furniture" might be divided into basic levels and further subdivided into subcategories.

Furniture

Beds   Tables   Chairs   Etc.   ] Basic level

Dining room tables   End tables   Etc.   ] Sub-categories

often mentioned is not the robin—it is the chicken. The term *chicken* is by no means unfamiliar, but it does not *typify* our concept of a bird. We are more likely to put chicken in the category of "food." A robin is more prototypical, "more of a bird" than a chicken is, at least in the human mind.

One way to study how people categorize things is to see how quickly they can make a judgment. One study found that the sentence "A robin is a bird" is recognized *more quickly* than the sentence "A chicken is a bird." In another study, Rosch (1975) asked people to fill in the blanks in the sentence "——— is virtually ———" with the numbers 100 and 103. There was a clear preference for "103 is virtually 100" over the reverse, "100 is virtually 103." It appears that 100 is a more prototypical number than 103. Our preference for "round numbers" and multiples of 10 is an example of our use of prototypes and categories.

Similarity

Members of a category are by definition similar in some ways to other members of the category. They share a number of attributes. The more shared attributes, the more similar the objects are judged to be. However, similarity is not that simple. Nearly everything in the external world has its varying attributes: some of these may be similar to other objects and some different. Two things can thus be both similar and different at the same time.

Consider these statements: Jamaica is like Cuba; Cuba is like Russia; Jamaica is like Russia. These form a loose kind of syllogism. The first two statements make sense. Jamaica and Cuba are both Caribbean countries. Cuba and Russia have Communist governments. But the third proposition, that Jamaica is like Russia, is odd because they have almost *no* attributes in common. The two other similar relationships lead to a confusion.

Another characteristic of similarity is that it is not always symmetrical: "A is like B" is not necessarily the same as "B is like A." In the first instance, A is the subject, B is the *reference;* when these roles are reversed, the meaning is often changed. Consider the sentence, "A rattlesnake is like lightning," which indicates that rattlesnakes are fast and may strike quickly. "Lightning is like a rattlesnake" conveys that lightning is dangerous, perhaps deadly. In both cases the attributes of the reference are attributed to the subject (Glass, Holyok, & Santa, 1984).

Judgments of similarities are quite complex (Tversky, 1977). Figure 10-2 shows the relationship between two entities. Similarity occurs where the circles overlap; the nonoverlapping areas represent the distinctive features of the two. Judgments of similarity are based on *shared attributes,* and differences, on *distinctive attributes.* The more familiar we are with something, the more we know about it, which means that two things *can* be both more similar and more different than are another pair. In these diagrams this is represented by larger circles. For example, how similar is China to Japan and how different is it? How similar (or different) is Sri Lanka to Nepal? Tversky and Gati (1978) found that because people tend to know more about the prominent countries of China and Japan, they also judge them to be both *more similar* and *more different* than the pair of less prominent countries.

Heuristics

Heuristics are simplifying strategies that are used to make judgments and solve problems; they could be called the "fast paths" of the mind. There is a trade-off in the use of heuristics: accuracy may be sacrificed for speed. We must usually rely on incomplete information to make judgments, to reason, and to solve problems. Heuristics are the rules of thumb that guide our decisions. Three heuristics often used in thinking are representativeness, availability, and comparison.

Representativeness

The judgment that an object is *typical* of its category is called **representativeness.** This heuristic involves matching prototypes: a robin, for instance, is quickly judged to be a bird; it is *representative* of birds. A chicken is less so. However, using representativeness as a heuristic can lead to mistakes or overgeneralization. We often tend to judge *concrete* or *vivid* examples of a category as representative

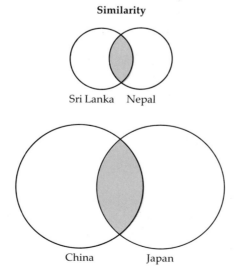

Similarity

Sri Lanka   Nepal

China   Japan

FIGURE 10-2
Similarity
The area where two circles overlap represents similarity. The overlapping areas represent dissimilar, distinctive features of each entity.

Current Information

Among the simplifying heuristics is the tendency to analyze everything as an immediate, personal phenomenon: "What does this mean to me?" A personal insult dominates attention, yet in time the insult is forgotten. Whatever gets close to us, in space, time, and thought, is immediately overemphasized. Viewers of violent movies believe there is more violence in the world than those who do not see such films.

Thus, whether it is an emotional slight, a change in the weather, or a matter of government policy, current information is automatically given higher weight in making decisions. During the Geneva summit between Reagan and Gorbachev, the Secretary of Defense wrote a letter to the President opposing summit accords. It was front-page news in international media, and many commentators felt that it threatened the talks. The letter, however, contained no real change in policy or new information, that is, no "news" of any kind—it simply restated already known positions. Yet is was *perceived* as potentially damaging because it was leaked close to the time of the talks. Thus, the letter was perceived wrongly as "current" information; had the letter been made public two weeks earlier, it probably would have had no effect.

This incident (and thousands of others like it) are misapplications of a mental system that is basically designed, like a frog's, to respond to immediate and local phenomena. The newly released warning that the artificial sweetener aspartame is bad for health is "news" and gets full scrutiny, while the enormous, constant dangers of cigarettes are well known and ignored.

Insensitivity to Old Problems

Consider an ordeal of the sort that happens 20 times per day in the United States, yet has little effect on decisions. Sarah Wilson will be forever brain injured as the result of hitting the windshield of her parent's car when it careened into a dump truck. Sarah is 3 years old and is now an orphan. Her mother and father are dead, killed in the collision. The tires on the family car were not able to grip the road and brake properly when the truck abruptly pulled into the road ahead.

In 1986 about 500 people were severely injured or killed each month in the United States because of underinflated tires and other results of poor car maintenance. This is a far greater, ongoing, and more important tragedy than a single terrorist murder, yet tire inflation is scarcely as exciting as the Symbionese Liberation Army or the hijacking of the *Achille Lauro*.

Little is done about the chronic dangers of highway safety or the 300 murders per week or the 100 billion cigarettes smoked each year—because they are familiar problems. A single "new event," such as a terrorist strike, is immediately on the front page of newspapers all over the world. We conscript jet fighters to apprehend terrorists who have killed a single man, but little is done to save thousands of lives like the Wilsons' or to improve the lives of many, such as Sarah, who are permanently injured and lost to society. It seems senseless, absurd, and bizarre, but the mental system ignores large daily dangers, even dangers that threaten death.

Sensitivity to Scarcity

A sensitivity to an immediate scarcity of resources—especially a sudden change leading to scarcity—is a default program in all animals. It is part of how all organisms evolved. Before the agricultural revolution, food supplies were not under human control. A sudden decrease in the number of game animals or a drought that resulted in a decline in the fruit supply needed immediate attention and action. Because such short-term changes are recorded quickly by the nervous system, our human ancestors probably avoided famine by

Because we tend to overemphasize the immediate, a sudden new event, such as a plane hijacking, will dominate headlines the world over. Here passengers from a hijacked TWA 727 return home.

responding to shortage immediately, by changing their diet or foraging in a new area.

This human tendency, to respond readily to scarcity, is sometimes exploited in interesting ways in modern-day society. Columnist Jon Carrol of *The San Francisco Chronicle* took over as headwaiter for one day in an Oakland restaurant. He learned about scarcity quickly. The title of his article (November 13, 1986) was "Only a Few Clams Left."

About halfway through my one-night tenure as the substitute maitre d' (or host) at the Bay Wolf, an Oakland restaurant of sole and heart, I checked in with the kitchen.

"The clams aren't moving," said Stephen, chef in charge of first courses. "Tell them about the clams."

Why not? The clams were swell; they just weren't selling. East Bay diners had developed an unaccountable craving for spinach salad. So the next five times I did my small tap dance at the beginning of the meal—"Let me direct your attention to a few special items on the menu"—I described the clams in loving detail. Still nothing.

With the next party, I tried a different approach. "The clams are very popular tonight," I said, "so if you want to start with them, I suggest you tell me now."

Marketing heaven. The clams began walking out the door like little soldiers. Rebecca, one of the waitresses told me: "Gold star on your chart. My whole table ordered clams."

I walked into the kitchen again. "I've got a great way to sell anything," I told Lee, the head chef, "just say it's going fast."

Lee considered carefully. Finally, she said: "Gee, do you think I could sell myself that way?"

(She probably could because "hard to get" people are usually thought to be quite attractive.)

The mental system automatically amplifies short-term scarcity. It makes us liable in the modern world to manipulations of scarcity. The best daily evidence comes from advertising, where the weak points of the mind get illuminated. About 20 years ago, I decided to get my car painted. I noticed a trifling price in an ad for Earl Scheib Auto Painting. The ad listed a "special low price" for paint jobs and then said "last three days" for this price. I went right out and had the job done.

Recently, I was looking for a new paint job on another car and happened to notice the current ad for Earl Scheib Auto Painting. The price was still low (in the context of 20 years of inflation), but what had not changed was the sales pitch: it still said "last three days" for the low price. This must be the longest three days in history! The pitch works because of our propensity to rush to a sudden scarce situation, the scarcity here being *time*.

Another example is the "special, limited time" offer that attracts us as a result of the defaults of the mind. One portrait company urges parents to buy as many poses as possible because "stocking limitations force us to burn the unsold pictures of your children within 24 hours." Of course, stocking limitations do not really exist, but this ploy has evolved because it works on the limitations of the purchaser's mind. When something is available for a limited period, people are more likely to value it. A limited performance of a stage play often attracts a larger audience than an extended run.

In a simple "consumer preference" study (Worchel et al., 1975), individuals were given a chocolate chip cookie taken from a jar. They were then asked to rate its quality, its probable price, and how tasty they thought it was. In the first study, half the people got cookies drawn from a jar containing ten cookies, half from a jar containing two cookies. The cookie in short supply was thought to be of higher quality and more costly than the abundant cookie.

This is bad enough, but we can go a step further. What about *sudden* scarcity of a previously *(continued)* abundant cookie? Worchel then ran the experiment again. One group of people first were given their cookie from the jar of two and the second group were given a cookie from the jar containing ten. But then the jar containing ten was immediately removed and replaced with a jar of two. Which was valued more? The subjects valued the *newly* scarce cookies more highly than the *previously* scarce cookies, estimating that the newly scarce cookies would be 20 percent more expensive than the old scarce cookies.

This experiment demonstrates some fundamental characteristics of the way the mental system evolved: notice the short-term and maximize gain. The same kinds of actions influence all sorts of decisions, in business as well as in cookie evaluation.

In 1973, ABC decided to pay the unheard of sum of $3.3 million for a showing of a movie, *The Poseidon Adventure.* It was an amount that ABC and other networks admitted, at the time, could not be justified. ABC stood to lose $1 million on the deal. Why did they do it?

The selling of this movie was different than previous sales of films to television. It was the subject of an open bid auction, the first of its kind. In an auction, the commodity, in this case a single showing of a film, automatically becomes scarce. Like the cookies, something scarce gets an automatically higher value within the mind. One competing bidder, CBS president Robert Wood, said, "Logic goes right out the window."

Wood described the feeling:

We were very rational at the start. We priced the movie out, in terms of what it could bring in for us, we allowed a certain value on top of that for exploitation.

But then the bidding started. ABC opened with $2 million. I came back with $2.4. ABC went to $2.8. And the fever of the thing caught us. Like a guy who had lost his mind, I kept bidding . . . there came a moment when I said to myself, "Good grief, if I get it, what the heck am I going to do with it?"

The "winner's" reaction was expressed later: "ABC has decided regarding its policy for the future that it would never again enter into an auction situation." The manipulation of this short-term spotlight on something rare is a way of life, from the crush of shoppers at opening hour specials ("prices good for the first hour") to the continuance of auction houses. It costs us daily, this vestige of the past. And it also determines how we judge other people.

Comparisons and Categories

Categories can affect comparisons. We seem to possess cutoff points for categories. Retailers are aware of this when they price goods at $99.98 rather than $100.00. They know people may be looking for something "under $100.00." The shifting nature of our comparisons is shown in the effect the rise in the cost of gasoline had on American drivers. There was little decline in gasoline consumption as gas rose from 38¢ to 60¢ to 90¢ and even 95¢ per gallon, but once gasoline was more than $1.00 a gallon, there was a marked decrease in usage. Later, as prices continued to remain above $1.00 a gallon, consumption rose again.

when they are not. Something that we see or hear firsthand overpowers other evidence. When there was a nearly catastrophic accident at the Three Mile Island nuclear reactor in 1979, its effect on influencing people to protest against nuclear power was dramatic. The accident was judged to be representative of nuclear power plants, and it entirely overwhelmed the generally good safety records of these plants. A single case has a striking influence; statistics are readily ignored.

The natural human sensitivity to scarcity is exploited effectively at sales and auctions where an artificial "shortage" can cause prices to rise quickly.

Our tendency to use representativeness is so strong that at the beginning of a movie or novel, a disclaimer usually appears that warns against its overuse: "Any resemblance to persons living or dead is purely coincidental."

Availability

Another heuristic we use to make judgments is **availability** — the ease with which relevant instances come to mind (Tversky & Kahneman, 1973). Recall from Chapter 9 on memory that events that occur more frequently are more easily retrieved from memory since they are more accessible for use. The availability heuristic is used when we are asked to guess the frequency or the probability of events. In general it is useful; things that occur more frequently are more available.

See Chapter 9, section on Memory Organizes and Makes Past Experience Accessible.

But availability can lead to error. A man from Indiana may remark, "Haven't you noticed how many famous Hoosiers [people from Indiana] there are?" Because he is a Hoosier himself, he finds more Hoosiers available, causing a bias or error in his judgment. People out of work may overestimate the rate of unemployment (Nisbett & Ross, 1981). In one experiment this question was asked: Are there more words in English that start with K or in which K is the third letter? Two-thirds of the people asked this question felt that more words begin with K; however, they are wrong. Why? Probably because of the way we index and categorize words; it is much easier to remember those that *begin* with K. Judgments are most often based on the *available* evidence (Kahneman & Tversky, 1973).

Comparison

The comedian Henny Youngman was asked, "How do you like your wife?" "Compared to what?" he responded. As we saw in Chapter 1, Youngman's

See Chapter 1, "box" on Some Universal Psychological Characteristics: Priorities and Policies.

See Chapter 5, section on Adaptation Level Theory.

answer points out two psychological processes: we judge by comparison and our standard of comparison constantly shifts. An outside air temperature of 50 degrees Fahrenheit is judged as "warm" in winter but as "cold" in summer; a salary of $500 a week is enormous to a college student but might insult an executive. A 200-gram weight in a series of weights ranging from 100 to 200 grams is experienced as heavy, while in a series of weights from 200 to 500 grams it is experienced as light. It is important to note that *the same procedures underlie judgments of sensory, cognitive, and social matters.*

One common effect of comparisons is **anchoring:** once a standard has been used in trying to solve a problem, a person is less likely to change or adjust, even if compelling new data are present or common sense would dictate a change. A person becomes "anchored" in his or her strategy.

Changing Standards of Comparison

We may apply different standards of comparison to different situations at different times. A friend of mine, who usually complains about paying more than $100 for a sport jacket, recently bought a jacket for $250. He really liked it because it was a unique blue linen blazer, something no one else had. But how did he justify the price? He told me, "It isn't one of [the famous designer's] signature models. Do you know, they cost $600!"

What is enough money at one time is not enough at another. Tversky and Kahneman conceptualize these changing standards as *psychological accounting,* that is, people shift into different "accounts." Suppose you were going to a play and lost $10 on the way. Would you still pay $10 for a ticket? Most people say they would. Now suppose you had already bought your $10 ticket and lost it on the way. Would you pay $10 for another ticket? Most people say no. *The loss in both of these situations is exactly the same:* $10. But they are not the same in "psychological accounting" terms. In the first case the loss is not "applied" to our "ticket account"; in the second case, the account has been used up (Tversky & Kahneman, 1981).

Would you drive 20 minutes to save $5? Whether you would or not depends upon comparison. If you were going to buy a toaster and a store close to you has it for $25 and another store 20 minutes away has it on sale for $20, would you drive? Most people say that they would. Suppose you are going to buy a jacket at a nearby store for $165 and a store 20 minutes away has the same one for $160. Most people say that they would not drive the extra miles. They are less likely to drive when the savings represent a smaller amount of the total. The savings are equal, but how they are compared is not (Tversky & Kahneman, 1981).

DECISION MAKING AND JUDGMENT

Which car should you buy? Which job offer should you accept? What should you have for lunch? Life is an endless series of decisions, one after another. Although in a sense every decision is a problem and every problem requires decision making, psychologists distinguish between the two. Problems require finding a series of steps that allow you to reach a goal. Decisions require making a choice among several options. In this section we will consider decision making; in the next, problem solving.

Elements of Decision Making

There are four basic elements in every decision:

1. A set of *alternatives* to choose from.
2. A set of possible *outcomes*.
3. The decision maker's *preferences* among the different outcomes.
4. The decision maker's judgments of the *probabilities* that a particular choice will lead to a particular outcome.

Suppose you have to decide whether or not to buy collision insurance for your car at $300 a year. Your *alternatives* are to buy or not buy the insurance. The *outcomes* are that you do or do not have a collision. Your *preference* is the outcome that will cost the least, but you are not sure which choice will lead to that outcome. This uncertainty can be represented as *probabilities*.

Assume you project that you have a 10 percent chance of having a collision in a year that would cost about $2,000. In this example, you can quantify the various factors since the numbers are specified; you can compute the expected value of each alternative by multiplying the probabilities by the values of the outcomes. According to these numbers, you should not buy the insurance since it costs $300 a year and your expected loss without it would be only $200 a year (10 percent of $2000). Obviously, the decision would not be this simple in reality. There may be other factors involved in your choice than just the amount of money, such as the "peace of mind" of having insurance. Also, there is no way to know for sure whether or not you will have a car accident.

Even though many decisions are more complex than this, the four basic elements — alternatives, outcomes, preferences, and probabilities — are always present in decision making in some form. Often just thinking about decisions in this way can help clarify decision making. Suppose that you were having trouble getting along with your roommate; you might make a list of alternative actions you could take and the possible outcomes of each choice. Then you could consider which outcomes seem most likely from each choice and which outcomes you would prefer most. This way of thinking about decisions is called **decision analysis.**

Biases in Decision Making

As discussed previously, we use heuristics to make decisions. These "shortcuts" probably result in more efficient decision making overall, but they also lead to systematic **biases** preventing impartiality in certain kinds of judgments that people make (Einhorn & Hogarth, 1981). Knowing about these common biases may help you avoid them in your judgments and decision making.

Availability

When people are asked to judge the relative frequency of different causes of death, they overestimate the frequency of well-publicized causes such as homicide, tornadoes, and cancer, and they underestimate the frequency of less remarkable causes such as diabetes, asthma, and emphysema. This is an example of how people's judgments are biased by *how easily they can recall specific examples.* This bias was also demonstrated in an experiment by Tversky and Kahneman (1973) in which they read subjects lists of names of well-known people of both sexes. In each list the people of one sex were more famous than those of the other sex. When the subjects were asked to estimate the proportion of men and women on the lists, they overestimated the proportion of the sex having more famous people on the list. If the list contained very famous women (such as Elizabeth Taylor) and only moderately well-known men (such as Alan Ladd), then subjects overestimated the proportion of women on the list. How available memories are affects our judgment.

Representativeness

People often overestimate the probability that something belongs in a particular category. Kahneman and Tversky (1973) told subjects to read the following passage and that this description of Tom W. was written by a psychologist when Tom was in his senior year of high school:

> Tom W. is of high intelligence, although lacking in true creativity. He has a need for order and clarity, and for neat and tidy systems in which every detail finds its appropriate place. His writing is rather dull and mechanical, occasionally enlivened by somewhat corny puns and by flashes of imagination of the sci-fi type. He has a strong drive for competence. He seems to have little feel and little sympathy for other people and does not enjoy interacting with others. Self-centered, he nonetheless has a deep moral sense.

Then they were told to imagine that Tom W. is now a graduate student and to rank the following categories in order of the likelihood that they are Tom's area of graduate specialization:

business administration	library science
computer science	medicine
engineering	physical and life sciences
humanities and education	social science and social work
law	

If you are like the people Kahneman and Tversky studied, you probably chose computer science or engineering as Tom's most likely area of specialization and thought that humanities, education, social science and social work were least likely. The character description probably fits your *prototype* of what "typical" computer science or engineering students are like. The representativeness heuristic leads you to think these are likely categories for his field of study. But there are many more graduate students in humanities, education, social science, and social work than there are in computer science or engineering. Even people who know these base rates of students in different fields and who have very little faith in the predictive value of the character sketch disregard the base rates in making their predictions.

Vivid Information

One particularly important consequence of availability and representativeness is that concrete or vivid information is very influential in judgment. The tendency to disregard statistical information and to overemphasize vivid examples extends even to some of society's most important decision makers. Nisbett and Ross (1981) described an acquaintance of theirs

> who often testifies at congressional committees on behalf of the Environmental Protection Agency. . . . She reported that the bane of her professional existence is the frequency with which she reports test data such as EPA mileage estimates based on samples of ten or more cars, only to be contradicted by a congressman who retorts with information about a single case: "What do you mean, the Blatzmobile gets twenty miles per gallon on the road?" he says. "My neighbor has one, and he only gets fifteen." His fellow legislators then usually respond as if matters were at a stand-off — one EPA estimate versus one colleague's estimate obtained from his neighbor.

People are continuously involved in problem solving. Some of the problems we deal with may be simple and unstructured, such as "What should I make for dinner?"; some may be chronic, such as "How can I get along better with my boss?"; and some may be formal, such as an intricate move in chess. Different problems demand different kinds of solutions and approaches. Many everyday problems are fairly simple and may be dealt with by simple trial and error, and some life problems involve hypothesis testing. More formal problems may draw on both of these methods, but also may involve structured analyses and strategies, some of which involve heuristics. Earlier we emphasized how heuristics interfere with judgment; here we will see how they help in solutions. Also examined here is how people go beyond problem solving to the creative invention of new ways to deal with unexpected situations.

PROBLEM SOLVING

Solving Simple Problems

We are faced with problems so constantly that we often do not notice that they are problems until they are solved. Trivial ones, such as how to open a tightly closed jar or how to get the sofa through the door, are usually solved by trial and error. Some problems are more substantial (although not formal), such as "How do I get a checkmate?" or "Why isn't my car working?" We may use hypothesis testing for the solution to these problems.

Trial and Error

Suppose you arrive in your hotel room in Tibet. There are three faucets in the shower with strange markings on them. How do you turn the hot water on? The only way to find out is to turn the faucets and see what happens. This is **trial and error** (Johnson-Laird, 1983). Trial and error is the most basic problem-solving strategy. When we are stuck in a situation and do not know how to get out of it, we start trying things to get unstuck. Trial and error usually involves a series of different actions aimed at solving a problem to which there seems to be no logical solution. What do you do to stop a car going downhill if the brakes fail?

Hypothesis Testing

Suppose one night you come home and find all the lights out. You check all the switches, turn them on and off and still no light. You call the electric company and find out that there has not been a power failure. You check the fuse box and all the fuses are OK. Then you check the main switch to the house — it is off. You switch it on and the lights brighten your house. What you did, even in this simple situation, was to entertain a series of hypotheses about the problem in a systematic and structured way. Using **hypothesis testing,** you eliminated each hypothesis until the solution was found. To do this you must have a *set of possible hypotheses* stored, each of which could account for the situation. In this case it could have been something wrong with the fuse box or the power line. You must also be able to take appropriate *actions* to test and *eliminate* certain hypotheses; in this case, turning on switches in different rooms eliminated the hypothesis that the lights were out in only one room.

Even animals use hypotheses. David Krechevsky (1932) had rats run a maze with four choice points. At each one the rats could turn left or right. Behind each choice point there was a door that could be opened or closed and that either blocked the rats or allowed them to continue. The rats did not treat the situation in a trial-and-error way but seemed to test hypotheses. They would try a series of all right turns or all left ones until they had arrived at a satisfactory solution.

Problem-Solving Strategies

Situations that can be solved by simple trial and error or hypothesis testing are not that common because most human actions and interactions are more complex than mazes or home electrical problems. In chess there are literally millions of possible moves. Players would be stymied unless they used some simplifying strategies and procedures (heuristics).

The variety of problems we face in life are too numerous to allow a neat classification. However, most problems are similar in having three basic elements:

1. The *initial state* or starting point of the problem.
2. A set of *operations* or actions that the problem solver can use to change the state of the problem.
3. A *goal* or a description of the states that would be solutions to the problem.

The game of tic-tac-toe, although simple, provides a good example of these three elements. The initial state is a set of nine empty squares. The operations are marking an X or an O in the squares and all the possible ways the squares can be marked. The goal is to get three of your marks in a row before your opponent does. Most puzzles and mathematical problems are similarly well defined, but most problems in life are not. If your problem is to write a paper for an English class, you might say that the initial state of the problem includes a blank sheet of paper and all your knowledge about the subject of the paper. The operations are researching and writing words on the page, and the goal is a completed paper.

However, in this example, and in most other real-life problems, it is difficult to specify all the possible states, operations, and especially, goals. But even though many real problems are not completely well defined, it still may be useful in solving problems to distinguish these elements.

Sequence of Problem Solving

The process of problem solving involves four basic steps (Polya, 1957):

1. Understanding the problem.
2. Planning a solution.
3. Carrying out the plan.
4. Checking the results.

You must first *understand* the elements discussed locational—the starting point, the operations, and the goal. Then you *plan* a sequence of operations to change the initial state into a goal. Finally, you *carry out* the operations and judge whether the solution is correct by *checking* the results. Of course, you may have to repeat the cycle many times before you reach a solution.

Problem Representation

At each step in problem solving there are a number of choices to be made. Two of the most important parts of solving problems are how to *represent* the problem and what *strategy* to use in solving it. **Problem representation,** the way you think about or represent a problem, may make it harder or easier to solve. Although logical reasoning often helps solve problems, sometimes it makes solutions more difficult. Consider the following problem:

> One morning, exactly at sunrise, a Buddhist monk began to climb a tall mountain. A narrow path, no more than a foot or two wide, spiraled around the mountain to a glittering temple at the summit. The monk ascended at varying rates of speed, stopping many times along the way to rest and eat dried fruit he carried with him. He reached the temple shortly before sunset. After several days of fasting and meditation, he began his journey back along the same path, starting [at] sunrise and again walking at variable speeds with many pauses along the way. His average speed descending was, of course, greater than his average climbing speed. Show that there is a spot along the path that the monk will occupy on both trips at exactly the same time of day. (Glass, 1980)

Try to think about this problem verbally and mathematically. Most people find the solution difficult: how can we be sure the monk would find himself at the same spot at the same time on two different days, when we do not know how fast he walked? The best way to *represent* this problem is visually. One woman describes her solution: "When you graph the position of the monk on the mountain for the two different days, there must be a point at which they cross, and this is the solution to the problem" (Glass et al., 1980).

However, visual solutions do not always work. Here is another problem. Suppose you take a piece of paper 0.02 inch thick and fold it on itself 50 times.

How high is it? Most people, visually estimating the solution, say "five inches" or "two feet," or perhaps "ten feet." They all underestimate the height greatly. Now attack the problem mathematically: we find that 50 folds increases the height by two multiplied by two 50 times, or 2^{50} times 0.02 inch. When the problem is solved mathematically, the answer is surprising—the thickness of the paper would reach from the earth nearly to Jupiter! Successful problem-solving strategy may require visual, verbal, mathematical, and other kinds of representation.

Algorithms

After you have a representation for a problem, there are several different strategies that can be used to solve it. Some strategies guarantee that you will find the solution if you keep working long enough. These strategies are called **algorithms.** If you follow the procedure exactly, you will reach a correct answer to the problem. One algorithm is a strategy for playing tic-tac-toe, in which you consider all the possible moves you could make, then all the possible replies your opponent could make to that move, then all the possible next moves you could make, and so on. Then you select a move that cannot lead to a win for your opponent. This strategy is called *generate and test* because at each point you *generate* a set of alternative moves and *test* each one to see if it works. Looking at many alternative actions in this way is called *searching the test* (or problem) *space.*

See section on The Computer and the Mind, this chapter.

Algorithms are used extensively in solving problems in the structured language of computer programs. For example, computer chess programs are based on the use of algorithms. The computer generates and tests a huge number of possible moves and selects the best one. The number of moves they test determines the level of difficulty of the chess game. However, computers can do this incredibly fast; it would take us far too long to play chess this way. People have the advantage of using heuristics and insight in solving complex problems such as chess.

Because computer chess games are based on algorithms, they can be programmed to match any level of ability.

Heuristics

People use heuristics as shortcuts in complex situations. They do not guarantee a solution in all cases, but are often very useful in reaching a solution. Some examples of chess-playing heuristics might be "Capture any piece you can" and "Never expose your king." This drastically reduces the amount of information that needs to be considered in solving a problem.

One heuristic that is often useful is called "hill climbing." For example, if your goal were to reach the top of a hill, a good strategy would be to walk uphill from where you were. Using this heuristic you would always apply operations that would bring the state of the problem more in line with the goal state. As a simplifying strategy in complex problems, this heuristic might help: someone with a poor sense of direction would remember that in California you always drive west to reach the ocean. But this strategy can sometimes get you into trouble if used blindly. In checkers the goal is to capture all the opponent's pieces. Using the hill-climbing strategy, you would try to capture any piece you could because this would bring you closer to the goal. But if done indiscriminately, this could lead you into a trap in which more of your own pieces were captured.

Another heuristic that is often useful is to break a larger problem into **subgoals.** Consider the algebraic problem $2x + y = 8$ and $x - y = 1$. To solve this, you might first set the subgoal of finding x and look for a way to reach it. The two equations added gives $3x = 9$ or $x = 3$; now y can be easily derived. Breaking a problem into pieces makes it easier to solve (Wickelgren, 1977).

Means-End Analysis. A particularly useful way of breaking a problem into subgoals is called **means-end analysis.** This heuristic involves working backward from the goal through the things needed to achieve it. If the goal is to cook spaghetti, you need a kitchen to cook in and all the ingredients for spaghetti. Suppose you need to buy the ingredients, but you have no transportation to the store. Your new subgoal is to get to the store. You might ask to borrow your roommate's car. If you get permission to use it, then your next subgoal is to find the keys. If permission is denied, then you may have to consider other means of transportation.

Insight

Not all problems are necessarily solvable using only systematic, step-by-step methods such as those treated thus far. Often a crucial **insight** is needed to solve a problem, a vision of how all the parts fit together or of how to represent the problem differently. Deciding to visually represent the Buddhist monk problem is one example of an insight (see section on Problem Representation). "Aha, that's it!" is the feeling of insight when all the different elements of a problem suddenly come together. This experience can come at the end of a directed process of hypothesis testing or seemingly out of the blue. The mathematician Poincare (1921) described his insight into a mathematical formula on which he had worked constantly for 15 days, after which he went on a trip:

> Just at this time I left Caen, where I was living, to go on a geologic excursion under the auspices of the School of Mines. The changes of travel made me forget my mathematical world. Having reached Coutances, we entered an omnibus to

go some place or other. At the moment when I put my foot on the step, the idea came to me, without anything in my former thoughts seeming to have paved the way for it . . . I did not verify the idea . . . as upon taking my seat in the omnibus I went on with a coversation already commenced, but I felt a perfect certainty. On my return to Caen, for conscience's sake, I verified the result at my leisure. (Poincare, 1921)

An insight is often visual and seems to consist of a simultaneous vision of the total problem. Some of the earliest experimental work on insight was done by Wolfgang Köhler. Köhler (1925) demonstrated that insight can even occur in animals. Recall Chapter 8 on learning that Köhler hung a bunch of bananas from the ceiling just out of reach of a chimpanzee (Figure 10-3). He also randomly arranged a set of boxes in the cage. After exhausting various approaches in a trial-and-error manner, the chimp suddenly stopped, perused the situation, and then appeared to see the solution: he stacked the boxes one on top of another, stood on the boxes, and reached the bananas. This is insight: the sudden arrangement of a set of elements in a new way.

See Chapter 8, section on Insight.

Studying Problem Solving

Protocol Analysis

How do psychologists study problem solving? One of the most obvious ways is by asking people to *introspect* (literally "look within") and talk about how they solve problems. It is usually best to have people do this while they are actually solving the problem. If they wait until they are finished, their memory may distort what they actually did to solve the problem.

The use of this "thinking aloud" technique is called **protocol analysis.** Newell and Simon (1972) used this technique to study how people solved puzzles in which each letter stood for a digit and the goal was to figure out which digit each letter stood for. Newell and Simon analyzed such protocols by means of a *problem behavior graph* that showed the path the person followed in solving the problem, including all the false starts and backtracking.

FIGURE 10-3
Problem Solving
This chimpanzee had a flash of insight and was thus able to solve the problem of how to reach the bananas.

Problems of "Set" in Problem Solving

One important problem in problem solving (and thinking in general) is that people tend to repeat actions that have been successful in other circumstances. In other words, they get "set" into a pattern of thought or behavior by activating stored schemata. Sometimes this can lead to inefficiency and difficulty in solving new problems. The classical demonstration of this problem involving "set" is in a series of experiments by Luchins (1942). Luchins tested more than 9,000 people on this "water jar" problem. For example, start with three jars; jar A holds 21 quarts, B holds 127 quarts, and C holds 3 quarts. How can you measure out 100 quarts? Most likely you would fill the 127-quart jar, then pour 21 quarts into jar A, then 3 quarts into jar C twice (Figure 10-4). The participants were asked to solve the five problems shown in Table 10-1, which begin with different quantities of water in each jar.

All of these problems can be solved using the formula

$$\text{Goal} = B - A - 2C$$

However, look again at the fifth problem in the table. A much simpler solution is $A - C$. People who work through the first four problems tend to use the more complicated formula ($B - A - 2C$) for the fifth problem and usually fail to see the simpler solution at all. Thus, success and efficiency using one approach with certain kinds of problems can be responsible for difficulty and inefficiency in solving other problems.

TABLE 10-1 Water Jar Problems

Problem	Jar A	Jar B	Jar C	Goal
		(IN QUARTS)		
1.	2	40	4	30
2.	1	27	6	14
3.	2	16	3	8
4.	7	59	12	28
5.	23	49	3	20

SOURCE: Adapted from Luchins & Luchins, 1959.

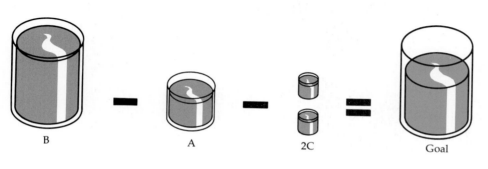

FIGURE 10-4
The Luchins Water Jar Problem

CREATIVITY

Life is more than solving problems. People go beyond normal problem solving to *inventing* solutions. One characteristic of creativity is that it may involve things as simple as cooking a new dish or as grand as a new scientific theory. The need for human beings to create is quite basic. We have been inventing ways to deal with unexpected situations for at least a million years.

Generation and Evaluation

Campbell (1960) proposed that creativity works this way: ideas are generated at random and some are retained (selected) because they are useful or have adaptive value. Creativity is thus considered a process similar to natural selection, in which there are random variations, some of which prove useful and are "selected" by the environment. The idea is that people generate many ideas, almost at random, and a few of them are appropriate and become selected. Chance plays a great role in both the generation and the evaluation of ideas. *Generation* of ideas is the primary stage. People who have a lot of ideas are more likely to have creative ones. A *useful* creative idea is rare. Campbell (1960) emphasizes:

> [The tremendous amount of nonproductive thought] must not be underestimated. Think of what a small proportion of thought becomes conscious, and of conscious thought what a small proportion gets uttered, what a still smaller fragment gets published, and what a small portion of what is published is used by the next intellectual generation. There is a tremendous wastefulness, slowness and rarity of achievement.

Thousands of small and wrong ideas help prepare the way for an occasional useful one. Thomas Edison evaluated his progress on an invention by supposedly saying that he now knew a hundred ways that wouldn't work.

Thomas Edison at work on one of his many creative inventions.

THE CREATIVE PERSON

People are not totally "creative" or "noncreative." However, there are certain human characteristics that may make it easier for some people to express ideas creatively. It seems that people who think unusual thoughts often lead lives different from the rest of us. Isaac Newton, for example, spent almost 16 hours a day locked up in his rooms at Cambridge working on his ideas. The conclusion is that if you spend too much time being like everybody else, you *decrease* your chances of coming up with something different.

Creativity involves hard work and the relentless generation of ideas and thoughts to produce a few that pass evaluation. *Evaluation* is the assessment of the worth of an idea. In an important passage, the psychologist Wickelgren (1979) wrote that "it is perhaps more important to *recognize* a good idea than it is to possess one."

Process of Creation

There have been many analyses of creativity and most have come to generally similar conclusions. It is thought that creativity involves four processes: preparation, generation, evaluation, and implementation (Johnson, 1972). *Preparation* involves immersion in the subject and often an especially intense period just before the solution. The mathematician Poincare, in the previous example of insight, began his discussion by saying that the problem had occupied him constantly for 15 days. Generation and evaluation have already been discussed. *Implementation* involves actually carrying out the idea, after the assessment of its worth. Only a few useful ideas get implemented because only rarely is anyone willing and able to do the further work needed to carry them out. Thomas Edison once said that genius is 1 percent inspiration and 99 percent perspiration.

LANGUAGE

The primary way we express our thoughts, share our ideas, and reveal our solutions and decisions is through speech. Language is probably the greatest human achievement. Talking makes it possible for a group to plan and carry out a very complex activity together; it makes it possible to teach and to transmit to a new generation what happened in the past. In our society and most civilized countries, history and culture are passed down in books. But even among illiterate primitive people, the primary vehicle for the transmission of culture is words. Every human culture has a language; every normal human being has the ability to speak.

Language is creation; every sentence we utter is an on-the-spot invention. Unless you are giving a prepared speech, everything you say is instantly put together in response to a new situation. *All children as they grow up can recognize millions of sentences and exclamations that they have never heard before!*

Education increases our store of knowledge, and most of that knowledge is stored in words. Every profession has its own vocabulary, or jargon, which speeds up communication among colleagues. Words such as *schema, cognitive,* and *neurotransmitter pathways* used in psychology ought to contain meaning for you now (I hope!).

Even a 3-year-old child, with little complex language ability, can communicate basic needs, ideas, and questions. A single word such as "hungry" will serve as important communication. "Where's Daddy?" communicates a different, more complex thought. Sentences can be extraordinarily complex in structure, but "I wonder where father might possibly have gone today?" is not much more complex than "Where's Daddy?"

Elements of Language

Speech Acts

The different forms of language are termed *speech acts* (Austin, 1962). Three important speech acts are associated with different kinds of sentences. A *declarative sentence* conveys specific information, such as "Jamaica is a country in the Caribbean." A *question* demands information, as in "Do you have any quarters?" or "Will you give me a kiss?" An *imperative* conveys a command: "Please pass the salad."

Phonemes

The individual sounds of a language are called **phonemes.** A particular sound is considered a phoneme only if it is used in language. The sound of *d* is used in words and is a phoneme; the grumbling sound we make when we clear our throat is not. A way to isolate a phoneme is to say a word and systematically change one of the sounds until the word changes into a different word. If a change in a single sound transforms one word into another, this identifies a phoneme. There are three phonemes in the word *bat* (b/a/t). A change in the first phoneme can give pat or vat; a change in the second phoneme can give bit or bet; a change in the third can give ban or bad. The phonemes in standard American English are listed

TABLE 10-2   Phonemes in General American English

Vowels		Consonants	
ee as in heat	*ʌ* as in ton	*t* as in tee	*s* as in see
I as in hit	*uh* as in the	*p* as in pea	*sh* as in shell
ε as in head	*er* as in bird	*k* as in key	*h* as in he
ae as in had	*oi* as in toil	*b* as in bee	*v* as in view
ah as in father	*au* as in shout	*d* as in dawn	*th* as in then
aw as in call	*ei* as in take	*g* as in go	*z* as in zoo
U as in put	*ou* as in tone	*m* as in me	*zh* as in garage
oo as in cool	*ai* as in might	*n* as in no	*l* as in law
		ng as in sing	*r* as in red
		f as in fee	*y* as in you
		θ as in thin	*w* as in we

SOURCE: Denes & Pinson, 1963.

in Table 10-2. Note that phonemes within words differ between different dialects; for example, merry, marry, and Mary are pronounced identically in parts of the midwestern United States.

Morphemes

Phonemes are as meaningless as individual letters. The phoneme *b* in *bet, bat,* and *bit* has no common meaning. Phonemes combine to make units of meaning, called **morphemes.** A morpheme can be a whole word, such as car, but, or teach, or it can be a word fragment. Prefixes and suffixes are themselves morphemes, such as *pre, dis, un, ing, es,* and *est.*

Words such as "dis+em+body" are made up of three morphemes; the spelling bee favorite, antidisestablishmentarianism, is made up of seven morphemes (anti+dis+establish+ment+ari+an+ism). English has only 26 letters, but they combine to make more than 90,000 morphemes, which in turn combine to make about 600,000 words, which can be made into an almost infinite number of sentences.

Grammar and Syntax

A word is the normal unit of meaning. Words form sentences and spoken sentences form conversations. We speak without being conscious of the elements; children learning to talk often do not actually know they are speaking words (Donaldson, 1978). However, written language is by nature more formal and self-conscious. The thought contained in a sentence is meaningful only if it follows the specific rules of language. **Grammar** is the study of those rules of language, and how words are arranged to convey meaning is called **syntax.** Although syntax and grammar are the bane of most students in school, most of us actually speak fairly grammatically all the time.

There are specific rules in language, both written and spoken. For example, "The boy the ball the road hit on" is meaningless; it is not a sentence. But "The boy hit the ball on the road" conveys a thought. When children begin to speak they utter *essentially* grammatical sentences, and although children's sentences are simple and not in perfect syntax, almost every sentence is original, not an imitation of other sentences they have heard.

Deep and Surface Structure

When children begin to speak they are naturally adept and make relatively few grammatical errors. Thus, many scientists characterize the grammar of language as being innate. The leading proponent of this view, called **transformational grammar,** is Noam Chomsky (1966). He believes there is important distinction in syntax between "deep" and "surface" structure. *Deep structure* is the underlying network of thought conveyed in a sentence, and *surface structure* is the actual sentence that carries the deep structure. A *transformation* occurs that changes the deep structure (or meaning) into the surface structure (the expression in words). Because there are many ways to say the same thing, a single deep structure has many possible variations in surface structure. "The large elephant saw the small mouse" and "The small mouse was seen by the large elephant" have the same deep structure but a different surface structure.

FIGURE 10-5
Transformational Grammar Analysis
Analysis A indicates that some people are paying a visit to firemen, whereas analysis B identifies "they" as firemen who are visiting.
(After Chomsky, 1966)

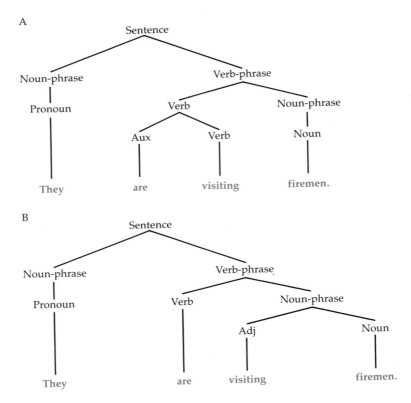

Sometimes the surface structure can be confusing and can derive from two different deep structures. In this case, knowing the deep structure is the only way to understand the sentence. In other words, you must have an idea of what the person is talking about. The following sentence is ambiguous: "They are visiting firemen." Figure 10-5 shows transformational grammar analyses of the sentence that show the two possible deep structures. A similar analysis of the two sentences about the large elephant and the small mouse would reveal that they share one deep structure.

Meaning in Language

Mental activities search for order and meaning and go beyond the information given, to fill in the gaps. This tendency is called *active processing*. When we listen and when we read, we attend selectively and "fill in" an enormous amount of information. The meaning of something causes us to complete the gaps in the elements of language—words and letters. As we read text, we are able to make good predictions the words we expect to see. These predictions, for example, were probably good enough to allow you to fill in the missing word "about" in the preceding sentence.

Context determines what we hear. "I went to the new display last night" can get a shocked reaction from someone who heard "I went to the nudist play," because the sounds are the same. When I was very young, my father told me that the "Prince of Whales" was coming to the United States. I asked him for weeks if we could go to the aquarium to see this royal marine mammal. Active processing is the way we analyze specific sounds and language patterns and how we search for meaning. When the sounds are ambiguous or difficult to hear, we fill in the gaps.

Warren and Warren (1920) did an interesting study on this process. People heard the following: "It was found that the —eel was on the ———." Different subjects were given four different words to end the sentence: axle, orange, shoe, table. They were then asked to repeat what they had heard. Those who had heard "axle" recalled the sentence as "It was found that the *wheel* was on the axle." Those who had heard "orange" inserted *peel*, those who had heard "shoe" inserted *heel*, and those who had heard "table" inserted *meal*. The subjects did not *think* that they were *guessing* the word, but that they had *actually heard* the sentence. They "filled in" the sentence with the most likely element.

Conversational Maxims

It is a long leap to go from the elements of language, such as phonemes and surface structure, to an understanding of how we actually communicate in daily speech. Consider the following exchange:

SARAH: I think I have a headache.
JANE: Well, there's a store open around the corner. (Miller, 1981)

Now, what are these people doing? What is the relationship between the first and second statements? The relationship between two speakers follows what is called the **cooperativeness principle:** each speaker tries to understand *why* the other said what he or she did. In this case, the implication is that the store sells something that might relieve the headache. Otherwise the exchange makes no sense.

Following the cooperativeness principle, there are four **conversational maxims** that speakers usually obey when they speak (Grice, 1967):

1. *Quantity.* Make your contribution as informative as required, but not more so. If someone asks, "Where do you live?", the answer will depend on where you are. If you live in San Francisco, California, and you are in your neighborhood, you may say "Green Street." If you are in London, you may say "The United States" or "California." It would be idiotic to tell someone in London that you live on "Green Street," and likewise, if you are in San Francisco, you would never say "I live in the United States." Both of these violate the maxim of quantity.

   However, sometimes this maxim is deliberately violated.

   BILL: How did you like your date last night?
   BOB: Well, she had nice shoes.

   Here Bob is not being as informative as is usually required and therefore implies something about his date. Since he says nothing about her personality, it most likely means that he did not like her much.

2. *Quality.* Try to be truthful in conversation. This maxim is often violated in the use of metaphor and in sarcasm. If you say, "I hated the movie," and your friend responds, "Swell, wasn't it," he or she is signaling agreement by violating the principle.

3. *Relation.*   Contributions should be relevant to the conversation. Suppose you are a building engineer and your boss says, "It's warm in here." Your response in relation to the situation might be "Yes, it's time for a mainte-nance check on the air conditioning." But if your date that night in your apartment says "It's warm in here," it is doubtful that you would respond the same way!

4. *Manner.*   Be clear and orderly. When this maxim is violated, the underlying intention usually is still clear. For example, here is a critique of a would-be singer's audition: "Ms. Mallam managed to produce a number of sounds that seemed to resemble the song 'How're You Gonna Keep 'em Down on the Farm after They've Seen Paree.'" The implication is clear (after Grice, 1967; Miller, 1981).

The perception of meaning in language, like all perception, is complex and arises from a combination of specific elements, their organization, and the "invisi-ble rules" that guide our conversation.

Language and Thought

It is nearly impossible for us to separate language and thinking; so many of our hypotheses are formed in language when we solve a problem, we often actively think it out in words. But language is not the only vehicle for thought; thoughts can be expressed in gestures and movement as well as in music, art, and many other ways. Still, the nature of the relationship of thinking and language has been an important and controversial one in psychology.

Benjamin Lee Whorf, an insurance man by trade and linguist by vocation, proposed that language determines the structure of thinking. He wrote:

> We dissect nature along lines laid down by our native language. The catego-ries and types that we isolate from the world of phenomena we do not find here because they stare every observer in the face; on the contrary, the world is presented in a kaleidoscopic flux of impressions which has to be organized by our minds—and this means largely by the linguistic systems in our minds. We put nature up, organize it into concepts, and ascribe significances as we do, largely because we are parties to an agreement to organize it this way—an agreement that holds throughout our speech community and is codified in the patterns of our language. The agreement is, of course, an implicit and unstated one, but its terms are absolutely obligatory; we cannot talk at all except by subscribing to the organization and classification of data which the agreement decrees. (Whorf, 1942)

The Arab, for example, has several words for camel; the Eskimo has many words for snow. Certain languages, like the Hopi, have no words for past and future. Whorf's hypothesis, in its strongest form — that language reflects the structure of our reality — has excited many psychologists and anthropologists and has created a great controversy. Eleanor Rosch studied this hypothesis on the Dani, a New Guinean culture, who have only two words for color; one roughly corresponds to black, the other to white. If Whorf's proposition were right, then the Dani would not be able to discriminate among colors such as gray, blue, and hot pink. When carefully questioned, however, the Dani *do* show the ability to perceive colors as we see them (Rosch, 1973). Thus, language does not *entirely* determine thought. Color perception is strongly determined by the innate receptive characteristics of the eye, presumably common to all cultures.

So, a diluted version of Whorf's hypothesis would be that language *influences* thought, not that it determines it. A particular language makes certain ideas more available than others. There are words in all languages that are not translatable into other languages. *Gemütlichkeit* and *gestalt* are German words that have no direct English equivalents. There is no word for *consciousness* in French.

It is, however, just as likely that languages are the way they are because our thinking is the way it is. The Eskimo may need hundreds of words for snow because they encounter it daily and need fine distinctions for survival. If it were necessary, we could learn them too. The more specialized we become in a field, the finer the linguistic distinctions we make. For instance, physicians learn a vocabulary that *follows*, not precedes, their thought. As we become more expert in an area, the nature of our category system changes; categories become more intricate and complex, and language develops along with them. An automobile enthusiast may see "a Jaguar XK 120 drophead"; an uninitiated person may notice "an old sports car."

Consider intelligence, artificial and natural. The goal of making an "artificial person" is one that has tantalized humanity for centuries. In recent years, scientists have made important progress toward one of the most important parts of this goal—building machines that do "intelligent" things. As we will see in Chapter 11, it is very hard to even define precisely what we mean by "intelligence," but most of us have a general idea of what it means for a person to seem intelligent. One useful way of defining **artificial intelligence** is the study of ideas that enable computers to do the things that make people seem intelligent (Winston, 1979).

Goals of Artificial Intelligence

From its inception in the late 1950s, artificial intelligence inquiry has combined two different goals. The first is to get computers to do intelligent things using whatever techniques succeed. The second goal is to get computers to do intelligent things in the same way that people do them. Both of these approaches have been successful.

The first approach has led to programs that now have commercial applications in such fields as factory automation, geological interpretation, and computer configuration (Winston & Prendergast, 1984). Computer programs are now being used to help geologists interpret the complex readings they receive from various instruments (such as seismographs) and predict the location of petroleum and mineral deposits.

The second approach has contributed to many of the insights discussed throughout this book about how people think, reason, communicate, and solve problems. Consider trying to program computers to understand language. The problem of getting computers to understand "natural languages" (like English and French) instead of "artificial languages" (like computer programming languages) has turned out to be much more difficult than researchers initially expected. One of the most important reasons for this difficulty is that understanding language requires knowing much more than just the rules of grammar and the definitions of words. A great deal of detailed knowledge about the world is also required.

For example, consider again the exchange we saw in the last section:

SARAH: I think I have a headache.
JANE: Well, there's a store open around the corner. (Miller, 1981)

Understanding this simple dialogue requires knowledge about the relationship between headaches and medications, about the kinds of medications that are sold in stores, and about regular business hours. There is so much knowledge like this that is potentially relevant to understanding language that no one has yet succeeded in representing more than a tiny fraction of it in a computer program. Also, computers still have very limited language-understanding capabilities. Trying to program computers to understand sentences such as this one has helped us to realize how much "world knowledge" is used everyday by people to understand the same sentences.

Similarities Between the Computer and the Mind

One of the reasons why research in artificial intelligence is important to psychologists is because comparing how people's minds work with how computers work can help us learn more about both. The ultimate degree of similarity between minds and computers, however, is an issue about which many people disagree.

Many researchers believe that both human beings and computers can be comprehended as physical systems that process meaningful symbols (Arkes & Hammond, 1986). People and computers do the same kinds of things: they receive information from the world, they "process" it in some way, and then they perform some action. The detailed ways in which this occurs may be very different in the two cases. Most computers have limited ways of receiving information and performing actions (for example, typewriter keyboards and television screens). Certainly the "hardware" in the two kinds of systems is very different: neurons in one case, silicon in the other. But since the same general kinds of behavior *can* occur in both cases, perhaps much of human thought can be analyzed in terms of how a computer might do the same thing.

A test of whether a computer is sufficient as a model of human intelligence is whether a computer can actually produce the same kind of behavior a human being can. In many cases, computer programs today can pass this test. For example, as mentioned before, there are computer programs that can play chess at the level of a good college chess team member, although the best human players can still beat these programs.

An extreme version of this kind of test is called the "Turing test," after Alan Turing who proposed a similar test (Turing, 1950). A person communicates by typing on a computer console with two other "people." One of the other "people" is in fact a computer program, and the other is a real person. The test is to see whether the first person can distinguish the human from the computer program by asking questions and looking at the answers. In part because of the difficulties of understanding natural language, no computer program today is close to being able to pass the most general form of this test.

Differences Between the Computer and the Mind

There are certainly differences in the things people and computers can now do and in how the two kinds of systems do the things of which both are capable. Computers can perform well-defined sequential calculations much more rapidly than people. People are much better than modern computers at understanding the ambiguous: seeing analogies or learning new concepts.

Some of these differences are simply because a human brain is many orders of magnitude more complex than even the largest of today's computers. There are also other important ways in which the basic processes of present-day computers may differ from human minds. Two of these involve analog vs. digital processing and serial vs. parallel processing.

Analog versus Digital Processing

Almost all computers used today are *digital* computers. This means that their basic processing occurs in terms of exact categories: a switch is either on or off. Thus, a number may be 4.1397 or 4.1396, but it is always *exactly* something. Human brains, on the other hand, seem to depend at least in part on what are called *analog* properties of the behavior of neurons. This means that there are not always exact categories; instead there may be "shades of gray" that gradually change from one thing to another without sharp boundaries. This distinction is a complicated one because either kind of system can behave like the other. Given enough time and storage capacity, digital systems can represent gradations, just like they represent decimal digits, with as much precision as necessary. Also, analog systems can be constructed to detect sharp boundaries. For example, the voltage potential on a neuron may change very gradually, but at some point, the neuron "fires." Nevertheless, these differences between what is easy and what is hard to accomplish in the two different kinds of systems may have important consequences for their overall behavior (Haugeland, 1985).

Serial versus Parallel Processing

Most computers today use primarily *serial processing,* which means that even when they do things very rapidly, they still do them one step at a time, one after another. Human brains, in contrast, appear to use a great deal of *parallel processing.* Even though you usually cannot pay attention to more than one thing at a time, much processing in your brain is occurring simultaneously. For example, your brain is constantly regulating your breathing and heartbeat while you think about other things. Even the processes of which you are conscious, like trying to remember someone's name, seem to occur with many different neurons in many different parts of the brain, all being involved at once. Here, too, the issue is complicated because both serial and parallel systems can ultimately do the same kinds of things, but processing that is very rapid and easy in one kind of system may be very time consuming and difficult in the other.

Some researchers feel that, because the basic processes by which humans and computers do things are so different, the resulting behavior must be fundamentally different, too. According to this view, even if computers behaved exactly like people, we would still not call what computers do "thinking." A somewhat less extreme position holds that, because the basic processes are so different, we will never be able to reproduce much interesting human behavior using computers. Therefore, according to this view, computers will not turn out to be very useful in explaining most human behavior because of practical rather than philosophical reasons.

SUMMARY

1. Helping us to cut through the complicated world are the simplifying mental structures that underlie thought. An important structure of thinking is *classification,* which simplifies mental processes. The function of categories is to give the most information with the least effort. Categories are not random and arbitrary but reflect the world: wings are more likely to have feathers than fur, and legs are found on animals, not trees. Categories aid in interacting with the world. An important distinction is made between natural and artificial categories—*natural categories* (such as color) reflect the structure of the physical world and *artificial categories* (such as money) do not.

2. Categories are arranged in different levels. The *basic level category* is the one in which we normally organize our experience. Furniture is a broad category, but a basic level of furniture would be table or chair. Below the basic level are still smaller levels or subcategories, such as different types of tables. Basic level categories are the categories first learned by children. Categories are arranged around a core of best examples or *prototypes.* Typical examples of a category are closest to the prototype.

3. *Heuristics* are simplifying strategies that we use to make judgments and solve problems. They are like rules of thumb. Important heuristics that have been studied are *representativeness* (the degree to which an object is typical of its category), *availability* (the ease with which relevant examples come to mind), and *comparison* (which involves shifting standards). The use of these strategies aids and simplifies thought, but can lead to common mistakes. A man from Indiana may remark, "Haven't you noticed how many famous Hoosiers there are?"

4. Decisions are important aspects of mental life, from what you will major in to what job you will accept. The four basic elements in decisions are alternatives, outcomes, preferences, and probabilities. Often just breaking down decisions into these elements can help clarify decision making. For example, if you have trouble getting along with your roommate, you could make a list of alternative things you could do. You could then consider the outcome most likely from each choice, which outcome you would prefer most, and how likely each of them is to occur.

5. We use heuristics in making decisions, and these usually lead to useful shortcuts in decision making, but they often lead to *biases.* When people are asked to judge the relative frequency of different causes of death, they overestimate the frequency of well publicized causes and underestimate the frequency of less vivid causes. An important consequence of availability and other heuristics is that concrete or vivid

information is influential in judgment. It is difficult to refute the evidence of one vivid case, even on the basis of statistical evidence. It seems human beings are not designed to think statistically.

6. Solving simple problems can be done by trial and error, which involves working through a series of different actions until a problem is solved. The search in this method is not systematic, and there are usually no organizing principles. A more organized form of simple problem solving is *hypothesis testing,* in which you entertain a series of hypotheses about a problem in a systematic and structured way and each is eliminated until the solution is found. To do this you must have a set of possible hypotheses stored, each of which could account for the situation. Even animals have been shown to use hypotheses.

7. It is useful to think of problems as having these elements: (a) the initial state or starting point of the problem, (b) a set of operations or actions that the problem solver can use to change the state of the problem, and (c) a goal or a description of the states that would be solutions to the problem. The sequence of problem solving has four basic steps: (1) understanding the problem, (2) planning a solution, (3) carrying out the plan, and (4) checking the results.

8. Two systematic ways of solving problems are using algorithms and means-end analysis. *Algorithms* use the strategy of generate and test, and they will always give you an answer if you work them through to the end. Computer programming involves algorithms. *Means-end analysis* is a way of breaking a problem into subgoals. With this method you work backward from your goal through the things you need to achieve it. For example, if your goal is to cook spaghetti, you need a kitchen to cook in and all the ingredients for spaghetti.

9. Not all problems are necessarily solvable using only systematic, step-by-step means described thus far. Often a crucial *insight* is needed to solve a problem, a vision of how all the parts fit together or of how to represent the problem differently. An insight is often visual and seems to consist of a simultaneous vision of the total problem.

10. One fundamental feature of human thought is *creativity*—ways to deal with unexpected situations. In an influential paper, Campbell proposed that creativity works this way: ideas are generated at random, and some are retained (selected) because they are useful or because (as in Darwinian natural selection) they have some adaptive value.

11. The specific sounds of a language are called *phonemes.* Phonemes are meaningless as individual letters but combine to make units of meanings called *morphemes.* A morpheme can be a whole word or a word fragment, such as a prefix or suffix. A word is the normal unit of meaning. Words form sentences, and spoken sentences form conversation. *Grammar* is the study of specific rules of language; how words are arranged to convey meaning is called *syntax.*

12. An influential theory of language by Chomsky, called *transformational grammar,* proposes that the grammar of language is innate. In this view there is an important distinction made in syntax between deep and surface structure. Deep structure is the underlying network of thought conveyed in a sentence; surface structure is the sentence that carries the deep structure. A transformation occurs that changes the deep structure (meaning) into the surface structure (the expression in words).

13. An important aspect of language is our ability to determine meaning in a sentence by going beyond the information given. This tendency is called *active processing*. When we listen and when we read, we attend selectively and fill in an enormous amount of information. Another aspect of language is that it is very creative. As children develop language, they recognize and utter millions of sentences, newly created, that they have never heard before.

14. Artificial intelligence programs now exhibit impressive capabilities in performing limited tasks that were previously thought to require human intelligence. However, we are still a long way from building computers that are even close to being as intelligent as people are in a wide range of situations. It is difficult to say how far we will be able to go with this in the future. For example, some researchers are now experimenting with computers that make heavy use of the kind of highly parallel, analog processing that occurs in the human brain. These computers may ultimately be able to reproduce some human mental behaviors that are difficult to produce using present-day computers.

15. Regardless of our eventual success in building artificially intelligent machines, comparisons between people and computers have already been the primary inspiration for the "cognitive" or "information processing" view of human mental functioning. This view has contributed a great deal to our understanding of how human minds work, and it seems to be increasingly influential in many areas of psychology and related fields.

TERMS AND CONCEPTS

active processing
algorithms
anchoring
artificial category
artificial intelligence
availability
basic level category
biases
conversational maxims
cooperativeness principle
decision analysis
grammar
heuristics
hypothesis testing
insight

means-end analysis
morpheme
natural category
phoneme
problem representation
protocol analysis
prototype
representativeness
speech acts
subgoals
syntax
taxonomy
transformational grammar
trial and error
typicality

SUGGESTIONS FOR FURTHER READING

Arkes, H. R., & Hammond, K. R. (1986). *Judgment and decision making.* New York: Cambridge University Press.

An up-to-date summary of research in the field with articles on rationality, expert judgment, decisions in clinical practice, and the like.

Kahneman, D., Slovic, P., & Tversky, A. (Eds.). (1982). *Judgment under uncertainty.* New York: Cambridge University Press.

A compilation of much of the classic work on how we use heuristics in judgment, how we make mistakes, and the nature of the mental system that underlies these processes. Technical, but interesting and worthwhile.

Johnson-Laird, P. N. (1983). *Mental models.* Boston: Harvard.

A recent and interesting account of problems in the nature of the mind, such as "Why do we have to think everything in order, not at once?"

Miller, G. A. (1981). *Language and speech.* San Francisco: W. H. Freeman.

An elegant, entertaining, and witty introduction to the question and the problem of understanding language.

Haugeland, J. (Ed.). (1985). *Mind design: Philosophy, psychology, and artificial intelligence.* Cambridge, MA: MIT Press.

An excellent collection of readings by leading computer scientists and philosophers about such questions as whether machines really "think" and whether people are really "information processors."

Intelligence and the Mind

It seems so simple: to be intelligent is to use the mind well. But this deceptively simple statement can have many different interpretations. One person may be considered intelligent for working out an elegant proof in mathematics, while another for something as mundane as maneuvering a sofa through a small door. There are brilliant chess moves, dress designs, mathematical proofs, football plays, main dishes, and stock buys. The concept of intelligence, as straightforward as it might seem, is perhaps the single most controversial subject in psychology.

Many people think that intelligence is a single, fixed quantity and that people are "smart" in almost all things or not at all. From the analysis presented in this book, you will find that this viewpoint is clearly wrong. Rather, intelligence is a *varied array* of abilities and talents. The common element is that someone acts with excellence and originality — as defined by those judging — in the best way.

Different societies can have very different concepts of intelligence. In most societies the group of people who are most useful are the most intelligent. Western society highly values verbal and rational thinking. In formal assessment of other minds, it is here that these values have cost our society so much. It has often been overlooked that mental abilities are diverse and multiple, but now psychologists are beginning to produce a new description of the mind.

Our society judges someone who thinks logically and communicates effectively as "intelligent." We would be more likely to call a lawyer intelligent than a riverboat guide. But a society does exist in which the mark of an intelligent person is one who can guide a boat down a river well. How would that society judge the intelligence of our lawyer if he was totally incapable of steering a boat? We judge people as intelligent because they possess or have developed a few of the many talents of mind that we value.

Because of the differences in the goals of individuals and societies, there is very little that is regarded in *all* cultures as intelligent. However, "intelligence" in general does aid us in adapting to different environments and to changing societies. David Wechsler's definition of intelligence is probably best: *the ability to understand the world and to cope with the challenges of the environment.*

STUDYING AND MEASURING INTELLIGENCE

There was a conference in 1921 of the prevailing experts at that time on intelligence. Seventeen people were there, and seventeen definitions of intelligence were offered. Finally, Edwin Boring, an influential Harvard psychologist, wrote an exasperated joke: "[Intelligence] is what intelligence tests measure."

Intelligence is a concept that varies with the individual (Neisser, 1979). Thus, it is not surprising that both experts and nonexperts alike do not know how to measure it.

For centuries, psychologists and other scientists have attempted to quantify intelligence. Some analyzed the accuracy of visual acuity, the force of grip strength, and the speed of auditory tracking. Others examined the growth rate and size of hair follicles and eye color. There have been tests of the speed of tapping, the ability to copy a figure, and the comprehension of a paragraph. Psychologists have analyzed the ability of people to draw, to extract a hidden figure from many, and to assemble blocks. People have looked at muddy inkblots, had their EEGs read, had their heads measured, performed mathematical calculations, even given blood. All this effort has been to discover the ''key'' that will somehow easily characterize the true nature of intelligence and allow us to quantify it.

History of Intelligence Testing

Perhaps the most important endeavor in the history of intelligence testing has been the search for a single intelligence. Psychologists have always hoped to develop a ''universal'' standard by which to measure minds. The history shows how difficult it has been to decide what is intelligence. Until quite recently, it has been difficult to come up with anything more useful than the early, simplified approaches.

In 1858 Charles Darwin published *The Origin of Species* and began the modern scientific era in biology and related sciences. In psychology, his theory of evolution provoked great interest in variations in human mental abilities. It was thought that if survival depends on adaptation to the environment, then the superior intelligence of human beings must have been important in human evolution. The most intelligent human beings, because of their superior adaptability, would have been selected. These new ideas ignited a great interest in measuring intelligence.

Darwin's cousin, Francis Galton (1822–1911), was the first modern scientist to try systematically to determine what intelligence was. What is obvious to us now was the result of a great deal of hard work! Galton tried hard to measure the key elements in intelligence, and some of what he did may seem strange to us now.

Galton examined the concepts of head size and **sensory acuity** as the primary indicators of intelligence. Thus, he began by measuring heads until he found that, in contrast to the popular supposition, a big head does not mean a big mind. He reasoned that ''the more perceptive the senses are of differences, the larger is the field upon which our judgment and intelligence can act.'' Thus, to measure intelligence, Galton devised tests of sensory acuity. He studied reaction times in response to sound, the speed in naming colors, the ability to perceive two close points on the skin, and so on.

This approach seemed plausible at the time. However, there is no proven relationship between simple sensory judgments and more complex cognitive abilities, such as mathematics. And so this initial intellectual approach foundered.

Binet: The Beginnings of Modern Intelligence Testing

The next great attempt to measure intelligence took place in France. It eventually led to the intelligence testing of millions of children, which greatly affected

Alfred Binet
(1857–1911)

the course of their lives. Before the late nineteenth century, only the rich could afford to educate their children. But in the late nineteenth century universal public education became compulsory. Suddenly, teachers did not know how to teach all these children from different backgrounds and different degrees of preparation for school. The testing that became necessary was to have a profound effect on our ideas of intelligence.

In 1904 the French government asked Alfred Binet to devise a test to predict which children would be least likely to succeed in school. In the preceding years, Binet and his colleagues had charted an important new approach to intelligence, an approach still in use today. Among the insights of Binet's group were these:

1. Why not directly test actions that teachers and school administrators regard as intelligent? No one had ever done that before. Binet and his associates designed tests of sentence comprehension, visual memory, reasoning, and the ability to detect errors in thinking.

2. Intelligence testing would have to be applicable to ranking large numbers of children into "bright," "average," and "below average" groups. To get an idea of how to do this, Binet first tested children who were *already known* to be performing at these levels in schools. The tests developed using these children were then used to test other children whose scholastic abilities were unknown.

3. Binet noted that *as children age, their intellectual abilities increase* (Figure 11-1). Thus, he developed tests to measure cognitive development. The measurements were converted into scores to identify which children were exceptionally intelligent, which were normal, and which were retarded. In this testing scheme, a bright child is one whose *mental age* is greater than his or her chronological age and a slow child is one whose mental age is less than his or her chronological age.

The French education system benefited from Binet's work. The tests were given individually by one examiner to one student, and it took hours to attain a score. The French schools then used the results of these tests to assign children to classes. Below average children were either given special training or were released from attendance.

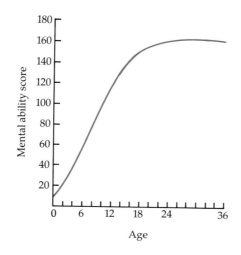

FIGURE 11-1
Increased Mental Abilities in Childhood
There is a rapid increase in intelligence in childhood and a leveling off in early adulthood.
(After Bayley, 1970)

Intelligence testing was first used on a mass scale at the beginning of World War I to test untrained recruits.

Intelligence testing is even done on babies to discover the cognitive capabilities of the very young.

Mass Testing

A few years later, another profound change in society directly affected intelligence testing: World War I broke out. This was a war vastly different from any waged previously. It was the first war in modern times in which millions of men from the general population were required to fight. In the United States, the Army needed to know the capability of its unknown, untrained, and untried soldiers.

Psychologists were called upon to develop intelligence tests that could be given to large groups and which could be scored quickly. The quantified scores took on more importance than they had in Binet's original tests. They were used directly to determine the assignments of soldiers. Unfortunately, the wartime necessity of group administration of tests and the strong reliance on the obtained test score as the primary measure of a person's "intelligence" *remained the norm even after the war ended.*

Modern Intelligence Testing

Currently used intelligence tests measure the **intelligence quotient** or **IQ** and most of them are modeled after Binet's original tests. They predict a child's success in the existing school system and act as a predictor of success in society. However, these tests have come to mean more than merely a test score. Many people believe that IQ is a genuine and almost physical characteristic of a person, like height. The futures of many young people's educations are often determined on the basis of one test, using only pencil and paper, that lasts only a few hours.

Since so much depends on IQ, the test has to be reliable, meaning that the test scores must be reproducible and consistent. The scores also have to be valid and measure what they purport to measure. The current IQ tests are reliable, but the question that remains is whether they are *valid.* Now we examine the most popular standardized tests of intelligence.

The original Binet test was adapted by Lewis Terman of Stanford University who standardized it on American students in 1916. This **Stanford–Binet test** was restandardized many times. Sample items appear in Table 11-1. Figure 11-2 shows the distribution used to standardize it in 1937. The IQ was originally a ratio that related a person's mental age to chronological age. It is derived by dividing the mental age by the chronological age (MA/CA) and then multiplying by 100. The *mental age* was a concept of Binet's that signified increasing amounts of intelligence. Thus, a child who tests at a mental age of 10 when he or she is 8 years old has an IQ of 125.

The Stanford–Binet test introduced the *deviation IQ*. Individuals are scored according to their relationship to their age group's average score on the test. The current test is standardized at a norm of 100 with a *standard deviation* of 16. An individual who scores one standard deviation above the norm is assigned an IQ of 116, two above the norm 132, and so on. The test is continually being modified to assess people at the low end of the range more adequately.

See Appendix—Statistics: Making Sense of Fallible Data, for an explanation of standard deviation.

TABLE 11-1   Descriptions of Items from the 1986 Stanford–Binet Intelligence Scale

Verbal Reasoning

Vocabulary   Defines words, such as "dollar" and "envelope."

Comprehension   Answers questions, such as "Where do people buy food?" and "Why do people comb their hair?"

Absurdities   Identifies the "funny" aspect of a picture, such as a girl riding a bicycle in a lake or a bald man combing his head.

Verbal Relations   Tells how the first three items in a sequence are alike and how they differ from the fourth: scarf, tie, muffler, shirt.

Quantitative Reasoning

Quantitative   Performs simple arithmetic tasks, such as selecting a die with six spots because the number of spots equals the combination of a two-spot and a four-spot die.

Number Series   Gives the next two numbers in a series, such as

$$20 \quad 16 \quad 12 \quad 8 \quad \text{—} \quad \text{—}.$$

Equations Building   Builds an equation from the following array:

$$2 \quad 3 \quad 5 \quad + \quad =.$$ One of several correct responses would be $2 + 3 = 5$.

Abstract/Visual Reasoning

Pattern Analysis   Copies a simple design with blocks.

Copying   Copies a geometrical drawing demonstrated by the examiner, such as a rectangle intersected by two diagonals.

Short-Term Memory

Bead Memory   Shown a picture of different-shaped beads stacked on a stick. Reproduces the sequence from memory by placing real beads on a stick.

Memory for Sentences   Repeats after the examiner sentences such as "It is time to go to sleep" and "Ken painted a picture for his mother's birthday."

Memory for Digits   Repeats after the examiner a series of digits, such as 5-7-8-3, forward and backward.

Memory for Objects   Shown pictures of individual objects, such as a clock and an elephant, one at a time. Identifies the objects in the correct order of their appearance in a picture that also includes extraneous objects; for example, a bus, a clown, an *elephant*, eggs, and a *clock*.

Note: These are typical items for 6- to 8-year-olds.

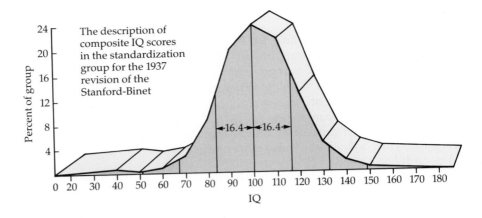

FIGURE 11-2
IQ Scores
This graph shows the normal distribution of the standardized IQ scores on the Stanford–Binet intelligence scale.
(After Terman & Merrill, 1973)

The description of composite IQ scores in the standardization group for the 1937 revision of the Stanford-Binet

Percent of group

IQ

Wechsler Test

David Wechsler devised another test, the Wechsler Adult Intelligence Scale (WAIS-R) (Table 11-2) and the Wechsler Intelligence Scale for Children (WISC-R) (Figure 11-3). Their advantage over the Binet tests is that they test two major areas of intelligence: *verbal* and *performance.* This test yields three scores: verbal, performance, and combined. This separation of abilities gives a slightly better portrait of the dimensions of intellectual abilities. Recent developments have gone even further in this regard.

Stability and Validity

Suppose that IQ reflects a constant and general faculty of a unitary and constant "intelligence." A child's IQ should thus be the same when he or she is age 2, 7, 14, and so on. How stable is the IQ? An IQ test given to a 2-year-old child does not predict well what the IQ will be later on in life. For example, the correlation between the IQ at 2 years and the IQ at 14 years is very low. At older ages the correlation is better. For example, the IQ at 14 years of age is fairly well predicted by the IQ at 7 years. As one moves into adulthood, the IQ appears to stabilize (see Figure 11-1).

Do IQs predict later success in school and in society? This is an important question because it relates to the purpose for which the test was designed. A review of data on IQ scores and school grades found that it *does:* the higher the IQ, the better the school grades. This finding has caused many defenders of the single intelligence idea to promote the use of the IQ. However, this correlation may result because school success depends on taking tests that are similar to IQ tests.

As expected, the IQ is less predictive of achievements outside of school. IQs in the normal range do predict success in society. On the average, accountants have higher IQs than sales clerks, and sales clerks higher than miners. However, some miners have much higher IQs than the average for accountants and lawyers. Adults take many different tests instead of IQ. Students take the SAT® to qualify for college, would-be lawyers take the dreaded law exams, and doctors take board certifications in different specialities. These are all evidence that the IQ test is not as useful as specialized tests.

TABLE 11-2 Tests Used in the Wechsler Adult Intelligence Scale

Test	Description
VERBAL SCALE	
Information	Questions tap a general range of information; for example, "How many nickels make a dime?"
Comprehension	Tests practical information and ability to evaluate past experience; for example, "What is the advantage of keeping money in a bank?"
Arithmetic	Verbal problems testing arithmetic reasoning.
Similarities	Asks in what way certain objects or concepts (for example, *egg* and *seed*) are similar; measures abstract thinking.
Digit span	A series of digits presented auditorily (for example, 7-5-6-3-8) is repeated in a forward or backward direction; tests attention and rote memory.
Vocabulary	Tests word knowledge.
PERFORMANCE SCALE	
Digit symbol	A timed coding task in which numbers must be associated with marks of various shapes; tests speed of learning and writing.
Picture completion	The missing part of an incompletely drawn picture must be discovered and named; tests visual alertness and visual memory.
Block design	Pictured designs must be copied with blocks (see Figure 11-3); tests ability to perceive and analyze patterns.
Picture arrangement	A series of comic-strip pictures must be arranged in the right sequence to tell a story; tests understanding of social situations.
Object assembly	Puzzle pieces must be assembled to form a complete object; tests ability to deal with part-whole relationships.

SOURCE: Wechsler Adult Intelligence Scale and Wechsler Adult Intelligence Scale-Revised. Copyright © 1955, 1981 by The Psychological Corporation. All rights reserved.

**FIGURE 11-3
The Wechsler Intelligence Scale for Children**
This scale uses modified versions of the tests in the adult scale, such as the block design test shown being taken by this child.

The best use of IQ seems to be close to Binet's original purpose: to identify those children who are most likely to profit from different types of schooling. In its original intent it was a great step forward. It could quickly sort children as to what kind of education they might need. Educators are greatly in Binet's debt for this. Notwithstanding, the IQ has taken on a meaning far beyond just another test for school achievement. It has come to mean a true assessment of intelligence. However, the IQ is just another test, not a measure of something essential about a person. How much we should rely on a test such as IQ as the sole measure of intelligence is a serious question.

Testing for General versus Specific Intelligence

Search for a General Intelligence

There has been a lot of effort expended on the search for a single, *general* intelligence. Charles Spearman's (1927) investigations sprang from his belief that general intelligence, which he called *g*, represented an entity related to "cerebral energy." Spearman assumed that a single, general intelligence would characterize each individual. Unfortunately, the scores on different mental tests are not close enough to calculate a single "quantity" of intelligence. Spearman, although quite brilliant, was too simplistic in his early analysis.

The notion of a single, general intelligence is too limited for an animal as complex as a human being. Too many things are considered "intelligent" to calculate a single number. Individuals are as different in the nature of their intelligence as they are in their memory, perceptions, and ability to learn. People have a great variety of abilities, and the abilities do not always relate to one another. One person may perform well on verbal tasks, while another may be good at fitting objects together; a third may write well. When children take several different tests of mental ability, some excel on some measures, others on different ones.

These and other findings have led psychologists to consider that there are many *different kinds* of abilities that make up intelligence.

The Search for Specific Intellectual Abilities

Going further than Spearman, Raymond Cattell (1971) has divided intelligence into two major kinds of abilities. **Fluid abilities** involve perception of the world and are thought to be genetically based and independent of culture. **Crystallized abilities** derive from *specific* cultural experiences. They represent the store of gradually accumulating knowledge: vocabulary, mathematics, and social reasoning.

Guilford and his colleagues (1971) conceive of intelligence as being a *very large set of independent abilities,* each different and distinct from the other. In Guilford's view the different mental factors are included under three categories:

1. *Contents* describe the information in the mind.
2. *Operations* are the working rules of the mind.
3. *Products* are units, systems, relationships, and so on that have to do with how things are related to one another in the mind.

This model may not be accurate in detail, but it is important in its general concept: a person's intelligence is best considered as a mosaic of specific intellectual abilities and talents that form an individual portrait of intelligence. For example, one person may be good at art and bad at math, another the reverse, and a third good or bad at both. One person is "smart" who picks the right stock, another "smart" who proposes a new theory. Intelligence is a judgment based on many *separate* abilities. People are much more individual in their assortment of characteristics than we normally give them credit for.

There are people with good memories for faces, and others who are good with names but not good with faces. There are people who are good at finding their way around in new surroundings, but who have trouble thinking abstractly. There are those who have great musical abilities but who have little intelligence in the area that Howard Gardner (1983) calls the "personal." Remember the comment, "You may know a lot about psychology, but you sure don't know anything about people!" This sums up many of the early approaches to the testing of intelligence.

People also differ in the way in which they *use* their talents. Some people seem able to keep many things in their minds at once, while others attend more deeply to one thing at a time. Cultures have radically differing approaches to the training and the cultivation of the mind.

The use of the Binet-type intelligence test has caused more controversy than any other product of psychology. The IQ tests are used to classify children in schools, and those who score low, 60 to 70, for example, may be placed in classes of "educable mentally retarded" (EMR). Here the scholastic program is much less challenging than that for people with higher IQs. Sometimes this division is warranted and humane. There are some severely retarded or disturbed people who could not make it in a traditional public school. However, much of the time, the standard tests discriminate against children whose backgrounds differ from the norm.

The issue of race and intelligence is a controversial topic that must be addressed squarely. We need to clarify the genetic basis of intelligence, understand what is meant by "intelligence" and "race," and analyze the extreme claims of some experts. These issues touch on everyone in society, of all skin colors, ages, and educational levels.

Inheritance of IQ and Intelligence

There *is* an inherited component to the elusive qualities we call intelligence. It is the nature of that inheritance that is in question. Compare the relationship of IQ to genetic similarity. If IQ is inherited, then the more similar people's genetic structures are, the more similar their IQs should be. Table 11-3 shows the correlation of IQ and genetic relationship. Note that the more genetically similar individuals are, the more similar are their IQs. Identical twins have an identical genetic

TABLE 11-3   IQ and Genetic Relationship

Relationship	Correlation
Identical twins	
Reared together	0.86
Reared apart	0.72
Fraternal twins	
Reared together	0.60
Siblings	
Reared together	0.47
Reared apart	0.24
Parent/child	0.40
Foster parent/child	0.31
Cousins	0.15

SOURCE: Bouchard & McGue, 1981.

The identical genetic makeup of monozygotic (identical) twins makes them uniquely valuable in research on the relative influence of heredity and environment factors on IQ.

makeup, and they also have the closest IQ resemblance. Next in similarity come fraternal twins and siblings; their similarity is less, but is still substantial. Parents and children also show a relationship, but as the genetic similarity decreases, so does the correspondence between their IQs.

Still, the environment has an overriding effect. Genetically related children reared together have much more similar IQs than similarly related children reared apart. The correlation of IQs of identical twins reared apart is 0.72; together it is 0.86. The correlation between foster parents and children is about 0.30, a good indicator that the environment is important.

A precise study of the IQs of adopted children compared the IQs of the biological parents with that of the adoptive parents (Horn, Loehlin, & Willerman, 1982). The relationship between the natural mother and the child was stronger (correlation = 0.32) than between the adoptive mother (0.19) or the adoptive father (0.17) and the child. This indicates a small but definite inherited component to IQ.

Problems with Studying Heredity and IQ

Most studies that attempt to relate heredity with IQ do seem to indicate *some* relationship between them, but the precise estimate of heritability of intelligence is still in great dispute. The studies themselves are fraught with problems and have been criticized on several grounds (Kamin, 1979).

Consider the problems of the adoptive studies and the studies of twins raised apart. Any precise estimate of heritability from these studies is wrong because adoptions are often not random. Usually, the environments of two separated twins are similar; sometimes they are raised by relatives, often close relatives. Many times twins know each other, and know that they are twins.

Adoption agencies go to great lengths to place children in homes that are not only stable and middle class, but "compatible" with their biological parents.

Many times a black family adopts a black child, an Oriental family adopts an Oriental one, and so on (Kamin, 1979). This matching of children and family is laudable from the point of view of the child and the family, but it makes precise measurement of the heritability of IQ very difficult. The adoptive family is often similar to the biological family. Thus, the influence of the similar environment makes the observed correlation between the IQs of the biological parents and that of the child appear greater than it is.

Matters are made even worse by cases of fraudulent studies. Much of the evidence amassed in support of the genetic viewpoint came from Sir Cyril Burt in England. Burt's work with his two colleagues was, for a time, the basis for many respectable scientists' positions. Burt had apparently documented a strong association between inheritance and IQ. But the work turned out to be a complete fraud. Burt had made up whole studies and had even invented his two famous colleagues!

Overall, it is very difficult to estimate precisely the exact relationship between heritability and the IQ. Jensen (1980) believes that 81 percent of IQ is inherited, but another important study estimates the heritability of the biological mother's IQ with the adopted child at only 25 percent.

Most investigators agree there is some heritability of IQ; indeed, it would be surprising if there were *no* genetic component to IQ. The information encoded in the genes could fill approximately 1,700 full-sized pages. It seems reasonable that some of that information might relate to the reasoning and problem-solving skills that are so important in human evolution.

Racial Differences in IQ

No issue in psychology is more controversial than the question of inherited differences in intelligence among the different races. The evidence is straightforward, but it has been subject to different interpretations. The average IQ for black Americans is 85 to 90, whereas for whites it is 100.

In 1916 Lewis Terman of Stanford, the adaptor of the Stanford–Binet test, stated that "high grade moronity [was] very common among Spanish, Indian, and Mexican families . . . and also among Negroes."

In a celebrated article in 1969, Arthur Jensen argued that compensatory education programs that attempt to improve the intelligence of black children fail because the difference in IQ is innate. Richard Herrnstein thinks that the United States will eventually develop into a "meritocracy" based on heredity.

> As the wealth and complexity of human society grow, there will be precipitated out of the mass of humanity a low capacity [group of people] that . . . cannot compete for success and achievement and are more likely to be born to parents who have similarly failed. . . . The tendency to be unemployed may run in the genes of the family about as certainly as bad teeth do now. (Herrnstein, 1973)

Every ethnic group that has migrated to the United States has been the subject of these arguments (Willerman, 1979). When the descendants of the people of the Italian Renaissance first came to the United States, they too were considered to be of inferior intelligence.

Misconceptions about Race and IQ

The claim that certain races are *genetically* inferior in intelligence rests on several inaccurate assumptions:

1. *The IQ score is intelligence.* The IQ is a *test score* developed by Terman from Binet's test. It was designed to discriminate groups of children who could and could not profit from normal schooling. The idea that intellect is a *composite* of different abilities replaces the simpler early idea. There is no single number that can adequately indicate a complex human intelligence.

2. *IQ represents a fixed capacity.* Change in the environment strongly affects IQ. A severely impoverished early experience stunts intellectual growth. However, when children in an impoverished environment get more stimulation, their IQ increases. The IQ is not a measure of a fixed aptitude, but rather a measure of *current achievement* in certain tasks. The quality of education, coaching on test taking, and improvements in motivation and in facility with language all increase test scores. Less educated people score less well on IQ tests. A low score probably means that the individual needs some compensatory education, as Binet originally intended.

3. *Racial differences exist and are important.* The division of the human species into races was first formally classified by Linneaus (1707–1778). He believed that races differed not only in color but also in personality characteristics. However, Linneaus's "racial" classifications were essentially arbitrary. There are many ways to categorize and classify human beings into so-called races. One could differentiate them on the basis of height, hair color, blood type, eye color, hand or head size, and much more. A person's skin color tells you nothing more about intelligence than hair color.

See Chapter 17, section on Prejudice.

   The problem is the nature of the mind doing the judging: as in attractiveness and personal perception, surface appearances dominate. In truth, the major characteristic differences between races are skin deep: they consist of superficial adaptations such as skin color, eye folds, and sweat glands. There is no evidence of differences in brain size, shape, organization, or structure between races.

4. *The difference between blacks and whites is due to heredity.* There is a profound confusion between the ideas that genes can influence IQ and the inference that the matter is "racial." Just because individual mental predispositions can be inherited does not mean that the characteristics of a specific group are inherited. *People get their genes from their parents, not from a group.* There is no way to extrapolate from individual differences to group differences. There are many times more differences among individuals within a "racial group" than there are among group averages.

See Chapter 4, section on Genetics: Influence on Evolution.

Investigations of Racial Differences and IQ

The evidence is scanty regarding there being any real differences between "black" and "white" genes with respect to IQ. A study of heredity and IQ compared the ancestry of a group of blacks with their IQ scores. If whites are innately more intelligent than blacks, then blacks having more "white" genes should have higher IQs. This was not the case: more white genes did not increase IQ (Scarr, 1981).

Consider the results of interracial marriages, in which the genes for intelligence should be approximately equal. It has been found, however, that the IQs are not equal (Scarr, 1981). Children of a black father and a white mother have higher IQs than children of a white father and a black mother. This only makes sense if we consider the environment: White women on the average seem to talk to their children more than black mothers do. The home environment, especially the mother–child relationship, seems to have an important influence on IQ.

Many other factors can influence IQ. Educators in Israel noted large IQ differences between Jews of European ancestry and Jews from Arabic countries. European Jews scored higher. These differences were larger than the black versus white differences in the United States. However, when both European and Arabic Jewish children are raised communally on the kibbutzim, where they get the same opportunities and education, the IQ differences disappeared and the children's IQ rose to average above 100 (Smilansky, 1974).

There are many other influences on IQ in the United States. Early experiences and nutrition have long-lasting effects on intelligence; environmental deprivations, if continuous, can be devastating to the child. Blacks on the average live in poorer environments and have more nutritional deficiencies than whites. The larger the size of the family, the more IQ decreases (Zajonc, 1986); blacks on the whole have larger families than whites. Even when blacks have the same income as whites, they often cannot live where they choose or go to the schools they choose.

There are many reasons to doubt that there are *important* genetic differences in intelligence among racial and ethnic groups. Intelligence is not just a single IQ score, and it is still not adequately defined. Furthermore, although biological differences among races are superficial, environmental differences are profound, at least in the United States.

It is not productive to conclude that blacks are *genetically* inferior in intelligence to whites. Asian students obtain better grades than whites in schools in the United States and score higher on IQ tests. Is it productive to conclude that Asians are superior to whites?

It is more productive for all concerned to use the concept of IQ to enrich the environment of children who score low on intelligence tests. Psychologists are working to develop other measures of "intelligence" than the IQ alone. Perhaps we should return to Binet's earliest notion: to use the IQ solely to aid children whose environment has been deficient and to identify those with organic deficits.

Sandra Scarr

M any programs and studies attempt to develop various components of intelligence. Experiences in the environment seem to be the important factor that affects the IQ differences between whites and blacks in the United States. Fortunately, the environment can be changed: improved nutrition and more stimulating environments have systematically been shown to increase IQ test scores. Preschools and Head Start programs in the United States and an ambitious program in Israel are currently attempting to increase the IQs of disadvantaged children.

ENHANCING INTELLIGENCE

Influence of Nutrition

Different brain structures underlie different parts of the mind, and its growth and development influence our array of mental abilities. During gestation and in the first year of life, the brain is the fastest-growing organ in the body. It consumes nutrients at twice the rate of the adult brain and is thus heavily dependent upon dietary intake. A severe deficiency in nutrition in the very first months of pregnancy can cause lasting and irremediable damage to the brain. Severe childhood malnutrition can produce many effects lasting seven or eight years (Kagan, 1984).

Some effects of early deprivation, however, can be overcome by later improvements in nutrition. A specific program of nutritional supplements can increase IQ. In one study, iron and B-complex vitamins were given to one group of pregnant black women, while another group received a placebo. When the children were 4 years old, the mean IQ of those whose mothers had received supplements was 102. Those whose diets were unsupplemented had an average IQ of 94 (Harrell et al., 1956).

In cases where there is a specific dietary deficiency, food supplements can increase IQ. A group of students deficient in ascorbic acid were regularly given some orange juice. In six months the IQs of those who had been low in ascorbic acid increased an average of 3.5 points. There was no change in IQ for a control group who had no ascorbic acid deficiency.

Nutrition has a profound effect on the brain both in its development and in its day-to-day operation. Food affects neurotransmission within hours of being eaten. Improvements in nutrition could have a great effect on intelligence. Perhaps differences between what two individuals have eaten within hours of taking an IQ test could explain some differences in IQ scores.

Stimulation in Early Experience

Most of the brain's growth (75 percent of its weight) occurs outside the womb. Therefore, certain early experiences can have a strong effect on brain growth and, consequently, on intelligence. Rats reared in "enriched" environments have enlarged brain size, as measured by the depth of the cortex. Cortical growth can continue into very old age if the environment remains stimulating. The brain is quite responsive to changes in the outside environment. Thus, changes in early experience can affect the brain and perhaps intelligence.

For instance, some rural Guatemalan children are reared in windowless huts, have no toys, and are rarely spoken to for the first year of life; they show extreme retardation at the end of the year (Kagan & Klein, 1973). When the environment is changed and they are allowed to explore, communicate, and eat better, their development begins to proceed more normally, although it takes many years for them to catch up to children whose first year of life was more stimulating. There is much less difference between them and normal children at 10 years of age than at 1 year of age (Kagan, 1978).

The human brain is remarkably resilient. Early traumas and deprivations can be overcome if later experience is more benign. Changed diet can overcome the effects of poor nutrition on intelligence. Intelligence, which suffers in a deprived environment, improves in a normal environment.

Orphanage Studies

Orphanages can have a negative effect on a child's mind. They are often bleak places that offer little human contact and minimal external stimulation. In a Lebanese orphanage, the average IQ of the orphans was 63; in a well-baby clinic,

the average was 101 (Dennis & Najarian, 1957). When the orphans were simply propped up in their cribs for an hour a day, they could see what was going on and showed dramatic improvement.

Howard Skeels (1966) decided to find out whether stimulation and attention (tender loving care) is important in the development of intelligence. He placed 13 orphanage children with an average IQ of 64 (range 35–85) in an institution for retarded adults. An older woman "adopted" each orphan. All the adoptees became favorites of and were doted on by the patients and staff. A control group of children between 1½ and 6 years of age remained in the same or similar orphanage. The control group's IQ *dropped* an average of 20 IQ points, while the "adopted" orphans *gained* an average of 28 points.

Programs to Develop IQ

General Enrichment

Skeels's results encouraged development of various enrichment programs aimed at increasing IQ. For example, many parents now send their children to preschools in the hope that such early training will enhance intellectual development. Children in preschools typically show an initial increase in IQ followed by a decline to the norm at around the second grade. Children in programs that emphasize only academic skills are most likely to show a later decline in IQ. Those preschools that emphasize *curiosity* and *self-motivation,* such as the Montessori schools, show the greatest long-term gains. Clearly, there are different parts of the mental structure that develop by different means. For example, students from well-motivated families will test as more intelligent than students from families who prize other abilities, such as serving others.

Head Start. In 1965 a large-scale experimental program of preschool enrichment began in underprivileged areas called **Head Start.** It was one of many

The environmental deprivations experienced by children raised in poverty or in institutions can produce extreme retardation. But if the quality of their environment is improved, such children begin to show more normal development and they can eventually catch up to those who have enjoyed the benefits of a stimulating environment and a good diet from the first year of life.

FIGURE 11-4
Head Start Program
Children in the Head Start preschool enrichment program tend on the average to get better grades and score higher on achievement tests. Although there is some controversy over whether their IQs increase, they do show improved health and nutrition and they benefit from their parents' increased involvement in their education.

general enrichment programs that sought to increase general stimulation and interaction with a child. All over the country many preschools began trying to enrich the environment of 4-year-olds, particularly racial minorities. There were many different curricula at each Head Start center (Figure 11-4). This ensured that programs might more closely fit a community's needs, and research could discover which programs were the most successful. The results followed a pattern similar to the study of more traditional preschools. There is an initial increase in intellectual functioning, followed by a decline almost back down to the level of the norm (Berger, 1980).

A major setback to the Head Start program came in 1969 when the Westinghouse Report claimed that Head Start did not work because children in the program showed no improvement in IQ over non–Head Start children. That report prompted Arthur Jensen to conclude that blacks cannot benefit from an improved environment. Jensen proposed that the reason Head Start did not work was because blacks are inferior intellectually to whites and that it was a waste of time and money to try to develop compensatory education programs. However, while Jensen's view has gained some acceptance, it is extreme and shared by very few people in psychology or in education.

With respect to the original goals of Head Start, it *has* been effective. Extremes of cultural differences and deprivations can't be completely overcome by a few hours a day of enrichment during one summer. Two major goals of Head Start are improvements in health and nutrition and encouraging parental involvement in their children's education. Also, the programs are different in different areas and are of uneven quality. However, children in Head Start programs on the average get better grades at school and score higher on achievement tests. In addition, the evaluation of the program probably had unrealistic expectations. The Westinghouse study evaluated the Head Start program after only a few years of operation while it was still in a very experimental phase.

Toy Demonstrators Program. Successful interventions to improve IQ, at least in the United States, can change the pattern of mother–child interaction. The most successful of these was devised by Phyllis Levenstein (1970). In this program, a "toy demonstrator" visits mother and children at home. Usually she visits twice a week for two years, beginning when the child is between 24 and 28 months old. The visitor brings a toy or a book as a gift (Figure 11-5). She demonstrates to the mother how to play games with the child, especially those involving language.

The IQs of the children involved in this program increased during the two years of the program. The improvement lasted for a long time. Three years after the program ended, the "toy demonstrator" children had IQs 13 points higher than a comparable group not visited. Further, nonprofessionals were equally successful as demonstrators as the original ones who had been professionals. Some of the first mothers who had been visited later joined the project.

The success of this program is probably because many intellectual skills important in schooling depend on language. Language skills develop within the family. The mother spends much more time with her child than do teachers. She is the primary "teacher" of language (at least in the pretelevision age) (Bruner, 1978). *Improving mother–child interaction seems to be an important intervention in increasing intelligence.*

Instrumental Enrichment

In addition to the general enrichment programs discussed thus far, many new programs to improve intelligence are in the works. **Instrumental enrichment (I.E.)** is a recent experimental approach in Israel. Reuven Feuerstein (1980), the developer of I.E., makes several important distinctions and points out certain concepts that may well aid in the effort to improve intelligence.

FIGURE 11-5
Toy Demonstrator's Program
Increasing the meaningful interaction between mothers and children—especially in games involving the development of language skills—seems to contribute to increasing a child's intelligence.

1. *There is a difference between* **cultural deprivation** *and* **cultural differences.** Individuals who are culturally *deprived* lack something in their own culture; those who are culturally *different* may belong to a culture that is different from the one they are living in. Cultural differences can lead to a deficiency or an improvement in the *content* of intelligence, while cultural deprivation in this analysis can lead to a deficiency in the *structure* of the mind. Testers often confuse these differences. A wrong answer on a test by the culturally different person might simply be due to not knowing the language, whereas a culturally deprived person may lack the reasoning and thinking skills necessary to answer. These two varieties of mistakes are very different and indicate very different needs of the person taking the test.

2. *Intelligence has to do with making adaptive responses in new situations.* The Binet-type tests are tests of current *achievement* rather than tests of an underlying mental structure. A testee should *learn* something during the test rather than simply recalling information. Instrumental enrichment thus attempts to measure the learning ability of the individual directly.

3. *Cognitive Modifiability.* The ability to *change* one's mental structure and contents is called **cognitive modifiability.** Learning, for instance, involves a change in contents; thinking involves a change in the structure of information in consciousness. Since the function of all the mental processes is adaptation to the environment, it should also be the focus of testing.

4. *Mediated Learning Experience.* Interaction with people in their environment gives children **mediated learning experience.** This means that other people, usually parents or siblings, interpret experience and give meaning to events. Consider a child who sees a growling dog and approaches it, but the mother says "Watch out!" The child learns to avoid growling animals through its mother's *mediation.* "The mediator selects the stimuli that are most appropriate and then frames, filters, and schedules them; . . . he determines the appearance or disappearance of certain stimuli and ignores others" (Feuerstein, 1980).

Learning Potential Assessment Device (LPAD). The main target group for instrumental enrichment programs is people who are below the norm on standard tests of intellectual skills like IQ. The aim is remediation of retarded individuals. When testing retarded people, the aim is to identify their specific deficits and point to possible remediation. This is the subject of the **learning potential assessment device (LPAD).** The LPAD differs from other tests in the way it is used and scored, but is similar in the tasks employed. The premise of LPAD design is that if a test is to measure human intelligence, it must be representative of real life. In life we are rarely called upon to recall one paragraph or select a number that fits into a progression, but we are often called upon, in collaboration with other people, to learn. The "tester" in the LPAD is involved in teaching the retarded performer new tasks: the measure of success is how well, under these conditions, the person learns and modifies his or her abilities — that is, demonstrates "cognitive modifiability" (Figure 11-6). This is done in a "test – train – retest" paradigm (how the testee improves or gets worse between the first test and the retest). The tasks are varieties of "content free" intelligence tests. The training consists of exercise sheets designed to guide the testee into learning successful strategies for solving the problem. The tester in the LPAD situation is not an examiner but a "committed teacher." When the student makes a new response or tries a different approach to a problem, the teacher tries to make it happen again.

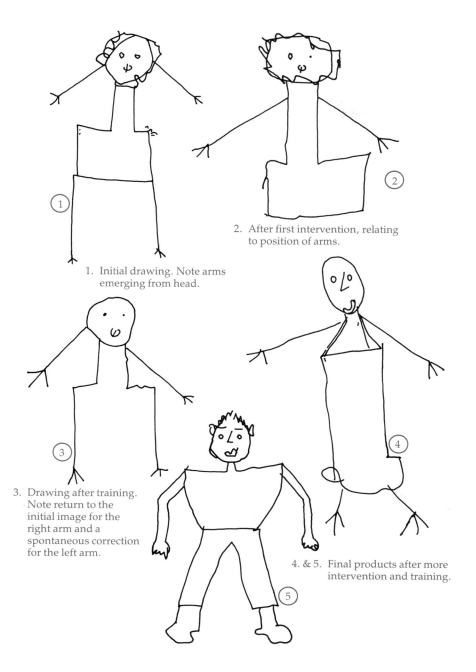

FIGURE 11-6
Instrumental Enrichment
Using LPAD
LPAD procedures helped an intellectually retarded, culturally deprived 10-year-old show progressive improvement in drawing a human figure.
(After Feuerstein, 1979)

1. Initial drawing. Note arms emerging from head.

2. After first intervention, relating to position of arms.

3. Drawing after training. Note return to the initial image for the right arm and a spontaneous correction for the left arm.

4. & 5. Final products after more intervention and training.

Assessment of Instrumental Enrichment. While general enrichment programs improve overall performance on intelligence tests among people who are substandard, the instrumental enrichment program attempts to pinpoint the *process* of enrichment. The program is designed to provide remedial mediated learning experiences so that retarded children can learn how, in the future, to learn from their own experience. The specific program consists of a wide variety of tasks to be completed under the guidance of a specially trained instructor. The tasks range from the inference of geometric figures in dot patterns to spatial orientations to syllogisms.

How well does it work? The appropriate comparison for instrumental enrichment is a program of general enrichment. With a sample of Israeli children, the I.E. program shows significant, though not immense, improvement over controls in a general enrichment program, using as assessments the LPAD and other measures such as the Stanford-Binet test. An assessment of I.E. programs by the Israeli military reveals impressive gains. The results show that, after I.E., formerly retarded service-age youths are equal to controls from the general population (Feuerstein & Rand, 1977).

ANALYSIS OF THE COMPONENTS OF THE MIND

To understand the mind we need to analyze the different components of thought and intelligence. This type of analysis derives from the knowledge of brain function, sensation, perception, learning, memory, and cognition. It is perhaps the most promising new trend in the difficulties of understanding intelligence. Several new all-encompassing theories of the mind and intelligence are presented here.

Triarchic Theory of Intelligence

Robert J. Sternberg's **triarchic theory of intelligence** consists of three parts. The first is intelligence and the internal world of the individual; second is the point of critical involvement of intelligence; and third is how the external world affects intelligence. Sternberg is attempting to discover which aspects of intelligence are universal and which are relative to individuals and groups.

Information-Processing Components

The first part of Sternberg's theory considers **information-processing components.** These are the mental mechanisms that translate sensory or mental representations (Sternberg, 1985, 1986). According to Sternberg, there are three such components:

1. *Metacomponents.* These are "executive" or "higher order processes" such as planning or evaluating that are responsible for working out task strategy. They keep in touch with the other components and modify the strategy as the need arises.

   There is a pervasive Western assumption that speed is a measure of intelligence. The "smart is fast" assumption has influenced most intelligence tests. Sternberg calls this function "speed selection"—the ability to judge the appropriate speed at which to think or act depending on the situation.

   Everyday experience, according to Sternberg, supports this view. We might need to make instant decisions when driving a car, but snap judgments are not necessarily always intelligent judgments. For example, it is smart to alphabetize bookshelves to avoid wasting hours looking for a title on a disorganized shelf. When studying for an exam we might give more time to reading important passages and less time reading passages that are less likely to be asked.

2. *Performance components.* These components are used in performing tasks and carrying out decisions made by the metacomponents. Binet tests mea-

sure these, but they are not adequately differentiated. Tests do evaluate one type of performance component, inductive reasoning, which includes inferring or applying relationships, but people use many other performance components in carrying out tasks. Linguistic and spatial strategies are two types of performance components people use in solving problems.

Developing a method to test more performance components would be an important diagnostic tool for the assessment and improvement of intelligence. It would show up individual weaknesses and strengths. It would reveal the difficulties experienced by someone who reasoned well, but who had difficulty reading or lacked education. Existing tests that result in a total score hide rather than elucidate a person's strengths and weaknesses.

3. *Knowledge–acquisition components.* These work to help us learn new things. They assess previous experience relevant to the task at hand, rather than the quantity of experience one has had in the area. An individual may have the knowledge required, but if he fails to employ this experience in a new context, he is less intelligent. If he has the same amount of experience as another person, but has learned more from it, he is more intelligent. More intelligent people are better able to acquire information in context, as shown in vocabulary tests.

Coping and Automatizing

The ability to deal with novelty and the ability to cope in extraordinary situations are measures of intelligence. Sternberg describes this process in terms of "insights" that are of three kinds.

1. *Selective encoding* — distinguishing between irrelevant and relevant information. A less intelligent scientist than Fleming would merely have thrown away the spoiled culture, bemoaning a failed experiment. Fleming noticed the mold had killed the bacteria and used this to provide the basis for his discovery of penicillin.
2. *Selective combination* — taking this encoded information and processing it in a novel but productive way. Recall the theory of evolution: it was Darwin's ability to combine information available for a long time that produced the theory of natural selection.
3. *Selective comparison* — the ability to relate new information to old information. The chemist Kekule dreamed of a snake who bit its tail. When he awoke, he realized that his dreamed image formed the geometric shape for the structure of the benzene ring.

Sternberg proposes that the extent of an individual's ability to automatize information processing is a measure of intelligence. A complex task works by automatizing the operations involved. The ability to automatize information may frequently affect the ability to deal with novel tasks or situations. The more efficient the person is at the one, the more the resources there are left over for the other. This experiential view reveals difficulties in judging intelligence, particularly across members of different sociocultural groups. A fair comparison between groups must have equivalent degrees of novelty and automatization of test items and comparable processes and strategies.

Adaptability

The theory defines intelligence as "mental activity involved in purposive adaptation to shaping of, and selection of, real-world environments relevant to one's life." Accordingly, we can only judge intelligence within a given culture. Again, the shortcomings of our ability to measure intelligence appear with regard to adaptive skills. For example, one cannot ignore the ingenuity used by retarded individuals to camouflage their problems. One individual who could not tell time wore a broken watch and would often look at it. He would then say to a passerby, "Excuse me. I see my watch is broken; could you tell me the correct time?"

Adaptability is also culture dependent. Being on time can be maladaptive in cultures where everyone is late. According to U.S. standards, sorting things "intelligently" is done by taxonomic category: Fruit sorts with fruit, animals with animals, cars with cars, and so on. The Kpelle tribe in Nigeria prefer a functional sorting, but are easily able to sort our way when asked to sort the way "stupid" people would!

There are instances in which it is actually maladaptive to be adaptive. One might prefer to leave a boring job rather than adapt to it. Intelligence also enables us to shape our environment in preference to adapting to it. Rather than divorce, a couple might decide to reshape their environment.

Intelligence is not a single thing: it comprises a very wide array of cognitive and other skills. We ought to define these skills and to learn how best to assess and train them, not combine them into a single but possibly meaningless number. Many educators welcome Sternberg's views as a step toward more of a "real world" intelligence test. Many psychologists think it is not entirely adequate as to portray the mind's operations.

The ingenuity of some retarded adults to adapt to the real-world environment enables many of them to fit well into the mainstream of society.

Frames of Mind

Another view expands on Sternberg's divisions of intelligence. Howard Gardner postulates six major "frames of mind." He believes that the many mental activities of human beings are separate and potentially independent abilities. His divisions are summarized here (Gardner, 1983):

Linguistic intelligence. The fundamental use of language, especially creative language, as in poetry.

Musical intelligence. One of the most striking early talents. Composing the sounds of music has a logic of its own, quite distinct from that of language.

Logical-mathematical intelligence. The ability to manipulate quantities, which is separate from the abilities of language and music. Mathematicians often show their talents early in life as well.

Spatial intelligence. The ability to design and build a table, to assemble a model airplane, to design an office floor plan, or to find your way around town. All of these are independent of the "intellectual" abilities above. This spatial ability is most likely linked to the right hemisphere of the brain.

Bodily-Kinesthetic Intelligence. The ability to use one's body in skilled ways for expressive purposes, like a dancer, including the capacity to work skillfully with objects using the fine motor movements of the fingers and hands, like an artist. People with a high degree of "body intelligence" may excel in sports or dance, but this ability does not necessarily preclude intelligence in other areas.

Personal intelligence. The ability to read another's feelings and intentions. Human beings are bonded to one another from birth, thus, this ability is very important. Is he angry? Will I hurt her if I say that? Is this a good time to ask for a raise? Our survival in the modern world depends on an understanding of other people's intentions and feelings. As we will see in the chapter on psychotherapy, some people are good "empathetic" judges of others and some are not. Gardner considers this ability to be a separate form of intelligence.

Gardner's theory is important for psychologists because it is the first modern cognitive approach that has broadened the concept of IQ. The inclusion of personal and spatial intelligences further extends the view of the mind. However, a focus on such high-level abilities such as music and mathematics is not conducive to an analysis of the mind because these are not typical human activities. More fundamental are the ordinary objects of our perception, physiology, and cognition, as discussed throughout this book.

Multimind: A Description of Mind and Intelligence

My own theory of the mind is called **multimind.** It is an attempt to reconcile the divisions of the mind, the different selves, as well as the obvious changeability of the mind. It does not compete with a theory of intelligence testing like Sternberg. Instead, it provides a summary of many of the topics in this book regarding brain–mind relationships and the diverse calculations within the brain "behind the scenes" of experiences.

The mental apparatus is an amalgam of different circuits, of different priorities, and even of the evolutionary developments of different eras. The human brain,

See Chapter 1, "box" on Some Universal Psychological Characteristics: Priorities and Policies.

whose structures underlie the functioning of the mind, is constructed of a variety of elements. It is a collection of circuits piled atop one another, each developed to serve a short-term purpose in millennia past. Evolution does not, unfortunately, work for the long term, but rather for the immediate exigencies of survival for individual animals.

The system of the mind works by "wheeling in" and "wheeling out" ideas and schemata in consciousness. This control system is associated with a person's sense of "self." It probably resides in the frontal lobes (Nauta et al., 1973; Ornstein, 1986). It is not an omnipotent manipulator, but a semiorganized center in the mind.

According to the multimind theory, the "mental operating system" of the mind is divided into different levels of operation (Figure 11-7). Some are fixed and rigid, some flexible, some innate, some learned. Some have direct access to consciousness, while others do not.

Reflexes and Basic Neural Transformation

The most elementary level is the most similar in almost all animals. This includes our base reflexes, such as jerking our hand away from fire, and *basic neural processes*. These processes transform incoming information from its "raw" form to a form manageable by the brain. We don't "see" anything directly.

See Chapter 5, section on Vision.

Here's what happens first in the brain. Information, say, electromagnetic radiation in the visible light band, must first be transduced into the language of the brain, that is, neural firing. The retina and the visual system do this. Although this process in all sensory systems is basic and relatively hardwired, they seem like "miracles," but ones that occur each moment of our lives.

FIGURE 11-7
Multimind Theory
According to Ornstein's multimind theory, the mental system of operation is divided into levels of operation which "wheel" in and out somewhat independently to operate thoughts and actions, depending on the situation. (From Ornstein, 1986)

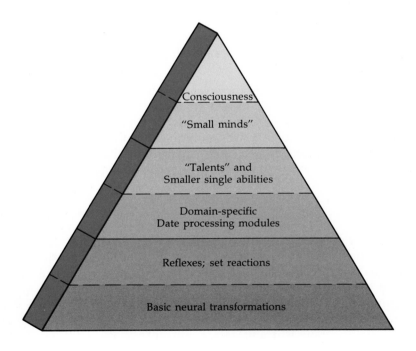

Consciousness

"Small minds"

"Talents" and
Smaller single abilities

Domain-specific
Date processing modules

Reflexes; set reactions

Basic neural transformations

Modules and Talents

After the "miracles," the transformed information must be further converted into something sensible. For example, various pressure waves in the air transform into the neural language of sound. How does the mind determine what is being said, or if anything is being said? Likewise, how does it know that an apple is red, or that an apple is there at all? This occurs in each sensory system by separate data processing *modules* which are probably specific to each sense. These modules allow us to make distinctions among sounds, sights, smells, touches, and tastes.

In these modules extraction of meaning from converted sounds, sights, and so on takes place. It may be simple, such as the consistent perception of red color under bright sunlight versus dusk. It may be perceptual, such as the realization that a building that is now blocking the view is the same building that appeared as a speck from three miles away. All these perceptions and more probably have their own private special-purpose computational modules designed to extract information. These are the "quick and dirty" analysis systems of the mind. In my view, they are not flexible, but they do a lot of automatic "grunt" work for us.

What I call the *talents* and similar abilities are slower but brighter than the modules. They are general and flexible and have much more capacity for change than do the modules. While we "automatically" respond to much of what goes on in the world through our reflexes and modules, at the same time we retain several higher level capacities to evaluate and act upon and sometimes to override the automatic analysis. These capacities make up our individual abilities and talents.

But this is where the modern understanding of the mind comes in: we do not have access to all of our talents at once. *Our consciousness manipulates only a few items at a time.* For example, although the "self" retains a privileged place in the mind, it is more isolated than we ordinarily imagine. It is just another independent talent of the mind, located in a specific portion of the brain. It has less special access to other equally important parts of the brain than we think! We never operate with a "full deck" but only with a small selection of our total mental apparatus at any one time. This means that *all our faculties of mind are never available at once.* Thus, at any given time we are both narrow-minded and much more changeable than we might otherwise believe of ourselves.

Small Minds and Consciousness

The mind is made up of many individual "small minds" that become active at different times and are thus specific to different situations and which change quickly. One moment your mind might contain a set reaction, such as a food avoidance "program." You might find yourself not wanting to eat food in a restaurant in which you were poisoned. Or a general policy might swing in: you become extra careful about the chemical plant in your area after reading about the disaster in Bhopal, India. At one moment one talent like talking may fill the small mind, or the current small mind might join different talents or may involve a piece of each talent. It is not a consistent system.

Most likely there are different varieties of learning and knowledge that coexist simultaneously within the mind and different accesses to intelligence. It is the job of consciousness to select the appropriate one. Most people think that once a person has learned something he knows it. A view that recognizes the different components of mind would ask, "Where is the knowledge in the mind?" *Something learned in one small mind doesn't mean that the whole mind knows it.* New learning, in school, in political ideas, or in psychotherapy, is not always a matter of just developing new abilities or skills. Often it is more of a matter of *using* that ability ("wheeling in" the right small mind) at a given time. Many writers find that they can't sit down to write a book, but gaily go on writing other things all the time! One well-known writing instructor advises these writers to write their books as they would a letter!

The theory of a multiple mind, which I call *multimind*, may help us understand many mysteries of the mind. Why do we misjudge people so often? Why are we so inconsistent? Why do moods, once they occur, spread to color other thoughts, then pass away? Why are people sometimes obsessed with things? Why do people act and speak so unusually when they are drunk, or angry, or elated? Because various "small minds" control each of these thoughts, actions, and functions at different times. It is not a neat or an accurate system, this mental "system" of ours. It is not predominantly rational. The *same* neural processes that were originally developed to judge brightness, taste, and weight now judge prices, politics, and personalities.

Intelligence and the Multimind

The mental system of human beings and other animals simplifies and "makes sense" out of an enormous amount of shifting and chaotic external and internal information. It helped us and our ancestors to adapt to the world well enough to survive. It didn't have to be perfect. It is best understood as a system evolved to have *extreme sensitivity to recent information*. It simplifies by registering only sharp changes in the information reaching it, so it has the ability to organize many bits of information into simple meaningful patterns, which allow us to act quickly.

The important component lacking in intelligence tests is the "wheeling and dealing" aspect of intelligence. Just because we have one ability does not mean that we will use it in the proper circumstance! Each person's intelligence is best considered as a *mosaic of specific intellectual abilities and talents that form an individual portrait of intelligence.*

Transforming information, modular analysis, interpreting, and judgments operate "behind the scenes" of the mind. Each of us is aware of the specific contents of the mind, but we are most often unaware of the wheeling and dealing, the assembling and disassembling of the mind's work. I hope the analysis presented so far in this book has made some of the complexities of your own mind more familiar.

SUMMARY

1. Intelligence and the nature of the mind has always been a difficult problem to define. Not only do different societies have their own concepts of intelligence, but different individuals have different ideas of what it is. One definition that is most useful is from David Wechsler: intelligence is the ability to understand the world and to cope with the challenges of the environment.

2. Alfred Binet laid out an important approach to studying intelligence that included several insights: (a) He felt that abilities of intelligent students, such as comprehension

and reasoning, should be directly tested. (b) He made intelligence testing applicable to large numbers of children by sorting them into bright, average, and below average ranks. (c) He recognized that as children age, their intellectual abilities increase. The brightest 3-year-old is hardly a match for an average 9-year-old. Therefore, age is critical in testing intelligence.

3. The intelligence quotient (IQ) was originally defined as the mental age divided by the chronological age times 100. The modern Stanford–Binet intelligence test uses an efficient and precise statistical measure of a student's score, called the deviation IQ. It scores individuals according to their relationship to their age group's average score on the test. The current test is now standardized with a norm of 100 with a standard deviation of 16. An individual who scores one standard deviation above the norm thus has an IQ of 116.

4. The primary usefulness of IQ tests seems to be close to Binet's original intention. It sorts children on skills that our culture values and identifies those who are likely to profit from schools. The IQ does appear to discriminate better at the low rather than the high end of the scale. Many people have criticized the IQ test as too heavily relied upon as the sole measure of intelligence, yet it remains the *single* best instrument for measuring the ability to do well in school.

5. One of the first questions in analyzing intelligence is whether it is a general faculty, that is, a trait characteristic of an individual. Spearman used *factor analysis* to determine if there was a general intelligence or *g*. Such notions of a single general intelligence are probably too limited to characterize the diversities of human beings. In contrast, Cattell divides intelligence into two major *kinds* of abilities. (a) *Fluid abilities* involve the perception and registration of the world and are genetically based and independent of cultural learning. (b) *Crystallized abilities* are derived from specific cultural experiences. They represent the store of gradually accumulating knowledge.

6. There is much concern with the question of how much intelligence is genetically based. Studies that attempt to measure the heritability of intelligence disagree. Even if there is a genetic basis for intelligence or specific intelligence skills, this does not necessarily mean that one race or another is superior or inferior in these traits. People get their genes from their parents, not from a group. In the United States there can be great differences between the races in early nutrition, early environment, and culture. It is unwise to conclude from current evidence that there are any significant differences in intelligence between racial and ethnic groups.

7. Because of extreme differences in the early environment of different groups, psychologists are turning their attention to ways to change the environment and thus intellectual abilities. Among areas now being investigated are nutrition and more stimulating early environments. Preschools and Head Start programs in the United States and recent programs in Israel and Venezuela are currently attempting to increase IQ.

8. The effects of severe malnutrition in childhood can last many years, but some effects of early deprivation can be overcome by later improvements in nutrition. Lack of stimulation in early experience also has a profound effect on intelligence, but can be overcome. Rural Guatemalan children, reared with little stimulation, show extreme retardation at the end of their first year, but when they are allowed to explore, communicate, and eat better, development begins to proceed more normally.

9. A successful program to improve intelligence attempts to change the pattern of mother–child interaction. In this program a "toy demonstrator" visits mothers and

children at home twice a week and brings a toy or book as a gift and demonstrates to the mother how to play language games with the child. IQs of the children increased during the two years of the program, but more important, the effect lasted for a long time.

10. One new and innovative attempt to increase intelligence is *instrumental enrichment*. It includes these concepts. (a) There is a difference between *cultural deprivation* and *cultural differences*. Individuals who are culturally deprived lack something in their own culture. Those who are culturally different may belong to a culture that is different from the one they are living in. (b) Intelligence has to do with making *adaptive* responses in new situations. Binet tests evaluate current achievement rather than the underlying mental structure. The testee learns something during the test rather than just recalling information. (c) *Cognitive modifiability* is the ability to change one's mental structure and contents. (d) Interaction with people provides children with a *mediated learning experience*. This means that others interpret information about events in the world.

11. The *learning potential assessment device* (LPAD) involves a testee learning something new in the presence of a tester. The premise of the LPAD is that, in life, people rarely recall a paragraph or select a number that fits into a progression. People often have to learn in collaboration with other people.

12. Modern analyses of intelligence attempt to relate it to knowledge about the mind and to analyze the components of mental abilities. Sternberg's *triarchic theory* of intelligence consists of three parts: intelligence and the internal world of the individual which includes information-processing components; the point of critical involvement of intelligence; and intelligence and the external world. Gardner postulates six separate and possibly independent mental abilities: linguistic, musical, logical, spatial, bodily, and personal.

13. Ornstein's *multimind* model attempts to describe the workings of the entire "mental operating system." At the lowest level are the reflexes, then come the transformation processes of sensation. Above that are the modules, fixed purpose systems for analyzing different domains of information. *Talents* comprise the innate abilities to talk, to reason, to see color and form. These large systems come together to form "small minds," which "wheel" in and out of consciousness. A small portion of the mind is active at any moment. Intelligence involves the components of the mind themselves and the ability to select the correct one at any given moment.

TERMS AND CONCEPTS

Binet
cognitive modifiability
crystallized abilities
cultural deprivation
cultural differences
deviation IQ
factor analysis
fluid abilities
general enrichment
Head Start
information-processing components
instrumental enrichment (I.E.)
intelligence quotient (IQ)

learning potential assessment device (LPAD)
mediated learning experience
mental age
multimind theory
reliability
sensor acuity
Stanford–Binet test
structure of intellect
triarchic theory
validity
Wechsler test

Feuerstein, R. (1980). *Instrumental enrichment.* Baltimore: University Park Press.
An important early statement about the possibility of improving intelligence.

Gardner, H. (1983). *Frames of mind.* New York: Basic Books.
A good introduction to the theory of "multiple intelligence."

Glaser, R., & Bond, L. (Eds.). (1981). Testing: Concepts, policy, practice and research [Special issue]. *American Psychologist, 36* (10).
Introduction to many of the different aspects of testing.

Ornstein, R. (1986). *Multimind.* Boston: Houghton Mifflin.
A further description of the complexity and "wheeling and dealing" of the mind. It includes intelligence and multiple personality.

Scarr, S. (1982). *Race, social class, and individual differences in IQ.* Hillsdale, NJ: Lawrence Erlbaum.
A presentation of evidence for inheritance of individual differences.

*W*e are a puzzle to ourselves and to others.

Some people seem like different people at different times. Someone is rude when you thought her nice; another surprises you with his generosity. You may have this same experience with yourself: you are different to your lover than to your boss.

Is someone "emotional," "money motivated," "generous," or "cynical," we may ask. We discuss it with others and try to come up with a single simple description.

It is the same puzzle as understanding intelligence. People cannot be characterized by a single number or phrase. We are a mosaic of abilities, predispositions, moods, and quirks. We are not the same person at all times.

Each of us is a number of people.

Part III

The World
of the Individual

Chapter 12

Emotions and Feelings

One summer evening I was stuck in traffic on the way home from the beach. The man ahead of me got out of his car and walked over to the car next to him. A pretty young woman in a bathing suit sat behind the wheel. He swaggered toward the car. She said nothing, but first frowned, then snarled and almost hissed at him. There was no verbal communication, but the man ''got the message'' without any doubt! He returned quickly to his car. The woman smiled in relief.

Emotions are intense experiences, and they communicate our own feelings to other people quite immediately. They can also, in a very real sense, protect us from harm. The woman, as she hissed, quickly tensed to defend herself, although she might not have been aware of this. There is an *automatic* and *involuntary* quality to emotions that sets them apart from thinking and reasoning. When frightened, we are almost automatically ''primed'' to run or to defend ourselves. You may decide to be calm when someone embarrasses you, but your blush may give you away. To borrow from the poet e. e. cummings, ''Feelings is first.''

Emotions—such as fear, anger, joy, surprise—are basic and immediate. We hear a strange noise and feel afraid instantly; we then determine in a logical way if there is something to be afraid of. Emotions were around even before human beings were; most of our emotions are common to other animals.

We get angry and embarrassed often when we don't want to, and we ''fall'' in love almost by accident. Emotions are similar among all peoples of the world and even between human beings and other animals. Emotions embody relatively automatic patterns of responding to different situations. They are *involuntary* and seem to be outside conscious control (Averill, 1978). They simplify an organism's experience by preparing it for action. They almost certainly evolved before language and other forms of human knowledge.

WHAT EMOTIONS ARE AND WHAT THEY DO

Function of Emotions

The word *emotion* has roots in the Latin word for ''movement,'' originating from the idea that emotions both guide and goad our actions. Basic emotions and expressions coincide in many species of animals. However, human emotional experience is far more complex than that of any other animal. We are the only animal that laughs when happy, and almost the only one that cries when sad (the bear is the other).

Why do we have emotions? Emotions *arouse* us, help *organize* experience, *direct* and *sustain* actions, and *communicate* actions.

Arousal

Emotions move us into action; they signal that something important is happening. An animal who becomes fearful and excited about an approaching attacker is more ready to respond and to defend itself. It would, therefore, be more likely to survive. A human being who experiences sexual love is more likely to reproduce than one who does not. Emotions give action its intensity. Emotions as opposite as elation and anger arouse the emergency system of the body.

Organization

Emotions help organize experience. Our emotional state colors perception of ourselves and of others. If your professor is in a grumpy mood, you know it is not the time to ask if you can hand in your paper late. His or her grumpy mood might follow a family argument the night before or a traffic tie-up on the way to work. The emotions spread and organize the professor's opinion of other events.

Emotions, then, can serve as schemata that aid in organizing consciousness (Bower, 1981). If one is in a good mood, everything seems right with the world: one sees it through "rose-colored glasses." In a bad mood, everything from foreign policy to friendships seems more negative. Recall from the chapter on memory that when an event enters consciousness, *all associated schemata* actuate as well. So it is with feelings: a feeling in consciousness influences perception. When you are angry, you see others as angry as well, even if they are not (Bower, 1981).

In one experiment people were hypnotized to feel anger and were later taught something. They remembered what they had learned better in the angry emo-

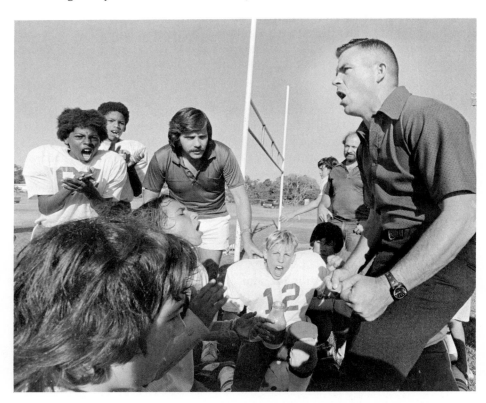

FIGURE 12-1
Sustaining and Engaging Action
A football coach gets his players "pumped up" emotionally by giving them a pregame pep talk to initiate, direct, and sustain their actions on the field.

tional state than in other emotional states (Bower & Gilligan, 1980). However, recent evidence (Bower, personal communication, 1986) has thrown some doubt on the evidence about mood effects on memory, so it is wise to remain cautious about these specific studies.

Directing and Sustaining Actions

An enraged animal may attack. A fearful one may immediately flee. A joyous one is willing and eager. Emotions are simplifying guides to behavior, and they have adaptive roles. Consider the pleasure we derive from eating sweet-tasting foods: it encourages us to search for and find sweet things to eat. A sweet tooth has adaptive value because natural sweet fruits are nutritious and unlikely to be poisonous. Psychologist Silvan Tomkins (1979) described this adaptive value colorfully. He wrote, "If, instead of pain, we had an orgasm to injury, we would . . . bleed to death."

Emotions not only initiate and direct action but *sustain* and engage action. If you are fearful, you will probably run longer and faster than if you are bored. This reaction is useful in avoiding danger. Coaches recognize this by giving pregame "pep" talks, making the team emotionally involved (Figure 12-1). Athletes use the expression "pumped up," one case in which slang is quite accurate.

Communication

Most animals have evolved effective display signals, such as odors, postures, facial expressions (Figure 12-2), and gestures, that communicate information

A

B

C

D

E

**FIGURE 12-2
Facial Expressions Chimpanzees Use to Communicate Emotions** These diagrammatic drawings, done from photographs and descriptions, illustrate "glare," anger (A); "scream calls," fear–anger (B); infant's "cry face," frustration–sadness (C); "play face," playfulness (D); "hoot face," excitement–affection (E). (After Ekman, 1973)

PSYCHOLOGICAL TERMS USED TO DESCRIBE EMOTIONAL LIFE

Affect refers to the feeling dimension of life. It is part of the general outward emotional expression. Someone with a *flat affect* displays little or no emotion.

Emotions are relatively specific and automatic patterns of short-lived physiological and mental responses. They arouse, communicate, direct, and sustain behavior.

Feelings are the subjective experience of emotions; they can be complex experiences. Jealousy is not, then, an emotion but a feeling comprised of many different emotions, including envy and anger.

Moods are relatively long-lasting states of feeling. A mood sets the emotional backdrop of experience.

People who are in a good mood are more likely to help others than someone in a bad mood. Moods color experience. Color words describe moods: blue mood, black mood, rosy or sunny mood.

Temperament is the most permanent and characteristic aspect of emotional life. Temperament is a predisposition to specific emotional reactions in certain situations. One person will become angry at social injustice, another will be sad, a third indifferent. One person has a sunny disposition, and usually sees the bright side of things. Another is a sourpuss and sees misfortune in the same things. (From Ekman, 1984)

---

about probable behavior to other animals. These signals and gestures are "social releasers." A dog cannot say "please go away" and so it snarls. The message gets across. Emotional signals like facial expression, tone of voice, and body posture convey meaning "between the lines." A person may verbally express interest in what you are saying, but blank stares, yawns, and passivity signify boredom.

Basic Emotions

We rarely experience a "pure emotion," just as we rarely see primary colors. Emotions mix. Some psychologists hypothesize several basic or pure emotions similar to the primary colors. These emotions then combine in different mixtures to make complex emotional experiences. Many theories concern the origin of emotional experience and are in general agreement over basic emotions (see Izard et al., 1986; Plutchik, 1984; Tomkins, 1984; Ekman, 1985; Scherer et al., 1986).

See Chapter 5, section on Basis of Color Vision.

Robert Plutchik's theory of emotions compares them to color experience. Recall that the psychological primary colors (red, green, yellow, and blue) exist because of the receptive characteristics of the eyes. All other colors are combinations of these primary colors. Based on evidence from extensive scaling of subjective responses, Plutchik postulates that there are eight *primary emotions*. They include joy, acceptance, fear, surprise, sadness, disgust, anger, and anticipation. These basic emotions produce new combinations in the way they vary in three dimensions:

1. They may vary in *intensity*. Surprise intensified is amazement; intense anger is rage; intense disgust is loathing. Less intense fear is apprehension, less intense disgust is boredom.

2. They may vary in *similarity*. Disgust is more similar to sadness than it is to joy.

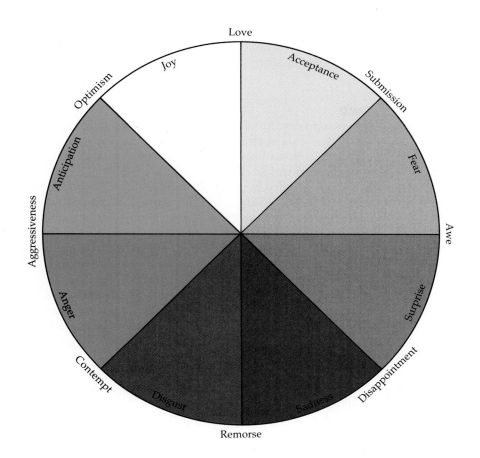

FIGURE 12-3
Plutchik's Emotion Wheel
This model has the eight primary emotions arranged in a circle of opposites. More complex emotions (dyads) resulting from combinations of adjacent primaries are shown just outside the wheel. Additional combinations, of primary emotions once removed on the wheel, produce such emotions as despair (from fear and sadness) and pride (from anger and joy).
(After Plutchik, 1980)

3. Emotions also vary in the dimension of *polarity*. Love is the opposite of hate, sadness is the opposite of joy.

Emotion Wheel and Emotion Solid

Plutchik (1984) proposes a general model of emotions called the **emotion wheel** (Figure 12-3). Here the eight primary emotions form a circle of opposites. Simple emotions combine to make complex ones. For example, the mix of the adjacent pair of joy and acceptance yields love. The composite of emotions that are once-removed from one another, such as fear and sadness, results in despair; anger and joy make pride.

The intensity dimension underlies the **emotion solid.** Plutchik's view is that emotions are most distinct from one another at the highest levels of intensity (at the top of the model) and they are least distinguishable at the lowest levels. Loathing and grief, both being very intense, are very different, while disgust is only slightly different from sadness. Boredom and pensiveness are very similar.

Are Emotions Universal?

Does everyone have the same emotions? Different things make different people happy, obviously, but is the *experience* of happiness the same for everyone? You have probably noticed individual differences in the role one emotion or another

FIGURE 12-4
**Universality of Emotional
Expression**
People in different cultures
all over the world express
emotion in very similar
ways. This suggests there
is an innate component to
emotion. You can notice
this yourself: you
immediately know what
these people are feeling.
The women in A are
obviously expressing grief.
The facial expression of
the man in B is completely
recognizable as disgust,
although he is not part of
our culture. One look at
the girl and guy in C
reveals they are flirting.
And people from any
culture would instantly
realize that the man in D is
very angry.

plays in different people's lives. One person is easily angered, another apprehensive. Some people give their emotions more weight in actions and in decision making than others; these people are sometimes called "emotional."

Studies on Universality of Emotion

The evidence for the universality of emotion rests on several different observations. They include the striking similarities of emotional expression among different species, among different human groups with no contact, and among blind infants, normal infants, and adults (Scherer et al., 1986).

Charles Darwin (1872) observed that all peoples of the world express grief by contracting the facial muscles in the same way. This is true from an Oxford don to an aborigine. It is the same for other emotions as well. In rage, the lips retract and the teeth clench. Similar are the snarl and disgust. All over the world, flirting is signaled by a lowering of the eyelids or the head, followed by direct eye contact. All over the world embarrassed people turn their heads away or cover their faces. And anger is easily recognizable in all cultures (Figure 12-4 and Plate 14).

In human beings, emotions are primarily displayed by the face (Ekman, 1984; Tomkins, 1984). The facial muscles of most animals do not permit much more than an opening and closing of the mouth and eyes. Mammals, especially primates and human beings, have further complicated patterns of muscles that allow a variety of facial expressions.

Gorillas, chimpanzees, and human beings have an upright posture. Thus, their faces are much more conspicuous to others than in lower animals. The eyes are in the front of the head, and human beings have stereoscopic vision. Central eyesight leads to a sharper focus on other animal's faces. Facial hair is relatively lacking in human beings and is further accentuated by the framing of head hair. The face is the primary organ of human social communication, followed by bodily gestures (Ekman, 1984).

Emotional Expression in Infants.   Emotional expression develops naturally in a predictable sequence. Like motor skills, it begins as undifferentiated and disorganized and gradually becomes more refined and precise.

Bridges (1932) observed the progressive differentiation of emotions in a study of 62 Canadian babies over a period of several months. At first, infants show "general excitement" to all stimuli; signs of this include increased muscle tension, quickness of breath, and increased movements. This general arousal gradually becomes differentiated into expressions of distress (at 3 weeks) and anger (3 months). Later are disgust (3–6 months), fear of strangers (7–8 months), and jealousy and envy (15–18 months). The predictable, reliable sequence of these changes indicates an innate maturational component to emotions.

Crying occurs earlier than smiling, perhaps because crying serves immediate survival needs. In addition, *attachment* seems to be an inborn biological and emotional bond between the mother and the child (Ainsworth, 1982).

See Chapter 3, section on Attachment.

Eibl-Eibesfeld (1970) filmed children born deaf and blind. He found that basic facial expressions—smiling, laughing, pouting, crying, surprise, anger—occurred in appropriate situations. Blind children show the same pattern of development of smiling as sighted children. The difference is that around 6 months of age social smiling becomes increasingly responsive to the mother's voice and touch instead of to her face (Fraiberg, 1971).

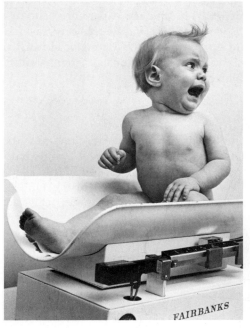 

The universality of emotional expression extends to infants (even infants born blind). The forms of emotional expression that babies gradually develop are similar to those seen in adults.

See Chapter 6, Figure 6-2.

See Chapter 18, section on Mechanisms of Stress.

HOW WE EXPERIENCE EMOTIONS

Emotional reactions involve the autonomic nervous system. Interestingly, the actual bodily response pattern in emotions closely matches the cliche expressions: "My heart leapt when I saw her" or "I've got butterflies in my stomach." Most emotional reactions involve the cardiovascular and gastrointestinal systems and signify emergency arousal in the sympathetic nervous system. Similar patterns are common to all emotions. That we differentiate emotions, and experience one as fear, another as lust, means that we must *interpret* our physical reactions. Just as ambiguous figures and illusions can fool our perceptual processes, emotions can be mislabeled and misunderstood.

It happened to me once. A few years ago, I flew to Los Angeles to give a lecture. I enjoy lecturing and was looking forward to the meeting. I was listening to the speaker who preceded me, waiting for my turn, when a most bizarre thing happened. I began to feel shaky, worried, uneasy. When I noticed this, I began to berate myself, silently: "I should have prepared more. I should have written out my speech. Why didn't I fly in last night and get a good night's sleep before the talk?" And there were more worries and ideas about what I should have done.

What was most surprising was that I had never felt like this before in my life. I lecture often on subjects I know well and I *was* prepared. But was I nervous! Then it began to dawn on me, slowly. I truly felt "shaky." My arms were shaking, so was my hand. Then I looked around. The *table* was shaking, the glasses on it almost spilled their water. The podium was shaking. I turned around, and there it was. The old air conditioner was rumbling and vibrating everything around it, including me. As soon as I saw what was actually happening, I wasn't nervous anymore.

What happened to me was almost a classic experiment in emotion. It is similar to what happened to you when you looked at the cube in the perception chapter: your hypothesis about the cube became your *experience* of the cube. I explained my thinking in this way: "I can feel myself shaking. Why? I'm delivering an important lecture, that must be it. Why didn't I . . ." and so on. The hypothesis about why I was shaking (that I was nervous) *became* my experience. The hypothesis "The whole room is shaking" is very unlikely, but when I saw this was the case, my experience changed. I had appraised myself wrongly. However, most times our appraisals are accurate, and it is only in unusual circumstances such as this one that we can observe them go wrong.

Activation of Emergency Reaction

The strongest physiological effect of emotion is **activation.** Emotions turn on (activate) the body's **emergency reaction,** allowing us to prepare for immediate action such as the "fight-or-flight" response (see Figure 18-1). Most of the "reactions" involved in emotions involve the activating mechanisms of the sympathetic nervous system. They underlie most strong feelings such as anger, fear, and joy.

The process works in several steps. An increase in the secretion of norepinephrine in the bloodstream by the adrenals activates the internal organs. Then heart rate, blood pressure, and blood volume increase. This allows more blood to flow to the muscles and the face; this is the origin of the expression "flushed with excitement." Skin resistance decreases; respiration, sweating, salivation, and gastric motility all increase; pupil size increases. As is becoming apparent, there seems to be nothing in the physical arousal system *alone* that defines what the emotion is.

Patterns of Activation

It seems that different emotions are grossly similar in their activating capacity, but is the "go–no go" system the only important aspect of emotion? This is too much of an oversimplification. Different emotions, such as grief and elation, anger and joy, *feel* different, so it seems logical that our brains are being activated differently, too. New research shows that there are also differences in physiology during different emotions.

We can call up different emotions using only simple poses of the face, somewhat like method acting. In one study Ekman (1984) asked people to assume different facial expressions, such as raising the eyebrows and lowering the lips. When they did, they *felt* the emotions they were expressing, such as anger and happiness. Ekman was able to consistently record different patterns of autonomic nervous system activity for different emotions, especially anger. This research points to the possibility that people can begin to learn to control their emotions using deliberate techniques. As one can see, this could have great effects on health (Ekman, 1984). However, no one has yet discovered specific structures in the brain that correspond to specific emotions.

What *has* been found is that each of us show *characteristic* emotional responses to certain situations. For example, one person flushes with anger as well as joy, another sweats with both, while a third may have stomach reactions (Lacey & Lacey, 1958). In other words, the pattern of activation is different among people experiencing the same emotion. In one study of students' anxiety over an examination, some sweated while others had increased heartbeat (Lacey, Bateman, & Van Lehn, 1953). The only specific body pattern that universally relates to all people's emotions is facial expression.

Emotions and the Brain

Two major divisions of the brain act differently with regard to the emotions. The limbic system is largely responsible for many emotional reactions. Stimulation of the pleasure center in the hypothalamus yields intense awareness of pleasure. Other areas of the limbic system, when stimulated, can produce rage and attack reactions (Delgado, 1969).

Yet in many emotional situations there is conscious control from the cortex. The "emergency reaction" releases hormones into the bloodstream. It can often occur involuntarily, as when trembling with fright before a job interview. Some scientists speculate that there is a discord between our "old" emotional brain and the "new" thinking brain. This clash is at the root of many conflicts between rational thought and our "gut" feelings (Koestler, 1974).

However, most recent analysis about the brain and emotions concerns the two cerebral hemispheres. They seem to be specialized for emotions, as they are for thought. The left hemisphere responds to the verbal content of emotional expression and the right to the tone and gesture (Kolb & Milner, 1980). Since the right

See Chapter 4, section on The Two Hemispheres.

HOW TO READ FACES

The face of emotion is complex. The brain's control of the facial muscles is exquisite. There is more area devoted to the control of the face than to any other surface of the body. This very detailed control serves a purpose: to express feelings. What a person's feelings are can be directly "read" as patterns of muscle movements on the face.

We continually send emotional messages to others by our facial expression: a raise of the eyebrows here, a downward turn of the mouth there. Our facial expressions are a large part of the impression we communicate to others. Sometimes we are unaware of the messages we are sending to others and of the messages others send to us. However, since many expressions of emotion are universal, it is possible to learn how to identify the emotions in various facial expressions.

The face provides three types of signals: *static* (such as skin color), *slow* (wrinkles), and *rapid* (a smile). Emotions communicate by the rapid movements of the facial muscles, which constantly alter the appearance of the face. These changes flash over the face in a matter of seconds. It is rare for a facial expression of emotion to last more than 5 to 10 seconds, and some are much faster. The accompanying pictures illustrate several facial expressions of emotion and the specific characteristics of the emotional expression.

Surprise

Surprise is a sudden experience (Figures 12-5A and B):

- The brows raise and are curved.
- Horizontal wrinkles mark the forehead.
- The eyelids open and the white of the eye is more prominent, particularly above the iris.
- The jaw drops open, but there is no tension in the mouth.

However, each one of these clues may express part of the feeling. And since our perception fills in the gaps, the rest of the face may seem to convey the emotion as well. A face may seem to express "mild surprise," but only the raised brows give that impression (Figure 12-5C).

FIGURE 12-5A

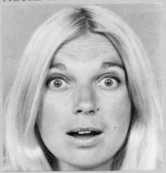

FIGURE 12-5B

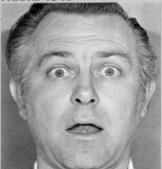

FIGURE 12-5C

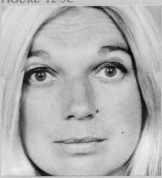

Fear

- The brows raise and draw together.
- The forehead wrinkles in the center, not sides.
- Both the upper and lower eyelids raise.
- The mouth opens and the lips tense slightly (Figures 12-6A and B).

Fear may occur with other emotions as well. Fear and surprise blend in when someone looks afraid, but not as afraid as in outright fear.

FIGURE 12-6A

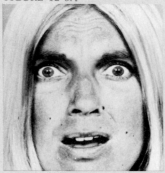

FIGURE 12-6B

Disgust

Disgust usually involves a response of getting away or getting rid of something offensive. Disgust is shown largely in the lower face and eyelids (Figures 12-7A and B).

- The upper lip raises, as does the lower lip.
- The nose wrinkles.
- The cheeks raise.
- The brow lowers.

If we mix disgust and surprise we get a new expression that seems to be disbelief or skepticism (Figure 12-7C).

FIGURE 12-7A

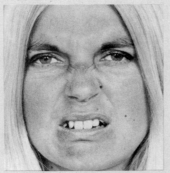

FIGURE 12-7B

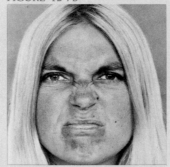

FIGURE 12-7C

(cont.)

FIGURE 12-10A
Mona Lisa's Smile
The celebrated ambiguity of the smile of Leonardo da Vinci's *Mona Lisa* might be attributable to the fact that she is smiling only on the left side, the side controlled by the right hemisphere of the brain. To aid you in considering whether or not this could be the source of the enigma, look at the related picture in Figure 12-10B.

HOW TO READ FACES *(continued)*

Anger

The expression of anger is strong and direct, and the emotion conveys strong displeasure. It is easy to read. There is much redundancy in the anger message, making it clear to all.

- The brows lower and draw together, causing vertical lines to appear.
- The eyes may have a hard stare and may bulge out.
- The lips may press together or open into a squarish shape as in shouting.

Anger often blends with disgust. Here the wrinkled nose blends with the angry eyes and brows: "How dare you do this to me?" (Figures 12-8A and B).

FIGURE 12-8A

FIGURE 12-8B

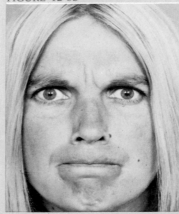

FIGURE 12-9A

FIGURE 12-9B

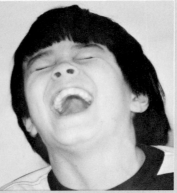

Happiness

Happiness is welcome after all these difficult emotions. It shows in the lower face and eyelids.

- The corners of the lips draw back and up.
- The mouth is upturned in a smile, either open or not.
- The cheeks raise, causing a wrinkle from the outer edges of the mouth to the nose.
- "Laugh lines" or crow's feet wrinkle outward from the outer corners of the eye (Figures 12-9A and B).

Anger can blend with happiness into a gleeful "gotcha" expression.

This section was adapted in large part from the work of Ekman and Friesen (1983).

hemisphere controls the left side of the body and the left hemisphere the right side, are there differences in the expression of emotions on both sides of the body? Look at Leonardo da Vinci's *Mona Lisa* (Figure 12-10A). She has a smile described as enigmatic, puzzling, ambiguous. Why? Look carefully at each side of her face, then look at the reversed image in Figure 12-10B. Only the left side is smiling, the side controlled by the right hemisphere! Perhaps this is why the expression is so ambiguous.

As another demonstration, look at the three faces in Figure 12-11. Which of the faces seems to express the emotion of disgust most strongly? These three photographs were specially created: the one on the left is a normal photograph of a man expressing disgust. The middle photograph is a double image, a composite of two *right* sides of the man's face. The one on the far right is a double image of the *left* side of the face. Most people feel that the far-right photograph, which expresses the right cerebral hemisphere, shows the emotions strongest. The results are the same with eye movements (Schwartz, Davidson, & Maer, 1975) and with interpreting a facial expression. We seem to express emotion on the left side more than the right (at least in deliberate expressions), and we interpret emotions better on the left than the right (Campbell, 1978).

You should note that in both of these demonstrations, the expressions were *posed.* You may have noticed that a posed smile is not the same as a genuine smile. It is often easy to tell if another's facial expression is not a genuine one. Ekman and colleagues point out that a forced smile is more asymmetrical than a normal one, and this may account for the results shown here.

However, there have also been studies on asymmetry of spontaneous expressions. Moscovitch and Olds (1980) unobtrusively recorded the asymmetry of facial expressions of people seated in restaurants. They found the same result: the right hemisphere controls the left side of the face, the side seen better by the viewer's right hemisphere. In a social situation there may be two kinds of messages sent—one from the left hemisphere to the left through words, and right to right through facial and other expressions.

In an intriguing series of studies, Davidson (1984) showed that the left hemisphere may involve different emotions than the right. The left seems to involve "positive" emotions, such as happiness, and the right, "negative" ones such as anger.

FIGURE 12-10B
Look at the smile on this reversed *Mona Lisa.* Is her smile as enigmatic, as ambiguous? Here, because she is smiling only on the right side of her face, the impact is different. Your response may be different because the smile is on the side controlled by the left hemisphere of the brain.

FIGURE 12-11
Expressing Emotion: The Two Sides of the Face and the Brain
The far left photo shows a man expressing disgust. The middle photo is a composite of two right sides of the man's face, and the one on the right is a composite of two left sides of his face. Do you agree with most people that the photograph on the right—a double image of the side of the face controlled by the right side of the brain—shows disgust most strongly?

 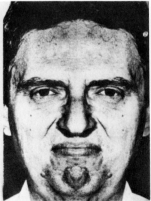 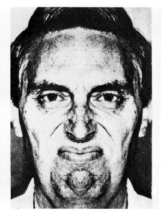

KNOWING WHAT WE FEEL

A basic emotional reaction such as fear is probably innate, a shortcut to action. In the long course of evolution emotions probably evolved to match well the needs of most organisms. Fear of snakes probably saved many lives. However, the situation for human beings is different: the dangers of the modern world are unprecedented in our evolutionary history. The fear of nuclear war is not as palpable as fear of snakes. For a war, there is no identifiable stimulus, no obvious and immediate course of action. The *meaning* of a situation and its *appraisal* are major components in human emotional life.

Appraisal and Reappraisal

Appraisal is the understanding of the meaning of an event. There are three basic dimensions to the appraisal process. The first is *evaluation:* is the situation good or bad, benign or threatening? The second is *potency:* is it alive or dead, strong or weak, fast or slow? The third is *activity:* is it active or passive? Osgood and colleagues (1971), who proposed these dimensions of emotions, describe their value:

> What is important to us now, as it was way back in the age of Neanderthal Man, about the sign of a thing is: First, does it refer to something *good* or *bad* for me (is it an antelope or a saber-toothed tiger)? Second, does it refer to something that is *strong* or *weak* with respect to me (saber-toothed tiger, or a mosquito)? And third . . . does it refer to something which is *active* or *passive* (is it a saber-toothed tiger or merely a pool of quicksand, which I can simply walk around)?

Emotions are not a succession of isolated, unrelated feelings and reactions to situations. Perception, consciousness, and memory operate in a cycle; emotions do too. The cycle involves a primary appraisal of the situation, feedback of that information, and continuous reappraisals, and feedback. Feelings change as new information comes in.

One night I awakened to the sound of a strange noise upstairs in my house. I became aroused and fearful. What could the sound be? Did I lock the door? Was the roof falling? With each thought something inside me immediately prepared me to act differently. Then I remembered that a friend of mine had asked to stay over. He must have noticed that I was asleep and then let himself in. Once I realized what had happened, I went back to sleep.

My first reaction was the primary appraisal: "Something's happening." I awoke, aroused. This *primary appraisal* first arouses the organism. *Reappraisal* considers whether an event is *benign* or *threatening* and what actions to take. When I decided that the noise was only my friend's footsteps, all my plans vanished. I did not want to call the police; the desire to run like mad from the roof caving in went away. The result of my reappraisal was that I went back to sleep.

Almost every situation is complex enough to require continuous appraisal. When a man sees that his wife prepared his favorite dish, his primary appraisal is benign. When the dish is set in front of him, he sees that the dish is burnt. This new information causes a reappraisal: disappointment. This may lead to an action such as complaining to his wife or going to a restaurant, which results in a new cycle of feelings (Lazarus & Folkman, 1986).

Interpretation of Emotions

Because the internal states of many different emotions are similar, situations need to be appraised and a conscious interpretation of their meaning must be made. Most times these appraisals are accurate and serve us well. Someone may insult us, so we get angry. Another person may snuggle up to us, and we become activated in a blizzard of lustful joy.

The *cognitive appraisal theory of emotion* (Schachter & Singer, 1962) states that the interpretation of the physiological state leads to different emotional experiences. In this view, our interpretation occurs in the same way as most perceptual interpretations: "What is the simplest explanation for my excitement?" But, as with perception, the interpretation can be difficult when the circumstance is ambiguous.

One factor that may cause confusion in our lives is that arousal is common to quite different emotions. When the situation is ambiguous we may misinterpret our own emotional state. Although this happens infrequently in life, psychologists can design experiments to test it in the lab. My experience of shaking before a lecture is an example from real life. I *interpreted* my shaking as nervousness. Once I understood the situation, I was no longer nervous. My interpretation had real consequences: I *felt* worried.

The conscious interpretation can affect the internal state itself. In one study, students saw a very arousing film while psychologists measured autonomic nervous system arousal during the viewing (Speisman, Lazarus, Davidson, & Mordkoff, 1964). The measure of arousal used was a standard measure of skin resistance, called the *galvanic skin response* (GSR). The film was of a ceremony an aboriginal tribe used to mark manhood. The rituals included the subincision of the penis with a knife. Most people find these scenes quite negatively arousing.

One group saw the film silently. A second group heard a narration that emphasized the cruelty of the ritual. Two other groups heard narrations that minimized the cruelty by denying or intellectualizing it. GSR measures of arousal increased in the narration that emphasized the cruelty, whereas arousal decreased in the narrations that minimized it (Figure 12-12).

To test interpretation of emotion, Schachter and Singer (1962) injected epinephrine into students who were told it was a vitamin. Half of the students were placed in a situation with a euphoric person (a confederate of the experimenters). He tossed paper airplanes, and used the wastebasket to shoot baskets with wads of paper. These students later reported feeling euphoric. The other half of the students confronted an insulting and irritated person. They later reported being angry. Schachter and Singer concluded that these results confirm the theory that emotional experiences depend upon the interpretation of arousal.

Abundant studies support Schachter's hypothesis, but there are problems with his experiments. Many people have tried with little success to replicate the result of this experiment (Marshall & Zimbardo, 1979). Since it is no longer permissible to conduct experiments with epinephrine injections, there will be no further replication attempts. However, many other studies indicate that the interpretation of inner states can have profound effects on emotional experience.

One way to test the theory is to offer *false feedback* on the internal state itself. If emotional experience depends on interpretation, then false information should also have an effect on experience. In one study men were shown photographs of

FIGURE 12-12
Cognitive Influences or
Emotional Reactions
In the experiment charted
in this graph, different
groups of people watched
a stress-provoking movie.
Those who heard a
narration that denied or
intellectualized the
distressing parts of the
film, or who saw the film
without any narration, had
less stressful emotional
reactions than people in
the group that heard a
narration intended to
increase stress.
(After Speisman, Lazarus,
Davidson, & Mordkoff, 1964)

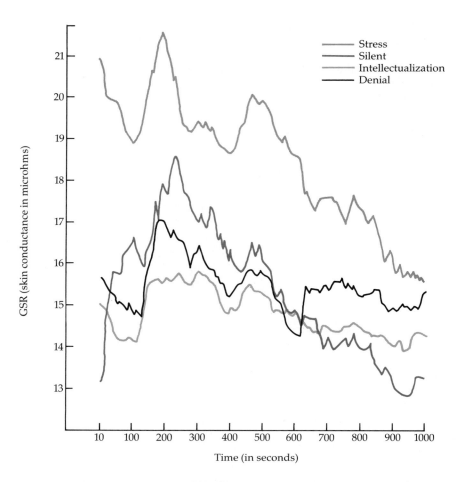

nude women while listening to their own heartbeat. What each actually heard, however, was not his own heart beating, but a recording. One group heard a recording in which the heart rate increased when five of the ten slides were shown. A second group heard the heart rate decrease for these five slides. Later they rated the attractiveness of the nudes. The group who heard the rapid heartbeat rated the women in the five slides as more attractive. The ones whose heart rate decreased found the other five more appealing (Valins, 1966).

In another experiment, women were shown slides of people who had experienced violent death. Some "heard" their heart rate increase in reaction to the slides. These women rated them as significantly more unpleasant and discomforting than those who had not been misinformed.

The study of sexual attraction on a wobbly bridge that we discussed in Chapter 1 is an example of this misinterpretation. The arousal caused by crossing a dangerous bridge was misinterpreted as sexual excitement upon seeing a woman. Other studies have shown similar results, and similar phenomena occur in life. For example, many people find that exercise with a partner of the opposite sex is very provocative. Why? In one study (Cantor, Zillman, & Bryant, 1974) people were asked to exercise for a period of time. The activation resulting from the exercise diminished with time. Soon after exercise one no longer *feels* activated. However, subtle measures of autonomic activation such as blood pressure are still elevated.

If people see erotic stimuli during this phase, they are more easily aroused than when they have fully recovered from the exercise. The interpretation of the unexplained activation is sexual excitement. So activation, especially in contrived or ambiguous situations, is subject to misinterpretation (Mandler, 1980). However, most situations are *not* ambiguous, and our emotions are usually an accurate and immediate guide for us.

Frustration and Conflict

Consequences of Frustration

Frustration is a normal reaction to stress. It results when a desired outcome is thwarted or delayed (Lazarus, 1976). A person may also feel threatened if he or she anticipates harm or frustration.

At one time psychologists thought that *all* frustrations increase the probability of *aggressive* behavior, and that all aggression was due to frustration. This was the "frustration–aggression hypothesis" proposed by Dollard and associates (1939). Aggression *is* a common response to frustration (Bandura, 1965), but frustration may lead to many things besides aggression (Mischel, 1976). A frustrated person may become depressed, or may feel guilty, disappointed, apathetic, anxious, or fearful — to mention only a few.

Conflicts

There are different types of conflicts that may result in threats or frustration. Needs or motives may be in opposition or may be incompatible, or an internal need or motive may oppose an external demand (Lazarus, 1976). Obviously, if the motivation or demands are weak, little threat or frustration may be felt. However, when they are strong, the conflict may be severe.

An example of *internal conflicting demands* is found in combat stress (Grinker & Spiegel, 1945). A soldier has a very strong need to survive, but he may also need to be respected by others, which requires that he live up to their expectations — that is, go into combat. Usually, the soldier overcomes or at least puts aside his fear of death and completes his combat tour of duty. Sometimes the conflict is so severe that it results in neurotic symptoms.

A person may also be subject to *external conflicting demands*. This may happen, for example, when one parent insists a child become an athlete and the other demands excellence in music to the exclusion of athletics. The frustration and threat of failure may be so great that the child ends up doing neither.

Finally, most people experience *internal demands* or desires that *conflict with external ones*. A child may want to eat nothing but junk food, but the parents will forbid it and insist vegetables also be eaten.

Feeling and Thinking

How do feelings relate to thinking and decision making? Many psychologists consider that mental functions such as perception, consciousness, memory, and thinking come before emotions. We first analyze and appraise information, then evaluate it and experience it emotionally. Recently, however, Robert Zajonc has proposed that feelings come first, or to use his phrase, "Preferences need no inferences" (Zajonc, 1980).

Zajonc argues that mental functions often service emotions, not the reverse. We evaluate first and think of the reasons second. He offers many examples of his theory. Consider a woman trying to decide rationally whom to marry: "Let's see, Jack has more money, one point for him. He wants to live where I do, another point in his favor. He's handsomer than Bill. . . . Wait a minute, this isn't coming out right, I want to marry Bill. Let's see . . ." In a contest between emotion and reason, emotion is more likely to win, according to this view.

It may be that the question, "Which comes first, emotions or cognitions?" is similar to asking about the chicken and the egg. It is perhaps more profitable to view emotions and thoughts as part of the same feedback system. Each influences the other, and appraisals and reappraisals follow each other. Sometimes emotional evaluation may come first: "I like wine" is an evaluation. Sometimes the evaluation may well come after a long analysis: "I don't like this white wine after all, it's too sweet." Emotions probably influence every mental process. They may cause us to seek out different information, remember differently, think and evaluate differently.

EMOTIONS AND HEALTH

In everyday language we assume an association between the expression of emotions and health. We may urge someone to let out their anger by saying "get it off your chest." The assumption seems to be that the release of "bottled-up" feelings is helpful. Many people believe that the expression of positive feelings is healthy. For years the *Reader's Digest* has run a column called "Laughter — The Best Medicine."

Norman Cousins, the editor of the *Saturday Review*, described treatment of an incurable illness (an undetermined blood disease) he contracted in Russia. After his doctors gave up, Cousins moved from the hospital to a hotel room and "prescribed" humor for himself. He watched films providing a dose of the Marx Brothers and administered round-the-clock Laurel and Hardy. He got better. While there is some anecdotal evidence for laughter as a cure for disease, single cases do not provide adequate scientific evidence.

However, there may be a link between emotional expression and cancer. In a long series of studies, Kissen (1966) found that people with lung cancer are people who characteristically suppress their emotions. Cancer patients seem to ignore their negative feelings, such as hostility, depression, and guilt (Zegans & Temoshok, 1985).

In a recent study comparing long-term survivors of breast cancer with those who do not survive, Derogatis and colleagues (1979) found the same pattern. The long-term survivors express much higher levels of anxiety, hostility, alienation, and other negative emotions than short-term survivors. They have more negative moods and expressed more negative feelings about their illness.

The link between expressing feelings and reduced cancer is fairly well established, but why this is so is not known. One link may be hormonal. Hormones can influence the growth of cancerous tumors, and since emotions involve sympathetic activation, it may alter hormonal levels in the body. In any case, "venting" emotions may cause difficulty in social situations (Tavris, 1982), but keeping feelings to yourself may be injurious to your health.

Denial of One's Own Feelings

Sometimes active coping through direct problem solving is not possible even for the hardiest. Some events cannot be avoided or changed by confronting them directly. The mind may become flooded with anxious thoughts. Memories or anticipations of threatening situations intrude into consciousness. Fortunately, psychological mechanisms clear the deck and make possible other thoughts and actions.

One such mechanism is denial, the mental operation by which thoughts, feelings, acts, threats, or demands are minimized or negated. Unfortunately, denial has often been misinterpreted as a negative defense mechanism that leads to pathology. It is thought that people must face reality, "get in touch with one's feelings," and be honest about them. Illusion, self-deception, and denial are thought by some to be unhealthy and must be rooted out, perhaps in therapy. Yet this traditional view is not consistent with newer information about how the brain works. Sometimes we need our illusions.

Psychologist Richard Lazarus (1979) argues that illusion has positive value in a person's psychological economy:

> The fabric of our lives is woven in part from illusions and unexamined beliefs. There is, for example, the collective illusion that our society is free, moral, and just, which, of course, isn't always true. Then there are the countless idiosyncratic beliefs people hold about themselves and the world in which they live: we are better than average, or doomed to fail, or that the world is a benign conspiracy, or that is rigged against us. Many such beliefs are passed down from parent to child and never challenged. Despite the fixity with which people hold such beliefs, they have little or no basis in reality. One person's beliefs are another's delusions. In effect, we pilot our lives in part by illusions and by self-deceptions that give meaning and substance to life.

Mental processes construct a small reality from a narrow trickle of information received, reduced, and filtered through our senses. These constructed beliefs, many based on denial and illusion, have adaptive value.

It should not come as a surprise that the brain has adaptive mechanisms to block painful feelings, whether due to physical injury or psychological trauma. The elaborate intrinsic pain relief system, in part mediated by endorphins, has evolved to be able to block transmission of pain stimuli. This system appears to be turned on during acutely stressful situations when the organism must prepare to flee or fight. For example, numbing pain during an attack by a charging wild animal would allow an organism to ignore physical trauma and handle the immediate threat (Goleman, 1985).

Analogously, the brain has developed certain adaptive mechanisms such as denial to help block perception of certain threatening information when attending to it will only arouse unnecessary anxiety and contribute little to changing the situation. Therefore, whether denial is healthy or not depends on the circumstances and the outcome.

Denial can interfere with necessary actions and thereby undermine health. The diabetic who needs to carefully regulate insulin dosages, the patient with kidney disease who needs to undergo dialysis, or the woman who discovers a breast lump all need to pay attention to information about their health to preserve it. Denying a breast lump can lead to delays in treatment for breast cancer. The patient with chest pain who does push-ups or runs up and down stairs to prove he is not having a heart attack clearly illustrates the danger of unhealthy denial.

But denial can be helpful. Frances Cohen and Richard Lazarus (1984) studied 61 patients about to undergo elective surgery for conditions like hernia and gall bladder disease. They were asked about how much they knew or wanted to know about the disease, the operation, and so on. Two basic coping strategies were avoidance and vigilance.

The avoiders denied the emotional or threatening aspects of the surgery and were not interested in thinking about or listening to anything that was related to their illness or surgery. They would say things like, "All I know is that I have a hernia. I just took it for granted. It doesn't disturb me one bit. I have not thought at all about it."

In contrast, the vigilant were alert to the emotional and threatening aspects of their upcoming medical event. They attempted to cope by trying to control every detail of the situation and were aroused to every danger. One vigilant patient commented after a detailed description of the operation: "I have all the facts, my will is prepared. It is major surgery. It's a body opening. You're put out, you could be put out too deep, your heart could quit, you can have a shock. I go not in lightly."

When compared, the avoiders seemed to fare better in the postsurgical recovery period than the vigilant. The avoiders left the hospital sooner, had fewer headaches, fevers, and infections. They required less pain medication and showed less distress. Of course, some of these differences may have been due to the different way the vigilant were treated by the doctors. Since they were more likely to notice and report symptoms after the operation, the doctors were perhaps more likely to conclude that the patient was not ready to go home.

There are other situations in which denial may be healthy. Immediately following an acute crisis or catastrophic illness, such as a miscarriage or a severe burn, the victim may be able to "buy" some time by denying the implications of the trauma. Denying the severity of an incapacitating disease or event may be a helpful first step in coping with it. A temporary disavowal of reality helps the person get through the devastating early period of loss and threat when there is in truth little he or she can do. Later the person can face the facts at a gradual, more manageable pace and mobilize other means of coping.

From the viewpoint of the brain and body, arousal, fear, and vigilance are useful to alert the brain to remediate the threat and instability. But when there is nothing that can be done to aid survival, then denying or ignoring the threat protects the stability and health of the person. And it leaves room for hope.

Stress Emotions: Fear and Anxiety

An important emotion resulting from stress is anxiety, apparently at the root of a variety of psychological disorders. Fear and anxiety are closely related, but there are differences.

Fear is an immediate and specific emotional reaction to a specific threatening stimulus. Young birds show fear if the shadow of a hawk — even a wooden one — passes over them. However, as we go up the phylogenetic scale, fear may become abstract.

Anxiety is a more general reaction that occurs in higher animals and human beings that may develop in response to the anticipation that something harmful *may* occur in the future. This harm may not be just physical but also psychological, as in a threat to a person's self-esteem. The stimulus for fear is usually clear and immediate. When a situation is ambiguous and the person is not sure what is going to occur, he or she may feel a vague sense of apprehension and become anxious (Lazarus, 1976).

The stress emotions, while unpleasant, usually alert a person that something is (potentially) wrong and that action is necessary. A student who is anxious about an exam is more likely to study harder than another who is not particularly anxious. Healthy fear may keep someone from walking alone at night in dangerous sections of town. However, when emotional reactions become too great, they disrupt. The student may be too anxious to study for the test, or a person may become too afraid to leave the house even during the day.

Antianxiety drugs, such as alcohol, barbiturates, and Valium, may be useful in helping a person to function. However, these drugs lessen anxiety at a cost. They seem to interfere with complex learning (Gray, 1984) and they inhibit REM sleep and dreaming (Greenberg & Pearlman, 1974). Antianxiety drugs may reduce the fear of the consequences of action without lessening a person's aggression. In some situations this can be useful, but in others it can be harmful. For example, giving Valium to an anxious parent with a tendency toward child abuse may actually increase the parent's aggression toward the child (Gray, 1978). Thus, such drugs should be used sparingly and with full consideration of the consequences of using them.

Benefits of Crying

It may seem strange to think of crying as useful. Yet, many people say that a good cry makes them feel better. The belief that crying has positive effects is of ancient origin. More than 2,000 years ago, Aristotle theorized that crying at a drama

See Chapter 16, section on Transference.

"cleanses the mind" of suppressed emotions. It works by a process called catharsis. **Catharsis** is the reduction of emotional distress by releasing the emotion in controlled circumstances.

Crying in response to a sad movie is a textbook case. Some people seem to seek out movies and plays that are "elicitors of psychogenic lacrimation," or simply, "tearjerkers." Such people cry freely at these movies. If their crying is the release of suppressed grief, perhaps the crying is therapeutic.

There are some studies of the effects of crying. Borquist (1906) obtained reports of the effects of crying, including the observation that 54 out of 57 respondents felt that crying had positive results. Weiner (1977) found from reports that asthma attacks—long thought to be largely psychosomatic—cease as a result of crying. Grinker (1953) noted that depressed persons do not cry and the development of the ability to cry aids recovery.

Research on the benefits of crying is intriguing but hardly decisive. However, other strands of evidence are becoming available. It has been found that tears produced by emotional crying differ in chemical content from those caused by irritants such as onion juice (Frey, 1982). Emotional tears contain more protein than tears induced by irritants. Frey contends that emotional crying is an eliminative process in which tears actually *remove toxic substances from the body*. Crying may "cleanse the mind" more than even the catharsis theorists imagine. Other researchers are now examining the contents of emotional tears for endorphins and growth hormone, which result from stress. The research on psychoactive substances in tears is just beginning. It is possible that emotional tears contribute to the maintenance of physical health and emotional balance.

Recent research has begun to show that crying may be more than just a moment of weakness but rather your body's way of literally cleansing your mind.

Human sexuality is very difficult to study because the feelings involved with it are the most intimate of all human experiences. Until the last few decades, cultural and personal taboos have made it impossible to study this important aspect of life. For example, many questions about women's orgasms were not settled until the mid-1960s when social mores had relaxed enough to permit laboratory investigation.

People are, simply, very sexual animals. We have sex more than any other primates do. Our love of sex is one of the reasons for the success of our species. In evolutionary terms, the "survival of the fittest"—those who have the most surviving offspring—determines how a population grows, changes, and develops. Survival is related more to sex than to aggression. Because we make love, not war, we have been successful.

Sex is different for human beings than for other animals in that the signals for sex are mental as well as biological. Recall that other female animals are sexually receptive to the males only for brief periods, during the estrus cycle. But human beings are biologically prepared to have sex at any time. More significant in human beings, however, is the role of emotions and our mental interpretation of love experiences, which are closely related to sexual feelings. Because how we feel depends on our interpretation of physical arousal, sexual attraction has mental components that include both love and attachment.

The Sexual Animal

Female human beings can have sex at any time of the year. While this might seem obvious and routine, it is not typical of most animals who have sex only to produce offspring. Human beings like to have sex much more often than the strict demands that reproduction requires. This style of continual sexual activity forms the basis of the family, and the cooperative human society.

The human being's anatomy by "design" calls attention to the sexual characteristics. Upright posture has transferred emphasis from odor to visual signs of sexuality. There is no reason for a woman's breasts to be large except when nursing—except that they are visually appealing and arousing to the male. The male penis is much larger, relative to body size, than that of the great apes. In addition, human genitalia are accented with pubic hair. Publications like *Playboy* magazine have not *created* a need for men to look at women sexually; they have merely taken advantage of a natural inclination (Symons, 1979).

See Chapter 2, section on Evolution of Love.

Sexual Response Cycle

There are regular physiological changes involved in sexual intercourse and sexual activity (Masters, Johnson, & Kolodney, 1986). The four major phases of the **sexual response cycle** (Figure 12-13) are excitement, plateau, orgasm, and resolution.

1. In the *excitement phase,* there is a general arousal reaction combined with an increase of blood flow *(vasocongestion)* to the genitals. There is increasing muscular tension in the genital area. The penis becomes erect, and the vagina lubricates through vaginal sweat glands.
2. In the *plateau phase,* vasocongestion and muscle tension level off but sexual and general excitement remain high. This is the phase when intercourse

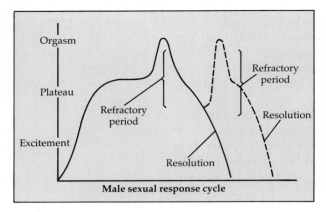

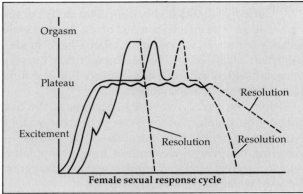

FIGURE 12-13
Human Sexual Response Cycles
These graphs show how males and females differ in their patterns of physiological response during sexual activity.
(After Masters & Johnson, 1966)

occurs. The plateau may be long or short depending on many factors, including the nature of the sexual act itself, the stimuli, and the training and control of the individual. One person may reach orgasm quickly, while another may wish to (and be able to) delay orgasm.

3. The third phase is *orgasm*, which is the briefest and most intense phase. Arousal, muscle tension, heart rate, and respiration increase rapidly to a peak. Then there is a sudden reduction of tension accompanied by orgasm. While sexual excitement can begin by purely mental means, such as fantasies, orgasm usually results from the stimulation of the genitals. Almost every male has orgasm. During orgasm men ejaculate semen, which contains sperm. From 10 to 30 percent of women never have orgasms, but about 14 percent report that they always have one or more climaxes during intercourse. The pattern of orgasm differs between the sexes. Men have orgasms more often over all, but women can have multiple orgasms during one sexual act.

4. In the *resolution phase,* the participants rest; arousal has subsided. There is mental and physical relaxation and a feeling of well-being. During resolution, a man cannot have an erection. After resolution, the cycle can begin again. There is, however, a physical limit to the number of times a day a man can have sexual intercourse. This number decreases as he gets older. Theoretically, there is no limit to the number of times a woman can have sex.

Homosexuality

In the past decade, many long-standing attitudes toward sexuality have been changed. Explicit sexual material, once relegated to the underworld, can now be checked out at the local video shop. In 1914 over 80 percent of males practiced premarital intercourse, while only 30 percent of women did. Current figures are almost equal (Hunt, 1974). Earlier characterizations of homosexuality are changing. About 10 percent of males are homosexual and about half of that for females (Kinsey, 1979).

Why do people become homosexual? Until 1973, the American Psychiatric Association considered homosexuality a disorder, but this designation was removed at that time. The aim of psychiatric treatment is no longer to quash a person's homosexuality. Instead, an attempt has begun to understand its causes. Is it a family problem, with the stereotypical idea of a lack of intimacy with parents and a lack of a strong relationship with the father? Some studies confirm this (Stephan, 1973), but a recent study found no relationship (Bell et al., 1981). Many other ideas are proposed. Biological factors such as response to hormones have been proposed (Gladue et al., 1984), but the evidence is yet scant.

Internal Arousal and Imprinting

One new approach draws from the general findings of the interpretation of arousal. This idea is that a crucial factor is the age of sexual maturity (Storms, 1981). Those who mature early would find their sexual drives prominent while they are in the company of companions of the same sex. Boys in our culture typically have close relationships with other boys until about age 13 or 14. The internal arousal, in this view, gets associated with one's surroundings and attached to them. Note how this is similar to many other bonding processes: the human baby bonds or attaches to its mother, and the baby duckling imprints on any moving object during a critical time. Men aroused in the company of others associate the arousal with those of like sex.

See Chapter 2, section on Imprinting.

Many of our sexual desires may well be formed in this manner. People form attachments not only to one sex or another, but to a certain look, smell, or ideal person if he or she appears at the right time. This view predicts that early sexual maturers would be more likely to be homosexual, and this seems to be the case (Goode & Haber, 1977). Feelings, even intimate ones, transfer, associate, and combine according to the principles of psychology.

How important is the feeling dimension to our lives? It warns us of danger, stirs us to actions, directs our thought. It is no wonder that the word *emotion* comes from the same root as movement. This leads us to the next chapter—on what "moves" us.

SUMMARY

1. Emotions are similar among all peoples of the world and even between human beings and other animals. Emotions comprise relatively automatic and involuntary patterns of responding to different situations. This might account for why "getting emotional" about something usually means our responses seem beyond conscious control. Emotions have several functions. They arouse us, help organize experience, direct and sustain actions, and communicate our actions to others. Most animals have evolved display signals, such as odors, postures, facial expressions, and gestures, that communicate information about probable behavior to other animals. These primitive communications are common also to human beings.

2. Some psychologists hypothesize that there are several primary, *basic emotions*. One viewpoint considers these emotions to be joy, acceptance, fear, surprise, sadness, disgust, anger, and anticipation. They produce new combinations of emotions in the way they vary in intensity, similarity, and polarity. Research initiated by Darwin and continued in various cultures by Ekman and others has established that the basic emotions are universal. People in widely different cultures have similar emotional expressions.

3. *Activation* of the body's *emergency reaction* underlies most strong feelings, such as anger, fear, and joy. It is controversial in psychology whether different emotions cause different bodily reactions. A new study shows that different patterns of autonomic nervous system activity characterize different emotions. Also, different people seem

to show characteristic autonomic patterns of emotional responses to situations, such as people who blush when they are joyful, embarrassed, or angry.

4. Sometimes active emotional coping with hardship through direct problem solving is not possible even for the hardiest. Fortunately, psychological mechanisms clear the deck and make possible other thoughts and actions. One such mechanism is denial, the mental operation by which thoughts, feelings, acts, threats, or demands are minimized or negated. Denial can help block perception of certain threatening information when attending to it will only arouse unnecessary anxiety. Therefore, whether denial is healthy or not depends on the circumstances and outcome.

5. Various emotional consequences follow upsets. *Frustration* is a normal reaction to stress that results when a desired outcome is thwarted or delayed. There are three types of conflicts that may result in threat or frustration: (1) when needs or motives are in opposition, (2) when external demands are incompatible, and (3) when an internal need or motive opposes an external demand.

6. The consequences of frustration or threat include the stress emotions, fear and anxiety, which can be modified by the taking of antianxiety drugs, such as alcohol or barbiturates. However, these drugs lessen anxiety at a cost—they seem to interfere with complex learning and inhibit REM sleep and dreaming. There are two ways to cope with anxiety: *problem-focused* coping includes such strategies as making and executing plans, asking for advice, and getting information. *Emotion-focused* coping is trying not to think about a problem, expressing your feelings to someone, or trying to look on the bright side.

7. The two cerebral hemispheres seem specialized differently for emotions. The left hemisphere responds to the verbal content of emotional expression and the right to tone of voice and gesture. The left side of the face (the side controlled by the right hemisphere) seems to express emotion more strongly than the right. In addition, we seem to judge people's left side of the face as the side expressing emotion. Davidson showed that the left hemisphere may actually involve different emotions than the right. The left seems to involve positive emotions, and the right, negative ones.

8. There are three basic dimensions to the *appraisal* process of emotions. The first is *evaluation:* is the situation good or bad, benign or threatening? The second is *potency:* is it alive or dead, strong or weak? The third is *activity:* is it active or passive? Emotions, like perception, consciousness, and memory, operate in a continuous cycle of appraisal, feedback, and reappraisal. The first, primary appraisal arouses the organism. Reappraisal considers whether an event is benign or threatening and directs which action to take.

9. In several studies, emotional expression decreases certain illnesses, such as cancer. One common characteristic of lung cancer patients is that they suppress their emotions. They also seem to ignore their negative feelings, such as hostility, depression, and guilt. Long-term survivors of breast cancer display anxiety, hostility, alienation, and other negative emotions and seem to be healthier for it. It is not yet clear why there is a link between "getting it off your chest" and reduced cancer. One link may be hormonal. Hormones can influence the growth of cancerous tumors.

10. Conscious interpretation can affect one's internal state. Schachter and Singer injected epinephrine into students who were told it was a vitamin. Half the students were placed with a euphoric person, the others with an insulting and irritated person. The first half reported feeling euphoric, while those confronted by the insulting person reported being angry. These results may show that an emotional experience depends

upon the interpretation of arousal, but there are problems with these experiments. Normally, activation requiring interpretation occurs in only contrived situations. Most life situations are not ambiguous, and our emotions guide us accurately.

11. Sex is very different for human beings than for other organisms. Sex signals for human sexuality are often mental rather than biological. However, there is a regular pattern of physiological changes involved in sexual intercourse and activity. Four major phases comprise the *sexual response cycle*, including excitement, plateau, orgasm, and resolution.

12. Recent research shows that homosexuality may occur in people who mature sexually at an early age when they are close to people of their own sex. This arousal thus becomes associated with people of their own sex and they become "attached" to them sexually.

TERMS AND CONCEPTS

activation
affect
anxiety
appraisal
arousal
catharsis
denial
emergency reaction
emotions
emotion solid
emotion wheel

fear
feelings
frustration
homosexuality
moods
orgasm
primary (basic) emotions
reappraisal
sexual response cycle
temperament
vasocongestion

SUGGESTIONS FOR FURTHER READING

Ekman, P. (1985). *Telling lies.* New York: Norton.
  A psychologist's attempt to explain how to detect deceit in business and in life. The book explains how difficult it is.

Ekman, P., & Friesen, W. (1983). *Unmasking the face.* Palo Alto, CA: Consulting Psychologists Press.
  The complete test of facial expression of emotions.

Goleman, D. (1985). *Vital lies, simple truths.* New York: Simon & Schuster.
  A popular and well thought out book about how the nervous system by design denies feelings.

Izard, C. E. et al. (1986). *Emotions, cognition and behavior.* New York: Cambridge.
  A definitive collection of essays on the relationship of emotions to other psychological processes.

Lazarus, R., & Folkman, S. (1986). Coping and adaptation. In W. Gentry (Ed.). *Handbook of behavioral medicine.* New York: Guilford.
  How emotions, stress, and coping all relate.

Scherer, K., Wallbott, H., & Summerfield, A. (1986). *Experiencing emotion: A cross-cultural study.* New York: Cambridge.
  How emotion is displayed in different social locales. A different approach to that taken in this text and in psychology.

Needs and Goals

A woman stops going out in the evening; she studies late, works extra hours at a waitress job, and saves all her money. Why? She has decided to go to medical school. At every moment we face an almost infinite number of choices. We can do things enthusiastically, halfheartedly, persistently, or lackadaisically. "Well-motivated" people do better on intelligence tests than others less motivated. People will give up their lives for their country. They may work all night tending the wounded, or eat nothing but bread and cheese to save for something special. People act in very different ways depending on what *motivates* them.

Motives are much more variable and individual than any other process we have considered so far. They can determine the course of your life. A person motivated by love may forgo the possibility of making a scientific contribution. Another motivated by achievement may have little time for a family.

Not only do different people have different motives, but each person has different *levels* of motivation within. Motives range from the basic and universal, such as hunger and thirst, to the ethereal, such as the desire for self-actualization. Motives build upon one another in a progression, from the simple to the complex.

As far as we know, we are the only animals aware of our own existence. It seems that this awareness, perhaps coupled with the awareness of death, leads to wondering about the purpose of life. We create our life in the pursuit of our goals, be they financial, intellectual, family, or others. This chapter considers motives common to all animals, such as basic hunger and thirst, and those such as creativity that create individuality.

<table>
<tr><td>AN OVERVIEW OF
NEEDS AND
GOALS</td><td>We share with other animals certain purely biologic needs that are basic to the survival of the individual and the species. Thirst, hunger, and temperature regulation are examples. But we do not live by bread and water alone. We also need to be safe and warm, to care and be cared for. People also look for meaning and strive for specific goals in life. To be "driven by ambition" is to be moved by a goal, be it the construction of a building or a symphony.</td></tr>
</table>

Some Definitions

Needs

There are two different groups of motives: needs and goals. **Needs** are specific deficits that any animal must satisfy, such as hunger and thirst. We have needs for food, water, rest, safety, and protection, among many others. Needs give rise to drives. The need itself is a deficiency that drives the organism into action to satisfy it.

Drives

Drives are physiologically based goads to behavior: they literally move us to action. A hungry person feels "driven" to find food. A drive is often experienced as a specific feeling such as thirst, hunger, or sex. At one time psychologists hypothesized that all behavior resulted from the reduction of a drive (Hull, 1943). The hunger drive increases when the organism has not fed. After eating that drive is reduced, and the motivation to seek food is lessened (Figure 13-1). Much of animal and human action is certainly "driven" in this way.

Nevertheless, the concept of drive *reduction* only accounts for behavior associated with very basic needs, such as hunger and thirst. It does not account for

FIGURE 13-1
Drive Reduction

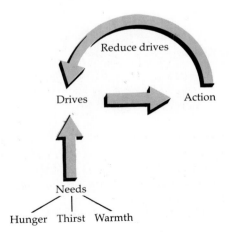

much that is characteristically human, such as curiosity and exploration. It hardly explains some behaviors that *increase* drives, such as watching pornographic movies, not to mention jumping out of airplanes for "fun."

Instincts

Psychologists once thought that all behaviors, animal and human, could be understood by innate patterns of behavior called **instincts** which "programmed" the animal to satisfy needs. An instinct is a behavior typical of every member of a species, and it appears without learning on the first occasion the appropriate situation occurs.

Today, there is less emphasis on instincts (McClelland, 1985b). It is generally accepted that certain *predispositions* are inherited as part of the human genetic program. Some are specific, such as the patterns of mother–infant attachment, while others are general, such as learning a language. Behavior is a mixture of innate and environmental factors. Most humans learn a language; their culture determines the specific language they learn.

Goals

What is unique about human motivation is the creation of goals. A **goal** is a desired outcome that has not yet occurred. Human beings do not merely adjust to the demands of their environment: they adapt the environment to suit themselves. If the satisfaction of needs is homeostatic adaptation, then the satisfaction of goals is "creative adaptation." Creative adaptation changes the environment to meet the goals of the organism (Dubos, 1978). It brings about the construction of cities, human culture and art, science and technology, books, and businesses. What makes human beings unique is our ability to go beyond our inheritance.

Maslow's Pyramid of Motivation

Human motives can be thought of as a "pyramid" of different needs and goals (Frager & Fadiman, 1987). At the bottom are the most basic needs. As one progresses to the top, human needs and the goals become more complex (Figure 13-2).

Prepotence

What distinguishes the different levels of Maslow's hierarchy is **prepotence:** the *relative strength* of the different needs. In this view, the "stronger" needs are lower on the hierarchy. Given the lack of both friendship and water, the need for water is stronger, that is, *prepotent.* The need for water preempts consciousness until it is satisfied. The general rule, then, is *once the lower needs are satisfied, the higher ones can be.*

Keys and colleagues did a study of 32 conscientious objectors during World War II. The volunteers had their caloric intake reduced from 3,500 to 1,600 per day for six months. During this time they lost an average of 24 percent of their body weight. The thought of food completely "preempted" their consciousness. They talked, dreamed, and read about it more than anything else. They were extremely disturbed by the slightest waste of available food and even licked their

Abraham Maslow
(1908–1970)

FIGURE 13-2
Maslow's Pyramid of
Motivation

Efforts must be made to
satisfy needs lower in the
hierarchy before needs
and goals at higher levels
can be expected to
motivate action.
(After Maslow, 1970)

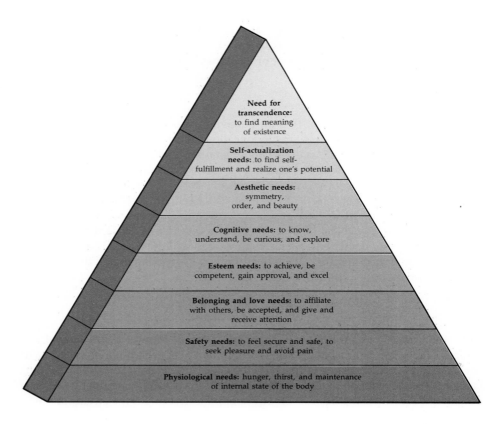

Need for
transcendence:
to find meaning
of existence

Self-actualization
needs: to find self-
fulfillment and realize one's potential

Aesthetic needs:
symmetry,
order, and beauty

Cognitive needs: to know,
understand, be curious, and explore

Esteem needs: to achieve, be
competent, gain approval, and excel

Belonging and love needs: to affiliate
with others, be accepted, and give and
receive attention

Safety needs: to feel secure and safe, to
seek pleasure and avoid pain

Physiological needs: hunger, thirst, and maintenance
of internal state of the body

plates clean. The motivation for anything not associated with food vanished (Keys, Brozek, Henschel, Mickelson, & Taylor, 1950).

Maslow's pyramid of motivation is a general and somewhat idealistic scheme. While thirst is certainly more basic than self-actualization, people may often satisfy many different needs at one time. The hierarchy does not really work for the higher end. Esteem, knowledge, and the like are much more equivalent to one another than Maslow presumed.

Also, the prepotence of the different levels may vary from individual to individual. The need for transcendence may be so strong that a person may forget friendship and esteem. Sometimes even survival needs are forgotten; religious figures such as Moses, Buddha, and Christ are examples. Still, the hierarchy is a useful way to organize the enormous range of human motives. This chapter begins with basic and well-understood motives, such as temperature regulation, thirst, and hunger, and it continues with needs for other people, curiosity, knowledge, achievement, and religious motives.

PHYSIOLOGICAL NEEDS

The primary motivation for all organisms is survival. Enough oxygen must be inspired, and ample food and liquid must be consumed for animals to stay alive and healthy. All animals, too, try to avoid pain and injury and seek shelter and safety. These needs operate via homeostasis. A deficiency in any of them leads to actions designed to correct the deficiency and a return to the original state.

Because these needs are so important, they have been the subject of much research and there is a great understanding of the complex and precise regulation of these processes. Many of our experiences seem quite simple: we are thirsty and we drink; we are hungry and we eat. However, much work and organization goes on within our bodies "behind the scenes" without our awareness.

Keeping Stable

What the entire mental system and brain does is to adapt continuously to keep the body stable (but not *static*) in a changing world. Neither the world nor we remain the same. We need more strength as an adult than we did as a child. Blood supply that is adequate for resting does not suffice for running. Metabolic processes that keep the energy supply adequate in winter do not do so in spring.

Countless systems within the brain harmonize this moving stability, as the world changes, as the organism changes, as needs change. Think about how much must be organized behind the scenes! We need to control blood flow through heartbeat, blood pressure, blood composition, and volume. Metabolism involves breathing, entrance of oxygen into the bloodstream, and the production, combination, and distribution of thousands of chemicals. Safety involves the integrity of the internal organs, the detection of danger, and mobilizing the emergency system. Social life depends on stable attachments to family, to friends, and to society. Internal stability depends, too, on those perceptual processes that generate constancy of perception.

Homeostasis — The Stability of the Body

Mental processes maintain constancy in the perceived world, and we also maintain constancy in the internal world. **Homeostasis** is the tendency to keep the organism in a constant (stasis) state. The regulatory systems of the body seek to maintain constant internal processes — constant temperature, water content, and food supply. This constancy must be maintained during extremes of temperature and during long periods without food or drink (Toates, 1986).

See Chapter 2, section on Feedback and Systems.

Homeostasis operates by the process of feedback. If the set point of a thermostat is 68°, higher temperatures cause the cooling systems to come on. Temperatures below 68° will result in heat production. Any deviation from the desired state is minimized by the thermostatic control of heat and cooling.

See Chapter 2, Figure 2-3.

Homeostatic principles underlie many bodily processes. We eat when we are hungry; we are hungry when our body needs more fuel. When we are cold, we shiver, which warms us up. Sweat cools us off when we are hot.

Temperature Regulation

One of the body's most basic homeostats is the mechanism of temperature regulation. In human beings the "set point" temperature of 98.6°F (37°C) is maintained by **thermometer neurons** in the hypothalamus of the brain that measure blood temperature. If there is a discrepancy of about 1°C from the set point, they alter their firing rate which triggers actions either to warm or cool the blood. Warming is accomplished by increased muscle tone, shivering, and constriction of the peripheral blood vessels, which decreases heat loss. Cooling is attained by sweating and vasodilation in the arms, legs, and head (Toates, 1986).

A fever occurs when the hypothalamic set point itself is raised. There is some evidence that the development of a fever itself may be beneficial. The increased body temperature during fever may kill viruses that cause common febrile diseases such as influenza (Dinarello & Wolfe, 1979).

Thirst

Fluids are essential: every cell of the body is bathed in them. They have the approximate mineral concentration of seawater, and they constitute 75 percent of body weight. The maintenance of proper fluid intake and regulation is an extremely important and intricate job, since a small loss of fluid or change in concentration of the electrolytes in the body fluids can kill us.

When your mouth feels dry, you drink — it seems so simple. However, there is a complicated brain-directed system that regulates body fluids. Your mouth becomes dry because the water content of the blood has dropped, which dries out the salivary glands (Figure 13-3). Usually the glands dry out gradually, but this drying may occur suddenly, as when you exercise on a hot day.

However, thirst can be quenched in several ways, only one of which is wetting the salivary glands. Water placed directly into the stomach through a tube reduces thirst. Thus, there is a more central mechanism for fluid control than the glands in the mouth. When the water content outside the cells (primarily in the blood) drops, the concentration of salt (which is usually 0.9 percent) in bodily fluids increases. That causes fluid from the cells to be released into the bloodstream, increasing blood volume and hence blood pressure (Figure 13-4). Pressure receptors in blood vessels also detect even the smallest reduction in the water content of

FIGURE 13-3
Thirst
A drop in the water content of your blood, which dries out your salivary glands and makes your mouth dry, is only part of what is involved in thirst. The extremely complex system for regulating body fluids is explained in the accompanying text and Figure 13-4.

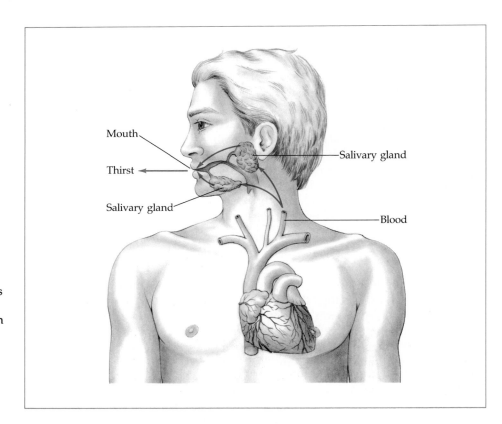

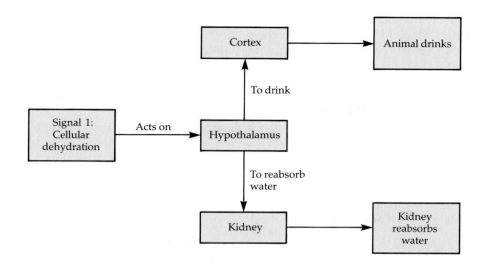

FIGURE 13-4
Regulation of Water Intake
In the upper flow chart cellular dehydration signals the hypothalamus to tell the kidney to reabsorb water and the cerebral cortex to have the animal drink. In the lower flow chart decreased blood volume prompts the kidney to trigger constriction of the blood vessels and to signal the hypothalamus of the need for water intake.

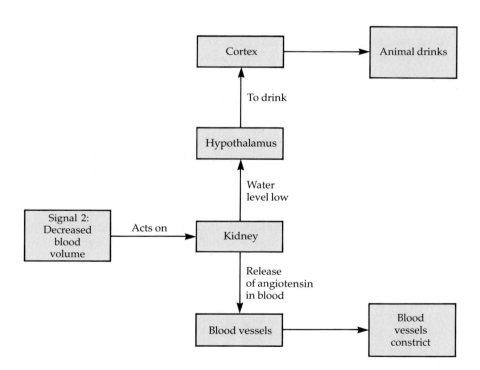

the blood (Toates, 1986). This leads, by means of messages transmitted from the vessels by the sympathetic nervous system, to the release of renin, an enzyme produced by the kidney. Renin changes blood protein into a new compound, a "thirst substance," which acts on receptors in the hypothalamus and other parts of the limbic system. This activates the sensation of thirst.

See Chapter 4, section on The Limbic System.

How we know to stop drinking is less clear than why we start, because we stop before the fluid has time to enter the cells of the body. Pressure receptors in the blood vessels detect entering fluid; they then reduce renin production, which diminishes the activity in the area of the hypothalamus concerned with thirst. This cannot be the whole story, though, because much of the liquid is still unabsorbed when we cease drinking. Perhaps increased stomach volume is used as a feedback signal as well.

If there is no fluid intake, as occurs in sleep, and the fluid content within cells is too low, then a hormonal feedback system is activated. The anterior hypothalamus produces antidiuretic hormone (ADH), which signals the kidneys to divert some of the water in the urine to the bloodstream. The absence of ADH, which may result from damage to the hypothalamus, as in the disease *diabetes insipidus*, leads to an increase of 10 to 15 times the normal amount of urine and almost constant thirst and drinking (Bellows, 1939).

Hunger

Thirst regulation is more complex than temperature regulation, and the processes regulating hunger are even more complex than those regulating thirst. So, while disorders of temperature regulation and thirst are unusual, hunger disorders such as obesity are common.

How Do We Know We Are Hungry?

When you "feel" hungry, you eat — as with thirst, it seems so simple. But there is an even more complex system underlying our experience of hunger. *Gastric* and *metabolic* factors are at work telling us when to eat and when to stop.

Gastric Factors. Walter Cannon, who pioneered much research on the wisdom of the body, emphasized the gastric (stomach) component of hunger. He cajoled his research assistant into swallowing a balloon attached to a graph that recorded the changes in size of the balloon. When the stomach expanded or contracted, so did the balloon. The assistant's reports of hunger pangs coincided with contractions of the balloon (Cannon, 1929). Thus, Cannon proposed that stomach contractions were the primary signal of hunger.

Metabolic Factors. There is more to hunger than stomach contractions and more to stomach contractions than simple stomach emptiness. Stomach contractions stop when sugar is injected into the bloodstream, even though the stomach is empty.

Metabolic factors relate hunger to the maintenance of energy and body weight. They are registered in the brain in terms of level of blood sugar and the amount of fat deposited in the body. We get hungry when blood sugar (glucose) is low (Mayer, 1953). However, we do not stop eating only because blood sugar is restored to the proper level (Thompson, 1986). Although the control of eating is complex, it involves several brain structures, especially the hypothalamus (Le Magnen, 1986). Consider what happens when the lateral hypothalamus of a rat is destroyed. The rat will stop eating and will actually starve to death without tube feeding (Anand & Brobeck, 1951). If these rats *are* tube fed, their normal eating and drinking patterns are gradually restored (Figure 13-5). This means that the lateral hypothalamus is not the "eating and drinking center."

Destruction of some areas of the hypothalamus leads to very specific deficits. There may be an inability to regulate blood sugar level, but response to food

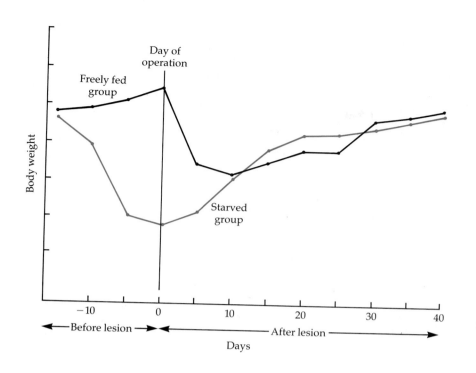

Day of operation

Freely fed group

Body weight

Starved group

−10 0 10 20 30 40

← Before lesion → ← After lesion →

Days

FIGURE 13-5
The Lateral Hypothalamus and the Control of Eating
When their lateral hypothalamus is destroyed, rats will not eat or drink. If tube fed, such animals usually resume eating and drinking on their own in time. But those that were starved before the operation increase their eating, and those freely fed prior to the operation eat less. Eventually, the two groups' weight and eating and drinking patterns will stabilize at about the same relatively normal level.

deprivation is untouched (Blass & Kety, 1974). The hypothalamus is intimately involved in feeding, but in a complex way. Also, disruption of eating and drinking is associated with lesions in a number of other brain areas (Grossman, 1979).

How Do We Know When to Stop Eating?

Destruction of the ventromedial nuclei (VMN) of the hypothalamus results in **hyperphagia** or extreme overeating. This produces some extremely fat rats that are unable to stop eating (Figure 13-6) (Hetherington & Ranson, 1942). Teitelbaum (1957) discovered that these rats are picky eaters. They consume an enormous amount, but are more sensitive to the taste of the food than normal rats. They only eat a lot of what they like.

This is also true of obese human beings. Obese people and rats with VMN lesions have lost internal mechanisms or cues that control eating, such as stomach contractions or low blood sugar. They seem to eat more because of external cues such as a lunch whistle or the appearance of food (Schachter, 1971; Schachter & Rodin, 1974).

Rats with VMN lesions do not go on eating until they explode. They simply maintain a new, higher body weight (King & Gaston, 1977) (Figure 13-7). When the VMN is damaged, growth hormone, which modulates the effect of insulin, decreases. Circulating insulin increases, which decreases the burning of fatty acids. The result is increased deposits of fat. Normally, circulating insulin increases as soon as the organism begins to eat (Struble & Steffens, 1975). When the VMN is damaged, this normal process may be exaggerated (Toates, 1986; Steffens, Mogenson, & Stevenson, 1972).

How does the VMN work when it is working well? It might be a direct sensory process. Food passing through several stages of digestion may be signaled to the VMN—or perhaps the production of insulin is the cue.

FIGURE 13-6
Eating Itself to Death
When part of its hypothalamus was destroyed, this rat had no way to tell when it was satiated, so it gorged itself to a weight three to four times normal.

RESISTING DISEASE

Maintaining the stability of fluids and nourishment are important motivators, and so is the stability to resist diseases from outside. How are we motivated to repel outside attacks from viruses and bacteria? The immune system defends the body; it has similarities to the nervous system. Both respond to a variety of outside information and regulate the body; both receive and transmit either excitatory or inhibitory signals. But most important and most revolutionary is that both learn and remember. The immune system identifies and recognizes what is foreign (not of the body) and what is not.

Mechanisms of Immunity

Antigens are "foreign" cells or large molecules of origin outside the body. Their intrusion into the body stimulates the immune responses to defend the organism. At the same time, the immune system must not attack the cellular and molecular constituents of the body itself. The ability of the immune system to recognize and keep track of millions of different substances is another "miracle" of our bodies. However, the immune system isn't perfect. If it overreacts to harmless antigens, this causes allergies. It can also fail to recognize the body's own cells attacking itself—as in autoimmune diseases.

Natural immunity involves general inflammatory processes for reacting to tissue damage. When most cells are damaged, they release molecules that increase the permeability of the capillaries. This allows cells and large molecules to enter the tissues that help to neutralize bacteria and viruses. Other molecules, such as interferon, inhibit viruses from spreading by "replicating" themselves.

Acquired immunity works through a type of white blood cell known as *lymphocytes*. Lymphocytes patrol the bloodstream and are ideally suited for the recognition and destruction of millions of different antigens. Here is how they work. Embryonic cells and (later in life) the bone marrow give rise to lymphocytes which then undergo further specialization. Some are carried by the circulation to the thymus where they undergo maturation to T-cells (the T is from thymus). Other lymphocytes called B-cells mature in the fetal liver and later in bone marrow. Other cell types in the immune army include *macrophages* (Greek for "big eaters"). These are large scavenger cells that ingest and destroy antigens, natural killer cells that attack tumors, and virus-infected cells.

The system has to patrol constantly and be able to make millions of duplicate cells upon demand. It can work this way because the lymphocytes mutate wildly very early in embryonic life and produce a vast range of cells. Each one, like the transmission of neural impulses, has different shapes of surface receptors. These cells remain available for defense against practically any kind of invader.

It works through the lock-and-key principle (see Chapter 4). The antigen through its own molecular shape automatically selects its worst enemy from an army of potential defenders. When the lymphocyte cell pool is exposed to a foreign antigen, a battle follows in rapid succession. Cells matching the pattern reproduce and generate an enormous army of identical lymphocytes. These instant defenders produce specific antibodies that combine with and inactivate the antigen. At the same time, other sensitized T-cells migrate to the source of the antigen (say a tumor). There they secrete chemicals called lymphokines, which are toxic to the foreign tissue.

The state of the immune system motivates the resistance of the organism. This motivation is perhaps more important in the development of diseases than exposure to actual disease entities (viral or bacterial) or toxins. Some viruses such as herpes simplex are always present but become active only when something goes wrong with the immune system.

The Brain and the Immune System

Recall the study in Chapter 1 in which the death of a spouse in a train wreck resulted in decreases in immune system functioning. Recent scientific efforts are beginning to track the many influences on the immune system. They range from laughter to empathy, from bereavement to anger.

But how do mental factors or even specific brain processes affect the immune system? Answering this question has barely begun, yet there are many important and promising new indications. It is known that there are extensive connections between the nervous system and the immune system. The immune system is regarded as the center of the defense against disease. It is of current interest also because AIDS is a disorder of the immune system.

Removal of certain areas in the hypothalamus leads to suppression while stimulation leads to enhanced immune system response. In an early study in Hungary in the 1950s two researchers first sensitized guinea pigs to allergic substances. When the hypothalamus was lesioned, those animals did not respond to the allergen. The intact animals responded with standard violent allergic reactions. Later research revealed that damage to certain areas of the hypothalamus resulted in decreased function in the thymus gland. Recall that the thymus is responsible for the maturation of the T-cells that control immune surveillance and antibody production.

Not only does the hypothalamus communicate with the immune system but the immune system talks back. Besedovsky et al. (1977) recorded the rate of firing of neurons in the hypothalamus when an animal was challenged by foreign and virulent antigens. The rate increased greatly. This indicates that information about

the immune system is registered, if not organized, in the hypothalamus.

The stronger the immune reaction, the stronger is the brain response. Since the hypothalamus controls the pituitary, the pharmacy of the brain, there were also significant changes in levels of the neurotransmitter norepinephrine. All this evidence suggests that the immune system can change brain function and vice versa.

Emotions and Immunity

As discussed in other chapters, research is beginning to show that mental factors influence resistance to disease. Kasl et al. (1979) studied the development of infectious mononucleosis in West Point cadets. The cadets were given blood tests to screen for antibodies to Epstein—Barr virus which causes infectious mono. In addition the investigators reviewed interview data about the cadets, which included information about their expectations and family backgrounds.

Each year about one-fifth of the cadets were infected but only about one-fourth of them developed mono. What predicted those who were likely to become ill? Cadets who wanted a military career but were doing poorly academically were most likely to develop symptoms. The combination of high expectation and poor performance was reflected in increased susceptibility to infectious disease.

Even mild upsets have effects on the immune system. Medical students were observed for the number of their "life change events" in the previous months as well as their loneliness. Both loneliness and the mild amount of life stress these students had (they were doing well on exams) preceded decreased natural killer immune cells (Kiecolt-Glaser, 1985).

The immune system responds directly to a break in the mother—infant attachment. Christopher Coe and his colleagues (1985) separated squirrel monkeys from their mothers at 6 months of age. Immune function (decreased antibody response   *(cont.)*

and levels of complement and immunoglobulins) were suppressed in those suffering maternal loss. However, this separation-induced immune suppression was less when the infant was placed in a familiar home environment or with familiar peers.

Anxiety and depression affect natural killer cell activity, which is a measure of cellular immune function. Stephen Locke studied a group of 114 Harvard undergraduates. "Good copers"—those who reported few psychiatric symptoms in the face of high levels of stress—had significantly higher cell activity than "poor copers" (Locke et al., 1984). Poor coping in the face of stressful life changes may adversely affect immunity.

Psychoimmunology

Can positive states of mind enhance the functioning of the immune system? This is the subject of a growing amount of research. There is some evidence that an individual can voluntarily improve immune functions. Hall and colleagues studied 20 healthy people to assess the response of the lymphocytes in the immune system to positive suggestions during hypnosis (Hall et al., 1981; Hall, 1986). While under hypnosis, they were told to visualize their white blood cells as strong powerful "sharks" swimming through the bloodstream attacking weak confused germs. They were given a posthypnotic suggestion that these "sharklike" cells would protect their body against germs. They did self-hypnosis two times each week and told themselves the shark story. The result was that the younger subjects showed an actual increase in the responsiveness of their immune systems following hypnosis. Those who were easily hypnotized showed *increased numbers* of lymphocytes after their hypnotic sessions!

There seems to be a benefit from laughing, as well. Ten students viewed a humorous videotape (*Richard Pryor Live*) and a didactic control tape. Their levels of salivary IgA were measured before and after each videotape. (Salivary IgA is a type of antibody that appears to defend against viral infections of the upper respiratory tract.) Viewing Richard Pryor's antics temporarily boosted the average concentrations of this antibody (Dillon et al., 1985–1986).

The immune system may be the central point of the motivation to resist disease, and research in this field promises to link mental and physical components of motivation. (Ornstein & Sobel, 1987)

FIGURE 13-7
The Ventromedial Hypothalamus and Hyperphagia
Destruction of the ventromedial area of a rat's hypothalamus causes hyperphagia—extreme overeating. The weight of such rats eventually stabilizes at a new, obese level that is only temporarily influenced by either force feeding or starvation.
(After Hoebel & Teitelbaum, 1966)

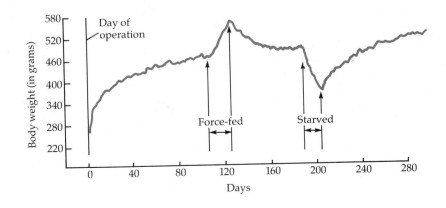

Obesity

The search for the edible and the delicious is constant and continues in modern culture with new cuisines, new restaurants, and new food crazes. Some foods are thought to be aphrodisiacs. Food is strongly associated with feelings: an image of daily love and togetherness might be a family gathered around a holiday table. People believe "the way to a man's heart is through his stomach." Jewish mothers cure everything with chicken soup.

> Humans will swallow almost anything that does not swallow them first. The animals they relish range in size from termites to whales; the Chinese of Hunan Province eat shrimp that are still wriggling, while North Americans and Europeans eat live oysters. . . . Strong preferences have been shown for the fetuses of rodents, the tongues of larks, the eyes of sheep, the spawn of eels, the stomach contents of whales, and the windpipes of pigs. (Farb & Armelagos, 1980)

Our love of and preoccupation with food has had, until recently, great adaptive value. When the food supply was insecure, people who gorged themselves when food was plentiful had more chance of survival later. When most work required strenuous manual labor, huge meals were needed as fuel. Until recently, unheated homes made it necessary for people to produce heat from what went into their stomachs, not a furnace.

Temperature and Food Intake Regulation

The body operates like a furnace: metabolism is a process in which fuel (food) is burned to make heat to keep the body warm and to provide energy. When there is more fuel than can be metabolized, it is stored as fat, to be used when needed.

The regulation is dishearteningly accurate. Each of us eats, over a lifetime, more than 45 tons of food, yet our weight varies little. Suppose you ate just 200

Humans are truly omnivorous, able and willing to eat large quantities of any and all kinds of food. This has generally been of great adaptive value to our species.

calories a day more than you burn (one small chocolate bar), and didn't increase other activities. If there was no adaptation in the body, you would gain about 20 pounds a year!

In Western modern culture, there is a drastic increase in the availability of food, a decrease in strenuous activities, and central heating. The end product is often great human stores of fat. In some contemporary Western European countries, such as Germany, more than 75 percent of the population is overweight.

The "Set Point"

Weight is gained when there are more calories taken in than are expended. A calorie is a measure of heat production: it is the amount of energy required to increase the temperature of one gram of water by 1°C. Losing and gaining weight is *not* simply a matter of decreasing calorie intake because the homeostatic mechanisms of the body regulate weight around a set point. The **set point** is the body weight around which the brain attempts to maintain homeostasis (Cabanac, 1971). The hypothalamus can control appetite, absorption of food into the body, and metabolic level to change caloric expenditure (Le Magnen, 1986; Bennett, 1984).

It is this set point, not primarily our conscious decisions, that keeps our weight around a predetermined level. It is almost impossible to consciously regulate food intake to a few hundred calories a day. Even a nutritionist could not estimate caloric intake that precisely (Bennett, 1984). The "set point" makes it more difficult both to *gain* and *lose* weight than we would predict by merely counting calories.

Here are some common excuses for being overweight:

1. "I've lost hundreds of pounds in my life" (the implication being that it is always gained back).
2. "It doesn't matter how much I eat—I am just naturally fat."
3. "I can gain weight by just looking at food."

Recent evidence suggests that these clichés are true.

Our ideas of obesity and beauty change through time and from culture to culture. People who are fat can be considered healthy and attractive in their own culture. But in our culture today, thinness is equated with health and beauty, while obesity is viewed as unattractive and unhealthy.

Innate Factors in Obesity

Here is a sad fact: some people *are* born to be fat. The set point for weight is simply higher in these people. This, as is well known, makes losing weight to a desired ideal difficult, if not impossible.

Fatness is related to the number and size of the body's fat cells, called **adipocites.** Obese people have three times the number of these fat cells as do people of normal weight (Bjorntorp, 1972). Fat cells are established in the first two years of life. Overfeeding in those years results in an increased number of fat cells. No amount of weight loss after that age lessens the number of fat cells. They abide inside the unfortunate person, waiting to be bloated. Critical periods of fat cell production are from the ages 6 to 10 and during adolescence (Nisbett, 1972).

A person with too many fat cells has a high set point for food consumption and will continue to be hungry even when his or her weight is at the supposed "norm." The problem for the "constitutionally obese" is that their own set point is higher than the cultural norm. They then face two bleak alternatives: either constant hunger or being thought of as overweight. So these people lose and gain weight constantly; their diets do not work. The reason is that they are fighting a powerful biological enemy.

The Losing Battle

There are many sophisticated ways the brain handles incoming food. It is not a matter of simple "calories in and calories out" as was once thought. There is a much more sophisticated system for dealing with intake. Not all calories are equally fattening. Fat in food leads to more fat deposit in the body since it deposits directly in the tissue. An equal amount of calories of carbohydrates has to be metabolized first and does not contribute as much to deposited fat.

Calories are handled with great precision. After eating too large a meal the brain lights an internal fire, using brown adipocite cells. People with a lot of this "brown fat" sweat out the excess calories overnight and return to a good weight in the morning (Rothwell & Stock, 1979).

The stabilizing mechanisms of the body also serve to discourage weight loss. At the beginning of an attempt to lose weight, when one may be high above the real set point, weight loss is easier; as one approaches the set point, however, weight loss is more difficult. This causes many people to go off their diet and return to the original weight. Also, people try to establish a new, lower set point; when this cannot be reached, they abandon all discipline. This reaction is known in technical terms as the "what the hell" effect (Polivy & Herman, 1983).

The body has a built-in protection against famine that lowers the "set point" drastically when the food supply is low. Then weight loss may be extremely difficult. The limits to which the body can conserve were determined by Jewish doctors during the Nazi occupation of Poland. The caloric intake of the residents of the Warsaw ghetto was decreased by the Nazis from about 2,400 per day to about 300. Protein intake was cut to about 10 percent of normal (Winnick, 1979). The record these doctors made of the human body was of an organism struggling heroically to adapt. Body temperature dropped, blood pressure decreased, and blood circulated at a slower rate. The body burned fuel in the most efficient way possible. Only as a last resort was the stored protein in muscles, including the heart, burned. The human body's ability to slow its metabolism to conserve

Sometimes a young person, most often a woman, simply refuses to eat and begins to waste away. Why does this happen? How are they treated? Here is one case and the way it was treated.

Ellen West had great artistic abilities, wrote poetry, and kept a diary, before and after she became sick. . . . After graduation from high school she took up horseback riding and attained great skill, doing it in the same over-intense way with which she approached every task. In her nineteenth year, she noticed the beginning of a new anxiety, *namely the* fear of becoming fat. *She had developed an enormous appetite and grew so heavy that her friends would tease her. Immediately thereafter she began to castigate herself, denying herself sweets and other fattening foods, dropping supper altogether, and went on long exhausting walks. Though she looked miserable, she was only* worried about getting too fat *and continued her endless walks. Parallel to this fear of becoming fat, her desire for food increased. The persisting conflict between the dread of fatness and the craving for food overshadowed her whole life. After many years of illness she wrote: "It is this external tension between wanting to be thin and not to give up eating that is so exhausting. In all other aspects I am reasonable, but I know on this point I am crazy. I am really ruining myself in this endless struggle against my nature. Fate wanted me to be heavy and strong, but I want to be thin and delicate."*

In the treatment of this case, reconditioning was used and was often effective. All meals were brought to her by a nurse and were to be taken in her room. The experimenters set up a reinforcement schedule that consisted of verbal rewards for any movements associated with eating. For example, when she lifted her fork to move toward spearing a piece of food, the experimenter would talk to her about something in which the patient was interested. The required response was then shaped by reinforcing successive movements associated with raising or lifting food toward her mouth,

chewing, and so on.

The same reinforcement procedures were followed to increase the amount of food consumed. At first, any portion of the meal that was eaten would be rewarded by having the nurse come into her room with a radio, TV set, or phonograph. If she did not touch any of the food before her, she received no reinforcement, and she would be left alone until the next meal. As time went on, more and more of her meal had to be eaten, until eventually she had to finish everything on the plate in order to be reinforced. Her meals were slowly increased in caloric value, with the cooperation of the dieticians, and her weight gradually rose to a level of 85 pounds.

After discharge from the hospital, the question became, "How does one generalize the eating response that was acquired under controlled conditions to a situation where such controls are lacking?" This problem was solved by enlisting the help of the patient's family. They were instructed specifically: (1) to avoid reinforcing any irrelevant behavior or complaints; (2) not to make any issue of eating; (3) to reinforce maintenance of her weight gain by complimenting with comments about her beginning to fill out her clothes; (4) not to prepare any special diet for her; (5) to refrain from weighing her at home because this was to be recorded only when she made periodic visits to see the medical student; (6) to discuss only pleasant topics at meal times; (7) never to allow her to eat alone; (8) to follow a rigid schedule for meals, with an alarm clock to be present for each meal; (9) to use a purple table cloth initially as a discriminative stimulus for mealtime table behavior associated with eating; and (10) to encourage her to dine out with other people under enjoyable conditions. (Ullman & Krasner, 1965)

In anorexia, we see how many "rules" are normally taken care of by the body's stabilizing systems. Specifying all these conditions to make a person eat helps to make us aware of the complexity of the regulation within.

resources saved lives in the concentration camps. This routine probably did the same when our ancestors were confronted with famine.

In less extreme circumstances deliberately eating less is one means of adjusting weight. However, to maintain weight loss, *food intake must be continually decreased as the diet goes along*, since our caloric needs decrease at lower weights. A diet low enough in calories to decrease weight early in dieting may cause no weight loss or even a weight gain later on. The brain makes a new stabilizing point.

An alternative is to increase exercise, which reduces appetite. Exercise increases the caloric consumption (heat production) during the exercise itself, and it also increases heat production *after* a meal. More importantly, the increase in calories burned during exercise *continues during the day*. The "set-point" regulation mechanism evolved in a setting in which our ancestors habitually engaged in a moderate amount of physical activity during the course of the day. There are substantial weight benefits for those who walk about 25 to 30 miles per week. An amount of exercise about equivalent to this seems to reset the set point since this is about the work load that our ancestors adapted to, and it is probably the average stabilizing point of the system.

There is a consolation for those who will never match the ideal figure in the jeans ads. Remember that the average weight gain is a little less than one pound per year for people of average height. A man who weighed 165 at age 30 will usually weight about 185 at age 60. Millions of people gain weight through their lives. This gain plagues the middle aged; it is the boon for fitness centers, fad diets, and diet aids.

But from the point of view of keeping the body stable, why should this occur? It is for health. It is usually assumed that thin people are healthier, and for years, actuarial tables have been built around this assumption. But new research, especially by Reuben Andres, shows that people who are of average weight for their ages or slightly overweight are the healthiest (Figure 13-8) (Andres et al., 1985).

Most of the social advice about weight is more likely advice about appearance (looking thin means looking young) rather than useful health information. Brain

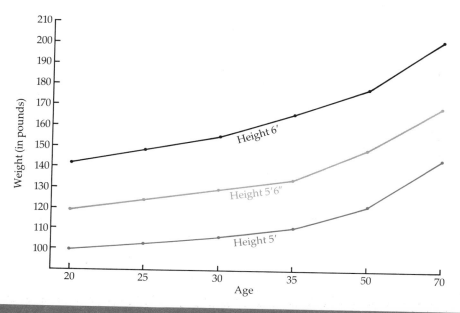

FIGURE 13-8
"Natural Weight"
The most recent research indicates that natural weight depends only on your height and age. This table graphs the natural weight for people of three heights at different ages in their lives. Weight within 15 pounds of each of these points should not interfere with health. For example, a 25-year-old woman who is 5'6" can weigh between 110 and 140 with little effect on her health.
(After Andres et al., 1985)

processes, having evolved over millions of years to adjust weight for health, are wiser than our current cultural ideal. So being "overweight" for those who are not grossly obese may not be such a losing battle after all.

BELONGING AND SAFETY

When the most basic and immediate physiological needs are met, others then need to be satisfied. Safety must be maintained, pain must be avoided, and pleasures are usually sought. There are human needs to belong to groups and social networks and to give and receive attention.

Pain and Pleasure

Avoiding pain and seeking pleasure guide the behavior of most animals. There exist well-defined pain and pleasure centers in the nervous system. These serve as a feedback system about actions that may be injurious or helpful to the organism's survival or reproductive success. An organism's feelings are a guide to action. It is here that emotions and motives are most closely related (Mook, 1986).

There are different networks for sending pain information to the brain. Sudden pain preempts consciousness. This happens when you put your hand on something hot. The lemniscal system quickly transmits sudden pain information. The spinothalamic system transmits slow pain information, like that of an old back problem.

There is a part of the brain's limbic system that is probably the final common pathway of the feeling of pleasure. Animals with electrodes in the "pleasure center" will perform almost any action to keep that center stimulated. They even forego food and drink under certain conditions (Routenberg, 1976).

Belonging

One element that runs through our evolutionary history is cooperation. At first glance you might be surprised to find "belonging" as a human need. After all, we have defined a need as something that if not satisfied, results in harm to the organism, such as starvation from lack of food. Why, then, is belonging a need? Recent evidence suggests that when people are deprived of belonging to a group, they may suffer health consequences. Human beings are social animals.

In one Australian aboriginal tribe, a person may become the victim of "bone pointing" when a powerful witch casts a spell condemning the unfortunate person to death. The people in the tribe then treat such individuals as if they were actually dead. They do not speak to them or acknowledge their presence, and they act as if they cannot see them. Unless the "spell" is lifted, the condemned often do die.

Is this extreme example just superstition? One study in our society partially repeated these extreme conditions. Experimenters at a military base instructed a group of soldiers to ignore one man completely and to act as if he literally were not there. The man lost his appetite, became apathetic, and withdrew. He began to develop a "thousand-mile stare" (looking far into the distance, noticed in prisoners of war). The effect was so surprising and devastating that the experiment was soon called off.

Cases of people deprived of normal social interaction show significant negative effects on intelligence and on health. Recall that children in a Lebanese

See Chapter 11, section on Enhancing Intelligence.

orphanage who were neglected showed much lower intelligence (Dennis & Dennis, 1948). When some children in an orphanage were "adopted" by caring people, their intelligence increased (Skeels & Dye, 1939).

So *people need people* and *need the attention of others.* In an extensive study of the effect of social networks on health, Syme and others found that healthy people have a more extensive network of friends than those less healthy. Syme often begins his lectures by saying, "When I was young and felt bad, my grandmother used to tell me, 'Go out and play with your friends'; now I find there is good evidence for this" (Syme, 1984).

When people who lack friends or a group are encouraged to join one, their health improves. A large project is under way in San Francisco's "Tenderloin" area seeking to improve the health of the impoverished elderly residents by forming neighborhood associations. The results show significant health improvements when people belong to a group (Minkler, 1984). Almost any improvement in "belonging" seems to help, whether there is a person involved or not. Patients in a nursing home who were given a plant to care for showed improvements in health (Rodin & Langer, 1978). To belong and to be needed by a family, group, or club is more of a basic human need that we might expect.

People Need to Belong
Taking a class, being a member of a team, joining a social organization, or just "gettin' together with the boys" provides a sense of belonging that can improve an individual's health and outlook on life.

Maternal Care

Maternal care in female rats seems largely under hormonal control. Some experiments have transferred hormones in the blood from a mother rat to another rat. The receptor rat later will begin to exhibit the characteristic maternal behavior pattern of rats. This includes nesting, licking, retrieving, and nursing the young rats. In humans, hormonal regulation probably does not completely determine maternal behavior. However, hormones under the control of the pituitary do play a specific role in lactation and nursing.

Male rats never care for their offspring. Human males may come to take an active role in child care, and some women abandon their children. The hormones associated with lactation may predispose the mother toward loving and caring for the child (Newton & Modahl, 1978). More likely it is the closeness involved in the activity of nursing itself that cements the love bond.

HUMAN GOALS

Many needs are common to all animals: food, drink, avoiding pain, and safety. Belonging needs and needs for attention are common to social animals such as human beings and chimpanzees. But what is uniquely human is not out needs but our *goals*. Human beings are not only motivated by biological *deficits* but by the invention of *possibilities* (Dubos, 1978). Homeostatic adaptation is important to all organisms, and it is to us as well. However, our most important inheritance is the ability to go beyond our inheritance.

Goals all serve the function of creative adaptation: the ability to create a new world to suit ourselves. These motives are more "mental" than biological. They are highly individual and are capable of being expressed differently by different people. If we had no goals, we would have no civilization and no world built of cities.

What makes us unique also makes us difficult to study. Why someone creates or is "driven" to form a new company is not as anatomically clear as the thirst drive. Thus, *some of the most important human experiences are not as well understood as the most basic.*

Competence and Excellence: Esteem

Competence is how well we can carry out an intended action. It earns us the esteem of others and builds our self-respect. Early in life, competence may involve simple tasks, such as getting food into the mouth or lifting a cup. At around age 2, a child smiles when he or she is able to perform a task successfully. Competence is a part of the emerging human consciousness.

Later on there are other challenges to competence—learning new tasks such as riding a bike, reading, making friends, and being liked. Challenges to one's competence appear throughout life, especially to people of high aspiration. The desired *level* of competence increases with age, from the toddler to the student to the worker to the executive.

Achievement

Competence produces its own reward: achievement. The sense of achievement is so reinforcing that it is itself a motivating force. David McClelland, a major investigator of human motivation, defines the drive for achievement as "competition with a standard of excellence" (McClelland, 1985b).

McClelland and his associates have concentrated their study on what they call the need for achievement. **Achievement motivation** is what enables us to carry through and complete the goals we set for ourselves. Many human goals are long-term and not immediately attainable. You can quench thirst right away, but it takes years to become a great pianist. The need to achieve keeps you on the path toward a distant goal.

Achievement motivation is different at different times. The value placed on achievement itself and the kinds of achievements that are valued vary within cultures and across time. In nineteenth-century America, the folklore was dominated by stories of remarkable achievements. They described inventions, mastery over the wild environment, and people making huge fortunes. "Success stories" are not as popular today. This idea of achievement has never been central in such cultures as those of the Egyptians and the American Indians. The rise and fall of a civilization can sometimes be correlated with the achievement level in literature. "Striving" is a major theme in early Greek literature, but by the time of the peak of the civilization, it had declined (McClelland, 1985a, b).

Revolutions bring forth changes in achievement. There was a higher level of achievement in children's books in Russia and China after their communist revolutions than before. High achievers were the heroes in stories in the early years following the American Revolution.

Characteristics of Achievers

The *need* for achievement is a characteristic component of a person's personality (McClelland, 1985a). There are striking differences between people in whom the need for achievement is high versus low.

People with a high level of *n-Ach* (a measure of the strength of the achievement motive) set *moderately high, realizable* goals. High achievers are more likely to succeed. They do not worry so much about avoiding failure. This activity includes a willingness to take some risks. They are more internally motivated than low achievers. They make decisions and judgments on their own, independently of the opinion of others. They are more likely to associate with others on the basis of their competence than on the basis of friendship. Their fantasies often concern unique accomplishments (McClelland, 1985b). They like concrete feedback and criticism, and they prefer to direct activities with definable goals and clear-cut results.

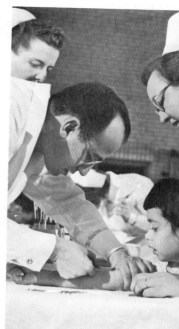

McClelland suggests that this tendency may be why high achievers are more attracted to business careers than academic ones. A business usually has a definable outcome: "the bottom line." An academic contribution is often difficult to evaluate.

The need for achievement is determined by environmental factors. But achievement does seem to breed achievement. The standards parents set for their children and the parents' accomplishments themselves are critical in the development of a high level of n-Ach. Parental training and expectations are the most important factors, specifically reliance in their children from an early age and allowing them to do things well on their own (McClelland, 1985b).

Upper- and middle-income homes produce twice as many high achievers as lower income homes. Middle- and upper-class parents are high achievers and set

Noble prizewinning geneticist Barbara McClintock (top) and Jonas Salk, developer of the vaccine for polio (bottom), are examples of high achievers who have contributed much to society.

AVOIDING BOREDOM

The brain appears to have another "set point" like the one that determines body weight. This one is for the amount of information, stimulation, and change that is optimal for the organism. What is stressful noise to one person may be another's Beethoven; what is delightful peace and quiet to one may drive another up the wall.

We are motivated to regulate the amount of information we receive within our own set range just as we regulate temperature and weight. The brain apparently has a need for a certain amount of stimulation and information to maintain its organization. When there is either too much or too little, instability results and illness may follow.

As the brain evolved, its ability to handle the world became increasingly comprehensive. It developed increasingly sophisticated cortical and subcortical systems for receiving, decoding, analyzing, and reducing the varied and complicated flow of information. And the individual brain follows a similar pattern of development throughout the life span.

Remember at age 5 what a delight it was to discover what a letter meant, then to discover that these letters go together to make whole words, and later that words go together to make sentences, sentences go together to make paragraphs, and paragraphs go together to make stories. But now that you are older, you can sit reading the newspaper for half an hour and when the question is asked, "What's in the paper today?" you answer "Nothing, really." The world becomes organized, automatized, and familiar.

The paradox is that as the human brain matures and develops it both enormously increases its ability to find out new things and, at the same time, develops an enormous capacity for getting bored. It is easy for us to adapt, to learn, and to develop and so we are in the crux of a two-horned dilemma —too much too soon, too little too late, and both at the same time.

On one hand we must deal with the destabilizing challenges of "life changes" (see Chapter 18) and, on the other, the destabilization that can result when the brain is understimulated. Stop lights all the same, repetitive conversations, stereotyped relationships, and a world that can become too familiar, too routine. Out of this need to stimulate themselves, people have produced great works of art, while other attempts, such as thrill-seeking, fast cars, and drugs, can be maladaptive. Cartoonist Sol Steinberg, discussing his art, said, "Avoiding boredom is one of our most important purposes."

Compared to a less experienced or

higher standards for their children. Over the past few decades, opportunities for advancement have become more available to blacks. Consequently, there has been an increase not only in their income, but also in their level of n-Ach (Banks, McQuarter, & Hubbard, 1977; Rokeach, 1973; Rosen, 1959).

Achievement motivation can be easily and quickly learned, even in adulthood. In one study, businessmen in India took an achievement motivation course. Later they made more investments, employed more people, and made more money than before they took the course (McClelland, 1985a).

Knowledge

A most important human motive is the search for knowledge and understanding of the world. Systems of education and philosophical, scientific, and fictional works all serve to further our understanding. What might not be so evident is this:

developed brain, the more experienced brain does receive less sensory information because we have learned to extract out just those bits of information that we need. We need only catch a glimpse of a spouse's expression to know whether they are angry or not. We only need to see a tiny bit of a scarf down the street to know whether someone is home. We only need to hear the beginning of someone's tone of voice to know whether we are welcome or not.

At each step we need less and less and we need to attempt less and less. As we age we get more and more needful of strong stimuli. Young children are prone to be frightened by unfamiliar stimulation, and any parent of a young child knows that they seem to enjoy repetition of the familiar more than older children or adults (Ornstein & Sobel, 1987).

The maturing brain develops the capacity to better organize the world, reducing unnecessary information so that critical threats and instabilities can be recognized and responded to. This process of brain organization begins at the earliest moments of life. Even in the first days of life, the stabilizing tendencies of motivation—to seek stimulation and to reduce complexity —are apparent.

People try to keep a stable level of stimulation going into consciousness. It seems that different people like different "levels" of stimulation, just as different people prefer their music at different loudness or different amounts of spice in their food. Much research has been done on changing levels of sensory stimulation since, as you might expect, this would change consciousness. Remember from Chapter 7 that when a person is put into sensory deprivation, he will immediately try to seek stimulation by moving about, brushing his hand against his leg, or making noises. It seems that consciousness, accustomed to a supply of "news," needs its fix to keep going.

What happens when people are prevented from stimulating themselves? They rapidly become disorganized and they lose their intellectual ability, concentration, and coordination.

People constantly need stimulation to develop, grow, and maintain an organization of the world, and not get bored with it. There is even some speculation among psychologists that lack of proper information flow can result in disease such as cancer. (de la Peña, 1984)

the search for how the world is organized is so basic that health suffers when our understanding of the world is in disarray (Antonovsky, 1984, 1987).

Organization

Recall from Chapter 6 that our nervous system organizes the world. It selects only a few meaningful elements from all the stimuli that reach us. It organizes them into the most likely occurrence, and remembers only a small organized sample of what has occurred. At each step the world becomes more organized and simplified in the mind. A network of schemata develops to represent the world. The external world, so chaotic and changing, becomes stable, simplified, and seemingly coherent in the mind. What is presented to us are thousands of reflecting bits of glass, gray stone, and scores of doors opening and closing. But we *perceive one building*; the parts fit together as a whole.

See Chapter 6, section on Processes of Perception.

There is a sense of organization, or of coherence, to things. When this sense of coherence regarding a person's world is disrupted, he or she is more likely to become ill (Antonovsky, 1987). If the world is disorganized, it is not clear what appropriate action to take in any situation.

Curiosity and Exploration

The other side of our voracious organizational ability is that we become restless when things get too organized. We get bored, we need to change, we need to create something new. We explore our environment as much to find what it is like as to find something in particular. Other organisms are also curious. Monkeys will work for the reward of the sight of another monkey or a stimulating toy (Figure 13-9). Indeed, even rats are motivated by curiosity: they will choose a more complex environment over a less complex one (Dember, Earl, & Paradise, 1957).

Curiosity increases mental activity by conveying more stimulation from the outside environment (Berlyne, 1960). If you had to eat your favorite meal every day, you would soon wince at the sight of it. A friend of mine was once a confirmed chocoholic. When she was in college, the job she was most excited about taking was in a candy store selling chocolates. She could eat all the chocolate she wanted, and for the first few days she was in paradise. After two weeks, however, she never wanted to see chocolate again! We are restless, "stimulus-hungry" creatures, even at the most basic physiological level of our nervous system.

Optimal Level of Arousal

Curiosity keeps us stimulated, but when the arousal level is too low — just before sleep or in a boring situation — the level of performance suffers. Likewise, overarousal — being highly excited at bedtime, or restless when you are trying to study — hurts performance. Each of us has an optimum level of arousal. Many psychologists use an n-shaped curve (sometimes called an "inverted-U") to describe this (Figure 13-10). The optimum level is in the middle of an organism's

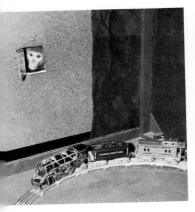

FIGURE 13-9
Curious Monkeys
Experiments have shown that monkeys and other animals are motivated by curiosity and prefer stimulating, complex environments.

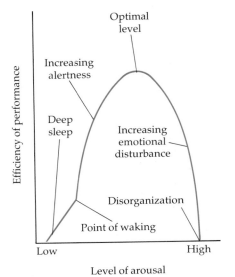

FIGURE 13-10
Arousal and Performance
As this n-shaped curve shows, arousal helps performance but overarousal can lower efficiency of performance.
(After Hebb, 1972)

Sensation seeking is a common human activity.

response range. Here pleasure is greatest, reinforcement is most efficient, and the processing of information is most efficient.

Many of our behaviors are motivated by the need to achieve our optimum level. Some people cannot study without loud music on; they need to increase their activation level. Others cannot be in a room with any distractions; they need to decrease their level. It is probable that individual differences in optimum level of arousal are relatively stable characteristics in individuals. Many actions during the day—working hard, exercising, resting, having a cup of coffee, playing music—change arousal level. The maintenance of the optimum level is another feedback process in human motivation. It is more complex but similar to the homeostatic mechanisms in the body.

But many people also seek to upset homeostasis and try to move their arousal level up, even if it is unpleasant. They do this presumably for the pleasure that occurs when that stimulation is reduced. People "sensation-seek" by riding roller coasters, driving quickly, eating spicy food, jumping out of airplanes, going to horror movies, and watching erotic films (Zuckerman, 1984).

H uman beings do not live for bread alone, nor for safety nor love nor their work. Abraham Maslow felt that there is a goal to develop oneself, called self-actualization, and a goal to go beyond the normal range of knowledge, that is, to "transcendence" (Maslow, 1970).

BEYOND KNOWLEDGE

Self-Actualization

Maslow was concerned that psychologists restrict their study to problems and breakdowns because these issues are more easily studied. It is easier and more fun to study mistakes in thinking than errorless thinking. It is easier to study a need such as hunger or belonging than a goal that makes people strive for years to achieve excellence.

Maslow used the term **self-actualization** to refer to the growth motivation of the healthy individual. He believed this motive to be natural, that every person, unless obstructed, tends toward growth and health. He thought that once the lower motives are fulfilled, people begin to feel the need to expand their inner lives. He studied such great people as Eleanor Roosevelt, Albert Einstein, and Gandhi to isolate those common characteristics that might be the defining characteristics of the self-actualized individual. Maslow identified the following as the distinguishing features of self-actualized individuals:

1. Creativity and inventiveness.
2. Problem centering rather than ego centering; capacity for concern about larger problems of society and humankind.
3. Strong purpose to life.

Gandhi (top left), Eleanor Roosevelt (top right), Martin Luther King, Jr. (bottom left), and Albert Einstein (bottom right) are among the rare individuals who Maslow calls *self-actualizers,* people who have reached the pinnacle of human motivation.

4. Objectivity and detachment; acceptance of self and others.
5. High tolerance of the unknown and of ambiguity.
6. Mystical or peak experiences of a special quality that serve to organize and give direction to one's life.
7. Freedom from prejudice and cultural conventions; an unconventional morality about what is right and wrong (Frager & Fadiman, 1987).

Transcendence

We seek meaning, from the meaning of sensory stimulation to the remembrance of actions that mean the most to us. At the highest level, the search for meaning involves the search for the order of the world and the meaning of life. This is generally termed the *spiritual* aspect of life, and it is embodied in organized religions such as Christianity, Judaism, and Islam, and by spiritual groupings such as Sufism (Shah, 1982).

Transcendence, then, means to go beyond the ordinary understanding of life. Some of the questions that lead to this search are "What is the meaning of life?" or "What is God?" There has been little attention given to transcendence in psychology since William James's *The Varieties of Religious Experience* appeared in 1900, but it nevertheless is a major organizing principle in the lives of many throughout the world. More than 2.5 billion people belong to the major religious groups of the world. Religions guide motivation; they determine morality, what one eats, whom one can marry, and many of the "lower" motives we have considered.

Many aspects of religions serve social functions. However, the foremost purpose of religious activity is to attain a direct knowledge of how the world is organized and the purpose of human life. This knowledge may take the form of a "born again" experience in contemporary Christianity or a mystical experience, either deliberately stimulated or accidental, or it may take the form of a continuously deepening understanding of the nature of human life. In any case, it is a powerful motivator. For millennia people have fasted, prayed, meditated, given up their possessions, and even gone to war in the service of religious knowledge.

The Motives Combined

At any moment we are doing many things. The brain monitors body temperature and food and fluid intake on the most basic level. At the same time, we may be angling to join a club or trying to understand a new concept. Sometimes needs combine: a person may combine the need for food with that of exploration and become a chef. Another combines achievement with understanding and becomes a rich inventor.

Some people *may* move up the hierarchy of motives during their lives in the idealized way Maslow describes. They first satisfy basic physiological and safety needs, belonging, and gaining esteem. They then develop competence and understanding and, finally, become self-actualized. However, few people follow this strict sequence.

The art collector Hirschorn described his motive for collecting: "After the first million, money doesn't make much difference. I tried eating four meals a day and I got sick. I can't change my suits more than three times a day. So I collect art." Sometimes an individual may become dominated by one particular motive. This occurs, for example, when the lower needs are not satisfied. All thoughts turn to food or drink or to the maintenance of other body processes.

Functional Autonomy

Some motives seem to persist even after they are satisfied. Students may work hard to obtain the esteem of their peers and may find it so rewarding that they continue to seek esteem for the rest of their lives. In doing so, they may neglect achievement and understanding. Politicians may find that they love to run for office and win, but they give little attention to the process of governing later on, as they continually run for office.

An important determinant of the motives an individual expresses is **functional autonomy**, which is the tendency for any action repeated often enough to become a motive in its own right (Allport, 1961). Functional autonomy may cause an individual to stay at one level of motivation or may lead him or her upward on the hierarchy. The motive to earn money may be prepotent when one is poor. Nevertheless it may continue for life, even when the person has enough money or is very rich. Habits persist. A child may learn to play a musical instrument simply to gain approval, but might later develop a true love for music.

However, some may skip stages on the way up; some may stay at one level. Some people may operate in a way contrary to Maslow's scheme. A person may ignore needs such as esteem and belonging in the search for achievement or for transcendence.

It is in the particular motives that a person expresses that we find the roots of individual personality.

SUMMARY

1. *Needs* are specific deficits that any animal must satisfy, such as hunger and thirst. We have needs for food, water, rest, safety, and protection, among many others. Needs give rise to *drives*, which are physiologically based goads to behavior. They move us, literally, to action. *Goals* are desired outcomes that have not yet occurred. It is characteristic of human motivation that we seek to create new situations and cause them to come into existence. Dubos calls this aspect of human motivation *creative adaptation.*

2. Instincts are patterns of behaviors that are (a) typical of every member of a species and (b) must appear without learning the first time the appropriate situation occurs. Examples of animal instincts are the specific songs of birds and the homing instincts of the salmon. In the human genetic program it is generally accepted that certain *predispositions* are inherited, not specific instincts. An example would be the attachment between mother and infant.

3. An important concept in motivation is the hierarchy proposed by Abraham Maslow. At the bottom of this *pyramid of motivation* are physiological needs, then safety, then love and belonging. Higher up are needs for esteem, cognition, aesthetics, self-actualization, and transcendence. What distinguishes the different levels on this hierarchy is the concept of *prepotence*. Once the lower (stronger) needs are satisfied, the higher ones can be. Maslow believed that a starving organism will not be able to do anything about its higher needs without first satisfying the strong, lower need for food.

4. *Homeostasis* is the tendency of an organism to try to maintain a constant (stasis) state. The regulatory systems of the body seek to maintain constant internal processes such

as temperature, food supply, and water content. Homeostasis operates by the process of feedback. Temperature regulation is maintained by a system of *thermometer neurons* located in the hypothalamus of the brain.

5. Thirst can be quenched in many ways, only one of which is wetting down the salivary glands. Water placed directly into the stomach through a tube reduces thirst. Thirst operates like this: when the fluid content outside the cells drops, pressure receptors in the veins detect the reduction in the water content of the blood. This sets a biochemical process in motion that activates the sensation of thirst. Why we stop drinking is more complicated because we stop drinking before the fluid has time to enter the cells. Venous pressure receptors detect entering fluid, reducing renal production, and eventually the activity in the hypothalamus concerned with thirst is reduced.

6. Hunger is more complex than thirst or temperature regulation. One consequence of this complexity is that hunger disorders are quite common. Two major ways we know when to eat and when to stop are the gastric and metabolic components of hunger. Although the control of eating is complex, we know that it is mediated by the hypothalamus. When the lateral hypothalamus of a rat is destroyed, the rat will stop eating. It will actually starve to death without tube feeding. However, if these rats are tube fed, their normal eating and drinking patterns are gradually restored. Destruction of another area of the hypothalamus results in *hyperphagia* or extreme overeating. Disruption of eating and drinking relate to lesions in many parts of the brain, not only the hypothalamus.

7. One important disorder of food regulation is obesity. The body operates like a furnace: when there is more fuel than can be metabolized, it is stored as fat and used when needed. Although the regulation is accurate, in some countries more than 75 percent of the population is overweight. The *set point* is a specific body weight around which the brain attempts to maintain homeostasis. It is more difficult both to gain and to lose weight by merely counting calories than people think. Important in obesity are the number of *adipocites* (fat cells) that people are born with. Obese people have three times more fat cells than normal people. Surprisingly, being slightly overweight is actually the healthiest weight for most people. Fighting against a ''set point'' that is higher than you would like may not be worth doing. Some people will always be unhappy with their weight, but this is more of a social concern than a physiological one. Exercise and calorie intake seem to be the only relevant factors affecting set point.

8. When the most basic and immediate physiological needs, such as hunger and thirst, are met, other ''higher'' ones need to be satisfied. Safety must be maintained, pain avoided, pleasure sought, and social needs met. Belonging is perhaps the most surprising of human needs. When people are deprived of belonging to a group, they may suffer specific health consequences. To belong to and be a part of something, such as a family, group, or club, is an important human need. It is more of a basic need than we might expect. Another social need is maternal care. In rats it has been discovered that maternal care seems to be under hormonal control. If the hormones in the blood from a mother rat are transferred to another rat, the latter exhibits maternal behavior. In humans it is undoubtedly true that this hormonal regulation is less strict. For example, human males may come to take an active role in child care, and some women abandon their children.

9. *Achievement motivation* has been studied extensively by McClelland and his associates. They have correlated different levels of achievement imagery in a culture with the subsequent success of that culture. For example, in nineteenth-century America the folklore was dominated by stories of remarkable achievements. The achievement

motive is a *need* for achievement and is a relatively consistent and characteristic component of personality. Personality profiles differ in people in whom the need for achievement is high versus low. High achievers set moderately high, realizable goals. They more actively pursue success rather than simply avoid failure and are more willing to take some risks. Low achievers are much less internally motivated. Achievement motivation can be easily and quickly learned even in adulthood.

10. At a higher level are cognitive needs for knowledge, for organizing the world, for curiosity, and exploration. Curiosity keeps us stimulated, but when our arousal level is too low the level of performance suffers. The highest level of performance is in the middle of an organism's response range. Many behaviors may be motivated by the need to achieve a personal optimum level of arousal. For instance, some people need loud levels of music to study by; others cannot be in a room with any distraction.

11. The highest levels of motivation described by Maslow are self-actualization and transcendence. Distinguishing features of self-actualized individuals are creativity, inventiveness, objectivity, detachment, tolerance of the unknown, and peak experiences. Transcendence means to go beyond the ordinary understanding of life and to develop a search for knowledge at the highest level. Included in this are religious, mystical, and other endeavors that are not often studied in contemporary psychology. Nevertheless, they claim the allegiance of billions of people throughout the world.

12. Maslow's view is one, idealized view. Some people may come up the hierarchy of motives during their lives. However, it is more likely that people do not follow a strict sequence. Some motives are described more by the process of *functional autonomy*. This is the tendency for any action repeated often enough to become a motive in its own right.

TERMS AND CONCEPTS

achievement motivation
adipocites
anorexia nervosa
antigens
drives
functional autonomy
goals
homeostasis
hyperphagia
instincts
Maslow

motives
natural immunity
needs
obesity
prepotence
pressure receptors
pyramid of motivation
self-actualization
set point
thermometer neurons
transcendence

SUGGESTIONS FOR FURTHER READING

Antonovsky, A. (1987). *Unraveling the mystery of health.* San Francisco: Jossey-Bass.
  The most recent discussion of how coherence affects health, and how psychological factors pertain.

Bennett, W. S., & Gurin, J. (1982). *The dieter's dilemma.* New York: Basic Books.
  A good read and synopsis of the "set point" approach to weight regulation.

Frager, R., & Fadiman, J. (1987). *Maslow's motivation and personality.* New York: Harper & Row.
  One of the few texts which gives a version of Maslow's approach to psychology.

McClelland, D. (1985a). How motives, skills, and values determine what people do. *American Psychologist, 40,* 812–825.

> *A leading theorist of motivation tries to explain how it operates in the person.*

McClelland, D. (1985b). *Human motivation.* Chicago: Scott, Foresman.

> *Perhaps the best statement of, as McClelland told me, "All I know about motivation."*

Mook, D. E. (1986). *Motivation, the organization of action.* New York: Norton.

> *An important text which helps outline the different components of motivation.*

Zuckerman, M. (1984). Sensation-seeking: A comparative approach to a human trait. *Behavioral and Brain Sciences. 73,* 413–433.

> *A recent account of the sensation-seeking theory, with responses from other professionals.*

The Puzzle of Personality

W̲e have analyzed separate components of a person—learning, thinking, intelligence, emotions. But to discover the nature of a *whole* person is like putting pieces of an enormous puzzle together. A divorce lawyer once said to me, "I've seen hundreds of divorces in my career. I can understand why people get divorced. What I don't understand is when someone, after 5, 10, or even *20* years of marriage, says 'I really never knew him.' How is it that someone can live with someone else every day and *never know them*?" This problem occurs for the rest of us, too. We wonder, "How could he do that? I always thought he was so conscientious," or "She's not *herself* today."

It would be nice to have an answer to the puzzling question of why other people are so difficult to know. But it is this very difficulty that has made the scientific study of personality so fascinating. It is an area of psychology that, like intelligence, involves characterizing and assessing people. It is understandable that both intelligence and personality are areas of great controversy in psychology. Part of the problem lies in the makeup of other people and part in our own tendency to simplify. People are certainly the most complex "objects" we ever perceive. They have different genetic predispositions and different histories. They seem different depending on our own individual personality and perceptions.

Two women may discuss the same man; one says, "He's so domineering," while the other says, "He's so sweet." People have different identities within, and they change with different people and different situations. Remember Indiana Jones in *Raiders of the Lost Ark*, who was both a swashbuckling adventurer and a meek professor.

None of us are simple, but the way we understand the world involves a great deal of simplifying. This simplifying costs us more in the perception of other people than it does in the perception of the outside world. We try hard to make other people be perfectly stable, like our perception of a rock. We categorize or "type" individuals as a "hot-tempered redhead" or the "strong, silent type." We are often surprised when people do not behave as we believe they "should."

Here are a few pieces of the puzzle of personality and how we experience ourselves and others. This chapter covers psychological theories of personality and whether we are really consistent. It also presents dimensions of personality —are boys more aggressive than girls and do some people try to control everything while others act helplessly?

Keep in mind a scene from Lawrence Durrell's *The Alexandria Quartet*. This set of novels is about a group of people living in Alexandria, Egypt, and how they come to know one another. The novels focus on a woman named Justine and how

others see her. To one man, Justine is a selfish lover; to another, she is a committed revolutionary. All through the books, we wonder who she *really* is.

But Durrell has anticipated some of the lessons in psychology. Near the end, he portrays a scene of Justine dressing in front of a mirror like those in clothing stores. It is a mirror with several panels, in which she can see herself reflected differently from all angles. We show, he seems to say, different "sides" of ourselves depending upon the point of view of the observer and the situation (Plate 13).

OURSELVES AND OTHER PEOPLE

It is a surprising experience the first time we hear our voice on tape. The taped voice sounds high-pitched and squeakier than your own. You protest, "That's not *me*, I hope." When we hear ourselves on tape, we are experiencing ourselves the same way we experience others. *There are great differences in how we experience ourselves and how we experience others.* The *self* may be very different from *personality*, which is how we present ourselves to others and how they experience us. However, the self and personality are related.

> A man has as many social selves as there are individuals who recognize him and carry an image of him in their mind. . . . He has as many different social selves as there are distinct groups of persons about whose opinions he cares. He generally shows a different side of himself to each of these different groups. . . . We do not show ourselves to our children as to our club companions, to our masters and employers as to our intimate friends. (James, 1890)

Many centuries ago, Socrates proclaimed "Know thyself," but how do we do this? It is unlikely that we are born with a "real" self that we later "discover." We construct a self-concept. Through interaction with others we learn to label our feelings and our behaviors. Suppose Sarah is disapproving of her friends who use cocaine. They may say "Sarah doesn't like drugs." She then learns to label that particular feeling as dislike. Similarly, we learn consequences of our behaviors and that certain ones are kind or naughty, rude or polite.

Perception of Ourselves

The perceptual processes allow us to experience a familiar, stable world of objects. Everything from line drawings to facial expressions, from cubes to buildings, is organized and interpreted by perception. The processes of perception also influence our experience of ourselves. We make many unconscious inferences about our own behavior and feelings.

See Chapter 6 on Perception.

Self-schemata and Observation

Self-schemata are the schemata about the self. They guide the processing of information and interpretation about the possible different selves that compose us (Markus, 1986; Markus & Smith, 1985). One man may regard himself as the "strong, silent type," while another as "oriented to achievement." Obviously, there are limits to these interpretations. In a dangerous situation, trying to label one's feelings as "pleasant tingling" may be fruitless if not actually harmful.

We learn about the self through observation of our internal states and behavior. Most of the time we know how we feel about something. We like or dislike a person, are excited about or dread an upcoming event. But sometimes there is ambiguity — we have mixed feelings or are unaware of some part of them. There may often be discrepancies: how we expect to feel versus how we actually feel and how we want to behave versus what we do.

Interpreting Inner Feelings

We are frequently unaware of interpreting inner feelings, as we are unaware of the organization and interpretation that guide perception. A parachutist about to jump out of a plane does not think, "My heart is beating rapidly, therefore I am afraid." He or she simply feels "afraid." In experiments it is fairly easy to demonstrate that interpretation does occur. If you speed up heart rate it can make a person feel more aroused sexually, or more afraid in a threatening situation.

In one experiment, Valins (1966) showed nude photographs in *Playboy* magazine to young men as they listened to the sound of heartbeats. They were told that this sound was their own heartbeat. It was not. For some pictures, the experimenters speeded up the rate of the "heartbeat" sounds. Later, the men judged those pictures of women to be the most attractive. This is likely to have occurred because of an unconscious interpretation: "My heart is beating fast, therefore I'm attracted."

Self-monitoring

It's a sunny summer afternoon. You're trying to decide whether to play tennis — one of your favorite games — with your friend Paul or with your friend Mike. You know that you like Paul more than Mike, but you also know that Mike is a better tennis player than Paul. What do you do? How you solve this dilemma may reflect your approach to friendship.

The photographs on this page and the next suggest some of the many social selves each of us may have. The woman pictured shows different sides of herself to different people in her life: she is a wife and lover to her spouse; a mother and homemaker to her child; a professional to people with whom she does business; an athlete to those who see her jogging.

If you choose Paul, chances are that you choose your friends on the basis of your feelings for them and that you keep the same friends for most of your social activities. . . .

If you choose Mike, you probably choose your friends on the basis of their skills in particular areas and you are likely to have different partners for different activities. (Snyder, 1987)

People differ in the kind of information they select for their self-concept, called **self-monitoring** (Snyder, 1987). A person's self-monitoring orientation relates to which approach you use to friendship.

High self-monitors are particularly concerned about how they appear to *others* and how appropriately they behave. They are sensitive to the wishes of others and use others' behavior as a guideline. If a high self-monitor went to a meeting where everyone was serious and staid, he or she will try to act appropriately sedate. They agree with these kinds of statements:

I would probably make a good actor.
In different situations and with different people, I often act like very different persons.
I'm not always the person I appear to be.

Low self-monitors are not so concerned about others and look to their own standards as a guide. If a low self-monitor feels good, he or she may think, "I'm really giddy tonight, I'd better go to a party." Low self-monitors claim the following:

I have trouble changing my behavior to suit different people and different situations.
I can argue only for ideas in which I already believe.
I would not change my opinion (or the way I do things) just to please people or to win their favor (Snyder, 1987).

Many studies under the direction of Mark Snyder confirm these different approaches of people. In one study, people were asked to characterize their friends. High self-monitors wrote essays characterizing their friends in terms of their activities, while low self-monitors did so in terms of their feelings about them.

The differences in self-monitoring offer a beginning to the puzzles of personality that we encounter. James' graphic statement, about showing different "selves" is backed up by research. However, it is most true of high self-monitors, who display their "selves" most often. Many people, less conscious of their appearance, show a more consistent self to the world. Part of the puzzle of personality is that the grand pronouncements about ourselves do not always hold up for everybody. We need to find more and smaller pieces to fill the puzzle: the large ones don't fit.

Perception of Other People

In general, we perceive others the same way we perceive everything else. We pick up sensory information, we have selective schemata, and we interpret actions and events. In the case of the cube (see Figure 6-2), we experience our *interpretations* about external events. This is even more true of our experience of people: we may interpret someone as "overbearing" and from then on select and notice only those actions consistent with our interpretation.

Impressions of People

When we first meet someone, we form a "snap judgment" about his or her basic characteristics. Although we generally have very limited information upon meeting someone, we nevertheless tend to form a coherent *impression*. We "fill in the gaps." Solomon Asch (1946) suggested that this occurs because we assume that people's "traits" form consistent patterns. An industrious person is more likely to be considered intelligent and skillful than frivolous.

Some traits are more central than others; they dominate and organize the impression. Asch (1946) gave subjects lists of traits and asked them to write a paragraph describing the characteristics of that person. Group A heard the person described as intelligent, skillful, industrious, *warm*, determined, practical, and cautious. Group B heard the person described similarly as intelligent, skillful, industrious, *cold*, determined, practical, and cautious. The two groups formed quite different impressions of the person, suggesting that *warm* and *cold* are central, organizing traits. Thus, if we think a person is warm, we are likely to infer specifically different characteristics than if we think he or she is cold. Certain traits seem to go better with other traits. How traits are grouped forms a naive, *implicit personality theory* that guides impression formation, that is, the characteristics we infer about others.

Prototypes

Not only do we make inferences about traits, but we also associate traits and behavior around a prototype formed of different individuals' behavior (Cantor & Niedenthal, in press). A **prototype** is a typical set of features that exemplify a person or an object. For example, a robin is a prototypical bird with which we associate birdlike qualities, such as chirping, flying, and pulling up worms. An "extrovert" is a common prototype of a person who is likely to be outgoing, boisterous, gregarious, and loud.

We use these common prototypes in our experience of others. In one study, people were shown a list of traits regarding a person. Some of these fit a prototype and some did not. Subjects recalled more of the traits that fit the prototype (for example, "loud" for an extrovert) and "remembered" traits not presented that fit the prototype (Cantor & Mischel, 1977, 1979). We are more likely to remember having heard that someone is "excitable" if he is an extrovert than if he is an introvert. We fill in the gaps with other people, just as we do with objects and events.

Special Features of Perception of Others

However, people are much more complicated than most objects we encounter. They vary greatly in personality, appearance, and circumstances. Although we organize and simplify them, perception of people has some special features (Mischel, 1986):

1. *People are causal agents.*   We perceive the movement of objects as caused by external forces, but we perceive the behavior of people as caused from within.
2. *We see other people as similar to ourselves.*   The inner goals and intentions of others are not directly observable. Because we assume that other people are similar to us, we infer something about their inner workings, emotions, goals, and intentions by reference to our own.
3. *Social interactions are dynamic.*   We act upon objects, but do not experience objects as acting on us. However, interactions with other people are dynamic and involve a feedback system. Other people respond to our actions and change their behavior. This changes our own behavior toward another person.

See Chapter 9, section on Importance of Context.

The diverse formal theories of personality are often derived from radically different assumptions about human nature. Sigmund Freud thought that primitive unconscious conflicts were the driving force behind personality. He felt that much of civilization arose primarily to check these sexual and aggressive urges. Maslow and Rogers felt that there is a tendency toward self-actualization and that personality results from conscious choices. Social learning theorists examine the effect of the social environment on behavior. They are likely to see both aggression and cooperation as deriving from models (Ross, 1987).

Some psychologists believe traits are important. Others feel that traits are products of the perceiver's tendency to simplify. Are actions chosen or determined, malleable or unchanging, consistent or inconsistent? These are some of the questions of personality (Monte, 1987).

Psychoanalysis

Sigmund Freud (1856–1939) is one of the most influential figures in modern psychology, and many consider him to be the most influential in twentieth-century thought. His theory of personality, **psychoanalysis**, is the most complete and detailed theory in psychology. It incorporates what motivates people and the development and structure of personality. It is a grand theory of another era, a time when it seemed possible to combine evolutionary, developmental, and social components of human nature. The appeal of Freud is his breathtaking ambition and his startling insights.

See Chapter 16, section on Psychoanalysis.

Freud studied medicine in the nineteenth century and began a research career in neurology. He later switched to clinical practice and became interested in the relationship between biology, psychological processes, and civilization. It was not until he was in his 40s that he began formulating theories of psychoanalysis.

There is no single and definitive statement of his psychology; Freud's ideas developed and changed over the course of his career. His early work emphasized the determining inherited biological instincts, and later it was more concerned with *higher mental functions*—in short, conscious processes.

Determinism

Freud sought to discover the underlying psychological structure that determines behavior and to understand how events in the past determine present behavior. Freud's viewpoint was based upon his conviction that personality is rooted in biology and is determined by *inherited instincts*.

The Unconscious

Freud used several metaphors to describe personality. In one he likened personality to an iceberg. Only the tip is above water and visible; the vast part of it is unseen. The rational "conscious" personality is like the small, visible part above water. Underlying it is a much larger, hidden **unconscious** (Figure 14-1).

As such, the unconscious cannot be observed *directly*, but only through processes that relate to the unconscious, such as dreams or slips of the tongue. In dreams, conscious control lessens, and the unconscious can more directly express its desires. Similarly, slips of the tongue (known as "Freudian slips") also reveal

Sigmund Freud
(1856–1939)

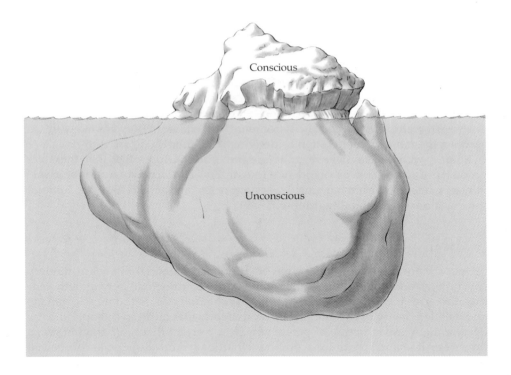

See Chapter 7, section
on Conscious and
Subconscious Levels of
Awareness.

unconscious processes. Suppose a woman calls her husband by the name of an old lover. She might unconsciously wish that her old lover was her husband, no matter how much she denies it.

Freud also compared personality to a horse and rider. The horse is like the unconscious: it has a "mind of its own," but seemingly submits to the direction of the rider, the conscious. But sometimes the horse takes the bit between his teeth and goes off in the direction it pleases. The rider may try to control the horse, but if unable to, he or she may try to *rationalize* the event, for example, by saying "I really meant to go that way in the first place." Alternatively, the rider may unconsciously alter his or her understanding of what happened.

Instincts and Psychic Energy

With the advent of Darwin's theory of evolution, scientists began to assume that animals are dominated by inherited instincts that improve reproduction. Freud felt that these "animal" instincts (which he likened to the horse) provide the "energy" that fuels actions. In human beings, this biological energy is transformed into psychic energy Freud called **libido**.

The primary source for libido is the *sexual instinct*, or **Eros**. There are many different sex instincts linked to *erogenous zones*. They are parts of the body that, when stimulated, produce pleasure. The oral, anal, and genital regions are the primary erogenous zones. In developing his theory, Freud developed the concept of *many different life instincts* subsumed under one category.

Eros comprises the positive, pleasurable, growth-oriented instincts. These instincts form the **pleasure principle,** which states that organisms seek to reduce tension created by a build-up of libido. Reducing tension is pleasurable, and in

Freud's theory, the motivation for all behavior. However, Eros is balanced by **Thanatos,** the *death instinct.* Freud felt that organisms seek a quiescent state such as death, a state of greatly reduced tension! "The aim of life," Freud wrote in a famous passage, "is death." The death instinct is the source of aggression—self-destructiveness turned outward.

Freud thought that all psychological processes reflect how psychic energy is channeled and how it directs behavior. One of the most important of these functions is **cathexis**, which is the investment of energy in an object, action, individual, image, or idea that will gratify an instinct. How a personality develops is largely a matter of the distribution of the psychic energy, or changes in what is "cathected."

The Structure of Personality

Freud divided personality into the *id,* the *ego,* and the *superego.* The **id** is the initial, infant personality. It is composed of the primary instincts (those largely concerned with survival) and other inherited psychological characteristics. It is the "reservoir" of psychic energy for the ego and superego, which derive from the id.

The pleasure principle guides the id, but the id cannot act directly on the outside world to avoid pain and obtain pleasure. It can only operate through reflexes and *primary processes.* Primary processes are irrational, unconscious attempts to fulfill wishes, often by creating mental images or hallucinations; dreams are the best example. To fulfill its wishes, the id needs an intermediary through which to operate on the outside world.

The **ego** comes into existence to do this. It mediates between the demands of the id and the reality of external constraints. It is guided by the **reality principle,** feedback from action. The ego prevents the "discharge of tension" or action until an appropriate object is found.

The **superego,** the last part of the personality to develop, is the internal representation of society's values and morals. The main functions of the superego restrain the aggressive and sexual impulses of the id and pressure the ego to substitute moralistic goals for realistic ones. While the ego is rational, both the id and the superego are irrational.

Civilization and Neuroses

For Freud, a central problem in human life was the conflict between biological inheritance and the demands of human society—an analysis much influenced by Darwin's ideas on evolution. Other animals express instincts for sex and aggression. However, for human beings to coexist in civilization, these must be restrained. Personality develops for purposes of restraint—people cannot have sex with anyone at any time nor can they kill their rivals.

Freud thought that almost all that is noble in our culture—religion, justice, family—exists primarily to *control* animal instincts. This conflict puts a tremendous strain on the individual, which may result in neuroses. **Neuroses** are unconscious conflicts between the desires of the id and the demands of the superego. They often occur as a result of *traumatic experiences* in early childhood. Normally the ego can control these conflicts. But when it cannot, too much tension or anxiety may result, which threatens to destroy the ego.

Defense Mechanisms

Defense mechanisms are unconscious processes used by the ego to distort the image of reality to ward off anxiety. The source of the anxiety is either separated from consciousness or distorted. There are many kinds of defense mechanisms.

Freud observed that his patients were unable to recall many hurtful childhood events. He hypothesized that this was deliberately done by the ego—it *represses* the memory of the event into the unconscious. Repression "defends" the person from having to be hurt over again. Repression is the primary defense mechanism: the anxiety-producing stimulus is first repressed before the other defenses operate.

Rationalization justifies our unacceptable actions. It is not a conscious process; attitudes simply appear in consciousness that defend our actions. We may take pencils home for work and cheat on our income tax because we believe that "the system" is unfair. Freud's analysis turns this around. Our belief that the system is unfair probably defends our otherwise unacceptable actions.

Threats of anxiety can simply be *denied* directly. For example, attraction to a friend's spouse can be denied and ignored. But sometimes attraction such as this may be *displaced* in the unconscious and reappear as dislike. In **displacement,** a person unable to display certain feelings may transfer them to another object.

Projection radiates inward threats into the external world; for example, a person afraid of erotic impulses may believe that society has gone sex-mad.

Reaction formation is a switch in the mind. It substitutes the opposite for the anxiety stimulus. It defends by making the person unaware of the original apprehension. For example, someone concerned about his thieving impulses may become a policeman.

In *regression,* a person returns to one of the early stages of development after a threat (Liebert & Spiegler, 1987).

Evaluation of Freud's Theory of Personality

Freud was a genius. He brilliantly integrated many turn-of-the-century ideas from biology, medicine, philosophy, and psychology. Some of his radical ideas stemmed from the evolutionary idea of his time that we share most of our characteristics with other animals. He was able, in a plausible way, to connect these ideas to the psychological problems of his patients. It remains a brilliant synthesis.

Freud focused attention on many of the most fundamental questions about personality and human nature. How much of our personality is inherited and how much is determined by early childhood experiences? Do we know what motivates us? Why and how do personality and civilization develop? How much conscious control can a person have over life? However, Freud's specific concepts are difficult to test experimentally. When this has been possible, they do not seem to hold up well.

There is little evidence that specific disorders, such as impotence, can be traced to difficulties in early childhood experience. Most important, it does not seem to be true that our psychological problems are so deeply rooted that removing one symptom (such as fear of snakes) may lead to "symptom substitution." If you remove a symptom it does not always reappear in a new form (Mischel, 1986). Further, the idea that all our personality stems from sexual "energy" is too simplistic. There are obviously many determinants of personality.

Freud's work *was* an astonishing synthesis and it has set the agenda for psychologists, especially those involved in psychotherapy and personality. In some ways our situation is worse than Freud imagined, in some ways better. It is not only sex that controls our lives but many other forces beyond our control. The food we eat affects thought processes. The structure of our nervous system is a profound barrier to adaptive thought. Even the weather and the electrical current in the air affect brain processes.

There has, however, been some confirmation of his theories. For example, it has been found that subliminal suggestions do affect conscious processes (Silverman, 1983). Some of Freud's ideas are being tested by those interested in the effects of schemata on the mind (Erdelyi, 1985). The conception of an unconscious defense system is generally thought to be a useful description of many mental processes. But, even after almost a century, it remains lacking in scientific proof. The ideas that schemata outside consciousness have great influence receives support from cognitive psychology. However, attempts to find genuine confirmation of Freud's theories in the modern analysis of the mind are exaggerated. There is little direct relationship between the two, although the same terms are used in both (Liebert & Spiegler, 1987; Mischel, 1986; however, see Erdelyi, 1985, for a different view).

But from the perspective of current scientific knowledge, it is most clear that *Freud greatly underestimated the human ability to continue to develop and change throughout life.* Aggressive and sexual "instincts" can be modified more than Freud thought (Bandura, 1986). Personality is certainly not fixed by age 5 but develops throughout the life span. The horse's "rider" (conscious capacity for development and change) has much more control than Freud thought.

Neo-Freudians

Much behavior does not seem to be linked to unconscious forces of sex and aggression nor to the id/superego conflicts. Infants playing with their hands seem to be motivated more by curiosity and new knowledge than by the release of "tension." Exploration does not serve tension reduction, but rather "higher" mental needs, such as achievement. Furthermore, Freud neglected some major social influences on behavior. Later psychologists, called **Neo-Freudians,** sought to modify Freud's theories about the important determinants of personality. They de-emphasized determinism, emphasized higher mental functions, and included social influence.

Ego Psychology

One group of Neo-Freudians was called *ego psychologists.* They emphasized that the ego, the conscious part of the personality, plays a large role in personality. The ego is thought to be responsible for such behaviors as exploration and mastery.

Other Neo-Freudians, such as Adler and Sullivan, minimized the importance of instincts in favor of social interactions and processes. Adler assumed that humans are motivated primarily by *social urges,* such as participation and cooperation, and Sullivan defined personality in terms of interpersonal interactions. Personality was thought to result from the observation of social interactions with others. It is "the relatively enduring pattern of recurrent interpersonal situations which characterize a human life" (Adler, 1929).

Erik Erikson

See Chapter 3, section on Erikson's Stages.

Erik Erikson considered the formative effect of social interaction on personality. His theory of psychosocial stages demonstrated the shift to ego processes and social influences in psychoanalytical thought.

Erikson's theory differs from Freud's in two basic ways. First, he suggested that the ultimate goal of people is *not* to reduce tension, but rather to *become integrated human beings.* Secondly, although early childhood experiences are important, Erikson emphasized that *development continues throughout the life span* (Erikson, 1986). People encounter a widening range of human relationships. Thus, Erikson described psycho*social* rather than psycho*sexual* stages. Personality develops through the resolution of the crises associated with each stage.

Jung's Analytical Psychology

Carl Jung was an early disciple of Freud's who was also interested in the role that instincts and the transformation of energy play in the development of personality. However, Jung disagreed with Freud on a number of important points. First, Jung rejected Freud's strong emphasis on sexuality as the *primary* motivator. Second, Jung also rejected Freud's extreme determinism, that all behavior is determined by unconscious forces from the past. He emphasized that humans also strive toward goals and are thus motivated by future events.

Jung formed his own school of thought called **analytical psychology**. It studied *individuation*, that is, development of the self through the process by which the unconscious and the conscious unite. Jung divided personality into the *ego,* the *personal unconscious,* and the *collective unconscious.*

The Ego

According to Jung, the ego is the conscious mind and is composed of thoughts, feelings, perceptions, and memories. It is the center of consciousness and forms the basis for our sense of identity and continuity.

The Personal Unconscious

The **personal unconscious** consists of memories that have been forgotten, suppressed, or were too weak to enter consciousness in the first place. Within the personal unconscious are **complexes**—organized groups or constellations of memories, thoughts, feelings, and perceptions. For example, experiences with a domineering mother may cause a mother complex. That person's thoughts, feelings, and actions will be guided by his or her conception of the mother. If the complex becomes strong enough, it may even take control of the personality.

The Collective Unconscious

The **collective unconscious** is the most innovative and significant of Jung's contributions. It is the inherited foundation of personality, the racial (in the sense

Carl Jung
(1875–1962)

of the human race) experience common to all people. It consists of *archetypes,* which are the inherited predispositions to have certain experiences or to react to the world in a certain way. Archetypes include such universal images as God, birth, rebirth, the hero, the child, the wise man, and the earth mother. These archetypes are found all over the world in legends and literature. They may contribute to the formation of complexes in the personal unconscious. The archetypes provide energy for the personality and a fund of wisdom and creativity that the ego can draw on.

Jung agreed with Freud that dreams are meaningful. However, he felt that dreams are the way in which both the personal and collective unconscious seek to provide information to the conscious. Jung's viewpoint has been significant as a bridge between the Western psychoanalytic viewpoint and the Eastern esoteric viewpoints on the great range of influences on personality.

Humanistic Psychology

Psychologists criticize psychoanalysis because it is based on emotionally disordered people. The resulting theory is thus pessimistic and limited in its conception of people. The proponents of **humanistic psychology** argue that psychology should study the healthy, growth-oriented facet of human nature.

Abraham Maslow

Maslow proposed a hierarchic theory of motivation, including basic needs of hunger and security and the psychosocial needs of belonging and esteem. Maslow's theory also encompasses the higher needs of self-actualization and transcendence. This conception extends the psychoanalytic and ego psychology to one that includes basic social curiosity and achievement as determinants of personality (Frager & Fadiman, 1987).

See Chapter 13, section on Maslow's Pyramid of Motivation.

Rogers' Self Theory

Carl Rogers exemplifies the humanistic view that each person has the possibility for healthy, creative growth. His theory rejects Freud's historical determinism to emphasize the *immediacy* of a person's experience at the moment. Rogers divided the personality into the *organism,* the locus of all experience, and the *self.* The self is part of the organism that becomes differentiated into the "I" or "me." In addition to the self, there is an *ideal self,* which is what the person would like to be.

In this view, the primary motivational force is self-actualization. But people also have two needs: the need for positive regard from others and the need for self-regard. However, these two needs are sometimes at odds. Others evaluate a person's behavior both positively and negatively, which sets up conditions for self-regard.

Both the organism and the self have related, but separate, self-actualizing tendencies. If the self is relatively congruent with the total experience of the organism, then the actualizing tendency is unified. But if not, the self and the organism may oppose each other. This results in the person becoming unhappy and dissatisfied. Incongruence results in part from differences between the self as perceived and the self as experienced (organism). Rogers (1959) writes:

If an individual should experience only unconditional positive regard, then no conditions of worth would develop, self-regard would be unconditional. The need for positive regard would never be at variance with organismic evaluation. The individual would continue to be psychologically adjusted, and would be fully functioning.

Rogers (1980) emphasized that personality develops through conscious choices based on the understanding of the self. When self-perceptions are no longer congruent with external reality, maladjustment results.

Social Learning Theory

Social learning theory emphasizes that most behavior is learned rather than instinctually determined. Its advocates generally reject the idea of an unconscious in favor of an analysis of immediate, situational influences on behavior. Social learning theorists currently emphasize cognitive influences on behavior, such as:

1. Competencies: both cognitive and social.
2. Encoding strategies and personal constructs.
3. Expectancies: anticipated outcomes in particular situations.
4. Subjective values: likes and dislikes.
5. Self-regulatory systems and plans: rules for the performance and the organization and evaluation of complex behavior sequences (after Mischel, 1986).

See Chapter 8, section on Observational Learning.

Social learning is more an *approach* to personality than a theory of it. It stresses the social situations that make us what we are. We are more likely to be aggressive if we see another person acting aggressively. We can be made to torture others by a seemingly bland set of circumstances (Milgram, 1974). People put in an imitation prisonlike environment immediately take on assigned social roles: "guards" become brutal, "prisoners" oppressed (Zimbardo, 1972).

Social learning theory's piece of the personality puzzle is the effect of situations in the outside world. It is an important and valuable addition (Bandura, 1986; Mischel, 1986).

Concluding Remarks

To recap, the tradition of theories of personality began with Sigmund Freud. Many of the later theories were reactions to and developments of Freud. Freud's theory about human personality was startling, especially in the context of the nineteenth century. He saw us doomed to live within society as the prisoners of our outmoded instincts of sex and aggression. Later theorists reacted to this bleak description and put more pieces back into the puzzle of our personality.

Some felt that the ego was stronger than Freud did. Some thought we have access to a deeper collective unconscious than Freud thought. Some believed that our personality develops socially with other people and continues to develop through the life span. Each theorist seems to have a piece of the puzzle — biology, consciousness, environment, our capacity for growth. It is like the protagonists in the story of the "Elephant in the Dark." No one has yet been able to fit these pieces together; human beings may just be too complex for that.

PLATE 13
Ourselves and Others
Each of us is a number of people, the many facets of our personality reflecting back from those around us.

PLATE 14
Universal Emotions

About 20 years ago, Paul Ekman traveled to New Guinea to take these photographs of a culture who had never before seen Westerners. His purpose was to see if they express emotions in the same way that we do. The emotions displayed here are readily identifiable, showing that emotions are universal, probably innate, and not culturally learned.

PLATE 15
This painting by Edvard Munch, entitled *The Scream*,
brilliantly portrays the anguish of disturbed people.

PLATE 16
Stages of Mental Illness
Artist Louis Wain (1860–1939) was well known for his
paintings of cats before he was institutionalized for mental
illness. These paintings were made during progressive stages
of Wain's psychosis and reflect perceptual distortions and
mental deterioration associated with schizophrenia.

Some personality theorists have devised ways to accurately describe personality characteristics and *individual differences*. Instead of grand conceptions about the structure of personality, some psychologists have tried to determine how people's personalities differ. The research parallels that of intelligence — from a general approach to more and more detailed analyses. There is a movement toward an understanding of the different abilities that constitute a person. The search has progressed through very general personality *types*, to specific traits, to measures of abilities.

Types

A *type* of person is one with consistent characteristics. One of the best known personality typologies is introversion versus extroversion (Jung, 1921). *Introverted* people are oriented toward the inner, subjective world, while *extroverted* ones are oriented toward the external, outer world. An introverted person prefers to be alone, tends to avoid others, and is shy. The extrovert is sociable and outgoing, and under stress, seeks the company of others. We all use type descriptions when describing others, like the "strong, silent type."

Type A versus Type B Behavior

Personality research progresses from simple and grand schemes to more scientific and detailed assessments. This direction in research is similar to that of intelligence in which more detailed components are analyzed over time. Here we begin with the first studies of the Type A and Type B personalities.

Rosenman and Friedman (1959) originally reported that people who are "coronary prone" seem to have certain personality characteristics. They are time urgent, show excessive devotion to work, have excessive hostility, deny fatigue, and are competitive. These "coronary-prone" people were twice as likely to get coronary artery disease as those who do not behave this way.

Jung felt that most people fall into either of two psychological types: introverts, such as this man who has withdrawn into his game of solitaire, and extroverts, such as this socially oriented cheerleader.

These Type A people have been characterized as the overbusy type of person who is always trying to do many things simultaneously.

> Type As may be found attempting to view television, read a newspaper or trade journal, and eat lunch or dinner all at the same time. "When the commercials come on, I turn down the volume and read my newspaper," is a statement we hear repeatedly. It is not unusual for a Type A to view two football games on two different television sets as he irons a shirt or treads an exercise bicycle. (Friedman & Ulmer, 1984)

Type A behavior is "an action–emotion complex that can be observed in any person involved in an incessant struggle to achieve more and more in less and less time." Type A was originally thought to be a very general characteristic of a person. This type reacts to challenge with aggressiveness, impatience, and time urgency.

Type B people, in contrast, are placid and speak slowly. They do not try to do several things at once, but are just as successful as Type A people.

Structured Interview. To discriminate between Type A and Type B, the "structured interview" was developed (Friedman & Ulmer, 1984; Friedman & Rosenman, 1974). Since Type A people respond to challenge with time urgency, the best test was to challenge them.

Friedman and Rosenman designed the interview to be irritating. They had people take time off from work to come to their hospital. The interviewer kept them waiting without explanation, and then asked questions about being hostile and pressed for time. How did they respond to waiting in bank lines and supermarket lines? How did they like driving behind someone who was going too slowly and whom they couldn't pass? The interviewer interrupted, challenged, irritated, and threw in nonsequiturs.

Many of these commuters appear aggressive, impatient, and overly busy, all characteristics of Type A personalities.

INTERVIEW WITH A TYPE A PERSONALITY

The following extract is from an interview with a strong Type A personality by Professor Charles Swencionis of the Albert Einstein College of Medicine.

Q: Do you ever feel rushed or under pressure?

MR. A: At all times.

Q: How would your wife describe you, as ambitious and hard-driving, or relaxed and easy-going?

MR. A: Ambitious and hard-driving.

Q: When your children were young, say around six or eight, did you ever play competitive games with them, cards, checkers, Monopoly?

MR. A: Yes.

Q: Did you ever let them win on purpose?

MR. A: No, I would beat the hell out of them. [embarrassed]

Q: You mean you would beat a six-year-old child?

MR. A: I would play with you and try to beat you. I'm always competitive. I'm sorry, it's just the way I am.

Q: Are you competitive off the job?

MR. A: Yes, everywhere. [Sigh, horizontal smile, tight lips and jaw]

Q: When you have an appointment to be somewhere at, say 2:00, are you on time?

MR. A: Definitely. I would always be there 15 to 20 minutes ahead.

Q: What's so important about being on time?

MR. A: I can't answer that. It's just important.

Q: Do you resent it if someone else is late?

MR. A: Do I. I hate it. [emotional]

Q: Would you say anything to them?

MR. A: Yes.

Q: What would you say?

MR. A: All according to the way I felt at the time. I'd say, "What the hell's the matter with you? Can't you keep your appointments? Do you have to keep me waiting?" [loudly]

Q: You would let them know?

MR. A: Yes, definitely. [angry tone]

Q: Do you remember a time when that happened?

MR. A: Yes. Just before my heart attack. I had to wait for my sister-in-law. I had called her up about an hour and two hours before and I told her, I said, "———, be ready." I had to come (about an hour's drive) and I had to wait about 20 minutes or so, almost a half hour. When she finally got to the car, I was muttering a few things. I was trying not to be too abusive, because my father-in-law was there, he's an older man. But boy, I let her know. [angry]

Q: What did you say?

MR. A: I said, "———, I had to come here, I had to wait for you, can't you make it on time? What's the matter with you? [angry] I said a lot of things I shouldn't have really said." (Swencionis, 1987)

Just as important as the interviewers' questions was the challenging manner in which they asked the questions. A challenge such as an implied criticism evokes vigorous and explosive speech in coronary-prone individuals. The interview was scored more on the manner in which the person answered the question rather than the answer itself.

The voice of the extreme Type A in the interview was very strong. There was much word emphasis and explosive, bombastic, staccato, and loud talk. The Type A tried to control the interview, and jumped in abruptly when the interviewer stopped talking; he or she talked more loudly to talk over the interviewer and couldn't be interrupted.

The classic Type A has clipped, telegraphic speech and sighs frequently; he or she sits in a tense manner, smiles a tight-lipped horizontal smile, and has a nervous laugh. Perhaps the hallmark of Type A people is that they describe hostile incidents with such emotional intensity that they seem to be reliving them.

The classic Type B, in contrast, speaks in a monotone, rambles, seems subdued and lethargic, speaks slowly and softly, and is easily interrupted. They don't raise their voices, and they sit in a relaxed manner. The Type B smiles with a round mouth and laughs a deep belly laugh.

Type A and Hostility

Like many other major dimensions of personality, the idea of an all-encompassing and complete behavior pattern, such as the Type A personality, has not held up to further research. Too many behaviors are massed under a single heading. More recent research has analyzed the components of the Type A personality in the same way that later research has analyzed the components of the mind, brain, and intelligence.

Dunbar, Matthews, and many others noticed that people who have coronary artery disease are frequently hostile. Easily provoked hostility is a more important indicator of heart disease than the Type A pattern. This has been known for centuries. John Hunter, an influential English physician (1729–1793) suffered from both hostility and angina pectoris. He noted the relationship between his emotions and his heart when he said, "My life is in the hands of any rascal who chooses to annoy me." Dr. Hunter died after a heated argument at a board meeting at St. George's Hospital in London.

Anything can cause this irritable eruption. Horn-honking in traffic is a favorite pastime for the hostile person. But they do not like it much when it is done to them. W. Gifford-Jones was driving with a hostile Type A surgeon who was slow to step on the gas pedal of his car after the signal at the intersection had turned green.

> "The result was a sudden and loud horn honk from the car behind us. Immediately the Irish temper flared. My friend jumped up, walked to the car behind us, opened the door, grabbed the keys out of the ignition, and with a mighty toss threw them into a snowbank." (Friedman & Ulmer, 1984)

Hostility is currently the most popular candidate in the search for the destructive Type A component. It links with blood pressure reactivity, severity of coronary artery disease, and death from all causes including coronary heart disease. But what are the reasons for hostility? One possibility is the degree of self-involvement. People who are very self-involved often think of themselves as better than others. These people are vulnerable to anyone who confronts such claims or who looks better than them. Hostility may be a strategy for coping with such challenges by saying, "Who do you think you are to challenge me like this!"

To the self-involved, many events are the cause for a threat: the success of a friend, the turn of the stock market, the prospects for one's company, the insurance crisis.

Those who were hostile during the Type A interview used more self references (use of "me, my, mine, I") (Dembrowski et al., 1983). In one study students recalled an incident that made them angry and later described it (Leventhal, Berton, & Scherwitz, 1977). The most important predictor of heart activation was *the number of times the students referred to themselves.* Self-involved individuals had the strongest emotional and physical reactions to challenge. They expressed anger more intensely and had much higher blood pressure, at levels that would qualify for hypertension.

Do people become more self-involved after developing heart disease? This has not been found to be the case. Self-involvement and the severity of coronary artery disease was most correlated with those who did not have a heart attack. And in an earlier study, Powell found that people with great self-involvement were more likely to have a second heart attack.

Scherwitz and colleagues (1985) speculate that it is not the activity of people that is dangerous to the heart, nor the hurry, but the *selfishness* that underlies it. "If individuals are ambitious, competitive, or time urgent for purely selfish reasons, they may be at greater risk than if they are ambitious or competitive to serve others or higher ideals."

Here, in the study of Type A behavior, is a progression in understanding. It begins with an overarching concept like a general personality type. It is analyzed into a specific reaction, hostility, which causes heart trouble. This process reflects the increasing understanding of psychologists, psychiatrists, and physicians in the puzzle of personality.

Traits

Although the concept of personality type is useful, people are generally not so consistent. They may be friendly and outgoing on one occasion, shy and withdrawn on another. Thus, most psychologists prefer to describe personalities in terms of **traits**, which are discrete characteristics assumed to be relatively stable, such as resourceful or conscientious.

Allport (1937) divided traits into:

1. **Cardinal traits**, which are highly generalized dispositions that organize the whole personality. John McEnroe's cardinal trait could be said to be competitiveness.
2. **Secondary traits,** which occur in only a few specific situations. A person may be generally calm, but become anxious on airplanes, so anxiety is a secondary trait.

Some traits are more closely related to others; cardinal traits organize other traits. One way to test this idea is to construct a *correlational matrix.* This shows the strength of relationships on a scale from −1 (completely opposite) to 0 (no relationship) to +1 (identity). Wishner (1960) found there was a high (0.48) correlation between warmth and imaginativeness, but no correlation between strength and warmth. But there are 18,000 adjectives in the English language to describe people (Allport & Odvert, 1936), so a correlational matrix can become too complicated. In these circumstances, a *factor analysis*, which reduces a correlation matrix to a few basic dimensions, is useful.

Measures

Raymond Cattell (1971), who also analyzed intelligence, gathered personality traits from many different sources. They included lists of adjectives, personality tests, and observations of behavior in real-life situations. Through a series of

---

TABLE 14-1   Cattell's Basic Trait Dimensions

	Low score description	Average	High score description	
A	1　　2　　3　　4 Reserved, cool impersonal	5　　6	7　　8　　9　　10 Warm, easygoing, likes people	WARM
B	1　　2　　3　　4 Concrete-thinking	5　　6	7　　8　　9　　10 Abstract-thinking	INTELLIGENT
C	1　　2　　3　　4 Easily upset, emotional, impatient	5　　6	7　　8　　9　　10 Emotionally stable, mature, patient	EMOTIONALLY STABLE
E	1　　2　　3　　4 Submissive, accommodating	5　　6	7　　8　　9　　10 Dominant, assertive, opinionated	DOMINANT
F	1　　2　　3　　4 Serious, sober, prudent, quiet	5　　6	7　　8　　9　　10 Cheerful, expressive, enthusiastic	CHEERFUL
G	1　　2　　3　　4 Expedient, disregards rules	5　　6	7　　8　　9　　10 Conforming, persevering, rule-bound	CONSCIENTIOUS
H	1　　2　　3　　4 Shy, timid, threat-sensitive	5　　6	7　　8　　9　　10 Socially bold, unafraid, can take stress	BOLD
I	1　　2　　3　　4 Tough-minded, insensitive, rough	5　　6	7　　8　　9　　10 Sensitive, tender-minded, refined	SENSITIVE
L	1　　2　　3　　4 Trusting, adaptable, accepting	5　　6	7　　8　　9　　10 Suspicious, hard-to-fool, skeptical	SUSPICIOUS
M	1　　2　　3　　4 Practical, "down to earth," conventional	5　　6	7　　8　　9　　10 Imaginative, absent-minded, impractical	IMAGINATIVE
N	1　　2　　3　　4 Forthright, unpretentious, open	5　　6	7　　8　　9　　10 Shrewd, polished, calculating	SHREWD
O	1　　2　　3　　4 Confident, self-satisfied, complacent	5　　6	7　　8　　9　　10 Insecure, apprehensive, self-blaming	GUILT PRONE
Q$_1$	1　　2　　3　　4 Conservative, traditional, resists change	5　　6	7　　8　　9　　10 Liberal, innovative, open to change	EXPERIMENTING
Q$_2$	1　　2　　3　　4 Group-oriented, sociable	5　　6	7　　8　　9　　10 Self-sufficient, resourceful, self-directed	SELF-SUFFICIENT
Q$_3$	1　　2　　3　　4 Undisciplined, uncontrolled, impulsive	5　　6	7　　8　　9　　10 Controlled, socially precise, compulsive	SELF-DISCIPLINED
Q$_4$	1　　2　　3　　4 Relaxed, composed, has lower drive	5　　6	7　　8　　9　　10 Tense, restless, has high drive	TENSE

SOURCE: From Cattell, R. B. (1986) *The handbook for the 16 personality factor questionnaire.* Champaign, IL: Institute for Personality and Ability Testing.

complex factor analyses he developed 16 *factors* that he believes are the basic trait dimensions. Each factor is represented by two expressions, one indicating a high score, the other a low score (Table 14-1). For this he developed the Sixteen Personality Factor Questionnaire, a list of 100 yes-or-no questions. By plotting a person's test score on a graph, a psychologist can discover that individual's *personality profile.*

There are literally hundreds of other personality tests, most based on various trait assumptions. The Minnesota Multiphasic Personality Inventory (MMPI) is a personality "atlas" consisting of more than 500 items. It was originally devised to distinguish between normal people and those with psychiatric difficulties such as paranoia, anxiety, and depression. It also reveals personality profiles and is the most used test in personality psychology.

The description and measurement of traits and their corresponding behavior play a central role in understanding personality. However, some psychologists question the usefulness of even a trait approach. They believe that people's behavior is very flexible and is modified in various situations.

People learn their social behavior mostly from direct reinforcement by others. However, learning can also be observational (vicarious), or reinforcement may be self-administered (Bandura, 1986). Actions in a given situation depend upon the situation, appraisal of the situation, and observation of others' behavior in similar situations. Behavior will be consistent only to the extent to which a person *generalizes* across situations. But more often, people *discriminate* between situations and adjust their behavior accordingly. For example, some students may be intellectually aggressive around their peers but very meek with their professors.

S. o personality remains a puzzle, both in our everyday lives and in formal theories in psychology. We all have our own implicit theories of personality. We use them not only to type other people (Joe is an honest person), but also to predict (Marie is generous so I'll ask her if I can borrow a dollar).

People assume that others are consistent and their behavior is understandable. Most theorists assume that concepts of personality structures, motivation, and conflicts can explain behavior. Furthermore, some studies have shown that most people's self-descriptions are very stable through time, even over decades (Block & Block, 1980).

Sex Differences in Personality and Behavior

There are clear-cut differences in the general behavior and personality of men and women. Obviously this does not hold true for *all* men and *all* women. These characteristics may partly be based in biological differences, but it is clear that differences in socialization contribute heavily to them.

Recently, Jean Block (1981), in an extensive review of the literature, has identified seven dimensions along which men and women differ.

1. *Aggression.* Male animals, including humans, are consistently more aggressive than females. Males on the average engage in more rough-and-tumble play and use more physical aggression. They try to dominate peers more and are more likely to engage in antisocial behavior. Males generally prefer television programs with more aggressive content.

2. *Activity level.* Males as a whole are more active than females, are more curious, and engage in more exploratory behaviors. They have more accidents requiring emergency medical treatment than females do. They also perceive themselves as more daring and adventurous.

3. *Impulsiveness.* Being impulsive is the inability to delay gratification and to control impulses. Males are more impulsive, and they are more mischievous than females. They are generally more likely to have temper tantrums, engage in disruptive behaviors, and overreact to frustration. Men operate machinery such as automobiles more impatiently and impulsively than women do.

4. *Susceptibility to anxiety.* However, females on the average are more likely to be fearful, anxious, and less self-confident than males. They generally have a less favorable attitude toward their own competence, score higher on measures of social desirability, and are more compliant. In group situations characterized by uncertainty, they are more influenced by peer pressure than males are.

5. *Achievement.* Sex differences with regard to achievement behavior are more complex. Women as a whole feel less confident in problem-solving situations and tend to underestimate their level of performance. However, they are no less likely to be persistent or motivated in achievement-related situations. Instead, they may be differently motivated than males. Challenging, ego-involving situations may stimulate male achievement, but generally do not effect or may even impair the performance of females. Social approval may enhance female achievement motivation.

6. *Potency of self-concept.* Men generally have greater feelings of personal efficacy than women. They are more interested in feelings of control and describe themselves as more powerful, ambitious, and energetic than females. Women, however, are more likely to describe themselves socially;

Typically males tend to choose activities that are more aggressive, active, and impulsive than those chosen by women.

they see themselves as more generous, sensitive, nurturing, and considerate than males.

Females, on the whole, tend to be more nurturing and tend to develop more intense social relationships than men.

7. *Social orientation.* Women on the whole are more empathetic than men. They are more accurate in discerning emotions from nonverbal cues than males are. They are more involved in pro-social activities, while men engage more in political-social dissent and protest. Friendship patterns also differ. Women are generally more affiliative and develop more intensive social relationships than men, who have more "extensive" relationships — more numerous and less involved. In all cultures, women express more interest in babies and engage in more nurturing activities.

Recall the discussions of statistical differences in Chapter 1. Just because there is an overall difference between groups does not mean that the same is true for individuals. Certain men may have extensive social relationships, while certain women may be aggressive. On the grand average, however, *there are overall differences*, although the magnitude of them is open to interpretation (Fausto-Sterling, 1986).

See Chapter 1, "box" on Individual and Group Differences.

Personal Control

People have a basic tendency to attribute either situational or dispositional causality to behavior (Rodin, 1986). However, people differ in their tendency to perceive their own behavior as internally or externally controlled. Julian Rotter (1966) did a systematic investigation into this perceived *locus of control* by devising the Internal-External (I-E) scale. This questionnaire examines a person's sense of control over personal achievement, social events, and political events. The subject must choose between two items such as:

Becoming a success is a matter of hard work; luck has little or nothing to do with it.

or

Getting a good job depends mainly on being in the right place at the right time.

Another example is:

No matter how hard you try, some people just don't like you.

or

People who can't get others to like them don't understand how to get along with others.

People who perceive events as situationally caused or due to luck are *externals*, whereas *internals* believe that events are under personal control. An internal person would most likely pick "Becoming a success is a matter of hard work . . . " and "People who can't . . . "

There are some very interesting differences between externals and internals. Externals are less likely to delay gratification, are more susceptible to manipulation, and are less likely to notice their environment (Lefcourt, 1976). Demographically, men are more internal than women. Internality increases with age, and minorities and lower socioeconomic groups are more external than higher socioeconomic groups.

Consider two people at the extremes. An older, white, wealthy male most likely believes that he has personal control over events. He feels that he has built his empire with his own hard work. A young, poor, black woman, however, is less likely to perceive a personal control over life. She is likely to believe that what happens to her is a matter of luck or external forces. And unfortunately, both of them are likely to be correct!

Are People Consistent?

This search for single descriptors of people causes us (the perceivers) much trouble. We think that someone who is honest does not lie to friends, does not cheat, and doesn't steal. But what would happen if you actually followed a child around for several days and kept a record of whether his or her actions were honest?

Hartshorne and his colleagues (Hartshorne & May, 1929) did just that. They studied over 8,000 children and assessed their "moral character" by looking at their behavior in a number of diverse circumstances: cheating in the classroom and on exams, stealing money, lying, and cheating during games. They found surprisingly little **consistency** of behavior across situations. They concluded that being honest in one situation does not mean that a person will be honest in another. This finding has been demonstrated repeatedly (Bem & Allen, 1974).

Errors in Perception

Perhaps people really are not so consistent. Perhaps consistency lies largely in the beholder's eye. Bem and Allen (1974) describe four reasons for such mistakes:

1. People hold implicit personality theories that lead us to generalize beyond observations. Like the rest of perception, we fill in the missing data with consistent data of our own manufacture.

2. We overestimate the degree to which behavior can be attributed to internal dispositions and underestimate the influence of the situation, which also leads to overgeneralization.

3. People assess unrepresentative samples. How we act tends to shape how others respond to us. You may think that your professor is a very nice person because you are usually nice to her and she responds in kind.

4. We tend to overgeneralize from the few behaviors that are consistent due to the similarities in situations. You may think Anne is a "competent person" because you only see her in class and in the laboratory. She may be completely incompetent in the kitchen.

Mischel (1984) proposes that people perceive some traits as linked, using prototypes (Cantor & Mischel, 1977, 1979). We are likely to see other's behavior as consistent because we usually see them in the same place — at work, at school, or on an outing. But if we see them in other roles, their behavior may be very different.

Granted that these processes do exist and that we do tend to overgeneralize about others, still our intuition *feels* correct. We see that our friendly psychology professor *is* indeed friendly to others as well. She makes special efforts to help people with problems and really seems to be *generally* a nice person.

Consistent and Inconsistent People

Some people actually *are* more consistent than others (Snyder, 1987). Epstein (1979) found that some people are almost completely consistent, with average correlation coefficients higher than 0.90, while others are much more inconsistent. Furthermore, people are quite accurate in predicting how consistently they (themselves) demonstrate certain traits across situations. Bem and Allen (1974) studied consistent and inconsistent people. Then they measured their behavior across situations in three ways:

1. The subjects filled out a questionnaire about friendly behavior in specific situations.
2. Their parents and friends rated their friendliness.
3. The subjects' behavior was observed while in the waiting room and in a group discussion.

All three measures showed the same results. Individuals who said they were friendly *were* more friendly in specific situations and were judged friendly by their parents and peers. However, these findings were much weaker for the trait "conscientious." Thus, "being friendly" means about the same thing to most people, but people have very different conceptions about what "being conscientious" entails. However, even Bem and Allen's "highly consistent" individuals responded *differently* in different situations, but they nevertheless gave the overall impression of being consistent. How is that possible?

Consistency across Situations and Time

As mentioned earlier, most people's self-descriptions are remarkably stable across years or even decades (Block & Block, 1980). This gives us a possible solution to this dilemma. Perhaps being consistent *across situations* is not as important as being consistent *across time*. Lutsky and colleagues (1978) measured consistency in conscientiousness both across time and situations. People were consistent over time in the same situations, but not in different situations.

As an example, let's look at the common behavior of hot temper. Some people seem just to burst out in emotions throughout their lives. Is this just our perception of them, or does it reflect something stable? Caspi (in press) is analyzing a 50-year study of people with data gathered in Berkeley. He finds that people who are explosive in early childhood stay that way throughout the course of their lives. This trait shapes their lives to some extent: they are the first in their jobs to be fired, they are twice as likely to become divorced, and they get less education. Whether temper is inherited is still unclear, but it might relate to activity level in infancy. Although this may be a small dimension of personality, it is important to those who have it! As a general case, it shows that people can be consistent in certain behaviors.

The Eye of the Beholder

One problem with the scientific data on consistency is that it mixes people and situations. Looking at people in different situations can blur the real consistency that comes in life because people often remain in the same kinds of situations throughout life. Clergymen have different surroundings than assembly workers; both differ from financiers. The pressures, problems, and pursuits all differ. Thus, people might be inconsistent if situations throughout their lives varied, but many people live unchanging lives and have little chance to exhibit inconsistency (Ross & Nisbett, in press).

Another important key comes from the recent work of Walter Mischel and his colleagues (Mischel, 1984, 1986). We probably judge other people in much the same way that we judge other objects. We try to *make* them more stable than they are. We may quickly judge someone as a prototypical "kindly old man," then we try to fit his actions into this "correct" category that we have established. Or more likely, we *select* a few "key features" that go along with being kindly, and then we restrict our observation to the few key features that mainly occur *in the same situation* over time.

Because behavior *is* consistent in the same situation over time, we maintain simplicity ("honest" or "conscientious") and ignore other behaviors of that person. Thus, we *impose* a primitive consistency on other people through our perceptual processes. Some consistency, of course, must actually be there, but some is contributed by ourselves. This is why people *are actually less consistent than they seem to us.* Perhaps consistency may lie, as does beauty, in the eye of the beholder.

A Concluding Note

Each approach to the puzzle of personality that has been discussed has something to contribute. But I want to make another point, one that is more personally relevant. The assumption that other people can be easily understood, and that

Co-workers who know this man as an executive who is "all business" may have a difficult time imagining him as a playful and loving father.

they are consistent, is an assumption that causes much trouble. And if there is one lesson to be learned from the study of personality, it is that *the human personality is quite complex and people are very difficult to categorize simply.*

So the next time someone you think well of does something that you do not like, you do not have to change your overall impression of them. If you thought he was kind and find that he acts heartlessly, there may be reasons for it. You may not have enough information; *he* may not consider the action unkind. Keep in mind that he is human and that human beings are inconsistent; there may be other parts of his personality operating. People do act very differently to other people, at different times, and in different situations.

Psychologists have the same problem in attempting to characterize personality. Some people show many sides of themselves, some few (Snyder, 1987). There are many independent components that make up a person, and some day an adequate research-based description may come along. Some important differences include male and female, firstborn and later born, fast and slow temperament, high and low self-monitoring, left- and right-handed. Each of these, plus different upbringings, all have their effects, and psychology is just beginning to assemble the pieces of the puzzle.

We have not yet mentioned another important issue that is now getting attention. Psychologists usually ask people to describe themselves as they *are*. But what about the self people want to *become*? A person may feel withdrawn now, but may expect to be happy later on; unworthy at the moment, but perhaps estimable at another time (Markus & Nurvus, 1986). And how we see others also depends upon how we see ourselves at any moment; our point of view shifts with different possible selves operating (Markus, Smith, & Hall, 1985). For example, an up-and-coming politician may see only danger in another's behavior, but when more successful, he may regard it as just misguided.

This very complexity, however, is probably what keeps most of us interested in one another, as well as puzzled, as we try to piece each other together.

SUMMARY

1. Personality is a puzzle, both to individuals and to psychologists. There are great differences between how we experience ourselves versus other people. The self may be very different from personality, which is how we present ourselves to others and how they experience us. Important to self-observation are *self-schemata* — cognitive generalizations that synthesize information about the self. We also develop and learn about the self through observation of our own internal states and behavior. People seem to differ in the kind of information they select for their self-concept. One dimension is *self-monitoring*. High self-monitoring individuals are particularly concerned with others' opinions, while low self-monitoring individuals are not so concerned about others and look to their own standards for a guide.

2. We do not perceive other people's behavior as random; rather, we try to judge other people's actions and attribute them to a simplifying *prototype*. In perceiving other people, we use the same processes that we do in perceiving objects and events. However, there are differences: we think of the behavior of others as intentional, of people being similar to us, and of social interactions as dynamic. People's inner goals and intentions are not directly observable, but we infer their workings. Somehow we group certain traits with others to form a naive, *implicit personality theory* that guides our impression of other people.

3. The most important theory of personality is that of Sigmund Freud. His theory, *psychoanalysis,* is the most complete and detailed explanation of what motivates people, how the personality develops, and how it is structured. Its general characteristics include determinism and the postulation of the unconscious, a system below consciousness that cannot be observed either by the person or other people, but which determines personality. Freud compared personality to a horse with the rider atop to describe how the unconscious and conscious parts function. Freud felt that animal instincts, which he likened to the horse, provided the energy which fuels action. The primary source of this energy, called *libido,* are the sexual instincts that are linked to erogenous zones.

4. Freud developed the general concept of many different life instincts subsumed under one category. *Eros* contains the positive, pleasurable, growth-oriented instincts and is balanced by *Thanatos,* the death instinct. The structure of personality for Freud is divided into three parts. The *id* is the initial, infant personality unconcerned with the demands of the world. The *ego* mediates between the demands of the id and the reality of external constraints and is guided by the *reality principle.* The *superego,* the last part of the personality to develop, is the internal representation of society's values and morals. *Defense mechanisms* are unconscious processes used by the ego to distort the image of reality to ward off anxiety. Among defense mechanisms are denial, repression, displacement, projection, reaction formation, and sublimation.

5. Freud was a genius and considered to be one of the most influential psychologists of all time, but his ideas have been less influential in scientific psychology because they are very difficult to test experimentally. He was able, in a plausible way, to connect the ideas of evolution and our continuity with other animals to current psychological problems and current mental life. He raised many of the most fundamental questions about personality and human nature. Are we the prisoners of animal instincts? How much of personality is inherited? Will we ever be able to know what motivates us? Freud underestimated people's ability to continue to develop and change throughout life.

6. The *Neo-Freudians* developed personality theories that emphasize those aspects of the person that have little to do with unconscious drives or conflicts. One group was called ego psychologists, who emphasized that the ego, the conscious part of the personality, plays a large role in personality. Erikson was interested in the formative effect of social interaction on personality. He suggested that the ultimate goal of people is not to reduce tension in the way that Freud described, but rather to become integrated human beings. He also emphasized that development continues throughout the life span and described psychosocial rather than psychosexual stages.

7. Jung was an early disciple of Freud's who emphasized that the determinants of personality are more extensive than Freud believed and formed his own school, called *analytical psychology*, which studied individuation, the process by which the unconscious and the conscious unite. Jung divided personality into the ego, the personal unconscious, and the *collective unconscious*, the last of which is the most innovative and significant of Jung's contributions. It is the inherited foundation of personality, and it consists of archetypes, which are inherited predispositions to have certain specific experiences or to react to the world in a certain way. Archetypes include such universal images as God, birth, and the hero and are found all over the world in legends and literature. They may contribute to the formation of complexes in the personal unconscious.

8. *Humanistic psychology* emphasizes the study of positive aspects of human nature, not the more pessimistic viewpoint of Freudian psychology. Rogers self theory exemplifies the humanistic view that each person has the possibility for healthy, creative growth. His theory rejects Freud's historical determinism to emphasize the immediacy of a person's experience at the moment. Rogers divides personality into three structures: the organism, the self, and the ideal self. In this view, the primary force for motivation is self-actualization. Rogers emphasizes that personality develops through people making deliberate and conscious choices based on their understanding of their self.

9. Social learning theorists emphasize that most behavior is learned rather than instinctually determined. They include: (1) competencies, (2) encoding strategies and personal constructs, (3) expectancies, (4) subjective values, and (5) self-regulatory systems and plans. Social learning is a way of studying personality emphasizing the social situations and the contingencies of a person's life.

10. Type A personalities are identified as the overbusy type of person, trying to do everything simultaneously, who has clipped speech, sighs frequently, sits in a tense manner, smiles a tight-lipped horizontal smile, and has a nervous laugh. The hallmark of the Type A is that he describes hostile incidents with such emotional intensity that he seems to be reliving them. In contrast, the Type B speaks in a monotone, rambles, seems subdued and lethargic, speaks slowly and softly, and is easily interrupted. He doesn't raise his voice and sits in a relaxed manner. The Type B smiles with a round mouth and laughs a deep belly laugh.

11. Like other major dimensions of personality, the idea of an absolute behavior pattern, such as Type A, has not held up to further research. Researchers noticed that people who have coronary artery disease are frequently hostile. Hostility is currently the most popular candidate in the search for the destructive Type A component. It may be caused by a higher degree of self-involvement, measured by the number of self-references. The scrutiny of Type A behavior shows a typical progression in understanding. Psychologists begin with an overarching concept like a general personality type,

which is then analyzed into a specific reaction, hostility, which causes heart trouble. This process reflects the increasing understanding of psychologists in the puzzle of personality.

12. A *type* of person is one with many consistent characteristics—a person being either male or female, extrovert or introvert. However, people are not so consistent; they may be friendly and outgoing on one occasion, shy and withdrawn on others. Thus, most psychologists prefer to describe personality in terms of *traits*, which are characteristics that seem to be relatively stable, like "resourceful." Allport divided traits into (a) *cardinal traits*, which are highly generalized dispositions, and (b) *secondary traits*, which occur in only a few instances, such as specific anxieties. Some traits seem to be more closely related to others; central traits seem to organize other traits.

13. One important dimension is sex differences in personality and behavior. Block identified seven dimensions along which men and women differ: aggression, activity level, impulsivity, susceptibility to anxiety, achievement, potency of self-concept, and social orientation. Another important dimension in personality is how much personal control people have over their lives. People who perceive events as situationally caused or due to luck are called externals. Internals believe that events are under personal control.

14. How consistent is personality and behavior? People are much less consistent than we would like to believe: behavior is situation specific. However, some people are more consistent than others. Mischel and his associates emphasize that we probably judge other people in much the same way that we judge other objects. We try to make them more stable than they are, or we select a few key features that go along with the prototype we have selected. If we judge someone as kindly, we restrict observations to those samples in which a person is kind, largely in the same situation over time. Behavior *is* consistent in the same situation over time, but is inconsistent in different situations at the same time. Because of this we can maintain our consistent perception by simply ignoring different contingencies. This is why people are actually less consistent than they seem to us. Consistency, in addition to beauty, may lie in the eye of the beholder.

TERMS AND CONCEPTS

analytical psychology
archetypes
attribution cardinal traits
cardinal traits
cathexis
collective unconscious
complexes
consistency
defense mechanisms
determinism
ego
egocentric bias
Eros
fixation
Freud
fundamental attribution error
humanistic psychology
id

implicit personality theory
Jung
libido
Neo-Freudians
neuroses
pleasure principle
prototypes
psychoanalysis
reality principle
regression
secondary traits
self-monitoring
self-schemata
social learning theory
superego
Thanatos
Type A personality
unconscious

Dilman, I. (1986). *Freud and human nature*. New York: Basil Blackwell.

A modern assessment of Freud's important viewpoint, more easily read than most.

Freud, S. (1962). *New introductory lectures on psychoanalysis*. London: Hogarth Press.

Perhaps the best statement of Freud's ideas. However, Freud changed his theory throughout his career, and there is no single definitive work.

Mischel, W. (1984). Convergences and challenges in the search for consistency. *American Psychologist, 39,* 351-364.

An up-to-date summary of the emerging research on consistency.

Rogers, C. R. (1980). *A way of being*. Boston: Houghton Mifflin.

A more personal but still definitive statement of Rogers' view of human nature.

Snyder, M. (1987). *Public appearances, private realities*. New York: Freeman.

A recent description of self-monitoring research.

Psychological Disorders

The crisis of mental illness appeared as a nuclear explosion in my life. All that I had known and enjoyed previously was suddenly transformed, like some strange reverse process of nature, from a butterfly's beauty into a pupa's cocoon. There was a binding, confining quality to my life, in part chosen, in part imposed. Repeated rejections, the awkwardness of others around me, and my own discomfort and self-consciousness propelled me into solitary confinement.

My recovery from mental illness and its aftermath involved a struggle — against my own body, which seemed to be without energy and stamina, and against a society that seemed reluctant to embrace me. It seemed that my greatest needs — to be wanted, needed, valued — were the very needs which others could not fulfill. At times, it felt as though I were trying to swim against a tidal wave. (Houghton, 1980)

Sometimes, problems in life become too great and people's ability to adapt can snap. When this happens, all or almost all efforts focus on problems, fears, and distorted thoughts. There remains little in life that is undisturbed, and a *disorder* results. Many psychological disorders are simply *exaggerations* or *extremes* of normal patterns of thought, action, emotions, personality, and coping. Part of the difference between normal psychological health and a disorder is this: although everyone sometimes does "crazy" things, the normal order in life returns; but when it is impossible to control daily life, a person may need help.

The distinction between a normal reaction to adversity and a disturbed one is not, in truth, clear. It is like the difference between a brief bout with the flu and a chronic illness. It is one thing to cry when a love affair ends or to feel sadness when a parent dies, but it is another thing to be so disturbed that for three years you cannot go out with friends. It is one thing to be anxious about going to a party but another to be so afraid of meeting people that you cannot go outside your house at all.

Some disorders are mild: they may interfere with work, mood, or relationships. Others are more extreme: the person seems to lose all contact with the world. Certain people can be incapacitated by their condition, some are just incongruous, while some are even dangerous to others or to themselves.

Psychological disorders affect all of us at some time and take an enormous toll on society. Scores of millions are so depressed that they cannot function adequately. Hundreds of thousands are paralyzed because of their fear of crowds, snakes, or elevators. Ten million alcoholics in the United States cannot live without a drink. More than a million are schizophrenic, a condition closest to the common concept of "crazy."

This chapter contains many direct case histories of people in trouble and in different states of mind. Reading these first-person accounts (along with the current diagnostic information) about being manic, schizophrenic, depressed, or homeless conveys the experience better than any psychologist could.

Characteristics

While any single case is not typical of all disorders, there are a few characteristics common to many disturbances (Goldstein, Baker, & Jamison, 1986).

Loss of Control. Feelings and thoughts seem beyond one's competence. Life seems meaningless, one's actions do not matter. Helplessness and lack of control is one aspect of this. In earlier ages, the idea that people were "possessed" by the devil or a spirit was popular. When one is possessed, one has no control.

Unhappiness or Distress. There is a romantic notion that mad people are happy to be different from others or have made a breakthrough. However, the experience is more of a *breakdown.* They are almost always unhappy about it. People who are considered disordered often make other people unhappy as well. They may be dangerous or so unable to function that others' lives are disturbed, as in families or jobs.

Isolation from Others. The individuals may physically separate themselves from others or feel withdrawn while in company.

Causes

There is no single cause for psychological disorders; they may arise from biological, mental, and situational factors.

Biological. Genetic inheritance may predispose a person to certain disorders, such as depression or antisocial actions. Other biological disorders, such as inadequate sensory input, may predispose a person to certain types of disorder.

Mental. Unique experiences influence each person's life. A person may grow up under extreme conditions: being beaten by the father or never receiving affection from either parent. He or she may have a strange series of accidents that create an unusual view of the world. Everyone in the family might have been murdered or had terrible luck in business. The person may take this unusual experience as representative and may overgeneralize from it.

Situational. In everyone's life there are times when one is more vulnerable and less able to cope with the problems of living. Violence and riots occur more during heat waves. Mental hospitals admit more people during times of economic hardship and recessions. We cannot predict with assurance an *individual's* disorder.

Classification of Disorders

Psychological disorders are difficult to isolate, for they are complex and more subject to interpretation than are medical disorders. Homosexuality was considered a disorder until the early 1970s and is no longer.

The most widely used classification system is the American Psychiatric Association's *Diagnostic and Statistical Manual of Mental Disorders (DSM)*. The *DSM* was first published in 1952, and there have been two major revisions, in 1968 and 1980. Although the *DSM* classification has been criticized for being too medical, we follow the general guidelines of *DSM-III* (its third edition) here. It provides an acceptable way of discussing disorders, both the mild and the severe (Table 15-1).

TABLE 15-1   *DSM-III* Diagnostic Categories

Disorders usually first evident in infancy, childhood, or adolescence
Organic mental disorders
Substance use disorders
Schizophrenic disorders
Paranoid disorders
Psychotic disorders not elsewhere classified
Affective disorders
Anxiety disorders
Somatoform disorders
Dissociative disorders (hysterical neuroses, dissociative type)
Psychosexual disorders
Factitious disorders
Disorders of impulse control not elsewhere classified
Adjustment disorders
Psychological factors affecting physical condition
Personality disorders

SOURCE: American Psychiatric Association, 1980.

The term **disorder** is used here in a neutral sense: the problems described are neither diseases nor alternative lifestyles. Something is definitely wrong with many people described here, and they need help (Plate 15).

A nxious people recognize and are disturbed by the symptoms they experience. There is generally no disturbance of thought processes, and behavior is not way out of line with normal social conventions. These disorders become part of the "background noise" of the individual's life. They are not normally precipitated by a specific stressful life event. Finally, there is no evidence that any genetic or organic factors contribute to the development of these disorders. Here is a fairly typical case:

MILD DISORDERS: ANXIETY AND SOMATOFORM

> A 25-year-old married salesman arrives at the emergency room for the fourth time in a month. He insists that he is having a heart attack and is admitted to the hospital by his internist. The cardiologist's workup is completely negative.
>
> The patient states that his "heart problem" started six months ago when he had a sudden episode of terror, chest pain, palpitations, sweating, and shortness of breath while driving across a bridge on his way to visit a prospective client. His father and uncle had both had heart problems, and the patient was sure he was developing a similar illness. Not wanting to alarm his wife and family, he initially said nothing; but when the attacks began to recur several times a month, he consulted his internist. The internist found nothing wrong, and told him he should try to relax, take more time off from work, and develop some leisure interests. In spite of his attempts to follow this advice the attacks recurred with increasing intensity and frequency.

The patient claims that he believes the doctors who say there is nothing wrong with his heart, but during an attack he still becomes concerned that he is having a heart attack and will die. (Spitzer, Skodol, Gibbon, & Williams, 1981)

Before the *DSM-III*, such disorders were classified as "neurotic disorders." Although people use the word *neurotic* in everyday speech, psychologists have no useful definition of it. In *DSM-III*, five disorders formerly called neurotic include *affective, anxiety, somatoform, dissociative,* and *psychosexual*. This section introduces anxiety and somatoform. Mild affective disorder is discussed in the section on depression. Dissociative disorders were briefly discussed in Chapters 7 and 14.

Causes of Mild Disorders

The causes of mild disorders seem to be entirely psychosocial. Typical examples are maladaptive coping strategies, learning of inappropriate contingencies, and difficulty in interpersonal relationships, especially those in the family.

Anxiety and somatoform disorders exist in Western civilization, but there is no recorded case history of these disorders among primitive tribes, such as the aborigines of Australia (Kidson & Jones, 1952). In our own culture anxiety disorders are more often experienced by middle and upper class people. They express general dissatisfaction with life and complain of being unhappy; these people are often called "the worried well." They experience dissatisfaction in the rather abstract, pervasive feeling of anxiety. People in lower income groups who experience mild disorders are more likely to experience somatoform disorders (*soma* refers to the body). The major symptoms are physical complaints that have no physical cause.

Anxiety Disorders

Generalized Anxiety Disorder

People suffering from **generalized anxiety** live in constant tension and worry. They seem uneasy when they are around people and are unusually sensitive to comments and criticisms. Often they are so terrified of making a mistake that they cannot concentrate or make decisions. Their posture is often strained and rigid, resulting in sore muscles (especially in the neck and shoulders). They may have chronic insomnia and gastrointestinal problems (such as diarrhea), perspire heavily, and experience high blood pressure, heart palpitations, and breathlessness. Irrespective of how well they are actually doing, they are worried that something will go wrong. Here is one case:

A 27-year-old married electrician complains of dizziness, sweating palms, heart palpitations, and a ringing of the ears of more than eighteen months' duration. He has also experienced dry throat, periods of uncontrollable shaking, and a constant "edgy" and watchful feeling that often interfered with his ability to concentrate. These feelings have been present most of the time over the previous two years; they have not been limited to discrete periods. . . .

For the past two years he has had few social contacts because of his nervous symptoms. Although he has sometimes had to leave work when the symptoms became intolerable, he continues to work for the same company for which he has worked since his apprenticeship following high-school graduation. He tends to hide his symptoms from his wife and children, to whom he wants to appear "perfect," and reports few problems with them as a result of his nervousness. (Spitzer et al., 1981)

Causes. There are several possible causes of generalized anxiety. It may be an extreme reaction to an early trauma. For example, whenever a young housewife heard a siren or accident reports, she experienced severe anxiety that someone in her family was hurt. Such people often feel anxious because they are afraid they will not be able to control dangerous impulses. A young man had persistent fantasies about strangling his girl friend. "When we are alone in the car, I can't get my mind off her nice white throat and what it would be like to choke her to death" (Coleman et al., 1980). Learning is also important: overanxious parents tend to have overanxious children.

Obsessive-Compulsive Disorders

Scientists or artists may be "obsessed" with their work and allow few intrusions. You may check many times throughout the day to see that you have bought the tickets for this evening's concert. But this behavior is normal — it actually may enhance daily life. **Obsessive-compulsive disorders,** however, are clear-cut exaggerations of feelings. In an obsession the mind is flooded with a specific thought. In a compulsive disorder the person feels compelled to repeat a certain action over and over. But this behavior does not enhance the obsessive–compulsive's life, it interferes with it. Davison and Neale (1986) report a client who washed her hands more than 500 times a day to prevent contamination from germs.

Phobic Disorders: The Fears

Phobia is Greek for "fear." In psychology the term refers to an extreme or unfounded fear of an object or place. In general, fear is adaptive, an efficient warning system that gets us out of dangerous situations. For example, fear of

snakes is very common, and justifiably so, since many snakes are poisonous, and it is wise to avoid them while hiking. However, if your fear of snakes is so great that you cannot leave your apartment on the 34th floor in New York City, then it is a disordered fear, or phobia.

The most common phobias are *zoophobia* (fear of animals), *claustrophobia* (fear of closed spaces), and *acrophobia* (fear of heights). *DSM-III* classifies **agoraphobia** separately. Agoraphobia is the fear of being alone in public places that might be difficult to escape. Phobics experience anxiety whenever they try to confront their fear.

Age is important in phobias. Most children are naturally phobic: afraid of the dark or of a certain kind of animal. Many parents of preschoolers have to check their children's closets to get rid of all the gorillas and monsters. These fears are not considered pathological in early childhood.

However, *schoolphobia* (the child experiences stomachaches whenever he or she has to go to school) may require help. Phobias usually originate in late teens or early adulthood. Women are more likely to suffer from a phobia than men. Simple phobias (those directed toward a specific object) are quite common.

See Chapter 8, section on Conditions of Conditioning.

Causes. A person can become phobic through faulty learning. Recall the case of little Albert, who became afraid of white furry things because they were associated with a frightening, loud noise. The child generalized incorrectly from a specific trauma. A fear is also likely to continue if it is acceded to by a child's parents.

A phobia may also be used as a defense mechanism to counteract dangerous impulses. A man avoids speaking in public because he is afraid he will expose his genitals. A woman avoids skyscrapers because she is afraid she will jump off.

There are also real gains from phobia. They may relieve individuals of anxiety and responsibilities or gain them increased attention. A child who has school-phobia may actually fear separation from his or her mother. By refusing to go to school, the child gets to stay home with her.

Somatoform Disorders

Somatoform disorders are those in which the individual complains of a physical ailment or pain for which there is no organic or physiological explanation. *DSM-III* classifies several kinds of somatoform disorders: somatization, conversion, psychogenic pain, hypochondriasis, and atypical.

Hypochondriasis

Hypochondriasis is characterized by an individual's misinterpretation of body functions. They can interpret heartbeat, perspiration, minor coughing, or even irregular bowel movements as symptoms of a serious disease. Sometimes the person is afraid of contracting a disease. At other times the hypochondriac believes that he or she has a specific disease. The belief that he or she already has a disease continues even in the face of medical evidence to the contrary. The feigned "illness" may cause serious restrictions in social, work, and home activities.

Hypochondriacs are famous for "doctor shopping." They go to doctor after doctor with their list of symptoms and medical knowledge picked up from popular journals and previous physicians. They search for the doctor who can find the serious disease they know they have.

Causes. Hypochondria can stem from early childhood learning. Overanxious parents, who pamper their children unduly when they are sick may be unwittingly teaching hypochondriacs how to gain love and attention.

People who become hypochondriacs later in life (men in their 30s and women in their 40s) may do so in reaction to a sense that they have not made much of their lives. They may feel that they have not achieved what they wanted professionally or that they are dissatisfied with their marriage. Hypochondria is the maladaptive behavior they "choose" over what they perceive to be a life full of wrong choices.

Again, there is the gain: hypochondriacs gain attention from families, friends, and doctors. They are reinforced and sometimes encouraged to persist in their behavior. These individuals will not have to worry about disappointing people because they are too "sick" to live up to the expectations of others.

PERSONALITY DISORDERS

People with personality disorders perceive, relate to, and think about themselves and their environment in maladaptive ways. The symptoms are "acted out" in the world rather than simply in the mind of the person. The entire personality seems to be imbued with the disorder. Here is one case:

> Charles Clay, aged 45, owned what had been a successful 24-hour-a-day grocery store. . . . Until 5 years ago he had been a cheerful, friendly merchant. Then his wife died, and his personality seemed to undergo a change. Increasingly he worried that people were trying to shoplift his merchandise. . . . As time

went on, he began to confront customers with his suspicions and even to demand that some of them submit to a search. . . .

Mr. Clay's business began to decline. When this happened, he got very angry and even more suspicious. The culminating event was an attempt he made to search a woman who entered the store, walked around for a few minutes, and then bought a newspaper. When he tried to search her (at the same time yelling, "Don't tell me you were just looking around!"), she ran from the store and summoned the police. The police investigation led Mr. Clay to seek advice from his lawyer, who had been a friend since high school. Although Mr. Clay insisted that "there is nothing the matter with me," his anger and suspiciousness bothered the lawyer. With deft touches of tact and persuasion, the lawyer got Mr. Clay to agree to visit a psychiatrist. Unfortunately, the visit did not work out well. Mr. Clay was reluctant to talk about his concerns and was angered by what he thought of as the psychiatrist's inquisitiveness. . . . several months later Mr. Clay was arrested and convicted of physically attacking another customer. (Sarason & Sarason, 1984)

People with personality disorders do not usually want treatment. They do not think anything is wrong, and often it is the people who live with them who do.

Types and Causes

Here is a list of major personality disorders and brief definitions from *DSM-III*.

Paranoid: pervasive and unwarranted suspiciousness and mistrust of people, hypersensitivity.

Schizoid: a defect in the capacity to form social relationships, evidenced by the absence of warm, tender feelings for others, indifference to praise, criticism, and the feelings of others.

Histrionic: overly dramatic, reactive, and intensely expressed behavior and characteristic disturbances in interpersonal relationships.

Narcissistic: a grandiose sense of self-importance or uniqueness.

Borderline: instability in a variety of areas, including interpersonal behavior, mood, and self-image; no single feature is invariably present.

Avoidant: hypersensitivity to potential rejection, humiliation, or shame; an unwillingness to enter into relationships unless given unusually strong guarantees of uncritical acceptance.

Dependent: the individual passively allows others to assume responsibility for major areas of his or her life because of a lack of self-confidence and an inability to function independently.

Compulsive: restricted ability to express warm and tender emotions; excessive devotion to work and productivity to the exclusion of pleasure; and indecisiveness (goodbye, I think).

Passive–Aggressive: resistance to demands for adequate performance in work and social functioning; the resistance is expressed indirectly rather than directly and the result is pervasive and persistent social or occupational ineffectiveness.

Antisocial: a history of continuous and chronic antisocial behavior in which the rights of others are violated.

Causes.   There is little information about why people develop personality disorders or why they develop the specific ones that they do. Because individuals with such disorders have little desire to change, treatment is rarely successful.

Antisocial Behavior: Sociopathic Personality

Suppose you saw this advertisement:

> Are you adventurous? Psychologists studying adventurous carefree people who've led exciting impulsive lives. If you're the kind of person who'd do almost anything for a dare and want to participate in a paid experiment, send name, address, phone number and short biography proving how interesting you are.

This ad appeared in several newspapers in Boston. It attracted people whose psychological tests later revealed fit the clinical picture of an **antisocial personality** (ASP), also called *psychopath* or *sociopath* (Wisdom, 1977). Most antisocial personalities studied by psychologists are institutionalized, usually in prisons or reformatories. Wisdom wanted to see if ASPs within society were similar to those institutionalized. They are. (One respondent determined the true purpose of the ad; he wrote: "Are you looking for hookers or are you trying to make a listing of all the sociopaths in Boston?")

The pattern of antisocial behavior usually begins before age 15. The individual is unable to feel either positive emotions or guilt. Such people also have superficial charm and average or above average intelligence. They have little sense of responsibility about anything, big or small. They tell lies and have no guilt or regret about any antisocial actions.

Causes of Antisocial Personality

Psychosocial Factors

Three percent of American men and less than one percent of American women have ASP disorder. The psychosocial factors thought to be important are:

1. Extreme poverty and poor education.
2. Poor family background; if the father suffers from the disorder the child is removed from the home and gets little discipline.

Biological Factors

Dan F., the antisocial personality described in the box on the next page, describes his own situation:

> I can remember the first time in my life when I began to suspect I was a little different from most people. When I was in high school my best friend got leukemia and died and I went to his funeral. Everybody else was crying and feeling sorry for themselves and as they were praying to get him into heaven I suddenly realized that I wasn't feeling anything at all. He was a nice guy but what the hell. That night I thought about it more and found out that I wouldn't miss my mother and father if they died and that I wasn't too nuts about my brothers and sisters, for that matter. I figured there wasn't anybody I really cared for but, then, I didn't need any of them anyway so I rolled over and went to sleep. (McNeil, 1967)

A CASE OF AN ANTISOCIAL PERSONALITY

Psychologist Elton McNeil described an antisocial personality (Dan F.) whom he knew, not as a patient, but as a friend.

One night, a colleague of Dan's committed suicide. My phone started ringing early the next morning with the inevitable question, "Why?" The executives at the station called but Dan F. never did. When I did talk to him, he did not mention the suicide. Later, when I brought it to his attention, all he could say was that it was "the way the ball bounces." At the station, however, he was the one who collected money for the deceased and presented it personally to the new widow. As Dan observed, she was really built and had possibilities. . . .

Dan F. has been married twice before, a fact he had failed to communicate to his present wife, and, as he described it, was still married only part time. He was currently involved sexually with girls ranging from the station manager's secretary (calculated) to the weather girl (incidental, based on a shared interest in Chinese food). The females of the "show biz" species seemed to dote on the high-handed treatment he accorded them. They regularly refused to believe he was "as bad as he pretended to be," and he was always surrounded by intense and glamorous women who needed to own him to feel complete as human beings.

Dan F. had charm plus. He always seemed to know when to say the right thing with exactly the proper degree of concern, seriousness, and understanding for the benighted victim of a harsh world. *But, he was dead inside* [italics added]. People amused him and he watched them with the kind of interest most of us show when examining a tank of guppies. Once, on a whim, he called each of the burlesque theaters in town and left word with the burlesque queens that he was holding a party beginning at midnight with each of them as an honored guest. He indeed held the party, charging it to the station as a talent search, and spent the evening pouring liquor into the girls. By about 3 a.m. the hotel suite was a shambles, but he thought it was hilarious. He had invited the camera and floor crew from the television station and had carefully constructed a fictional identity for each: one was an independent film producer, another a casting director, a third an influential writer, and still another, a talent agent. This giant hoax was easy to get away with since Dan had read correctly and with painful accuracy the not so secret dreams, ambitions, drives, and personal needs of these entertainers. What was staggering was the elaborateness of the cruel joke. He worked incessantly, adding a touch here and a touch there to make it perfect. (McNeil, 1967)

The antisocial personality has *decreased emotional response*, especially to unpleasant stimuli. In studies measuring autonomic system reactions, ASPs have less activation to shock (Wilson & Herrnstein, 1985). When a child is punished or slapped for doing the wrong thing, it activates a feeling of hurt and guilt and makes it less likely that the child will repeat the action. People with "flat" emotions would not feel the hurt and would be less likely to learn law-abiding behavior. Thus, one characteristic of these people is extreme calm, perhaps due to the underarousal. There is a constant search in these people for excitement. They attack others verbally or set up wild scenes, such as Dan F.'s burlesque queen party. This may be due to a characteristic underarousal and the need for extreme stimulation.

Genetic Factors

There is evidence for genetic factors in this disorder. Children of criminal fathers have less reactive autonomic nervous system response than do children of noncriminals. In a very large study, Wadsworth noted the pulse rate of 11-year-old boys just before a mild stress. He compared these to later pulse rates and records of delinquency. Those with low increases in pulse rate were much more likely to become delinquent (Mednick, 1977). Biological relatives of adopted criminals show a higher rate of criminality and antisocial behavior than does the general population (Wilson & Herrnstein, 1985). In studies of the antisocial personality, the same relationship holds: the transmission is significant from the biological father (Schulsinger, 1972). What might be inherited, then, is an autonomic nervous system that is less responsive to stimulation. In the appropriate situation this could lead to some deficiencies in learning law-abiding behavior, to less responsiveness to others' feelings, and to the need to create excitement. These are all characteristic of the antisocial personality.

The use of mood- or consciousness-altering drugs is common in every culture. Alcohol is the most common recreational drug in our society. The use of illegal drugs such as marijuana and heroin is widespread in certain subcultures of American society. **Substance use disorder** means that there is a *consistent pattern of excessive use resulting in impairment of social or occupational functioning.* Disordered individuals are dependent on the drug (substance), and they may not be able to get through the day without it nor can they stop or restrict their use even if they know that they should.

Some disorders may be minor, such as caffeine intoxication:

> A 35-year-old secretary sought consultation for "anxiety attacks." A thorough history revealed that the attacks occurred in the mid-to-late afternoon, when she became restless, nervous, and easily excited and sometimes was noted to be flushed, sweating, and, according to co-workers, "talking a mile a minute." In response to careful questioning, she acknowledged drinking five or six cups of coffee each day before the usual time the attacks occurred. (Spitzer et al., 1981)

The patient must experience a disturbance in behavior for at least one month before the *DSM-III* will classify him or her as having a drug disorder. There are two forms of substance use disorders: abuse and dependence. *Dependence* is more severe: the drug-dependent person begins to show increased tolerance. He or she requires greater amounts of the drug over time, and experiences specific physiological symptoms if the drug is withdrawn.

There are five categories of substances that may invite abuse or dependence: *alcohol*; barbiturates or other *sedatives*; *analgesics* such as painkillers or narcotics, which include heroin; *stimulants* such as amphetamines; and *psychoactive drugs* such as marijuana and LSD.

Incidence

About 16 percent of Americans report alcohol-related problems. More men than women have a substance use disorder with alcohol. Abuse and dependence do not usually appear until adulthood. Alcoholic disorder usually appears between

SUBSTANCE USE DISORDERS

See Chapter 7, sections on Drugs and Psychoactive Drugs.

the ages of 20 and 50, whereas problems with marijuana, cocaine, heroin, and other narcotics start earlier, in late teens and early 20s. Substance abuse and dependence may lead to physical problems such as malnutrition or hepatitis. A major complication of alcohol abuse is traffic accidents. Half of all highway deaths in America involve either a driver or pedestrian who has been drinking. About one-fourth of all suicides and more than one-half of all murderers *and* their victims are drunk at the time of the death.

Causes

The use of a drug may begin for recreational purposes and to alleviate fear and anxiety in social settings. Lessening anxiety is the reinforcer that maintains the abuse. The factors that contribute to the abuse of different drugs vary. Alcoholism often runs in families, and there is some evidence for genetic predisposition to alcoholism. However, the important factors seem to be psychosocial, such as stress, marital problems, and tension reduction. Also, rapid changes in socioeconomic status (especially downward) may lead to alcoholism.

PSYCHOLOGY AND THE HOMELESS

In the past several years, advances in drug treatments have launched a surge of people into the streets of almost every major city. What are they like? What is being done for them? In this extract, psychologist Daniel Goleman writes of some new programs in New York City.

A central concept [in helping the homeless] . . . is "supportive housing." That phrase embodies a concept of many layers of support. Mental health workers must make sure that their clients eat, take their medicine, keep appointments, work their way through bureaucratic red tape, get training in basic social skills and find work when possible. The clients' condition must be monitored and psychiatric help sought when necessary. The total vigilance of a caring family has to come into play. In some instances, it means that when a client heads off for a new job he is accompanied by a guardian who will take over if the client fails. . . .

The key has been to combine the compassion of nonprofessional guardians, who bear most of the day-to-day burden, with a tight link to professional psychiatry, which is called in as needed. . . . The St. Francis Residence was found to be six times

more effective than the prevailing facilities—including state mental hospitals and shelters—in keeping the most seriously disturbed of the homeless mentally ill from drifting back to a life on the streets.

Most of the mentally ill on the streets suffer from schizophrenia. . . . For some, schizophrenia is a lifelong condition whose symptoms alternately worsen and improve. For others, a single psychotic episode is followed by complete remission.

The new approach means creating a surrogate family including someone who will help the schizophrenic past the obstacles of agencies that offer stipends but only to people with an address, a birth certificate or identity card. . . .

In recent days I accompanied Timothy—his name has been changed to protect his identity—when he moved into the St. Francis Residence.

Last January, when a phone call brought him to the attention of the workers at Project Reachout, Timothy had spent two months huddled in a heap of garbage in the stairwell of a brownstone on West 68th St., hearing voices telling him his life was threatened by the Mafia.

Timothy shunned public shelters, and insisted he needed a job, not a

In narcotic addiction there is some evidence of neurological causes. Recall that the brain produces its own painkillers and mood modulators called endorphins. Specific endorphins fit, as a key does into a lock, specific receptors in the brain, especially in the limbic system. Morphine (of which heroin is a derivative) fits these locks as well. Some researchers hypothesize that morphine addiction may occur in people whose brain produces too few endorphins (Coleman et al., 1980).

However, in narcotic addiction sociocultural factors are more important. In the United States, heroin addiction is more common in lower economic groups. Fortunately, heroin addiction is often short-lived; this is not true of alcohol or the other narcotics. But the death rate among heroin users is high, due in large part to impurities and continual injections without proper hygiene. If a person survives, dependence rarely lasts more than nine years.

See Chapter 4, section on The Healing Brain.

Depression

Depression is the "common cold of psychological disorders" (Rosenhan & Seligman, 1985). We often use the word *depressed* to mean sad, upset, or in a bad

psychiatrist. But months of patient efforts eased Timothy out of his stairwell and into psychiatric care. His bizarre ideas faded. Then he was lucky enough to be accepted into a program at Fountain House, a combination clubhouse and job training center for the mentally ill whose places, far too few for those who need them, are awarded by lottery. Through Fountain House, Timothy got a job as a messenger at a bank.

The day he moved into his own small room at the St. Francis Residence, Timothy, who is still painfully shy and who mumbles when he talks, said he was, at last, very happy. Timothy's journey from a garbage heap to a job and room of his own shows the possibilities for those apparently hopeless schizophrenics one sees—or tries to avoid seeing— huddled on the city's streets. . . .

In a recently completed study, Dr. Frank Lipton, director of the psychiatric emergency unit at Bellevue, studied a group of homeless schizophrenics who had been brought in by the police because they were threatening other people or in danger of suicide. Some had been homeless for as long as five years.

After treatment at Bellevue, half the group were discharged to the usual settings, ranging from state hospitals and city shelters to adult homes. And half the group, assigned at random, were sent to the St. Francis Residence. A year later, the difference between the groups was dramatic. Those sent to the St. Francis Residence spent an average of 20 nights of the following year homeless again; most of the small number who left the residence did so in the first few weeks. For those sent elsewhere, the number of homeless nights during that year was 121. . . .

Many more people could be brought off the streets almost immediately if there were enough workers to contact them, enough proper places to bring them and enough caring people to help manage their lives. New York City boasts some of the nation's finest programs and facilities for the homeless mentally ill. One of the best and largest is the St. Francis Residence. It houses 215 people.

In the entire city, there are just 2,020 beds in such supervised residences; the state plans to add 5,245 by 1995. And, by the best estimates, there are at this moment roaming the streets of the city 15,000 homeless mentally ill. (Dan Goleman, "For mentally ill on the street a new approach shines." *The New York Times*, Nov. 11, 1986)

mood. "I'm depressed—the store is out of chocolate chip cookies and I was thinking about them all day." **Depression** is judged to be a severe mental disorder when the person suffers from an overwhelming sadness that immobilizes and arrests the entire course of his or her life. Here is a case of a college student suffering from severe depression:

> Nancy entered the university with a superb high-school record. She had been president and salutatorian of her class, and a popular and pretty cheerleader. Everything she wanted had always fallen into her lap; good grades came easily and boys fell over themselves competing for her attentions. She was an only child, and her parents doted on her, rushing to fulfill her every whim; her successes were their triumphs, her failures their agony. Her friends nicknamed her Golden Girl.
>
> When I met her in her sophomore year, she was no longer a Golden Girl. She said that she felt empty, that nothing touched her any more; her classes were boring and the whole academic system seemed an oppressive conspiracy to stifle her creativity. The previous semester she had received two F's. She had "made it" with a succession of young men, and was currently living with a dropout. She felt exploited and worthless after each sexual adventure; her current relationship was on the rocks, and she felt little but contempt for him and for herself. She had used soft drugs extensively and had once enjoyed being carried away on them. But now even drugs had lost their appeal.
>
> She was majoring in philosophy, and had a marked emotional attraction to Existentialism: like the existentialists, she believed that life is absurd and that people must create their own meaning. This belief filled her with despair. Her despair increased when she perceived her own attempts to create meaning—participation in the movements for women's liberation and against the war in Vietnam—as fruitless. When I reminded her that she had been a talented student and was still an attractive and valuable human being, she burst into tears: "I fooled you, too." (Seligman, 1975)

Characteristics of Depression

Depression is classified in *DSM-III* as an **affective disorder**—a disturbance of *mood.* There are two categories of serious depressive disorders. In *unipolar depression* an individual suffers only from depression, whereas in *bipolar depression* a person suffers from depression, but also experiences the "polar" opposite emotion of **mania,** which is excessive elation. An individual in a manic episode is in a frenzy of overexcitability and activity; it is a happiness that is as out of control as the sadness. Both forms of the illness vary from mild to extremely severe. A severely depressed or manic person may need to be hospitalized. All of the affective disorders involve either mania or depression or both. Here we will describe the essential characteristics of both, and in the following sections begin to examine the causes of the disorder.

Although we use the word "depressed" loosely, before a clinician would diagnose a person as depressed, at least four of the following symptoms have to be present *every day* for two weeks:

1. *Loss of interest and pleasure.* This is almost universal. The individual is indifferent to the activities that usually provide interest and pleasure. This loss of interest extends to friends and family. The depressed person often withdraws from people and activities.

2. *Appetite disturbance.* The most common appetite disturbance is loss, al-

though some people experience an increase in appetite, causing a significant change in the person's normal weight. A fairly accurate description of a depressed person is that he or she is "wasting away." One sign that a person is pulling out of a depressive episode is weight gain.

3. *Sleep disturbance.* The most common sleep disturbance is insomnia, although sometimes there is the opposite, hypersomnia.

4. *Psychomotor disturbance.* They may be agitated, and cannot sit still; they pull their hair, pace up and down the floor, and wring their hands. They may be retarded, with slower and monotonous speech. They move slowly as if carrying a heavy weight.

5. *Decrease in energy level.* A virtually universal trait. People feel tired consistently, although they have slept or done nothing physically taxing. The prospect of having to do even the smallest task is overwhelming.

6. *Sense of worthlessness.* The degree of worthlessness varies from general feelings of inadequacy and negative self-evaluations to feelings of delusional proportion.

7. *Difficulty in concentrating.* Thinking is slower. The depressed person has trouble making decisions and often complains of memory disturbances. They are easily distracted.

8. *Thoughts about death.* A depressed person often seems preoccupied with death. They may be afraid of it, wish for it, or plan or attempt suicide.

9. *Miscellaneous associated symptoms.* Other features that depressed persons may experience are anxiety, phobias, overconcern with health, tearfulness, and irritability.

Manic Episodes

The attributes of mania are the mirror image of depression. *DSM-III* characterizes the mood as predominantly elevated, expansive, or irritable. Patients often experience elevated moods as pure euphoria, and those who know the disturbed people will recognize that the euphoria is a bit excessive. Their friends are "not themselves." The happiness has no specific cause and is not under the person's control.

The manic person has unbounded enthusiasm for everyone and everything. The two qualities of euphoria and expansiveness, if not too extreme, are infectious. They enable some manics to be very effective manipulators. Here is a manic expressing this:

"You look like a couple of bright, alert, hard working, clean-cut, energetic, go-getters and I could use you in my organization! I need guys that are loyal and enthusiastic about the great opportunities life offers on this planet! It's yours for the taking! Too many people pass opportunity by without hearing it knock because they don't know how to grasp the moment and strike while the iron is hot! You've got to grab it when it comes up for air, pick up the ball and run! You've got to be decisive! decisive! decisive! No shilly-shallying! Sweat! Yeah, sweat with a goal! Push, push, push, and you can push over a mountain! Two mountains, maybe. It's not luck! Hell, if it wasn't for bad luck I wouldn't have any luck at all! Be there firstest with the mostest! My guts and your blood! That's the system! I know, you know, he, she, or it knows it's the only way to travel! Get'em off balance, baby, and the rest is leverage! Use your head and save your heels! What's

SEASONAL AFFECTIVE DISORDER (SAD)

Almost everyone experiences mood change in the presence or absence of sunlight. On bright, sunny days we feel better, perhaps more energetic and "sunny." On dull gray days, we may feel moody, blue, and out of sorts. For some light-sensitive people, changes in light exposure can generate mood swings.

Mr. P., a sixty-three-year-old scientist, started experiencing unexplained depressive episodes at thirty-five. After many years, he began to notice a pattern: toward the end of June he would begin to become depressed. He would feel anxious, reluctant to go to work, and fearful of interacting with others. He had difficulty developing new ideas, and his sexual energy declined. He slept fitfully and became reluctant to get out of bed.

Mr. P. remained depressed until about the end of January when he would switch dramatically into a hypomanic state. His energy level surged and he required less sleep, sometimes as little as two to three hours per night. He had taken without success a variety of antidepressant medications.

Mr. P. suffers from seasonal affective disorder (SAD). This newly identified

disorder is common. Symptoms begin in the teens and twenties. The symptoms appear directly related to the amount of sunlight which reaches the brain. For people in the northern hemisphere the depressive symptoms usually start between September and October and last into March. One patient living in Chile experienced her depressive episodes between June and September, which are the winter months in the southern hemisphere. (Rosenthal, 1984)

Norman Rosenthal and his colleagues at the National Institute of Health have developed a novel approach to treating such patients. Reasoning that the symptoms were due to an extreme reaction of the brain to light deprivation, they prescribed "light therapy." Patients sit directly in front of a bright, full spectrum fluorescent light source for three hours before dawn and three hours after dusk. A control group sat an equal amount of time in front of a dim yellow light. The high intensity light treatment dramatically lessened depression, as does diet. (Rosenthal et al., 1984; Rosenthal, 1986)

this deal? Who are these guys? Have you got a telephone and a secretary I could have instanter if not sooner? What I need is office space and the old LDO [long-distance operator]." (McNeil, 1967)

Incidence.   Affective disorders afflict five to eight percent of all people at some time in their lives. Of these people six percent of the women and three percent of the men have an episode serious enough to require hospitalization.

Bipolar disorder (depression with both depressive and manic periods) is experienced by 0.4 to 1.2 percent of the population. Women are more likely than men to suffer from unipolar disorder (only depression). However, there is no sex difference in the bipolar form. A major depression can occur at any age. A person with bipolar form of the disorder often experiences his or her manic episode before the age of 30. The average age of onset for bipolar is 28 and for unipolar, 36.

Causes of Depressive Disorder

The causal factors of both unipolar and bipolar disorder can be divided to factors *within* (*endogenous*) and those from *without* (*exogenous*). Endogenous factors include genetic predisposition and biochemical components, whereas exogenous factors include undue stress, a precipitating event, and psychosocial factors such as helplessness, personality predispositions, and sociocultural factors. It is unlikely that endogenous factors alone can account for a severe disorder, but it is possible that depression may be caused by exogenous factors alone.

Endogenous Factors. One way to separate genetic and learned factors is to compare two kinds of twins. Fraternal twins are the product of two eggs; they are no more alike genetically than any normal brother and sister. Identical twins, in contrast, are both from the same egg and have an identical genetic makeup. A "concordance rate" indicates the degree to which when one twin has the disorder so does the other. There is an extremely high concordance rate in both unipolar and bipolar forms of the disorder in identical twins. In bipolar disorder the concordance rate for identical twins is 72 percent, but for fraternal twins, it is 14 percent; in unipolar disorder, the rate is 40 percent for identical twins but only 11 percent for fraternal twins (Kessler, 1980). This finding is particularly interesting because the bipolar form of the disorder is rarer than the unipolar.

There is probably more of a predisposing genetic factor in bipolar depression. Studies of families of bipolar depressives reveal that 11 percent of close relatives also had experienced bipolar depression, whereas only 0.5 percent had the unipolar form. Of the close relatives of people with unipolar depression 7 percent also had experienced a major depression, but only 0.4 percent had experienced the bipolar form (Winokur, Clayton, & Reich, 1969). Other severe psychological disorders and suicide are more prevalent in families of people with bipolar disorder.

Winokur was able to locate and interview the close relatives of 61 bipolar patients. He found that there was a risk of an affective disorder in 56 percent of the mothers and 13 percent of the fathers. He found a much lower incidence in a similar study of unipolar patients. The evidence so far points to a probable genetic component in bipolar disorder, but it is not so clear in unipolar disorder.

Some studies (Cadoret, Winokur, & Clayton, 1971) suggest that a predisposition to bipolar depression might be transmitted as a dominant gene on the X chromosome. Geneticists have traced specific X chromosome traits, such as red-green color blindness, through several generations of families. They have also traced bipolar depression. However, this finding has not always been reproduced and is controversial. Even if they can prove it conclusively, it would indicate only inherited vulnerability to, not a certainty of, depression.

Exogenous Causes. Stress and other precipitating causes are important factors in the onset of depression. Depressed patients report two to three times as many disruptive events as normal in the period just before a depression. The kinds of events reported are threatening, for example, marital separation and children leaving home. Marital separation increases the probability of depression by five to six times (Deykin, Klerman, & Armor, 1966). Still, fewer than 10 percent of people who separate from their spouse become clinically depressed. Women who develop depression often do so after menopause.

There also seem to be personality characteristics that predispose one to depression. They are often successful, hard working, and conscientious to the point of obsessiveness. The typical family background of bipolar depressed individuals includes parents who used their children to gain social acceptance for themselves. The children were told that they had to behave better and do better than other kids. Consequently, the children felt they had to earn their parents' love by superior effort. As adults, these people are inclined to be dependent on others and work hard to make other people like them. They still believe that they cannot be loved without extra effort.

An Interesting Finding about Realism. Most people—psychologists among them—believe that a depressed person has a negative perception of how others feel about him or her. However, one study shows that depressed people are *more* realistic in their self-perception than nondepressed people. Normal people overestimate how much others like them, while depressives are fairly accurate in this regard. One sign that depression is abating is that the *realism decreases*, and depressives begin to think people view them more favorably than they do (Lewinshohn, Mischel, & Barton, 1980).

Suicide

The most serious and tragic outcome of depression is suicide. Three-fourths of suicides are committed by people who are depressed at the time of death (Leonard, 1971). Suicide is among the ten leading causes of death in Western countries. Over 200,000 people attempt suicide each year in the United States alone. This means that five million living Americans have tried to kill themselves. Each year about 15 percent of those who attempt it succeed. Three times as many women as men attempt to kill themselves, but three times as many men as women are successful. This fact may have something to do with the way they choose to commit suicide. Women are more likely to try to overdose on drugs, especially barbiturates; men are more likely to use firearms.

Most commonly a person who commits suicide is in the 24 to 44 age group. However, in recent years there has been an enormous increase in the number of young adults 15 to 24 years of age who have tried. In the next year we estimate that 80,000 of this group will attempt suicide and about 4,000 will succeed. One characteristic of this group of suicides is that they often come from privileged backgrounds. The rate is higher at larger, more prestigious colleges and universities (Peck & Schrut, 1971).

Multiple Personality

Remember the case of Billy Milligan in Chapter 1? While unusual, the breakup of the mind reveals its normally separate components. The number of cases are small, so we can't be sure about the cause. But it seems to occur in people whose parents were violent and sadistic to them as children and who were extremely inconsistent—nice one day, harsh the next; sweet one day, horrible the next. Often there are almost unspeakable sexual assaults in childhood, followed by aloofness. The child simply cannot understand what is happening, and does not know how to think, how to act, or what to do.

See Chapter 1, section on Clinical Approach.

For some who cannot bear the pain, the solution is to give full and independent voices to those different minds. Then distinct personalities emerge which are unaware of one another; this may help in avoiding consciousness of the pain and horror of their life. Sometimes two personalities coexist, and later a third one may emerge, one who has all the memories of the independent first two. Normally there is coherence and order maintained by the mental system under most conditions, but under the daily violence that these children are exposed to, it seems to break down, revealing the splits.

In addition to brutality and sexual degradation of disordered families, multiple personalities can also result from violence experienced later in life. Here is the case of Charles Poultney, in which a third personality of a former soldier comes forward after severe wartime trauma. This case is described by the psychologist Ernest Hilgard in his book *Divided Consciousness,* which also describes the therapy.

> . . . it was found that he had first been picked up in Los Angeles in 1919 in a dazed condition, wandering the streets. Although he had identification papers made out to Charles Poulting of Florida and had British and French war medals with him, he did not know who he was. He spoke with an Irish accent, thought he might be a Canadian, and Michigan seemed to have some importance to him. He was tattooed with Buffalo Bill and an American flag. He had traveled widely since World War I, trying to find himself, for he had lost all memories prior to February 1915. . . .
>
> The police again found him wandering in a dazed condition in March 1930, now having regained the memories and identity of Charles Poultney from birth to 1915, but having lost all recent memories. He now thought he was back to 1914 and looked on newspapers with the 1930 dates as some strange 'futuristic' sheets because they gave no war news. He missed his uniform and, when seeking to return things to a pocket, automatically fumbled for the breast pocket of his uniform, where there was no pocket in his civilian clothes.
>
> In this second state, as Charles Poulting, it was possible to "introduce him" to the memories of the first state, as Charles Poultney, by way of the biography that he had written while in that state. This did not help him much, until with a map of

Africa before him, two personal memories were integrated in a flood of emotion. The place name of Voi proved to be the trigger. [He was able to recall two events.] About one he felt no guilt, but the other burdened his conscience. Out in the forest with another soldier in leopard country, his companion refused to climb a tree and tie himself there to spend the night. During the night he was attacked and eaten by leopards. This did not bother Poultney; he had seen many battle deaths, and this was the companion's fault for not taking the precaution that he had recommended and himself taken. However, the other event was different. He had a monkey with him when nightfall occurred in the same territory. He tied the monkey to the base of the tree, while he found his own secure place up in the tree. During the night the monkey was attacked and eaten; had Poultney not tied him at the bottom of the tree he could have escaped. By contrast with the death of the human companion, the death of the monkey — his fault — was an intolerable burden and he became amnesic for the event and the other events surrounding it. (Hilgard, 1977)

Once the monkey episode came to light, all the subsequent memories of Poulting and Poultney became fused, and the man felt essentially cured, even though there were still some memory gaps.

Schizophrenia

Schizophrenia is the name for a group of disorders that involve *severe deterioration of mental abilities*. Here is one case:

> Mary Waverly was in her late 20s. A university graduate, she had run a successful boutique in a large western city before her marriage and until shortly before the birth of her daughter, who is now 2. During the year before Mary's daughter was born, Mary's mother had been treated for cancer. She died when Alice, her granddaughter, was 14 months old. During the baby's first year and a half, Mary was also under pressure because her daughter had surgery several times to correct a birth defect.
>
> Recently, Mary's husband attempted to have her committed to a psychiatric hospital. He said he was concerned about their daughter's welfare. Mary had become a religious fanatic. Although she came from a very religious family, her behavior had not seemed unusual until recently, when she joined a cult group. Since joining the group she refused to have sexual relations with her husband because he was not a "believer." Although she seemed to take good care of her child, she made all decisions only after listening to the "voice of the Lord." (Sarason & Sarason, 1984)

This fundamental disorganization causes disturbances in every area of life: social functioning, feelings, and behavior. The characteristics of these disturbances are listed here, although no single feature is *always* present.

1. *Content of thought delusions.* These are the most common disturbances of thought. Common delusions are the belief that someone is spying on the individual or spreading rumors. Often the schizophrenic gives inappropriate, unusual, or impossible significance to events. One man was convinced that Ronald Reagan was instructing him on one of his television broadcasts. Other common delusions include: *thought broadcast,* the belief that others hear one's thoughts; *thought insertion,* that others are inserting thoughts into one's mind; *thought withdrawal,* the sensation that one's thoughts are

"INTERFERENCE PATTERNS" IN A SCHIZOPHRENIC

Here is a recent account by Carol North, a woman who was schizophrenic, who then recovered to become a psychiatrist. This is an extract from her book *Welcome, Silence* (North, 1987).

After supper, I sat quietly in the dayroom trying to watch TV. The medication was slowing me down considerably, and even the simplest movement seemed to take forever.

The voices gathered behind me, keeping up a running commentary on everything that was happening.

A nurse breezed through the dayroom on her way down another hallway. "There goes the nurse," said a voice.

A flash of light zoomed across the dayroom, burning out and disappearing into thin air. Had I really seen that?

"There goes another comet," said a voice.

Okay, I did see it. This could only mean one thing: further leakage of the Other Worlds into this world. The comet had been a sign.

"It's all right," Hal reassured me with his sugary voice. "We're here with you."

Interference Patterns began to materialize in the air. I stared at their colorful swirls, watching new patterns emerge in response to every sound in the room. When the voices spoke, the patterns shifted, just as they did with other sounds. It was like the vampire test: vampires don't have reflections in mirrors; nonexistent voices shouldn't affect the patterns the way other sounds did. That was scientific proof that the voices were just as real as everything else in the world; actually, they seemed even more real.

Frightening. I didn't know whether existence in the Other Worlds would be divinely magnificent, beyond human description, like heaven, or whether it would be like the worst imaginable hell. I was ambivalent about whether I wanted it to happen. On one hand, I didn't want to stop the emergence of goodness, yet if it threatened to be hellish, I would have to try to prevent it.

I froze, not wanting to produce further patterns from the stimulation of my bodily movement. I didn't want to be responsible for encouraging such change in the world. Live your life as a prayer, I reminded myself.

I heard a news announcer on TV parrot my words: "Live your life as a prayer."

Yes, that was good advice for the world to know. The newscaster had broadcast my own thought. The communication systems brought in from the Other Worlds were incredibly sophisticated, more than I could understand. The whole world was now praying with me.

A nurse sat down next to me on the couch and put her hand on my arm. "Carol, what's going on with you? You're just sitting there doing nothing. Are you bored?"

The sound of her voice created new waves of Interference Patterns, sent hurtling through the air in front of us.

Hush! Don't you understand what you're doing? For God's sake, don't help the Other Side. [Italics in original]

She shook my arm gently. "Why, Carol, I believe you look scared. Am I right?"

Oh, no, now you've done it, you've inadvertently hurled us into that bottomless pit. With the force of your movement you've made us start to fall again. [Italics in original]

The nurse got up and went for help. She returned with two male aides, who picked me up off the couch, carried me to my bed, and left me lying there alone in the dark. The whole time, the patterns swirled through the air, crashing over my head like a tidal wave. Would any of us survive this ordeal?

On my bed, undisturbed, unmoving, I applied the powers of my concentration, gradually settling the turbulent waters of the Other Side. The Interference Patterns began to fade back into the air. If I could only lie still indefinitely, I might have a chance. (North, 1987) being stolen from one's mind; and *delusions of being controlled,* the belief that one's actions and thoughts are being controlled.

2. *Form of thought.* This disturbance involves unusual patterns of formal thought. Typically, this involves loosening of associations, and ideas shift from one topic to another with no apparent connections. The speaker typically is unaware of the bizarreness of this thought process. Often the associations are so loose as to make speech incoherent and incomprehensible. Also, although the person speaks a lot, there is little content.

3. *Perception hallucinations.* These are the most characteristic perceptual disturbance. Auditory hallucinations ("voices") are the most common, although visual and olfactory ones do occur. Many investigators believe that a breakdown in perceptual filtering is also characteristic of people with schizophrenic disorder (Plate 16).

4. *Affect.* There are three kinds of affect: blunt, flat, or inappropriate. A blunt affect means there is little intensity in feeling. A flat affect means there are virtually no signs of emotions. An inappropriate affect is that the emotion expressed does not fit the situation (giggling at a funeral).

5. *Sense of self.* There is severe disturbance in the sense of self. The person has the delusion of being controlled or of their most private thoughts being public. Laing (1959) writes that the schizophrenic "may say that he is made of glass, of such transparency and fragility that a look directed at him splinters him to bits and penetrates straight through him."

6. *Volition.* There is often an impairment in goal-directed activity. The reasons for this are either lack of interest, inability to complete something, or lack of initiative.

7. *Relationship to the external world.* The tendency of individuals with schizophrenia is to withdraw from the world. Often their strange behavior may cause other people to withdraw from them. In the withdrawn state they become totally immersed in their own fantasies, delusions, and illogical conclusions.

8. *Psychomotor behavior.* There are several different patterns of psychomotor disturbance. In extreme cases, a person may maintain a rigid posture for hours. In others he or she may assume bizarre postures or make strange gestures. Often there is a "waxy flexibility" to body and muscle movements.

9. *Associated features.* Almost any other symptom of any psychological disorder may be present in the schizophrenic. These may include *anhedonia* (a defect in the capacity for pleasure), depression, anxiety, and memory impairment.

It is estimated that about one percent of all populations suffer from a form of schizophrenic disorder. It is far more likely in urban than rural areas. As mentioned before, Farris and Dunham (1965) and others have found a greater instance of people hospitalized for schizophrenia in the lower socioeconomic sections of a city. There is no sex difference in schizophrenia.

Types of Schizophrenic Disorders

Bleuer first classified schizophrenia as a separate disorder. He chose the term to indicate that "the splitting of the different psychic functions" was the most important characteristic. (*Schiz* means splitting, *phren* refers to the mind). Although we use the single term schizophrenia, it is really a group of disorders. Most psychologists divide them into the following categories:

Hebephrenic. This is the most severely disorganized form of schizophrenia, characterized by extreme disturbance of affect. Most often the hebephrenic appears silly. There is more disintegration of personality in hebephrenia than any other form of schizophrenia. It also has the worst prognosis for recovery. It often begins in childhood.

Paranoid. This type is dominated by delusions of being persecuted. The person is extremely suspicious. Speech is generally coherent. Sirhan Sirhan, who assassinated Bobby Kennedy, was diagnosed as a paranoid schizophrenic.

Catatonic. This type is characterized by unusual motor activity: either excitement or stupor. In catatonia with stupor a person might maintain a single posture for days, usually one that a normal person would find difficult to maintain for more than a few minutes (Figure 15-1). One woman explained that the reason that she held her arm outstretched in front of her, palm outstretched, was that the forces of good and evil were warring on the palm of her hand and she did not want to upset the balance in favor of evil.

Undifferentiated. This type is a rapidly changing mix of all or most of the primary symptoms of schizophrenia. Many people exhibit signs of the undifferentiated type in the beginning stages of the disorder.

Sirhan Sirhan, here shown in custody after his assassination of Bobby Kennedy, was diagnosed as a paranoid schizophrenic.

Causes of Schizophrenia

Genetic Factors. Genes are a necessary cause in the development of schizophrenic disorder, but they are not the only explanation. Kringlen (1967) in a study in Norway found a 38 percent concordance rate in identical twins and only 10 percent in fraternal twins. U.S. studies have also shown high concordance rates. Gottesman and Shields (1972) found 42 percent concordance for identical twins, but only 9 percent for fraternal twins. Thus, although the concordance rate is high, it is not perfect. It indicates a predisposition, not a certainty.

Heston (1966) found that 16.6 percent of children reared apart from their schizophrenic parents developed schizophrenic disorder. Schizophrenics often have retarded, neurotic, or psychopathic children (Heston, 1966). They have unusual peer relations, are suspicious, and exhibit strange mental activity and group behavior.

The risk of developing schizophrenia is 5 to 15 times higher in siblings of schizophrenics than in the general population. The risk for developing schizophrenia is less than one percent in the general population. It is less than 5 percent in parents of schizophrenics, averages 10 percent in siblings, and 11 percent in the children. If both parents are schizophrenic, a child has a 35 to 45 percent or more chance of developing the disorder.

In studies of twins reared apart, identical twins showed a concordance rate of 50 to 60 percent, while fraternal twins showed 10 to 15 percent (Rosenthal, 1970). Although the evidence for genetic factors is impressive, the biochemist Solomon Snyder offers a caution: "Schizophrenia runs in families, but so does attendance at Harvard." The great majority of people who become schizophrenic do *not* have a schizophrenic relative.

See Chapter 4, section on Neurotransmitters.

Biochemical and Neurophysiological Factors. Certain chemical agents, such as LSD and mescaline, present in the bloodstream can evoke schizophrenic symptoms. Researchers established this in the 1950s. They were excited by the possibility of discovering a substance produced in the body that might be the dominant causal factor. So far there have been no breakthroughs, but there is one promising theory called the **dopamine hypothesis**. Schizophrenia is caused by a surplus of dopamine, a neurotransmitter of the catecholoamine group, at important synapses. Alternatively, there may be a surplus of dopamine receptor sites. The very effective antipsychotic drugs given to patients to control their schizophrenic symptoms work by blocking dopamine at synapse receptor sites (Snyder, 1979). This supports the dopamine hypothesis.

There are other neurophysiological abnormalities that might be causal factors. One hypothesis is that the disturbance might be due to imbalances in the exciting and inhibiting processes, leading to inappropriate arousal. Disturbances of these processes would interfere with the normal attentional process (Wynne, Cromwell, & Mattysse, 1978). A woman who had suffered a schizophrenic episode later became a psychiatric nurse. She writes: "I had very little ability to sort the relevant from the irrelevant. The filter had broken down. Completely unrelated events became intricately connected in my mind." These attentional deficiencies often occur before the onset of the episode.

FIGURE 15-1
The withdrawn immobility of catatonic schizophrenics may arise from a combination of many factors.

Another predisposing factor is the adequacy of sensory information. Tests show that paranoids are found to have poorer hearing than normals. In an ingenious experiment based upon these findings, Zimbardo and colleagues (1981) studied the relationship between paranoia and deafness. They gave subjects under hypnosis the suggestion that they would experience partial deafness and would be unaware of the suggestion. When subjects awoke, they began to develop paranoid tendencies because they could not hear the conversations going on around them. Presumably, they reasoned that people they were talking to were excluding them by talking so low.

Why Does Schizophrenia Persist in Populations?

Jarvick and Deckard (1977) propose an interesting explanation. The personality of nonpsychotic relatives of schizophrenics might represent "a selective advantage." Their outlook of general suspiciousness and distrust of peers might make them better candidates for survival in difficult circumstances. Their improved chances of survival mean that they are more likely to contribute to the gene pool of the species.

"They, rather than their trusting peers, are the ones more likely to survive long enough to ensure the survival of their progeny." Other evidence suggests that the genes that predispose schizophrenia may be double-edged. There is some correlation between giftedness and social prominence among relatives of schizophrenics. They often show schizoid tendencies and are slightly detached in relationships. This detachment allows them to pursue with greater intensity their chosen vocations. Such people often achieve great success in science, art, or the pursuit of power.

I t is possible to classify someone as "disordered," but does this do justice to the person? McNeil (1967) writes:

IMPORTANCE OF BEING NORMAL

> Each of us is neurotic in one sense or another. Each of us carries through life a set of unsolved problems, prejudices, and biases in response to our fellow human beings. Since neurosis so often disguises itself as normality and so often is indistinguishable from it, a major problem of adjustment is focused on the correct or incorrect diagnosis each of us makes of the other. The disorder of a single life usually has repercussions in the lives of others, and that is the issue. Normality, then, becomes a very relative term, and its limits are more elastic than most of us suspect. We are all, simultaneously, normal and abnormal.

A person who deviates too far from social standards is often considered abnormal. There are two different kinds of norms. One is *statistical*; it refers to the most common or average incidence of a particular quality. The second is *ethical* — qualities considered by the majority to be desirable or valuable. Isaac Stern is not a normal violin player; Eric Heiden is not a normal skater. Great artists, athletes, scientists, inventors, politicians, and entrepreneurs are all "abnormal" in a sense. But these abnormalities are not worrisome. In psychology, *abnormal* refers to patterns of thought and behavior that interfere with a desirable, useful, or healthy conduct of life.

The "dividing line" between normal and abnormal is not absolute. It is often a subjective determination, and abnormality is often in the eye of the beholder. Society's idea of what is normal changes over time. A century ago it was considered abnormal for a woman to have premarital sex, now it is not. Homosexuality was once classified as a disease, now it is not. Society relaxes or restricts the boundaries of what behaviors it will accept and tolerate. Behavior perfectly fitting for a 2-year-old would be highly inappropriate for a 20- or 40-year-old. To be depressed when someone you love dies or stops loving you is quite normal, but it is abnormal when the depression persists and becomes the pervasive life experience over an extremely long period of time. It is normal to be neat and clean, but it is abnormal to wash one's hands 500 times a day.

Often the labels that society places on certain behavior can have serious consequences in a person's life. Individuals who have been diagnosed as schizophrenic are considered "in remission" for five years before a diagnosis of "no mental disorder" is made. Aside from the debilitating effect this may have on these people psychologically, it may also interfere with their ability to find work and with their personal relationships. For instance, friends and family may treat them as "disturbed." Often this is a self-fulfilling judgment.

What happens to people so labeled is in part determined by how their disorders are treated. It is to this that we now turn.

SUMMARY

1. Psychological disorders are not restricted to a few people; they occur in all of us at some time in our lives. In the United States, hundreds of thousands are paralyzed because of phobias, ten million are alcoholics, and more than one million are schizophrenics. Disorders differ from person to person, but several qualities are common to all disorders: (a) loss of control, (b) unhappiness or distress, and (c) isolation from others. The most widely used classification system for disorders is in the *Diagnostic and Statistical Manual of Mental Disorders (DSM)* of the American Psychiatric Association. The *DSM-III* (1980 edition) characterizes mild and severe disorders.

2. Mild disorders include anxiety and somatoform disorders. The cause of mild disorders seems to be entirely psychological. People have maladaptive coping strategies, learn inappropriate contingencies, and have difficulty in family or personal relationships. People suffering from *generalized anxiety* live in constant tension, are uneasy around people, and are unusually sensitive to criticism from others.

3. Another anxiety disorder is *phobia*, the Greek word for "fear." In psychology, a *phobic* disorder means an extreme or unfounded fear of an object or a place. There are many varieties of phobias, including zoophobia (fear of animals), claustrophobia (fear of closed spaces), and acrophobia (fear of heights). Three primary factors contributing to

the development of phobias are faulty learning, displacement of anxiety, and the development of a defense mechanism to counteract dangerous impulses.

4. *Somatoform* disorders are those in which an individual complains of a physical ailment or pain, but there is no organic or physiological explanation. There are several kinds of somatoform disorders: somatization, conversion, psychogenic pain, hypochondriasis, and atypical. *Hypochondriasis* is characterized by an individual's misinterpretation of body functions, usually leading to the belief that one has a disease. Three predisposing factors to hypochondriasis are early childhood learning, dissatisfaction with life, and reinforcement of the behavior.

5. Personality disorders are quite common. People with personality disorders perceive, relate to, and think about themselves and their environment in maladaptive ways. They often have symptoms that are "acted out" in the world rather than simply in their minds. Some major personality disorders are *paranoid*, pervasive and unwarranted suspiciousness and mistrust of people; *schizoid*, defect in the capacity to form social relationships; *avoidant*, hypersensitivity to potential rejection; *compulsive*, restricted ability to express warm and tender emotions; and *antisocial*, history of chronic and continuous antisocial behavior in which the rights of others are violated.

6. The *antisocial personality* (also called psychopath or sociopath) typically develops in an individual with an inability to feel either positive emotions or guilt. They have insensitivity to the needs of other people. They seem to have an autonomic nervous system that is less likely to react to punishment, so they do not seem to develop the normal social conscience. Loud parties, extreme manipulation of others, and a consistent disregard for other people's feelings are illustrations of the antisocial personality. There is evidence for genetic factors in this disorder.

7. Substance use disorders are those disturbances in behavior that result from abuse or dependence on a drug. Five categories of these substances are alcohol; barbiturates or other sedatives; analgesics, painkillers, or narcotics; stimulants such as amphetamines; and psychoactive drugs such as marijuana and LSD. It is more common for men than women to have a substance use disorder, and dependence does not usually appear until adulthood. The causes of disorders may be genetic as well as psychosocial and sociocultural.

8. A severe mental disorder of great importance to Americans is *depression*, which consists of an overwhelming sadness that immobilizes and arrests the entire course of a person's life. There are two kinds: *unipolar depression*, in which the person experiences only depression, and *bipolar depression*, in which the person also suffers the "polar" opposite, *mania*. The characteristics of mania are the mirror image of depression. The mood is characterized as predominantly elevated, expansive, or irritable. There are large swings between euphoria and extreme annoyance.

9. Symptoms of clinical depression include loss of interest and pleasure; appetite, sleep, and psychomotor disturbances; decrease in energy level; sense of worthlessness; difficulty in concentrating; and thoughts about death. There are *endogenous* (from within) causes of depression. The concordance rate is very high for this disorder in identical twins. *Exogenous* (from without) causes include stress and tragic events. Depressives are usually conventional, well behaved, often successful, conscientious people. The most serious outcome of depression is suicide, which is one of the top ten causes of death in Western countries. Most suicides are attempted between the ages of 24 and 44, but there has recently been a sharp rise in the 15 to 24 age group.

10. Schizophrenia is a uniquely human disorder. It is the name for a group of disorders that involve severe deterioration of mental abilities. This fundamental thought disorganization causes disturbances in every area of life: social functioning, feeling, and behavior. The schizophrenic may be disturbed in any of the following ways: content of thought delusions, form of thought, perception hallucinations, affect, sense of self, volition, relationship to the external world, and psychomotor behavior. Categories of schizophrenic disorders include *hebephrenic,* the most severely disorganized form of schizophrenia, characterized by extreme disturbance of affect; *paranoid*, dominated by delusions of being persecuted; *catatonic,* unusual motor activity, either excitement or stupor; and *undifferentiated*, rapidly changing mix of all or most of the primary symptoms of schizophrenia.

11. There is a strong genetic component to schizophrenia. One study showed a 38 percent concordance rate in identical twins. The risk of developing schizophrenia is 5 to 15 times higher in siblings of schizophrenics than in the general population; its incidence is about one percent in the general population. The causes of schizophrenia may also include biochemical and neurophysiological factors. One theory states that it is caused by a surplus of the neurotransmitter dopamine in the brain.

12. About being normal: it is possible to classify someone as disordered, but does this do justice to the person? The dividing line between normal and abnormal is not often easy to determine. It is normal to be depressed when someone you love dies, but it is abnormal when that feeling becomes the pervasive experience over a very long period. Exaggeration of normal behavior can become abnormal. Neatness is normal, but having to clean every room every time you enter it is not. Normality is a reflection of society and culture at a particular time. Homosexuality used to be classified a disease, but now it is not.

TERMS AND CONCEPTS

abnormal
affective disorders
agoraphobia
antisocial personality
anxiety disorders
bipolar depression
depression
dopamine hypothesis
DSM-III
endogenous causes
exogenous causes

generalized anxiety
hypochondriasis
mania
multiple personality
norms
obsessive-compulsive disorders
phobia
schizophrenia
sociopath
somatoform disorders
substance use disorders

Houghton, J. F. (1980). One personal experience: Before and after mental illness. In J. G. Rabkin, L. Gelb, & J. B. Lazar (Eds.), *Attitudes toward the mentally ill: Research perspectives.* Rockville, MD: National Institute of Mental Health.

Houghton, J. F. (1982). First person account: Maintaining mental health in a turbulent world. *Schizophrenia Bulletin, 8,* 548-549.

What it is like to experience schizophrenia, from someone who did.

Rosenhan, D., & Seligman, M. (1985). *Abnormal psychology.* New York: Norton.

An important text, especially because it is written by two of the top investigators.

Wilson, J., & Herrnstein, R. (1985). *Crime and human nature.* New York: Simon & Schuster.

A massive summary of the literature on the possible inherited tendencies to criminality.

Psychotherapies

My mother and I sat next to each other in the waiting room while my father investigated admission procedures. A young man was seated near us. Perspiration dripped across his brow and down his cheeks. In silence I took a tissue from my purse, moved close to him and gently wiped the moisture from his face. I reassured him that everything would be fine.

Soon my father rejoined us. We went together to a small room where I met Kay, the psychiatric social worker assigned to my case, and a psychiatrist (whose name I don't recall). We talked a few minutes. I was presented with a piece of paper and instructed to sign my name. Obediently, I wrote "Saint Joan" on the paper, not realizing that I was voluntarily admitting myself to a state mental hospital. . . . At the time of my hospitalization I had both a sense of death and a rebirth about me. My first psychotic episode appeared as a private mental exorcism, ending with the honor of sainthood and the gifts of hope and faith. (Houghton, 1980)

As long as people suffer, others undertake to relieve that suffering and to restore adaptive functioning. Throughout history there have been many forms of psychotherapy, reflecting differing beliefs about mental disorder. If society believes that psychological disorder is caused by demons that invade a person, the treatment may include getting the demons out. If the culture thinks that psychological disorder originates in early childhood experiences, the treatment may attempt to root out these experiences. If it is thought that disorders result from learning inappropriate responses, the treatment may involve teaching a new, more adaptive set of responses.

If society contends that the problem is essentially biological, drugs may be administered or surgery performed. If the problem is perceived as a difficulty in cognitive patterns, the person may be helped to restructure his or her ways of thinking. If a psychological problem is thought to be the result of blockage in the normal development of self, treatment would seek to find out where the block is and what caused it and then would try to unblock it.

Although all psychotherapies have as their goal the restoration of normal functioning, they vary in method, approach, and assumptions. Thus, there are many controversies about therapy and about which ones work best, and whether any of them work at all. This question is a difficult one. The last section in this chapter evaluates the evidence of the effectiveness of psychotherapy.

Early Approaches

One widespread prescientific belief during Medieval times was that mental disorder was caused by demons who entered and possessed the victim. One treatment that followed from that idea was **trephining** (Figure 16-1), in which holes were drilled into a person's head to let the demons out. Other treatments following from the concept of demon possession included floggings, burnings, and

FIGURE 16-1
Trephining
In this medieval treatment, holes were cut into a mentally disturbed person's head in the hope that the demons would pass out through them.

other forms of torture. These treatments were not intended to be cruel to the victim—but rather to the devil.

During the Industrial Revolution, mental disorders were believed to be a moral problem. Disorders were considered to be a result of idleness or bad character. Mad people were lumped together with criminals and vagrants, chained and thrown into dungeons. The "insane" were considered dangerous nuisances to society and were also used as warnings. They were often put on view so that young people would see the consequences of deviant behavior. In this period, there was confinement, not treatment.

Then, in the nineteenth century, Philippe Pinel (1745–1826) began a series of reforms in France during the French Revolution. Dorothea Dix (1802–1887) and others started them later in America. Finally, research and advances in biology, medicine, and neurology encouraged a conception of insanity as a disease. This paradigm led to more humane treatment; the onus of blame was off the victim. A doctor treated the disease, usually with a certain amount of compassion.

A great advance in the late nineteenth century was the discovery of the cause of one disorder called **general paresis,** which is a slow, degenerative disease that eventually erodes mental faculties. They discovered that syphilis causes paresis. Understanding the cause of the disease led to an effective treatment: the administration of the drug salvarsan. The elimination of paresis is one of the few decisive victories in the war against mental disorder. That victory spurred important research: mental disorders began to receive more attention from medical and scientific researchers.

Classification of Disorders

See Chapter 15, section on Classification.

As more investigation was done by researchers on the malfunctioning of the mind, classification of disorders became more precise. One of the major contributors to the biomedical point of view was Emil Kraepelin (1856–1926). He noted

that mental disorder was not a monolithic entity, but several *distinct* disorders with their own particular patterns of symptoms. He devised the first classification system of mental disorders. His system was the basis for the *DSM* classification system (discussed in Chapter 15) used today by clinicians. Kraepelin believed that a specific brain pathology is responsible for each mental disturbance. Many have joined him in that belief, but there has been no success as spectacular as the victory over general paresis.

Modern Psychotherapists

Today there are many different kinds of psychotherapists. A **psychiatrist** is a medical doctor whose specialty is the treatment of psychological problems. He or she has a license to dispense drugs as part of the treatment. A **psychoanalyst** is a psychotherapist trained in the psychoanalytic techniques first formulated by Sigmund Freud. Almost all psychoanalysts are physicians.

A **clinical psychologist** holds a Ph.D. in psychology and may specialize in a specific psychotherapy, such as behavior modification or sex therapy. Some clinical psychologists are also involved in testing and research. But many concentrate on therapy and guidance counseling in schools or industry. A **psychiatric social worker** holds an advanced degree (M.S. or Ph.D.) and usually concentrates on social or community-based problems.

Psychoanalysis is a "psychology of conflict": the conflict between the biological and social (or civilized) selves. Freud believed that inherited "instincts" underlie the state of the mind and that psychological distress arises from basic conflicts of the id and the ego. Unconscious wishes and desires cause anxiety and fear, so they are repressed and forced out of consciousness. Freud believed that the roots of disorder lie in early childhood.

PSYCHOANALYSIS

See Chapter 14, Formal Theories of Personality.

One of Freud's cases concerned "Little Hans," a boy who was so afraid of horses that he would not leave his house. (Freud based his analysis, by the way, on letters from Hans's father; he only met the boy once.) Before Hans became so afraid of horses, he was a perfectly normal boy in every respect. But he did show an "uncommon" interest in his penis.

Once his mother caught him playing with it. She told him she would cut it off if she ever caught him at it again. At four he tried to "seduce" his mother. About six months later he was out walking with his nurse when a horse and carriage rolled over in front of them. He began crying and said that he wanted to go home to hug his mother.

From that day on, he was terrified of horses and would not leave the house. Freud's analysis was that Hans' real fear was that he so desired his mother that he subconsciously wanted his father out of the way. Since he really feared his impulses, he transferred his fear to horses to relieve himself of guilt. Freud hypothesized that even though his mother had actually threatened to castrate him, it was his father who represented that threat. By avoiding horses, he thus avoided his fear of castration, and by staying home, he got to stay close to his mother.

Psychoanalytic Method

From this previous example, you can see that Freud believed that therapy should bring unconscious desires into consciousness where they can be analyzed. However, the unconscious does not give up its secret desires easily or without struggle. The ego "edits" and represses those desires. Thus, Freud at first used hypnosis in his therapy to bring the unconscious to the surface.

Later he developed the technique of **free association.** The psychiatrist asks the patient to say anything that comes into his or her mind. There is no criticism or editing of the patient's thoughts — no matter how obscene, unimportant, or silly the thought. Free association is difficult because people characteristically exercise control and are modest about personal subjects.

To aid in this process, the patient lies on a couch facing away from the analyst. Removing normal eye-to-eye contact usually removes some reticence. The analyst usually listens passively, but occasionally may interrupt the patient's free flow of ideas. He or she may highlight or suggest connections among things that the patient has said. A psychoanalyst often asks the patient to recall dreams and uses the content of dreams as a starting point for free association. Thus, the interpretation of dreams is a cornerstone of Freudian analysis.

The patients who seek psychoanalysis commit themselves to a very long process of self-evaluation, criticism, and examination. Psychoanalysis usually requires four to five 50-minute sessions a week for one to several years. These conditions exclude a great number of people from treatment, including most psychotics, people with personality disorders who are not highly motivated to change, nonverbal people, and poor people.

Resistance

The *opening* phase of treatment usually lasts from three to six months. In this time, the analyst begins to learn the patient's history and the general nature of his or her unconscious conflicts. One of the greatest signals of an unconscious conflict in the

opening phase is **resistance,** which is the characteristic way that the patient resists or works against revealing feelings or thoughts. For example, every time some patients start to talk about their mothers, they may change the subject; they might tell a joke or say that the thought is too silly. Another sign of resistance to therapy is when the patient "forgets" an appointment or is late. Resistance serves to reduce the anxiety of the patient by not allowing anxiety-producing thoughts to surface.

Transference

An important concept in psychoanalytic therapy is how the patient perceives the analyst. At a certain point in treatment, **transference** takes place: the patient "tranfers" onto the *analyst* attitudes toward people about whom he or she has conflicting feelings. For example, a male patient who has difficulty getting along with people in authority may have had a domineering father who demanded perfection from his son and strict obedience to all his rules. At a certain point in therapy, the patient may begin to show anger at the analyst for requiring him to follow the rules of analysis. The analyst comes to play a role in the patient's life whose significance is all out of proportion with reality. Freud believed that transference is extremely important. It is the patient's way of recreating and reenacting forgotten or repressed memories from earliest childhood. Instead of recalling events, the patient repeats them.

The therapist then proceeds to an analysis of the transference. This is a very critical stage. The patients begin to see the nature of their misconceptions, maladaptive responses, and misinterpretations. They have "transferred" them to the analyst, and thus they can see them in a very concrete way. Patients can then begin to evaluate their situation more realistically.

The analysis of the transference should offer patients some insight into the nature of their unconscious conflicts. Usually during this phase the patients recall some extremely important event, desire, or fantasy of their youth. The recollection and their ability to express it produces in them a **catharsis,** which is the release of stored up or held back feelings. It is an intensely emotional experience. The immediate result of a catharsis is pleasurable relief.

Resolution of the transference is the last phase of the treatment, in which the patients and therapist agree that they have accomplished their goals. This means that the patients ought to be behaving in different ways. They should no longer experience anxiety in situations that used to make them very anxious.

BEHAVIOR
THERAPY

The behavioristic viewpoint is that psychological disorders are the result of "faulty learning." Psychotherapy then is a process of relearning. A behaviorist would view Freud's analysis of little Hans as too complex: Hans' fear could be better explained by respondent conditioning. Recall from Chapter 8 the story of little Albert: a loud noise presented at the same time as a white rat caused Albert to be afraid of anything white and furry. In Hans' case, it is conceivable that the commotion associated with the accident frightened him. Because his parents reinforced the fear by letting him stay home, the fear was maintained.

Behavior therapy proceeds from the assumption that the behavior that is causing the person distress is the problem. Psychoanalysis assumes that it is only the symptom of an underlying neurosis. A prominent behavior therapist, Hans Eysenck, wrote, "There is no neurosis underlying the symptom, but merely the symptom itself. Get rid of the symptom . . . and you have eliminated the neurosis."

This is probably an overstatement. Most behaviorists would agree there are many mental components of fear and anxiety. However, it is probably also true that a change in overt behavior may realign the person's underlying problems. Two varieties of therapy are related to two primary modes of learning: the form called *behavior therapy* is based on *respondent* conditioning, while the other, called *behavior modification,* is based on the theory of *operant* conditioning.

Behavior therapy aims to reduce the anxiety that the person experiences in response to certain key external stimuli (Wolpe, 1958). Anxiety is thought to be the underlying cause of the "neurotic" behavior. Behavior therapy techniques are based on respondent conditioning, and they decondition those anxiety-producing autonomic responses. In contrast, behavior therapists base **behavior modification** on operant conditioning. They attempt to change behaviors by changing the stimuli and conditions. Someone who feels helpless or trapped may feel depressed. If a person is punished, he or she may become fearful. A person who cannot fight back or is frustrated by others may feel anger. Behavior modification may employ reinforcement or extinction to alter such situations and people's responses to them.

Behavior therapy has a wide range of applications and methods. The person is called a *client,* not a patient. Therapy may be for an individual, a group, a family, or even a community. Therapy may last for a single session or for a lifetime (as in the cases of autistic children). Behavior therapists treat problems that include test anxiety, sexual dysfunctions, phobias, addictions, interpersonal difficulties, and personality problems.

Methods of Behavior Therapy

A first step in a successful therapeutic program is beginning a good relationship between the therapist and the client. Unlike psychoanalysis, the therapist does not "do" therapy on a "patient," but instead they work together to accomplish agreed-upon outcomes. In the first phase of treatment, the therapist often asks the client to give an account of the history of the problem.

The behavior therapist's purpose in knowing the client's history is fundamentally different from that of the psychoanalyst. Behaviorists do not believe that solving the problems of early childhood will solve the problems of adult life. Instead, the aim is to *discover where and how the inappropriate conditioning was acquired.* The therapist also tries to find out how the problem now arises.

To get an accurate account, the therapist may not rely only on the client's own verbal report. The client may be asked to keep diaries of events and feelings during the week. The therapist may interview members of the client's family or engage the client in role playing. In **role playing** the therapist creates a hypothetical situation; the chosen situation is likely to cause the client anxiety and they act it out together.

See box: One Problem, Four Treatments.

Reconditioning Techniques

Once the client achieves an understanding of the problem, reconditioning proceeds. There are several behavior therapy techniques to do this. Here we will mention systematic desensitization, flooding, and assertiveness training.

Systematic Desensitization.   This technique is based on the phenomenon of *counterconditioning.* The idea is to eliminate an unwanted conditioned response by conditioning the client to another stimulus. The stimulus elicits a response (usually relaxation) incompatible with the original response.

Systematic desensitization is very effective in helping people overcome phobias. The therapist asks the client to imagine or role play an anxiety-provoking situation. When the client begins to be anxious, the therapist instructs him or her in relaxation techniques. When the client is able to relax, the therapist presents a situation *more* likely to produce anxiety. The client again learns to relax. The therapist arranges the situations in a progression, and the client reduces fear step by step. The therapist may first ask a person who is afraid of elevators to imagine an elevator, then to imagine being alone in the elevator. Later, he or she may go and stand beside the elevator, then may stand inside it. Finally, the client will ride it.

Flooding.   In this technique, the therapist literally "floods" the client's mind. He or she incessantly presents situations that evoke fear and anxiety. The person begins to experience anxiety. The therapist, aware of being on the right track, elaborates on the story to make the person more and more anxious.

Take the case of a woman with agoraphobia who is afraid to leave the house. The therapist might begin by asking her to close her eyes and to imagine going out of the house. Then she imagines meeting someone in the street, imagines a group of children running down the sidewalk bumping into her, and imagines getting on a public bus at rush hour. Eventually, the client will notice that her anxiety diminishes even if she does not run away. Then the therapist may ask the client to try to imagine going places on her own. Finally, she actually imagines going to specific places on her own. Flooding is extremely intense. There is no letup until the client begins to feel the fear and anxiety dissipate. But it is an effective therapy for phobias.

Assertiveness Training.   This technique is often used in relationships. It teaches people that they have a right to their own feelings and opinions and that they can be themselves as long as they do not hurt others. The therapist may use role playing. He or she may assign clients tasks to force them to confront and overcome their inability to assert themselves.

Behavior Modification

Behavior modification techniques, which are based on operant conditioning, treat a wide range of problems. They break maladaptive habits such as compulsive gambling or antisocial behavior. For example, the popular Smokenders program uses behavior modification. People who sign up come to a group meeting where the therapist allows them to smoke. But they agree on a date six weeks in advance as the day when they will quit smoking. The therapist gives each person a little card and a pencil that fits into a pack of cigarettes. They are then free to smoke as much as they want for the first week, but they must make a note of every cigarette.

In later weeks the therapist asks them to cut back on their smoking and to notice the situations when they want to smoke. Group support emerges and becomes an important reinforcer. By the time of their "quit date," they have cut back substantially on their smoking. They see that they can live without cigarettes in many situations that they previously thought impossible. The therapist brings each person's family into the reinforcing circle by encouraging them to be demonstrative in their support.

Cognitive or Cognitive-Behavior Therapy

Cognitive or cognitive-behavior therapies combine many of the techniques of behaviorism with cognitive psychology. The main emphasis is on the *effects of thought on behavior.* There are three forms of cognitive therapy: rational-emotive, cognitive restructuring, and stress inoculation. These therapies differ in method and emphasis, but they share two major assumptions: (1) cognitive processes influence behavior and (2) restructuring of the individual's cognitive system can change behavior, by the individual becoming conscious of thought processes and analyzing them. The method of cognitive therapy is hypothesis testing. As in the

Behavior modification therapy was used successfully to help these people quit smoking.

behavior therapies, the client and therapist work together and the therapist takes an active role.

Rational-Emotive Therapy

Rational-emotive therapy (RET) was developed by Albert Ellis (1970), who bases his therapy on the assumption that a person's perceptual interpretation becomes his or her "world." In this view, a well-adapted person is one in whom there is a good match between behaviors, self-perception, and reality. Maladaptive behavior can result from unrealistic beliefs or expectations. A person might believe that he or she must be loved by everyone, must always show perfect control, or must be good at everything. Because these are unrealistic goals, they are self-defeating. A person may feel a failure and thus no good. This feeling is a consequence of the *interpretation,* not of any external event.

In **rational-emotive therapy** the therapist determines what the underlying belief system of the individual is. In contrast to psychoanalysis and behavior therapy, the therapist confronts the client with his or her belief system and *directly* forces him or her to examine it against reality. For example, a woman's lover breaks a date with her. She interprets this to mean that he does not love her and is trying to avoid her. A RET therapist might point out that her lover might have had a good reason for his behavior.

In RET the awareness of the client is constantly directed to the *inconsistencies* between his or her beliefs and external reality. At first the therapist is quite active in disputing the beliefs. There has been some criticism of RET on this point. A person might hold very strict religious beliefs, which may be at the core of the problem. If the religion says that sex is bad, the client may feel sinful every time he or she has sex. The therapist may attack the religious belief.

RET holds a generally humanistic view of human nature. It is founded on belief in the worth and value of human beings and their potential for growth and self-understanding and self-acceptance.

Cognitive Restructuring Therapy

Cognitive restructuring therapy was developed by Beck (1976), who assumes that disorders result from individuals' negative beliefs about events in the world and about themselves. Because people tend to set unrealistic goals for themselves, their efforts are usually self-defeating, and thus their negative beliefs are reinforced. Beck proposed four major areas where a person's thought processes make the beliefs self-fulfilling.

1. Absolute thinking; everything is black or white, all or nothing.
2. Generalizing a few negative events to every aspect of life.
3. Magnifying the importance of negative events.
4. Being overselective in perception, noticing only those events that confirm the negative beliefs.

The therapist in cognitive restructuring therapy does not dispute clients' beliefs directly (as does the RET therapist). Rather, he or she encourages clients to engage in experiments that will help them to confirm or disconfirm their beliefs. The

ONE PROBLEM, FOUR TREATMENTS

With all the types of therapies available today (over 250 of them), no wonder people are confused. This extract is presented as a unique opportunity for you to compare how four common therapies work. Perry Turner (1986) asked four therapists to treat a fictional patient named George and each in turn offered a solution to the problem. Here is the scenario they were given:

George is 31 years old and has been married for five year. . . . His wife, who is 30, is four months pregnant with their first child.

George came in complaining of insomnia, "testiness," and anxiety caused by fantasies about another woman and by fears that he would prove inadequate as a father, husband, and musician. George reports no history of significant acute or chronic physical illness. He takes no prescribed or over-the-counter medications. His last physical was seven months ago; all findings were normal.

His childhood was "as happy as anyone's," he says, and his parents were loving and fair. There is no mental illness in the family. . . . His mother, a housewife, was a quiet, passive woman whose principle disciplinary tactic was a doleful look used mostly when George neglected to practice his bassoon and when his sister dated unsuitable boys.

. . . About seven months ago, a new typist named Laura started working in George's office. Laura, a poor typist and a very pretty young woman, behaved quite seductively around George. He found this amusing at first and planned to tell Ann about it—they had always prided themselves on sharing more of their lives than other couples. The night he planned to tell her they had a fight—George thinks it has to do with who would be using the car that evening, but he can't remember with certainty. He ended up not telling Ann about Laura, and he remembers feeling a moment of satisfaction in keeping this part of his life to himself. He and Ann made up

shortly, but he "never got around to telling her" about Laura, who made it progressively clearer to George that she wanted to sleep with him.

About two months after she had started working in his office, George played a noontime concert in a nearby park with a quintet made up of several co-workers. Laura and Ann showed up, though separately. When he saw them, he felt suddenly humiliated by his "artistic pretensions." . . . One night, having awakened at 4:00 A.M., he resolved to get his life in order: the next day he began suggesting to Ann that they start a family, and he asked a co-worker to complain about Laura's performance to the office manager and see about getting her transferred. Within three weeks, Laura had been reassigned to an office on another floor and Ann had conceived.

But George didn't feel any happier, and he began to grow frustrated. He started waking up regularly in the middle of the night and could not fall asleep. He feared Laura would discover he had engineered her transfer and considered taking her out to lunch to "set the record straight." He soon abandoned this idea, as it made him too nervous. He grew irritated at his wife's "sickliness"—she was by this time frequently nauseous —and he began taking different elevators to avoid running into [Laura] at the office. He threw himself into his music and decided if he was going to make anything of himself as a musician, he would need a new bassoon. But there was no extra money now that a baby was on the way, which aggravated his "testiness" with Ann.

He did run into Laura several times at work and was disconcerted because she continued to behave seductively around him, though now he wondered if she was mocking him. One night while making love to Ann he fantasized he was with Laura, and subsequently he has been unable to stop doing this whenever he and Ann make love.

George sought help three weeks

after the fantasies commenced. He spoke of finding "self-discipline" to be a good husband, father, and musician. He does not want to resent his child as an intrusion in his life, but fears that he might. And he wants to sleep through the night.

Behavioral Therapy

"What I would first try to do," says behavior therapist Marcia Chambers, "is 'operationalize' George's complaints—get him to define them as specifically as possible. What does 'self-discipline' mean? Does 'testiness' mean he can't sit in a chair for more than three minutes, does he lose his temper more quickly? Once we had defined behaviors he would like to change, I would have him monitor what he's doing that's a problem. In behavioral therapy, everything is measurable and you can see change. It's important for the person to see the change visually, so clients chart their progress on lots of different kinds of graphs and three-by-five cards.

"In George's case, probably the easiest behavior to monitor would be sleep—what time he wakes up, and either how many times he wakes up in the middle of the night or how long those times were. Sometimes just monitoring a behavior makes it drop out—it just stops happening. For instance, one of the best ways to lose weight is to write down everything you eat. . . .

"I would spend maybe four sessions teaching George relaxation. A very deep relaxation takes 30 to 35 minutes. Once he'd learned that, we could really use it for many different things. For instance, what I could do is once he's very relaxed, have him think about being in bed and having sex with Ann. And then see if he could do it again at home. You first have to train him to have positive thoughts about being with Ann; it gives him a good feeling, and you want to get as much 'positive' in him as possible. So if he starts thinking about Laura, he could signal to me—by closing his eyes tighter, or moving his elbow—

and I'd say, 'Stop—think about Ann.' If he can't get into an 'Ann scene' or gets anxious in it, I could get him back to the neutral relaxing scene I taught him earlier, and then ease him back into thinking about Ann."

With practice, George would come to relax when he made love to Ann, and the deeper his relaxation, the higher his resistance to distress—to thoughts of Laura, specifically. As Chambers points out, "It's physiologically impossible to feel relaxed and anxious at the same time." . . . And she would encourage him to devise his own incentives, especially ones that he could work into his day-to-day routines, such as taking Ann to dinner after a week of faithfully practicing his bassoon. "My goal," she explains, "is to put myself out of business."

Cognitive Therapy

Each session, as George recounted the bad moments of the week before, cognitive therapist Dean Schuyler would mark off three columns on a lap-sized blackboard and jot down the critical events and the accompanying thoughts and feelings. He might, for example, record the noontime concert episode this way: *Laura and Ann at concert/"I'm a lousy musician and just fooling myself"/Humiliation.* He would also get George to track his responses in a journal between sessions, either at the time of, or as soon as possible after, an emotional upset.

Schuyler claims that careful monitoring would soon reveal how George's thoughts—thoughts he might not have even been aware of— were setting off feelings of distress. "The therapy," says Schuyler, "would then consist of disputing these thoughts," a process dramatized in the following exchange between Schuyler and George (who appeared via the writer):

s: *What is so bad about thinking of someone else while making love to your wife?*
G: *Your marriage is a hoax—this person [Ann] isn't who you wanted.* (cont.)

ONE PROBLEM, FOUR TREATMENTS (continued)

s: *So what if your marriage is a hoax?*

g: *Well—then you're destroying someone's chances for happiness because—you bound her into this arrangement under false pretenses.*

s: *So what if you did that?*

g: *It's hard enough for each person in the world to be happy—why drag someone else down with your lies?*

s: *Okay, so all of this miserable stuff that you're doing has resulted from your having thought about someone else while making love to your wife?*

g: *No, no, but—*

s: *(smiling a little): Certainly seems what you've been saying. . . .*

[This therapy is] "not for everyone. The people who do best in cognitive therapy are the kind who do best with psychoanalytic therapy: psychologically minded, generally bright, verbal individuals who are comfortable dealing with concepts and looking at themselves. For George to get relief from the symptoms presented, six months of once-a-week therapy is not an unreasonable expectation."

Family Therapy

"What I would do in the first session," says family therapist Joseph Lorio, "is talk to George a little bit about the presenting symptoms, maybe for as little as 10 or 15 minutes. Then I would get a history of the relationship between him and his wife, going back to when they first met, and how the relationship developed, what the big events in it were, and how they each reacted to those events. I would be looking for any changes in the relationship's tone that could have been significant as a trigger for stirring up the anxieties he has." . . .

Lorio would also try to involve Ann in therapy as soon as possible. "I may see George alone the first two times and then try to get his wife in by the third session. I might then spend one session just with her, or see the two of them together, then see her individually, then go back to seeing them together—just depends on what the problem is and how they're dealing with it. . .

"You can let them know that when families are in this kind of situation, her distancing from him is pretty typical. And when he understands what's going on between him and his wife, he can understand that what he's reacting to is her distancing, and that what he needs to do is be more available to her emotionally.

"The key thing is to change from being an emotional reactor to a better observer. The better you can observe and learn about the interplay between self and relationships, the less you react emotionally to it and the faster you make progress. Oftentimes people with just six sessions feel less anxious, calmer, better in control of their lives. But he could be in therapy a year or two, or even longer, if I could get him to bridge his current situations to his extended family. . . ."

Psychodynamic Theory

[Psychoanalyst Robert Winer responded]: "I'm struck by the kind of

client and therapist may develop a hypothesis, and then the client has the assignment of gathering information to support or demolish it. For example, a depressed man may decide to wallpaper his living room. His wife papers one side, and he does the other. He predicts that he will not be as good as his wife at the job. When he finishes the papering, he may point out all the places on his side where the pattern does not exactly match or the seams are slightly off kilter. He may point to the excellent job on his wife's side of the room. His therapist may counter that no work George does, to begin with — he manages other people's development, but he's having some problem managing his own. It's sort of like that cliche, 'Those who can, do; those who can't, teach.' Then there's his complaint of 'testiness' — the more I thought about that word, the more it struck me that that's not a word that somebody would use about himself. People call *other* people testy, but since he's saying it about himself, I'd think he was reporting someone else's complaint about himself. . . . And his childhood was 'as happy as anyone's — *that* struck me as an odd statement; it implies some oversensitivity to other people's opinions, something in his early family life about keeping up with the Joneses.

"He says his parents were 'loving and fair.' Well, 'fair' isn't a word a person normally used to describe his parents, unless fairness was some kind of an issue. . . . George [had] as a model a father who is frightened of assertion, who to a degree hides behind his wife's skirts and had failed to make claims for himself on life. . . .

"This is getting me to think about the baby representing some further injury to his sense of masculinity. That's unusual — becoming a father usually helps men feel more phallically potent, more full of themselves. In George's case, it's more as if Ann's growing and he's shrinking. . . . You wonder if he feels some threat to his security with his wife.

"And the whole business of getting Laura transferred represents an overriding concern with his own security and a lack of a reasonable effort to be concerned with someone else's. Laura is nothing to get nervous about. She's being flirtatious, that's all. She's entitled to that in life. He can always say. . . . 'Look I'm a married man, we're not going to have anything happen.' I did think getting her transferred is a strikingly aggressive act for him — though again, it's passively done; like his father, he won't do it himself, he gets someone else to do it. . . .

"And now he becomes obsessed with Laura. Usually obsessions are a way of controlling aggression. You wonder how much anger toward his wife about the pregnancy is tied up in that. And men can experience intercourse with a pregnant wife as an attack on the baby, if they're already feeling aggression toward it, so maybe the obsessive thoughts about Laura are some way of blocking out that aggression.

"He does say that he doesn't want to resent the child as an intrusion so he has some capacity for self-awareness. And he takes the initiative to seek help, which leads me to think that he also has the capacity to make more active decisions. It may be that just seeing him through the end of the pregnancy will be enough to help him make some kind of adjustment around the baby. But if his goal is to realize himself more fully as a man, given that he's been ducking that all his life," concludes Winer, "you're talking about analysis: four or five sessions a week, probably for several years." (Excerpted from: "The Shrinking of George," Perry Turner, *Science '86*, 7(5), 38–44.)

one can notice the small mistakes if they are not pointed out. Eventually, this type of feedback may make it possible for the man to change his perception of himself.

An important part of cognitive restructuring therapy, especially in the treatment of depression, is the assignment or scheduling of tasks that interfere with the "conduct" of the disorder. For example, a depressed person might find no pleasure in doing things that once gave pleasure. The therapist may ask him or her to list those things: going to a movie, listening to records, going for walks, cooking meals. The "assignment" may be to engage in a certain number of these activities before the next session. The client will feel he or she has accomplished something by completing such assignments, and may even begin to discover the pleasure once felt in participating in these activities. As part of the therapy, the client is called upon to monitor his or her thoughts and to question constantly whether they are realistic.

Stress Inoculation Therapy

See Chapter 18, section on Stress as the Failure to Adapt.

Stress inoculation therapy is based on Meichenbaum's theory of stress inoculation. Meichenbaum proposes that by altering the way people talk to themselves, the way they approach stressful problems will be changed. The training takes place in three phases. First, the therapist and client *examine the situations* causing stress and try to uncover the beliefs and attitudes being carried into these situations. The therapist focuses attention on how what the clients say to themselves in these situations affects their behavior. For example, a graduate student experiences great stress every time he has to give a lecture. Often the effects of the stress are so overpowering that he begins to stutter; his mind has gone blank on occasion. Before he enters the classroom he says to himself, "I know I am going to do a lousy job. I am not well enough prepared. What if a student asks a question I cannot answer?" When the client realizes how damaging his self-statements are, he and the therapist can work up a new set of statements that will be more constructive.

The second phase is called *acquisition and rehearsal.* The client rehearses and learns a new set of statements. Meichenbaum (1974) suggests certain self-statements that are helpful for a person who feels overwhelmed by the task he or she must do. Some examples of these include, "When the fear comes, just pause"; or "It will be over shortly"; or "Just think about something else."

Application and practice are the third phase of the training. The client begins to use the new set of statements in real situations. Usually he or she begins with situations that are only slightly stressful and gradually works up to increasingly stressing situations. Stress inoculation training is most helpful in cases where the situations that cause distress are clearly defined: for example, fear of speaking in front of crowds. Some believe that stress inoculation training may prove to be an effective preventive treatment. Maladaptive behaviors may be prevented from developing if a person has the stress inoculation coping strategy in his or her behavioral repertoire (Mahoney & Arnkoff, 1978).

HUMANISTIC THERAPY: PERSON-CENTERED

Humanistic therapies are based on the positive assumption that human beings, if unobstructed, tend toward growth, health, and realization of potentials. In this view (Rogers, 1959, 1980), psychological disorders arise from a blocking of a person's natural inclination toward self-actualization. These blocks arise because of unrealistic demands people make on themselves. Individuals might believe that it is wrong to feel anger or hostility toward others. Rather than admit to feeling these "wrong" emotions, they deny and suppress them. In denying these feelings, people may actually numb themselves emotionally or lose touch with these feelings. When individuals lose touch with their real experience, the self is necessarily more fragmented and less integrated. This state makes relationships and a whole variety of behaviors difficult and maladjusted.

The purpose of this form of psychotherapy is to release "an already existing capacity in a potentially competent individual" (Rogers, 1959). Under the proper conditions, clients can learn to unblock themselves and allow their self-actualizing capacity to emerge. In **person-centered therapy** (formerly called *client-centered*), perhaps the most important element is the relationship between the therapist and client. The client's perception of the therapist is particularly important. The client has to perceive in the therapist three qualities: genuineness, empathy, and unconditional positive regard.

Person-centered therapy is *nondirective.* The therapist gains the trust of clients. He does this by showing that he bases his concern for them on his ability to accept them unjudgmentally. The therapist respects the client's feelings, privacy, and reluctance. A psychoanalyst directs, interferes, and (to some extent) shapes the patient's revelations and the connections they make. A person-centered therapist does not probe. Unless it is necessary, he or she does not express either approval or disapproval and does not interpret what clients say. More often, he or she repeats and paraphrases what clients have said. These restatements should help clients further clarify their feelings. They demonstrate that the therapist understands the clients because he or she is experiencing what they are experiencing.

Here is an example of a typical session between a person-centered therapist (T) and a client (C).

Carl Rogers

T: Just kind of fell, sunk way down deep in these lousy, lousy feelings, hum? Is that something like it?

C: No.

T: No? (Silence of 20 seconds.)

C: No. I just ain't no good to nobody, never was, and never will be.

T: Feeling that now, hum? That you're just no good to yourself, no good to anybody. Never will be any good to anybody. Just that you're completely worthless, huh? Those really are lousy feelings. Just that you're no good at *all,* hm?

C: Yeah. (Muttering in a low, discouraged voice.) That's what this guy I went to town with just the other day told me.

T: This guy that you went to town with really told you that you were no good? Is that what you're saying? Did I get that right?

Carl Rogers, who developed person-centered therapy, is shown here (upper right corner) conducting one of his early group therapy sessions.

C: M-hm.

T: I guess the meaning of that if I get it right is that here's somebody that meant something to you and what does he think of you? Why, he's told you that he thinks you're no good at all. And that just really knocks the props out from under you. (C weeps quietly.) It just brings the tears. (Silence of 20 seconds.)

C: I don't care though. (Rather defiantly.)

T: You tell yourself you don't care at all, but somehow I guess some part of you cares because some part of you weeps over it. (Rogers, 1970)

Rogers found that therapy usually progresses in three stages. In the first stage the clients express predominantly negative feelings toward themselves, the world, and the future. In the second stage they begin to feel and express a few glimmers of hope. They show a few tenuous signs that they are beginning to accept themselves. Finally, positive feelings emerge which allow them to care about others. They develop more self-confidence and start to make plans for the future. The therapist then concludes the treatment because the person has allowed his or her natural "self-actualizing capacity" to emerge.

BIOLOGICAL THERAPY

The evidence on possible biological factors in disorders comes from two sources. First, patients first feel and experience many disorders as *somatic* complaints, that is, complaints related to the body. Modern psychotherapy began with Freud's discovery of the power that the mind has over the body. His first patients were primarily *hysterics*, people who complained of a *physical* problem that had no underlying physical cause. For example, they would suffer from paralysis or loss of some other sensory modality.

Second, as discussed elsewhere in this book, mood and thought can greatly influence body state and vice versa. Stress can cause physical disease, but it is also possible for *physical disease* to cause *psychological distress*. Of 100 patients who were about to be committed to a state mental hospital, 46 percent had undiagnosed medical illnesses. These were specifically related to their psychiatric symptoms or exacerbated them significantly. When treated for their medical ailments, 61 percent had reduced psychiatric symptoms. The most common illnesses were Addison's disease, Wilson's disease, low levels of arsenic poisoning, and dietary deficiencies (Hall, Gardner, Stickney, LeCann, & Popkin, 1980).

Certain diseases and medical treatments can have mood-altering side effects. Depression is a side effect of the degenerative blood disease lupus and of the strong chemotherapy used in the treatment of cancer. In this section, we will examine the two main kinds of biological therapy: electroconvulsive shock and drugs.

Electroconvulsive Therapy

Shock treatments began as a result of an observation that later proved to be wrong: that epileptics do not suffer schizophrenia. Psychiatrists thought that the intense electrical activity that causes epileptic convulsions was incompatible with schizophrenia. In 1938 two Italian psychiatrists, Cerletti and Bini, developed a method whereby an electrical current of about 160 volts was passed through the patient's head from one hemisphere to the other. The patient first loses consciousness and then undergoes convulsive seizures. When the patient wakes up, he or she has amnesia for the period immediately preceding the administration of the shocks. He or she may be disoriented and experience loss of memory for a period lasting up to a few months.

A patient undergoing **electroconvulsive therapy** (ECT) may receive a series of several (usually fewer than 12) shocks. At the completion of the treatment, there is often a cessation of disordered symptoms. In the early days of ECT, the convulsions were often so severe that bones were fractured. However, people are now premedicated with a muscle relaxant, which has obliterated that side effect. A new method of ECT, called *unilateral ECT*, passes the electrical current through only one side of the brain (usually the right hemisphere). This results in fewer of the disorienting verbal side effects of bilateral ECT (Lynch et al., 1984).

Sometimes the cure seems miraculous. Other times the effects are short-lived. Since the development of antipsychotic drugs, the use of ECT has been in decline. It is an extremely violent and drastic intervention, and the overadministration of ECT may cause significant brain damage.

Furthermore, no one really knows why shock therapy works. The mechanism may simply be the increased amount of electrical firing it induces in the brain, which may in turn facilitate and stimulate the release of greater amounts of neurotransmitters. The inhibition of certain neurotransmitters might underlie severe disorders such as depression and schizophrenia. Today, only in the most severe cases of depression or schizophrenia is ECT used. But it still is the *most effective treatment* (Snyder, 1980).

Pharmacotherapy: Administering Drugs

A major change in the treatment of mental disorders came in the 1950s. This was the development of drugs that relieve the major symptoms of several different psychological disorders. **Pharmacotherapy** involves administering drugs from four main categories: antipsychotics, antidepressants, antianxiety drugs, and lithium compounds. Lithium is used exclusively to resolve manic episodes and to control mood swings in bipolar depressive disorder.

Antipsychotic Drugs

Psychiatrists use **antipsychotic drugs** in the treatment of severe disorders such as schizophrenia. They serve to calm the patient (they are often called the *major tranquilizers*), and they reduce the experience of some of the major symptoms of the disorder, namely, the hallucinations and delusions. It is important to realize what a tremendous impact the use of these drugs has had in mental hospitals. Here is the experience of one psychologist regarding the change that drugs make:

> [I] worked several months in the maximum security ward of (a mental) hospital immediately prior to the introduction of this type of medication in 1955. The ward patients fulfilled the oft-heard stereotypes of individuals "gone mad." Bizarreness, nudity, wild screaming, and the ever present threat of violence pervaded the atmosphere. Fearfulness and a near-total preoccupation with the maintenance of control characterized the attitudes of staff. Such staff attitudes were not unrealistic in terms of the frequency of occurrence of serious physical assaults by patients, but they were hardly conducive to the development or maintenance of an effective therapeutic program.
>
> Then, quite suddenly—within a period of perhaps a month—all of this dramatically changed. The patients were receiving antipsychotic medication. The ward became a place in which one could seriously get to know one's patients on a personal level and perhaps even initiate programs of "milieu therapy," and the like, promising reports of which had begun to appear in the professional literature. A new era in hospital treatment had arrived, aided enormously and in many instances actually made possible by the development of these extraordinary drugs. (Coleman, Butcher, & Carson, 1980)

The first antipsychotic drug used in the United States was *reserpine.* It had a calming effect on patients and helped to reduce manic and schizophrenic symptoms. However, it has severe side effects, such as producing low blood pressure and sometimes depression; it may also be carcinogenic. Reserpine is no longer in widespread use because of the introduction of new antipsychotic drugs.

One such drug is *chlorpromazine* (trade name, Thorazine). Because it has fewer side effects than reserpine, it became the most widely prescribed drug in the treatment of schizophrenia. Different drug companies manufacture several other compounds of the phenothiazine group, which are all basically variants of chlorpromazine. Chlorpromazine and the other antipsychotics have side effects such as jaundice, stiffness in the muscles, and dryness of the mouth. The most serious side effects are those that affect the motor control areas of the brain. The facial muscles may become so rigid as to make eating difficult and tremors resembling Parkinson's disease may result. With extended use these drugs may also cause infertility and cessation of menstruation.

An important result of the use of antipsychotic drugs has been a drastic reduction in the number of people in mental hospitals. Many people who might have remained in institutions for the rest of their lives are able now to live fairly normally. After the development of antipsychotic drugs, the number of people in

state and county mental hospitals decreased each year. In 1955 there were almost 560,000; in 1980 there were only 132,000 (Coleman et al., 1980). However, an unfortunate consequence of reducing the number of people hospitalized has been a dramatic increase in the number of released mental patients without homes. They have no jobs and live as street people in our major cities.

In recent years, antipsychotic drugs and other advances have made it possible for mental institutions to become more open therapeutic communities (left). They have also allowed many former mental patients to live in half-way houses and become involved with society (right).

The antipsychotic drugs treat schizophrenia but do not cure it. A schizophrenic taking an antipsychotic drug no longer shows overt signs of abnormal behavior, but the evidence suggests that the symptoms are merely "suppressed" or masked by the drug. It may be that the way they work is analogous to the way insulin controls diabetes. As long as diabetics receive doses of insulin, their disease is under control. But if they stop taking insulin, it will reappear. This analogy is not perfect, because it is not yet clear exactly how the antipsychotics work. We do not know if they work on the basic mechanism of schizophrenia. They may perhaps supplement a short supply of some chemical agent in the brain, or they may only reduce the intensity of the internal experience or inhibit the overt symptoms.

See Chapter 15, section on Schizophrenia.

The dopamine hypothesis described in the last chapter presumes that the drugs work by inhibiting the production of dopamine at the synapse receptor sites (see Figure 4-26). In one study, half of a group of schizophrenics were given a placebo and the other half were maintained on their antipsychotic drug. At the end of six months, the placebo group showed a relapse rate of 60 percent compared to 30 percent of the group on the drugs (Hogarty & Goldberg, 1973). It is still too early to know what the long-term side effects of prolonged treatment with these drugs might be.

Antidepressants

Biochemical abnormalities play an important role in depression. Evidence for this is the effectiveness of drugs used to treat depressive symptoms and the action of these drugs on the neurotransmitters (Snyder, 1980). Serotonin and norepinephrine are two important transmitters that operate, among other places, along

See Chapter 4, section on The Limbic System.

Alcohol remains the most widely used antianxiety drug, usually self-prescribed.

limbic system pathways. Recall that the limbic system of the brain governs emotions, thus depressive symptoms may relate to levels of serotonin and norepinephrine.

To see how researchers arrived at this conclusion, let's look at how two types of **antidepressant** drugs work. One class of drugs are *monoamine oxidase* (MAO) *inhibitors*. They work by blocking the work of an enzyme, monoamine oxidase, which destroys both neurotransmitters. Thus, MAO inhibitors allow serotonin and norepinephrine concentrations to build up. *Tricyclics* are another class that work by *preventing the inactivation* of serotonin and norepinephrine in the synapse. Recall that neurotransmitters are normally inactivated during the absolute refractory period following transmission across the synapse. During this time, the re-uptake mechanism brings the chemicals back into the presynaptic neuron. Tricyclics block the re-uptake mechanism, allowing the released serotonin and norepinephrine to go to work. Tricyclics have side effects; they are sedatives and cause dryness in the mouth, blurry vision, and difficulty in urinating.

Antianxiety Drugs

People suffering from any one of the mild disorders have in common the experience of anxiety. Although there are a variety of ways to relieve anxiety, the most common method of treatment is with drugs. The oldest and most widely used antianxiety drug is alcohol, and it is usually self-prescribed.

Before the 1950s, the tranquilizers most often prescribed by doctors were sedatives. Today two drugs of the benzodiazepine group are the most popular: Librium and Valium. These drugs work very effectively to reduce the experience of anxiety. People are able to return to work, to sleep, and to confront situations that used to give rise to anxiety reactions.

Antianxiety drugs are the most prescribed drugs in America (Coleman et al., 1980). There is a growing concern over the overuse of these drugs, first, because

**FIGURE 16-2
Antianxiety Drugs and Electrical Activity in the Brain**
Antianxiety drugs such as Librium (chlordiazepoxide) alter the rhythm of theta brain waves, and this rhythm can be artificially "driven" to test how such drugs work. The graph here shows that the drug raises the minimum threshold needed to drive the theta rhythm. (After Gray, 1978)

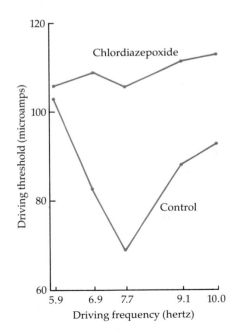

they are addicting, and second, because their indiscriminate use may prevent people from developing coping strategies from within to handle their fears (Gray, 1984).

How the antianxiety drugs work is not fully known. One promising approach is Jeffrey Gray's. Gray proposes that the brain represents anxiety by increased electrical activity (Figure 16-2). This activity is in the parts of the brain that contain the neurotransmitters norepinephrine and serotonin. This increased activity may stimulate increased firing of the neurons and hence the flow of the transmitters. Antianxiety drugs may block synthesis of norepinephrine and serotonin at the receptor sites (Gray, 1984).

A bout one out of every seven (30 million) people in the United States will consult a professional for a psychological problem during their lifetime. What will be the outcome? Do therapies work? Does one work better than another? If they work, do we know why? What does "work" mean in this context? The question of the effectiveness of psychotherapy is very difficult to answer. Circumstantial evidence would say that it does work. Why else would 30 million people spend so much time and money seeking it out? But there are hundreds of therapies available — which ones work and for whom?

Psychotherapists worry about the situation being like the verdict of the Dodo bird in Lewis Carroll's *Alice's Adventures in Wonderland,* who exclaimed, "Everybody has won and all must have prizes" (Stiles, Shapiro, & Elliott, 1986). Is this the case for all the therapies?

Empirical evidence is still hard to come by. We still do not know what causes psychological disorder. It is equally difficult to assess why we become "ordered" again. There are many variables to consider. For example, the cause and nature of the disorder, the particular experience and personality of the individual seeking help, the therapist, and the nature of the interaction.

It is difficult to obtain an objective measure of effectiveness. Suppose that individuals enter therapy when they are troubled and that therapy is finished when they feel better. Would we then judge that the therapy was effective? Suppose they sought additional therapy six months later? What if they went to another psychotherapist?

Early Outcome Studies

There was virtually no objective data on the effectiveness of psychotherapy until the mid-1940s. Freud and most followers of the psychoanalytic school maintained that the outcome of psychoanalysis was too complex to be studied. Carl Rogers was the first pioneer in the gathering of psychotherapy outcome data. With the development of behavioral therapies, data collection became customary.

In 1952 Hans Eysenck initiated research on the question of psychotherapy's effectiveness. His paper was called "The Effects of Psychotherapy: An Evaluation" (Eysenck, 1952). Eysenck separated people seeking psychotherapy into two groups. The members of one group were put on a waiting list; the others received psychotherapy. At the end of the study, he found that "roughly two-thirds of a group of neurotic patients will recover or improve to a marked extent within about two years of the onset of their illness."

This improvement took place whether the person had received therapy or not. He called this two-thirds figure the rate of **spontaneous remission,** meaning that the patient perceived that the neurosis vanished without psychiatry. This figure then would be a baseline to compare the effectiveness of any therapy. At the time he wrote his report Eysenck claimed that there was no evidence of the usefulness of psychotherapies. However, about 80 percent of the studies since then have shown positive results (Smith, Glass, & Miller, 1980). Thus, the questions that remain are which ones work better, on whom, and why.

Psychoanalysis

Psychoanalysis is the most difficult of all therapies to evaluate. First, few psychoanalysts undertake research on outcomes. Second, psychoanalysis is available to a very few individuals and suitable for only a few disorders. Freud felt that psychoanalysis was effective in the treatment of mild or "neurotic" disorders only. So more serious disorders—schizophrenia, personality disorders, and depressions—are not usually treated by psychoanalysis. Because of the time and expense, psychoanalysis is a route open to a very few. A study conducted by the Menninger Foundation found, however, that psychoanalysis is effective for individuals who scored high on scales of ego strength at the beginning of therapy (Smith et al., 1980).

Behavior Therapy

The advent of behavior therapy had several important advantages for the study of outcomes. Primarily, the methods are precise and thus easily measured. Second, the desired outcome is explicit at the beginning—the modification of a certain behavior. How close one is to that predetermined goal at the end is a good measure of success. The outcome of studies shows that behavior therapy is most useful when someone has a specific behavior to change, such as specific phobias and breaking habits like smoking, overeating, addictions, and sexual dysfunctions. Like psychoanalysis and most other therapies, behavior therapy is not usually successful with severe disorders.

Cognitive–behavioral therapies are so new that the results are naturally more tentative. However, the first results are promising enough that this area of psychotherapy is growing rapidly (Coleman et al., 1980). Although Rogers initiated outcome research, evidence on the humanistic therapies is extremely difficult to quantify. The goals of the therapy are often hard to evaluate.

Drug Therapy

The only therapies that show a consistent advantage over other types are drug therapies. Drugs can be used in the treatment of a wide range of disorders, particularly the severe ones such as depression and schizophrenia. In one important study, Hogarty and Goldberg (1973) divided 374 recently released schizophrenics into four groups: (1) those who received chlorpromazine alone, (2) those who received a placebo alone, (3) those who received chlorpromazine and psychotherapy, and (4) those who received a placebo and psychotherapy.

At the end of one year, the hospitalization rate was as follows: for the first group, 33 percent; for the second, 72.5 percent; for the third, 26 percent; and for the fourth, 63 percent. Thus, drug therapy with psychotherapy was only slightly more effective than drug therapy alone. Both were substantially more effective than psychotherapy or minimal (counting placebo treatment as minimal).

Factors Affecting Therapy

Many studies (summarized in Frank, 1983) make it clear that *the most important factor in therapeutic success is the therapist–client relationship.* If there is a successful outcome, it is not because one theory or another has the right answer. The approach and treatment hardly seem to matter. What *does* matter is that each therapy recognizes the importance of the therapist establishing a good trusting relationship with the client (or patient) at the start of therapy.

Therapists

What makes a good therapist? One area of research compared the effects of experienced and inexperienced therapists. There have been many studies in which researchers compared experienced therapists with: (a) undergraduates, (b) housewives, (c) graduate students, and (d) inexperienced but trained therapists. In general, inexperienced or nonprofessional people are far more directive and less interpretive; they act the way most nonprofessionals would imagine a therapist to act. But a panel of experts can pick out experienced from inexperienced therapists. However, are professional therapists always more effective than amateurs? In a comparison of twelve outcome studies using inexperienced versus experienced therapists, only *five* showed that patients of experienced therapists achieved better outcomes (Smith et al., 1980). This suggests that something on a personal level seems to happen between the people involved in therapy, something beyond just the formal training.

Placebos: Are They for Real?

Frank (1983) states that "the placebo *is* psychotherapy." This may seem like an exaggeration, but it points out the power of the placebo and the great importance of mental phenomena. Researchers often compare all kinds of therapies to placebos. However, the placebo itself is an important aspect of therapy. For example, consider Lourdes, the most famous Western religious healing shrine where each year over two million pilgrims come to be healed by the springs where in 1858 Marie Bernadette Soubrious (St. Bernadette) had her vision. Thousands of the pilgrims are chronically ill and, having failed medical treatment, turn to the shrine as a last resort. Even before arriving at the shrine, the ailing pilgrim's hopes are raised by the elaborate preparation. And once there, the ill people are overcome with religious faith and hope. These strong, positive emotions may well act as powerful placebos to cure many of the pilgrims' illnesses.

The word *placebo* itself comes from the Latin, meaning "I shall please," and the implications are intriguing. Does this refer to the doctor or healer? A **placebo** is a substance that a doctor may give to please or placate a patient even though it has no specific pharmacological activity for the ailment. Does it refer to the patient's own decision to get better, possibly to please the doctor? In either case, researchers have historically viewed the placebo as a nuisance, something to be shunted aside and "controlled for" rather than something to be understood in its own right (White, Tursky, & Schwartz, 1985).

Placebos have been shown to be effective against postoperative wound pain, seasickness, headaches, coughs, anxiety, and other disorders of nervousness. Subsequent studies have also shown improvements in high blood pressure, angina, depression, acne, asthma, hay fever, colds, insomnia, arthritis, ulcers, gastric acidity, migraine, constipation, obesity, blood counts, and lipoprotein levels from using placebos (Frank, 1982; Buckalew & Ross, 1981). But not all the results of placebos are positive and therapeutic. Placebos can produce an entire range of symptoms including palpitations, drowsiness, headaches, diarrhea, and nausea (Agras, Horne, & Taylor, 1982).

A recent British study has also found that brand names add to the placebo response. Women who regularly suffered from headaches were given either aspirin or a placebo (a sugar pill, in this case). The wrapping was either a familiar and well-known branded packet or an unfamiliar one. Approximately 40 percent of the group receiving the unbranded placebos reported that the pain was considerably better. However, 50 percent reported relief with branded placebos, 56 percent with unbranded aspirin, and 60 percent with branded aspirin. Thus, while the active ingredient in aspirin was slightly more effective than the sugar pill, the packaging (and thus the patients' expectations) also increased the effectiveness (Branthwaite & Cooper, 1981).

See Chapter 4, section on Endorphins.

Although we have known and used the placebo for centuries, its mechanism has seemed inexplicable and mysterious. An experiment (mentioned in Chapter 4) suggests that endorphins may mediate at least one aspect of the placebo effect — placebo-induced pain relief. Recall that Levine and Fields studied postoperative pain and selected 51 men and women undergoing surgical removal of impacted wisdom teeth. The patients consented to postoperative treatment with either morphine, placebo, or naloxone (which might increase pain) (Fields & Levine, 1981). They had their wisdom teeth removed under standard anesthesia. Then the patients spent several hours in a recovery room where the researchers administered the experimental drugs and measured the pain. Two hours after anesthesia had begun, all patients received a randomly selected injection of either morphine, naloxone, or placebo. One hour later the researchers gave them another injection. Neither patients nor researchers knew which substances had been administered until after the experiment (this is called a *double blind* experiment). Of the patients, 17 received placebo both times, 23 received placebo followed by naloxone, and 11 received naloxone followed by placebo.

Patients receiving placebo as the first injection were divided into two groups: placebo responders and nonresponders. Responders were patients who reported less pain one hour after receiving placebos. Nearly 40 percent of the patients were classified as responders by this definition.

When responders received a high dose of naloxone as the second injection, they reported significantly increased levels of pain. When nonresponders received naloxone as the second injection, they reported no changes in pain levels. Pain ratings for responders after naloxone were approximately the same as those for nonresponders. Since naloxone blocks the effects of opiates and endorphins, a major part of placebo analgesia must be mediated by the release of endorphins.

Placebos result in many effects other than pain relief, so it is unlikely that endorphins mediate the whole range of responses to placebos. But findings such as these have led many researchers to wonder whether psychological factors and the doctor – patient relationship may not be as important as drugs in medicine and may form part of the basis of therapy itself. Remember that physical symptoms sometimes display as psychological ones. The reverse may be true, and it may well be possible to interrupt problems in a variety of ways.

Attention

The need to belong is quite basic to us. It follows then that some people are helped by the "attention" they receive from the therapist. In one study Paul divided a sample of college students seeking therapy for "performance anxiety" into two groups. One group became involved with an insight-oriented therapy (for example, psychoanalysis and person-centered). The other group received "attention-placebo" treatment, which means that a person was merely convinced that a therapist was interested in him or her but received no actual treatment. At the end of two years, both groups showed the same rate of improvement (Paul, 1965).

Many other analyses have shown that the therapeutic situation, regardless of methodology, has many elements in common. People come in without feeling control over their lives, and they leave with some hope (Frank, 1982).

"Meta-analysis" of the Outcome of Psychotherapy

The controversy over whether psychotherapy works has stimulated some recent comprehensive studies. Smith and colleagues (1980) analyzed the results of many different studies of effectiveness of psychotherapy. This *meta-analysis* (so-called

because it is the analysis of many analyses) finds these effects (Smith, Glass, & Miller, 1980):

1. The *average* effect of psychotherapy is *positive* in almost all kinds of therapies.
2. The amount of effect is fairly large, enough to move a person who is at the mean (50th percentile) of a population up to the 80th percentile rank.
3. Cognitive therapies seem to be the most effective of all therapies, but all are effective.
4. There is a significant positive effect of "attention-placebo," but it is not as strong as psychotherapy.
5. Drug therapy is as effective as psychotherapy, and the effects of drug therapies and psychotherapy add to one another. Thus, drug plus psychotherapy is the most effective treatment on the average.

Thus, although certain therapies seem to be slightly more beneficial than others, three decades of research and almost a century of treatment show that most therapies are largely effective. Some may be due simply to attention, some to the specific technique, some to drugs. The main point is that psychotherapy, on the average, can help people, if right factors are applied to the right people.

There remain many problems, however. Berman, Miller, and Massmann (1984) found that the allegiance of the investigators predicts which therapy is judged better, even in the meta-analysis studies! A more fundamental problem is that there is no real matching of problem to therapy. The chance to compare alternative therapies, as in the case of George (One Problem, Four Treatments) is rare. Often people who are in trouble do find a sincere, competent therapist who wants to help. Yet this help may be lacking simply because the problem is not matched to the therapy. It is as if someone broke his arm and went to a heart surgeon to get it fixed. Clearly, there is much research now to be done in diagnosis, evaluation of treatment, and referral of problems to therapists before psychotherapy is able to approach its full capacity.

The elements of treatment and technique are there. But as with research on intelligence, personality, and the nature of the mind, the need for a complex analysis of multiple components of the mind is becoming clear. This analysis of the components of successful therapy is an initial step toward scientific psychology becoming more capable of resolving complex human problems.

SUMMARY

1. In the late eighteenth century a series of humane reforms allowed disordered people to be treated as victims of disease instead of as if something "possessed" them. A great advance in the late nineteenth century was the discovery of the cause of one type of disorder, *general paresis,* which is a slow degenerative disease that eventually erodes mental faculties. It was discovered to be caused by syphilis. The elimination of syphilis by medical means is one of the few decisive victories in the war against mental disorder. That victory led to the hope that researchers would find a specific biological cause for every pathology.

2. A most important innovation in the history of mental disease was the development of classifications of mental disorders. Kraepelin noted that mental disorder was not a monolithic entity, but several distinct disorders, each with its own particular pattern of symptoms. His system remains the foundation of the modern classification of disorders. Currently, much treatment of mental disease is administered by psychotherapists. A *psychiatrist* is a medical doctor whose specialty is the treatment of psychological problems. A *psychoanalyst* is a psychotherapist trained in psychoanalytic techniques first formulated by Freud. A *clinical psychologist* holds a Ph.D. in psychology and may specialize in a particular form of psychotherapy. A *psychiatric social worker* concentrates on social or community-based problems.

3. The psychoanalytic method of treatment is based on the theories of Freud. He believed that disorders are caused by conflicts between conscious and unconscious desires. In this system, therapy brings these desires into consciousness where the patient can acknowledge and analyze them. Freud developed the technique of *free association* in which the psychotherapist asks the patient to say anything that comes to mind, without criticism or editing. The idea is that the thoughts, images, and connections in therapy must come from within the patient. Psychoanalysis is usually very expensive and lasts from one to several years.

4. There are several phases of treatment in psychoanalysis. In the opening phase, resistance in the patient emerges, which is the way the patient unconsciously works against revealing feelings or thoughts. At a certain point in treatment, patients transfer their feelings toward people in their lives onto the analyst (an important process called *transference*) and these feelings thus come to the surface. The therapist then proceeds to an analysis of this transference. Patients begin to see, in a concrete way, the nature of their misconceptions, having transferred them to the analyst. The transference is then resolved in the last phase of the treatment, in which patients and the therapist agree that they have achieved their goals.

5. In behavior therapy, the approach is to work directly on problems, which are the result of "faulty learning." Psychotherapy, then, is the process of relearning. Two varieties of behavior therapy relate to the two primary modes of learning. The form called *behavior therapy* is based on respondent conditioning and aims to reduce the anxiety that a person experiences in response to certain key external stimuli. Since anxiety is the underlying cause of neurotic behavior, behavior therapy aims to decondition those anxiety-producing autonomic responses. *Behavior modification* is based on operant conditioning and attempts to change behaviors by changing the stimuli and conditions. Therapy may involve an individual, group, family, or community. This form of therapy has been useful in treating test anxiety, sexual dysfunctions, phobias, addictions, and interpersonal problems.

6. Some important reconditioning techniques in behavior therapy include the following. (a) *Systematic desensitization* eliminates unwanted conditioned responses and conditions the client to another stimulus that elicits a response (usually relaxation) incompatible with the original one. (b) *Flooding* is similar to systematic desensitization in that the therapist deliberately presents the client with fear or anxiety-provoking stimuli. Flooding, however, is more intensive and does not rely on relaxation; it is most effective in severe phobias. (c) *Assertiveness training* is used when a person's problem involves difficulties in interpersonal relationships and teaches people that they have a right to their own feelings as long as they do not hurt others.

7. Cognitive-behavior therapy is a new and very effective form of therapy. In one type, *rational-emotive therapy* (RET), the therapist determines what the underlying belief

system of the individual is, and the client is confronted directly with this belief system and examines it against reality. The therapist is quite active in the disputing of these beliefs. Another type of cognitive-behavior therapy is *cognitive-restructuring therapy*, which is similar to RET in that it works on beliefs. This therapy contends that there are four major areas where people's thought processes make their beliefs self-fulfilling: (a) absolute thinking; (b) generalizing negative events to every aspect of their lives; (c) magnifying the importance of negative events; and (d) selective perception, noticing only those events that confirm negative beliefs about themselves.

8. In person-centered psychotherapies, psychological disorders are thought to arise from a blocking of a person's natural inclination toward self-actualization. The purpose of psychotherapy is to release an already existing capacity in a potentially competent individual. This therapy is nondirective. It usually progresses in three stages: (a) the client expresses predominantly negative feelings both inwardly and toward the world and the future, (b) the client begins to feel hope, and (c) impromptu feelings emerge that allow the client to have more self-confidence and to plan for the future.

9. A different approach to therapy is biological. Recent research has shown that the areas of the "mental" and "physical" are not as unrelated as previously thought. Brain states affect mental states and body states affect brain states. This is why placebos work so well. Therefore, the relationship between the biology of the body and therapy is potentially quite important.

10. One important form of therapy is *electroconvulsive therapy* (ECT) in which a patient receives a series of several shock treatments. When completed, there is often a complete cessation of disordered symptoms, especially those of depression. Since the invention of antipsychotic drugs, the use of ECT has been in decline because it is a violent and drastic intervention. Today, only in the most severe cases of depression or schizophrenia is ECT used. Still, it is the most effective treatment of such severely disordered cases.

11. *Pharmacotherapy* has perhaps been the most revolutionary change in the treatment of mental disorder. Three types of drugs have been developed that relieve the major symptoms of several different psychological disorders. *Antipsychotic* drugs treat severe disorders, such as schizophrenia. They serve to calm the patient and reduce the experience of delusions and hallucinations. Examples of antipsychotic drugs are reserpines and chlorpromazine. *Antidepressants* are an effective class of drugs used to treat depressive symptoms. These drugs seem to act on the neurotransmitters, especially serotonin and norepinephrine. *Antianxiety* drugs are widely used in our culture. Among the most popular are Librium and Valium. These drugs work effectively to reduce the experience of anxiety. There is growing concern because they are addicting and their indiscriminate use may prevent people from developing coping strategies from within to handle their fears.

12. It is controversial how effective psychotherapy is. Early outcome studies showed that patients improved as much without therapy as with it. Among therapies, psychoanalysis is the most difficult to evaluate; there is little emphasis on successful outcome. Behavior therapy is much easier to evaluate because its procedures and the criteria for successful outcome are quite specific. Behavior therapy is effective with specific phobias and habits. Cognitive–behavioral therapies are also successful in certain well-defined situations. On the average, people in therapy are statistically better off than people in matched situations who do not enter therapy. Not everyone is helped by every form of psychotherapy to the maximum extent. Psychotherapy is still in its infancy, and much research still needs to be done.

assertiveness training
behavior modification
behavior therapy
catharsis
clinical psychologist
cognitive-restructuring therapy
electroconvulsive therapy
flooding
free association
general paresis
meta-analysis
person-centered therapy

pharmacotherapy
placebo
psychiatric social worker
psychiatrist
psychoanalyst
rational–emotive therapy
resistance
spontaneous remission
stress inoculation therapy
systematic desensitization
transference
trephining

London, P. (1986). *The modes and morals of psychotherapy.* New York: Harper & Row.

The most influential study of therapy of the past period, now revised after 22 years. Recommended.

Smith, M. L., Glass, G. V., & Miller, T. I. (1980). *The benefits of psychotherapy.* Baltimore: Johns Hopkins University Press.

A technical account of how the different methods of therapy are evaluated and analyzed. Useful to look at.

VandenBos, G. A. (1986). Psychotherapy research [Special issue]. *American Psychologist,* 41 (2).

A special issue of the journal, concerning many of the current problems of therapy research. They include its evaluation, and the help computers may bring. Also included are some of the difficulties.

White, L., Tursky, B., & Schwartz, G. (1985). *Placebo.* New York: Guilford.

A recent compendium on the many effects and the importance of placebos.

*I*f our earliest development is primarily biological, our later development is social. Other people often determine how and where we work, what we like to eat, and how we think. We conform, obey, accept. We may make extreme decisions, such as whether or not to kill, while in a group.

The experiences of adulthood — marriage, becoming a grandparent, work — make many people aware that they are part of something larger than their individual selves. We are workers, citizens, members of a political party. Some people become "citizens of the world," concerned with life on the planet as a whole.

So, we expand away from our biology during our adulthood.

Until the end, when our biology reclaims us once again.

Part IV

The Social World of the Adult

Social Psychology

Imagine you are alone in a room and you hear someone cry for help next door. Would you help? Probably. Now imagine that you are sitting with a few other people when you hear a cry for help. Would you go to help? Yes again? Probably not. You are three times *less* likely to help if there are six people in the room than if you are alone. The group we are in has a profound effect on our behavior, attitudes, and experience.

Human beings are "social animals." Not all human doings spring directly from our biology. Social situations are also crucial. The presence of other people *intensifies* and *directs* our behavior. This phenomenon has been known since the early days of psychology as the **coaction effect.** Bicyclists ride faster against other people than alone against the clock; children reel in their fishing lines faster in groups than alone (Triplett, 1897).

We make social judgments by comparing ourselves to a standard *reference group.* Here is an example. I was once a member of a local touch-football team, and I was a good quarterback. I could throw longer and better than anyone I knew. I was also a 49er fan, and at the time, the quarterback of the 49ers was being pilloried in the press — he was too old, his arm was no good, and so on. I was as down on him as anyone and agreed that he couldn't throw.

He retired. He lived across the street from me, and an enterprising friend asked if he would join our team; he agreed. And you should have seen him throw! One doesn't realize until something like this happens just how different our standards can be, and how easily different ideas are held apart. Here was this retired quarterback, who I thought was "all washed up," throwing sensational passes and making me (in my mind, a good passer) look terrible by comparison.

We are all changed by the groups in which we live and the situations we experience. Social psychology is the study of how people and situations affect us. This book began with a narration of how human ancestors evolved specific adaptations to suit their original world. But for human beings, the "worlds" — the specific life situations — are diverse and constantly change.

People are adaptable and thus they change (more than we would like to think) to adjust to different situations. So the complexity of the human story continues; a person can become cruel in one situation, generous in another. Social situations have their own life within the mind. When one person commits suicide, others are more likely to do so. When one person obeys, others obey. Person see, person do. Attractiveness is contagious too, and we act very differently toward those who are attractive to us.

Many of the important principles studied in this book thus far now combine in this chapter on social judgment and influence. Such principles include

THE PERSON IN THE SITUATION

Because we use the behavior of our peers as a guide to our own behavior, these teenagers (at the funeral of a friend who committed suicide) are more likely to consider suicide now than they would have before.

selectivity, comparison, and schemata. But social psychology is more than just a combination of other factors. It has its own unique principles, as recent research has begun to show (Ross & Nisbett, in press).

It is now realized how malleable human behavior is and how compelling specific situations are in which people find themselves. For example, college, prisons, bureaucracies, size of a city, and events in the daily newspaper all have very strong effects on us, much greater effects than most people would have believed before they studied social psychology. Also, and this is similar to other principles in this book, our perception of any situation is what is so important (Ross & Nisbett, in press).

What follows are four situations in which people find themselves that we can examine to gain some insight into the social nature of human beings.

Situation 1: Response to Suicide

Imagine you are flying to Chicago to visit your parents. In the morning's paper you read that a prominent banker has killed himself. Too bad, you think, then you dismiss it from your mind. It has nothing to do with you. That would be true if people did not respond so immediately and strongly to the actions of others. Little do you realize that the suicide you just read about may actually affect the safety of your plane ride!

Suicides of prominent people are often given front page space in the newspaper. Immediately after a highly publicized suicide, the suicide rate increases (Phillips, 1979). After Marilyn Monroe killed herself, the suicide rate was eight times the normal rate for months (Cialdini, 1985). Suicide is contagious and becomes "more available" as an option when it receives publicity. In fact, statistics show that every publicized suicide stimulates an average of 58 more "copycat suicides"! The more space given to a suicide story in the media, the more subsequent suicides. This is called the "Werther effect" after Goethe's hero who committed suicide in *The Sorrows of Young Werther* (Phillips, 1974). This eighteenth century novel became immediately popular in Europe and stimulated suicides in every country where it was read. It caused such devastating reactions to its readers that the book was banned for a time in France.

But what does this have to do with your plane ride? More chilling than the copycat suicides are dramatic increases later in airplane crashes and auto accidents. Phillips (1979, 1980) points out that these surplus accidents and disasters are probably suicides by the operators done in a way to conceal the intent. People often don't wish it known that they have killed themselves so they may simply drive off the road in a dangerous area. Or a pilot may crash the plane deliberately in an area which is known to be hazardous (Phillips, 1980).

If people do copy immediate behaviors, we would expect certain evidence. For example, crashes of commercial airliners within a few days of a publicized suicide should be more lethal than usual. And this seems to be the case. Phillips presents convincing evidence that fatalities are three times greater in these crashes than normal. This indicates that there is probably a deliberate element in them.

It is hard to believe that one would have to be careful when flying after a recently publicized suicide, or that someone driving on the freeway could be affected by it. But such is the complicated result of the nature of social judgments (Phillips, 1983).

Situation 2: A "Shocking" Experiment

In certain situations ordinary people will follow the commands of an authority figure, even when they are extreme and uncalled for and when there is no threat of punishment.

In a study by Milgram (1960–1963), men responded to a newspaper advertisement for "participants in a psychology experiment" at Yale University. The ad said it would take about one hour and they would be paid $4.50. When each subject arrived for the experiment, he was introduced to the experimenter and another "subject" (actually a confederate of the experimenter). The real subjects were told that the experiment was "an investigation of the effects of punishment on learning."

The subject and confederate drew lots to see who would be the "teacher" and who would be the "learner." The drawing was rigged, however, so that the confederate was always the learner and the real subject was always the teacher. The experimenter said that the teacher's job was to administer an electric shock every time the learner made a mistake.

The experimenter took the teacher and learner to an adjoining room and strapped the learner into a chair and attached electrodes to his wrist (Figure 17-1). The learner (the confederate) then expressed concern about receiving shocks, stating that he had a heart condition (this was not true). The experimenter assured him and the teacher that there were no physical risks in the experiment. The teacher and the experimenter then returned to the original room.

The experimenter asked the teacher first to read a series of word pairs to the learner, then to read the first word of each pair along with four word choices. For each pair, the learner was to recall which word had been the second in the original pair. When the learner answered correctly, the teacher was to press a switch that

FIGURE 17-1
Milgram Experiment
These photos show some of the actual events in the Milgram experiment on obedience to authority in which subjects (designated as "teachers") gave electric shocks to "learners" (see text).

lit a light in the learner's room. When the learner was wrong, the teacher was supposed to read the correct answer aloud. He was also to punish the learner by pressing a switch that delivered an electric shock to the learner.

There were 30 switches ranging from 15 volts (labeled Slight Shock) to 420 volts (labeled Danger: Severe Shock). The two final switches, for 435 and 450 volts, were simply labeled XXX. Each time the learner made a mistake, the teacher was to administer a shock and each time it would be one level higher (15 more volts) than the last shock.

Unbeknown to the subject (teacher), the experimenter instructed the learner to make mistakes. He never actually received any shocks. Following a prearranged script, the learner complained about the shocks. He expressed concern over his heart condition and begged for release. After the teacher administered 300 volts, the learner began to pound the walls. Then, ominously, he no longer responded.

Whenever the teacher showed hesitation about giving a shock, the experimenter simply instructed the "teacher" to follow the directions. He did not threaten or display force. Now, consider this question honestly: how much shock would *you* have given? Almost no one says they would have given the maximum shock (Aronson, 1984).

The results are (forgive the pun) shocking (Figure 17-2). The "teachers" knew that the learner had a heart condition and heard him beg to be released. Nevertheless, *62.5 percent* of the teachers in the experiment complied completely and gave the *maximum* shock of 450 volts. Even more startling, only 22.5 percent gave less than 300 volts. In one variation of the experiment *no one* gave less than 300 volts.

This experiment, extreme though it is, shows how strongly human beings can be influenced by a social situation. The subjects gave the maximum shock because they were in a situation where pressure to comply with an authority figure outweighed their own judgment. But think how abstract and subtle the pressure was. The subjects agreed to be in an experiment, they accepted money for their

FIGURE 17-2

Obedience to Authority
In the Milgram experiment, all subjects followed instructions and administered what they thought were painful shocks of up to 300 volts. Only above 300 volts did some subjects refuse to go on administering shocks to the protesting "learner."
(After Milgram, 1963)

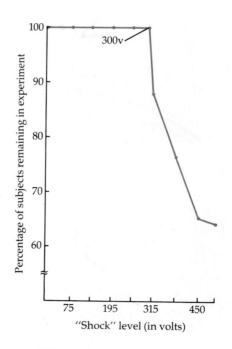

participation, and they felt an obligation to the experimenter. The experimenter assured them that there was no danger, even when they first heard the screams, then the silence.

The subjects may have felt that the scientists, dressed in doctor-like white coats, would not ask them to do anything really dangerous. Perhaps they felt that whatever happened was the researcher's responsibility. This experiment by no means proves that people are weak willed and always obedient. It does point out, however, that it is hard not to obey or conform when there is social "pressure" urging us on.

Situation 3: A Mock Prison Study

Philip Zimbardo sought to investigate the degree to which brutal behavior can be situationally determined. In one of psychology's most important studies, he simulated a "prison" in the basement of the psychology building at Stanford University (Haney, Banks, & Zimbardo, 1973; Zimbardo, 1972).

He randomly assigned male students to the roles of prisoner and guard. The local police even cooperated by picking up the prisoners in squad cars, complete with siren. Prisoners were treated realistically. They were fingerprinted, stripped, "skin searched," and given demeaning uniforms. The uniforms were dresses, with no underclothing, intended to "emasculate" the male prisoners. The prisoners also wore a chain locked around one ankle. Guards were uniformed and were given handcuffs, cell and gate keys, and billy clubs. But they were told physical violence was prohibited. The guards were to maintain "law and order" and to be stern with the prisoners (Figure 17-3).

Soon the experiment took an unsettling turn. Some of the guards identified with their roles and began to enjoy their power over the prisoners. The prisoners rebelled at first. After the rebellion was put down, the guards became more

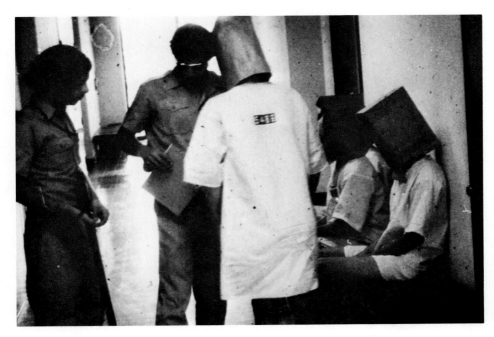

FIGURE 17-3
The Stanford "Prison" Study
Students playing their roles as prisoners and guards in the mock prison in the basement of the psychology building at Stanford University.

aggressive and the prisoners became more passive. Five prisoners were released early because of their severe anxiety and rage reactions. The experiment was originally scheduled to last for two weeks. It had to be terminated after only six days due to the distress of the prisoners. Because this was just an experiment, the "prisoners" could have left at any time. But they did not, having assumed the role of weak and submissive prisoners, accepting punishment.

The guards, on the other hand, were disappointed with the early termination of the experiment. They quickly grew to enjoy their power roles. Outside the situation the guards were normal, nondestructive people, as measured by standard psychological tests. The apparently complete power over the prisoners resulted in arrogant, aggressive, and cruel behavior.

Not *all* the guards behaved in a "corrupt" manner. Only one-third were described as "quite inventive in their techniques of breaking the spirit of the prisoners." The rest were described as "tough but fair." They were "good guards from the prisoner's point of view since they did small favors and were friendly" (Zimbardo, 1972).

Situation 4: Conforming in College

Social pressure can change behavior, but can it actually change beliefs? A classic study was begun in 1935 at Bennington College, then a small expensive college for women in Vermont. The college had just graduated its first senior class, and it had not yet gained a wide reputation. The professors were liberal, but the bulk of the students came from very conservative families. Thus, there was a wide difference in beliefs between the attitudes of new students and the attitudes of their new reference group (the faculty). The stage was set for a real-life study of conformity pressure on beliefs. Theodore Newcomb and his colleagues (1943) charted its effects on these students for over a quarter of a century.

Over the four years in college the once-conservative students increasingly adopted the liberal attitudes of their new reference group: 62 percent of the freshman class were Republican, 43 percent of the sophomore class, but only 15 percent of the juniors and seniors.

How did these changes come about? First, many of the students reported that they made a deliberate shift in their choice of reference group. They threw over the attitudes of their conservative parents and took up the attitudes of the liberal students and faculty that they wanted to be like. Second, the liberal faculty and students tended to reject conservative students, labeling them immature and "not intellectual." Third, there was an intellectual influence: the liberal environment provided students with new information on issues and events.

Even after 25 years, most of the students were still politically liberal. The change that had been initiated by the college reference group persisted (Newcomb, Koenig, Flacks, & Warwick, 1967). Newcomb explained this persistence by noting that after college, the students actively sought out other liberals. They joined liberal groups which then became their new reference groups and provided a continuing source of liberal information and identification. Many of the reference group changes that many of us make in college become important for life. But in this extreme case, in only eight months some of the most conservative people in America became the most liberal — without dramatic brainwashing and with nothing but a change in reference group.

The four examples in the last section show the great effect that social situations have on behavior, but how does this work? The mechanism social psychologists identify is an internal perception and comparison process. We constantly interact with other people who belong to a variety of groups: large ones, such as business, professional, political, or social groups, and small groups, such as family, friends, a club, or a team. A fundamental part of our lives is determining how we stand compared to the rest of the group and how we fit into the group.

Social Comparison

You can easily determine if you are taller or heavier than someone else by a simple measurement. But most social situations are very complex. There is no objective scale to tell you whether your attitudes or behavior are normal for a particular group.

Leon Festinger, one of the leading social psychologists, proposed an important theory of **social comparison** (1954) which states: if there is no objective measure of comparison, we seek out other people and compare our attitudes or behaviors to theirs.

We compare ourselves to those we admire or whom we believe are like us. Most of us would not compare our political beliefs to a group of drunks, unless we aspire to inebriation. Assume that you are opposed to investment in South Africa and want to find out if your opposition is "normal." You probably would not compare your opinion to the Ambassador of South Africa. You are more likely to pick someone who is like you in many ways, such as another college student.

The group we choose to compare ourselves to is called the **reference group.** When attitudes and behavior agree with the reference group, we consider ourselves part of it. When we do not fit in, there is often a heavy price to pay. The members of the group may dislike us, reject us, or treat us badly. When there are

differences between our attitudes and the group's, there may be pressure to change attitudes and to *conform*. The pressure that forces us to try to be like everyone else is **social pressure** or **conformity pressure**.

SCARCITY AND COMPARISON: USING SOCIAL PSYCHOLOGY TO MAKE MONEY

Because of all the simplification processes of social judgment, we do not use all the information that is available to us. Sometimes the results are disastrous, such as in the case of the Milgram and Zimbardo experiments. But sometimes it causes a hilarious manipulation of our desires and our money. In the book *Influence* Cialdini (1984) describes how his cousin put himself through college by buying and selling cars. He created a situation so that people would ignore important information.

For a car he had purchased on the prior weekend, he would place an ad in the Sunday paper. Because he knew how to write a good ad, he usually received an array of calls from potential buyers on Sunday morning. Each prospect who was interested enough to want to see the car was given an appointment time—the same appointment time. So, if six people were scheduled, they were all scheduled for, say, 2:00 that afternoon. This little device of simultaneous scheduling paved the way for . . . [sales] . . . because it created an atmosphere of competition for a limited resource.

Typically, the first prospect to arrive would begin a studied examination of the car and would engage in standard car-buying behavior such as pointing out any blemishes or deficiencies and asking if the price were negotiable. The psychology of the situation changed radically, however, when the second buyer drove up. The availability of the car to the prospect became limited by the other. Often the earlier arrival, inadvertently stoking the sense of rivalry, would assert his right to primary consideration. "Just a minute, now, I was here first." If he didn't assert that right, Richard would do it for him. Addressing the second buyer, he would say, "Excuse

me, but this other gentleman was here before you. So, can I ask you to wait on the other side of the driveway for a few minutes until he's finished looking at the car? Then, if he decides he doesn't want it or if he can't make up his mind, I'll show it to you."

Richard claims it was possible to watch the agitation grow on the first buyer's face. His leisurely assessment of the car's pros and cons had suddenly become a now-or-never, limited-time-only rush to a decision over a contested resource. If he didn't decide for the car—at Richard's asking price—in the next few minutes, he might lose it for good to that . . . that . . . lurking newcomer over there. The second buyer would be equally agitated by the combination of rivalry and restricted availability. He would pace about the periphery of things, visibly straining to get at this suddenly desirable hunk of metal. . . . [And] the trap snapped securely shut when the third 2:00 appointment arrived on the scene. According to Richard, stacked-up competition was usually too much for the first prospect to bear.

So Richard went through college selling cars quickly and for a good profit. He did this by creating a situation in which very little of the available information was brought into mind. He was clever enough to create a situation in which the process of comparison called up another specific reaction. "Compete and win for scarce resources" it might be called. If you are ever buying a car, another trick to try is to have a friend call the seller before you do. Your friend should offer the seller a very low price, then your offer will look quite good. Thus, scarcity affects comparisons.

Social Conformity

A single individual can sometimes pressure us to change our behavior. More often, however, our judgments, attitudes, and actions are influenced by groups, as we saw in the situation of the college students who became liberal. The more desirable and important we find the group, the more difficult it is to resist its pressure.

Opinions and Social Influence

It is difficult to resist such demands even with a random collection of strangers and no inducement to comply. Solomon Asch conducted a classic study of the social influences of conformity. Volunteers were requested for a psychology experiment on visual perception. One real subject and six other subjects (actually confederates of the experimenters) were seated around a circular table and shown a board with a vertical line on it. The experimenter then showed a second board that had three vertical lines, one the same length as the first board and two obviously different in length (Figure 17-4).

The subjects were asked to identify which line on the second board was the same length as the one on the first. The subjects answered in turn; the real subject responded last. All of the confederates picked the same obviously incorrect line, but there was no overt demand for group unanimity of response. Common sense tells you it would be very easy to resist this pressure. However, 32 percent of the real subjects conformed to the group pressure and gave the incorrect answer. The pressure of even a group formed of a random collection of people that one has never met can be considerable.

Factors in Conformity

People in different groups conform to different rules. Indians dress like Indians, Americans like Americans — when in Rome, you do as the Romans do. When you change your reference group, you change many things about yourself. A recent law school graduate who takes a job in a prestigious New York law firm may find he or she needs an entirely new wardrobe. It would be different from

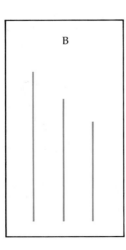

FIGURE 17-4
Social Influence
In the Asch study, subjects viewed display A and then were asked to choose the line in display B that matched it.
(After Asch, 1956)

Social life is characterized by many interactions involving both cooperation and competition among members of groups large and small.

one needed by a lawyer in a small town in the Sierras. Several factors determine to what extent we conform.

One factor is *group unanimity*. People are most likely to conform when faced with unanimous group opinion. In the Asch experiment conformity was 32 percent. If, however, there is even *one* other person who does not go along, conformity drops drastically to about 8 percent. It does not even matter if the other dissenter's answer is wrong (Wilder & Allen, 1973).

Group size is important, too. If you are sitting with someone in a lecture who says that it is boring, you may or may not agree. But if 10 other people say it is boring, you may begin to agree. In the Asch experiment, only 2.8 percent conformed with one other person in the room, while 12.8 percent conformed with two other people, and about 30 percent with four. Conformity does not increase with groups over four (Asch, 1951). We take a consensus of opinion from other people to define social reality. Once defined, further confirmation seems to be surplus.

ATTITUDES AND PREJUDICE

There is a subtle effect of all this pressure to change. Conformity pressures directed at attitudes can indirectly produce other types of change. One of the major areas of investigation in this field in the 1960s was how to change attitudes and behavior. It was a time of important new legislation guaranteeing civil rights to blacks. Many minority groups have followed the leadership of the blacks, demanding a fair and equal share. Social psychologists were approached to help devise ways to counter long-held attitudes of majority groups that resisted the changes.

Attitudes

Attitudes consist of several components. An attitude about another person (say, a negative one) has a *cognitive* component (belief that the person is conceited and domineering), an *emotional* component (dislike), and a *behavioral* component (avoid that person).

Consistency of Attitudes

We hold many different attitudes at once, but we are motivated to make all of our attitudes simpler and consistent with one another. **Cognitive consistency** theories classify how we achieve consistency among attitudes.

Balance theory (Heider, 1946, 1958) describes the relationship between an attitude about a person and attitudes about other things. The basic formulation of this theory is simple. If you like someone, you want to have all the same attitudes as that person. If you dislike someone, you want the opposite attitudes. Both of these two statements are "balanced" or "consistent."

Suppose in the Bennington College experiment, a student liked a certain professor and suppose that both the student and the professor had liberal political attitudes (a shared positive attitude about politics). This state is balanced because the student likes both the professor and his politics. An unbalanced state would be if the student liked the professor but held political attitudes that were the opposite of the professor's.

This was exactly the case for many of the Bennington freshmen. They admired and liked the liberal professors, but held conservative attitudes. According to Heider, this unbalanced state is psychologically uncomfortable. Thus, it motivated the students to create balance by changing their attitudes about politics to be consistent with the professor's.

Balance can be achieved in one of two ways. In our example, a student could change her attitude about the professor and decide she disliked him. The other way (which was chosen by most of the Bennington students) was to change their political attitudes from conservative to liberal. The importance of social reality explains much that seems to baffle political commentators. Ronald Reagan was personally very popular and was reelected by a wide majority. However, not many people liked his policies as much as they liked him.

Relationship Between Attitudes and Behavior

There is another relationship between attitudes and behavior that seems appealing and obvious—that an attitude about a person, object, or event can influence our *behavior* toward it. Everyday experience is full of examples of attitudes affecting behavior. If you like one political candidate more than another, you are more likely to say positive things about that candidate. You will most likely vote for him or her in the election. If someone you like enjoys foreign movies, you may catch yourself finding that foreign film festivals are fascinating!

The relationship between attitudes and behavior has been controversial in social psychology. But this controversy is centered on the definitions and measurements of attitude and behaviors. The ordinary view that attitudes can and do cause behaviors is supported when researchers have properly measured both (Azjen & Fishbein, 1974).

Cognitive Dissonance

Not only can attitudes affect behavior, but the opposite is also true: behavior can influence attitudes. This relationship involves **cognitive dissonance,** which like balance theory, assumes the need for cognitive consistency (Festinger, 1957). Cognitive dissonance occurs whenever an individual holds two cognitions (that is, beliefs, attitudes, or knowledge of behaviors) that are *inconsistent* with each other. A dissonance (literally, *disharmony*) is a discrepancy, and we try constantly to resolve discrepancies.

Consider these two statements: (1) I know cigarette smoking causes cancer; (2) I smoke. A rational person would be uncomfortable trying to live with these two contradictory facts. So the discrepancy could be solved in several ways. She could give up smoking, or consider cancer not a bad thing. She could assume that researchers will find a cure by the time she gets the disease. In the extreme, she could ignore the data. (Festinger jokingly suggested that the person could give up reading!)

Dissonance would also occur if a person liked someone but had insulted that person in public. Dissonance arises because he would not usually harm or insult someone that he liked. As in any state of disequilibrium, dissonance is uncomfortable and motivates the person to reduce it. Dissonance can be reduced by changing one of the cognitions so that it is no longer inconsistent with the second cognition, or by attempting to reduce the importance of one of the dissonant cognitions. He could decide he really doesn't like the person he insulted, or that what he said was a joke, not an insult. Dissonance can also be reduced by *adding* other cognitions that are consistent with one of the beliefs. He could compensate for the insult by doing something especially nice for the slighted person.

The following experiment was the first, and remains the most eminent, demonstration that behavior can change attitudes (Festinger & Carlsmith, 1959). Sixty undergraduates were randomly assigned to one of three experimental conditions. Experimenters first asked each subject to perform a dull, repetitive task. They were to place 12 spools in a tray, empty the tray, place the spools in the tray, empty it, and repeat this for one hour.

A rational person who smokes may have a hard time justifying his or her habit in the face of the strong arguments against smoking, such as the one presented here by the core of the New York Giant's defense.

Afterward, one third of the subjects were paid $1. They were asked to tell a waiting subject (who was in cahoots with the experimenters) that the task was enjoyable and interesting. Another third of the subjects were paid $20 to say the same thing. The final third simply performed the repetitive task and were not asked to tell anyone how they liked the job. Later, the subjects were asked to fill out a questionnaire that they thought was unrelated to the purpose of the experiment and were asked to rate how much they had actually enjoyed the task. In reality all subjects initially thought that the task was extremely dull.

Festinger and Carlsmith predicted that subjects in the $1 condition would experience dissonance and would change their attitude about the task and that subjects in the $20 condition would not experience dissonance and would not change their attitude. They felt that the $1 subjects' unconscious reasoning would be, "I wouldn't lie about such a silly thing for $1, so I must have really enjoyed it." The $20 subjects would think, "Heck, for $20 it's no skin off my back to lie about such an insignificant thing." The $20 would give them a *valid* reason for the inconsistency.

The results confirmed this prediction (Figure 17-5). After the experiment, someone other than the experimenter (the questionnaire) asked them to rate their "true" attitude toward the task. The $1 subjects evaluated the task as significantly more enjoyable than did the $20 subjects and the control subjects. In this case, the behavior (the statement to the confederate) produced a change in attitude. The inconsistency between the behavior and initial attitude produced an uncomfortable state. This prompted them to change their *attitude* so that it was consistent with their *behavior.*

This phenomenon may explain why a teacher whose income is far less than that of a banker friend may conclude that making money is "selling out." A starving artist might claim that successful artists aren't "pure." It also may explain why when few inducements are provided to someone to do something, the more likely it is to create attitude change. Chronically underpaid nurses, teachers, and social workers often describe the "psychic income" of their jobs; they have changed their attitude to work and value it more highly.

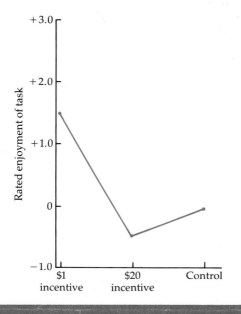

FIGURE 17-5
Behavior, Incentive, and Attitude Change
Paid to perform what they knew would be a boring task, those paid only $1 had more reason to change their attitude about the work to make it consistent with their behavior than did those paid $20, an amount that gave them sufficient reason to perpetuate the inconsistency.
(After Festinger & Carlsmith, 1959)

Self-Perception Theory

Daryl Bem (1972), however, characterized these and similar phenomena differently in his *theory of self-perception.* Bem argues that our justification in situations such as the Festinger and Carlsmith experiment are produced by a search for self-understanding and not by a need to reduce dissonance.

Bem hypothesizes that in judging our *own* attitudes we put ourselves into the role of an outside observer who witnesses his own behavior. In the Festinger and Carlsmith study, the observer sees himself perform a task that appears dull and uninteresting. He then sees himself tell someone that it is interesting after being paid only $1. The observer then probably infers that this must be his own true attitude. However, if the observer sees the subject being paid $20, his reasoning would be different. He could well think that for $20 he would probably be willing to lie about his enjoyment of the task.

When a person is asked to describe his *own* attitudes, he bases his judgment on the same evidence as an outside observer would. This is the assumption of the self-perception theory. Comparing the dissonance and self-perception interpretations, we see that both assume that behavior can influence attitudes. People often rely on their behavior and their circumstances to infer what their internal experience attitude is. "I didn't realize I liked X so much until I defended him to my friends" or "I must like chemistry because I got an A on the exam."

The theories differ only in the specific mechanisms postulated to explain how behavior influences attitudes. Dissonance theory assumes that the attitude was produced by the attempt to reduce discrepancy, while the self-perception theory assumes that the attitude was produced by the subjects' attempt to infer or discover their true beliefs.

Both theories offer interesting and compelling explanations for the link between behavior and attitudes. Many psychologists have assumed that only one explanation can be adequate. But both have advantages. "Dissonance" helps us understand that constancy and consistency are important. Self-perception is useful in that it emphasizes that sometimes we must *infer* or calculate what is happening to us, just as subjects in the Schacter and Singer experiment did. Although this self-perception theory seems appealing, it overlooks an important point. We usually *do* know what our attitudes and feeling are. Perhaps in some ambiguous situations we infer attitudes, but it is unlikely that we do so very often. Some psychologists advocate a more reasonable position: both theories have applications. They merely emphasize two different paths that lead to the same conclusion.

Personal Influence: "Machiavellianism"

Do people differ in how much they try to influence others? One dimension psychologists have identified is the manipulative techniques of the sixteenth-century writer Machiavelli, in his book *The Prince,* written in 1532. While this book does not really condone manipulations except in extenuating circumstances, psychologists and the public use the term *machiavellian* to describe someone who exploits others.

People who are called "high machs" would agree with statements like the following: "Never tell anyone the reason you do something," or "Don't get too close to someone because they could hurt you." In contrast, people called "low machs" would say, "Honesty is the best policy" (Christie & Geis, 1970).

High machs are likely to be good leaders and to play dominant roles, but they don't really use the normal kinds of social influence we have been discussing. Neither are they like high self-monitors (Snyder, 1987) who are more concerned with getting people to *like* them than exploiting others. The difference is described by Ickes and his colleagues (1986) as being as plain as the difference between "me" and "you." One is concerned with how others see you, the other with how much you can get out of a situation for yourself. So, the degree to which one tries to influence others for purely personal aims is a dimension of both personality and the social network of influences.

See Chapter 14, section on Self-Monitoring.

Prejudice

One of the major problems in society is prejudice. Some people are denied jobs, housing, and basic civil and human rights just because other people hold different attitudes. Thus, it is important for us to know the origins of prejudice. The word *prejudice* literally means "to prejudge" (Worchel, Cooper, & Goethals, 1987).

The study of sensation, perception, and thought shows that people come to most situations primed to prejudge. Our attitudes "prejudice" us naturally. For example, we can be prejudiced against eating steak, for capital punishment, and against women's rights. However, the basis of prejudice in the mind is not what most people mean by prejudice in society. **Prejudice** in this sense is a *negative judgmental attitude toward an identifiable group of people, based on a simplistic overgeneralization.*

Stereotypes

Prejudice derives from mechanisms similar to those that we use to experience the world and develop our ideas and attitudes. We are able to judge many different objects and people because of our efficient simplification processes. We sort the infinite variety of things we come across into simpler categories, and we assume all members of a category are similar. The problem comes when we overextend our simplifying strategies.

Central to categories are prototypes. However, when a prototype is overextended it becomes a *stereo*type. A **stereotype** is a generalized assumption attributing identical characteristics to all members of a group: for example, Americans are materialistic, blondes are dumb, the elderly are wise, and the Irish are drunks.

When we judge someone according to a stereotype, we attempt to fit all of an individual's actions and qualities into a consistent personality. Gordon Allport, in *The Nature of Prejudice* (1954), gives this example:

MR. X: The trouble with Jews is that they only take care of their own group.

MR. Y: But the record of the Community Chest campaign shows that they give more generously, in proportion to their numbers, to the general charities of their community than do non-Jews.

MR. X: That shows they are always trying to buy favor and intrude into Christian affairs. They think of nothing but money, that is why there are so many Jewish bankers.

MR. Y: But a recent study shows that the percentage of Jews in the banking business is negligible, far smaller than the percentage of non-Jews.

MR. X: That's just it: they don't go in for respectable businesses. They are only in the movie business or run night clubs.

Jane Elliot did an experiment to study the effects of prejudice. As a teacher, she announced to her class that brown-eyed people were superior to blue-eyed people. She said that they were more intelligent and better behaved. Brown-eyed children were given many more privileges; blue-eyed children had to sit in the back of the room and wait at the end of lines. Blue-eyed children began to falter at their lessons and began describing themselves in negative terms, such as bad, sad, and stupid. The brown-eyed children became nasty, vicious, and discriminating.

The next day, Elliot said that she had made a mistake: in fact, blue-eyed people were superior. The moods and actions of the two groups quickly reversed. Friendships that had previously existed between brown- and blue-eyed children vanished and were replaced with hostility. On the third day, she told the students what she had done and reassured them that they were all equal (Elliot, 1977).

In our society, there has long been a stereotype that women are intellectually inferior to men. In one study, male college students were asked to judge the accomplishments of highly successful physicians, male and female. Even though the accomplishments were equal, the males rated the females as less competent than the males (Feldman-Summers & Kiesler, 1974). Women also seemed to believe the female stereotype. A number of female students were asked to read several scholarly articles and to evaluate them. The articles were signed by either John T. McKay or Joan T. McKay. The articles were rated more highly when written by John than by Joan (Goldberg, 1968).

Some Causes and Cures of Prejudice

There is a general tendency to simplify and oversimplify the world and those in it. But prejudice arises more regularly in certain situations and in certain groups.

Conformity.   People want to fit in well with the groups they belong to. One way to fit in is to adopt and conform to many of the existing attitudes of that group and to do it without questioning or examining these attitudes. Unfortunately, many of a group's "attitudes" may be prejudices.

The opposite can also happen: conformity of attitude can also work to reduce prejudice. When prejudiced people join less prejudiced groups, they adopt more tolerant attitudes (Aronson, 1984). This occurred in the study of the liberals at Bennington College. Another way to reduce prejudice is to increase contact with the prejudged group; this increases the availability of positive thoughts and decreases the availability of negative ones.

The rule is this: *the more you know about someone, the less likely you are to make sweeping judgments about him or her.* This fact holds true in our judgments about groups of people. Because society has become less segregated in the past 40 years, we should expect less prejudice toward minorities. Indeed, there is less prejudice among people in public housing, where black and white families live together, than among people who live in segregated areas.

Competition and Conflict within a Group.   Scarcity is important in judging everything from cookies to other people (Cialdini, 1984). When there is intense competition for limited resources, prejudice and discrimination are likely to flourish. Greely and Sheatsly (1971) found that the strongest antiblack prejudice was in people who were one step above blacks on the socioeconomic scale. It was most severe when the two were in close competition for jobs.

One interesting study shows both how prejudice can develop and how we might change it (Sherif, Harvey, White, Hood, & Sherif, 1961). Twenty-two boys came to summer camp at Robbers Grave, Oklahoma. They were divided into two different groups, the "eagles" and the "rattlers." The experimenters encouraged each group to cooperate and to work together as a team toward goals, such as making improvements to the campgrounds. The first phase of the experiment was to create strong group affiliation and cohesion of a random grouping of individuals.

Once each group had become a cohesive unit, they were pitted against one another in competitive sports events. Initially, the boys showed good sportsmanship, but gradually there arose resentment, hostility, and discrimination between the teams.

In the second phase of the experiment, the goal was to decrease the ill will between the groups. Simply eliminating competition did not work. The experimenters found that when both groups worked together toward a common goal, hostility decreased and cooperation and fellowship increased. Once, a truck broke down and all the campers were needed to tow it up a hill (pulling on a large rope). The cooperative effort reduced the feelings of differences between the groups and allowed the two groups to share a sense of accomplishment and to discover similarities.

The Jigsaw Classroom.   Another systematic attempt at reducing prejudice through cooperation is the "jigsaw classroom technique" developed by Eliot Aronson. Classrooms often stress individual competition, but in this technique the stress is on interdependence. Students are divided into groups, and each group is assigned a project. Each member of the group is given information about

Prejudice seems to be reduced through increased cooperative contact with members of the prejudged group.

one part of the assignment, that is, one puzzle piece. The only way the assignment can be completed is if each member teaches and shares his or her information with the others. Thus, each person is an important and invaluable resource. In addition, the teacher gives grades based on group cooperation rather than individual effort (Aronson, 1984).

Thus, two major psychological principles can work to reduce prejudice:

1. Stereotypes can be overcome by increasing the availability of information about the groups, especially by increasing direct knowledge of a variety of individuals within the group.
2. Association and cooperation with members of a discriminated group as equals.

ATTRIBUTION

Olympic gold medal winner Mary Lou Retton promoted a certain camera. Why did she do it? Does she *really* think the camera is terrific or was she paid a large amount of money to make the commercial? The reasons we give for our own or others' behavior are **attributions.** "To what do you attribute your success?" There are, broadly, two kinds of attribution:

Dispositional: We judge that a person does something because of who he or she is. (In our example, the athlete likes the camera.)
Situational: A person does something because of his or her situation. (In our example, she wants the money.)

In Ross and Nisbett's (in press) terms, in making attributions people are "charitable," that is, we tend to overestimate the power of the person and underestimate the power of the situation.

Discounting and Covariance

What do we base attributions on? Harold Kelley (1967), in his *attribution theory,* argues that people use one of two logical rules. The first is the **discounting principle.** This is used in cases where one is forced to attribute the behavior of a single person in a single situation on a single occasion. Take the case of the Olympic medal winner's endorsement of a camera. If you explain her behavior using the discounting principle, you include only the most simple causal factors. Thus, other plausible causes or determinants are not identified. If you find that the situation is a "sufficient" explanation, you will not make a dispositional attribution.

A second principle, the **covariation principle,** is used in cases were one has multiple observations rather than a single one. For example, you may have observed Mary Lou in a number of commercials talking about a variety of products. In this case, you apply the covariation principle. You assess the degree to which her behavior occurs in the presence of, but fails in the absence of, each possible cause. You might see that she always says positive things when she is paid large sums of money but never says positive things when she is not paid money. So you might infer that money was the cause of her behavior.

Errors in Attribution

The most frequent "charitable" error in attribution is called the **fundamental attribution error** (Ross, 1977; Ross & Nisbett, in press). This is the tendency to underestimate the impact of situational forces and to overestimate the role of dispositional forces in controlling behavior. Jones and Harris (1967) found that listeners were willing to attribute a subject's pro-Castro statement to that subject's private opinions even when the listeners knew the subject was being influenced by a situational force. He was reading a prepared speech given him by the experimenter.

Recall the results of the "shocking" experiment discussed earlier. Most people (perhaps you included) are stunned by the results of this study mainly because they infer that the "teachers" who gave the maximum amount of punishment were (dispositionally) "evil." What the experiment actually demonstrates, however, is that the behavior was almost totally controlled by situational forces.

A particular type of situational force that individuals commonly overlook when making attributions are how social roles determine behavior. Social roles typically are unequal in situations; the dominant one is usually "in control." This control allows a person to display knowledge or skills while concealing various deficiencies. In these situations, people overgeneralize and make dispositional rather than situational attributions.

Ross, Amabile, and Steinmetz (1977) set up an experiment in which they randomly assigned the role of "questioner" in a "college bowl" quiz to one subject. They assigned another subject the role of "answerer." The questioner was to compose a set of challenging questions from his or her store of knowledge and to pose these questions to the answerer. Later, both subjects were asked to rate the general knowledge of both the questioner and answerer.

Before looking at the results of this experiment, note that the questioners had an advantage in this situation. They were able to *display* their own "wealth of knowledge" by composing difficult questions to which they knew the answers. (It is always easier to make up difficult questions than to answer them.) The role also guaranteed that the questioners could *conceal* their lack of knowledge in many other areas. The answerers, on the other hand, were prevented any such display. Did the subjects make allowance for this "role-based situational cause" of behavior? No. They overlooked it and inferred instead that the questioner was smarter than the answerer — a *dispositional* rather than a *situational* attribution. We charitably view the person as triumphant, when actually it is just the circumstances.

Reasons for the Fundamental Attribution Error

Although one would not expect it, there is a difference between attributions about oneself and others in at least some situations. One explanation calls on Kahneman and Tversky's principle of availability. It emphasizes that the information available to an individual performing a behavior is different from that of an observer witnessing that behavior. For example, let's use the case of an actor. The actor knows what he or she is thinking at any given moment and knows how he or she has behaved in the situation in the past. The observer is unaware of this information. This difference in information in turn can produce the differing tendency to commit the fundamental attribution error. It was shown that the more well known an actor is to an observer, the more likely the observer is to attribute the actor's behavior to situational rather than dispositional causes (Nisbett & Ross, 1981). This implies that the more information we have, the less likely we are to make the fundamental attribution error.

False Consensus

False consensus is another error; it is the tendency of individuals to *overestimate* the commonness of their own responses in a situation and to *underestimate* the commonness of the responses of others who acted differently (Ross, Greene, & House, 1977). In one study, subjects were asked to complete a questionnaire containing such questions as "Are you shy?" and "Where do you prefer to live?" The experimenters then asked them to estimate the percentage of people who responded as they did on each question. The subjects consistently overestimated the percentage of people who agreed with them.

One explanation of this error emphasizes the biased information available to each person. Much of our knowledge about the behavior of others comes from those we know and associate with. But we tend to know and associate with people who share our interests, background, and attitudes. These people usually do respond as we do in many circumstances. So we have a biased sample of information about the behavior of others. Given this, it is not surprising that we believe our behavior to be more common and representative than it actually is. Thus, according to Ross, the specific behaviors we have chosen, or would choose, are likely to be more readily retrievable from memory. They would be more easily imagined than opposite behavior. In Kahneman and Tversky's terms, the behavior choices we favor may be more cognitively "available." We are apt to be misled by this ease or difficulty of access in estimating the likelihood of relevant behavioral options (Ross, 1977).

Why Do We Make Errors in Attribution?

Occasionally the attributions people make are different than those they would make if they used the principles of discounting and covariation. Why? One obvious answer is that using these rules requires more resources and information than the individual usually has. The discounting rule requires that we have extensive knowledge of characteristics of individuals and that we can accurately assess the impact of specific situational factors such as money, social roles, and so on. We seek simple and quick judgments of everything and this information burden is just too much. It also requires a lot of time to sift through all the alternatives. In an experiment, people are usually given sufficient information and time, but in life we usually have neither. An attribution about Mary Lou Retton's behavior is a snap judgment about someone you do not know much about. You do not know how much she was paid, what she was thinking, or if she uses the products she endorses.

The covariation rule has similar limitations: it requires an individual to perform a logical and statistical task. However, in life we are not usually provided with all relevant information. There are many possible causes for each of the many behaviors we witness each day. When judging a celebrity endorsement, we do not know how the person has acted in other situations or in the same situation on other occasions. Nor do we know how other people have acted in the same situation. Lack of information and the principle of simplicity leads us to rely on the available information, which may be biased or unrepresentative.

So we follow the *same* principles in judging others as we do in thinking, feeling, and remembering. We *select* and *simplify* and use the information *available* to come to the best and quickest assessment. We use comparison and interpretation. Luckily, the simplifying system probably helps us more than it hurts. Most of us seem successful in our ordinary judgments for the most part. Psychologists are, of course, interested in the errors and distortions because they allow us to study the process of judgment and attribution.

Love

LOVE AND ATTRACTION

Of all our relationships with others, those involving love probably inspired the most comment. It is easy to see why: being in love is among the best and most treasured experiences of life. Being without love is often dismal. The experience of love is complex and involves intense feelings of ecstasy, despair, and uncertainty. We do not know when love will strike or why it goes away. Love is a complicated, private experience, involving intense and intimate feelings. Therefore, it is tricky to study and difficult to analyze scientifically. Many people do not want any of the secrets of love subjected to the ''cold eye'' of science. In 1975, Senator William Proxmire of Wisconsin denounced the federal government for funding research on love:

> I believe that 200 million other Americans want to leave some things in life a mystery, and right at the top of things we don't want to know is why a man falls in love with a woman and vice versa. . . . So National Science Foundation — get out of the love racket. Leave that to Elizabeth Barrett Browning and Irving Berlin. Here, if anywhere, Alexander Pope was right when he observed, ''If ignorance is bliss, 'tis folly to be wise.''

However, the senator is wrong, on many accounts. Love relationships are central in people's lives, and disruption of them is a major cause of personal distress. The most common precipitating factor in severe depression and suicides is disruption of a love relationship. People are hungry for information. Why do we fall in love with a certain person? Why does love turn to hate? Do opposites attract? Love stories are best-selling books; songs exalt or lament over love. Newspaper columnists and advisors to the lovelorn prosper by the thousands. A scientific analysis, flawed as it might be, would begin to expose some of the essential components of love.

In addition, one might want to study love out of sheer curiosity about the hows and whys of a most prized human emotion. It is no less interesting or important than how and why memory works. In a world troubled by wars and discord in national and private affairs, learning how love works seems an important task.

Characteristics of People in Love

Something dramatic happens to us when we are in love (Argyle & Henderson, 1985). When you love someone, that person is suddenly unique, the central person in your world. You may act differently around your lover than around anyone else. The language we use to describe love uses images of movement and distance. We "fall" in love, lovers are "inclined" toward one another, lovers are "close," "as one." The physical and verbal expressions of closeness are related. It is quite easy to tell who are the lovers and who are not. There are three characteristics that researchers have observed as indicators of interest: inclination, closeness, and eye contact.

"Inclination" toward Another.   Francis Galton in 1884 first proposed that the ordinary metaphors of speech are useful for the scientific student of love. He wrote: "When two persons have an 'inclination' to one another they visibly incline or slope together when sitting side by side. . . ." Galton never got around to testing this idea empirically, but experimenters recently have done so. They measured the posture of people in situations in which they confront people they like and dislike. They found that we lean toward those we like and away from those we dislike.

Closeness.   When we are in love, we feel "close" to the other person. Couples walking with distance between them seem less in love than those entwined arm in arm. In one study, men and women students were introduced and sent off for a coke on a 30-minute "blind date." When they returned they were asked to rate their date's attractiveness. Unknown to the students, the psychologists also rated how closely the couples stood when they returned. There was a high relationship. The more the couple reported liking one another, the closer they stood to each other (Hatfield & Sprecher, 1986).

Gaze.   When two people are close to one another, each looks more often into the other's eyes. People who like one another more look more into each other's eyes than those who do not (Argyle & Henderson, 1985).

Excitement of Sexual Love

Love is a grand stirring up of feeling and probably depends on activation more than most other experiences. Walster and her colleagues (1966) sent a group of men on blind dates. They then asked them to come to the lab to fill out a questionnaire. While they were waiting, half were given fairly boring reading material and half were given *Playboy* and other similar magazines. The experimenters thought that the *Playboy* magazines would be more arousing and would lead to a higher rating of attractiveness of the "blind date." This hypothesis was confirmed (Hatfield & Sprecher, 1986).

See Chapter 1, section on Thinking Like an Experimental Psychologist.

Many studies confirm the importance of arousal in sexual attraction. The men on the wobbly bridge in the Dutton and Aron experiment interpreted their arousal (from the danger) as attraction. In other experiments, those given false feedback on their heart rates and those aroused by exercise also showed increased attraction. The arousal component of love can help make sense of a common problem that occurs when love ends. Many people report that they strongly hate someone they once loved. At first glance that seems odd, but perhaps it is due to the arousal component of sexual love. When the affair ends, the strong positive feelings are replaced by equally strong negative feelings that have been *amplified* by the arousal.

Obstacles to love, such as short separations and the exciting effects of dangerous exploits, heighten intensity. Women who are hard to get are often thought to

Each of these couples has the look of people who are passionately in love.

be the most desirable. One man, after kidnapping his former lover, said, "The fact that she rejected me only made me want to love her more." The philosopher Bertrand Russell (quoted in Tennov, 1979) wrote: "The belief in the immense value of the lady is a psychological effect of the difficulty of obtaining her, and I think it may be laid down that when a man has no difficulty in obtaining a woman, his feeling toward her does not take the form of romantic love."

Passionate and Companionate Love

The strong form of "being in love" is **passionate love.** It is a state of intense absorption, arousal, and longing for another. This experience seems to have some similar aspects among many people. It is involuntary and there are times when many people wish they were not in love. The French writer Stendahl once commented that if he were murdered while he was in the throes of an unrequited passion, he would thank the murderer before he died. The experience often includes these "systems":

1. Thinking of the object of desire almost all the time. The person involved intrudes into thinking; attention is narrowed to him or her. One so involved wrote: "Love is a human religion in which another person is believed in."
2. Longing for reciprocation.
3. Dependency of mood on the other's reactions.
4. Inability to react in the same way to more than one person at a time.
5. Fear of rejection.
6. Intensification through adversity.
7. Emphasis and focus on positive qualities of the person, ignoring all negative ones (Tennov, 1979).

In time, however, most passionate relationships fade. Arousal is dependent on novelty, so it is probably impossible to maintain such intense feeling for long. When the initial passion fades, there are two possibilities. Either the relationship is burned out and over, or it develops into the more sober kind of "everyday" love, **companionate love** (Walster & Walster, 1980). This involves less arousal and excitement, but more friendly affection and deep attachment. Companionate love, to be sure, has its moments of passion, but these do not usurp all other concerns.

Falling in Love

What causes us to fall in love, and what are the characteristics of this "fall"? Each love experience is different, yet there are some similarities of all love experiences.

It is commonly thought that women are the romantics; their lives are said to be organized more around love, while men are thought to be more concerned with work, money, and other activities. But here the data contradict that common assumption. Hobart (1958) asked hundreds of men and women questions about romance. He found that men are much more likely to be romantics than women are. Men fall in love faster and have a more romantic view of love relationships than women do. In another study, 20 percent of men fell in love before their fourth date, while 15 percent of women did. Also, it is usually the woman who ends the affair and the men who suffer more (Walster, Walster, & Traupmann, 1978).

Relationship between Attractiveness and Loving

We want someone to love us for ourselves—not for external qualities such as a pretty face. However, physical attractiveness is very important in the initial tumble into love. In one study (Walster, Aronson, Abrahams, & Rottmann, 1966), a panel of college students rated the physical attractiveness of 752 college freshmen. Afterward other information regarding their intelligence, personality, and attitudes was also assembled.

Then the experimenters staged a dance at which the freshmen were randomly assigned a date. The freshmen were later asked how satisfied they were with their date. They were asked how eager they were for another date, and whether they would ask the person out. *The only determinant of interest was physical attractiveness.* Another study found that physical attractiveness was more related to a woman's popularity than to a man's. There was a strong correlation between a woman's physical attractiveness and the number of dates, but the relationship was slight for men (Hatfield & Sprecher, 1986).

Physical attractiveness may be most important at the beginning of a love relationship; with time other "more real" factors come into play. However, the evidence so far disagrees with those who believe that "love" does not depend upon "mere physical" attributes.

Attractiveness

Human sensitivity to scarcity makes anyone who is difficult to meet seem more valuable. In one study of a singles bar, researchers in Virginia randomly selected customers. They asked them to rate the attractiveness of individuals of the opposite sex who were present three hours, two hours, and then one-half hour before closing. The results were surprising. Those remaining one-half hour before clos-

Many older couples still retain a deep sense of warm affection called companionate love.

SHOPLIFTING AND GOOD LOOKS

In one study (Mace, 1972), 440 young men and women were asked to shoplift merchandise from ten markets in a large city. Clerks were less likely to accuse shoplifters who were well-groomed and neatly dressed than those who were sloppily groomed. Customers were also more likely to report shoplifters of undesirable appearance. In two grocery stores and a discount department store, an accomplice blatantly shoplifted in the presence of customers. The shoplifter looked like a typical professional out on a shopping break. Very few people reported the thefts.

In contrast, a "hippie" shoplifter (this study took place in the mid-1970s) was described in great detail in the following way: "He wore soiled patched blue jeans, blue workman's shirt, and blue denim jacket; well-worn, scuffed shoes with no socks. He had long and unruly hair with a ribbon tied around his forehead. He was unshaven and had a small beard" (Stefensmeyer & Terry, 1973). Thus, hippie shoplifters were not only more likely to be reported, but they were reported with more enthusiasm. "That [expletive] hippie over there stuffed a banana down his coat." Apparently, good looks pay off, even when committing a crime. We are less suspicious of attractive people.

What other effects does a person's attractiveness have on others? In another study people were asked to watch a well-dressed or a slovenly woman shoplifting. The "detectives" were asked how upset the woman would probably be if she were caught, tried, and convicted of shoplifting. Observers felt that the well-dressed woman would suffer most if she were convicted of shoplifting. They thought she would be emotionally upset and concerned about what her family and friends would think of her than the scruffy woman would be (Deseran & Chung, 1979).

---

ing were judged the best looking. This is when the chances to meet and strike up a conversation were becoming less and less, scarcer and scarcer (Pennebacker et al., 1979).

One of the quickest ways to judge people is by their appearance. Clothes, manner of speech, skin color, and sex often overwhelm other considerations. So many long-held stereotypes may be influenced by the overwhelming amount of exterior information (appearance) we receive about people.

It is easy to misconstrue the applicability of the immediate impressions from the physical features of others. One survey of college graduates showed that those six feet two inches tall and over had starting salaries of $125 per week higher than those shorter than six feet. Tall people are judged more trustworthy and generous as well (Deck, 1968).

Unfortunately, this bias affects more than just trivial matters. The same processes are at work in judging job worth and political capabilities. Consider this: in all presidential elections from 1900 to 1968, the taller candidate won. So impressed was the Carter campaign by this fact that when Jimmy Carter had to meet Gerald Ford in debate, he insisted that their lecturns be placed far apart. Even the ritual handshake was analyzed. Carter stood far away and extended his hand as far as possible, then walked away, minimizing the time they were on the screen together (Keyes, 1980).

Surface attractiveness is important to us in selecting a mate and planning a family, especially to males (Argyle & Henderson, 1985). Beauty is slightly more than skin deep. It indicates good health and thus good reproductive potential. A clean skin may signify freedom from disease. And someone who is not fat is more likely to be healthy.

Attractiveness and Criminals

While most of us believe that attractiveness is important for sex and loving, we do not think that attractiveness should play a role in the courtroom. But there is clear evidence that most people are unable to put their default positions aside and to act on their convictions. Criminologists have collected evidence showing that if defendants are good-looking people, they are less likely to get caught at illicit activities. If caught, they are less likely to be reported. And if the case comes to court, judges and jurors are more likely to be lenient with them.

Whenever juries decide, they are presumed to use all the information they acquire to come to the right decision. Because of the tendency of the mind to ignore the familiar, unusual or incongruous information may have great influence. Solomon and Schopler (1978) hypothesized that we might judge unusually attractive defendants most leniently. We assume that "what is beautiful is good." Homely defendants may also be judged compassionately out of pity. An average-looking defendant, however, does not get the benefit of the doubt for either reason. Thus, he or she may get the harshest sentence.

Students at the University of North Carolina evaluated a fake case of a young woman accused of hustling $10,000. The woman was presented to the "jury" as attractive, average-looking, or unattractive. The attractive woman got the most magnanimous sentence of 12 months. The unattractive women had an average prison sentence of 18 and a half months. The average-looking woman, however, received the most restrictive sentence of all — the men wanted to lock her up for 19 and a half months (Solomon & Schopler, 1978).

Do you think the attractiveness of John and Christina Delorean (shown here after his acquittal) influenced the outcome of the trial?

The sentencing of a rapist may depend not only on his crime, but also on his looks. Test yourself on this. Suppose you heard a description such as the following (Jacobsen, 1981, adapted from Jones & Aronson, 1973).

> It was ten o'clock at night and Judy W. was getting out of an evening class at a large Midwestern university. She walked across the campus toward her car, which was parked two blocks off campus. A man was walking across the campus in the same direction as Judy W. and began to follow her.
>
> Less than a block from Judy W.'s car, the man accosted her. In the ensuing struggle, he stripped her and raped her. A passerby heard her screams and called the police. They arrived at the scene within minutes.
>
> Judy W. told the police that she had never seen her attacker before that night. Based on her description, the police arrested Charles E., a student whom they found in the vicinity of the attack. Judy W. positively identified Charles E. as the man who raped her. Charles E. swore that he was innocent. He testified that he was just taking a break from studying by going out for a walk and that it was just a coincidence that he was in the vicinity and that it was a coincidence that he matched Judy W.'s description of her attacker.

Again, in a psychology experiment Charles E. was depicted as either good-looking or ugly. When described as a handsome man, both men and women "judges" (subjects in the experiment) were likely to think he was just out for a walk and that his resemblance to the rapist was coincidental. Not so if Charles E. was described as ugly: then they saw him as guilty.

The subjects were also asked how long a prison sentence they would recommend for Charles E. if he were found guilty. The good-looking Charles E. was given a 10-year sentence, but the homely version was given almost 14 years in prison! Ugliness may be dangerous to your freedom.

The looks of the victim were also important. Judges were more likely to assume Charles E. was guilty when Judy W. was alluring. They were less sympathetic to a rapist of an attractive woman than to a rapist of an unattractive woman (Jacobsen, 1981; Hatfield & Sprecher, 1986). The snap judgments of prejudice and attractiveness are difficult to overcome.

AGGRESSION AND VIOLENCE

Aggression is intentionally harming another. The injury caused by aggression can be psychological (for example, due to verbal abuse) as well as physical (Bandura, 1986). Aggression is an attribution as well as an act. Whether one judges an act to be aggressive depends on one's values. This, in turn, partly depends on one's culture and place in it. Some types of harm-causing behavior are almost universally considered legitimate and not "aggressive," for example, self-defense. The harm caused by favored members of society is usually attributed to accident or circumstance, but when harm is caused by disfavored members it is attributed instead to personal intent (Bandura, 1986). A peace march may be considered "nonviolent protest" or "aggressive provocation" depending on the interpretation.

It is possible to distinguish two basic types of aggression. *Hostile aggression* is motivated by anger or hatred and is intended only to make the victim suffer. *Instrumental aggression* is motivated by an incentive, usually economic. The victim may be injured incidentally, as when a purse snatcher causes an old lady to

fall, breaking her hip. Undoubtedly, hostile and instrumental aggression are often combined in the same act.

Approaches to Aggression

Freud

Freud held that aggression is an instinct. He called it *Thanatos* or the death instinct. This is a destructive energy that accumulates until it is discharged either inwardly or outwardly, as in self-destructive behavior or in the destruction of others. He believed that, as an instinct, aggression could never be eliminated from human beings. "The aim of life," he wrote, "is death." As with other instincts, our innate aggression was more useful in the days before settled society. Then killing one's enemies was important for survival. Civilization puts curbs on aggression and makes it necessary for us to redirect these instinctual urges (Ibister, 1986).

See Chapter 14, section on Psychoanalysis.

Ethology

Like Freud, ethologists contend that aggression is instinctive. Lorenz (1966) and others proposed a complex theory of aggression. Here is a simplified version. In animals, aggression is most often directed at other species. Animals have evolved innate *inhibitions* against fatal aggression toward members of their *own* species. These inhibitions involve either behavior patterns or physical characteristics. Coloration "turns off" an aggressor before he can do serious damage. *The strength of the inhibition corresponds to the strength of a species' offensive weapons.* Thus, wolves, as predators, are well equipped for violence and also have strong inhibitions against killing other wolves.

However, the human inheritance has provided us with very weak "natural" instruments of physical aggression. We are weak for our size and we do not have the strength of a tiger nor the jaws of a shark. Since we inherit weak weapons, we also *inherit weak inhibitions* on personal aggression. However, human beings can go beyond their inheritance. We have invented weapons that are vastly more destructive than any inherited ones. But we have not evolved corresponding inhibitions.

Our lack of inhibition against violence toward members of our own species explains why we have become so dangerous to ourselves. A whole city can be destroyed by the push of a button by someone in an underground fortification.

Social Learning Theory

According to social learning theory, there is no simple aggressive instinct (Bandura, 1986). The biological basis of aggression is the same as that of all learning. Organisms, especially human beings, have the ability to learn vicariously. They learn by observing the behavior of models, especially people who are perceived as important controllers of reward and punishment (Bandura, 1986). Thus, nonaggressive models are useful in reducing aggression in others (Baron & Kepner, 1970) and appear to be more effective than threats of retaliation. Threatened punishment works to subdue aggression, but only if certain conditions are satisfied (Baron, 1977):

1. The instrumental value of the aggression is low, that is, there is little to be gained by aggression.
2. The threatened punishment is severe.
3. The potential aggressor understands that punishment is highly likely.
4. The potential aggressor is not very angry.

Aggressive behavior is not elicited merely by learning how to do it, but by rewards and punishments, both experienced and anticipated. It is based on what the learners observe to be the consequences of others' behavior, as well as of theirs (Bandura, 1986).

Factors That Affect Aggression

There are several factors that affect the aggressive response.

1. *Arousal.*   In addition to incentives and provocation, environmental factors that affect arousal also can influence the likelihood of aggressive behavior. Physiological arousal increases the probability of aggression, but only when aggression has become a dominant response (Zillman, Johnson, & Day, 1974). A high level of sexual arousal increases aggression, and a low level inhibits it, presumably by simply distracting attention from the provocation (Bandura, 1986).
2. *Crowding* is an intensifier of feelings, pleasant or unpleasant. If one is in an aggressive mood, crowding is likely to make one feel more aggressive (Freedman, 1975).
3. *Noise* increases the chance of aggressive behavior when aggression is dominant in the response hierarchy (Bandura, 1986).
4. *High temperatures* also facilitate violence. The long, hot summer has been implicated in the precipitation of urban riots. Riots occur relatively more frequently in very hot weather (Carlsmith & Anderson, 1979).

5. *Alcohol* in small amounts tends to reduce aggression, while larger amounts make aggression more likely (Taylor, Gammon, & Capasso, 1976).
6. *Marijuana* in large amounts inhibits aggression (Taylor, Vardaris, Rawitch, Gammon, Cranston, & Lubetkin, 1976).
7. *Tranquilizers* surprisingly do not lessen aggressive behavior. In fact, they may even increase it. Tranquilizing drugs seem to work by interfering with the transmission of the neurotransmitter norepinephrine, associated with general arousal. They provide evidence that aggression is not a function of mere arousal. Cognitive interpretation of physiological state is crucial (Bandura 1986).

There are also personality differences in aggression. Comparatively low aggression is found among people with a high need for social approval (Taylor, 1970). People who feel that they have some control over what happens to them (internal locus of control) are more likely to use aggression as a means to an end. Those who feel that they cannot affect what happens to them no matter what they do probably will not use aggression as much. Persons with Type A personalities —highly competitive, "driven" types—exhibit more aggression when strongly provoked than Type B personalities (Carver & Glass, 1977).

Urban Environments

See Chapter 18, section on The Built Environment.

An important determinant of violence is *city size.* Large cities are more prone to violence and crime than small cities and rural areas (Fischer, 1976). Does this mean that city violence is due to the large number of violence-prone individuals who dwell in cities?

A member of a *large crowd* may tend to act with less inhibition than an individual alone. Similarly, residents of large cities seem more likely to indulge in vandalism than those who live in less urban areas. Zimbardo (1973) demonstrated this by abandoning a car in New York City (large urban area) and a similar car in Palo Alto, California (a much smaller urban area) (Figure 17-6). In New York, the car was systematically looted and vandalized, beginning within 10 minutes. Surprisingly, this violence was not started by juvenile delinquents, but by a middle-class family who stripped the car of valuable parts. In Palo Alto, however, the car stood untouched for a week, except for one thoughtful passerby who lowered the hood to prevent the engine from getting wet during a rainstorm! Zimbardo did not

**FIGURE 17-6
Environment and Aggression**
A car abandoned in New York City, as part of an experiment in the motives for vandalism, began being stripped within minutes by various people, including a "respectable" middle-class family (far right). When a car was similarly abandoned on a street in Palo Alto, California—a much smaller urban area—it went untouched for a week.

conclude that New Yorkers are inherently more violent than Californians, but that large, urban environments disinhibit aggression.

Television and Violence

Since television is so available to all, any situation it portrays is amplified. There have been many instances of violence, some quite brutal, which were imitated from television. Television shows the world as a violent place, and the content of programs exaggerates the amount of crime in society. The viewing of so much crime has its effects. The heavy television viewer perceives society as more violent than the light viewer (Gerbner & Gross, 1976).

Adults as well as children appear to learn violent behavior from television. The wide television exposure of the first airplane hijacking in the United States was followed quickly by a number of hijackings. In another case, a child put ground glass into his parents' dinner. He said he wanted to see if it would work as well as it did on television (Liebert & Baron, 1972). When reports of Tylenol being laced with cyanide were shown on news programs, a series of other tamperings and poisonings followed. The movie "The Doomsday Flight" was a story about a bomb threat to an airliner. In the week following its airing, there were 12 bomb threats to airlines. This was an 800 percent increase from the previous month (Liebert & Baron, 1972).

The exact imitation of aggressive models on television has also been observed in the laboratory. Children observed an adult beat up a bobo doll. They imitated the behavior almost exactly when given the opportunity (Bandura, Ross, & Ross, 1961). The photographs in Figure 1-2 indicate the extent of the imitation. The children exhibited the same amount of violence whether the aggressive model was a film actor or a cartoon character. Comparable results have been obtained from older children and young adults viewing movies of actual violence or television programs. The viewing of violent programs, as indicated in many studies, increases the general aggressiveness of the viewers (Baron, 1977).

See Chapter 1, Figure 1-2.

Because children learn much of their behavior through imitation, those who watch violent television shows are more likely to exhibit aggressiveness in their own behavior.

The exact imitation of an aggressive model on television is comparatively rare. However, continuous observation of aggressive models as on television can lead to more *generalized* aggressiveness (Bandura, 1986). This is accomplished by such mechanisms as:

1. Increasing arousal, especially among children (Osborn & Endsley, 1971).
2. Lowering restraint, making aggression more likely in conjunction with provocation or an aggressive model.
3. Desensitization: Adults who view a lot of violent television have a lower physiological response to violent scenes than those who watch less violence.

We cannot directly blame television *itself* for violent behavior. The *content* of television programs responds to demand; programs with aggression and violence are popular. However, many studies and reports of the effect of television on violence are clear: televised violence does increase the probability of violent behavior among viewers.

LEARNING TO CHANGE HARMFUL SITUATIONS

Milgram, Zimbardo, and others have demonstrated the complaisant way ordinary people can harm others. How can we learn to avoid doing harm? Social learning theory and ethology provide us with two important possibilities.

1. Through observation people can learn not only antisocial behavior, but also **prosocial behavior.** For instance, the presence of two disobedient models removed the obedience of most subjects in Milgram's "shocking" experiment (Milgram, 1974).
2. Ethologists believe that the more closely we observe the suffering of others, the less likely we are to harm them. The Milgram experiment illustrates this: when the "teachers" (subjects) heard more of the suffering of the "students," the level of the maximum shock they delivered tended to be lower. The closer they were, the less they shocked them (Milgram, 1974).

And consider this: if it takes only a short time to turn a person into a harmful guard (as in the mock prison study), what would it take to make a hero? Now that social psychologists have demonstrated how much harm can be caused, they may turn to how they can help society (Lynn & Oldenquist, 1986).

SUMMARY

1. The theory of how we judge ourselves in relation to others is called *social comparison,* which states that if there is no objective measure of comparison, we seek out other people and compare our attitudes or behaviors to theirs. We compare ourselves to those we admire or whom we believe are like us. The group we choose to compare ourselves to is the *reference group.* The pressure that forces us to try to be like everyone else is *social pressure* or *conformity pressure.*

2. An important experiment on obedience to authority was performed by Milgram in which men responded to an ad for participants in a psychology experiment. These subjects were given the role of "teacher" and were told to administer an electric shock (from 15 to 450 volts) to a "learner" each time he made a mistake. (In reality, the learner was a confederate of the experimenters, received no actual shocks, and merely acted out being shocked.) The results were astounding. More than 60 percent of the "teachers" in the experiment complied completely with the experimenter's request and gave the maximum shock. In one variation of the experiment no one gave less than 300 volts.

3. Opinions and social influence in a group cause us to conform. In a study by Asch, volunteers were solicited for an experiment on visual perception. When six observers, who were confederates of the experimenter, all denied that one line length was the same as another, their obviously incorrect answer influenced the real subject of the experiment, the new member of the group. Of these real subjects, 32 percent conformed and also gave the wrong answer. The pressure of even a group formed by a random collection of strangers is considerable. In other studies it has been shown that social pressure can change people's beliefs. Important factors in conformity are group unanimity and group size. The more unanimous the other people's opinions and the larger the group, the more likely you are to conform.

4. Attitudes typically consist of several components: cognitive, emotional, and behavioral. *Cognitive consistency* theories attempt to define exactly how we achieve consistency among our attitudes. *Cognitive dissonance* occurs whenever an individual holds two cognitions (e.g., beliefs, attitudes, or knowledge of behaviors) that are inconsistent with one another. In an important experiment, people were asked to perform an extremely boring task and to tell another waiting person that they liked the task. People who were paid $1 for the experiment experienced dissonance and actually believed that the task was pleasant, whereas another group, which was paid $20, persisted in believing the task was dull. This finding may have general implications: perhaps the fewer inducements that are provided for someone to do something, the more likely an attitude change will occur.

5. *Prejudice* is a negative judgmental attitude toward an identifiable group of people based on a simplistic overgeneralization. Prejudice derives from mechanisms similar to others we use to experience the world, such as simplification and creation of prototypes. However, when a prototype is overextended it becomes a *stereotype,* and we then attribute identical characteristics to all members of a group. If a stereotype is widely accepted, it can have lasting effects on the group so labeled. One way to overcome prejudice is to increase contact with the prejudged group. The more you know about people, the less likely you are to make sweeping judgments about them. A systematic attempt to use the principle of cooperation between groups, also known to reduce prejudice, is called *cooperative interdependence.*

6. An important factor in developing *attributions* is the *discounting principle,* used in cases in which one is forced to attribute the behavior of a single person in a single situation on a single occasion. If you find that a celebrity was paid a large amount of money to endorse a product, you may discount the importance of other information. But if the celebrity's endorsement occurred in spite of situational forces and the commercial was done for free, you might believe the endorser really did like the camera. A second principle, *covariation,* is used in cases where we have multiple observations. If you observe a celebrity in a number of commercials endorsing a variety of products, you may note that the endorser always says positive things when paid a sum of money. Then, you might correctly infer that money was the cause of this behavior.

7. The *fundamental attribution error* is the tendency to underestimate the impact of situational forces and to overestimate the role of dispositional forces in controlling behavior. We typically overlook the degree to which social roles determine behavior and overgeneralize from a small bit of evidence. The reason for this error is that the information available to the person behaving is different from the person observing the behavior. We tend to make attribution errors because avoiding them requires more resources and information than we usually have. As with everything else we do, in making judgments about other people we select, simplify, and use the available information to come to the best and quickest assessment.

8. *Aggression* is intentionally harming another. It is an attribution as well as an act because what one judges to be aggressive depends on one's culture and one's place in it. There are two types of aggression. Hostile aggression is motivated by anger and hatred, and instrumental aggression is motivated by an incentive, usually economic. The two often are combined in the same act. Freud considered aggression an instinct, calling it *Thanatos* or the death instinct. Because civilization puts curbs on aggression, Freud contended that it becomes necessary for us to redirect our destructive instinctual urges.

9. Ethologists also see aggression as instinctual. Animals have evolved innate inhibitions against fatal aggression toward members of their own species, and the strength of this inhibition corresponds to the strength of a species' offensive weapons. However, the human inheritance has provided us with weak natural instruments of physical aggression. We are weak for our size, and since we inherit weak weapons, we also inherit weak inhibitions on personal aggression. Human beings have developed weapons that are vastly more destructive than any inherited ones, but we have not evolved corresponding inhibitions. This lack of inhibition against violence toward members of our own species explains why, under the circumstances, we have become so dangerous to ourselves.

10. *Social learning theory* holds that there is no necessarily aggressive instinct and that a threatened punishment usually works to subdue aggression. Factors that affect aggressive response are arousal, crowding, noise, hot weather, and use of drugs such as alcohol, marijuana, and tranquilizers. Watching televised aggression can also lead to more generalized aggressiveness. This is accomplished by such means as: (a) increasing arousal, especially among children, (b) lowering restraint, and (c) desensitization. Adults who view a lot of violent television have a lower physiological response to violent scenes than those who watch less violence.

11. Psychologists have devoted some study to specific situations that cause people to behave aggressively. In an important study, Zimbardo sought to investigate the degree to which behavior can be situationally determined. He simulated a "prison" in the basement of Stanford University and found that student subjects soon took on their assigned social roles of prisoners and guards. The "prisoners" assumed a weak and submissive role, and many of the "guards" behaved in a corrupt and threatening manner. The experiment caused so much distress that it had to be terminated after only six days.

12. Two important ways that we may learn to avoid aggression and develop *prosocial behavior* are (a) through observation of other people behaving in a prosocial way and (b) by more closely observing the suffering of others. We are then less likely to harm them. It seems a human being needs feedback from other individuals that harm is being done.

aggression
attitudes
attractiveness
attribution
coaction effect
cognitive consistency
cognitive dissonance
companionate love
conformity pressure
covariation principle

discounting principle
fundamental attribution error
machiavellian
passionate love
prejudice
prosocial behavior
reference group
social comparison
social pressure
stereotype

TERMS AND CONCEPTS

Argyle, M., & Henderson, M. (1985). *The anatomy of relationships.* New York: Penguin Books.

> *Information about attraction, marriage, friendship, and life as it unfolds. The conclusions are not always compelling, but the evidence is intriguing.*

Cialdini, R. (1984). *Influence.* Chicago: Scott Foresman.

> *An excellent book about how social psychological principles influence our decisions. Well worth reading and important.*

Hatfield, E., & Sprecher, S. (1986). *Mirror, mirror: The importance of looks in everyday life.* New York: SUNY Press.

> *An excellent summary of research on attractiveness, second only in value to Cialdini's book.*

Milgram, S. (1974). *Obedience to authority: An experimental view.* New York: Harper & Row.

> *The famous study, well presented by its author.*

SUGGESTIONS FOR FURTHER READING

Chapter 18

Living in a High-tech World

Life did not start out well for Mary. Her mother's pregnancy developed after many unsuccessful attempts to conceive. Her mother was very overweight and had medical problems during pregnancy; she was hospitalized three times for severe false labor and was in labor for 20 hours. During childhood her parents had money problems and her mother had to work outside the home. Between Mary's fifth and tenth birthdays, her mother had several major illnesses and surgeries. She had two hospitalizations for "unbearable tension," nervousness, annoyance with her children, and fears that she might harm them.

At 18 Mary described herself. "If I say how I am it sounds like bragging—I have a good personality and people like me. I don't like it when people think they can run my own life—I like to be my own judge. I know right from wrong, but I feel I have a lot more to learn and go through. Generally, I hope I can make it—I hope." She planned to enroll in college and was keeping her future career goals open. She had high self-esteem and was outgoing, persistent, and concerned for others.

Mary was one of 700 children growing up in Hawaii who were tracked from birth into their early 20s. They came of age during the years from 1955 to 1979—a time of unprecedented social change. They had to confront war in Southeast Asia and, later, a huge influx of tourists into Hawaii. They witnessed the assassination of one president and the resignation of another. They were the first generation encountering television, contraceptive pills, and mind-altering drugs. By all standards these children were at high risk. They were born and raised in poverty and reared by mothers with little education. They had many learning and behavioral problems in childhood and adolescence.

Yet some endured and thrived while challenging stresses. They developed into competent, autonomous adults who worked well, played well, loved well, and expected well. How were these people able to adapt? Furthermore, how do *any* of us adapt to the modern world? (See Plate 17.) The changes Mary encountered are not really unusual. Many people who are alive today were born when the automobile was a curiosity and there were no airplanes, televisions, radios, refrigerators, freeways, frozen dinners, paperback books, tape recorders, computers, antibiotics, or nuclear weapons.

Anyone who is now over 50 was born into a world where a majority of the present countries did not even exist, and there were less than half the number of people on earth than there are today. At the time of the birth of those who are now over 75, there had never been a world war, electricity and pasteurization were rare, and one out of every three people died in childhood.

All of us in current society live in an unprecedented world. No one can visualize two billion people dying within one-half hour from a nuclear war. For much more than 99 percent of its history, humanity never faced a problem of this magnitude. We did not evolve to comprehend the problems of the colossal number of people (five billion human beings) who are alive today. We face problems of a scale and speed of change for which history and biology has left us poorly prepared. Senses, perception, memory, thought, and social judgment evolved in a stable, small, simple, and slow world, now long gone. The "problems" pose unprecedented, even incalculable dangers. You are only a few hundred generations away from the agricultural revolution, and only about 2,000 generations from Neanderthal.

Because these changes are so new, they are also new to the study of psychology. But understanding them is important. Thus, this chapter is presented as an essay and an introductory look at the present world around us. Time is running out on us as a species, so it is now vital that we learn to comprehend how different our world is from the world that made us. This mismatch in the worlds, *the world that made us* and *the world we made,* is in part responsible for many of our misjudgments about current events. It creates stress and the problems of forging a new world. Psychologists are attempting to help in the adaptation by confronting stress and analyzing the mental mismatches. A new psychology of health has been developed and the "new world" of computers, buildings, and travel is being studied.

ADAPTING TO CHANGES IN THE WORLD

Emergency Reaction

Imagine that you are a nurse who works in the evening. To get home you must walk a few blocks to your car through a dangerous area. It's dark, and only a few people are around. You begin to hear footsteps behind you, but when you turn around, there's no one there. You start walking faster, but the footsteps keep pace. You remember that a nurse was mugged last week not too far from here and you begin to feel afraid. Your heart starts to pound, your mouth gets dry, and your hands get clammy. The footsteps get closer, and you can't decide if you should run for it or turn and face the "mugger."

Suddenly you whirl around and you see a person in the shadows who seems huge and menacing. A man steps into the light and then you realize that it's just the security guard, who offers to escort you to your car. Although you feel relieved, you worry about the next night and wonder if you shouldn't switch to the day shift.

This is an example of our most basic and immediate reaction to stress, called the **emergency reaction.** It includes both the fight-or-flight reaction and the general adaptation syndrome.

Fight-or-Flight

See Chapter 12, section on Activation of Emergency Reaction.

If our prehistoric ancestors were confronted by a charging animal, it would be adaptive if they were instantly aroused. They would be ready for action — to fight or to flee (Cannon, 1929). This **fight-or-flight** emergency reaction (Figure 18-1) is mediated by the sympathetic nervous system and includes these changes:

1. The rate and strength of the heartbeat increase, allowing oxygen to be pumped more rapidly.
2. The spleen contracts, releasing stored red blood cells to carry this oxygen.
3. The liver releases stored sugar for the use of the muscles.
4. The blood supply is redistributed from the skin and viscera to the muscles and brain.
5. Respiration deepens.
6. The pupils dilate.
7. The blood's ability to seal wounds is increased (Gray, 1984).

Thus, there are a variety of physiological systems at work within us that respond directly to immediate stress.

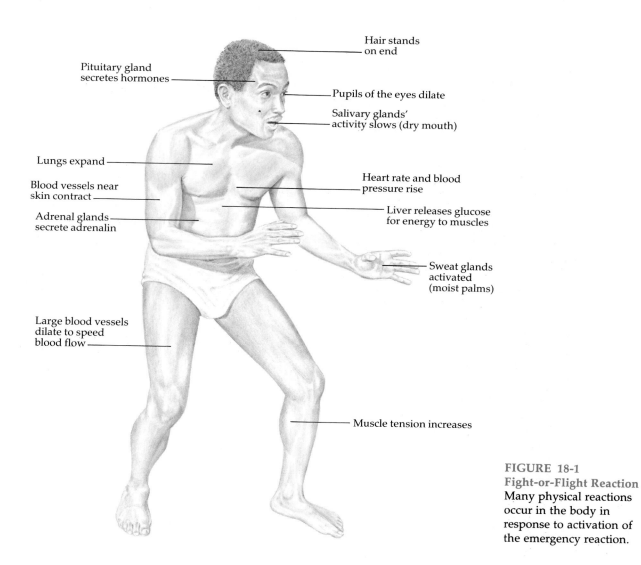

FIGURE 18-1
Fight-or-Flight Reaction
Many physical reactions occur in the body in response to activation of the emergency reaction.

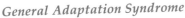

Hans Selye

General Adaptation Syndrome

As a medical student in the 1920s, Hans Selye, the main proponent of the stress concept, noticed something that eluded his professors. No matter what type of illness a patient had, one thing was common to all—they all *looked* sick.

Selye called this response the **general adaptation syndrome** and identified three stages. First is the *alarm reaction,* which prepares the organism for immediate flight or fight. Then comes the *resistance* stage in which many of the physiological changes associated with the alarm reaction are reversed. The organism has increased resistance to the stressor. Selye subjected rats to prolonged cold for five weeks. These animals, having developed resistance, withstood colder temperatures than rats that had been kept at room temperatures. The third stage, *exhaustion,* occurs when the body's ability to adapt runs out. After several months of cold, the rats lost their resistance and became less tolerant of the cold than ordinary rats. At this point they were very prone to sickness and death.

To explain this, we need to look at how the emergency reaction is mediated by the sympathetic nervous system (SNS). Its synapses directly stimulate the heart to beat faster and direct the peripheral blood vessels to clamp down. Chemical neurotransmitters at these synapses are epinephrine and norepinephrine. The SNS stimulates the adrenal medulla to secrete epinephrine and less norepinephrine, which are doubly assured of reaching the target organs.

If the emergency reaction is extreme or occurs over a long period, it brings on the general adaptation syndrome. Then the hypothalamus stimulates the pituitary gland to release an important hormone called ACTH into the blood, which stimulates the adrenal cortex to release other hormones. These hormones stimulate the immune system to attack and stimulate the liver to fight the stressor. If glucocorticoids are produced, the body has made the decision to peacefully coexist with the stressor.

Stress as the Failure to Adapt

Described above was our immediate reaction to stress. It includes *physiological* changes in heart rate, respiration, and skin conductance, as well as more subtle, hormonal changes. It also involves *psychological* reactions, such as fear, anger, guilt, and anxiety. In our example the reaction was *adaptive* in the modern world, even though the danger was not real. But a similar reaction to a TV murder or a divorce is not adaptive. There is no need to mobilize mind and body to deal with these events.

People now face new challenges equipped with a brain and biology suited to a different and more stable world than that of today. The flight-or-fight response, which evolved to mobilize the body to cope with physical threats, is now regularly elicited by symbolic ones. Financial difficulties, an unsympathetic boss, traffic jams, and unemployment are met with increased adrenaline, rapid heart rate, increased respiration, moist palms, and tense muscles. Many of these biological reactions are inappropriately elicited. Do you need to escape or flee from a bounced check?

The current popular view of stress is that people are passive, helpless victims. Stressors of all sorts, from loss of a loved one to loss of car keys, attack us. The answer would seem to be to avoid all stress, change, and challenge. Yet stress does not result simply from exposure to events in the environment. The way we

perceive and appraise the event has more to do with the outcome than the event itself.

Stress, and its negative impact on health, derives from a mismatch between *perceived* environmental demands and *perceived* resources to adapt. **Stress** is the failure of adaptability. It occurs when the environment or internal demands exceed the adaptive resources of an organism (Lazarus & Launier, 1978). These situations are of several types: *catastrophes,* such as earthquakes, wars, and fires; *major life changes,* such as the death of a spouse or unemployment; *chronic life strains,* such as poor working conditions; and *minor "hassles,"* such as having a check bounce.

Catastrophes

Human adaptation can be overwhelmed by too much change, such as in the catastrophic effects of war. The study of stressful situations began with men in combat who suffer extreme psychological distress. This was called "shell shock" in World War I, "combat fatigue" in World War II, and "acute combat reaction" in the Vietnam war.

Under combat conditions, a soldier may have to make extreme demands on his body, going without sleep, food, or shelter for many days. He may be called upon to commit extreme acts such as killing, and he may see his buddies become injured, disfigured, or die, and may fear for his own life. World War II veterans who had combat stress for prolonged periods still have major psychological problems four decades later.

Major Life Changes

Major alterations in the world should cause major upsets within because the mental system detects instability and change. The connection between the predictability of life and illness deserves emphasis. *People are more likely to become ill after extensive life changes* (Figure 18-2).

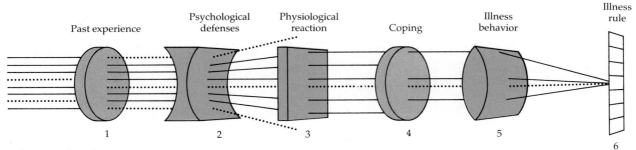

Past experience | Psychological defenses | Physiological reaction | Coping | Illness behavior | Illness rule

1　　2　　3　　4　　5

6

FIGURE 18-2
Dealing with Stressful Life Events

Illness is not the inevitable reaction to life changes and stress. Each of us has various ways of deflecting, defusing, or interpreting stressful events to permit coping and possibly to prevent physiological reactions and illness. How such physiological defenses can filter upsets and upheavals is shown diagrammatically above.
(After Rahe, 1974)

In the 1960s, Thomas Holmes, Richard Rahe, and colleagues developed scales that measure **major life changes** in the recent past (Holmes & Rahe, 1967). These life events include positive events, such as marriage, vacations, and outstanding personal achievements, and negative events, such as marital separation, death of a close friend, and jail terms. It also includes neutral events, such as changes in work hours, recreation, or number of family get-togethers. Increases in life changes parallel such problems as increased risk of traffic accidents (Rahe & Arthur, 1978). People who score high on this scale are more likely to have certain diseases, including diabetes, leukemia, cardiovascular disease, schizophrenia, depression, and difficulties in pregnancy (Schwartz & Griffen, 1986).

It is difficult to rate life events as to how stressful they are. Holmes and Rahe (1967) asked people how much adjustment certain events would require. The relative rankings are shown in Table 18-1. They set marriage at a value of 50 *life*

TABLE 18-1　Ratings of Stressful Life Events

LIFE EVENT	Life Change Units[1]		
	AMERICAN	EUROPEAN	JAPANESE
Death of spouse	100 (1)	66 (1)	108 (1)
Divorce	73 (2)	54 (3)	63 (3)
Marital separation	65 (3)	49 (5)	46 (7)
Jail term	63 (4)	57 (2)	72 (2)
Death of close family member	63 (5)	31 (18)	57 (4)
Personal injury or illness	53 (6)	39 (8)	54 (5)
Marriage	50 (7)	50 (4)	50 (6)
Being fired from job	47 (8)	37 (9)	37 (8)
Marital reconciliation	45 (9)	40 (7)	27 (15)
Retirement	45 (10)	31 (17)	29 (11)
Change in health of family member	44 (11)	30 (20)	33 (9)
Pregnancy	40 (12)	43 (6)	27 (13)
Sexual difficulties	39 (13)	32 (15)	31 (10)
Addition of new family member	39 (14)	34 (13)	18 (23)
Major business readjustment	39 (15)	34 (11)	28 (12)

[1] Ranking is shown in parentheses.
SOURCE: Ornstein & Sobel, 1987.

change units (LCU). Mild stress occurs at an LCU score of 150–199, moderate stress at 200–299, and high at 300 LCU or more. These early findings were startling. However, some researchers began questioning some of the assumptions of the scale and the way it was used.

Negative life events relate to illness, but positive events relate weakly. Few who experience major life changes get sick. The *nonoccurrence* of a desired event may also be stressful, as when a person would like to marry someone but does not. Life events are not necessarily *discrete* episodes that occur at once. They are often events that take place over a span of time, with far-reaching consequences for many areas of a person's life. The effects of a bad job or an unhappy marriage endure.

Much of the problem stems from the simplified nature of the early investigations. Obviously, not everyone finds marriage as relating in the same way to other events as did the original sample. Also, the loss of a spouse is very different for men versus women. There are also cultural differences: for Americans, the death of close family members is fifth on the scale, but for a European, it is eighteenth.

Chronic Life Strains

Chronic conditions such as an unhappy marriage or poor working conditions are not really "events" per se, but may be very stressful (Pearlin, 1980). **Chronic life strains** can be produced by the way in which a society is organized and by a person's position in that society. For example, a society that accepts some unemployment (for the greater economic good) assures that some of its members will be under the great stress of unemployment. Consequently, how a society is structured and what sorts of demands are placed upon its members may increase stress.

In one study, chronic conditions that people find stressful were found to come under four different roles in life: marriage, parenthood, household economics, and work. The work environment in particular involves stresses that seem to outstrip our capacity to adapt to them. Certain aspects of work add to stress, such as the type of work, the work load, and relationships with co-workers and bosses.

However, being out of work may be even more stressful than having work that one doesn't like. When unemployment increases, mental hospital admissions and deaths also increase (Brenner, 1976). Also, the cost of unemployment, in increased use of physical and mental health services, is surprisingly high (Cobb & Kasl, 1977). Each time the unemployment rate increases by 1 percentage point, 4 percent more people commit suicide, 5.7 percent more commit murder, and nearly 2 percent more die of cirrhosis of the liver or cardiovascular disease (Gore, 1978).

Hassles and Uplifts

Stressful life events are relatively uncommon compared to daily **hassles.** What about all the frustrating, irritating, and annoying common events? There are traffic jams, waiting in lines, foul-ups at work, arguments, misplacing things, concerns about weight and rising prices, and other daily hassles (see Table 18-2). Even major life events are accompanied by minor hassles. Getting a divorce unbalances people partly because of the added extra hassles: fixing the car,

TABLE 18-2   Ten Most Common Hassles

College Sample (n = 34)	% of Times Checked	Middle-aged Sample (n = 100)	% of Times Checked
1. Troubling thoughts about future	76.6	1. Concerns about weight	52.4
2. Not getting enough sleep	72.5	2. Health of a family member	48.1
3. Wasting time	71.1	3. Rising prices of common goods	43.7
4. Inconsiderate smokers	70.7	4. Home maintenance	42.8
5. Physical appearance	69.9	5. Too many things to do	38.6
6. Too many things to do	69.2	6. Misplacing or losing things	38.1
7. Misplacing or losing things	67.0	7. Yard work or outside home maintenance	38.1
8. Not enough time to do the things you need to do	66.3	8. Property, investment, or taxes	37.6
9. Concerns about meeting high standards	64.0	9. Crime	37.1
10. Being lonely	60.8	10. Physical appearance	35.9

SOURCE: Kanner, Coyne, Schaefer, & Lazarus (1981).

TABLE 18-3   Ten Most Common Uplifts

College Sample (n = 34)	% of Times Checked	Middle-aged Sample (n = 100)	% of Times Checked
1. Completing a task	83.7	1. Relating well with your spouse or lover	76.3
2. Relating well with friends	81.6	2. Relating well with friends	74.4
3. Giving a present	81.3	3. Completing a task	73.3
4. Having fun	81.3	4. Feeling healthy	72.7
5. Getting love	81.3	5. Getting enough sleep	69.7
6. Giving love	80.0	6. Eating out	68.4
7. Being visited, phoned, or sent a letter	79.0	7. Meeting your responsibilities	68.1
8. Laughing	79.0	8. Visiting, phoning, or writing someone	67.7
9. Entertainment	78.4	9. Spending time with family	66.7
10. Music	78.0	10. Home (inside) pleasing to you	65.5

SOURCE: Kanner, Coyne, Schaefer, & Lazarus (1981).

cooking meals, arranging child care, and so on. Hassles better predict psychosomatic and physical symptoms than major life events (Lazarus, 1984).

Stress alone does not predict illness; perhaps positive events, **uplifts,** can balance out negative ones. A person with a very active life may have hassles because of it, but may also be doing something that gives great pleasure. Take the example of someone who is preparing for the Olympics. Trying to balance school and workouts, watching weight, scrounging up money to go to competitions, and so on may be a lot of hassle, but the joy of mastery, winning matches, and maybe being the best in the world much more than compensates for the hassles.

Kanner and his colleagues (1981) devised an "uplifts scale" to assess positive experiences. Not unexpectedly, people of different ages and occupations have different patterns of hassles and uplifts (Tables 18-2 and 18-3). College students were found to be "struggling with the academic and social problems typically associated with attending college (wasting time, concerns about meeting high standards, being lonely)." Middle-aged subjects found pleasure and satisfaction primarily in their family and in good health. However, the students preferred hedonic ("fun") activities such as laughing, entertainment, music, and the like. This research is just at its beginning, and there is little solid evidence yet developed to link uplifts with improved health. However, this approach is probably on the right track.

The stresses and difficulties of modern life in part result from living in a modern world that is different from the world we originally adapted to. Thus, psychologists are currently applying their knowledge to aid in a fresh adaptation: to learn to be healthy in our new circumstances. Some of these new studies are examining those who are "better selected" to withstand the difficulties of the modern world. Identifying what makes them "hardy" may make it easier for others. Other studies are developing new treatments and new ways to understand relationships among the mind, the brain, the body, and society, some of

HEALTH
PSYCHOLOGY

which have already been presented, such as the new field of "psychoimmunology." Still others consider the surprising changes in the environment that aid health. For example, simply providing a view out of a window may help to heal patients. All these studies hold great promise.

Hardiness in the Face of Stress

In *Vulnerable, but Invincible* Emmy Werner and Ruth Smith (1982) recount their study of 72 resilient children, such as Mary who was described in the beginning of this chapter. The children's mothers reported that they were active and "socially responsive" even when they were infants. Other observers reported that they had positive social orientations as young children. They seemed to have a strong concept of themselves and could follow their interests where they led. In the description of the study, they had

These children and others like them who have suffered from life's adversity show a resilience that gives testimony to the amazing ability of human beings to adapt.

> a more positive self-concept, and a more nurturant, responsible, and achievement-oriented attitude toward life than peers who developed serious coping problems. At the threshold of adulthood, the resilient men and women had developed a sense of coherence in their lives and were able to draw on a number of informal sources of support. They also expressed a desire to "improve themselves," i.e., toward continued psychological growth.

This study, and others of children with schizophrenic parents and of children surviving war, abuse, and adversity, give testimony to the enormous adaptability of people. These investigations are beginning to reshape our thinking about stress and resistance to disease.

A current belief of many experts is that "stress equals disease"—that all the stressors of modern life inevitably take their toll and wear us down. It is thought stress as a rule makes us more vulnerable to all disorders from cancer to heart attacks, infections to depression. However, this simple equation—that stress (whether it be psychological trauma or microbes) equals disease—doesn't really work. Most people exposed to stressors don't become ill. Different people confronting the same stressor react differently: some break down while others thrive.

The popular view, supported by many researchers, therapists, and certainly the media, is that stress kills. Watch out for stressors and try to avoid them at all costs. But this pessimistic view of people as passive victims of stress doesn't really make sense. If we really followed this advice and tried to avoid stressors, no one would ever marry, have children, take a job, write a book, or invent anything. And how would the modern world have come about?

Most people need change and challenge. They seek out novelty and stimulation. Many come through stressful experiences not with illness but with better strength and health. For many people, disease is not inevitable in the face of difficulty.

Although the relationship between "life change events" (as discussed in the last section) and subsequent disease is important, the correlations are modest and may hide more than they reveal. If you try to predict who will become ill based on a tally of major life events, you are likely to be correct only about 15 percent of the time. This means that there is a large group of people who are not exposed to high stress but still become ill.

Commitment, Challenge, and Control

More interesting are those who survive changes and challenges in their lives. When confronted with a stressor, some people seem to be able to cope with it without becoming anxious and aroused in a harmful way. Some people appraise the potential stressor in such a way as to avoid stress. The charging lion may elicit a very different reaction in you than in an experienced animal trainer. Some people are able to take action in the face of a stressor that minimizes or eliminates the threat.

Suzanne Kobasa and colleagues (1982) identified the components of psychological hardiness. She studied middle- and upper-level business executives at Illinois Bell Telephone Company at a time of great stress and uncertainty in the company. Two hundred were selected from those who had high stress. About half of them had high levels of illness, while the other half remained healthy. The executives were similar in income, job status, educational level, age, ethnic background, and religious practice, but they were opposite in their attitudes about themselves, their jobs, and the people around them.

Those executives with a low incidence of illness were shown to have a strong *commitment* to self, work, family, and other important values. They had a sense of *control* over their life, and they saw change as a *challenge* rather than a threat. They accepted that change, rather than stability, is the norm in life and they welcomed it as an opportunity for growth. They sought novelty, tolerated ambiguity, and demonstrated a cognitive flexibility and a strong sense of purpose in approaching life's problems. They would agree with statements like: "I would be willing to sacrifice financial stability in my work if something really challenging came along."

In contrast, those executives with a high incidence of illness were threatened by change and suffered in the face of uncertainty. They would tend to agree with this statement: "It bothers me when I have to deviate from the routine or schedule I have set for myself." Here is an extract from Kobasa's (1987) study of a man who told her:

> "I'm thinking of making a major change. I'm thinking of leaving the phone company and going to this little electronics company that's a much more risky operation. I figure if what you're going to do is free, I'll come and get the advice. Maybe it'll be helpful."
>
> This man's protocol showed high stress and high illness. He was only in his thirties, but he had hypertension, peptic ulcer, and migraine headaches: many symptoms as well as diseases. He arrives forty-five minutes late, trenchcoat flying behind him, papers under his arm. Then he makes a beeline for my secretary's desk and begins calling people. He's got to call many people to let them know where he's going to be in the next forty-five minutes. All the time I'm in my office waiting, hearing all these phone calls. He comes in and I've prepared what's going to be a fairly difficult conversation with him about his alienation from other people. However it's difficult to do that because the phone keeps ringing and every time it does he jumps up because he's convinced it's for him. He can't talk in my office so he has to run out to the secretary's office. This happens three times and we're not getting anywhere.
>
> He says to me, "Look, I really need to take all these calls, they're very crucial. But you may have something here. So why don't you talk into my tape recorder?" So he pulls out a tape recorder, puts it on my desk and says, "I'll listen to it at night when I have a chance." (Kobasa, 1987)

Here, in contrast, is a description of one of the low-illness executives.

Although he has a clear sense of the importance of broader social issues concerning his work, and certainly feels that his role requires innovative planning, it is the moment-to-moment activities of the day that intrigue him the most. He claims to learn fairly continuously, even when the task appears at first to be routine.

When asked his views about the company reorganization, he expresses a clear sense of the magnitude of the changes in the offing. But he shows no signs of the panic we saw in other subjects. He is not more certain than they are about what the changes will mean to him specifically. But he is so involved and interested in the evolutionary process going on that he almost welcomes it. Whatever his new role turns out to be, he is sure he will find a way to make it meaningful and worthwhile. He recognizes the hard work and possible frustrations involved in the company's reorganization, but he treats it as all in a day's work. He looks forward to rolling up his sleeves, working hard, and learning new things — he is involved with the company and wants to help with its reorganization. (Kobasa, 1987)

These differences in appraisal can result in enormous differences in how people respond to potentially stressful events. Hardy people transform problems into opportunities and thereby do not elicit a stress response in the first place. Those who cannot handle stress (the "unhardy") distract themselves from the problem with drugs, television, or social interaction.

The findings correlating hardiness with health in the face of stress were confirmed in a prospective study. Over 250 business managers were surveyed three times over a two-year period. The characteristics of challenge, commitment, and control predicted which of the stressed executives would get ill and which would remain well. The hardy executives were only half as likely to get sick as less hardy people confronting similar stressors (Kobasa, Maddi, & Kahn, 1982).

Hardiness Induction

Can one learn to become more hardy? Kobasa and Maddi identified childhood experiences that foster hardiness. Commitment seems to emerge from strong parental encouragement and acceptance. Control is cultivated in children successfully encountering a variety of tasks that are neither too simple nor too difficult. A challenge orientation develops when the child perceives the confusing environment as rich and full rather than chaotic. These features also appear to foster hardiness in adults. A work environment that encourages self-mastery and includes encouragement from superiors assists in the breeding of hardiness (Kobasa, Maddi, & Kahn, 1982).

Maddi and Kobasa (1984) developed "hardiness induction groups," which are small group sessions to encourage commitment, control, and challenge. Group members are taught how to focus on their bodies and mental sensations in response to stressful situations. They are encouraged to ask themselves such questions as "What's keeping me from feeling terrific today?" This focusing increases the person's sense of control over stress.

People are also encouraged to think about a recent stressful episode and imagine three ways it might have been worse and three ways it could have gone better. In addition, group members plan action when they face a stressor they cannot

PLATE 17
Adapting to Change
This bustling modern downtown intersection in San Diego, California, is the same intersection photographed in 1938. The contrast between these two scenes exemplifies the enormous increase in density in our world over the last 50 years, both in numbers of people and the built environment. Small wonder that so many of us have trouble adapting to the modern world.

PLATE 18
**Impact of Computers
on Everyday Life**
The enormous information
processing power of computers
has become an everyday
routine in our lives, from
computerized scanners in
grocery stores and automated
bank tellers to the ubiquitous
home computer.

PLATE 19
Development in Adulthood
These photographs of Katherine Hepburn taken at different stages of her illustrious career give a glimpse of the enduring qualities of her adult life.

1941, age 34

1967, age 60

1981, age 74

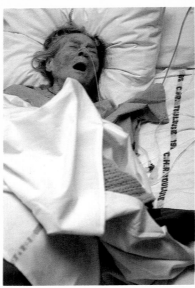

PLATE 20
Old Age
Depending on how involved people are in life with
activities and others, old age can either be an exhilarating
or demoralizing time.

avoid or control, such as the death of a spouse or a serious illness. They are encouraged to refocus on another area of their lives in which they can master a new challenge and restore their sense of control and competence. They might learn a new skill like swimming or offer their services in tutoring.

The preliminary result of this hardiness training is encouraging. A group of eight high-stress, hypertensive executives attended eight weekly group sessions. At the end, not only were their hardiness scores higher, but they reported fewer symptoms of psychological distress and their blood pressures were lower in comparison to an untreated control group.

"Mind-made" Health

How would you rate your health overall (poor, fair, good, excellent)? Surprisingly, this simple question better predicts a person's health status than objective assessments made by his or her doctor. People who tend to rate their health poorly die earlier and have more disease than their counterparts who view themselves as healthy. Even people with objective disease seem to do better when they believe themselves to be healthy than when they believe themselves weak.

In Manitoba, Canada, more than 3,500 senior citizens were interviewed at the outset of a seven-year study. They were asked this question: "For your age would you say, in general, your health is excellent, good, fair, poor, or bad?" In addition, their objective health status was determined by reports from their physicians on medical problems and how often they required hospitalization or surgery (Mossey & Shapiro, 1982).

Mental attitudes have a direct effect on a person's physical well-being

Those people who rated their health as poor were almost three times more likely to die during the seven years of the study than those who perceived their health as excellent. Was this because those who rated themselves as unhealthy were, in fact, so? The evidence is against it. Surprisingly, subjective self-reported health was more accurate in predicting who would die than the objective health measures from physicians. Those who were in objectively poor health according to physician reports survived at a higher rate as long as *they believed their own health to be good.*

Nearly 15 percent of the people who rated their health as fair or poor had good or excellent health according to the objective health measures. These "health pessimists" had a slightly greater risk of dying than the "health optimists" who viewed themselves as healthy in spite of negative reports from their doctors. The predictive power of self-rated health was the same for male or female, older or younger, objectively sick or well. Only greater age appears to have a more powerful influence on death rates than self-rated health.

Another study of 7,000 adults in Alameda County in California confirmed the importance of the way a person views his or her health. Men with poor self-rated health were 2.3 times more likely to die than those who saw their health as excellent. For women the difference was five times greater. The importance of self-reported health remained even when smoking, drinking, exercising, marriage, social contacts, happiness, and depression were controlled for (Kaplan & Camacho, 1983).

Optimistic attitudes seem to bolster an individual's ability to resist disease: those with better self-reported health are less likely to die from any cause. Whatever the mechanism, the message is clear that how people view their own health significantly influences health outcomes. Quickly assessing a person's overall perception of their health may help us identify people at greater risk. By encouraging more positive self-perceptions, we may eventually be able to affect physiological processes and improve health outcomes.

A Room with a View

Visual stimulation can also effect health. According to a recent controlled study of hospitalized patients, those who had a room with a view recovered more quickly than those who stared out at a brick wall. Roger Ulrich from the University of Delaware studied 46 patients who had undergone gall bladder surgery. Half the patients had hospital rooms with a window looking out onto a small stand of deciduous trees, while the matched controls had a view of a brown brick wall.

The patients with a view of the trees spent fewer days in the hospital after surgery (by nearly one day), had fewer negative evaluations in the nursing notes, and took fewer doses of moderate and strong pain medications. They also had slightly fewer postoperative complications. The view of a wooded scene thus apparently had a therapeutic effect, at least when compared with a view of a brown brick wall. Whether similar salutary effects could be achieved by pictures or murals depicting outdoor scenes is not known but worth considering. Ulrich remarks:

> The conclusions cannot be extended to all built views, nor to other patient groups, such as long-term patients, who may suffer from low arousal or boredom rather than from the anxiety problems typically associated with surgeries. Perhaps to a chronically understimulated patient, a built view such as a lively city

street might be more stimulating and hence more therapeutic than many natural views. These cautions notwithstanding, the results imply that hospital design and siting decisions would take into account the quality of patient window views. (Ulrich, 1984)

A New Approach to Heart Disease

Blaise Pascal wrote in 1670, *"La coeur a ses raisons qui la raison ne connait pas"* ("The heart has reasons that reason knows not"). When the circulatory system was discovered, it was immediately suggested that the mind can have profound effects on the heart. In 1628, Sir William Harvey, discoverer of the circulation of the blood, wrote about the heart and mind. "Every affection of the mind that is attended with either pain or pleasure, hope or fear, is the cause of an agitation whose influence extends to the heart."

Social Pressure and Blood Pressure

In *The Language of the Heart* (1985), James Lynch describes his problem with blushing:

> Even as a young boy, I blushed almost as easily as the wind blows across the open sea. Not the everyday, home-grown garden variety of blushing, mind you; not the subtle shift in color that you often see in people, a slight reddening around the cheeks and eyes, a charming glow. . . . As a boy and adolescent, and even today as a middle-aged professor in a medical school, when embarrassed I light up with all the splendor of a harvest moon rising to defeat the blackness of a frosty autumn evening. No pumpkin in all its resplendent autumnal glory could even begin to match the glow of my face when it decides to give me away.
>
> My firefly face was a dead giveaway. It was a fink, a bodily appendage that simply refused to hide my inner secrets. If I was embarrassed—bingo, on came the red. If I was angry, my chameleon surface quickly revealed me to the enemy. No one ever had to ask me what mark I got on a test: an A was gray-white; and F, bright red; and C—well, that was the usual color. If I was frightened, then I had to head for the dark.

No one blushes when they are alone, and the act of blushing immediately connects other people to one's own distress. "I cannot recall ever blushing in the dark by myself, no matter what devilish fantasy was coursing through my brain. As near as I can recall, my blushing occurred only when other people were present. How often I wished it was the other way around," Lynch writes.

Lynch theorizes that one of the causes of high blood pressure is that people "blush internally" in social situations. External blushing is noticed by other people immediately; it is understood as a reaction to what others might be thinking of us. High blood pressure is, in this view, partly social: internal blushing.

Lynch (1982, 1985) found that there were surges in recorded blood pressure when people talked. He was struck by the contrast between these hidden reactions (the rising in blood pressure) and the person's apparent calm. Perhaps both blushing and blood pressure elevations when we speak are communications, both to the outside world and within ourselves (Lynch, 1985).

These observations began an important line of research on the relationship of social pressure with that of blood pressure. When a person is talking with another person who is equal in status, his or her blood pressure goes up very little.

However, when a person is being interviewed by someone with higher status, for example, a physician or a prospective employer, blood pressure goes up dramatically.

Blood pressure taken in a physician's office is almost always higher than recorded at home. An Italian study demonstrated that within four minutes of a

BLOOD PRESSURE, HYPERTENSION, AND HEART DISEASE

Blood pressure is the force (the "pressure") with which blood pushes against the walls of the blood vessels. When the heart beats, it pumps about three ounces of blood into the aorta, the major artery leaving the heart. The aorta divides into smaller arteries that lead into a system of tiny vessels—arterioles—which open and shut. The peak pressure when the heart is contracting is the *systolic* pressure, the low point when the heart relaxes is the *diastolic* (Figure 18-3).

Arteries squeeze their liquid content into the arterioles the way water goes through a hose. When water is turned on, it enters the hose. If a valve at the other end of the hose is closed, the pressure in the hose will rise, but no water will go through. As you open the closed end of the hose, water flows out and the pressure will then fall. In the bloodstream, the tiny arterioles are like millions of valves. When they *constrict,* the pressure behind them (in the arteries) increases. Blood pressure is determined by the amount of blood pumped from the heart ("cardiac output") and by the resistance the blood meets in its passage throughout the peripheral circulation (Figure 18-4).

Blood pressure normally changes from heartbeat to heartbeat. People in whom the pressure is consistently high have the disease **hypertension.** Hypertension, or sustained elevated blood pressure, contributes to stroke and heart attacks. Hypertensives are two to three times more likely to develop coronary artery disease than are those with normal blood pressure, and four times more likely to suffer from a stroke.

Sixty million Americans are hypertensive, and about half remain untreated, a potentially dangerous condition because high blood pressure injures the blood vessels, which can later damage the brain, heart, kidneys, and eyes. Hypertension usually is not noticeable until there is a stroke, eye failure, or heart attack.

Heart diseases cause more than 50 percent of deaths in the United States (Figure 18-5). Forty million Americans suffer from diseases of the heart and blood vessels. The economic costs of cardiovascular disorders, including loss of productivity and health expenditures, exceed $80 billion annually in the United States alone.

High blood pressure forces the heart to work harder. The increased pressure in the arteries can cause enlargement of the heart muscle, especially of the left ventricle, which pumps blood into the body. In addition, the high pressure and turbulent flow of blood can damage the walls of arteries, contributing to the establishment of fatty deposits, which can block the blood flow further.

Such changes place the person under ever-increasing risk of a heart attack. In the brain, the constant strain of high pressure within the blood vessels can cause them to tear or to explode suddenly, leading to a stroke. Brain hemorrhages and other forms of blood vessel blockages are four times more common in people with hypertension.

Except for the few cases of hypertension that are due to kidney abnormalities, the vast majority of hypertension is called "essential hypertension," which means we do not know the essential cause. The search for causes has been restricted to the physician's normal categories of "somatic etiologies," such as too much sodium, too little calcium, too much of this hormone, too little of that. Hypertension is viewed as a matter of the hydraulics of the system; the person has been by and large ignored.

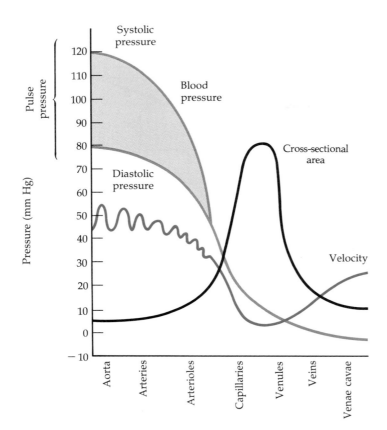

Systolic pressure

Blood pressure

Diastolic pressure

Pulse pressure

Cross-sectional area

Velocity

Pressure (mm Hg)

Aorta　Arteries　Arterioles　Capillaries　Venules　Veins　Venae cavae

FIGURE 18-3
Blood Pressure
This graph shows the relationship between blood pressure (both systolic and diastolic), velocity of blood flow, and cross-sectional area in the blood vessels. Note that when the vessels are less constricted (high cross-sectional area), the blood pressure is lower.

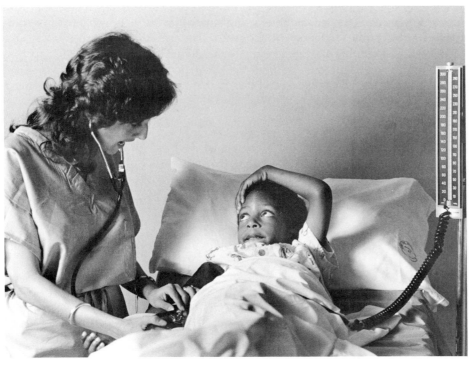

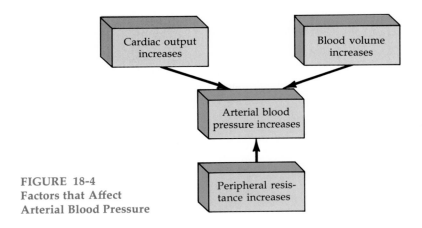

FIGURE 18-4
Factors that Affect
Arterial Blood Pressure

doctor walking into a patient's room, the patient's blood pressure jumps higher. A clinical observation often made is that hypertensive patients frequently mention status problems in their job. They have much conflict with people in positions of authority, and they often discuss their low self-esteem. Are they responding to status in a way that affects cardiovascular health?

Lynch and his research group studied 40 college students with normal blood pressure. They were asked to be quiet, then to talk to an experimenter, to be quiet once again, then to read a book aloud. For half the students, the experimenter dressed in jeans and portrayed himself as a graduate student. For the rest, he dressed in a shirt and tie and the laboratory jacket of a resident in internal medicine. He also told this group of students that he was an internist conducting a research project in blood pressure. The blood pressure of all 40 students rose when they spoke. The rise and the resting level of pressure, however, was significantly higher for the students who spoke to the internist than for those who spoke to the fellow graduate student (Lynch, 1985; Lynch et al., 1982).

Blood pressure is lowest when people talk with someone with whom they are intimate, such as their spouse, and it is highest when a person is addressing a group of unfamiliar people.

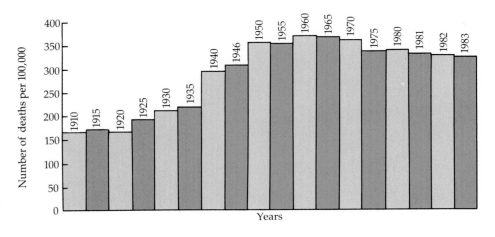

FIGURE 18-5
Deaths due to Heart
Disease from 1910 to 1983
in the United States

Transactional Psychophysiology:
A Computer-based Treatment for the Heart

If Lynch is correct that the link between human communication and blood pressure is strong, then a change in communication could cause a change in blood pressure. Lynch and his colleagues have developed such a treatment which tries to link the social world with the internal world. It is called *transactional psychophysiology*—measuring how the heart responds to other people.

In this kind of therapy a patient comes into a room and is seated next to a table with a box-shaped automated blood pressure device and an Apple computer. The therapist attaches a standard blood pressure cuff to her arm. "Sit quietly for a few minutes," he says.

Then he pushes a key on the computer and her blood pressure is shown to her as a graph on the computer's screen. "Now, talk about anything," he says to her. She begins to speak about the weather, and he again pushes a key on the computer. Her blood pressure is shown to her in comparison to when she was quiet, only two minutes before. It is much higher now, in the range for which a physician would treat it aggressively with medication.

"Be quiet again," he requests. She sits quietly again for three minutes, and amazingly, when he pushes the key again, her blood pressure is back in the normal range. In successive sessions for six months, once every week or two, she will watch her blood pressure response on the graph, compared to that of minutes, weeks, and months before. She will learn how it goes up when she speaks rapidly and breathes shallowly, and how it goes down when she speaks slowly, pauses for breath, and breathes deeply. She will learn subtle physical signals, too small to be considered symptoms, such as her forehead feeling tense or perspiration on her upper lip, that warn her when her pressure is rising. This is a complex form of biofeedback.

Most difficult, she will learn to connect these subtle signals to her social interactions. She will learn to change her interactions with people and situations that consistently make her blood pressure go up. In a sense she will learn how to have a healthy dialogue with herself and others, and how she is a part of society.

See Chapter 7, section on Self-Regulation.

A Sense of Coherence and Health

Aaron Antonovsky, an Israeli medical sociologist, was first struck by the importance of resistance resources when he was conducting a study of how women from different ethnic backgrounds experienced and adapted to menopause. He identified a group of women who had been in Nazi concentration camps during World War II. Not surprisingly, he found that the concentration camp survivors, as a group, were in poorer emotional and physical health than other comparable women who had not been in the camps.

This is where such studies most often end, but Antonovsky looked more deeply. He was intrigued that some women survived the concentration camps and were healthy by all measures of physical, psychological, and social functioning. As he remarked, "Despite having lived through the most inconceivably inhuman experience, some women were reasonably healthy and happy, had raised families, worked, had friends, and were involved in community activities." How was this possible?

Later, Antonovsky proposed that resistance resources that promote health, whether they be money, friends, education, or coping strategies, all worked to forge and reinforce a certain way of looking at the world, a way of perceiving the stimuli and demands that bombard the person. He originally defined this as a *sense of coherence:*

> A sense of coherence is a global orientation that expresses the extent to which one has a pervasive, enduring though dynamic feeling of confidence that one's internal and external environments are predictable and that there is a high probability that things will work out as well as can reasonably be expected. (Antonovsky, 1984)

Antonovsky (1987) later refined the sense of coherence to include three basic attributes: comprehensibility, manageability, and meaningfulness. *Comprehensibility* means that the demands made on the person seem ordered, consistent, structured, clear, and hence predictable, as opposed to random, chaotic, disordered, and unpredictable. *Manageability* refers to the extent to which people feel that they have resources at their disposal adequate to meet the demands made upon them. This does not mean that they have to control the resources—they could be controlled by friends, relatives, benevolent leaders, or God—but one way or another, they will have access to adequate resources to help them cope. *Meaningfulness* refers to the feeling that the demands posed by living are viewed as worth investing in and worthy of commitment and engagement. The demands are meaningful in the sense that they are viewed as worthwhile challenges, not threats or unwelcome burdens (Antonovsky, 1987).

A strong sense of coherence can function in many ways to strengthen health. The beliefs that life is meaningful, that one has the resources to manage, and that life is ordered and predictable may allow one to engage in activities that are more health promoting and to avoid those that endanger health. This way of appraising the world may permit a person to see unavoidable stressors as challenges rather than as threats and thereby short-circuit a stress reaction. Further, people with a stronger sense of coherence may be more likely to use friends, material resources, and coping skills to deal with potentially stressful situations.

See Chapter 6, section on Rules of Organization.

Coherence is basic to perception and cognition. At each step the world becomes more organized and simplified in the mind. Schemata represent the chaotic and changing external world, so that it becomes stable, simplified, and seemingly coherent. Instead of thousands of reflecting bits of glass, gray stone, scores of doors opening and closing, and several high ceilings, we perceive *one* building. The parts fit together; it makes sense.

We develop this simple stable organization (coherence), and it is basic to us in our connections to others. When this sense of coherence regarding a person's world is disrupted, he or she is more likely to become ill. If the world is disorganized, it is not clear what appropriate action to take in any situation nor is it clear that we can control our lives to any extent.

PROBLEMS OF JUDGMENT IN THE MODERN WORLD

Human beings have gone outside their original home in subtropical East Africa and now live all over the earth. We can even live for brief periods away from the earth itself. From the moment our ancestors stood upright, they began to explore unexpected places and to create unanticipated conditions. As a result, we have to adapt to unprecedented challenges.

The technology of our modern world, including our ability to destroy ourselves with nuclear weapons, has made it difficult for many of us to adapt.

Until recently these changes in the relatively stable environments to which we were adapted were gradual. This is no longer true. The world we are creating is constantly and rapidly changing. Travel that was unimaginable, such as visiting the moon, is possible. Such phenomena as nuclear power and nuclear weapons, unimagined by our predecessors, now threaten our existence. Much of what is newly invented or created now is done by a lone genius or a small group. Therefore, our technology can leap way ahead of the ability of the remaining billions of us to adapt.

The first atomic bomb exploded, and Albert Einstein wrote: "Everything has now changed except for our way of thinking." More destructive power can now be carried by a single submarine than has been used in all the wars in human history.

Next month the population will increase by more than the number of human beings who lived on the planet 100,000 years ago. In the next two years, more people will be *added* to the earth's population than lived at the time of Christ.

At the end of the chapter on evolution, we mentioned that many of society's current difficulties are rooted in our past evolution. There were no radical changes in the brain in the course of vertebrate, primate, and human evolution. We carry the remains of our long history inside our own heads. And then suddenly, we changed things completely. Our cultural evolution has proceeded enormously faster than our genetic evolution.

All nonhuman species have evolved to survive in their physical habitat. Human beings originally evolved to do this as well. Now, we have turned the tables on the physical environment and made our physical world change to fit *us*.

Clothing, fire, dwellings, and agriculture all enable people to live where none could before. The world of prehistoric human beings was a world bounded by a few miles rather than continents. It contained small groups perhaps of 50 to 500 individuals isolated from other small groups. The tribal network originally designed to accommodate 200 people now tries to deal with a population of five billion. Early human beings led a nomadic life, moving through familiar terrain but subject to many short-term threats and opportunities.

See Chapter 4, section on The Changing Brain.

Our "mental structure" evolved in large part to deal with those changes in the environment. The human brain evolved to aid the *survival of individuals,* individuals who had to live in circumstances very different from our own. They lived in small groups, in a stable situation, with only short-term threats to safety and security. The "environment," both natural and cultural, remained relatively constant for very long periods, for hundreds of thousands of years. When long-term changes occurred, our ancestors could do little or nothing about it. At the time of the agricultural revolution, about 10,000 years ago, this stability gradually began to disappear. The great civilizations of our historical era then arose from the "roots" of the agricultural revolution. Human societies and cultures evolved rapidly.

When people began to settle down to till the soil, they started on the road to cities, to overpopulation, to smog, and to nuclear weapons. The "trip" down that road was slow at first. Even in the 10,000 years from the agricultural revolution to the Middle Ages, there was no *great* change in the nature of human lives.

In the industrial revolution the number of inventions greatly increased: printing presses, factories, steam engines, mass production, railroads, electric power, telegraphs, and more. In this new era, development piled on development and the pace of change picked up. Human society moved faster and faster until it took off into a new and unknown world.

Where there were once only prairies and deserts, now farms and factories thrive. Where there were swamps and forests, now laboratories and launching pads are built.

Many of today's serious problems have their roots in our ability to make a new world that is beyond our ability to live within it. Improvements in agriculture and health make it possible for almost all children to survive infancy, grow to adulthood, and reproduce. There has been no balancing reduction in birth rates. As a result, the world is now badly overpopulated, resources are depleted, and life-support systems are damaged.

We have immigrated to a strange New World, but it has been an invisible immigration, across time, not space. Almost unnoticed on this scale, people have changed the world more in the past 10,000 years than their ancestors did in the preceding four million.

Mistakes and Mismatches in Judgment

Remember that people were more afraid of the first few small atomic bombs than they are of the tens of thousands of much more powerful nuclear weapons that are now in U.S. and Soviet arsenals. When the wife of President Ford was reported to have breast cancer, all over the country women went to their physicians to get examined. Both actions are misapplications of new information to immediate and local phenomena.

This emphasis on new and exciting changes in the world makes individuals and society as a whole vulnerable to anyone who can exploit this component of the mind. It leads to the effectiveness of terrorism, to violence spreading as a result of watching brutality in the cinema, and to ignoring the dangers resulting from acid rain.

See Chapters 1, 10, and 17 for other examples.

Consider these events of the mid-1980s and the responses to them. A chemical spill in a Union Carbide plant in Bhopal, India, exposed hundreds of thousands of people to toxic fumes. It caused severe damage to the health of at least 20,000 people. Soon after the spill, stories appeared in the press describing the dangerous storage procedures in similar chemical plants in the United States. This event stimulated an investigation of such chemicals in the air in the United States and western Europe that would have been done sooner were it not for the way human beings evolved to receive information. The slow release of toxins stays out of mind because the changes are slight. Then a disaster occurs, and all attention is fixed on it and similar problems.

Movie star Rock Hudson revealed that he had AIDS. Funds for research were increased dramatically only a few days later. An announcer on ABC news said, "AIDS has received more attention in the few weeks after Rock Hudson's announcement than in the previous four years." AIDS, growing slowly and continuously, was suddenly noticed as a problem when a single famous person contracted it.

Misplaced Comparisons

Recall from Chapters 5, 10, and 17 that we constantly judge things by comparison and our judgment shifts constantly. For example, an automobile ad may say, "BMW prices range from $60,000 to $24,950." This ad makes your comparison shift, and you begin telling yourself that the $24,950 car is actually quite cheap for a BMW. Since our judgments of reality are comparative, this is taken advantage of in the modern world. For example, this shortcut of mind works in sales. Here is an extract about selling pool tables.

> If you were a billiard-table dealer, which would you advertise — the $329 model or the $3,000 model? The chances are you would promote the low-priced item and hope to trade the customer up when he comes to buy. But G. Warren Kelley, new business promotion manager at Brunswick, says you would be wrong. . . . To prove his point, Kelley has actual sales figures from a representative store. . . . During the first week, customers were shown the low end of the line . . . and then encouraged to consider more expensive models — the traditional trading-up approach. . . . The average table sale that week was $550. However, during the second week, customers . . . were led instantly to the $3,000 table, regardless of what they wanted to see. [They were] then allowed to shop the rest of the line, in declining order of price and quality. The result of selling down was an average sale of over $1,000. (Cialdini, 1985)

The policy of comparison judges the brightness of light, the temperature of water, how you buy things, and whether you harm or help someone. To repeat: the same neural procedures that originally developed to judge brightness, weight, and pressure now preside over the life and death of us all. We retain primitive processes of judgment, appropriate to an era long gone. In the modern world important decisions about the lives and death of millions and political campaigns also funnel through the ancient system, and it sometimes has incalculable consequences.

THE TALE OF WATERGATE

The misjudgments people make by the comparison process helped to bring down a U.S. president. In 1972 there was a break-in at the head of the opposition party's headquarters which came to be known as "Watergate"— an elaborate, extensive plan to spy and harass the opposition. How could an experienced group of politicians have approved such a ridiculous operation?

The Watergate break-in was proposed by G. Gordon Liddy following the strategy of the billiard table salesman—start very high and then lower your demands until something that at first would seem outlandish now appears reasonable.

Liddy went to planning sessions of the Committee to Re-Elect the President. He first proposed an outlandish program of compromising the Democrats by spying on them using walkie-talkies. He also proposed selective kidnappings, break-ins at Democratic headquarters, and other "dirty tricks" on the Democrats during the entire year, culminating with the live confessions at the Democratic convention in Miami. This plan, which he proposed would cost $1 million, was rejected by the Attorney General.

Liddy later halved the plan, eliminating the most offensive element —no kidnapping, only a few whores. His cutdown plan costing $500,000 was also rejected. Finally, for "only" $250,000, Mr. Liddy proposed a simple and comparatively mild "break-in" at the Democratic headquarters in the Watergate office building.

Jeb Magruder, one of the members of the committee, wrote:

. . . *after starting at the grandiose sum of $1 million, we thought that probably $250,000 would be an acceptable figure. . . . We . . . signed off on it in the sense of saying "Okay, let's give him a quarter of a million dollars and let's see what he can come up with." A quarter of a million looked small after the initial proposals, as did the simple break-in compared to the wild scheme. It brought down the government.*

With a view less clouded by the comparative pressures of the moment, Magruder later wrote:

If he had come to us at the outset and said "I have a plan to burglarize and wiretap Larry O'Brien's office," we might have rejected the idea out of hand. Instead he came to us with his elaborate kidnapping/mugging/sabotage/ wiretapping scheme. He had asked for the whole loaf when he was quite content to settle for half or even a quarter. (Magruder, 1974)

ADAPTING TO COMPUTERS

Nothing has increased the pace of change more than computers. A small personal computer on an executive's desk now has more power than was available to all of the Allied forces in World War II. Fifty years ago, computers did not exist. Twenty-five years ago, people who had seen a computer were rare. Today, it is hard to live in society without coming into daily contact with computers. We use computers when we withdraw money from our bank accounts using automated teller machines, when we play video games, and every time we make a long distance telephone call. We use word processing programs to write everything from business letters to term papers to this textbook. In the future, computers may be used as often as telephones to send "electronic mail," to access "expert" knowledge in making decisions, and in many other ways that we cannot predict (Plate 18).

The widespread application of computers is the most recent in a series of technological changes that have affected our lives in complex ways. For example,

the personal automobile not only enables us to travel long distances more quickly and easily, it has also led to the development of suburbia, smog, and the decay of our inner cities. When the telephone was first invented, many people thought it would be used primarily to broadcast entertainment into people's homes (Pool, 1977). Instead, it has given us new opportunities for convenient (and sometimes inconvenient) social and business communications.

Unlike some areas of psychology where there are "right answers" that most people agree on, no one really knows what the effects of computers wil be. Most of the evidence so far is inconclusive and contradictory (Attewell & Rule, 1984). In spite of this uncertainty, some people think that computers will have some inevitable "impacts" on people and that it is up to us to adapt to these changes (or to resist the use of computers altogether). In fact, the adaptation works both ways. There are many choices that we, as a society, can make about the ways we use computers. Understanding the possibilities for how computers can affect people will help us make these choices wisely.

Quality of Work Life

Many people in our society spend a large portion of their waking hours for most of their adult lives at work, and computers may have profound effects on the experiences that people have during this time.

Deskilling versus Upgrading

The views are at two extremes: *deskilling* and *upgrading* (Attewell & Rule, 1984). Some observers claim that computers will lead to deskilling of many jobs. If this occurs, jobs will decrease in status and much of their satisfying content will

AN EXPERT SYSTEM

Artificial intelligence programs that are used to help make decisions ordinarily made by human experts are often called *expert systems*. One of the first and best known expert systems was the MYCIN program developed at Stanford University in the early 1970s (Davis, 1984). This program helps physicians diagnose and treat certain kinds of infectious diseases. First, it asks the physician dozens of questions about the patient's age, sex, and symptoms and about the results of previous laboratory tests. Then, using its knowledge of diseases and treatments, the program guesses which diseases are present and suggests drugs to treat them. Most of MYCIN's knowledge about diseases and treatments is stored in the form of approximately 500 "rules" such as this one:

Rule 27:
    IF (1) the gram stain of the organism
    is gram negative, and (2) the
    morphology of the organism is rod,
    and (3) the aerobicity of the

organism is anaerobic,
THEN there is suggestive evidence
(0.7) that the identity of the
organism is bacteriodes.

If physicians want to know how the program arrived at its suggestions, they can ask for explanations like this one:

Q: How did you decide that
    ORGANISM-1 was *E. coli?*
A: I used rule 084 to conclude that
    the identity of ORGANISM-1 is *E.
    coli.* This gave a cumulative
    certainty factor of 0.41. I used rule
    003 to conclude that the identity
    of ORGANISM-1 is *E. coli.* This
    gave a cumulative certainty factor
    of 0.43.

Because of MYCIN's extensive knowledge about this small part of medicine, its suggestions are often as good as those of human experts. The range of its knowledge, however, is quite limited. It knows nothing about broken legs or psychiatric conditions.

---

be lost (Braverman, 1974; Glenn & Feldberg, 1977). The conceptual and judgmental content of these jobs will be transferred to computer programs or to a smaller number of high-level specialists assisted by computers. Only the routine, uninteresting, and subservient parts will be left. For instance, if banks use computer programs to tell their credit officers which loan applications to accept, the role of the loan officer will become more clerical and less judgmental.

In contrast, some observers believe that the primary effect of computers will be to upgrade jobs. These observers argue that computers are most often used to do the repetitive and uninteresting parts of jobs, leaving people more time to concentrate on conceptual and decision-making tasks (Giuliano, 1982). A secretary who uses a word-processing program no longer has to spend hours retyping entire documents to make changes. The result of this time saving will be that secretarial positions will be upgraded to involve less clerical work and more administrative responsibility.

We do not know for sure which of these possibilities, deskilling or upgrading, will be the most common effect of computers. There are situations in which each has occurred, and opinion surveys show that people generally feel that their jobs have been improved somewhat by computers. However, no large-scale studies of actual job changes in the economy as a whole have been made (Attewell & Rule,

1984). In many ways, the technology is changing faster than researchers can study it. For instance, most studies of the effects of computers on work life were done when large "mainframe" computers were used. People now use personal computers in many new ways, and the effects of this newer version of technology may be very different from the old.

Unemployment

Computers might eliminate jobs altogether and cause large-scale unemployment. There have been waves of fear since at least the 1950s that automation would put many people out of work. These fears have not materialized for previous technologies, and there is no evidence yet that they will be realized for computers either (Attewell & Rule, 1984).

Organizational Structures and Decision Making

Since computers can process and distribute information in new ways, many people have predicted that computers will affect how organizations are structured and decisions are made. Leavitt and Whisler (1958) predicted that whole levels of middle management would be eliminated as improved information technology led to centralized decision making at higher levels of the corporate hierarchy. Others have argued that computers may lead to greater decentralization of decision making because lower level managers have more access to information or because their decisions can be more easily monitored from above (Pfeffer, 1978).

Here, too, case studies show both kinds of changes, but we do not know what overall effect, if any, computers will have on the distribution of authority and control in organizations. In many cases, either organizational structures do not change when computers are used or the existing structure is reinforced (Robey, 1981). Where changes do occur, centralization may be more common than decentralization, but computerized information systems are used in many different kinds of power relationships (Attewell & Rule, 1984).

Much of the research in this area has studied the use of large mainframe computers for such tasks as accounting. Personal computers and new uses of computers for communication tasks, including electronic mail and computer conferencing, may have very different effects (Hiltz & Turoff, 1978). For instance, in some laboratory studies, groups of people who communicate via computers to make decisions participate more equally in the decision-making process but take longer to come to a consensus than face-to-face groups. They also engage in more "uninhibited verbal behavior" such as swearing and expressing strong opinions (Kiesler, Siegel, & McGuire, 1984).

Computers in Education

The primary "work" of many people is learning, and computers may have important effects on this process (Taylor, 1980). By giving students highly individualized instruction and immediate feedback, computers can sometimes significantly increase learning speeds (Suppes & Morningstar, 1969). Computers can also be used to create highly motivating instructional environments (Plate 12).

When some of the motivational characteristics of computer games are used in designing instructional programs, they may lead students to give more time and higher quality attention to their educational tasks (Malone, 1981).

Depending on how these motivational characteristics are used, however, they might distract students from their educational tasks or lead students to be less interested in academic material when it is later presented in a less motivating fashion (Lepper, 1985).

One of the most common uses of computers in education is to teach students how to program computers. This is certainly a skill that will be useful in its own right in our increasingly computerized society. Many people also believe that students can be taught to program in a way that helps them learn more general thinking and problem-solving skills (Papert, 1980). The results of research on this topic are still inconclusive, but some early work indicates that transferring problem-solving skills from programming tasks to other domains is not as simple as proponents would argue (Pea & Kurland, in press).

ADAPTING TO DENSITY

Crowding

Recall from the section on heart disease that Lynch's patients learned that they were part of a larger "social body." People and things around us become part of ourselves. The "self" extends beyond the body. Anything that we control we consider to be part of us (Miller, 1980). For instance, when someone hits our car, we say "he hit *my* rear end" not "the car's rear end."

The space we live in is also a medium of communication. How close we approach another person may indicate what culture we come from, how much we like the other person, and whether our meeting is casual or for business. Too many people in the same space produces crowding and loss of privacy, but both individuals and cultures differ on what is "too many people."

Personal Space

Edward T. Hall wrote, "We treat space somewhat as we treat sex. It is there but we don't talk about it." Hall developed a method of analysis called **proxemics,** which makes our spatial habits explicit. This analysis begins with the concept of *personal space,* which Hall defines as a "small, protective sphere or bubble that an organism maintains between itself and others." *Individual distance,* in contrast, is the basic minimum distance members of a species keep between themselves. The maintenance of a fixed individual distance seems innate in most animals, but is different in different human cultures. Such distance is classified into four basic types (Hall, 1969):

- *Intimate:* from actually touching to 18 inches
- *Personal:* up to 4 feet
- *Social:* 4 to 12 feet
- *Public:* more than 12 feet

Distances that may be considered "invasions" depend on one's culture, and this can easily lead to misunderstandings. People from the Middle East and southern Europe interact with each other at close range, touching frequently and gazing intently into each other's eyes (Figure 18-6). North Americans and the English tend to find this very disconcerting. One person interacting with another whose cultural distance is less than his or her own can be driven across a room trying to avoid this "rude pursuer."

However, the English and Americans differ between themselves in their concept of "proper" space. The English are accustomed to less exclusive space than Americans, so they learn ways to enhance mutual privacy when they are with others. The technique of "reserve" serves this function. English people often

FIGURE 18-6
Personal Space
Westerners would not feel comfortable as close to one another as these Middle Easterners are; personal territorial demands are larger here.

speak quietly and diplomatically and interact less with the people in their immediate environment than do Americans (Hall, 1969).

Members of different cultures appear to need widely varying amounts of space. In Hong Kong, the world's most densely populated city, low-cost housing provides only 35 square feet of living space per person. One architect reports:

> When the construction supervisor of one Hong Kong project was asked what the effects of doubling the amount of floor area would be upon the living patterns, he replied, "with 60 square feet per person, the tenants would sublet!" (*American Institute of Planners Newsletter*, 1967)

Privacy

Privacy is the need to be alone when desired. We can enhance privacy by different means: behavior, words, and body language (the English "reserve"); space (a large house on spacious grounds); and security measures (locks and alarms).

Privacy is sought in different ways throughout the world. Americans create physical barriers, while the English specialize more in psychological barriers. The Japanese developed the movable wall to make space multifunctional while preserving situational privacy (Hall, 1969).

The Experience of Crowding

Crowding is having more people around than one desires. It might seem that the experience of crowding would simply be a function of the number of people in a given amount of space—the population density (a physical measure of the number of people in a given area) (Aiello & Thompson, 1980; Freedman, 1975; Stokols, 1972). Yet this is not always the case. The *experience* of crowding depends on many factors: population density as well as the individual and social *interpretation* of that density.

The experience of crowding can be triggered in a number of ways, only some of which are related to density. The effect of density in social pathology has been studied in rats and mice (Calhoun, 1973). In an experimental situation, populations of these animals were allowed to increase without external restraint by predators, disease, or lack of food and water. These colonies grew rapidly at first, then leveled off, and finally declined. The mouse population eventually died out completely.

In the process, several curious patterns developed. Dominant males staked out the favorable areas, and the females in their territories produced more offspring than others. As population grew, territorial defense broke down, females became more aggressive to protect their litters, but maternal behavior and live births declined. A large population of nonreproducing females developed along with nonviolent and asexual males, which Calhoun called the "beautiful ones." They only ate, drank, slept, and groomed. When mice from this environment were transferred to one of low density, most could not establish a society or reproduce (Marsden, 1972).

Yet density is not the principal cause of deterioration of this mouse society nor of any human society. Rather, as Calhoun notes, *rate and quality of social interaction are paramount issues*. The same factors are important in human life. Despite the thousandfold increase in human numbers since the beginning of culture, some forty to fifty thousand years ago, there has been no change in effective density'' (Calhoun, 1973).

Responses to Population Density

When an animal population in the wild becomes too large, it may suddenly decline or ''crash.'' For instance, the victims of a population crash among Sika deer were not sick or undernourished in general, but they did have enlarged adrenal glands, indicating an extreme stress reaction (Christian, Flyger, & Davis, 1960). This is consistent with the evidence from other animal studies: the adrenal glands of lone mice in very small enclosures do not enlarge (Freedman, 1975).

The human response to density is much more flexible. Males and females may differ in response to density. In a mock jury deliberation, women became less aggressive and gave lighter sentences in small rooms than in large ones, but men tended to do just the reverse. Similar effects have been found for competition in all-girl and all-boy groups (Freedman, Levy, Buchanan, & Price, 1972). Although this type of relationship has not always been found, it has occurred often enough to suggest that men and women may respond differently to high-density situations.

In general, crowding *amplifies* what is occurring (as do other parts of our social life), whether this is positive or negative (Freedman, 1975). Parties and football games are crowded environments most of us seek out for pleasure — the excitement of the crowd increases ours. Going to a crowded bar after an irritating day at the office may result in a sudden lifting of a bad mood. People who are put into situations that violate their distance preferences react physiologically and become less creative than under preferred conditions (Aiello & Thompson, 1980).

The Built Environment

''We shape our buildings, and thereafter our buildings shape us.'' When he said this, Winston Churchill was referring to the reconstruction of the sixteenth-century House of Commons. The Commons was destroyed by bombing in World War II, and many in England wanted to reconstruct the building along more modern lines. Churchill, however, felt that the design of the building had, in some part, determined the course of British politics. The oblong shape of the Commons room encouraged the existence of two opposed parties that had a number of leaders rather than just one. It encouraged confrontation rather than cooperation. The building was rebuilt as it had been, brick by brick.

Although Churchill was speaking of a political institution, his observation ''our buildings shape us'' is universally applicable. Our built environment has a profound effect on how well we live and work. Failure to recognize this can lead good intentions into disaster.

The Pruitt–Igoe housing project in St. Louis was built in the 1950s as a radical new approach to improving life. The hope was to replace the slums of the black ghetto (Jacobs, 1959). It was assumed that new housing would automatically be better. So a large high-rise project was built that effectively and instantly ''replaced'' the slum. However, it did not include any of the *benefits* of the ghetto. Twenty years later, part of it was torn down because people would not live in it any longer (Figure 18-7). Why?

FIGURE 18-7
The Pruitt–Igoe Housing Project

Many housing projects contain design flaws that a knowledge of human needs and of the relationship of spatial arrangements to behavior could have prevented. High rises such as the Pruitt–Igoe project, are usually set off in an open space (Figure 18-8). This seems like a good, humane idea at first glance, but on closer inspection, it is clearly the opposite. In poor neighborhoods, there is frequently a network of affiliation that makes an area a true community, even if it is run down. The streets are safe because so many people are on them, and other people keep an eye on the street from their windows. In high rises with spacious grounds, full

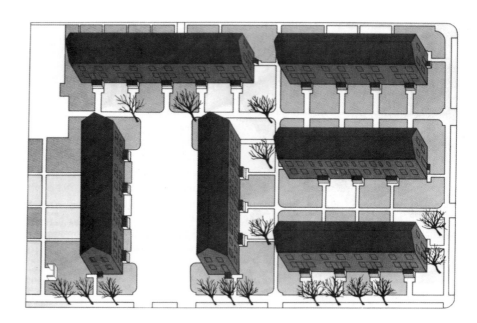

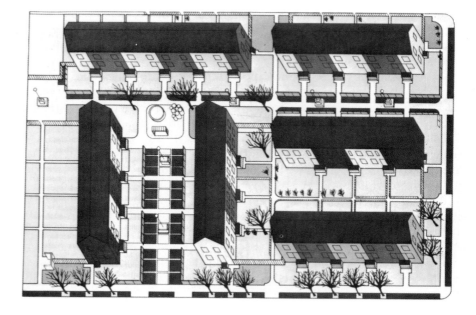

FIGURE 18-8
Modifying the Built Environment
Before the Clason Point housing project in New York City was modified (top), the crime rate was rising and the buildings were deteriorating. The modification (bottom) assigned parts of the grounds to the residents to treat as their own front and rear yards. This ended the totally open access from all directions and, along with other modifications and increased community interest that developed, contributed to lowering the crime rate and improving the residents' attitudes about both their built environment and their social environment.
(After Newman, 1979)

surveillance by occupants is not possible, and from about the fourth floor up, keeping an eye out for trouble is not very effective anyway. The open spaces therefore become a "no man's land" in which people are justifiably afraid to walk (Jacobs, 1959).

ADAPTING TO
THE MODERN
WORLD:
STABILITY

An essential component of health seems to be the maintenance of a stability inside one's body and a sense of stability about the external world. The human brain evolved to organize the world so that critical instabilities that represent threats to health and survival might be identified.

The brain reduces the ever-changing, "blooming, buzzing confusion" of the real world to a stable, organized model. It does so by radically selecting sensory information, refining and processing it, and organizing it into a workable set of routines that can encompass the world. Against this backdrop the brain then attempts to note changes or instabilities such as an irregular beating of the heart or a bear approaching—irregularities that may signal danger.

However, one's approach to stability should not include the assumption that the world is static. Friends come and go, people move, people die, ideas change, people change. If one's entire sense of stability rests on such shifting sands, one is likely to be highly vulnerable. It is possible to find stability and learn to live in a rapidly changing world by regarding *change* as what is stable. When changes are immediately perceived as threats, this upsets the stability of the organism because the change cannot be comfortably incorporated into one's view of themselves or the world. However, changes understood as challenges and opportunities for growth can be incorporated into a stable, yet flexible, sense of the world. This requires an enormous cognitive and emotional flexibility. The ability to attach and strongly bond with others needs to be counterbalanced by the ability to detach and shift one's perspective.

If this approach is beginning to sound familiar, it is because it has been a part of traditional philosophies and religious teachings since earliest times. The medical

Activities involving other people draw us out of ourselves and into a larger involvement with life, which can be a very effective coping mechanism.

systems of many ancient and traditional societies were proponents of this perennial philosophy.

Relationships with people, pets, and plants; activities that draw us out of a narrow concern with ourselves into a larger involvement with life; philosophies, cultural beliefs, and religions that enable us to see how our lives fit into a larger picture—all of these things may protect our health. These explorations shift one's organization of the world away from a focus on the scurryings of daily events and toward a more stable, complete view of life. It is a view in which there will always be change, separation loss, and death of individuals, but life itself and our contribution to it will continue.

People can learn to transcend the normal range of human reactions and human knowledge. In many ways this achieves stability at a more organized level. Religious and spiritual figures describe a view of life as an organized process, and our local hysteria, fads, and concerns as deviations and minor disruptions. Again, this is not such an esoteric perception as one might think, and it is not far off of much contemporary thought about health. Robert Eliot, who worked with heart attack-prone patients ("hot reactors"), advises just such a shift in perspective. He taught his heart patients two points to remember:

1. Don't sweat the small stuff.
   and
2. It's all small stuff (Eliot & Breo, 1984).

These recommendations, common to health professionals as well as traditional and modern psychologists, may point to well-developed adaptations leading to a stabler, healthier way to view ourselves, our lives, and our place in society. That the words "whole," "heal," and "holy" come from the same root is not an accident. *Seeing things as whole makes them organized and stable.* Idries Shah recently observed:

> The human being is, almost by definition, one who doesn't know what is going to happen tomorrow—whether he is going to be run over by a streetcar in two minutes or drop dead in five.
> The human being does, in fact, live a transient life. But what he tries to do is to pretend that life is constant. What he can actually do is recognize that life is not constant—even solid objects are not solid and so on. He can be prepared for change so that change does not cause stress reactions, ulcers and worse. (Shah, 1986)

It all works together: the countless adjustments of the heart, the control of the immune system, the secretion of chemicals to allow communication between the brain and the organs, the stability of the body's internal environment, and the stability of the person in the world. Cell to self to society. But we are just at the beginning of a view that brings such psychological, medical, and physiological knowledge together. This is the promise and the payoff of health psychology. A sense of connectedness and responsibility seems to draw something within us out of ourselves and link us to the larger world. The predisposition to communicate with others, to bond, appears to be vital to our health. It is also deeply rooted in human evolution.

1. *Stress* is the failure of adaptability. There are numerous situations that cause the environmental or internal demands to exceed the adaptive resources of an organism. These include catastrophes, major life events, chronic life strains, and everyday hassles.

2. Stressful life events have been studied extensively in their relationship to health. People are more likely to become ill after experiencing major changes in their lives. A scale of *life change units* has been developed that assesses *major life changes* a person has experienced in the recent past, including positive, negative, and neutral events. Other important stressors include those of the working environment: workload, work relationships, and unemployment. It has also recently been found that the number of daily hassles also seems to strongly affect health.

3. The *emergency reaction* is the basic reaction to stress. It includes the *fight-or-flight* emergency reaction and the *general adaptation syndrome.* The emergency reaction includes an increase in the rate and strength of the heartbeat, contraction of the spleen, release of stored sugar from the liver for use by the muscles, redistribution of the blood supply, deepening of respiration, dilation of the pupils, and an increase in the blood's ability to seal wounds. The general adaptation syndrome occurs in three stages: (1) an alarm reaction similar to the fight-or-flight reaction; (2) increased resistance to the stressor; and (3) exhaustion in which the body's adaptation energy runs out.

4. An important new area of psychological research is learning to improve one's health. Many diseases can be modified by individual's actions. Psychologists are currently applying their knowledge to aid in a fresh adaptation: to learn to be healthy in new circumstances. Some people are better able to withstand the difficulties of the modern world. Identifying what makes them ''hardy'' may make it easier for others. When confronted with a stressor, some people seem to be able to cope without becoming anxious and aroused in a harmful way. These people appraise the potential stressor in such a way as to avoid stress. Kobasa identified the components of psychological hardiness as commitment, challenge, and control. Hardy executives were only one-half as likely to get sick as less hardy people confronting similar stressors.

5. In a new kind of therapy, called *transactional psychophysiology,* Lynch tries to link the social world with physiology. Patients learn how their blood pressure goes up when they speak rapidly and how it goes down when they pause for breath. They learn subtle physical signals, too small to be considered symptoms, that warn them when their blood pressure is rising.

6. Antonovsky proposes that resistance to disease also depends on a sense of *coherence* —a global orientation that expresses the extent to which one has a pervasive, enduring, though dynamic feeling of confidence that one's internal and external environments are predictable and that there is a high probability that things will work out as well as can reasonably be expected. People with a strong sense of coherence may be more likely to mobilize and effectively use resistance resources, such as friends and coping skills, to deal with potentially stressful situations. When this sense of coherence in a person's world is disrupted, he or she is more likely to become ill. If the world is disorganized, it is not clear what appropriate action to take in a given situation.

7. Many of society's current difficulties are rooted in the past evolution of human beings. There were no radical changes in the brain throughout human evolution, but our

cultural evolution has proceeded at an enormous rate. This leads to a built-in bias to misapply the processes of the mind. Because of the characteristics of the sensory–brain system, current information is automatically given high weight in making decisions. For example, people were more afraid of the first few small atomic bombs than they are of the tens of thousands of much more powerful nuclear weapons that are now in U.S. and Soviet arsenals.

8. We constantly judge things by comparison and our judgment shifts constantly. An automobile ad says: "BMW prices range from $60,000 to $24,950." This ad makes your comparisons shift, and you begin telling yourself that the $24,950 car is actually quite cheap for a BMW. Comparison processes contribute to many major miscalculations, even the Watergate scandal.

9. Computers may have profound effects on the experiences that people have during work, especially deskilling and upgrading. People generally feel that their jobs have been improved somewhat by computers, but there have been no large-scale studies of actual job changes in the economy as a whole. Computers may also have important effects on learning. By giving students highly individualized instruction and immediate feedback, computers can sometimes significantly increase learning speeds. Computers can also be used to create highly motivating instructional environments, which may lead students to give more time and higher quality attention to their educational tasks.

10. Hall developed proxemics, a method of making our spatial habits explicit. This analysis begins with the concept of *personal space,* a small, protective "sphere" that an organism maintains between itself and others. Distances that may be considered "invasions" depend on one's culture, and this can easily lead to misunderstandings. A person meeting with another whose cultural distance is less than his or her own can be driven across a room trying to avoid this "rude pursuer."

11. Our built environment has a profound effect on how well we live and work. Failure to recognize this can lead good intentions into disaster. Many housing projects contain design flaws that a knowledge of human needs and of the relationship of spatial arrangements to behavior could have prevented. High rises in the Pruitt–Igoe housing project were torn down because people would not live in it because they were not designed with the idea of a close community space in mind.

TERMS AND CONCEPTS		
	adaptation	health psychology
	blood pressure	hypertension
	cardiovascular health	life change units (LCU)
	chronic life strains	major life changes
	coherence	population density
	deskilling	proxemics
	emergency reaction	psychoimmunology
	expert system	somatic etiologies
	fight-or-flight	stress
	general adaptation syndrome	transactional psychophysiology
	hardiness	upgrading
	hassles	uplifts

Advances: Journal of the Institute for the Advancement of Health (Institute for the Advancement of Health, 16 East 53rd Street, New York, NY 10022).

This professional quarterly journal, initiated in 1983, examines important developments of how mind-body interactions affect health and disease.

Eliot, R., & Breo, D. (1984). *Is it worth dying for?* New York: Bantam.

Perhaps the most readable of all the "save your heart" books. It gives a good overview and the evidence about "hot reactors."

Frank, J. (1973). *Persuasion and Healing.* Baltimore: Johns Hopkins Press.

In this highly readable book, Frank investigates such diverse therapeutic approaches as shamanism, faith healing, religious revivalism, placebo effect, and the modern psychotherapies. He finds some striking commonalties including the ability of the healer to mobilize expectant faith, restore morale, and alter the beliefs of the patient.

Locke, S., & Colligan, D. (1986). *The healer within.* New York: E. P. Dutton.

An account of the roots and modern emergence of psychoneuroimmunology, the scientific study of the mind, the nervous system, and the immune system.

Lynch, J. (1977). *The broken heart.* (1985). *The language of the heart.* New York: Basic Books.

Perhaps the most seminal contribution of how the mind, the heart, and the social world are related.

Winston, P., & Prendergast, K. (Eds.). (1984). *The AI business.* Cambridge, MA: MIT Press.

Haugeland, J. (Ed.). (1985). *Mind design: Philosophy, psychology, and artificial intelligence.* Cambridge, MA: MIT Press.

Two important books on how computers are changing the world we live in.

Chapter 19

Development in Adulthood

George Orwell wrote: "At 50 you have the face you deserve." If early development is a series of *stages of growth,* then later development is primarily a series of *choices,* in other words, *self-development.*

The process of choice and self-development continues as long as we live. In middle age people change careers, leave unhappy marriages, and form new friendships. The new study of adult development challenges many of the common stereotypes about the "declines" in aging (Plate 19).

There is little decline in brain functioning in the aged with normal levels of stimulation. Barring illness, this decline is not seen until we are very old. I once watched a friend direct a film that had a part in it for a woman 65 years old. The actress engaged for the part was herself about 65. The director told her to act like a 65-year-old woman in the scene. Since she was one, she acted like she normally did. She smiled, almost leaped around the room, and walked with a spring in her step. This did not satisfy my friend. The woman was acting too young for him. Finally, because expensive time on the set was adding up, he got an idea. He told her, "Act like you are 110 years old." Then he got the effect he wanted.

You will spend more than three-quarters of your life as an adult. The majority of successes, joys, and sorrows lie ahead. You will fall in love, probably marry,

The well-known American painter Georgia O'Keeffe remained vital and active up to her death at the age of 93.

achieve some important goals, and fail at others. There are transitions you may face: becoming a professional, getting married, becoming a parent. Nearly half of you will get divorced. You will also probably face your parents' death and, certainly, your own.

In this chapter we pick up the threads of our discussion on early development that were woven in Chapter 3.

THEORIES OF ADULT DEVELOPMENT

Jung

Jung (1953) speculated that different developmental stages have different problems. In *puberty*, prohibitions and limitations become internalized and conflict with the self begins. *Youth* runs from puberty to about age 35. During this time the person confronts problems of sexuality, widening horizons, and establishing oneself in the world. Around age 35 or 40, subtle changes begin.

There may be changes in character; traits and interests long suppressed from childhood may begin to assert themselves. Often, men who have buried themselves in their careers may find themselves becoming more interested in their families. Women who took time off for child rearing may now look forward to starting a career. Conversely, a person may become more rigid in his or her convictions and principles, as if they are becoming endangered and it is now more necessary to reinforce them.

Jung characterized a person's values in the first half of life as expanding in an *outward* direction. In the second half of life, he felt the values become more *inward* directed. These include self-knowledge, cultural concerns, and preparation for death.

Erikson

See Chapter 3, section on Erikson's Stages.

Erikson recognized that development processes occur in a social context, hence his term *psychosocial development.* As we saw in Chapter 3, Erikson viewed the life course as a series of eight successive stages. Each stage has a particular *developmental task,* a dialectical conflict that the person must resolve. The adult developmental tasks are (1) identity versus role confusion, (2) intimacy versus isolation, (3) generativity versus self-absorption, and (4) integrity versus despair. The resolution of each task forms the basis for the next stage. If the task is not resolved, damaging consequences result, which interfere with the successful completion of the next stage. An adolescent who has not successfully negotiated the identity crisis cannot establish intimate bonds with another in early adulthood.

Erikson's (1986) writings provide a rich descriptive framework for understanding the life cycle. But unfortunately they are difficult to translate into "objective" measures. Vaillant (1977) simplified the concepts of the stages to measure them and found some evidence for this hierarchical concept. In a large longitudinal study, men judged as "best outcomes" in terms of socioeconomic success, length of marriage, status in the community, and so on had resolved Erikson's developmental tasks. Those judged as "worst outcomes" had not. Men who achieved intimacy were more likely to be involved in tasks that reflected generativity. The worst outcomes often had childhoods that were rated not conducive to developing basic trust, autonomy, and initiative. As adolescents, they had less integrated and secure identities, and later, they were less likely to achieve intimacy in marriage and tended to reject responsibility for others in midlife.

Erik Erikson

Social Factors in Development

Social psychologists and sociologists view the life span in terms of progression through successive *roles* and *statuses.* A woman may be a toddler, school child, adolescent, college student, wife, mother, working mother, chemist, grandparent, and retiree all at different life stages. The process of learning *norms*—behavior appropriate to a given role—is termed **socialization.** This is a continuous process throughout the life span.

Within a culture, there are *timetables,* generally agreed upon times for entering or completing certain roles. Neugarten and associates asked a middle-aged, middle-class sample about the appropriate ages for a number of events. They found a very high consensus. Furthermore, there are different timetables for different roles; for example, there is a wider range of ages at which it is acceptable to become a father than to graduate from college. These timetables may vary according to social class, ethnicity, sex, and so on.

The higher the social class, the later the age for various roles (Neugarten & Hagestad, 1976). Working-class women tend to marry and have children earlier than middle-class women. Cultures may also have different timetables for roles. In the United States, a 15-year-old boy is still in school with few adult responsibilities, but in traditional cultures, he may be considered a man and have a family to support.

Much research in the past two decades has been directed at biological and cognitive changes in aging. This investigation has emphasized individual differences in how people age.

BIOLOGICAL AND COGNITIVE CHANGES

Biological Development

When we are young, we cannot imagine not being able to bend over easily or trot across the street. As we grow older, we first experience subtle changes in our bodies and then may face increasing physical limitations.

Age- and Disease-Related Changes

Age-related changes in bodily functioning are different from disease-related changes. Birren and his associates (1963) studied 47 men aged 67 to 91 who appeared healthy. They were given lengthy and extensive examinations of medical, physiological, psychological, and social functioning. They were divided into two groups: those in Group A were optimally healthy on every measure, but those in Group B, who appeared healthy, actually had subclinical diseases, such as the beginnings of diabetes, heart disease, and the like. Many of the decrements associated with being old were absent in the healthy men but were present in the men in Group B. This is an indication that impairments are often more a function of *disease* than of *age.*

Why Do We Age?

Aging results from many different processes, some of which are genetically controlled. In shorter lived species, genetics is more important than it is in human beings (Medvedev, 1975). Earlier theories of aging in human beings focused on genetic mechanisms such as limitations on cell division or breakdown in DNA repair mechanisms. Recent studies instead focus on changes in the immune and neuroendocrine systems as the basic mechanisms of aging in human beings.

The immune system distinguishes between what is "us" and what is "foreign." As we age, our immune systems become less competent. We are less able to fight off foreign invaders or *antigens* such as infections and cancers. We literally lose the ability to recognize ourselves. We then develop *autoantibodies* which can attack our own organs and joints. One study showed that elderly people with impaired immune functioning die much earlier than elders who maintain more normal immune system functioning. However, immune system changes may either cause or result from other aging processes (Hausman & Weksler, 1985).

Research on the *neuroendocrine* systems holds great promise for understanding the effects of aging. The neuroendocrine system, controlled by the hypothalamus and the pituitary, is responsible (among other things) for starting and stopping menstruation in women. Researchers think that these neural structures may play a role in other aging processes as well. Overproduction of or artificially increasing the levels of certain neuroendocrines can lead to accelerated aging in fish and rats. Much more research is needed to find out if there are similar mechanisms in humans (Finch & Landfield, 1985).

Changes in the Brain

There is *less* change in the aging brain than in the rest of the body. Many people think that the brain loses cells as we age. However, we came into the world with more brain cells than we need. One result of development is the "pruning" of brain cells (Greenough, 1982), possibly for more efficient functioning. Studies of rats under controlled conditions show that most brain cells are actually lost in the first years of life and that relatively fewer brain cells are lost in later life (Diamond, 1980).

As many as two million people in the United States suffer from Alzheimer's disease.

Encouraging results from brain physiology show that the cortex of the brain in older rats can increase in size if they are put in an enriched environment that has a lot of sensory stimulation and activities that the rats can engage in. So the brain continues to adapt and develop throughout life depending on the environment. Thus, the elderly in bland institutional settings seem disoriented or confused, whereas elderly justices of the Supreme Court may be at the height of their mental abilities. As Diamond (1984) reminds us, "Use it or lose it."

Alzheimer's Disease

The ability to permanently store new information begins to decline when people reach their 60s. About 10 to 15 percent of people over 65 suffer from mild to severe symptoms of senility or senile dementia. Much of this is a normal part of growing old, but more than 50 percent of these senile people (two million in the United States) actually have **Alzheimer's disease,** a severe form of senility that can attack its victim earlier in life, even before age 65.

The symptoms of Alzheimer's disease include marked defects in thought or cognitive processes, memory, language, and perceptual abilities. In some people the onset is slow and gradual, but in others it can be quite rapid. The first and most obvious symptom is loss of the ability to remember recent experience and things learned. The cause seems to be linked to abnormalities in the hippocampus and certain regions of the cerebral cortex. These are the brain systems most dedicated to complex cognitive processes and memory functions.

There may soon be a breakthrough in treatment of Alzheimer's disease, involving the neurotransmitter ACh. Nerve cells near the hypothalamus in the *nucleus basalis* contain ACh neurons that radiate to the cortex and hippocampus. Coyle and associates (1983) examined the brains of a number of people who died from Alzheimer's disease and found loss of cells in the nucleus basalis and lower levels of chemicals associated with the ACh system in the cerebral cortex and hippocampus. It is not known whether the loss of ACh neurons is a *cause* of Alzheimer's disease, but now that a relationship between the disease and loss of ACh neurons has been established, many new treatments are possible.

Choline can improve memory performance in animals and seems to do the same for normal young adult humans. Drugs that are precursors of ACh or substances that contain choline (such as egg yolks) can be therapeutic tools with patients who are only mildly senile. Perhaps diet can impede or even prevent Alzheimer's. Some soup companies plan to add lecithin to powdered mixes (Wurtman & Wurtman, 1984), so now chicken soup might help memory as well as illness!

How Long Can We Live?

The average life span in the United States today is in the 70s, although men and minorities have shorter life spans than this. White women are the longest-lived group in our country; half of them can expect to live beyond 78. The over 80 group is the fastest growing segment of the population (Figure 19-1).

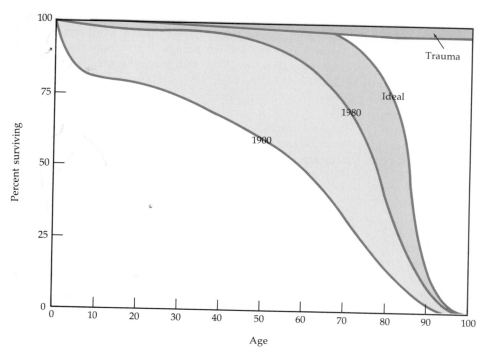

FIGURE 19-1
Survival Curve
If premature death from disease were eliminated in the United States, the population would attain the ideal survival curve. By 1980, more than 80 percent of the discrepancy between the 1900 curve and the ideal curve had been eliminated.
(From Fries & Crapo, 1981)

FIGURE 19-2
Maximal Life Span
The Caucasus villagers in this photo claim to be well over 100 years old.

Maximal life span, or how long a person *can* live, is a matter of debate. Some villagers in the Caucasus Mountains in Russia and Turkey claim to be 120, 130, and even 150 years old (Figure 19-2) (Medvedev, 1974). Many of these elderly people indeed do live a long time and are exceptionally healthy. However, there is very little evidence such as birth certificates to back up these claims.

People who live long lives often had parents and grandparents who also lived a long time. This indicates that genes may play a large role in the aging process. But life choices also play an important role. Smoking and heavy alcohol consumption shorten lives, as does eating too many fatty foods and refined sugars. Mice kept on a calorie-restricted diet age much slower than rats who gain a lot of weight. It is not yet clear that the same is true for human beings. It has been shown that exercise is very important in staying healthy and living longer. People who exercise retain muscle and bone mass, have faster reflexes, and show better neurological and cognitive functioning in later life. They also live longer (Buskirk, 1985; Paffenbarger, 1986).

Kyucharyants (1974) asked one elderly woman in the Caucasus who claimed to be 138 years old whether a fountain of youth existed in her village. She replied, "Of course, it exists, young man. It is inside each of us. Only not everyone knows how to use it."

Changes in Cognition

Intelligence

See Chapter 11, section on Modern Intelligence Testing.

If we were to take a cross section of people aged 20, 40, 60, and 80, we would find that IQ scores decrease with age. We might be tempted to conclude that people lose cognitive function after age 20. However, this conclusion does not take into account that in this century, each successive generation has been better educated. This is a major factor in IQ scores known as the *cohort* effect—the apparent decline in intelligence is due to *historical* rather than *aging* factors.

Longitudinal studies attempt to control for this problem. A group or panel of people is selected and studied over a number of years or decades. Data from longitudinal studies show *increases* in IQ scores with age — that we *gain* cognitive function after age 20. However, longitudinal studies also have a problem: the *survivor* effect. People who are more intelligent tend to live longer and to continue as participants in longitudinal studies. So the survivors in longitudinal studies make it appear as if intelligence increases.

What does happen to our intellectual capacity as we age? There appears to be very little actual change, at least not until very late in life. Verbal abilities, or *crystallized intelligence,* seem to remain relatively constant or increase slightly with age. *Fluid intelligence,* or measures of performance, decline. However, these declines are often not found before age 50 or 60, and even then they are relatively small (Botwinick, 1977).

Memory

We may, however, become more forgetful as we age. The main problem appears to be with long-term memory. Older people tend to take longer to learn new things. They seem to learn them in a less organized fashion, which makes retrieval difficult (Poon, 1985). Again, this finding may in part be a function of education or the cohort effect rather than age differences. Elders with good verbal skills often do not show many decrements in secondary memory with age (Bowles & Poon, 1982). Still, older adults report more memory problems than younger ones, especially when doing things out of their normal daily routine or when they need to remember information not used recently (Cavanaugh, Grady, & Pertmutter, 1983).

There are many different theories of why memory declines with age. There may be decreases in neuroendocrine functioning (Hines & Fozard, 1980), loss of neurons (Kinsbourne, 1980), or damage in the frontal cortex with age (Albert & Kaplan, 1980). On the other hand, Botwinick et al. (1980) assert the reason is that neurological processes slow with age. Because memory is often time-dependent, this general slowing may account for many of the cognitive deficits found in the elderly. It is also true that memory declines can be reversed by teaching elders mnemonics, or memory aids (Poon et al., 1980).

See Chapter 9, section on Mnemonics.

A dolescence is a time of exploration. If individuals do not burden themselves prematurely with adult responsibilities and commitments, this pattern of exploration continues into early adulthood. College or military service can provide a hiatus of a sort, in which young persons may be physically separate from their parents, while not completely independent. They have time to build a basis for living in the adult world.

While there is no definite biological event that signals the beginning of early adulthood, for most people there are several hallmarks of this period: beginning a career, getting married, and becoming a parent.

EARLY ADULTHOOD: WORK AND MARRIAGE

Work and Career

People assume that in their early 20s they must decide on an occupation and "settle down." Actually, the process of "forming a career" is very complicated

Early adulthood is usually a time of deciding on a career, getting married, setting up a household, and starting a family.

and may take several years or even decades. Kimmel (1980) identifies six factors that influence occupational choice: background factors, role models, experience, interests, personality, and research.

Background factors include socioeconomic status, ethnic origin, intelligence, race, sex, and education. These may set boundaries or limitations on the range of occupational choice.

A person may choose an occupation on the basis of identification with a *role model*. A woman may decide to become a dentist like her uncle. Of course, such a person may be more than a role model; he or she may also provide entry opportunities. An important figure in this regard is a *mentor*, someone who eases the youth into adulthood (Levinson, 1978). A mentor ideally aids a person in developing his or her own autonomy, interests, and commitment to an occupation. The mentor may be a teacher, an older colleague, or a family friend.

A person's *experience* is also an important factor. Pre-med students often mention that they want to become a doctor because of the care given to them during a serious illness as a child. Of course, a person's *personality* and *interests* may be better expressed in or matched to a particular field. Finally, a person may *research* the job market and decide that the best opportunities exist in computer programming or in setting up a mail order business, for example, and then obtain the specialized training needed in those fields.

Marriage

Marriage generally has a profound impact on a person's development and is considered to be a major developmental milestone. If you ask a person why he or she marries, the automatic answer will often be, "Because I love so-and-so." However, if one probes a little deeper, other reasons for marriage become more apparent.

People may marry to get out of a difficult situation with their parents, to show that they are now "adults." They may do so simply because it "feels like the right time." Nearly half (in some samples) marry because the woman became pregnant (Rubin, 1976).

Whatever the reason, marriage responsibilities may seem huge, especially when people marry very young. When asked if there was a period of adjustment after getting married, a young person gave this response:

> Was there? Wow! Before I got married, I only had to do for myself; after, there was somebody else along all the time. . . . Then, I suddenly found I had to worry about where we'd live and whether we had enough money, and all those things like that. Before, I could always get a job and make enough money to take care of me and give something to the house. Then, after we got married, I suddenly had all those responsibilities. Before, it didn't make any difference if I didn't feel like going to work sometimes. Then, all of a sudden, it made one hell of a difference because the rent might not get paid, or, if it got paid, there might not be enough food money. (Rubin, 1976)

Becoming a Parent

Having a baby has a profound effect not only on the mother, but on the whole family. It is not so much a crisis as a developmental stage — it is disruptive, with some possibility of harm, but also the possibility of growth (Grossman, Eichler, & Winickhoff, 1980).

Becoming a parent for the first time signals that the person is adult. He or she has adult responsibilities for caring and providing for someone else. A woman may begin to identify herself exclusively as a mother, instead of as other identities (wife, writer, gourmet cook, and so on). She often becomes more sympathetic to her own mother (Cowan et al., 1978).

Having a very young infant is time-consuming and tiring, and sheer exhaustion may account for low morale. A woman who shifts from full-time employment to full-time motherhood may find this disruptive (Cowan et al., 1978).

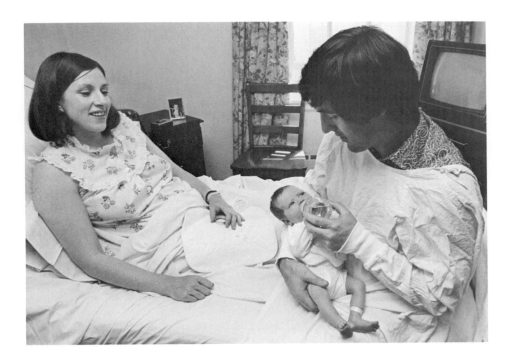

Furthermore, loss of her income may produce financial strain at a time when expenses increase.

But all this may be offset by the sheer exhilaration of becoming a parent. Many have described the joy, awe, and sense of fulfillment a woman feels upon giving birth. Men may also experience similar feelings. Asked to describe his reaction during his wife's delivery, one man said:

> It was very powerful. There we were—my wife pushing and I pushing with her—then the baby slipped out. The doctor suctioned her and cut the cord, and the nurse cleaned her up and brought her to me. She was crying, and her color changed from blue to pink. I held her, my bright-eyed little child, and she looked right at me and quieted in my arms. (Fein, 1978)

Whether motherhood is positive or negative depends on the mother's characteristics, the child's, and the husband's. The mother's satisfaction is likely to be very low under certain circumstances. The marital relationship may be poor, the husband may be anxious, or the mother may have a history of anxiety or depression. The infant could be difficult, sick, handicapped, or temperamental (Grossman et al., 1980). The woman may feel frustrated, depressed, and resentful, and her relationship with her husband and with the child may deteriorate. However, if these three elements are in reasonably good order, then becoming a parent is likely to be an enriching, rewarding experience for both parents. The woman may become more self-assured, and the marital relationship may become closer (Cowan et al., 1978).

Marital Satisfaction

A good marriage is material to health and well-being. Married people, especially men, live longer and may be less likely to develop mental illness. Wives are often the most important source of social support for men. After being laid off work, men with supportive wives show fewer negative effects of stress (Cobb & Kasl, 1977).

Being married (even a bad marriage) appears better than no relationship at all. An Israeli study of 10,000 marriages found that those who reported a happy marriage had lower death rates than those who said they were unhappy with their relationship. Other studies show that being married, whether satisfying or not, offers more protection than no relationship at all (Gerstel & Riesman, 1981).

In fact, getting a divorce can seriously affect one's health. One study showed that the effect of divorce on the death rate was about the same as smoking a pack of cigarettes a day (Moscowitz, 1975).

	Death Rate	
	NONSMOKERS	SMOKERS
Married	796	1,560
Divorced	1,420	2,675

Divorce may merit a warning from the Surgeon General: divorce may be hazardous to your health!

"His and Her" Marriages

Marriage appears to be clearly beneficial, *especially for men*. Compared to men who are divorced, widowed, or never married, married men live much longer, have fewer mental and physical illnesses, and appear happier. Divorced and widowed men also remarry very quickly. However, married *women* have higher rates of depression than married men. Marriage, in general, may be unfavorable to women. Married women have higher rates of mental illness than married men, while single women have lower rates of mental illness than single men. And when a spouse dies, it is the man who suffers more than the woman, indicating that he was more dependent on the wife than she on him (Longino & Lipman, 1981).

Part of the reason for the different reactions to the loss of a spouse lies in the different social relationships men and women form in our culture. In American society male friendships are not lifelong but are related to specific situations: school chums, sports or fishing buddies, and work colleagues. Men do not usually find their main emotional source of support in these relationships. They do not usually have a close confidant outside of their marriage, and their friends change more often than do women's.

COMMUNICATION AND MARITAL SATISFACTION

There is a high correlation ($r = 0.82$) between how well couples communicate and their marital satisfaction (Gottman, 1979). Happy couples talk to each other more about a wider range of subjects than unhappy pairs. They show more sensitivity to each other's feelings and convey the sense that they understand what is being said to them. Happily married couples try to keep open verbal and nonverbal communication, and when angry, express their dissatisfaction. When there is a serious problem, the main indicator of whether a marriage will succeed is the amount of expressed anger and unhappiness, indicating that communication in marriage is important (Gottman, in press).

In contrast, unhappily married people use less "give and take" in resolving differences and tend to distort nonverbal communication. They fail to develop a private communication system (Gottman, in press). Instead, they tend to "mirror" each other's behavior sequences. Complaint is met with complaint, proposals with counterproposals, negative feelings with more negative feelings.

By contrast, women's friendships have, at least historically, been quite different. They maintain close ties with friends of youth and their families, and they are more likely to keep up long and permanent friendships even after an old friend has moved or remarried. They have more close, long-lasting confidants, whom they tend to keep even after marriage. Because of these strong social bonds, a woman is less vulnerable to the loss and less likely to suffer from the pain of bereavement.

For men the increased illness following divorce relates mainly to the loss of a confidant, loneliness, and the loss of the social networks that the marriage provided. For women the increases in symptoms and mental health problems after divorce correlates most significantly to the increased financial strain coupled with child care responsibilities. Divorced women also suffer as a consequence of loneliness, but women confide in a variety of friends. So adverse affects of divorce are buffered somewhat.

Divorce

If a marriage becomes unhappy enough, the couple may decide to divorce. The rate of divorce is now at an all-time high. Between 1970 and 1979, the divorce rate nearly doubled. Currently, one-third of all marriages can expect to end in divorce. The rate has increased to nearly half of all new marriages.

Some people are more likely to divorce than others. People who were married when they were teenagers and have little education and low incomes are most likely to divorce (Glick & Norton, 1977). A low income is likely to put a great strain on a marriage. People who marry very young are less likely to have the maturity necessary to cope with the various problems of a marital relationship, household economics, and child rearing.

Obviously, such a widespread phenomenon has attracted a great deal of attention. There is legitimate concern for what effect divorce has on individuals and on society. How stressful is divorce? Is it harder on men or on women? What are the problems divorced men and women are likely to face? Which is worse, living with a "bad" marriage or divorcing? What are the best strategies for coping with divorce? And perhaps most important of all, what does it do to the children?

Effects of Divorce on Adults

There are four periods of the divorce process: marital distress, the decision to divorce, separation, and postdivorce. There is no doubt that the whole process is very painful: people who are separating are often lonely, anxious, angry, depressed, feel rejected, and have low self-esteem. Separated and divorced individuals have high rates of illness and disability (White & Bloom, 1981).

See Chapter 3, section on Effects of Divorce on Children.

The separation period is more stressful than either the preceding marital distress or the postdivorce period. The process of separation is just as painful whether one is leaving a relatively good marriage or a relatively bad one (Bloom & White, 1981). However, in postdivorce, both men and women are likely to state that their situation is better than it was before the divorce (Albrecht, 1980). Nevertheless, it still takes approximately three years after a divorce for adults to regain their sense of equilibrium.

Indeed, women are more likely than men to report divorce as being traumatic and stressful (Albrecht, 1980). However, assessments of emotional distress and psychosomatic symptoms show that divorce is as painful for men, if not more so. Women are distressed at the beginning of the divorce process, while men's distress appears later (Argyle & Henderson, 1985).

Coping with Divorce

Getting divorced, especially when there are children, may bring about a host of problems. They involve contacts with the former spouse, problems with interpersonal relationships, loneliness, practical problems, financial concerns, and problems with parent–child interaction (Berman & Turk, 1981). Income generally drops precipitously, although this may be more true for women than for men (White & Bloom, 1981). Only about one-third of ex-husbands contribute to the financial support of their children and former wives (Brandwein, Brown, & Fox, 1974). Half of all households headed by single women are at or below the poverty level (U.S. Bureau of the Census, 1975).

There are practical problems of taking over the tasks previously done by the ex-spouse, such as cooking, household and car maintenance, and child care and discipline. Men with primary custody of children are especially likely to feel disorganized and have problems coping with practical demands. Social adjustment is also difficult. A person may discover that some friends were actually closer to the other spouse, and social networks become disrupted. Women with children may have an especially hard time dating, but men usually enter into a "flurry" of social activity (Hetherington et al., 1977). Contacts with former spouses are often distressing. Problems with parent–child combinations may increase, especially when mothers must discipline male children (Argyle & Henderson, 1985).

The establishment of a new satisfying sexual relationship, for both men and women, helps the most in recovering from divorce (Berman & Turk, 1981). This underlines the importance of interpersonal relationships in our lives.

Settling Down

For people who have followed the traditional family and career patterns, the beginning of middle adulthood in the 30s is often a time of "settling down" (Levinson, 1978). If the marriage has survived the tumultuous beginnings, the husband and wife have largely learned how to accommodate to each other.

With the children a little older, parenthood is a little easier. Jobs have become more stable, and financial security is a little better. A person has often developed some skills and acquires some seniority at work. He or she is less likely to be fired or laid off. He or she may have had some rewarding promotions and may feel on the way to becoming established in the field.

For others, the 30s are a time for crucial decisions. A woman who has intentionally forgone having children for the sake of a career must now make the decision whether or not to become a mother. The "biological clock" is running out. Past the age of 35, a woman faces increasing risk of difficulty in pregnancy. After she is 40, her child has an increased risk of birth defects, especially Down's syndrome.

If a person has not yet settled into a career, he or she may feel time pressure to find one that better suits his or her needs or interests. Women who have been full-time homemakers may start going back to school or working.

Middle Age

Middle age is more of a social stage of life than a specific biological event. Most researchers set its boundaries from about age 40 to about 65, although today age 60 is still part of the prime of life. However, since it is socially influenced, the boundaries of middle age differ in different groups. In the upper middle class, the 40s are considered the prime of life, and middle age is considered to start at about age 50. In the lower income groups, the 30s are the prime of life, and middle age starts at age 40. Marriage and parenthood begin earlier in lower income groups, thus children leave the home when the parents are younger. The earnings and prestige of blue collar jobs peak in the 30s, while for the upper middle class, the peak is usually in the 40s and sometimes 50s (Kimmel, 1980).

Midlife Crisis

At this time people review and assess their early adulthood. They may try to change those facets of their life with which they are dissatisfied. They may attempt to resolve the psychological issues introduced by entering the final half of life (Levinson, 1978).

A *midlife crisis* occurs when a person discovers that he or she is not happy with life, and that goals either have not been attained or do not bring the expected satisfactions. The awareness of one's own mortality—that a whole lifetime no longer lies ahead—may also prompt radical changes (Golan, 1986).

Two personality types are prone to depression in midlife (Block, 1971). Early maturing, socially gregarious men may have a hard time with the passing of their youth. They are often athletically oriented and nonintellectual. Lonely, independent women, on the other hand, may become depressed as their chance to have a family fades. They have often primarily invested in their intellect to the exclusion of social relationships. The woman who remains strongly involved with her children may have difficulty in the "empty nest" stage (see the next section) (Argyle & Henderson, 1985). Finally, it may not be the high-flying executive who has a midlife crisis; poorer people are actually more likely to become depressed at this time.

Of course, it may not be possible to equate depression with midlife crisis. Midlife is a time of transition for many, and transitions are often stressful (Lowenthal, Fiske, Thurner, & Chiriboga, 1974). However, many of these transitions are eagerly anticipated and provide opportunities for growth as well as crisis. Middle age may be a spicier time of life than youth realize.

Menopause and the "Empty Nest"

Not all of the important events in middle age cause a crisis. Menopause and the "empty nest" are good examples of this. Menopause generally occurs between the ages of 48 and 51 (Talbert, 1977). It may be associated with hot flashes, irritability, crying spells, and depression. However, in a study of over 700 Japanese and American women, 75 percent reported none of the symptoms usually associated with menopause (Goodman, Stewart, & Gilbert, 1977).

It is primarily younger women who feel that menopause is a disagreeable event. Older women (aged 45–55) were more likely to feel that menopause creates no major changes (Neugarten, Wood, Kraines, & Loomis, 1963). Loss of fertility may have a profound effect on a woman's self-esteem, but many women feel that not having to worry about menstruation or getting pregnant is positive.

Similarly, the *empty nest period,* when children leave home and become independent, is often thought to be a time of crisis for the family. A woman who is no longer a mother and who has no other interests may become depressed (Bart, 1971). However, not all women become despondent. In an analysis of ethnic differences, Bart found that Jewish mothers had the highest rate of depression, WASPs an intermediate rate, and blacks the lowest. This may reflect differences in family patterns in these groups.

Other responsibilities may also keep a woman at home at this stage of her life. With increasing age, the middle-aged person's own parents are likely to become more dependent and may need extensive assistance. This responsibility usually falls to the woman (Robinson & Thurner, 1979). It may entail great sacrifices of time and money. Having an active, healthy parent may be a source of comfort and reassurance in middle age, but having to care for parents who show increasing signs of mental deterioration may be a source of great stress.

For many, however, the empty nest period is a time of great satisfaction. Once the adolescent rebellion is over, families may have improved relationships with their children. Parents may take great pride in the accomplishments of their offspring and may delight in becoming grandparents (Neugarten & Weinstein, 1964). Also, for a woman, the empty nest period may be a time of decreased responsibility and a time when she can finally pursue her own interests (Deutscher, 1964). Couples may find that they have time again not only for themselves but also for each other. The increased privacy and leisure time may improve their sexual relationship. Many start saving and planning for their retirement and look forward to various leisure activities such as traveling (Figure 19-3).

FIGURE 19-3
Joys of Middle Age
Many people find that the departure of their grown children brings them new freedom and an increased satisfaction with their marriage.

Late Adulthood

Toward the end of life our biology begins to claim us once again. There are certainly some declines in mental and physical functions. But if a person remains active, these are often minimal until very late in life. People who are *forced* to retire may begin to decline in functioning. Others, who find retirement a time of pleasure, may flourish.

For most older people, the traditional "frail old person" stereotype does not apply. Due to better nutrition and medical care, today many elderly people are active and vigorous well into their 70s. Neugarten (1974) suggested that the elderly be divided into two groups: the "young-old" and the "old-old." The young-old, aged 55 to 75, have good health, relative economic security, and leisure time resulting from a decrease in traditional work and family responsibilities. The old-old are more likely to be frail and in ill health.

Another myth about old age is that most adult children abandon their parents to nursing or old age homes. Actually only 4 to 5 percent of the elderly are institutionalized; families go through great sacrifices to maintain their parents at home (Lowenthal, 1964). However, nearly 23 percent of people over age 80 are in nursing homes. Most elderly, however, live near their children and have constant contact with them (Shanas, 1979).

There are some inescapable facts of life that everyone faces in late adulthood. Bereavement and grief are a part of this phase of life. Just before death, we decline, although we might cling to life for a while. We may want to reach another birthday or to live to see an important (say, 50th) wedding anniversary. Everyone dies and yet, until recently, research on death has been as taboo as research on sex. The early evidence indicates that people go through a series of stages of dying, and it is not all that unpleasant.

Retirement

Retirement at the end of life, with its implications of leisure time, is a recent phenomenon. Previously, most people worked until they were too ill to continue. Now, with better health and more economic security, many people look forward to (or dread) their retirement years.

The people who most look forward to retirement have an adequate income and are not overinvolved with their work. Retirement is perceived as a chance to have fun and perhaps practice a skill or hobby that work left little time for. People who dread retirement are those who have erratic work histories who will not have enough funds for an adequate income after retirement. Incomes are generally halved upon retirement.

Professional people, or those who have a great deal invested in their work and derive much satisfaction from it, often keep working longer. Even after retirement they may continue to work part-time or consult. Most people's lives are structured by the demands of their jobs. Work provides an income and satisfaction from a sense of having done something well, from practicing a skill or helping others. It also provides opportunities for social interaction and friendships. In retirement, people are removed from many of their previous social patterns and sources of satisfaction. Retired spouses tend to see a lot more of each other (which may or may not be a good thing).

The most important things that affect a person's adjustment to retirement are health and an adequate income. Some elderly may feel useless and regret the lack of responsibility. Others may have parents in their 80s and 90s who require a good deal of care. Or they may assume major responsibility for raising their grandchildren, especially if their adult children are single parents. Others may start new careers.

Aging and Personality

There are very few well-documented changes in personality with age. A most consistent finding was noted by Jung in the 1930s. In later life people compensate for those aspects of their personality that were neglected in the first half. Men begin to express the more feminine, or nurturant and receptive, tendencies, and women begin to express the more masculine, or aggressive and dominant, aspects. Lowenthal, Thurnher, and Chiriboga (1975) noted:

> The preretired men are mellow—and significantly less dissatisfied and unhappy—compared to men at earlier stages . . . they see themselves as less hostile and more reasonable. They feel less ambitious but also less restless than any of the younger men. Unlike the middle-aged, they do not seem to feel the need to control others or to drive themselves. Rather, they manifest a concern for warm interpersonal relations. . . . In sum, the preretired men seem the group most comfortable, not only with others, but with themselves as well.
>
> It is in the preretirement stage that women seem finally to hit their stride. The problems with competence, independence, and interpersonal relations . . . appear resolved. The preretired women seem themselves as less dependent and helpless and as more assertive: "I don't have the fears and tragedies that I had when I was younger. I can say what I feel, I am not embarrassed by many things any more, and my personality is better."

Some become less concerned with themselves, and less egocentric:

> I've become more tolerant of people, tolerant of their faults or objectionable features. I'll admit I have faults of my own and that I've made mistakes. I realize that other people have the same privilege. I don't carry my worries home from the plant any more. I used to worry, wake up in the night, but I don't do that anymore (Reichard, Livson, & Peterson, 1962).

Integrity Versus Despair

Erikson (1953) suggested that in midlife, the developmental crisis is *generativity versus stagnation.* We either reach out to others, our adult children, grandchildren, or parents, and continue to grow and develop as people, or we can focus in on ourselves and stagnate. In later life, the self has one last developmental task: *integrity versus despair.* In this ''crisis,'' a person evaluates his or her life and what meaning it may have had. Out of this may come integrity and wisdom. Alternatively, a person may despair at the realization that there is no time left to start again. Butler (1963) has suggested that life review may facilitate the resolution of this crisis. Reminiscence may be related to adaptive functioning in the elderly (Havighurst & Glaser, 1972). The achievement of integrity may allow a person to face his or her own death and that of friends and family members with more equanimity.

Bereavement and Widowhood

In the past, people of all ages had very frequent contact with death. The death of infants was more common than not, and longer lived people could expect to bury two or three spouses. However, in modern society we have much less experience with death. The death of a loved one at any age is a great loss for us. This is especially true for very young children whose parent dies or for parents who lose a child. But the most traumatic bereavement may be the loss of a spouse.

Most women live longer than men and marry men older than themselves. There are far more widowed women than widowers in old age. If a woman marries a man 10 years older than herself, she stands an 80 percent chance of being widowed by age 55.

The stressful effect of losing a spouse is reflected in health and mortality statistics. The bereaved person's health generally deteriorates, along with loss of weight, sleeplessness, depression, and general irritability. There is an increased use of tranquilizers, alcohol, and cigarettes. The bereaved visit their physicians more often and face an increased risk of death in the first year after bereavement.

There are many reasons why widowhood is so traumatic. A widow's income often drops dramatically. As in divorce, the widow must now learn many new roles and skills formerly handled by the spouse. She may now have to face taking care of the car and managing the budget. The woman's social life changes—in a couple-oriented society, a woman may feel "like a fifth wheel" if she goes out with married friends. As a consequence, she may gradually lose contact with them. Also, many cultures place severe restrictions on widows (Lopata, 1979).

The loss of the person you have loved and spent many years with is undoubtedly the hardest to bear. A person's identity may become so entwined with that of the spouse that many people feel as if they have lost a part of themselves. "I feel as if half of myself was missing," said one widow, and another spoke of "a great emptiness" (Parkes, 1972).

Many widowed men and women sense the "presence" of their spouse. They may actually feel that they have seen, heard, or spoken to their spouse. Nearly 50 percent of people in both a British sample (Morris, 1958) and Welsh one (Rees, 1971) had such experiences. Yamamoto and his colleagues (1969) found this in 90 percent of their sample of 20 Japanese widows. Such experiences are most likely to occur to people who had happy marriages. Most found the experience helpful, although some were disturbed by "seeing" their spouse (Morris, 1974).

Grief of Widowhood

Many other aspects of the grief reaction are similar the world over (Glick et al., 1974). The initial reaction is one of shock and disbelief, especially if the death was unexpected. For many, the shock is so great that they feel "numb." This prevents them from being overwhelmed by grief and allows them to carry on, at least briefly. But the numbness lasts only a few hours or days and gives way eventually to overwhelming grief and despair. Lindemann (1944) describes the "pangs of grief" this way:

> The picture showed by persons in acute grief is remarkably uniform. Common to all is the following syndrome: sensations of somatic distress occurring in waves lasting from twenty minutes to an hour at a time. There is a feeling of tightness in the throat, choking with a shortness of breath, need for sighing, an empty feeling in the abdomen, lack of muscular power, and an intense subjective distress described as tension or mental pain.

While such intense mourning generally lasts only a few weeks, the effects of bereavement last much longer, including exhaustion, loss of appetite, and inability to initiate activity. Feelings of emptiness, guilt, apathy, hostility, and that life has no meaning are common. The person may feel unable to surrender the past.

He or she may brood over memories or refuse to let go of possessions. The bereaved may have feelings of unreality. It should be emphasized that these characteristics are not pathological, but rather *normal* reactions to bereavement, which can continue for as long as a year.

DEATH AND DYING

The death of others close to us reminds us of our own mortality. Everyone goes through specific life stages, from the egg, embryo, and fetus, to the infant, the adolescent, and finally, the adult. These periods are marked by specific maturational changes. Adulthood is less dominated by biology, as conscious choices determine how our adulthood develops. But we are never free of our physical nature. As the end of life approaches, the last state is biological and is common to us all.

These photos of Frank Tugend, from the book *Gramp*, written by his grandsons Mark and Dan Jury, are part of the record of this 81-year-old man's final weeks of life and of his death, which took place at home and was witnessed by his family. Gramp's physical and mental decline put great stress on his family, but they maintained that the experience taught them a lot about life and themselves.

The Years before Death

Most people believe, somehow, that death is something that happens to others, not to them. But in late age, "cues" remind a person of his or her own death. Parents and friends may die, health may deteriorate, and so on. People may begin to think in terms of how many years left to live rather than how many years since birth (Neugarten, 1964).

People who are close to death may experience subtle psychological changes before they experience any obvious physical decline. There can be a marked decrease in intelligence scores a few months or a year before death. Riegel and Riegel (1972) term this a *terminal drop*. There is some controversy about the timing and size of the decline. Botwinick, West, and Starandt (1978) found that slower response, slower learning and memory, depression, lessened sense of control, and lower self-rated health strongly indicate people who are going to die.

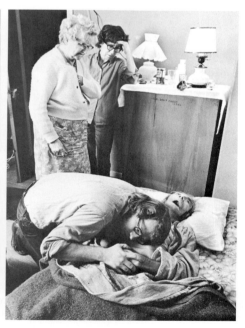

The effect of psychological and personal processes on health and mortality in the elderly should not be underestimated. Kastenbaum and his colleagues have done a series of studies on raising the morale on geriatric wards in hospitals (Kastenbaum, 1965). Even beer and wine parties for patients and staff have a remarkable effect. They influence both the morale of the staff and the physiological and psychological well-being in the elderly. They even effect the severely impaired. On one "hopeless" ward, elderly who had gross impairment showed marked gains, such as reduced incontinence.

There is also some clinical and anecdotal evidence that psychological factors can affect the timing of a person's death. The person can die prematurely — "losing the will to live" (Pattison, 1977) — or postpone death until a special occasion. Statistically, there are fewer deaths before birthdays, before presidential elections, and before important holidays (Phillips & Feldman, 1973). They concluded that this *anniversary effect* results from a person postponing death.

Social Support for the Elderly

The elderly are often isolated. Social isolation and disconnection somehow increase susceptibility to disease in general. The death rates for people not stable socially are higher for all types of disease, including heart disease, cancer, infections, and accidents. Perhaps changing the social world can change health.

Berkman and Syme (1979) studied 7,000 residents of Alameda County in California over nine years to distinguish why some people get ill and die younger than others. Although most of the questions were about smoking, physical exercise, eating habits, and history of disease, several questions asked how well the people were connected with others. They were asked whether they were married, how many close friends and relatives they had, and how much contact they had with these people, and if they were members of community organizations.

Those who were single, widowed, or divorced, those with few close friends or relatives, and those who tended not to join or participate in community organizations died at a rate two to five times greater than those with more extensive social ties. This was true for men and women, old and young, rich and poor. The more social connectedness, the lower the death rate (Plate 20).

Comparison with Other Societies

We know that males have a less structured support system than females, and suffer for it. What about different societies? Compare people living in Japan with those in the United States. Both countries are highly industrialized, urbanized, polluted, and exhibit a fast pace of life. Yet Japan has the highest life expectancy in the world and one of the lowest rates of heart disease, only one-fifth the rate in the United States. Yet this low rate of heart disease seems to hold only for the Japanese who live in Japan. Those Japanese who migrate to Hawaii or California have much higher heart disease rates than Japanese remaining in Japan. How can these different death rates be explained? Is it diet?

Apparently not. Marmot studied Japanese migrants in California who had low rates of heart disease similar to those who remained in Japan. Japanese migrants who maintained strong links to the traditional community had less heart disease. In spite of eating Western foods, having high serum cholesterol, smoking cigarettes, and having high blood pressures, those Japanese with close ties to the traditional Japanese community had rates of heart disease only one-fifth as high as those who adopted a Western pattern of social relationships.

Those with very low heart disease rates lived a traditional Japanese life. As children, they had lived in Japanese neighborhoods and had attended Japanese language schools. As adults their friends were Japanese, and they identified with the Japanese community, they visited Japanese doctors, and they most often attended Japanese cultural events and Japanese political and social gatherings (Marmot et al., 1975).

Forms of Social Support

Social support appears to offer a stability that protects people in times of transition and stress. Losing one's job, particularly when it is unanticipated, is understandably stressful and is associated with the development of subsequent illness. But not everyone gets ill when there is a recession or when a company folds.

Social support comes in many forms: intimate relationships with friends and family, casual contacts in the community, memberships in religious and other community organizations, and work relationships with bosses, employees, and co-workers (Figure 19-4). These relationships help the elderly in different ways. They can obtain emotional support such as reassurance, empathy, and someone to rely on and to confide in, as well as the feeling that they are loved and cared about. They can be encouraged by others to adopt healthier behaviors: to stop smoking, eat regularly, exercise, take prescribed medications, or seek medical care. Friends can provide an invaluable source of information on how to do things, find a job, or locate services. Social support can be a source of money, goods, or services.

In a study of the degree of atherosclerosis of the coronary arteries, Seeman (1985) found that a lower occurrence of the disease was *not* associated with the number of friends or contacts or the degree of intimacy. Instead, people who felt they had someone they could turn to for help, money, or support were the ones with less coronary artery disease.

Consider for a moment the strong and enduring relationships people cultivate with pets. Medical dogma paints a sad picture for pet owners. You can be bitten,

FIGURE 19-4
Social Support
Being part of a group, having a friend, or engaging in social interaction can provide a sense of belonging that can improve an elderly person's health and outlook on life.

scratched, or clawed; you can get rabies, ringworm, cat-scratch fever, or even a rare lung disease from parrots. Nevertheless, people persist in owning pets. Over one-half of American homes have one or more pets.

But now there is good news on the health front for pet owners. A study of victims of a heart attack one year later revealed that pet owners had one-fifth the death rate when compared with the petless. It didn't seem to matter what kind of pet the person owned. Since most people don't walk their fish, increased exercise doesn't account for the difference. It may have something to do with the sense of control experienced by pet owners. They may have an added incentive to survive in order to continue to care for their animal companions, who depend upon them (Fitzgerald, 1986; Friedman et al., 1980).

Effects of Having Control

In a recent review, Rodin (1986) notes that the connection between health and sense of control is strong in the elderly. She gives three reasons why this should be so. First, control is important to older people who seek to organize their lives more than do the young. Second, the physiological changes mentioned in this chapter, such as alterations of the immune system, make psychological effects more potent. Third, since there is more conscious attention to health, the influence of directed behaviors (such as seeing the physician) is much greater.

Rodin cites much of the evidence covered in this and the previous chapter that enhancements of social support, self-efficacy, hardiness, and the attainment of a sense of coherence can have striking effects on health. In one of her own studies, Rodin and Langer simply gave plants to the elderly in nursing homes. Some were asked to take care of their own plants, as opposed to being instructed that the staff would have that responsibility. They were significantly happier, more alert, and spent more time interacting with others.

A follow-up study showed that in a given period the responsibility-induced group was healthier than the comparison group that less than half as many of them died (Rodin & Langer, 1977). Rodin feels that psychological interventions can (if the need for self-determination is taken into account) greatly enhance the lives of the elderly (Rodin, 1986). This point is echoed by Erik Erikson in his recent book *Vital Involvement in Old Age* (1986).

This new research on the study of social support, control, aging and health is a good example of how psychology is beginning to integrate. Here, research on the mind, health psychology, and adult development come together.

Stages of Death

A recent study describes five stages that a dying person goes through. We should not think of these as necessarily sequential, but rather that they reflect common characteristics of the terminally ill (Kubler-Ross, 1969, 1975).

The first stage is *denial* and *isolation*. This may function positively to keep the person from being overwhelmed with grief and to maintain hope. The second stage, *anger,* is a natural reaction to disrupted plans and loss of personal control. It is also one's way of asserting that he or she is still alive. In the third stage, the person may *bargain with fate,* that is, he or she may offer to devote the remaining life to God in exchange for a little more time. *Depression,* the fourth stage, is an

Recent studies have confirmed what animal lovers have always known: having a pet can actually help to keep you young and healthy.

understandable reaction to increasing debilitation. It may include the tremendous financial burden of hospitalization and fear of losing loved ones. A dying person may sometimes be unable to communicate with his or her family or may feel rejected by them. In the final stage, some may *accept* impending death. This is sometimes aided by religious faith or by the understanding that one has lived a full and meaningful life. Kubler-Ross believes that if one has accepted his or her death, it is easier to die in peace and dignity.

While acknowledging the importance of Kubler-Ross's work, some researchers caution against a too literal interpretation (Kastenbaum, 1977). They point out that these "stages" are not sequential. A person may go from anger to denial to hope to fear, and so on. There are many questions not addressed. For example, what factors affect the way a person handles death? Are age, type of illness, and setting important? Are there personality, sex, or ethnic differences? We know that people do not die in the same manner. Hinton (1967) found that about half of his sample of patients openly acknowledged and accepted their death, but only one-fourth showed a high degree of acceptance and composure. Another one-fourth expressed distress, and the remainder said very little about it.

Paradise, by Hieronymous Bosch

Experience of Dying

The *dying process* may be more or less painful or distressing. However, intriguing clinical reports show that the *experience of death* may be quite different. Ring (1980) studied 102 men and women who had "near-death experiences" — they had all been very close to death or had actually been clinically dead and then revived. The results were fascinating. These people reported experiencing *intense feelings of peace* or *joy,* or felt that they had *left their bodies* and had traveled through a dark tunnel. In addition, they reported *seeing a brilliant light* or beautiful colors. A few reported *speaking with deceased relatives* or friends or a *"presence"* who convinced the person to return to life. Some felt that they had taken stock of their life by reviewing all or parts of it; this was sometimes seen in the form of a movie.

This "core experience" seems to be ordered in five distinct stages: (1) feelings of peace and affective well-being, (2) body separation, (3) entering darkness, (4) seeing a light, and (5) entering the light. People who experienced the first stage reported a cessation of pain and intense feelings of joy, peace, or calm. This was usually unlike anything they had previously experienced. This has led to some speculation that production of endorphins in the brain are involved (Thomas, 1982). In the second stage, some people reported a sense of being detached from their bodies. Some even felt they were somehow looking down at their own bodies. Those who did also reported an unusual brightness of the environment.

The next stage seems to be one of transition. People experienced moving through a dark space, sometimes described as a tunnel. At the end of the "tunnel," there was often a brilliant light. Although very bright, it did not hurt the eyes. They described it as very comforting and beautiful. Finally, a very few people reported entering the light. This light was somehow a different land — a field or valley, always very bright and beautiful, and indescribable.

There are other elements of the core experience, which cut across these stages, such as the life review, meeting with a "presence" or deceased loved ones, and the decision to return to life. In the life review, a person may experience all or part of

The Soul Hovering Over the Body Reluctantly Parting with Life, **by William Blake**

his or her life in visual, instantaneous images. This experience is usually positive. People report a sense of detachment and sometimes also an ability to "edit" — to move backward or forward to skip certain parts.

One-fifth of the people in Ring's sample experienced a "presence," which was rarely seen. It somehow communicated directly with the person, offering him or her the opportunity to go back. This presence was sometimes interpreted within a religious framework; for example, God or Jesus for Christians and Krishna for Hindus (Osis & Hanalosen, 1977). Alternatively, a person may "be greeted" by the "spirits" of deceased loved ones, usually relatives, who inform the person that it is not time yet, and that he or she must go back to life.

While not everyone in Ring's sample experienced all or any of these phenomena, *not one person had a negative experience.* The experience of nearly dying almost always had a positive effect on the person's life. Everyone who had a brush with death came away a different person. Ring stated:

> The typical near-death survivor emerges from his experience with a heightened sense of appreciation for life, determined to live life to the fullest. He has a purpose in living, even though he cannot articulate just what this purpose is.

As one young man said:

> [I had an] awareness that something more was going on in life than just the physical part of it. . . . It was just a total awareness of not just the material and how much we can buy. . . . There's more than just consuming life. There's a point where you have to *give* to it and that's real important. And there was an awareness at that point that I had to give more of myself *out* of life. That awareness has come to me.

Some psychologists have argued that these experiences are little more than hallucinations (Siegel, 1980). And Ring (1984) himself in a recent book has begun

The Organization of This
Book and of Human
Experience: The Story
and the Cycle Completed

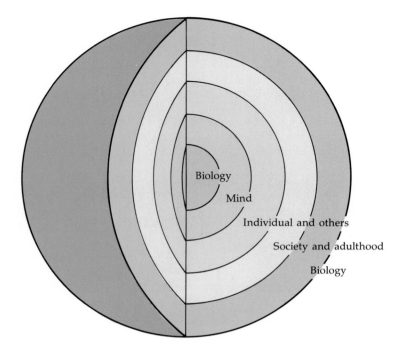

Biology

Mind

Individual and others

Society and adulthood

Biology

to rather blur the point, and become vague about his findings. But hallucinations or not, they indicate that the experience of dying is not as terrible as we once thought.

So, at the end, our biology reclaims us once again, quietly and pleasantly. It completes the story begun before we were born.

SUMMARY

1. Important theories of adult development include those of Jung and Erikson. Jung felt that different developmental stages have different problems and that values in the first half of life are directed inward and in the second half, outward. Erikson recognized eight stages in the developmental process that occur in a social context, called *psychosocial development.* Each stage involves a conflict that must be resolved.

2. There are several biological changes that predictably occur in adulthood, but it is not really known why we age. Aging apparently results from many different processes, some of which are genetically controlled. Recent research shows that impairments such as diabetes and heart disease normally associated with growing old are actually more a function of disease than age. Recent studies show that changes in the immune and neuroendocrine systems are the basic mechanisms of aging in human beings.

3. There is less change in the aging brain than in the rest of the body. It is commonly thought that the brain loses cells as we age, but this is not the case. Most brain cells are lost in the first few years of life. One study put very old animals into an enriched environment and found that this increased the size of their brains. Thus, the old maxim "use it or lose it" seems to hold true for mental capacity.

4. Alzheimer's disease is a severe form of senility afflicting two million people in the United States alone. Symptoms include defects in thought processes, memory, lan-

guage, and perceptual abilities. The cause seems to be linked to abnormalities in the hippocampus and regions of the cerebral cortex. Drugs that are precursors of the neurotransmitters ACh seem to aid in the treatment of Alzheimer's disease.

5. If IQ is measured in a cross-sectional sample, IQ scores decline with age. However, if we control for *cohort* effects and examine IQ in a *longitudinal sample,* the results are different—the older the person, the higher the IQ. What *really* happens is that verbal abilities seem to remain relatively constant or increase slightly with age and that the elderly perform worse than younger groups if the tasks involve long-term memory. Elderly people also do not learn as well as younger people.

6. The hallmarks of early adulthood are beginning a career, getting married, and becoming a parent. Marriage has a profound impact on a person's development, but few people enter marriage with realistic expectations about what it is like. Some experts regard the needs of males and females as so different that they refer to "his" and "her" marriages. However, the first year of marriage is often remembered as the happiest time of people's lives. Statistically speaking, marriage is very beneficial, especially for men. Compared to men who are divorced, widowed, or who have never married, married men live longer. They have fewer mental and physical illnesses and appear happier. Married women have higher rates of depression than married men. Characteristics of satisfying marriages include (a) commitment to the relationship, (b) communication, (c) role flexibility, and (d) having a separate identity and greater acceptance of oneself as a unique person while accepting the partner's growth and autonomy.

7. The rate of divorce is at an all-time high; one-half of all marriages currently can expect to end in divorce. There are four periods of the divorce process: marital distress, the decision to divorce, separation, and postdivorce. The separation period is the most stressful. It is just as painful whether one is leaving a "good" or "bad" marriage. However, in postdivorce both men and women are likely to state that their situation is better than it was before the divorce. The social adjustment after divorce can be difficult. Friendships and other social networks may become disrupted. Women with children may have an especially hard time dating, although men usually enter into a "flurry" of social activity. Overall, stable sexual and social relationships appear to be the best resource for coping with the stress of divorce.

8. For people who have followed traditional family and career patterns, the 30s— middle adulthood—are generally a time of "settling down." Middle age is more of a social stage in life than a specific biological event, but most researchers set it from about age 40 to about 65. Some people experience a *midlife crisis,* which is when a person discovers dissatisfaction with life and goals that have not been attained. Women may have difficulty with the *empty nest period* when children leave home and become increasingly independent. Menopause generally occurs between the ages of 48 to 51 and may be associated with hot flashes, irritability, crying spells, and depression. However, one study reported that 75 percent of women did not have any of these symptoms.

9. Retirement is a recent phenomenon and is either anticipated with excitement or dread, depending on a person's health and level of income. Elderly people who have kept active are the most satisfied with their lives and with their retirement.

10. Social support for the elderly is a much more important factor in the health and happiness of the elderly than was previously imagined. Social support can come in the form of relationships with friends, family, community, church, work, or even pets. A

recent comparative study shows that Japanese migrants who have maintained close ties with the traditional Japanese community have less heart disease than those who have adopted Western ways.

11. As people age, their friends tend to age, and older people begin to have more contact with death and dying. Most women live longer than men and marry men older than themselves, thus they have a much higher chance of being widowed than men do. The stressful effect of losing a spouse is reflected in health and mortality statistics. The bereaved person's health generally deteriorates. There are many reasons why widowhood is so traumatic. The widow's income generally drops dramatically, and she must learn many new roles and skills formerly handled by the spouse.

12. The death of others close to us reminds us of our own mortality. In late age, there are many "cues" that remind people of their own death. Parents and friends may die, or health may deteriorate. People may shift their thinking. They now consider how many years they have left to live rather than how many years since birth. There is a marked decrease in intelligence scores very close to death, called the *terminal drop*.

13. A recent study describes five stages that a dying person goes through: denial and isolation, which may function positively to keep the person from being overwhelmed with grief; anger, a natural reaction to disrupted plans and loss of personal control; trying to bargain with fate; depression; and finally, for some people, acceptance of their impending death. These stages are not sequential, but they do reflect common characteristics of the terminally ill. There are also tentative reports that while the *dying process* may be painful or distressing, the *experience of death* may actually be quite pleasant. So, in the end, it is our biology that reclaims us once again.

TERMS AND CONCEPTS

Alzheimer's disease
anniversary effect
cohort effect
disengagement theory
empty nest period
false assumptions
longitudinal study
mentor

midlife crisis
neuroendocrine system
psychosocial development
stages of death
terminal drop
timetables
widowhood

SUGGESTIONS FOR FURTHER READING

Blythe, R. (1979). *The view in winter: Reflections on old age.* New York: Harcourt Brace Jovanovich.
> *How people see themselves as they age, in their own words. Wonderful reading.*

Erikson, E. (1986). *Vital involvement in old age.* New York: Norton.
> *The most recent view of this eminent psychologist about enhancing older age.*

Ring, K. (1980). *Life at death.* New York: Coward, McCann, & Geoghegan.
> *A study of people who have clinically died and were revived. It is quite controversial, but raises important questions about the nature of life itself. His more recent book is less valuable.*

Rodin, J. (1986). Aging and health: effects of the sense of control. *Science, 233,* 1271–1276.
> *A well-written integrated view on the new research about health, control, and age.*

Statistics: Making Sense of Fallible Data

Geoffrey Iverson

INTRODUCTION

Take a long hard look at the world. Try to describe what you see—all of it, as precisely, as completely as you can.

You will soon give up in frustration. There is just too much going on, too much detail, too much change, too much that appears arbitrary. No two peas, no two people, no two pearls are exactly alike. Sometimes dogs chase cats, sometimes they do not.

Fortunately, we spend little time bogged down in this mire of detail. The world, as it actually is, as it really occurs, is something we hardly notice. Individual detail is sacrificed for lucidity; attention is confined to trends, tendencies, and regularities.

Suppose you want to describe (in a precise way) the direction that the wind is blowing. You know the importance of this if you have ever gone sailing. For gauging wind direction, a small flag or wind sock is usually used. Despite the fact that the flag never stays put and is never in exactly the same position twice, it serves well as a directional indicator. We see constancy in its motion that is unaffected by irregular, moment-to-moment fluctuations. Such regularity emerges in our eyes almost automatically, a useful end-product of visual processing and short-term memory. No conscious calculations are involved and none are needed.

We have inherited an amazingly powerful and flexible visual system that, as long as our eyes are open, provides us with the information needed to navigate our way successfully through a world seething with inconsequential detail. How do we extract stability from the irregular, unpredictable motion of a flag? This question is for the psycho-physicists and physiologists. But here we are asking a different, less specific question—one that does not require a knowledge of vision: How can we describe things so as to reveal, on a piece of paper, the hidden regularity in "fallible" (that is, variable) data?

Suppose we can measure the direction of the tip of the flag at any designated time. We might take a movie of the flag—a sequence of still shots, each of which yields an instantaneous measurement. Let us record these measurements as compass directions, that is, in degrees with respect to the fixed direction north (Figure 1).

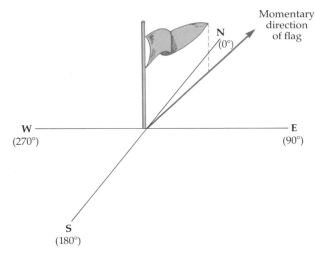

FIGURE 1   Direction of flag (degrees of compass direction).

We have recorded 20 such measurements as they occur in our movie, frame by frame. These are given in Table 1. But there is no simple, unitary direction of wind peering up at us from Table 1, just a bunch of different numbers. Perhaps a graph would help to visualize the data better. In Figure 2 the measurements of Table 1 are plotted as flag positions for each movie frame number. This graph is a history of the flag position over time, exactly as it was recorded in the sequence of movie frames.

Does Figure 2 remind you of anything? If you have any interest in the stock market, it might occur to you that the graph of Figure 2 looks like the Dow–Jones industrial average. To make this analogy clearer, in Figure 3 we have plotted typical Dow–Jones averages for a typical week. Although the units in Figures 2 and 3 are different (Figure 2 plots position, while Figure 3 plots the Dow–Jones index), the appearance of each figure is essentially the same. If one graph is clear, can we understand the other in the same way? Note that in Figure 3 each day's trading has been divided into four separate values, taken in succession: an opening figure, a morning figure, an afternoon figure, and a closing figure.

Here is a description of Figure 3 in terms of events on Wall Street. In a run that showed only a minor correction after lunch, the Dow dropped 22 points on Monday. A rally early on Tuesday was not sustained, though by Tuesday's close there was a hint of recovery. This promise persisted, somewhat nervously, through Wednesday and Thursday, but on Friday the market began to slide again. By the week's end, the Dow had dropped 16 points altogether.

Can we profit from this blow-by-blow description of the stock market in gauging wind direction? I

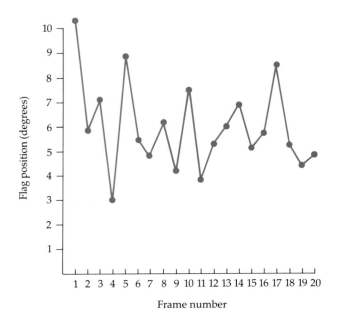

FIGURE 2 Motion of a flag depicted graphically (based on data from Table 1).

suggest not. There ought to be a better way of visualizing the data of Table 1 than that conveyed by Figure 2. So let's try another way of representing the data. Figure 4 shows each of the 20 measurements given in Table 1 by a cross (x) on a line.

The picture is easy to interpret. While the x's are scattered, this scatter is limited to about a 7° range

Movie frame	1	2	3	4	5	6	7	8	9	10
Direction of flag (degrees)	10.2	5.8	7.1	3.0	8.9	5.4	4.8	6.2	4.1	7.4
Movie frame	11	12	13	14	15	16	17	18	19	20
Direction of flag (degrees)	3.8	5.3	6.0	6.9	5.1	5.7	8.3	5.2	4.3	4.9

Table 1 Twenty instantaneous measurements of flag direction.

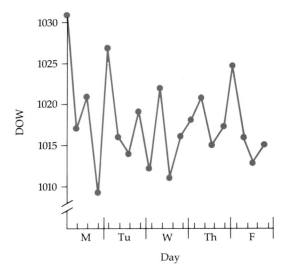

FIGURE 3 Hypothetical weekly record of Dow–Jones industrial average (based on data from Figure 2).

1　2　3　4　5　6　7　8　9　10

Flag direction (degrees)

FIGURE 4　A visual representation of data from Table 1.

Direction	1	2	3	4	5	6	7	8	9	10
Frequency	0	0	1	3	6	4	3	1	1	1

Table 3　Frequency with which each direction occurs in Table 2.

(3° to about 10°). Moreover, there is a marked concentration of crosses between 4° and 6°. So we can generalize the data in the following way: the wind direction is approximately 5° east of north.

However, Figure 4 is not visually pleasing. Perhaps we can achieve a more pleasing representation of the data by sacrificing unnecessary precision. We therefore round the measurements of Table 1 to the nearest whole degree. Thus, the first measurement, 10.2°, becomes 10°; the next, 5.8°, becomes 6°; and so on. In this way we obtain the list of rounded measurements shown in Table 2.

Many of the measurements are now identical. This suggests the following strategy: count the number of times each of the rounded measurements occurs in Table 2 and record these counts in a new table (like taking an inventory), as has been done in Table 3. This inventory allows a simple, elegant picture to emerge in the alternative visual form of a bar graph, or *histogram* (Figure 5). The first 20 measurements of wind direction combine into a visual form that displays their regularity. Like vision and our other senses, this regularity was achieved by excluding detail. *Thus, statistics is similar in principle to the kind of simplification processes the mind performs.*

The process we just went through is a rudimentary example of a *statistical analysis*. This is a process of organizing evidence, typically numerical, so as to reveal tendencies, trends, regularities, and so on that are often present in collections of measurements but that are quite difficult, even impossible, to detect in any individual measurement.

A major benefit of a statistical description of data

is the simple, clear picture that often emerges. The forest is emphasized at the expense of the individual trees. Should we always analyze information this way? We rejected the "Wall Street" description of the motion of a flag in favor of the simplicity manifested in a histogram. Should we then use a histogram to describe the Dow–Jones fluctuations?

A full answer is complicated, and we content ourselves with a simple "no." To appreciate the difference between the stock market and a piece of cloth flapping in a steady breeze, we need to free ourselves from the shackles of mechanical habit, of blindly following a recipe. The recipe, "construct a histogram," applied to the data of Figure 2, leads to the highly interpretable representation of Figure 5. If applied to the similar data of Figure 3, it would lead to a similar picture, but one that most stock market analysts would label as worthless.

There seems to be a paradox here. To resolve it, let us examine in more detail what one preserves in a histogram, and more important, what one throws away.

It is useful to go back to the source of our data, namely, a movie, a sequence of individual photographs, each of which gives rise to an individual measurement. Suppose we ran our movie backward. Would the average wind direction change?

Frame number	1	2	3	4	5	6	7	8	9	10
Direction	10	6	7	3	9	5	5	6	4	7
Frame number	11	12	13	14	15	16	17	18	19	20
Direction	4	5	6	7	5	6	8	5	4	5

Table 2　Data of Table 1 rounded to nearest whole number.

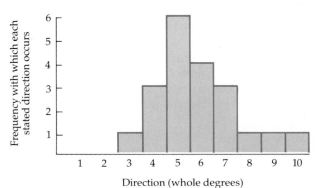

FIGURE 5　A histogram showing the frequency with which each direction occurs in Table 2.

Of course not. Even more drastically, suppose we arbitrarily shuffled the order of the frames that make up our movie, thereby creating a new one. Would the average wind direction change? Again, the answer is no. While the momentary fluctuations of the flag are different for each of the (roughly) 2.4 billion movies that could be created by shuffling the order of 20 individual frames, the histogram and estimate of average wind direction accompanying each such movie would remain exactly the same.

But this is not so for the stock market descriptions. Taking into account the *sequence* of events in the stock market is of indisputable importance for deciding when to buy and when to sell. Similar considerations of order are irrelevant when one is out sailing. Thus, to follow the recipe, "construct a histogram," is to assume that *the order of measurements is irrelevant* to the object or system under study. We do not usually care if a big cloud follows a little one, or vice versa; only that it might rain. But we behave and feel very differently if the prime lending rate is on the increase rather than on the decline.

In psychology, as in any science, we place a premium on "stable," replicable measurements. Is there any reason to distinguish between the abilities of two students who in a course receive respective homework grades of A, B, B, C, A, B, B, B, C and C, B, B, A, B, B, A, C, B? Each student's performance would be characterized by the same histogram, and each averages to a solid B.

This is not to say that people do not learn, do not change their behavior, do not adopt new habits — of course they do. But to understand learning or to measure a behavior change requires us to calibrate "before and after" learning or change. Those "before and after" measurements are critical, because it is through comparison (just as with the senses) that we detect change or recognize that learning has taken place. Statistics is used for the *description* of stable, practical measurement, but just as important is its related role in *detecting change.*

The question "Has the wind changed?" requires *statistical inference.* However, at least in some circumstances, the issue may not be settled with the mere detection of change. If the wind changes direction by 1°, do we (usually) care? What we do with the outcome of a statistical analysis, what actions we take, is an issue for *decision theory.* Decision theory is still in its infancy, and we will not say much about it here.

In summary, statistics divides into three major areas: *descriptive statistics, statistical inference,* and *decision theory.* These form a hierarchy in which issues that are unresolved at one level become the dominant focus at the next.

DESCRIPTIVE STATISTICS

The purpose of descriptive statistics is to *accurately* represent a set of observations of the world in as condensed a form as seems appropriate. Weather reports, the Dow–Jones average, baseball "stats," grade point averages, IQs, and Nielsen ratings are all examples of the use of descriptive statistics.

Condensing a large set of measurements of facts without destroying their collective integrity is termed *data reduction.* It is characterized by a number of useful procedures, called *algorithms,* of wide applicability. We have already seen one of the most widely used algorithms—"form a histogram." However, blind application of this algorithm may lead nowhere, or worse, to potential misrepresentation. Yet a sensitive, informed descriptive analysis can be of great power and beauty. A good description often allows data to "speak for themselves."

A common form of data reduction is supplied by a *table.* Baseball statistics are usefully represented in this form. Tables are very desirable devices for collecting information related to some specific issue. The visual format of a sensibly organized table allows the eye to quickly pick out clusters of related information that might otherwise go unnoticed. Indeed, important questions and hypotheses often emerge from a scrutiny of tabulated information.

Tables are most commonly used to list categories of some focus of interest; for example, diseases and other causes of death are listed in a historically interesting table from the year 1632 (Table 4). Typically, numerical information accompanies each category; for instance, we see from Table 4 that 62 Londoners died "suddenly" (perhaps by a heart attack?), while 46 were "kil'd by several accidents."

The algorithms "form a table" and "form a bar graph" are sometimes equivalent. For example, there is no more (nor less) information in Table 3 than in the histogram of Figure 5. However, it would not be natural nor helpful to represent a gro-

The Diseases, and Casualties this year being 1632.

Abortive, and Stillborn	445	Grief	11
Affrighted	1	Jaundies	43
Aged	628	Jawfaln	8
Ague	43	Impostume	74
Apoplex, and Meagrom	17	Kil'd by several accidents	46
Bit with a mad dog	1	King's Evil	38
Bleeding	3	Lethargic	2
Bloody flux, scowring, and flux	348	Livergrown	87
Brused, Issues, sores, and ulcers	28	Lunatique	5
Burnt, and Scalded	5	Made away themselves	15
Burst, and Rupture	9	Measles	80
Cancer, and Wolf	10	Murthered	7
Canker	1	Over-laid, and starved at nurse	7
Childbed	171	Palsie	25
Chrisomes, and Infants	2268	Piles	1
Cold, and Cough	55	Plague	8
Colick, Stone, and Strangury	56	Planet	13
Consumption	1797	Pleurisie, and Spleen	36
Convulsion	241	Purples, and spotted Feaver	38
Cut of the Stone	5	Quinsie	7
Dead in the street, and starved	6	Rising of the Lights	98
Dropsie, and Swelling	267	Sciatica	1
Drowned	34	Scurvey, and Itch	9
Executed, and prest to death	18	Suddenly	62
Falling Sickness	7	Surfet	86
Fever	1108	Swine Pox	6
Fistula	13	Teeth	470
Flocks, and small Pox	531	Thrush, and Sore mouth	40
French Pox	12	Tympany	13
Gangrene	5	Tissick	34
Gout	4	Vomiting	1
		Worms	27

Christened { Males ... 4994, Females . 4590, In all ... 9584 } Buried { Males ... 4932, Females . 4603, In all ... 9535 } Whereof, of the Plague.8

Increased in the Burials in the 122 Parishes, and at the Pesthouse this year 993
Decreased of the Plague in the 122 Parishes, and at the Pesthouse this year..... 266

Table 4 A mortality table for the year 1632 in London. (Source: John Graunt, "Natural and Political Observations made upon the Bills of Mortality," 1662)

cery list (with prices) as a bar graph. (If you are not sure why, try it.)

In many applications, categories are artificially formed by grouping measurements (of a single entity) that fall into a narrow range, *bin*, or *interval* of values. Rounding measurements creates categories in this manner (recall the transition from Table 1 to Table 3). When categories of a single quantity, such as wind direction, reaction time, height, or weight, are involved, a histogram is often preferred to a table (compare Table 3 with the visual clarity of Figure 5). Our next example, which requires some preamble, is a beautiful illustration of the power of a well-constructed histogram.

As you know, the nervous system is composed of billions of neurons grouped into bundles according to function. Information is transmitted by these neurons both electrically and chemically. The easiest, most direct way to measure the activity of neurons is to do it electrically. Not surprisingly, recordings of neural events (action potentials, or "spikes") from a single cell are of great importance in neurophysiology. It is possible to record the activity induced in a primary auditory neuron by an externally applied tone of fixed frequency and intensity.

Our ability to hear, particularly, to distinguish one sound from another, strongly suggests that the nervous activity induced by physical sound is a sort of "code," a running record of those aspects of a physical stimulus that are crucial for its recognition and eventual meaning. Physiologists spend a good deal of effort attempting to decode neural activity, especially the activity produced in response to simple stimuli such as pure tones. To a physicist, however, a tone is an undulating pressure wave, as depicted in Figure 6. An obvious feature of a tone is its *period*, the time between two consecutive peaks of physical pressure.

The question naturally arises: is periodicity present in the activity of a single auditory neuron? The answer is "yes," but this is not obvious at first glance. A spike train recorded in response to a tone looks something like that depicted in Figure 7. Disappointingly, no semblance of periodic behavior is apparent, even though it is present. The way to see it is to form an *interval histogram*, that is, an inventory of intervals between successive spikes. (Presenting a tone over and over again allows the inventory to grow arbitrarily large.) Such a histogram is displayed in Figure 8. The intervals between neural spikes are clustered at precise multiples of the stimulus period. In other words, each cluster is separated by exactly one stimulus period. The activity of a single auditory neuron is locked in synchrony with the stimulus (at least at moderate to low

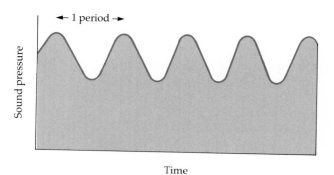

FIGURE 6 According to physics, a representation of a pure tone.

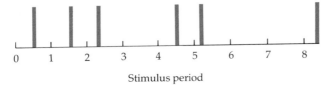

FIGURE 7   Neural responses to a pure tone.

frequencies), thus preserving (or "coding") the periodicity of the stimulus.

It is not uncommon to reduce the information in a histogram or table even further. We did this in our discussion of how to use a flag to measure the direction of a steady breeze. Recall that we reduced 20 individual measurements first to a histogram and then to a single summary statement: "The wind direction is approximately 5° east of north." There are two key issues here; one having to do with the term "approximately," the other being the numerical value "5 degrees." Let's look at the latter first.

Frequently it is useful to condense a set of data or histogram into a single number, which is a measure of *location* or *central tendency*. When we look at the histogram of Figure 5, it is apparent that the data are fairly evenly distributed at a value of about 5°. We can be even more systematic than this.

There are a number of useful indices of location employed in practice, and of these, three are usually singled out at having the widest application. They are the *mode,* the *mean,* and the *median.* The mode is easy to define: it is the most frequently occurring category (the tallest bar in a histogram). In Figure 5, the category "5°" occurs more often than any other, so the mode of that histogram is 5°.

The median of a set of measurements is the value that divides the set in two: half the measurements fall below the median, half above. The median of the set of directions recorded in Table 1 is between 5.3° and 5.7°, and it suffices to record the median as 5.5°.

Finally, the mean of a set of measurements is simply their arithmetic average. If we compute the arithmetic average of the 20 values listed in Table 1, we find that it is 5.9°. These three numerical values, 5°, 5.5°, and 5.9° are different but sufficiently close in magnitude that no one would (usually) care which was selected. The close agreement of these three values will occur whenever a histogram is approximately "heaped symmetrically" about its mode.

However, there are many examples of data that do not distribute themselves in this ideal way. Income provides a notorious example. The average income of people who work in a factory is dramatically influenced by a few large managerial salaries together with many much smaller salaries paid to workers on the production line. The average of one $100,000 salary and ten $10,000 salaries is $18,182, which is not representative of anyone's income. However, both the modal and median salaries in this case are $10,000, which are more reasonable reflections of reality.

A histogram can be a combination of two or more histograms. It is not uncommon for such histograms to have two or more distinct modes. Notice in Figure 9, the bimodal nature of a "living histogram" of men and women arranged according to height. This could be broken down into two histograms, one for

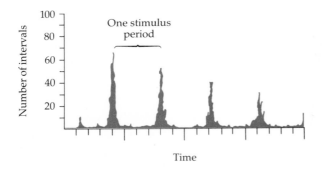

FIGURE 8   Interval histogram of a single auditory neuron driven by a pure tone with a period of 4,060 microseconds—roughly middle C. (Source: Rose et al., 1967)

FIGURE 9   A living bimodal histogram of college students arranged by height.

each sex, each being characterized by a single mode.

This example should not be taken as indicating that more than one mode necessarily indicates the presence of more than one underlying structure. It can certainly occur that a single system is naturally characterized by several modes. An example is provided by gambling. Have you ever noticed that when playing poker you are either "hot" or "cold"? In fact, in a simple game between two players involving the tossing of a fair (unbiased) coin, it is common for one player to be ahead for the entire duration of the game! Despite this, over many such games of the same length, the average winnings will eventually even out. An appropriately constructed histogram for tossing a coin would be diagrammatically U-shaped, showing two pronounced modes (always ahead and always behind), with a mean of zero in between. Both the modes and the mean are reflections of a single underlying mechanism: pure chance.

An additional comment is in order before we proceed. The calculation of a mean requires the arithmetic operations of addition and multiplication. These operations may be inappropriate, indeed meaningless, if applied without thought. We could facetiously classify the major interests of teenagers into three categories: sex, drugs, and rock 'n' roll. What is the average category of interest? The answer cannot be found in averaging. There simply is no answer, for the question as posed is meaningless. Likewise, to compute a median requires that a meaningful *order* be established for the category values or labels. Only the mode remains unaffected by such considerations of meaningfulness (or *scale type* in statistical jargon). One can always sensibly ask, What is the most frequent category? Unfortunately, the answer may be none, many, or worse, irrelevant.

A histogram is often not well represented by a mere measure of location because such measures are essentially blind to the "width" or dispersion of the histogram. It is one thing to know that the modal direction of a breeze is 5° east of north, but quite another to know that it varies over a 7° range. To state the mean direction of the Mississippi River is to ignore its incredible meandering.

To compensate for the deficiencies of measures in location, measures of *variability* (scatter, spread, and dispersion) are introduced. The *range* of a set of measurements is one such measure. This is simply the difference between the largest and smallest of a set of measurements. The range of the data listed in Table 1 is 7.2° (10.2° − 3.0°).

Just as there are several useful indices of location, there are also a number of measures of variability in use. The most commonly used of these are *variance* and the closely related *standard deviation*. Like the mean, variance is an arithmetic average, not a set of raw measurements, but of squared *deviations*. A deviation is computed for each raw measurement by subtracting from it the value of the common mean. These deviations are squared so as to eliminate the distinction between positive and negative values, and they are subsequently averaged to produce the variance. In Table 5 these arithmetic operations are illustrated for the data of Table 1.

The variance of the data of Table 1 is given by the average of the squared deviations listed in the right-hand column of Table 5. We see that

$$\text{variance} = \frac{60.644}{20} = 3.032$$

Original measurement (Flag directions)	Deviations (Measurement − Mean)	Squared deviations
10.2	4.28	18.318
5.8	−0.12	0.014
7.1	1.18	1.392
3.0	−2.92	8.526
8.9	2.98	8.880
5.4	−0.52	0.270
4.8	−1.12	1.254
6.2	0.28	0.078
4.1	−1.82	3.312
7.4	1.48	2.190
3.8	−2.12	4.494
5.3	−0.62	0.384
6.0	0.08	0.006
6.9	0.98	0.960
5.1	−0.82	0.672
5.7	−0.22	0.048
8.3	2.38	5.664
5.2	−0.72	0.518
4.3	−1.62	2.624
4.9	−1.02	1.040
Average = $\frac{118.4}{20}$	Average = 0	Average = $\frac{60.644}{20}$
= 5.92		= 3.032
= Mean		= Variance

Table 5   Calculating a variance (based on data in Table 1)

Note that the average of the middle column, that is, the average of the (unsquared) deviations is zero. This is no accident—it is a simple algebraic consequence of the definition of a deviation and provides a useful check on intermediate calculations.

Standard deviation arises from variance by extracting a square root; thus, for the above data,

$$\text{standard deviation} = \sqrt{3.032} = 1.74$$

Why bother with standard deviation when variance will do? The answer is convenience; a standard deviation possesses the same units as the original data and may be pictured as a "distance" from the mean value. Standard deviation provides a gauge of how discrepant individual values are from the mean, and hence how discrepant they are from each other. A rule of thumb for histograms is this: nearly all measurements fall within ± 2 standard deviations from the mean. In other words, one can expect the range of a typical set of data to be a total of about four standard deviations. For example, for the data of Table 1, we noted above that the range was $7.2°$. This is close to 6.96, which is 4×1.74 (one standard deviation), in accord with the rule of thumb.

So far we have exclusively considered univariate data, that is, measurements pertaining to a single numerical quantity such as time, direction, salary, and so on, or to a single qualitative variable such as sex, occupation, or marital status. Inventories of such measurements lend themselves to organization in tables, bar graphs, and histograms, which allows for further reduction to a measure of location and one of variability. Sometimes this is enough, especially if all that is required is an assertion of simple fact: "The life expectancy of a Saudi Arabian is presently 42 years"; or "The percentage of 15- to 18-year-olds enrolled in education in the United States was 84% in 1976"; or "The infant mortality rate is 15 per 1000 births in the United States."

However, there are many classes of statements that are more complex: "From 1973 to 1980, average verbal scores on the Scholastic Aptitude Test dropped over 50 points, and average mathematics scores dropped nearly 40 points"; or "Warning: The Surgeon General has determined that cigarette smoking is dangerous to your health"; or "Psychologists have shown a connection between viewing violence on TV and aggressive behavior." When dissected, such statements are seen to involve two

or more variables or two or more sets of measurements. The Surgeon General's warning means that there is a difference between the incidence of various diseases (for example, lung cancer, emphysema, and heart ailments) for those who smoke cigarettes and those who do not and, moreover, that such differences cannot reasonably be attributed to other possible sources (for example, alcohol, place of domicile, or anxiety).

The ability to detect change, to recognize differences, and to notice that one variable (say, height) is linked to another (say, weight) are all crucial for what is perhaps the major ambition of science: to provide a simple yet highly precise description of the world. No encyclopedia of bare facts is adequate to this task.

The question "Does juvenile delinquency increase with population density?" is one that typifies many research efforts in the social sciences. It is often dealt with by using *correlational algorithms*, two of which we deal with below. They are distinguished by the type of variables involved (whether the variables are quantitative or qualitative), but their purpose remains the same: to decide if two or more variables *covary* (vary together).

Suppose 40 high school seniors, 20 male and 20 female, are submitted to a battery of tests designed to assess "ability in mathematics." The results of these 40 individual ability scores are compiled and the median is computed. Why the median? This allows individuals of both sexes to be classified as "above the median" or "below the median." In short, we record the number of students falling into each of the four categories "male-above," "male-below," "female-above," and "female-below." It is convenient to record these counts in a "2 × 2" table (Table 6).

Those who score above the median are typically male, while those who score below are typically

	Male	Female	Totals
Above	13	7	20
Below	7	13	20
Totals	20	20	

Table 6   A 2 × 2 cross classification of 20 male and 20 female students according to mathematics ability.

female. In other words, the variables "gender" and "mathematics ability" are positively *associated*. We can go further and compute an index of *strength* and *direction* of association, designated by the Greek letter ϕ (phi). The index ϕ varies between two extreme values: -1 (complete negative association) and $+1$ (complete positive association). Speed and accuracy are usually negatively associated (quickness begets sloppiness), whereas motivation and effort are often positively correlated. Values of ϕ near zero indicate little or no association.

The algorithm for computing ϕ for any 2×2 table is given in Table 7. Applying the algorithm to the data of Table 6, we compute $\phi = 0.3$, confirming what our eye told us already, that there is a modest positive association between gender and mathematics ability.

Now, women, do you accept this conclusion without protest? Surely not. There is good reason to believe that the observed association may be a byproduct of complex social circumstances that conspire to the detriment of women. (To what extent this more complex and subtle explanation is true is an area of current investigation.) As this example suggests, it is a mistake to confuse association with the notion of cause. Although no one doubts anymore that cigarette smoking is a causal agent for a number of horrible diseases, it took about ten years of research to replace the phrase "may be" with the definitive "is" in the warning that appears on the side of every pack of cigarettes on sale in the United States. Why? Because taking into account other relevant factors can change an observed association between two variables quite dramatically, turning a large value of ϕ into a small one, or even reversing its sign.

When covariation is suspected between a pair of quantitative variables, a simple *scatter plot* is useful. The data recorded in Table 8 are *pairs* of measure-

County	Index of exposure	Cancer mortality per 100,000 person-years
Clatsop	8.34	210.3
Columbia	6.41	177.9
Gilliam	3.41	129.9
Hood River	3.83	162.3
Morrow	2.57	130.1
Portland	11.64	207.5
Sherman	1.25	113.5
Umatilla	2.49	147.1
Wasco	1.62	137.5

Table 8 Radioactive contamination and cancer mortality. (Source: Fadeley, 1965, cited in Anderson & Sclove, 1986)

ments taken in a few counties in Oregon following leakage of radioactive contaminated waste into the Columbia River. One measurement is an index of exposure; large values indicate more serious exposure than small values. The other is the mortality rate due to various forms of cancer. These pairs of measurements have been plotted on a graph to form a scatter plot (Figure 10), in which the two measurements are used as the horizontal and vertical axes.

The relationship between death from cancer and radioactive exposure is obvious from this plot. An index called *coefficient of correlation*, denoted r, is often employed for the same purpose as the measure ϕ. The coefficient r, like ϕ, also ranges between -1 and $+1$ and has roughly the same

	B		
	B_1	B_2	Totals
A A_1	a	b	$a + b$
A_2	c	d	$c + d$
Totals	$a + c$	$b + d$	

$$\phi = \frac{ad - bc}{\sqrt{(a + b)(c + d)(a + c)(b + d)}}$$

Table 7 Computation of coefficient of association ϕ for an arbitrary 2×2 frequency table.

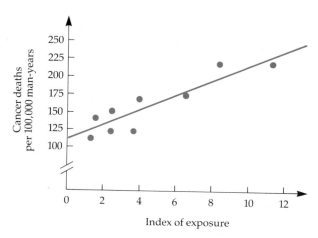

FIGURE 10 Scatter plot of data of Table 8. (Source: After Fadeley, 1965, cited in Anderson & Sclove, 1986)

interpretation. More precisely, r is a measure of how well the relationship between two quantitative variables conforms to a simple straight line (see Figure 10). The value of r for the present data turns out to be about 0.93, a value which again bolsters what we see by eye in the scatter plot.

Correlations can be very misleading if accepted uncritically. For example, the scatter plot of Figure 11 shows a definite linear relationship between human population size and stork population size in the German city of Oldenburg. The value of r for these data is 0.95. But does this mean that storks bring babies? The answer is surely "no"—in fact, it is closer to the truth to say that babies bring storks. As the Oldenberg population increases, more housing is built, a by-product of which are chimneys, ideal nesting sites for storks. The large correlation between the populations of inhabitants and storks would drop to zero if the number of chimneys was kept constant and not allowed to increase with new housing.

Problems with the interpretation of indices such as r and ϕ make the task of the social scientist quite difficult. It is not a problem so much for statistics as it is for scientific explanation. There *is* a large positive correlation between the number of storks and the number of babies; that is all that a statistical index is required to report. But the scientific explanation of covariation is not to be found in accepting such indices at face value. Other nonmeasured or

hidden variables (e.g., chimneys) may be responsible for superficial appearances.

Problems of interpreting data are usually traced to lack of *control*. It is often difficult to control natural events, so science has invented the laboratory, a place where the individual scientist can, in theory, have the last word as to what will vary and what will remain fixed. A good deal of technology, common sense, intuition, and creative effort goes into a well-controlled scientific experiment. Each scientist brings to bear one or more techniques from a bag of tricks called *scientific method* so as to achieve as much control as he or she can. When successful, scientific explanation and statistical interpretation practically coincide. But in psychology, as in other social sciences, control may not always be possible without disturbing important features of the system being studied. And even in the context of a laboratory, control is often only partially achieved. While scientific method is a branch of metaphysics, statistics is a branch of applied mathematics. They should never be confused.

STATISTICAL INFERENCE

Descriptive techniques are helpful in the preliminary search for regularity in variable data. But there are a number of vexing questions that remain unanswered, indeed unanswerable, without further consideration. Suppose we ask the simple question: Has the wind changed? We might mean a number of things by this: Has the breeze shifted its mean direction from 5.9° east of north to a new value? Has the breeze become more variable than before? Or we may be asking both of these questions.

The issue can be stated more clearly and scientifically this way: if the data represented in the histogram of Figure 5 were collected at 10 A.M., for example, and we take another set of measurements on the same flag at 2 P.M. and construct a new histogram from those measurements, can we tell the difference between the two histograms? Large differences will show up quite clearly; one needs no elaborate statistical apparatus to distinguish two clearly different sets of measurements. But what about the two histograms shown in Figure 12? While they are actually different, would you be willing to attribute this difference to a genuine trend?

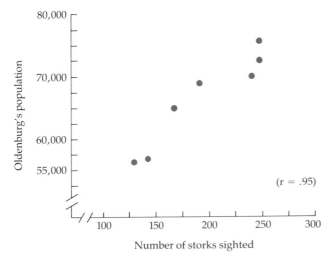

FIGURE 11   The population of Oldenburg, Germany, and the corresponding stork population for the years 1930–1936. (Source: Glass & Hopkins, 1984)

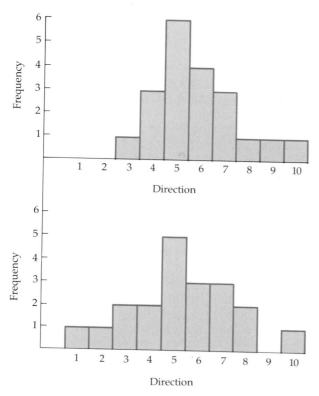

FIGURE 12   Are these histograms representative of the same breeze, or has the breeze changed its direction?

The problem of detecting change, especially small differences that are difficult to discern, is common in scientific research. Its resolution calls for a new language, supplied by the theory of probability. We do not have the space here to enter into this mathematical theory in any serious way, so we shall content ourselves with the briefest indication of the role it plays.

Probability theory is used by statisticians as a framework for modeling *inherently* variable measurements. Regardless of researcher's attempts to control matters, variability of measurement, especially in the behavioral sciences, cannot be eliminated. Sometimes this may be attributed to "individual differences" among people, but such inherent variation is also present in the behavior of each one of us. For instance, do you chew your food or blink your eyes at precisely regular intervals? The sun rises each morning at the correct time and in the right place, but can you say the same about your own behavior or that of anyone else? Even for people who pride themselves on being punctual, the

best we can say is something like "There is a 90% chance that Mr. Discipline will be in the shower between 7:00 and 7:05 A.M. on any given day."

To be sure, not all variability is due to chance, and it is the responsibility of each scientist to attempt the difficult job of partitioning it into two components, one that is controllable and one that is uncontrollable (chance events). A characteristic signature of chance is that its effects disappear in *large* batches of independently repeated measurements; this is called the "law of averages." It is no empirical law or phenomenon, but a mathematical theorem, an inevitable consequence of averaging out the annoying obfuscations of chance. It is testimony to the appropriateness of probability theory for application to data that batches of empirical observations do behave in the manner dictated by that theory.

Not to be outdone by nature, science has exploited the theory of probability to good end in the process of *sampling*. The Nielsen ratings, which greatly influence the television advertising industry, are based on measurements taken in 1,000 households. This is a tiny proportion of the approximately 100 million dwellings in the United States. Political polls, famous for a few outstanding blunders, also deserve to be credited with an otherwise flawless track record. (In fact, they may be "too" good. These days it is not uncommon for the results of an election to be announced before the voting has ended.)

While there are various forms of sampling, that is, of selecting a few from a larger *population* of possible measurements, the most useful forms are those called *probability sampling*, in which chance is injected *deliberately* by the scientist or pollster. This is done so that the result of a scientific endeavor, survey, or poll may be subject to the description afforded by probability theory and so that it may gain from the precision offered by that theory.

The simplest form of probability sampling is known as *random sampling*. Here, all samples of a given size (that is, all samples containing a specified number of measurements) are conceptually laid out on a table, and just one of these is chosen "at random" without bias or emotion. It is usually the failure to carry out this conceptual random selection that causes problems in practice. For example, a convenient practical way to research people for survey purposes is to call them on the phone. But this excludes people who do not own telephones, who have limited access to them, and who have unlisted numbers. Such departures from the strict requirements of random sampling can and do lead to unwarranted conclusions in research or to incorrect predictions in a close political contest. For related reasons, psychology has sometimes been dubbed (not entirely without justification) as the "science of college sophomores."

Let us pick some simple notion to examine, such as the average height of 10-year-old American males. This measure is not entirely frivolous. For example, the federal Department of Health and Human Services might be interested in determining whether providing free milk in schools has a measurable effect on mean height. The cost of locating, measuring, and recording *all* 10-year-old males would be about $1 million, so a random sample of 1,000 is selected. The average value of these 1,000 measurements is computed. Now the question arises: to what extent is this sample average indicative of the true, but unknown, population mean? The answer turns out to depend on the *variance of the population,* an unknown quantity, and on the size of the sample. In fact, the "error" of our sample mean falls within

$$\pm 2 \times \frac{\text{unknown population standard deviation}}{\sqrt{\text{sample size}}}$$

We can take a rough guess at the value one would expect of the unmeasured population standard deviation. Remember the rule of thumb mentioned earlier: almost all the measurements of a single numerical quantity fall between ± 2 standard deviations of the mean. Common experience tells us that the range of heights of typical 10-year-old boys is surely no more than 2 feet, so a reasonable guess at the unknown population standard deviation should be no more than 6 inches. Using the above formula, the "error" incurred by quoting our sample mean as if it were the true population mean is

$$\frac{2 \times 6 \text{ inches}}{\sqrt{1000}} \times 0.38 \text{ inches}$$

Our sample mean (whatever its value) is seen to be an excellent *estimate* of the true population value. We could improve our accuracy farther by increasing sample size to, say, 10,000; the error now drops to 0.12 inches. If we were not interested in such

precision, a sample size of 100, incurring an error of 1.2 inches, might be tolerable and would certainly be cheaper to obtain.

The use of sample means as estimates of population means is widespread in scientific and commercial enterprises. Similar sample quantities are available for estimating other *parameters* of populations; for instance, it is intuitively reasonable, and theory confirms, that a sample variance provides a good estimate of population variance, at least for large samples.

Now that we know how to estimate the mean height of 10-year-old American males with an accuracy that improves with sample size, we are close to being able to address more serious matters. First, let's look at the question that prompted the measurement of height: Does the school milk program have the effect of increasing height? To address this question requires two samples — one taken just before the program is instituted and one taken, say, five years later. Entirely different 10-year-olds characterize each sample, and each sample typifies different populations, one who received milk and one who did not.

The question can be put this way: Do these populations differ in their means? This question is handled by *statistical inference,* the major application of which involves *hypothesis* testing. Briefly, this means that a skeptical attitude is adopted and the hypothesis of "no effect" (that is, "no difference in height") is made. The hypothesis allows the observed difference in the (undoubtedly different) sample averages to be evaluated under the assumption that all one really has are two samples from the *same* population.

Imagine that the heights from each sample are listed side-by-side in long columns of 1,000 entries each. Suppose the initial sample is listed in the left-hand column and the final sample on the right. Proceeding line by line, imagine subtracting the left-hand number from the right, recording the 1,000 differences in yet a third column. What do you expect the average of those 1,000 differences would be? According to the skeptical hypothesis of no difference, each sample average provides a good estimate of the same population mean; so their difference should be close to zero. Simple algebra tells us that an average of differences is the same as a difference of averages. Thus, we have answered our question: the average of the 1,000 differences should be close to zero, if indeed the sample means are estimating a common population value.

However, what if the hypothesis is wrong; what if milk does in fact have an effect on height? We should then expect many more of our 1,000 differences to be positive and consequently the average difference to be positive. The only question that remains unanswered is this: How discrepant from zero is a *significant* positive difference? This question can be put another way: How likely is it to observe a positive difference of any stated amount?

Such questions are answered by probability theory. We can now use the rule of thumb about the scatter of any distribution of numerical data. Differences are numerical data, so we can apply our rule to them. We expect almost all differences to fall within ± 2 standard deviation of their mean (which we are temporarily assuming is zero). We have to somehow come to terms with the standard deviation of differences, and once again it is probability theory that provides the answer: the "error" of our sample differences is $\sqrt{2}$ times the error incurred by either sample mean alone. For samples of size 1,000, we saw above that this latter error was at most 0.38 inches. Multiplying by 2 we find that almost all average differences in height would lie in the interval -0.54 to $+0.54$ inches, provided that milk has no effect. Thus, if we observe an average difference of 0.25 inches, for example, we attribute it to chance and give up on the milk program (at least insofar as it affects height). However, if we observe a mean difference of 1 inch, we stay with the program and maybe hire some more high school basketball coaches.

While this example is fictitious, it does illustrate a common design strategy. Another more realistic example along similar lines is provided by the 1954 Salk vaccine trials, which constituted possibly the largest public health experiment ever conducted in the world.

The Salk vaccine greatly reduced the incidence of poliomyelitis, a crippling disease to which young children were especially prone. Two very large random samples of young children were chosen, roughly equal in number. One group, the "control" group, received a placebo—each child received injections of a harmless substance. Each child in the "treatment" group received injections of the new vaccine. No child, parent, or administering medical staff had any knowledge of the true nature of the

	Placebo	Vaccine	Totals
Children contracting polio	110	33	143
Children not contracting polio	201,119	200,712	401,831
Totals	201,229	200,745	

Table 9 Incidence of poliomyelitis. (Source: Francis et al., 1957, cited in Anderson & Sclove, 1986)

substance being injected into any individual; that is, the study was a *double-blind* experiment. This very useful device helps to offset any bias that might otherwise contaminate the interpretation of results.

Partial data from this experiment are given in Table 9. Notice the large sample size, about 200,000 for each group. Why so large? The answer is partially contained in the "placebo" column: the rate of the naturally occurring disease is estimated as 110 per 201,229, or about one case per 2,000 children. A sample of 1,000 children would not be expected to reveal a single case of polio. To obtain an accurate estimate of the incidence of any rare event, such as contracting polio, calls for large sample sizes.

There is another reason for the large number of children studied. While it is important to be conservative in evaluating differences between treatment and control groups, so that small differences are not inappropriately interpreted as an effect of treatment, it is also important to pick up genuine effects of treatment when they do in fact exist. The ability of a statistical test to satisfy the latter requirement involves the notion of *power*. To achieve a high likelihood of detecting genuine effects of vaccine in the polio trials calls for high power, which in the present context, is also achieved by employing very large sample sizes.

We have a tool for evaluating the effect of the vaccine, namely, the coefficient of association ϕ introduced in Table 7. Calculation reveals that $\phi = 0.01$, a shocking result that, taken at face value, would seem to implicate the vaccine as worthless. But this conclusion is unwarranted. Tiny as it is, the 0.01 value of ϕ is wildly significant; that is, it could not have been produced by chance (except in about 1 in every 200 experiments). This example points to the often dramatic difference between a purely descriptive use of statistical indices and a more refined

Fear

Rage

FIGURE 13 The joint effects of fear and rage on aggressiveness. (Source: Zeeman, 1976)

statistical analysis of the same data. A value of ϕ close to zero may be highly significant, but in contrast, it may be routine in smaller scale experiments to observe nonsignificant values of ϕ equal to about 0.5.

There are extensions of the above simple design. One common extension involves two or more *levels* of some treatment. For example, the vaccine may be available in two or more concentrations; all concentrations may be effective, but is one more effective than another?

A more important extension involves the simultaneous experimental manipulation of two or more *independent* variables, so as to study their *joint* effect on a single *dependent* variable. For example, age could have been incorporated into the vaccine trials so that the effectiveness of the vaccine on adults as well as children could have been assessed simultaneously.

When two or more variables influence a third, their joint effect is not predictable in any simple way from the effect of each of them taken alone. Con-

sider the influence of fear and rage on the aggressiveness of an animal. We probably expect a frightened animal to be passive, while on the contrary, we would expect an enraged animal to be relatively dangerous. What then can we expect of a frightened, enraged animal? It is possible that the situation depicted in Figure 13 may occur. Notice that a dog in a state of moderate fear and moderate rage (center) appears more vicious than one in a state of no fear and moderate rage. This is contrary to what would have been anticipated from our earlier conjecture about the effect of increasing fear alone. In the jargon of *analysis of variance*—statistical machinery developed for analyzing the effects of two or more variables on a single dependent measure—we say that fear and rage *interact* in their influence on aggressiveness.

CONCLUDING REMARKS

Contrary to popular impression, statisticians do not normally spend much of their time scratching out arithmetic calculations on a piece of paper. Computers compute, but statisticians occupy themselves with "good" methods for organizing data, "good" methods for estimating population quantities, and "good" inferential procedures. The emphasis is always on the term *good* and what it means in a given context.

The advantages of an informed data analysis are obvious and many. Such an analysis is tailored to the requirements of some set of specific data and keeps in prominent view questions that arise naturally from the empirical context generating those data. All too frequently the conservative ("no effect") *null hypothesis* of the working scientist is confirmed. Usually this occurs not because an effect is absent, but as a by-product of an insensitive analysis chosen naively for reasons of convenience or tradition. A competent statistician can often turn an apparently uninteresting set of data into a highly revealing, thought-provoking one. If for no other reason, I leave you with the following advice: support your local statistician.

A

absolute threshold The least amount of physical energy necessary to register a stimulus. It is defined as the minimum strength for a stimulus to be noticed by an observer 50 percent of the time. See also **difference threshold.**

accommodation When a new event cannot be easily assimilated into one's knowledge structure, the knowledge structure must be disrupted and changed—accommodated to the new event. See also **assimilation.**

acetylcholine (ACh) One of the major chemical transmitters in the nervous system, it is involved in the arousal of the organism and is most concentrated in the brain during sleep. See also **neurotransmission.**

achievement motivation The form of motivation, postulated by McClelland, that enables us to carry through and complete the goals we set for ourselves. Achievement motivation varies in different cultures and in different subgroups within a culture. In many experiments, it has been found that achievement motivation can be developed. See also **goals.**

acquired immunity A component of the body's defense system that works through a type of white blood cell called lymphocytes which oversee the bloodstream. They recognize and destroy millions of different antigens.

action potential The electrical impulse of the neuron, which releases its stored energy. The action potential sweeps down the axon and releases the neurotransmitters, which complete the process.

activation The major physiological effect of emotion. See also **emergency reaction.**

activation synthesis An influential theory of dream interpretation proposed in 1977 by Hobson and McCarley. It assumes that the brain is activated in REM sleep and that dreams are a conscious *interpretation* or *synthesis* of the bizarre varieties of information available during dream states; this information may come from the internal state of the dreamer and from events of the day and long-term preoccupations.

adaptation The process wherein an organism changes to fit better in its environment. Varieties of adaptation include sensory adaptation, perceptual adaptation, and biological adaptation through the long processes of evolution.

adaptation level The adjustment an organism makes to respond to differences in its external environment. It is determined by three factors: focal stimuli, background stimuli, and residual stimuli. The general finding in adaptation level research is that we adjust perceptions to match the average of external surroundings. Thus, if we are watching a group of very tall people such as basketball players, those "only" 6'2" seem short.

adaptive value Any trait is said to have adaptive value if it enables an organism to function better in its environment. See also **adaptation.**

adipocite A fat cell in the body, the number and size of which are genetically determined. Fat cells are established in the first two years of life, and overfeeding in those years results in an increased number of fat cells.

affect A term used by psychologists to refer to the feeling dimension of life. Someone with a *flat affect* displays little or no emotion.

affective disorder A psychological disorder in which a disturbance of mood is the distinguishing feature, such as depression, manic depression, and mania.

affordance The rich source of information offered by each object in the environment about its nature.

aggression The intentional harming of another. According to Freud, aggression is an instinct, but according to social learning theory, it is learned behavior. In social psychology, the *situation* is analyzed to determine how people can be coerced to become aggressive.

algorithm A thought strategy for guaranteeing a solution if one keeps working at it long enough; if you follow the procedure exactly, you will reach a correct solution to the problem.

altruism Behavior characterized by kindness and concern for others, which in extreme situations may extend to sacrificing one's life for others. Since natural selection is presumed to operate on individuals, the question for evolutionary biologists is why an individual would give up his or her life for another. See also **sociobiology.**

amnesia A sudden loss of memory caused by a blow to the head or similar injury.

amniocentesis A prenatal test in which a small amount of amniotic fluid (the liquid surrounding the fetus inside the womb) is withdrawn and subjected to chromosome analysis.

amygdala A small structure between the hypothalamus and the hippocampus. Its functions are not completely understood, but it seems to have to do with the maintenance and gratification of internal bodily needs and the storage of some memory processes.

analgesic A drug, such as morphine, that reduces the experience of pain; also called a painkiller.

analytical psychology An offshoot of psychoanalysis, developed by Jung, that studies individuation, the development of the person through the process by which the unconscious and the conscious unite.

anchoring A common effect of comparisons, by which once a standard has been used to solve a problem, it becomes less likely that the problem solver will change or adjust his or her approach, having become "anchored" in that particular strategy.

anniversary effect The apparent postponing of death until after a special occasion—such as a birthday, election, or special holiday—by persons very near death who might otherwise not be expected to live that long.

antigen A "foreign" cell or large molecule of origin outside the body. It stimulates immune responses.

antipsychotic drug A substance, often called a major tranquilizer, used in the treatment of severe mental disorders. See also **pharmacotherapy.**

antisocial personality A personality disorder that is characterized by an extremely calm mood, no sense of responsibility or shame, and a lack of genuine concern or caring for other people. Also called *psychopath* or *sociopath.*

anxiety A general emotional reaction that develops in response to the anticipation that something unpleasant or frightening may occur in the future. This could be something physical or psychological, such as a threatened insult or embarrassment.

aphasia The disruption of the ability to use language caused by damage to the temporal lobes.

appraisal The understanding of the meaning of an event. Among the many dimensions by which people evaluate events is whether there is harm or loss and whether the situation is threatening, challenging, or benign.

arousal General physiological activation or excitement.

artificial category A system of classification that refers to attributes of constructed objects, such as chairs or buildings.

assertiveness training A form of behavior therapy used when the problem entails difficulties in interpersonal relationships. It generally teaches people that they have a right to their own feelings and opinions, which matter as much as anyone else's.

assimilation The incorporation of a new event into one's existing knowledge structure. See also **accommodation.**

association The postulated bond that forms in the mind when two events occur often enough together: for example, a dinner bell and the taste of food.

attachment The special bond between an infant and the mother or other major caregiver. It probably is an innate bond that develops due to the necessity for mother love, the gratification of needs, the infant's cognitive development, and the communication between the caregiver and the child.

attribution The process by which we explain the causes of our own or others' actions or behavior. We try to determine whether people's actions are attributed to a specific situation or whether their behavior reflects something enduring about their personal disposition.

Australopithecus A hominid, dating from 3 to 4 million years ago, that might be considered the earliest direct ancestor of human beings.

automatization When a series of movements or actions are repeated many times, as in writing or walking, the behavior is accomplished automatically or "without thinking." Automatization is an important aspect of cognitive functioning; without it we would have to "pay attention" to all the many actions we must take during the day.

autonomic nervous system (ANS) A division of the peripheral nervous system primarily responsible for running the internal organs, such as the heart, kidneys, liver, and gastrointestinal tract. Its processes are *autonomic,* that is, they seem to work without conscious control. See also **somatic nervous system.**

availability A thought judgment that refers to the ease with which relevant instances come to mind. We use availability to judge the frequency or the probability of events. See also **heuristics.**

awareness Keeping track or monitoring a set of activities, actions, or behaviors.

axon A part of a neuron that extends outward from the cell body. The axon is the transmitter end of the neuron. See also **dendrites; neurotransmission.**

B

basic level category That part of a categorization system that children learn first, such as table, apple, and house, and the level at which we most naturally divide the world.

basilar membrane A structure in the ear at the base of the cochlea. It moves like a whip being cracked and creates a traveling wave that is transduced into sound.

behavioral repertoire A set of abilities that each organism is born with. This repertoire varies greatly among species: some can fly, some cannot; some can swim, some cannot.

behaviorism Growing out of a desire in the late nineteenth century to make psychology objective, it is an approach that studies external, observable behavior of organisms and attempts to infer what caused that behavior.

behavior modification A form of therapy based on operant conditioning, which attempts to change behaviors by changing the stimuli and conditions. Behavior modification may employ reinforcement or extinction to teach people new learned responses and to alter problem situations.

behavior therapy A form of psychotherapy, based primarily on classical conditioning. It attempts to "decondition" anxiety-producing responses.

bias A factor in the decision-making process that prevents impartiality in certain kinds of judgments; includes availability, representativeness, and vivid information.

binaural disparity The difference in sound information received by each ear that provides us with cues to distance, since a sound slightly to our left will strike the left ear before the right and vice versa.

binocular disparity The difference in information received by the left versus right eye, which is analyzed by the brain to provide cues to distance.

biofeedback A method of training people to control internal processes not normally controlled by consciousness, such as glandular and muscular activity, brain waves, blood pressure, and heart rate.

biological adaptation See **adaptation; evolution.**

biological approach The approach to psychology that emphasizes the relationship of the brain and nervous system to human experience.

bipedalism Walking on two legs instead of all four limbs. Human beings are the only organisms that typically walk on the hindlimbs, enabling them to carry, to share, to use their delicate forelimbs to manipulate objects, and to accomplish many other tasks that contribute to human uniqueness.

birth order An individual's rank in age in the family, which seems to influence personality and psychosocial development.

brain stem The oldest and deepest area of the brain, which evolved over 500 million years ago. It sets the general level of alertness and warns the organism of important incoming information.

C

case history A psychologist's report of a person's life in the attempt to reconstruct how patterns of behavior have developed.

catharsis An ancient idea, first proposed by the Greeks, that strong emotional experience will "cleanse the mind" and release some form of stored energy. In more technical terms, catharsis is the reduction of emotional stress by releasing emotions in controlled circumstances.

cathexis According to Freud, the investment of energy in an object, action, individual, image, or idea that will gratify an instinct.

central nervous system (CNS) The system comprising the brain and the spinal cord that forms the overall network wherein brain activity is relayed through nerve junctions in the spinal cord to the body. See also **peripheral nervous system.**

chromosome A tiny but complex structure in every cell in the body on which the genes are arranged. They carry an individual's entire genetic program and are the basic mechanism of human heredity.

chronic life strain An ongoing condition that persists in someone's life, such as an unhappy marriage or poor working conditions, that may be very stressful. It can also be produced by the way a society is organized.

chunking A memory process that reorganizes individual bits of items into larger "chunks" of information by using a code or an easily remembered pattern.

classical conditioning See **respondent conditioning.**

client-centered therapy See **person-centered therapy.**

coaction effect A phenomenon in which the presence of other people intensifies and directs an individual's behavior.

cochlea The part of the inner ear that contains an ideal medium for the transmission of sound waves.

cognitive consistency A common theory in social psychology that postulates that we are motivated to make attitudes more simple and more consistent with one another. We do not, in this view, like to have discrepant cognitive attitudes.

cognitive dissonance A social cognition theory stating that whenever an individual holds two cognitions (such as beliefs, attitudes, or behaviors) that are inconsistent with one another, a disharmony results. There is then a desire to reduce this disharmony by changing either attitudes or behaviors. This theory has been influential in social psychology and has led to many imaginative experiments. See also **cognitive consistency.**

cognitive psychology The study of the mind, which is not an observable entity like the brain. It involves many hidden activities, such as thinking, memory, language, and consciousness.

coherence A pervasive feeling of confidence that the environment is predictable and that there is a high probability that things will work out as well as can reasonably be expected. Coherence contains the components of comprehensibility, manageability, and meaningfulness.

cohort effect The distorting effect of different environmental experiences caused by sampling people from different age groups, that is, groups that begin at different times. To avoid this effect, people in psychological studies are grouped into cohorts (same age groups).

collective unconscious Perhaps the most important of Jung's contributions to psychology, it is considered to be the inherited foundation of personality and contains the common reservoir of experience available to all human beings. It consists largely of archetypes, which are inherited predispositions toward certain experiences or reactions to the world.

companionate love After passionate love fades, it is often replaced (especially in successful relationships) with this more sober, "everyday" kind of love, in which there is less arousal and excitement but more friendly affection and deep attachment.

competence One of the indicators (along with planning and concern for standards) that a child has developed consciousness of himself or herself.

complex In the usage developed by Jung, it is an organized group of constellations of one's memories, thoughts, feelings, and perceptions that can influence or even control a person's personality.

concrete operation The stage of cognitive development, according to Piaget, that lasts from age 7 to 12 years during which thinking is no longer dominated by sensory information. Children begin to reason abstractly, and they become more organized and more able to focus and direct attention for longer periods.

conditioned response (CR) A response that comes to be associated with a conditioned stimulus, such as Pavlov's dog salivating at the dinner bell. See also **respondent conditioning.**

conditioned stimulus (CS) In classical conditioning, something that has no inherent meaning (such as a sound) that comes to acquire meaning through a specific learning situation. A sound may always be paired with eating food, thus the sound will become a conditioned stimulus to the food. See also **respondent conditioning.**

conditioning The study of the *conditions* under which simple associations are formed. Extensive experiments in conditioning in psychology have been conducted by Pavlov and Skinner, among others. See also **operant conditioning; respondent conditioning.**

cone A photoreceptor in the retina that is responsible for color vision and is less sensitive than rods (it needs bright light to be activated). Three kinds of cones exist, each of which responds primarily to a different range of wavelengths: one responds best to red/orange, one to green, and one to blue/violet. See also **photoreceptors.**

conformity pressure See **social pressure.**

conservation The understanding that a certain volume is the same, even if it has a different shape. A ball of clay is the same whether it is spread out into a disc or made into a cylinder. Piaget felt that children under 3 years of age do not understand this principle.

consistency The degree to which a person's behavior is the same from situation to situation.

constancy The goal of the perceptual process to achieve a stable, constant world. We experience surprisingly little change, even though the sensory information changes radically. For example, a building may first appear as a small dot, then larger than anything on the horizon, but you still see it as the same constant building. There are three varieties of constancy: shape, size, and brightness.

constructivist approach The view that maintains that sensory information reaching the brain is chaotic and disorganized, thus perception must be a process of constructing a representation or model of the world. In this view, the information from the senses merely "sparks off" the creation of what could have caused a sensation.

continuous reinforcement (CRF) A form of reinforcement in operant conditioning in which each time the animal makes the correct response, it is reinforced. See also **operant conditioning; partial reinforcement.**

control group That part of the sample similar in every way to the experimental group except that it is observed in the absence of the independent variable. See also **experimental group; sample; variables.**

conventional morality In Kohlberg's theory of moral development, the level of moral reasoning that goes beyond individual considerations and takes the view of society as whole. See also **postconventional morality; premoral level.**

conversational maxim According to Grice, one of four maxims that speakers usually obey when they speak, which are quantity, quality, relation, and manner. The existence of these maxims makes it possible to understand the general rules people follow when they have a conversation. See also **cooperativeness principle.**

cooperativeness principle The principle that describes the relationships between two speakers: each speaker tries to understand *why* the other said what he or she did.

coping Thought or behavior that is directed at managing a problem or an emotional situation or stress.

cornea A transparent membrane that covers the front of the eye.

corpus callosum A large structure in the brain of 300 million neurons that connects the two separate cerebral hemispheres. Fibers in the corpus callosum run from one area in the left hemisphere to corresponding areas in the right, serving as an important network of communication.

correlation A statistic that measures the relationship between two sets of numbers. Usually used in psychology to measure the relationship between two factors, such as years of drinking and decline in intelligence.

cortex This is the "executive branch" of the brain. In human beings the cerebral cortex constitutes about 85 percent of the brain's weight. It contains more unspecialized neurons than the rest of the brain. These neurons can be programmed in many different ways, thus accounting for human flexibility and creativity.

counterconditioning A method of therapy using extinction and generalization, often used to help people overcome their fears. In this method, an unwanted conditioned response is eliminated by conditioning the subject to another stimulus (a conditioned stimulus) that elicits a new conditioned response, less disruptive than the unwanted conditioned response.

covariation principle A method of understanding how we attribute other people's behaviors; it involves multiple observations rather than a single one. In this view, developed by Kelly, we assess the degree to which the other person's behavior occurs in the presence of every possible cause. If we know a person always says positive things when paid large sums of money, we may infer that money is the dispositional cause of that individual's behavior. See also **discounting principle.**

Cro-Magnon The first modern human beings, members of our species, *Homo sapiens.*

crystallized abilities Mental abilities hypothesized by Cattell to derive from specific cultural experiences. See also **fluid abilities.**

cultural deprivation A concept of Feuerstein's, that individuals who are culturally *deprived* are lacking something in their own culture.

cultural difference The culturally *different* have different ideas of the answer to a question than those who are culturally deprived. A wrong answer on a test to the culturally different may simply be due to not knowing the language or the usual usage of a word.

cultural evolution The rapid development of human civilization, including science, arts, humanities, and technology. Biological evolution may take millennia or even millions of years to produce changes, but cultural evolution can produce profound changes in weeks.

D

decentration According to Piaget, the process at each stage of development, of children and adults becoming increasingly aware of the world outside of themselves and less focused on themselves. They become progressively less and less egocentric.

decision analysis Thinking about decisions in terms of alternatives, outcomes, preferences, and probabilities.

deconstruction The process of perceiving the external world in which stimuli are broken up, or *decomposed*, into elements that the nervous system can deal with, and later composed into the kinds of representations an organism needs to survive.

defense mechanism An unconscious way of distorting reality to ward off unpleasant facts that might produce anxiety. Among defense mechanisms are denial, repression, rationalization, displacement, projection, and reaction formation.

dendrite Part of a neuron, named after the Greek word for *tree*, indicating that the branch of one neuron connects with another. It receives information from the axon of another neuron. See also **neurotransmission.**

dependent variable See **variable.**

depression A severe mental disorder consisting of an overwhelming sadness that immobilizes and arrests the entire course of a person's life. See also **affective disorder; mania.**

deviation IQ In the Stanford–Binet IQ test, a precise statistical method for defining the relative position of an individual testee in comparison with others. Currently, tests are standardized with a norm of 100, so that someone who scores 116 is one standard deviation above the norm.

dexterity The ability in human beings to use the forelimbs (hands) in a delicate manner. Human dexterity, allowed by bipedalism, encouraged toolmaking and other factors important to human evolutionary development.

difference threshold The minimum increase in a physical stimulus necessary for us to notice a difference; also called the *just noticeable difference (j.n.d.).* It is not constant; the experience of a stimulus is always relative to its surroundings. See also **absolute threshold.**

discounting principle A rule of attribution developed by Kelly to describe how people attribute the behavior of a single person in a single situation or a single occasion. In this view, people discount one factor in favor of another. See also **covariation principle.**

discrimination The ability to notice differences between stimuli. See also **generalization.**

disengagement theory The proposal that it is normal for the elderly to withdraw or disengage from society. This is a controversial theory that inspired numerous studies showing that the elderly who keep active are the most satisfied with their lives.

dissociation A division of consciousness, described by Janet, in which certain experiences can only be recovered under specific conditions. Under hypnosis people can be made either to forget or to remember certain experiences that are not accessible to the remainder of consciousness.

distress From the Latin *dis*, meaning *bad*, the form of stress that is usually thought to last a long time and to become physically harmful. Selye divided stress into distress and *eustress*, the bad and good forms of stress.

DNA Deoxyribonucleic acid, which is formed into molecules made up of two chains twisted into a spiral. The chains consist of four chemical building blocks (amino acids): adenine, thymine, guanine, and cytosine. Virtually every living thing is made up of this substance.

dominant gene A gene that governs a trait that appears in the individual's physical makeup. See **recessive gene.**

dopamine An important chemical neurotransmitter whose pathway connects the limbic system to the cortex; it also participates in the brain's reward system and in the control of motor activity. The lack of dopamine causes Parkinson's disease.

dopamine hypothesis The theory that schizophrenia is caused by a surplus of dopamine, a neurotransmitter of the catecholamine group. Alternatively, it is proposed that there may be a surplus of dopamine receptor sites.

double-bind A situation in which a person is called on to respond to a message that contains two opposite meanings, such as "I love you" and "I hate you," which is thought to contribute to the development of schizophrenia.

double-blind procedure An experimental procedure in which the experimenter as well as the subjects are unaware, or "blind," of which is the experimental group and which is the control group, and are thus unable to influence the results.

drives Physiologically based goads to behavior, which literally move us to action, such as a hungry person is "driven" to find food. A drive is often experienced as a specific need, such as thirst, hunger, or sex. See also **goals; needs.**

E

ecological approach A theory of perception that emphasizes the richness of the information available to be "picked up" by the perceiver. In this view, perception is a direct function of stimulation.

ego An important part of the personality as described by Freud. It mediates between the demands of the *id* and the reality of the external world. See also **id; superego.**

egocentric bias A bias in judgment of other people and ourselves. We tend to overestimate our own contribution to a situation, mainly because we know everything that *we* have done, but do not know everything about the other person.

egocentrism An important principle in psychology emphasizing that individuals' experience tends to be centered upon themselves. With normal development a human being becomes progressively less egocentric from childhood to adulthood. See also **decentration.**

electroconvulsive therapy (ECT) A form of therapy for severe cases of schizophrenia and depression, which involves the passing of an electric shock through one of the hemispheres of the brain. In many cases, it is extremely effective, but in other cases it is of marginal use.

electroencephalogram (EEG) A record of voltage that the brain produces, usually recorded on the scalp. The voltages recorded are typically small (millionths of a volt). Variations in the EEG often relate to changes in arousal and alertness.

embryonic period The first period of the development of the embryo in the uterus, lasting until about the ninth week of pregnancy. It is the critical stage of development for the central nervous system of an organism.

emergency reaction The activation reaction of the body, preparing us to respond to the unexpected; also called *fight-or-flight* response. It involves stimulating the mechanisms of the sympathetic nervous system: increases in norepinephrine, heart rate, blood pressure, and blood volume. Skin resistance decreases; respiration, sweating, salivation, gastric motility, and pupil size increase.

emotions Relatively specific involuntary and autonomic patterns of short-lived physiological and mental responses.

emotion solid A theoretical analysis proposed by Plutchik, which describes that emotions are most distinct from one another at the highest levels of intensity and least distinguishable at the lowest level of intensity. See also **emotion wheel.**

emotion wheel A theoretical approach to how emotions are organized. In this framework, proposed by Plutchik, the eight primary emotions are arranged in a circle of opposites. See also **emotion solid; primary emotions.**

empty nest period The period for a woman in which the children leave home and become increasingly independent.

endorphins Stemming from the word meaning "the morphines within," they are a class of neurochemicals (peptides) that serve as modulators of nervous system activity and seem to be involved in pain and healing and in relief from unpleasant stimulation.

episodic memory A record of individual and personal experiences; memories that are unique to ourselves, such as a special event, a relationship, or a learning experience.

Eros According to Freud, the sexual instinct, the primary source of libido.

estrus The period during which most female animals are sexually receptive and communicate their sexual receptivity to others. See also **ovulation.**

eustress From the Greek *eu*, meaning *good*, the stress associated with the exhilaration of a change in one's life. Eustress is thought to be less harmful than distress.

evoked potential The sum of electrical activity in the brain associated with a specific event.

evolution The long series of physical changes through which species develop specific characteristics that allow them to adapt to their environment. See also **adaptation.**

exosystem In Bronfenbrenner's view of development, those elements of society that affect the individual: the media, jobs, and political movements. Changes in the exosystem can affect the microsystem and mesosystem, which are below it. For example, how much time a mother spends with her child can be affected by social trends and attitudes toward women at work.

experimental group That part of the sample with whom the researcher intervenes by manipulating the independent variable and observing this group's reactions. See also **control group; sample; variables.**

experimenter bias An experimenter's subtle and often unconscious influence of the results of an experiment.

extinction The process whereby a conditioned response gradually decreases as a result of it no longer being reinforced, because of the conditioned stimulus being presented without the unconditioned stimulus. See also **reinforcement.**

extrasensory perception (ESP) The ability to communicate and acquire information about the world by means other than those familiar to us.

F

factor analysis A technique devised by Spearman in 1929 to measure the relationship of different test scores. Spearman developed it because he assumed that a single factor would be found that would correspond to general intelligence.

false assumption The characterization by Gould that major life stages in adulthood are characterized by misconceptions about one's identity and intimacy. At different ages, there are different false assumptions to be challenged.

false consensus An error in attribution; the tendency of individuals to overestimate the commonness of their own responses and to underestimate the commonness of the responses of others who acted differently.

fear An immediate and specific emotional reaction to a threatening stimulus. For example, young birds show fear if the shadow of a hawk passes over them.

feature analyzer A cell in the visual area of the cerebral cortex that responds best to a certain feature in the environment. See also **receptive field.**

feedback Information about the operation of a system, used within the system to attain its goal.

feedback loop The cyclic action by which information from one part of a system affects another, which in turn affects the part of the system that initiated the cycle of feedback. See also **feedback; negative feedback; positive feedback.**

fetal alcohol syndrome An ailment suffered by babies born of alcoholic mothers. These newborns have cone-shaped heads and may be mentally retarded.

fight-or-flight See **emergency reaction.**

fixation In Freud's view, many individuals' personalities become *fixed* at a given stage of mental development. Therefore, their adult personality will reflect this tendency. A person who is overly dependent and derives much satisfaction from oral activities, such as eating, is said to be fixated at the oral stage. See also **regression.**

fixed-action pattern Unlearned behavior, generic to a species, which appears or is released in the presence of certain sign stimuli. The attack of the stickleback fish to a red stimulus is an example.

fixed interval (FI) One of the four kinds of partial reinforcement schedules, in which reinforcement is presented at regular intervals after the correct response. See also **variable interval (VI); fixed ratio (FR); variable ratio (VR).**

fixed ratio (FR) In this schedule of reinforcement, the reward is given after a certain number of responses.

flooding A form of behavior therapy similar to systematic desensitization. In flooding, the therapist fills (literally "floods") the client's mind with a continuing narrative of situations that evoke fear and anxiety.

fluid abilities Mental abilities hypothesized by Cattell to be involved in the perception and registration of the world. These are thought to be genetically based. See also **crystallized abilities.**

formal operation A stage from age 12 to adulthood, in Piaget's framework for cognitive development in which higher order, abstract thinking begins, complex scientific experiments can be followed, and hypotheses can be formulated and tested.

fovea An area at the center of the retina that contains the greatest concentration of cones and no rods.

fraternal twin Developed when the mother releases two eggs and each is fertilized by different sperms. The individuals are no more alike biologically than any two siblings would be.

free association A fundamental feature of psychoanalytic therapy developed by Freud in which the patient is asked to say anything that comes into his or her mind, without criticism or editing. Free association is designed to allow normally "forbidden" thoughts to arise to the surface of consciousness.

frontal lobes A part of the cortex intimately connected to the limbic system, and regarded by some psychologists as part of the limbic system. They are also involved in forward planning and seem to contain different emotions: the left side seems to be involved in positive or "happy" emotions, and the right, negative or "sad" ones.

frustration Results when a desired outcome is thwarted or delayed. It is a normal reaction to stress and to the hassles of everyday life.

functional autonomy The tendency for any action repeated often enough to become a motive in its own right. For example, a person who initially strives to make money may continue to try to make money even after becoming very rich.

fundamental attribution error A mistake that people often make in judgment: what little information is available is overused. In judging other people, we tend to overgeneralize from this small sample we have and to underestimate situational forces and overestimate dispositional forces.

G

ganglion cells The third layer of nerve cells in the retina. Each ganglion has a long axon and all these axons exit the eye at the same point, where they are bundled together and form the optic nerve that carries visual information to the brain. See also **retina.**

gender identity When a child knows and identifies with what sex he or she is.

gene The basic unit of heredity in all living things. Genes are made of a substance called DNA (deoxyribonucleic acid). See also **chromosome; genetic code.**

general adaptation syndrome The physiological reactions to extreme change, which occur in three stages: (1) alarm reaction, (2) resistance, and (3) exhaustion. It was first identified by Selye, who set out to study the phenomena that occur in all illnesses. See also **emergency reaction.**

generalization Once a specific stimulus has become a conditioned stimulus, similar stimuli can elicit the conditioned response. For example, someone who has an aversion to eating a hamburger may also avoid eating steak. See also **discrimination.**

generalized anxiety A common anxiety disorder in which people live in constant tension and worry. They are uneasy around people and are sensitive to comments and criticism. They are often so terrified of making a mistake that they cannot concentrate or make decisions.

general paresis A slow degenerative disease that eventually erodes mental faculties. A scourge in the late nineteenth century, it was discovered to be caused by syphilis. This understanding of the biological roots of a supposedly mental disorder gave psychiatrists the hope that other biological causes would be found for many mental disorders.

genetic code The sequence of instructions contained in the four chemical building blocks in the DNA of the genes, which guides the construction of any particular organism. The essential differences between, for example, human beings and turtles at the molecular level is only the arrangement of the chemical substances on the DNA molecule. See also **DNA; gene.**

genetic potential The specific genetic endowment that may predispose an individual to an ability or a trait. See also **range of reaction.**

genetics The study of how specific characteristics are passed physically from one generation to the next.

genotype The entire complement of an individual's genetic inheritance. See also **phenotype.**

Gestalt Literally, to "create a form." In psychology, it is an immediate organizing of the form of an object. One of the principles of Gestalt psychology is that the whole is greater than the sum of its parts.

goals Desired outcomes that have not yet occurred. See also **achievement motivation; needs.**

grammar The study of the rules for formation of a specific language. See also **syntax.**

H

hassles Common, daily annoyances, such as traffic jams, waiting in long lines, and computer foulups, that add measurably to emotional conflict and stress.

Head Start A large-scale experimental program of preschool enrichment in underprivileged areas of the United States, which was initiated in 1965.

health psychology Psychologists are currently applying knowledge to teach people to learn to be healthy. Some research involves those who are "hardy" and can resist disease and others whose behavior makes them susceptible to disease.

heuristics Simplifying strategies that we use to make judgments and to solve problems; our usual mental "rules of thumb."

hidden observer The idea that many experiences below consciousness enter consciousness through hypnosis. In a demonstration, a person was instructed that he would feel no pain during hypnosis. While his conscious report indicated that he felt no pain, through "automatic writing," his hidden observer, operating below consciousness, reported the experience of pain, indicating that this experience was simply dissociated from consciousness.

hippocampus A structure in the limbic system that seems to be involved in three related functions: learning, the recognition of novelty, and the storage of memory.

homeostasis Literally, "a return to the same state." It describes the general principle whereby the body maintains a constant environment. Changes in one direction are neutralized, and body functions remain at a constant. For instance, changes in blood flow, heartbeat rate, blood temperature, and breathing rate are all regulated to maintain constant internal processes. The best known of these is the normal body temperature of 98.6°F. See also **negative feedback.**

hominids All human beings and their humanlike ancestors.

Homo erectus Probably one of the first true human beings, this upright man stood fully erect and walked much as we do, had a relatively large brain, and had developed a complex culture and technology that included mastery of fire.

Homo habilis Literally "handy man," this hominid was a maker and user of tools, and an efficient worker and hunter who was probably a direct ancestor of later human beings.

Homo sapiens Literally "intelligent man," the species of modern human beings. See also **Cro-Magnon.**

homunculus A representation of how various portions of the brain correspond to different parts of the body.

hormones Chemicals manufactured and secreted by special glands in the body, such as the endocrine glands; they are carried through the blood to specific target cells in the body.

human adaptation The simultaneous development, in a positive feedback loop, of all those characteristics that set human beings apart from other animals. See also **adaptation.**

humanistic approach An attempt to analyze human experience by understanding important, positive aspects of life, such as growth and development.

humanistic psychology A field of psychology that studies primarily the healthy, growth-oriented side of human nature.

hunter-gatherers The typical human society throughout most of evolutionary history in which there are two main activities: the search for meat and the gathering of available fruits, vegetables, and grains.

hyperphagia Extreme overeating resulting from damage to the hypothalamus.

hypertension A chronic condition of high blood pressure, caused by constriction of blood vessels.

hypnagogic state Borderline state entered just before sleep. See also **hypnopompic state.**

hypnopompic state Borderline state entered just before complete awakening in which consciousness is receptive. Images in the mind have qualities of vividness, originality, independence of conscious control, and changeability.

hypnosis A form of dissociation in which individuals relinquish the normal control of their consciousness to another person. People under hypnosis have been able to recall events otherwise inaccessible to their waking consciousness. They can also withstand pain and follow detailed suggestions.

hypochondriasis An individual's

misinterpretation of bodily functions, leading usually to fear of disease or belief that one is already suffering from a disease.

hypothalamus A small organ in the brain that weighs about 4 grams. It is located in the limbic system and regulates many activities relating to survival: eating, drinking, sleeping, waking, body temperature, balance, heart rate, hormones, sex, and emotions.

hypothesis A specific statement about what will happen if certain events take place: "if A, then B." For a hypothesis to be scientific, it should be able to be confirmed or disconfirmed.

hypothesis testing The systematic consideration of a series of hypotheses until all are eliminated except the one solution.

I

id According to Freud, it is the initial, infant personality and is composed of the primary instincts (those largely concerned with survival) and other inherited psychological characteristics. See also **ego; superego.**

identical twins See **monozygotic twins.**

immaturity The state of the human infant not being fully developed at birth. The human mother and father need to care for the human infant longer than in other species. The many learning experiences that occur throughout their long childhood make human beings more distinct from one another than other animals.

immunity The body's natural and complex defenses against foreign substances such as viruses.

imprinting The process of a very young animal seeing an object, usually its mother, and following it. This is a prepared reaction that leads to a greater chance of survival.

independent variable See **variable.**

innate Inborn, unlearned, and fixed at birth. Usually applied to such characteristics as instincts. See also **instincts.**

insight A vision of how all the parts of a problem fit together or of how to represent a problem differently. The experience of insight can come at the end of a long process of hypothesis testing or suddenly and unexpectedly.

instinctive drift A phenomenon identified by Breland and Breland that various organisms have difficulty learning arbitrary responses because learned behavior "drifts" toward instinctive behavior.

instincts Innate, fixed patterns of behavior typical of every member of a given species, which are thought to be "programmed" to satisfy needs and which appear without learning as soon as they are needed. The salmon's inevitable return to the river of its birth is instinctual.

instrumental conditioning See **operant conditioning.**

instrumental enrichment (I.E.) A program devised by Feuerstein in Israel, which attempts to develop a special set of techniques to increase intelligence and to assess increases in intelligence.

intelligence quotient (IQ) A term first used by Binet when testing individuals for their suitability for either normal or remedial school. Determined by dividing a person's mental age by the chronological age. The IQ test is probably psychology's most visible contribution to society, and its most controversial.

intermediate layer One of the three main layers of nerve cells in the retina, comprising bipolar cells, horizontal cells, and amacrine cells. See also **ganglion cells; photoreceptors; retina.**

interneurons Nerve cells in the spinal cord that connect afferent and efferent neurons. See also **afferent neuron; efferent neuron.**

interposition A cue to depth, provided when one object stands in front of another and blocks part or all of the other object.

interpretation After organization, interpretation is the second step in discovering meaning. A question we answer when we interpret phenomena is: what is the simplest meaningful stimulus that gives rise to my experience?

introspection The primary research method used by late nineteenth-century psychologists, involving study of their own minds and examination of the contents of their own experience.

invariance A constant pattern of stimulation. From every perspective we can see that a post has right angles and is always perpendicular to the horizon.

J

jigsaw classroom technique A technique developed by Aronson to teach interdependence in which students are divided into groups and assigned a project. Each member is given information about one part of the assignment, one "puzzle piece." The only way the assignment can be completed is if each member teaches and shares his or her information with the others; thus, each person is an important and invaluable resource.

just noticeable difference (j.n.d.) See **difference threshold.**

K

kinesthesis The feedback from the joints of the body that allows us to know and coordinate the movement of different body parts (where limbs are, what their angle is, and what they are doing).

knowledge acquisition Components of Sternberg's theory of intelligence; our ability to learn new things using previous experience relevant to the task at hand, not general experience. An individual may have general knowledge, but if he fails to employ this specific ability to get new knowledge he is considered less intelligent. More intelligent people can deal with novelty and can cope in extraordinary situations.

L

latent learning Learning that can occur without being manifested in an observable performance improvement.

lateral inhibition Retinal cells fire and affect one another. The brighter the light, the more they fire. Whenever a cell fires, it inhibits the firing of a cell next to it (laterally). This mechanism sharpens perception of sharp changes, like corners and edges, but sometimes makes edges appear where there are none.

learned helplessness The discovery that one has no control over events and that actions do not lead to goals. This can decrease motivation, decrease the ability to learn new responses, and increase emotional disturbance.

learning potential assessment device (LPAD) An intelligence testing and enrichment program aimed at remediation of retarded individuals.

levels of awareness The steps in our awareness of the world, from full consciousness, such as a deliberate action, to preconscious, nonconscious, and unconscious processes.

levels of processing A theory of memory stating that all information presented to us is processed at different depths or levels. According to this theory, the greater the depth of processing, the more likely something is to be remembered. The "deepest" processing is that which relates information to oneself.

libido In Freud's theory, the "animal" instincts provide the fuel for actions and for the human mind. In human beings, this biological fuel is transformed into "psychic energy," or libido.

life change units (LCU) The major life changes a person has experienced in the recent past. Certain events are set on this scale at arbitrary values, such as marriage at 50 life change units. Different experiences, such as divorce, the birth of a child, and changing a job, are also assigned values in relation to marriage. The number of life change units a person experiences during a year is strongly related to one's propensity for becoming ill.

limbic system A group of cellular structures between the brain stem and the cortex, which evolved about 150 million years ago. It is the area of the brain that helps maintain constant environment in the body. Its activities include regulating the maintenance of body temperature, blood pressure, heartbeat rate, and levels of sugar in the blood. See also **homeostasis.**

lock-and-key principle The principle recently discovered about transmission in the nervous system. Each neuron transmitter has a specific shape, and the shape of its molecule forms a "key" that fits a receptor whose shape matches it, as a key fits into a lock. This relationship describes how chemical messages of the body can connect with their target cells.

longitudinal study Research in which a group or panel of people are studied over a number of years or even decades. See also **cohort effect.**

long-term memory A kind of memory thought by many psychologists to store permanent records of experiences, including both episodic and representational memory.

M

macrosystem According to Bronfenbrenner, the cultural norms that guide behaviors. These include the age at which a child is considered responsible, how much care each parent gives to the child, and what constitutes a "good child."

mania A serious psychological disorder characterized by excessive elation and a frenzy of overexcitability and activity. Grandiose and impossible plans may be made during manic episodes.

maturation The emergence of individual characteristics through normal growth processes. It is controlled by the information contained in the genes, is relatively unaffected by learning or experience, and follows a universal pattern.

mean The arithmetic average of a set of numbers.

means-end analysis A method of problem solving in which one works backward from the goal through actions and materials needed to achieve it.

median From the Latin word for *middle,* the middle figure in a distribution of numbers.

mediated learning experience Information about the world, events, and experiences as *interpreted* by others, usually a parent or sibling. Thus, the *meaning* of events is given to us by other people. In Feuerstein's theory of instrumental enrichment, the hypothesis is made that the roots of intelligence will be found in the adequacy of the mediated learning experience.

meditation A system of mental training that often involves relaxation and an attempt at knowledge of oneself and one's place in the world. It is a different form of knowledge than the intellectual and academic knowledge taught in schools.

menarche The onset of first menstruation.

mental age Based on the concept that intellectual abilities increase with age, it attributes various levels of attainment (ages) to different IQ test scores.

mentor Someone who eases a youth into adulthood. A mentor ideally aids a person in developing his or her own autonomy and interests.

mesosystem In Bronfenbrenner's view of child development, the family structure at different stages of development. The world of the infant expands; the world of the family then widens to include school friends, athletic groups, and social clubs in late childhood. The network of relationships grows.

meta-analysis The analysis of analyses. This technique has been used to analyze the results of many different studies of effectiveness of psychotherapy and has shown that the *average* effect of psychotherapy is positive and fairly large.

metacomponents In Sternberg's analysis of intelligence, the higher order processes such as planning and evaluating. These work out task strategies and allow communication with the other components.

method of loci A memory method developed by the Greeks which is to create a new and different association to improve recall by visualizing the items to be recalled.

microsystem In the view of Bronfenbrenner, those relationships of everyday life, home, and family that constitute the child's immediate world and greatly affect the child.

midlife crisis A hypothesized stage in middle adulthood when people review and assess their early adulthood. They may try to change the facets of life with which they are dissatisfied in an attempt to resolve the psychological issues introduced by entering the final half of life. It may be triggered by awareness of their own mortality and by discovery that they are not happy with life, and this may lead to radical changes, such as job and family disruptions.

mitosis The process of cell division that underlies normal organism growth.

mnemonics A technique for aiding memory that involves making up a context in which certain meaningless items can be remembered. For example, "Spring forward, fall back" is a mnemonic to remember which way to change the clocks for daylight savings time.

modules Sensory "programs" in the brain designed to analyze specifically one type of information. They are *encapsulated,* that is, they do not communicate with other modules, and *domain specific,* that is, the analysis routine for smell may be different from the analysis for shape or language.

monozygotic twins Identical twins developed from the same fertilized egg. See also **fraternal twins.**

moods Long-lasting states of feeling. See also **affective disorders.**

morality The knowledge of what is right and what is wrong. According to Kohlberg, morality develops in several stages, from the premoral stage, through the conventional moral stage, to the postconventional stage. These stages parallel developments in cognition and are based on them.

morpheme The smallest unit of meaning in language; it can be a word or a word fragment, such as a prefix or suffix.

motion parallax The differences in apparent speed and direction of movement by objects at varying distances from a moving observer.

motivational processes In Bandura's analysis of observational learning, the drive for the acquisition of knowledge. The kinds of motivation that affect observational learning depend on the level of development. Young children are motivated by immediate consequences of their actions, but older children are increasingly motivated by abstract incentives such as personal satisfaction and a sense of self-efficacy.

multimind Ornstein's theory of the mind, in which the mind is seen as an incoherent mixture of diverse processes, from reflexes to modules to "small minds," which underlies the inconsistency of personality and mental processing.

multiple personality A condition in which different "selves" exist separately.

mutation A spontaneous change in the structure of a gene.

myelin sheath A fatty substance coating the axons of many neurons. It serves to insulate, to accelerate neuronal transmission, and to isolate neurons from one another.

N

natural categories Systems of classification that reflect the structure of the physical world; for example, the categories of color.

natural selection A theory first described by Darwin in 1859 to elucidate how populations can change over time. It involved two insights: (1) individuals who survive are more fit and better able to live in and adapt to their environment; and (2) offspring differ in important respects from the parents. Therefore, differences that are passed on to the offspring are ones that usually enable them to fit better in their environment. See also **adaptation.**

nature–nurture The controversy in psychology over whether we are more determined by innate characteristics or by experiences in the environment. Most human behavior is the product of both factors.

Neanderthal The caveman of popular folklore, but with mental abilities and a culture far more advanced than was once suspected and much like modern human beings in many ways.

needs In psychological terms, the specific deficits that any animal must satisfy, such as hunger and thirst. See also **goals.**

negative feedback A form of feedback in which information triggers changes in the opposite (negative) direction; for example, low blood sugar signals us to increase blood sugar levels. It is important to the maintenance of the body's internal state. See also **homeostasis; positive feedback.**

neuroendocrine system The system comprising the autonomic nervous system (ANS) and the endocrine glands, which is one of the means through which the brain controls the body.

neuron The nerve cells that are the building blocks of the brain and nervous systems. The nucleus of the neuron is called the *cell body.* There are approximately 10 billion neurons in the human brain, each one having thousands of different interconnections.

neurosis In the definition of Freud, an unconscious conflict between the desires of the id and the demands of the superego. He felt it often occurred as the result of a traumatic experience in early childhood.

neurotransmission The largely chemical process by which nerve cells in the brain and other parts of the body communicate with one another. When a neuron fires, it releases chemicals at its axon, which then migrate across the synoptic cleft to a second cell.

nonconscious A level of awareness that is primarily concerned with the autonomic functioning of the body, such as the pumping of the heart, blood circulation, breathing, digestion, and other biochemical and neurological activities.

norepinephrine Formerly called *adrenaline,* this neurotransmitter is important in coding of memory and in the reward system of the brain.

norms Standards of permissible thought and behavior shared by members of a group.

O

object permanence An important demonstration, first pointed out by Piaget, that children, at about 8 months, begin to be able to form a representation of an object not present. They will follow an object that they have previously seen and attempt to find it. Younger babies will not look for such a vanished object.

observational learning The process of learning through watching others and modeling or imitating their behavior; also called *social learning.*

obsessive-compulsive disorders In an obsession the mind is flooded with a specific thought. In a compulsive disorder the person feels compelled to repeat a certain action over and over again.

occipital lobes The area at the back of the brain that is devoted entirely to vision.

ocular accommodation The change in the width of the lens in the eye to focus light on the retina.

olfactory cilia The receptors for smell, located at the end of the nasal cavity.

olfactory epithelium Literally "smell skin," the end of the nasal cavity containing the receptors for smell.

operant conditioning Also called *instrumental conditioning,* a type of conditioning developed by Skinner in the 1930s in which the organism's *operations* or actions are conditioned. It is very useful for teaching organisms new responses and the contingencies of different situations. See also **conditioning; reinforcement; respondent conditioning.**

operant level In operant conditioning, the number of times a specific response is made before the conditioning trials begin.

operant strength In operant conditioning, the measure of the rate of response after conditioning and the strength of association between a behavior and its reinforcement. See also **operant level.**

operations In Piaget's theory of cognitive development, rules for transforming and manipulating information in the world. A simple arithmetic operation is: If you have two and add two, you will have four.

optical expansion The so-called looming effect, which creates the impression that, as you approach a scene, objects closer to you are moving toward you faster than those far away.

organization See **perceptual organization.**

organizational stress The combination of tension, pressure, and danger that impinge upon people in their work environment and that may outstrip their capacity to adapt to it.

orgasm The most brief and intense phase of the sexual response cycle, during which arousal, muscle tension, heart rate, and respiration increase rapidly to a peak, which for males also involves ejaculation.

orienting reflex The physiological changes that prepare the organism for action: muscles tense, neurotransmitters increase, and sensory acuity sharpens. See also **emergency reaction.**

ovulation The time when the female egg is developed and released from the ovary and can thus be fertilized. In human females this takes place every month, rather than only during estrus.

P

pair bonding The sexual bond that is the basis of the family, that encourages fathers to stay with and care for their mates and their offspring, permitting families to expand faster through the sharing of food and child-rearing responsibilities.

parapsychology The study of extrasensory communication.

parasympathetic nervous system A division of the autonomic nervous system, it acts to return the body to normal after emergencies. See also **sympathetic nervous system.**

parietal lobe The area of the brain between the frontal lobe and the occipital lobe, which is thought to be involved in the integration and analysis of sensory input.

parental investment Any "investment" (of care, food, support, risk, or resources) that enhances the survival potential of an offspring. Its analysis is similar to economic cost–benefit analyses.

partial reinforcement In this form of reinforcement, each time the animal makes a correct response, the reinforcement does not always occur. See also **continuous reinforcement; operant conditioning.**

passionate love This is the strong form of being in love; a state of intense absorption in another person. It includes arousal, longing, and activation of many different emotions.

perceptual cycle A concept of Neisser that helps to explain how perception is an active process guided by schemata. When something is seen, it stimulates direct exploration; then the sensory information provided by these exploratory movements modifies the view of the world and the schemata change again. New movements are directed and exploration begins anew. This is why different people have different perceptual experiences of the same scene; each of us selects the world differently.

perceptual organization The connection and coordination of separate sensory stimuli into something meaningful. When something becomes organized as an illusion, it is difficult to disorganize it.

perceptual-motor memory This form of memory is sometimes called "skill memory." It contains the rules for operating certain routine actions, such as throwing a ball, getting dressed, or playing a game.

performance components In Sternberg's analysis of intelligence, strategies used in the performance of tasks and in carrying out decisions made by the metacomponents, such as linguistic and spatial strategies.

peripheral nervous system (PNS) Nerves from the spinal cord that conduct commands to the muscles and organs of the body and gather information about body states, muscle position, limb position, and internal states of organs. See also **central nervous system.**

person-centered therapy An influential form of psychotherapy developed by Rogers. In this humanistic therapy, the most important element is the relationship between the therapist and client. Clients are encouraged by means of *nondirective* statements to explore and reveal their feelings about themselves and their life situations. Once these situations can come to consciousness, it is hoped that a clarification of beliefs and action will follow.

pharmacotherapy An attempt to treat psychological problems by administering drugs in four major categories: antipsychotics, antidepressants, antianxiety drugs, and lithium compounds.

phenotype The portion of the genotype (genetic inheritance) that is expressed in the organism.

pheromones Chemical substances found in insects and mammals that convey information, usually relating to sex. For example, female mice secrete a substance called *copulin* that arouses the male. Smell is important in human sexual behavior; scent glands in the armpits seem to be part of a human pheromone system.

phobia From the Greek word for *fear,* in psychology the term refers to an extreme or unfounded fear of an object or place.

phonemes The specific sound elements of language; a particular sound is considered a phoneme only if it is used in language.

photoreceptors The rods and cones in the eye, which are the nerve cells containing photochemicals that respond to light. They constitute the main layer of the retina. See also **retina.**

pituitary The control gland of the neuroendocrine system, it lies below the hypothalamus in the limbic system.

placebo The result of a drug or therapy that is not due to its intrinsic physiological effect.

pleasure principle In Freud's theory of personality, the principle that organisms seek to reduce tension created by the build-up of libido.

polarity In Plutchik's theory of emotions, the variation between emotions that makes them opposites, such as love being the opposite of hate, sadness the opposite of joy. See also **emotion solid; emotion wheel.**

pontine reticular formation A network of cells located in the pons of the brain that activates eye movement neurons during REM sleep. During this period, these cells also inhibit another part of the brain, which in turn blocks muscle movements.

positive feedback A process by which changes in one element of a system change the rest of the system in the same direction. Increases in grumpiness, hostility, or happiness lead to further increases in the same direction. See also **negative feedback.**

postconventional morality In Kohlberg's theory of moral development, moral reasoning based on an individual's principles of conscience, which respect both the moral rights of individuals and the welfare of the community. See also **conventional morality; premoral level.**

potency A component of emotional appraisal proposed by Osgood in which a person judging an emotional experience asks, "Is it alive or dead, strong or weak, fast or slow?"

Power Law A principle of sensation described by Stephens, which shows that the different senses transform the information they select differently. Within each sensory system, equal ratios of stimulus intensity produce equal ratios of change in experience. See also **Weber's Law.**

preconscious A level of awareness that includes memories that enable us to operate in the world.

prehuman beings Creatures having both apelike and humanlike characteristics. See also **hominids.**

prejudice A negative judgmental attitude toward an identifiable group of people, which is usually based on a simplistic overgeneralization.

premoral level In Kohlberg's theory of moral development, moral reasoning in which individuals consider only their own interest. See also **conventional morality; postconventional morality.**

preoperational stage In Piaget's view of cognitive development, the state (from 2 to 7 years) during which a child begins to be able to represent objects in drawings or words and schemata become more integrated and coordinated.

preparedness An influential concept developed by Seligman, which hypothesized that certain animals are more predisposed (prepared) to learn certain responses better than other animals.

prepotence In Maslow's hierarchy of motivation, prepotence denotes the relative strength of different needs. In this view, the "stronger" needs are lower on the hierarchy. The need for water, for example, is a stronger need than the need for friendship.

pressure receptors Specific receptors in the veins that detect even the smallest reduction in water content of the blood. This is an important mechanism in the transmission of thirst signals to the brain.

primacy The phenomenon that the first parts of things are easier to remember than the later parts. For example, the first lessons of a course are easier to learn and remember than the later ones. See also **recency.**

primary emotions The recent hypothesis that there are several primary emotions, as there are primary colors. Plutchik further states that there are eight of these: joy, acceptance, fear, surprise, sadness, disgust, anger, and anticipation.

proactive interference This occurs when previous knowledge interferes with present memory. See also **retroactive interference.**

problem representation The way a person thinks about or *presents* a problem may make it harder or easier to solve. Some problems need to be represented visually, some purely mathematically. The wrong representation of a problem may dramatically change how it works.

production processes In Bandura's analysis of learning, the components of behavior and the knowledge of how to organize them into action. The processes primarily compare sensory feedback with conceptions or mental models.

proprioception The sense that allows us to know where each part of the body is in relationship to all other parts.

prosocial behavior Behaving in such a way as to enhance social integration and to enhance the actions of others.

prototype The sample that most typifies a category.

proxemics An analysis of personal space developed by Hall. Personal space is classified into intimate, personal, social, and public.

psychiatric drugs Substances, such as antidepressants, antipsychotics, antianxiety drugs, and lithium, that help to "normalize" consciousness by correcting neurochemical imbalances.

psychiatric social worker The holder of an advanced degree in the psychiatric field who concentrates on social and community-based problems.

psychiatrist A medical doctor whose specialty is the treatment of psychological problems and who is licensed to dispense drugs.

psychoactive drugs Substances such as marijuana, mescaline, and LSD that change the overall structure of consciousness.

psychoanalysis The most famous and one of the most influential theories in psychology. Proposed by Freud and developed from the late nineteenth century until 1940, it is a complete theory of personality and a method of treatment. It specifies what motivates people, how personality develops, and how it is built. Its primary aim is to show that the relationship between conscious and unconscious processes is often the root of much behavior, especially behavior that causes difficulties.

psychoanalyst A psychotherapist trained in the psychoanalytic techniques formulated by Freud; almost all psychoanalysts are physicians.

psychoimmunology A new branch of psychology that traces the effects of mental states on the immune system. For instance, the grieving of a spouse after an accident is associated with a significant loss of health; the connecting link is the immune system.

psychokinesis The ability to affect the physical world by mental force alone. A demonstration of this would be transporting objects merely by willing them to move, although such demonstrations have not been scientifically verified.

psychopath See **antisocial personality.**

psychosocial development The individual relationship with various groups—family, community, nation—and the socialization and development of the individual. Erikson recognized that development processes occur in a psychosocial context; he viewed the life course as a series of eight successive stages, each with a characteristic crisis to be resolved.

pyramid of motivation A theoretical description of motivation by Maslow, which places emotions in an ascending pyramid of relative strength. At the bottom are physiological needs, such as hunger and thirst. Following those are safety and belonging needs, such as the need for shelter and friendship. Above those are the goals of competence and self-esteem, knowledge, self-actualization, and transcendence.

Q

qualitative In psychology, the type of measurement that points to the qualities or characteristics of an individual; for example, she is aggressive, he is friendly.

quantitative In psychology, the type of measurement that is a numerical value or quantity and that usually gives the degree of difference between two measurements; for example, group X is 5 inches taller on average than group Y.

questionnaire A formal method for asking specific questions that provide researchers dependable written answers on which to base their judgments.

R

range of reaction The portion of an individual's genetic potential that predisposes him or her to a certain ability or trait. Whether the predisposition develops into a reality depends on experience and environmental factors.

rapid eye movement. See **REM sleep.**

rational-emotive therapy (RET) A form of therapy, developed by Ellis, in which the therapist determines what the underlying belief system of the individual is, confronts the client with that belief system, and directly forces him or her to examine it against reality.

reality principle The principle, postulated by Freud, in which the ego operates. It specifies that actions are tested against reality, and the feedback from those actions modifies behavior. See also **ego.**

recall The ability to summon up stored information in the memory in the absence of the actual object or event.

recency Enhanced recall of the most recent thing learned or experienced. See also **primacy.**

receptive field The area of stimulation that a retinal cell responds best to. Different cells have been found to have differently shaped receptive fields.

recessive gene A gene that governs a trait that is not expressed unless both parents contribute it. See **dominant gene.**

recognition The ability to correctly identify an object or an event.

reference group The group we

choose to compare ourselves to on a number of dimensions, often a group of peers or appropriate individuals.

reflexes Inborn, unlearned responses of newborns, many of which involve sophisticated motor skills. Reflexes include sucking and head turning in response to noise.

regression Under stress, according to Freud, a person may regress to earlier stages of personality. Thus, people will act more as they did when they were younger, when the foundations of their personality were formed. See also **fixation.**

reinforcement Any event that strengthens the possibility that a certain response will reoccur. When something is given to an animal after a desired response, this is called *positive reinforcement.* When something unpleasant is taken away from the animal after a desired response, this is called *negative reinforcement.*

reliability The necessity that test scores be reproducible and consistent. See also **validity.**

REM sleep Rapid eye movements (REM) during sleep were first discovered in the 1950s. Since then, they have been taken as an unequivocal sign that the sleeper is in a dream state, and hundreds of experiments have shown a consistent association between REM sleep and dreaming.

replication The ability of psychological experiments to be repeatable by others. If the findings of a second experiment confirm those of the first, then the findings of the first experiment are more likely to be accepted.

representational memory A record of general knowledge of the world, such as how to speak, how to ride a bicycle, and where Chicago and Scotland are. Representational memory is generally assumed to be common to all members of a culture. See also **episodic memory.**

representational thought At about 18 months, children begin to develop the capacity to represent objects in their minds. One important kind of symbol is language.

representativeness The judgment that an object is *typical* of its cate-

gory. Because we tend to judge vivid examples of a category as representative, a single case, considered representative, can have a disproportionate influence on us.

resistance In psychoanalysis, a characteristic way that the patient unconsciously works *against* revealing his or her feelings or thoughts. For instance, every time a patient might start to talk about his or her mother, he or she might change the subject or say that the thought is too silly.

respondent conditioning Also called *classical conditioning,* the process whereby a previously neutral stimulus (NS) comes to have a significant effect on an organism's behavior. See also **conditioned response; conditioned stimulus; unconditioned response; unconditioned stimulus.**

retention A process in memory in which new information must be stored and kept. This is a hypothetical stage in the cycle of memory used by many psychologists. See also **retrieval.**

retention process In Bandura's analysis of observational learning, a process that helps to reproduce observed behavior, which involves forming a mental model of the behavior. Cognitive rehearsal is one means of increasing retention of observational learning.

reticular activating system (RAS) A system in the brain that arouses the cortex to important incoming stimulation. It seems to serve a general alarm function—it tells the cortex that something visual, auditory, or olfactory is on its way. The RAS controls the existence and the intensity of consciousness.

retina The center of the process of vision in the eye; it is composed of neural tissues and cones and rods. See **cones; photoreceptors; rods.**

retrieval A process hypothesized by many psychologists in which stored information is brought forward into consciousness at the appropriate time. See also **retention.**

retroactive interference This occurs when new information interferes with older memories. See also **proactive interference.**

risky shift The concept that people

are more likely to take risks in an extreme position when they are in groups than when alone; also called the *extremity shift.*

rods Photoreceptors in the retina of the eye that respond most to light energy at low levels, particularly those at a wavelength of about 480 nanometers. There are about 120 million rods distributed over the retina, with the heaviest concentration at the sides. See also **cones; photoreceptors.**

S

sample The group of subjects in an experiment or study that is representative of an entire population.

schema (schemata, pl.) The unit of mental life; the internal, mental organization of how actions relate to one another, how different internal stimuli relate to one another, and how outside stimuli relate to specific actions. Schemata are the cognitive generalizations about oneself that guide the processing information and interpretation about oneself.

schizophrenia The group of psychological disorders that involve severe deterioration of mental abilities; fundamental disorganization that causes disturbances in every area of life, including social functioning, feelings, and behavior.

seasonal affective disorder (SAD) Winter-time depression in the absence of sunlight. For some of these light-sensitive people, changes in light exposure can generate mood swings. Rosenthal developed a novel "light therapy" to treat such patients.

secondary traits In Allport's theory of personality, these are traits that only occur in a few specific situations. A person may be generally calm but may become anxious on airplanes. See also **cardinal traits.**

sedatives Drugs, such as barbiturates, that induce relaxation and sleep.

self-actualization Maslow theorized that we all have within us certain "potentials" and that we strive to make those potentials "actual." Thus, self-actualization is the drive within individuals to actualize their potential.

self-awareness The typically human consciousness of existence and mortality—the knowledge of who we are and the sense of personal self.

self-involvement A characteristic of people who think of themselves as better than others and who are vulnerable to anyone who confronts such claims or who looks better than them. Hostility may be used to cope with difficulty. Studies show that self-involved people have high risk of heart attacks and high blood pressure.

self-monitoring The dimension on which people differ in the kind of information they select for their self-concept. *High self-monitors* are chiefly interested in how they appear to others and how correctly they behave. They are sensitive to the wishes of others and use others' behavior as a guideline. *Low self-monitors* look more to their inner selves for guidelines.

self-schemata Cognitive generalizations that guide the processing of information and interpretation about the self.

semantic memory The knowledge of a specific language and of what words mean and how they are used within a specific culture. The average college student has a vocabulary of about 50,000 words in semantic memory.

sensorimotor stage In Piaget's view of cognitive development, the stage (up to 2 years of age) during which a child learns primarily through motor and sensory play, begins to develop a sense of self, and starts to be capable of representational or symbolic thought. See also **object permanence.**

sensory acuity Used by Galton in the late nineteenth century to judge a person's intelligence, it is measured by such tests as reaction time for sound, speed in naming colors, how tightly the hand can squeeze, and other measures of the efficiency of the senses.

sensory adaptation See **adaptation.**

sensory deprivation A technique of eliminating all input to the senses,

resulting in hallucinations and distortions of perceptions.

sensory–motor areas The part of the cortex of the brain located at the juncture of the frontal and parietal lobes. Sensory areas receive information about body position, muscles, touch, and pressure from all over the body.

separation anxiety The extreme distress shown by some infants, usually beginning about 8 months of age, when the mother leaves them in the care of someone else. See also **attachment.**

serotonin A chemical neurotransmitter that connects the brain stem and reticular activating system to the cortex and limbic system. It is thought to be involved in sleep and sleep regulation.

set point The weight that the body tends to maintain for a given individual, set as the temperature on a thermostat is. The hypothalamus controls eating and drinking and metabolic level to raise or lower caloric expenditure. The implications of the set point are that weight is more difficult to gain or lose than we would like and that people's normal weight is likely to be higher than the current social norm. See also **homeostasis.**

sex roles Society's expectations of how a male or female should behave.

sexual response cycle The regular physiological changes involved in sexual intercourse and sexual activity, described by Masters and Johnson as comprising four phases: excitement, plateau, orgasm, and resolution.

short-term memory The process by which information is thought to be stored for temporary retention of only a few seconds. Its capacity is about seven items, such as a seven-digit phone number.

sleep spindles The appearance of 12–14 hertz rhythms on the electroencephalogram during stage 2 sleep. See also **electroencephalogram.**

social comparison An important theory in social psychology by Festinger, which states that if there is no objective measure of comparison, we tend to seek out other people, whom we admire or believe are like us, and compare attitudes and behavior to theirs. The only way to achieve such comparisons as "How smart am I?" is to compare oneself to others. See also **reference group.**

social environmental perspective The study of how other people and our environment affect us.

social learning See **observational learning.**

social learning theory An outgrowth of the learning theory analyses of conditioning in the 1930s, it emphasizes that most behavior is learned rather than instinctually determined. It generally rejects the idea of an unconscious and favors an analysis of the situational and immediate determinants of behavior.

social pressure Pressure inherent in many group situations that forces us to be like everyone else.

social support The company and attention of others. Many studies have shown that the more social support a person has, the less likely he or she is to become ill when under stress.

sociobiology A new field of study that attempts to account for much social behavior in biological terms. Important questions dealt with by sociobiologists are altruism, male and female sex differences, and territoriality.

sociopath See **antisocial personality.**

somatic nervous system (SNS) A division of the peripheral nervous system that controls voluntary movements of the body.

somatoform disorders Disorders in which the individual complains of a physical ailment for which there is no organic or physiological explanation.

somesthetic system Part of the vestibular senses, it conveys to the brain information concerning sensations in the internal environment (body), such as deep pain or nausea.

species-specific behavior See **instincts.**

split brain In this surgical operation devised by Sperry and his colleagues, the corpus callosum in the brain is severed, producing a person or animal whose hemispheres can no longer communicate with one another. Studies performed on split-brain people have revealed the dramatic differences between the two hemispheres.

spontaneous remission The process by which people "spontaneously" recover from psychological disorders without the intervention of psychotherapy. This is now used as a control in studies evaluating the outcome of specific therapies.

SQ3R The method of remembering, which stands for "survey, question, read, recite, review." It involves surveying and questioning material before you read it, reading the material after a framework for remembering is in place, reciting what you have learned, and reviewing the material.

statistics The formal, mathematical set of rules for the evaluation of evidence that enables scientific judgments to be more precise and quantitative than ordinary judgments.

stereotype A generalized, inaccurate assumption attributing identical characteristics to all members of a group, such as blondes being dumb or Americans being materialistic.

stimulants Drugs, such as amphetamines and cocaine, that elevate mood and increase alertness.

storage space The amount of memory capacity taken up by given experiences, which helps us construct a sense of time, because we judge periods of time by how much is remembered about them, that is, by how much storage space they take up.

stranger anxiety Infants' fear of strangers, which often develops around the last quarter of the first year and may cause them to scream and cry if a stranger approaches. See also **attachment.**

strange situation In this experiment, developed by Ainsworth, a stranger enters the room where a baby and mother are playing with toys. The mother leaves the room so that the child is alone with the stranger. The experimenter observes how the baby reacts to the mother's departure. See also **attachment; separation anxiety.**

stress The failure of adaptability that occurs when environmental or internal demands exceed the adaptive resources of an organism. Also defined by Selye as the general reaction of the body to change. See also **emergency reaction; general adaptation syndrome.**

structure of intellect A model of the mind hypothesized by Guilford, which describes human intelligence as a set of abilities, each different and distinct from one another. In this model, the abilities are arranged in a cube, each side of which represents a different function of the mind.

subgoals A method of thinking that is useful in problem solving involving breaking a large problem into shorter problems and setting intermediate or subgoals.

subjects The people or animals whose behavior is observed as part of an experiment. See also **control group; experimental group; sample.**

substance use disorders Psychological disorders in which there is a consistent pattern of excessive use of substances, such as food, alcohol, or drugs, resulting in impairment of social or occupational functioning and that may involve physical dependence on the substance.

superego In Freud's theory, the last part of the personality to develop. It is the internal representation of society's values and morals. The superego restrains aggression and sexual impulses of the *id*, pressures the *ego* to act in a more moralistic than realistic way, and encourages the individual to strive for perfection. See also **ego; id.**

symbolic thought See **representational thought.**

sympathetic nervous system A division of the autonomic nervous system, it prepares internal organs for emergencies. It operates "in sympathy" with the emotions, telling the body to "go." See also **parasympathetic nervous system.**

synapse The point at which two neurons meet—usually between the axon of one and the dendrite of the other—where the chemicals involved in neurotransmission pass from the transmitting to the receiving neuron.

syntax How words in a specific language are arranged to convey meaning. See also **grammar.**

system Any group of things that function together for a common purpose. A system can be as wide ranging and complex as the educational system or as specific as the visual system.

systematic desensitization A form of behavior therapy based on the phenomenon of counterconditioning. In this therapy, the aim is to *eliminate* an unwanted conditioned response by conditioning the client to another stimulus that elicits a response (usually relaxation) that is incompatible with the original response.

T

tactile sensory replacement (TSR) A technique using a device that impresses "televised" images onto the skin so that blind persons can feel the pattern of stimulation and recognize objects in front of them.

taxonomy A system of classification; an orderly organization of things by similarities and differences.

teaching story A story form predominant in the Sufi tradition, which aims to entice the mind into operating in an unfamiliar manner. Examples of such tales include "The Elephant in the Dark" and "The Man with the Inexplicable Life" by Idries Shah.

temperament The enduring emotional characteristics of a person's life.

temporal lobe The area on the side of the brain devoted in part to hearing as well as perception, memory, and dreaming. Damage to these lobes may result in a condition known as *aphasia*. See also **aphasia.**

terminal drop A marked decline in intelligence and other measures of cognitive and biological functioning a few months to a year before death.

Terra Amata The site in southern France where archaeologists uncovered a well-preserved *Homo erectus* settlement and unlocked many of the secrets of *Homo erectus* culture.

tests In psychology, formal measurements of such psychological abilities as intelligence, verbal and spatial skills, and the ability to get along with others.

texture gradient As you look over a uniform surface, the density of the texture increases with distance; this is analyzed by the brain for information about distance and the angle of the surface.

thalamus The brain stem structure that relays information to the appropriate areas of the cortex. It appears that certain areas of the thalamus are specialized for specific kinds of sensory information, such as auditory and visual, and that these forms of sensory information are sent to the cortex.

Thanatos In Freud's theory, the death instinct: organisms seek a quiescent state, and death is the ultimate of this. "The aim of life," Freud wrote in a famous passage, "is death." See also **Eros.**

thermometer neurons Nerve cells that measure blood temperature and can alter their firing rate to trigger actions either to warm or cool the blood. See **homeostasis.**

tool use The characteristic of human adaptation made possible by the dexterity of hands freed for such use by bipedalism. Although largely confined to humans, tool use is attributed to prehumans and other species, notably chimpanzees.

transactional psychophysiology A heart therapy devised by James Lynch which emphasizes the link between human communication and blood pressure and, by changing communication, attempts to change blood pressure. In this kind of therapy a patient is connected to an automated blood pressure device and observes the reactions of his or her heart to different emotional situations.

transcendence The form of motivation that drives people to go beyond the ordinary understanding of life. Many people try to search for knowledge at the highest level and ask questions, such as "What is the meaning of life?" or "What is God?"

transduction A sensory process that transforms each particular kind of physical energy into neural firing. For example, the eye transduces light, the ear transduces sound waves, and the nose transduces gaseous molecules.

transference An important concept of psychoanalytic theory in which the patient tends to *transfer* his or her general feelings about life onto the therapist. For example, a person who has difficulty getting along with people in authority may suddenly start to have that problem with the therapist. Clarifying the transference is thought to reveal fundamental ways in which the patient acts in the world. Psychoanalysis then proceeds to work through the transference.

transformational grammar An influential theory that holds that there is a distinction in syntax between *surface* and *deep structure.* This theory presupposes that the human brain is designed to produce language and that the structure of language is in some way innate.

trephining A medieval method of treatment of mental disorder in which holes were drilled into a person's head to let out the demons who were thought to be causing the disorder. It is not a current method of treatment.

Type A personality The behavior of individuals who have specific reactions to the stresses of life: they tend to be aggressive, hostile, competitive, time-urgent, fast-paced, impatient, and irritable. They are deeply involved in their work and often deny failure, fatigue, and illness. They are twice as likely to develop heart disease as type B people, who may be as successful but tend to be calmer.

typicality Having characteristics of a category that make something an example of that category closest to the prototype.

U

unconditioned response (UCR) A response that is made without any specific sort of learning, such as salivation to food.

unconditioned stimulus (UCS) A stimulus, such as food or a loud noise, that elicits an unconditioned response, such as salivation or being startled.

unconscious A level of awareness, postulated by Sigmund Freud, in which memories and thoughts that are difficult to deal with are supposedly hidden.

unconscious inferences The automatic process performed by a perceiver of filling in gaps in the information reaching him or her. These inferences transform a set of disconnected images into the living world of objects.

uplifts Positive life events that give a great deal of pleasure and may, in some instances and to varying degrees, balance out the impact of negative events.

V

validity A required characteristic of tests, such as intelligence tests, assuring that they measure what they are intended to measure. See also **reliability.**

variable interval (VI) In this reinforcement schedule, the intervals between reinforcement vary randomly around an average.

variable ratio (VR) In this reinforcement schedule, the reward occurs after a randomly varying number of responses.

variables In experiments, the factors that are allowed to change and vary. Variables are of two kinds: *independent variables* are those the experimenter may attempt to manipulate, such as how many hours an animal is deprived of food, and *dependent variables* are those the experimenter measures, which change after the experimenter's manipulations, such as how much the animal might eat.

vasocongestion The increase of blood flow to the genitals, which is one of the physical changes during the excitement phase of the sexual response cycle.

vestibular system This consists of organs sensitive to motion, position, and balance.

visual cliff A structure developed by Gibson to test whether depth perception develops only when a baby can move around. It is the effect created by two surfaces under glass, both of which have a checkerboard pattern, and it gives the illusion of a visual drop.

W

Weber's Law The first major principle of sensation, discovered by Weber (1834), which states that there is a consistent proportional relationship between a physical stimulus and the psychological response to it.

Werther effect An effect named after Goethe's hero who committed suicide in *The Sorrows of Young Werther*, a popular European eighteenth century novel, which stimulated suicides in every country where it was read.

References

Many of the discussions in the text, such as the basics of learning, hunger and thirst, motives, social behavior, intelligence, and disorders, draw on a great variety of sources. Some of these references are not cited directly in the text, but provide further background material for the student wishing to deepen her or his knowledge. Also, not all worthy lines of research can be covered in an introductory text. Thus, in addition to the cited references, I include here "classic" references in psychology. Here you will find classic studies about schizophrenia, circadian rhythms, aggression, learning and memory, the myth of mental illness, aging, divorce, health and disease, feelings, the birth of cognitive science, problem-solving, sex roles, the psychology of being witty, play, the costs of adaptation to stress, love and hate, anger, and much more. I hope these sources prove useful to you in further studies.

ADAM, K., & OSWALD, I. (1977). Sleep is for tissue restoration. *Journal of the Royal College of Physicians, 11*, 376–388.

ADAMOWITZ, S. I. (1969). Locus of control and self-reported depression among college students. *Psychological Reports, 25*, 149–150.

ADER, R. (Ed.). (1984). *Psychoneuroimmunology.* New York: Academic Press.

ADER R., & COHEN, N. (1985). CNS-immune system interactions: Conditioning phenomena. *Behavioral and Brain Sciences, 8*, 379–426.

ADLER, A. (1929). *The practice and theory of individual psychology.* New York: Harcourt, Brace.

ADORNO, T. W., FRENKEL-BRUNSWICK, E., LEVINSON, D. S., & SANFORD, R. N. (1950). *The authoritarian personality.* New York: Harper & Row.

AGRAS, W. S., HORNE, M., & TAYLOR, C. B. (1982). Expectation and the blood-pressure-lowering effect of relaxation. *Psychosomatic Medicine, 44*, 389–395.

AIELLO, J. R., DE RISI, D. T., EPSTEIN, Y. M., YAKOV, M., & KARLIN, R. A. (1977). Crowding and the role of interpersonal distance preference. *Sociometry, 40*, 271–282.

AIELLO, J. R., & THOMPSON, D. E. (1980). When compensation fails: Mediating effects of sex and locus of control at extended interaction distances. *Basic and Applied Social Psychology, 1*, 65–82.

AINSWORTH, M. D. S. (1982). Attachment: Retrospect and prospect. In C. M. Parkes & J. Stevenson-Hinde (Eds.), *The place of attachment in human behavior.* New York: Basic Books.

AINSWORTH, M. D. S., & BELL, S. M. (1970). Attachment, exploration and separation: Illustrated by the behavior of one-year-olds in a strange situation. *Child Development, 41.*

AINSWORTH, M. D. S., BLEHAR, M., WATERS, E., & WALL, S. (1978). *Patterns of attachment: A psychological study of the strange situation.* Hillsdale, NJ: Erlbaum.

AINSWORTH, M. D. S., & WHITTIG, B. A. (1965). Attachment and exploratory behavior of one year olds in a strange situation. In B. M. Foxx (Ed.), *Determinants of infant behaviour: Vol. 4* (pp. 54–61). London: Methuen.

ALBERT, M. A., & OBLER, L. K. (1978). *The bilingual brain.* New York: Academic Press.

ALBERT, M. S., & KAPLAN, E. (1980). Organic implications in neuropsychological deficits in the elderly. In Poon, L. et al. (Eds.), *New directions in memory and aging.* Hillsdale, NJ: Erlbaum.

ALBRECHT, S. (1980). Reactions and adjustments to divorce: Differences in the experiences of males and females. *Family Relations, 29*, 59–68.

ALEXANDER, R. D., HOOGLAND, J. L., HOWARD, R. D., NOONAN, K. M., & SHERMAN, P. W. (1979). Chapter 6. In N. A. Chagnons & W. G. Irons (Eds.), *Evolutionary biology and human social behavior* (pp. 101–128). North Scituate, MA: Duxbury.

ALLEN, I. M. (1951). Cerebral injury with shock treatment. *New Zealand Medical Journal, 50*, 356–364.

ALLISON, R. (1980). *Minds in many pieces.* New York: Rawson-Wade.

ALLPORT, G. W. (1937). *Personality: A psychological interpretation.* New York: Holt, Rinehart & Winston.

ALLPORT, G. W. (1954). *The nature of prejudice.* Cambridge, MA: Addison-Wesley.

ALLPORT, G. W. (1955). *Becoming.* New Haven, CT: Yale University Press.

ALLPORT, G. W. (1961). *Pattern and growth in personality.* New York: Holt, Rinehart & Winston.

ALLPORT, G. W., & ODVERT, H. S. (1936). Trait-names: A psycholexical study. *Psychological Monographs, 47*, 1–171.

ALLPORT, G. W., & ROSS, J. M. (1967). Personal religious orientation and prejudice. *Journal of Personality and Social Psychology, 5*, 432–443.

ALPER, T. G. (1974). Achievement motivation in college women: A now-you-see-it-now-you-don't phenomenon. *American Psychologist, 29*, 194–203.

ALPERS, B. J., & HUGHES, J. (1942). Changes in the brain after electrically induced convulsions in cats. *Archives of Neurology and Psychiatry, 47*, 385–398.

ALTROCCHI, J. (1980). *Abnormal behavior.* New York: Harcourt Brace Jovanovich.

AMERICAN INSTITUTE OF PLANNERS NEWSLETTER, 1967 (p. 91). Baltimore.

AMERICAN PSYCHIATRIC ASSOCIATION. (1980). *Diagnostic and statistical manual of mental disorders* (3rd ed.). Washington, DC: Author.

ANAND, B. K., & BROBECK, J. R. (1951). Hypothalamic control of food intake in rats and cats. *Yale Journal of Biology and Medicine, 24,* 123–140.

ANDERSON, T. W., & SCLOVE, S. L. (1986). *An introduction to the statistical analysis of data.* Palo Alto, CA: Scientific Press.

ANDRES, R., ELAHI, D., TOBIN, J. D., MULLER, D. C., & BRANT, L. (1985). Impact of age on weight goals. *Annals of Internal Medicine, 103* (6, part 2), 1030–1033.

ANTONOVSKY, A. (1984). The sense of coherence as a determinant of health. In J. D. Matarazzo, S. M. Weiss, J. A. Herd, & N. E. Miller (Eds.), *Behavioral Health.* New York: John Wiley.

ANTONOVSKY, A. (1987). *Unraveling the mystery of health.* San Francisco: Josey-Bass.

ARCHER, D., ARONSON, E., PETTIGREW, T. (1983). *An evaluation of the energy conservation research of California's major energy utility companies, 1977–1980.* (Report to the California PUC). Santa Cruz: University of California.

ARCHER, D., PETTIGREW, T., COSTANZO, M., IRITANI, B., WALKER, L., & WHITE, L. *Energy conservation and public policy: The mediation of individual behavior.* Unpublished manuscript.

ARGYLE, M. (1978). *The psychology of interpersonal behavior.* New York: Penguin.

ARGYLE, M., & HENDERSON, M. (1985). *The anatomy of relationships.* New York: Penguin.

ARIES. P. (1962). *Centuries of childhood.* London: Jonathan Cape.

ARKES, H. R., & HAMMOND, K. R. (1986). *Judgment and decision making.* New York: Cambridge University Press.

ARON, A. (1977). Maslow's other child. *Journal of Humanistic Psychology, 17*(2), 9–24.

ARONSON, E. (1958). The need for achievement as measured by graphic expression. In J. W. Atkinson (Ed.), *Motives in fantasy, action and society* (pp. 249–265). Princeton: Van Nostrand-Reinhold.

ARONSON, E. (1984). *The social animal.* San Francisco: Freeman.

ARONSON, E., BLANEY, N., STEPHAN, C., SIKES, J., & SNAPP, M. (1978). *The jigsaw classroom.* Beverly Hills: Sage.

ARONSON, E., & O'LEARY, M. (1983). The relative effects of models and prompts on energy conservation. *Journal of Environmental Systems, 12,* 219–224.

ARONSON, E., & OSHEROW, N. (1980). Cooperation, prosocial behavior, and academic performance: Experiments in the desegregated classroom. In L. Bickman (Ed.), *Applied social psychology annual: Vol. 1.* Beverly Hills: Sage.

ASCH, S. E. (1946). Forming impressions of personality. *Journal of Abnormal and Social Psychology, 41,* 258–290.

ASCH, S. E. (1951). Effects of group pressure upon the modification and distortion of judgments. In H. Guetzkow (Ed.), *Groups, leadership, and men* (pp. 177–190). Pittsburgh: Carnegie Press.

ASCH, S. E. (1956). Studies of independence and conformity, a minority of one against a unanimous majority. *Psychological Monographs, 70*(9, Whole No. 416).

ASCHOFF, J. (1965). *Circadian clocks.* Amsterdam: North-Holland.

ASCHOFF, J. (1967). Human circadian rhythms in activity, body temperature, and other functions. In A. H. Brown & F. G. Favoite (Eds.), *Life sciences and space research: Vol. 5.* (pp. 159–173). Amsterdam: North-Holland.

ASERINSKY, E., & KLEITMAN, N. (1953). Regularly occurring periods of eye motility and concomitant phenomena during sleep. *Science, 118,* 273–274.

ATTEWELL, P., & RULE, J. (1984). Computing and organizations: What we know and what we don't know. *Communications of the ACM, 27,* 1184–1192.

AUSTIN, J. L. (1962). *How to do things with words.* Oxford: Oxford University Press.

AVERILL, J. R. (1980). A constructivist view of emotions. In R. Plutchik (Ed.), *Theories of emotion.* New York: Academic Press.

AYLLON, T., & AZRIN, N. (1968). *The token economy: A motivational system for therapy and rehabilitation.* New York: Appleton-Century-Crofts.

AZJEN, I., & FISHBEIN, M. (1977). Attitude-behavior relations: A theoretical analysis and review of empirical research. *Psychological Bulletin, 84,* 888–918.

BAASTRUP, P. C. (1980). Lithium in the treatment of recurrent affective disorders. In F. N. Johnson (Ed.), *Handbook of lithium therapy.* Baltimore: University Park Press.

BADDELEY, A. (1986). *Working memory.* New York: Oxford University Press.

BAGCHI, B. K., & WENGER, M. A. (1957). Electrophysiological correlates of some yogi exercises. *Electroencephalography and Clinical Neurophysiology, 7,* 132–149.

BAHNSON, C. B., & BAHNSON, M. B. (1964). Cancer as an alternative to psychosis: A theoretical model of somatic and psychological regression. In D. M. Kissen & L. L. Leshan (Eds.), *Psychosomatic aspects of neoplastic disease.* London: Pitman.

BAHNSON, M. B., & BAHNSON, C. B. (1969). Ego defenses in cancer patients. *Annals, New York Academy of Science, 164,* 546–559.

BAHRICK, H. P., BAHRICK, P. O., & WHITTLINGER, R. P. (1976). Fifty years of memory for names and faces: A cross-sectional approach. *Journal of Experimental Psychology: General, 104,* 54–75.

BAKAN, P. (1977). Left-handedness and birth order revisited. *Neuropsychology, 15.*

BANDURA, A. (1965). Vicarious processes: A case of no-trial learning. In L. Berkowitz (Ed.), *Advances in experimental social psychology: Vol. 2.* New York: Academic Press.

BANDURA, A. (1973). *Aggression: A social learning analysis.* Englewood Cliffs, NJ: Prentice-Hall.

BANDURA, A. (1977). *Social learning theory.* Englewood Cliffs, NJ: Prentice-Hall.

BANDURA, A. (1978). Social learning theory of aggression. *Journal of Communication, 28,* 12–29.

BANDURA, A. (1979). *Aggression: A social learning analysis* (2nd ed.). Englewood Cliffs, NJ: Prentice-Hall.

BANDURA, A. (1982). Self-efficacy mechanism in human agency. *American Psychologist, 37*, 122–147.

BANDURA, A. (1986). *Social foundations of thought and action.* Englewood Cliffs, NJ: Prentice-Hall.

BANDURA, A., & ADAMS, N. E. (1977). Analysis of self-efficacy theory of behavioral change. *Cognitive Therapy and Research, 1*(4), 287–310.

BANDURA, A., & McDONALD, F. D. (1963). The influence of social reinforcement and the behavior of models in shaping children's moral judgments. *Journal of Abnormal and Social Psychology, 67*, 274–281.

BANDURA, A., ROSS, O., & ROSS, S. A. (1961). Transmission of aggression through imitation of aggressive models. *Journal of Abnormal and Social Psychology, 63*, 575–582.

BANDURA, A., TAYLOR, C. B., WILLIAMS, S. L., MEFFORD, I. N., & BARCHAS, J. D. (1985). Catecholamine secretion as a function of perceived self-efficacy. *Journal of Consulting and Clinical Psychology, 53*, 406–414.

BANE, M. S. (1976). *Here to stay: American families in the twentieth century.* New York: Basic Books.

BANKS, W. C., McQUARTER, G. V., & HUBBARD, J. L. (1977). Task-liking and intrinsic-extrinsic achievement orientations in black adolescents. *Journal of Black Psychology, 3*(2), 61–71.

BARASH, D. (1986). *The Tortoise and the hare,* New York: Viking.

BARKER, R. G., & WRIGHT, H. F. (1951). *One boy's day: A specimen record of behavior.* New York: Harper.

BARON, R. A. (1977). *Human aggression.* New York: Plenum.

BARON, R. A., & KEPNER, C. R. (1970). Model's behavior and attraction toward the model as determinants of adult aggressive behavior. *Journal of Personality and Social Psychology, 14*, 335–344.

BARR, J., LANGS, R., HOLT, T., GOLDBERGER, L., & KLEIN, G. (1972). *LSD: Personality and experience.* New York: John Wiley.

BARSLEY, M. (1979). *Left-handed people.* Los Angeles: Wilshire.

BART, P. (1971). Depression in middle-aged women. In V. Goinich & B. K. Moran (Eds.), *Women in sexist society.* New York: Basic Books.

BARTLETT, F. C. (1932). *Remembering: A study in experimental and social psychology.* Cambridge: Cambridge University Press.

BARTHROP, R. W., LAZARUS, L., LUCKHURST, E., KILOH, L. G., & PENNY, R. (1978). Depressed lymphocyte function after bereavement, *Lancet, 1*, 834–839.

BATESON, G. (1959). *The double bind.* Palo Alto, CA: Science & Behavior Books.

BATESON, G., JACKSON, D. D., HALEY, J., & WEAKLAND, J. H. (1972). Toward a theory of schizophrenia. *Behavioral Science, 1* (4).

BATESON, C. D., NAIFEL, S. V., & PATE, S. (1978). Social desirability, religious orientation and racial prejudice. *Journal for the Scientific Study of Religion, 17*, 31–41.

BECK, A. T. (1976). *Cognitive therapy and the emotional disorders.* New York: International Universities Press.

BECK, A. T., & KATCHER, A. (1983). *Between pets and people: The importance of animal companionship.* New York: Putnam.

BECK, A. T., RUSH, A. J., SHAW, B., & EMERY, G. (1979). *Cognitive therapy of depression: A treatment manual.* New York: Guilford.

BEE, H. (1978). *The developing child* (2nd ed.). New York: Harper & Row.

BEECHER, H. W. (1885). *Evolution and religion.* New York: Holt, Rinehart.

BEER, R., JR. (1979). *Mechanisms of pain and analgesic compounds.* New York: Raven Press.

BELL, A. P., WEINBERG, M. S., & HAMMERSMITH, S. K. (1981). *Sexual preference: Its development in men and women.* Bloomington: Indiana University Press.

BELLAH, R. N. (1973). Evil and the American ethos. In N. Sanford & C. Comstock (Eds.), *Sanctions for evil* (pp. 187–188). San Francisco: Jossey-Bass.

BELLER, S., & PALMORE, E. (1974). Longevity in Turkey. *Gerontologist, 14*(5), 373–376.

BELLOWS, R. T. (1939). Time factors in water drinking in dogs. *American Journal of Physiology, 125*, 87–97.

BELOFF, J. (1978). Why parapsychology is still on trial. *Human Nature, 1*(12), 68–76.

BEM, D. J. (1967). Self-perception: An alternative interpretation of cognitive dissonance phenomena. *Psychological Review, 74*, 183–200.

BEM, D. J. (1970). *Beliefs, attitudes and human affairs.* Belmont, CA: Brooks/Cole.

BEM, D. J. (1972). Self-perfection theory. In L. Berkowitz (Ed.), *Advances in experimental social psychology: Vol. 6.* New York: Academic Press.

BEM, D. J., & ALLEN, A. (1974). On predicting some of the people some of the time: The search for cross-situational consistencies in behavior. *Psychological Review, 81*, 506–520.

BENNETT, W. (1984). *Set point regulation of body weight* (Cassette Recording). Los Altos, CA: Institute for the Study of Human Knowledge.

BENNETT, W., & GURIN, J. (1982). *The dieter's dilemma: Eating less and weighing more.* New York: Basic Books.

BENSHOOF, L., & THORNHILL, R. (1979). The evolution of monogamy and concealed ovulation in humans. *Journal of Social and Biological Structures, 2*(2), 95–105.

BERDYSHEV, G. D. (1966). *Ecologic and genetic factors of aging and longevity.* Moscow: Nauka.

BERGER, H. (1984). *The developing person.* New York: Worth.

BERGER, P. A., WATSON, S. J., AKIL, H., BARCHAS, J. D., & LI, C. H. (1980). Clinical studies with naloxone and beta-endorphin in chronic schizophrenia. In E. Usdin et al. (Eds.). *Neurotransmitters in schizophrenia.* New York: MIT Press.

BERKMAN, L., & SYME, S. L. (1979). Social networks, host resistance, and mortality: A nine-year follow-up study of Alameda County residents. *American Journal of Epidemiology, 109*, 186–204.

BERKMAN, L. F. (1984). Assessing the physical health effects of social networks and social support. *Annual Review of Public Health, 5,* 413–432.

BERKOWITZ, L. (1970). Aggressive humor as a stimulus to aggressive responses. *Journal of Personality and Social Psychology, 16,* 710–717.

BERLIN, B., & KAY, P. (1969). *Basic color terms: Their universality and evolution.* Berkeley and Los Angeles: University of California Press.

BERLYNE, D. E. (1960). *Conflict, arousal, and curiosity.* New York: McGraw-Hill.

BERLYNE, D. E. (1966). Curiosity and exploration. *Science, 153.* 25–33.

BERLYNE, D. E. (1967). Arousal and reinforcement. *Nebraska Symposium of Motivation* (pp. 1–110). Lincoln: University of Nebraska Press.

BERLYNE, D. E. (1972). Humor and its kin. In J. H. Goldstein & P. E. McGhee (Eds.), *The psychology of humor* (pp. 43–60). London: Academic Press.

BERMAN, J. S., MILLER, R. C., & MASSMAN, P. J. (1984). Cognitive therapy versus systematic desensitization: Is one treatment superior? In J. S. Berman (Ed.), *Meta-analytic reviews of psychotherapy outcome research.* New York: Longmans, Green.

BERMAN, W., TURK, D. (1981, February). Adaptation to divorce: Problems and coping strategies. *Journal of Marriage and the Family,* 179–189.

BERNARD, J. (1973). *The future of marriage.* New York: Bantam.

BESEDOVSKY, H. O., DEL REY, A., & SORKIN, E. (1983). What do the immune system and the brain know about each other? *Immunology Today, 4,* 342–346.

BESEDOVSKY, H. O., DEL REY, A., SORKIN, E., DAPRADA, M., & KELLER, H. H. (1979). Immunoregulation mediated by the sympathetic nervous system, *Cellular Immunology, 48,* 346–355.

BESEDOVSKY, H. O., SORKIN, R., FELIX, D., & HAAS, H. (1977). Hypothalamic changes during the immune response. *European Journal of Immunology, 7,* 325–328.

BETCHER, R. (1981). Intimate play and marital adaption. *Psychiatry, 44,* 13–33.

BETTELHEIM, B. (1960). *The informed heart: Autonomy in a message.* Glencoe, IL: Free Press.

BIBRING, G. (1959). Some consideration of the psychological processes in pregnancy. *Psychoanalytic Study of the Child, 14,* 113–121.

BINFORD, S. R., & BINFORD, L. R. (1969, April). Stone tools and human behavior. *Scientific American, 96.*

BIRREN, J. E., BUTLER, R. N., GREENHOSE, S. W., SOKOLOFF, L., & HARROW, M. R. (Eds.). (1963). *Human aging: A biological and behavioral study.* (Publication No. HSM 71-9051). Washington, DC: U.S. Government Printing Office.

BIRREN, J. E. et al. (1981). *Developmental psychology: A life-span approach.* Boston: Houghton Mifflin.

BJORK, R. A., & LANDAUER, T. K. (1979). On keeping track of the present status of people and things. In M. M. Gruneberg, P. E. Morris, & R. N. Sykes (Eds.), *Practical aspects of memory.* New York: Academic Press.

BJORNTORP, P. (1972). Disturbances in the regulation of food intake. *Advances in Psychosomatic Medicine, 7,* 116–147.

BLACK, S., HUMPHREY, J. H., & NIVEN, J. S. F. (1963). Inhibition of Mantoux reaction by direct suggestion under hypnosis. *British Medical Journal, 1,* 1649–1652.

BLANCHARD, F. A., ADELMAN, L., & COOK, S. W. (1975). Effect of group success and failure upon interpersonal attraction in cooperating interracial groups. *Journal of Personality and Social Psychology, 31,* 1020–1030.

BLANCHARD, F. A., WEIGEL, R. H., & COOK, S. W. (1975). The effect of relative competence of group members upon interpersonal attraction in cooperating interracial groups. *Journal of Personality and Social Psychology, 32*(3), 519–530.

BLASI, A. (1980). Bridging moral cognition and moral action: A critical review of the literature. *Psychological Bulletin, 88,* 1–45.

BLASS, E. M., & KETY, F. S. (1974). Medial forebrain bundle lesions: Specific loss of feeding to decreased glucose utilization in rats. *Journal of Comparative and Physiological Psychology, 86,* 679–692.

BLOCK, J. (1971). *Lives through time.* Berkeley: Bancroft Books.

BLOCK, J. (1981). Some enduring and consequential structures of personality. In A. I. Rabin, J. Aronoff, A. M. Barclay, & R. A. Zucker (Eds.), *Further explorations in personality.* New York: Wiley-Interscience.

BLOCK, J. H. (1978). Another look at sex differences in the socialization of mothers and fathers. In J. Sherman & F. Denmark (Eds.), *The psychology of women: Future directions in research.* New York: Psychological Dimensions.

BLOCK, J. H. (1979). Socialization influences on personality development in males and females. In M. M. Parkes (Ed.), *American Psychological Association master lecture series on issues of sex and gender in psychology.* Washington, DC: American Psychological Association.

BLOCK, J. H., & BLOCK J. (1980). The role of ego-control and ego resiliency in the organization of behavior. In W. A. Collins (Ed.), *Minnesota Symposium on Child Psychology: Vol. 13.* Hillsdale, NJ: Erlbaum.

BLOOM, B. L., ASHER, S. J., & WHITE, S. W. (1978). Marital disruption as a stressor: A review and analysis. *Psychological Bulletin, 85,* 867–894.

BLOOM, B. L., & WHITE, S. W. (1981). Factors related to the adjustment of divorcing men. *Family Relations, 30,* 349–360.

BLUMENTHAL, H., & BURNS, A. (1964). Autoimmunity in aging. In B. Strehler (Ed.), *Advances in gerontological research: Vol. 1.* New York: Academic Press.

BLYTH, R. (1979). *The view in winter: Reflections on old age.* New York: Harcourt Brace Jovanovich.

BOLLES, R. C. (1970). Species-specific defense reactions in avoidance learning. *Psychological Review, 71*, 32–48.

BOLLES, R. C. (1974). Cognition and motivation: Some historical trends. In B. Weiner (Ed.), *Cognitive views on human motivation* (pp. 1–32). New York: Academic Press.

BOLLES, R. N. (1972). *What color is your parachute: A practical manual for job-hunters and career-changers.* Berkeley: Ten Speed Press.

BORGES, J. L. (1966). Funes the memorius. In D. A. Yates & J. E. Irbt (Eds.), *Labyrinths.* New York: New Directions.

BORQUIST, A. (1906). Crying. *American Journal of Psychology, 17*, 149–205.

BORYSENKO, J. Z. (1985). Healing motives: An interview with David McClelland. *Advances, 2*, 29–41.

BOTWINICK, D. E., WOODS, A. M., & WILLIAMS, M. V. (1980). Behavioral slowing of age: Causes, organization, and consequences. In Poon, L. W. (Ed.), *Aging in the 1980's: Psychological issues.* Washington, D.C.: APA.

BOTWINICK, J. (1977). Intellectual abilities. In J. E. Birren & K. W. Schaie (Eds.), *Handbook of the psychology of aging.* New York: Van Nostrand-Reinhold.

BOTWINICK, J., WEST, R., & STARANDT, M. (1978). Predicting death from behavioral test performance. *Journal of Gerontology, 33*, 755–762.

BOUCHARD, T., & McGUE, R. (1981). Familial studies of intelligence: A review. *Science, 212*, 1055–1059.

BOWER, G. H. (1978). Improving memory. *Human Nature, 7*, 62–67.

BOWER, G. H. (1981). Mood and memory. *American Psychologist, 36*, 129–148.

BOWER, G. H., & GILLIGAN, S. G. (1980). Remembering information related to one's self. *Journal of Research in Personality, 13*, 420–432.

BOWER, G. H., GILLIGAN, S. G., & MONTEIRO, K. P. (1981). Selectivity of learning caused by affective states. *Journal of Experimental Psychology: General, 110*(4), 451–473.

BOWER, G. H., & HILGARD, E. R. (1981). *Theories of learning* (5th ed.). Englewood Cliffs, NJ: Prentice-Hall.

BOWER, T. G. R. (1974). *Development in infancy.* San Francisco: Freeman.

BOWLBY, J. (1969). *Attachment: Vol. 1. Attachment and loss.* New York: Basic Books.

BOWLES, N., & POON, L. (1982). An analysis of the effect of aging on memory. *Journal of Gerontology, 37*, 212–219.

BRADY, J. V. (1958). Ulcers in "executive" monkeys. *Scientific American, 199*, 95–100.

BRAINERD, C. (1978). *Piaget's theory of intelligence.* Englewood Cliffs, NJ: Prentice-Hall.

BRAINERD, C., KINGMAN, J., & HOWE, M. L. (1985). On the development of forgetting. *Child Development, 56*, 1103–1119.

BRANCH, A. Y., FINE, G. A., & JONES, J. M. (1973). Laughter, smiling, and rating scales: An analysis of responses to tape recorded humor. *Proceedings of the 81st Annual Convention of the American Psychological Association.*

BRAND, R. J., ROSENMAN, R. H., SHOLTZ, R. I., & FRIEDMAN, M. (1976). Multivariate prediction of coronary heart disease in the Western Collaborative Group Study compared to the findings of the Framingham Study. *Circulation, 43*(2), 348–355.

BRANDWEIN, R. A., BROWN, A., & FOX, S. M. (1974). Women and children last: The social situation of divorced mothers and their families. *Journal of Marriage and the Family, 36*, 495–514.

BRANSFORD, J. D., & JOHNSON, M. K. (1974). Contextual prerequisites for understanding: Some investigations of comprehension and recall. *Journal of Verbal Learning and Verbal Behavior, 11*, 717–726.

BRANTHWAITE, A., & COOPER, P. (1981). Analgesic effect of branding in treatment of headaches. *British Medical Journal, 282*, 1576–1578.

BRAVERMAN, H. (1974). Labor and monopoly capital: The degradation of work in the twentieth century. *Monthly Review, 37*, 211–216.

BRAY, G. A. (1974). Endocrine factors in the control of food intake. *Federal Proceedings, 33*, 1140–1145.

BRECHER, E. M., & CONSUMER REPORTS (Eds.). (1974). *Licit and illicit drugs.* Boston: Little, Brown.

BRELAND, H. (1977). Family configuration and intellectual development. *Journal of Individual Psychology, 31*, 86–96.

BRELAND, K., & BRELAND, M. (1961). The misbehavior of organisms. *American Psychologist, 16*, 661–664.

BRENNER, M. H. (1973). *Mental illness and the economy.* Cambridge, MA: Harvard University Press.

BRENNER, M. H. (1976). *Estimating the social costs of economic policy.* Paper No. 5, report to the Congressional Research Service of the Library of Congress. Washington, DC: U.S. Government Printing Office.

BRENNER, M. H. (1980). Importance of the economy to the nation's health. In L. Eisenberg & A. Kleinman (Eds.), *The relevance of social science for medicine.* Dordrecht, Holland: Reidel.

BRESNITZ, S. (Ed.). (1983). *The denial of stress.* New York: International Universities Press.

BRETHERTON, J., & WATERS, L. (1985). *Growing points of attachment theory and research.* SRCD monographs.

BREUER, J., & FREUD, S. (1955). Studies in hysteria. In J. Strachey (Ed.), *The standard edition of the complete psychological works of Sigmund Freud.* London: Hogarth Press. (Original work published 1895)

BREWER, V., & HARTMANN, E. (1973). Variable sleepers: When is more or less sleep required. *Sleep Research, 2*, 128.

BRICKMAN, P. (1975). Adaptation level determinants of satisfaction with equal and unequal outcome distributions in skill and chance situations. *Journal of Personality and Social Psychology, 32*, 191–198.

BRIDGES, D. (1927). Occupational interests of three-year-old children. *Journal of Genetic Psychology, 34*, 415–423.

BRIDGES, K. M. B. (1932). Emotional development in early infancy. *Child Development, 3,* 324–341.

BRIM, O. G., JR. (1976). Theories of the male mid-life crisis. *Counseling Psychologist, 6*(1), 2–9.

BROADBENT, D. E. (1961). *Behavior.* New York: Basic Books.

BROADHEAD, W. E., KAPLAN, B. H., WAGNER, E. H., SCHOENBACH, V. J., GRIMSON, R., HEYDEN, S., TIBBLIN, G., & GEHLBACH, S. H. (1983). Epidemiological evidence for a relationship between social support and health. *American Journal of Epidemiology, 117,* 521–537.

BROADHURST, P. L. (1957). Emotionality and the Yerkes-Dodson law. *Journal of Experimental Psychology, 84,* 345–352.

BROBECK, J. R. (1946). Mechanics of the development of obesity in animals with hypothalamic lesions. *Physiological Review, 26,* 541–559.

BRONFENBRENNER, U. (1970). *Two worlds of childhood.* New York: Russell Sage.

BRONFENBRENNER, U., & CROUTER, A. C. (1983). The evolution of environmental models in developmental research. In P. H. Mussen (Ed.), *Handbook of child psychology: Vol. 1.* (4th ed.). New York: John Wiley.

BROOKS, C. McC., & LAMBERT, E. F. (1946). A study of the effect of limitation of food intake and the method of feeding on the rate of weight gain during hypothalamic obesity in the albino rat. *American Journal of Physiology, 147,* 695–707.

BROOKS, G. W., & MUELLER, E. (1966). Serum urate concentrations among university professors: Relation to drive, achievement, and leadership. *Journal of the American Medical Association, 195*(6), 415–418.

BROWN, G. W., & HARRIS, T. (1978). *Social origins of depression.* New York: Free Press.

BROWN, J. (1977). *Mind, brain and consciousness.* New York: Academic Press.

BROWN, J. B., & STERNBERG, J. (1986). *Teaching thinking skills.* New York: Freeman.

BROWN, L. B. (1964). Classifications of religious orientation. *Journal for the Scientific Study of Religion, 4,* 91–99.

BROWN, R. (1965). *Social psychology.* New York: Free Press.

BROWN, R., & HERRNSTEIN, R. J. (1975). *Psychology.* Boston: Little, Brown.

BROWN, R. W., & LENNEBERG, E. H. (1954). A study in language and cognition. *Journal of Verbal Learning and Verbal Behavior, 49,* 454–462.

BRUN, J. (1984). Therapeutic value of hope. *Southern Medical Journal, 77,* 215–219.

BRUNER, J. S. (1978). Learning the mother tongue. *Human Nature, 1,* 52–59.

BRUNER, J. S. (1986). *Actual minds, possible worlds.* Boston: Harvard University Press.

BRUNER, J. S., & GOODMAN, C. C. (1946). Value and need as organizing factors in perception. *Journal of Abnormal and Social Psychology, 42,* 33–44.

BRUNER, J. S., & TAGIURI, R. (1954). Person perception. In G. Lindzey (Ed.), *Handbook of social psychology: Vol. 2.* Reading, MA: Addison-Wesley.

BRYAN, J. H., & TEST, M. (1967). Models and helping: Naturalistic studies in aiding behavior. *Journal of Personality and Social Psychology, 6,* 400–407.

BRYDEN, M. P. (1973). Auditory-visual and sequential-spatial matching in relation to reading ability. *Child Development, 43*(3), 824–832.

BUCKALEW, L. W., & ROSS, S. (1981). Relationship of perceptual characteristics to efficacy of placebos. *Psychological Reports, 49,* 955–961.

BUDZYNSKI, T. (1977). Biofeedback and the twilight states of awareness. In G. Schwartz & D. Shapiro (Eds.), *Consciousness and self-regulation.* New York: Plenum.

BUDZYNSKI, T. (1981). Lecture at "The Healing Brain," University of California, San Francisco.

BUFFREY, A., & GRAY, J. (1972). Sex differences in the development of spatial and linguistic skills. In C. Ounsted & D. Taylor (Eds.), *Gender differences, their ontogeny and significance.* New York: Churchill Livingstone.

BURNES, K., BROWN, W. A., & KEATING, G. W. (1971). Dimensions on control: Correlations between MMPI and I-E scores. *Journal of Consulting and Clinical Psychology, 36,* 301.

BUSKIRK, E. R. (1985). Health maintenance and longevity: Exercises. In C. E. Finch & E. L. Schneider, (Eds.), *Handbook of the biology of aging.* New York: Van Nostrand-Reinhold.

BUTLER, R. N. (1963). The life review: An interpretation of reminiscence in the aged. *Psychiatry, 26,* 65–76.

CABANAC, M. (1971). Physiological role of pleasure. *Science, 173*(4002), 1103–1107.

CADORET, R. J., WINOKUR, G., & CLAYTON, P. J. (1971). Family history studies: VI. Depressive disease types. *Comprehensive Psychiatry, 12,* 148–155.

CALHOUN, J. B. (1973). Population density and social pathology. *Scientific American, 206,* 139–148.

CAMPBELL, B. G. (1982). *Humankind emerging* (3rd ed.). Boston: Little, Brown.

CAMPBELL, D. T. (1960). Blind variation and selective retention in creating thought as in other knowledge processes. *Psychological Review, 67,* 380–400.

CAMPBELL, D. T. (1963). Social attitudes and other acquired behavioral dispositions. In S. Koch (Ed.), *Psychology: A study of a science: Vol. 6.* New York: McGraw-Hill.

CAMPBELL, R. (1978). Asymmetries in interpreting and expressing a posed facial expression. *Cortex, 14,* 327–342.

CANGEMI, J. J. (1976). Characteristics of self-actualizing individuals. *Revista de Psicologia General Aplicada, 31,* 88–90.

CANNON, W. (1929). *Bodily changes in pain, hunger, fear and rage: An account of recent researches into the function of emotional excitement* (2nd ed.). New York: Appleton-Century-Crofts.

CANNON, W. B. (1977). "Voodoo"

death. In A. Monat & R. S. Lazarus (Eds.), *Stress and coping*. New York: Columbia University Press.

CANTOR, J., ZILLMAN, D., & BRYANT, J. (1974). Enhancement of humor appreciation by transferred excitation. *Journal of Personality and Social Psychology, 30,* 812–821.

CANTOR, N., & MISCHEL, W. (1977). Traits and prototypes: Effects on recognition memory. *Journal of Personality and Social Psychology, 35,* 38–48.

CANTOR, N., & MISCHEL, W. (1979). Prototypes in person perception. In L. Berkowitz (Ed.), *Advances in social experimental psychology: Vol. 12*. New York: Academic Press.

CANTOR, N., & NIEDENTHAL, P. (in press). Affective responses as guides to category based inferences. *Motivation and Emotion*.

CARLSMITH, J. M., & ANDERSON, C. A. (1979). Ambient temperature and the occurrence of collective violence: A new analysis. *Journal of Personality and Social Psychology, 37,* 337–344.

CARMICHAEL, L., HOGAN, H. P., & WALTERS, A. (1932). An experimental study of the effects of language on the reproduction of visually perceived form. *Journal of Experimental Psychology, 16,* 73–86.

CARROL, J. (1986, November 13). Only a few clams left. *San Francisco Chronicle*.

CARVER, C., & GLASS, D. (1977). *The coronary prone behavior pattern and interpersonal aggression*. Unpublished manuscript, University of Texas.

CASPI, A. (in press). Moving against the world: Life course patterns for explosive people.

CASPI, A., & ELDER, G. H., JR. (in press). Childhood precursors of the life course. In E. M. Hetherington, R. M. Lerner, & M. Perlmutter (Eds.), *Child development in life-span perspective*.

CASSEL, J. C. (1976). The contribution of the social environment to host resistance. *American Journal of Epidemiology, 104,* 107–123.

CASSILETH, B. R., LUSK, E. J., MILLER, D. S., BROWN, L. L., &

MILLER, C. (1985). Psychosocial correlates of survival in advanced malignant disease? *New England Journal of Medicine,* 14–18.

CATTELL, R. B. (1971). *Abilities: Their structure, growth and action*. Boston: Houghton Mifflin.

CAVANAUGH, J. C., GRADY, J. G., & PERTMUTTER, M. P. (1983). Forgetting and using memory aids in 20- to 70-year-olds' everyday life. *International Journal of Aging and Human Development, 14,* 238–246.

CHANCE, P. (1987). *Learning and behavior* (2nd ed.). San Francisco: Wadsworth.

CHAPMAN, A. J. (1976). Social aspects of humorous laughter. In A. J. Chapman & H. C. Foot (Eds.), *Humour and laughter: Theory, research and applications*. London: John Wiley.

CHASE, W. G., & SIMON, N. A. (1973). The mind's eye in chess. In W. G. Chase (Ed.), *Visual information processing*. New York: Academic Press.

CHESNEY, M., & ROSEMEAN, R. H. (Eds.). (1985). *Anger and hostility in cardiovascular and behavioral disorders*. Washington, DC: Hemisphere Publishing.

CHESS, S., & THOMAS, A. (1987). *Know your child*. New York: Basic Books.

CHIRIBOGA, D. (1977). Life event weighting systems: A comparative analysis. *Journal of Psychosomatic Research, 21,* 415–422.

CHIRIBOGA, D. (1981). The developmental psychology of middle age. In J. Howells (Ed.), *Modern perspectives in the psychiatry of middle age*. New York: Brunner/Mazal.

CHIRIBOGA, D., & CUTLER, L. (1977). Stress responses among divorcing men and women. *Journal of Divorce, 1*(2), 95–106.

CHIRIBOGA, D., ROBERTS, J., & STEIN, O. (1978). Psychological well-being during marital separation. *Journal of Divorce, 2*(1), 21–35.

CHOMSKY, N. (1966). *Aspects of the theory of syntax*. Cambridge, MA: MIT Press.

CHOMSKY, N. (1980). *Rules and representations*. Cambridge, MA: MIT Press.

CHRISTIAN, J. J., FLYGER, V., & DAVIS, D. C. (1960). Factors in the mass mortality of a herd of Sika Deer, Cervus Nippon. *Chesapeake Science, 1,* 79–95.

CHUKOVSKY, K. (1963). *From two to five*. Berkeley: University of California Press.

CIALDINI, R. (1985). *Influence*. Chicago: Scott, Foresman.

CLARK, K., & CLARK, M. (1947). Racial identification and preference in Negro children. In T. M. Newcomb & E. L. Hartley (Eds.), *Readings in social psychology*. New York: Holt, Rinehart & Winston.

CLARK, M. S., & FISKE, S. T. (Eds.). (1982). *Affect and cognition*. Hillsdale, NJ: Erlbaum.

CLECKLEY, H. (1954). *The mark of sanity*. St. Louis: Mosby.

COBB, S., & KASL, S. V. (1977, June). *Termination: The consequences of job loss* (Report No. 76-1261). Cincinnati: National Institute for Occupational Safety and Health, Behavioral and Motivational Factors Research.

COBB, S., & ROSE, R. M. (1973). Hypertension, peptic ulcer, and diabetes in air traffic controllers. *Journal of the American Medical Association, 224,* 489–492.

COE, C. L., ROSENBERG, L. T., & LEVINE, S. (1985). Effect of maternal separation on humoral immunity in infant primates. In Spector, N. H. (Ed.), *Proceedings of the First International Workshop on Neuroimmunomodulation*. Bethesda, MD.

COFER, C. N., & APPLEY, M. H. (1964). *Motivation: Theory and research*. New York: John Wiley.

COGEN, M., BAKER, G., COHEN, R. A., FROMM-REICHMANN, F., & WEIGERT, E. V. (1954). An intensive study of twelve cases of manic-depressive psychosis. *Psychiatry, 17,* 103–137.

COHEN, F., & LAZARUS, R. (1973). Active coping processes, coping dispositions, and recovery from surgery. *Psychosomatic Medicine, 35,* 375–389.

COHEN, S., GLASS, D. C., & SINGER, J. E. (1973). Apartment noise, auditory discrimination, and reading ability in children. *Journal* of Experimental Social Psychology, 9, 407–422.

COHEN, S., & SYME, S. L. (Eds.). (1985). *Social support and health.* New York: Academic Press.

COLBY, A., & KOHLBERG, L. (1986). *The measurement of moral behavior.* New York: Cambridge University Press.

COLEMAN, J. C., BUTCHER, J. N., & CARSON, R. C. (1980). *Abnormal psychology and modern life.* Glenview, IL: Scott, Foresman.

COLEMAN, P. O. (1974). Measuring reminiscence: Characteristics from conversation as an adaptive feature of old age. *International Journal of Aging and Human Development, 5,* 281–294.

COLLINS, A. M., & QUILLIAN, M. R. (1972). Experiments on semantic memory and language comprehension. In L. W. Gregg (Ed.), *Cognition and learning.* New York: John Wiley.

COMFORT, A. (1974). *The joy of sex.* New York: Simon & Schuster.

CONDRY, J., & CONDRY, S. (1976). Sex differences: A study in the eye of the beholder. *Child Development, 47,* 812–819.

CONDRY, J., & DYER, S. (1976). Fear of success: Attribution of cause to the victim. *Journal of Social Issues, 32*(3), 63–83.

CONNORS, J. R., & DIAMOND, M. C. (1982). A comparison of dendritic spine number and type on pyramidal neuron of the visual cortex of old adult rats from social and isolated environments. *Journal of Comparative Neurology, 210,* 99–106.

COOPER, C., & MARSHALL, J. (1976). Occupational sources of stress: A review of the literature relating to coronary heart disease and mental ill health. *Occupational Psychology, 94,* 11–28.

COOPER, J. E., KENDELL, R. E., GURLAND, B. J., SHARPE, L., COPELAND, J. R. M., & SIMON, R. (1972). *Psychiatric diagnosis in New York and London.* London: Oxford University Press.

CORAH, N., & BOTTA, J. (1970). Perceived control, self-observation, and response to aversion stimulation. *Journal of Personality and Social Psychology, 16*(1), 1–4.

COREN, S., PORAC, C., & WARD, L. M. (1984). *Sensation and perception.* New York: Academic Press.

CORSO, J. (1977). Auditory perception and communication. In J. Birren & K. Schaie (Eds.), *Handbook of the psychology of aging.* New York: Van Nostrand-Reinhold.

COSMIDES, L., & TOOBY, J. (1986). From evolution to behavior: Evolutionary psychology as the missing link. In J. Dupre (Ed.), *The latest on the best: Essays on evolution and optimality.* Cambridge, MA: MIT Press.

COSTA, P. T., & McCRAE, R. R. (1980). Still stable after all these years: Personality as a key to some issues in adulthood and old age. In P. Baltes & O. Brim (Eds.), *Life span development and behavior: Vol. 3.* New York: Academic Press.

COSTA, P. T., McCRAE, R. J., & ARENBERG, D. (1980). Enduring dispositions in adult males. *Journal of Personality and Social Psychology, 38,* 793–800.

COSTANZO, M., ARCHER, D., ARONSON, E., & PETTIGREW, T. (1986). Energy conservation behavior: The difficult path from information to action. *American Psychologist, 41,* 521–528.

COTMAN, C., & McGAUGH, J. (1980). *Behavioral neuroscience.* New York: Academic Press.

COWAN, C., COWAN, P. COIE, L., & COIE, J. (1978). Becoming a family. In W. Miller & L. Newman (Eds.), *The first child and family formation.* Chapel Hill, NC: Carolina Population Center.

COYLE, J., PRICE, D., & DELONG, M. (1983). Alzheimer's disease: A disorder of cortical cholinergic innervation. *Science, 219,* 1184–1190.

COYNE, J., ALDWIN, C., & LAZARUS, R. S. (1981). Depression and coping in stressful episodes. *Journal of Abnormal Psychology, 90,* 439–447.

CRAIK, F. (1977). Age differences in human memory. In J. Birren & K. Schaie (Eds.), *Handbook of the psychology of aging.* New York: Van Nostrand-Reinhold.

CRAIK, F., & LOCKHART, R. R. (1972). Levels of processing: A framework for memory research.

Journal of Verbal Learning and Verbal Behavior, 12, 599–607.

CRAIK, F., & TULVING, E. (1975). Depth of processing and the retention of words in episodic memory. *Journal of Experimental Psychology: General, 104,* 268–294.

CSIKSZENTMIHALYI, M. (1975). *Beyond freedom and anxiety.* San Francisco: Jossey-Bass.

CUMMING, E., & HENRY, W. (1961). *Growing old: The process of disengagement.* New York: Basic Books.

CUMMINGS, S. (1977). Family socialization and fatalism among black adolescents. *Journal of Negro Education. 46*(1), 62–75.

CURTIS, H. J. (1966). *Biological mechanisms of aging.* Springfield, IL: Charles C Thomas.

CUSTANCE, J. (1951). *Wisdom, madness, and folly: The philosophy of a lunatic.* New York: Pellegrini Cudahy.

CZEISLER, C., WEITZMAN, E. D., MOORE-EDE, M. C., ZIMMERMAN, J. C., & KNAUER, R. S. (1980). Human sleep: Its duration and organization depend on its circadian phase. *Science, 210,* 1264–1267.

DARBY, W. J. (1978). The benefits of drink. *Human Nature, 1,* 30–37.

DARLEY, J. M., & BATSON, C. D. (1973). From Jerusalem to Jericho: A study of situational and dispositional variables in helping behavior. *Journal of Personality and Social Psychology, 27,* 100–108.

DARLEY, J. M., & LATANÉ, B. (1968). Bystander intervention in emergencies. *Journal of Personal and Social Psychology, 8,* 377–383.

DARWIN, C. (1872). *The expression of the emotions in man and animals.* London: Longmans, Green.

DARWIN, C. (1968). *The origin of species.* New York: Penguin. (Original work published 1859)

DAVIDSON, R. (1984). Hemispheric asymmetry and emotion. In K. Scherer & P. Ekman (Eds.), *Approaches to emotion.* Hillsdale, NJ: Erlbaum.

DAVIS, R. (1984). Expert systems: Where are we and where do we go from here? In P. Winston & K. Prendergast (Eds.), *The AI business.* Reading, MA: Addison-Wesley.

DAVISON, G. (1976). Homosexuality: The ethical challenge. *Journal of Consulting and Clinical Psychology*, 44, 156–162.

DAVISON, G., & NEALE, J. (1986). *Abnormal psychology* (3rd ed.). New York: John Wiley.

DAWKINS, R. (1986). *The blind watchmaker*. New York: Norton.

DAWSON, J. (1975). Socio-economic differences in size judgments of discs and coins by Chinese primary VI children in Hong Kong. *Perceptual and Motor Skills*, 41, 107–110.

DECHARMS, R. (1968). *Personal causation*. New York: Academic Press.

DECI, E. L. (1975). *Intrinsic motivation*. New York: Plenum.

DECK, L. (1968). Untitled report in *Journal of College and University Personnel Association*, 19, 99–137.

DEIKMAN, A. (1966). Deautomatization and the mystic experience. *Psychiatry*, 29, 329–343.

DE LA PENA, A. (1984). *The psychobiology of cancer*. New York: Praeger.

DELGADO, J. M. R. (1969). *Physical control of the mind*. New York: Harper & Row.

DELONGIS, A., COYNE, J. C., DAKOF, G., FOLKMAN, S., & LAZARUS, R. S. (1982). Relationship of daily hassles, uplifts and major life events to health status. *Health Psychology*, 1, 119–136.

DE LUMLEY, H. (1969). A Paleolithic camp at Nice. *Scientific American*, 220(5), 47–59.

DEMBER, W. N. (1974). Motivation and the cognitive revolution. *American Psychologist*, 29, 161–168.

DEMBER, W. N., EARL, R. W., & PARADISE, N. (1957). Response by rats to differential stimulus complexity. *Journal of Comparative and Physiological Psychology*, 50, 514–518.

DEMBROWSKI, T. M., MacDOUGALL, J. M., ELIOT, R. S., & BUELL, J. C. (1983). Moving beyond Type A. *Advances*, 3(2), 16–78.

DEMENT, W. C. (1974). *Some must watch while some must sleep*. San Francisco: Freeman.

DEMENT, W. C., & WOLPERT, E.

(1958). The relation of eye movements, bodily motility and external stimuli to dream content. *Journal of Experimental Psychology*, 55, 543–553.

DENES, P. B., & PINSON, E. N. (1963). *The speech chain*. New York: ATT Technologies.

DENGERINK, H. A., O'LEARY, M. R., & KASNER, K. H. (1975). Individual differences in aggressive responses to attack: Internal-external locus of control and field dependence-independence. *Journal of Research in Personality*, 9(3), 191–199.

DENNIS, W. (1960). Causes of retardation among institutional children: Iran. *Journal of Genetic Psychology*, 96, 47–59.

DENNIS, W., & DENNIS, S. G. (1948). Development under controlled environmental conditions. In W. Dennis (Ed.), *Readings in child psychology*. New York: Prentice-Hall.

DENNIS, W., & NAJARIAN, P. (1957). Infant development under environmental handicap. *Psychological Monographs*, 71(7).

DENTON, D. A. (1967). Salt appetite. In C. F. Code (Ed.), *Handbook of physiology: Alimentary canal: Vol. 1* (pp. 433–459). Washington DC: American Physiological Society.

DEREGOWSKI, J. B. (1973). Illusion and culture. In R. L. Gregory & G. H. Gombrich (Eds.), *Illusion in nature and art* (pp. 161–192). New York: Scribners.

DEREGOWSKI, J. B. (1987). Unpublished manuscript, Behavioral and Brain Sciences.

DEROGATIS, L., ABELOFF, M., & MELISARATOS, N. (1979). Psychological coping mechanisms and survival time in metastatic breast cancer. *Journal of the American Medical Association*, 112, 45–56.

DERRINGTON, A. M., & FUCHS, A. F. (1981). The development of spatial-frequency selectivity in kitten striate cortex. *Journal of Physiology*, 316, 1–10.

DESERAN, F. A., & CHUNG, C. S. (1979). Appearance, role-taking, and reactions to deviance. *Social Psychology Quarterly*, 42, 426–430.

DEUTSCHER, I. (1964). The quality of post-parental life. *Journal of*

Marriage and the Family, 26(1), 263–268.

DEVALOIS, R. L., ALBRECHT, D. G., & THORELL, L. G. (1982). Spatial frequency selectivity of cells in macaque visual cortex. *Vision Research*, 22, 545–559.

DEYKIN, E. Y., KLERMAN, G. L., & ARMOR, D. J. (1966). The relatives of schizophrenic patients: Clinical judgment of potential emotional resourcefulness. *American Journal of Orthopsychiatry*, 36(3), 518–528.

DIAMOND, M. C. (1978, January/February). The aging brain: Some enlightening-optimistic results. *American Scientist*, 46–51.

DIAMOND, M. C. (1980, June). Environment, air ions and brain chemistry. *Psychology Today*, 31–38.

DIAMOND, M. C., & CONNORS, J. R. (1981). A search for the potential of the aging cortex. In M. Diamond (Ed.), *Brain neurotransmitters and receptors in aging and age related disorders*. New York: Raven Press.

DILLON, K., MINCHOFF, B., & BAKER, K. H. (1985–1986). Positive emotional states and enhancement of the immune system. *International Journal of Psychiatry in Medicine*, 15, 13–17.

DILMAN, I. (1986). *Freud and human nature*. New York: Basil Blackwell.

DINARELLO, C., & WOLFE, S. (1979). Fever. *Human Nature*, 2(2), 66–74.

DOBRZECKA, C., & KONOROWSKI, J. (1968). Qualitative versus directional cues in differential conditioning. *Acta Biologiae Experimentale*, 28, 61–69.

DOBZHANSKY, T. (1962). *Mankind evolving*. New Haven, CT: Yale University Press.

DODSON, J. D. (1917). Relative values of reward and punishment in habit formation. *Psychobiology*, 1, 231–276.

DOHRENWEND, B. S., & DOHRENWEND, B. P. (1974). A brief historical introduction to research on stressful life events. In B. S. Dohrenwend & B. P. Dohrenwend (Eds.), *Stressful life events: Their nature and effects*. New York: John Wiley.

DOLLARD, J., DOOB, L. W., MILLER, N. E., MOWRER, O. H., & SEARS, R. R. (1939). *Frustration and aggression.* New Haven, CT: Yale University Press.

DONALDSON, M. (1978). *Children's minds.* London: Croom Helm.

DONER, J. F., & LAPPIN, J. S. (1980). Commentary in S. Ullman, Against direct perception. *Behavioral and Brain Sciences, 3*(3).

DOOLING, D. J., & LACHMAN, R. (1971). Effects of comprehension on retention of prose. *Journal of Experimental Psychology, 88,* 216–222.

DOUVAN, E. (1956). Social status and success striving. *Journal of Abnormal and Social Psychology, 52,* 219–223.

DOYLE, G., & GENTRY, W. (Ed.). (1984). *Handbook of behavioral medicine.* New York: Guilford.

DUA, P. S. (1970). Comparison of the effects of behaviorally oriented action and psychotherapy reeducation on introversion-extroversion, emotionality, and internal-external control. *Journal of Counseling Psychology, 17,* 567–572.

DUBOS, R. (1968). *So human an animal.* New York: Scribners.

DUBOS, R. (1978). Health and creative adaptation. *Human Nature, 1*(1), 14–21.

DUBOS, R. (1979, April). The price of adapting to work. *Human Nature, 2,* 29–35.

DUNN, J. P., BROOKS, G. W., MAUSNER, J., RODMAN, G. P., & COBB, S. (1963). Social class gradient of serum uric acid levels in males. *Journal of the American Medical Association, 185*(6).

DURKEIM, E. (1951). *Suicide.* New York: Free Press.

DUTTON, D., & ARON, A. (1974). Some evidence for heightened sexual attraction under conditions of high anxiety. *Journal of Personality and Social Psychology, 30,* 510–517.

DWORKIN, E. S., & EFRAN, J. S. (1967). The angered: Their susceptibility to varieties of humor. *Journal of Personality and Social Psychology, 6,* 233–236.

DYER, W. G. (1962). Analyzing marital adjustment using role theory. *Marriage and Family Living, 24*(4), 371–375.

EBBINGHAUS, H. (1969). *Über das gedächtnis (Memory).* (H. A. Ruger & E. Bussenius, Trans.) New York: Dover. (Original work published 1885)

ECKERMAN, J., WHATLEY, J., & KUTZ, S. (1975). The growth of social play with peers during the second year of life. *Developmental Psychology, 11,* 42–49.

ECKHOLM, E. (1978). Vanishing firewood. *Human Nature, 1*(5), 58–67.

EGBERT, L. D. (1985). Postscript. *Advances, 2,* 56–59.

EHRHARDT, S. A., & MEYER-BAHLBURG, H. (1981). Effects of prenatal sex hormones on gender-related behavior. *Science, 211,* 1312–1318.

EHRLICH, P., & FELDMAN, S. (1977). *The race bomb.* New York: Quadrangle.

EHRLICH, P., HOLDREN, J., & EHRLICH, A. (1977). *Ecoscience.* San Francisco: Freeman.

EHRLICH, P., & ORNSTEIN, R. (in press). *New world new mind.* New York: Doubleday.

EIBL-EIBESFELDT, I. (1970). *Ethology, the biology of behavior.* New York: Holt, Rinehart & Winston.

EIBL-EIBESFELDT, I. (1971). *Love and hate: The natural history of behavior patterns* (G. Strachan, Trans.). New York: Holt, Rinehart & Winston.

EIBL-EIBESFELDT, I. (1972). Similarities and differences between cultures in expressive movements. In R. A. Hinde (Ed.), *Non-verbal communication.* Cambridge: Cambridge University Press.

EIBL-EIBESFELDT, I. (1980). Strategies of social interaction. In R. Plutchik & H. Kelerman (Eds.), *Emotion: Theory, research, and experience.* New York: Academic Press.

EINHORN, H. J., & HOGARTH, R. M. (1981). Behavioral decision theory: Processes of judgment and choice. *Annual Review of Psychology, 32,* 53–88.

EINSTEIN, A. (1956). My life as a scientist. In J. Bronowski (Ed.), *The structure of science.* New York: Doubleday.

EKMAN, P. (Ed.). (1982). *Emotion in the human face* (2nd ed.). Cambridge: Cambridge University Press.

EKMAN, P. (1984). Expression and the nature of emotion. In K. Scherer & P. Ekman (Eds.), *Approaches to emotion.* Hillsdale, NJ: Erlbaum.

EKMAN, P. (1985). *Telling lies.* New York: Norton.

EKMAN, P., & FRIESEN, W. (1983). *Unmasking the face.* Palo Alto, CA: Consulting Psychologists Press.

ELIOT, R., & BREO, D. (1984). *Is it worth dying for?* New York: Bantam.

ELKIND, D. (1974). *Children and adolescents: Interpretive essays on Jean Piaget* (2nd ed.). New York: Oxford University Press.

ELKIND, D. (1978). *A sympathetic understanding of the child: Birth to sixteen* (2nd ed.). Boston: Allyn & Bacon.

ELLIOTT, J. (1977). The power and pathology of prejudice. In P. G. Zimbardo & F. L. Ruch (Eds.), *Psychology and life* (9th ed.). Glenview, IL: Scott, Foresman.

ELLIS, A. (1970). *Reason and emotion in psychotherapy.* New York: Lyle Stuart.

ENGEL, G. (1971). Sudden and rapid death during psychological stress: Folklore or folk wisdom. *Annals of Internal Medicine, 74,* 771–782.

ENGEN, T. (1977). Taste and smell. In J. E. Birren & J. W. Schaie (Eds.), *Handbook of the psychology of aging.* New York: Van Nostrand-Reinhold.

ENGEN, T., & ROSS, B. M. (1973). Long term memory of odors with and without verbal descriptions. *Journal of Experimental Psychology, 100,* 221–227.

EPSTEIN, S. M. (1967). Toward a unified theory of anxiety. In B. A. Maher (Ed.), *Progress in experimental personality research: Vol. 4.* New York: Academic Press.

EPSTEIN, S. M. (1979). The stability of behavior: I. On predicting most of the people much of the time. *Journal of Personality and Social Psychology, 37,* 1097–1126.

EPSTEIN, S., & SMITH, R. (1956). Repression and insight as related to reaction to cartoons. *Journal of*

Consulting Psychology, 20, 391–395.

ERDELYI, M. H. (1986). *Psychoanalysis: Freud's cognitive psychology.* New York: Freeman.

ERICSSON, K. A., & SIMON, H. A. (1980). Verbal reports as data. *Psychological Review, 87,* 215–251.

ERIKSON, E. (1986). *Vital involvement in old age.* New York: Norton.

ESTES, W. K. (1980). Is human memory obsolete? *American Scientist, 68,* 62–69.

EYSENCK, H. J. (1952). The effects of psychotherapy: An evaluation. *Journal of Consulting Psychology, 16,* 319–324.

FANTZ, R. L. (1961). The origin of form perception. *Scientific American, 204,* 66–72.

FARB, P., & ARMELAGOS, G. (1980). *Consuming passions: The anthropology of eating.* Boston: Houghton Mifflin.

FARIS, R. E. L., & DUNHAM, H. W. (1965). *Mental disorders in urban areas.* Chicago: University of Chicago Press. (Original work published 1939)

FARR, L. E. (1967). Medical consequences of environmental noises. *Journal of American Medical Association, 202,* 171–174.

FAUSTO-STERLING, A. (1986). *Myths of gender: Biological theories about women and men.* New York: Basic Books.

FEIN, R. A. (1978). Consideration of men's experiences and the birth of a first child. In W. Miller & L. Newman (Eds.), *The first child and family formation.* Chapel Hill, NC: Carolina Population Center.

FELDMAN-SUMMERS, S., & KIESLER, S. B. (1974). Those who are number two try harder: The effect of sex on attributions of causality. *Journal of Personality and Social Psychology, 30,* 846–855.

FERENCZI, S. (1954). *Thalassa: A theory of genitality.* New York: Norton.

FESTINGER, L. (1954). A theory of social comparison processes. *Human Relations, 7,* 117–140.

FESTINGER, L. (1957). *A theory of cognitive dissonance.* Stanford: Stanford University Press.

FESTINGER, L., & CARLSMITH, J. M. (1959). Cognitive consequences of forced compliance. *Journal of Abnormal and Social Psychology, 58,* 203–211.

FESTINGER, L., SCHACHTER, S., & BACK, K.(1950). *Social pressures in informal groups: A study of human factors in housing.* New York: Harper & Row.

FEUERSTEIN, R. (1979). *The dynamic assessment of retarded performers.* Baltimore: University Park Press.

FEUERSTEIN, R. (1980). *Instrumental enrichment.* Baltimore: University Park Press.

FEUERSTEIN, R., & RAND, Y. (1977). *Studies in cognitive modifiability. Instrumental enrichment: Redevelopment of cognitive functions of retarded early adolescents.* Jerusalem: Hadassah-Wizo-Canada Research Institute.

FIELDS, H. L., & LEVINE, J. D. (1981). Biology of placebo analgesia. *American Journal of Medicine, 70,* 745–746.

FINCH, C. E., & LANDFIELD, P. W. (1985). Neuroendocrine and autonomic functions in aging mammals. In C. E. Finch & E. L. Schneider, (Eds.), *Handbook of the biology of aging.* New York: Van Nostrand-Reinhold.

FISCHER, C. S. (1976). *The urban experience.* New York: Harcourt Brace Jovanovich.

FITZGERALD, F. T. (1986). The therapeutic value of pets. *Western Journal of Medicine, 144,* 103–105.

FLAVELL, J. H. (1977). *Cognitive development.* Englewood Cliffs, NJ: Prentice-Hall.

FLINN, M. W. (1966). *The origins of the industrial revolution.* London: Longmans, Green.

FODOR, J. (1983). *The modularity of mind.* Cambridge, MA: MIT Press.

FOLKMAN, S., & LAZARUS, R. (1980). An analysis of coping in a middle-aged population. *Journal of Health and Social Behavior, 21,* 219–239.

FORT, J. (1970). *The pleasure seekers: The drug crisis, youth and society.* New York: Grove.

FOUCAULT, M. (1978). *The history of sexuality: Vol 1: An introduction* (R. Hurley, Trans.). New York: Random House.

FOZARD, J., WOLF, E., BELL, B.,

FARLAND, R., & PODOLSKY, S. (1977). Visual perception and communication. In J. Birren & K. Schaie (Eds.), *Handbook of the psychology of aging.* New York: Van Nostrand-Reinhold.

FRAGER, R., & FADIMAN, J. (1987). *Maslow's motivation and personality.* New York: Harper & Row.

FRAIBERG, S. (1971). Blind infants and their mothers: An examination of the sign system. In M. Lewis & L. A. Rosenblum (Eds.), *The effect of the infant on its care-giver* (pp. 215–232). New York: John Wiley.

FRANK, J. D. (1982). Therapeutic components shared by all psychotherapies. In J. H. Harvey & M. M. Parks (Eds.), *Psychotherapy research and behavior change.* Washington, DC: American Psychological Association.

FRANK, J. D. (1983). The placebo is psychotherapy. *Behavioral and Brain Sciences, 6,* 291–292.

FRANQUEMONT, C. (1979). Watching, watching, counting, counting. *Human Nature, 2,* 82–84.

FREEDMAN, D. (1979). Ethnic differences in babies. *Human Nature, 2,* 36.

FREEDMAN, J. L. (1975). *Crowding and behavior.* New York: Viking.

FREEDMAN, J. L. (1986). Television violence and aggression: A rejoinder. *Psychological Bulletin, 100,* 372–378.

FREEDMAN, J. L., LEVY, A. S., BUCHANAN, R. W., & PRICE, J. (1972). Crowding and human aggressiveness. *Journal of Experimental Social Psychology, 8,* 528–548.

FREEDMAN, J. L., SEARS, D. O., & CARLSMITH, J. M. (1984). *Social psychology.* Englewood Cliffs, NJ: Prentice-Hall.

FREEMAN, N., & COX, C. (1986). *Visual order.* Boston: Cambridge University Press.

FRENCH, E., & LESSER, G. S. (1964). Some characteristics of the achievement motive in women. *Journal of Abnormal and Social Psychology, 68,* 119–128.

FRENCH, J., & CAPLAN, R. (1970). Psychosocial factors in coronary heart disease. *Industrial Medicine, 39,* 383–397.

FREUD, S. (1896). *Further remarks on the neuro-psychoses of defense. In Standard edition: Vol. 3* (p. 159). London: Hogarth Press.

FREUD, S. (1920). *Beyond the pleasure principle. In Standard edition: Vol. 18.* London: Hogarth Press.

FREUD, S. (1955). *The interpretation of dreams.* London: Hogarth Press. (Original work published 1900)

FREUD, S. (1962). *New introductory lectures on psychoanalysis.* London: Hogarth Press.

FREY, A. (1982). Personal communication.

FREY, W. H., II, DESOTA-JOHNSON, D., HOFFMAN, C., & McCALL, J. T. (1981). Effect of stimulus on the chemical composition of human tears. *American Journal of Opthalmology, 92*(4), 559–567.

FRIEDL, E. (1978). Society and sex roles. *Human Nature, 1*(4), 68–75.

FRIEDMAN, M., & ROSENMAN, R. (1974). *Type A behavior and your heart.* New York: Knopf.

FRIEDMAN, M., & STRICKER, E. M. (1976). The psychological psychology of hunger: A psychological perspective. *Psychological Review, 83,* 409–431.

FRIEDMAN, M., THORESON, C. E., & GILL, J. J. (1982). Feasibility of altering Type A behavior pattern after myocardial infarction. *Circulation, 66,* 83–92.

FRIEDMAN, M., & ULMER, D. (1984). *Treating type A behavior and your heart.* New York: Knopf.

FRIEDMANN, E., KATCHER, A., LYNCH, J. J., & THOMAS, S. A. (1980). Animal companions and one-year survival of patients after discharge from a coronary care unit. *Public Health Reports, 95,* 307–312.

FROHMAN, L. A., & BERNARDI, L. L. (1968). Growth hormone and insulin levels in weanling rats with ventromedial hypothalamic lesions. *Endocrinology, 82,* 1125–1132.

FROMM, E. (1941). *Escape from freedom.* New York: Holt, Rinehart & Winston.

GALANTER, E. (1962). Contemporary psychophysics. In R. Brown, E. Garlanter, E. Hess, & G. Mandler (Eds.), *New directions in psychology* (pp. 85–157). New York: Holt, Rinehart & Winston.

GALIN, D., & ORNSTEIN, R. (1972). Lateral specialization of cognitive mode: An EEG study. *Psychophysiology, 9,* 412–418.

GALIN, D., ORNSTEIN, R. E., & ADAMS, J. (1977). Midbrain stimulation of the amygdala. *Journal of States of Consciousness, 2,* 34–41.

GALIN, D., ORNSTEIN, R. E., HERRON, J., & JOHNSTONE, J. (1982). Sex and handedness differences in EEG measures of hemispheric specialization. *Brain and Language, 16*(1), 19–55.

GALLUP, G. G. (1977). Self-recognition in primates: A comparative approach to the bi-directional properties of consciousness. *American Psychologist, 32,* 329–338.

GALLUP, G. G. (1979). Self-awareness in primates. *American Scientist, 67,* 417–421.

GALTON, F. (1979). *Hereditary genius.* New York: St. Martin's Press. (Original work, *British men of science,* published 1875)

GARCIA, J., & KOELLING, R. (1966). Relation of cue to consequence in avoidance learning. *Psychonomic Science, 4,* 123–124.

GARDNER, H. (1975). *The shattered mind.* New York: Knopf.

GARDNER, H. (1983). *Frames of mind.* New York: Basic Books.

GARDNER, H. (1985). *The mind's new science.* New York: Basic Books.

GARNER, W. R. (1974). *The processing of information and structure.* Potomac, MD: Erlbaum.

GARRISON, W. (1971, March). Tears and laughter. *Today's Health,* 29–32.

GARVEY, C. (1977). *Play.* Cambridge, MA: Harvard University Press.

GAZZANIGA, M. (1985). *The social brain.* New York: Basic Books.

GELMAN, R., & GALISTEL, C. R. (1986). *The child's understanding of number.* Boston: Harvard University Press.

GENDLIN, E. T. (1986). What comes after traditional psychotherapy research? *American Psychologist, 41,* 131–137.

GERBNER, G., & GROSS, L. (1976). The scary world of TV's heavy viewer. *Psychology Today, 89,* 41–45.

GERSTEL, N., & RIESMAN, C. (1981). Social networks in a vulnerable population: The separated and divorced. Paper presented at the American Public Health Association Meetings, Los Angeles.

GESCHWIND, N. (1972). Language and the brain. *Scientific American, 226*(4), 76–83.

GESCHWIND, N., & GALABURDA, A. (Eds.). (1984). *Biological foundations of cerebral dominance.* Cambridge, MA: Harvard University Press.

GESCHWIND, N., & LEVITSKY, W. (1976). Left-right asymmetries in temporal speech region. *Science, 161,* 186–187.

GIBSON, E., & WALK, R. (1960). The visual cliff. *Scientific American, 202,* 64–71.

GIBSON, J. J. (1960). *The perception of the visual world.* Boston: Houghton Mifflin.

GIBSON, J. J. (1966). *The senses considered as perceptual systems.* Boston: Houghton Mifflin.

GIBSON, J. J. (1970). On theories for visual space perception: A reply to Johansson. *Scandinavian Journal of Psychology, 11,* 73–79.

GIBSON, J. J. (1979). *The ecological approach to visual perception.* Boston: Houghton Mifflin.

GIBSON, J. J., OLUM, P., & ROSENBLATT, F. (1955). Parallax and perspective during aircraft landings. *American Journal of Psychology, 68,* 372–385.

GIEDION, S. (1948). *Mechanization takes command.* New York: Norton.

GILLIGAN, C. (1982). *In a different voice: Psychological theory and women's development.* Cambridge, MA: Harvard University Press.

GIULIANO, V. (1982). The mechanization of office work. *Scientific American, 247,* 148–165.

GLADUE, B. A., GREEN, R., & HELLMAN, R. E. (1984). Neuroendocrine response to estrogen and sexual orientation. *Science, 225,* 1496–1499.

GLASER, R., & BOND, L. (Eds.). (1981). Testing: Concepts, policy, practice, and research [Special issue]. *American Psychologist, 36*(10).

GLASS, A. L., HOLYOAK, K. J., & SANTA, J. L. (1984). *Cognition.* Reading, MA: Addison-Wesley.

GLASS, D. C., & SINGER, J. E. (1972). *Urban stress: Experiments on noise and social stressors.* New York: Academic Press.

GLASS, D. C., SINGER, J. E., & FRIEDMAN, L. N. (1969). Psychic cost of adaptation to an environmental stressor. *Journal of Personality and Social Psychology, 12,* 200–210.

GLASS, G. V., & HOPKINS, K. D. (1984). *Statistical methods in education and psychology.* Englewood Cliffs, NJ: Prentice-Hall.

GLEESON, P. A., BROWN, J. S., WARING, J. J., & STOCK, M. J. (1979). Thermogenic effects of diet and exercise. *Proceedings of the Nutrition Society, 38,* 82.

GLENN, E., & FELDBERG, R. (1977). Degraded and deskilled: The proletarianization of clerical work. *Social Problems, 25,* 52–64.

GLICK, F. O., WEISS, R. S., & PARKES, C. M. (1974). *The first year of bereavement.* New York: John Wiley.

GLICK, P. C., & NORTON, A. J. (1977). Marrying, divorcing and living together in the U.S. today. *Population Bulletin, 38,* 106–124.

GMELCH, G. (1978). Baseball magic. *Human Nature, 1,* 32–40.

GOLAN, N. (1986). *The perilous bridge: Helping clients through midlife transitions.* New York: Free Press.

GOLDBERG, S., & LEWIS, M. (1969). Play behavior in the year-old infant: Early sex differences. *Child Development, 40,* 21–31.

GOLDBERG, P. (1968, April). Are women prejudiced against women? *Trans-Action, 28*–30.

GOLDSTEIN, A. (1980). Thrills in response to music and other stimuli. *Physiological Psychology, 8,* 126–129.

GOLDSTEIN, J. H., DAVIS, R. W., & HERMAN, D. (1975). Escalation of aggression: Experimental studies. *Journal of Personality and Social Psychology, 31*(1), 162–170.

GOLDSTEIN, K. (1974). *Human nature in the light of psychopathology.* Cambridge, MA: Harvard University Press.

GOLDSTEIN, M. J. (1959). The relationship between coping and avoiding behavior and response to fear-arousing propaganda. *Journal of Abnormal and Social Psychology, 58,* 247–252.

GOLDSTEIN, M. J., BAKER, B. L., & JAMISON, K. R. (1986). *Abnormal psychology: experiences, origins, and interventions* (2nd ed.). Boston: Little, Brown.

GOLEMAN, D. (1984a, December). Denial and hope. *American Health, 3,* 54–61.

GOLEMAN, D. (1984b, December). To dream the impossible dream. *American Health, 3,* 60–61.

GOLEMAN, D. (1985). *Vital lies, simple truths: The psychology of self-deception.* New York: Simon & Schuster.

GOLEMAN, D. (1986, November 11). For mentally ill on the street, a new approach shines. *The York Times.*

GOMBRICH, E. H. (1961). *Art and illusion* (2nd ed.). Princeton: Princeton University Press.

GOODCHILDS, J. D. (1972). On being witty: Causes, correlates and consequences. In J. H. Goldstein & P. E. McGhee (Eds.), *The psychology of humor.* London: Academic Press.

GOODE, E., & HABER, L. (1977). Sexual correlates of homosexual experience: An exploratory study of college women. *Journal of Sex Research, 13,* 12–21.

GOODE, W. (1956). *Women in divorce.* New York: Free Press.

GOODMAN, M. J., STEWART, G. J., & GILBERT, F., JR. (1977). A study of certain medical and physiological variables among Caucasian and Japanese women living in Hawaii. *Journal of Gerontology, 32*(3), 291–298.

GOODY, J. (1976). *Production and reproduction.* Cambridge: Cambridge University Press.

GORDON, B. (1979). *I'm dancing as fast as I can.* New York: Harper & Row.

GORE, S. (1978). The effect of social support in moderating the health consequences of unemployment. *Journal of Health and Social Behavior, 19,* 157–165.

GOSS, A., & MOROSKO, I. E. (1970). Relations between a dimension of internal-external control and the MMPI with an alcoholic population. *Journal of Consulting and Clinical Psychology, 34,* 189–192.

GOTTESMAN, I. I., & SHIELDS, J. (1972). *Schizophrenia: A twin study vantage point.* New York: Academic Press.

GOTTESMAN, I. I. (1974). Developmental genetics and ontogenetic psychology. *Minnesota Symposia on Child Psychology, 8.* Minneapolis: University of Minnesota Press.

GOTTMAN, J. M. (1979). *Marital interaction: Experimental investigations.* New York: Academic Press.

GOTTMAN, J. M. (in press). Marital communication.

GOULD, R. L. (1978). *Transformations: Growth and change in adult life.* New York: Simon & Schuster.

GOULD, S. J. (1979). *Ever since Darwin.* New York: Norton.

GOVE, W. R. (1972). Sex roles, marital roles, mental illness. *Social Forces, 51,* 34–44.

GRABOYS, T. B. (1981). Celtic fever: Playoff-induced ventricular arrythmia. *New England Journal of Medicine, 305,* 467–468.

GRAFF, H., & STELLAR, E. (1962). Hyperphagia obesity and finickiness. *Journal of Comparative and Physiological Psychology, 55,* 418–424.

GRANICH, S., & PATTERSON, R. (Eds.). (1971). *Human aging II: An eleven year follow-up biomedical and behavioral study* (Publication No. HSM 71-9037). Washington, DC: U.S. Government Printing Office.

GRASTYAN, E., KARMOS, G., VORECZKEY, L., MARTIN, J., & KELLENYI, L. (1965). Hypothalamic motivational processes as reflected by their hippocampal electrical correlates. *Science, 149,* 91–93.

GRAUNT, J. (1986). Natural and political observations made upon the bills of mortality. In J. R. Newman (Ed.), *The world of mathematics: Vol. 3.* New York: Simon & Schuster.

GRAVELLE, K. (1985). Can a feeling of capability reduce arthritis pain? *Advances, 2,* 8–13.

GRAVES, C. W. (1966). Deterioration of work standards. *Harvard Business Review, 44,* 117–128.

GRAY, J. A. (1984). *The neuropsychology of anxiety.* New York: Oxford University Press.

GRAY, R., & SMITH, T. (1960). Effect of employment on sex differences in attitudes toward the parental family. *Marriage and Family Living, 22,* 36–38.

GREELY, A., & SHEATSLEY, P. (1971). The acceptance of desegregation continues to advance. *Scientific American, 225*(6), 13–19.

GREENBERG, R., & PEARLMAN, C. A. (1974). Cutting the REM nerve: An approach to the adaptive role of REM sleep. *Perspectives in Biology and Medicine, 19,* 513–521.

GREENOUGH, S. (1975). Experimental modification of the developing brain. *American Scientist, 63,* 37–46.

GREENOUGH, W. T. (1982). Lecture to the Developmental Psychology Research Group, Estes Park, CO.

GREER, H. S. (1981, August). *Psychological response to breast cancer and eight-year outcome.* Paper presented at the Annual Meetings of the American Psychological Association, Los Angeles.

GREER, H. S., & MORRIS, T. (1975). Psychological attributes of women who develop breast cancer. *Psychosomatic Research, 19,* 147–153.

GREER, H. S., MORRIS, T., & PETTINGALE, K. W. (1979). Psychological response to breast cancer: Effect on outcome. *Lancet 11,* 785–787.

GREGORY, R. L. (1973, 1977). *Eye and brain* (2nd & 3rd eds.). New York: McGraw-Hill.

GRICE, G. R. (1948). The relation of secondary reinforcement to delayed reward in visual discrimination learning. *Journal of Experimental Psychology, 38,* 1–16.

GRICE, H. P. (1967). Utterer's meaning, sentence-meaning and word-meaning. *Foundations of Language, 4,* 225–242.

GRIFFITH, R. M., MIYAGI, O., & TAGO, A. (1958). The universality of typical dreams: Japanese vs. American. *American Anthropologist, 60,* 1173–1179.

GRINKER, R. R. (1953). *Emotions and emotional disorders.* New York: Hoeber.

GRINKER, R. R., & SPEIGEL, J. P. (1945). *Men under stress.* Philadelphia: Blackiston.

GRINSPOON, L., & BAKALAR, J. B. (1979). *Psychedelic drugs reconsidered.* New York: Basic Books.

GRIVES, P. M., & THOMPSON, R. F. (1973). A dual process theory of habituation: Neural mechanisms. In H. M. S. Pecks & M. J. Herz (Eds.), *Habituation, physiological substrates II.* New York: Academic Press.

GROSS, C. G., ROCHA-MIRANDA, C. E., & BENDER, D. B. (1972). Visual properties of neurons in inferotemporal cortex of the macaque. *Journal of Neurophysiology, 35,* 96–111.

GROSSMAN, F. K., EICHLER, L. S., & WINICKHOFF, S. A. (1980). *Pregnancy, birth, and parenthood.* San Francisco: Jossey-Bass.

GROSSMAN, S. (1979). The biology of motivation. *Annual Review of Psychology, 30,* 209–242.

GUILFORD, J. P. (1967). *The nature of human intelligence.* New York: McGraw-Hill.

GUILFORD, J. P., & HOEPFNER, R. (1971). *The analysis of intelligence.* New York: McGraw-Hill.

HAAN, N. (1977). *Coping and defending.* New York: Academic Press.

HABER, R., & STANDIG. L. G. (1966). Direct measures of short-term visual storage. *Quarterly Journal of Experimental Psychology, 21,* 43–54.

HAITH, M. M. (1980). *Rules that babies look by: The organization of newborn visual activity.* New York: Erlbaum.

HALDANE, J. B. S. (1932). *The causes of evolution.* London: Longmans, Green.

HALDANE, J. B. S. (1986). *On being the right size.* London: Oxford University Press.

HALER, R. N. (1958). Discrepancy from adaptation level as a source of affect. *Journal of Experimental Psychology, 56,* 360–375.

HALL, C. (1966). *The meaning of dreams.* New York: McGraw-Hill.

HALL, E. (1978). *Why we do what we do: A look at psychology.* Boston: Houghton Mifflin.

HALL, E. T. (1969). *The hidden dimension.* New York: Anchor Press.

HALL, H. (1983). Hypnosis and the immune system: A review with implications for cancer and the psychology of healing. *American Journal of Clinical Hypnosis.*

HALL, H. (1986). Hypnosis, suggestion, and the psychology of healing: A historical perspective. *Advances, 3,* 29–37.

HALL, H., LONGO, S., & DIXON, R. (1981). Hypnosis and the immune system: The effect of hypnosis on T and B cell function. Paper presented to the Society for Clinical and Experimental Hypnosis, 33rd Annual Workshops and Scientific Meeting.

HALL, R. C., GARDNER, E. R., STICKNEY, S. K., LECANN, A. F., & POPKIN, M. K. (1980). Physical illness manifesting as psychiatric disease: II. Analysis of a state hospital inpatient population. *Archives of General Psychiatry, 37*(9), 989–995.

HAMILTON, C. L. (1963). Interactions of food intake and temperature regulation in the rat. *Journal of Comparative and Physiological Psychology, 56,* 476–488.

HAMILTON, W. D. (1964). The genetical evolution of social behavior. *Journal of Theoretical Biology, 7,* 1–52.

HAMMOND, B. L., & SCHEIRER, C. J. (1986). *Psychology and Health (Vols. 1–4).* Washington, DC: American Psychological Association.

HANDAL, P. S. (1965). Immediate acceptance of sodium salts by sodium deficient rats. *Psychorem. Sci., 3,* 315–316.

HANEY, C., BANKS, C., & ZIMBARDO, P. G. (1973). Interpersonal dynamics in a simulated prison. *International Journal of Criminology and Penology, 1,* 69–97.

HARE, R. D., & CRAIGEN, D. (1974). Psychopathy and physiological activity in a mixed-motive game situation. *Psychophysiology, II,* 197–206.

HARLOW, H., & HARLOW, M. H.

(1966). Learning to love. *American Scientist, 54,* 244–272.

HARLOW, H. F. (1950). Learning and satiation of response in intrinsically motivated complex puzzle performance by monkeys. *Journal of Comparative and Physiological Psychology, 43,* 289–294.

HARRELL, R. F., WOODYARD, E. R., GATES, E. R., & GATES, I. A. (1956). The influence of vitamin supplementation in the diets of pregnant and lactating women on the intelligence of their offspring. *Metabolism, 5,* 555–562.

HARRINGTON, D. M., BLOCK, J. H., & BLOCK, B. (1978). Intolerance of ambiguity in preschool children: Psychometric considerations, behavioral manifestations and parental correlates. *Developmental Psychology, 14,* 242–256.

HARRIS, M. (1971). *Culture, people, nature.* New York: Thomas Y. Crowell.

HARTLINE, H. K., & RATLIFF, F. (1957). Inhibitory interaction of receptor units in the eye of Limulus. *Journal of General Physiology, 40,* 357–376.

HARTMANN, E. (1973). *The functions of sleep.* New Haven, CT: Yale University Press.

HARTON, J. J. (1938). An investigation of the influence of success and failure on the estimation of time. *Journal of General Psychology, 21,* 51–62.

HARTSHORNE, H., & MAY, M. A. (1928). *Studies in the nature of character: Studies in deceit.* New York: Macmillan.

HARTSHORNE, H., & MAY, M. A. (1929). *Studies in the nature of character: Studies in self-control.* New York: Macmillan.

HASKELL, W. (1979). Physical activity in health maintenance. In D. Sobel (Ed.), *Ways of health.* New York: Harcourt Brace Jovanovich.

HASTORF, A. H. (1950). The influence of suggestion of the relationship between stimulus, size and perceived distance. *Journal of Psychology, 19,* 195–217.

HASTORF, A. H., & CANTRIL, H. (1954). They saw a game: A case study. *Journal of Abnormal and Social Psychology, 49,* 129–134.

HATFIELD, E., & SPRECHER, S.

(1986). *Mirror, mirror: The importance of looks in everyday life.* New York: SUNY Press.

HAUGELAND, J. (Ed.). (1985). *Mind design: Philosophy, psychology, and artificial intelligence.* Cambridge, MA: MIT Press.

HAUSMAN, P. B., & WEKSLER, M. C. (1984). Changes in the immune response with age. In C. E. Finch & E. L. Schneider (Eds.), *Handbook of the biology of aging.* New York: Van Nostrand-Reinhold.

HAVIGHURST, R. J., & GLASER, R. (1972). An exploratory study of reminiscence. *Journal of Gerontology, 27,* 245–253.

HAVIGHURST, R. J., NEUGARTEN, B. L., & TOBIN, S. S. (1968). Disengagement and patterns of aging. In B. L. Neugarten (Ed.), *Middle age and aging.* Chicago: University of Chicago Press.

HAYES-ROTH, F. (1980). Comment regarding ''Against direct perception.'' *Behavioral and Brain Sciences, 3*(3), 367–368.

HAYFLICK, L. (1980). The cell biology of human aging. *Scientific American, 242*(1), 58–65.

HAYFLICK, L., & MOORHEAD, P. S. (1961). The serial cultivation of human diploid cell strains. *Experimental Cell Resources, 25,* 585–621.

HEATH, R. G. (1963). Electrical self-stimulation of the brain in man. *American Journal of Psychiatry, 120,* 571–577.

HEATH, R. G., & MICKLE, W. A. (1960). Evaluation of seven years' experience with depth electrode studies in human patients. In E. R. Ramey & D. S. O'Doherty (Eds.), *Electrical studies of the unanesthetized brain.* New York: Holber.

HEBB, D. O. (1949). *The organization of behavior.* New York: John Wiley.

HECKHAUSEN, H. (1967). *The anatomy of achievement motivation.* New York: Academic Press.

HEIDER, F. (1946). Attitudes and cognitive organization. *Journal of Psychology, 21,* 107–112.

HEIDER, F. (1958). *The psychology of interpersonal relations.* New York: John Wiley.

HEILMAN, K. M., & SATZ, P. (Eds.). (1984). *Neuropsychology of human emotion.* New York: Guilford.

HELD, R., & HEIN, A. (1963). Movement produced stimulation in the development of visually guided behavior. *Journal of Comparative and Physiological Psychology, 56,* 872–876.

HELSON, H. (1964). *Adaptation level theory: An experimental and systematic approach to behavior.* New York: Harper & Row.

HENRY, J. P., & STEPHENS, P. M. (1977). *Stress, health and social environment: A sociobiological approach to medicine.* New York: Springer-Verlag.

HENRY, W. (1956). *The analysis of fantasy.* New York: John Wiley.

HERBERT, M. J., & HARSH, C. M. (1944). Observational learning by cats. *Journal of Comparative and Physiological Psychology, 37,* 81–95.

HERRMANN, D. J., & NEISSER, U. (1978). An inventory of everyday memory experiences. In M. M. Gruneberg, P. E. Morris, & R. N. Sykes (Eds.), *Practical aspects of memory.* New York: Academic Press.

HERRNSTEIN, R. J. (1973). *IQ in the meritocracy.* Boston: Little, Brown.

HERRON, J. (1980). *Neuropsychology of left-handers.* New York: Academic Press.

HERZBERG, F. (1966). *Work and the nature of man.* Cleveland: World Publishing.

HESS, E. H. (1973). *Imprinting.* New York: Van Nostrand-Reinhold.

HESS, E. H. (1975). *The tell-tale eye: How your eyes reveal hidden thoughts and emotions.* New York: Van Nostrand-Reinhold.

HESTON, L. (1966). Psychiatric disorders in foster home reared children of schizophrenic mothers. *British Journal of Psychiatry, 112,* 819–825.

HETHERINGTON, A. W., & RANSON., S. W. (1942). The spontaneous activity and food intake of rats with hypothalamic lesions. *American Journal of Physiology, 136,* 609–617.

HETHERINGTON, E., COX, M., & COX, D. (1977). Divorced fathers. *Family Coordination, 25,* 417–428.

HILGARD, E. R. (1966). *The experience of hypnosis.* New York: Harcourt Brace Jovanovich.

HILGARD, E. R. (1977). *Divided consciousness: Multiple controls in human thought and action.* New York: Wiley-Interscience.

HILGARD, E. R. (1978). Hypnosis and consciousness. *Human Nature, 1,* 42–51.

HILGARD, E. R. (1986). *Psychology in America: A historical survey.* San Diego: Harcourt Brace Jovanovich.

HILGARD, E. R., & MARQUIS, D. G. (1940). *Conditioning and learning.* New York: Appleton-Century.

HILTZ, S. R., & TUROFF, M. (1978). *The network nation.* Reading, MA: Addison-Wesley.

HINES, T., & FOZARD, J. (1980). Memory and aging: Relevance of recent developments for research and application. In *Annual Review of Gerontology and Geriatrics (Vol. 1).* New York: Springer.

HINTON, J. (1967). *Dying.* Baltimore: Penguin.

HIRST, W., NEISSER, U., & SPELKE, E. (1978). Divided attention. *Human Nature, 1,* 54–61.

HOBART, C. W. (1958). The incidence of romanticism during courtship. *Social Forces, 36,* 362–367.

HOBSON, J. A., & McCARLEY, R. W. (1977). The brain as a dream state generator: An activation-synthesis hypothesis of the dream process. *American Journal of Psychiatry, 134*(12), 1335–1348.

HOCHBERG, J. E. (1978). *Perception* (2nd ed.). Englewood Cliffs, NJ: Prentice-Hall.

HOCKETT, C. F., & ASHER, R. (1964). Human revolution. *Current Anthropology, 135,* 142.

HOEBEL, B., & TEITELBAUM, P. (1962). Hypothalamic control of feeding and self-stimulation. *Science, 135,* 375–376.

HOFFMAN, A. (1968). Psychotomimetic agents. In A. Burger (Ed.), *Drugs affecting the central nervous system: Vol. 2.* New York: Dekker.

HOFFMAN, L. W. (1974). Fear of success in males and females: 1965 and 1972. *Journal of Consulting and Clinical Psychology, 42,* 353–358.

HOFSTADTER, R. (1959). *Social Darwinism in American thought.* New York: George Braziller.

HOGARTY, G. E., & GOLDBERG, S. C. (1973). Drug and sociotherapy in the aftercare of schizophrenic patients. *Archives of General Psychiatry, 28,* 54–63.

HOLLAND, J. L. (1973). *Making vocational choices: A theory of careers.* Englewood Cliffs, NJ: Prentice-Hall.

HOLMES, L. (1978). How fathers can cause the Down Syndrome. *Human Nature, 1*(10), 70–73.

HOLMES, T. H., & RAHE, R. H. (1967). The social readjustment rating scale. *Journal of Psychosomatic Research, 11,* 213–218.

HONORTON, C. (1974). Psi-conducive states of awareness. In E. Mitchell & J. White (Eds.), *Psychic exploration: A challenge for science* (pp. 611–638). New York: Putnam.

HORN, J. L., & KNAPP, J. R. (1973). On the subjective character of the empirical base of Guilford's structure of intellect model. *Psychological Bulletin, 80,* 33–43.

HORN, J. M., LOEHLIN, J. C., & WILLERMAN, L. (1982). Personality resemblances between unwed mothers and their adopted-away offspring. *Journal of Personality and Social Psychology, 42*(6), 1089–1099.

HORNER, M. S. (1968). *Sex differences in achievement motivation and performance in competitive and noncompetitive situations.* Unpublished doctoral dissertation, University of Michigan. (University Microfilms No. 69-12, 135).

HORNEY, K. (1950). *Neurosis and human growth.* New York: Norton.

HOUGHTON, J. F. (1980). One personal experience: Before and after mental illness. In J. G. Rabkin, L. Gelb, & J. B. Lazar (Eds.), *Attitudes toward the mentally ill: Research perspectives.* Rockville, MD: National Institute of Mental Health.

HOUGHTON, J. F. (1982). First person account: Maintaining mental health in a turbulent world. *Schizophrenia Bulletin, 8,* 548–549.

HOUSE, J. S., ROBBINS, C., & METZNER, H. L. (1982). The association of social relationships and activities with mortality. *American Journal of Epidemiology, 116,* 123–140.

HUBEL, D. H. (1979). The brain. *Scientific American, 241,* 44–53.

HUBEL, D. H., & WIESEL, T. N. (1962). Receptive fields, binocular interactions and functional architecture in the cat's visual cortex. *Journal of Physiology, 160,* 106–154.

HUBEL, D. H., & WIESEL, T. N. (1979). Brain mechanisms of vision. *Scientific American, 241,* 150–162.

HUDSON, W. (1960). Pictorial depth perception in sub-cultural groups in Africa. *Journal of Social Psychology, 52,* 183–208.

HULICKA, I. M., & GROSSMAN, J. L. (1967). Age group comparisons for the use of mediators in paired associate learning. *Journal of Gerontology, 22,* 46–51.

HULL, C. L. (1943). *Principles of behavior.* New York: Appleton-Century-Crofts.

HUMPHREY, N. K. (1978). The origins of human intelligence. *Human Nature, 1* (12), 42–49.

HUNT, J. McV. (1965). Intrinsic motivation and its role in psychological development. *Nebraska Symposium on Motivation 1965,* (pp. 189–282). Lincoln: University of Nebraska Press.

HUNT, M. (1974). *Sexual behavior in the 1970's.* New York: Dell.

HURVICH, L. M., & JAMESON, D. (1957). An opponent-process theory of color. *Psychological Reviews, 64,* 384–404.

HURVICH, L. M., & JAMESON, D. (1974). Opponent processes as a model of neural organization. *American Psychologist, 29,* 88–102.

HUTCHINGS, B., & MEDNICK, S. A. (1974). Registered criminality in the adoptive and biological parents of registered male adoptees. In S. A. Mednick, F. Schulsinger, J. Higgins, & B. Bell (Eds.), *Genetics, environment and psychopathology.* New York: Elsevier.

HUXLEY, A. (1971). Fifth philosopher's song. In D. Watt (Ed.), *The collected poetry of Aldous Huxley.* New York: Harper & Row.

ICKES, W., REIDHEAD, S., & PATTERSON, M., (1986). Machiavellianism and self-monitoring: As different as me and you. *Social Cognition, 400*(1), 58–74.

ISBISTER, J. N. (1986). *Freud.* New York: Polity/Blackwell.

ISEN, A. M. (1984). Affect, cognition, and social behavior. In R. S. Wyer & T. K. Srull (Eds.), *Handbook of social cognition* (Vol. 3, pp. 179–236). Hillsdale, NJ: Erlbaum.

ITTLESON, H. (1952). The constancies in perceptual theory. In F. R. Kilpatrick (Ed.), *Human behavior from the transactional point of view*. Hanover, NH: Institute for Associated Research.

IZARD, C. E., KAGAN, J., & ZAJONC, R. B. (Eds.). (1986). *Emotions, cognition and behavior*. New York: Cambridge University Press.

JACOBS, B., & MOSS, H. (1976). Birth order and sex of sibling as determinants of mother-infant interaction. *Child Development, 47*, 315–322.

JACOBS, J. (1959). *Death and life of great American cities*. New York: Vintage.

JACOBS, J. (1971). *Adolescent suicide*. New York: John Wiley.

JACOBSON, J. (1977). *The development of peer play and cautiousness toward peers in infancy*. Unpublished doctoral dissertation, Harvard University.

JACOBSON, M. B. (1981). Effects of victim's and defendant's physical attractiveness on subjects' judgments in a rape case. *Sex Roles, 4*, 169–174.

JACQUES, E. (1951). *The changing culture of a factory*. London: Travistock.

JACQUES, E. (1965). Death and the midlife crisis. *International Journal of Psychoanalysis, 46*, 502–514.

JAHODA, M., & WEST, P. (1951). Race relations in public housing. *Journal of Social Issues, 7*, 132–139.

JAMES, S., & KLEINBAUM, D. G. (1976). Socioecologic stress and hypertension: Related mortality rates in North Carolina. *American Journal of Public Health, 66*, 354–358.

JAMES, W. (1970). *The principles of psychology: Vol 1*. New York: Dover. (Original work published 1890)

JAMES, W. (1980). *The varieties of religious experience*. New York: Longmans, Green. (Original work published 1917)

JANNIS, I. L., & MANN, L. (1977). *Decision-making*. New York: Free Press.

JARVICK, L. F., & DECKARD, B. S. (1977). The Odyssean personality: A survival advantage for carriers of genes predisposing to schizophrenia. *Neuropsychobiology, 3*(2–3), 179–191.

JEMMOTT, J. B., BORYSENKO, J. Z., BORYSENKO, M., McCLELLAND, D. C., CHAPMAN, R., MEYER, D., & BENSON, H. (1983). Academic stress, power motivation, and decrease in secretion rate of salivary secretory immunoglobulin A. *Lancet*, 1400–1402.

JEMMOTT, J. B., & LOCKE, S. E. (1984). Psychosocial factors, immunologic mediation and human susceptibility to infection: How much do we know? *Psychological Bulletin, 95*, 78–108.

JENKINS, J. G., & DALLENBACH, K. M. (1924). Oblivescence during sleep and waking. *American Journal of Psychology, 35*, 605–612.

JENKINS, R. L. (1966). Psychiatric syndromes in children and their relation to family background. *American Journal of Orthopsychiatry, 36*, 450–457.

JENKINS, R. L. (1969). Classification of behavior problems of children. *American Journal of Psychiatry, 125*(8), 1032–1039.

JENSEN, A. R. (1969). How much can we boost IQ and scholastic achievement? *Harvard Educational Review, 39*, 1–123.

JENSEN, A. R. (1980). *Bias in mental testing*. New York: Free Press.

JESSOR, R., & JESSOR, S. L. (1977). *Problem behavior and psychosocial development: A longitudinal study of youth*. New York: Academic Press.

JESSOR, S. L., & JESSOR, R. (1975). Transition from virginity to non-virginity among youth: A social-psychological study over time. *Developmental Psychology, 11*, 473–484.

JOHANSEN, D., & EDEY, M. (1981). *Lucy: The beginnings of humankind*. New York: Simon & Schuster.

JOHNSON, A. (1978). In search of the affluent society. *Human Nature, 1*(9), 50–60.

JOHNSON, D. M. (1972). *Systematic introduction to the psychology of thinking*. New York: Harper & Row.

JOHNSON-LAIRD, P. N. (1983). *Mental models*. Boston: Harvard University Press.

JOHNSON-LAIRD, T. N., & WASON, P. C. (Eds.). (1977). *Thinking: Readings in cognitive science*. New York: Cambridge University Press.

JOHNSTON, T. (1981). Contrasting approaches to a theory of learning. *Behavioral and Brain Sciences, 4*, 125–139.

JOINER, B. L. (1975). Living histograms. *International Statistical Review, 43*, 339–340.

JONES, C., & ARONSON, E. (1973). Attribution of fault to a rape victim as a function of responsibility of the victim. *Journal of Personality and Social Psychology, 26*, 415–491.

JONES, E. E., & HARRIS, V. A. (1967). The attribution of attitudes. *Journal of Experimental Social Psychology, 3*, 1–24.

JONES, E. E., & NISBETT, R. E. (1971). *The actor and the observer: Divergent perception of the causes of behavior*. Morristown, NJ: General Learning Press.

JONES, M. C. (1924). A laboratory study of fear: The case of Peter. *Journal of Genetic Psychology, 31*, 308–315.

JOSEPH, S. A., & KNIGGE, J. M. (1968). Effects of VMH lesions in adult and newborn guinea pigs. *Neuroendocrinology, 3*, 309–331.

JULIEN, R. M. (1978). *A primer of drug action*. San Francisco: Freeman.

JUNG, C. (1921). Psychological types. In *Collected works: Vol. 6*. Princeton: Princeton University Press.

JUNG, C. (1953). *Collected works*. H. Read, M. Fordham, & G. Adler (Eds.). New York: Bollingen Series/Pantheon Books.

KAGAN, J. (1978). *The growth of the child: Reflections on human development*. New York: Norton.

KAGAN, J. (1981). *The second year: The emergence of self-awareness*. Cambridge, MA: Harvard University Press.

KAGAN, J. (1984). *The nature of the child*. New York: Basic Books.

KAGAN, J., & KLEIN, R. E. (1973). Cross cultural perspectives on early development. *American Psychologist, 28*, 947–961.

KAHN, M. (1970). Non-verbal communication and marital satisfaction. *Family Process, 9,* 449–456.

KAHN, R. L., HEIN, K., HOUSE, J., McLEAN, A., & KASL, S. (1980, July). *Stress in organizational settings.* Paper prepared for the National Academy of Sciences, Institute of Medicine, Committee on Stress in Health and Disease.

KAHNEMAN, D., SLOVIC, P., & TVERSKY, A. (Eds.). (1982). *Judgment under uncertainty.* New York: Cambridge University Press.

KAHNEMAN, D., & TVERSKY, A. (1973). On the psychology of prediction. *Psychological Review, 80,* 237–251.

KALISH, R. A. (1976). Death and dying in a social context. In R. H. Binstock & E. Shanas (Eds.), *Handbook of aging and the social sciences.* New York: Van Nostrand-Reinhold.

KAMIN, L. (1979, April). Psychology as social science: The Jensen affair, ten years after. Presidential address to Eastern Psychological Association, Philadelphia.

KAMIN, L. (with H. J. Eysenck). (1981). *The intelligence controversy.* New York: John Wiley.

KANNER, A. D., COYNE, J. D., SCHAEFER, C., & LAZARUS, R. S. (1981). Comparison of two modes of stress measurement: Daily hassles and uplifts versus major life events. *Journal of Behavior Medicine, 4*(1), 1–39.

KAPLAN, E. A. (1960). Hypnosis and pain. *Archives of General Psychiatry, 2,* 567–568.

KAPLAN, G. A., & CAMACHO, T. (1983). Perceived health and mortality: A one-year follow-up of the Human Population Laboratory cohort. *American Journal of Epidemiology, 117,* 292–304.

KAPLEAU, P. (1980). *The three pillars of Zen.* New York: Anchor Press.

KASAMATSU, A., & HIRAI, T. (1963). An electroencephalographic study on the Zen meditation (Zazen). *Folia Psychiatria et Neurologia, 20,* 315–336.

KASL, S. V., EVANS, A. S., & NEIDERMAN, J. C. (1979). Psychosocial risk factors in the development of infectious mononucleosis. *Psychosomatic Medicine, 41,* 445–466.

KASTENBAUM, R. (1965). Wine and fellowship in aging: An exploratory action program. *Journal of Human Relations, 13,* 266–275.

KASTENBAUM, R. (1977). Is death a crisis? In N. Daton & R. Ginsberg (Eds.). *Life-span developmental psychology.* New York: Academic Press.

KASTENBAUM, R., & AISENBERG, R. (1972). *Psychology of death.* New York: Springer.

KATCHER, A., & BECK, A. (Eds.). (1983). *New perspectives on our lives with companion animals.* Philadelphia: University of Pennsylvania Press.

KATZ, M. L. (1973). *Female motive to avoid success: A psychological barrier or a response to deviancy?* Princeton, NJ: Educational Testing Service.

KAUFMAN, L. (1974). *Sight and mind: An introduction to visual perception.* New York: Oxford University Press.

KEESEY, R., & POWLEY, T. (1975, September-October). Hypothalamic regulation of body weight. *American Scientist, 63,* 558–565.

KELLEY, H. H. (1967). Attribution theory in social psychology. In D. Levine (Ed.), *Nebraska Symposium on Motivation, 15,* 192–238. Lincoln: University of Nebraska Press.

KENNEDY, J. M. (1974). *A psychology of picture perception.* San Francisco: Jossey-Bass.

KESSEN, W., HAITH, M., & SALAPATEK, P. H. (1970). Infancy. In P. H. Mussen. (Ed.), *Charmichael's manual of child psychology* (3rd ed.). New York: John Wiley.

KESSLER, S. (1980). *Schizophrenic families.* New York: Raven Press.

KEYES, D. (1982). *The minds of Billy Milligan.* New York: Bantam.

KEYES, R. (1980). *The height of your life.* New York: Warner.

KEYS, A., BROZEK, J., HENSCHEL, A., MICKELSON, O., & TAYLOR, H. (1950). *The biology of human starvation (Vols. 1–2).* Minneapolis: University of Minnesota Press.

KIDSON, M. A., & JONES, I. H. (1952). Psychiatric disorders among aborigines of the Australian western desert. *Archives of General Psychiatry, 38,* 58–62.

KIECOLT-GLASER, J. K., GARNER, W., SPEICHER, C., PENN, G. M., HOLLIDAY, J., & GLASER, R. (1984). Psychosocial modifiers of immunocompetence in medical students. *Psychosomatic Medicine, 46,* 7–14.

KIECOLT-GLASER, J. K. et al. (1985). Psychosocial enhancement of immunocompetence in a geriatric population. *Health Psychology, 4,* 25–41.

KIESLER, S., SIEGEL, J., & McGUIRE, T. W. (1984). Social psychological aspects of computer-mediated communication. *American Psychologist, 39,* 1123–1134.

KIMBLE, G. A. (1961). *Hilgard and Marquis' conditioning and learning* (2nd ed.). New York: Appleton-Century-Crofts.

KIMMEL, D. C. (1980). *Adulthood and aging: An interdisciplinary developmental view* (2nd ed.). New York: John Wiley.

KIMURA, D. (1963). Right temporal lobe damage. *Archives of Neurology, 8,* 264–271.

KING, B. M., & GASTON, M. G. (1977). Reappearance of dynamic hyperphagia during the static phase in medial hypothalamic lesioned rats. *Physiology and Behavior, 18,* 463–473.

KINSBOURNE, M. (1980). Attentional dysfunctions in the elderly: Theoretical models and research proceedings. In L. Poon et al. (Eds.), *New directions in memory and aging.* Hillsdale, NJ: Erlbaum.

KINSEY, A., POMEROY, W., & MARTIN, C. (1948). *Sexual behavior in the human male.* Philadelphia: Saunders.

KINSEY, A., POMEROY, W., & MARTIN, C. (1953). *Sexual behavior in the human female.* Philadelphia: Saunders.

KISSEN, D. M. (1966). The significance of personality in lung cancer in men. *Annals of the New York Academy of Science, 125,* 820–826.

KLEINKE, C. (1978). *Self-perception: The psychology of personal awareness.* San Francisco: Freeman.

KOBASA, S. C. (1984, September). How much stress can you survive? *American Health, 3,* 64–77.

KOBASA, S. C. (in press). *The stress resistant personality.* In R. Ornstein & C. Swencionis (Eds.), *The healing brain: A scientific reader.* New York: Guilford Press.

KOBASA, S. C., MADDI, S., & KAHN, S. (1982). Hardiness and health: A prospective study. *Journal of Personality and Social Psychology, 42,* 168–177.

KOBASA, S. C., MADDI, S., & PUCCETTI, M. C. (1982). Personality and exercise as buffers in the stress-illness relationship. *Journal of Behavioral Medicine, 4,* 391–404.

KOBASA, S. C., & PUCCETTI, M. C. (1983). Personality and social resources in stress-resistance. *Journal of Personality and Social Psychology, 45,* 839–850.

KOESTLER, A. (1974). *The heel of Achilles: Essays 1968–1973.* London: Hutchinson.

KOGAN, N., & WALLACH, M. A. (1967). Risk taking as a function of the situation, the person, and the group. In G. Mandler (Ed.), *New directions in psychology: Vol. 3.* New York: Holt, Rinehart & Winston.

KOHLBERG, L. (1969). Stage and sequence: The cognitive developmental approach to socialization. In D. A. Goslin (Ed.), *Handbook of socialization theory and research.* Chicago: Rand McNally.

KOHLER, I. (1962). Experiments with goggles. *Scientific American, 206,* 62–86.

KOHLER, W. (1925). *The mentality of apes.* New York: Harcourt, Brace.

KOHN, B., & DENNIS, M. (1974). Selective impairments of visual-spatial abilities in infantile hemiplegics after right hemidecortication. *Neuropsychologia, 12,* 505–512.

KOLB, B., & MILNER, B. (1980). Observations on spontaneous facial expression in patients. In B. Kolb & I. Whishaw (Eds.), *Fundamentals of human neuropsychology.* (2nd ed.). San Francisco: Freeman.

KOLB, B., & WHISHAW, I. (Eds.). (1984). *Fundamentals of human neuropsychology.* (2nd ed.). San Francisco: Freeman.

KOSSLYN, S. (1986). *Image and mind.* Boston: Harvard University Press.

KRECHEVSKY, D. (1932). "Hypotheses" in rats. *Psychological Review, 39,* 516–532.

KRECH, D., ROSENZWEIG, M., & BENNETT, E. L. (1962). Relations between brain chemistry and problem-solving among rats raised in enriched and impoverished environments. *Journal of Comparative and Physiological Psychology, 55,* 801–807.

KRINGLEN, E. (1967). *Heredity and environment in the functional psychosis: An epidemiological-clinical twin study.* Oslo: Universitsferlaget.

KRUEGER, A. (1978). Ions in the air. *Human Nature, 1*(7), 46–53.

KUBLER-ROSS, E. (1969). *On death and dying.* New York: Macmillan.

KUBLER-ROSS, E. (1975). *Death: The final stage of growth.* Englewood Cliffs, NJ: Prentice-Hall.

KUHN, T. S. (1962). *The structure of scientific revolutions.* Chicago: University of Chicago Press.

KURLAND, D. M., PEA, R. D., CLEMENT, C., & MAWBY, R. (in press). A study of the development of programming ability and thinking skills in high school students. *Journal of Educational Computing Research.*

KURTINES, W., & GRIEF, E. B. (1974). The development of moral thought: Review and evaluation of Kohlberg's approach. *Psychological Bulletin, 81,* 453–470.

KUTAS, M., & HILLYARD, S. A. (1980). Reading senseless sentences: Brain potentials reflect semantic incongruity. *Science, 207,* 203–204.

KYUCHARYANTS, V. (1974). Will the human life-span reach one hundred? *Gerontologist, 14*(5), 66–68.

LABERGE, S. (1985). *Lucid dreaming.* New York: Ballantine.

LABERGE, S., NAGEL, L. E., DEMENT, W. C., & ZARCONE, V. P. (1981). Lucid dreaming verified by volitional communication during REM sleep. *Perceptual and Motor Skills, 52,* 727–732.

LACEY, J. I. (1950). Individual differences in somatic response patterns. *Journal of Comparative and Physiological Psychology, 43,* 338–350.

LACEY, J. I., BATEMAN, D. E., & VAN LEHN, R. (1953). Automatic response specificity and Rohrschach color responses. *Psychosomatic Medicine, 14,* 256–260.

LACEY, J. I., & LACEY, B. C. (1958). Verification and extension of the principle of autonomic response stereotypy. *American Journal of Psychology, 71,* 50–73.

LAING, R. D. (1959). *The divided self.* London: Travistock.

LAMARK, J. B. DE. (1951). Evolution through environmentally produced modifications. In *A source book in animal biology* (Trans. of original statement of hypothesis by Lamark).

LANCASTER, J. L. (1978). Carrying and sharing in human evolution. *Human Nature, 1*(2), 82–89.

LANGER, E. J., & ABELSON, R. P. (1974). A patient by any other name. *Journal of Consulting and Clinical Psychology, 42,* 4–9.

LANGLOIS, J. H., & DOWNS, A. C. (1980). Mothers, fathers and peers as socialization agents of sex-typed behaviors. *Child Development, 51,* 1237–1247.

LATANÉ, B., & DARLEY, J. M. (1970). *The unresponsive bystander: Why doesn't he help?* New York: Appleton-Century-Crofts.

LATANÉ, B., & RODIN, J. (1969). A lady in distress: Inhibiting effects of friends and strangers on bystander intervention. *Journal of Experimental Social Psychology, 5,* 189–202.

LAZARUS, R. S. (1976). *Patterns of adjustment* (3rd ed.). New York: McGraw-Hill.

LAZARUS, R. S. (1979, November). Positive denial: The case for not facing reality. *Psychology Today,* 44–60.

LAZARUS, R. S. (1984). Puzzles in the study of daily hassles. *Journal of Behavioral Medicine, 7,* 375–389.

LAZARUS, R. S., & FOLKMAN, S. (1986). Coping and adaptation. In W. Gentry (Ed.), *Handbook of behavioral medicine.* New York: Guilford.

LAZARUS, R. S., & LAUNIER, R. (1978). Stress-related transactions between the person and the environment. In L. A. Pervin & M. Lewis (Eds.), *Internal and external determinants of behavior.* New York: Plenum.

LEAHEY, T. H., & HARRIS, R. J. (1985). Human learning. Englewood Cliffs, NJ: Prentice-Hall.

LEAKEY, R., & LEWIN, R. (1977). *Origins.* New York: Dutton.

LEAVITT, H., & WHISLER, T. (1958). Management in the 1980s. *Harvard Business Review, 36,* 41–48.

LEFCOURT, H. (1976). *Locus of control.* New York: John Wiley.

LEHMAN, H. C. (1953). *Age and achievement.* Princeton, NJ: Princeton University Press.

LEHMAN, H. C. (1966). The psychologist's most creative years. *American Psychologist, 21*(4), 363–369.

LEIBOWITZ, S. F. (1976). In D. Novin, W. Wyrwicka, & G. A. Bray, *Hunger: Basic mechanisms and clinical implications* (pp. 1–18). New York: Raven Press.

LEMAGNEN, J. (1986). *Hunger.* New York: Cambridge University Press.

LENNEBERG, E. H. (1967). *The biological foundations of language.* New York: John Wiley.

LEONARD, C. B. (1971). Depression and suicidality. *Journal of Consulting and Clinical Psychology, 42,* 98–104.

LEPPER, M. (1985). Microcomputers in education: Motivational and social issues. *American Psychologist, 40,* 1–18.

LETTVIN, J. Y., MATURANA, H. R., McCULLOCH, S. W., & PITTS, W. H. (1959). What the frog's eye tells the frog's brain. *Proceedings of the Institute of Radio Engineers, 47,* 140–151.

LEUTENEGGER, W. (1977). Scaling of sexual dimorphism in body size and breeding system in primates. *Nature, 272,* 610–611.

LEVENSTEIN, P. (1970). Cognitive growth in pre-schooler through verbal interaction with mothers. *American Journal of Orthopsychology, 40,* 426–432.

LEVINE, J. D., & FIELDS, H. (1979). Role of pain in placebo analgesia. *Proceedings National Academy of Science,* 3528–3531.

LEVINE, J. D., & GORDON, N. C. (1984). Influence of the method of drug administration on analgesic response. *Nature, 312,* 755–756.

LEVINE, J. D., GORDON, N. C., BORNSTEIN, J. C., & FIELDS, H. L. (1979). Role of pain in placebo analgesia. *Proceedings of the Na-*
tional Academy of Sciences, 76, 3528–3531.

LEVINE, S., & URSIN, H. (1980). *Coping and health.* New York: Plenum.

LEVINSON, D. J. (1977). The midlife transition: A period in adult psychosocial development. *Psychiatry, 40,* 208–226.

LEVINSON, D. J. (with C. Darrow, E. B. Klein, M. H. Levinson, & B. McKee). (1978). *The seasons of a man's life.* New York: Knopf.

LEVY, S. M. (1984). Emotions and the progression of cancer: A review. *Advances, 1,* 10–15.

LEWINSHOHN, P. M., MISCHEL, W., & BARTON, R. (1980). Social competence and depression: The role of illusory self-perceptions. *Journal of Abnormal Psychology, 89*(2), 203–212.

LEWIS, C. N. (1971). Reminiscing and self-concept in old age. *Journal of Gerontology, 26,* 240–243.

LEWIS, M., & FREEDLE, R. (1973). Mother-infant dyad: The cradle of meaning. In P. Pliner, L. Kramer, & T. Alloway (Eds.), *Communication and affect: Language and thought.* New York: Academic Press.

LIEBER, R. M., & SPIEGLER, M. D. (1987). *Personality: Strategies and issues* (5th ed.). Chicago: Dorsey.

LIEBERMAN, M. A., & FALK, J. (1971). The remembered past as a source of data for research on the life cycle. *Human Development, 14,* 132–141.

LIEBERT, R. M., & BARON, R. A. (1972). Some immediate effects of televised violence on children's behavior. *Developmental Psychology, 6,* 469–478.

LIFTON, R. J. (1963). *Thought reform and the psychology of totalism: A study of "brainwashing" in China.* New York: Norton.

LINDEMANN, E. (1944). The symptomatology and management of acute grief. *American Journal of Psychiatry, 101,* 141.

LINDSAY, P. H., & NORMAN, D. A. (1977). *Human information processing* (2nd ed.). New York: Academic Press.

LIVINGSTON, R. B., CALLAWAY, D. F., MacGREGOR, J. S., FISCHER, G. J., & HASTINGS, A. B. (1971). U.S. poverty impact on
brain development. In M. A. B. Brazier (Ed.), *Growth and development of the brain.*

LOCKE, H. J. (1951). *Predicting adjustment in marriage: A comparison of a divorced and a happily married group.* New York: Henry Holt.

LOCKE, J. (1964). *An essay concerning human understanding.* New York: Meridian.

LOCKE, S., & COLLIGAN, D. (1986). *The healer within.* New York: Dutton.

LOCKE, S. E., KRAUS, L., LESERMAN, J., HURST, M. W., HEISEL, J. S., & WILLIAMS, R. M. (1984). Life change stress, psychiatric symptoms, and natural killer cell activity. *Psychosomatic Medicine, 46*(5), 441–453.

LOFTUS, E. F. (1978). Shifting human color memory. *Memory and Cognition, 5,* 696–699.

LOFTUS, E. F., MILLER, D. G., & BURNS, H. J. (1978). Semantic integration of verbal information into a visual memory. *Journal of Experimental Psychology, 4,* 19–31.

LOFTUS, E. F., & PALMER, J. C. (1974). Reconstruction of automobile destruction: An example of the interaction between language and memory. *Journal of Verbal Learning and Verbal Behavior, 13,* 585–589.

LOFTUS, G. R., & LOFTUS, E. F. (1974). The influence of one memory retrieval on a subsequent memory retrieval. *Memory and Cognition, 3,* 467–471.

LOFTUS, G. R., & LOFTUS, E. F. (1975). *Human memory: The processing of information.* New York: Halsted Press.

LONDON, P. (1986). *The modes and morals of psychotherapy.* New York: Harper & Row.

LONGINO, C. F., & LIPMAN, A. (1981). Married and spouseless men and women in planned retirement communities: Support network differentials. *Journal of Marriage and the Family, 43,* 169–177.

LOPATA, H. Z. (1973). *Widowhood in an American city.* Cambridge, MA: Schenkman.

LOPATA, H. Z. (1979). *Women as widows: Support systems.* New York: Elsevier.

LORENZ, K. (1966). *On aggression*

(M. K. Wilson, Trans.). New York: Harcourt Brace Jovanovich.

LORENZ, K. (1943). Die angeborenen Formen moeglicher Erfahrung. *Zeitschrift Fur Tierpsychologie, 5,* 276.

LORIG, K., LAURIN, J., & HOLMAN, H. (1984). Arthritis self-management: A study of the effectiveness of patient education for the elderly. *Gerontologist, 24,* 455–457.

LORIG, K., LAURIN, J., HOLMAN, H., BRAINERD, C., KINGMAN, J., & HOWE, M. L. (1985). On the development of forgetting. *Child Development, 56,* 1103–1119.

LOVEJOY, C. O. (1974). The gait of Australopithecines. *Yearbook of Physical Anthropology, 17,* 147–161.

LOVEJOY, C. O. (1981). The origin of man. *Science, 211,* 128–130.

LOWENSTEIN, W. R. (1960). Biological transducers. *Scientific American, 203,* 98–108.

LOWENTHAL, M. F. (1964). *Lives in distress.* New York: Basic Books.

LOWENTHAL, M. F., TURNER, M., & CHIRIBOGA, D. (1975). *The four stages of life.* San Francisco: Jossey-Bass.

LOWN, B., DESILVA, R. A., REICH, P., & MURAWSKI, B. J. (1980). Psychophysiologic factors in sudden cardiac death. *American Journal of Psychiatry, 137,* 1325–1335.

LOWN, B., VERRIER, R. L., & RABINOWITZ, S. H. (1977). Neural and psychologic mechanisms and the problem of sudden cardiac death. *The American Journal of Cardiology, 39,* 890–902.

LUBORSKY, L., SINGER, B., & LUBORSKY, L. (1975). Comparative studies of psychotherapies. *Archives of General Psychiatry, 32,* 995–1008.

LUCE, G. (1970). *Biological rhythms in psychiatry and medicine.* U.S. Public Health Service Publication No. 2088.

LUCE, G., & SEGAL, J. (1966). *Sleep.* New York: Lancet.

LUCERO, M. (1970). Lengthening of REM sleep duration consecutive to learning in the rat. *Brain Research, 20,* 319–322.

LUCHINS, A. (1942). Mechanization in problem solving. *Psychological Monographs, 54*(248).

LUCHINS, A. S., & LUCHINS, E. H.

(1959). *Rigidity of behavior: A variational approach to the effect of Einstellung.* Eugene, OR: University of Oregon Books.

LUDEL, J. (1978). *Introduction to sensory processes.* San Francisco: Freeman.

LURIA, A. R. (1968). *The mind of a mnemonist.* New York: Basic Books.

LURIA, A. R. (1973). *The working brain.* New York: Penguin.

LUTSKY, N., PEAKE, P. K., & WRAY, L. (1978). *Inconsistencies in the search for cross-situational consistencies in behavior: A critique of the Bem and Allen study.* A paper presented to the Midwestern Psychological Association, Chicago.

LYNCH, J. J. (1977). *The broken heart: The medical consequences of loneliness.* New York: Basic Books.

LYNCH, J. J. (1985). *The language of the heart.* New York: Basic Books.

LYNCH, G., McGAUGH, J., & WEINBERGER, N. (1984). *Neurobiology of learning and memory.* New York: Guilford.

LYNCH, J. J. et al. (1974). The effects of human contact on the heart activity of curarized patients in a shock-trauma unit. *American Heart Journal, 88,* 160–169.

LYNCH, J. J. et al. (1977). Psychological aspects of cardiac arrhythmia. *American Heart Journal, 93,* 645–657.

LYNCH, J. J. et al. (1982). Blood pressure changes while talking. *Israeli Journal of Medical Science, 18*(5), 575–579.

LYNN, M., & OLDENQUIST, A. (1986, May). Egoistic and non-egoistic motives in social dilemmas. *American Psychologist,* 456–463.

MacCOBY, E. (1980). *Social development: Psychological growth and the parent-child relationship.* New York: Harcourt Brace Jovanovich.

MacCOBY, E. E., & JACKLIN, C. N. (1974). *The psychology of sex differences.* Stanford: Stanford University Press.

MACE, K. C. (1972). The "overt-bluff" shoplifter: Who gets caught? *Journal of Forensic Psychology, 4,* 26–30.

MacFARLANE, A. (1978). What a baby knows. *Human Nature, 1,* 74–81.

MacLEAN, P. (1978). The triune

brain. *American Scientist, 66,* 101–113.

MADDI, S. R., & KOBASA, S. C. (1984). *The hardy executive: Health under stress.* Homewood, IL: Dow Jones-Irwin.

MAGRUDER, J. S. (1974). *An American life: One man's road to Watergate.* New York: Atheneum.

MAHONEY, M., & ARNKOFF, D. (1978). Cognitive and self-control therapies. In S. Garfield & A. Bergin (Eds.), *Handbook of psychotherapy and behavior change: An empirical analysis.* New York: John Wiley.

MAIER, S. F., & LAUDENSLAGER, M. (1985, August). Stress and health: Exploring the links. *Psychology Today,* 44–49.

MAIN, M. (1973). *Exploration, play and level of cognitive functioning as related to child-mother attachment.* Unpublished doctoral dissertation, Johns Hopkins University.

MAKINODAN, T. (1977). Immunity and aging. In C. Finch & L. Hayflick (Eds.), *Handbook of the biology of aging.* New York: Van Nostrand-Reinhold.

MALINOWSKI, B. (1955). *Sex and repression in savage society.* New York: Meridian. (Original work published 1928)

MALONE, T. W. (1981). Toward a theory of intrinsically motivating instruction. *Cognitive Science, 4,* 333–369.

MALONE, T. W., & LEPPER, M. R. (1987). Making learning fun. In R. E. Snow & M. J. Farr, *Aptitude, learning, and instruction: III. Cognitive and affective process analysis.* Hillsdale, NJ: Erlbaum.

MANDLER, G. (1980). *Mind and emotion.* New York: John Wiley.

MARKUS, H., & NURVUS, P. (1986). Possible selves. *American Psychologist, 41*(9), 954–969.

MARKUS, H. (1977). Self-schemata and processing information about the self. *Journal of Personality and Social Psychology, 35,* 63–78.

MARKUS, S., SMITH, J., & HALL, C. (1985). Role of self-conception in the perception of others. *Journal of Personality and Social Psychology, 49,* 1494–1512.

MARMOT, M. G., SYME, S. L., KAGAN, A., KATO, H., COHEN, J. B., & BELSKY, J. (1975). Epidemiological studies of coronary heart disease and stroke in Japanese men living in Japan, Hawaii, and California. *American Journal of Epidemio, 102,* 514–525.

MARMOT, M. G., & SYME, S. L. (1976). Acculturation and coronary heart disease in Japanese-Americans. *American Journal of Epidemiology, 104,* 225–247.

MARR, D. (1982). *Vision.* New York: Freeman.

MARSDEN, H. M. (1972). Crowding and animal behavior. In J. F. Wohlwill & D. H. Carson (Eds.), *Environment and the social sciences: Perspectives and applications.* Washington, DC: American Psychological Association.

MARSHAK, A. (1978). The art and symbols of Ice Age man. *Human Nature, 1*(9), 32–41.

MARSHALL, G. D., & ZIMBARDO, P. G. (1979). Affective consequences of inadequately explained physiological arousal. *Journal of Personality and Social Psychology, 37*(b), 970–988.

MASLOW, A. H. (1970). *Motivation and personality* (2nd ed.). New York: Harper & Row.

MASLOW, A. H. (1971). *The farther reaches of human nature* (2nd ed.). New York: Viking.

MASTERS, W. H., & JOHNSON, V. E. (1966). *Human sexual response.* Boston: Little, Brown.

MASTERS, W. H., JOHNSON, V. E., & KOLODNY, R. C. (1986). *Human sexuality* (2nd ed.). Boston: Little, Brown.

MATARAZZO, J., WEISS, S. M., HERD, J. A., & MILLER, N. E. (Eds.). (1984). *Behavioral health.* New York: John Wiley.

MATAS, L., AREND, R., & SROUFE, L. A. (1978). Continuity of adaptation in the second year: The relationship between quality of attachment and later competence. *Child Development, 49,* 547–556.

MAWHINNEY, V. T., BOSTON, D. E., LAWS, D. R., BLUMENFELD, G. J., & HOPKINS, B. L. (1971). A comparison of students studying: Behavior produced by daily, weekly, and three-week testing schedules. *Journal of Applied Behavioral Analysis, 4,* 257–264.

MAYER, A. D., & ROSENBLATT, J. S. (1979). Hormonal influences during the ontogeny of maternal behavior in female rats. *Journal of Comparative and Physiological Psychology, 93,* 879–898.

MAYER, J. (1953a). Genetic, traumatic and environment factors in the etiology of obesity. *Physiological Review, 33,* 472–508.

MAYER, J. (1953b). Glucostatic mechanism of regulation of food intake. *New England Journal of Medicine, 249,* 13–16.

MAYNARD SMITH, J. (1978). The evolution of behavior. In Scientific American, *Evolution.* San Francisco: Freeman.

McCLELLAND, D. C. (1971). *Motivational trends in society.* Morristown, NJ: General Learning Press.

McCLELLAND, D. C. (1975). *Power: The inner experience.* New York: Irvington.

McCLELLAND, D. C. (1984). *Achievement motivation.* New York: Free Press.

McCLELLAND, D. C. (1985a). How motives, skills, and values determine what people do. *American Psychologist, 40*(7), 812–825.

McCLELLAND, D. C. (1985b). *Human motivation.* Chicago: Scott, Foresman.

McCLELLAND, D. C., ATKINSON, J. W., CLARK, R. A., & LOWELL, E. L. (1953). *The achievement motive.* New York: Appleton-Century-Crofts.

McCLELLAND, D. C., FLOOR, E., DAVIDSON, R. J., & SARON, C. (1980). Stressed power motivation, sympathetic activation, immune function, and illness. *Journal of Human Stress, 6,* 11–19.

McCLELLAND, D. C., & JEMMOTT, J. B. (1980). Power motivation, stress and physical illness. *Journal of Human Stress, 6,* 6–15.

McCLELLAND, D. C., & KIRSHNIT, C. *The effect of motivational arousal through films on salivary immune function.* Unpublished manuscript.

McCLELLAND, D. C., ROSS, G., & PATEL, V. (1985). The effect of an academic examination on salivary norepinephrine and immunoglobulin levels. *Journal of Human Stress, 11,* 52–59.

McCLELLAND, D. C., & WINTER, D. G. (1971). *Motivating economic achievement: Accelerating economic development through psychological training.* New York: Free Press.

McCLINTOCK, M. K. (1971). Menstrual synchrony and suppression. *Nature, 229,* 244–245.

McCONNELL, P., & BERRY, M. (1978). The effects of undernutrition on Purkinje cell dendritic growth in the rat. *Journal of Comparative Neurology, 177,* 159–171.

McGLONE, J. (1980). Sex differences in human brain asymmetry: A critical survey. *Behavioral and Brain Sciences, 3*(2), 215–263.

McLEAN, A. (1979). *Work stress.* Reading, MA: Addison-Wesley.

McNEIL, E. B. (1967). *The quiet furies: Man and disorder.* Englewood Cliffs, NJ: Prentice-Hall.

MEDICAL WORLD NEWS (1986, February 24). Certain jobs linked to hypertension.

MEDNICK, S. A. (1977). A bio-social theory of the learning of law-abiding behavior. In S. A. Mednick & K. O. Christiansen (Eds.), *Biosocial bases of criminal behavior.* New York: Gardner.

MEDVEDEV, Z. A. (1974). Caucasus and Altay longevity: A biological or. social problem. *Gerontologist, 14*(5), 31–37.

MEDVEDEV, Z. A. (1975). Aging and longevity: New approaches and new perspectives. *Gerontologist, 15*(3), 196–201.

MEICHENBAUM, D. (1977). *Cognitive behavior modification: An integrative approach.* New York: Plenum.

MELLEN, S. L. W. (1981). *The evolution of love.* San Francisco: Freeman.

MELNECHUK, T. (1985). Why has psychoneuroimmunology been controversial? *Advances, 2,* 22–38.

MENNINGER, K. A. (1945). *The human mind* (3rd ed.). New York: Knopf.

MICHAELS, C. F., & CARELLO, C. (1981). *Direct perception.* Englewood Cliffs, NJ: Prentice-Hall.

MILGRAM, S. (1970). The experience of living in cities. *Science, 13,* 1461–1468.

MILGRAM, S. (1974). *Obedience to authority.* New York: Harper & Row.

MILLER, E. (1971). Handedness and the pattern of human ability. *British Journal of Psychology, 62,* 111–112.

MILLER, G. A. (1951). *Language and*

communication. New York: McGraw-Hill.

MILLER, G. A. (1981). *Language and speech.* San Francisco: Freeman.

MILLER, G. A., & BUCKHOUT, R. (1973). *Psychology: The science of mental life* (2nd ed.). New York: Harper & Row.

MILLER, G. A., GALANTER, E., & PRIBRAM, K. H. (1960). *Plans and the structure of behavior.* New York: Holt, Rinehart & Winston.

MILLER, J. (1978). *General systems theory.* New York: McGraw-Hill.

MILLER, J. (1980). *The body in question.* New York: Holt, Rinehart & Winston.

MILLER, N. (1978). Biofeedback and visceral learning. *Annual Review of Psychology, 29,* 421–452.

MILLER, N. (1980). Lecture at "The Healing Brain," Albert Einstein College of Medicine.

MINEKA, S., & SUOMI, S. J. (1978). Social separation in monkeys. *Psychological Bulletin, 85,* 1376–1400.

MINKLER, M. (1984). Social networks and health: People need people (Audio tape). Los Altos, CA: Institute for the Study of Human Knowledge.

MISCHEL, W. (1981). *Personality and assessment* (3rd ed.). New York: John Wiley.

MISCHEL, W. (1984). Convergences and challenges in the search for consistency. *American Psychologist, 39,* 351–364.

MISCHEL, W. (1986). *Introduction to personality* (4th ed.). New York: Holt, Rinehart & Winston.

MISCHEL, W., & PEAKE, P. K. (1982). Beyond deja vu in the search for cross-situational consistency. *Psychological Review, 89,* 730–755.

MONAGAN, D. (1986). Sudden death. *Discover, 7*(1), 64–71.

MONTE, C. F. (1987). *Beneath the mask: An introduction to the theories of personality* (3rd ed.). Lavellette, NJ: Holt, Rinehart & Winston.

MOOK, D. E. (1986). *Motivation, the organization of action.* New York: Norton.

MORISKY, D. E., DEMUTH, N. M., FIELD-FASS, M., GREEN, L. W., & LEVINE, D. M. (1985). Evaluation of family health education to build social support for long-term control of high blood pressure.

Health Education Quarterly, 12, 35–50.

MORISKY, D. E., LEVINE, D. M., GREEN, L. W., SHAPIRO, S., RUSSELL, R. P., & SMITH, C. R. (1983). Five-year blood pressure control and mortality following health education for hypertensive patients. *American Journal of Public Health, 73,* 153–162.

MORRIS, P. (1958). *Widows and their families.* London: Routledge.

MORRIS, P. (1974). *Loss and change.* New York: Pantheon Books.

MOSCOVITCH, M., & OLDS, J. (1980). *Asymmetries in spontaneous facial expressions and their possible relation to hemispheric specialization.* Paper presented at the meeting of the International Neuropsychology Society, Holland.

MOSCOWITZ, H. (1975, August). Hiding in the Hammond report. *Hospital Practice,* 35–39.

MOSSEY, J. M., & SHAPIRO, E. (1982). Self-rated health: A predictor of mortality among the elderly. *American Journal of Public Health, 72,* 800–807.

MOUNTCASTLE, V. B. (1976). The world around us: Neural command functions for selective attention. *Neurosciences Research Program Bulletin, 14*(Suppl.), 1–47.

MUMFORD, L. (1970). *The pentagon of power.* New York: Harcourt Brace Jovanovich.

MYERS, D. G., & LAMM, H. (1976). The group polarization phenomenon. *Psychological Bulletin, 83,* 602–627.

MYERS, R. D. (1971). Hypothalamic mechanisms of pyrogen action in the cat and monkey. In G. E. V. Wolstenholme & J. Birch (Eds.), *Ciba Foundation symposium on pyrogens and fever* (pp. 131–153). London: Churchill.

NAGLE, J. J. (1979). *Heredity and human affairs* (2nd ed.). St. Louis: Mosby.

NAUTA, W. J. H. (1971). The problem of the frontal lobe: A reinterpretation. *Journal of Psychiatric Research, 8,* 167–187.

NAUTA, W. J. H. (1973). Connections of the frontal lobe with the limbic system. In L. V. Laitinen & R. E. Livingston (Eds.), *Surgical approaches in psychiatry.* Baltimore: University Park Press.

NAVRAN, L. (1967). Communication and adjustment in marriage. *Family Process, 6,* 173–184.

NEBES, R. (1972). Dominance of the minor hemisphere in commissurotomized man in a test of figural unification. *Brain, 95,* 633–638.

NEISSER, U. C. (1976). *Cognition and reality.* San Francisco: Freeman.

NEISSER, U. C. (1979). *Cognitive psychology.* New York: Appleton-Century-Crofts.

NEISSER, U. C. (1982). *Memory observed: Remembering in natural context.* San Francisco: Freeman.

NELSON, T. O. (1976). Reinforcement and human memory. In W. K. Estes (Ed.), *Handbook of learning and cognitive processes* (Vol. 3). Hillsdale, NJ: Erlbaum.

NESER, W. B., TYROLER, H. A., & CASSEL, J. C. (1971). Social disorganization and stroke mortality in the Black population of North Carolina. *American Journal of Epidemiology, 93,* 166–175.

NEUGARTEN, B. L. (1964). Summary and implications. In B. L. Neugarten et al., *Personality in middle and late life.* New York: Atherton.

NEUGARTEN, B. L. (1974, September). Age groups in American society and the rise of the young-old. *The Annual of the American Academy of Political and Social Science,* 187–198.

NEUGARTEN, B. L. (1977). Personality and aging. In J. E. Birren & K. W. Schaie (Eds.), *Handbook of the psychology of aging.* New York: Van Nostrand-Reinhold.

NEUGARTEN, B. L., & HAGESTAD, G. O. (1976). Age and the life course. In R. H. Binstock & E. Shanas (Eds.), *Handbook of aging and the social sciences.* New York: Van Nostrand-Reinhold.

NEUGARTEN, B. L., HAVIGHURST, D. J., & TOBIN, S. S. (1968). Personality and patterns of aging. In B. L. Neugarten (Ed.), *Middle age and aging.* Chicago: University of Chicago Press.

NEUGARTEN, B. L., MOORE, J. W., & LOWE, J. C. (1965). Age norms, age constraints, and adult socialization. *American Journal of Sociology, 70*(6), 710–717.

NEUGARTEN, B. L., & PETERSON, W. (1957). A study of the American age-grade system. *Fourth Congress of the International Association of Gerontology, Vol. 3.* Florence, Italy: Tito Mattiolo.

NEUGARTEN, B. L., & WEINSTEIN, K. (1964). The changing American grandparent. *Journal of Marriage and Family, 24*(2), 199–204.

NEUGARTEN, B. L., WOOD, V., KRAINES, R. J., & LOOMIS, B. (1963). Women's attitudes toward the menopause. *Vita Humana, 6*(3), 140–151.

NEVILLE, H. (1977). EEG testing of cerebral specialization in normal and congenitally deaf children: A preliminary report. In S. J. Segalowitz & F. A. Gruber (Eds.), *Language development and neurological theory.* New York: Academic Press.

NEWCOMB, T. M. (1943). *Personality and social change.* New York: Dryden.

NEWCOMB, T. M., KOENIG, K. E., FLACKS, R., & WARWICK, D. P. (1967). *Persistence and change: Bennington College and its students after twenty-five years.* New York: John Wiley.

NEWELL, A., & SIMON, H. A. (1972). *Human problem solving.* Englewood Cliffs, NJ: Prentice-Hall.

NEWELL, A., & SIMON, H. A. (1976). Computer science as empirical enquiry: Symbols and search. *Communications of the ACM, 19,* 113–126.

NEWMAN, B. N., & NEWMAN, P. R. (1987). *Development through life.* Chicago: Dorsey.

NEWMAN, J., & McCAULEY, C. (1977). Eye contact with strangers in city, suburb, and small town. *Environment and Behavior, 9*(4), 547–558.

NEWMAN, O. (1979). Community of interest. *Human Nature, 2*(1).

NEWTON, N., & MODAHL, C. (1978). Pregnancy: The closest human relationship. *Human Nature, 1*(3), 40–50.

NISAN, M., & KOHLBERG, L. (1982). Universality and variation in moral judgment: A longitudinal and cross-sectional study in Turkey. *Child Development, 53,* 865–876.

NISBETT, R. E. (1968). Taste, deprivation, and weight determinants of eating behavior. *Journal of Personality and Social Psychology, 10,* 107–116.

NISBETT, R. E. (1972). Hunger, obesity, and the ventromedial hypothalamus. *Psychological Review, 79*(6), 433–453.

NISBETT, R. E., CAPUTO, C., LEGANT, P., & MARACEK, J. (1973). Behavior as seen by the actor and as seen by the observer. *Journal of Personality and Social Psychology, 27,* 154–164.

NISBETT, R. E., & ROSS, L. (1981). *Human inference: Strategies and shortcomings of social judgment.* Englewood Cliffs, NJ: Prentice-Hall.

NORMAN, D. (1983). *Learning and memory.* San Francisco: Freeman.

NORTH, C. (1987). *Welcome, Silence.* New York: Simon & Schuster.

NUCKOLLS, K. B., CASSEL, J., & KAPLAN, B. H. (1972). Psychosocial assets, life crisis, and the prognosis of pregnancy. *American Journal of Epidemiology, 95,* 431–441.

OLDS, J. (1958). Self-stimulation of the brain. *Science, 127,* 315–323.

OLDS, J., & MILNER, P. (1954). Positive reinforcement produced by electrical stimulation of septal area and other regions of rat brain. *Journal of Comparative Physiological Psychology, 47,* 419–427.

O'LEARY, A. (1985). Self-efficacy and health. *Behavioral Research and Therapy, 23,* 437–451.

OMARK, D. R., & EDELMAN, M. (1973). *Peer group social interactions from an evolutionary perspective.* Paper presented at the meetings of the Society for Research in Child Development, Philadelphia.

ORNSTEIN, R. (1969). *On the experience of time.* London: Penguin Books.

ORNSTEIN, R. (Ed.). (1973). *The nature of human consciousness.* San Francisco: Freeman.

ORNSTEIN, R. (1976). *The mind field.* London: Octagon Press.

ORNSTEIN, R. (1986a). *Multimind.* Boston: Houghton Mifflin.

ORNSTEIN, R. (1986b). *The psychology of consciousness* (3rd ed.). New York: Penguin.

ORNSTEIN, R., HERRON, J., JOHNSTONE, J., & SWENCIONIS, C. (1979). Differential right hemisphere involvement in two reading tasks. *Psychophysiology, 16*(4), 398–401.

ORNSTEIN, R., & SOBEL, D. (1987). *The healing brain.* New York: Simon & Schuster.

ORNSTEIN, R., & SWENCIONIS, C. (1985). Analytic and synthetic problem-solving strategies in hemispheric asymmetry. *Neuropsychologia.*

ORNSTEIN, R., THOMPSON, R., & MACAULAY, D. (1984). *The amazing brain.* Boston: Houghton Mifflin.

OSGOOD, C., SUCI, G. J., & TANNENBAUM, P. H. (1971). *The measurement of meaning.* Urbana, IL: University of Illinois Press.

OSIS, K., & HANALOSEN, E. (1977). *At the hour of death.* New York: Avon Books.

OSWALD, I. (1962). *Sleeping and waking.* Amsterdam, NY: Elsevier.

OZER, D. J. (1986). *Consistency in personality: A methodological framework.* New York: Springer-Verlag.

PAFFENBERGER, R. (1986). *The American way of life is dangerous to your health.* San Francisco: Freeman.

PAPERT, S. (1980). *Mindstorms: Children, computers, and powerful ideas.* New York: Basic Books.

PAPEZ, J. W. (1937). A proposed mechanism of emotion. *Archives of Neurology and Psychiatry, 38,* 725–743.

PARKES, C. M. (1972). *Bereavement: Studies of grief in adult life.* New York: International Universities Press.

PARKES, C. M., BENJAMIN, B., & FITZGERALD, R. G. (1969). Broken heart: A statistical study of increased mortality among widows. *British Medical Journal, 1,* 740.

PATTISON, E. M. (1977). The will to live and the expectation of death. In E. M. Pattison (Ed.), *The experience of dying* (pp. 61–74). Englewood Cliffs, NJ: Prentice-Hall.

PAUL, G. L. (1965). Effects of insight, desensitization, and attention-placebo treatment of anxiety: An approach to outcome research in psychotherapy. *Dissertation Abstracts, 25*(9), 5388–5389.

PAVLOV, I. P. (1927). *Conditioned reflexes.* London: Oxford University Press.

PAVLOV, I. P. (1928). *Lectures on conditioned reflexes.* New York: International Publishers.

PAVLOV, I. P. (1941). *Conditional reflexes and psychiatry*. (W. H. Gantt, Ed. and Trans.). New York: International Publishers.

PAXTON, A. L., & TURNER, E. J. (1978). Self-actualization and sexual permissiveness, satisfaction, prudishness, and drive among female undergraduates. *Journal of Sex Research, 14*(2), 65–80.

PEA, R. D., & KURLAND, D. M. (in press). On the cognitive effects of learning computer programming: A critical look. *New Ideas on Psychology.*

PEARLIN, L. (1980). Life strains and psychological distress among adults. In N. J. Smelser & E. H. Erikson (Eds.), *Themes of work and love in adulthood.* Cambridge, MA: Harvard University Press.

PEARLIN, L., & JOHNSON, J. (1977). Marital stress, life strains and depression. *American Sociological Review, 42,* 704–715.

PECK, M. A., & SCHRUT, A. (1971). Suicidal behavior among college students. *HSMHA Health Reports, 86*(2), 149–156.

PECK, R., & BERKOWITZ, H. (1964). Personality and adjustment in middle age. In B. L. Neugarten et al., *Personality in middle and late life* (pp. 15–43). New York: Atherton.

PENFIELD, W. (1975). *The mystery of the mind.* Princeton: Princeton University Press.

PENNEBAKER, J. W., DYER, M. A., CAULKINS, R. S., LITOWITZ, D. L., ACKERMAN, P. L., ANDERSON, D. B., & McGRAW, K. M. (1979). Don't the girls get prettier at closing time. *Personality and Social Psychology Bulletin, 5,* 122–125.

PETTIGREW, J. (1961). Social psychology and desegregation research. *American Psychologist, 15,* 61–71.

PHILLIPS, D. P. (1974). The influence of suggestion on suicide: Substantive and theoretical implications of the Werther effect. *American Sociological Review, 39,* 340–354.

PHILLIPS, D. P. (1979). Suicide, motor vehicle fatalities, and the mass media: Evidence toward a theory of suggestion. *American*

Journal of Sociology, 84, 1150–1174.

PHILLIPS, D. P. (1980). Airplane accidents, murder, and the mass media: Towards a theory of imitation and suggestion. *Social Forces, 58,* 1001–1024.

PHILLIPS, D. P. (1983). The impact of mass media violence on U.S. homicides. *American Sociological Review, 48,* 560–568.

PHILLIPS, D. P., & FELDMAN, K. A. (1973). A dip in deaths before ceremonial occasions: Some new relationships between social integration and mortality. *American Sociological Review, 38,* 678–696.

PIAGET, J. (1952). *The origins of intelligence in children.* New York: International Universities Press.

PIAGET, J. (1960). *The moral judgment of the child.* Glencoe, IL: Free Press. (Original work published 1932)

PILBEAM, O. (1972). *The ascent of man.* New York: Macmillan.

PILISUK, M., & MINKLER, M. (1980). Supportive networks: Life ties for the elderly.*Journal of Social Issues, 36*(2), 95–116.

PINKER, S. (Ed.). (1985). *Visual cognition.* Cambridge, MA: MIT/Bradford.

PLUTCHIK, R. (1980). *Emotion: A psychoevolutionary synthesis.* New York: Harper & Row.

PLUTCHIK, R. (1984). Emotions: A general psychoevolutionary theory. In K. Scherer & P. Ekman (Eds.), *Approaches to emotion.* Hillsdale, NJ: Erlbaum.

POINCARÉ, H. (1921). The value of science. In G. B. Halstead (Trans.), *The foundations of science.* New York: Science Press.

POLIVY, J., & HERMAN, P. (1983). *Breaking the diet habit: A natural weight alternative.* Boston: Houghton Mifflin.

POLYA, G. (1957). *How to solve it.* Garden City, NY: Doubleday/Anchor.

POOL, I. DE S. (Ed.). (1977). *The social impact of the telephone.* Cambridge, MA: MIT Press.

POON, L. W. (1985). Memory skill training for the elderly. *Psychological Reports, 45,* 345–349.

POON, L. W. et al. (Eds.). (1980).

New directions in memory and aging. Hillsdale, NJ: Erlbaum.

PREMACK, D. (1965). Reinforcement theory. *Nebraska symposium on motivation.* Lincoln: University of Nebraska Press.

PREMTICE, N. M. (1972). The influence of live and symbolic modeling on promoting moral judgment of adolescent delinquents.*Journal of Abnormal Psychology, 80*(2), 157–161.

PRETI, G. et al. (in press). Male pheromones and the menstrual cycle. *Hormones and Behavior.*

PREVOST, F. (1975). An indication of sexual and aggressive similarities through humour appreciation. *Journal of Psychology, 91,* 283–288.

PRICE, J. S. (1968). The genetics of depressive disorder. In A. Coppen & A. Walk (Eds.), Recent developments in affective disorders. *British Journal of Psychiatry, Special Publication, 2.*

PROSSER, H. A. (1978). Social factors affecting the timing of the first child. In W. Miller & L. Neuman (Eds.), *The first child and family formation.* Chapel Hill, NC: Carolina Population Center.

QUAY, H. C. (1965). Psychopathic personality as pathological stimulation-seeking. *American Journal of Psychiatry, 122,* 180–183.

RABKIN, J. G., GELB, L., & LAZAR, J. B. (Eds.). (1980). *Attitudes toward the mentally ill: Research perspectives.* Rockville, MD: National Institute of Mental Health.

RABKIN, S. W., MATHEWSON, F., & TATE, R. B. (1980). Chronobiological cardiac sudden death in men. *Journal of the American Medical Association, 244,* 1357–1358.

RACHMAN, S. (1978). *Fear and courage.* San Francisco: Freeman.

RADLOFF, L. (1975). Sex differences in depress: The effect of occupation and marital status. *Sex Roles, 1,* 249–265.

RAHE, R. H., & ARTHUR, R. J. (1978, March). Life change and illness studies: Past history and future directions. *Journal of Human Stress,* 24–39.

RAHULA, W. (1969). *What the Buddha taught.* New York: Grove.

RANDI, J. (1975). *The magic of Uri Geller.* New York: Ballantine.

RAUDICH, A., & LOLORDO, V. M. (1979). Associative and nonassociative theories of the UCS preexposure phenomenon: Implications for Pavlovian conditioning. *Psychological Bulletin, 86*, 523–548.

RAZRAN, G. (1939). A quantitative study of meaning by conditioned salivary technique (semantic conditioning). *Science, 90*, 89–91.

REDMOND, D. E., HUANG, Y. H., BAULU, J., SNYDER, R. V., & MAAS, J. W. (1971). In R. A. Vigersky (Ed.), *Anorexia nervosa*, 81–96. New York: Raven Press.

REES, W. D. (1971). The hallucinations of widowhood. *British Medical Journal, 4*, 37–41.

REICH, J., & ZAUTRA, A. (1981). Life events and personal causation: Some relationships with satisfaction and distress. *Journal of Personality and Social Psychology, 41*, 1002–1012.

REICHARD, S., LIVSON, F., & PETERSON, P. (1962). *Aging and personality: A study of eighty-seven older men.* New York: John Wiley.

REID, D. K. (1977). *Early identification of children with learning disabilities.* New York: Regional Access Project, Region 11, New York University.

REISMAN, D., GLAZER, N., & DENNEY, R. (1950). *The lonely crowd: A study of the changing American character.* New Haven, CT: Yale University Press.

REITE, M., & FIELDS, T. (Eds.). (1985). *The psychobiology of attachment and separation.* New York: Academic Press.

REST, J. R., DAVISON, M. L., & ROBBINS, S. (1978). Age trends in judging moral issues: A review of cross-sectional, longitudinal, and sequential studies of the defining issues test. *Child Development, 49*, 263–279.

REVUSKY, S., & GARCIA, J. (1970). Learned associations over long delays. In G. H. Bower (Ed.), *The psychology of learning and motivation: Advances in research in theory: Vol. 4.* New York: Academic Press.

RICHARDS, M., & LIGHT, P. (1986). *Children of social worlds.* Boston: Harvard University Press.

RIEGEL, K. F., & RIEGEL, R. M. (1972). Development, drop, and death. *Developmental Psychology, 9*, 306–319.

RING, K. (1980). *Life at death: A scientific investigation of the near-death experience.* New York: Coward-McCann.

RING, K. (1984). *Heading toward omega.* New York: Morrow.

ROAZIN, P. (1986). *Erik Erikson.* New York: Free Press.

ROBEY, D. (1981). Computer information systems and organizational structure. *Communications of the ACM, 24*, 679–687.

ROBINSON, B., & THURNER, M. (1979). Taking care of aged parents: A family cycle. *Transition Gerontologist, 19*(6), 67–82.

ROCK, I. (1985). *Perception.* New York: Scientific American.

RODIN, J. (1986). Aging and health: Effects of the sense of control. *Science, 233*, 1271–1276.

RODIN, J., & LANGER, E. (1977). Long-term effects of a control-relevant intervention with the institutional aged. *Journal of Personality and Social Psychology, 35*(12), 897–902.

ROGERS, C. R. (1951). *Client-centered therapy.* Boston: Houghton Mifflin.

ROGERS, C. R. (1959). A theory of therapy, personality and interpersonal relationships, as developed in the client-centered framework. In S. Koch (Ed.), *Psychology: A study of a science: Vol. 3* (pp. 184–256). New York: McGraw-Hill.

ROGERS, C. R. (1970). *On becoming a person: A therapist's view of psychotherapy.* Boston: Houghton Mifflin.

ROGERS, C. R. (1972). Some social issues which concern me. *Journal of Humanistic Psychology, 12*(2), 45–60.

ROGERS, C. R. (1974). In retrospect: Forty-six years. *American Psychologist, 29*, 115–123.

ROGERS, C. R. (1980). *A way of being.* Boston: Houghton Mifflin.

ROGERS, T. B., KULPER, N. A., & KIRKER, W. S. (1977). Self-reference and the encoding of personal information. *Journal of Personality and Social Psychology, 35*, 677–688.

ROKEACH, M. (1960). *The open and closed mind.* New York: Basic Books.

ROKEACH, M. (1973). *The nature of human values.* New York: Free Press.

ROSCH, E. (1973). Natural categories. *Cognitive Psychology, 4*, 328–350.

ROSCH, E. (1975). Cognitive representation of semantic categories. *Journal of Experimental Psychology, 104*, 192–233.

ROSCH, E., & MERVIS, C. (1975). Family resemblances: Studies in the internal structure of categories. *Cognitive Psychology, 7*, 573–605.

ROSCH, E., MERVIS, C., GRAY, W., JOHNSON, D., & BOYES-BRAEM, P. (1976). Basic objects in natural categories. *Cognitive Psychology, 8*, 382–439.

ROSEKRANS, M. A., & HARTUP, W. W. (1967). Imitative influences of consistent and inconsistent response consequences to a model on aggressive behavior in children. *Journal of Personality and Social Psychology, 7*, 429–434.

ROSEN, B. C. (1959). Race, ethnicity, and the achievement syndrome. *American Sociological Review, 24*, 47–60.

ROSEN, G. (1946). Mesmerism and surgery: A strange chapter in the history of anaesthesia. *Journal of the History of Medicine, 1*, 527–550.

ROSENHAN, D. L. (1973). On being sane in insane places. *Science, 179*, 250–258.

ROSENHAN, D. L., & SELIGMAN, M. (1985). *Abnormal psychology.* New York: Norton.

ROSENMAN, R. H., BRAND, R. J., JENKINS, C. D., FRIEDMAN, M. et al. (1975). Coronary heart disease in the Western Collaborative Study: Final follow-up experience of eight and one-half years. *Journal of the American Medical Association, 223*, 872–877.

ROSENMAN, R. H., & FRIEDMAN, M. (1980). The relationship of Type A behavior pattern to coronary heart disease. In H. Selye (Ed.), *Selye's guide to stress research: Vol. 1.* New York: Van Nostrand-Reinhold.

ROSENTHAL, D. (Ed.). (1963). *The Genain quadruplets.* New York: Basic Books.

ROSENTHAL, D. (1970). *Genetic*

theory and abnormal behavior. New York: McGraw-Hill.

ROSENTHAL, N. E. (1986, August). *Seasonal affective depression.* Paper delivered at American Psychological Association meeting.

ROSENTHAL, N. E., SACK, D. A. et al. (1984). Seasonal affective disorder: A description of the syndrome and preliminary findings with light therapy. *Archives of General Psychiatry, 41,* 72–80.

ROSENTHAL, R. (1966). *Experimenter effects in behavioral research.* New York: Appleton-Century-Crofts.

ROSENTHAL, R., & ROSNOW, R. (1985). *Contrast analysis: Focused comparisons in the analysis of variance.* New York: Cambridge University Press.

ROSS, A. O. (1987). *Personality: The scientific study of complex human behavior.* Lavallette, NJ: Holt, Rinehart & Winston.

ROSS, L. (1969). *Cue- and cognition-controlled eating among obese and normal subjects.* Unpublished doctoral dissertation, Columbia University.

ROSS, L. (1977). The intuitive psychologist and his shortcomings: Distortions in the attribution process. In L. Berkowitz (Ed.), *Advances in experimental social psychology: Vol. 10.* New York: Academic Press.

ROSS, L., AMABILE, T. M., & STEINMETZ, J. L. (1977). Social roles, social control, and biases in social-perception process. *Journal of Personality and Social Psychology, 35,* 485–494.

ROSS, L., GREENE, D., & HOUSE, P. (1977). The false consensus phenomenon: An attributional bias in self-perception and social perception processes. *Journal of Experimental Social Psychology, 13,* 279–301.

ROSS, L., & NISBETT, R. (in preparation) *The person and the situation.*

ROTHWELL, N. J., & STOCK, M. J. (1979). Regulation of energy balance in two models of reversible obesity in the rat. *Journal of Comparative and Physiological Psychology, 93(6),* 1024–1034.

ROTTER, J. B. (1966). Generalized expectancies of internal versus external control of reinforcement. *Psychological Monographs, 81*(1 Whole No. 609).

ROUTENBERG, A. (1976). The reward system of the brain. *Scientific American, 239,* 154–164.

RUBIN, D. C. (1977). Very long-term memory for prose and verse. *Journal of Verbal Learning and Verbal Behavior, 16,* 611–621.

RUBIN, J. Z., PROVENZANO, F. J., & LURIA, Z. (1974). The eye of the beholder: Parents' view on sex of newborns. *American Journal of Orthopsychiatry, 44,* 512–519.

RUBIN, L. B. (1976). *Worlds of pain.* New York: Basic Books.

RUBIN, Z. (1980). *Children's friendships.* Cambridge, MA: Harvard University Press.

RUMBAUT, R. G., ANDERSON, J. P., & KAPLAN, R. M. (in press). Stress, health and the "sense of coherence." In M. J. Megenheim (Ed.), *Geriatric medicine and the social Sciences.* Philadelphia: Saunders.

RUSSELL, B. (1929). *Marriage and morals.* New York: Liveright.

RUSSELL, B. (1979). In D. Tennov, *Love and limerance* (p. 56). New York: Stein & Day.

SACKHEIM, H. A., GUR, R. C., & SAUCY, M. C. (1978). Emotions are expressed more intensely on the left side of the face. *Science, 202(4366),* 434–436.

SACKS, O. (1986). *The man who mistook his wife for a hat.* New York: Simon & Schuster.

SAHLINS, M. (1972). *Stone Age economics.* Chicago: Aldine.

SALAPATEK, O., & KESSEN, W. (1966). Visual scanning of triangles by the human newborn. *Journal of Experimental Child Psychology, 3,* 111–122.

SARASON, I. G., & SARASON, B. G. (1984). *Abnormal psychology.* New Jersey: Prentice-Hall.

SAUTER, S. L., GOTTLIEB, M. S., JONES, K. C., DODSON, V. N., & ROHRER, K. M. (1983). Job and health implications of VDT use: Initial results of the Wisconsin-NIOSH study. *Communications of the ACM, 26,* 284–294.

SCARR, S. (1981). *Race, social class, and individual differences in IQ.* Hillsdale, NJ: Erlbaum.

SCARR, S. (1984). *Mothercare/othercare.* New York: Basic Books.

SCARR, S., & CARTER-SALTZMANN, L. (1983). Genetic differences in intelligence. In R. A. Sternberg (Ed.), *Handbook of intelligence.* Cambridge, MA: Harvard University Press.

SCARR, S., & WEINBERG, R. A. (1978). Attitudes, interests, and IQ. *Human Nature, 1(4),* 29–37.

SCHACHTER, S. (1959). *The psychology of affiliation: Experimental studies of the sources of gregariousness.* Stanford: Stanford University Press.

SCHACHTER, S. (1971). Some extraordinary facts about obese humans and rats. *American Psychologist, 26(2),* 129–144.

SCHACHTER, S., & RODIN, J. (1974). *Obese humans and rats.* Potomac, MD: Erlbaum.

SCHACHTER, S., & SINGER, J. (1962). Cognitive, social, and physiological determinants of emotional state. *Psychological Review, 69,* 379–399.

SCHAFFER, H. R., & EMERSON, P. E. (1964). The development of social attachments in infancy. *Monographs of the Society for Research in Child Development, 29(3,* Serial No. 94).

SCHANK, R. C., & COLBY, K. M. (Eds.). (1973). *Computer models of thought and language.* San Francisco: Freeman.

SCHERER, K., WALLBOTT, H., & SUMMERFIELD, A. (1986). *Experiencing emotion: A cross-cultural study.* New York: Cambridge University Press.

SCHERWITZ, L., BERTON, K., & LEVENTHAL, H. M. (1984). Type A behavior, self-involvement and cardiovascular response. *Psychosomatic Medicine, 40,* 593–609.

SCHERWITZ, L., GRAHAM, L. E., & ORNISH, D. (1985). Self-involvement and the risk factors for coronary heart disease. *Advances, 2,* 6–18.

SCHERWITZ, L., McKELVAIN, R., LAMAN, C. et al. (1983). Type A behavior, self-involvement, and coronary atherosclerosis. *Psychosomatic Medicine, 45,* 47–57.

SCHLIEFER, S. J., KELLER, S. E., CAMERINO, M., THORNTON,

J. C., & STEIN, M. (1983). Suppression of lymphocyte stimulation following bereavement. *Journal of the American Medical Association, 250,* 374–377.

SCHMALE, A., & IKER, H. (1966). The affect of hopelessness and the development of cancer: I. Identification of uterine cervical cancer in women with atypical cytology. *Psychosomatic Medicine, 28,* 714–721.

SCHMALE, A., & IKER, H. (1971). Hopelessness as a predictor of cervical cancer. *Social Science and Medicine, 5,* 95–100.

SCHMALLEGER, F. (1979). World of the career criminal. *Human Nature, 2*(3), 50–58.

SCHMIDT, D. D., ZYZANSKI, S., ELLNER, J., KUMAR, M. L., & ARNO, J. (1985). Stress as a precipitating factor in subjects with recurrent herpes labialis. *Journal of Family Practice, 20,* 359–366.

SCHULSINGER, F. (1972). Psychopathy, heredity, and environment. *International Journal of Mental Health, 1,* 190–206.

SCHWARTZ, G. E., DAVIDSON, R. J., & MAER, F. (1975). Right hemispheric lateralization for emotion in the human brain: Interactions with cognition. *Science, 190*(4211), 286–288.

SCHWARTZ, S., & GRIFFIN, T. (1986). *Medical thinking: The psychology of medical judgment and decision making.* New York: Springer-Verlag.

SEARLE, J. (1984). *Minds, brains and science.* Boston: Harvard University Press.

SEEMAN, T. (1985). Social support and angiography. Unpublished doctoral thesis, University of California, Berkeley.

SEGAL, M. H., CAMPBELL, D. T., & HERSKOVITS, M. J. (1963). Cultural differences in the perception of geometric illusions. *Science, 139,* 769–771.

SELFE, L. (1977). *Nadia, a case of extraordinary drawing ability in an autistic child.* London: Academic Press.

SELIGMAN, M. E. P. (1970). On the generality of the law of learning. *Psychological Review, 77,* 406–418.

SELIGMAN, M. E. P. (1973). Fall into hopelessness. *Psychology Today, 7*(1), 43–48.

SELIGMAN, M. E. P. (1975). *Helplessness: On depression, development and death.* San Francisco: Freeman.

SELIGMAN, M. E. P., & HAGER, J. (1972). *Biological boundaries of learning.* New York: Appleton-Century-Crofts.

SELYE, H. (1956). *The stress of life.* New York: McGraw-Hill.

SELYE, H. (1978). They all looked sick to me. *Human Nature, 1*(2), 58–63.

SHAH, I. (1970). *Tales of the dervishes.* New York: Dutton.

SHAH, I. (1971). *The pleasantries of the incredible Mulla Nasrudin.* New York: Dutton.

SHAH, I. (1982). *Seeker after truth.* San Francisco: Harper & Row.

SHAH, I. (1986). *The exploits and subtleties of Mulla Nasrudin.* London: Octagon Press.

SHANAS, E. (1979). Social myth as hypothesis: The case of the family relations and old people. *Gerontologist, 19*(1), 3–9.

SHANAS, E., TOWNSEND, D., WEDDERBURN, D., FRIIS, H., MILHOJ, P., & STENOUWER, J. (1968). *Older people in three industrial societies.* New York: Atherton Press.

SHANON, B. (1979). Yesterday, today and tomorrow. *Acta Psychologica, 43,* 469–476.

SHATAN, C. (1978). Stress disorders among Vietnam veterans: The emotional context of combat continues. In C. R. Figley, *Stress disorders among Vietnam veterans.* New York: Brunner/Mazel.

SHEDLER, J., & MANIS, M. (1986). Can the availability heuristic explain vividness effects? *Journal of Personality and Social Psychology, 51,* 26–36.

SHEPARD, R. (1967). Recognition memory for words, sentences, and pictures. *Journal of Verbal Learning and Verbal Behavior, 6,* 156–163.

SHEPARD, R. (1984). Ecological constraints in internam representation. *Psychological Review, 94*(4), 417–447.

SHEPARD, R., & SHEENAN, M. M. (1963). Immediate recall of numbers containing a familiar prefix or postfix. *Perceptual and Motor Skills, 21,* 263–273.

SHERIF, M., HARVEY, O. J., WHITE, B. J., HOOD, W., & SHERIF, C. (1961). *Intergroup conflict and cooperation: The robbers' cave experiment.* Norman: University of Oklahoma Institute of Intergroup Relations.

SHIRLEY, M. N. (1933). The first two years. *Institute of Child Welfare Monograph, 7.* Minneapolis: University of Minnesota Press.

SIEGEL, R. K. (1980). The psychology of life after death. *American Psychologist, 35,* 911–931.

SIEGEL, R. K. (1981). Accounting for "afterlife experiences." *Psychology Today, 15,* 64–75.

SIEGEL, S. (1976). Morphine analgesic tolerance: Its situational specificity supports a Pavlovian conditioning model. *Science, 193,* 323–325.

SILVERMAN, L. H. (1983). The subliminal psychodynamic activation method. *Empirical studies of psychoanalytic theories.* J. Masling (Ed.). Hillsdale, NJ: Erlbaum.

SIMON, W., BERGER, A. S., & GAGNON, J. S. (1972). Beyond anxiety and fantasy: The coital experiences of college youth. *Journal of Youth and Adolescence, 1,* 203–222.

SINCLAIR-GIEBEN, A. H. C., & CHALMERS, D. (1959). Evaluation of treatment of warts by hypnosis. *Lancet, 11,* 480–482.

SINGER, B., & LUBORSKY, L. (1975). Comparative studies of psychotherapies: Is it true that "everyone has won and all must have prizes?" *Archives of General Psychiatry, 32*(8), 995–1008.

SINGER, J. L. (1976). *The inner world of daydreaming.* New York: Harper & Row.

SINGER, J. L. (1984). *The human personality.* New York: Harcourt Brace Jovanovich.

SINGER, S., & HILGARD, H. (1978). *The biology of people.* San Francisco: Freeman.

SINGER, J. L., & SINGER, D. G. (1981). *Television, imagination and aggression.* Hillsdale, NJ: Erlbaum.

SKEELS, H. M. (1966). Adult status of children with contrasting early life experience. *Monographs of the*

Society for Research in Child Development, 31(3), 1–65.

SKEELS, H. M., & DYE, H. B. (1939). A study of the effects of differential stimulation of mentally retarded children. *Proceedings of the American Association on Mental Deficiency, 44*, 114–136.

SKEELS, J. M., & HAMS, I. (1948). Children with inferior social histories; their mental development in adoptive homes. *Journal of Genetic Psychology, 72*, 283–294.

SKINNER, B. F. (1938). *The behavior of organisms*. New York: Appleton-Century-Crofts.

SKINNER, B. F. (1972). *Cumulative record: A collection of papers* (3rd ed.). New York: Appleton-Century-Crofts.

SKINNER, B. F. (1981). Selection by consequences. *Science, 213*, 501–504.

SKINNER, B. F. (1982). *Notebooks.* R. Epstein (Ed.). Englewood Cliffs, NJ: Prentice-Hall.

SKINNER, B. F. (1986). What is wrong with daily life in the western world? *American Psychologist, 41*(5), 568–574.

SKOLNICK, A. (1986). *The psychology of human development*. San Diego: Harcourt Brace Jovanovich.

SLATER, E., & COWIE, V. (1971). *The genetics of mental disorders*. London: Oxford University Press.

SLOBIN, D. I. (1970). Universals of grammatical development in children. In G. B. Flores d'Arcais & W. J. M. Levelt (Eds.), *Advances in psycholinguistics.* Amsterdam: North-Holland Publishing.

SMILANSKY, B. (1974). Paper presented at the meeting of the American Educational Research Association, Chicago.

SMITH, M. L., GLASS, G. V., & MILLER, T. I. (1980). *Benefits of psychotherapy*. Baltimore: Johns Hopkins University Press.

SNOW, R. E., & FARR, M. J. (Eds.). (in press). *Aptitude, learning, and instruction: III. Conative and affective process analysis*. Hillsdale, NJ: Erlbaum.

SNYDER, M. (1987). *Public appearances/private realities*. New York: Freeman.

SNYDER, S. H. (1980a). *Biological aspects of mental disorder.* New York: Oxford University Press.

SNYDER, S. H. (1980b). Brain peptides and neurotransmitters. *Science, 209*, 976–983.

SOLOMON, G. F., & AMKRAUT, A. A. (1981). Psychoneuroendocrinological effects on the immune response. *Annual Review of Microbiology, 35*, 155–184.

SOLOMON, M. R., & SCHOPLER, J. (1978). The relationship of physical attractiveness and punitiveness: Is the linearity assumption out of line? *Personality and Social Psychology Bulletin, 4*, 483–486.

SOLOMON, R. L. (1980). The opponent-process theory of acquired motivation: The costs of pleasure and the benefits of pain. *American Psychologist, 35*, 691–712.

SOLOMON, R. L., & CORBIT, J. D. (1973). An opponent-process theory of motivation: I. Cigarette addiction. *Journal of Abnormal Psychology, 81*, 158–171.

SOLOMON, R. L., & CORBIT, J. D. (1974). An opponent-process theory of motivation: II. Temporal dynamics of affect. *Psychological Review, 81*, 119–145.

SOLOMON, S., & SAXE, L. (1977). What is intelligent, as well as attractive, is good. *Personality and Social Psychology Bulletin, 3*, 670–673.

SPANIER, G. B., & GLICK, P. C. (1981). Marital instability in the U.S.: Some correlates and recent changes. *Family Relations, 31*, 329–338.

SPEARMAN, C. (1927). *The abilities of man*. New York: Macmillan.

SPEISMAN, J. C., LAZARUS, R. S., DAVIDSON, L., & MORDKOFF, A. M. (1964). Experimental analysis of a film used as a threatening stimulus. *Journal of Consulting Psychology, 28*(1), 23–33.

SPENCE, D. (1983). The paradox of denial. In S. Bresnitz (Ed.), *The denial of stress*. New York: International Universities Press.

SPERRY, R. (1982). Some effects of disconnecting the cerebral hemispheres. *Science, 217*, 1223–1226, 1250.

SPERRY, R. W. (1952). Neurology and the mind-brain problem. *American Scientist, 40*, 291–312.

SPITZER, R. L., SKODOL, A. E., GIBBON, M., & WILLIAMS, J. B. (1980). *Diagnostic and statistical manual of mental disorders* (3rd ed.). (DSM-III). Washington, DC: American Psychiatric Association.

SPITZER, R. L., SKODOL, A. E., GIBBON, M., & WILLIAMS, J. B. (1981). *DSM-III Casebook* (3rd ed.). Washington, DC: American Psychiatric Association.

SPRECHER, S., & HATFIELD, E. (1985). Interpersonal attraction. In G. Stricker & R. H. Keisner (Eds.), *From research to clinical practice* (pp. 179–217). New York: Plenum.

SPRINGER, S., & DEUTSCH, G. (1984). *Left brain, right brain* (2nd ed.). San Francisco: Freeman.

SQUIRE, L. (1987). *Memory and the brain*. New York: Oxford University Press.

SQUIRE, L., & COHEN, N. J. (1984). Human memory and amnesia. In G. Lynch et al. (Eds.), *Neurobiology of learning and memory*. New York: Guilford.

STAUDENMAYER, H., KINSMAN, R. A., DIRKS, J. F., SPECTOR, S. L., & WANGAARD, C. (1979). Medical outcome in asthmatic patients: Effects of airways hyperactivity and symptom-focused anxiety. *Psychosomatic Medicine, 41*, 109–118.

STEFFENS, A. B., MOGENSON, G. J., & STEVENSON, J. A. F. (1972). Blood glucose, insulin, and free fatty acids after stimulation and lesions of the hypothalamus. *American Journal of Physiology, 222*, 1446–1452.

STEFFENSMEIER, D. J., & TERRY, R. M. (1973). Deviance and respectability: An observational study of reactions to shoplifting. *Social Forces, 51*, 417–426.

STEIGLEDER, M. K., WEISS, R. F., BALLING, S. S., WENNINGER, V. L., & LOMBARDO, J. P. (1980). Drivelike motivational properties of competitive behavior. *Journal of Personality and Social Psychology, 38*, 93–104.

STEIN, M., SCHLEIFLER, S. J., & KELLER, S. E. (1981). Hypothalamic influences on immune responses. In R. Ader (Ed.), *Psychoneuroimmunology*. New York: Academic Press.

STEPHAN, W. G. (1973). Parental relationships and early social experiences of activist male homosexuals and male heterosexuals. *Journal of Abnormal Psychology, 82*, 506–513.

STERMAN, M. B. (1978). Effects of sensorimotor EEG feedback training on sleep and clinical manifestations of epilepsy. In J. Beatty & H. Legewie (Eds.), *Biofeedback and behavior*. New York: Plenum.

STERNBERG, R. J. (1985). *Beyond IQ: A triarchic theory of human intelligence*. New York: Cambridge University Press.

STERNBERG, R. J. (1986). *Intelligence applied: Understanding and increasing your intellectual skills*. Orlando, FL: Harcourt Brace Jovanovich.

STEVENS, S. S. (1956). The direct estimation of sensory magnitudes-loudness. *American Journal of Psychology, 69*, 1–25.

STEVENS, S. S. (1957). On the psychophysical law. *Psychological Review, 64*, 153–181.

STEVENS, S. S. (1961). The psychophysics of sensory functions. In W. A. Rosenblith (Ed.), *Sensory communication* (pp. 1–33). Cambridge, MA: MIT Press.

STEVENS, S. S., WARSHOFSKY, F., & STAFF. (1965). *Sound and hearing*. New York: Time-Life Books. (Original work published 1906)

STILES, W. B., SHAPIRO, D. A., & ELLIOTT, R. (1986). Are all psychotherapies equivalent? *American Psychologist, 41*(2), 165–180.

STOKOLS, D. (1972). On the distinction between density and crowding: Some implications for future research. *Psychological Review, 79*, 275–277.

STORMS, M. S. (1981). A theory of erotic orientation development. *Psychological Review, 88*, 340–353.

STRATTON, G. M. (1896). Some preliminary experiments on vision without inversion of the retinal image. *Psychological Review, 3*, 611–617.

STRUBLE, J. H., & STEFFENS, A. B.

(1975). Rapid insulin release after ingestion of a meal in the unanesthetized rat. *American Journal of Physiology, 229*, 1019–1022.

SUNDSTROM, E. (with M. G. Sundstrom). (1986). *Work places*. New York: Cambridge University Press.

SUPPES, P., & MORNINGSTAR, M. (1969). Computer-assisted instruction. *Science, 166*, 343–350.

SURMAN, O. S., GOTTLIEB, S. K., HACKETT, T. P., & SILVERBERG, E. L. (1973). Hypnosis in the treatment of warts. *Archives of General Psychiatry, 28*, 439–441.

SWENCIONIS, C. (in press). Type A behavior and the brain. In R. Ornstein & C. Swencionis (Eds.), *Scientific papers on the healing brain*. New York: Guilford Press.

SYME, S. L. (1984). Sociocultural factors and disease etiology. In W. Doyle Gentry (Ed.), *Handbook of behavioral medicine*. New York: Guilford.

SYMONS, D. (in preparation). A critique of Darwinian anthropology. Department of Anthropology, University of California.

SYMONS, D. (1980). Precis of the evolution of human sexuality. *Behavioral and Brain Sciences, 3*, 171–214.

SZASZ, T. (1961). *The myth of mental illness*. New York: Harper & Row.

TALBERT, G. B. (1977). The aging of the reproductive system. In C. Finch & L. Hayflick (Eds.), *Handbook of the biology of aging*. New York: Van Nostrand-Reinhold.

TANNER, J. M. (1962). *Growth at adolescence* (2nd ed.). Oxford: Blackwell Scientific Publications.

TARG, R., & PUTHOFF, H. (1977). *Mind reach: Scientists look at psychic ability*. New York: Delacorte.

TART, C., PUTHOFF, H. E., & TARG, R. (Eds.). (1979). Mind at large. *Institute of Electrical and Electronics Engineers Symposia on the Nature of Extra-sensory Perception*. New York: Praeger.

TART, C. T. (1971). *On being stoned*. Palo Alto, CA: Science & Behavior Books.

TASKIN, D. P., CALVERESE, B. M., SIMMONS, M. S., & SHAPIRO, B. J. (1978). *Respiratory status of 74 habitual marijuana smokers*. Paper

presented at the annual meeting of the American Thoracic Society, Boston.

TAVRIS, C. (1982). Anger defused. *Psychology Today, 16*, 25–35.

TAYLOR, R. P. (Ed.). (1980). *The computer in the school: Tutor, tool, tutee*. New York: Teachers College Press.

TAYLOR, S. (1970). Aggressive behavior as a function of approval motivation and physical attack. *Psychonomic Science, 18*, 195–196.

TAYLOR, S. E., & THOMPSON, S. C. (1982). Stalking the elusive "vividness" effect. *Psychological Review, 89*, 155–181.

TAYLOR, S. P., GAMMON, C. B., & CAPASSO, D. R. (1976). Aggression as a function of the interaction of alcohol and threat. *Journal of Personality and Social Psychology, 34*(5), 938–941.

TAYLOR, S. P., VARDARIS, R. M., RAWITCH, A. B., GAMMON, C. B., CRANSTON, J. W., & LUBETKIN, A. I. (1976). The effects of alcohol and delta-9-tetra hydrocannabinal on human physical aggression. *Aggressive Behavior, 2*, 153–161.

TEITELBAUM, P. (1957). Random and food-directed activity in hyperphagic and normal rats. *Journal of Comparative and Physiological Psychology, 50*, 486–490.

TENNOV, D. (1979). *Love and limerence*. New York: Stein & Day.

TERMAN, L. M., & MERRILL, M. A. (1937). *Measuring intelligence*. Chicago: Riverside.

TEYLER, T. (1978). *A primer of psychobiology*. San Francisco: Freeman.

THOMAS, L. (1982). *The youngest science*. New York: Viking.

THOMAS, S. A. et al. (1984). Blood pressure and heart rate changes in children when they read aloud in school. *Public Health Reports, 99*(1), 77–84.

THOMPSON, R. (1986). *The brain*. New York: Freeman.

THOMPSON, R. F. (1967). *Foundations of physiological psychology*. New York: Harper & Row.

THOMPSON, R. F. (1975). *Introduction to physiological psychology*. New York: Harper & Row.

THORNDIKE, E. L. (1911). *Animal intelligence.* New York: Macmillan.

THORNDIKE, R. L. (1954). The psychological value systems of psychologists. *American Psychologist, 9,* 787–789.

THURSTONE, L. L. (1938). Primary mental abilities. *Psychometrika Monographs, 1.*

TINBERGEN, N. (1951). *The study of instinct.* Oxford: Clarendon.

TOATES, F. (1986). *Motivational behavior.* New York: Cambridge University Press.

TOCH, H. (1969). *Violent men.* Chicago: Aldine.

TOLMAN, E. C., & HONZIK, C. H. (1930). "Insight" in rats. *University of California Publications in Psychology, 4,* 215–232.

TOMKINS, S. S. (1962). *Affect, imagery, consciousness: Vol. 1. The positive affects.* New York: Springer-Verlag.

TOMKINS, S. S. (1963). *Affect, imagery, consciousness: Vol. 2. The negative affects.* New York: Springer-Verlag.

TOMKINS, S. S. (1979). Script theory: Differential magnification of affects. In H. E. Howe & R. A. Dienstbier (Eds.), *Nebraska Symposium on Motivation, 1978, 26.* Lincoln: University of Nebraska Press.

TOMKINS, S. S. (1984). Affect theory. In K. Scherer & P. Ekman (Eds.), *Approaches to emotion.* Hillsdale, NJ: Erlbaum.

TREVARTHEN, W. R. (1981). Maternal touch at first contact with the newborn infant. *Developmental Psychology, 14*(6), 549–558.

TRIPLETT, N. (1897). The dynamogenic factors in pace making and competition. *American Journal of Psychology, 9,* 507–533.

TRIVERS, R. L. (1978). The evolution of reciprocal altruism. *Quarterly Review of Biology, 46,* 35–57.

TULVING, E. (1972). Episodic and semantic memory. In E. Tulving & W. Donaldson (Eds.), *Organization and memory.* New York: Academic Press.

TURNBULL, C. (1961). Some observations regarding the experiences and behavior of the Bambuti pygmies. *American Journal of Psychology, 74,* 304–308.

TURNER, J. S., & HELMS, D. B. (1987). *Lifespan development* (3rd ed.). Lavallette, NJ: Holt, Rinehart & Winston.

TURNER, P. (1986, June). The shrinking of George. *Science '86, 7*(5), 38–44.

TURVEY, M. T., & SHAW, R. (1979). The primacy of perceiving. In G. Nillson (Ed.), *Perspectives on memory research essays in honor of Uppsala University's 500th anniversary.* Hillsdale, NJ: Erlbaum.

TVERSKY, A. (1977). Features of similarity. *Psychological Review, 84,* 327–352.

TVERSKY, A., & GATI, I. (1978). Studies of similarity. In E. Rosch & B. B. Lloyd (Eds.), *Cognition and categorization.* Hillsdale, NJ: Erlbaum.

TVERSKY, A., & KAHNEMAN, D. (1973). Availability: A heuristic for judging frequency and possibility. *Cognitive Psychology, 5,* 207–232.

TVERSKY, A., & KAHNEMAN, D. (1981). The framing of decisions and the psychology of choice. *Science, 211,* 453–458.

ULLMAN, L., & KRASNER, L. (1965). *Case studies in behavior modification.* New York: Holt, Rinehart & Winston.

ULLMAN, M., KRIPPNER, S., & VAUGHN, A. (1973). *Dream telepathy.* New York: Macmillan.

ULLMAN, S. (1980). Against direct perception. *Behavioral and Brain Sciences, 3,* 373–381.

ULRICH, R. S. (1984). View through a window may influence recovery from surgery. *Science, 224,* 420–421.

U.S. BUREAU OF THE CENSUS. (1975, March). *Current population reports. Marital status and living arrangements* (Series P-20, No. 287). Washington, DC.: U.S. Government Printing Office.

VALINS, S. (1966). Cognitive effects of false heart-rate feedback. *Journal of Personality and Social Psychology, 4,* 400–408.

VALLIANT, G. (1977). *Adaptation to life.* Boston: Little, Brown.

VALLIANT, G., & MILOFSKY, E. (1978). Natural history of male psychological health: IX. Empirical evidence for Erikson's model of the life cycle. *American Journal of Psychiatry, 137*(11).

VANDELL, D., WILSON, K., & BUCHANAN, N. (1980). Peer interaction in the first year of life: An examination of its structure, content, and sensitivity to toys. *Child Development, 41,* 481–488.

VANDENBOS, G. A. (1986). Psychotherapy research. *American Psychologist, 41*(2).

VIERLING, J. S., & ROCK, J. (1967). Variations in olfactory sensitivity to Exaltolide during the menstrual cycle. *Journal of Applied Physiology, 22,* 311–315.

VOGEL, G. W. (1978). An alternative view of the biology of dreaming. *American Journal of Psychiatry, 135*(12), 1531–1535.

VON BEKESY, G. (1949). *Experiments in hearing.* New York: McGraw-Hill.

WADDINGTON, C. H. (1957). *The strategy of the genes.* New York: Macmillan.

WALLERSTEIN, J. S., & KELLY, J. B. (1980). *Surviving the breakup: How children and parents cope with divorce.* New York: Basic Books.

WALSTER, E., ARONSON, V., ABRAHAMS, D., & ROTTMANN, L. (1966). The importance of physical attractiveness in dating behavior. *Journal of Personality and Social Psychology, 4,* 508–516.

WALSTER, E., & WALSTER, G. W. (1978). *A new look at love.* Boston: Addison-Wesley.

WALSTER, E., WALSTER, G. W., & TRAUPMANN, J. (1978). Equity and premarital sex. *Journal of Personality and Social Psychology, 37,* 82–92.

WARREN, R. M., & WARREN, R. P. (1972). Auditory illusions and confusions. *Scientific American, 223,* 30–36.

WASHBURN, S. (1960). Tools and human evolution. *Scientific American, 203*(3), 67–73.

WATSON, J. B. (1914). *Behavior, an introduction to comparative psychology.* New York: Henry Holt.

WATSON, J. B. (1925). *Behaviorism.* New York: Norton.

WATSON, J. B., & RAYNOR, R. (1920). Conditioned emotional reactions. *Journal of Experimental Psychology, 3,* 1–14.

WEBER, E. H. (1834). *De pulsu, resorptione, auditu et tactu: Annotationes anatomical et physiological.* Leipzig: Koehler.

WEINER, H. (1977). *Psychobiology and human disease.* New York: Elsevier.

WENEGRAT, B. (1984). *Sociobiology and mental disorder: A new view.* Boston: Addison-Wesley.

WERNER, E. E., & SMITH, R. S. (1982). *Vulnerable, but invincible: A study of resilient children.* New York: McGraw-Hill.

WHITBOURNE, S. K. (1986). *The me I know: A study of adult identity.* New York: Springer-Verlag.

WHITE, L., TURSKY, B., & SCHWARTZ, G. E. (Eds.). (1985). *Placebo: Theory, research and mechanisms.* New York: Guilford.

WHITFIELD, I. C. (1976). *The auditory pathway.* London: Arnold.

WHORF, B. (1942). *Language, thought, and reality: Selected writings of Benjamin Lee Whorf.* J. B. Caroll (Ed.). New York: John Wiley.

WHYTE, W. H. (1956). *The organization man.* New York: Simon & Schuster.

WICKELGREN, W. (1977). *Learning and memory.* Englewood Cliffs, NJ: Prentice-Hall.

WICKELGREN, W. (1979). *Cognitive psychology.* Englewood Cliffs, NJ: Prentice-Hall.

WILDER, D. A., & ALLEN, V. L. (1973). Veridical dissent, erroneous dissent, and conformity. Unpublished master's thesis. University of Waterloo.

WILLEMSEN, E. (1979). *Understanding infancy.* San Francisco: Freeman.

WILLERMAN, L. (1979). *The psychology of individual and group differences.* San Francisco: Freeman.

WILLIAMS, R. B., JR. (1983). Hostility and hormones: New clues to why Type A's have more heart disease. Paper presented to American Heart Association's 10th Science Writers Forum, Tucson.

WILSON, C. P. (1979). *Jokes: Form, content, use and function.* London: Academic Press.

WILSON, E. O. (1975). *Sociobiology.* Cambridge, MA: Harvard University Press.

WILSON, J. & HERRNSTEIN, R. (1985). *Crime and human nature.* New York: Simon & Schuster.

WINNICK, M. (1979). Starvation studies. *Human Nature Manuscript Series, 4.*

WINOGRAD, T. (1980, February). Face savings memory. *Psychology Today,* 81.

WINOKUR, G. (1981). *Depression: The facts.* New York: Oxford University Press.

WINOKUR, G., CLAYTON, P. J., & REICH, T. (1969). *Manic-depressive illness.* St. Louis: Mosby.

WINSTON, P. H. (1984). *Artificial intelligence.* (2nd ed.). Reading, MA: Addison-Wesley.

WINSTON, P H., & PRENDERGAST, K. A. (Eds.). (1984). *The AI business: Commercial uses of artificial intelligence.* Cambridge, MA: MIT Press.

WISDOM, C. S. (1977). A methodology for studying noninstitutionalized psychopaths. *Journal of Consulting and Clinical Psychology, 45,* 674–683.

WISHNER, J. (1960). Reanalysis of "impressions of personality." *Psychological Review, 67,* 96–112.

WITELSON, S. F. (1976). Sex and the single hemisphere: Specialization of the right hemisphere for spatial processing. *Science, 193,* 425–427.

WOLFE, J. B. (1936). Effectiveness of token-rewards for chimpanzees. *Comparative Psychology Monograph, 12,* 5.

WOLMAN, B. (Ed.). (1982). *Handbook of developmental psychology.* Englewood Cliffs, NJ: Prentice-Hall.

WOLMAN, B. B., & ULLMAN, M. (Eds.). (1986). *Handbook of states of consciousness.* New York: Van Nostrand-Reinhold.

WOLPE, J. (1958). *Psychotherapy by reciprocal inhibition.* Stanford: Stanford University Press.

WOLPE, J. (1981). The experimental model and treatment of neurotic depression. *Behavior Research and Therapy, 17*(6), 555–565.

WORCHEL, S., COOPER, J., & GOETHALS, G. R. (1987). *Understanding social psychology* (4th ed.). Chicago: Dorsev.

WORCHEL, S., LEE, J., & ADEWOLE, A. (1975). Effects of supply and demand on ratings of object value. *Journal of Personality and Social Psychology, 32,* 906–914.

WRIGHT, J. C., & VLEITSTRA, A. G. (1975). The development of selective attention: From perceptual exploration to logical search. In H. W. Reese (Ed.), *Advances in child development and behavior: Vol. 10.* New York: Academic Press.

WURTMAN, R., & WURTMAN, J. (1984). *Nutrition and the brain* (Vol. 7). New York: Raven Press.

YAMAMOTO, J., OKONOGI, K., IWASAKI, T., & YOSHIMURA, S. (1969). Mourning in Japan. *American Journal of Psychiatry, 125*(12), 1660–1665.

YARROW, L. J., RUBENSTEIN, J. L., PEDERSEN, F. A., & JANKOWSKI, J. J. (1972). Dimensions of early stimulation and their differential effects on infant development. *Merrill-Palmer Quarterly, 18,* 205–218.

YATES, S., & ARONSON, E. (1983). A social-psychological perspective on energy conservation in residential buildings. *American Psychologist, 38,* 435–444.

ZAHN-WAXLER, C. et al. (Eds.). (1986). *Altruism and aggression: Social and biological origins.* New York: Cambridge University Press.

ZAJONC, R. B. (1980). Feeling and thinking: Preferences need no interferences. *American Psychologist, 35*(2), 151–175.

ZAJONC, R. B. (1986). The decline and rise of Scholastic Aptitude scores. *American Psychologist, 41*(8), 862–867.

ZAJONC, R. B., MARKUS, H., & MARKUS, G. P. (1979). The birth order puzzle. *Journal of Personality and Social Psychology, 37,* 1325–1341.

ZEGANS, L., & TEMOSHOK, L. (Eds.). (1985). *Emotions and health.* San Diego: Grune & Stratton.

ZILLMAN, D., JOHNSON, R. C., & DAY, K. D. (1974). Attribution of apparent arousal and proficiency of recovery from sympathetic activation affecting activation transfer to aggressive behavior. *Journal of Experimental Social Psychology, 10,* 503–515.

ZIMBARDO, P. G. (1972). The tactics and ethics of persuasion. In B. T. King & E. McGinnis (Eds.), *Attitudes, conflict and social change.* New York: Academic Press.

ZIMBARDO, P. G. (1973a). The psychological power and pathology of imprisonment. *Catalog of Selected Documents in Psychology, 30,* 45.

ZIMBARDO, P. G. (1973b). A field experiment in auto-shaping. In C. Ward (Ed.), *Vandalism.* London: Architectural Press.

ZIMBARDO, P. G., ANDERSEN, S. M., & KABAT, L. G. (1981). Induced hearing deficit generates experimental paranoia. *Science, 212*(4502), 1529–1531.

ZUCKERMAN, M. (1984). Sensation-seeking: A comparative approach to a human trait. *Behavioral and Brain Sciences, 7,* 413–433.

Copyrights and Acknowledgments

Photos

Part one opener: © Lennart Nilsson, *Behold Man*. Little, Brown and Co., Boston, 1974; **Part two opener:** © Richard Wood/The Picture Cube; **Part three opener:** © Joel Gordon, 1982; **Part four opener:** Emilio A. Mercado/The Picture Cube. **Page 12:** Charles Gatewood/Image Works; **21:** New York Port Authority; **35 (left):** © Harry Crosby/Photophile; **(right)** Bob Glasheen/Photophile; **63 (top):** Photo F. D. Schmidt, © Zoological Society of San Diego; **(bottom):** © Howard Dratch/Image Works; **76 (left):** Bruce Roberts from Rapho/Photo Researchers; **(right):** © Elizabeth Crews; **93 (bottom):** Karyl Gatteno/Taurus Photos; **98–99:** © Gerry Cranham/Photo Researchers; **111:** World Health Organization; **113 (bottom):** Phillips Collection, Washington, D.C.; **117:** © Joel Gordon; **178:** Alan Carey/Image Works; **184:** George Bellerose/Stock, Boston; **203:** © Judy Porter, 1974/Photo Researchers; **259:** Philadelphia Museum of Art. Given by Mr. and Mrs. Rodolphe M. de Schauensee; **266:** Christopher Brown/Stock, Boston; **267:** Alan Carey/Image Works; **271:** © 1980 Susan Berkowitz/Taurus Photos; **274:** Charles Gatewood/Image Works; **276 (left):** Rhoda Sidney/Monkmeyer Press Photo Service; **(right):** Arthur Tress © 1977/Photo Researchers; **277:** Barbara Steinberg/Zephyr Pictures; **279:** Charles Gatewood/Image Works; **289:** Bill Blass, Inc.; **302:** Frank Siteman/The Picture Cube; **304:** UPI/Bettmann Newsphotos; **309:** Janet Robertson; **312 (left):** © George Gardner; **(right):** Jeffery W. Meyers/Stock, Boston; **313:** Paul S. Conklin; **322:** © Imogen Cunningham Trust; **324 (left):** © Vivienne della Grotta, 1980/Photo Researchers; **(right):** Alan Carey/Image Works; **326:** Multigravitational Aerodance Group/Photo by Ken Karp; **348:** Mimi Forsyth from Monkmeyer Press Photo Service; **364:** Wide World Photos; **367:** Rick Mansfield/Image Works; **378:** HBJ Collection; **374:** © Tom McHugh/Photo Researchers; **396 (top):** Bettmann Archive; **(bottom left):** Judith Sedwick/The Picture Cube; **402:** Harvey Stein, **407 (left):** Paul S. Conklin; **(right):** © Elizabeth Crews; **414:** Lionel J. M. Delevigne/Stock, Boston; **431 (left):** Standard Oil Company; **(right):** George Zimbel/Monkmeyer Press Photo Service; **441:** © Marcia Weinstein; **446:** David S. Strickler/The Picture Cube; **453:** David E. Kennedy/TexaStock; **466 (left):** Robert Kalman/Image Works; **466 (middle):** Peter Paul Rubens, *The Judgement of Paris*. National Gallery; **(right):** Elizabeth Crews/Stock, Boston; **471 (top left):** © Joel Gordon, 1979; **471 (top right):** © Kolvoord/TexaStock; **(bottom left):** © Alan Carey/Image Works; **(bottom right):** © John W. Manos/The Picture Cube; **473 (top):** Nik Kleinberg/Picture Group; **(bottom):** National Foundation; **477:** Ron Cooper/EKM-Nepenthe; **478 (top left):** UPI/Bettmann Newsphotos; **(top right):** UPI/Bettmann Newsphotos; **(bottom left):** Flip Schulke/Black Star; **(bottom right):** Fritz Goro/Black Star; **488 and 489 (all):** © Erika Stone/Peter Arnold Inc.; **499 (left):** © Steve Takatsuno/The Picture Cube; **(right):** Tom Cheek/Stock, Boston; **500:** Alan Carey/Image Works; **506 (left):** National Safety Council. Photo by Al Henderson; **(right):** Gerhard Gscheidle/Peter Arnold Inc.; **507 (left):** Paul S. Conklin; **(right):** © Hazel Hankin; **511:** Frank Siteman/Stock, Boston; **517:** Mikki Ansin Ehrenfeld/The Picture Cube; **520:** © Jean-Claude Lejeune; **521:** © Harvey Stein; **522:** © Pamela Price/The Picture Cube; **528:** © Richard Hutchings/Photo Researchers; **530:** Paul S. Conklin; **531:** Norman Mosallem/FPG; **534:** Nancy Hayes/Monkmeyer Press Photos Service; **539:** UPI/Bettmann Newsphotos; **549 (left):** Bettmann Archive; **(right):** Culver Pictures; **551:** © Edmund Engleman; **544:** Hazel Hankin/Stock, Boston; **561:** Michael Rougier. Life Magazine © 1968 Time, Inc.; **563:** Will McIntyre, Duke University Medical Center/Photo Researchers; **565 (left):** Vista Hill Foundation; **(right):** Lionel J. M. Delevigne/Stock, Boston; **566:** Dean Abramson/Stock, Boston; **571:** © Ken Robert Buck/Stock, Boston; **580:** A. Tannenbaum/Stock, Boston; **585:** Klaus Francke/Peter Arnold, Inc.; **588 (left):** Werner Muller/Peter Arnold, Inc.; **(right):** Audrey Topping/Photo Researchers; **590:** Wide World Photos; **595:** Michael D. Sullivan/TexaStock; **602:** Robert V. Eckert/EKM-Nepenthe; **601 (left):** Alan Carey/The Image Works; **(middle):** Sandra Weiner/The Image Works; **(right):** Paul S. Conklin; **604:** Bart Bartholomew/Black Star; **609:** Charles Gatewood/The Image Works; **618:** P. Damien/Click, Chicago; **619 (top):** George Bellerose/Stock, Boston; **(bottom):** National Archives; **621:** Alan Carey/The Image Works; **623 (left):** Earl Dotter/Archive; **(right):** Melanie Kaestner/Zephyr Pictures; **624:** Carey Wolinsky/Stock, Boston; **627:** Stan Levy/Photo Researchers; **631:** Jennifer Bishop/Stock, Boston; **635:** Wide World Photos; **639:** Alan Glauberman/Photo Researchers; **642:** © Joel Gordon; **647 (both):** © Joel Gordon; **656:** Michael D. Sullivan/TexaStock; **660 (left):** © Joel Gordon; **(middle):** John Maher/Stock, Boston; **(right):** Alan Carey/The Image Works; **661:** Frederick D. Bobin/Stock, Boston; **663:** Erika Stone/Peter Arnold; **669:** Jaye R. Philips/Picture Cube; **675:** Julie O'Neil/Picture Cube.

Figures

CHAPTER ONE: Page 3: Donna Salmon from Ornstein, R. E., *The psychology of consciousness*, Second Edition. New York: Harcourt Brace Jovanovich, Inc., 1977; **Figure 1-1b:** Sea World Photo; **1-2:** Courtesy, Dr. Albert Bandura; **1-3:** Penfield, W., *The mystery of the mind*. Princeton University Press, 1975; **1-4:** Hirst, W., Neisser, U., and Spelke, E., Divided attention. *Human Nature* 57, June, 1978. Copyright © 1978 by Human Nature. Reprinted by permission of the publisher; **1-5 (left):** © Teri Leigh Stratford/Photo Researchers; **(right):** © Robert Goldstein/Photo Researchers; **1-6:** Selfe, L., *Nadia, a case of extraordinary drawing ability in an autistic child*. London: Academic Press, 1977; **1-7:** Grives, P. M., and Thompson, R. F., A dual process theory of habituation: neural mechanisms, in Pecke, H. M. S. and Herz, M. J., (eds.) *Habituation, psychological substrates II*. New York: Academic Press, 1973; **1-10:** Bob Kreuger/Photo Researchers; **1-12:** Metzger, Wolfgang, *Gesetze des sehens*. Frankfurt: Verlag Waldemar Kramer, 1953.

CHAPTER TWO: Pages 44–45 and Figure 2-8: Leakey, R. E. and Lewin, R., *Origins*. New York: E. P. Dutton, 1977; **2-1:** Peter Jones © National Geographic Society; **2-7:** From Hubel, D., The brain, in *The Brain*. San Francisco: W. H. Freeman, 1979, p. 5; **2-9:** Colorphoto Hans Heinz, Basel; **2-13:** Based on Kinsey, Pomeroy and Martin, 1953, Table 153. Adapted by permission of the Kinsey Institute for Research in Sex, Gender and Reproduction; **2-14:** Campbell, B. G., (ed.), *Humankind emerging*, Second Edition. Boston: Little, Brown and Co., 1979; **2-15:** Hess, E. H., *Imprinting*. New York: Van Nostrand-Reinhold, 1973; **2-16:** Nina Leen, Life Magazine © Time, Inc.; **2-18a:** © Walt Disney Productions; **2-18b:** From *Studies in animal and human behavior*, Vol. II, by Konrad Lorenz. © 1971 by Methuen & Co., Ltd.; **2-22 and 2-23:** Cytogenics Laboratory, University of California, San Francisco; **2-24:** Culver Pictures; **2-25:** Gottesman, I. I., Developmental genetics and ontogenetic psychology, from Pick, A. D. (ed.) *Minnesota symposia on child psychology*, Vol. 8. Minneapolis: University of Minnesota Press, 1974; **2-26:** Wenegrat, B., *Sociobiology and mental disorder: A new view*. Boston: Addison-Wesley, 1984.

CHAPTER THREE: Figure 3-1: © David Scharf/Peter Arnold, Inc.; **3-2:** After Waddington, C. H., *The strategy of the genes*. New York: Macmillan Publishing Co., 1957; **3-3 (top left):** Barbara Alper/Stock, Boston; **(top right):** © Jason Laure/Woodfin Camp and Associates; **3-4:** Franz, R. L., The origin of form perception, *Scientific American*, 204, May 1961; **3-5:** Shirley, Mary, N., The first two years, *Institute of Child Welfare Monograph No. 7*. Minneapolis: University of Minnesota Press, 1933; **3-6:** Hall, Elizabeth, et al., *Child Psychology Today*. New York: Random House, 1982; **3-7:** Cowan, W. Maxwell, The development of the brain, in *The brain*. San Francisco: W. H. Freeman and Co., 1979, p. 59; **3-8:** Goren, Carolyn, *Form perception*, 1970: Innate form preferences and visually mediated head-turning in human neonates. Unpublished doctoral dissertation, Committee on Human Development, University of Chicago; **3-9:** Braun, J. and Lindner, D., *Psychology today: An introduction*, Fourth Edition. New York: CRM Books, a Division of Random House, Inc., 1979; **3-10:** Zimbel/Monkmeyer Press Photo Service; **3-11 (top left):** Colin Graham Young; **(top right):** Eric McNaul; **(bottom):** From Gaitskell, Hurwitz and Day, *Children and their art*. New York: Harcourt Brace Jovanovich, Inc. © 1984. Reprinted by permission of the publisher; **3-12:** © Marcia Weinstein; **3-14:** © Carol Palmer/Picture Cube; **3-15:** © Sponholtz/University of Wisconsin Primate Lab; **3-16:** Ainsworth, M. D. S., and Bell, S. M., Attachment, exploration and separation: Illustrated by the behavior of one-year-olds in a strange situation, *Child Development* 41, 1970. By permission of the Society for Research in Child Development, Inc.; **3-17:** © Elizabeth Crews; **3-18:** Tanner, J. M., *Growth at adolescence*, Second Edition. Oxford: Blackwell Scientific Publications, 1962; **3-19 and page 127:** Csikszentmihalyi, M. and Larson, R., *Being adolescent: Conflict and growth in the teenage years*. New York: Basic Books, 1984.

CHAPTER FOUR: Figure 4-2: Thompson, R. F., *Foundations of physiological psychology*. New York: Harper and Row, 1967. © 1967 by Richard F. Thompson. Reprinted by permission of Harper and Row; **4-4:** Vannini, V. and Pogliani, G., *The color atlas of human anatomy*. New York: Harmony Books, 1979; **4-6:** National Library of Medicine; **4-8:** Truex, R. C. and Carpenter, M. B., *Human neuroanatomy*. Baltimore: Williams and Wilkins, 1964; **4-9:** Penfield W., and Rasmussen, T., *The cerebral cortex of man*. New York: Macmillan Publishing Company, 1950. Copyright renewed 1978 by Theodore Rasmussen. Adapted with permission of Macmillan Publishing Company; **4-10:** Woolsey and Van der Loos, *Brain research*. Elsevier Science Publishing Company, 1970; **4-15:** Sperry, R. W., *The great cerebral commissure*, Scientific American, Inc., 1964; **4-16:** Levy, J., Trevarthen, C. and Sperry, R. W., Perception of bilateral chimeric figures following hemispheric disconnection, *Brain* 95: 68, 1972; **4-17:** Bogen, J., The other side of the brain, I, *Bulletin of the Los Angeles Neurological Societies*, 34, July, 1969; **4-18:** Eric Arneson, from Ornstein, R. E., *The psychology of consciousness*, Second Edition. © 1977 Harcourt Brace Jovanovich, Inc. Used by permission of the publisher; **4-21:** © Manfred Kage/Peter Arnold, Inc.; **4-22 and 4-29:** Adapted from Ornstein, R. and Thompson, R. F., *The amazing brain*. Boston: Houghton-Mifflin Company, 1984; **4-31:** © Robin Risque.

CHAPTER FIVE: Figure 5-2: Stevens, S. S., the psychophysics of sensory function, in Rosenbluth, W. A. (ed.), *Sensory communication*. Cambridge: MIT Press, 1961; **5-4, 5-16, and 5-17:** Cornsweet, T. N., *Visual perception*. New York: Academic Press, 1970; **5-8:** Hurvich, L. M., and Jameson, D., Opponent processes as a model of neural organization, *American Psychologist* 29: 88–102, 1974; **5-11, 5-13, and 5-14:** Hubel, D. H. and Weisel, T. N., *Journal of Psychology* 160: 106–154, 1962; **5-19:** A. L. Yarbus/Plenum Publishers; **5-22:** Lindsay, P. H., and Norman, D. A., *Human information processing*, Second Edition. New York: Academic Press, 1977; **5-24 and 5-26:** Ludel, J., *Introduction to sensory processes*. New York: W. H. Freeman and Co., 1978; **5-27:** Snyder, S. H., Opiate receptors and internal opiates, *Scientific American* 51, March 1977; **5-28:** © Hazel Hankin.

CHAPTER SIX: Figures 6-1 and 6-4: Thurston, J. and Carraher, R. G., *Optical illusions and the visual arts*. New York: Litton Educational Publishing Co., 1966; **6-2:** Hochberg and McAllister, *Perception*, Second Edition. Englewood Cliffs, NJ: Prentice-Hall, 1953; **6-3, 6-20, and 6-32:** © Susan Holtz; **6-11:** Coren, S. Subjective contours and apparent depth, *Psychological review* 79: 359–367, 1972; **6-13:** Norman Snyder; **6-14:** Neisser, U., *Cognition and reality: principles and implications of cognitive psychology*. New York: W. H. Freeman and Company. Used by permission; **6-18:** From Coren, S., Porac, C. and Ward, L., *Sensation and perception*, Second Edition, © 1984, Academic Press, p. 179; **6-23:** © Robin Risque; **6-24:** William Vandievert; **6-25:** R. L. Gregory, *Eye and brain*. © 1977, McGraw-Hill and Company; **6-26:** Kennedy, J. M., *A psychology of picture perception*. San Francisco: Jossey-Bass, Inc., 1974; **6-27:** Ralph Crane, Life Magazine © Time, Inc.; **6-28:** British Information Services; **6-29:** Hudson, W., Pictorial perception and education in Africa, *Psychologia Africana* 9: 226–239, 1962; **6-34 (top):** Vincent Van Gogh, *Hospital Corridor at Saint Remy*, 1889. Gouache and watercolor, 24⅛ × 18⅝". Collection, the Museum of Modern Art, New York. Abby Aldrich Rockefeller Bequest; **(bottom):** M. C. Escher, *The Waterfall*, 1961. © M. C. Escher heirs, c/o Cordon Art, Baarn, Holland. Collection, Haags Gemeentemuseum, The Hague; **6-35:** Chase Manhattan Bank; **6-36:** U.S. Department of Agriculture; **6-37:** Alan Pitcairn from Grant Heilman; **6-38:** Gibson, J. J., Kaplan, G. A., Reynolds, H. V., and Wheeler, K., The change from visible to invisible: A study of optical transitions, *Perception and Psychophysics* 1969, 5: 113–116.

CHAPTER SEVEN: Figure 7-1: UPI/Bettmann Newsphotos; **7-2 (left):** S. Hurok; **(right):** Mimi Forsyth/Monkmeyer; **7-3:** © Robin Risque; **7-6:** Van de Castle, R., *The psychology of dreaming*. Morristown, NJ: General Learning Corporation, 1971; **7-7:** Hartmann, E., *The biology of dreaming*. Springfield, IL: Charles Thomas, 1967; **7-8:** Hilgard, E. R., Hypnosis and consciousness, *Human Nature* 48, January 1978. Copyright © 1977 by Human Nature, Inc. Reprinted by permission of the publisher; **7-9:** *Triangle*, Sandoz Journal of Medical Science, Vol. II, No. 3, 1955. Copyright Sandoz, Ltd., Basel, Switzerland; **7-10:** UPI/Bettmann Newsphotos; **7-11:** Owen Franken/Stock, Boston.

CHAPTER EIGHT: Figure 8-1: Gale Zucker/Stock, Boston; **8-5:** Harvard University; **8-7 and 8-8:** Yerkes Regional Primate Center, Emory University; **8-11:** Garcia, J. and Koelling, R. A., Relation of cue to consequence in avoidance learning, *Psychometric Science* 4: 123–214, 1966.

CHAPTER NINE: Figure 9-1: Nickerson, R. S. and Adams, M. J., Long-term memory for a common object, *Cognitive Psychology* 11: 297, 1979; **9-3:** Shannon, B., Yesterday, today and tomorrow, *Acta Psychologica* 43: 469–76, 1979. Reprinted by permission of North-Holland Publishing Company; **9-5 (top):** Bahrick, H. P., Bahrick, P. O., and Wittlinger, R. P., Fifty years of memory for names and faces, *Journal of Experimental Psychology* 74: 81–99; **(bottom):** 1963 yearbook, *The Tartan*. Helix High School, La Mesa, CA. Courtesy, Candy Young; **9-6:** Rubin, D. C, Very long term memory for prose and verse, *Journal of Verbal Learning and Verbal Behavior* 16: 611–12; **6-7:** Shepard, R. N., Recognition memory for word, sentences, and pictures, *Journal of Verbal Learning and Verbal Behavior* 6: 156–163; **9-11:** Loftus and Loftus, Reconstruction of automobile destruction: An example of the interaction between language and memory, *Journal of Verbal Learning and Verbal Behavior* 13: 585–89, 1974; **9-12:** Rogers, T. B., Kulper, N. A., and Kirker, W. S., Self-reference and the encoding of personal information, *Journal of Personality and Social Psychology* 35: 677–88, 1977.

CHAPTER TEN: Figure 10-3: Lilo Hess/Three Lions; **10-5:** Chomsky, N., *Aspects of the theory of syntax*. Cambridge: MIT Press, 1966.

CHAPTER ELEVEN: Figure 11-1: Bayley, N., Development of mental abilities, in Mussen, P., (ed.), *Carmichael's manual of child psychology*, Vol. 1. New York: John Wiley and Sons, 1970; **11-2:** Adapted from Terman and Merrill, *Manual for the third revision of the Stanford-Binet intelligence scale*. Boston: Houghton Mifflin Co., 1973. Reprinted by permission of the Riverside Publishing Company, Chicago; **11-3:** Judith Sedwick/The Picture Cube; **11-4:** © Alan Carey/The Image Works; **11-5:** Jean-Claude Lejeune; **11-6:** Feuerstein, R., *The dynamic assessment of retarded performers*. Baltimore: University Park Press, 1979. Reprinted by permission of the publisher.

CHAPTER TWELVE: Figure 12-1: Melanie Carr/Zephyr Pictures; **12-2:** Ekman, Paul (ed.), *Darwin and facial expression*. New York: Academic Press, 1973; **12-3:** Plutchik, R., *Emotion: A psychoevolutionary synthesis*. New York: Harper & Row, 1980. Copyright © 1980 by Robert Plutchik. Reprinted by permission of Harper & Row, Inc.; **12-4 (top left):** Earl Dotter/Archive; **(top right):** © 1977 by Paul Ekman; **(bottom left):** Stock, Boston; **(bottom right):** Robert V. Eckert/EKM-Nepenthe; **12-5 and 12-6:** Dr. Paul Ekman; **12-7 (top right and middle):** Dr. Paul Ekman; **(bottom right):** UPI/Bettmann Newsphotos; **12-8:** Dr. Paul Ekman; **12-9 (top right):** HBJ Collection; **(bottom right):** Pam Hasegawa/Taurus Photos; **12-10:** Art Resource; **12-11:** Sackheim, H. A., Gur, R. C., and Saucy, M. C., Emotions are expressed more intensely on the left side of the face, *Science* 202: 434–36, 1978; **12-12:** Speisman, J. C., Lazarus, R. S., Davison, L., and Mordkoff, A. M., Experimental reduction of stress based on ego-defense theory, *Journal of Abnormal and Social Psychology* 68: 367–80, 1964; **12-13:** Masters, W. H., and Johnson, V. E., *Human sexual response*. Boston: Little, Brown and Company, 1966.

CHAPTER THIRTEEN: Figure 13-2: Maslow, A. H., *Motivation and personality*, Second Edition. Data based on Hierarchy of Needs in "A Theory of Human Motivation." Copyright © 1970 by Abraham Maslow. Reprinted by permission of Harper and Row, Inc. **13-5:** Powley, T. L. and Keesey, R. E., Relationship of body weight to the lateral hypothalamic feeding syndrome, *Journal of Comparative and Physiological Psychology* 70: 25–36, 1970; **13-6:** Dr. Neal Miller/Rockefeller University; **13-7:** Hoebel, B. G. and Tietelbaum, P., Effects of force-feeding and starvation on food intake and body weight of a rat with ventromedial hypothalamic lesions, *Journal of Comparative and Physiological Psychology* 61: 189–93, 1966; **13-9:** © Sponholtz/University of Wisconsin Primate Laboratory; **13-10:** Hebb, D. O., Emotion arousal and performance. *Textbook of psychology*, Third Edition. Philadelphia: W. B. Saunders, 1972.

CHAPTER FIFTEEN: Figure 15-1: Jack Manning/NYT Pictures.

CHAPTER SIXTEEN: Figure 16-1: Museo del Prado; **16-2:** Gray, J. A., Anxiety, *Human Nature* 43, July 1978. Copyright © 1978 by Human Nature, Inc. Reprinted by permission of the publisher.

CHAPTER SEVENTEEN: Figure 17-1: © 1965 by Stanley Milgram, from the film *Obedience*, distributed by Pennsylvania State University PCR. Estate of Stanley Milgram, Alexandra Milgram, executrix; **17-2:** Milgram, S., Behavioral study of obedience, *Journal of Abnormal and Social Psychology* 7: 371–78, 1963; **17-3 and 17-6:** Phillip Zimbardo; **17-4:** Asch, S. E., Effects of group pressure upon modification and distortion of judgements, in Maccoby, E. E., Newcomb, T. M., and Hartley, E. L., (eds.), *Readings in social psychology*, Third Edition. New York: Holt, Rinehart and Winston, 1958; **17-5:** Festinger, L., and Carlsmith, J. M., Cognitive compliance, *Journal of Abnormal and Social Psychology* 58: 203–10, 1959.

CHAPTER EIGHTEEN: Figure 18-2: Rahe, R. H., The pathway between subjects' recent life changes and their near-future illness reports: Representative results and methodological issues, in Dohenwend, B. S., and Dohenwend, B. P., (eds.), *Stressful life events: Their nature and effects*. New York: John Wiley and Sons, 1974; **18-3:** Tortora and Anagastobos, *Principles of anatomy and physiology*. New York: Harper and Row, p. 487. **18-6:** Esaias Baitel/VIVA 1980/Woodfin Camp and Associates; **18-7:** Wide World Photos; **18-8:** Newman, O., Community of interest, *Human Nature*, January 1979, 58–9.

CHAPTER NINETEEN: Figure 19-1: From Fries, J. F. and Crapo, L. M., *Vitality and aging*. 1981, W. H. Freeman and Company; **19-2:** Wide World Photos: **19-3:** © Joel Gordon 1978; **19-4 (right):** Abigail Hayman/Archive; **(left):** Paul S. Conklin.

APPENDIX: Figure 8: Rose, J. E., Brugge, J. F., Anderson, K. J., & Hind, J. E., Phase-locked response to low frequency tones in single auditory nerve fibers of the squirrel monkeys, *Journal of Neural Physiology 30:* 769, 1967; **9:** Pearce, T. V., in Kendall, *Advanced statistics*, 1930. Reproduced in Moroney, M. J., *On the average and scatter*, Chapter 5, Vol. 3. New York: Simon & Schuster; **10:** Joiner, B. L., Living histograms, *International Statistical Review* 43: 339–340, 1975; **11:** Fadeley, R. C., Oregon malignancy pattern physiographically related to Hanford, Washington radioisotope storage, *Journal of Environmental Health 27:* 883–897, 1965. As quoted by Anderson, T. W., & Sclove, S. L., *An introduction to the statistical analysis of data*. Boston: Houghton Mifflin, 1978, p. 592; **12:** Glass, G. V., and Hopkins, K. D., *Statistical methods in education and psychology*, 2nd ed. Englewood Cliffs, NJ: Prentice Hall, 1984, p. 105. Reprinted by permission of the publisher; **19:** Zeeman, E. L., Catastrophe theory, *Scientific American* April 1976, p. 67.

Color Plates

Plate la: Dr. Sundstroem/© Gamma; **1b and 1c:** C. Edelman/Black Star, 1980; **4:** Clint Powell/Photophile; **5:** Dr. Robert Livingstone, University of California, San Diego Medical School; **6:** Isaac Geib/Grant Heilman; **7 and 8:** © Lennart Nilsson from *Behold Man*. Little, Brown & Co., 1974; **9:** Martin M. Rotker/Taurus Photos; **10:** Joan Miró, *Woman, Bird by Moonlight*, 1949. Tate Gallery, London; **11 (top):** Salvador Dali, *Apparition of a Face and a Fruit Dish on a Beach*, 1938. Wadsworth Atheneum, Hartford. The Ella Gallup Sumner and Mary Catlin Sumner Collection; **11 (bottom):** Giorgio de Chirico, *The Anguish of Departure*, c. 1913–1914. Oil on canvas, 33½ × 27¼". Albright-Knox Art Gallery, Buffalo, New York. Room of Contemporary Art Fund, 1939; **12 (bottom):** © Rob Nelson/Picture Group; **12 (top right):** Courtesy of International Business Machines Corporation; **12 (top left):** Commodore- Amiga, Inc.; **13:** Reed Kaestner/Zephyr Pictures; **14:** Courtesy, Dr. Paul Ekman; **15:** Edvard Munch, *The Scream*, 1893. Nasjonalgaleriet, Oslo; **16:** Guttmann-Maclay Collection, The Bethlem Royal Hospital and the Maudsley Hospital; **17 (top):** © Susan Holtz; **17 (bottom):** San Diego Historical Society, TICOR Collection; **18 (top right):** National Semiconductor Corporation; **18 (top left):** Bank of America NT & SA; **18 (bottom):** PPS: Werner Kalber; **19:** Wide World Photos: **20 (top left):** David Weintraub/Photo Researchers; **20 (bottom left):** F. le Diascorn/Rapho, Photo Researchers; **20 (right):** Bill Gallery/Stock, Boston.

Table Credits

Table 2-1 From Bernard G. Campbell, *Humankind Emerging*, 3rd ed., p. 148. Copyright © 1982 by Bernard G. Campbell. Reprinted by permission of Little, Brown and Company.

Table 2-2 Berger, K. S. (1980). *The developing person*. Adapted tables from McMillen (1979) and Nagle (1979). New York: Worth Publishers, Inc.

Table 2-3 Gottesman, I. I., & Sheilds, J. *Schizophrenia: A twin study vantage point.* NY: Academic Press © 1972.

Table 2-4 Slater, E., & Cowie, V. (1971). *The genetics of mental disorders.* London: Oxford University Press.

Table 2-4 Rosenthal, D., *Genetic theory and abnormal behavior.* Copyright © 1970, McGraw-Hill Book Co.

Table 3-1 Lenneberg, E. H. *Biological foundations of language.* Copyright © 1967. New York: John Wiley & Sons, Inc. By permission of the publisher.

Table 7-1 Griffith, R. M., Miyagi, O., & Tago, A. (1958). The universality of typical dreams: Japanese vs. American. Reproduced by permission of the American Anthropological Association from *American Anthropologist.* 60:6, Part 1, 1958. Not for further reproduction.

Table 10-1 Adapted from A. S. Luchins & E. H. Luchins, *Rigidity of behavior: A variational approach to the effect Einstellung.* University of Oregon Books, 1959, p. 109.

Table 10-2 Denes, P. B., & Pinson, E. N. (1963). *The speech chain.* Bell Laboratories and Murray Hill News Publishing Company.

Table 11-1 Stanford-Binet materials reproduced by permission of the Riverside Publishing Company, Chicago.

Table 11-2 Reproduced by permission from the Wechsler Adult Intelligence Scale and the Wechsler Adult Intelligence Scale—Revised. Copyright © 1955, 1981 by The Psychological Corporation. All rights reserved.

Table 11-3 Bouchard, T. J., & McGue, M. Familial studies of intelligence. A review. *Science,* 212, 1055–1059. Figure. 29 May 1981. Copyright © 1981 by the American Association for the Advancement of Science.

Table 14-1 Adapted from Cattell, R. B. (1986). *The handbook for the 16 Personality Factor Questionnaire.* Champaign, Ill.: Institute for the Personality and Ability Testing, p. 425. Reprinted by permission of the author.

Table 15-1 American Psychiatric Association. *Diagnostic and statistical manual of mental disorders,* 3rd ed. Washington, D.C.: APA, 1980. Used with permission.

Table 18-1 Ornstein, R., & Sobel, D. (1987). *The healing brain.* New York: Simon & Schuster. Copyright © 1987 by The Institute for the Study of Human Knowledge. Reprinted by permission of Simon & Schuster, Inc.

Tables 18-2 and 18-3 Kanner, A. D., Coyne, J. C., Schaefer, C., and Lazarus, R. S. (1981). Comparison of two modes of stress measurement: Daily hassles and uplifts versus major life events. *Journal of Behavior Medicine,* 4(1), p. 1–39. Reprinted by permission of the publisher.

Appendix Table 7 Fadeley, Robert C. (1965). Oregon malignancy pattern physiographically related to Hanford, Washington, radioisotope storage. *Journal of Environmental Health 27:* 883–897. As adapted by Anderson, T. W., and Sclove, S. L. (1986). *The Statistical analysis of data,* 2nd ed. Copyright © 1986 The Scientific Press, Redwood City, CA.

Appendix Table 8 Francis, Thomas, Jr., *et al.* (1957). *Evaluation of 1954 Field Trial of Poliomyelitis Vaccine: Final Report.* Poliomyelitis Vaccine Evaluation Center, University of Michigan, Ann Arbor, Michigan. As adapted by Anderson, T. W., and Sclove, S. L. (1986). *The statistical analysis of data,* 2nd ed, Copyright © 1986 The Scientific Press, Redwood City, CA.

Text Credits

Page 3 Adapted from *Tales of the Dervishes* by Idries Shah. Copyright © 1967 by Idries Shah. Reprinted by permission of the publisher, E. P. Dutton, a division of NAL Penquin Inc.

Pages 12–13 and 637 *From Influence: Science and practice* by Robert B. Cialdini. Copyright © 1985 by Scott, Foresman and Company. Reprinted by permission.

Pages 16–18 Adapted from *Multimind* by Robert Ornstein. Copyright © 1986 by Robert Ornstein. Reprinted by permission of Houghton Mifflin Company.

Page 65 "General Review of the Sex Situation" from *The Portable Dorothy Parker,* edited by Brendan Gill. Copyright 1926, renewed 1954 by Dorothy Parker. Reprinted by permission of Viking Penquin Inc.

Pages 142–143 Sacks, Oliver (1985). *The man who mistook his wife for a hat.* New York: Simon & Schuster. Copyright © 1970, 1981, 1983, 1984, 1985 by Oliver Sacks. Reprinted by permission of Summit Books, a division of Simon & Schuster, Inc.

Pages 238–239 Nancy Hechinger Lowe, "Seeing without eyes." Reprinted by permission of author through ISHK.

Pages 268–269 Nancy Hechinger Lowe, "Seeing without eyes." Reprinted by permission of author through ISHK.

Pages 268–269 "Teaching Stories" from Idries Shah, *The Exploits and Subtleties of Mulla Nasrudin,* Octagon Press, 1986.

Page 343 Bartlett, F. C., The war of the ghosts. *Remembering.* Cambridge University Press © 1932.

Page 365 Carroll, Jon (1986, November 13). Only a few clams left. *San Francisco Chronicle.* © San Francisco Chronicle, 1986. Reprinted by permission.

Pages 434–436 Ekman, P., & Friesen, W. V., *Unmasking the face.* Reprint edition, 1975, Palo Alto, CA: Consulting Psychologists Press.

Page 468 Adapted from Ullman, L. — Krasner, L. (1965). *Case Studies in Behavior Modification.* New York: Holt Rinehart & Winston.

Page 501 Swencionis, C. (1987). Type A behavior and the brain. In R. Ornstein & C. Swencionis (Eds.), *Scientific papers on the healing brain.* New York: Guilford Press.

Pages 517, 547 From Houghton, J. F. (1980). One personal experience: before and after mental illness. In Rabkin, J. G., et al. (Eds.), *Attitudes toward the mentally ill: Research perspectives.* Washington, D.C.: National Institute of Mental Health.

Pages 519–521, 527 Spitzer, R. L., Skodol, A. E., Gibbon, M., & Williams, J. B. (1981). *DSM-III Casebook* (3rd ed.) Copyright © 1981 American Psychiatric Association, Washington, D.C.

Pages 525, 526, 531–532, 541 Elton B. McNeil, *The quiet furies: Man and disorder.* 1967. Reprinted by permission of Prentice-Hall, Inc. Englewood Cliffs, New Jersey.

Pages 528–529 Goleman, D. (1986, November 11). For mentally ill on the street a new approach shines. Copyright © 1986 by The New York Times Company. Reprinted by permission.

Page 530 Seligman, M. E. (1975). *Helplessness: On depression, development and death.* San Francisco: W. H. Freeman.

Pages 535–536 Hilgard, E. R., 1977, *Divided consciousness: Multiple controls in human thought and action.* New York: Wiley-Interscience.

Page 537 North, C. S. (1987). *Welcome, silence.* New York: Simon & Schuster. Copyright © 1987 by Carol S. North. Reprinted by permission of Simon & Schuster, Inc.

Pages 556–559 Excerpted from: Turner, P. (1986). The Shrinking of George. Vol. 7, No. 5, pp. 38–44. Reprinted by permission from the June issue of *Science '86.* Copyright © 1986 by the American Association for the Advancement of Science.

Pages 625 and 626 Kobasa, S. (1987). The stress resistant personality. In R. Ornstein & C. Swencionis (Eds.), *The healing brain: A scientific reader.* New York: Guilford Press.

Color Plate 1A From "Fifth Philosopher's Song" in *The Collected Poetry of Aldous Huxley* edited by Donal Watt. Copyright © 1971 by Laura Huxley. Reprinted by permission of Harper & Row, Publishers, Inc.

Index

Page references in *italics* indicate figures, tables, or other illustrative material. Plate numbers refer to the color sections.

A

P

Pacinian corpuscle, 205, *205*
Paffenbarger (1986), 658
Pain
    curve, 184, *184*
    and learning, 28–29
    pathways, *206*
    and placebos, 570
    and pleasure, 470
    relief system, in brain, 165–68
    in sensory experience, 183–84
Pair bonding, 63–64
Papert (1980), 642
Papillae, 204, *204*
Paranoid personality, 524
Paranormal (psi) abilities, 281, 282
    extrasensory perception (ESP), 281–82
    psychokinesis (PK), 282
Paranormal phenomena, 281
Parapsychology
    described, 281–82
    experiments, 282–83
    research difficulties, 283
Parasympathetic system, *163*, 164
Parental investment, 82, *83*
Parenting, 661–62
Parietal lobes, *143*
    of cortex, 144
    damage to, *147*
Parker, Dorothy, 65
Parkes (1972), 671
Partial reinforcement schedules, 301–3. *See also*
        Reinforcement
    fixed interval (FI), 301
    fixed ratio (FR), 302
    variable interval (VI), 301–2
    variable ratio (VR), 302, *302*
Pascal, Blaise, 629
Passive-aggressive personality, 524
Pattison (1977), 673
Pavlov, Ivan, 291, *291. See also* Respondent (classical)
        conditioning
    association experiments, 291–93, *291*, *292*
    on basic conditioning, 293
    conditioning apparatus, *291*
Pavlov (1927), 293, 295
Pavlov (1928), 314
Pea & Kurland (in press), 642
Pearlin (1980), 621
Peck & Schrut (1971), 535
Penfield, Wilder
    electrical stimulation of brain experiments, 8–9,
        9, 146
Penfield (1975), 8–9, *9*
Penfield & Rasmussen (1950), *145*
Pennebacker et al. (1979), 603
Perception, 215–16. *See also* Perceptual cycle; Person
        perception
    cultural effects on, 238–40
    depth (distance) cues
        binaural disparity, 242
        binocular disparity, 241–42, *241*
        internal, 241
    errors, 508–9
    Gestalt, 219–20, *219*
    innate, 236–38
    invariance of, 218, *218*
    learned, 238–40
    and meaning, 215–16
    and memory, 240
    organization, 216, *216*
    of others, 489–90
    of ourselves, 487–89
    process, 217–31
        adapting to distortion, 235

        adapting to environment, 235
        affordance, 218
        and assumptions, 223, *224*
        constancy in, 231–34
        and environmental characteristics, 217–18
        illusions, 233–34, *234*
        interpretation, 214, 221–22, *221*, *222*
        invariance, 218, *218*
        needs and values, 224
        rules of organization, 219–23, *219*, *220*, *221*
        unconscious inferences, 222–23, *224*
    relativity of, 233
    of self, 487–89
    sensory simplification, 216, *217*
    of space, 240–46
    subliminal, 266–67
    theories, 227–31
        constructivist approach, 227–28
        deconstruction, computation, and
            reconstruction, 228–31
        ecological approach, 227
        Marr's, 228–30, 231
    visual
        in babies, 236–37, *236*
        and blindness, 237–39, *237*, *238*, *239*
    of the whole, *219*
Perceptual adaptation, 45
Perceptual cycle, 224–25, *225*
    accommodation, 226
    assimilation, 225–26, *226*
    defined, 224, *225*
Perceptual encoding, in memory, 329
Peripheral nervous system (PNS), 161–64, *161*, *162*,
        163. See also Central nervous system
        (CNS)
    autonomic nervous system in, 162–64, *162*, *163*
    in brain function, 154
    somatic nervous system in, 162, *162*, *163*
Personal control, and Internal-External (I-E) scale,
        507–8
Personal influence, 592–93
Personality, 485–511. *See also* Personality disorders
    and aging, 669–70
    antisocial, 524, 525–27
    behavior consistency, 508–10
    consistent and inconsistent, 509
    Erikson's theories of, 496
    measures, 504–5
    and psychosocial development, 122–23
    self and others, 486–90, Plate 13
    self-monitoring, 487–89
    sex differences in, 505–7
    structure
        Freud's theory of, 493
        Jung's theory of, 496–97
        in psychoanalysis, 491
    summarized, 511
    theories, 491–98
        of Freud, evaluated, 494–95
        of humanistic psychology, 497–98
        of Jung, 496–97
        of neo-Freudians, 495–96
        psychoanalysis (Freud), 491–95
        social learning theory, 498
    traits, 503–4, *504*
        cardinal, 503
        and correlational matrix, 503
        secondary, 503
    types, 499
        extroverts vs. introverts, 499–503
Personality disorders, 523–27. *See also* Antisocial
        personality (ASP)
    antisocial personality (ASP), 525–27
    causes, 525
    types, 524

Personal space, 643, *643*
    concept of, 643
    in different cultures, 643–44
    individual distance in, 643
Personal unconscious, 496
Person-centered (nondirective) psychotherapy
    described, 560–62
    self-actualization in, 560, 562
    stages of progress, 562
    and therapist-client relationship, 561–62
Person perception, 489–90
    impressions, 489–90
    prototypes in, 490
    special features of, 490
Perspective
    as depth (distance) cue, 242–43, *243*
    rules of, *24*
Pert, Candace, 166
Pfeffer (1978), 641
Pharmacotherapy, 563–67
    antianxiety drugs, 566–67
    antidepressant drugs, 565–66
    antipsychotic drugs, 564–65
    lithium, 278, 564
Phenotype, 74, 79
Pheronomes, 203–4
Phillips (1974), 580
Phillips (1979), 580
Phillips (1980), 580
Phillips (1983), 580
Phillips & Feldman (1973), 673
Phobias. *See* Phobic disorders
Phobic disorders, 521–23
    and age, 521–23
    agoraphobia, 522
    causes, 522–23
    flooding technique for, 553
    and systematic desensitization, 553
Phonemes, 380–81, *380*
Photoreceptors. *See also* Cones; Retina; Rods
    dark adaptation, 189–90, *189*
    in retina, 186–91, *187*, *189*, *190*
Physical attractiveness, 602–5
    and criminals, 604–5
    and loving, 602
    and shoplifters, 603
Physical development. *See* Development, physical
Physiological reinforcers, 300, *300*
Piaget, Jean, *100. See also* Cognitive development
    theory of cognitive development, 100–106
        accommodation, 100–101, *101*
        assimilation, 100, *101*
        assumption and terms, 100–102
        concrete operational stage, 105
        criticism of, 106–7
        decentration, 105–6
        egocentrism, 105–6
        formal operational stage, 105
        object permanence, 102–3, *102*
        operations, 101–2
        preoperational stage, 103–5
        representational (symbolic) thought, 102
        schemata, 100, *101*
        sensorimotor stage, 102–3
        stages of development in, 102–5
Piaget (1932), 107, 115
Piaget (1952), 92
Pinel, Phillipe, 548, *549*
Pinna (ear), 199
Pituitary gland, *134*, 137–38, 164. *See also*
        Neuroendocrine system
PK (psychokinesis), 282, *282*
Placebos, 569–71
Planum temporale, 149, *150*
Plateau stage, of sexual response cycle, 447–48, *448*

Somatoform disorders, 523
Somesthetic system, 206
Sound waves, 199
Space, perception of, 240–46
Spatial frequency, 230, 231
Spearman (1927), 400–401
Species-specific defense reactions (SSDRs), 314
Speech. See also Language
    acts, 380
    Cro-Magnon, 54
    development, 53, 96–97
Speisman, Lazarus, Davidson, & Mordkoff (1964),
    439, 440
Sperry (1982), 151, 151, 152
Spinal cord, 134, 160
    Spinothalamic system, 205, 206
Spitzer, Skodol, Gibbon, & Williams (1981), 520, 521,
    527
Split brain hemispheres. See Brain, hemispheres
Spontaneous remission versus psychotherapy, 568
Spreading effect, Plate 3
SQ3R, 348–49
Squire (1987), 339
Stability and adaptation, 647–48
Stabilized images, 197
Stanford-Binet Intelligence Scale, 397, 397, 398
    controversy over, 401
    sample items from, 397
Stanford "prison" study, 583–84, 583
Starvation, and weight set point, 467–69
Statistics, 30–34
Stefensmeyer & Terry (1973), 603
Steffens, Morgenson, & Stevenson (1972), 461
Steinberg, Sol, 474
Stendahl, on passionate love, 601
Stephan (1973), 449
Stereotypes
    defined, 593
    effects on groups, 594
    and prejudice, 593–94
Sterling-Smith (1976), 279
Sterman (1978), 283
Stern & Aronson (1984), 589
Sternberg, Robert
    triarchic theory of intelligence, 412–13
Sternberg (1985, 1986), 412, 413
Stevens (1956), 183, 199
Stevens (1961), 184
Stevens, Warshofsky, & Staff (1965), 199
Stevens's Power Law, 183
Stiles, Shapiro, & Elliott (1986), 567
Stimulants, 275, 277–78, 527. See also Substance use
    disorders
    amphetamines, 277
    cocaine, 277–78, 277
Stimulation, levels of, 474–75
Stimuli, in conditioning
    frequency of, 294
    recency of, 294
    timing of, 293–94
Stimulus comparison, 181
stimulus difference, in preparedness continuum,
    315, 315
Stimulus response
    and brain growth, 169
Stimulus simplification, 180–81
Stirrup, in ear structure, 200, 200
Stokols (1972), 644
Storms (1981), 449
Stranger anxiety, 114
Strange situation, in attachment anxiety experiment,
    115–16, 115
Stratton (1896), 235
Stress
    and catastrophes, 619

chronic life strains, 621–23
and control of one's life, 625–26
defined, 619
and depression, 533
emergency (fight-or-flight) reaction, 616–18, 617
emotions
    anxiety, 445
    fear, 445
as failure to adapt, 618–23
in everyday life, 621–23
general adaptation syndrome, 618
and hardiness, 624–27
hassles, 621–23, 622
and heart disease, 629–33
and illness, 625
inoculation, 560
life change units, 620–21, 620
major life changes, 619–21
natural disasters, 619
physiological reactions, 616–18, 617
uplifts, 621–23, 622
and wars, 619
work-related, 621
Stress inoculation therapy, 560
Struble & Steffens (1975), 461
Subconscious awareness, 256–57, 257
Subliminal perception, 266–67
Substance use disorders, 527–29
    causes, 528–29
    incidence of, 527–28
Suedfield (1983), 266
Suicide
    and depression, 534–35
    and LSD, 281
    response to, 580, 580
    statistics, 534–35
    Werther effect in, 580
Sullivan, Harry Stack, 495
Superego, 493
Superstitious behavior, 304, 304
Suppes & Morningstar (1969), 641
Surface structure, in language, 381–82
Surman, Gottlieb, Hackett, & Silverberg (1973), 272
Survival of the fittest, 57–58
Swencionus (1987), 501
Syme (1984), 471
Symons (1979), 447
Symons (in press), 64, 65–66
Sympathetic system, 163–64, 163
Synapse, 157–58, 158
Synaptic cleft, 158, 158
Synaptic vesicles, 157, 158
Syntax, 381
Systematic desensitization, 553
Systems, defined, 46

T

Tactile Sensory Replacement (TSR), 238–39, 239
Talbert (1977), 667
Tanner (1962), 124
Targ & Puthoff (1977), 282
Tart (1971), 24, 279
Tart (1977), 282
Tart, Puthoff, & Targ (1979), 282
Taskin, Calvarese, Simmons, & Shapiro (1978), 279
Taste, sense of, 204–5, 204
Taste buds, 204–5, 205, Plate 7
Tavris (1982), 443
Taxonomy, 360
Taylor, R. (1980), 641
Taylor, S. (1970), 608
Taylor, S., Gammon, & Capasso (1976), 608
Taylor, Vadaris, Rawitch, Gammon, Cranston, &
    Lubetkin (1976), 608

Teaching stories, 268–69
Technology, adapting to new, 638–41
Teitelbaum (1957), 461
Television, and violence, 609–10, 609
Temperament, 428
Temperature regulation, and fever, 457–58
Temporal lobes
    of cortex, 144, 148
    damage, 145–48
Tennov (1979), 601
Terman, Lewis, 403
Terman & Merrill (1973), 398
Terminal drop, 672
Terra Amata, 53
Tests, as formal observations, 23–24, 53
Texture gradients, 242, 244
Thalamus, 134, 136
Thanatos, 493, 606
THC (marijuana), 278–79, 608
Therapies. See Psychotherapies
Thermometer neurons, 457
Thinking. See Thought
Thirst, 458–60, 458, 459
Thomas (1982), 339
Thompson (1986), 23, 23, 135, 140, 143, 156, 460
Thorazine, 565
Thorndike (1954), 296–97, 314
Thought
    categories of, 359–62, 362
        characteristics, 361–62
        function of, 360
        natural and artificial, 360–61
        prototypes, 361
        similarities, 362–63, 363
        typical, 361
    characteristics of, 359–68
    decision making and judgment, 368–77
    forms, in schizophrenia, 538
    generalization in, 358–59
    heuristics, 363–67
    and language, 384–85
    overgeneralization, 358–59
    standards of comparison, 368
Thresholds, 182
Thyroid gland, 164, 164
Thyroid releasing hormone (TRH), 164, 164
Thyroxin, 164, 164
Time
    evolutionary, 49
    experience of, 246–48
    and memory experiment, 248, 248, 250
    past, duration, 247
    present, 247
    storage space of, 247–48, 247
Timing of stimuli, in conditioning, 293–94
Tinbergen (1951), 69, 70
Tinkelberg & Darley (1975), 279
Tiredness, mental and physical, 259
Toates (1986), 457, 458–59, 461
Tolerance, in substance use disorders, 527
Tolman (1930), 307, 307
Tolman & Honzik (1930), 306, 306
Tomkins (1979), 427
Tomkins (1984), 428, 430
Tongue, 204–5
    basic tastes, 205
Toolmaking, 67
Tool use, 66, 67
    in bipedal animals, 60
    Cro-Magnon, 54, 67, 67
    Homo erectus, 67
    Homo habilis, 50
    specialization, 65–67
Touching and feeling, 205–6, 205
Toy demonstrators program, 409, 409